I0299765

Alexander Grant

The Ethics of Aristotle

Illustrated with Essays and Notes

Alexander Grant

The Ethics of Aristotle
Illustrated with Essays and Notes

ISBN/EAN: 9783742826435

Manufactured in Europe, USA, Canada, Australia, Japa

Cover: Foto ©Klaus-Uwe Gerhardt /pixelio.de

Manufactured and distributed by brebook publishing software (www.brebook.com)

Alexander Grant

The Ethics of Aristotle

THE

ETHICS OF ARISTOTLE

ILLUSTRATED WITH

ESSAYS AND NOTES.

BY

SIR ALEXANDER GRANT, BART., M.A., LL.D.

PRINCIPAL AND VICE-CHANCELLOR OF THE UNIVERSITY OF EDINBURGH; HON.
MEMBER OF THE DEUTSCHE MORGENLÄNDISCHE GESELLSCHAFT; SOMETIME
DIRECTOR OF PUBLIC INSTRUCTION IN THE BOMBAY PRESIDENCY;
AND FORMERLY FELLOW OF ORIEL COLLEGE, OXFORD.

THIRD EDITION, REVISED AND PARTLY REWRITTEN.

IN TWO VOLUMES.

VOLUME THE SECOND.

LONDON:
LONGMANS, GREEN, AND CO.
1874.

THE NICOMACHEAN ETHICS.

BOOKS III.—X.

PLAN OF BOOK III.

IT has been already assumed without proof, that virtue implies purpose (*Eth.* II. iv. 3, II. v. 4, II. iv. 15), and therefore of course will and freedom. Before proceeding to the analysis of particular virtues, Aristotle begins by examining the generic conception of the Voluntary, with a view chiefly to the comprehension of its species, Purpose.

The first five Chapters of Book III. are accordingly devoted to this subject, and stand so much apart from what goes before and after, that some have been led to the conclusion that they were written as a separate treatise (see Vol. I. Essay I. p. 45). That several parts of these chapters are unnecessarily repeated in Book V. c. xiii., and that certain points in them do not agree with the psychology of Books VI. and VII., is no argument against the present chapters having formed part of Aristotle's original draft and conception of his *Ethics*, but only tends to show that Books V. VI. VII. were written later. It is more to the purpose to notice that in Chapter v. § 10, there is an apparent ignoring of the whole discussion upon the formation of moral states which occupies the commencement of Book II., and that no allusion occurs to 'the mean' or to 'happiness.' But this is only a specimen of the way in which Aristotle concentrated his mind on each new subject as it arose, and in writing upon it frequently neglected to refer to other cognate passages. The same thing is observable in the treatise on Friendship (VIII. i. 1). The treatise on the Voluntary is neatly fitted on to the general ethical treatise by §§ 21, 22 of the fifth chapter of this book. There is no reason to suspect these sections of being other than the work of Aristotle.

It must not be supposed that the present disquisition on the Voluntary is a disquisition on Free Will. The latter question

Aristotle would certainly have assigned to πρώτη φιλοσοφία, or metaphysics, and would have thought out of place in a system of ethics. Some remarks upon his views of Free Will, so far as they can be gathered, will be found in Vol. I. Essay V. The ensuing chapters assume that man is the ἀρχὴ of his own actions, and with this assumption treat of the Voluntary under its various aspects in relation to virtue and vice, praise and blame, reward and punishment. From this practical point of view these chapters furnish to some extent a psychology, though not a metaphysic, of the Will. Their contents are as follows:—

(1.) The general definition of the Voluntary. Ch. i.

(2.) The special account of Purpose, that it is distinct from desire, wish, opinion; its relation to the process of deliberation. Ch. ii.—iii.

(3.) Some consideration of the question whether Wish is for the absolute or the apparent good. Ch. iv.

(4.) An attack upon the position that while virtue is free, vice is involuntary. Ch. v.

The remainder of the book is occupied with a discussion of the two first virtues upon Aristotle's list—Courage and Temperance. With regard to Courage the following heads are treated of:—(1.) Its proper objects; Ch. vi. (2.) That it is a mean; Ch. vii. (3.) That true courage is to be distinguished from five spurious kinds of courage; Ch. viii. (4.) That it is particularly related to pain, and implies making great sacrifices for the sake of what is noble; Ch. ix. The objects and the nature of Temperance are treated of in Chapters x. and xi. And the book ends with two remarks on Intemperance: (1.) that it is more voluntary than cowardice; and, (2.) that its character is shown in its etymology; Ch. xii.

ΗΘΙΚΩΝ ΝΙΚΟΜΑΧΕΙΩΝ III.

ΤΗΣ ἀρετῆς δὴ περὶ πάθη τε καὶ πράξεις οὔσης, καὶ ἐπὶ μὲν τοῖς ἑκουσίοις ἐπαίνων καὶ ψόγων γινομένων, ἐπὶ δὲ τοῖς ἀκουσίοις συγγνώμης, ἐνίοτε δὲ καὶ ἐλέου, τὸ ἑκούσιον καὶ ἀκούσιον ἀναγκαῖον ἴσως διορίσαι τοῖς περὶ ἀρετῆς ἐπισκοποῦσι, χρήσιμον δὲ καὶ τοῖς νομοθετοῦσι πρός τε 2

I. 1—2 Τῆς ἀρετῆς δὴ—κολάσεις] 'Virtue then being concerned with feelings and actions; and praise and blame being bestowed on acts which are voluntary, while pardon and sometimes even pity are conceded to involuntary ones,—it will surely be necessary for the philosopher who treats of virtue to define the voluntary and involuntary; and moreover this will be useful for the legislator with a view to the rewards and punishments with which he has to deal.' In the *Eudemian Ethics*, which contain generally speaking a reproduction of these *Ethics*, for the most part compressed, but also occasionally expanded and supplemented, we find (*Eth. Eud.*, II. vi.) a more definite and reasoned statement of the voluntariness of virtue and vice. The reasoning of Eudemus is briefly as follows: --All οὐσίαι are ἀρχαί, and tend to reproduce themselves; and only those ἀρχαί are properly so called (κύριαι) which are primary causes of motion, as is especially the case with regard to immutable motions, whose cause is doubtless God. Mathematical ἀρχαί are called so only by analogy, not being causes of motion. We have hitherto only mentioned necessary consequences: but there are many things which may happen or may not, and whose causes therefore must be, like themselves, contingent. All human actions being contingent, it is obvious that man is a contingent cause, and that the reason of the contingency in his actions is his ability to will one way or the other, as is farther manifest from our praise or blame of actions.—A deeper ground than that which Aristotle has taken might surely have been found for the position that morality implies freedom. But though philosophy even before Aristotle had dealt to some extent with the ideas of necessity and freedom, it remained for the Stoics to open the question more decisively. It is plain that the discussions on the Will in this place are never metaphysical. An appeal to language and common opinions sums up nearly the whole. The scope of the argument is

3 τὰς τιμὰς καὶ τὰς κολάσεις. δοκεῖ δὴ ἀκούσια εἶναι τὰ βίᾳ ἢ δι' ἄγνοιαν γινόμενα. βίαιον δὲ οὗ ἡ ἀρχὴ ἔξωθεν, τοιαύτη οὖσα ἐν ᾗ μηδὲν συμβάλλεται ὁ πράττων ἢ ὁ πάσχων, οἷον εἰ πνεῦμα κομίσαι ποι ἢ ἄνθρωποι κύριοι
4 ὄντες. ὅσα δὲ διὰ φόβον μειζόνων κακῶν πράττεται ἢ διὰ καλόν τι, οἷον εἰ τύραννος προστάττοι αἰσχρόν τι πρᾶξαι κύριος ὢν γονέων καὶ τέκνων, καὶ πράξαντος μὲν σώζοιντο, μὴ πράξαντος δ' ἀποθνήσκοιεν, ἀμφισβήτησιν ἔχει πότερον

---

limited to a political, as distinguished from a theological point of view (ἀναγκαῖον τοῖς περὶ ἀρετῆς ἐπισκοποῦσι, χρήσιμον δὲ καὶ τοῖς νομοθετοῦσι).

3 δοκεῖ δὴ—γινόμενα] 'Now those acts seem to be involuntary which are done under compulsion or through ignorance.' In asking what is the Voluntary, Aristotle does not pursue a speculative method of inquiry. Such a method might have commenced with the deep-lying ideas of personality and consciousness, of the individuality of the subject, &c. But he is content with defining the voluntary by a contrast to the common notions (δοκεῖ) of what constitutes an involuntary act. It might be said that this is giving a merely negative conception of freedom. But in fact the conception given is positive, only the analysis of it is not pushed very far. The voluntariness of an act Aristotle represents to be constituted in this—that the actor is in every case the ἀρχή, or cause, of his actions, except in cases of compulsion, where there really is a superior ἀρχή (Kant's 'heteronomy'), or of ignorance, where he does not know what his action is, and can only be held to be the cause of what he meant to do. In what sense and how the individual is an ἀρχή, is the point where Aristotle stops short in the inquiry.

βίαιον δὲ—ὄντες] 'That is compulsory, whose cause is external to the agent, and is of such a nature that the agent (or patient) contributes nothing towards it; as, for instance, if a wind were to carry you to any place, or men in whose power you are.' Ἀρχή seems here equivalent to ἀρχὴ κινήσεως, the efficient cause. Aristotle attributes spontaneity so decisively to the individual act, that he confines the term compulsion as only applicable to cases of absolute physical force, where a man's limbs are moved or his body transported, as if he were inanimate, by some external power. The compulsion of threats, fear, and such like, he will not call compulsion without qualification, because still the individual *acts* under it. He has already spoken of the life of money-making as being βίαιός τις, 'in a sort compulsory' (*Eth.* i. v. 8). With ὁ πράττων ἢ ὁ πάσχων cf. v. viii. 3: πολλὰ γὰρ τῶν φύσει ὑπαρχόντων εἰδότες καὶ πράττομεν καὶ πάσχομεν—οἷον τὸ γηρᾶν ἢ ἀποθνήσκειν.

4—9 The cause of the act must be entirely from without, for in some cases men are forced, not to an act, but to an alternative. They may do what is grievous for the fear of what is worse. Such acts, then, are of a mixed character, partaking of the nature both of voluntariness and involuntariness. Relatively to the moment, they come from the choice and will of the individual. Abstractedly and in themselves they are contrary to the will. But as

ἀκούσιά ἐστιν ἢ ἑκούσια. τοιοῦτον δέ τι συμβαίνει καὶ 5
περὶ τὰς ἐν τοῖς χειμῶσιν ἐκβολάς· ἁπλῶς μὲν γὰρ οὐδεὶς
ἀποβάλλεται ἑκών, ἐπὶ σωτηρίᾳ δ' αὑτοῦ καὶ τῶν λοιπῶν
ἅπαντες οἱ νοῦν ἔχοντες. μικταὶ μὲν οὖν εἰσὶν αἱ τοιαῦται 6
πράξεις, ἐοίκασι δὲ μᾶλλον ἑκουσίοις· αἱρεταὶ γάρ εἰσι
τότε ὅτε πράττονται, τὸ δὲ τέλος τῆς πράξεως κατὰ τὸν

---

every act aims at something in reference to the particular moment, and is thus entirely dependent on it, so these must be judged as acts done and chosen voluntarily, and according to circumstances must obtain blame or praise. There seem to be four cases which Aristotle conceives as possible: (1) Praise is deserved where pain or degradation is endured for the sake of some great and noble end; (2) but blame, where what is degrading is endured without a sufficiently great and noble end. (3) Pardon is conceded where human nature succumbs, under great extremities, to do what is not right; (4) except the action be such as no extremities ought to bring a man to consent to, in which case pardon is withheld. In these distinctions we may recognise a practical and political wisdom such as might be found in the speeches of Thucydides, but the discussion does not rise to the level of philosophy.

6 *μικταὶ—οὐδέν*] 'Now it may be said that such actions are of a mixed character, but they are more like things voluntary, for at the particular moment when they are done they are such as one would choose, and the moral character of an action depends on the circumstance of the moment; hence also the terms "voluntary" and "involuntary" must be predicated in reference to the moment when a person is acting. Now, in the supposed case (*ἐν τοιαύταις πράξεσι*), the individual acts voluntarily; for the efficient cause of the movement of the accessory limbs is in himself, and where the cause is in a person, it rests with him to act or not. Therefore such things are voluntary, though abstractedly perhaps, involuntary, for in themselves no one would choose any of such things as these.'

τὸ δὲ τέλος τῆς πράξεως] The phrase is general, not referring only to the cases under dispute, but to action universally. In this sense we may translate *τῆς πράξεως* 'of *an* action.' *Τέλος* is used here in a peculiar sense to denote the 'moral character of an action.' This sense arises out of a combination of associations, 'final cause,' and 'motive,' being combined with 'end-in-itself,' 'perfection,' 'completeness.' A precisely similar use of the word occurs, *Eth.* III. vii. 6: *Τέλος δὲ πάσης ἐνεργείας—ὁρίζεται γὰρ ἕκαστον τῷ τέλει* (on which see note). The Paraphrast, in accordance with the above explanation, states the argument thus:—'Because the character of an action as good or bad is judged in reference to the mind of the actor at the moment of action, so also must the voluntariness of an action be judged.' *Ἐπεὶ καὶ τὸ ἑκάστης πράξεως τέλος κατὰ τὸν καιρὸν αὐτῆς ἐστί, καὶ ἀπὸ τοῦ καιροῦ ἢ ἀγαθὸν ἢ πονηρὸν γίνεται· ἔστι καὶ τὸ ἑκούσιον, ἢ τὸ ἀκούσιον, κατὰ τὸν καιρὸν ὅτε πράττεται, ζητητέον.* Of course the interpretation of Muretus is wrong which attributes a merely popular and un-Aristotelian sense to *τέλος*—'actio terminatur eo ipso tempore quo agimus.'

καιρόν ἐστιν. καὶ τὸ ἑκούσιον δὴ καὶ τὸ ἀκούσιον, ὅτε πράττει, λεκτέον. πράττει δὲ ἑκών· καὶ γὰρ ἡ ἀρχὴ τοῦ κινεῖν τὰ ὀργανικὰ μέρη ἐν ταῖς τοιαύταις πράξεσιν ἐν αὐτῷ ἐστίν· ὧν δ' ἐν αὐτῷ ἡ ἀρχή, ἐπ' αὐτῷ καὶ τὸ πράττειν καὶ μή. ἑκούσια δὴ τὰ τοιαῦτα, ἁπλῶς δ' ἴσως ἀκούσια· οὐδεὶς γὰρ ἂν ἕλοιτο καθ' αὑτὸ τῶν τοιούτων οὐδέν.
7 ἐπὶ ταῖς πράξεσι δὲ ταῖς τοιαύταις ἐνίοτε καὶ ἐπαινοῦνται, ὅταν αἰσχρόν τι ἢ λυπηρὸν ὑπομένωσιν ἀντὶ μεγάλων καὶ καλῶν· ἂν δ' ἀνάπαλιν, ψέγονται· τὰ γὰρ αἴσχισθ' ὑπομεῖναι ἐπὶ μηδενὶ καλῷ ἢ μετρίῳ φαύλου. ἐπ' ἐνίοις δ' ἔπαινος μὲν οὐ γίνεται, συγγνώμη δ', ὅταν διὰ τοιαῦτα πράξῃ τις ἃ μὴ δεῖ, ἃ τὴν ἀνθρωπίνην φύσιν ὑπερτείνει καὶ
8 μηδεὶς ἂν ὑπομείναι. ἔνια δ' ἴσως οὐκ ἔστιν ἀναγκασθῆναι, ἀλλὰ μᾶλλον ἀποθανατέον παθόντι τὰ δεινότατα· καὶ γὰρ τὸν Εὐριπίδου Ἀλκμαίωνα γελοῖα φαίνεται τὰ ἀναγ-
9 κάσαντα μητροκτονῆσαι. ἔστι δὲ χαλεπὸν ἐνίοτε διακρῖναι ποῖον ἀντὶ ποίου αἱρετέον καὶ τί ἀντὶ τίνος ὑπομενετέον, ἔτι δὲ χαλεπώτερον ἐμμεῖναι τοῖς γνωσθεῖσιν· ὡς γὰρ ἐπὶ τὸ πολύ ἐστι τὰ μὲν προσδοκώμενα λυπηρά, ἃ δ' ἀναγκάζονται αἰσχρά, ὅθεν ἔπαινοι καὶ ψόγοι γίνονται περὶ τοὺς

ὅτε πράττει] The omission of τις, especially after conjunctions like εἰ, ὅτι, &c., is common in Aristotle, though not peculiar to him. Cf. *Eth.* III. ix. 5: *πλὴν ἐφ' ὅσον τοῦ τέλους ἐφάπτεται.* *Pol.* VII. xiii. 8: *ὥσπερ εἰ τοῦ κιθαρίζειν λαμπρὸν καὶ καλῶς αἴτιοιτο τὴν λύραν μᾶλλον τῆς τέχνης.*

τὰ ὀργανικὰ μέρη] The 'subservient,' or 'instrumental' limbs. The modern word 'organised,' which has grown out of the Aristotelian conception of *ὀργανικὸν σῶμα*, does not exactly represent it. 'Organisation' implies multeity in unity, the co-existence and interjunction of physical parts under a law of life. But in *ὀργανικὸς* originally nothing more was implied than 'that which is fitly framed as an instrument,'—according to Aristotle's principle, that the body is the means to the life, mind, or soul, which is the end. Cf. *De An.* II. i. 6: *ψυχή ἐστιν ἐντελέχεια ἡ πρώτη σώματος φυσικοῦ δυνάμει ζωὴν ἔχοντος. τοιοῦτο δέ, ὃ ἂν ᾖ ὀργανικόν.* *De Part. An.* I. i. 41: *οὕτως καὶ ἐπεὶ τὸ σῶμα ὄργανον (ἕνεκά τινος γὰρ ἕκαστον τῶν μορίων, ὁμοίως δὲ καὶ τὸ ὅλον), ἀνάγκη ἄρα τοιονδὶ εἶναι καὶ ἐκ τοιωνδὶ εἰ ἐκεῖνο ἔσται.*

8 *καὶ γὰρ τὸν Εὐριπίδου—μητροκτονῆσαι*] 'For the things which compelled the Alcmæon of Euripides to kill his mother appear absurd,' i. e. the curses threatened by Amphiaraus, who, when departing for Thebes, enjoined his son to put Eriphyle to death. Aspasius preserves the lines:—

Μάλιστα μὲν μ' ἐπῆρ' ἐπισκήψας πατήρ,
ὅθ' ἅρματ' εἰσέβαινεν εἰς Θήβας ἰών.

ἀναγκασθέντας ἢ μή. τὰ δὴ ποῖα φατέον βίαια; ἢ ἁπλῶς
μέν, ὁπότ' ἂν ἡ αἰτία ἐν τοῖς ἐκτὸς ᾖ καὶ ὁ πράττων μηδὲν 10
συμβάλληται; ἃ δὲ καθ' αὑτὰ μὲν ἀκούσιά ἐστι, νῦν δὲ καὶ ἀντὶ τῶνδε αἱρετά, καὶ ἡ ἀρχὴ ἐν τῷ πράττοντι, καθ' αὑτὰ μὲν ἀκούσιά ἐστι, νῦν δὲ καὶ ἀντὶ τῶνδε ἑκούσια. μᾶλλον δ' ἔοικεν ἑκουσίοις· αἱ γὰρ πράξεις ἐν τοῖς καθ' ἕκαστα, ταῦτα δ' ἑκούσια. ποῖα δ' ἀντὶ ποίων αἱρετέον, οὐ ῥᾴδιον ἀποδοῦναι· πολλαὶ γὰρ διαφοραί εἰσιν ἐν τοῖς καθ' ἕκαστα.
εἰ δέ τις τὰ ἡδέα καὶ τὰ καλὰ φαίη βίαια εἶναι (ἀναγκάζειν 11
γὰρ ἔξω ὄντα), πάντα ἂν εἴη οὕτω βίαια· τούτων γὰρ χάριν πάντες πάντα πράττουσιν. καὶ οἱ μὲν βίᾳ καὶ ἄκοντες λυπηρῶς, οἱ δὲ διὰ τὸ ἡδὺ καὶ καλὸν μεθ' ἡδονῆς. γελοῖον δὴ τὸ αἰτιᾶσθαι τὰ ἐκτός, ἀλλὰ μὴ αὑτὸν εὐθήρατον ὄντα ὑπὸ τῶν τοιούτων, καὶ τῶν μὲν καλῶν ἑαυτόν, τῶν δ'
αἰσχρῶν τὰ ἡδέα. ἔοικε δὴ τὸ βίαιον εἶναι οὗ ἔξωθεν ἡ 12
ἀρχή, μηδὲν συμβαλλομένου τοῦ βιασθέντος.

---

10 ποῖα δ' ἀντὶ ποίων αἱρετέον, οὐ ῥᾴδιον ἀποδοῦναι] These words repeat what has been already said in the preceding section. Ἔστι δὲ χαλεπὸν ἐνίοτε κ.τ.λ., but they add the reason 'because each particular case has its own special diversity:' cf. διαφορὰν καὶ πλάνην, I. iii. 2.

11–12 In these sections Aristotle guards his definition against a possible misconception. Having defined the compulsory to be that whose cause is external, he disallows the supposition that the two great inducements to all action, the pleasant and the noble, because external to us, make the actions they induce compulsory. His arguments against this supposition are: (1) It would make all action compulsory, and thus imply more than any one would wish to support. (2) Compulsory actions are painful; those done for the pleasant or the noble are pleasurable. (3) It leaves out of account the internal susceptibility of the agent (αὑτὸν εὐθήρατον ὄντα). His own definition, then, is sufficiently qualified by the addition of the words, 'the person under compulsion in nowise consenting' (μηδὲν συμβαλλομένου τοῦ βιασθέντος).

τὰ ἡδέα καὶ τὰ καλά] Aspasius reads τὰ ἡδέα καὶ τὰ λυπηρά. The commentators, Victorius, Muretus, Giphanius, and Zell, get over the difficulty by taking τὰ καλά to mean 'non honesta, sed formosa, pulchra.' It is plain, however, that the same classification of inducements is here referred to as that given *Eth.* II. iii. 7, the συμφέρον being a means either to the ἡδὺ or the καλόν. The καλόν is in short 'the noble,' or 'the good, viewed as morally beautiful.' A concise definition of it is given in *Rhet.* I. ix. 3: καλὸν μὲν οὖν ἐστιν, ὃ ἂν δι' αὑτὸ αἱρετὸν ὂν ἐπαινετὸν ᾖ, ἢ ὃ ἂν ἀγαθὸν ὂν ἡδὺ ᾖ, ὅτι ἀγαθόν. It is used in the present passage not at all emphatically, but simply to denote that form of inducement which consists in our wishing to do a thing

13 Τὸ δὲ δι' ἄγνοιαν οὐχ ἑκούσιον μὲν ἅπαν ἐστίν, ἀκούσιον δὲ τὸ ἐπίλυπον καὶ ἐν μεταμελείᾳ· ὁ γὰρ δι' ἄγνοιαν
πράξας ὁτιοῦν, μηδὲν δὲ δυσχεραίνων ἐπὶ τῇ πράξει, ἑκὼν
μὲν οὐ πέπραχεν, ὅ γε μὴ ᾔδει, οὐδ' αὖ ἄκων, μὴ λυπούμενός
γε. τοῦ δὴ δι' ἄγνοιαν ὁ μὲν ἐν μεταμελείᾳ ἄκων δοκεῖ, ὁ
δὲ μὴ μεταμελόμενος, ἐπεὶ ἕτερος, ἔστω οὐχ ἑκών· ἐπεὶ
14 γὰρ διαφέρει, βέλτιον ὄνομα ἔχειν ἴδιον. ἕτερον δ' ἔοικε
καὶ τὸ δι' ἄγνοιαν πράττειν τοῦ ἀγνοοῦντα ποιεῖν· ὁ γὰρ
μεθύων ἢ ὀργιζόμενος οὐ δοκεῖ δι' ἄγνοιαν πράττειν, ἀλλὰ

---

because it is right. A little examination shows that the writing here is vague, for presently it is said to be absurd to assign the cause of the good things to oneself, and of the bad things to pleasure (*αἰτιᾶσθαι—τῶν μὲν καλῶν ἑαυτόν, τῶν δ' αἰσχρῶν τὰ ἡδέα*); whereas consistently the 'good things' would have been assigned to 'the good' as an external cause by those who maintained the position, *εἰ δέ τις τὰ ἡδέα κ.τ.λ.* Also would Aristotle say that what is done *διὰ τὸ καλόν*, is always done *μεθ' ἡδονῆς*? This goes strangely against *Eth.* III. ix. 4—5, where the higher satisfaction of the *καλὸν* is represented as purchased by great pain. There is a vagueness also in the use of *βίαιον*, which first stands for that which compels, and secondly for that which is compelled. The principle, however, is well brought out, that the objective inducement to an action cannot be separated from the subjective apprehension of this in the will.

13 *τὸ δὲ δι' ἄγνοιαν—ἔχειν ἴδιον*] 'Now that which is done through ignorance is always non-voluntary, but it is involuntary only when followed by pain, and when it is a matter of regret. For he who has done something through ignorance, but without feeling any dislike at the action, has not, it is true, acted voluntarily, inasmuch as he did not know he was doing it, but, on the other hand, not involuntarily, since he is not sorry. With regard, therefore, to actions done through ignorance we may say that he who repents has been an involuntary agent, while him who does not repent we may distinguish as having been a non-voluntary one; for where there is a real difference, it is proper to have a distinctive name.' Aristotle begins the discussion of ignorance as modifying volition by this refined distinction, that an action may be done through ignorance, and yet not against the will. It may in short be neither with the will nor against it. He then goes on to consider the precise meaning of *δι' ἄγνοιαν*.

14—16 *ἕτερον δ' ἔοικε—ἀκουσίως πράττει*] 'There seems to be a farther difference between acting through ignorance and doing a thing in ignorance. Common opinion pronounces that the drunken or the angry man acts not through ignorance, but in consequence of drunkenness or anger, and yet that he does not act wittingly, but in ignorance. Without doubt every depraved man is in ignorance of what he ought to do, and of that from which he ought to refrain, and it is

διά τι τῶν εἰρημένων, οὐκ εἰδὼς δὲ ἀλλ' ἀγνοῶν. ἀγνοεῖ μὲν οὖν πᾶς ὁ μοχθηρὸς ἃ δεῖ πράττειν καὶ ὧν ἀφεκτέον, καὶ

---

in consequence of this error that men become unjust, or bad generally. But the term involuntary is not meant to cover ignorance of man's true interest. Ignorance which affects moral choice, and ignorance of the universal, are the causes, not of involuntary action, but of wickedness, and it is precisely for this ignorance that wicked men are blamed. The ignorance which causes involuntary action is ignorance of particulars, which are the circumstances and the objects of actions. With regard to these particulars, pity and pardon may be proper, for the man who acts in ignorance of some particular is an involuntary agent.' The connexion of this somewhat compressed passage is as follows. An act is involuntary when caused by ignorance. But ignorance cannot be said to be the cause of an act if the individual be himself the cause of the ignorance. In that case ignorance rather accompanies the act (ἀγνοῶν πράττει) than causes it (δι' ἄγνοιαν πράττει). We see this (1) in instances of temporary oblivion, as from anger, or wine; (2) in those of a standing moral ignorance or oblivion (εἴ τις ἀγνοεῖ τὸ συμφέρον—ἡ ἐν τῇ προαιρέσει ἄγνοια—ἡ καθόλου ἄγνοια). The only ignorance, then, which is purely external to the agent, so as to take away from him the responsibility of the act, is some chance mistake with regard to the particular facts of the case. A great deal of trouble has been expended upon the endeavour to distinguish and explain the various terms, ἀγνοοῦντα πράττειν—ἀγνοεῖν τὸ συμφέρον—ἡ ἐν τῇ προαιρέσει ἄγνοια—ἡ καθόλου ἄγνοια. But a closer examination shows that these different terms are not opposed to each other, but rather are all different ways for expressing the same thing, being opposed to the ἡ καθ' ἕκαστα, ἐν οἷς ἡ πρᾶξις. This is the way in which the Paraphrast understands the passage, for he renders it: Αἱ δὴ τοιαῦται πράξεις οὐκ εἰσὶν ἀκούσιοι· ἡ γὰρ ἐν τῇ προαιρέσει ἄγνοια, ἥτις ἐστὶν αἰτία τῶν κακιῶν, οὐκ ἔστιν αἰτία τοῦ ἀκουσίου, ἀλλὰ τῆς μοχθηρίας. Οὐ γὰρ τὸ καθόλου περὶ τῆς μέθης ἀγνοεῖν ὅτι πονηρόν, αἴτιον γίνεται τοῦ ἀκουσίου, ἀλλὰ τὸ ἀγνοῆσαι μερικῶς τήνδε τὴν μέθοδον· οἷον, φέρε εἰπεῖν, οὐκ εἰδέναι μέχρι πόσου πίνοντας ἔστι μεθύειν. Aristotle strictly confines ignorance, as a cause of involuntary action, to mistakes about particulars. Before proceeding to this particular ignorance, he separates from it that kind of ignorance which is faulty, because caused by the agent himself. Of this there are two kinds, the temporary, as for instance that caused by intoxication, and the permanent, such as that caused by any vicious habit. 'Ignorance of the universal' is not different from 'ignorance of our real interest,' but serves to point the antithesis of 'ignorance of the particular': nor is it opposed to ignorance as shown in wrong moral choice, but to ignorance of external facts. It goes to constitute ignorance in the purpose, for in every moral act there is a universal conception, as well as a particular application of this. But Aristotle does not here enter upon the psychology of the subject, as is afterwards done, *Eth.* VII. iii. The word συμφέρον is used, *Politics*, I. ii. 11, to include and denote all kinds of good, ὁ δὲ λόγος ἐπὶ τῷ δηλοῦν ἐστὶ τὸ συμφέρον καὶ τὸ βλαβερόν, ὥστε καὶ τὸ δίκαιον καὶ τὸ ἄδικον.

14 διά τι τῶν εἰρημένων] Some refer

διὰ τὴν τοιαύτην ἁμαρτίαν ἄδικοι καὶ ὅλως κακοὶ γίνονται.
15 τὸ δ' ἀκούσιον βούλεται λέγεσθαι οὐκ εἴ τις ἀγνοεῖ τὸ συμφέρον· οὐ γὰρ ἡ ἐν τῇ προαιρέσει ἄγνοια αἰτία τοῦ ἀκουσίου ἀλλὰ τῆς μοχθηρίας, οὐδ' ἡ καθόλου (ψέγονται γὰρ διά γε ταύτην) ἀλλ' ἡ καθ' ἕκαστα, ἐν οἷς καὶ περὶ ἃ ἡ πρᾶξις·
16 ἐν τούτοις γὰρ καὶ ἔλεος καὶ συγγνώμη· ὁ γὰρ τούτων τι ἀγνοῶν ἀκουσίως πράττει. ἴσως οὖν οὐ χεῖρον διορίσαι αὐτά, τίνα καὶ πόσα ἐστί, τίς τε δὴ καὶ τί καὶ περὶ τί ἢ ἐν τίνι πράττει, ἐνίοτε δὲ καὶ τίνι, οἷον ὀργάνῳ, καὶ ἕνεκα τίνος, οἷον σωτηρίας, καὶ πῶς, οἷον ἠρέμα ἢ σφόδρα.
17 ἅπαντα μὲν οὖν ταῦτα οὐδεὶς ἂν ἀγνοήσειε μὴ μαινόμενος, δῆλον δ' ὡς οὐδὲ τὸν πράττοντα· πῶς γὰρ ἑαυτόν γε; ὃ δὲ πράττει, ἀγνοήσειεν ἄν τις, οἷον λέγοντές φασιν ἐκπεσεῖν αὐτούς, ἢ οὐκ εἰδέναι ὅτι ἀπόρρητα ἦν, ὥσπερ Αἰσχύλος τὰ μυστικά, ἢ δεῖξαι βουλόμενος ἀφεῖναι, ὡς ὁ τὸν καταπέλτην. οἰηθείη δ' ἄν τις καὶ τὸν υἱὸν πολέμιον εἶναι ὥσπερ ἡ Μερόπη, καὶ ἐσφαιρῶσθαι τὸ λελογχωμένον δόρυ, ἢ τὸν λίθον κίσσηριν εἶναι· καὶ ἐπὶ σωτηρίᾳ παίσας ἀποκτεῖναι ἄν· καὶ δεῖξαι βουλόμενος, ὥσπερ οἱ ἀκροχειριζόμενοι,

---

this to § 11, τὰ ἡδέα καὶ τὰ καλά, but it appears simply to mean 'not from ignorance, but from one of the things now specified,' (*i. e.* drunkenness or anger). Cf. III. iii. 11, τὸν εἰρημένον τρόπον, which refers to the passage immediately preceding.

16–17 The particulars connected with an action are as follows. (1) The person doing it, about which ignorance is impossible to the doer. (2) The thing done, which may not be known, *e.g.*, Æschylus did not know he was revealing the mysteries. (3) The thing or person made the object of the action (*περὶ τί ἢ ἐν τίνι*), *e.g.*, Merope did not know it was her son. (4) The instrument, *e.g.*, one might fancy one's spear had a button on it. (5) The purpose, or tendency of the act (*ἕνεκα τίνος*), *e.g.*, one wishing to preserve might kill. (6) The manner (*πῶς*), *e.g.* one might strike harder than one wished.

ὥσπερ Αἰσχύλος τὰ μυστικά] Referring to the well-known story that Æschylus was summoned before the Areopagus on the charge of having revealed the mysteries, against which charge he pleaded that he had never himself been initiated. Ælian, *Var. Hist.* v. 19.

ὥσπερ ἡ Μερόπη] This same incident is alluded to by Aristotle in the *Poetics*, c. xiv. 19: *Κράτιστον δὲ τὸ τελευταῖον*, (*i.e. τὸ μέλλοντα ποιεῖν τι τῶν ἀνηκέστων δι' ἄγνοιαν, ἀναγνωρίσαι πρὶν ποιῆσαι*), *λέγω δὲ οἷον ἐν τῷ Κρεσφόντῃ ἡ Μερόπη μέλλει τὸν υἱὸν ἀποκτείνειν, ἀποκτείνει δὲ οὔ, ἀλλ' ἀνεγνώρισεν*.

καὶ δεῖξαι βουλόμενος, ὥσπερ οἱ ἀκροχειριζόμενοι, πατάξειεν ἄν] 'And wishing to show the way, as those do who box with the open hand, a man

πατάξειεν ἄν. περὶ πάντα δὴ ταῦτα τῆς ἀγνοίας οὔσης ἐν 18
οἷς ἡ πρᾶξις, ὁ τούτων τι ἀγνοήσας ἄκων δοκεῖ πεπραχέναι,
καὶ μάλιστα ἐν τοῖς κυριωτάτοις· κυριώτατα δ' εἶναι
δοκεῖ ἐν οἷς ἡ πρᾶξις καὶ οὗ ἕνεκα. τοῦ δὴ κατὰ 19
τὴν τοιαύτην ἄγνοιαν ἀκουσίου λεγομένου ἔτι δεῖ τὴν
πρᾶξιν λυπηρὰν εἶναι καὶ ἐν μεταμελείᾳ. ὄντος δ' 20
ἀκουσίου τοῦ βίᾳ καὶ δι' ἄγνοιαν, τὸ ἑκούσιον δόξειεν
ἂν εἶναι οὗ ἡ ἀρχὴ ἐν αὐτῷ εἰδότι τὰ καθ' ἕκαστα ἐν
οἷς ἡ πρᾶξις. ἴσως γὰρ οὐ καλῶς λέγεται ἀκούσια εἶναι 21
τὰ διὰ θυμὸν ἢ δι' ἐπιθυμίαν. πρῶτον μὲν γὰρ οὐδὲν ἔτι 22
τῶν ἄλλων ζῴων ἑκουσίως πράξει, οὐδ' οἱ παῖδες· εἶτα 23
πότερον οὐδὲν ἑκουσίως πράττομεν τῶν δι' ἐπιθυμίαν καὶ
θυμόν, ἢ τὰ καλὰ μὲν ἑκουσίως τὰ δ' αἰσχρὰ ἀκουσίως; ἢ
γελοῖον ἑνός γε αἰτίου ὄντος; ἄτοπον δὲ ἴσως τὸ ἀκούσια 24
φάναι ὧν δεῖ ὀρέγεσθαι. δεῖ δὲ καὶ ὀργίζεσθαι ἐπί τισι
καὶ ἐπιθυμεῖν τινῶν, οἷον ὑγιείας καὶ μαθήσεως. δοκεῖ δὲ 25
τὰ μὲν ἀκούσια λυπηρὰ εἶναι, τὰ δὲ κατ' ἐπιθυμίαν ἡδέα.
ἔτι δὲ τί διαφέρει τῷ ἀκούσια εἶναι τὰ κατὰ λογισμὸν ἢ 26

---

might give another a blow.' Aspasius explains ἀκροχειρίζεσθαι thus: ἔστι τὸ πυκτεύειν ἢ παγκρατιάζειν πρὸς ἕτερον ἄνευ συμπλοκῆς ἢ ὅλως ἄκραις ταῖς χερσὶ μετ' ἀλλήλων γυμνάζεσθαι, *i.e.* it is what we call 'sparring.' This same phrase δεῖξαι βουλόμενος was applied before to 'the man who was showing the catapult,' and was given as an instance of one being ignorant of the nature of his act. Here it is an instance of ignorance of the tendency of an act. The different kinds of ignorance are not very distinct from one another.

18 περὶ πάντα δὴ—ἕνεκα] 'Ignorance then being concerned with all these circumstances of the action, he that was ignorant of some one of these is held (δοκεῖ) to have acted involuntarily, and especially (if ignorant) with regard to the most important; and the most important seem to be the objects of the action and the tendency of it.' The words ἐν οἷς are used at the beginning of the section in a general sense, as before (§ 15); afterwards they correspond with περὶ τί καὶ ἐν τίνι (§ 16). There is an awkwardness about οὗ ἕνεκα. A person knows with what end or view he is acting (and this is what οὗ ἕνεκα legitimately expresses). But he is mistaken about the means which he uses. Hence wishing to produce one result he produces another. But what he mistakes, is not the end (οὗ ἕνεκα) but the means (τὰ πρὸς τὸ τέλος). The phrase here would imply that an action had an end, or aim of its own (οὗ ἕνεκα) independent of the doer,—in other words a tendency, of which therefore the doer might be ignorant.

20–27 Having separated off the involuntary in its two forms of compulsion and mistake, there remains to us the conception of the voluntary, as that whose cause is in an agent know-

27 θυμὸν ἁμαρτηθέντα; φευκτὰ μὲν γὰρ ἄμφω, δοκεῖ δὲ οὐχ ἧττον ἀνθρωπικὰ εἶναι τὰ ἄλογα πάθη. αἱ δὲ πράξεις τοῦ ἀνθρώπου ἀπὸ θυμοῦ καὶ ἐπιθυμίας. ἄτοπον δὴ τὸ τιθέναι ἀκούσια ταῦτα.

2 Διωρισμένων δὲ τοῦ τε ἑκουσίου καὶ τοῦ ἀκουσίου, περὶ

---

ing the circumstances of the action. This definition requires justification, owing to a false notion (οὐ καλῶς λέγεται) that acts done from anger or desire (which are 'in the agent') are involuntary. This notion is refuted by the following arguments: (1) It would prove too much, and would make all the actions of brutes and of children involuntary. (2) Some acts prompted by desire or anger are right and good. We must either call these involuntary, or say that, while these are voluntary, bad acts similarly prompted are involuntary. Either supposition is absurd. (3) There is a feeling of obligation (δεῖ), attaching sometimes to these emotions; we *ought* to desire some things and be angry at some. This feeling of 'ought' implies freedom. (4) Acts prompted by desire are pleasant; involuntary acts, painful. (5) We have as strong a feeling about errors of passion, as about errors of reason, that they are to be eschewed (φευκτά). The passions are as much part of the man as the reason, therefore acts prompted by them are acts of the man.

The polemic in these arguments does not seem to be directed against any philosophical school, but rather against a popular error. Aristotle does not deal with the maintainers of the doctrine of necessity as a whole, but only with those who, allowing that half our actions are free, would argue that the other half are not free. Such reasoners are comparatively easy to answer. The most important argument adduced by Aristotle is the third, where he implies that the idea of freedom is contained in that of duty. He does not draw out this principle, nor could he have done so without anticipating the philosophy of later times. The last argument seems to come to this, that you cannot separate a man from his passions, or say the reason is the man's self and the passions not. Elsewhere Aristotle says ὁ νοῦς αὐτὸς ἕκαστος. And in truth the relation of a man's desires to his individuality might be more deeply investigated than is here done.

φευκτὰ μὲν γὰρ ἄμφω] This seems a counterpart to the former argument, ἄνευ ἴσως τὸ λυπεῖσθαι φαίνεται ὧν δεῖ ὀρέγεσθαι. The passions are proved to be voluntary on account of the feeling of reprehension we have for errors of passion. On the emphatic opposition between φευκτόν and αἱρετόν, cf. *Eth.* x. ii. 5.

II. Having given a generic account of the voluntary, Aristotle proceeds to examine the special form of it which he calls προαίρεσις. This does not mean the will as a whole (for which, indeed, Aristotle has no one name), but a particular exhibition of it, namely, a conscious, determinate act of the will. 'Purpose' or 'determination' is perhaps the nearest word in our language, but in fact no word exactly corresponds. The contrasts and distinctions made in this chapter might at first seem unnecessary, until we observe that Aristotle is himself founding a new psychology. The

προαιρέσεως ἕπεται διελθεῖν· οἰκειότατον γὰρ εἶναι δοκεῖ
τῇ ἀρετῇ καὶ μᾶλλον τὰ ἤθη κρίνειν τῶν πράξεων. ἡ 2
προαίρεσις δὴ ἑκούσιον μὲν φαίνεται, οὐ ταὐτὸν δέ, ἀλλ' ἐπὶ
πλέον τὸ ἑκούσιον· τοῦ μὲν γὰρ ἑκουσίου καὶ παῖδες καὶ
τἆλλα ζῷα κοινωνεῖ, προαιρέσεως δ' οὔ, καὶ τὰ ἐξαίφνης
ἑκούσια μὲν λέγομεν, κατὰ προαίρεσιν δ' οὔ. οἱ δὲ λέγον- 3
τες αὐτὴν ἐπιθυμίαν ἢ θυμὸν ἢ βούλησιν ἤ τινα δόξαν οὐκ
ἐοίκασιν ὀρθῶς λέγειν. οὐ γὰρ κοινὸν ἡ προαίρεσις καὶ
τῶν ἀλόγων, ἐπιθυμία δὲ καὶ θυμός. καὶ ὁ ἀκρατὴς

---

word προαίρεσις only once occurs in Plato, and then not in its present psychological sense, but merely denoting 'selection' or 'choice.' *Parmenides*, p. 143 B: τί οὖν; ἐὰν προελώμεθα αὐτῶν εἴτε βούλει τὴν οὐσίαν καὶ τὸ ἕτερον εἴτε τὴν οὐσίαν καὶ τὸ ἓν εἴτε τὸ ἓν καὶ τὸ ἕτερον, ἆρ' οὐκ ἐν ἑκάστῃ τῇ προαιρέσει προαιρούμεθά τινε ὣ ὀρθῶς ἔχει καλεῖσθαι ἀμφοτέρω; It is true that the verb προαιρεῖσθαι is of frequent occurrence in Plato, but generally in the sense of 'selecting' or 'preferring,' and not 'purposing' or 'determining.' As in other cases, then, Aristotle takes up a floating term from common language, and gives it scientific definiteness, so that it becomes henceforth a psychological formula. His account of προαίρεσις in the present chapter is, that it is a species of the voluntary (ἑκούσιον μὲν φαίνεται, οὐ ταὐτὸν δέ, ἀλλ' ἐπὶ πλέον τὸ ἑκούσιον), and that it differs from anger, desire, wish, and any form of opinion. (1) It differs from desire or anger as not being shared by irrational creatures, as being often opposed to desire, &c. (2) It is still less like anger than like desire, anger excluding the notion of purpose or deliberate choice (ἥκιστα γὰρ τὰ διὰ θυμὸν κατὰ προαίρεσιν εἶναι δοκεῖ). (3) It is not wish, because we often wish for what is impossible, or beyond our control, and because, speaking generally, wish is of the end, whereas purpose is of the means, and restricts itself to what is in our power. (4) Nor is it opinion, which may be about anything, the eternal or the impossible, and which is characterised as true or false, not, like purpose, as good or bad. Nor is it opinion on matters of action. For opinion on good and evil does not constitute the moral character in the way that purpose does; again, the use of these terms in common language points out a difference between purpose and opinion.

Purpose then, being a species of the voluntary, implies also intellect (μετὰ λόγου καὶ διανοίας) and deliberation. It is a deliberate desire of what is within our own power (βουλευτικὴ ὄρεξις τῶν ἐφ' ἡμῖν, *Eth.* III. iii. 19).

1 οἰκειότατον γὰρ—πράξεων] 'For it seems most closely bound up with virtue, and to be a better criterion of moral character than even actions.' Cf. *Eth.* X. viii. 5: ἀμφισβητεῖται δὲ πότερον κυριώτερον τῆς ἀρετῆς ἡ προαίρεσις ἢ αἱ πράξεις, ὡς ἐν ἀμφοῖν οὔσης. The importance of this position as a ground-work for the whole doctrine of morality must be estimated by the advance which is made in it beyond what Plato had arrived at.

3 οἱ δὲ λέγοντες] There is a tendency in Plato to merge the distinctions of will and reason: whether some of his school are here alluded

ἐπιθυμῶν μὲν πράττει, προαιρούμενος δ' οὔ· ὁ ἐγκρατὴς
δ' ἀνάπαλιν προαιρούμενος μέν, ἐπιθυμῶν δ' οὔ. καὶ
προαιρέσει μὲν ἐπιθυμία ἐναντιοῦται, ἐπιθυμίᾳ δ' ἐπιθυμία
οὔ. καὶ ἡ μὲν ἐπιθυμία ἡδέος καὶ ἐπιλύπου, ἡ προαίρεσις
6 δ' οὔτε λυπηροῦ οὔθ' ἡδέος. θυμὸς δ' ἔτι ἧττον· ἥκιστα
7 γὰρ τὰ διὰ θυμὸν κατὰ προαίρεσιν εἶναι δοκεῖ. ἀλλὰ μὴν
οὐδὲ βούλησίς γε, καίπερ σύνεγγυς φαινόμενον· προαίρεσις
μὲν γὰρ οὐκ ἔστι τῶν ἀδυνάτων, καὶ εἴ τις φαίη προαιρεῖσθαι,
δοκοίη ἂν ἠλίθιος εἶναι· βούλησις δ' ἐστὶ τῶν ἀδυνάτων,
8 οἷον ἀθανασίας. καὶ ἡ μὲν βούλησίς ἐστι καὶ περὶ τὰ
μηδαμῶς δι' αὐτοῦ πραχθέντα ἄν, οἷον ὑποκριτήν τινα νικᾶν
ἢ ἀθλητήν· προαιρεῖται δὲ τὰ τοιαῦτα οὐδείς, ἀλλ' ὅσα
9 οἴεται γενέσθαι ἂν δι' αὐτοῦ. ἔτι δ' ἡ μὲν βούλησις τοῦ
τέλους ἐστὶ μᾶλλον, ἡ δὲ προαίρεσις τῶν πρὸς τὸ τέλος,
οἷον ὑγιαίνειν βουλόμεθα, προαιρούμεθα δὲ δι' ὧν ὑγιανοῦμεν,
καὶ εὐδαιμονεῖν βουλόμεθα μὲν καὶ φαμέν, προαιρούμεθα δὲ
λέγειν οὐχ ἁρμόζει· ὅλως γὰρ ἔοικεν ἡ προαίρεσις περὶ
10 τὰ ἐφ' ἡμῖν εἶναι. οὐδὲ δὴ δόξα ἂν εἴη· ἡ μὲν γὰρ δόξα
δοκεῖ περὶ πάντα εἶναι, καὶ οὐδὲν ἧττον περὶ τὰ ἀΐδια καὶ
τὰ ἀδύνατα ἢ τὰ ἐφ' ἡμῖν· καὶ τῷ ψευδεῖ καὶ ἀληθεῖ
διαιρεῖται, οὐ τῷ κακῷ καὶ ἀγαθῷ, ἡ προαίρεσις δὲ τούτοις
11 μᾶλλον. ὅλως μὲν οὖν δόξῃ ταὐτὸν ἴσως οὐδὲ λέγει οὐδείς.

---

to, or whether it is a merely popular confusion of terms that Aristotle attacks, is not clear.

5 καὶ προαιρέσει μὲν ἐπιθυμία ἐναντιοῦται, ἐπιθυμίᾳ δ' ἐπιθυμία οὔ] It might be said that desires are really contrary to each other, and contradict each other as much as purpose contradicts any desire, *e.g.* the desire for money is thwarted by that for pleasure. But the psychology is not very explicit here, and Aristotle seems to imply, without definitely expressing it, that in the moral will there is an element contradicting the desires in a manner different from that in which one desire interferes with another.

7 βούλησις δ' ἐστὶ τῶν ἀδυνάτων, οἷον ἀθανασίας] 'But wish is for impossibilities, as, for instance, immortality.' This is not a passage that can be cited as an indication of Aristotle's opinion with regard to a future life. 'Ἀθανασία here means 'exemption from death,' and does not touch the question as to the imperishability of the soul. It seems to have been a stock instance of an impossible wish. Dr. Cardwell quotes Xenophon's *Symposium* (1. § 15): οὔτε γὰρ ἔγωγε σπουδάσαι ἂν δυναίμην μᾶλλον, ἤπερ ἀθάνατος γενέσθαι.

11–13 ὅλως μὲν οὖν—ἴσμεν] 'Now that purpose is identical with opinion as a whole, perhaps no one maintains at all. But neither is it identical with any special kind of opinion

ἀλλ' οὐδέ τινι· τῷ γὰρ προαιρεῖσθαι τἀγαθὰ ἢ τὰ κακὰ
ποιοί τινές ἐσμεν, τῷ δὲ δοξάζειν οὔ. καὶ προαιρούμεθα 12
μὲν λαβεῖν ἢ φυγεῖν ἤ τι τῶν τοιούτων, δοξάζομεν δὲ τί
ἐστιν ἢ τίνι συμφέρει ἢ πῶς· λαβεῖν δ' ἢ φυγεῖν οὐ πάνυ
δοξάζομεν. καὶ ἡ μὲν προαίρεσις ἐπαινεῖται τῷ εἶναι οὗ 13
δεῖ μᾶλλον ἢ τῷ ὀρθῶς, ἡ δὲ δόξα τῷ ὡς ἀληθῶς. καὶ
προαιρούμεθα μὲν ἃ μάλιστα ἴσμεν ἀγαθὰ ὄντα, δοξάζομεν
δὲ ἃ οὐ πάνυ ἴσμεν. δοκοῦσί τε οὐχ οἱ αὐτοὶ προαιρεῖσθαί 14
τε ἄριστα καὶ δοξάζειν, ἀλλ' ἔνιοι δοξάζειν μὲν ἄμεινον,
διὰ κακίαν δ' αἱρεῖσθαι οὐχ ἃ δεῖ. εἰ δὲ προγίνεται δόξα 15
τῆς προαιρέσεως ἢ παρακολουθεῖ, οὐδὲν διαφέρει· οὐ τοῦτο
γὰρ σκοποῦμεν, ἀλλ' εἰ ταὐτόν ἐστι δόξῃ τινί. τί οὖν ἢ 16
ποῖόν τι ἐστίν, ἐπειδὴ τῶν εἰρημένων οὐθέν; ἑκούσιον μὲν
δὴ φαίνεται, τὸ δ' ἑκούσιον οὐ πᾶν προαιρετόν. ἀλλ' ἆρά 17
γε τὸ προβεβουλευμένον; ἡ γὰρ προαίρεσις μετὰ λόγου
καὶ διανοίας. ὑποσημαίνειν δ' ἔοικε καὶ τοὔνομα ὡς ὂν
πρὸ ἑτέρων αἱρετόν.

Βουλεύονται δὲ πότερα περὶ πάντων, καὶ πᾶν βουλευτόν 3

For in purposing what is good or bad our moral character consists,—not in opining it. And we purpose to take or avoid, or something of the kind, but we opine what a thing is, or for whom it is good, or how; but we do not exactly opine to take or avoid. And while purpose is praised rather by the epithets, "of the right object," or "rightly," opinion is praised by the epithet "truly." And we purpose on the one hand things that we know for certain to be good, but we opine what we do not exactly know for certain.'

οὐδέ τινι] i.e. purpose is not identical with an opinion as to moral matters. The first argument to prove this is characteristic of Aristotle as opposed to Plato. He says, 'our moral character does not consist in our opinions on good and evil, but in the deliberate acts of our will.' This is guarded afterwards by the limitation (§ 15) that 'opinion may go to form purpose, and may again be reacted on by it;' but the question is, are they identical?

12—13. The arguments in these sections consist in an appeal to language—we cannot speak of 'opining to take,' &c.

μᾶλλον ἢ τῷ ὀρθῶς] Ἢ is of course not connected with *μᾶλλον*. It simply means 'or.' Ὀρθῶς, which should properly go with a verb, seems used because the verb *προαιρεῖσθαι* was much commoner before Aristotle than the abstract form *προαίρεσις*. Ὀρθή is applied to ὄρεξις (the element of desire in *προαίρεσις*), *Eth.* VI. ii. 2.

III. Since Purpose implies deliberation, this latter is now analysed, and an account is given, first of its object, secondly of its mode of operation. The object of deliberation is determined by an exhaustive process. All things are either eternal or mutable; we do *not* deliberate about things

ἐστιν, ἢ περὶ ἐνίων οὐκ ἔστι βουλή; λεκτέον δ' ἴσως βου-
2 λευτὸν οὐχ ὑπὲρ οὗ βουλεύσαιτ' ἄν τις ἠλίθιος ἢ μαινόμενος,
3 ἀλλ' ὑπὲρ ὧν ὁ νοῦν ἔχων. περὶ δὲ τῶν ἀϊδίων οὐδεὶς
βουλεύεται, οἷον περὶ τοῦ κόσμου ἢ τῆς διαμέτρου καὶ τῆς
4 πλευρᾶς, ὅτι ἀσύμμετροι. ἀλλ' οὐδὲ περὶ τῶν ἐν κινήσει,
ἀεὶ δὲ κατὰ ταὐτὰ γινομένων, εἴτ' ἐξ ἀνάγκης εἴτε καὶ φύσει
ἢ διά τινα αἰτίαν ἄλλην, οἷον τροπῶν καὶ ἀνατολῶν. οὐδὲ
5 περὶ τῶν ἄλλοτε ἄλλως, οἷον αὐχμῶν καὶ ὄμβρων. οὐδὲ
6 περὶ τῶν ἀπὸ τύχης, οἷον θησαυροῦ εὑρέσεως. ἀλλ' οὐδὲ

---

eternal. Of things mutable, we do not deliberate about those things which are regulated by necessity, by nature, or by chance. Hence it remains that we deliberate about mutable things within the power of man, and not about all such, but about those within our own power, and not about ends, but about means, and where there is room for question. The mode of operation in deliberating is a kind of analysis. Assuming as desirable some end, we first ask what means will immediately produce this end, what again will produce those means, and so on till we have brought the last link of the chain of causation to ourselves, when we commence acting at once, the last step in the analysis being the first in the productive process. If any step occurs which is on the one hand necessary for the given end, and on the other hand unattainable by us, the chain cannot be completed; the deliberation is relinquished. But if all the steps are feasible, that which was indefinite before at once becomes definite, and purpose succeeds deliberation. A discussion of the nature of *εὐβουλία* as related to *φρόνησις* occurs *Eth.* vi. ix., but is evidently written quite independently of the present chapter, on which it improves by employing the formula of the moral syllogism, and by inquiring after the faculty which perceives ends. We might have expected Aristotle to say that in the deliberation which precedes an action some account should always be taken of the right or wrong of the action. But here the only question is represented to be, how a given end is to be obtained? What action will serve as a means to it? Hence while the present discussion must be considered a subtle piece of elementary psychology, and of great merit in the infancy of the science, on the other hand it seems incomplete as regards the theory of morals.

3—5 *περὶ δὲ τῶν ἀϊδίων—εὑρέσεως*] 'No man deliberates about eternal things, such as the universe, or the incommensurability of the diagonal and the side in a square; nor indeed about things in motion, if the motion takes place invariably in the same way, whether of necessity, or by nature, or from any other cause, as in the instance of the solstices and the risings of the sun: nor about things entirely variable, like droughts and rains: nor about matter of chance, like the finding of a treasure.' The opposition to τὰ ἀΐδια is τὰ *ἐν κινήσει*. The more exhaustive division of objects would have been that which is given *Eth.* vi. i. 6, into τὰ *ἐνδεχόμενα ἄλλως ἔχειν* and τὰ *μὴ ἐνδεχόμενα*. But there is an absence of logical formulæ in the present book which is observable. The instances here given

περὶ τῶν ἀνθρωπικῶν πάντων, οἷον πῶς ἂν Σκύθαι ἄριστα
πολιτεύοιντο οὐδεὶς Λακεδαιμονίων βουλεύεται. οὐ γὰρ
γένοιτ' ἂν τούτων οὐθὲν δι' ἡμῶν. βουλευόμεθα δὲ περὶ 7
τῶν ἐφ' ἡμῖν πρακτῶν· ταῦτα δὲ καὶ ἔστι λοιπά. αἴτια
γὰρ δοκοῦσιν εἶναι φύσις καὶ ἀνάγκη καὶ τύχη, ἔτι δὲ νοῦς
καὶ πᾶν τὸ δι' ἀνθρώπου. τῶν δ' ἀνθρώπων ἕκαστοι
βουλεύονται περὶ τῶν δι' αὑτῶν πρακτῶν. καὶ περὶ μὲν 8
τὰς ἀκριβεῖς καὶ αὐτάρκεις τῶν ἐπιστημῶν οὐκ ἔστι βουλή,
οἷον περὶ γραμμάτων (οὐ γὰρ διστάζομεν πῶς γραπτέον)·
ἀλλ' ὅσα γίνεται δι' ἡμῶν, μὴ ὡσαύτως δ' ἀεί, περὶ τούτων
βουλευόμεθα οἷον περὶ τῶν κατὰ ἰατρικὴν καὶ χρηματι-

---

of the eternal are (1) the universe, (2) a particular mathematical truth—that the diagonal of a square is incommensurate with its side. That the universe is eternal, being uncreated, indestructible, and, as a whole, immutable, was part of Aristotle's physical philosophy. Cf. *de Cælo* I. x. 10: Ὅλως δ' εἰ τὸ ὅλον σῶμα συνεχὲς ὂν ὁτὲ μὲν οὕτως ὁτὲ δ' ἐκείνως διατίθεται καὶ διακεκόσμηται, ἡ δὲ τοῦ ὅλου σύστασίς ἐστι κόσμος καὶ οὐρανός, οὐκ ἂν ὁ κόσμος γίγνοιτο καὶ φθείροιτο, ἀλλ' αἱ διαθέσεις αὐτοῦ.—The above mathematical truth is called 'eternal,' *De Gen. An.* II. vi. 15: ἐπεὶ καὶ τὸ τρίγωνον ἔχειν δυσὶν ὀρθαῖς ἴσας ἀεὶ καὶ τὸ τὴν διάμετρον ἀσύμμετρον εἶναι πρὸς τὴν πλευρὰν ἀΐδιον. It is mentioned as one of those things which philosophy begins by wondering at, and ends by feeling their universal necessity. *Metaphys.* I. ii. 15: καθάπερ τῶν θαυμάτων ταὐτόματα τοῖς μήπω τεθεωρηκόσι τὴν αἰτίαν, ἢ περὶ τὰς τοῦ ἡλίου τροπὰς ἢ τὴν τῆς διαμέτρου ἀσυμμετρίαν· θαυμαστὸν γὰρ εἶναι δοκεῖ πᾶσιν, εἴ τι τῷ ἐλαχίστῳ μὴ μετρεῖται. δεῖ δὲ εἰς τοὐναντίον—ἀποτελευτῆσαι·—οὐθὲν γὰρ ἂν οὕτω θαυμάσειεν ἀνὴρ γεωμετρικὸς ὡς εἰ γένοιτο ἡ διάμετρος μετρητή. Two kinds of eternity seem here placed in juxtaposition—one physical, the other mathematical. But eternity or necessity can only exist in relation to the laws of the mind that perceives it. Therefore we might say that these two kinds of eternity find their meeting-point in a metaphysic above the division of the sciences. Aristotle however is writing οὐ κατ' ἀκρίβειαν.

7 αἴτια γὰρ—ἀνθρώπου] 'For the causes of things seem to be as follows, nature, and necessity, and chance, and again reason and all that depends on man.' A similar classification of causes is implied *Eth.* I. ix. 5, VI. iv. 4. The relation of necessity and chance, as causes, to nature, forms the subject of Aristotle's *Physics*, Book II. Chapters IV.—IX. See Vol. I. Essay V.

8 καὶ περὶ—γραπτέον] 'And on the one hand there is no deliberation about sciences that are fixed and complete in themselves, as for instance about writing—for we do not doubt how we ought to write.' The ἀκριβεῖς ἐπιστῆμαι here meant are not the 'exact sciences,' as we may judge from the instance given. Ἀκριβὴς seems equivalent to 'fixed' (cf. the note on *Eth.* I. vii. 18), and ἐπιστήμη is used in a sense equivalent to τέχνη, though the words are immediately afterwards distinguished.

στικήν, καὶ περὶ κυβερνητικὴν μᾶλλον ἢ γυμναστικήν, ὅσῳ
9 ἧττον διηκρίβωται, καὶ ἔτι περὶ τῶν λοιπῶν ὁμοίως, μᾶλλον
δὲ καὶ περὶ τὰς τέχνας ἢ τὰς ἐπιστήμας· μᾶλλον γὰρ
10 περὶ αὐτὰς διστάζομεν. τὸ βουλεύεσθαι δὲ ἐν τοῖς ὡς ἐπὶ
τὸ πολύ, ἀδήλοις δὲ πῶς ἀποβήσεται, καὶ ἐν οἷς ἀδιόριστον.
συμβούλους δὲ παραλαμβάνομεν εἰς τὰ μεγάλα, ἀπι-
11 στοῦντες ἡμῖν αὐτοῖς ὡς οὐχ ἱκανοῖς διαγνῶναι. βουλευόμεθα δ' οὐ περὶ τῶν τελῶν ἀλλὰ περὶ τῶν πρὸς τὰ τέλη.
οὔτε γὰρ ἰατρὸς βουλεύεται εἰ ὑγιάσει, οὔτε ῥήτωρ εἰ
πείσει, οὔτε πολιτικὸς εἰ εὐνομίαν ποιήσει, οὐδὲ τῶν λοιπῶν
οὐδεὶς περὶ τοῦ τέλους· ἀλλὰ θέμενοι τέλος τι, πῶς καὶ
διὰ τίνων ἔσται σκοποῦσι, καὶ διὰ πλειόνων μὲν φαινομένου
γίνεσθαι διὰ τίνος ῥᾷστα καὶ κάλλιστα ἐπισκοποῦσι, δι'
ἑνὸς δ' ἐπιτελουμένου πῶς διὰ τούτου ἔσται κἀκεῖνο διὰ
τίνος, ἕως ἂν ἔλθωσιν ἐπὶ τὸ πρῶτον αἴτιον, ὃ ἐν τῇ εὑρέσει
ἔσχατόν ἐστιν· ὁ γὰρ βουλευόμενος ἔοικε ζητεῖν καὶ
12 ἀναλύειν τὸν εἰρημένον τρόπον ὥσπερ διάγραμμα. φαίνεται
δ' ἡ μὲν ζήτησις οὐ πᾶσα εἶναι βούλευσις, οἷον αἱ μαθημα-
τικαί, ἡ δὲ βούλευσις πᾶσα ζήτησις, καὶ τὸ ἔσχατον ἐν τῇ
13 ἀναλύσει πρῶτον εἶναι ἐν τῇ γενέσει. κἂν μὲν ἀδυνάτῳ

11 οὔτε γὰρ—διάγραμμα] 'The physician does not deliberate whether he is to cure, nor the orator whether he is to persuade, nor the statesman whether he is to produce law and order. The end is not the subject of deliberation in any science. An end being assumed, we consider how and by what means it can be brought about; if it appear that there are more ways than one, we inquire which is the easiest and best; if it can be accomplished by one mean alone, we inquire how this produces the end, and by what it is itself produced, until we come to that which as a cause is first, but is the last thing to be discovered; for such deliberation as we describe is like seeking the solution of a geometrical problem by analysis of the diagram.' The process of deliberation is analytical, proceeding backwards ἐπὶ τὴν ἀρχήν. It ends with the πρῶτον αἴτιον, i.e. the individual will. 'Will,' says Kant, 'is that kind of causality attributed to living agents, in so far as they are possessed of reason, and freedom is such a property of that causality as enables them to originate events independently of foreign determining causes.' That each man is, as regards his own acts, an originating cause not determined by other causes, is Aristotle's view throughout. Kant's definition throws light upon this.

κἀκεῖνο] Refers to ἑνὸς and διὰ τούτου.

ὥσπερ διάγραμμα] Aristotle compares deliberation with the analysis of mathematical problems. Given a

ἐντύχωσιν, ἀφίστανται, οἷον εἰ χρημάτων δεῖ, ταῦτα δὲ μὴ οἷόν τε πορισθῆναι· ἐὰν δὲ δυνατὸν φαίνηται, ἐγχειροῦσι πράττειν. δυνατὰ δὲ ἃ δι' ἡμῶν γένοιτ' ἄν· τὰ γὰρ διὰ τῶν φίλων δι' ἡμῶν πως ἐστίν· ἡ γὰρ ἀρχὴ ἐν ἡμῖν.
ζητεῖται δ' ὁτὲ μὲν τὰ ὄργανα, ὁτὲ δ' ἡ χρεία αὐτῶν. 14
ὁμοίως δὲ καὶ ἐν τοῖς λοιποῖς ὁτὲ μὲν δι' οὗ, ὁτὲ δὲ πῶς ἢ
διὰ τίνος. ἔοικε δή, καθάπερ εἴρηται, ἄνθρωπος εἶναι ἀρχὴ 15
τῶν πράξεων· ἡ δὲ βουλὴ περὶ τῶν αὐτῷ πρακτῶν, αἱ δὲ
πράξεις ἄλλων ἕνεκα. οὐκ ἂν οὖν εἴη βουλευτὸν τὸ τέλος 16
ἀλλὰ τὰ πρὸς τὰ τέλη. οὐδὲ δὴ τὰ καθ' ἕκαστα, οἷον εἰ
ἄρτος τοῦτο ἢ πέπεπται ὡς δεῖ· αἰσθήσεως γὰρ ταῦτα.
εἰ δὲ ἀεὶ βουλεύσεται, εἰς ἄπειρον ἥξει. βουλευτὸν δὲ καὶ 17
προαιρετὸν τὸ αὐτό, πλὴν ἀφωρισμένον ἤδη τὸ προαιρετόν· τὸ γὰρ ἐκ τῆς βουλῆς προκριθὲν προαιρετόν ἐστιν. παύεται γὰρ ἕκαστος ζητῶν πῶς πράξει, ὅταν εἰς αὑτὸν ἀναγάγῃ τὴν ἀρχήν, καὶ αὑτοῦ εἰς τὸ ἡγούμενον· τοῦτο γάρ τό

---

problem in geometry, *e.g.*, to find the method of constructing some figure. Assume it as constructed, and draw it accordingly. See what condition is immediately necessary, and what again will produce this, &c.

14 ζητεῖται δ'—διὰ τίνος] 'The question is sometimes what instruments are necessary, sometimes how they are to be used; and, speaking generally, we have to find sometimes the means by which, sometimes the manner or the person by whom.' Michelet makes a difficulty about ἐν τοῖς λοιποῖς, explaining it 'in reliquis categoriis;' but the Paraphrast renders it simply καὶ ἄλλως.

15 ἔοικε δή—ἕνεκα] 'It seems, therefore, that man is, as we have said, the cause of his actions; that deliberation is about the things to be done by ourselves, and that actions are means to something else.' In one sense, and so far as deliberation is concerned, actions must be regarded as means. Cf. *Rhetoric*, I. vi. 1: πρόκειται τῷ συμβουλεύοντι σκοπὸς τὸ συμφέρον, βουλεύονται δὲ οὐ περὶ τοῦ τέλους ἀλλὰ περὶ τῶν πρὸς τὸ τέλος, ταῦτα δ' ἐστὶ τὰ συμφέροντα κατὰ τὰς πράξεις. But in another sense, and from a moral point of view, each action is an end-in-itself. Cf. *Eth.* VI. ii. 5: Οὐ τέλος ἁπλῶς—τὸ ποιητόν. 'Αλλὰ τὸ πρακτόν· ἡ γὰρ εὐπραξία τέλος, ἡ δ' ὄρεξις τούτου.

16 εἰς ἄπειρον ἥξει] 'It will go on to infinity'—impersonal. Cf. I. ii. 1, I. vii. 7.

17 παύεται γὰρ—προαιρούμενον] 'For every one stops inquiring how he shall act, when he has brought home the first link in the chain to himself and to the guiding principle in himself; that is to say, to that which purposes.' Throughout these discussions we find a striking clearness of expression for some of the ordinary phenomena of consciousness; on the other hand, evident tokens that the psychology is new and tentative; and again, a want of deeper inquiry into

18 προαιρούμενον. δῆλον δὲ τοῦτο καὶ ἐκ τῶν ἀρχαίων
πολιτειῶν, ἃς Ὅμηρος ἐμιμεῖτο· οἱ γὰρ βασιλεῖς ἃ προ-
19 έλοιντο ἀνήγγελλον τῷ δήμῳ. ὄντος δὲ τοῦ προαιρετοῦ
βουλευτοῦ ὀρεκτοῦ τῶν ἐφ' ἡμῖν, καὶ ἡ προαίρεσις ἂν εἴη
βουλευτικὴ ὄρεξις τῶν ἐφ' ἡμῖν· ἐκ τοῦ βουλεύσασθαι γὰρ
20 κρίναντες ὀρεγόμεθα κατὰ τὴν βούλευσιν. ἡ μὲν οὖν
προαίρεσις τύπῳ εἰρήσθω, καὶ περὶ ποῖά ἐστι, καὶ ὅτι τῶν
πρὸς τὰ τέλη.

4 Ἡ δὲ βούλησις ὅτι μὲν τοῦ τέλους ἐστίν, εἴρηται,

---

the nature of personality and of the will.

18 δῆλον δὲ—δήμῳ] 'Now this is exemplified from the old polities which Homer depicted; for the kings used to announce to the people the course they had selected.' Cf. the conduct of Agamemnon, *Iliad* ii. 53, sqq. A modern illustration is furnished by the French Parliaments, which used to register the edicts presented to them by the king as a matter of course. The Paraphrast explains the comparison by making the people represent the προαίρεσις—*Εἰσάγει γὰρ τοὺς βασιλεῖς μετὰ τὴν βουλὴν τὸ προκριθὲν ἀναγγέλλοντας τῷ δήμῳ ὥσπερ τῇ προαιρέσει, ὥστε πραχθῆναι.* The people were required to acquiesce in and carry out the decisions of the kings, which else would have remained unratified. So the reason announces its decisions to the will or purpose, i.e. the active powers in the mind. Metaphors of this sort never accurately represent mental distinctions. The present comparison has many flaws. For the προαίρεσις is here called τὸ ἡγούμενον, which does not answer to the people, distinguished from the king. Again, it is the individual (ἕκαστος), not the reason, that announces his deliberations to the leading part in himself. What constitutes the individual as separate from the will or purpose? And, is not reason part of purpose, how then can it be distinguished from it?

19 ὄντος δὲ—βούλευσιν] 'If the object of purpose is that, which, being in our power, we desire after deliberation, purpose will be a deliberate desire of things in our power. After deliberating we decide, and form a desire in accordance with our deliberation.' The Paraphrast here reads κατὰ τὴν βούλησιν at the end of this passage. There might seem to be something plausible in the change, because βούλευσις is represented as confining itself to means; hence how can we be said to desire κατὰ τὴν βούλευσιν? Consistently, our desires must depend on something else, namely, βούλησις—deliberation is the faculty for attaining them. On the other hand, the phrases βουλευτοῦ ὀρεκτοῦ, and βουλευτικὴ ὄρεξις, run the consideration of means and ends together.

IV. Hitherto every act has been regarded as a means, and has been accounted voluntary because originating in the individual. Deliberation and purpose have been restricted in their function to the mere choice and taking of means. A great question therefore remains to be mooted, whence do we get our conception of ends? What is the nature of the faculty called βούλησις, which has

δοκεῖ δὲ τοῖς μὲν ἀγαθοῦ εἶναι, τοῖς δὲ τοῦ φαινομένου ἀγαθοῦ. συμβαίνει δὲ τοῖς μὲν τὸ βουλητὸν τἀγα- 2

---

been assumed to be the faculty of ends? Are we as free in the choice of these, as we are in that of the means? Aristotle contents himself with mentioning in the present chapter that there are two extreme opinions, the one (that of Plato) that wish is always for the good; the other (that of some of the sophists) that it is for the apparent good. He rejects both of these, the first as contradicting facts, the second as ignoring any true object of wish. He takes a position between them, that, abstractedly and ideally, as appealing to the universal reason (ἁπλῶς μὲν καὶ κατ' ἀλήθειαν) the good is the object of wish, while to the individual mind only what appears good can seem desirable; hence, although the good man, who has the *mens sana*, and is thus in accordance with the universal reason, and is its exponent in particular cases (τἀληθὲς ἐν ἑκάστοις ὁρᾷ, ὥσπερ κανὼν καὶ μέτρον αὐτῶν ὤν), wishes for the good alone, others are deceived by false appearances and by pleasure, and choose what is not truly good. In the statement that the morally good man (σπουδαῖος) wishes aright, there is implied the doctrine, afterwards developed by the Peripatetics, that it is Virtue that gives a right conception of ends. *Cf. Eth. Eud.* II. xi. 1, and *Eth. Nic.* VI. xii. 8, and see Vol. I. Essay I. p. 57.

1 δοκεῖ δὲ τοῖς μὲν ἀγαθοῦ εἶναι] This doctrine is found stated at length in the *Gorgias* of Plato, p. 466, sqq. Polus having argued that the position of a tyrant or orator is enviable, because 'he can do what he wishes,' Socrates answers that 'the tyrant or orator does nothing that he wishes:' φημὶ γάρ, ὦ Πῶλε, ἐγὼ καὶ τοὺς ῥήτορας καὶ τοὺς τυράννους δύνασθαι μὲν ἐν ταῖς πόλεσι σμικρότατον—οὐδὲν γὰρ ποιεῖν ὧν βούλονται, ὡς ἔπος εἰπεῖν· ποιεῖν μέντοι ὅ τι ἂν αὐτοῖς δόξῃ βέλτιστον εἶναι. Then follows an account of βούλησις, that it is of ends not means. Πότερον οὖν σοι δοκοῦσιν οἱ ἄνθρωποι τοῦτο βούλεσθαι, ὃ ἂν πράττωσιν ἑκάστοτε, ἢ ἐκεῖνο οὗ ἕνεκα πράττουσι τοῦθ' ὃ πράττουσιν; By which it can be demonstrated that βούλησις is of the absolute good. The difference between Plato's account and the one above is, that Plato distinguishes βούλησις from ἐπιθυμία, while Aristotle does not. The βούλησις of Plato is the higher will, or desire of the Universal. In this higher sense of the word wish, no one wishes except for what is good, that is, in his best moments, in the deepest recesses of his nature, if the true bearings of his wish be pointed out to him. In this sense the wish of the individual is in accordance with universal reason, and is an expression of it. In a lower sense, we wish with different parts of our nature, and thus wish for all sorts of things, bad as well as good. But to this latter kind of wish the name 'desire' is appropriate. The tenet ὅτι ἀγαθοῦ βούλησίς ἐστιν is of great importance for morals. It implies much that modern systems would convey in other terms, such as the 'supremacy of conscience,' the 'autonomy of the will,' &c. Elsewhere Aristotle distinctly maintains it. *Cf. Metaphys.* XI. vii. 2: τὸ ὀρεκτὸν καὶ τὸ νοητὸν κινεῖ οὐ κινούμενα. τούτων τὰ πρῶτα τὰ αὐτά (transcendentally the objects of reason and of longing are identical). Ἐπιθυμητὸν μὲν γὰρ τὸ φαινόμενον καλόν, βουλητὸν δὲ πρῶτον τὸ ὂν καλόν. In

θὸν λέγουσι μὴ εἶναι βουλητὸν ὃ βούλεται ὁ μὴ ὀρθῶς
αἱρούμενος (εἰ γὰρ ἔσται βουλητόν, καὶ ἀγαθόν· ἦν δ', εἰ
3 οὕτως ἔτυχε, κακόν), τοῖς δ' αὖ τὸ φαινόμενον ἀγαθὸν τὸ
βουλητὸν λέγουσι μὴ εἶναι φύσει βουλητόν, ἀλλ' ἑκάστῳ
τὸ δοκοῦν· ἄλλο δ' ἄλλῳ φαίνεται, καὶ εἰ οὕτως ἔτυχε,
4 τἀναντία. εἰ δὲ δὴ ταῦτα μὴ ἀρέσκει, ἆρα φατέον ἁπλῶς
μὲν καὶ κατ' ἀλήθειαν βουλητὸν εἶναι τἀγαθόν, ἑκάστῳ δὲ
τὸ φαινόμενον; τῷ μὲν οὖν σπουδαίῳ τὸ κατ' ἀλήθειαν
εἶναι, τῷ δὲ φαύλῳ τὸ τυχόν, ὥσπερ καὶ ἐπὶ τῶν σωμάτων
τοῖς μὲν εὖ διακειμένοις ὑγιεινά ἐστι τὰ κατ' ἀλήθειαν
τοιαῦτα ὄντα, τοῖς δ' ἐπινόσοις ἕτερα. ὁμοίως δὲ καὶ
πικρὰ καὶ γλυκέα καὶ θερμὰ καὶ βαρέα καὶ τῶν ἄλλων
ἕκαστα· ὁ σπουδαῖος γὰρ ἕκαστα κρίνει ὀρθῶς, καὶ ἐν
5 ἑκάστοις τἀληθὲς αὐτῷ φαίνεται. καθ' ἑκάστην γὰρ ἕξιν
ἴδιά ἐστι καλὰ καὶ ἡδέα, καὶ διαφέρει πλεῖστον ἴσως ὁ
σπουδαῖος τῷ τἀληθὲς ἐν ἑκάστοις ὁρᾶν, ὥσπερ κανὼν καὶ
μέτρον αὐτῶν ὤν. τοῖς πολλοῖς δὲ ἡ ἀπάτη διὰ τὴν ἡδονὴν
ἔοικε γίνεσθαι· οὐ γὰρ οὖσα ἀγαθὸν φαίνεται· αἱροῦνται
οὖν τὸ ἡδὺ ὡς ἀγαθόν, τὴν δὲ λύπην ὡς κακὸν φεύγουσιν.

De Animâ, III. x. 4. he makes the wish (or will) side with reason, in opposition to desire. Ἡ γὰρ βούλησις ὄρεξις· ὅταν δὲ κατὰ τὸν λογισμὸν κινῆται, καὶ κατὰ βούλησιν κινεῖται. ἡ δ' ὄρεξις κινεῖ παρὰ τὸν λογισμόν· ἡ γὰρ ἐπιθυμία ὄρεξίς τίς ἐστιν. In other parts of the *Ethics* also (which may hence be concluded to have been composed at a different period from this chapter) this distinction between βούλησις, the general wish, and any particular desire or determination, is observed. Cf. *Eth.* v. ix. 6: οὐθεὶς γὰρ βούλεται οὐδ' ὁ ἀκρατής, ἀλλὰ παρὰ τὴν βούλησιν πράττει. οὔτε γὰρ βούλεται οὐδεὶς ὃ μὴ οἴεται εἶναι σπουδαῖον. VIII. xiii. 8: τοῦτο δὲ συμβαίνει διὰ τὸ βούλεσθαι μὲν πάντας ἢ τοὺς πλείστους τὰ καλά, προαιρεῖσθαι δὲ τὰ ὠφέλιμα.

τοῖς δὲ τοῦ φαινομένου ἀγαθοῦ] This is a corollary of the doctrine of Protagoras. If the individual could only know what 'seemed' to him, he could only wish for what seemed good. Thus the objective distinction between good and evil is done away with (συμβαίνει μὴ εἶναι φύσει βουλητόν). Cf. *Metaphys.* x. vi. 1: Ἐκεῖνος (ὁ Πρωταγόρας) ἔφη πάντων χρημάτων εἶναι μέτρον ἄνθρωπον, οὐδὲν ἕτερον λέγων ἢ τὸ δοκοῦν ἑκάστῳ τοῦτο καὶ εἶναι παγίως. τούτου δὲ γιγνομένου τὸ αὐτὸ συμβαίνει καὶ εἶναι καὶ μὴ εἶναι, καὶ κακὸν καὶ ἀγαθὸν εἶναι.

4 ὁ σπουδαῖος γὰρ ἕκαστα κρίνει ὀρθῶς] The good man is made here again, as above (II. vi. 15), that standard of right and wrong, that exponent of the universal reason, by which Aristotle escapes being forced into an utterly relative system of morals.

5 οὐ γὰρ οὖσα ἀγαθὸν φαίνεται] The 'pleasant' is characterised as 'the seeming good' in the Peripa-

Ὄντος δὴ βουλητοῦ μὲν τοῦ τέλους, βουλευτῶν δὲ καὶ 5
προαιρετῶν τῶν πρὸς τὸ τέλος, αἱ περὶ ταῦτα πράξεις κατὰ
προαίρεσιν ἂν εἶεν καὶ ἑκούσιοι. αἱ δὲ τῶν ἀρετῶν ἐνέργειαι
περὶ ταῦτα. ἐφ' ἡμῖν δὲ καὶ ἡ ἀρετή, ὁμοίως δὲ καὶ ἡ 2

---

telic book *De Motu Animal.* vi. 5: δεῖ δὲ τεθέναι καὶ τὸ φαινόμενον ἀγαθὸν ἀγαθοῦ χώραν ἔχειν, καὶ τὸ ἡδύ· φαινόμενον γάρ ἐστιν ἀγαθόν.

V. Aristotle winds up his account of the voluntary, by arguing that virtue and vice are free (ἐφ' ἡμῖν δὲ καὶ ἡ ἀρετή, ὁμοίως δὲ καὶ ἡ κακία). As before remarked, this must not be taken as a metaphysical discussion of the question of free-will. Partly, the question had never yet been fully started; partly, Aristotle would have thought it foreign to an ethical treatise; partly, we find in the present chapter that same elementary and tentative character which marks the previous discussions in this book. In dealing with one of the real difficulties of the question at the end of the chapter, Aristotle contents himself with a very qualified and moderate assertion of freedom, which contrasts with the dogmatic statements on the same subject in the *Ethics* of Eudemus. The discussion here is evidently suggested by, and directed against, the doctrine of the Platonists, that 'vice is involuntary,' since it consists in ignorance. The arguments are as follows: (1) All action implies the possibility of its contrary, hence if to act rightly be in our power, to act wrongly must be in our power also. (2) That an individual is the originating cause of his actions, is a conception which it is difficult to get rid of. This implies freedom. (3) We all act as if vice were free as well as virtue. It is punished by the state. Even for ignorance and carelessness producing vice, men are held to be responsible. (4) Men must not charge their acts upon their natural character—rather their character is produced by their acts. (5) The analogy of bodily infirmities shows us that if some vices are congenital, some, at all events, are self-produced. (6) The great difficulty of the question is as follows: If, as was said above (Chapter IV.), we each of us desire what seems good; if our conception of the end, that is, our idea of good, depends not on our own will, but on nature, or our character and tendency from birth; and if all our acts are determined by this conception of the end, how can they be called free? Aristotle answers by putting various alternatives: (α) you may either accept this position in its full extent. It will then apply to virtue as well as vice. Both will be equally under a law of nature. Neither will be voluntary. But this the mind seems to revolt against. (β) Or, you may say that while the end is absolutely determined, the means to it are all free as springing from the will of the individual. Thus, virtue and vice are free, because all their parts are free. (γ) Or, you may modify the doctrine by admitting that there is something self-produced and self-determined in the character as a whole, and therefore in the idea of good, which is to determine our actions.

1—2 Ὄντος δὴ—ἡ κακία) 'The end then being the object of wish, while the means are the objects of

κακία. ἐν οἷς γὰρ ἐφ' ἡμῖν τὸ πράττειν, καὶ τὸ μὴ πράττειν, καὶ ἐν οἷς τὸ μή, καὶ τὸ ναί· ὥστ' εἰ τὸ πράττειν καλὸν ὂν ἐφ' ἡμῖν ἐστί, καὶ τὸ μὴ πράττειν ἐφ' ἡμῖν ἔσται αἰσχρὸν ὄν, καὶ εἰ τὸ μὴ πράττειν καλὸν ὂν ἐφ' ἡμῖν, καὶ
3 τὸ πράττειν αἰσχρὸν ὂν ἐφ' ἡμῖν. εἰ δ' ἐφ' ἡμῖν τὰ καλὰ πράττειν καὶ τὰ αἰσχρά, ὁμοίως δὲ καὶ τὸ μὴ πράττειν, τοῦτο δ' ἦν τὸ ἀγαθοῖς καὶ κακοῖς εἶναι, ἐφ' ἡμῖν ἄρα
4 τὸ ἐπιεικέσι καὶ φαύλοις εἶναι. τὸ δὲ λέγειν ὡς

οὐδεὶς ἑκὼν πονηρὸς οὐδ' ἄκων μάκαρ,

ἔοικε τὸ μὲν ψευδεῖ τὸ δ' ἀληθεῖ· μακάριος μὲν γὰρ οὐδεὶς

---

deliberation and purpose, the actions that are concerned with the means must depend on purpose and must be voluntary. But every calling out of the virtues into play is concerned with the means; virtue accordingly is in our power, and in like manner so is vice.'

αἱ περὶ ταῦτα πράξεις] The words *περὶ ταῦτα* are ambiguous. The paraphrast confines them to 'the means,' which rendering is supported by *κατὰ προαίρεσιν ἂν εἶεν*. Actions were above said to be means (III. iii. 15).

αἱ δὲ τῶν ἀρετῶν ἐνέργειαι] This is an unusual expression. We find it again, *Eth.* x. iii. 1: *οὐδὲ γὰρ αἱ τῆς ἀρετῆς ἐνέργειαι ποιότητές εἰσιν*. Aristotle's usual formula is *ἐνέργεια κατ' ἀρετήν*, *i.e.* the evocation of the internal nature into consciousness or action, under the regulation of the moral law. He seems averse to considering *ἀρετή* as a *δύναμις*, or latent quality that might be so evoked. The psychology of this passage is different from that of *Eth.* vi. xii. 8–10. *Here* it is said that *βούλησις* gives us the idea of the end, and that virtue consists in *προαίρεσις* and *βούλευσις* taking the means; *there* that virtue gives the end, and an intellectual faculty (*φρόνησις*) the means. But see above, note on iv. 1.

2 *ἐν οἷς γὰρ ἐφ' ἡμῖν τὸ πράττειν καὶ τὸ μὴ πράττειν*] Elsewhere (*Metaphys.* viii. ii. 2) Aristotle states in more philosophical form this first step in the doctrine of free-will, namely, that every psychical *δύναμις* is a capacity of contraries, see Vol. I. Essay IV.

3 *τοῦτο δ' ἦν τὸ ἀγαθοῖς καὶ κακοῖς εἶναι*] 'And this is, according to our hypothesis,—being good and bad.' *ἦν* = 'is as we have said,' referring to the preceding section. Trendelenburg in his paper on *τὸ τί ἦν εἶναι* (*Rheinisches Museum*, 1828) tells us that *ἀγαθοῖς* in the present passage is by attraction to *ἡμῖν*. It is therefore to be distinguished from the logical expression *τὸ ἀγαθῷ εἶναι*, 'the essential idea of goodness.'

τὸ δὲ λέγειν ὡς—ἀληθεῖ] 'But to say that "No man prefers a crime or spurns a bliss" seems half false and half true.' The line here quoted, on which the discussion in this chapter turns, is of uncertain authorship. It is quoted in the ninth book of the *Laws of Plato*, p. 374. A. which passage is referred to here. *Πότερον δὲ ἑκόντας οἴει ἔχειν τοῦτο τὸ ἄδικον τοὺς ἀνθρώπους ἢ ἄκοντας; ὧδε δὲ λέγω,*

ἄκων, ἡ δὲ μοχθηρία ἑκούσιον. ἢ τοῖς γε νῦν εἰρημένοις 5
ἀμφισβητητέον, καὶ τὸν ἄνθρωπον οὐ φατέον ἀρχὴν εἶναι
οὐδὲ γεννητὴν τῶν πράξεων ὥσπερ καὶ τέκνων. εἰ δὲ ταῦτα 6
φαίνεται καὶ μὴ ἔχομεν εἰς ἄλλας ἀρχὰς ἀναγαγεῖν παρὰ
τὰς ἐφ' ἡμῖν, ὧν καὶ αἱ ἀρχαὶ ἐν ἡμῖν, καὶ αὐτὰ ἐφ' ἡμῖν
καὶ ἑκούσια. τούτοις δ' ἔοικε μαρτυρεῖσθαι καὶ ἰδίᾳ ὑφ' 7
ἑκάστων καὶ ὑπ' αὐτῶν τῶν νομοθετῶν· κολάζουσι γὰρ
καὶ τιμωροῦνται τοὺς δρῶντας μοχθηρά, ὅσοι μὴ βίᾳ ἢ δι'
ἄγνοιαν ἧς μὴ αὐτοὶ αἴτιοι, τοὺς δὲ τὰ καλὰ πράττοντας
τιμῶσιν, ὡς τοὺς μὲν προτρέψοντες, τοὺς δὲ κωλύσοντες.
καίτοι ὅσα μήτ' ἐφ' ἡμῖν ἐστὶ μήθ' ἑκούσια, οὐδεὶς προ-

Ἑκόντας οἴει ἀδικεῖν καὶ ἀδίκους εἶναι ἢ ἄκοντας; Ἑκόντας ἔγωγε, ὦ Σώκρατες· πονηροὶ γάρ εἰσιν. Ἑκόντας ἄρα σὺ οἴει πονηροὺς εἶναι καὶ ἀδίκους ἀνθρώπους; Ἔγωγε· σὺ δ' οὔ; Οὐκ, εἴ γέ τι δεῖ τῷ ποιητῇ πείθεσθαι. Ποίῳ ποιητῇ; Ὅστις εἶπεν

οὐδεὶς ἑκὼν πονηρὸς οὐδ' ἄκων μάκαρ.

Ἀλλά τοι, ὦ Σώκρατες, εὖ ἡ παλαιὰ παροιμία ἔχει, ὅτι πολλὰ ψεύδονται ἀοιδοί. The answer to this is, an argument to shew that injustice is δι' ἀμαθίαν, and therefore involuntary. Οὐκ ἄρα ἐψεύσατο τοῦτό γε ἀοιδός. The original saying was probably a mere truism, πονηρός meaning not 'wicked,' but 'wretched.' This play on the word rendered the line peculiarly suitable for Plato's argument. The same quotation occurs in the spurious Platonic dialogue περὶ Δικαίου.

5 γεννητὴν τῶν πράξεων ὥσπερ καὶ τέκνων] The analogy here given, when looked at closely, does not imply any very strong assertion of free-will (though Aristotle meant it to be so). For the father inherits, or receives by nature, qualities that he transmits to his children. Analogously the will might be regarded as an effect, as well as a cause, of circumstances.

7 τούτοις δ' ἔοικε—νομοθετῶν] 'This seems to be supported by the testimony both of individuals and of the great legislators themselves.' The argument drawn from the constitution of society, from the fact of rewards and punishments, goes so far as this. It proves that the mind is of a nature to be acted on by inducements. It, of course, does not touch the metaphysical difficulty as to the whole world being bound by a law of necessity. But it proves an instinctive belief existing in society, exactly coincident with the position of Aristotle, that the individual is the cause of particular acts. There is no natural tendency in criminals to disclaim responsibility for their crimes. If they do so, it is not from an instinctive feeling, but rather from a sophisticated mind. As before said, this fact is not sufficient to disprove a metaphysical system which would represent legislature, judge, criminal, and the whole world, as forced to do what they do by an irresistible succession of cause and effect. But ethically and politically it is sufficient to justify a practical assumption of freedom. And in any system it must at all events be taken account of.

τρέπεται πράττειν, ὡς οὐδὲν πρὸ ἔργου ὂν τὸ πεισθῆναι μὴ
θερμαίνεσθαι ἢ ἀλγεῖν ἢ πεινῆν ἢ ἄλλ' ὁτιοῦν τῶν τοιούτων·
8 οὐδὲν γὰρ ἧττον πεισόμεθα αὐτά. καὶ γὰρ ἐπ' αὐτῷ τῷ
ἀγνοεῖν κολάζουσιν, ἐὰν αἴτιος εἶναι δοκῇ τῆς ἀγνοίας, οἷον
τοῖς μεθύουσι διπλᾶ τὰ ἐπιτίμια· ἡ γὰρ ἀρχὴ ἐν αὐτῷ·
κύριος γὰρ τοῦ μὴ μεθυσθῆναι, τοῦτο δ' αἴτιον τῆς ἀγνοίας.
καὶ τοὺς ἀγνοοῦντάς τι τῶν ἐν τοῖς νόμοις, ἃ δεῖ ἐπίστα-
9 σθαι καὶ μὴ χαλεπά ἐστι, κολάζουσιν. ὁμοίως δὲ καὶ
ἐν τοῖς ἄλλοις, ὅσα δι' ἀμέλειαν ἀγνοεῖν δοκοῦσιν, ὡς ἐπ' αὐ-
10 τοῖς ὂν τὸ μὴ ἀγνοεῖν· τοῦ γὰρ ἐπιμεληθῆναι κύριοι. ἀλλ'
ἴσως τοιοῦτός ἐστιν ὥστε μὴ ἐπιμεληθῆναι. ἀλλὰ τοῦ
τοιούτους γενέσθαι αὐτοὶ αἴτιοι ζῶντες ἀνειμένως, καὶ τοῦ
ἀδίκους ἢ ἀκολάστους εἶναι, οἱ μὲν κακουργοῦντες, οἱ δὲ ἐν
πότοις καὶ τοῖς τοιούτοις διάγοντες· αἱ γὰρ περὶ ἕκαστα
11 ἐνέργειαι τοιούτους ποιοῦσιν. τοῦτο δὲ δῆλον ἐκ τῶν
μελετώντων πρὸς ἡντινοῦν ἀγωνίαν ἢ πρᾶξιν· διατελοῦσι
12 γὰρ ἐνεργοῦντες. τὸ μὲν οὖν ἀγνοεῖν ὅτι ἐκ τοῦ ἐνεργεῖν
13 περὶ ἕκαστα αἱ ἕξεις γίνονται, κομιδῇ ἀναισθήτου. ἔτι
δ' ἄλογον τὸν ἀδικοῦντα μὴ βούλεσθαι ἄδικον εἶναι ἢ τὸν
ἀκολασταίνοντα ἀκόλαστον. εἰ δὲ μὴ ἀγνοῶν τις πράττει

---

8 διπλᾶ τὰ ἐπιτίμια] Cf. *Politics*, II. xii. 13: Ἐγένετο δὲ καὶ Πιττακὸς νόμων δημιουργὸς ἀλλ' οὐ πολιτείας· νόμος δ' ἴδιος αὐτοῦ τὸ τοὺς μεθύοντας, ἂν τυπτήσωσι, πλείω ζημίαν ἀποτίνειν τῶν νηφόντων· διὰ γὰρ τὸ πλείους ὑβρίζειν μεθύοντας ἢ νήφοντας οὐ πρὸς τὴν συγγνώμην ἀπέβλεψεν, ὅτι δεῖ μεθύουσιν ἔχειν μᾶλλον, ἀλλὰ πρὸς τὸ συμφέρον. Drunkenness is self-caused ignorance of right and wrong. (Cf. *Eth.* III. i. 14.) The law of Pittacus is given in the *Rhetoric* to illustrate an ἔνστασις depending on an appeal to authority. (II. xxv. 7) Εἴ τις ἐνθύμημα εἴπειεν ὅτι τοῖς μεθύουσι δεῖ συγγνώμην ἔχειν, ἀγνοοῦντες γὰρ ἁμαρτάνουσιν, ἔνστασις ὅτι οὔκουν ὁ Πιττακὸς αἰνετός. οὐ γὰρ ἂν μείζους ζημίας ἐνομοθέτησεν ἐάν τις μεθύων ἁμαρτάνῃ.

10—12 αἱ γὰρ περὶ ἕκαστα—ἀναισθήτου] 'For the particular developments of the mind in each case give people their character. This may be illustrated by the case of those who are practising for some contest or action,—for they keep on exercising their powers. Now not to know that the several states of mind arise from particular developments of the powers is absolute idiocy.' This passage contains exactly the same theory of the formation of moral states as that given at the beginning of Book II. But it is written independently of the former passage—in that separate way, which must be called a marked peculiarity of Aristotle's writings.

13 ἔτι δ' ἄλογον — ἀκόλαστον] 'Again it is absurd to say that he who acts unjustly does not wish to be unjust, or he who acts intemperately

ἐξ ὧν ἔσται ἄδικος, ἑκὼν ἄδικος ἂν εἴη, οὐ μὴν ἐάν γε 14
βούληται, ἄδικος ὢν παύσεται καὶ ἔσται δίκαιος· οὐδὲ γὰρ
ὁ νοσῶν ὑγιής. καὶ εἰ οὕτως ἔτυχεν, ἑκὼν νοσεῖ, ἀκρατῶς
βιοτεύων καὶ ἀπειθῶν τοῖς ἰατροῖς. τότε μὲν οὖν ἐξῆν
αὐτῷ μὴ νοσεῖν, προεμένῳ δ' οὐκέτι, ὥσπερ οὐδ' ἀφέντι
λίθον ἔτ' αὐτὸν δυνατὸν ἀναλαβεῖν· ἀλλ' ὅμως ἐπ' αὐτῷ
τὸ βαλεῖν καὶ ῥῖψαι· ἡ γὰρ ἀρχὴ ἐπ' αὐτῷ. οὕτω δὲ καὶ
τῷ ἀδίκῳ καὶ τῷ ἀκολάστῳ ἐξ ἀρχῆς μὲν ἐξῆν τοιούτοις
μὴ γενέσθαι, διὸ ἑκόντες εἰσίν· γενομένοις δ' οὐκέτι ἔξεστι
μὴ εἶναι. οὐ μόνον δ' αἱ τῆς ψυχῆς κακίαι ἑκούσιοί 15
εἰσιν, ἀλλ' ἐνίοις καὶ αἱ τοῦ σώματος, οἷς καὶ ἐπιτιμῶμεν·
τοῖς μὲν γὰρ διὰ φύσιν αἰσχροῖς οὐδεὶς ἐπιτιμᾷ, τοῖς δὲ δι'
ἀγυμνασίαν καὶ ἀμέλειαν. ὁμοίως δὲ καὶ περὶ ἀσθένειαν καὶ
πήρωσιν· οὐθεὶς γὰρ ἂν ὀνειδίσειε τυφλῷ φύσει ἢ ἐκ νόσου
ἢ ἐκ πληγῆς, ἀλλὰ μᾶλλον ἐλεήσαι· τῷ δ' ἐξ οἰνοφλυγίας
ἢ ἄλλης ἀκολασίας πᾶς ἂν ἐπιτιμήσαι. τῶν δὴ περὶ τὸ 16
σῶμα κακιῶν αἱ ἐφ' ἡμῖν ἐπιτιμῶνται, αἱ δὲ μὴ ἐφ' ἡμῖν οὔ.
εἰ δ' οὕτω, καὶ ἐπὶ τῶν ἄλλων αἱ ἐπιτιμώμεναι τῶν κακιῶν
ἐφ' ἡμῖν ἂν εἶεν. εἰ δέ τις λέγοι ὅτι πάντες ἐφίενται τοῦ 17

---

to be intemperate.' Aristotle would not say himself that any one 'wished to be intemperate,' that is, wished it in the general, in the abstract, for its own sake. But here he points out that those who do not wish to be intemperate yet take the steps that lead inevitably to this. He argues that the means make the end free; the outset, the conclusion; the parts, the whole. Afterwards (§ 22) he allows that the general state is not so entirely in our power as the particular act. With regard to the former it is rather true to say that we are responsible for it, than that we choose it. A paradox then still remains, that men produce by voluntary acts that which they do not wish. The resolution of this is to be found in *Eth.* VII. iii., where it is shown that right moral acting consists in allowing the act of the moment to be sufficiently influenced by universal considerations. Error and vice, on the contrary, consist in suffering the universal idea, the general conception of what is good and desirable, to stand in abeyance.

14 *προεμένῳ δ' οὐκέτι*] 'But after he has thrown his health away, he has no longer a choice.' To 'give away' is the only sense in which *προΐεσθαι* is used in the *Ethics*. Cf. IV. i. 9, IX. i. 7, &c.

17—20 This complex argument will be perhaps made most clear, if divided into the following separate members. (1) *Εἰ δέ τις λέγοι—αὐτῷ* is the general protasis. Suppose it to be said that all aim at what appears to them good, but that their ideas and impressions are beyond their control, being dependent in each case on the character of the individual. (2) On this an alternative follows: *either* (εἰ

φαινομένου ἀγαθοῦ, τῆς δὲ φαντασίας οὐ κύριοι, ἀλλ' ὁποῖός ποθ' ἕκαστός ἐστι, τοιοῦτο καὶ τὸ τέλος φαίνεται αὐτῷ·

μὲν οὖν—αἴτιος) the individual is the cause of his own character, and so accordingly of his ideas, *or* (3) let us see what the consequences will be if we allow that the individual is not the cause of his own character (*εἰ δὲ μή—εὐφυΐα*). In this case no one will be responsible for doing wrong: wrong will reduce itself to mere ignorance, the knowledge of the good to a happy gift of nature. (4) But these extreme deductions are overthrown (*εἰ δὲ ταῦτ' ἐστὶν—*[illegible]) by its being shown that they will equally disprove the voluntariness of virtue, as well as that of vice. (5) The argument is concluded by summing up the results of the previous discussions (*εἴτε δὴ—ὁμοίως γάρ*). In whatever sense virtue is said to be free, whether as implying that the idea of the end is in our power, or only that there is something free and individual in the taking of means,—in exactly the same sense will vice be free, for these two opposite terms stand on exactly the same footing.

17 *τῆς δὲ φαντασίας οὐ κύριοι*] 'But are not masters of their impression.' *Φαντασία* is a special word, denoting something between sense and intellect (*φαντασία γὰρ ἕτερον καὶ αἰσθήσεως καὶ διανοίας· αὐτή τε οὐ γίγνεται ἄνευ αἰσθήσεως, καὶ ἄνευ ταύτης οὐκ ἔστιν ὑπόληψις. De An.* III. iii. 5). It denotes, in short, the sensuous impression of an object. Aristotle says that we may have a false *φαντασία* even where we have true opinions, as, for instance, our *φαντασία* of the sun makes it a foot in diameter, while our belief is that the sun surpasses in magnitude the habitable world (*φαίνεται δὲ καὶ ψευδῆ, περὶ ὧν ἅμα ὑπόληψιν ἀληθῆ ἔχει, οἷον φαίνεται μὲν ὁ ἥλιος ποδιαῖος, πιστεύεται δ' εἶναι μείζων τῆς οἰκουμένης. De An.* III. iii. 15). *Φαντασία* is closely allied with *μνήμη*, it belongs to the same part of the mind (*De Memor.* i. 9). Memory and *φαντασία* are something short of intellect: Aristotle attributed them to the lower animals. Cf. *Metaphys.* I. i. 3: *τὰ μὲν οὖν ἄλλα ταῖς φαντασίαις ζῇ καὶ ταῖς μνήμαις, ἐμπειρίας δὲ μετέχει μικρόν.* Cf. also *Eth.* VII. iii. 11. Brutes and the incontinent are said to follow their *φαντασίαι*, *De An.* III. iii. 21: *καὶ διὰ τὸ ἐμμένειν καὶ ὁμοίας εἶναι ταῖς αἰσθήσεσι, πολλὰ κατ' αὐτὰς πράττει τὰ ζῷα, τὰ μὲν διὰ τὸ μὴ ἔχειν νοῦν, οἷον τὰ θηρία, τὰ δὲ διὰ τὸ ἐπικαλύπτεσθαι τὸν νοῦν ἐνίοτε πάθει ἢ νόσοις ἢ ὕπνῳ, οἷον οἱ ἄνθρωποι.* Cf. *Eth.* VII. vii. 8. We find the word *φαντασία* not as yet settled into a psychological formula in Plato's *Theaetetus*, p. 152 c, where the doctrine of Protagoras is shown to imply that everything is as it appears, and that this appearing is identical with sensation. *Σ. τὸ δέ γε φαίνεται αἰσθάνεσθαί ἐστιν; Θ. Ἔστι γάρ. Σ. Φαντασία ἄρα καὶ αἴσθησις ταὐτὸν ἔν τε θερμοῖς καὶ πᾶσι τοῖς τοιούτοις, οἷα γὰρ αἰσθάνεται ἕκαστος, τοιαῦτα ἑκάστῳ καὶ κινδυνεύει εἶναι.* Aristotle, giving a scientific account of it in the *De Anima*, separates it, as we have seen, from sensation on the one hand, and reason on the other. The term does not correspond with any of our regular psychological terms. In relation to the fancy and the imagination, it represents the material for these, the brain-images out of which the creations of fancy (as well as the phantasmagoria of dreams) are con-

εἰ μὲν οὖν ἕκαστος ἑαυτῷ τῆς ἕξεώς ἐστί πως αἴτιος, καὶ
τῆς φαντασίας ἔσται πως αὐτὸς αἴτιος· εἰ δὲ μή, οὐθεὶς αὑτῷ
αἴτιος τοῦ κακὰ ποιεῖν, ἀλλὰ δι' ἄγνοιαν τοῦ τέλους ταῦτα
πράττει, διὰ τούτων οἰόμενος αὑτῷ τὸ ἄριστον ἔσεσθαι.
ἡ δὲ τοῦ τέλους ἔφεσις οὐκ αὐθαίρετος, ἀλλὰ φῦναι δεῖ ὥσπερ
ὄψιν ἔχοντα, ᾗ κρινεῖ καλῶς καὶ τὸ κατ' ἀλήθειαν ἀγαθὸν
αἱρήσεται. καὶ ἔστιν εὐφυὴς ᾧ τοῦτο καλῶς πέφυκεν· τὸ
γὰρ μέγιστον καὶ κάλλιστον, καὶ ὃ παρ' ἑτέρου μὴ οἷόν τε
λαβεῖν μηδὲ μαθεῖν, ἀλλ' οἷον ἔφυ, τοιοῦτον ἕξει, καὶ τὸ εὖ
καὶ τὸ καλῶς τοῦτο πεφυκέναι ἡ τελεία καὶ ἀληθινὴ ἂν εἴη
εὐφυΐα. εἰ δὴ ταῦτ' ἐστὶν ἀληθῆ, τί μᾶλλον ἡ ἀρετὴ τῆς
κακίας ἔσται ἑκούσιον; ἀμφοῖν γὰρ ὁμοίως, τῷ ἀγαθῷ 18
καὶ τῷ κακῷ, τὸ τέλος φύσει ἢ ὁπωσδήποτε φαίνεται καὶ
κεῖται, τὰ δὲ λοιπὰ πρὸς τοῦτ' ἀναφέροντες πράττουσιν
ὁπωσδήποτε. εἴτε δὴ τὸ τέλος μὴ φύσει ἑκάστῳ φαί- 19
νεται οἱονδήποτε, ἀλλά τι καὶ παρ' αὐτόν ἐστιν, εἴτε τὸ
μὲν τέλος φυσικόν, τῷ δὲ τὰ λοιπὰ πράττειν ἑκουσίως τὸν
σπουδαῖον ἡ ἀρετὴ ἑκούσιόν ἐστιν, οὐθὲν ἧττον καὶ ἡ κακία
ἑκούσιον ἂν εἴη· ὁμοίως γὰρ καὶ τῷ κακῷ ὑπάρχει τὸ δι'
αὐτὸν ἐν ταῖς πράξεσι καὶ εἰ μὴ ἐν τῷ τέλει. εἰ οὖν, 20
ὥσπερ λέγεται, ἑκούσιοί εἰσιν αἱ ἀρεταί (καὶ γὰρ τῶν ἕξεων
συναίτιοί πως αὐτοί ἐσμεν, καὶ τῷ ποιοί τινες εἶναι τὸ τέλος

---

structed. Aristotle, not entering at all into the philosophy of the imaginative faculties, merely speaks of φαντασία as furnishing a necessary element to thought (νοεῖν οὐκ ἔστιν ἄνευ φαντάσματος, *De Mem.* i. 5). From what has been said it is easy to see the special appropriateness of the word in the above passage to denote an impression or idea of the good received passively, and in itself erroneous.

19 εἴτε δὴ—τέλει] 'Whether, then, the conception to the end, of whatever kind, comes not to each individual by nature, but something also is contributed by himself (τι καὶ παρ' αὐτόν ἐστιν), or whether the end indeed is fixed by nature, but it is through the good man's voluntarily taking the means that virtue is voluntary; in either case, I say, vice will be not a whit less voluntary (than virtue), for the bad man, exactly as the good, has individuality (τὸ δι' αὐτὸν) in the particular actions, if not in the conception of the end.'

20 καὶ γὰρ τῶν ἕξεων συναίτιοί πως αὐτοί ἐσμεν] 'For we are ourselves joint causes, in a way, of our own states of mind.' The word συναίτιος, meaning not the primary, but a concomitant cause, is of not unfrequent occurrence in Plato. Cf. *Timaeus*, p. 46 D, where it is said of fire, &c., δοξάζεται δὲ ὑπὸ τῶν πλείστων οὐ

τοιόνδε τιθέμεθα), καὶ αἱ κακίαι ἑκούσιοι ἂν εἶεν· ὁμοίως
21 γάρ. κοινῇ μὲν οὖν περὶ τῶν ἀρετῶν εἴρηται ἡμῖν τό τε
γένος τύπῳ, ὅτι μεσότητές εἰσιν, καὶ ὅτι ἕξεις, ὑφ' ὧν τε
γίνονται, καὶ ὅτι τούτων πρακτικαὶ καθ' αὑτάς, καὶ ὅτι ἐφ'
ἡμῖν καὶ ἑκούσιοι, καὶ οὕτως ὡς ἂν ὁ ὀρθὸς λόγος προστάξῃ·
22 οὐχ ὁμοίως δὲ αἱ πράξεις ἑκούσιοί εἰσι καὶ αἱ ἕξεις· τῶν
μὲν γὰρ πράξεων ἀπ' ἀρχῆς μέχρι τοῦ τέλους κύριοί ἐσμεν,
εἰδότες τὰ καθ' ἕκαστα, τῶν ἕξεων δὲ τῆς ἀρχῆς, καθ'
ἕκαστα δὲ ἡ πρόσθεσις οὐ γνώριμος, ὥσπερ ἐπὶ τῶν ἀρρω-
στιῶν· ἀλλ' ὅτι ἐφ' ἡμῖν ἦν οὕτως ἢ μὴ οὕτω χρήσασθαι,
23 διὰ τοῦτο ἑκούσιοι. ἀναλαβόντες δὴ περὶ ἑκάστης, εἴπωμεν
τίνες εἰσὶ καὶ περὶ ποῖα καὶ πῶς· ἅμα δ' ἔσται δῆλον καὶ
πόσαι εἰσίν. καὶ πρῶτον περὶ ἀνδρείας.

ξυναίτια, ἀλλ' αὐτοὺς εἶναι τῶν πάντων.

21—22 These sections form the junction between the somewhat isolated treatise on the Voluntary and Aristotle's discussion of the separate virtues. They bear marks of having been added for the express purpose of forming a junction. For after a general statement of the theory of virtue in section 21 there is a *résumé* of some points with regard to the voluntariness of actions and habits, which is just what a man might have been likely to add after reading over his own treatise, and thinking that it required a word or two of elucidation.

22 *οὐχ ὁμοίως δὴ—ἀρρωστιῶν*] 'But actions and habits are not equally voluntary, for we are masters of our actions from the beginning to the end because we know all the particulars, but we can only control the beginning of our habits, while the gradual addition made by each particular step is unperceived, as is the case also with illnesses.'

23 *ἀναλαβόντες δὴ περὶ ἑκάστης—εἰσίν*] 'Let us therefore resume our discussion of the separate virtues, stating what they are, with what actions they are concerned, and in what manner. It will at the same time appear how many there are.' On the assumed completeness of Aristotle's list of the virtues, see note on *Eth.* II. vii. 1, and the plan of Book IV.; cf. also *Eth.* III. x. 1, note.

καὶ πρῶτον περὶ ἀνδρείας] Aristotle's admirable account of courage is to some extent indebted to the observations of Plato, while in some points again it is a protest against the Platonic theory. In the *Protagoras* (pp. 349—351, 359—361) courage is identified with the science of the truly safe and the truly dangerous. In the *Laches* (pp. 198—201), however, written previously, it is argued that, if danger be 'future evil,' courage cannot be the science of this, for a science excludes all consideration of time, so, if courage be a science at all, it must be the science of good and evil universally. Thus Plato merges courage in that universal wise consciousness, which he considered the true ground of morality. In the *Republic* (p. 430 B), courage is said to be the maintenance of

Ὅτι μὲν οὖν μεσότης ἐστὶ περὶ φόβους καὶ θάρρη, ἤδη 6
καὶ πρότερον εἴρηται, φοβούμεθα δὲ δῆλον ὅτι τὰ φοβερά, 2
ταῦτα δ' ἐστὶν ὡς ἁπλῶς εἰπεῖν κακά· διὸ καὶ τὸν φόβον
ὁρίζονται προσδοκίαν κακοῦ. φοβούμεθα μὲν οὖν πάντα 3
τὰ κακά, οἷον ἀδοξίαν πενίαν νόσον ἀφιλίαν θάνατον, ἀλλ'
οὐ περὶ πάντα δοκεῖ ὁ ἀνδρεῖος εἶναι· ἔνια γὰρ καὶ δεῖ
φοβεῖσθαι καὶ καλόν, τὸ δὲ μὴ αἰσχρόν, οἷον ἀδοξίαν· ὁ

---

right principles in spite of the distractions of danger. By Aristotle, courage is more definitely fixed as a condition of [illegible] moral side of man's nature, and [illegible] implying not only a consciousness, but a conscious choice of the highest moral good. Its sphere is limited to war, and thus a rather special and restricted character is given to the virtue. At the same time a reverence is shown for the nobleness of courage beyond what we find in Plato. And deep human observations are made which are in the best style of Aristotle's moral writing.

VI. 1—2 *περὶ φόβους καὶ θάρρη— ταῦτα δ' ἐστὶν ὡς ἁπλῶς εἰπεῖν κακά· διὸ καὶ τὸν φόβον ὁρίζονται προσδοκίαν κακοῦ*] These points are accepted from Plato, cf. *Protag.* p. 358 D: *προσδοκίαν τινὰ λέγω κακοῦ τοῦτο, εἴτε φόβον εἴτε δέος καλεῖτε.* *Laches*, p. 198 B: *ἡγούμεθα δ' ἡμεῖς δεινὰ μὲν εἶναι ἃ καὶ δέος παρέχει, θαρραλέα δὲ ἃ μὴ δέος παρέχει· δέος δὲ παρέχει οὐ τὰ γεγονότα οὐδὲ τὰ παρόντα τῶν κακῶν, ἀλλὰ τὰ προσδοκώμενα· δέος γὰρ εἶναι προσδοκίαν μέλλοντος κακοῦ. . . . τούτων δέ γε τὴν ἐπιστήμην ἀνδρείαν προσαγορεύεις; κομιδῇ γε.* The subject of the present chapter is the proper sphere of courage. *ἤδη καὶ πρότερον*, *Eth.* II. vii. 2.

3—8 *φοβούμεθα μὲν οὖν—κινδύνῳ*] These sections contain a protest against the doctrine represented in the *Laches*, p. 191 D, E, where courage is extended to all those objects which are here expressly excluded from it—dangers by sea, illness, political conflicts, even the encountering of temptation. *Βουλόμενος γάρ σου πυθέσθαι μὴ μόνον τοὺς ἐν τῷ ὁπλιτικῷ ἀνδρείους, ἀλλὰ καὶ τοὺς ἐν τῷ ἱππικῷ καὶ ἐν ξύμπαντι τῷ πολεμικῷ εἴδει, καὶ μὴ μόνον τοὺς ἐν τῷ πολέμῳ, ἀλλὰ καὶ τοὺς ἐν τοῖς πρὸς τὴν θάλατταν κινδύνοις ἀνδρείους ὄντας, καὶ ὅσοι γε πρὸς νόσους καὶ ὅσοι πρὸς πενίας ἢ καὶ πρὸς τὰ πολιτικὰ ἀνδρεῖοί εἰσι, καὶ ἔτι αὖ μὴ μόνον ὅσοι πρὸς λύπας ἀνδρεῖοί εἰσιν ἢ φόβους, ἀλλὰ καὶ πρὸς ἐπιθυμίας ἢ ἡδονὰς δεινοὶ μάχεσθαι, καὶ μένοντες ἢ ἀναστρέφοντες . . . εἰσὶ γάρ πού τινες, ὦ Λάχης, καὶ ἐν τοῖς τοιούτοις ἀνδρεῖοι.* Aristotle treats all such applications of the word *ἀνδρεῖος* as merely metaphorical (*λέγεται δ' ὑπό τινων ἀνδρεῖος κατὰ μεταφοράν*), to these he opposes the *proper* use of the word (*κυρίως δὴ λέγοιτ' ἄν*, § 10) as belonging peculiarly to war.

ἔνια γὰρ δεῖ φοβεῖσθαι καὶ καλόν] Cf. *Eth.* III. i. 24: *δεῖ δὲ καὶ ὀργίζεσθαι ἐπί τισι καὶ ἐπιθυμεῖν τινῶν, οἷον ὑγιείας καὶ μαθήσεως.* It admits of discussion how much, independently of a merely permissive attitude in the will and reason, the instincts of fear, anger, and desire may be positively called out and even created by considerations and suggestions of the reason, or how far their place

μὲν γὰρ φοβούμενος ἐπιεικὴς καὶ αἰδήμων, ὁ δὲ μὴ φοβούμενος ἀναίσχυντος. λέγεται δ' ὑπό τινων ἀνδρεῖος κατὰ μεταφοράν· ἔχει γάρ τι ὅμοιον τῷ ἀνδρείῳ· ἄφοβος
4 γάρ τις καὶ ὁ ἀνδρεῖος. πενίαν δ' ἴσως οὐ δεῖ φοβεῖσθαι οὐδὲ νόσον, οὐδ' ὅλως ὅσα μὴ ἀπὸ κακίας μηδὲ δι' αὑτόν. ἀλλ' οὐδ' ὁ περὶ ταῦτα ἄφοβος ἀνδρεῖος. λέγομεν δὲ καὶ τοῦτον καθ' ὁμοιότητα· ἔνιοι γὰρ ἐν τοῖς πολεμικοῖς κινδύνοις δειλοὶ ὄντες ἐλευθέριοί εἰσι καὶ πρὸς χρημάτων
5 ἀποβολὴν εὐθαρσῶς ἔχουσιν. οὐδὲ δὴ εἴ τις ὕβριν περὶ παῖδας καὶ γυναῖκα φοβεῖται ἢ φθόνον ἤ τι τῶν τοιούτων, δειλός ἐστιν· οὐδ' εἰ θαρρεῖ μέλλων μαστιγοῦσθαι, ἀνδρεῖος.
6 περὶ ποῖα οὖν τῶν φοβερῶν ὁ ἀνδρεῖος; ἢ περὶ τὰ μέγιστα; οὐθεὶς γὰρ ὑπομενετικώτερος τῶν δεινῶν. φοβερώτατον δ' ὁ θάνατος· πέρας γάρ, καὶ οὐδὲν ἔτι τῷ
7 τεθνεῶτι δοκεῖ οὔτ' ἀγαθὸν οὔτε κακὸν εἶναι. δόξειε δ' ἂν οὐδὲ περὶ θάνατον τὸν ἐν παντὶ ὁ ἀνδρεῖος εἶναι, οἷον εἰ
8 ἐν θαλάττῃ ἢ ἐν νόσοις. ἐν τίσιν οὖν; ἢ ἐν τοῖς καλλίστοις; τοιοῦτοι δὲ οἱ ἐν πολέμῳ· ἐν μεγίστῳ γὰρ
9 καὶ καλλίστῳ κινδύνῳ. ὁμόλογοι δὲ τούτοις εἰσὶ καὶ αἱ τιμαὶ αἱ ἐν ταῖς πόλεσι καὶ παρὰ τοῖς μονάρχοις.
10 κυρίως δὴ λέγοιτ' ἂν ἀνδρεῖος ὁ περὶ τὸν καλὸν θάνατον ἀδεής, καὶ ὅσα θάνατον ἐπιφέρει ὑπόγυια ὄντα· τοιαῦτα
11 δὲ μάλιστα τὰ κατὰ πόλεμον. οὐ μὴν ἀλλὰ καὶ ἐν θαλάττῃ καὶ ἐν νόσοις ἀδεὴς ὁ ἀνδρεῖος, οὐχ οὕτω δὲ ὡς οἱ θαλάττιοι· οἱ μὲν γὰρ ἀπεγνώκασι τὴν σωτηρίαν καὶ τὸν θάνατον τὸν τοιοῦτον δυσχεραίνουσιν, οἱ δὲ εὐέλπιδές εἰσι
12 παρὰ τὴν ἐμπειρίαν. ἅμα δὲ καὶ ἀνδρίζονται ἐν οἷς ἐστὶν ἀλκὴ ἢ καλὸν τὸ ἀποθανεῖν· ἐν ταῖς τοιαύταις δὲ φθοραῖς οὐδέτερον ὑπάρχει.

may be supplied by the reason itself. It is a similar question which is discussed by Kant. How far is it possible to obey in a positive sense the injunction, 'love your enemies'?

6 φοβερώτατον δ' ὁ θάνατος· πέρας γάρ] See Vol. I. Essay V.

10—12 κυρίως—ὑπάρχει] 'He then can be properly called brave who is fearless about the noble kind of death, and about things which suddenly (ὑπόγυια ὄντα) bring on death,—and such are especially the affairs of war. No doubt the brave man, when he is upon the sea, or upon a sickbed, will be brave: but his bravery will not be that of a sailor. Landsmen in danger of drowning give up all hope of safety, and feel repugnance at the thought of such a death;

Τὸ δὲ φοβερὸν οὐ πᾶσι μὲν τὸ αὐτό, λέγομεν δέ τι καὶ 7
ὑπὲρ ἄνθρωπον. τοῦτο μὲν οὖν παντὶ φοβερὸν τῷ γε νοῦν
ἔχοντι, τὰ δὲ κατ' ἄνθρωπον διαφέρει μεγέθει καὶ τῷ μᾶλλον
καὶ ἧττον· ὁμοίως δὲ καὶ τὰ θαρραλέα. ὁ δὲ ἀνδρεῖος 2
ἀνέκπληκτος ὡς ἄνθρωπος. φοβήσεται μὲν οὖν καὶ τὰ
τοιαῦτα, ὡς δεῖ δὲ καὶ ὡς ὁ λόγος ὑπομενεῖ, τοῦ καλοῦ
ἕνεκα· τοῦτο γὰρ τέλος τῆς ἀρετῆς. ἔστι δὲ μᾶλλον 3
καὶ ἧττον ταῦτα φοβεῖσθαι, καὶ ἔτι τὰ μὴ φοβερὰ ὡς
τοιαῦτα φοβεῖσθαι. γίνεται δὲ τῶν ἁμαρτιῶν ἡ μὲν 4
ὅτι οὐ δεῖ, ἡ δὲ ὅτι οὐχ ὡς δεῖ, ἡ δὲ ὅτι οὐχ ὅτε, ἤ τι τῶν
τοιούτων· ὁμοίως δὲ καὶ περὶ τὰ θαρραλέα. ὁ μὲν οὖν 5
ἃ δεῖ καὶ οὗ ἕνεκα ὑπομένων καὶ φοβούμενος, καὶ ὡς δεῖ καὶ
ὅτε, ὁμοίως δὲ καὶ θαρρῶν, ἀνδρεῖος· κατ' ἀξίαν γάρ, καὶ
ὡς ἂν ὁ λόγος, πάσχει καὶ πράττει ὁ ἀνδρεῖος. τέλος 6

---

while sailors are made confident by their experience. Besides, men put forth their courage on occasions where to die is helpful or glorious; but in death at sea or from sickness neither of these qualities is to be found.' This passage is a curious exemplification of Athenian feeling. In spite of the glorious traditions of Salamis, the Athenians had never attained those instincts which are inherited by the descendants of the Norsemen—the feeling that 'the deck' is their proper 'field of fame.'

VII. This chapter discusses courage as being a mean state with regard to daring and fearing. Setting aside terrors which are too great for human nature to bear, the brave man is calm (ἀνέκπληκτος), and endures or fears all things in their due measure according to the true standard, his aim being to attain the noble. Thus he is distinguished from the extremes by whom these proportions are violated. The extremes, by a refinement which Aristotle does not extend to the other virtues (cf. note on *Eth.* II. vii. 2), are fourfold. (1) Deficiency of fear, producing a character which has no name. (2) Excess of fear = cowardice. (3) Deficiency of daring = cowardice. (4) Excess of daring = rashness. Two of these terms are identical, and one is nameless, so that the extremes really reduce themselves to cowardice and rashness (§ 12). Some excellent remarks are introduced on the characters of the boastful man and the rash man.

1 τὸ δὲ φοβερὸν—θαρραλέα] Having said where fear and courage are to be looked for, we next observe that fear admits of degrees, so that courage is proportionate. 'Now the Fearful is different to different persons, independent of our calling some things fearful beyond human endurance. These latter are fearful to every man in his senses, but dangers that are not beyond human endurance differ both in magnitude and in degree, a difference found also in the things that give courage.'

6 τέλος δὲ—ἀνδρείαν] This difficult section must be taken in connexion with what has gone before.

δὲ πάσης ἐνεργείας ἐστὶ τὸ κατὰ τὴν ἕξιν. καὶ τῷ ἀνδρείῳ
δὲ ἡ ἀνδρεία καλόν. τοιοῦτον δὴ καὶ τὸ τέλος· ὁρίζεται
γὰρ ἕκαστον τῷ τέλει. καλοῦ δὴ ἕνεκα ὁ ἀνδρεῖος ὑπομένει
7 καὶ πράττει τὰ κατὰ τὴν ἀνδρείαν. τῶν δ' ὑπερβαλλόντων ὁ μὲν τῇ ἀφοβίᾳ ἀνώνυμος (εἴρηται δ' ἡμῖν ἐν τοῖς
πρότερον ὅτι πολλά ἐστιν ἀνώνυμα), εἴη δ' ἄν τις μαινόμενος ἢ ἀνάλγητος, εἰ μηθὲν φοβοῖτο, μήτε σεισμὸν μήτε
τὰ κύματα, καθάπερ φασὶ τοὺς Κελτούς. ὁ δὲ τῷ θαρρεῖν
8 ὑπερβάλλων περὶ τὰ φοβερὰ θρασύς. δοκεῖ δὲ καὶ
ἀλαζὼν εἶναι ὁ θρασὺς καὶ προσποιητικὸς ἀνδρείας. ὡς οὖν
ἐκεῖνος περὶ τὰ φοβερὰ ἔχει, οὕτως οὗτος βούλεται φαίνε-
9 σθαι· ἐν οἷς οὖν δύναται, μιμεῖται. διὸ καὶ εἰσὶν οἱ
πολλοὶ αὐτῶν θρασύδειλοι· ἐν τούτοις γὰρ θρασυνόμενοι
10 τὰ φοβερὰ οὐχ ὑπομένουσιν. ὁ δὲ τῷ φοβεῖσθαι
ὑπερβάλλων δειλός· καὶ γὰρ ἃ μὴ δεῖ καὶ ὡς οὐ δεῖ, καὶ

Aristotle is determining the characteristics of a brave act. He here says that 'the End-in-itself, or perfection, of a particular moral act will be identical with that which belongs to the formed moral character. The End-in-itself for courage, as a whole, is the idea of the beautiful. The idea of the beautiful, therefore, must be that End-in-itself which a man proposes to himself in each separate act of bravery in order to constitute it brave.' In short, the meaning comes to this, 'what makes an act truly brave, is that, like the perfect state of bravery, it aims at the beautiful.' The term *τέλος* is used in a sense between that of 'perfection' and 'motive,' or rather as implying both (see Vol. I. Essay IV., and cf. *Eth.* III. i. 6, note). Ἐνέργεια, in *πάσης ἐνεργείας*, is opposed to *ἕξις* as 'act' to 'state.' The phrase *τὸ κατὰ τὴν ἕξιν τέλος* occurs again III. ix. 3: *οὐ μὴν ἀλλὰ δόξειεν ἂν εἶναι τὸ κατὰ τὴν ἀνδρείαν τέλος ἡδύ.* The whole notion that a moral act can only be considered good when it exhibits the qualities of the formed moral character has been already brought forward, II. iv. 3.

καὶ τῷ ἀνδρείῳ δὲ—ἀνδρείαν] 'Now to the brave man courage is something morally beautiful. Of this nature, then, must be the end of courage, for it is the end of a thing which in each case determines its character. Therefore the beautiful is the end for the sake of which the brave man endures and does whatever is brave.' The argument is as follows: Moral beauty is what characterises bravery, therefore it is the end of bravery (because final and formal causes coincide), therefore it should be the end of each brave act. The above explanation agrees with that given by the Paraphrast, except that he does not appear to supply *τέλος* with *τὸ κατὰ τὴν ἕξιν*. His words are, *τοῦτο γὰρ τέλος ἐστὶ πάσης ἐνεργείας τῆς κατ' ἀρετήν, τὸ κατὰ τὸν λόγον τῆς ἕξεως γίνεσθαι· οἷον αἱ κατὰ δικαιοσύνην πράξεις τέλος ἔχουσι τὸ κατὰ τὸν λόγον τῆς ἕξεως τῆς δικαιοσύνης*

πάντα τὰ τοιαῦτα ἀκολουθεῖ αὐτῷ. ἐλλείπει δὲ καὶ τῷ
θαρρεῖν· ἀλλ' ἐν ταῖς λύπαις ὑπερβάλλων μᾶλλον κατα-
φανής ἐστιν. δύσελπις δή τις ὁ δειλός· πάντα γὰρ φο- 11
βεῖται. ὁ δ' ἀνδρεῖος ἐναντίως· τὸ γὰρ θαρρεῖν εὐέλπιδος.
περὶ ταὐτὰ μὲν οὖν ἐστὶν ὅ τε δειλὸς καὶ ὁ θρασὺς καὶ 12
ὁ ἀνδρεῖος, διαφόρως δ' ἔχουσι πρὸς αὐτά· οἱ μὲν γὰρ
ὑπερβάλλουσι καὶ ἐλλείπουσιν, ὁ δὲ μέσως ἔχει καὶ ὡς
δεῖ· καὶ οἱ μὲν θρασεῖς προπετεῖς, καὶ βουλόμενοι πρὸ τῶν
κινδύνων ἐν αὐτοῖς δ' ἀφίστανται, οἱ δ' ἀνδρεῖοι ἐν τοῖς
ἔργοις ὀξεῖς, πρότερον δ' ἡσύχιοι. καθάπερ οὖν εἴρηται, 13
ἡ ἀνδρεία μεσότης ἐστὶ περὶ θαρραλέα καὶ φοβερά, ἐν οἷς
εἴρηται, καὶ ὅτι καλὸν αἱρεῖται καὶ ὑπομένει, ἢ ὅτι αἰσχρὸν
τὸ μή. τὸ δ' ἀποθνήσκειν φεύγοντα πενίαν ἢ ἔρωτα ἤ τι
λυπηρὸν οὐκ ἀνδρείου, ἀλλὰ μᾶλλον δειλοῦ· μαλακία γὰρ
τὸ φεύγειν τὰ ἐπίπονα, καὶ οὐχ ὅτι καλὸν ὑπομένει, ἀλλὰ
φεύγων κακόν.

Ἔστι μὲν οὖν ἡ ἀνδρία τοιοῦτόν τι, λέγονται δὲ καὶ 8
ἕτεραι κατὰ πέντε τρόπους, πρῶτον μὲν ἡ πολιτική·

[illegible] καὶ αἱ κατὰ τὴν ἀνδρείαν κατὰ τὴν λέγουσαν τῆς ἕξεως τῆς ἀνδρείας, κ.τ.λ.

13 Aristotle denounces suicide committed on account of poverty, or love, or anything grievous, as the act rather of a coward than of a brave man. Taking a broad human view of life, he does not sympathise with or discuss the sentimental deaths of the Cynic philosophers (see Vol. I. Essay II.). Suicide was afterwards dignified by the Stoics with the name of ἐξαγωγή, 'ushering oneself out of the world.'

VIII. This chapter discusses the spurious kinds of courage, classified under five heads. (Of this classification we find the germ in Plato's *Protagoras*, p. 351 A: θάρσος μὲν γὰρ καὶ ἀπὸ τέχνης γίγνεται ἀνθρώποις καὶ ἀπὸ θυμοῦ τε καὶ ἀπὸ μανίας, ὥσπερ ἡ δύναμις, ἀνδρεία δὲ ἀπὸ φύσεως καὶ εὐτροφίας τῶν ψυχῶν γίγνεται. The five shades (τρόποι) mentioned by Aristotle are (1) apparent courage produced from a regard to the opinions of society, (2) from experience of the particular danger, (3) from anger, (4) from a sanguine mind, (5) from ignorance.

1 πρῶτον μὲν ἡ πολιτική] This phrase is to be found in Plato's *Republic*, p. 430 C, where it probably originates, but it is there used in a different sense from the present. Plato meant by the term 'civil courage' to distinguish the true courage of a civilized man from all merely brutal instincts. δοκεῖς γάρ μοι τὴν ὀρθὴν δόξαν περὶ τῶν αὐτῶν τούτων ἄνευ παιδείας γεγονυῖαν, τήν τε θηριώδη καὶ ἀνδραποδώδη, οὔτε πάνυ νόμιμον ἡγεῖσθαι, ἄλλο τέ τι ἢ ἀνδρείαν καλεῖν. Ἀληθέστατα, ἦν δ' ἐγώ, λέγεις. Ἀποδέχομαι τοίνυν τοῦτο ἀνδρείαν εἶναι. Καὶ γὰρ ἀποδέχου, ἦν δ' ἐγώ, πολιτικήν γε, καὶ ὀρθῶς

μάλιστα γὰρ ἔοικεν· δοκοῦσι γὰρ ὑπομένειν τοὺς κινδύνους οἱ πολῖται διὰ τὰ ἐκ τῶν νόμων ἐπιτίμια καὶ τὰ ὀνείδη καὶ διὰ τὰς τιμάς. καὶ διὰ τοῦτο ἀνδρειότατοι δοκοῦσιν εἶναι
2 παρ' οἷς οἱ δειλοὶ ἄτιμοι καὶ οἱ ἀνδρεῖοι ἔντιμοι. τοιούτους δὲ καὶ Ὅμηρος ποιεῖ, οἷον τὸν Διομήδην καὶ τὸν Ἕκτορα.

> Πουλυδάμας μοι πρῶτος ἐλεγχείην ἀναθήσει·

καὶ Διομήδης,

> Ἕκτωρ γάρ ποτε φήσει ἐνὶ Τρώεσσ' ἀγορεύων,
> 'Τυδείδης ὑπ' ἐμεῖο.'

3 ὡμοίωται δ' αὕτη μάλιστα τῇ πρότερον εἰρημένῃ, ὅτι δι' ἀρετὴν γίνεται· δι' αἰδῶ γὰρ καὶ διὰ καλοῦ ὄρεξιν (τιμῆς

ἐναθίζει. Aristotle meant by 'civil courage' that daring which is prompted, not by an independent desire for the beautiful, but by a regard to reputation, and to the fame or disgrace, and even punishment, awarded by society to brave or cowardly actions respectively.

διὰ τὰ ἐκ νόμων ἐπιτίμια] The laws relating to cowardice are alluded to, *Eth.* v. i. 14.

καὶ διὰ τοῦτο—ἔντιμοι] 'And for this cause men appear to be more brave in communities where cowards are held in dishonour, and the brave in honour.' Aristotle does not actually assert that real courage is capable of cultivation by the influence of society. But if we do not put too fine a meaning on the word courage, there is no doubt that it flourishes most in warlike ages and communities. And, in short, with all but the very few, individual virtue generally springs out of the feelings of society; what is first outward, afterwards takes root in the mind.

2 τοιούτους δὲ—ἐμεῖο] 'Now just such men does Homer depict, as, for instance, Diomed and Hector, (when the latter says,) "Polydamas will be the first to cast a reproach at me;" and so Diomed, "Hector will some day, haranguing among the Trojans, declare,—Tydides, by me terrified, fled to the ships."' Cf. *Iliad* XXII. 100, VIII. 148, sq., where the line ends φοβεύμενος ἵκετο νῆας.

3 ὡμοίωται δ'—ὄντος] 'But this courage is most like the kind which we described above, for it originates in virtue, namely, in a sense of honour (αἰδῶ), in a desire for the beautiful (since it aims at reputation), and in a fear of dishonour as of something base.' On the nature of αἰδώς, see *Eth.* IV. ix. and the note on II. vii. 14. Most admirably does Aristotle touch off here in a few words the spirit of honour which is the nearest approach to, and, at all events in many of the relations of life, the best substitute for, a genuine morality. In reading his words, we can hardly fail to be reminded of Burke's magnificent lament over the loss of the age of chivalry. 'The unbought grace of life, the cheap defence of nations, the nurse of manly sentiment and heroic enterprise, is gone! It is gone, that sensibility of principle, that chastity of honour,

γάρ) καὶ φυγὴν ἐπιδόους, αἰσχροῦ ὄντος. τάξαι δ' ἄν τις 4
καὶ τοὺς ὑπὸ τῶν ἀρχόντων ἀναγκαζομένους εἰς ταὐτό· χείρους δ', ὅσῳ οὐ δι' αἰδῶ ἀλλὰ διὰ φόβον αὐτὸ δρῶσι, καὶ φεύγοντες οὐ τὸ αἰσχρὸν ἀλλὰ τὸ λυπηρόν· ἀναγκάζουσι γὰρ οἱ κύριοι, ὥσπερ ὁ Ἕκτωρ

> ὃν δέ κ' ἐγὼν ἀπάνευθε μάχης πτώσσοντα νοήσω,
> οὔ οἱ ἄρκιον ἐσσεῖται φυγέειν κύνας.

καὶ οἱ προστάττοντες, κἂν ἀναχωρῶσι τύπτοντες τὸ αὐτὸ 5
δρῶσι, καὶ οἱ πρὸ τῶν τάφρων καὶ τῶν τοιούτων παρατάττοντες· πάντες γὰρ ἀναγκάζουσιν. δεῖ δ' οὐ δι' ἀνάγκην ἀνδρεῖον εἶναι, ἀλλ' ὅτι καλόν. δοκεῖ δὲ καὶ ἡ 6

---

which felt a stain like a wound, which inspired courage whilst it mitigated ferocity, which ennobled whatever it touched, and under which vice itself lost half its evil, by losing all its grossness' (*Reflections on the Revolution in France*, p. 149). Just as Plato placed the philosopher above the man of honour (θυμοειδής, cf. *Repub.* p. 547–9), so Aristotle conceives of a courage higher and purer than that which emanates from the spirit of honour.

4 'Civil courage' is of two kinds (1) that which depends on honour, (2) that which depends on fear. The latter may remind us of the description given by Plato (*Phaedo*, p. 68 D), where he speaks of most men being courageous from a sort of cowardice. There is a vast falling off between the first class and the second. To the second belongs the spirit of Asiatic slavery, which Burke contrasted with the spirit of chivalry (*l.c.*). The instances here given are the compulsory measures used by the princes in the Trojan war to make the people fight, and similar devices used by the Persians, &c.

ὁ Ἕκτωρ] This is a misquotation, the words are those of Agamemnon (*Iliad* II. 391), and stand thus in the original: Ὃν δέ κ' ἐγὼν ἀπάνευθε μάχης ἐθέλοντα νοήσω μιμνάζειν παρὰ νηυσὶ κορωνίσιν, οὔ οἱ ἔπειτα ἄρκιον ἐσσεῖται φυγέειν κύνας ἠδ' οἰωνούς.

τύπτοντες] As done by the Persians at Thermopylae, Herod. VII. 223.

6 δοκεῖ δὲ—εἶναι] 'Experience of particular dangers is also accounted a kind of courage; which gave Socrates occasion to think that courage was a science. Different men have experience in different dangers, and regular soldiers in the dangers of war. Now there are many unreal shows of danger in warfare, and professional soldiers, being perfectly accustomed to these, appear brave, because other men are deceived by appearances.' The second cause (after that of a regard for opinions) which gives rise to a semblance of courage, is experience, the quality of the practised veteran. The effects of this may be analysed and subdivided into (1) a familiarity with, and contempt for, much that is seemingly, but not really, terrible; (2) a skill of weapons, &c., giving both an offensive and a defensive superiority (ποιῆσαι καὶ μὴ παθεῖν μάλιστα δύνανται ἐκ τῆς ἐμπειρίας).

ἐμπειρία ἡ περὶ ἕκαστα ἀνδρεία τις εἶναι· ὅθεν καὶ ὁ
Σωκράτης ᾠήθη ἐπιστήμην εἶναι τὴν ἀνδρείαν. τοιοῦτοι δὲ
ἄλλοι μὲν ἐν ἄλλοις, ἐν τοῖς πολεμικοῖς δ' οἱ στρατιῶται·
δοκεῖ γὰρ εἶναι πολλὰ κενὰ τοῦ πολέμου, ἃ μάλιστα συνεωρά-
κασιν οὗτοι· φαίνονται δὴ ἀνδρεῖοι, ὅτι οὐκ ἴσασιν οἱ ἄλλοι
7 οἷά ἐστιν. εἶτα ποιῆσαι καὶ μὴ παθεῖν μάλιστα δύνανται ἐκ
τῆς ἐμπειρίας, δυνάμενοι χρῆσθαι τοῖς ὅπλοις καὶ τοιαῦτα
ἔχοντες ὁποῖα ἂν εἴη καὶ πρὸς τὸ ποιῆσαι καὶ πρὸς τὸ

ὅθεν καὶ ὁ Σωκράτης] Cf. *Memorab.* III. ix. 2, and Plato, *Protag.* p. 350, where it is agreed that those who dive most boldly are the professional divers, those who fight most boldly the professional soldiers, &c. This empirical view of courage forms one side, it is true, of the Socratic doctrine, but by no means the whole (see Vol. I. Essay II.), and the statement about Socrates in the text is accordingly unfair. The statement is corrected by Eudemus in his *Ethics* (III. i. 13), where he well sums up the present part of the subject: Ἔστι δ' εἴδη ἀνδρείας πέντε λεγόμενα καθ' ὁμοιότητα· τὰ αὐτὰ γὰρ ὑπομένουσιν, ἀλλ' οὐ διὰ τὰ αὐτά. Μία μὲν πολιτική· αὕτη δ' ἐστὶν ἡ δι' αἰδῶ οὖσα. Δευτέρα δ' ἡ στρατιωτική· αὕτη δὲ δι' ἐμπειρίαν καὶ τὸ εἰδέναι, οὐχ ὥσπερ Σωκράτης ἔφη, τὰ δεινά, ἀλλ' ὅτι (ἴσασι) τὰς βοηθείας τῶν δεινῶν.

πολλὰ κενὰ τοῦ πολέμου] This is the reading of Bekker, supported by a majority of the MSS., the Scholiast, the Paraphrast, Casaubon, &c. It is illustrated by Cicero, *Epist. ad Att.* v. 20: 'Scis enim dici quædam πανικά, dici item τὰ κενὰ τοῦ πολέμου,' where the *editio princeps* (Romana) has καινά, another instance of similar confusion. Another reading, supported by six MSS., is 'τὰ καινὰ τοῦ πολέμου,' which would mean 'the surprises of war.' The phrase occurs in Diodorus Siculus, xx. 30: ἀληθὲς εἶναι, ὅτι πολλὰ τὰ καινὰ τοῦ πολέμου. Cf. Thucyd. III. 30: καὶ μὴ ἀποκνήσωμεν τὸν κίνδυνον, νομίσαντες οὐκ ἄλλο τι εἶναι τὸ καινὸν τοῦ πολέμου ἢ τὸ τοιοῦτον, ὃ εἴ τις στρατηγὸς ἔν τε αὑτῷ φυλάσσοιτο καὶ τοῖς πολεμίοις ἐνορῶν ἐπιχειροίη, πλεῖστ' ἂν ὀρθοῖτο: where also the MSS. vary between καινὸν and κενόν. It would seem, then, that τὰ κενὰ τοῦ πολέμου, and τὰ καινὰ τοῦ πολέμου, were both received formulæ, only with different senses. In the text above, either phrase might have been substituted for the other, according as it was more familiar to the transcriber. But τὰ κενὰ alone makes good sense, for while the soldiers would get accustomed to the empty show, the noise and pageantry of war, it is not true to say that they would get accustomed to the surprises of war, these being exactly what not even the experienced could calculate upon. Perhaps there is no better setting forth of the κενὰ τοῦ πολέμου than in the speech of Brasidas, Thucyd. IV. 126, 4: οὗτοι δὲ τὴν μέλλησιν μὲν ἔχουσι τοῖς ἀπείροις φοβεράν· καὶ γὰρ πλήθει ὄψεως δεινοὶ καὶ βοῆς μεγέθει ἀφόρητοι, ἥ τε διὰ κενῆς ἐπανάσεισις τῶν ὅπλων ἔχει τινὰ δήλωσιν ἀπειλῆς· προσμῖξαι δὲ τοῖς ὑπομένουσιν οὐχ ὅμοιοι.

συνεωράκασιν] The συν here seems to mean not 'together,' or 'at a glance,' but as in συγγινώσκω, σύνοιδα, &c., 'intimately,' 'privily,' 'familiarly.'

μὴ παθεῖν κράτιστα. ὥσπερ οὖν ἀνόπλοις ὡπλισμένοι 8
μάχονται καὶ ἀθληταὶ ἰδιώταις· καὶ γὰρ ἐν τοῖς τοιούτοις
ἀγῶσιν οὐχ οἱ ἀνδρειότατοι μαχιμώτατοί εἰσιν, ἀλλ' οἱ
μάλιστα ἰσχύοντες καὶ τὰ σώματα ἄριστα ἔχοντες. οἱ 9
στρατιῶται δὲ δειλοὶ γίνονται, ὅταν ὑπερτείνῃ ὁ κίνδυνος
καὶ λείπωνται τοῖς πλήθεσι καὶ ταῖς παρασκευαῖς· πρῶτοι
γὰρ φεύγουσι, τὰ δὲ πολιτικὰ μένοντα ἀποθνήσκει, ὅπερ
κἀπὶ τῷ Ἑρμαίῳ συνέβη. τοῖς μὲν γὰρ αἰσχρὸν τὸ φεύγειν καὶ ὁ θάνατος τῆς τοιαύτης σωτηρίας αἱρετώτερος·
οἱ δὲ καὶ ἐξ ἀρχῆς ἐκινδύνευον ὡς κρείττους ὄντες, γνόντες
δὲ φεύγουσι, τὸν θάνατον μᾶλλον τοῦ αἰσχροῦ φοβούμε-
νοι· ὁ δ' ἀνδρεῖος οὐ τοιοῦτος. καὶ τὸν θυμὸν δ' ἐπὶ τὴν 10
ἀνδρείαν ἐπιφέρουσιν· ἀνδρεῖοι γὰρ εἶναι δοκοῦσι καὶ οἱ
διὰ θυμὸν ὥσπερ τὰ θηρία ἐπὶ τοὺς τρώσαντας φερόμενοι,
ὅτι καὶ οἱ ἀνδρεῖοι θυμοειδεῖς· ἰτητικώτατον γὰρ ὁ θυμὸς
πρὸς τοὺς κινδύνους, ὅθεν καὶ Ὅμηρος 'σθένος ἔμβαλε
θυμῷ' καὶ 'μένος καὶ θυμὸν ἔγειρε' καὶ 'δριμὺ δ' ἀνὰ
ῥῖνας μένος' καὶ 'ἔζεσεν αἷμα·' πάντα γὰρ τὰ τοιαῦτα
ἔοικε σημαίνειν τὴν τοῦ θυμοῦ ἔγερσιν καὶ ὁρμήν. οἱ 11

9 οἱ στρατιῶται δὲ—συνέβη] 'But regular troops lose heart when the danger is overpowering, and when they are inferior in numbers and equipment. In such cases they are the first to run away, while citizen troops remain and die, as actually happened at the Hermæum.'

ἐπὶ τῷ Ἑρμαίῳ] Of this affair the Scholiast gives the following account. Coronea had been betrayed to one Onomarchus of Phocis; an engagement took place in an open spot called the Hermæum; the Coronean citizens were killed to a man, while their Bœotian auxiliaries fled in a panic. Τὰ πολιτικά, by a common usage, is nearly equivalent to οἱ πολῖται. Cf. Æsch. *Persæ*, 1. τάδε μὲν Περσῶν—πιστὰ καλεῖται, &c. Στρατιῶται, or mercenaries, in the time of Aristotle had not a high name. As common fighting men, the machines of war, they are opposed to the independent heroism of the brave man; see below, III. ix. 6. The present passage contrasts the courage of the man of honour with the hardiness of the veteran, which under any extraordinary pressure gives way. 'Citizen courage' in the instance mentioned cannot externally be distinguished from the very highest kind of courage.

10 καὶ τὸν θυμὸν δ'—ὁρμήν] 'The spirit of anger, too, men reckon as courage, and they who act through anger (like brutes turning on those who have wounded them) get the character of being brave, because the converse is true, and brave men are spirited. The spirit of anger is most keen for the encountering dangers, and hence Homer wrote:

"(Apollo) put strength into his
spirit."

μὲν οὖν ἀνδρεῖοι διὰ τὸ καλὸν πράττουσιν, ὁ δὲ θυμὸς συνεργεῖ αὐτοῖς· τὰ θηρία δὲ διὰ λύπην· διὰ γὰρ τὸ πληγῆναι ἢ φοβεῖσθαι, ἐπεὶ ἐάν γε ἐν ὕλῃ ἢ ἐν ἕλει ᾖ, οὐ προσέρχονται. οὐ δή ἐστιν ἀνδρεῖα διὰ τὸ ὑπ' ἀλγηδόνος καὶ θυμοῦ ἐξελαυνόμενα πρὸς τὸν κίνδυνον ὁρμᾶν, οὐθὲν τῶν δεινῶν προορῶντα, ἐπεὶ οὕτω γε κἂν οἱ ὄνοι ἀνδρεῖοι εἶεν πεινῶντες· τυπτόμενοι γὰρ οὐκ ἀφίστανται τῆς νομῆς· καὶ οἱ μοιχοὶ δὲ διὰ τὴν ἐπιθυμίαν τολμηρὰ πολλὰ δρῶσιν.
12 οὐ δή ἐστιν ἀνδρεῖα τὰ δι' ἀλγηδόνος ἢ θυμοῦ ἐξελαυνόμενα πρὸς τὸν κίνδυνον. φυσικωτάτη δ' ἔοικεν ἡ διὰ τὸν θυμὸν εἶναι, καὶ προσλαβοῦσα προαίρεσιν καὶ τὸ οὗ ἕνεκα ἀνδρεία εἶναι. καὶ οἱ ἄνθρωποι δὴ ὀργιζόμενοι μὲν ἀλγοῦσι,

---

"He roused up his strength and spirit."
"Fierce strength in his nostrils."
"His blood boiled."

For all such things appear to signify the awakening and outbreak of anger.' These quotations are obviously made from memory, and none of them are quite accurate. The first seems to be compounded of *Il.* xiv. 151, μέγα σθένος ἔμβαλ' ἑκάστῳ καρδίῃ, and xvi. 529, μένος δέ οἱ ἔμβαλε θυμῷ. The second appears to be meant for *Il.* v. 470, ὄτρυνε μένος καὶ θυμὸν ἑκάστου. The third is *Od.* xxiv. 318, ἀνὰ ῥῖνας δέ οἱ ἤδη δριμὺ μένος προὔτυψε. The last is not in Homer at all. This passage illustrates the progress of psychology towards distinctness, for it is impossible to translate it simply into English; θυμὸς means more than anger, or than any one modern word, for even with Aristotle it includes what we should call 'spirit.' But with Homer it meant (1) life, (2) spirit, (3) wrath, (4) heart, (5) mind. Aristotle in quoting Homer fails to remember this great indefiniteness, though there is no doubt that in Homer a simple and physical account is given of the manifestations of courage.

12 φυσικωτάτη δ' ἔοικεν — εἶναι] 'Yet the sort that springs from anger appears most natural, and with purpose and motive added, it becomes genuine courage.' Taking this sentence in its context, it must be an apology for the ἀνδρεία διὰ θυμόν. Aristotle had said that anger makes a man brave only in the sense that a hungry ass is brave, obeying the goads of a blind instinct. He adds that the instinct of anger is part of our nature (cf. *Eth.* II. iii. 10, note, and VII. vi. 2), and that, rightly directed and brought under the control of the will and reason, it can be elevated into a moral state. It is remarkable on what a high level Aristotle places courage. It must be entirely, he says, prompted by a desire for what is morally beautiful (οἱ μὲν οὖν ἀνδρεῖοι διὰ τὸ καλὸν πράττουσιν); mere physical courage is only an assistance in realising this (ὁ δὲ θυμὸς συνεργεῖ αὐτοῖς), and the prompting of anger, &c., will make men pugnacious, but not brave (οἱ δὲ διὰ ταῦτα μαχόμενοι μάχιμοι μέν, οὐκ ἀνδρεῖοι δέ). Perhaps Aristotle makes almost too great a separation between true courage and this 'spirited element,' which must be its physical basis. This is to be attributed (1) to

τιμωρούμενοι δ' ἥδονται· οἱ δὲ διὰ ταῦτα μαχόμενοι
μάχιμοι μέν, οὐκ ἀνδρεῖοι δέ· οὐ γὰρ διὰ τὸ καλὸν οὐδ' ὡς ὁ
λόγος, ἀλλὰ διὰ τὸ πάθος· παραπλήσιον δ' ἔχουσί τι.
οὐδὲ δὴ οἱ εὐέλπιδες ὄντες ἀνδρεῖοι· διὰ γὰρ τὸ πολ- 13
λάκις καὶ πολλοὺς νενικηκέναι θαρροῦσιν ἐν τοῖς κινδύνοις.
παρόμοιοι δέ, ὅτι ἄμφω θαρραλέοι· ἀλλ' οἱ μὲν ἀνδρεῖοι
διὰ τὰ προειρημένα θαρραλέοι, οἱ δὲ διὰ τὸ οἴεσθαι κρείττους εἶναι καὶ μηδὲν ἀντιπαθεῖν. τοιοῦτον δὲ ποιοῦσι 14
καὶ οἱ μεθυσκόμενοι· εὐέλπιδες γὰρ γίνονται. ὅταν δὲ
αὐτοῖς μὴ συμβῇ τοιαῦτα, φεύγουσιν· ἀνδρείου δ' ἦν τὰ
φοβερὰ ἀνθρώπῳ ὄντα καὶ φαινόμενα ὑπομένειν, ὅτι καλὸν
καὶ αἰσχρὸν τὸ μή. διὸ καὶ ἀνδρειοτέρου δοκεῖ εἶναι τὸ 15
ἐν τοῖς αἰφνιδίοις φόβοις ἄφοβον καὶ ἀτάραχον εἶναι ἢ ἐν
τοῖς προδήλοις· ἀπὸ ἕξεως γὰρ μᾶλλον, ἢ καὶ ὅτι ἧττον
ἐκ παρασκευῆς· τὰ προφανῆ μὲν γὰρ κἂν ἐκ λογισμοῦ καὶ
λόγου τις προέλοιτο, τὰ δ' ἐξαίφνης κατὰ τὴν ἕξιν.
ἀνδρεῖοι δὲ φαίνονται καὶ οἱ ἀγνοοῦντες, καὶ εἰσὶν οὐ 16
πόρρω τῶν εὐελπίδων, χείρους δ' ὅσῳ ἀξίωμα οὐδὲν ἔχουσιν, ἐκεῖνοι δέ. διὸ καὶ μένουσί τινα χρόνον· οἱ δ'

---

his high moral tone, (2) to his analytical mode of treatment. In Shakespeare, as in Homer, courage is attributed to physical causes. It is made sometimes to depend on the action of the spleen, or it is connected with the gall. Cf. *King John*, Act II. Sc. 1:

> 'Rash, inconsiderate, fiery voluntaries,
> With ladies' faces and fierce dragons' spleens.'

And *Hamlet*, Act II. Sc. 2, quoted below on *Eth.* IV. v. 6.

13—15 The fourth kind of spurious courage is that which arises from a sanguine mind. This may be due to previous success, and gives a confidence like courage, but also like intoxication. Such confidence is liable to a collapse.

15 διὸ καὶ—ἕξιν] 'For this reason it seems braver to be fearless and untroubled in sudden perils than in such as may be anticipated. In the former case a man is brave more by habit, or in other words less by premeditation; for in foreseen dangers a man may calculate and reason out the course to be chosen, in sudden ones he must depend upon his habitual character.' This acute observation puts real courage in opposition to the case of a man puffed out with a sort of extraneous confidence. Take a man on a sudden, and you will find how brave he is. While Aristotle makes courage a quality of the moral will, he requires that it should be a settled habit, and a second nature of the mind, not prepared consciously to meet a particular emergency.

16 ἀνδρεῖοι δὲ—εὐελπίδων] 'In the

ἠπατημένοι, ἐὰν γνῶσιν ὅτι ἕτερον ἢ ὑποπτεύσωσι, φεύγουσιν· ὅπερ οἱ Ἀργεῖοι ἔπαθον περιπεσόντες τοῖς
17 Λάκωσιν ὡς Σικυωνίοις. οἵ τε δὴ ἀνδρεῖοι εἴρηνται ποῖοί τινες, καὶ οἱ δοκοῦντες ἀνδρεῖοι.

9 Περὶ θάρρη δὲ καὶ φόβους ἡ ἀνδρεία οὖσα οὐχ ὁμοίως περὶ ἄμφω ἐστίν, ἀλλὰ μᾶλλον περὶ τὰ φοβερά· ὁ γὰρ ἐν τούτοις ἀτάραχος καὶ περὶ ταῦθ' ὡς δεῖ ἔχων ἀνδρεῖος
2 μᾶλλον ἢ ὁ περὶ τὰ θαρραλέα. τῷ δὴ τὰ λυπηρὰ ὑπομένειν, ὡς εἴρηται, ἀνδρεῖοι λέγονται. διὸ καὶ ἐπίλυπον ἡ ἀνδρεία, καὶ δικαίως ἐπαινεῖται· χαλεπώτερον γὰρ τὰ
3 λυπηρὰ ὑπομένειν ἢ τῶν ἡδέων ἀπέχεσθαι. οὐ μὴν ἀλλὰ δόξειεν ἂν εἶναι τὸ κατὰ τὴν ἀνδρείαν τέλος ἡδύ, ὑπὸ τῶν κύκλῳ δ' ἀφανίζεσθαι, οἷον κἀν τοῖς γυμνικοῖς ἀγῶσι γίνεται· τοῖς γὰρ πύκταις τὸ μὲν τέλος ἡδύ, οὗ ἕνεκα, ὁ στέφανος καὶ αἱ τιμαί, τὸ δὲ τύπτεσθαι ἀλγεινόν, εἴπερ σάρκινοι, καὶ λυπηρόν, καὶ πᾶς ὁ πόνος· διὰ δὲ τὸ πολλὰ ταῦτ' εἶναι, μικρὸν ὂν τὸ οὗ ἕνεκα οὐδὲν ἡδὺ φαίνεται ἔχειν.

---

last place, men appear brave from not knowing their danger. Such persons are not far removed from the sanguine, but are inferior to them, because they have no self-confidence, as the sanguine have. This confidence enables the sanguine to stand their ground for a time; while those who have blundered into bravery, as soon as it appears that the danger is other than they had supposed, take to their heels, as was the case with the Argives, when they fell in with some Lacedæmonians whom they took for men of Sicyon.' The last and poorest semblance of courage is when something daring is done unknowingly, and from a mistake. The instance given is mentioned by Xenophon (*Hellenics*, IV. 10). Some Spartans assumed the shields of some vanquished Sicyonians, and were at first contemptuously encountered by the Argives, who, when they discovered their formidable enemies, took to flight.

IX. This interesting chapter is on the connection of courage with pain and loss. The nobleness of courage chiefly depends on the sacrifice which it implies (ἐπίλυπον ἡ ἀνδρεία καὶ δικαίως ἐπαινεῖται). The brave man by encountering death consciously makes a sacrifice of the greatest magnitude, since he runs the risk of relinquishing a life which is eminently valuable, and, by reason of his virtue, full of happiness. Courage, then, is not to be called pleasurable, except as attaining to a satisfaction above all pleasure, attaining, in short, to the end of one's being (οὐ δὴ ἐν ἁπάσαις ταῖς ἀρεταῖς τὸ ἡδέως ἐνεργεῖν ὑπάρχει, πλὴν ἐφ' ὅσον τοῦ τέλους ἐφάπτεται). The conscious heroism of the brave man distinguishes him from the recklessness of the mercenary; it disqualifies him, indeed, from becoming mere rank and file, a mere machine of discipline.

3 οὐ μὴν ἀλλὰ—ἔχειν] 'Without

εἰ δὴ τοιοῦτόν ἐστι καὶ τὸ περὶ τὴν ἀνδρείαν, ὁ μὲν 4
θάνατος καὶ τὰ τραύματα λυπηρὰ τῷ ἀνδρείῳ καὶ ἄκοντι ἔσται, ὑπομένει δὲ αὐτά, ὅτι καλὸν ἢ ὅτι αἰσχρὸν τὸ μή. καὶ ὅσῳ ἂν μᾶλλον τὴν ἀρετὴν ἔχῃ πᾶσαν καὶ εὐδαιμονέστερος ᾖ, μᾶλλον ἐπὶ τῷ θανάτῳ λυπηθήσεται· τῷ τοιούτῳ γὰρ μάλιστα ζῆν ἄξιον, καὶ οὗτος μεγίστων ἀγαθῶν ἀποστερεῖται εἰδώς· λυπηρὸν δὲ τοῦτο. ἀλλ' οὐδὲν ἧττον ἀνδρεῖος, ἴσως δὲ καὶ μᾶλλον, ὅτι τὸ ἐν τῷ πολέμῳ καλὸν

---

doubt the end that belongs to courage is pleasant in itself, but this pleasantness is neutralised by the attendant circumstances, as happens likewise in the contests of the arena. The end at which the boxers aim, the garland and the honours, is pleasant; but the blows, and indeed the whole exertion, are painful and grievous to flesh and blood; so that by the multitude of intervening pains the incentive, which is small in itself, loses all appearance of being pleasant.'

4 καὶ ὅσῳ—αἱρεῖται] 'And in proportion as a man possesses all excellence, and the happier he is, so much the more will he be pained at death, for to such a one life is especially valuable, and he will consciously be deprived of the greatest blessings. And this is painful. But he is not the less brave, nay, perhaps even more, because he chooses the noble in war in preference to those other goods.' These last words may remind us of the characteristic attributed by Wordsworth to his *Happy Warrior*, who is 'more brave for this, that he hath much to love.' The whole of Wordsworth's description may well be compared with that of Aristotle:

"Who, if he be called upon to face
Some awful moment to which Heaven has joined
Great issues, good or bad for human kind,
Is happy as a lover, and attired
With sudden brightness, like a man inspired;
And, through the heat of conflict, keeps the law
In calmness made, and sees what he foresaw;
Or if an unexpected call succeed,
Come when it will, is equal to the need:
He who, though thus endued as with a sense
And faculty for storm and turbulence,
Is yet a soul whose master-bias leans
To homefelt pleasures and to gentle scenes;
Sweet images! which wheresoe'er he be
Are at his heart, and such fidelity
It is his darling passion to approve;
More brave for this, that he hath much to love."

The consciousness of the sacrifice to be made appears rather more prominent in Aristotle's brave man than in Wordsworth's. In saying this we must not forget that the word 'sacrifice,' in the moral sense of the term, expresses an idea that has grown up in the human mind subsequently to Aristotle. How nearly Aristotle, by the force of his penetration, realised it, the present chapter shows most remarkably.

5 ἀντ᾽ ἐκείνων αἱρεῖται. οὐ δὴ ἐν ἁπάσαις ταῖς ἀρεταῖς τὸ ἡδέως ἐνεργεῖν ὑπάρχει, πλὴν ἐφ᾽ ὅσον τοῦ τέλους ἐφά-
6 πτεται. στρατιώτας δ᾽ οὐδὲν ἴσως κωλύει μὴ τοὺς τοιούτους κρατίστους εἶναι, ἀλλὰ τοὺς ἧττον μὲν ἀνδρείους, ἄλλο δ᾽ ἀγαθὸν μηδὲν ἔχοντας· ἕτοιμοι γὰρ οὗτοι πρὸς τοὺς κινδύνους, καὶ τὸν βίον πρὸς μικρὰ κέρδη καταλλάττονται.
7 περὶ μὲν οὖν ἀνδρείας ἐπὶ τοσοῦτον εἰρήσθω· τί δ᾽ ἐστίν, οὐ χαλεπὸν τύπῳ γε περιλαβεῖν ἐκ τῶν εἰρημένων.

Μετὰ δὲ ταύτην περὶ σωφροσύνης λέγωμεν· δοκοῦσι

---

5 *οὐ δὴ—ἐφάπτεται*] 'Therefore it is not the case that in all the virtues virtuous action is accompanied by pleasure, except in so far as one attains to the End-in-itself.' On the import of this passage, see Vol. I. Essay IV. With *ἐφάπτεται*, τις is to be understood; see above, III. i. 6, note.

6 *στρατιώτας δ᾽—καταλλάττονται*] 'After all, perhaps it is true that it is not brave men such as I have described who will make the best mercenaries, but fellows who, while they are less brave, have nothing to lose: for these are ready for dangers, and will sell their life for a trifling sum.' See above, ch. viii. 9, note. On the readiness of miserable wretches for danger and death, cf. Shakespeare, *Macbeth*, Act III. Sc. 1:

> *Second Murderer.*—I am one, my liege,
> Whom the vile blows and buffets of the world
> Have so incens'd, that I am reckless what
> I do, to spite the world.
> *First Murderer.*—And I another,
> So weary with disasters, tugg'd with fortune,
> That I would set my life on any chance,
> To mend it, or be rid on't.

X. *Μετὰ δὲ ταύτην—ἀρεταί*] 'Next let us speak of temperance, for these (namely, courage and temperance) seem to be the excellencies of the irrational parts of our nature.' This is almost the only indication which Aristotle gives of the system upon which he has arranged the several virtues in order; he places together, and first treats of, the development of the lower and more instinctive qualities. On the arrangement of the remaining virtues see the plan of Book IV. With regard to the first two, there is a want of any distinct principle in their arrangement. If it be said that they are based on *θυμός* and *ἐπιθυμία*, and that Aristotle begins at the bottom of the scale, why does he not begin with *σωφροσύνη*, since *θυμὸς* is higher than *ἐπιθυμία* (*Eth.* VII. vi.)? Again, as we have seen (ch. viii. § 12) *θυμὸς* is here considered rather as having an occasional connection with courage than as being the basis of it. But in fact Aristotle's *Ethics* are very little psychological in their character. In them psychology and morals are both in process of formation; we cannot therefore expect in so tentative and unfinished a work to find systematic arrangement. Aristotle probably began his list of the virtues with courage and temperance because they were two of the Greek cardinal virtues, and when he came to temperance, he said 'this comes

γὰρ τῶν ἀλόγων μερῶν αὗται εἶναι αἱ ἀρεταί. ὅτι μὲν οὖν μεσότης ἐστὶ περὶ ἡδονὰς ἡ σωφροσύνη, εἴρηται ἡμῖν· ἧττον γὰρ καὶ οὐχ ὁμοίως ἐστὶ περὶ τὰς λύπας· ἐν τοῖς αὐτοῖς δὲ καὶ ἡ ἀκολασία φαίνεται. περὶ ποίας οὖν τῶν ἡδονῶν, νῦν ἀφορίσωμεν. διῃρήσθωσαν δὲ αἱ ψυχικαὶ καὶ 2
αἱ σωματικαί, οἷον φιλοτιμία φιλομάθεια· ἑκάτερος γὰρ

---

next, since it also belongs to the irrational part of our nature.'

τῶν ἀλόγων μερῶν] The instincts, such as those of self-preservation, fear, desire, &c., can only be capable of excellence by being brought under a law (μεσότης, λόγος) of the intellect, having no law in themselves. This law of the intellect becomes the most important part of the conception of virtue, as form is more striking than matter. In Plato the law is put for virtue altogether, and thus, as we saw, he calls courage a science. Similarly in the *Charmides*, where temperance is discussed, the nearest definition that is given is 'self-knowledge,' though it is shown that mere 'self-knowledge' has no content, and would be a useless blank; therefore it is implied that knowledge of the good must be added to make the conception complete.

It is the extreme opposite of Plato's view to speak of temperance as 'a virtue of the instincts' (τῶν ἀλόγων μερῶν); the word μεσότης however in the next line implies what was omitted, namely, 'under a law of the intellect.' The formula of Aristotle attributes a worth to the bodily instincts which would be opposed to asceticism.

μεσότης ἐστὶ περὶ ἡδονὰς] Σωφροσύνη, which, in spite of the false etymology given in Plato's *Cratylus*, 411 E, and *Eth.* VI. v. 5, meant originally 'soundmindedness' (in German Besonnenheit), soon came to mean temperance with regard to pleasures. In this sense it is often popularly defined by Plato, cf. *Repub.* p. 430 E: κόσμος πού τις—ἡ σωφροσύνη ἐστὶ καὶ ἡδονῶν τινων καὶ ἐπιθυμιῶν ἐγκράτεια. *Sympos.* p. 196 C: εἶναι γὰρ ὁμολογεῖται σωφροσύνη τὸ κρατεῖν ἡδονῶν καὶ ἐπιθυμιῶν, &c. Aristotle's procedure in discussing it is first to ascertain definitely its object. Pleasures are either bodily or mental. With mental pleasures temperance and intemperance are not concerned. Nor again with all bodily pleasures—not those of hearing, nor of smell; but only the merely animal pleasures (ὧν καὶ τὰ λοιπὰ ζῷα κοινωνεῖ) of touch and taste. Even taste, as an object of intemperance, reduces itself to touch; and with regard to touch we must exclude the manly and human satisfaction felt in exercise, &c. (chapter xi.) Desires of the kind in question are either common, or special and acquired (ἴδιοι καὶ ἐπίθετοι); in the former, excess is the only kind of error possible; in the latter all kinds of errors are committed. The only pains with which temperance and intemperance can be concerned are pains arising from the want of certain pleasures; these pains the intemperate man feels to excess. While intemperance thus consists in excess, there is no such thing as deficiency in the sense for the above-named pleasures; thus there is no name for the opposite extreme to intemperance. With due regard to his health, and the means at his disposal, and acting under the law of the beautiful (xi. 8), the temperate man preserves a balance.

2 διῃρήσθωσαν - ψυχικαί] 'We must

τούτων χαίρει, οὐ φιλητικός ἐστιν, οὐθὲν πάσχοντος τοῦ σώματος, ἀλλὰ μᾶλλον τῆς διανοίας· οἱ δὲ περὶ τὰς τοιαύτας ἡδονὰς οὔτε σώφρονες οὔτε ἀκόλαστοι λέγονται. ὁμοίως δ' οὐδ' οἱ περὶ τὰς ἄλλας ὅσαι μὴ σωματικαί εἰσιν· τοὺς γὰρ φιλομύθους καὶ διηγητικοὺς καὶ περὶ τῶν τυχόντων κατατρίβοντας τὰς ἡμέρας ἀδολέσχας, ἀκολάστους δ' οὐ λέγομεν, οὐδὲ τοὺς λυπουμένους ἐπὶ χρήμασιν ἢ φίλοις.
3 περὶ δὲ τὰς σωματικὰς εἴη ἂν ἡ σωφροσύνη, οὐ πάσας δὲ
οὐδὲ ταύτας· οἱ γὰρ χαίροντες τοῖς διὰ τῆς ὄψεως, οἷον
χρώμασι καὶ σχήμασι καὶ γραφῇ, οὔτε σώφρονες οὔτε
ἀκόλαστοι λέγονται· καίτοι δόξειεν ἂν εἶναι καὶ ὡς δεῖ
χαίρειν καὶ τούτοις, καὶ καθ' ὑπερβολὴν καὶ ἔλλειψιν.
4 ὁμοίως δὲ καὶ ἐν τοῖς περὶ τὴν ἀκοήν· τοὺς γὰρ ὑπερβεβλημένως χαίροντας μέλεσιν ἢ ὑποκρίσει οὐθεὶς ἀκολά-
5 στους λέγει, οὐδὲ τοὺς ὡς δεῖ σώφρονας. οὐδὲ τοὺς
περὶ τὴν ὀσμήν, πλὴν κατὰ συμβεβηκός· τοὺς γὰρ χαίροντας μήλων ἢ ῥόδων ἢ θυμιαμάτων ὀσμαῖς οὐ λέγομεν
ἀκολάστους, ἀλλὰ μᾶλλον τοὺς μύρων καὶ ὄψων· χαίρουσι
γὰρ τούτοις οἱ ἀκόλαστοι, ὅτι διὰ τούτων ἀνάμνησις
6 γίνεται αὐτοῖς τῶν ἐπιθυμητῶν. ἴδοι δ' ἄν τις καὶ τοὺς
ἄλλους, ὅταν πεινῶσι, χαίροντας ταῖς τῶν βρωμάτων ὀσμαῖς.
τὸ δὲ τοιούτοις χαίρειν ἀκολάστου· τούτῳ γὰρ ἐπιθυμητὰ
7 ταῦτα. οὐκ ἔστι δὲ οὐδὲ τοῖς ἄλλοις ζῴοις κατὰ ταύτας

take a distinction between the bodily pleasures and such as are mental, like ambition and the desire of knowledge. The man who has either of these feelings takes pleasure in the object of his desire without the body being at all affected, but only the mind.' The writing is loose here, constituting a σχῆμα πρὸς τὸ σημαινόμενον. Transitions as from φιλοτιμία to φιλότιμος are common. Cf. below, ch. xi. § 3: διὸ λέγονται οὗτοι γαστρίμαργοι, where there is nothing preceding which answers to οὗτοι, only a general description of a course of action.

4–5 While Aristotle justly says that the words temperance and intemperance do not apply to the pleasure felt in colours, forms, painting, music, and acting, it is strange that he should have spoken of these at all as bodily pleasures. Such a way of speaking shows an early and immature psychology.

6 Pleasures of smell are not the objects of intemperance, except accidentally, as by association, reminding people of eating, &c. Eudemus quotes a witty remark on the subject. *Eth. Eud.* III. ii. 10: ἐμμελῶς ἔφη Στρατόνικος τὰς μὲν καλὸν ὄζειν, τὰς δὲ ἡδύ.

7 Brutes, says Aristotle, have no pleasures of hearing, or smell, or sight, except accidental ones, namely

τὰς αἰσθήσεις ἡδονὴ πλὴν κατὰ συμβεβηκός. οὐδὲ γὰρ ταῖς
ὀσμαῖς τῶν λαγωῶν αἱ κύνες χαίρουσιν, ἀλλὰ τῇ βρώσει·
τὴν δ' αἴσθησιν ἡ ὀσμὴ ἐποίησεν. οὐδ' ὁ λέων τῇ φωνῇ
τοῦ βοός, ἀλλὰ τῇ ἐδωδῇ· ὅτι δ' ἐγγύς ἐστι, διὰ τῆς
φωνῆς ᾔσθετο, καὶ χαίρειν δὴ ταύτῃ φαίνεται. ὁμοίως δ'
οὐδ' ἰδὼν ἢ εὑρὼν ἔλαφον ἢ ἄγριον αἶγα, ἀλλ' ὅτι βορὰν
ἕξει. περὶ τὰς τοιαύτας δὴ ἡδονὰς ἡ σωφροσύνη καὶ ἡ 8
ἀκολασία ἐστὶν ὧν καὶ τὰ λοιπὰ ζῷα κοινωνεῖ, ὅθεν
ἀνδραποδώδεις καὶ θηριώδεις φαίνονται· αὗται δ' εἰσὶν
ἁφὴ καὶ γεῦσις. φαίνονται δὴ καὶ τῇ γεύσει ἐπὶ μικρὸν ἢ 9
οὐθὲν χρῆσθαι· τῆς γὰρ γεύσεώς ἐστιν ἡ κρίσις τῶν χυμῶν,
ὅπερ ποιοῦσιν οἱ τοὺς οἴνους δοκιμάζοντες καὶ τὰ ὄψα
ἀρτύοντες. οὐ πάνυ δὲ χαίρουσι τούτοις, ἢ οὐχ οἵ γε
ἀκόλαστοι, ἀλλὰ τῇ ἀπολαύσει, ἣ γίνεται πᾶσα δι' ἁφῆς
καὶ ἐν σιτίοις καὶ ἐν ποτοῖς καὶ τοῖς ἀφροδισίοις λεγομένοις.
διὸ καὶ ηὔξατό τις ὀψοφάγος ὢν τὸν φάρυγγα αὐτῷ 10

---

when sounds or scents indicate to them their prey or their food. It may be questioned whether this is absolutely true, whether, for instance, brutes are not capable of some pleasure from musical sounds. This appears to be the case with lizards and snakes; and horses are fond of bells. It is said that the cat likes the smell of mint. Dogs like the smell of carrion, apparently for its own sake, this being their taste. With brutes the senses are the intellect, and thus by the well-known law that as an organ increases in fineness of perception, it decreases in sensitiveness to pleasure and pain,—we may conceive how it is that the fine perceptive organs of brutes are to them in a less degree the instruments of pleasure. See Sir W. Hamilton, *Reid's Works*, pp. 880 and 886.

εὑρὼν ἔλαφον] This alludes to Homer, *Il.* III. 23:

ὥστε λέων ἐχάρη μεγάλῳ ἐπὶ σώματι κύρσας,
εὑρὼν ἢ ἔλαφον κεραὸν ἢ ἄγριον αἶγα.

10 διὸ καὶ ηὔξατό τις ὀψοφάγος] The name of this glutton is recorded by Eudemus (III. ii. 10), who paraphrases the present passage as follows: διὸ οἱ ὀψοφάγοι οὐκ εὔχονται τὴν γλῶτταν ἔχειν μακρὰν ἀλλὰ τὸν φάρυγγα γεράνου, ὥσπερ Φιλόξενος ὁ Ἐρύξιδος. Athenaeus mentions the same story (VIII. 26), quoting the verses—

Φιλόξενός ποθ', ὡς λέγουσ', ὁ Κυθήριος
ηὔξατο τριῶν ἔχειν λάρυγγα πήχεων.

Aristotle uses the word φάρυγγα here in its loose sense for the 'throat,' as λάρυγξ (which properly meant the top of the windpipe) was also loosely employed by the ancients to mean the whole throat. Speaking scientifically Aristotle confined the term φάρυγξ to mean the *trachea* or windpipe, distinguishing it from the *oesophagus* or gullet, cf. *De Part. An.* III. iii. 1: ὁ μὲν οὖν φάρυγξ τοῦ πνεύματος ἕνεκεν πέφυκεν· ὁ δ' οἰσοφάγος ἐστὶ δι' οὗ ἡ τροφὴ πορεύεται εἰς τὴν κοιλίαν. The latter was the term properly required above. Aristotle seems to

μακρότερον γεράνου γενέσθαι, ὡς ἡδόμενος τῇ ἁφῇ. κοινοτάτη δὴ τῶν αἰσθήσεων καθ' ἣν ἡ ἀκολασία· καὶ δόξειεν ἂν δικαίως ἐπονείδιστος εἶναι, ὅτι οὐχ ᾗ ἄνθρωποί ἐσμεν
11 ὑπάρχει, ἀλλ' ᾗ ζῷα. τὸ δὴ τοιούτοις χαίρειν καὶ μάλιστα ἀγαπᾶν θηριῶδες. καὶ γὰρ αἱ ἐλευθεριώταται τῶν διὰ τῆς ἁφῆς ἡδονῶν ἀφῄρηνται, οἷον αἱ ἐν τοῖς γυμνασίοις διὰ τρίψεως καὶ τῆς θερμασίας γινόμεναι· οὐ γὰρ περὶ πᾶν τὸ σῶμα ἡ τοῦ ἀκολάστου ἁφή, ἀλλὰ περί τινα μέρη.

11 Τῶν δ' ἐπιθυμιῶν αἱ μὲν κοιναὶ δοκοῦσιν εἶναι, αἱ δ' ἴδιοι καὶ ἐπίθετοι. οἷον ἡ μὲν τῆς τροφῆς φυσική· πᾶς γὰρ ἐπιθυμεῖ ὁ ἐνδεὴς ξηρᾶς ἢ ὑγρᾶς τροφῆς, ὁτὲ δ' ἀμφοῖν, καὶ εὐνῆς, φησὶν Ὅμηρος, ὁ νέος καὶ ἀκμάζων· τὸ δὲ τοιᾶσδε
2 ἢ τοιᾶσδε, οὐκέτι πᾶς, οὐδὲ τῶν αὐτῶν. διὸ φαίνεται ἡμέτερον εἶναι. οὐ μὴν ἀλλ' ἔχει γέ τι καὶ φυσικόν. ἕτερα γὰρ ἑτέροις ἐστὶν ἡδέα, καὶ ἔνια πᾶσιν ἡδίω τῶν
3 τυχόντων. ἐν μὲν οὖν ταῖς φυσικαῖς ἐπιθυμίαις ὀλίγοι ἁμαρτάνουσι καὶ ἐφ' ἕν, ἐπὶ τὸ πλεῖον. τὸ γὰρ ἐσθίειν τὰ τυχόντα ἢ πίνειν ἕως ἂν ὑπερπλησθῇ, ὑπερβάλλειν ἐστὶ τὸ κατὰ φύσιν τῷ πλήθει· ἀναπλήρωσις γὰρ τῆς ἐνδείας ἡ φυσικὴ ἐπιθυμία. διὸ λέγονται οὗτοι γαστρίμαργοι, ὡς παρὰ τὸ δέον πληροῦντες αὐτήν. τοιοῦτοι δὲ γίνονται οἱ
4 λίαν ἀνδραποδώδεις. περὶ δὲ τὰς ἰδίας τῶν ἡδονῶν πολλοὶ

---

have considered that the pleasure of gluttony was not in *taste*, of which the tongue was the organ, but in the contact of food with the passage of the oesophagus.

XI. 1 καὶ εὐνῆς, φησὶν Ὅμηρος] *Iliad* XXIV. 129: μεμνημένος οὔτε τι σίτου, οὔτ' εὐνῆς, the remonstrance of Thetis to Achilles. It is plain what εὐνῆς means.

2 διὸ — τυχόντων] 'Hence (this choice of particular foods, &c.) appears merely factitious. In reality, however, it has something natural in it, for different things are pleasant to different people, and all men have their preferences.' Aristotle attributes the very diversity of tastes to a law of nature, which no doubt exists,—and to a wise purpose, else what a fearful rivalry there would be in the world. Some MSS. for πᾶσιν read τισιν. It seems common for transcribers, when they do not understand a sentence, to play fast and loose with πᾶς and τις: see below, *Eth.* v. vii. 4.

3 γαστρίμαργοι] 'Greedy-bellies' from μάργος, cf. Homer, *Od.* XVIII. 2, μετὰ δ' ἔπρεπε γαστέρι μάργῃ—and Euripides, *Cyclops* 310, πάρες τὸ μάργον σῆς γνάθου.

πληροῦντες αὐτήν] sc. τὴν γαστέρα, which is to be supplied from γαστρίμαργοι, according to the Aristotelian mode of writing.

καὶ πολλαχῶς ἁμαρτάνουσιν· τῶν γὰρ φιλοτοιούτων
λεγομένων ἢ τῷ χαίρειν οἷς μὴ δεῖ, ἢ τῷ μᾶλλον, ἢ ὡς οἱ
πολλοί, ἢ μὴ ὡς δεῖ, κατὰ πάντα δ' οἱ ἀκόλαστοι ὑπερ-
βάλλουσιν· καὶ γὰρ χαίρουσιν ἐνίοις οἷς οὐ δεῖ (μισητὰ
γάρ), καὶ εἴ τισι δεῖ χαίρειν τῶν τοιούτων, μᾶλλον ἢ δεῖ,
καὶ ὡς οἱ πολλοὶ χαίρουσιν. ἡ μὲν οὖν περὶ τὰς ἡδονὰς 5
ὑπερβολὴ ὅτι ἀκολασία καὶ ψεκτόν, δῆλον· περὶ δὲ τὰς
λύπας οὐχ ὥσπερ ἐπὶ τῆς ἀνδρείας τῷ ὑπομένειν λέγεται
σώφρων ἀκόλαστος δὲ τῷ μή, ἀλλ' ὁ μὲν ἀκόλαστος τῷ
λυπεῖσθαι μᾶλλον ἢ δεῖ ὅτι τῶν ἡδέων οὐ τυγχάνει (καὶ
τὴν λύπην δὲ ποιεῖ αὐτῷ ἡ ἡδονή), ὁ δὲ σώφρων τῷ μὴ
λυπεῖσθαι τῇ ἀπουσίᾳ καὶ τῷ ἀπέχεσθαι τοῦ ἡδέος. ὁ μὲν 6
οὖν ἀκόλαστος ἐπιθυμεῖ τῶν ἡδέων πάντων ἢ τῶν μάλιστα,
καὶ ἄγεται ὑπὸ τῆς ἐπιθυμίας ὥστε ἀντὶ τῶν ἄλλων ταῦθ'
αἱρεῖσθαι· διὸ καὶ λυπεῖται καὶ ἀποτυγχάνων καὶ ἐπιθυμῶν.
μετὰ λύπης γὰρ ἡ ἐπιθυμία· ἀτόπῳ δ' ἔοικε τὸ δι' ἡδονὴν
λυπεῖσθαι. ἐλλείποντες δὲ περὶ τὰς ἡδονὰς καὶ ἧττον ἢ 7
δεῖ χαίροντες οὐ πάνυ γίνονται· οὐ γὰρ ἀνθρωπική ἐστιν
ἡ τοιαύτη ἀναισθησία· καὶ γὰρ τὰ λοιπὰ ζῷα διακρίνει τὰ
βρώματα, καὶ τοῖς μὲν χαίρει τοῖς δ' οὔ· εἰ δέ τῳ μηθέν
ἐστιν ἡδὺ μηδὲ διαφέρει ἕτερον ἑτέρου, πόρρω ἂν εἴη τοῦ
ἄνθρωπος εἶναι· οὐ τέτευχε δ' ὁ τοιοῦτος ὀνόματος διὰ τὸ

4 *ἢ τῷ μᾶλλον, ἢ ὡς οἱ πολλοί*] It seems almost certain that ὡς here is an interpolation. It could not have been said that 'with regard to the special pleasures men are called "lovers of particular things" because they like them *as people in general do*.' What Aristotle wrote was, no doubt, *ἢ τῷ μᾶλλον ἢ οἱ πολλοί*, 'or because they like them more than people in general;' cf. *Eth.* IV. iv. 4, *ἐπαινοῦντες μὲν ἐπὶ τὸ μᾶλλον ἢ οἱ πολλοί, ψέγοντες δ' ἐπὶ τὸ μᾶλλον ἢ δεῖ*. The copyist must have taken *ἢ οἱ πολλοί* for a separate sentence, and so have thought it necessary to insert ὡς.

5 *καὶ τὴν λύπην δὲ ποιεῖ αὐτῷ ἡ ἡδονή*] 'And thus it is pleasure that produces him his pain.' This is stated as if it were a sort of disgraceful paradox, which takes place in intemperance.

7 *οὐ πάνυ γίνονται*] Aristotle, from his experience as a Greek, might have been justified in asserting that a deficiency in the sense for pleasures 'could hardly be said to exist.' It is not so certain that the same would be true in all periods of the world. It is not so certain that the monkish turn of mind does not occasionally diminish to an unhappy extent the natural and human feelings, so as to impair the kindliness, the geniality, and the good sense of mankind.

8 μὴ πάνυ γίνεσθαι. ὁ δὲ σώφρων μέσως περὶ ταῦτ' ἔχει· οὔτε γὰρ ἥδεται οἷς μάλιστα ὁ ἀκόλαστος, ἀλλὰ μᾶλλον δυσχεραίνει, οὐδ' ὅλως οἷς μὴ δεῖ οὔτε σφόδρα τοιούτῳ οὐδενί, οὔτ' ἀπόντων λυπεῖται οὐδ' ἐπιθυμεῖ, ἢ μετρίως, οὐδὲ μᾶλλον ἢ δεῖ, οὐδ' ὅτε μὴ δεῖ, οὐδ' ὅλως τῶν τοιούτων οὐθέν· ὅσα δὲ πρὸς ὑγίειάν ἐστιν ἢ πρὸς εὐεξίαν ἡδέα ὄντα, τούτων ὀρέξεται μετρίως καὶ ὡς δεῖ, καὶ τῶν ἄλλων ἡδέων μὴ ἐμποδίων τούτοις ὄντων ἢ παρὰ τὸ καλὸν ἢ ὑπὲρ τὴν οὐσίαν. ὁ γὰρ οὕτως ἔχων μᾶλλον ἀγαπᾷ τὰς τοιαύτας ἡδονὰς τῆς ἀξίας· ὁ δὲ σώφρων οὐ τοιοῦτος, ἀλλ' ὡς ὁ ὀρθὸς λόγος.

12 Ἑκουσίῳ δὲ μᾶλλον ἔοικεν ἡ ἀκολασία τῆς δειλίας. ἡ μὲν
γὰρ δι' ἡδονήν, ἡ δὲ διὰ λύπην, ὧν τὸ μὲν αἱρετόν, τὸ δὲ φευ-
2 κτόν. καὶ ἡ μὲν λύπη ἐξίστησι καὶ φθείρει τὴν τοῦ ἔχοντος

---

8 We see how indefinite after all Aristotle has left the standard of temperance, he refers it merely to the blank formula of *ὡς δεῖ* and *τὸ καλόν*. In so leaving it, however, he appeals to a sense in each man's own mind. There is a relative element to be considered, the health or fortune of the individual (*πρὸς ὑγίειαν*, *μὴ ὑπὲρ τὴν οὐσίαν*), and there is also something that appears absolute amidst all that is relative (*τὸ καλόν*).

ὁ γὰρ οὕτως ἔχων] This is an awkward piece of writing. *Οὕτως* refers to those phrases which have been negatived—*παρὰ τὸ καλὸν ἢ ὑπὲρ τὴν οὐσίαν*.

XII. Which is most voluntary, cowardice or intemperance? a suitable question to conclude a Book which opened with a theory of the voluntary and proceeded to discuss courage and temperance. Thus far there is method. Courage and temperance are considered very much throughout in relation to each other, and here they are considered in relation to the voluntary. On the other hand the subject of this chapter is closely connected with the theory of the formation of habits (*Eth.* II. i.—ii.), and also with the questions mooted above (*Eth.* III. v.) as to the voluntariness of vicious habits. Standing then as it does isolated, it forms an instance of the immaturity of Aristotle's moral investigations.

Intemperance is more voluntary than cowardice, inasmuch as it consists in *choosing* pleasure, while cowardice is under a sort of compulsion, flying from pain. (2) Again it is easier by practice to learn to resist temptation, than it is to learn to withstand danger, for the opportunities are frequent and *free from risk*. Hence intemperance is the more disgraceful of the two. (3) These vices are in a peculiar way different from each other, for cowardice as a whole is more voluntary than its parts. Intemperance as a whole is less voluntary than its parts.

The chapter ends with some remarks on the nature of *ἀκολασία* as connected with its etymology.

2 *καὶ ἡ μὲν λύπη—ποιεῖ*] 'And while pain distracts and overturns the

φύσιν, ἡ δὲ ἡδονὴ οὐδὲν τοιοῦτον ποιεῖ, μᾶλλον δ' ἑκούσιον·
διὸ καὶ ἐπονειδιστότερον· καὶ γὰρ ἐθισθῆναι ῥᾷον πρὸς αὐτά·
πολλὰ γὰρ ἐν τῷ βίῳ τὰ τοιαῦτα, καὶ οἱ ἐθισμοὶ ἀκίνδυνοι,
ἐπὶ δὲ τῶν φοβερῶν ἀνάπαλιν. δόξειε δ' ἂν οὐχ ὁμοίως 3
ἑκούσιον ἡ δειλία εἶναι τοῖς καθ' ἕκαστον· αὐτὴ μὲν γὰρ
ἄλυπος, ταῦτα δὲ διὰ λύπην ἐξίστησιν, ὥστε καὶ τὰ ὅπλα
ῥίπτειν καὶ τἆλλα ἀσχημονεῖν· διὸ καὶ δοκεῖ βίαια εἶναι.
τῷ δ' ἀκολάστῳ ἀνάπαλιν τὰ μὲν καθ' ἕκαστα ἑκούσια, 4
ἐπιθυμοῦντι γὰρ καὶ ὀρεγομένῳ, τὸ δ' ὅλον ἧττον· οὐθεὶς
γὰρ ἐπιθυμεῖ ἀκόλαστος εἶναι. τὸ δ' ὄνομα τῆς ἀκολασίας 5
καὶ ἐπὶ τὰς παιδικὰς ἁμαρτίας φέρομεν· ἔχουσι γάρ τινα
ὁμοιότητα. πότερον δ' ἀπὸ ποτέρου καλεῖται, οὐθὲν πρὸς
τὰ νῦν διαφέρει, δῆλον δ' ὅτι τὸ ὕστερον ἀπὸ τοῦ προτέρου. οὐ κακῶς δ' ἔοικε μετενηνέχθαι· κεκολάσθαι γὰρ 6
δεῖ τὸ τῶν αἰσχρῶν ὀρεγόμενον καὶ πολλὴν αὔξησιν ἔχον,
τοιοῦτον δὲ μάλιστα ἡ ἐπιθυμία καὶ ὁ παῖς· κατ' ἐπιθυμίαν γὰρ ζῶσι καὶ τὰ παιδία, καὶ μάλιστα ἐν τούτοις

---

mental balance of him who experiences it, pleasure does nothing of the kind.' Φύσις here denotes the perfect or normal state: see above, *Eth.* II. i. 3, note.

3 δόξειε δ' ἂν—ἐξίστησιν] 'But cowardice is not equally voluntary with (*i.e.* is more voluntary than) its particular acts, for in itself it is painless, while its particulars distract the mind with pain.' It seems curious to speak of cowardice in this abstract way as distinct from all particular acts of cowardice. It is, however, true that cowardice is not, like intemperance, a growing chain upon the mind. Each cowardly act, while it leaves the mind irresolute and so prone to fresh cowardice, on the other hand brings experience and renders the mind more familiar with danger. Thus cowardice, which at first was involuntary, tends to become more and more voluntary and deliberate, the more it is continued in; but intemperance, which at first was voluntary, becomes, the longer it lasts, more and more involuntary and a mere bondage.

5—6 τὸ δ' ὄνομα—ὄρεξις] 'Now the name intemperance (or unrestrainedness) we apply also to the faults of children, for these have some resemblance to it. *Which* is called from *which*, matters not for our present purpose; obviously that which is later in conception is called from that which is earlier. And it seems no bad metaphor, for that which hankers after what is base, and which has a mighty capacity for development, requires to be chastened, and this is just the character of desire and of the child. Children live entirely by desire, and have the longing for what is pleasant most strongly.' Eudemus (*Eth. Eud.* III. ii. 1) commences his account of intemperance with this etymology. He points out that ἀκόλαστος is capable of two meanings,

7 ἡ τοῦ ἡδέος ὄρεξις· εἰ οὖν μὴ ἔσται εὐπειθὲς καὶ ὑπὸ τὸ ἄρχον, ἐπὶ πολὺ ἥξει· ἄπληστος γὰρ ἡ τοῦ ἡδέος ὄρεξις καὶ πανταχόθεν τῷ ἀνοήτῳ, καὶ ἡ τῆς ἐπιθυμίας ἐνέργεια αὔξει τὸ συγγενές, κἂν μεγάλαι καὶ σφοδραὶ ὦσι, καὶ τὸν λογισμὸν ἐκκρούουσιν. διὸ δεῖ μετρίας εἶναι αὐτὰς καὶ
8 ὀλίγας, καὶ τῷ λόγῳ μηθὲν ἐναντιοῦσθαι. τὸ δὲ τοιοῦτον εὐπειθὲς λέγομεν καὶ κεκολασμένον· ὥσπερ γὰρ τὸν παῖδα δεῖ κατὰ τὸ πρόσταγμα τοῦ παιδαγωγοῦ ζῆν, οὕτω καὶ τὸ
9 ἐπιθυμητικὸν κατὰ τὸν λόγον. διὸ δεῖ τοῦ σώφρονος τὸ ἐπιθυμητικὸν συμφωνεῖν τῷ λόγῳ· σκοπὸς γὰρ ἀμφοῖν τὸ καλόν, καὶ ἐπιθυμεῖ ὁ σώφρων ὧν δεῖ καὶ ὡς δεῖ καὶ
10 ὅτε· οὕτω δὲ τάττει καὶ ὁ λόγος. ταῦτ' οὖν ἡμῖν εἰρήσθω περὶ σωφροσύνης.

'he that has not been chastened,' and 'he that cannot be chastened.' His account of the metaphor implied in the word appears to be lost. He says (§ 3), *διεγράψαμεν πρότερον νῦν τὴν ἀκολασίαν ὀνομάζοντες μεταφέρομεν*, but in *Eth. Eud.* II. iii., to which he alludes, there is apparently a lacuna. Aristotle declines to decide which is the primary and which the metaphorical use of the word; but there can be no doubt that the punishment and unrestrainedness of children is the more concrete and the primary idea.

7 *εἰ οὖν—ἐναντιοῦσθαι*] 'If then this thing be not obedient and subjected to the governing element, it will develop vastly; for the longing for what is pleasant is insatiable to him that is foolish, and it seeks satisfaction from all quarters; and the exercise of desire increases its native powers, and if the desires grow great and vehement, they expel all reasoning in the end. Wherefore the desires should be moderate and few, and nowise opposed to the law of reason.' *Εὐπειθές* is indefinite; it might refer either to *ἡ ἐπιθυμία* or *ὁ παῖς*. Aristotle speaking indistinctly had the idea of *ἐπιθυμία* most present to his mind. Out of this etymology of 'intemperance' he develops anew the relationship which ought to exist between the passions and the reason. The passions should be to the reason as a child to his tutor. This analogy was already suggested in *Eth.* I. xiii. 19: *διττὸν ἔσται καὶ τὸ λόγον ἔχον, τὸ μὲν κυρίως καὶ ἐν αὑτῷ, τὸ δ' ὥσπερ τοῦ πατρὸς ἀκουστικόν τι.*

PLAN OF BOOK IV.

WITH only two exceptions, this Book follows faithfully the programme drawn out in the seventh chapter of Book II. These exceptions are, that it inverts the order of the social virtues—Truth, Wit, and Friendship; and that, being at its close fragmentary or mutilated, it omits to discuss Indignation, and breaks off in the middle of a discussion upon Modesty.

The only question, then, that arises is—Can we find any logical sequence in Aristotle's list of the virtues as given in Book II. and followed out here? There are various principles on which a classification of the virtues might have been made; as, for instance, on a principle of psychological division, it might have been shown how the virtues are the proper development of man's nature in its various parts. Or, again, with a view to education, the virtues might have been arranged according to the most natural order of inculcation. Or, again, in point of excellence, the greater virtues might have taken precedence of the lesser ones. But no one broad principle of this kind is to be found in the arrangement made by Aristotle. It must always be remembered that his *Ethics*, while tending to advance psychology very greatly, are not composed upon a psychological system. Hence, though he said (*Eth.* III. x. 1) that Temperance must succeed Courage, because these both consisted in the regulation of the brute instincts, we do not find elsewhere any reference to a classification of the parts of man's nature. Aristotle, having clearly divided moral from intellectual excellence, does not carry out the same sort of division in discussing moral excellence. He seems to have taken up first the most prominent and striking qualities, according to the common notions in Greece—Courage, Temperance, and Liberality. Liberality suggested to him Magnificence—Magnificence, Great-souledness; and from this he proceeded to distinguish the more ordinary quality of Ambition. He then added, what had hitherto been omitted, the virtue of regulation of the temper; and pointed out that in social intercourse three excellent qualities are produced by bringing the demeanour under the control of the law of balance. Lastly, he was proceeding to show that even in the instinctive and untrained feelings of Modesty and Indignation, this same law exhibits itself, when, either from interruption, or from mutilation, the book came abruptly to a close.

ΗΘΙΚΩΝ ΝΙΚΟΜΑΧΕΙΩΝ IV.

ΛΕΓΩΜΕΝ δ' ἑξῆς περὶ ἐλευθεριότητος, δοκεῖ δ' εἶναι
ἡ περὶ χρήματα μεσότης· ἐπαινεῖται γὰρ ὁ ἐλευθέριος οὐκ ἐν τοῖς πολεμικοῖς, οὐδ' ἐν οἷς ὁ σώφρων,
οὐδ' αὖ ἐν ταῖς κρίσεσιν, ἀλλὰ περὶ δόσιν χρημάτων καὶ
λῆψιν, μᾶλλον δ' ἐν τῇ δόσει. χρήματα δὲ λέγομεν 2
πάντα ὅσων ἡ ἀξία νομίσματι μετρεῖται. ἔστι δὲ καὶ ἡ 3
ἀσωτία καὶ ἡ ἀνελευθερία περὶ χρήματα ὑπερβολαὶ καὶ
ἐλλείψεις. καὶ τὴν μὲν ἀνελευθερίαν προσάπτομεν ἀεὶ
τοῖς μᾶλλον ἢ δεῖ περὶ χρήματα σπουδάζουσι, τὴν δ'
ἀσωτίαν ἐπιφέρομεν ἐνίοτε συμπλέκοντες· τοὺς γὰρ ἀκρατεῖς καὶ εἰς ἀκολασίαν δαπανηροὺς ἀσώτους καλοῦμεν.
διὸ καὶ φαυλότατοι δοκοῦσιν εἶναι. πολλὰς γὰρ ἅμα 4
κακίας ἔχουσιν. οὐ δὴ οἰκείως προσαγορεύονται· βούλε- 5
ται γὰρ ἄσωτος εἶναι ὁ ἓν τι κακὸν ἔχων, τὸ φθείρειν τὴν
οὐσίαν· ἄσωτος γὰρ ὁ δι' αὑτὸν ἀπολλύμενος, δοκεῖ δ'

I. 1 Aristotle's excellent account of liberality represents it as the balance between illiberality and prodigality. On the characters produced by these different qualities the most discriminating and happy remarks are made in the present chapter.

1 οὐδ' αὖ ἐν ταῖς κρίσεσιν] 'Nor again in decisions.' The Paraphrast adds ὥσπερ ὁ δίκαιος. Κρίσις here is used in a general sense; it may or may not be a legal decision. Cf. *Eth.* v. vi. 4: ἡ γὰρ δίκη κρίσις τοῦ δικαίου καὶ τοῦ ἀδίκου.

2 χρήματα δὲ—μετρεῖται] 'Now we call "property" all things whose value is measured by money.' In other words 'all things with an exchangeable value.'

3 τὴν δ' ἀσωτίαν—καλοῦμεν] 'But the term "prodigality" we sometimes apply in a complicated sense, for we call those who are incontinent and who lavish money on intemperance—prodigals.' Exactly the same usage has been confirmed in modern language by the associations of the parable of 'the Prodigal Son.'

5 οὐ δὴ οἰκείως—ἐκδεχόμεθα]

ἀπώλειά τις αὐτοῦ εἶναι καὶ ἡ τῆς οὐσίας φθορά, ὡς τοῦ
ζῆν διὰ τούτων ὄντος. οὕτω δὴ τὴν ἀσωτίαν ἐκδεχόμεθα.
6 ὧν δ' ἐστὶ χρεία, ἔστι τούτοις χρῆσθαι καὶ εὖ καὶ κακῶς·
ὁ πλοῦτος δ' ἐστὶ τῶν χρησίμων· ἑκάστῳ δ' ἄριστα
χρῆται ὁ ἔχων τὴν περὶ τοῦτο ἀρετήν· καὶ πλούτῳ δὴ
χρήσεται ἄριστα ὁ ἔχων τὴν περὶ τὰ χρήματα ἀρετήν.
7 οὗτος δ' ἐστὶν ὁ ἐλευθέριος. χρῆσις δ' εἶναι δοκεῖ χρημάτων δαπάνη καὶ δόσις· ἡ δὲ λῆψις καὶ ἡ φυλακὴ κτῆσις
μᾶλλον. διὸ μᾶλλόν ἐστι τοῦ ἐλευθερίου τὸ διδόναι οἷς
δεῖ ἢ λαμβάνειν ὅθεν δεῖ καὶ μὴ λαμβάνειν ὅθεν οὐ δεῖ.
τῆς γὰρ ἀρετῆς μᾶλλον τὸ εὖ ποιεῖν ἢ τὸ εὖ πάσχειν, καὶ
τὰ καλὰ πράττειν μᾶλλον ἢ τὰ αἰσχρὰ μὴ πράττειν·
8 οὐκ ἄδηλον δ' ὅτι τῇ μὲν δόσει ἕπεται τὸ εὖ ποιεῖν καὶ τὸ
καλὰ πράττειν, τῇ δὲ λήψει τὸ εὖ πάσχειν ἢ μὴ
αἰσχροπραγεῖν. καὶ ἡ χάρις τῷ διδόντι, οὐ τῷ μὴ λαμ-
9 βάνοντι, καὶ ὁ ἔπαινος δὲ μᾶλλον. καὶ ῥᾷον δὲ τὸ μὴ

'This application of the name is improper; for "prodigal" ought to denote a man who has *one* fault, the habit of wasting his substance. The word literally means "he who destroys himself," and the wasting of one's substance may well be thought a kind of self-destruction, for life depends upon substance. This accordingly is the sense in which we take the word "prodigality."' Aristotle attributes some weight here to the etymology of ἄσωτος, arguing that the man who destroys his property, destroys himself, and he who destroys himself is beyond salvation (ἄσωτος). Βούλεται εἶναι is exactly analogous to the English word 'means.' Cf. *Eth.* III. i. 15. Τὸ δ' ἀκούσιον βούλεται λέγεσθαι κ.τ.λ. In *Eth.* V. v. 14, βούλεται is used in a slightly different sense to denote not the 'meaning' of a word, but a 'tendency' in things, ὅμως δὲ βούλεται μένειν μᾶλλον.

7 Liberality or 'the virtue connected with property' consists more in right giving and spending than in right receiving. The former is the positive and active side, the latter is the negative and passive side. Giving is the 'use' of money, receiving and keeping is more 'possession.' And 'use,' as Aristotle tells us in the *Rhetoric* (I. v. 7), constitutes wealth proper, as being a sort of life and reality (ἐνέργεια), which mere possession is not. Ὅλως δὲ τὸ πλουτεῖν ἐστὶν ἐν τῷ χρῆσθαι μᾶλλον ἢ ἐν τῷ κεκτῆσθαι· καὶ γὰρ ἡ ἐνέργειά ἐστι τῶν τοιούτων καὶ ἡ χρῆσις πλοῦτος.

8 οὐκ ἄδηλον δ' — αἰσχροπραγεῖν] 'It is not hard to see that giving is an avenue to the doing of good and to noble action, while in taking we only receive a benefit or at most keep clear of having to do base actions.' See below § 39, where it is said to be the excuse of the illiberal ἵνα μή ποτ' ἀναγκασθῶσιν αἰσχρόν τι πρᾶξαι.

9 καὶ ῥᾷον δὲ — ἀλλότριον] 'And it is easier too to abstain from taking than it is to give; for men are less

λαβεῖν τοῦ δοῦναι. τὸ γὰρ οἰκεῖον ἧττον προΐενται
μᾶλλον ἢ οὐ λαμβάνουσι τὸ ἀλλότριον. καὶ ἐλευθέριοι δὲ 10
λέγονται οἱ διδόντες· οἱ δὲ μὴ λαμβάνοντες οὐκ εἰς ἐλευθεριότητα ἐπαινοῦνται, ἀλλ' οὐχ ἧττον εἰς δικαιοσύνην·
οἱ δὲ λαμβάνοντες οὐδ' ἐπαινοῦνται πάνυ. φιλοῦνται δὲ 11
σχεδὸν μάλιστα οἱ ἐλευθέριοι τῶν ἀπ' ἀρετῆς. ὠφέλιμοι
γάρ, τοῦτο δ' ἐν τῇ δόσει. αἱ δὲ κατ' ἀρετὴν πράξεις 12
καλαὶ καὶ τοῦ καλοῦ ἕνεκα. καὶ ὁ ἐλευθέριος οὖν δώσει
τοῦ καλοῦ ἕνεκα καὶ ὀρθῶς· οἷς γὰρ δεῖ καὶ ὅσα καὶ ὅτε,
καὶ τἆλλα ὅσα ἕπεται τῇ ὀρθῇ δόσει. καὶ ταῦτα ἡδέως 13
ἢ ἀλύπως· τὸ γὰρ κατ' ἀρετὴν ἡδὺ ἢ ἄλυπον, ἥκιστα δὲ
λυπηρόν. ὁ δὲ διδοὺς οἷς μὴ δεῖ, ἢ μὴ τοῦ καλοῦ ἕνεκα 14
ἀλλὰ διά τιν' ἄλλην αἰτίαν, οὐκ ἐλευθέριος ἀλλ' ἄλλος τις
ῥηθήσεται. οὐδ' ὁ λυπηρῶς· μᾶλλον γὰρ ἕλοιτ' ἂν τὰ
χρήματα τῆς καλῆς πράξεως, τοῦτο δ' οὐκ ἐλευθερίου.
οὐδὲ λήψεται δὲ ὅθεν μὴ δεῖ· οὐδὲ γάρ ἐστι τοῦ μὴ τιμῶν- 15
τος τὰ χρήματα ἡ τοιαύτη λῆψις. οὐκ ἂν εἴη δὲ οὐδ' 16
αἰτητικός. οὐ γάρ ἐστι τοῦ εὖ ποιοῦντος εὐχερῶς εὐεργε-

---

willing to give away (ἧττον προΐενται μᾶλλον) what is their own, than they are to abstain from taking what belongs to others.' Μᾶλλον is redundant, it goes to strengthen the comparative force of ἧττον.—Οὐ λαμβάνουσι corresponds to μὴ λαβεῖν just before, and makes up a positive notion to 'abstain from taking.' Aristotle attributes to men in general a character the reverse of that attributed by Sallust to Catiline, 'alieni appetens, sui profusus.'

11 οἱ δὲ λαμβάνοντες οὐδ' ἐπαινοῦνται πάνυ] 'But they who receive are not praised at all.' Πάνυ means 'quite': οὐ πάνυ in the sense of 'hardly' is frequent in Aristotle; cf. *Eth.* III. ii. 12—13: λαβεῖν ἢ φυγεῖν οὐ πάνυ δοξάζομεν—δοξάζομεν ἃ οὐ πάνυ ἴσμεν: and οὐδὲ πάνυ appears to mean 'not at all,' the οὐδέ being joined with the verb.

16 οὐκ ἂν εἴη—εὐεργετεῖσθαι] 'Nor would he be ready to ask favours, for it does not belong to the benefactor to be easily a receiver of benefits.' This is a manifestation of the spirit which runs through the virtuous characters of Aristotle—the spirit of manliness and nobility (ἀνδρώδης καὶ φιλόκαλος, cf. *Eth.* IV. iv. 3). It appears most strongly in the character of the great-souled man; see below, ch. iii. § 24. The principle of individuality, a sense of life and free action (ἐνέργεια), are with Aristotle the basis of morality, and the first requisite to nobleness seems to be self-respect. Now, a slight difference in the way in which this truth is stated will make it appear a pure or a selfish principle. Christianity says, 'It is more blessed to give than to receive,' implying that to gratify a feeling of love and kindness is better than any pleasure that the sense of gain could afford. But the Christian sentiment of love and

17 τεῖσθαι. ὅθεν δὲ δεῖ, λήψεται, οἷον ἀπὸ τῶν ἰδίων κτημάτων, οὐχ ὡς καλὸν ἀλλ' ὡς ἀναγκαῖον, ὅπως ἔχῃ διδόναι.
οὐδ' ἀμελήσει τῶν ἰδίων, βουλόμενός γε διὰ τούτων τισὶν
ἐπαρκεῖν. οὐδὲ τοῖς τυχοῦσι δώσει, ἵνα ἔχῃ διδόναι οἷς δεῖ
18 καὶ ὅτε καὶ οὗ καλόν. ἐλευθερίου δ' ἐστὶ σφόδρα καὶ τὸ
ὑπερβάλλειν ἐν τῇ δόσει, ὥστε καταλείπειν ἑαυτῷ ἐλάττω·
19 τὸ γὰρ μὴ ἐπιβλέπειν ἐφ' ἑαυτὸν ἐλευθερίου. κατὰ τὴν
οὐσίαν δ' ἡ ἐλευθεριότης λέγεται· οὐ γὰρ ἐν τῷ πλήθει
τῶν διδομένων τὸ ἐλευθέριον, ἀλλ' ἐν τῇ τοῦ διδόντος ἕξει,
αὕτη δὲ κατὰ τὴν οὐσίαν δίδωσιν. οὐθὲν δὴ κωλύει ἐλευθεριώτερον εἶναι τὸν τὰ ἐλάττω διδόντα, ἐὰν ἀπ' ἐλαττόνων
20 διδῷ. ἐλευθεριώτεροι δὲ εἶναι δοκοῦσιν οἱ μὴ κτησάμενοι
ἀλλὰ παραλαβόντες τὴν οὐσίαν· ἄπειροί τε γὰρ τῆς

---

charity, though unselfish, is not selfless. For as all knowledge implies a subject as well as an object, so does every moral act or feeling imply the will and individuality of the actor. In the Christian sentiment there is so great a harmony between the object and subject, that the subjective side appears to be lost; but in reality it is only lost to be found again, it is diminished to be enhanced. Aristotle's statement would be, 'It is better to give than to receive, because it is more noble.' This has a slight tendency to give too much weight to the subjective side. In Aristotle's whole account we do not find a word about benevolence or love to others as prompting acts of liberality. We find no other motive but the 'splendour' (*καλόν*) of the acts themselves. What is said in the present section verges towards the selfish theory, which would ascribe such acts to the love of power inherent in man. In Hobbes (*Leviathan*, Book 1, Chap. xi.) we find a bitter statement of the feelings with which benefits may be received. 'To have received from one, to whom we think ourselves equal, greater benefits than there is hope to requite, disposeth to counterfeit love; but really secret hatred. For benefits oblige, and obligation is thraldom; and unrequitable obligation, perpetual thraldom, which is to one's equal, hateful.' Cf. *Eth.* IX. vii.

17—19 Points in the character of the liberal man: he will take care of his own property in order that he may have means for his liberality. Hence, too, he will be discriminating in the objects of his favours; yet his tendency is to forget himself, to give largely, to leave hardly anything for himself; yet again, liberality does not depend on the largeness of the gift, it is in proportion to the means of the giver—a less gift may be more liberal than a large one.

20 *ἐλευθεριώτεροι δὲ — ποιηταί*] 'We see that those are the most liberal who have not themselves acquired their property, but have inherited it; for they have never known what want is, nor are they restrained by that love of what we have ourselves produced, which belongs to all men, and is well exemplified in parents and poets.' On the philosophy of this remark, cf.

ἐνδείας, καὶ πάντες ἀγαπῶσι μᾶλλον τὰ αὑτῶν ἔργα, ὥσπερ
οἱ γονεῖς καὶ οἱ ποιηταί. πλουτεῖν δ' οὐ ῥᾴδιον τὸν ἐλευθέριον, μήτε ληπτικὸν ὄντα μήτε φυλακτικόν, προετικὸν
δὲ καὶ μὴ τιμῶντα δι' αὑτὰ τὰ χρήματα ἀλλ' ἕνεκα
τῆς δόσεως. διὸ καὶ ἐγκαλεῖται τῇ τύχῃ ὅτι οἱ μάλιστα 21
ἄξιοι ὄντες ἥκιστα πλουτοῦσιν. συμβαίνει δ' οὐκ ἀλόγως
τοῦτο· οὐ γὰρ οἷόν τε χρήματ' ἔχειν μὴ ἐπιμελούμενον
ὅπως ἔχῃ, ὥσπερ οὐδ' ἐπὶ τῶν ἄλλων. οὐ μὴν δώσει γε 22
οἷς οὐ δεῖ οὐδ' ὅτε μὴ δεῖ, οὐδ' ὅσα ἄλλα τοιαῦτα· οὐ γὰρ
ἂν ἔτι πράττοι κατὰ τὴν ἐλευθεριότητα, καὶ εἰς ταῦτα
ἀναλώσας οὐκ ἂν ἔχοι εἰς ἃ δεῖ ἀναλίσκειν. ὥσπερ γὰρ 23
εἴρηται, ἐλευθέριός ἐστιν ὁ κατὰ τὴν οὐσίαν δαπανῶν καὶ
εἰς ἃ δεῖ· ὁ δ' ὑπερβάλλων ἄσωτος. διὸ τοὺς τυράννους
οὐ λέγομεν ἀσώτους· τὸ γὰρ πλῆθος τῆς κτήσεως οὐ δοκεῖ
ῥᾴδιον εἶναι ταῖς δόσεσι καὶ ταῖς δαπάναις ὑπερβάλλειν.
τῆς ἐλευθεριότητος δὴ μεσότητος οὔσης περὶ χρημάτων 24
δόσιν καὶ λῆψιν, ὁ ἐλευθέριος καὶ δώσει καὶ δαπανήσει εἰς
ἃ δεῖ καὶ ὅσα δεῖ, ὁμοίως ἐν μικροῖς καὶ μεγάλοις, καὶ ταῦτα
ἡδέως· καὶ λήψεται δ' ὅθεν δεῖ καὶ ὅσα δεῖ. τῆς ἀρετῆς
γὰρ περὶ ἄμφω οὔσης μεσότητος, ποιήσει ἀμφότερα ὡς δεῖ·
ἕπεται γὰρ τῇ ἐπιεικεῖ δόσει ἡ τοιαύτη λῆψις, ἡ δὲ μὴ
τοιαύτη ἐναντία ἐστίν. αἱ μὲν οὖν ἑπόμεναι γίγνονται
ἅμα ἐν τῷ αὐτῷ, αἱ δ' ἐναντίαι δῆλον ὡς οὔ. ἐὰν δὲ παρὰ 25
τὸ δέον καὶ τὸ καλῶς ἔχον συμβαίνῃ αὐτῷ ἀναλίσκειν,
λυπήσεται, μετρίως δὲ καὶ ὡς δεῖ· τῆς ἀρετῆς γὰρ καὶ

Eth. IX. vii. 2-7. The remark itself comes almost *verbatim* from Plato's *Republic*, p. 330 B–C. Socrates asks Cephalus whether he made his money or inherited it, and gives as a reason for the question, οὔ τοι ἕνεκα ἠρόμην, ἦν δ' ἐγώ, ὅτι μοι ἔδοξας οὐ σφόδρα ἀγαπᾶν τὰ χρήματα. Τοῦτο δὲ ποιοῦσιν ὡς τὸ πολὺ οἳ ἂν μὴ αὐτοὶ κτήσωνται· οἱ δὲ κτησάμενοι διπλῇ ἢ οἱ ἄλλοι ἀσπάζονται αὐτά· ὥσπερ γὰρ οἱ ποιηταὶ τὰ αὑτῶν ποιήματα καὶ οἱ πατέρες τοὺς παῖδας ἀγαπῶσι, ταύτῃ τε δὴ καὶ οἱ χρηματισάμενοι περὶ τὰ χρήματα σπουδάζουσιν, ὡς ἔργον ἑαυτῶν, καὶ κατὰ τὴν χρείαν, ᾗπερ οἱ ἄλλοι. From another cause, however, merchants, with their large fluctuating gains, seem often more liberal than the landowners, with their fixed incomes.

21 With perfect good sense Aristotle says that a very natural explanation may be given of the common railings you hear against fortune for not making 'the right people' (*i.e.* the liberal) rich. People can't expect to be rich who have hardly any care for money, and this is the characte-

26 ἥδεσθαι καὶ λυπεῖσθαι ἐφ' οἷς δεῖ καὶ ὡς δεῖ. καὶ εὐκοινώ-
27 νητος δ' ἐστὶν ὁ ἐλευθέριος εἰς χρήματα· δύναται γὰρ ἀδικεῖσθαι, μὴ τιμῶν γε τὰ χρήματα, καὶ μᾶλλον ἀχθόμενος
εἴ τι δέον μὴ ἀνάλωσεν ἢ λυπούμενος εἰ μὴ δέον τι ἀνάλωσε,
28 καὶ τῷ Σιμωνίδῃ οὐκ ἀρεσκόμενος. ὁ δ' ἄσωτος καὶ ἐν
τούτοις διαμαρτάνει. οὔτε γὰρ ἥδεται ἐφ' οἷς δεῖ οὐδὲ ὡς
29 δεῖ οὔτε λυπεῖται· ἔσται δὲ προϊοῦσι φανερώτερον. εἴρηται
δ' ἡμῖν ὅτι ὑπερβολαὶ καὶ ἐλλείψεις εἰσὶν ἡ ἀσωτία καὶ ἡ
ἀνελευθερία, καὶ ἐν δυσίν, ἐν δόσει καὶ λήψει· καὶ τὴν δαπάνην
γὰρ εἰς τὴν δόσιν τίθεμεν. ἡ μὲν οὖν ἀσωτία τῷ διδόναι
καὶ μὴ λαμβάνειν ὑπερβάλλει, τῷ δὲ λαμβάνειν ἐλλείπει,
ἡ δ' ἀνελευθερία τῷ διδόναι μὲν ἐλλείπει, τῷ λαμβάνειν
30 δ' ὑπερβάλλει, πλὴν ἐπὶ μικροῖς. τὰ μὲν οὖν τῆς ἀσωτίας
οὐ πάνυ συνδυάζεται· οὐ γὰρ ῥᾴδιον μηδαμόθεν λαμβάνοντα
πᾶσι διδόναι· ταχέως γὰρ ἐπιλείπει ἡ οὐσία τοὺς ἰδιώτας
31 διδόντας, οἵπερ καὶ δοκοῦσιν ἄσωτοι εἶναι, ἐπεὶ ὅ γε τοιοῦτος
δόξειεν ἂν οὐ μικρῷ βελτίων εἶναι τοῦ ἀνελευθέρου. εὐίατός

---

ristic of the liberal.

26—27 καὶ εὐκοινώνητος—ἀρεσκόμενος] 'Farther, the liberal man is easy to deal with in business transactions; for there is no difficulty in cheating him, owing to his disregard of money, and he is more annoyed at having omitted any proper expense than vexed at spending what is needless, nor does he approve the precepts of Simonides.' These remarks show a penetrating knowledge of mankind, but they do not exhibit liberality in the highest light. The gratification of a personal feeling is made rather too prominent, hence we miss the beauty of 'charity seeketh not her own.' With the present passage we may compare the description of equity in the *Rhetoric* (I. xiii. 15-19), part of which is τὸ ἀνέχεσθαι ἀδικούμενον. Various sentiments are attributed to Simonides, all testifying to the solid advantage of riches. Cf. Ar. *Rhetoric*, II. xvi. 2: ὅθεν καὶ τὸ Σιμωνίδου εἴρηται περὶ τῶν σοφῶν καὶ πλουσίων πρὸς τὴν γυναῖκα τὴν Ἱέρωνος ἐρομένην πότερον γενέσθαι κρεῖττον πλούσιον ἢ σοφόν· πλούσιον εἰπεῖν· τοὺς σοφοὺς γὰρ ἔφη ὁρᾶν ἐπὶ ταῖς τῶν πλουσίων θύραις διατρίβοντας. Again, there is quoted by Plutarch a saying that 'the money-chest is always full, and the chest of the graces always empty;' and another, that 'avarice is the proper pleasure of old age.' On the philosophy of Simonides, see Vol. I. Essay II. pp. 94-95.

29 τῷ λαμβάνειν—μικροῖς] 'Illiberality exceeds in taking, only it must be in petty matters.' Grasping on a large scale gets another name than illiberality; cf. §§ 41-42.

30 τὰ μὲν οὖν—ἀνελευθέρου] 'The two sides of prodigality can hardly exist together; for it is not easy to give to everybody and receive from nobody; private persons, whom alone we reckon prodigals, soon find their substance failing them. For, in fact, the

τι γάρ ἐστι καὶ ὑπὸ τῆς ἡλικίας καὶ ὑπὸ τῆς ἀπορίας, καὶ ἐπὶ τὸ μέσον δύναται ἐλθεῖν. ἔχει γὰρ τὰ τοῦ ἐλευθερίου· καὶ γὰρ δίδωσι καὶ οὐ λαμβάνει, οὐδέτερον δ' ὡς δεῖ οὐδ' εὖ. εἰ δὴ τοῦτο ἐθισθείη ἤ πως ἄλλως μεταβάλοι, εἴη ἂν ἐλευθέριος· δώσει γὰρ οἷς δεῖ, καὶ οὐ λήψεται ὅθεν οὐ δεῖ. διὸ καὶ δοκεῖ οὐκ εἶναι φαῦλος τὸ ἦθος· οὐ γὰρ μοχθηροῦ οὐδ' ἀγεννοῦς τὸ ὑπερβάλλειν διδόντα καὶ μὴ λαμβάνοντα,
ἠλιθίου δέ. ὁ δὲ τοῦτον τὸν τρόπον ἄσωτος πολὺ δοκεῖ 32
βελτίων τοῦ ἀνελευθέρου εἶναι διά τε τὰ εἰρημένα, καὶ ὅτι
ὁ μὲν ὠφελεῖ πολλούς, ὁ δὲ οὐθένα, ἀλλ' οὐδ' αὑτόν.
ἀλλ' οἱ πολλοὶ τῶν ἀσώτων, καθάπερ εἴρηται, καὶ λαμ- 33
βάνουσιν ὅθεν μὴ δεῖ, καὶ εἰσὶ κατὰ τοῦτο ἀνελεύθεροι.
ληπτικοὶ δὲ γίνονται διὰ τὸ βούλεσθαι μὲν ἀναλίσκειν, 34

---

prodigal man may well be thought in no small degree superior to the illiberal.' The commentators, from not seeing the train of thought in this passage, have made a difficulty about *ἐπεὶ* which refers to the beginning of the sentence, the intermediate clauses *οὐ γὰρ ῥᾴδιον—εἶναι* being parenthetical. With *εἴπερ καὶ δοκοῦσιν*, cf. § 23.

31—32 Reasons are given why the prodigal is better than the illiberal man; namely, he may be cured by time, or by the failure of his means. His tendency to give is a principle which requires only to be harmonised to become a virtue. Lastly, he does more good than the illiberal man. Aristotle here is speaking of a better sort of prodigality (*τοῦτον τὸν τρόπον ἄσωτος*), which is only a slight overstepping of the bounds of liberality; but even with this restriction, it is much to be doubted whether prodigality does more good than illiberality. From wise acts of liberality much good may arise, but the common sort of prodigality, as Aristotle himself says, § 35, being prompted by folly and vanity, almost invariably goes to enrich the wrong people. If the case be even not so bad as this, the solid benefit which accrues from any tendency to capitalise money may surely be set against the chance good done by money given away indiscriminately or spent unproductively.

33 *ἀλλ' οἱ πολλοὶ—ἀνελεύθεροι*] 'But most prodigals, as we have implied already, take whence they ought not, and in this way are illiberal.' This is an instance of a phenomenon often to be observed in Aristotle's virtues and vices, that the 'extremes meet' (cf. IV. vii. 15, II. vii. 15). The *rationale* of this phenomenon appears to be that the extremes are both the result of the same principle, they are both different forms of selfishness. Selfishness can equally produce prodigal giving and meanness in receiving. Hence, if a man be selfish, though his tendency is to be prodigal, yet on occasion selfishness, which is his governing principle, will lead him to become illiberal. The fact is noticed by Eudemus, *Eth. Eud.* III. vii. 12: *Ἔστι δ' ἐναντιώτερον τοῖς ἄκροις τὸ μέσον ἢ ἐκεῖνα ἀλλήλοις, διότι τὸ μὲν μετ' οὐδετέρου γίνεται αὐτῶν, τὰ δὲ πολλάκις*

εὐχερῶς δὲ τοῦτο ποιεῖν μὴ δύνασθαι· ταχὺ γὰρ ἐπιλείπει αὐτοὺς τὰ ὑπάρχοντα. ἀναγκάζονται οὖν ἑτέρωθεν πορίζειν. ἅμα δὲ καὶ διὰ τὸ μηθὲν τοῦ καλοῦ φροντίζειν ὀλιγώρως καὶ πάντοθεν λαμβάνουσιν· διδόναι γὰρ ἐπιθυμοῦσι, τὸ
35 δὲ πῶς ἢ πόθεν οὐθὲν αὐτοῖς διαφέρει. διόπερ οὐδ' ἐλευθέριοι αἱ δόσεις αὐτῶν εἰσίν· οὐ γὰρ καλαί, οὐδὲ τούτου αὐτοῦ ἕνεκα, οὐδὲ ὡς δεῖ. ἀλλ' ἐνίοτε οὓς δεῖ πένεσθαι, τούτους πλουσίους ποιοῦσι, καὶ τοῖς μὲν μετρίοις τὰ ἤθη οὐδὲν ἂν δοῖεν, τοῖς δὲ κόλαξιν ἢ τιν' ἄλλην ἡδονὴν πορίζουσι πολλά. διὸ καὶ ἀκόλαστοι αὐτῶν εἰσὶν οἱ πολλοί· εὐχερῶς γὰρ ἀναλίσκοντες καὶ εἰς τὰς ἀκολασίας δαπανηροί εἰσι, καὶ διὰ τὸ μὴ πρὸς τὸ καλὸν
36 ζῆν πρὸς τὰς ἡδονὰς ἀποκλίνουσιν. ὁ μὲν οὖν ἄσωτος ἀπαιδαγώγητος γενόμενος εἰς ταῦτα μεταβαίνει, τυχὼν
37 δ' ἐπιμελείας εἰς τὸ μέσον καὶ τὸ δέον ἀφίκοιτ' ἄν. ἡ δ' ἀνελευθερία ἀνίατός ἐστιν· δοκεῖ γὰρ τὸ γῆρας καὶ πᾶσα ἀδυναμία ἀνελευθέρους ποιεῖν. καὶ συμφυέστερον τοῖς ἀνθρώποις τῆς ἀσωτίας· οἱ γὰρ πολλοὶ φιλοχρήματοι
38 μᾶλλον ἢ δοτικοί. καὶ διατείνει δ' ἐπὶ πολύ, καὶ πολυειδές ἐστιν· πολλοὶ γὰρ τρόποι δοκοῦσι τῆς ἀνελευθερίας εἶναι. ἐν δυσὶ γὰρ οὖσα, τῇ τ' ἐλλείψει τῆς δόσεως καὶ τῇ ὑπερ-

---

μετ' ἀλλήλων καὶ εἰσὶν ἐνίοτε οἱ αὐτοὶ θρασύδειλοι, καὶ τὰ μὲν ἄσωτοι τὰ δὲ ἀνελεύθεροι καὶ ὅλως ἀνώμαλοι κακῶς.

37 *καὶ συμφυέστερον—δοτικοί*] 'This vice runs more in our blood than prodigality: the mass of men love to keep money, rather than to give it.' It may be doubted whether this assertion is universally true. Would it, for instance, be true of the Irish? Again, Aristotle hardly acknowledges enough the *kindness* that exists among men, and which made Kant wonder that there was 'so much kindness and so little justice' in the world. Aristotle, from his dislike to all that is sordid, and his admiration for the brilliant and noble qualities, takes perhaps too favourable a view of the vice of prodigality. Its connexion with vanity, selfishness, and often utter heartlessness, he does not sufficiently notice, nor does he observe that lavish giving often proceeds from the want of a faculty—from an incapacity for estimating the worth of objects. Thus if illiberality be incompatible with a magnanimous spirit, prodigality is incompatible with absolute truth and justice.

38 Illiberality is widely spread, and has many forms; it contains two elements—excess of taking and defect of giving; but it does not always manifest itself in its entirety (*οὐ πᾶσιν ὁλόκληρος παραγίγνεται*), sometimes one element exists separately from the other.

βολῇ τῆς λήψεως, οὐ πᾶσιν ὁλόκληρος παραγίνεται, ἀλλ' ἐνίοτε χωρίζεται, καὶ οἱ μὲν τῇ λήψει ὑπερβάλλουσιν, οἱ
δὲ τῇ δόσει ἐλλείπουσιν. οἱ μὲν γὰρ ἐν ταῖς τοιαύταις 39
προσηγορίαις οἷον φειδωλοὶ γλίσχροι κίμβικες, πάντες τῇ δόσει ἐλλείπουσι, τῶν δ' ἀλλοτρίων οὐκ ἐφίενται οὐδὲ βούλονται λαμβάνειν, οἱ μὲν διά τινα ἐπιείκειαν καὶ εὐλάβειαν τῶν αἰσχρῶν. δοκοῦσι γὰρ ἔνιοι ἢ φασί γε διὰ τοῦτο φυλάττειν, ἵνα μή ποτ' ἀναγκασθῶσιν αἰσχρόν τι πρᾶξαι. τούτων δὲ καὶ ὁ κυμινοπρίστης καὶ πᾶς ὁ τοιοῦτος· ὠνόμασται δ' ἀπὸ τῆς ὑπερβολῆς τοῦ μηθενὶ ἂν
δοῦναι. οἱ δ' αὖ διὰ φόβον ἀπέχονται τῶν ἀλλοτρίων ὡς 40
οὐ ῥᾴδιον τὸ αὐτὸν μὲν τὰ ἑτέρων λαμβάνειν, τὰ δ' αὐτοῦ ἑτέρους μή· ἀρέσκει οὖν αὐτοῖς τὸ μήτε λαμβάνειν μήτε διδόναι. οἱ δ' αὖ κατὰ τὴν λῆψιν ὑπερβάλλουσι τῷ πάντοθεν λαμβάνειν καὶ πᾶν, οἷον οἱ τὰς ἀνελευθέρους ἐργασίας ἐργαζόμενοι, πορνοβοσκοὶ καὶ πάντες οἱ τοιοῦτοι, καὶ τοκισταὶ κατὰ μικρὸν ἐπὶ πολλῷ. πάντες γὰρ οὗτοι ὅθεν οὐ δεῖ λαμβάνουσι, καὶ ὁπόσον οὐ δεῖ. κοινὸν δ' ἐπ' αὐτοῖς ἡ αἰσχρο- 41
κέρδεια φαίνεται· πάντες γὰρ ἕνεκα κέρδους, καὶ τούτου
μικροῦ, ὀνείδη ὑπομένουσιν. τοὺς γὰρ τὰ μεγάλα μὴ ὅθεν 42
δὲ δεῖ λαμβάνοντας, μηδὲ ἃ δεῖ, οὐ λέγομεν ἀνελευθέρους, οἷον τοὺς τυράννους πόλεις πορθοῦντας καὶ ἱερὰ συλῶντας,

39—40 οἱ μὲν γὰρ—οὐ δεῖ] 'Men of one class, those who go by such names as "stingy," "close-fisted," "curmudgeons," all fall short in what they give away, but they neither covet their neighbours' goods, nor wish to take them. With some of them this arises from a certain sense of equity and shrinking from what is base; for their motive, either supposed or professed, in being careful of their means, is to prevent the possibility of their being compelled by want to do base actions. To this set belong the "skinflint," and all his like, a name derived from superlative unwillingness to give to anybody. But others again abstain from their neighbours' goods through fear, since it is not easy to take what belongs to others, and not have others take what belongs to oneself—they are content, therefore, neither to take nor give. A second class are excessive in taking everything and from all quarters, as for instance, those who ply illiberal trades, brothel-keepers, and all such like, and lenders of small sums at high interest. For all these take whence they ought not, and more than they ought.' This passage falls into two parts, *οἱ δ' αὖ κατὰ τὴν λῆψιν* corresponding to *οἱ μὲν γὰρ ἐν ταῖς τοιαύταις*. There are two subordinate divisions of the first part, namely, *οἱ μὲν διά τινα ἐπιείκειαν*, and *οἱ δ' αὖ διὰ φόβον*.

43 ἀλλὰ πονηροὺς μᾶλλον καὶ ἀσεβεῖς καὶ ἀδίκους. ὁ μέντοι κυβευτὴς καὶ ὁ λωποδύτης καὶ ὁ λῃστὴς τῶν ἀνελευθέρων εἰσίν. αἰσχροκερδεῖς γάρ. κέρδους γὰρ ἕνεκεν ἀμφότεροι πραγματεύονται καὶ ὀνείδη ὑπομένουσιν, καὶ οἱ μὲν κινδύνους τοὺς μεγίστους ἕνεκα τοῦ λήμματος, οἱ δ' ἀπὸ τῶν φίλων κερδαίνουσιν, οἷς δεῖ διδόναι. ἀμφότεροι δὴ ὅθεν οὐ δεῖ κερδαίνειν βουλόμενοι αἰσχροκερδεῖς, καὶ πᾶσαι δὴ αἱ τοιαῦται
44 λήψεις ἀνελεύθεροι. εἰκότως δὲ τῇ ἐλευθεριότητι ἀνελευθερία ἐναντίον λέγεται· μεῖζόν τε γάρ ἐστι κακὸν τῆς ἀσωτίας, καὶ μᾶλλον ἐπὶ ταύτην ἁμαρτάνουσιν ἢ κατὰ τὴν
45 λεχθεῖσαν ἀσωτίαν. περὶ μὲν οὖν ἐλευθεριότητος καὶ τῶν ἀντικειμένων κακιῶν τοσαῦτ' εἰρήσθω.

2 Δόξειε δ' ἂν ἀκόλουθον εἶναι καὶ περὶ μεγαλοπρεπείας

---

44 μεῖζόν τε γὰρ ἐστι κακὸν τῆς ἀσωτίας] Before (§ 32) Aristotle made the doubtful statement that prodigality does more good than illiberality. He now makes the positively untrue statement that illiberality does more harm than prodigality. His view is fallacious from an ignorance of the principles of political economy, and from not looking at the question with sufficient breadth. He regards prodigality as a short-lived evil which will be cured by time, and illiberality as inveterate. But in their consequences it is rather prodigality that is incurable, and illiberality transitory. Illiberality can always be remedied, and indeed it brings its own remedy, for saving produces wealth and capital, and these lift a man naturally and necessarily into a more expensive style of living, however much he may haggle over details. But prodigality causes personally, to the family, and to the nation, a loss of resources which is absolutely incurable.

II. Magnificence, the virtue next discussed, is a higher kind of liberality. It consists in spending money on a great scale with propriety (ἐν μεγέθει πρέπουσα δαπάνη ἐστίν). Thus there are two elements, greatness and propriety. The greatness is relative, being limited by the propriety, and the propriety is relative to the person, the circumstances, and the object. Magnificence will of course be prompted by a desire for what is noble. There will be something imaginative and striking about the effect it produces (τὸ δὲ μεγαλοπρεπὲς θαυμαστόν). Great and solemn occasions will be its proper sphere, the services of religion, the entertaining of foreigners, public works, gifts, and return-gifts. The well-born and illustrious will be the proper persons to exercise it. The house of the magnificent man will be of suitable splendour, everything he does will show taste and propriety: even in a gift to a child he will exhibit the idea of magnificence. The vulgar man, missing this happy nicety, will jar on our taste with his excessive splendour (λαμπρύνεται παρὰ μέλος), his object being evidently mere ostentation. The petty man, on the other hand,

διελθεῖν· δοκεῖ γὰρ καὶ αὐτὴ περὶ χρήματά τις ἀρετὴ
εἶναι. οὐχ ὥσπερ δ' ἡ ἐλευθεριότης διατείνει περὶ πάσας
τὰς ἐν χρήμασι πράξεις, ἀλλὰ περὶ τὰς δαπανηρὰς μόνον·
ἐν τούτοις δ' ὑπερέχει τῆς ἐλευθεριότητος μεγέθει. καθάπερ γὰρ τοὔνομα αὐτὸ ὑποσημαίνει, ἐν μεγέθει πρέπουσα
δαπάνη ἐστίν. τὸ δὲ μέγεθος πρός τι· οὐ γὰρ τὸ αὐτὸ 2
δαπάνημα τριηράρχῳ καὶ ἀρχιθεωρῷ. τὸ πρέπον δὴ πρὸς
αὐτόν, καὶ ἐν ᾧ καὶ περὶ ἅ. ὁ δ' ἐν μικροῖς ἢ ἐν μετρίοις 3
κατ' ἀξίαν δαπανῶν οὐ λέγεται μεγαλοπρεπής, οἷον τὸ
'πολλάκι δόσκον ἀλήτῃ·' ἀλλ' ὁ ἐν μεγάλοις οὕτως.
ὁ μὲν γὰρ μεγαλοπρεπὴς ἐλευθέριος, ὁ δ' ἐλευθέριος οὐθὲν
μᾶλλον μεγαλοπρεπής. τῆς τοιαύτης δ' ἕξεως ἡ μὲν 4
ἔλλειψις μικροπρέπεια καλεῖται, ἡ δ' ὑπερβολὴ βαναυσία
καὶ ἀπειροκαλία καὶ ὅσαι τοιαῦται, οὐχ ὑπερβάλλουσαι τῷ
μεγέθει περὶ ἃ δεῖ, ἀλλ' ἐν οἷς οὐ δεῖ καὶ ὡς οὐ δεῖ λαμ-

---

from timidity and constant fear of expense, will be always below the mark, and even after considerable expense will mar the whole effect by meanness in some point of detail.

2 τὸ δὲ μέγεθος—ἀρχιθεωρῷ] 'Now the greatness is relative, for there is not the same expense for a trierarch as for the head of a sacred legation.' This latter office would of course demand peculiar splendour. The λειτουργίαι at Athens were exactly fitted to exercise the magnificence of the citizens.

τὸ πρέπον δὴ πρὸς αὐτόν, καὶ ἐν ᾧ καὶ περὶ ἅ] 'The propriety accordingly must be relative to the person, the circumstances, and the object.' We have here nearly the same categories as were given, *Eth.* III. i. 16, where the points connected with an action are enumerated, τίς τε δὴ καὶ τί καὶ περὶ τί ἢ ἐν τίνι πράττει. On the suitableness of the person see below §§ 12—14. The circumstances are touched upon §§ 11, 15. The object (which cannot be definitely separated from the circumstances), §§ 16—18.

3 πολλάκι δόσκον ἀλήτῃ] Homer *Odyss.* XVII. 420.

4 ἡ δ' ὑπερβολὴ βαναυσία καὶ ἀπειροκαλία καὶ ὅσαι τοιαῦται] 'The corresponding excess is called "vulgarity," and "bad taste," and the like.' Βάναυσος is said to be derived from βαῦνος 'a forge' and αὔω. Thus it means a metal-worker, or artisan. From the contempt felt by the Athenians for this kind of craft, βάναυσος came to imply 'mean,' 'vulgar,' analogously to φορτικός. In Aristotle's *Politics*, there is a definition of what kind of work is strictly to be considered βάναυσος (VIII. ii. 4). Βάναυσον δ' ἔργον εἶναι δεῖ τοῦτο νομίζειν καὶ τέχνην ταύτην καὶ μάθησιν, ὅσαι πρὸς τὰς χρήσεις καὶ τὰς πράξεις τὰς τῆς ἀρετῆς ἄχρηστον ἀπεργάζονται τὸ σῶμα τῶν ἐλευθέρων ἢ τὴν ψυχὴν ἢ τὴν διάνοιαν. The word βαναυσία is applied here to denote vulgarity in expenditure.

5 πρυνόμεναι· ὕστερον δὲ περὶ αὐτῶν ἐροῦμεν. ὁ δὲ μεγαλοπρεπὴς ἐπιστήμονι ἔοικεν· τὸ πρέπον γὰρ δύναται θεω-
6 ρῆσαι καὶ δαπανῆσαι μεγάλα ἐμμελῶς. ὥσπερ γὰρ ἐν
ἀρχῇ εἴπομεν, ἡ ἕξις ταῖς ἐνεργείαις ὁρίζεται, καὶ ὧν ἐστίν.
αἱ δὴ τοῦ μεγαλοπρεποῦς δαπάναι μεγάλαι καὶ πρέπουσαι.
τοιαῦτα δὴ καὶ τὰ ἔργα· οὕτω γὰρ ἔσται μέγα δαπάνημα καὶ
πρέπον τῷ ἔργῳ. ὥστε τὸ μὲν ἔργον τῆς δαπάνης ἄξιον
δεῖ εἶναι, τὴν δὲ δαπάνην τοῦ ἔργου, ἢ καὶ ὑπερβάλλειν.
7 δαπανήσει δὲ τὰ τοιαῦτα ὁ μεγαλοπρεπὴς τοῦ καλοῦ ἕνεκα·
8 κοινὸν γὰρ τοῦτο ταῖς ἀρεταῖς. καὶ ἔτι ἡδέως καὶ προετι-
9 κῶς· ἡ γὰρ ἀκριβολογία μικροπρεπές. καὶ πῶς κάλλιστον
καὶ πρεπωδέστατον, σκέψαιτ' ἂν μᾶλλον ἢ πόσου καὶ πῶς
10 ἐλαχίστου. ἀναγκαῖον δὴ καὶ ἐλευθέριον τὸν μεγαλοπρεπῆ
εἶναι· καὶ γὰρ ὁ ἐλευθέριος δαπανήσει ἃ δεῖ καὶ ὡς δεῖ.
ἐν τούτοις δὲ τὸ μέγα τοῦ μεγαλοπρεποῦς, οἷον μέγεθος,
περὶ ταὐτὰ τῆς ἐλευθεριότητος οὔσης, καὶ ἀπὸ τῆς ἴσης
δαπάνης τὸ ἔργον ποιήσει μεγαλοπρεπέστερον. οὐ γὰρ ἡ
αὐτὴ ἀρετὴ κτήματος καὶ ἔργου· κτῆμα μὲν γὰρ τὸ πλείστου ἄξιον τιμιώτατον, οἷον χρυσός, ἔργον δὲ τὸ μέγα

---

5 *ὁ δὲ μεγαλοπρεπὴς—ἐμμελῶς*] 'The magnificent man is a kind of artist, because he has an eye for the becoming, and can spend great sums tastefully.' The word *ἐπιστήμονι* here conveys the association of those qualities which were said to belong to a perfect work of art, *Eth.* II. vi. 9: *Εἰ δὴ πᾶσα ἐπιστήμη οὕτω τὸ ἔργον εὖ ἐπιτελεῖ, πρὸς τὸ μέσον βλέπουσα*, κ.τ.λ.

6 *ὥσπερ γὰρ—τῷ ἔργῳ*] 'For as we said at the outset, a moral state is determined by its acts and its objects. Therefore the outlays of the magnificent man will be great and suitable. And the works on which he employs them will be of the same character, for only thus it will be possible to have a great outlay suitable to the work.'

ἐν ἀρχῇ] The allusion seems to be generally to the beginning of Book II.; perhaps *Eth.* II. ii. 8 is the nearest reference that can be given. But in the present place Aristotle is not speaking of the formation of habits out of acts, but rather of moral habits or states having a definite existence and reality only in acts and in the objective circumstances (*ὧν ἐστίν*) to which they (the moral states) refer. This view regards a moral state as a mere potentiality, which only attains definite and conscious reality by emerging into an act. The remark is apparently made to account for a *concrete* treatment of the virtue of magnificence. Elsewhere we have noticed (*Eth.* III. xii. 3 note) a complete separation made between the habit and the act.

10 *ἀναγκαῖον δὴ—ἐν μεγέθει*] 'It follows therefore that the magnificent

καὶ καλόν. τοῦ γὰρ τοιούτου ἡ θεωρία θαυμαστή, τὸ δὲ
μεγαλοπρεπὲς θαυμαστόν. καὶ ἔστιν ἔργου ἀρετὴ μεγαλοπρέπεια ἐν μεγέθει. ἔστι δὲ τῶν δαπανημάτων οἷα 11
λέγομεν τὰ τίμια, οἷον τὰ περὶ θεοὺς ἀναθήματα καὶ
κατασκευαὶ καὶ θυσίαι, ὁμοίως δὲ καὶ ὅσα περὶ πᾶν τὸ
δαιμόνιον, καὶ ὅσα πρὸς τὸ κοινὸν εὐφιλοτίμητά ἐστιν, οἷον
εἴ που χορηγεῖν οἴονται δεῖν λαμπρῶς ἢ τριηραρχεῖν ἢ καὶ
ἑστιᾶν τὴν πόλιν. ἐν ἅπασι δ' ὥσπερ εἴρηται, καὶ πρὸς 12
τὸν πράττοντα ἀναφέρεται τὸ τίς ὢν καὶ τίνων ὑπαρχόντων·

---

man must also be liberal, for the liberal man spends what he ought and in the way he ought. But it is in these same particulars, which are common to magnificence and liberality, that the element of greatness which there is in the magnificent man appears, as for example in vastness of proportions, and with the same expense he will make the result more splendid. For a work is not to be esteemed for the same qualities as a possession. That possession is most prized which is worth most, as for instance gold, but that work which is great and noble. When we contemplate such a work, we admire; but the magnificent is always admirable; and in short magnificence is—excellence of some work, which is on a scale of grandeur.' The words *οἷον μέγεθος* have vexed the commentators. One device that has been adopted is to omit the stop after *μέγεθος* and to translate the passage, 'Sed in his magnum est magnifici, veluti magnitudo liberalitatis circa haec (reading *ταῦτα*) versantis' (Michelet). Or, without altering the punctuation, we might construe, taking *οἷον μέγεθος* as epexegetic of *τὸ μέγα*, 'But the greatness of the magnificent man, as it were a certain grandeur of scale, appears in these same particulars, which are common to magnificence and liberality.' But the point Aristotle insists on is that magnificence differs from liberality not in degree, but in kind, being a display of more genius and imagination on the same objects, and thus with the same expense producing a more striking result. He gives as an instance of the means employed, 'vastness of size.' Τὸ *μέγα* is the moral greatness of the magnificent man, this takes as its exponent *μέγεθος* or physical bulk. Cf. Aristotle's definition of Tragedy (*Poetic.* vi. 2). Ἔστιν οὖν τραγῳδία μίμησις πράξεως σπουδαίας καὶ τελείας, μέγεθος ἐχούσης, κ.τ.λ., where *μέγεθος* implies bulk, or length of the story. Its limits are assigned *Ib.* vii. 12. ἀεὶ μὲν ὁ μείζων μέχρι τοῦ σύνδηλος εἶναι καλλίων ἐστὶ κατὰ τὸ μέγεθος, ὡς δὲ ἁπλῶς διορίσαντας εἰπεῖν, ἐν ὅσῳ μεγέθει κατὰ τὸ εἰκὸς ἢ τὸ ἀναγκαῖον ἐφεξῆς γιγνομένων συμβαίνει εἰς εὐτυχίαν ἐκ δυστυχίας ἢ ἐξ εὐτυχίας εἰς δυστυχίαν μεταβάλλειν, ἱκανὸς ὅρος ἐστὶ τοῦ μεγέθους.

11 εὐφιλοτίμητα] 'favourite objects of rivalry.' Dr. Cardwell (upon § 2 above) quotes Lycurgus, *Orat. contra Leocr.* p. 167: Οὐ γὰρ εἴ τις ἱπποτετρόφηκεν ἢ κεχορήγηκε λαμπρῶς — ἄξιός ἐστι παρ' ὑμῶν τοιαύτης χάριτος — ἀλλ' εἴ τις τετριηράρχηκε λαμπρῶς ἢ τείχη τῇ πατρίδι περιέβαλεν, ἢ πρὸς τὴν κοινὴν σωτηρίαν ἐκ τῶν ἰδίων συνευπόρησε.

ἄξια γὰρ δεῖ τούτων εἶναι, καὶ μὴ μόνον τῷ ἔργῳ ἀλλὰ καὶ
13 τῷ ποιοῦντι πρέπειν. διὸ πένης μὲν οὐκ ἂν εἴη μεγαλο-
πρεπής· οὐ γάρ ἐστιν ἀφ' ὧν πολλὰ δαπανήσει πρεπόντως·
ὁ δ' ἐπιχειρῶν ἠλίθιος· παρὰ τὴν ἀξίαν γὰρ καὶ τὸ δέον,
14 κατ' ἀρετὴν δὲ τὸ ὀρθῶς. πρέπει δὲ καὶ οἷς τὰ τοιαῦτα
προϋπάρχει δι' αὐτῶν ἢ διὰ τῶν προγόνων ἢ ὧν αὐτοῖς
μέτεστιν, καὶ τοῖς εὐγενέσι καὶ τοῖς ἐνδόξοις καὶ ὅσα
τοιαῦτα· πάντα γὰρ ταῦτα μέγεθος ἔχει καὶ ἀξίωμα.
15 μάλιστα μὲν οὖν τοιοῦτος ὁ μεγαλοπρεπής, καὶ ἐν τοῖς
τοιούτοις δαπανήμασιν ἡ μεγαλοπρέπεια, ὥσπερ εἴρηται·
μέγιστα γὰρ καὶ ἐντιμότατα· τῶν δὲ ἰδίων ὅσα εἰσάπαξ
γίνεται, οἷον γάμος καὶ εἴ τι τοιοῦτον, καὶ εἰ περί τι πᾶσα ἡ
πόλις σπουδάζει ἢ οἱ ἐν ἀξιώματι, καὶ περὶ ξένων δὲ ὑπο-
δοχὰς καὶ ἀποστολάς, καὶ δωρεὰς καὶ ἀντιδωρεάς· οὐ γὰρ
εἰς ἑαυτὸν δαπανηρὸς ὁ μεγαλοπρεπὴς ἀλλ' εἰς τὰ κοινά, τὰ
16 δὲ δῶρα τοῖς ἀναθήμασιν ἔχει τι ὅμοιον. μεγαλοπρεποῦς δὲ
καὶ οἶκον κατασκευάσασθαι πρεπόντως τῷ πλούτῳ· κόσμος γάρ τις καὶ οὗτος. καὶ περὶ ταῦτα μᾶλλον δαπανᾶν
ὅσα πολυχρόνια τῶν ἔργων· κάλλιστα γὰρ ταῦτα. καὶ ἐν
17 ἑκάστοις τὸ πρέπον· οὐ γὰρ ταὐτὰ ἁρμόζει θεοῖς καὶ ἀνθρώποις, οὐδ' ἐν ἱερῷ καὶ τάφῳ· καὶ ἐπὶ τῶν δαπανημάτων
ἕκαστον μέγα ἐν τῷ γένει, καὶ μεγαλοπρεπέστατον μὲν τὸ
18 ἐν μεγάλῳ μέγα, ἐνταῦθα δὲ τὸ ἐν τούτοις μέγα. καὶ
διαφέρει τὸ ἐν τῷ ἔργῳ μέγα τοῦ ἐν τῷ δαπανήματι·
σφαῖρα μὲν γὰρ ἢ λήκυθος ἡ καλλίστη ἔχει μεγαλοπρέπειαν
παιδικοῦ δώρου, ἡ δὲ τούτου τιμὴ μικρὸν καὶ ἀνελεύθερον.
19 διὰ τοῦτό ἐστι τοῦ μεγαλοπρεποῦς, ἐν ᾧ ἂν ποιῇ γένει,

14 πρέπει δὲ—ἀξίωμα] 'The undertaking of such expenses is proper for persons already distinguished by magnificence, either in themselves, or their ancestors, or their connections, and for the noble, the illustrious, and such like persons: for in all these cases greatness and dignity are present.' The use of προϋπάρχειν here to denote that which exists already as an achievement in one's family is not unlike its use, *Eth.* I. xi. 4, to denote those events which in a play are supposed to have been done before the commencement of the action.

18—19 καὶ διαφέρει—δαπανήματι] 'And the "greatness," which is exhibited in the work, differs from the "greatness" of the expense; for the most beautiful of balls or of bottles is magnificent as a present to a child, though its price be small and paltry. Hence the magnificent man, whatever kind of thing he be producing, will

μεγαλοπρεπῶς ποιεῖν· τὸ γὰρ τοιοῦτον οὐκ εὐυπέρβλητον,
καὶ ἔχον κατ' ἀξίαν τοῦ δαπανήματος. τοιοῦτος μὲν οὖν ὁ 20
μεγαλοπρεπής, ὁ δ' ὑπερβάλλων καὶ βάναυσος τῷ παρὰ τὸ
δέον ἀναλίσκειν ὑπερβάλλει, ὥσπερ εἴρηται. ἐν γὰρ τοῖς
μικροῖς τῶν δαπανημάτων πολλὰ ἀναλίσκει καὶ λαμπρύνεται παρὰ μέλος, οἷον ἐρανιστὰς γαμικῶς ἑστιῶν, καὶ κωμῳδοῖς χορηγῶν ἐν τῇ παρόδῳ πορφύραν εἰσφέρων, ὥσπερ οἱ
Μεγαρεῖς. καὶ πάντα τὰ τοιαῦτα ποιήσει οὐ τοῦ καλοῦ
ἕνεκα, ἀλλὰ τὸν πλοῦτον ἐπιδεικνύμενος, καὶ διὰ ταῦτα
οἰόμενος θαυμάζεσθαι, καὶ οὗ μὲν δεῖ πολλὰ ἀναλῶσαι,
ὀλίγα δαπανῶν, οὗ δ' ὀλίγα, πολλά. ὁ δὲ μικροπρεπὴς 21
περὶ πάντα ἐλλείψει, καὶ τὰ μέγιστα ἀναλώσας ἐν μικρῷ
τὸ καλὸν ἀπολεῖ, καὶ ὅ τι ἂν ποιῇ μέλλων, καὶ σκοπῶν
πῶς ἂν ἐλάχιστον ἀναλώσαι, καὶ ταῦτ' ὀδυρόμενος, καὶ

---

produce it magnificently; for the character of such work is that it cannot be easily outdone, its magnificence being always in proportion to the outlay;' *i.e.* the feeling about such works will never be merely 'how costly they are!' but 'how great they are!' from an imaginative point of view; cf. § 10. The 'ball' and the 'bottle' seem to have been common toys. Dr. Fitzgerald compares the description of Cupid's toy in Apollonius Rhodius, *Arg.* III. 135, and Plato, *Phædo*, p. 110 B, *ὥσπερ αἱ δωδεκάσκυτοι σφαῖραι, ποικίλη, χρώμασι διειλημμένη.* Also Theophrastus' *Characters*, Περὶ ἀρεσκείας, where the ἄρεσκος is said to purchase Θουριακὰς τῶν στρογγύλων ληκύθους—καὶ σφαιριστήριον.

20 τοιοῦτος—πολλά] 'Such now is the magnificent man, but he who exceeds and is vulgar—exceeds, as was said before, in that he spends more than is right. He spends much upon trifles, and preserves no harmony in his splendour; he entertains his club-fellows with a wedding-feast, and when he has charge of a comic chorus, he makes them appear in purple, as the Megarians do. In all this extravagance he never aims at the beautiful, but only seeks to parade his riches, in the hope of being stared at; where he should spend much, he draws his purse-strings, where he should spend little, he squanders.' The last sentence shows that in vulgarity extremes meet, selfishness prompting both too much expense and too little, see above, chap. I. § 33 note. With παρὰ μέλος we may compare Shakespeare, *Merry Wives*, Act I. sc. 3. 'His filching was like an unskilful singer: he kept not time.'

οἷον ἐρανιστὰς] ἔρανος being a club where each member entertained in turn, or an entertainment where each guest contributed, it was of course bad taste to eclipse the rest in splendour.

ἐν τῇ παρόδῳ] The parode was the first song of the chorus sung at its entry. Naturally the comic chorus would not require rich purple dresses. The expense of a comic chorus at Athens appears to have been sixteen minæ (64*l.*), that of a tragic chorus thirty minæ (120*l.*); see Bentley *on Phalaris*,

22 πάντ' οἰόμενος μείζω ποιεῖν ἢ δεῖ. εἰσὶ μὲν οὖν αἱ ἕξεις αὗται κακίαι, οὐ μὴν ὀνείδη γ' ἐπιφέρουσι διὰ τὸ μήτε βλαβεραὶ τῷ πέλας εἶναι μήτε λίαν ἀσχήμονες.

3 Ἡ δὲ μεγαλοψυχία περὶ μεγάλα μὲν καὶ ἐκ τοῦ ὀνόματος

---

p. 360. The Megarians were noted among the Greeks for stupidity.

22 εἰσὶ μὲν οὖν—ἀσχήμονες] 'Now these (*i.e.* vulgarity and pettiness) *are* vices, but they do not entail disgrace, because they are neither hurtful to one's neighbour, nor are they very unseemly.'

III. Aristotle's famous description of the virtue of great-souledness (which he places as a mean between vanity and want of spirit) throws light upon the whole bearing of his moral system.

We must notice in it rather an admiring picture of what *is* than an investigation into what ought to be. Great-souledness is nothing else than a certain loftiness of spirit possessed by great men. It can only (in its fullest sense) belong to great men, for unless accompanied by qualities superior to those of the rest of the world, it would be simply ridiculous.

Aristotle takes this loftiness of spirit, and, considering it fine and admirable, points out the various traits in which it exhibits itself. And nothing can be more subtle or felicitous than many of his observations on this head. But it is plain that great-souledness, as here represented, is not something which is prompted by duty, rather it stands quite beside the idea of duty. Greatness and the sense of moral obligation are essentially distinct, however much they may accidentally coincide.

The great-souled man has all virtues, says Aristotle (§§ 14—15). But we find on nearer inspection that this means that he is above all those minor interests which might induce to vice; he does not care about money, so he will never cheat; he does not value even life very high, so he will not be a coward. Here then there is no self-subjection to a law. The great-souled man does not avoid vice because it is 'wrong' (in the modern sense), but simply because it is unworthy of him. Thus he is most essentially a law to himself and above all other law. Aristotle spoke of great-souledness as being a sort of culmination of the virtues (§ 16), and justly so, for it is the culmination of his moral system. As we before remarked (ch. i. § 16, note), his system is based on the idea of self-respect. Loftiness of spirit is the highest form of self-respect (μεγάλων ἑαυτὸν ἀξιοῖ, ἄξιος ὤν). This principle goes a long way in elevating the character and purifying the conduct, but its natural development is also a dislike (§§ 24—26) of all limitations of the individuality; in short, its natural development is a sort of noble pride.

Great-souledness, however fine may be the qualities that go to make it up, is essentially not a human attitude. As we have observed already, it is something exceptional, and in Aristotle's account of it we have a psychological portrait of a great man. Yet still this account shows Aristotle not to have been familiar with that conception of 'moral goodness' which has arisen out of later associations.

ἔοικεν εἶναι, περὶ ποῖα δ' ἐστὶ πρῶτον λάβωμεν. διαφέρει 2
δ' οὐθὲν τὴν ἕξιν ἢ τὸν κατὰ τὴν ἕξιν σκοπεῖν. δοκεῖ δὲ 3
μεγαλόψυχος εἶναι ὁ μεγάλων αὑτὸν ἀξιῶν ἄξιος ὤν. ὁ
γὰρ μὴ κατ' ἀξίαν αὐτὸ ποιῶν ἠλίθιος, τῶν δὲ κατ' ἀρετὴν
οὐδεὶς ἠλίθιος οὐδ' ἀνόητος. μεγαλόψυχος μὲν οὖν ὁ
εἰρημένος. ὁ γὰρ μικρῶν ἄξιος καὶ τούτων ἀξιῶν ἑαυτὸν 4
σώφρων, μεγαλόψυχος δ' οὔ· ἐν μεγέθει γὰρ ἡ μεγαλο- 5
ψυχία, ὥσπερ καὶ τὸ κάλλος ἐν μεγάλῳ σώματι, οἱ μικροὶ
δ' ἀστεῖοι καὶ σύμμετροι, καλοὶ δ' οὔ. ὁ δὲ μεγάλων 6
ἑαυτὸν ἀξιῶν ἀνάξιος ὢν χαῦνος· ὁ δὲ μειζόνων ἢ ἄξιος
οὐ πᾶς χαῦνος. ὁ δ' ἐλαττόνων ἢ ἄξιος μικρόψυχος, ἐάν 7
τε μεγάλων ἐάν τε μετρίων, ἐάν τε καὶ μικρῶν ἄξιος ὢν ἔτι
ἐλαττόνων αὑτὸν ἀξιοῖ. καὶ μάλιστα ἂν δόξειεν ὁ μεγάλων
ἄξιος· τί γὰρ ἂν ἐποίει, εἰ μὴ τοσούτων ἦν ἄξιος; ἔστι 8
δὴ ὁ μεγαλόψυχος τῷ μὲν μεγέθει ἄκρος, τῷ δὲ ὡς δεῖ
μέσος· τοῦ γὰρ κατ' ἀξίαν αὑτὸν ἀξιοῖ. οἱ δ' ὑπερβάλλουσι καὶ ἐλλείπουσιν. εἰ δὲ δὴ μεγάλων ἑαυτὸν ἀξιοῖ ἄξιος 9
ὤν, καὶ μάλιστα τῶν μεγίστων, περὶ ἓν μάλιστα ἂν εἴη.
ἡ δ' ἀξία λέγεται πρὸς τὰ ἐκτὸς ἀγαθά. μέγιστον δὲ τοῦτ' 10
ἂν θείημεν ὃ τοῖς θεοῖς ἀπονέμομεν, καὶ οὗ μάλιστ' ἐφίενται
οἱ ἐν ἀξιώματι, καὶ τὸ ἐπὶ τοῖς καλλίστοις ἆθλον.

---

2 διαφέρει δ' οὐθὲν—σκοπεῖν] 'Now it does not make the least difference whether we consider the state of mind, or the character that is produced by the state of mind.' The procedure adopted by Aristotle throughout is that of describing virtues in the concrete, though in no other case does he give so complete a personality as in describing the great-souled man. This procedure, while it gives graphic liveliness to his discussions, tends to make us forget that these virtues are not so much different *kinds* of character as different *elements* in the same character. A later development of Aristotle's ethical system calls attention to this point (cf. *Eth.* vi. xiii. 6). It has been said that the picture of a great-souled man here given to us must have been taken from life. Probably Aristotle traced different manifestations of the great-souled element in different people, and has here combined them.

5 ἐν μεγέθει γὰρ—οὔ] 'For great-souledness implies greatness, just as beauty implies a large body; little people may be pretty and elegant, but not beautiful.' This was the Greek idea, cf. *Politics*, vii. iv. 8: τό γε καλὸν ἐν πλήθει καὶ μεγέθει εἴωθε γίνεσθαι. *Poetic*, vii. 8: τὸ γὰρ καλὸν ἐν μεγέθει καὶ τάξει ἐστί. Cf. also the story of Phye in Herodotus, i. c. 60. Against such critics of beauty as the Greeks, nothing is to be said.

τοιοῦτον δ' ἡ τιμή· μέγιστον γὰρ δὴ τοῦτο τῶν ἐκτὸς
ἀγαθῶν. περὶ τιμὰς δὴ καὶ ἀτιμίας ὁ μεγαλόψυχός ἐστιν
11 ὡς δεῖ. καὶ ἄνευ δὲ λόγου φαίνονται οἱ μεγαλόψυχοι
περὶ τιμὴν εἶναι· τιμῆς γὰρ μάλισθ' οἱ μεγάλοι ἀξιοῦσιν
12 ἑαυτούς, κατ' ἀξίαν δέ. ὁ δὲ μικρόψυχος ἐλλείπει καὶ
13 πρὸς ἑαυτὸν καὶ πρὸς τὸ τοῦ μεγαλοψύχου ἀξίωμα. ὁ δὲ
χαῦνος πρὸς ἑαυτὸν μὲν ὑπερβάλλει, οὐ μὴν τόν γε μεγαλό-
14 ψυχον. ὁ δὲ μεγαλόψυχος, εἴπερ τῶν μεγίστων ἄξιος,
ἄριστος ἂν εἴη· μείζονος γὰρ ἀεὶ ὁ βελτίων ἄξιος, καὶ
μεγίστων ὁ ἄριστος. τὸν ὡς ἀληθῶς ἄρα μεγαλόψυχον
δεῖ ἀγαθὸν εἶναι. καὶ δόξειεν δ' ἂν εἶναι μεγαλοψύχου τὸ ἐν
15 ἑκάστῃ ἀρετῇ μέγα. οὐδαμῶς τ' ἂν ἁρμόζοι μεγαλοψύχῳ
φεύγειν παρασείσαντι, οὐδ' ἀδικεῖν· τίνος γὰρ ἕνεκα πράξει αἰσχρά, ᾧ οὐθὲν μέγα; καθ' ἕκαστα δ' ἐπισκοποῦντι
πάμπαν γελοῖος φαίνοιτ' ἂν ὁ μεγαλόψυχος μὴ ἀγαθὸς
ὤν. οὐκ εἴη δ' ἂν οὐδὲ τιμῆς ἄξιος φαῦλος ὤν· τῆς
ἀρετῆς γὰρ ἆθλον ἡ τιμή, καὶ ἀπονέμεται τοῖς ἀγαθοῖς.
16 ἔοικε μὲν οὖν ἡ μεγαλοψυχία οἷον κόσμος τις εἶναι τῶν
ἀρετῶν· μείζους γὰρ αὐτὰς ποιεῖ, καὶ οὐ γίνεται ἄνευ
ἐκείνων. διὰ τοῦτο χαλεπὸν τῇ ἀληθείᾳ μεγαλόψυχον

10—11 τοιοῦτον δ'—κατ' ἀξίαν δέ] 'Such a prize is honour, which is the greatest of all outward goods. Therefore the great-souled man bears himself as he ought with regard to honour and dishonour. But why should we prove what is obvious, that the study of magnanimous minds is honour? And great men lay especial claim to honour, yet according to their desert.' Aristotle here fixes external honour as the object with which great-souledness deals. Afterwards he sets it above all external honour (§ 17), ἀρετῆς γὰρ παντελοῦς οὐκ ἂν γένοιτο ἀξία τιμή. Honour is not good enough, but the world has nothing better to give.

15 οὐδαμῶς—παρασείσαντι] 'It would never suit the great-souled man to fly in ungraceful haste.' Παρασείειν (i.e. τὰς χεῖρας) means 'to work the hands in running.' Cf. *De Incess. Animal.* iii. 4, where the principle of the lever is shown to be involved in this motion. Διὸ καὶ οἱ πένταθλοι ἅλλονται πλεῖον ἔχοντες τοὺς ἁλτῆρας ἢ μὴ ἔχοντες, καὶ οἱ θέοντες θᾶττον θέουσι παρασείοντες τὰς χεῖρας· γίνεται γάρ τις ἀπέρεισις ἐν τῇ διατάσει πρὸς τὰς χεῖρας καὶ τοὺς καρπούς.

16 ἔοικε μὲν οὖν—καλοκἀγαθίας] 'Now great-souledness appears to be, as it were, a sort of crown of the virtues; it enhances them, and it cannot come into existence without them. Hence it is hard to be great-souled in the true sense of the term, for this is impossible without nobleness and virtue.' The word 'magnanimity' is the conventional

εἶναι· οὐ γὰρ οἷόν τε ἄνευ καλοκἀγαθίας. μάλιστα μὲν 17
οὖν περὶ τιμὰς καὶ ἀτιμίας ὁ μεγαλόψυχός ἐστι, καὶ ἐπὶ
μὲν ταῖς μεγάλαις καὶ ὑπὸ τῶν σπουδαίων μετρίως ἡσθή-
σεται, ὡς τῶν οἰκείων τυγχάνων ἢ καὶ ἐλαττόνων· ἀρετῆς
γὰρ παντελοῦς οὐκ ἂν γένοιτο ἀξία τιμή· οὐ μὴν ἀλλ' ἀπο-
δέξεταί γε τῷ μὴ ἔχειν αὐτοὺς μείζω αὐτῷ ἀπονέμειν. τῆς
δὲ παρὰ τῶν τυχόντων καὶ ἐπὶ μικροῖς πάμπαν ὀλιγωρήσει·
οὐ γὰρ τούτων ἄξιος. ὁμοίως δὲ καὶ ἀτιμίας· οὐ γὰρ
ἔσται δικαίως περὶ αὐτόν. μάλιστα μὲν οὖν ἐστίν, ὥσπερ 18
εἴρηται, ὁ μεγαλόψυχος περὶ τιμάς, οὐ μὴν ἀλλὰ καὶ περὶ
πλοῦτον καὶ δυναστείαν καὶ πᾶσαν εὐτυχίαν καὶ ἀτυχίαν
μετρίως ἕξει, ὅπως ἂν γίνηται, καὶ οὔτ' εὐτυχῶν περιχαρὴς
ἔσται οὔτ' ἀτυχῶν περίλυπος. οὐδὲ γὰρ περὶ τιμὴν οὕτως
ἔχει ὡς μέγιστον ὄν. αἱ γὰρ δυναστεῖαι καὶ ὁ πλοῦτος
διὰ τὴν τιμήν ἐστιν αἱρετά· οἱ γοῦν ἔχοντες αὐτὰ τιμᾶσθαι δι' αὐτῶν βούλονται. ᾧ δὴ καὶ ἡ τιμὴ μικρόν ἐστι,
τούτῳ καὶ τἆλλα. διὸ ὑπερόπται δοκοῦσιν εἶναι. δοκεῖ 19
δὲ καὶ τὰ εὐτυχήματα συμβάλλεσθαι πρὸς μεγαλοψυχίαν.
οἱ γὰρ εὐγενεῖς ἀξιοῦνται τιμῆς καὶ οἱ δυναστεύοντες ἢ οἱ
πλουτοῦντες· ἐν ὑπεροχῇ γάρ, τὸ δ' ἀγαθῷ ὑπερέχον πᾶν
ἐντιμότερον. διὸ καὶ τὰ τοιαῦτα μεγαλοψυχοτέρους ποιεῖ.
τιμῶνται γὰρ ὑπό τινων. κατ' ἀλήθειαν δ' ὁ ἀγαθὸς μόνος
τιμητέος· ᾧ δ' ἄμφω ὑπάρχει, μᾶλλον ἀξιοῦται τιμῆς. 20
οἱ δ' ἄνευ ἀρετῆς τὰ τοιαῦτα ἀγαθὰ ἔχοντες οὔτε δικαίως

---

representative of *μεγαλοψυχία*, but it does not really answer to it. 'Magnanimity' often implies rather generosity, and what Aristotle calls *ἐπιείκεια*, than that loftiness of spirit which he attributes to the *μεγαλόψυχος*.

καλοκἀγαθίας] This abstract noun does not occur in Plato, who frequently uses the words *καλός τε κἀγαθός* (written separately) in the common Athenian sense, denoting very much what we mean by 'a gentleman.' Aristotle uses the words *τῶν ἐν τῷ βίῳ καλῶν κἀγαθῶν* (*Eth.* I. viii. 9) to denote generally 'what is noble and excellent in life.' He also introduces the present form, *Eth.* x. ix. 3. *τοὺς δὲ πολλοὺς ἀδυνατεῖν πρὸς καλοκἀγαθίαν προτρέψασθαι.* In *Pol.* I. xiii. 4. he asks if both ruler and ruled must equally partake of *καλοκἀγαθία*. In these passages there is no special import given to the word. It seems to imply a sort of elevated virtue. Stahr translates the present place. "Es ist unmöglich ein Grossgesinnter zu sein, ohne die Totalität aller Tugenden." And St. Hilaire—"On ne peut l'être sans une vertu complète." This is, however, taking *καλοκἀγ.* in the Eudemian sense, on which see Vol. I. Essay I. p. 23–26.

ἑαυτοὺς μεγάλων ἀξιοῦσιν οὔτε ὀρθῶς μεγαλόψυχοι λέγον-
21 ται. ἄνευ γὰρ ἀρετῆς παντελοῦς οὐκ ἔστι ταῦτα. ὑπερόπται δὲ καὶ ὑβρισταὶ καὶ οἱ τὰ τοιαῦτα ἔχοντες ἀγαθὰ
γίγνονται. ἄνευ γὰρ ἀρετῆς οὐ ῥᾴδιον φέρειν ἐμμελῶς τὰ
εὐτυχήματα· οὐ δυνάμενοι δὲ φέρειν καὶ οἰόμενοι τῶν
ἄλλων ὑπερέχειν ἐκείνων μὲν καταφρονοῦσιν, αὐτοὶ δ' ὅ τι
ἂν τύχωσι πράττουσιν. μιμοῦνται γὰρ τὸν μεγαλόψυχον
οὐχ ὅμοιοι ὄντες, τοῦτο δὲ δρῶσιν ἐν οἷς δύνανται· τὰ μὲν
οὖν κατ' ἀρετὴν οὐ πράττουσι, καταφρονοῦσι δὲ τῶν
22 ἄλλων. ὁ δὲ μεγαλόψυχος δικαίως καταφρονεῖ (δοξάζει
23 γὰρ ἀληθῶς), οἱ δὲ πολλοὶ τυχόντως. οὐκ ἔστι δὲ
μικροκίνδυνος οὐδὲ φιλοκίνδυνος διὰ τὸ ὀλίγα τιμᾶν, μεγαλοκίνδυνος δέ, καὶ ὅταν κινδυνεύῃ, ἀφειδὴς τοῦ βίου ὡς οὐκ
24 ἄξιον ὂν πάντως ζῆν. καὶ οἷος εὖ ποιεῖν, εὐεργετούμενος
δ' αἰσχύνεται· τὸ μὲν γὰρ ὑπερέχοντος, τὸ δ' ὑπερεχομένου. καὶ ἀντευεργετικὸς πλειόνων· οὕτω γὰρ προσ-
25 οφλήσει ὁ ὑπάρξας καὶ ἔσται εὖ πεπονθώς. δοκοῦσι δὲ
καὶ μνημονεύειν οὓς ἂν ποιήσωσιν εὖ, ὧν δ' ἂν πάθωσιν
οὔ· ἐλάττων γὰρ ὁ παθὼν εὖ τοῦ ποιήσαντος, βούλεται
δ' ὑπερέχειν. καὶ τὰ μὲν ἡδέως ἀκούει, τὰ δ' ἀηδῶς· διὸ
καὶ τὴν Θέτιν οὐ λέγειν τὰς εὐεργεσίας τῷ Διί· οὐδ' οἱ
Λάκωνες πρὸς τοὺς Ἀθηναίους, ἀλλ' ἃ πεπόνθεσαν εὖ.

---

22 ὁ δὲ μεγαλόψυχος—τυχόντως] 'But the great-souled man despises justly (for his estimate is true), but most people do so at haphazard.' Throughout, the great man is justified in the high position he assumes by reason of the correctness of his estimate. Modern ideas of delicacy, to say the least, would proscribe this accuracy of self-appreciation, and the claims founded upon it.

24—26 He is glad to do a benefit and ashamed to receive one; he will wipe out a favour by doing a greater one in return; he will remember those whom he has benefited, but not those by whom he has been benefited; he will be in want of no one; he will serve any readily; he will be proud to the great, and easy with the lowly, &c. On the principle of independence, which appears here in an extreme form, see above, note on ch. i. § 16.

διὸ καὶ τὴν Θέτιν] Homer, *Iliad* I. 503—4. She only says—

εἴποτε δή σε μετ' ἀθανάτοισιν ὄνησα ἢ ἔπει ἢ ἔργῳ.

οὐδ' οἱ Λάκωνες] This is said to have been on the occasion of a Theban invasion into Laconia. Aspasius quotes from Callisthenes a mention of the circumstance. Xenophon is thought to allude to the same event (*Hell.* VI. v. 33), where, however, he makes the Spartans enumerate their services.

μεγαλοψύχου δὲ καὶ τὸ μηδενὸς δεῖσθαι ἢ μόγις, ὑπηρετεῖν 26
δὲ προθύμως, καὶ πρὸς μὲν τοὺς ἐν ἀξιώματι καὶ εὐτυχίαις
μέγαν εἶναι, πρὸς δὲ τοὺς μέσους μέτριον· τῶν μὲν γὰρ
ὑπερέχειν χαλεπὸν καὶ σεμνόν, τῶν δὲ ῥᾴδιον, καὶ ἐν ἐκείνοις
μὲν σεμνύνεσθαι οὐκ ἀγεννές, ἐν δὲ τοῖς ταπεινοῖς φορτικόν,
ὥσπερ εἰς τοὺς ἀσθενεῖς ἰσχυρίζεσθαι. καὶ εἰς τὰ ἔντιμα 27
μὴ ἰέναι, ἢ οὗ πρωτεύουσιν ἄλλοι· καὶ ἀργὸν εἶναι καὶ
μελλητὴν ἀλλ' ἢ ὅπου τιμὴ μεγάλη ἢ ἔργον, καὶ ὀλίγων
μὲν πρακτικόν, μεγάλων δὲ καὶ ὀνομαστῶν. ἀναγκαῖον δὲ 28
καὶ φανερόμισον εἶναι καὶ φανερόφιλον· τὸ γὰρ λανθάνειν
φοβουμένου. καὶ μέλειν τῆς ἀληθείας μᾶλλον ἢ τῆς δόξης,
καὶ λέγειν καὶ πράττειν φανερῶς· παρρησιαστὴς γὰρ διὰ
τὸ καταφρονεῖν. διὸ καὶ ἀληθευτικός, πλὴν ὅσα μὴ
δι' εἰρωνείαν· εἴρωνα δὲ πρὸς τοὺς πολλούς. καὶ πρὸς 29
ἄλλον μὴ δύνασθαι ζῆν ἀλλ' ἢ πρὸς φίλον· δουλικὸν γάρ,
διὸ καὶ πάντες οἱ κόλακες θητικοὶ καὶ οἱ ταπεινοὶ κόλακες.
οὐδὲ θαυμαστικός· οὐδὲν γὰρ μέγα αὐτῷ ἐστίν. οὐδὲ 30
μνησίκακος. οὐ γὰρ μεγαλοψύχου τὸ ἀπομνημονεύειν,
ἄλλως τε καὶ κακά, ἀλλὰ μᾶλλον παρορᾶν. οὐδ' ἀνθρω- 31
πολόγος· οὔτε γὰρ περὶ αὑτοῦ ἐρεῖ οὔτε περὶ ἑτέρου·
οὔτε γὰρ ἵνα ἐπαινῆται μέλει αὐτῷ οὔθ' ὅπως οἱ ἄλλοι
ψέγωνται, οὐδ' αὖ ἐπαινετικός ἐστιν· διόπερ οὐδὲ κακο-
λόγος, οὐδὲ τῶν ἐχθρῶν, εἰ μὴ δι' ὕβριν. καὶ περὶ 32
ἀναγκαίων ἢ μικρῶν ἥκιστα ὀλοφυρτικὸς καὶ δεητικός·

27—34 A list of characteristics follows, completing the picture of the great-souled man. He will not compete for the common objects of ambition (τὰ ἔντιμα); he will only attempt great and important matters, he will seem otherwise inactive; he will be open in friendship and hatred; really straightforward and deeply truthful, but reserved and ironical in manner to common people. Will live for his friend alone, will wonder at nothing, will bear no malice, will be no gossip (οὐκ ἀνθρωπολόγος), will not be anxious about trifles, and will care more to possess that which is fine, than that which is productive. His movements are slow, his voice is deep, and his diction stately.

28 εἴρωνα δὲ πρὸς τοὺς πολλούς] Bekker has introduced this reading on the authority of one MS. alone; all the rest read εἰρωνείᾳ. Εἴρωνα is not strictly grammatical, but it is in accordance with the Aristotelian mode of writing; it comes in despite the nominative ἀληθευτικός, as a carrying on of the accusatives before used, καὶ ἀργὸν εἶναι—καὶ ὀλίγων πρακτικόν, &c.

33 σπουδάζοντες γὰρ οὕτως ἔχειν περὶ ταῦτα. καὶ οἷος
κεκτῆσθαι μᾶλλον τὰ καλὰ καὶ ἄκαρπα τῶν καρπίμων καὶ
34 ὠφελίμων· αὐτάρκους γὰρ μᾶλλον. καὶ κίνησις δὲ βραδεῖα
τοῦ μεγαλοψύχου δοκεῖ εἶναι, καὶ φωνὴ βαρεῖα, καὶ λέξις
στάσιμος· οὐ γὰρ σπευστικὸς ὁ περὶ ὀλίγα σπουδάζων,
οὐδὲ σύντονος ὁ μηδὲν μέγα οἰόμενος· ἡ δ' ὀξυφωνία καὶ
35 ἡ ταχυτὴς διὰ τούτων. τοιοῦτος μὲν οὖν ὁ μεγαλόψυχος, ὁ
δ' ἐλλείπων μικρόψυχος, ὁ δ' ὑπερβάλλων χαῦνος. οὐ κακοὶ
μὲν οὖν δοκοῦσιν εἶναι οὐδ' οὗτοι· οὐ γὰρ κακοποιοί εἰσιν·
ἡμαρτημένοι δέ. ὁ μὲν γὰρ μικρόψυχος ἄξιος ὢν ἀγαθῶν
ἑαυτὸν ἀποστερεῖ ὧν ἄξιός ἐστι, καὶ ἔοικε κακὸν ἔχειν τι ἐκ
τοῦ μὴ ἀξιοῦν ἑαυτὸν τῶν ἀγαθῶν, καὶ ἀγνοεῖν δ' ἑαυτόν·
ὠρέγετο γὰρ ἂν ὧν ἄξιος ἦν, ἀγαθῶν γε ὄντων. οὐ μὴν
ἠλίθιοί γε οἱ τοιοῦτοι δοκοῦσιν εἶναι, ἀλλὰ μᾶλλον ὀκνηροί.

---

35 οὐ κακοὶ—ἡμαρτημένοι δέ] 'Now it is true that these again are not bad, for they do no harm, but are only in error.' Οὐδὲ refers to ch. ii. § 22. Vanity and want of spirit are, like pettiness and vulgarity, not very serious vices. Of the latter pair, speaking of the qualities and not the persons possessing them, he said they *are κακίαι*, but not disgraceful.

ὁ μὲν γὰρ—ἀγαθῶν] 'For the small-souled man, though worthy of good things, deprives himself of his deserts, and seems to be harmed by not appreciating his own claims, and by ignorance of himself; else he would have aimed at the good things he had a claim to. Such characters, however, are not to be called foolish, but it is rather their energy that is deficient. Still this way of thinking seems to have a bad effect upon the character: for men's aims are regulated by their opinions of their merits,—but these draw back from noble actions and pursuits, thinking themselves unworthy; and in the same way they cut themselves off from external advantages.' From these considerations, and from the whole tendency of his system, Aristotle decides that small-souledness is worse than vanity (§ 37), and he also asserts that it is more common. Want of elevated aims, want of effort, of will, of individuality, these are indeed fatal deficiencies as regards the attainment of what is fine and noble in character. The conception of 'humility' is of course quite beside the system of Aristotle, but we may observe that it does not come into necessary collision with a condemnation of *μικροψυχία*. For this latter implies a want of moral aspiration. Now it is desirable to combine with humility the greatest amount of moral aspiration.

ἀλλὰ μᾶλλον ὀκνηροί] Another reading, supported by several MSS., is *νωθροί*, which the Scholiast explains by *βραδεῖς καὶ* [illegible]. The Paraphrast, however, gives *ὀκνηροί*, which supports the present reading. *Νωθροί* makes good sense, since it is true that want of spirit often accompanies an intellectual turn of mind, men's 'native hue of resolution' being

ἡ τοιαύτη δὲ δόξα δοκεῖ καὶ χείρους ποιεῖν· ἕκαστοι γὰρ ἐφίενται τῶν κατ' ἀξίαν, ἀφίστανται δὲ καὶ τῶν πράξεων τῶν καλῶν καὶ τῶν ἐπιτηδευμάτων ὡς ἀνάξιοι ὄντες, ὁμοίως δὲ καὶ τῶν ἐκτὸς ἀγαθῶν. οἱ δὲ χαῦνοι ἠλίθιοι καὶ ἑαυτοὺς 36
ἀγνοοῦντες, καὶ ταῦτ' ἐπιφανῶς· ὡς γὰρ ἄξιοι ὄντες τοῖς ἐντίμοις ἐπιχειροῦσιν, εἶτα ἐξελέγχονται· καὶ ἐσθῆτι κοσμοῦνται καὶ σχήματι καὶ τοῖς τοιούτοις, καὶ βούλονται τὰ εὐτυχήματα φανερὰ εἶναι αὐτῶν, καὶ λέγουσι περὶ αὐτῶν ὡς διὰ τούτων τιμηθησόμενοι. ἀντιτίθεται δὲ τῇ 37
μεγαλοψυχίᾳ ἡ μικροψυχία μᾶλλον τῆς χαυνότητος· καὶ γὰρ γίγνεται μᾶλλον καὶ χεῖρόν ἐστιν. ἡ μὲν οὖν μεγα- 38
λοψυχία περὶ τιμήν ἐστι μεγάλην, ὥσπερ εἴρηται.

Ἔοικε δὲ καὶ περὶ ταύτην εἶναι ἀρετή τις, καθάπερ ἐν τοῖς 4
πρώτοις ἐλέχθη, ἣ δόξειεν ἂν παραπλησίως ἔχειν πρὸς τὴν μεγαλοψυχίαν ὥσπερ καὶ ἡ ἐλευθεριότης πρὸς τὴν μεγαλοπρέπειαν. ἄμφω γὰρ αὗται τοῦ μὲν μεγάλου ἀφεστᾶσι, περὶ δὲ τὰ μέτρια καὶ τὰ μικρὰ διατιθέασιν ἡμᾶς ὡς δεῖ. ὥσπερ δ' ἐν λήψει καὶ δόσει χρημάτων μεσότης ἐστὶ καὶ 2
ὑπερβολή τε καὶ ἔλλειψις, οὕτω καὶ ἐν τιμῆς ὀρέξει τὸ μᾶλλον ἢ δεῖ καὶ ἧττον, καὶ τὸ ὅθεν δεῖ καὶ ὡς δεῖ. τόν τε 3
γὰρ φιλότιμον ψέγομεν ὡς καὶ μᾶλλον ἢ δεῖ καὶ ὅθεν οὐ δεῖ τῆς τιμῆς ἐφιέμενον, τόν τε ἀφιλότιμον ὡς οὐδ' ἐπὶ τοῖς καλοῖς προαιρούμενον τιμᾶσθαι. ἔστι δ' ὅτε τὸν φιλότιμον 4

'sicklied o'er with the pale cast of thought.' Yet, on the other hand, it is possible that νωθροί has come to supplant ὀκνηροί from a mistake arising from a fancied antithesis to ἠλίθιοι.

IV. Descending now from what is extraordinary to the common level, Aristotle discusses another virtue which bears the same relation to greatsouledness as liberality does to magnificence, namely, the virtue of a laudable ambition. This is concerned with the desire for honour as it exists in ordinary men. There is no name for this virtue, but language testifies to the existence of extremes, hence we may infer a mean. There are two words, ambitious and unambitious; both these are made terms of reproach, thus implying that there must be a middle quality, in relation to which they are each extremes. Again, both are used as terms of praise, which shows that each in turn lays claim to the mean place, as setting itself off against its opposite.

1 καθάπερ ἐν τοῖς πρώτοις] Cf. *Eth.* II. vii. 8. This expression might seem to suggest that the present passage was written after an interval; it is repeated in § 4.

4 ἔστι δ' ὅτε—μέσον] 'But sometimes we praise the ambitious man as

ἐπαινοῦμεν ὡς ἀνδρώδη καὶ φιλόκαλον, τὸν δὲ ἀφιλότιμον ὡς μέτριον καὶ σώφρονα, ὥσπερ καὶ ἐν τοῖς πρώτοις εἴπομεν. δῆλον δ' ὅτι πλεοναχῶς τοῦ φιλοτοιούτου λεγομένου οὐκ ἐπὶ τὸ αὐτὸ ἀεὶ φέρομεν τὸν φιλότιμον, ἀλλ' ἐπαινοῦντες μὲν ἐπὶ τὸ μᾶλλον ἢ οἱ πολλοί, ψέγοντες δ' ἐπὶ τὸ μᾶλλον ἢ δεῖ. ἀνωνύμου δ' οὔσης τῆς μεσότητος, ὡς ἐρήμης ἔοικεν ἀμφισβητεῖν τὰ ἄκρα· ἐν οἷς δ' ἐστὶν ὑπερβολὴ καὶ
5 ἔλλειψις, καὶ τὸ μέσον. ὀρέγονται δὲ τιμῆς καὶ μᾶλλον ἢ δεῖ καὶ ἧττον, ἔστι δ' ὅτε καὶ ὡς δεῖ· ἐπαινεῖται γοῦν ἡ ἕξις αὕτη, μεσότης οὖσα περὶ τιμὴν ἀνώνυμος. Φαίνεται δὲ πρὸς μὲν τὴν φιλοτιμίαν ἀφιλοτιμία, πρὸς δὲ τὴν ἀφιλοτιμίαν φιλοτιμία, πρὸς ἀμφότερα δὲ ἀμφότερά πως.
6 ἔοικε δὲ τοῦτ' εἶναι καὶ περὶ τὰς ἄλλας ἀρετάς. ἀντικεῖσθαι δ' ἐνταῦθ' οἱ ἄκροι φαίνονται διὰ τὸ μὴ ὠνομάσθαι τὸν μέσον.

5 Πραότης δ' ἐστὶ μὲν μεσότης περὶ ὀργάς, ἀνωνύμου δ' ὄντος τοῦ μέσου, σχεδὸν δὲ καὶ τῶν ἄκρων, ἐπὶ τὸν μέσον

---

manly and noble-spirited, and sometimes we praise the unambitious man as moderate and soberminded, as mentioned in our first remarks. Now it is plain that as the term "lover of anything" is used in more senses than one, we do not always apply the term "lover of honour" to express the same thing, but when we praise, we praise that ambition which is more than most men's, and when we blame, we blame that which is greater than it should be. The mean state having no name, the extremes contend, as it were, for this unoccupied ground; but still it exists: for where there is excess and defect there must also be a mean.'

6 *ἔοικε δὲ τοῦτ' εἶναι καὶ περὶ τὰς ἄλλας ἀρετάς*] Cf. *Eth.* II. viii. 1-2.

V. The regulation of the temper (*πραότης περὶ ὀργάς*) is the next subject for discussion. Aristotle confesses that there is no name for this, but he provisionally calls it mildness, though this term is also used to express a deficiency in the feeling of anger. Excess in this feeling has various forms, and accordingly various names; the passionate (*ὀργίλοι*), the hasty (*ἀκρόχολοι*), the sulky (*πικροί*), the morose (*χαλεποί*), all come under the same category as showing excessive or ill-directed anger. Aristotle does not here enter upon the philosophy of anger, inquire its final cause, and in accordance with this determine its right manifestation. He says it is human to avenge oneself (§ 12), and not to resent certain things is slavish (§ 6) and a moral defect, hence we must have a certain amount of anger. This amount must be duly regulated, but where the true mean is cannot be laid down in the abstract (*οὐ ῥᾴδιον τῷ λόγῳ ἀποδοῦναι*): it depends on the particular circum-

τὴν πραότητα φέρομεν, πρὸς τὴν ἔλλειψιν ἀποκλίνουσαν,
ἀνώνυμον οὖσαν. ἡ δ' ὑπερβολὴ ὀργιλότης τις λέγοιτ' ἄν. 2
τὸ μὲν γὰρ πάθος ἐστὶν ὀργή, τὰ δ' ἐμποιοῦντα πολλὰ καὶ
διαφέροντα. ὁ μὲν οὖν ἐφ' οἷς δεῖ καὶ οἷς δεῖ ὀργιζόμενος, 3
ἔτι δὲ καὶ ὡς δεῖ καὶ ὅτε καὶ ὅσον χρόνον, ἐπαινεῖται· πρᾶος
δὴ οὗτος ἂν εἴη, εἴπερ ἡ πραότης ἐπαινεῖται. βούλεται
γὰρ ὁ πρᾶος ἀτάραχος εἶναι καὶ μὴ ἄγεσθαι ὑπὸ τοῦ
πάθους, ἀλλ' ὡς ἂν ὁ λόγος τάξῃ, οὕτω καὶ ἐπὶ τούτοις
καὶ ἐπὶ τοσοῦτον χρόνον χαλεπαίνειν. ἁμαρτάνειν δὲ δοκεῖ 4
μᾶλλον ἐπὶ τὴν ἔλλειψιν. οὐ γὰρ τιμωρητικὸς ὁ πρᾶος,
ἀλλὰ μᾶλλον συγγνωμονικός. ἡ δ' ἔλλειψις, εἴτ' ἀοργησία 5
τίς ἐστιν εἴθ' ὅ τι δή ποτε, ψέγεται. οἱ γὰρ μὴ ὀργιζόμενοι ἐφ' οἷς δεῖ ἠλίθιοι δοκοῦσιν εἶναι, καὶ οἱ μὴ ὡς δεῖ
μηδ' ὅτε μηδ' οἷς δεῖ· δοκεῖ γὰρ οὐκ αἰσθάνεσθαι οὐδὲ 6
λυπεῖσθαι, μὴ ὀργιζόμενός τε οὐκ εἶναι ἀμυντικός. τὸ δὲ
προπηλακιζόμενον ἀνέχεσθαι καὶ τοὺς οἰκείους περιορᾶν

---

stances, and must be left to the intuitive judgment of the mind (ἐν τῇ αἰσθήσει ἡ κρίσις).

3—6 βούλεται γὰρ—ἀνδραποδῶδες] 'For the term "mild man" means one that should be dispassionate and not carried away by his feeling, but should be angry in the way, at the things, and for so long a time, as the mental standard may have appointed. Yet this character seems rather to incline to error on the side of deficiency, for the mild man is more apt to pardon than to resent. But the deficiency is a moral fault (ψέγεται), whether it be called perhaps (τις) want of anger, or whatever else. For men seem fools who do not feel anger at things at which they ought to feel it, or in the manner they ought, or at the time they ought, or with the persons they ought. Such a man seems to be devoid of feeling and of the sense of pain, and since nothing provokes him, he seems not to know how to defend himself: but to suffer insult or to stand by and see one's friends insulted is servile.'

βούλεται γὰρ ὁ πρᾶος] βούλεται appears to be used here in a doubtful sense, something between 'the word mild means,' &c., and 'the mild man has a tendency to,' &c.; cf. ch. i. § 5, note.

τὸ δὲ προπηλακιζόμενον] Had the *Ethics* been composed on a psychological plan, what is said here might have been arranged under the head of θυμός, and would have been connected with the relation of θυμός to courage, which is discussed above, *Eth.* III. viii. 10—12. The present passage is admirably illustrated by Shakespeare's *Hamlet*, Act II. Scene 2:

'Am I a coward?
Who calls me villain? breaks my pate across?
Plucks off my beard and blows it in my face?
Tweaks me by the nose? gives me the lie i' the throat

7 ἀνδραποδῶδες. ἡ δ' ὑπερβολὴ κατὰ πάντα μὲν γίνεται·
καὶ γὰρ οἷς οὐ δεῖ, καὶ ἐφ' οἷς οὐ δεῖ, καὶ μᾶλλον ἢ δεῖ,
καὶ θᾶττον, καὶ πλείω χρόνον· οὐ μὴν ἅπαντά γε τῷ
αὐτῷ ὑπάρχει. οὐ γὰρ ἂν δύναιτ' εἶναι· τὸ γὰρ κακὸν
καὶ ἑαυτὸ ἀπόλλυσι, κἂν ὁλόκληρον ᾖ, ἀφόρητον γίνεται.
8 οἱ μὲν οὖν ὀργίλοι ταχέως μὲν ὀργίζονται καὶ οἷς οὐ δεῖ
καὶ ἐφ' οἷς οὐ δεῖ καὶ μᾶλλον ἢ δεῖ, παύονται δὲ ταχέως·
ὃ καὶ βέλτιστον ἔχουσιν. συμβαίνει δ' αὐτοῖς τοῦτο, ὅτι
οὐ κατέχουσι τὴν ὀργὴν ἀλλ' ἀνταποδιδόασιν ᾗ φανεροί
9 εἰσι διὰ τὴν ὀξύτητα, εἶτ' ἀποπαύονται. ὑπερβολῇ δ'
εἰσὶν οἱ ἀκρόχολοι ὀξεῖς καὶ πρὸς πᾶν ὀργίλοι καὶ ἐπὶ
10 παντί· ὅθεν καὶ τοὔνομα. οἱ δὲ πικροὶ δυσδιάλυτοι, καὶ

As deep as to the lungs? Who does me this?
Ha! why I should take it: for it cannot be
But I am pigeon-liver'd, and lack gall
To make oppression bitter.'

7 ἡ δ' ὑπερβολὴ—γίνεται] 'Now the excess is possible under all heads, the wrong people, the wrong things, more, quicker, longer, than is right. However, these excesses cannot all coexist in the same man. This would be impossible. For evil destroys even itself, and if it exist in its entirety, it becomes unbearable.' Psychological reasons might be assigned why the same person cannot be passionate, peevish, and sulky. But Aristotle here gives an abstract generalization—that the different forms of evil are mutually destructive, and that it is only by tempering evil with a certain admixture of good that its existence can be borne.

8 συμβαίνει δ'—ἀποπαύονται] 'This happens because they do not keep in their anger, but through their keenness make reprisals in an open way, and then they are done.' The words ᾗ φανεροί εἰσι can have nothing to do with the principle given in the *Rhetoric*, II. ii. 1, that anger desires to make itself manifestly felt, else we must have had ᾗ φανεροὶ ἂν εἶεν. The Paraphrast simply renders οὐ κατέχουσι τὴν ὀργήν, οὐδὲ κρύπτουσιν, ἀλλὰ ἐξάγονται καὶ ἀμύνονται εὐθύς.

9 οἱ ἀκρόχολοι] 'The hasty.' The older form of this word is ἀκράχολοι. The etymology appears to be ἄκρος and χολή, as if 'on the point' or 'extreme verge of anger.' On the same analogy we find the word ἀκροσφαλής, 'on the verge of being overturned,' 'ricketty,' cf. Plato, *Repub.* p. 404 A. Plato speaks of passionate and peevish people as having become so through the overrating of an originally noble and spirited temperament. Cf. *Repub.* p. 411 B—413: ἐὰν δὲ θυμοειδῆ (ἐξ ἀρχῆς λάβῃ), ἀσθενῆ ποιήσας τὸν θυμὸν ὀξύρροπον ἀπειργάσατο, ἀπὸ σμικρῶν ταχὺ ἐρεθιζόμενόν τε καὶ κατασβεννύμενον. ἀκράχολοι οὖν καὶ ὀργίλοι ἀντὶ θυμοειδοῦς γεγένηνται, δυσκολίας ἔμπλεῳ. κ.τ.λ.

10 οἱ δὲ πικροὶ—φίλοις] 'But the sulky are hard to bring round, and are angry a long time, for they keep

πολὺν χρόνον ὀργίζονται· κατέχουσι γὰρ τὸν θυμόν.
παῦλα δὲ γίνεται, ὅταν ἀνταποδιδῷ· ἡ γὰρ τιμωρία
παύει τῆς ὀργῆς, ἡδονὴν ἀντὶ τῆς λύπης ἐμποιοῦσα·
τούτου δὲ μὴ γινομένου τὸ βάρος ἔχουσιν· διὰ
γὰρ τὸ μὴ ἐπιφανὲς εἶναι οὐδὲ συμπείθει αὐτοὺς οὐδείς,
ἐν αὑτῷ δὲ πέψαι τὴν ὀργὴν χρόνου δεῖ. εἰσὶ δ'
οἱ τοιοῦτοι ἑαυτοῖς ὀχληρότατοι καὶ τοῖς μάλιστα
φίλοις. χαλεποὺς δὲ λέγομεν τοὺς ἐφ' οἷς τε μὴ 11
δεῖ χαλεπαίνοντας καὶ μᾶλλον ἢ δεῖ καὶ πλείω χρόνον,
καὶ μὴ διαλλαττομένους ἄνευ τιμωρίας ἢ κολάσεως. τῇ 12
πραότητι δὲ μᾶλλον τὴν ὑπερβολὴν ἀντιτίθεμεν· καὶ
γὰρ μᾶλλον γίνεται· ἀνθρωπικώτερον γὰρ τὸ τιμωρεῖσθαι.
καὶ πρὸς τὸ συμβιοῦν οἱ χαλεποὶ χείρους. ὃ δὲ καὶ ἐν 13
τοῖς πρότερον εἴρηται, καὶ ἐκ τῶν λεγομένων δῆλον· οὐ
γὰρ ῥᾴδιον διορίσαι τὸ πῶς καὶ τίσι καὶ ἐπὶ ποίοις καὶ
πόσον χρόνον ὀργιστέον, καὶ τὸ μέχρι τίνος ὀρθῶς ποιεῖ
τις ἢ ἁμαρτάνει. ὁ μὲν γὰρ μικρὸν παρεκβαίνων οὐ
ψέγεται, οὔτ' ἐπὶ τὸ μᾶλλον οὔτ' ἐπὶ τὸ ἧττον. ἐνίοτε
γὰρ τοὺς ἐλλείποντας ἐπαινοῦμεν καὶ πράους φαμέν, καὶ
τοὺς χαλεπαίνοντας ἀνδρώδεις ὡς δυναμένους ἄρχειν. ὁ δὴ
πόσον καὶ πῶς παρεκβαίνων ψεκτός, οὐ ῥᾴδιον τῷ λόγῳ
ἀποδοῦναι· ἐν γὰρ τοῖς καθ' ἕκαστα καὶ τῇ αἰσθήσει ἡ
κρίσις. ἀλλὰ τό γε τοσοῦτον δῆλον, ὅτι ἡ μὲν μέση 14
ἕξις ἐπαινετή, καθ' ἣν οἷς δεῖ ὀργιζόμεθα καὶ ἐφ' οἷς δεῖ
καὶ ὡς δεῖ καὶ πάντα τὰ τοιαῦτα, αἱ δ' ὑπερβολαὶ καὶ ἐλλείψεις ψεκταί, καὶ ἐπὶ μικρὸν μὲν γινόμεναι ἠρέμα, ἐπὶ
πλέον δὲ μᾶλλον, ἐπὶ πολὺ δὲ σφόδρα. δῆλον οὖν ὅτι

in their wrath. Now there is a natural termination, when one has wreaked one's resentment, since revenge stops anger by substituting a feeling of pleasure for that of pain. But if this does not take place, these people continue to feel their burden. Their feeling is not manifest, and so no one reasons them out of it, while to digest it internally requires time. Therefore such persons are exceedingly vexatious both to themselves and to their best friends.' An admirable account of sulkiness, on which nothing more need be said.

13 *ὃ δὲ καὶ ἐν τοῖς πρότερον εἴρηται*] This refers to *Eth.* II. ix. 7—9, which passage is with some amplification almost exactly repeated here. This part of the *Ethics* is written with a constant reference to Book II., and yet as if the subject had been taken up again to be worked out after an interval.

15 τῆς μέσης ἕξεως ἀνθεκτέον· αἱ μὲν οὖν περὶ τὴν ὀργὴν ἕξεις εἰρήσθωσαν.

6 Ἐν δὲ ταῖς ὁμιλίαις καὶ τῷ συζῆν καὶ λόγων καὶ πραγμάτων κοινωνεῖν οἱ μὲν ἄρεσκοι δοκοῦσιν εἶναι, οἱ πάντα
πρὸς ἡδονὴν ἐπαινοῦντες καὶ οὐθὲν ἀντιτείνοντες, ἀλλ'
2 οἰόμενοι δεῖν ἄλυποι τοῖς ἐντυγχάνουσιν εἶναι· οἱ δ' ἐξ
ἐναντίας τούτοις πρὸς πάντα ἀντιτείνοντες καὶ τοῦ λυπεῖν
οὐδ' ὁτιοῦν φροντίζοντες δύσκολοι καὶ δυσέριδες καλοῦν-
3 ται. ὅτι μὲν οὖν αἱ εἰρημέναι ἕξεις ψεκταί εἰσιν, οὐκ
ἄδηλον, καὶ ὅτι ἡ μέση τούτων ἐπαινετή, καθ' ἣν ἀποδέξεται
4 ἃ δεῖ καὶ ὡς δεῖ, ὁμοίως δὲ καὶ δυσχερανεῖ. ὄνομα δ' οὐκ
ἀποδέδοται αὐτῇ τι, ἔοικε δὲ μάλιστα φιλίᾳ· τοιοῦτος
γάρ ἐστιν ὁ κατὰ τὴν μέσην ἕξιν οἷον βουλόμεθα λέγειν τὸν
5 ἐπιεικῆ φίλον, τὸ στέργειν προσλαβόντα. διαφέρει δὲ
τῆς φιλίας, ὅτι ἄνευ πάθους ἐστὶ καὶ τοῦ στέργειν οἷς
ὁμιλεῖ· οὐ γὰρ τῷ φιλεῖν ἢ ἐχθαίρειν ἀποδέχεται ἕκαστα
ὡς δεῖ, ἀλλὰ τῷ τοιοῦτος εἶναι. ὁμοίως γὰρ πρὸς ἀγνῶτας
καὶ γνωρίμους καὶ συνήθεις καὶ ἀσυνήθεις αὐτὸ ποιήσει,
πλὴν καὶ ἐν ἑκάστοις ὡς ἁρμόζει. οὐ γὰρ ὁμοίως προσήκει

VI. The next subject is the regulation of one's deportment in society, with regard especially to complacency or the reverse. This also is a balance between extremes, avoiding on the one side surliness (τὸ δύσκολον), and on the other side the conduct both of the weak assentor (ἄρεσκος), and of the interested flatterer (κόλαξ). The balance has no name, it is most like friendship, but differs from it in being devoid of affection, and being extended to all in proper degrees. There is a slight departure here from Book II. vii. 11–13, and it may be said that the present treatment is an improvement. Before (*l.c.*) it was said, there are three virtues connected with speech and action in society: the first is about what is true, the others about what is pleasant. But here the quality which concerns the deportment and whole spirit of a man in society is rightly treated as most generic, and placed first. In Book II. the name φιλία is incorrectly given to the quality in question, but here no name is assigned, and only a resemblance to friendship is pointed out.

5 οὐ γὰρ ὁμοίως—λυπεῖν] 'For it is not fitting that we should pay the same regard to strangers as to familiars, nor again have we an equal title to put them to pain.' This latter clause is explained in §§ 7–9, where it is laid down that though the general object will be to give pleasure, yet that a man must bring himself to give pain on occasion, with a view to important moral consequences in the future. He would, of course, feel himself more bound to exercise this duty with regard to friends. Φροντίζειν is a

συνήθων καὶ ὀθνείων φροντίζειν, οὐδ' αὖ λυπεῖν. καθόλου 6
μὲν οὖν εἴρηται ὅτι ὡς δεῖ ὁμιλήσει, ἀναφέρων δὲ πρὸς τὸ
καλὸν καὶ τὸ συμφέρον στοχάσεται τοῦ μὴ λυπεῖν ἢ
συνηδύνειν. ἔοικε μὲν γὰρ περὶ ἡδονὰς καὶ λύπας εἶναι 7
τὰς ἐν ταῖς ὁμιλίαις γινομένας, τούτων δ' ὅσας μὲν αὐτῷ
ἐστὶ μὴ καλὸν ἢ βλαβερὸν συνηδύνειν, δυσχερανεῖ, καὶ
προαιρήσεται λυπεῖν. κἂν τῷ ποιοῦντι δ' ἀσχημοσύνην
φέρῃ, καὶ ταύτην μὴ μικράν, ἢ βλάβην, ἡ δ' ἐναντίωσις
μικρὰν λύπην, οὐκ ἀποδέξεται ἀλλὰ δυσχερανεῖ. διαφε- 8
ρόντως δ' ὁμιλήσει τοῖς ἐν ἀξιώμασι καὶ τοῖς τυχοῦσι, καὶ
μᾶλλον ἢ ἧττον γνωρίμοις, ὁμοίως δὲ καὶ κατὰ τὰς ἄλλας
διαφοράς, ἑκάστοις ἀπονέμων τὸ πρέπον, καὶ καθ' αὑτὸ μὲν
αἱρούμενος τὸ συνηδύνειν, λυπεῖν δ' εὐλαβούμενος, τοῖς δ'
ἀποβαίνουσιν, ἐὰν ᾖ μείζω, συνεπόμενος, λέγω δὲ τῷ καλῷ
καὶ τῷ συμφέροντι. καὶ ἡδονῆς δ' ἕνεκα τῆς εἰσαῦθις
μεγάλης μικρὰ λυπήσει. ὁ μὲν οὖν μέσος τοιοῦτός ἐστιν, 9
οὐκ ὠνόμασται δέ, τοῦ δὲ συνηδύνοντος ὁ μὲν τοῦ ἡδὺς εἶναι
στοχαζόμενος μὴ δι' ἄλλο τι ἄρεσκος, ὁ δ' ὅπως ὠφέλειά
τις αὐτῷ γίγνηται εἰς χρήματα καὶ ὅσα διὰ χρημάτων,
κόλαξ· ὁ δὲ πᾶσι δυσχεραίνων εἴρηται ὅτι δύσκολος καὶ

general expression, implying equally care to please, and care for the welfare of the persons in question.

6—7 καθόλου — δυσχερανεῖ] 'We have said generally that (the good man) will associate with people as he ought, but we may add (δὲ) that, with a constant reference to what is beautiful and what is expedient, he will aim at not giving pain, or at contributing pleasure. The province of his virtue lies among the pleasures and pains that arise out of social intercourse, and wherever in giving pleasure he would dishonour or injure himself, he will make a difficulty, and rather choose to give pain than such gratification. And if there be something which will bring, to any considerable degree, disgrace or harm on the doer, while opposition will give him slight pain, (the good man) will not approve it, but will show his repugnance.' (1) It may be derogatory to oneself to show complacency. (2) It may be hurtful to some member of the company. These cautions show the moral and thoughtful spirit by which Aristotle would have conduct in society regulated. The following section prescribes the bearing of a finished gentleman, giving to all their due. It must not be forgotten that Aristotle himself had played the part, not only of a philosopher, but also of a courtier.

9 δύσκολος] Eudemus uses the word αὐθάδης to denote this character (*Eth. Eud.* III. vii. 4), in which he is followed by Theophrastus (*Characters*, c. 15) and the author of the *Magna Moralia* (I. xxix.). Eudemus makes the mean state σεμνότης, which is a departure from the present treatment.

δύσερις. ἀντικεῖσθαι δὲ φαίνεται τὰ ἄκρα ἑαυτοῖς διὰ τὸ ἀνώνυμον εἶναι τὸ μέσον.

7 Περὶ τὰ αὐτὰ δὲ σχεδόν ἐστι καὶ ἡ τῆς ἀλαζονείας
μεσότης· ἀνώνυμος δὲ καὶ αὐτή. οὐ χεῖρον δὲ καὶ τὰς
τοιαύτας ἐπελθεῖν· μᾶλλόν τε γὰρ ἂν εἰδείημεν τὰ περὶ
τὸ ἦθος, καθ' ἕκαστον διελθόντες, καὶ μεσότητας εἶναι τὰς
ἀρετὰς πιστεύσαιμεν ἄν, ἐπὶ πάντων οὕτως ἔχον συνιδόντες.
ἐν δὴ τῷ συζῆν οἱ μὲν πρὸς ἡδονὴν καὶ λύπην ὁμιλοῦντες
εἴρηνται, περὶ δὲ τῶν ἀληθευόντων τε καὶ ψευδομένων
εἴπωμεν ὁμοίως ἐν λόγοις καὶ πράξεσι καὶ τῷ προσποιή-
2 ματι. δοκεῖ δὴ ὁ μὲν ἀλαζὼν προσποιητικὸς τῶν ἐνδόξων
3 εἶναι καὶ μὴ ὑπαρχόντων καὶ μειζόνων ἢ ὑπάρχει, ὁ δὲ
εἴρων ἀνάπαλιν ἀρνεῖσθαι τὰ ὑπάρχοντα ἢ ἐλάττω ποιεῖν,
4 ὁ δὲ μέσος αὐθέκαστός τις ὢν ἀληθευτικὸς καὶ τῷ βίῳ καὶ

VII. There follows another nameless excellence closely connected with the former, having still to do with demeanour in society: this, by a curious formula, is termed the regulation of boastfulness (ἡ τῆς ἀλαζονείας μεσότης). The boastful man lays claim to honourable qualities which he does not possess, or to a greater degree than he possesses them (δοκεῖ προσποιητικὸς τῶν ἐνδόξων εἶναι κ.τ.λ.), while the ironical man denies or understates his own merits. The balance between these two is found in the straightforward character (αὐθέκαστός τις), who in word and deed neither diminishes nor exaggerates his own good qualities. In *Eth.* II. vii. 12, the provisional name ἀλήθεια was given to this virtue, but here Aristotle points out that it is to be distinguished from 'truth,' in the more serious sense of the word,—that 'truth' which makes the difference between justice and injustice. What he is at present concerned with is merely a truthfulness of manner, though he confesses (§ 8) that this has a moral worth (ἐπιεικής), and that the man who is truthful in little things will also be truthful in more important affairs.

3 εἴρων] This is an excessively difficult word to express in English. 'Ironical' has acquired an association of bitterness and taunting,—'Dissembler' of craft. If we render it by 'over-modest' we trench upon the qualities of the μικρόψυχος, and imply too much that is connected with the whole character. Εἰρωνεία as here spoken of is simply an affair of the manner; there appear to be two forms of it, one that refined species exhibited by Socrates, the other an affectation of humility which is really contemptible. There is perhaps no one English word to express these two forms, the only resource appears to be to use the word 'Ironical' in a restricted sense. Εἴρων in Theophrastus (*Char.* I.) is used in a worse sense than in Aristotle, to denote one who dissembles for selfish motives, and whose whole life is artificial and deceitful.

αὐθέκαστος] probably from αὐτὸ ἕκαστον, 'everything exactly as it is,'

τῷ λόγῳ, τὰ ὑπάρχοντα ὁμολογῶν εἶναι περὶ αὑτόν, καὶ
οὔτε μείζω οὔτε ἐλάττω. ἔστι δὲ τούτων ἕκαστα καὶ ἕνεκά 5
τινος ποιεῖν καὶ μηθενός. ἕκαστος δ' οἷός ἐστι, τοιαῦτα
λέγει καὶ πράττει καὶ οὕτω ζῇ, ἐὰν μή τινος ἕνεκα πράττῃ.
καθ' αὑτὸ δὲ τὸ μὲν ψεῦδος φαῦλον καὶ ψεκτόν, τὸ δ' 6
ἀληθὲς καλὸν καὶ ἐπαινετόν. οὕτω δὲ καὶ ὁ μὲν ἀληθευτικὸς μέσος ὢν ἐπαινετός, οἱ δὲ ψευδόμενοι ἀμφότεροι μὲν
ψεκτοί, μᾶλλον δ' ὁ ἀλαζών. περὶ ἑκατέρου δ' εἴπωμεν,
πρότερον δὲ περὶ τοῦ ἀληθευτικοῦ. οὐ γὰρ περὶ τοῦ ἐν 7
ταῖς ὁμολογίαις ἀληθεύοντος λέγομεν, οὐδ' ὅσα εἰς ἀδικίαν
ἢ δικαιοσύνην συντείνει (ἄλλης γὰρ ἂν εἴη ταῦτ' ἀρετῆς),
ἀλλ' ἐν οἷς μηθενὸς τοιούτου διαφέροντος καὶ ἐν λόγῳ καὶ
ἐν βίῳ ἀληθεύει τῷ τὴν ἕξιν τοιοῦτος εἶναι. δόξειε δ' 8
ἂν ὁ τοιοῦτος ἐπιεικὴς εἶναι. ὁ γὰρ φιλαλήθης, καὶ ἐν
οἷς μὴ διαφέρει ἀληθεύων, ἀληθεύσει καὶ ἐν οἷς διαφέρει
ἔτι μᾶλλον. ὡς γὰρ αἰσχρὸν τὸ ψεῦδος εὐλαβήσεται,
ὅ γε καὶ καθ' αὑτὸ ηὐλαβεῖτο· ὁ δὲ τοιοῦτος ἐπαινετός.
ἐπὶ τὸ ἔλαττον δὲ μᾶλλον τοῦ ἀληθοῦς ἀποκλίνει· 9

---

and hence a 'matter-of-fact' or 'straightforward' man.

5—6 ἔστι δὲ—ἀλαζών] 'Now it is possible to practise both irony and boastfulness either with or without a particular motive. But in general a man speaks, acts, and lives, in accordance with his character, unless he have a particular motive. Falsehood is in itself base and reprehensible, and truth is noble and praiseworthy. And thus the truthful man, who occupies the mean, is praiseworthy, while those who strive to give a false impression of themselves are both reprehensible, and especially the boaster.' Aristotle first appears to assert that both irony and boastfulness are prompted generally by a particular motive, for, if it were not so, men would be simple and natural. Afterwards we are told that boastfulness is a condition of the will (ἐν τῇ προαιρέσει), that it aims at either gain or reputation,—that irony may spring from a motive of refinement, or again from vanity itself. These things however may aim at reputation and yet be instinctive, the desire for reputation forming part of men's natural impulses.

8 δόξειε δ' ἂν—ἐπαινετός] 'But this character appears to possess a moral excellence. For the lover of truth, who adheres to what is true even in things where it does not matter, will be still more truthful in affairs of importance, for he will surely avoid a lie when it appears as something base, when he avoided it before merely for its own sake.' The writing here is a little careless, since above, all lies were declared to be essentially base, but here a contrast seems to be drawn between the 'white lie' in society, and the base lie in affairs of importance. It throws great light upon the nature of Aristotle's table of the so-called 'virtues'

ἐμμελέστερον γὰρ φαίνεται διὰ τὸ ἐπαχθεῖς τὰς ὑπερ-
10 βολὰς εἶναι. ὁ δὲ μείζω τῶν ὑπαρχόντων προσποιούμενος
μηθενὸς ἕνεκα φαύλῳ μὲν ἔοικεν (οὐ γὰρ ἂν ἔχαιρε τῷ
11 ψεύδει), μάταιος δὲ φαίνεται μᾶλλον ἢ κακός. εἰ δ' ἕνεκά
τινος, ὁ μὲν δόξης ἢ τιμῆς οὐ λίαν ψεκτός, †ὡς ὁ ἀλαζών,
12 ὁ δὲ ἀργυρίου, ἢ ὅσα εἰς ἀργύριον, ἀσχημονέστερος. οὐκ
ἐν τῇ δυνάμει δ' ἐστὶν ὁ ἀλαζών, ἀλλ' ἐν τῇ προαιρέσει·
κατὰ τὴν ἕξιν γὰρ καὶ τῷ τοιόσδε εἶναι ἀλαζών ἐστιν,
ὥσπερ καὶ ψεύστης ὁ μὲν τῷ ψεύδει αὐτῷ χαίρων, ὁ δὲ
13 δόξης ὀρεγόμενος ἢ κέρδους. οἱ μὲν οὖν δόξης χάριν
ἀλαζονευόμενοι τὰ τοιαῦτα προσποιοῦνται ἐφ' οἷς ἔπαινος
ἢ εὐδαιμονισμός, οἱ δὲ κέρδους, ὧν καὶ ἀπόλαυσίς ἐστι τοῖς
πέλας καὶ ἃ διαλαθεῖν ἔστι μὴ ὄντα, οἷον μάντιν σοφὸν ἢ
ἰατρόν. διὰ τοῦτο οἱ πλεῖστοι προσποιοῦνται τὰ τοιαῦτα
14 καὶ ἀλαζονεύονται· ἔστι γὰρ ἐν αὐτοῖς τὰ εἰρημένα. οἱ
δ' εἴρωνες ἐπὶ τὸ ἔλαττον λέγοντες χαριέστεροι μὲν τὰ ἤθη
φαίνονται· οὐ γὰρ κέρδους ἕνεκα δοκοῦσι λέγειν, ἀλλὰ

---

to observe that he excludes from them truth proper, and admits truthfulness of manner.

10—12 *ὁ δὲ μείζω—κέρδους*] 'But the man who pretends to better qualities than he really possesses, if he has no motive, shows like a mean man, for else he would not have delighted in the falsehood, though he seems foolish rather than bad. Supposing there is a motive, if it be reputation or honour, the boaster is not to be severely blamed, but if it be money, directly or indirectly, his conduct is more discreditable. The boaster is not constituted by a given faculty, but by a particular condition of the will; for it is in accordance with his moral state, and by reason of his character, that he is a boaster, just as either from taking pleasure in falsehood itself, or from aiming at reputation or gain (in short, from the state of his will and moral character)—a man is called a liar.

†ὡς ὁ ἀλαζών] This makes no sense. The Paraphrast omits *ὡς* altogether, rendering the passage, *εἰ δὲ τινος ἕνεκα προσποιεῖται, εἰ μὲν δόξης ἢ τιμῆς οὐ λίαν ψεκτὸς ὁ ἀλαζών*. To follow his example seems the simplest remedy. One of the MSS. omits *ὁ*, which would give the sense 'he is not very blameable considering that he is a boaster.'

12 *οὐκ ἐν τῇ δυνάμει—ἀλλ' ἐν τῇ προαιρέσει*] Cf. the well-known passage *Rhet.* I. i. 14, where the Sophist is said to be distinguished from the Dialectician not intellectually but morally. *ὁ γὰρ σοφιστικὸς οὐκ ἐν τῇ δυνάμει ἀλλ' ἐν τῇ προαιρέσει.*

13 This is a very happy observation, that desire for reputation makes men pretend to virtue, power and the like; but desire for gain makes them pretend to useful arts the possession of which cannot be tested; thus a man will give himself out to be a clever soothsayer or doctor.

14—15 *οἱ δ' εἴρωνες—ἀλαζονικόν*]

φεύγοντες τὸ ὀγκηρόν. μάλιστα δὲ καὶ οὗτοι τὰ ἔνδοξα
ἀπαρνοῦνται, οἷον καὶ Σωκράτης ἐποίει. οἱ δὲ καὶ τὰ 15
μικρὰ καὶ τὰ φανερὰ προσποιούμενοι βαυκοπανοῦργοι
λέγονται καὶ εὐκαταφρόνητοί εἰσιν. καὶ ἐνίοτε ἀλαζονεία
φαίνεται, οἷον ἡ τῶν Λακώνων ἐσθής· καὶ γὰρ ἡ ὑπερβολὴ
καὶ ἡ λίαν ἔλλειψις ἀλαζονικόν. οἱ δὲ μετρίως χρώμενοι 16
τῇ εἰρωνείᾳ καὶ περὶ τὰ μὴ λίαν ἐμποδὼν καὶ φανερὰ εἰρωνευόμενοι χαρίεντες φαίνονται. ἀντικεῖσθαι δ' ὁ ἀλαζὼν 17
φαίνεται τῷ ἀληθευτικῷ· χείρων γάρ.

Οὔσης δὲ καὶ ἀναπαύσεως ἐν τῷ βίῳ, καὶ ἐν ταύτῃ 8

'Ironical persons, in depreciating themselves, exhibit it is true a certain refinement of character, for they do not appear to speak in that way for the sake of gain, but to avoid pomposity; but it must be confessed that these too especially disclaim qualities held in repute, as Socrates used to do. But they who make a pretence about things petty and obvious are called "humbugs," and are despised by every one. Sometimes this kind of conduct appears to be really pretension, as in the case of the Laconian dress; for both the excess and the extreme of deficiency are of the nature of boasting.'

There appears to be a slight antithesis between *χαριέστεροι μὲν*—and *μάλιστα δὲ καὶ οὗτοι*, as if the disclaiming of honourable qualities were not so much to the credit of the Ironical. *καὶ οὗτοι* seems to imply a reference to the great-souled man, who was described as having tendencies of the same kind, c. ii. § 27—28.

οἷον καὶ Σωκράτης] On the Irony of Socrates, see Vol. I. Essay II.

15 *προσποιούμενοι*] It is impossible to understand this in the sense of 'disclaiming' which the context requires. The Paraphrast supplies *μὴ δύνασθαι*, and explains it very clearly, as follows, *ὃς δὲ οὐ μόνον τὰ μεγάλα καὶ ἔνδοξα ἀλλὰ καὶ τὰ μικρὰ ἀπαρνεῖται, καὶ ἃ δῆλόν ἐστι δυνάμενος ταῦτα προσποιεῖται μὴ δύνασθαι*. But *προσποιούμενοι* can never have been consciously meant to stand for this. There must have been some slip about the writing. Two of the MSS. read *μὴ προσποιούμενοι*. This sort of variation in MSS. does not show what was the original reading, but only that the transcribers felt a difficulty.

VIII. 1 *Οὔσης δὲ—τοιούτων ἀκούειν*] 'Rest also being a part of human life, and an element of this being playful diversion, we find here likewise the sphere for a certain harmonious manner of intercourse, and the possibility of both speaking and hearing the right sort of things in the right way; though there will be a difference as to whether one is the speaker in such matters or listens to what is said.'

Aristotle considers the virtue of wit or tact (*εἴτ' ἐπιδέξιοι εἴτ' εὐτράπελοι λέγεται*) to be concerned with the amusing and sportive element in society, and to be a balance between buffoonishness that sacrifices all propriety to the ludicrous, and dulness that is incapable of either making or appreciating a joke. Aristotle does not here enter into the philosophy of the ludicrous, or inquire what is a

διαγωγῆς μετὰ παιδιᾶς, δοκεῖ καὶ ἐνταῦθα εἶναι ὁμιλία τις ἐμμελής, καὶ οἷα δεῖ λέγειν καὶ ὥς, ὁμοίως δὲ καὶ ἀκούειν. διοίσει δὲ καὶ τὸ ἐν τοιούτοις λέγειν ἢ τοιούτων ἀκούειν.
2 δῆλον δ' ὡς καὶ περὶ ταῦτ' ἐστὶν ὑπερβολή τε καὶ ἔλλειψις
3 τοῦ μέσου. οἱ μὲν οὖν τῷ γελοίῳ ὑπερβάλλοντες βωμολόχοι δοκοῦσιν εἶναι καὶ φορτικοί, γλιχόμενοι πάντως τοῦ γελοίου, καὶ μᾶλλον στοχαζόμενοι τοῦ γέλωτα ποιῆσαι ἢ τοῦ λέγειν εὐσχήμονα καὶ μὴ λυπεῖν τὸν σκωπτόμενον· οἱ δὲ μήτ' αὐτοὶ ἂν εἰπόντες μηθὲν γελοῖον τοῖς τε λέγουσι δυσχεραίνοντες ἄγριοι καὶ σκληροὶ δοκοῦσιν εἶναι. οἱ δ' ἐμμελῶς παίζοντες εὐτράπελοι προσαγορεύονται, οἷον εὔτροποι· τοῦ γὰρ ἤθους αἱ τοιαῦται δοκοῦσι κινήσεις εἶναι, ὥσπερ δὲ τὰ σώματα ἐκ τῶν κινήσεων κρίνεται, οὕτω καὶ
4 τὰ ἤθη. ἐπιπολάζοντος δὲ τοῦ γελοίου, καὶ τῶν πλείστων χαιρόντων τῇ παιδιᾷ καὶ τῷ σκώπτειν μᾶλλον ἢ δεῖ, καὶ οἱ βωμολόχοι εὐτράπελοι προσαγορεύονται ὡς χαρίεντες. ὅτι
5 δὲ διαφέρουσι, καὶ οὐ μικρόν, ἐκ τῶν εἰρημένων δῆλον. τῇ μέσῃ δ' ἕξει οἰκεῖον καὶ ἡ ἐπιδεξιότης ἐστίν· τοῦ δ' ἐπι-

---

joke and why it pleases. Nor does he lay down any canons for the regulation of wit, except such general ones as that 'nothing should be said which is unworthy of a gentleman' (πότερον οὖν τὸν εὖ σκώπτοντα ὁριστέον τῷ λέγειν ἃ πρέπει ἐλευθερίῳ;), that the hearer must not be shocked, &c. On the whole he leaves it indefinite, saying that tastes differ, and the educated man will be a law to himself. His account of wit then is negative, and abstract, though perfectly just as far as it goes.

διαγωγῆς μετὰ παιδιᾶς] διαγωγὴ is the passing of time, hence 'diversion.' Cf. *Metaphys.* I. i. 15: πλειόνων δ' εὑρισκομένων τεχνῶν, καὶ τῶν μὲν πρὸς τἀναγκαῖα τῶν δὲ πρὸς διαγωγὴν οὐσῶν. *Eth.* X. vi. 3: καταφεύγουσι δ' ἐπὶ τὰς τοιαύτας διαγωγὰς τῶν εὐδαιμονιζομένων οἱ πολλοί.

βωμολόχοι] This name seems originally to have belonged to the vile creatures who lay in wait at the altars to purloin the offerings, and hence to have been applied to those who thought nothing too low for them, buffoons who would descend to anything.

3 οἱ δ' ἐμμελῶς—τὰ ἤθη] 'But they whose jocularity is in good taste are called witty, by a name that implies their happy turns; for such motions of wit seem to belong to the moral character, and characters, like bodies, are judged by their movements.' Aristotle here calls attention to the etymology of εὐτράπελος, as he did before to that of ἄσωτος. Ch. i. § 5.

4 ἐπιπολάζοντος—χαρίεντες] 'But as the ludicrous meets us at every turn (ἐπιπολάζοντος, cf. *Eth.* I. iv. 4), and most people take pleasure in sport and jesting more than they ought, even buffoons get the name of witty just as though they were fine wits.'

δεξίου ἐστὶ τοιαῦτα λέγειν καὶ ἀκούειν οἷα τῷ ἐπιεικεῖ καὶ
ἐλευθερίῳ ἁρμόττει· ἔστι γάρ τινα πρέποντα τῷ τοιούτῳ
λέγειν ἐν παιδιᾶς μέρει καὶ ἀκούειν, καὶ ἡ τοῦ ἐλευθερίου
παιδιὰ διαφέρει τῆς τοῦ ἀνδραποδώδους, καὶ αὖ τοῦ πεπαιδευμένου καὶ ἀπαιδεύτου. ἴδοι δ' ἄν τις καὶ ἐκ τῶν 6
κωμῳδιῶν τῶν παλαιῶν καὶ τῶν καινῶν· τοῖς μὲν γὰρ ἦν
γελοῖον ἡ αἰσχρολογία, τοῖς δὲ μᾶλλον ἡ ὑπόνοια· διαφέρει δ' οὐ μικρὸν ταῦτα πρὸς εὐσχημοσύνην. πότερον 7
οὖν τὸν εὖ σκώπτοντα ὁριστέον τῷ λέγειν ἃ πρέπει ἐλευθερίῳ, ἢ τῷ μὴ λυπεῖν τὸν ἀκούοντα, ἢ καὶ τέρπειν; ἢ καὶ
τό γε τοιοῦτον ἀόριστον; ἄλλο γὰρ ἄλλῳ μισητόν τε καὶ
ἡδύ. τοιαῦτα δὲ καὶ ἀκούσεται· ἃ γὰρ ὑπομένει ἀκούων, 8
ταῦτα καὶ ποιεῖν δοκεῖ. οὐ δὴ πᾶν ποιήσει· τὸ γὰρ 9
σκῶμμα λοιδόρημά τί ἐστιν, οἱ δὲ νομοθέται ἔνια λοιδορεῖν
κωλύουσιν· ἔδει δ' ἴσως καὶ σκώπτειν. ὁ δὴ χαρίεις καὶ 10
ἐλευθέριος οὕτως ἕξει, οἷον νόμος ὢν ἑαυτῷ. τοιοῦτος μὲν
οὖν ὁ μέσος ἐστίν, εἴτ' ἐπιδέξιος εἴτ' εὐτράπελος λέγεται·
ὁ δὲ βωμολόχος ἥττων ἐστὶ τοῦ γελοίου, καὶ οὔτε ἑαυτοῦ

---

6 ἴδοι δ' ἂν—εὐσχημοσύνην] 'This we may see from a comparison of the old and the new comedy. In the former it is coarse language that provokes laughter, in the latter it is rather innuendo; which makes no small difference with respect to decorum.' This interesting remark is in accordance with what we know from other sources, of the comparative tameness of the new comedy in relation to the license of the old. Cf. Horace, *A. P.* 281 sqq.

9 οὐ δὴ πᾶν—σκώπτειν] 'Therefore he will not give utterance to every jest, for the jest is a sort of reviling, and the lawgivers forbid certain kinds of reviling—they ought perhaps to have forbidden (certain) jests.' Ἔνια must be understood as carried on from λοιδορεῖν to σκώπτειν. Aristotle could never have wished that jesting altogether should be forbidden by the law.

ὁ δὴ χαρίεις—ἑαυτῷ] 'This then will be the attitude of the refined and liberal man, he being as it were a law to himself.' Aristotle usually escapes from pure indefiniteness and relativity by asserting that the standard in each case is to be found in the good, the wise, the refined man. This standard is evidently the expression of the universal reason of man. It is not to be supposed that wit, beauty, or goodness are mere matters of taste, as Aristotle would seem for a moment to imply (ἢ καὶ τό γε τοιοῦτον ἀόριστον; ἄλλο γὰρ ἄλλῳ μισητόν τε καὶ ἡδύ). When he adds afterwards that the educated man must be the standard of appeal, he means that the laws of reason must decide. And these might, had Aristotle thought it worth his while, have been more drawn out in reference to the question under discussion.

10—12 These sections are an

οὔτε τῶν ἄλλων ἀπεχόμενος, εἰ γέλωτα ποιήσει, καὶ τοιαῦτα λέγων ὧν οὐδὲν ἂν εἴποι ὁ χαρίεις, ἔνια δ' οὐδ' ἂν ἀκούσαι. ὁ δ' ἄγριος εἰς τὰς τοιαύτας ὁμιλίας ἀχρεῖος· οὐδὲν γὰρ
11 συμβαλλόμενος πᾶσι δυσχεραίνει. δοκεῖ δὲ ἡ ἀνάπαυσις
12 καὶ ἡ παιδιὰ ἐν τῷ βίῳ εἶναι ἀναγκαῖον. τρεῖς οὖν αἱ εἰρημέναι ἐν τῷ βίῳ μεσότητες, εἰσὶ δὲ πᾶσαι περὶ λόγων τινῶν καὶ πράξεων κοινωνίαν. διαφέρουσι δ' ὅτι ἡ μὲν περὶ ἀλήθειάν ἐστιν, αἱ δὲ περὶ τὸ ἡδύ. τῶν δὲ περὶ τὴν ἡδονὴν ἡ μὲν ἐν ταῖς παιδιαῖς, ἡ δ' ἐν ταῖς κατὰ τὸν ἄλλον βίον ὁμιλίαις.

9 Περὶ δὲ αἰδοῦς ὥς τινος ἀρετῆς οὐ προσήκει λέγειν·

---

almost verbal repetition of what was said, *Eth.* II. vii. 11—13. They appear like an afterthought as compared with *Eth.* IV. vi. 1.

We perhaps ought hardly to quit the present subject without alluding to the remarks which Aristotle has elsewhere thrown out on the nature of wit and of the ludicrous. The most striking are *Rhet.* II. xii. 16, where he defines wit as 'chastened insolence,' ἡ γὰρ εὐτραπελία πεπαιδευμένη ὕβρις ἐστίν, and his account of the ludicrous, that it consists in a thing being out of place, anomalous, ugly and faulty, though not in such a way as to cause any sense of apprehension or pain. *Poet.* v. 2: Τὸ γὰρ γελοῖόν ἐστιν ἁμάρτημά τι καὶ αἶσχος ἀνώδυνον καὶ οὐ φθαρτικόν, οἷον εὐθὺς τὸ γελοῖον πρόσωπον αἰσχρόν τι καὶ διεστραμμένον ἄνευ ὀδύνης. This definition, which is to the highest degree penetrating, has been made by Coleridge the text for his admirable dissertations on wit and humour. See *Literary Remains*, Vol. I.

IX. 1—2 Περὶ δὲ αἰδοῦς—εἶναι] 'Modesty we can scarcely with propriety describe as a virtue; for it seems to be rather a feeling than a moral state; at least it is defined to be a kind of fear of evil report; and in its effects it greatly resembles the fear of danger, for persons who are ashamed blush, and those who are in terror of death grow pale. Both affections then appear to be in a manner corporeal, which is the mark rather of feelings than of states.' Aristotle, following out the programme given, *Eth.* II. vii. 14—15, arrives now at the place for discussing two instances of the law of the balance existing in the instinctive feelings of the mind (ἐν τοῖς πάθεσι μεσότητες), namely modesty and indignation. But from some cause his work is interrupted here; Indignation (Νέμεσις) is not treated of at all, and the discussion on modesty is left unfinished. There is no mention of the extremes, shamelessness (ἀναισχυντία) and shamefacedness (καταπλῆξις), which are specified in Book II. (*l. c.*) and in *Eth. Eud.* III. vii. 2. After stating that only to certain ages is 'modesty' suitable, and that only in a certain provisional sense (ἐξ ὑποθέσεως) can it be called a virtue, the chapter abruptly ends, a couple of sentences having been added by some later hand which give an appearance of finish to the book and awkwardly connect it with the opening of Book V.

πάθει γὰρ μᾶλλον ἔοικεν ἢ ἕξει. ὁρίζεται γοῦν φόβος τις
ἀδοξίας, ἀποτελεῖται δὲ τῷ περὶ τὰ δεινὰ φόβῳ παρα- 2
πλήσιον· ἐρυθραίνονται γὰρ οἱ αἰσχυνόμενοι, οἱ δὲ τὸν
θάνατον φοβούμενοι ὠχριῶσιν. σωματικὰ δὴ φαίνεταί
πως εἶναι ἀμφότερα, ὅπερ δοκεῖ πάθους μᾶλλον ἢ ἕξεως
εἶναι. οὐ πάσῃ δ' ἡλικίᾳ τὸ πάθος ἁρμόζει, ἀλλὰ τῇ νέᾳ· 3
οἰόμεθα γὰρ δεῖν τοὺς τηλικούτους αἰδήμονας εἶναι διὰ τὸ
πάθει ζῶντας πολλὰ ἁμαρτάνειν, ὑπὸ τῆς αἰδοῦς δὲ κωλύεσθαι. καὶ ἐπαινοῦμεν τῶν μὲν νέων τοὺς αἰδήμονας,
πρεσβύτερον δ' οὐδεὶς ἂν ἐπαινέσειεν ὅτι αἰσχυντηλός·
οὐδὲν γὰρ οἰόμεθα δεῖν αὐτὸν πράττειν ἐφ' οἷς ἐστὶν
αἰσχύνη. οὐδὲ γὰρ ἐπιεικοῦς ἐστὶν ἡ αἰσχύνη, εἴπερ γίγνε- 4
ται ἐπὶ τοῖς φαύλοις· οὐ γὰρ πρακτέον τὰ τοιαῦτα. εἰ 5
δ' ἐστὶ τὰ μὲν κατ' ἀλήθειαν αἰσχρὰ τὰ δὲ κατὰ δόξαν,
οὐδὲν διαφέρει· οὐδέτερα γὰρ πρακτέα, ὥστ' οὐκ αἰσχυντέον. φαύλου δὲ καὶ τὸ εἶναι τοιοῦτον οἷον πράττειν τι 6
τῶν αἰσχρῶν. τὸ δ' οὕτως ἔχειν ὥστ' εἰ πράξειέ τι τῶν
τοιούτων αἰσχύνεσθαι, καὶ διὰ τοῦτ' οἴεσθαι ἐπιεικῆ εἶναι,
ἄτοπον· ἐπὶ τοῖς ἑκουσίοις γὰρ ἡ αἰδώς, ἑκὼν δὲ ὁ ἐπιεικὴς οὐδέποτε πράξει τὰ φαῦλα. εἴη δ' ἂν ἡ αἰδὼς ἐξ 7
ὑποθέσεως ἐπιεικές· εἰ γὰρ πράξαι, αἰσχύνοιτ' ἄν. οὐκ
ἔστι δὲ τοῦτο περὶ τὰς ἀρετάς. εἰ δ' ἡ ἀναισχυντία
φαῦλον καὶ τὸ μὴ αἰδεῖσθαι τὰ αἰσχρὰ πράττειν, οὐδὲν
μᾶλλον τὸ τοιαῦτα πράττοντα αἰσχύνεσθαι ἐπιεικές. † οὐκ 8

3—5 αἰδὼς is the apprehension of shame, joined of course with a capacity for strongly feeling it; neither modesty nor any other English word seems adequately to convey the force of αἰδώς. Aristotle speaks of it as a desirable quality in tender age, before the character is formed. But in maturer life the necessity for it, and therefore its merit, ceases to exist. It might be said that sensibility to shame ought to be preserved with regard to acts that are conventionally (κατὰ δόξαν) and not really (κατ' ἀλήθειαν) disgraceful; but Aristotle says that any possibility of feeling shame must be avoided altogether, so that the former acts must not be done.

7 'Modesty can only be good hypothetically: if a person were to do so and so, he would be ashamed. But this is not the way with the virtues. Though shamelessness and the having no sensibility about base acts is bad, it does not follow that to do such things and feel shame is good.' Ἐξ ὑποθέσεως 'conditionally' is opposed to ἁπλῶς 'absolutely.' While the virtues are absolutely good, modesty is only conditionally so.

οὐκ ἔστι δὲ τοῦτο περὶ τὰς ἀρετάς] The same formula occurs before, *Eth.*

ἔστι δ' οὐδ' ἡ ἐγκράτεια ἀρετή, ἀλλά τίς μικτή· δειχθήσεται δὲ περὶ αὐτῆς ἐν τοῖς ὕστερον. νῦν δὲ περὶ δικαιοσύνης εἴπωμεν.

I. vii. 20: *ἱκανὸν ἔν τισι τὸ ὅτι δειχθῆναι καλῶς, οἷον καὶ περὶ τὰς ἀρχάς.*

† *οὐκ ἔστι δ' οὐδ' ἡ ἐγκράτεια ἀρετή, ἀλλά τις μικτή· δειχθήσεται δὲ περὶ αὐτῆς ἐν τοῖς ὕστερον. Νῦν δὲ περὶ δικαιοσύνης εἴπωμεν*] Aristotle's MS. of the fourth book having ended abruptly at the word *ἐπιεικής*, Nicomachus or the editor, whoever he was, in all probability added these clauses in order to give the book a seeming union with the three Eudemian books which were now to be grafted on.

PLAN OF BOOK V.

HITHERTO all has been perfectly coherent and regular in the *Ethics* of Aristotle. Down to the ninth Chapter of Book IV., though all the parts may not have been composed at the same time, yet all belong to the same plan, and bear every mark of being the work of the same author. But the MS. of Book IV. seems suddenly to have broken off in the middle of a subject. Whether this was owing to mutilation, or to original incompleteness, there is now no means of saying. What is clear to us from internal evidence is, that the editor has at this point commenced supplying a *lacuna*; and accordingly three whole books are now introduced, which, though bearing a close resemblance to the style of Aristotle, and probably conveying, with only slight modifications, his actual system, yet belong to the *Ethics* of Eudemus, Aristotle's disciple, and thus have only an imperfect coherence with the present work. The chief arguments by which it is demonstrated that Books V., VI., VII., are only 'copies' from Aristotle by one of his school have been given, Essay I. pp. 49–70, and need not here be recapitulated.

The present Eudemian book on Justice may bear the same relation to Aristotle's theory of Justice, now lost, as the Eudemian theory of Pleasure in Book VII. bears to Aristotle's theory of Pleasure given in Book X. Or, on the other hand, Aristotle's account of Justice may never have been actually written, and may only have existed as orally imparted to the School; in which case the present book would claim a slightly more original character, being built up by Eudemus out of Aristotelian materials, but not on the lines of any one treatise. The extent to which parts of this book appear to have been suggested by passages in the *Politics* of Aristotle (see ii. 11, iii. 1–14, v. 6, vi. 4–5, and notes) would rather favour the latter supposition. But we trace the same endeavour to slightly improve on the conclusions of the *Politics*, which Eudemus elsewhere so often exhibits to improve upon the *Ethics* of Aristotle. We observe here also indications that the Peripatetic School had been busy in working out the beginnings of political economy as made by Plato and Aristotle. The theory of money, value, and price, given in chap. v. is in its way excellent. The Eudemian books, however, have all a peculiar indistinctness which taxes the reader's thought to divine their exact bearing. But on consideration, the outlines of a method appear to show themselves through the mist. And accordingly, the following parts may perhaps be discerned in Book V.

(1.) Justice having been defined to be 'a state of mind that wills to do what is just,' the first part of the book is concerned with determining, what is the just? (*τὸ δίκαιον* as distinguished from *δικαιοσύνη*). The abstract principle of 'the just' may either be identified with all law and therefore with all morality; or it may be restricted to its proper sense, fair dealing with regard to possessions, &c. (*τὸ ἴσον*). In this restricted sense 'the just' finds its sphere either in distributions of the state, or in correcting the wrongs done in dealings between man and man. Though justice is not retaliation, yet in all commerce, &c., there is a sort of retaliation. Ch. I.—V. § 16.

(2.) Having settled the nature of 'the just,' it follows to discuss 'justice,' or this same principle manifested in the mind of the individual. This part of the subject is very imperfectly carried out. We miss the graphic impersonations of the virtues with which the fourth book of Aristotle's *Ethics* is filled. We find nothing but a few barren remarks on voluntariness as necessary to make an act unjust, and deliberate purpose to constitute an unjust character. There is a large digression here on the proper sense of the word 'justice.' Justice, it is said, can only properly exist between citizens; it is a mere metaphor to talk of justice in families, &c. Ch. v. § 17.—Ch. viii.

(3.) Certain questions are added, the answers to which go to supply deficiencies in the definition hitherto given of justice. The leading question is, Can one be injured voluntarily? and the answer to this shows that justice implies a relation between two distinct wills and interests. It is again repeated that justice must be a settled state of the character; thus the just man could not at will be unjust. The subject is concluded by an assertion that justice is essentially a human quality. Ch. ix.

(4.) An appendix follows on the nature of Equity, which is a higher and finer justice, dealing with exceptional cases and acting in the spirit not in the letter of the law. Ch. x.

(5.) Ch. xi. might be called superfluous and out of place. It touches on the already settled question, Can a man injure himself? But the want of a *lucidus ordo* is universally characteristic of the *Eudemian Ethics*; and this chapter adds some afterthoughts on suicide, as an act of injustice, and on the metaphor of justice between the higher and the lower faculties.

Owing, probably, to the want of distinctness in it, this book has not made so much impression on the world as some of the *Nicomachean* books with which it has been incorporated. The distinction between 'distributive' and 'corrective' justice is, however, sometimes referred to, as for instance by Lord Bacon in the 'Advancement of Learning.' This and the other distinctions which the book brings out belong rather to politics or political economy, than to morals. The remaining contributions to the subject, here made—such as the showing that injustice implies a conflict of wills—may have been useful as a clearing up of language at the time when the book was written.

ΗΘΙΚΩΝ [ΕΥΔΗΜΙΩΝ] V.

ΠΕΡΙ δὲ δικαιοσύνης καὶ ἀδικίας σκεπτέον, περὶ ποίας τε τυγχάνουσιν οὖσαι πράξεις, καὶ ποία μεσότης
2 ἐστὶν ἡ δικαιοσύνη, καὶ τὸ δίκαιον τίνων μέσον. ἡ δὲ σκέψις ἡμῖν ἔστω κατὰ τὴν αὐτὴν μέθοδον τοῖς προειρημέ-
3 νοις. ὁρῶμεν δὴ πάντας τὴν τοιαύτην ἕξιν βουλομένους

I. This chapter proposes and opens the discussion upon the nature of justice and injustice. The chief points it contains are as follows. (1) Justice and injustice must stand opposed to each other, as being two contrary states of mind. From the nature of one, we may infer its contrary the nature of the other, and if the one term be used in a variety of senses, the other term will be used in a corresponding variety of senses. (2) The term 'unjust man' is used in two senses, to denote one who is lawless, and one who is unfair. Therefore the term 'just' must denote both lawful and fair. (3) The lawful (*τὸ νόμιμον*) is simply all that the state has enacted for the welfare of its citizens. Therefore, in one sense, 'justice' means fulfilling all the requirements of law. Thus it is nothing else than perfect and consummate virtue. In this general sense justice is different from virtue only in the point of view which one would take in defining it.

1 *ποία μεσότης*] Aristotle proposed the question about the two kinds of justice, 'in what sense are they mean states?' *πῶς μεσότητές εἰσιν* (*Eth.* II. vii. 16), which is slightly different from the above. Cf. ch. v. § 17 of this book.

2 *ἡ δὲ σκέψις — προειρημένοις*] 'And let our inquiry be according to the same method as what has preceded.' This probably refers to the way in which the moral virtues have been treated in the preceding Book of the *Eudemian Ethics*. There is nothing distinctive about this method, or different from the procedure of Aristotle. What is most specially alluded to at present must be the fixing of the meaning of terms, which is now resorted to with regard to justice, and which was more or less employed before. Cf. *Eth. Eud.* III. v. 1—3, where the general method and the style of the writing has great affinity to the present opening. *Περὶ δὲ μεγαλοψυχίας ἐκ τῶν τοῖς μεγαλοψύχοις ἀποδιδομένων δεῖ διορίσαι τὸ ἴδιον* (e conj. Bonitz. Ceteri *αἴτιον*). *Ὥσπερ γὰρ καὶ τὰ ἄλλα κατὰ τὴν γειτνίασιν καὶ ὁμοιότητα μέχρι του λανθάνει πόρρω προϊόντα, καὶ περὶ*

λέγειν δικαιοσύνην, ἀφ' ἧς πρακτικοὶ τῶν δικαίων εἰσὶ καὶ
ἀφ' ἧς δικαιοπραγοῦσι καὶ βούλονται τὰ δίκαια· τὸν αὐτὸν
δὲ τρόπον καὶ περὶ ἀδικίας, ἀφ' ἧς ἀδικοῦσι καὶ βούλονται
τὰ ἄδικα. διὸ καὶ ἡμῖν πρῶτον ὡς ἐν τύπῳ ὑποκείσθω
ταῦτα. οὐδὲ γὰρ τὸν αὐτὸν ἔχει τρόπον ἐπί τε τῶν ἐπι- 4
στημῶν καὶ δυνάμεων καὶ ἐπὶ τῶν ἕξεων. δύναμις μὲν
γὰρ καὶ ἐπιστήμη δοκεῖ τῶν ἐναντίων ἡ αὐτὴ εἶναι,
ἕξις δ' ἡ ἐναντία τῶν ἐναντίων οὔ, οἷον ἀπὸ τῆς ὑγιείας οὐ
πράττεται τὰ ἐναντία, ἀλλὰ τὰ ὑγιεινὰ μόνον· λέγομεν
γὰρ ὑγιεινῶς βαδίζειν, ὅταν βαδίζῃ ὡς ἂν ὁ ὑγιαίνων.
πολλάκις μὲν οὖν γνωρίζεται ἡ ἐναντία ἕξις ἀπὸ τῆς ἐναν- 5
τίας, πολλάκις δὲ αἱ ἕξεις ἀπὸ τῶν ὑποκειμένων· ἐάν τε
γὰρ ἡ εὐεξία ᾖ φανερά, καὶ ἡ καχεξία φανερὰ γίνεται, καὶ
ἐκ τῶν εὐεκτικῶν ἡ εὐεξία καὶ ἐκ ταύτης τὰ εὐεκτικά. εἰ
γάρ ἐστιν ἡ εὐεξία πυκνότης σαρκός, ἀνάγκη καὶ τὴν καχεξίαν εἶναι μανότητα σαρκὸς καὶ τὸ εὐεκτικὸν τὸ ποιητικὸν
πυκνότητος ἐν σαρκί. ἀκολουθεῖ δ' ὡς ἐπὶ τὸ πολύ, ἐὰν 6
θάτερα πλεοναχῶς λέγηται, καὶ θάτερα πλεοναχῶς λέγε-

τὴν μεγαλοψυχίαν ταὐτὸ συμβέβηκεν. —Λέγομεν δὲ τὸν μεγαλόψυχον κατὰ τὴν τοῦ ὀνόματος προσηγορίαν, ὥσπερ ἐν μεγέθει τινὶ ψυχῆς καὶ δυνάμεως. κ.τ.λ.

4 οὐδὲ γὰρ τὸν αὐτὸν—μόνον] '(And I have specified them thus) for it is not the same with developed states as it is with sciences and faculties. A faculty or a science appears to be the same of contraries, but a contrary state does not include its contraries, as, for instance, from health only healthful things and not the contraries of health are produced.' Γὰρ refers to the mention of both justice and injustice separately, and as opposed to each other. The writer accounts for this by saying that a δύναμις admits of contraries, but a ἕξις not (see Vol. I. Essay IV.). The style above is somewhat careless, for we first have ἐπιστήμη τῶν ἐναντίων ἡ αὐτή, and then, to answer to it, ἕξις ἡ ἐναντία τῶν ἐναντίων οὔ.

5—6 Though a state does not include its contrary, yet its contrary may be inferred from it; and the state itself may be known by its particular manifestations (ἀπὸ τῶν ὑποκειμένων), just as a bodily condition is known from the symptoms. If the name of a state be used in more senses than one (πλεοναχῶς), it follows usually that the name of its contrary will be used in more senses than one.

ἀπὸ τῶν ὑποκειμένων] As we might say, 'from its facts,' the ὑποκείμενα being the singular instances in which a general notion is manifested. The meaning is, that τὰ δίκαια are to δικαιοσύνη as good symptoms are to good health. Τῶν ὑποκειμένων is an instance of the logical formulæ with which the writing of Eudemus abounds.

7 σθαι, οἷον εἰ τὸ δίκαιον, καὶ τὸ ἄδικον. ἔοικε δὲ πλεοναχῶς λέγεσθαι ἡ δικαιοσύνη καὶ ἡ ἀδικία, ἀλλὰ διὰ τὸ σύνεγγυς εἶναι τὴν ὁμωνυμίαν αὐτῶν λανθάνει καὶ οὐχ ὥσπερ ἐπὶ τῶν πόρρω δήλη μᾶλλον· ἡ γὰρ διαφορὰ πολλὴ ἡ κατὰ τὴν ἰδέαν, οἷον ὅτι καλεῖται κλεὶς ὁμωνύμως ἥ τε ὑπὸ τὸν αὐχένα τῶν ζῴων καὶ ᾗ τὰς θύρας κλείουσιν.
8 εἰλήφθω δὴ ὁ ἄδικος ποσαχῶς λέγεται. δοκεῖ δὲ ὅ τε παράνομος ἄδικος εἶναι καὶ ὁ πλεονέκτης καὶ ὁ ἄνισος, ὥστε δῆλον ὅτι καὶ ὁ δίκαιος ἔσται ὅ τε νόμιμος καὶ ὁ ἴσος. τὸ μὲν δίκαιον ἄρα τὸ νόμιμον καὶ τὸ ἴσον, τὸ δ'

Cf. Ar. *Met.* I. ii. 4 (ὁ ἔχων τὴν καθόλου ἐπιστήμην) οἶδέ πως πάντα τὰ ὑποκείμενα.

7 ἔοικε δὲ—κλείουσιν] 'Now the term "justice" appears to be used in more senses than one, and so does the term injustice, but, because there is a close resemblance between the ambiguous senses, the ambiguity escapes notice, and the case is not the same as with things widely differing, where the ambiguity is comparatively plain (δήλη μᾶλλον). A physical difference appealing to the eye (κατὰ τὴν ἰδέαν) is widest, as for instance the word "key" is used ambiguously to denote the clavicular bone of animals, and that with which men lock doors.' While the general upshot of this passage is clear enough, the writing is in itself very indistinct. Hence in translation it has been necessary to use expansion. To say that 'their equivocation escapes notice because it is close' goes beyond the legitimate bounds of compression. Cf. the obscure and probably corrupt passage above cited from *Eth. Eud.* III. v. 1: ὥσπερ γὰρ καὶ τὰ ἄλλα κατὰ τὴν γειτνίασιν καὶ ὁμοιότητα μέχρι τοῦ λανθάνειν πόρρω προϊόντα.

κατὰ τὴν ἰδέαν] This seems to mean 'in external form.' Cf. *Eth.* I. viii. 16: ὁ τὴν ἰδέαν παναισχής.

κλεῖς] There is a pun attributed to Philip of Macedon—cf. Plutarch, *Reg. et Imp. Apophth.*, *Philippi* 12.—which, it has been thought, may be here alluded to: τῆς κλειδὸς αὐτῷ κατεαγείσης ἐν πολέμῳ καὶ τοῦ θεραπεύοντος ἰατροῦ πάντως τι καθ' ἡμέραν αἰτοῦντος, Λάμβανε, ἔφη, ὅσα βούλει, τὴν γὰρ κλεῖν ἔχεις.

8—11 The word 'unjust' is used in three different senses to denote the lawless man, the greedy man, and the unfair man. The word 'just' may mean either the lawful man or the fair man. In this statement there is something illogical, for we notice at once that there are only two senses of the word 'just' to match the three senses of 'unjust.' We find in § 10, that unfairness (τὸ ἄνισον) is a generic term, including both greediness (πλεονεξία) and also the collateral notion of selfishly avoiding evil. In short, to divide 'unjust' into lawless, greedy, and unfair, is a cross division. Evidently there are on each side two terms: (1) justice is divided into lawfulness or universal justice, and (2) fairness about property, or particular justice. Injustice is divided into (1) lawlessness or universal injustice, and (2) unfairness about property, or particular injustice.

ἄδικον τὸ παράνομον καὶ τὸ ἄνισον. ἐπεὶ δὲ καὶ πλεονέ- 9
κτης ὁ ἄδικος, περὶ τἀγαθὰ ἔσται, οὐ πάντα, ἀλλὰ περὶ
ὅσα εὐτυχία καὶ ἀτυχία, ἃ ἐστὶ μὲν ἁπλῶς ἀεὶ ἀγαθά,
τινὶ δ' οὐκ ἀεί. οἱ δ' ἄνθρωποι ταῦτα εὔχονται καὶ διώ-
κουσιν· δεῖ δ' οὔ, ἀλλ' εὔχεσθαι μὲν τὰ ἁπλῶς ἀγαθὰ καὶ
αὐτοῖς ἀγαθὰ εἶναι, αἱρεῖσθαι δὲ τὰ αὐτοῖς ἀγαθά. ὁ δ' 10
ἄδικος οὐκ ἀεὶ τὸ πλέον αἱρεῖται, ἀλλὰ καὶ τὸ ἔλαττον ἐπὶ
τῶν ἁπλῶς κακῶν· ἀλλ' ὅτι δοκεῖ καὶ τὸ μεῖον κακὸν
ἀγαθόν πως εἶναι, τοῦ δ' ἀγαθοῦ ἐστὶν ἡ πλεονεξία, διὰ
τοῦτο δοκεῖ πλεονέκτης εἶναι. ἔστι δ' ἄνισος· τοῦτο γὰρ 11
περιέχει καὶ κοινόν. ἐπεὶ δ' ὁ παράνομος ἄδικος ἦν ὁ δὲ 12
νόμιμος δίκαιος, δῆλον ὅτι πάντα τὰ νόμιμά ἐστί πως
δίκαια· τά τε γὰρ ὡρισμένα ὑπὸ τῆς νομοθετικῆς νόμιμά
ἐστι, καὶ ἕκαστον τούτων δίκαιον εἶναί φαμεν. οἱ δὲ 13
νόμοι ἀγορεύουσι περὶ ἁπάντων, στοχαζόμενοι ἢ τοῦ
κοινῇ συμφέροντος πᾶσιν ἢ τοῖς ἀρίστοις ἢ τοῖς κυρίοις,

---

9 ἐπεὶ δὲ—ἀγαθά] 'Now, since the unjust man is greedy, he will be concerned with things good, not all, but the "goods of fortune," which abstractedly are always goods, but which are not so always to the individual. (Men pray for these and follow after them, but they ought not to do so; they ought to pray that what are abstractedly goods may be so to *them*, and they ought to choose the things which are good for them.)' The goods of fortune are those which all men desire, though it is not certain that they will prove goods to *them*. The phrase τὰ ἁπλῶς ἀγαθά is an Eudemian formula. See Vol. I. Essay I. p. 62. The difficulties connected with prayer, arising out of human ignorance, form the subject of Plato's *Second Alcibiades*. They are also alluded to, *Laws*, III. p. 687. At the end of *Phaedrus* is given the prayer of Socrates (279 B): Ὦ φίλε Πάν τε καὶ ἄλλοι ὅσοι τῇδε θεοί, δοίητέ μοι καλῷ γενέσθαι τἄνδοθεν· ἔξωθεν δ' ὅσα ἔχω, τοῖς ἐντὸς εἶναί μοι φίλια. πλούσιον δὲ νομίζοιμι τὸν σοφόν. τὸ δὲ χρυσοῦ πλῆθος εἴη μοι ὅσον μήτε φέρειν μήτε ἄγειν δύναιτ' ἄλλος ἢ ὁ σώφρων.

12—15. In one sense all that is lawful is just; the law aiming at the good of all, or of a part, of the citizens, speaks on *all* subjects, and more or less rightly enjoins the practice of all the virtues. Justice, then, in this sense, may be said to be the practice of entire virtue towards one's neighbour.

13 στοχαζόμενοι ἢ τοῦ κοινῇ συμφέροντος κ.τ.λ.] Cf. Ar. *Pol.* III. vii. 5: ἡ μὲν γὰρ τυραννίς ἐστι μοναρχία πρὸς τὸ συμφέρον τὸ τοῦ μοναρχοῦντος, ἡ δ' ὀλιγαρχία πρὸς τὸ τῶν εὐπόρων, ἡ δὲ δημοκρατία πρὸς τὸ συμφέρον τὸ τῶν ἀπόρων. The term νομοθετική (§ 12) occurs again in the Eudemian book, *Eth.* VI. viii. 2. The view given here of law, which is expressed still more strongly below, ch. xi. § 1, is quite different from modern views. Law is here represented as a positive system

κατ' ἀρετὴν ἢ κατ' ἄλλον τινὰ τρόπον τοιοῦτον· ὥστε ἕνα
μὲν τρόπον δίκαια λέγομεν τὰ ποιητικὰ καὶ φυλακτικὰ τῆς
εὐδαιμονίας καὶ τῶν μορίων αὐτῆς τῇ πολιτικῇ κοινωνίᾳ.
14 προστάττει δ' ὁ νόμος καὶ τὰ τοῦ ἀνδρείου ἔργα ποιεῖν,
οἷον μὴ λείπειν τὴν τάξιν μηδὲ φεύγειν μηδὲ ῥίπτειν τὰ
ὅπλα, καὶ τὰ τοῦ σώφρονος, οἷον μὴ μοιχεύειν μηδ' ὑβρίζειν, καὶ τὰ τοῦ πράου, οἷον μὴ τύπτειν μηδὲ κακηγορεῖν,
ὁμοίως δὲ καὶ κατὰ τὰς ἄλλας ἀρετὰς καὶ μοχθηρίας τὰ μὲν
κελεύων τὰ δ' ἀπαγορεύων, ὀρθῶς μὲν ὁ κείμενος ὀρθῶς,
15 χεῖρον δ' ὁ ἀπεσχεδιασμένος. αὕτη μὲν οὖν ἡ δικαιοσύνη
ἀρετὴ μέν ἐστι τελεία, ἀλλ' οὐχ ἁπλῶς ἀλλὰ πρὸς ἕτερον.
καὶ διὰ τοῦτο πολλάκις κρατίστη τῶν ἀρετῶν εἶναι δοκεῖ ἡ

(though the instances quoted of its formulæ are all negative, μὴ λείπειν τὴν τάξιν, &c.), aiming at the regulation of the whole of life, sometimes, however, with a bias of class-interests, and sometimes only roughly executed (ἀπεσχεδιασμένος). This educational and dogmatic character of the law was really exemplified to the greatest extent in the Spartan institutions. Athens rather prided herself (according to the wise remarks which Thucydides puts into the mouth of Pericles) on leaving greater liberty to the individual. But Plato and Aristotle both made the mistake of wishing for an entire state-control over individual life.

14 τὰ τοῦ ἀνδρείου] Cf. *Eth.* III. viii. 1—2. Enactments of the kind here mentioned form part of the system given in Plato's *Laws*, pp. 943—4. Modern statutes of military discipline against desertion, &c., furnish an exact parallel to these ancient laws, if we only consider that in the Greek cities the whole state was more or less regarded as an army.

15 αὕτη μὲν οὖν—ἕτερον] 'Now this justice is complete virtue, not absolutely, however, but in relation to one's neighbour.' There is a careless transition here from τὰ νόμιμα and τὰ δίκαια to ἡ δικαιοσύνη. Correct writing would have required ἡ κατὰ ταῦτα δικαιοσύνη or a similar phrase. Generally speaking, this first part of the Book is about τὰ δίκαια as distinguished from ἡ δικαιοσύνη (see Plan of Book V.).

15—20 Hence justice is often thought the best of the virtues, brighter than the evening or the morning star, the sum of all other excellence. It is the *use* of virtue, and not in relation to oneself alone, but also towards others. Hence it has been defined 'others' profit.' As he is the worst man who is bad both to himself and others, so he is the best who is good to himself and to others. This kind of justice is not a part of virtue, but the whole; it can only be distinguished from virtue when you come to define it, and discover that you must take a different point of view for each.

οὔθ' ἕσπερος κ.τ.λ.] This may have allusion to something in literature, now lost. At all events it is a fine saying.

ἐν δὲ δικαιοσύνῃ] Given among the

δικαιοσύνη, καὶ οὔθ' ἕσπερος οὔθ' ἑῷος οὕτω θαυμαστός· καὶ παροιμιαζόμενοί φαμεν

ἐν δὲ δικαιοσύνῃ συλλήβδην πᾶσ' ἀρετὴ ἔνι.

καὶ τελεία μάλιστα ἀρετή, ὅτι τῆς τελείας ἀρετῆς χρῆσίς
ἐστιν. τελεία δ' ἐστίν, ὅτι ὁ ἔχων αὐτὴν καὶ πρὸς ἕτερον
δύναται τῇ ἀρετῇ χρῆσθαι, ἀλλ' οὐ μόνον καθ' αὑτόν·
πολλοὶ γὰρ ἐν μὲν τοῖς οἰκείοις τῇ ἀρετῇ δύνανται χρῆσθαι, ἐν δὲ τοῖς πρὸς ἕτερον ἀδυνατοῦσιν. καὶ διὰ τοῦτο 16
εὖ δοκεῖ ἔχειν τὸ τοῦ Βίαντος, ὅτι ἀρχὴ ἄνδρα δείξει·
πρὸς ἕτερον γὰρ καὶ ἐν κοινωνίᾳ ἤδη ὁ ἄρχων. διὰ δὲ τὸ 17
αὐτὸ τοῦτο καὶ ἀλλότριον ἀγαθὸν δοκεῖ εἶναι ἡ δικαιοσύνη
μόνη τῶν ἀρετῶν, ὅτι πρὸς ἕτερόν ἐστιν· ἄλλῳ γὰρ τὰ
συμφέροντα πράττει, ἢ ἄρχοντι ἢ κοινωνῷ. κάκιστος μὲν 18
οὖν ὁ καὶ πρὸς αὑτὸν καὶ πρὸς τοὺς φίλους χρώμενος τῇ
μοχθηρίᾳ, ἄριστος δ' οὐχ ὁ πρὸς αὑτὸν τῇ ἀρετῇ ἀλλὰ
πρὸς ἕτερον· τοῦτο γὰρ ἔργον χαλεπόν. αὕτη μὲν οὖν 19
ἡ δικαιοσύνη οὐ μέρος ἀρετῆς ἀλλ' ὅλη ἀρετή ἐστιν, οὐδ' ἡ
ἐναντία ἀδικία μέρος κακίας ἀλλ' ὅλη κακία. τί δὲ διαφέ- 20
ρει ἡ ἀρετὴ καὶ ἡ δικαιοσύνη αὕτη, δῆλον ἐκ τῶν εἰρημένων.

---

verses of Theognis (147 sq.) in the following couplet:

ἐν δὲ δικαιοσύνῃ συλλήβδην πᾶσ' ἀρετή 'στιν,
πᾶς δέ τ' ἀνὴρ ἀγαθός, Κύρνε, δίκαιος ἐών.

It is however also attributed to Phocylides, and may have been the common property of many early moralists.

πρὸς ἕτερον] Fritzsche quotes Eurip. *Heracl.* 2:

ὁ μὲν δίκαιος τοῖς πέλας πέφυκ' ἀνήρ,
ὁ δ' εἰς τὸ κέρδος λῆμ' ἔχων ἀνειμένον,
πόλει τ' ἄχρηστος καὶ συναλλάσσειν βαρύς,
αὑτῷ δ' ἄριστος.

And Ar. *Pol.* III. xiii. 3: *κοινωνικὴν γὰρ ἀρετὴν εἶναί φαμεν τὴν δικαιοσύνην ᾗ πάσας ἀναγκαῖον ἀκολουθεῖν τὰς ἄλλας.*

16 *ἀρχὴ ἄνδρα*] The same sentiment is expressed by Sophocles, *Antig.* 175 sq.

17 *ἀλλότριον ἀγαθόν*] Repeated below, ch. vi. § 6. Cf. Plato's *Repub.* I. p. 343 C: *ἀγνοεῖς ὅτι ἡ μὲν δικαιοσύνη καὶ τὸ δίκαιον ἀλλότριον ἀγαθὸν τῷ ὄντι, τοῦ κρείττονός τε καὶ ἄρχοντος συμφέρον, οἰκεία δὲ τοῦ πειθομένου τε καὶ ὑπηρετοῦντος βλάβη* (see Vol. I. Essay II. p. 150). The sophistical and sneering definition of justice is here repeated without comment, being accepted as a testimony to the unselfish character of justice.

20 *τί δὲ διαφέρει—ἀρετή*] 'But what the difference is between virtue and this kind of justice is clear from what we have said already. They are the same, only conceived diffe-

ἔστι μὲν γὰρ ἡ αὐτή, τὸ δ' εἶναι οὐ τὸ αὐτό, ἀλλ' ᾗ μὲν πρὸς ἕτερον, δικαιοσύνη, ᾗ δὲ τοιάδε ἕξις ἁπλῶς, ἀρετή.

2 Ζητοῦμεν δέ γε τὴν ἐν μέρει ἀρετῆς δικαιοσύνην· ἔστι
γάρ τις, ὥς φαμέν. ὁμοίως δὲ καὶ περὶ ἀδικίας τῆς κατὰ
3 μέρος. σημεῖον δ' ὅτι ἔστιν· κατὰ μὲν γὰρ τὰς ἄλλας

---

really: viewed as a relation to others the state is justice, viewed as a state of the mind simply, it is virtue.'

τὸ δ' εἶναι οὐ τὸ αὐτό] This logical formula occurs again *Eth.* VI. viii. 1, where it is said that wisdom and politics are the same state of mind, only their essence is differently conceived (τὸ μέντοι εἶναι οὐ ταὐτὸν αὐταῖς). On the force of εἶναι, see *Eth.* II. vi. 17, note. In both of these Eudemian passages, where it is said of two things that 'they are the same, only their εἶναι is different,' we must understand that the results are the same, but the essential nature, the causes, and what the Germans would call the *Grund-begriff*, or fundamental conception, are different. Thus the first idea about justice (in the widest sense) is, that it is a relation to others. The first idea about virtue is, that it is a regulation of the mind. There is a slightly different application of the formula, Arist. *De Animâ*, III. ii. 4: ἡ δὲ τοῦ αἰσθητοῦ ἐνέργεια καὶ τῆς αἰσθήσεως ἡ αὐτὴ μέν ἐστι καὶ μία, τὸ δ' εἶναι οὐ ταὐτὸν αὐταῖς. 'Now the present existence of an object is identical with and inseparable from the present existence of the sensation of it, but yet in conception these differ from each other fundamentally.' Here we have two distinct sides or 'moments' represented as, though logically distinct, yet inseparable.

Plato in discussing justice had first to clear the subject of sophistical notions, and to prove that justice did not depend alone upon human institutions, but far more on the nature of the human soul. Thus he concluded by defining it to be a just balance in the mind itself. The Peripatetic starting-point is different. It is assumed that justice proceeds from the development of man's nature as a 'political creature.' Also it is assumed that in political institutions there is something which is absolute and not merely conventional (*Eth.* V. vii. 1—5). Then the only question is, what are the exact limits of justice itself? To which the answer is, that we may either regard it in the broadest sense as including the whole of right dealing with others, or, more restrictedly, as right dealing in respect of property and advantages of all kinds.

II. This chapter consists of three parts. (1) It brings arguments to prove the existence of a particular kind of injustice, relating chiefly to property, from which the existence of a particular kind of justice might also be inferred, §§ 1—6. (2) It sets aside universal justice as not being the object of discussion to the present book, §§ 7—11. (3) It divides particular justice into two kinds, distributive and corrective, §§ 12—13.

1—6 The arguments brought to prove the existence of a particular kind of injustice reduce themselves apparently to an appeal to language.

(1) We speak of the coward as 'doing wrongly' (ἀδικεῖν); also we speak of the man who takes more than his share, as 'doing wrongly;'

μοχθηρίας ὁ ἐνεργῶν ἀδικεῖ μέν, πλεονεκτεῖ δ' οὐδέν, οἷον ὁ
ῥίψας τὴν ἀσπίδα διὰ δειλίαν ἢ κακῶς εἰπὼν διὰ χαλεπότητα ἢ οὐ βοηθήσας χρήμασι δι' ἀνελευθερίαν· ὅταν δὲ
πλεονεκτῇ, πολλάκις κατ' οὐδεμίαν τῶν τοιούτων, ἀλλὰ
μὴν οὐδὲ κατὰ πάσας, κατὰ πονηρίαν δέ γε τινά (ψέγομεν
γάρ) καὶ κατ' ἀδικίαν. ἔστιν ἄρα γε ἄλλη τις ἀδικία 3
ὡς μέρος τῆς ὅλης, καὶ ἄδικόν τι ἐν μέρει τοῦ ὅλου ἀδίκου
τοῦ παρὰ τὸν νόμον. ἔτι εἰ ὁ μὲν τοῦ κερδαίνειν ἕνεκα 4
μοιχεύει καὶ προσλαμβάνων, ὁ δὲ προστιθεὶς καὶ ζημιούμενος δι' ἐπιθυμίαν, οὗτος μὲν ἀκόλαστος δόξειεν ἂν εἶναι
μᾶλλον ἢ πλεονέκτης, ἐκεῖνος δ' ἄδικος, ἀκόλαστος δ' οὔ·
δῆλον ἄρα ὅτι διὰ τὸ κερδαίνειν. ἔτι περὶ μὲν τἆλλα 5
πάντα ἀδικήματα γίνεται ἡ ἐπαναφορὰ ἐπί τινα μοχθηρίαν ἀεί, οἷον εἰ ἐμοίχευσεν, ἐπ' ἀκολασίαν, εἰ ἐγκατέλιπε
τὸν παραστάτην, ἐπὶ δειλίαν, εἰ ἐπάταξεν, ἐπ' ὀργήν· εἰ δ'
ἐκέρδανεν, ἐπ' οὐδεμίαν μοχθηρίαν ἀλλ' ἢ ἐπ' ἀδικίαν.

---

the latter use of the terms is evidently different from the former.

(2) A crime committed for the sake of gain is called a 'wrong' distinctively, rather than by the name it would have had, were this motive of gain not present.

(3) While all other wrongs (*ἀδικήματα*) are referred each to some evil principle, such as cowardice, intemperance, and the like; acts of unjust gain are referred to no other principle except 'injustice,' which accordingly must be used in a special sense and denote a special vice in the mind.

The statement of the first of these arguments in the text is extremely confused. It is put in such a way that it would as well prove any other vice as *πλεονεξία* to be particular injustice. Suppose we substituted 'idleness' in the text for 'grasping': it would then be true to say, 'When a man is idle, he often errs in none of the other vices, certainly not in all, but yet he acts with a certain faultiness (for we blame him) and wrongly (*κατ' ἀδικίαν*). Hence there is a kind of wrong separate from universal injustice,' &c. However this is only a matter of statement; there is no doubt that *ἀδικία* with regard to property means something special, and different from *ἀδικία* in the sense of wrong-doing in general. In English 'injustice' is not used to mean vice generally; though its opposite 'just' is occasionally used in the translation of the Bible as equivalent to 'righteous,' and in a sense answering pretty nearly to that of *νόμιμος*.

4 *ἔτι εἰ ὁ μὲν—κερδαίνειν*] 'Again if one man commits an adultery for the sake of gain, making a profit by it, and another man does the same for lust, lavishing money (*[illegible]*) and incurring loss; the latter would rather be deemed intemperate than covetous, the former would be called unjust, but not intemperate; evidently because of his gaining by it.' Fritzsche (upon l. 14) quotes Aeschines Socraticus, ii. 14: *δοκεῖ δ' ἄν σοι ἄνθρωπος εἰ μοιχεύει τὰς τῶν πέλας*

6 ὥστε φανερὸν ὅτι ἔστι τις ἀδικία παρὰ τὴν ὅλην ἄλλη ἐν
μέρει, συνώνυμος, ὅτι ὁ ὁρισμὸς ἐν τῷ αὐτῷ γένει· ἄμφω
γὰρ ἐν τῷ πρὸς ἕτερον ἔχουσι τὴν δύναμιν, ἀλλ' ἡ μὲν
περὶ τιμὴν ἢ χρήματα ἢ σωτηρίαν, ἢ εἴ τινι ἔχοιμεν ἑνὶ
ὀνόματι περιλαβεῖν ταῦτα πάντα, καὶ δι' ἡδονὴν τὴν ἀπὸ
τοῦ κέρδους, ἡ δὲ περὶ ἅπαντα περὶ ὅσα ὁ σπουδαῖος.
7 Ὅτι μὲν οὖν εἰσὶ δικαιοσύναι πλείους, καὶ ὅτι ἔστι τις
καὶ ἑτέρα παρὰ τὴν ὅλην ἀρετήν, δῆλον· τίς δὲ καὶ ὁποία
8 τις, ληπτέον. διώρισται δὴ τὸ ἄδικον τό τε παράνομον
καὶ τὸ ἄνισον, τὸ δὲ δίκαιον τό τε νόμιμον καὶ τὸ ἴσον.
κατὰ μὲν οὖν τὸ παράνομον ἡ πρότερον εἰρημένη ἀδικία
9 ἐστίν. ἐπεὶ δὲ τὸ ἄνισον καὶ τὸ πλέον οὐ ταὐτὸν ἀλλ'
ἕτερον ὡς μέρος πρὸς ὅλον (τὸ μὲν γὰρ πλέον ἅπαν
ἄνισον, τὸ δ' ἄνισον οὐ πᾶν πλέον), καὶ τὸ ἄδικον καὶ ἡ
ἀδικία οὐ ταὐτὰ ἀλλ' ἕτερα ἐκείνων, τὰ μὲν ὡς μέρη τὰ δ'
ὡς ὅλα· μέρος γὰρ αὕτη ἡ ἀδικία τῆς ὅλης ἀδικίας, ὁμοίως
δὲ καὶ ἡ δικαιοσύνη τῆς δικαιοσύνης. ὥστε καὶ περὶ τῆς ἐν
μέρει δικαιοσύνης καὶ περὶ τῆς ἐν μέρει ἀδικίας λεκτέον,
10 καὶ τοῦ δικαίου καὶ τοῦ ἀδίκου ὡσαύτως. ἡ μὲν οὖν κατὰ

γυναῖκας ἐπ' ἀργυρίῳ, ἀδικεῖν ἂν ἢ οὔ, καὶ ταῦτα μέντοι καὶ τῆς πόλεως καὶ τῶν νόμων κωλυόντων;

6 ὥστε—σπουδαῖος] 'So that it is plain that there is a particular kind of injustice distinct from the universal kind, having the same name by reason of a kindred nature (συνώνυμος), because its definition falls under the same genus. For both have their whole force consisting in a relation to others, but the one is concerned with honour, property, or safety (or by whatever one name one might sum up all such things), and is prompted by the pleasure of gain, but the other has to do with the whole sphere of virtue.'

συνώνυμος] What logic calls 'analogous.' We before had the word ὁμωνυμία to denote 'equivocation' (c. i. § 7), see *Eth.* i. vi. 12, and note; and cf. Ar. *Categor.* i. 3: Συνώνυμα δὲ λέγεται ὧν τό τε ὄνομα κοινὸν καὶ ὁ κατὰ τοὔνομα λόγος τῆς οὐσίας ὁ αὐτός.

9 ἐπεὶ δὲ—δικαιοσύνης] 'But as (ἐπεὶ) 'unequal' and 'more' are not the same, but stand related to each other as part to whole (for 'more' is a species of 'unequal'), so (καὶ) the unjust principle and habit belonging respectively to the two kinds we have mentioned are not the same but different, this from that, the one being as part, the other as whole. For this injustice (about property) is a part of universal injustice, and the correspondent justice is a part of universal justice.' The only way to give any meaning to this indistinct passage is to consider what is said about 'more' and 'unequal' to have nothing to do with πλεονεξία, but simply to be an illustration of a part included by a whole. Particular justice includes all the generic qualities of universal justice,

τὴν ὅλην ἀρετὴν τεταγμένη δικαιοσύνη καὶ ἀδικία, ἡ μὲν
τῆς ὅλης ἀρετῆς οὖσα χρῆσις πρὸς ἄλλον, ἡ δὲ τῆς κακίας,
ἀφείσθω. καὶ τὸ δίκαιον δὲ καὶ τὸ ἄδικον τὸ κατὰ ταύτας φανερὸν ὡς διοριστέον· σχεδὸν γὰρ τὰ πολλὰ τῶν
νομίμων τὰ ἀπὸ τῆς ὅλης ἀρετῆς πραττόμενά ἐστιν·
καθ' ἑκάστην γὰρ ἀρετὴν προστάττει ζῆν καὶ καθ' ἑκάστην μοχθηρίαν κωλύει ὁ νόμος. τὰ δὲ ποιητικὰ τῆς ὅλης 11
ἀρετῆς ἐστὶ τῶν νομίμων ὅσα νενομοθέτηται περὶ παιδείαν
τὴν πρὸς τὸ κοινόν. περὶ δὲ τῆς καθ' ἕκαστον παιδείας,
καθ' ἣν ἁπλῶς ἀνὴρ ἀγαθός ἐστι, πότερον τῆς πολιτικῆς
ἐστὶν ἢ ἑτέρας, ὕστερον διοριστέον· οὐ γὰρ ἴσως ταὐτὸν
ἀνδρί τ' ἀγαθῷ εἶναι καὶ πολίτῃ παντί. τῆς δὲ κατὰ 12
μέρος δικαιοσύνης καὶ τοῦ κατ' αὐτὴν δικαίου ἓν μέν ἐστιν

---

no less than as a particular virtue it includes all the generic qualities of universal virtue. Some MSS. read ἐπεὶ δὲ τὸ ἄνισον καὶ τὸ παράνομον, from not understanding the force of the illustration applied in ἐπεί. It is no wonder that confusion should have been caused when the writer was at so little pains to avoid it.

10—11 We may set aside justice in the wider sense as being identical with the exercise of virtue, and also the principle on which it depends (καὶ τὸ δίκαιον δὲ), this being simply the inculcation of virtue by the state. (The question as to whether private education is the same as public, whether the good man is the same as the good citizen, may be discussed hereafter).—This seems to be the train of thought, the whole of § 11. being parenthetical. σχεδὸν γὰρ τὰ πολλὰ κ.τ.λ. is a mere repetition of ch. i. § 14.

τὰ δὲ ποιητικὰ—παντί] 'Now the enactments productive of entire virtue are those which have been made with regard to education for public life. With regard to individual education, according to which one is not a good citizen, but simply a good man, we must afterwards determine whether it belongs to politics or some other province. For perhaps the idea of the good man is not the same as that of the citizen in every case.'

ὕστερον διοριστέον] This is an unfulfilled promise in the *Eudemian Ethics* as they stand. The question here started seems to have arisen out of the discussions in *Politics* III. iv. and III. xviii., as to whether the virtue of the man and the citizen is the same, which, on the whole, Aristotle would answer in the affirmative; and he also lays it down decisively that all education should be public, *i.e.* under the control of government and reduced to a common standard. Aristotle's treatise on education was however unfinished, the eighth book of the *Politics* being a fragment. Eudemus would seem to have wished to take up the question where Aristotle left it, and—with the view of giving a separate existence to Morals as a science—to ask whether there is not a kind of education, not falling within the province of Politics, which aims at producing the virtues of the individual man, as distinct from those of the citizen. But the *Eudemian Ethics*

εἶδος τὸ ἐν ταῖς διανομαῖς τιμῆς ἢ χρημάτων ἢ τῶν ἄλλων
ὅσα μεριστὰ τοῖς κοινωνοῦσι τῆς πολιτείας (ἐν τούτοις
γὰρ ἔστι καὶ ἄνισον ἔχειν καὶ ἴσον ἕτερον ἑτέρου), ἓν δὲ τὸ
13 ἐν τοῖς συναλλάγμασι διορθωτικόν. τούτου δὲ μέρη δύο·
τῶν γὰρ συναλλαγμάτων τὰ μὲν ἑκούσιά ἐστι τὰ δ' ἀκούσια, ἑκούσια μὲν τὰ τοιάδε οἷον πρᾶσις ὠνὴ δανεισμὸς
ἐγγύη χρῆσις παρακαταθήκη μίσθωσις· ἑκούσια δὲ λέγεται,
ὅτι ἡ ἀρχὴ τῶν συναλλαγμάτων τούτων ἑκούσιος. τῶν
δ' ἀκουσίων τὰ μὲν λαθραῖα, οἷον κλοπὴ μοιχεία φαρμακεία προαγωγεία δουλαπατία δολοφονία ψευδομαρτυρία,
τὰ δὲ βίαια, οἷον αἰκία δεσμὸς θάνατος ἁρπαγὴ πήρωσις
κακηγορία προπηλακισμός.

3 Ἐπεὶ δ' ὅ τ' ἄδικος ἄνισος καὶ τὸ ἄδικον ἄνισον,
2 δῆλον ὅτι καὶ μέσον τί ἐστι τοῦ ἀνίσου. τοῦτο δ' ἐστὶ τὸ
ἴσον· ἐν ὁποίᾳ γὰρ πράξει ἐστὶ τὸ πλέον καὶ τὸ ἔλαττον,

---

were also unfinished, or else mutilated. See Vol. I. Essay I. pp. 66–67.

ἀνδρί τ' ἀγαθῷ εἶναι] 'The essential idea of a good man.' On this formula, see *Eth.* II. vi. 17, note.

12–13 Particular justice is now divided into distributive and corrective justice. For all details connected with these two forms, see the following chapters. It is here said that 'voluntary transactions' (τὰ ἑκούσια συναλλάγματα), 'such as buying, selling, lending, pledging, using, depositing, and hiring,' come under the head of corrective justice, as well as 'involuntary transactions.' By this must be meant that the rectification of acts of injustice committed under these various heads falls to be made by corrective justice. Buying and selling, as we learn from ch. v., are, or ought to be, arranged on the principle of geometric proportion, and thus resemble cases of distributive justice. It is only where cheating or mistake has occurred, that buying and selling would be brought under corrective justice.

III. This chapter, without formally announcing its subject, treats of distributive justice. The main points with regard to it are as follows. Justice implies equality, and not only that two things are equal, but also two persons between whom there may be justice. Thus it is a geometrical proportion in four terms; if A and B be persons, C and D lots to be divided, then as A is to B, so must C be to D. And a just distribution will produce the result that A + C will be to B + D in the same ratio as A was to B originally. In other words, distributive justice consists in the distribution of property, honours, &c., in the state, according to the merits of each citizen.

With regard to this principle, though the text is not explicit, yet it appears to be (1) really applicable in all cases of awards made by the state, (2) ideally to be capable of a wider application as a regulative principle for the distribution of property and all the distinctions of society. As to the history of the

ἐστὶ καὶ τὸ ἴσον. εἰ οὖν τὸ ἄδικον ἄνισον, τὸ δίκαιον 3
ἴσον· ὅπερ καὶ ἄνευ λόγου δοκεῖ πᾶσιν. ἐπεὶ δὲ τὸ ἴσον 4

---

doctrine, we find it shadowed out by Plato in the great idea of a harmony and proportion ruling in the world; cf. *Gorgias*, p. 507 E: φασὶ δ' οἱ σοφοί, ὦ Καλλίκλεις, καὶ οὐρανὸν καὶ γῆν καὶ θεοὺς καὶ ἀνθρώπους τὴν κοινωνίαν συνέχειν καὶ φιλίαν καὶ κοσμιότητα καὶ σωφροσύνην καὶ δικαιότητα, καὶ τὸ ὅλον τοῦτο διὰ ταῦτα κόσμον καλοῦσιν, ὦ ἑταῖρε, οὐκ ἀκοσμίαν, οὐδὲ ἀκολασίαν. σὺ δέ μοι δοκεῖς οὐ προσέχειν τὸν νοῦν τούτοις, καὶ ταῦτα σοφὸς ὤν, ἀλλὰ λέληθέ σε ὅτι ἡ ἰσότης ἡ γεωμετρικὴ καὶ ἐν θεοῖς καὶ ἐν ἀνθρώποις μέγα δύναται· σὺ δὲ πλεονεξίαν οἴει δεῖν ἀσκεῖν· γεωμετρίας γὰρ ἀμελεῖς. There is a still nearer approach to the present doctrine in *Laws*, p. 757 B, where it is said that there are two kinds of equality; one is a mere equality of number and measure, the other is the 'award of Zeus,' the equality of proportion. Τὴν δὲ ἀληθεστάτην καὶ ἀρίστην ἰσότητα οὐκέτι ῥᾴδιον παντὶ ἰδεῖν. Διὸς γὰρ δὴ κρίσις ἐστί· καὶ τοῖς ἀνθρώποις ἀεὶ σμικρὰ μὲν ἐπαρκεῖ· πᾶν δὲ ὅσον ἂν ἐπαρκέσῃ πόλεσιν ἢ καὶ ἰδιώταις, πάντ' ἀγαθὰ ἀπεργάζεται. τῷ μὲν γὰρ μείζονι πλείω, τῷ δὲ ἐλάττονι σμικρότερα νέμει, μέτρια διδοῦσα πρὸς τὴν αὐτῶν φύσιν ἑκατέρῳ· καὶ δὴ καὶ τιμὰς μείζοσι μὲν πρὸς ἀρετὴν ἀεὶ μείζους· τοῖς δὲ τοὐναντίον ἔχουσιν ἀρετῆς τε καὶ παιδείας τὸ πρέπον ἑκατέροις ἀπονέμει κατὰ λόγον.

It is remarkable that the terms 'distributive and corrective justice' are not found in the *Politics* of Aristotle, though this distinction and the various points connected with it in reality belong much more to political than to ethical science. However, though the *name* of distributive justice does not occur, yet the *idea* of it is fully developed in *Politics*, III. c. ix.—a passage from which it is not improbable that the present chapter may be partly taken, though an interpolated reference (καθάπερ εἴρηται πρότερον ἐν τοῖς ἠθικοῖς) gives the passage in the *Politics* a fallacious appearance of having been written later, and of having accepted conclusions from the present book. Far rather it is likely that the conception of 'distributive justice,' having been received as a conception from Plato, and further worked out by Aristotle in his *Politics*, only became stereotyped into a phrase in the after-growth of his system, at the end of his own life, or in the exposition of his views made by Eudemus. It is in speaking of the 'oligarchical and democratical principles of justice' that Aristotle says: (§ 1) πάντες γὰρ ἅπτονται δικαίου τινός, ἀλλὰ μέχρι τινὸς προέρχονται, καὶ λέγουσιν οὐ πᾶν τὸ κυρίως δίκαιον. Οἷον δοκεῖ ἴσον τὸ δίκαιον εἶναι, καὶ ἔστιν, ἀλλ' οὐ πᾶσιν ἀλλὰ τοῖς ἴσοις. καὶ τὸ ἄνισον δοκεῖ δίκαιον εἶναι, καὶ γάρ ἐστιν, ἀλλ' οὐ πᾶσιν, ἀλλὰ τοῖς ἀνίσοις. οἱ δὲ τοῦτ' ἀφαιροῦσι, τὸ οἷς, καὶ κρίνουσι κακῶς. τὸ δ' αἴτιον ὅτι περὶ αὑτῶν ἡ κρίσις· σχεδὸν δ' οἱ πλεῖστοι φαῦλοι κριταὶ περὶ τῶν οἰκείων. Ὥστ' ἐπεὶ τὸ δίκαιον τισίν, καὶ διῄρηται τὸν αὐτὸν τρόπον ἐπί τε τῶν πραγμάτων καὶ οἷς, † καθάπερ εἴρηται πρότερον ἐν τοῖς ἠθικοῖς, τὴν μὲν τοῦ πράγματος ἰσότητα ὁμολογοῦσι, τὴν δὲ οἷς ἀμφισβητοῦσι. The conclusion is (*Pol.* III. ix. 15) that they who contribute most to the joint-stock of virtue and good deeds in the state are entitled to a larger share in the control of affairs than those who base their claims upon any other kind of superiority.

1—4 These sections are full of

μέσον, τὸ δίκαιον μέσον τι ἂν εἴη. ἔστι δὲ τὸ ἴσον ἐν
ἐλαχίστοις δυσίν· ἀνάγκη τοίνυν τὸ δίκαιον μέσον τε καὶ
ἴσον εἶναι [καὶ πρός τι] καὶ τισίν, καὶ ᾗ μὲν μέσον, τινῶν
(ταῦτα δ' ἐστὶ πλεῖον καὶ ἔλαττον), ᾗ δ' ἴσον ἐστί, δυοῖν,
5 ᾗ δὲ δίκαιον, τισίν. ἀνάγκη ἄρα τὸ δίκαιον ἐν ἐλαχίστοις
εἶναι τέτταρσιν· οἷς τε γὰρ δίκαιον τυγχάνει ὄν, δύο ἐστί,
6 καὶ ἐν οἷς τὰ πράγματα, δύο. καὶ ἡ αὐτὴ ἔσται ἰσότης,
οἷς καὶ ἐν οἷς· ὡς γὰρ ἐκεῖνα ἔχει τὰ ἐν οἷς, οὕτω κἀ-
κεῖνα ἔχει· εἰ γὰρ μὴ ἴσοι, οὐκ ἴσα ἕξουσιν, ἀλλ' ἐντεῦθεν
αἱ μάχαι καὶ τὰ ἐγκλήματα, ὅταν ἢ ἴσοι μὴ ἴσα ἢ μὴ
7 ἴσοι ἴσα ἔχωσι καὶ νέμωνται. ἔτι ἐκ τοῦ κατ' ἀξίαν
τοῦτο δῆλον· τὸ γὰρ δίκαιον ἐν ταῖς διανομαῖς ὁμολογοῦσι πάντες κατ' ἀξίαν τινὰ δεῖν εἶναι, τὴν μέντοι ἀξίαν
οὐ τὴν αὐτὴν λέγουσι πάντες ὑπάρχειν, ἀλλ' οἱ μὲν
δημοκρατικοὶ ἐλευθερίαν, οἱ δ' ὀλιγαρχικοὶ πλοῦτον, οἱ δ'
8 εὐγένειαν, οἱ δ' ἀριστοκρατικοὶ ἀρετήν. ἔστιν ἄρα τὸ
δίκαιον ἀνάλογόν τι. τὸ γὰρ ἀνάλογον οὐ μόνον ἐστὶ

---

confused writing. It is said 'since the unjust is unequal, there must be a mean, which is equal; justice must be equal; the equal is a mean, therefore justice must be a mean. As being equal justice implies two terms, as being a mean two extremes, as being just two persons, therefore it must be in four terms, &c.' The general meaning is clear, but the statement, especially in § 4, is very faulty. A confusion is made by the introduction of the idea of *μέσον* with regard to justice, which at the present part of the argument was not required.

6 *εἰ γὰρ μὴ ἴσοι, κ.τ.λ.*] Cf. Ar. *Pol.* III. ix. 1 sq. *l. c.*

7 *ἔτι ἐκ τοῦ—ἀρετήν*] 'Again this is clear from the principle of equality according to standard; for all agree that justice in distributions must be according to standard, but men are not unanimous in declaring the same standard. While the democrats declare freedom, those who are for an oligarchy declare wealth or birth, and those who are for an aristocracy (in the highest sense) declare virtue.' This is apparently taken from the saying in Aristotle's *Pol.* III. ix. 4: *Οἱ μὲν γὰρ ἂν κατά τι ἄνισοι ὦσιν, οἷον χρήμασιν, ὅλως οἴονται ἄνισοι εἶναι, οἱ δ' ἂν κατά τι ἴσοι, οἷον ἐλευθερίᾳ, ὅλως ἴσοι.* Cf. *Ib.* III. ix. 15. 'Freedom' here of course means being above the condition of a slave. To make this the ground for political claims would be analogous, from A.'s point of view, to instituting manhood suffrage. For a slave is less than man; cf. *Ib.* § 6, where it is said that slaves and the lower animals could not constitute a state διὰ τὸ *μὴ μετέχειν εὐδαιμονίας μηδὲ τοῦ ζῆν κατὰ προαίρεσιν.*

8–14 *ἔστιν ἄρα—ἀγαθοῦ*] 'The just then is something proportionate. The proportionate is not restricted to pure number alone, but applies to everything that admits the idea of number. Proportion is an equality of ratios, and implies four terms at the least. Now it is plain that "discrete proportion"

μοναδικοῦ ἀριθμοῦ ἴδιον, ἀλλ' ὅλως ἀριθμοῦ· ἡ γὰρ ἀναλογία ἰσότης ἐστὶ λόγων, καὶ ἐν τέτταρσιν ἐλαχίστοις.
ἡ μὲν οὖν διῃρημένη ὅτι ἐν τέτταρσι, δῆλον. ἀλλὰ καὶ ἡ 9
συνεχής· τῷ γὰρ ἑνὶ ὡς δυσὶ χρῆται καὶ δὶς λέγει, οἷον
ὡς ἡ τοῦ α πρὸς τὴν τοῦ β, οὕτως καὶ ἡ τοῦ β πρὸς τὴν
τοῦ γ. δὶς οὖν ἡ τοῦ β εἴρηται· ὥστ' ἐὰν ἡ τοῦ β τεθῇ
δίς, τέτταρα ἔσται τὰ ἀνάλογα. ἔστι δὲ καὶ τὸ δίκαιον 10
ἐν τέτταρσιν ἐλαχίστοις, καὶ ὁ λόγος ὁ αὐτός· διῄρηται
γὰρ ὁμοίως, οἷς τε καὶ ἅ. ἔσται ἄρα ὡς ὁ α ὅρος πρὸς τὸν 11
β, οὕτως ὁ γ πρὸς τὸν δ, καὶ ἐναλλὰξ ἄρα, ὡς ὁ α πρὸς τὸν
γ, ὁ β πρὸς τὸν δ. ὥστε καὶ τὸ ὅλον πρὸς τὸ ὅλον· ὅπερ
ἡ νομὴ συνδυάζει· κἂν οὕτως συντεθῇ, δικαίως συνδυάζει.
ἡ ἄρα τοῦ α ὅρου τῷ γ καὶ ἡ τοῦ β τῷ δ σύζευξις τὸ ἐν 12
διανομῇ δίκαιόν ἐστι, καὶ μέσον τὸ δίκαιον τοῦτ' ἐστὶ τοῦ
παρὰ τὸ ἀνάλογον. τὸ γὰρ ἀνάλογον μέσον, τὸ δὲ δίκαιον

---

is in four terms; but so also is "continuous proportion," for it uses the one of its terms as two, and names it twice over, thus,—as *a* is to *b*, so is *b* to *c*. *b* then is twice named, and if it be set down twice over, the proportionate terms will be four. But justice also implies four terms at least, and an equality of ratios: for the two persons and the two things are divided in similar proportion. (The formula) then will be, "as the term *a* is to *b*, so is *c* to *d*;" and *alternando*, "as *a* is to *c*, so is *b* to *d*," and so too the whole to the whole, which the distribution couples, and if the terms be thus united, it couples them justly. The joining therefore of *a* to *c* and of *b* to *d* in distribution is just, and this justice is a mean between violations of proportion. For proportion is a mean, and the just is proportionate. Mathematicians call this kind of proportion geometrical, for in geometrical proportion the whole is to the whole as each separate term is to each. This proportion is not "continuous," for it has no one term standing in a double relationship. Well then, the just is that which is thus proportionate, and the unjust is a violation of proportion, which takes place either on the side of more or less. And this is actually the case, for he that does an injury has more than his share, while he that is injured has less than his share of what is good.' This passage gives a formula for distributive justice in mathematical language, which comes in short to this, that in all awards of the state the result should be proportionate to the separate worth of the citizens.

8 *μοναδικοῦ ἀριθμοῦ*] 'number expressed in ciphers, 'abstract number,' in German, *unbenannte Zahl*. Fritzsche refers to Euclid *El.* vii. *def.* 1. The terms introduced in this chapter seem to be neither lines, nor numbers, but algebraic quantities.

9 *ἐὰν ἡ τοῦ β*] ἡ is indefinite and probably meant to be so. It may stand for *στιγμή*, *γραμμή*, or the like.

13 *γεωμετρικήν*] Cf. Plato, *Gorgias*, p. 508, quoted above, p. 109.

13 ἀνάλογον· καλοῦσι δὲ τὴν τοιαύτην ἀναλογίαν γεωμετρικὴν οἱ μαθηματικοί· ἐν γὰρ τῇ γεωμετρικῇ συμβαίνει
καὶ τὸ ὅλον πρὸς τὸ ὅλον ὅπερ ἑκάτερον πρὸς ἑκάτερον.
14 ἔστι δ' οὐ συνεχὴς αὕτη ἡ ἀναλογία· οὐ γὰρ γίνεται εἷς
ἀριθμῷ ὅρος, ᾧ καὶ ὅ. τὸ μὲν οὖν δίκαιον τοῦτο τὸ ἀνάλογον, τὸ δ' ἄδικον τὸ παρὰ τὸ ἀνάλογον. γίνεται ἄρα
τὸ μὲν πλέον τὸ δὲ ἔλαττον. ὅπερ καὶ ἐπὶ τῶν ἔργων
συμβαίνει· ὁ μὲν γὰρ ἀδικῶν πλέον ἔχει, ὁ δ' ἀδικούμενος
15 ἔλαττον τοῦ ἀγαθοῦ. ἐπὶ δὲ τοῦ κακοῦ ἀνάπαλιν· ἐν
ἀγαθοῦ γὰρ λόγῳ γίνεται τὸ ἔλαττον κακὸν πρὸς τὸ μεῖζον
16 κακόν· ἔστι γὰρ τὸ ἔλαττον κακὸν μᾶλλον αἱρετὸν τοῦ
17 μείζονος, τὸ δ' αἱρετὸν ἀγαθόν, καὶ τὸ μᾶλλον μεῖζον. τὸ
μὲν οὖν ἓν εἶδος τοῦ δικαίου τοῦτ' ἐστίν.

4 Τὸ δὲ λοιπὸν ἓν τὸ διορθωτικόν, ὃ γίνεται ἐν τοῖς συναλ-

15—16 A repetition of ch. i. § 10.

IV. This chapter is on corrective justice, which is said to apply to the transactions between men whether voluntary or involuntary. Corrective justice goes on a principle, not of geometrical, but of arithmetical proportion; in other words, it takes no account of persons, but treats the cases with which it is concerned as cases of unjust loss and gain, which have to be reduced to the middle point of equality between the parties. Justice is a mean, and the judge a sort of impersonation of justice, a mediator, or equal divider. The operation of justice, bringing plaintiff and defendant to an equality, may be illustrated by the equalizing of two unequal lines. The names, 'loss,' and 'gain,' are however often a mere metaphor borrowed from commerce.

The term 'corrective justice' (τὸ διορθωτικὸν or, as it is afterwards called, § 6, τὸ ἐπανορθωτικὸν δίκαιον) is itself an unfortunate name, because it appears only to lay down principles for restitution, and therefore implies wrong. Thus it has a tendency to confine the view to 'involuntary transactions,' instead of stating what must be the principle of the just in all the dealings between man and man. In the present chapter, it is remarkable that although we are told at first that 'voluntary transactions' belong to corrective justice, yet all that is said applies only to the 'involuntary transactions;' and at last we are told that the terms used are 'a metaphor from voluntary transactions'—as if these were something quite distinct. It may be said however that bargains, and voluntary dealings in general, have no respect of persons (κατὰ τὴν ἀριθμητ. ἀναλ.), and thus have something in common with civil and criminal law. Bacon, in the *Advancement of Learning*, Book II., refers to the two heads of Justice, here given, under the names '*commutative* and *distributive*.'

1 τὸ δὲ λοιπὸν ἓν] This excludes all possibility of the writer having conceived another kind of justice, to be called 'catallactic' or some such name, as it has been sometimes fancied. Τὸ διορθωτικὸν δικ. implies not merely 'regulative,' but strictly 'remedial'

λάγμασι καὶ τοῖς ἑκουσίοις καὶ τοῖς ἀκουσίοις. τοῦτο δὲ 2
τὸ δίκαιον ἄλλο εἶδος ἔχει τοῦ προτέρου. τὸ μὲν γὰρ
διανεμητικὸν δίκαιον τῶν κοινῶν ἀεὶ κατὰ τὴν ἀναλογίαν
ἐστὶ τὴν εἰρημένην· καὶ γὰρ ἀπὸ χρημάτων κοινῶν ἐὰν
γίγνηται ἡ διανομή, ἔσται κατὰ τὸν λόγον τὸν αὐτὸν ὅνπερ
ἔχουσι πρὸς ἄλληλα τὰ εἰσενεχθέντα. καὶ τὸ ἄδικον τὸ
ἀντικείμενον τῷ δικαίῳ τούτῳ παρὰ τὸ ἀνάλογόν ἐστιν.
τὸ δ' ἐν τοῖς συναλλάγμασι δίκαιον ἐστὶ μὲν ἴσον τι, καὶ 3
τὸ ἄδικον ἄνισον, ἀλλ' οὐ κατὰ τὴν ἀναλογίαν ἐκείνην
ἀλλὰ κατὰ τὴν ἀριθμητικήν. οὐθὲν γὰρ διαφέρει, εἰ
ἐπιεικὴς φαῦλον ἀπεστέρησεν ἢ φαῦλος ἐπιεικῆ, οὐδ' εἰ
ἐμοίχευσεν ἐπιεικὴς ἢ φαῦλος· ἀλλὰ πρὸς τοῦ βλάβους
τὴν διαφορὰν μόνον βλέπει ὁ νόμος, καὶ χρῆται ὡς ἴσοις,
εἰ ὁ μὲν ἀδικεῖ ὁ δ' ἀδικεῖται, καὶ εἰ ἔβλαψεν ὁ δὲ βέβλαπται. ὥστε τὸ ἄδικον τοῦτο ἄνισον ὂν ἰσάζειν πειρᾶται 4
ὁ δικαστής· καὶ γὰρ ὅταν ὁ μὲν πληγῇ ὁ δὲ πατάξῃ, ἢ
καὶ κτείνῃ ὁ δ' ἀποθάνῃ, διῄρηται τὸ πάθος καὶ ἡ πρᾶξις
εἰς ἄνισα· ἀλλὰ πειρᾶται τῇ ζημίᾳ ἰσάζειν, ἀφαιρῶν

---

justice; *διόρθωμα* is used to signify a remedy in Arist. *Pol.* III. xiii. 23, where it is said of ostracism, *βέλτιον μὲν οὖν τὸν νομοθέτην ἐξ ἀρχῆς οὕτω συστῆσαι τὴν πολιτείαν ὥστε μὴ δεῖσθαι τοιαύτης ἰατρείας· δεύτερος δὲ πλοῦς, ἂν συμβῇ, πειρᾶσθαι τοιούτῳ τινὶ διορθώματι διορθοῦν.*

2 τὸ μὲν γὰρ—εἰσενεχθέντα] 'For distributive justice deals always with the goods of the state according to the proportion we have described; for if the distribution be of common goods, it will be according to the proportion which the different contributions bear to one another.' Τὰ *εἰσενεχθέντα* is thus explained by the Paraphrast, *ἀναλόγως ἑκάστῳ δίδωσι κατὰ τὴν ἀξίαν ἑκάστου καὶ τὴν εἰσφοράν, ἣν εἰς τὸ κοινὸν συντέθεικεν· ἐπεὶ οὐ πάντες ἴσως, οὐδὲ πάντες ὁμοίως εἰσφέρουσιν.* Probably the remark in the text was taken from Aristotle, *Pol.* III. ix. 15: *διόπερ ὅσοι συμβάλλονται πλεῖστον εἰς τὴν τοιαύτην κοινωνίαν, τούτοις τῆς πόλεως μέτεστι πλεῖον.*

3 κατὰ τὴν ἀριθμητικήν] This term occurs *Eth.* II. vi. 7. 'Arithmetical proportion' denotes a middle term or point of equality, equidistant from two extreme terms, thus, 6 is the mean, according to arithmetical proportion, between 4 and 8. In *Eth.* II. (*l.c.*) it is called *μέσον τοῦ πράγματος*, which implies that it has no respect of persons. So corrective justice is here said to regard each case impersonally as an affair of loss and gain, and between these it strikes the middle point. It is the moral worth of persons that is ignored (*εἰ ἐπιεικὴς φαῦλον κ.τ.λ.*), for we find afterwards, ch. v. §§ 3—4, that a consideration of the position and circumstances of persons *does* come in to modify the estimate of the loss sustained from an indignity, &c.

5 τοῦ κέρδους. λέγεται γὰρ ὡς ἁπλῶς εἰπεῖν ἐπὶ τοῖς
τοιούτοις, κἂν εἰ μή τισιν οἰκεῖον ὄνομα εἴη, τὸ κέρδος,
6 οἷον τῷ πατάξαντι, καὶ ἡ ζημία τῷ παθόντι· ἀλλ' ὅταν
γε μετρηθῇ τὸ πάθος, καλεῖται τὸ μὲν ζημία τὸ δὲ κέρδος.
ὥστε τοῦ μὲν πλείονος καὶ ἐλάττονος τὸ ἴσον μέσον, τὸ δὲ
κέρδος καὶ ἡ ζημία τὸ μὲν πλέον τὸ δ' ἔλαττον ἐναντίως,
τὸ μὲν τοῦ ἀγαθοῦ πλέον τοῦ κακοῦ δ' ἔλαττον κέρδος, τὸ
δ' ἐναντίον ζημία· ὧν ἦν μέσον τὸ ἴσον, ὃ λέγομεν εἶναι
δίκαιον· ὥστε τὸ ἐπανορθωτικὸν δίκαιον ἂν εἴη τὸ μέσον
7 ζημίας καὶ κέρδους. διὸ καὶ ὅταν ἀμφισβητῶσιν, ἐπὶ
τὸν δικαστὴν καταφεύγουσιν· τὸ δ' ἐπὶ τὸν δικαστὴν ἰέναι
ἰέναι ἐστὶν ἐπὶ τὸ δίκαιον· ὁ γὰρ δικαστὴς βούλεται εἶναι
οἷον δίκαιον ἔμψυχον· καὶ ζητοῦσι δικαστὴν μέσον, καὶ
καλοῦσιν ἔνιοι μεσιδίους, ὡς ἐὰν τοῦ μέσου τύχωσι, τοῦ
8 δικαίου τευξόμενοι. μέσον ἄρα τι τὸ δίκαιον, εἴπερ καὶ ὁ
δικαστής. ὁ δὲ δικαστὴς ἐπανισοῖ, καὶ ὥσπερ γραμμῆς
εἰς ἄνισα τετμημένης, ᾧ τὸ μεῖζον τμῆμα τῆς ἡμισείας
ὑπερέχει, τοῦτ' ἀφεῖλε καὶ τῷ ἐλάττονι τμήματι προσέθηκεν. ὅταν δὲ δίχα διαιρεθῇ τὸ ὅλον, τότε φασὶν ἔχειν
9 τὰ αὑτῶν, ὅταν λάβωσι τὸ ἴσον. τὸ δ' ἴσον μέσον ἐστὶ
τῆς μείζονος καὶ ἐλάττονος κατὰ τὴν ἀριθμητικὴν ἀναλογίαν. διὰ τοῦτο καὶ ὀνομάζεται δίκαιον, ὅτι δίχα ἐστίν,
ὥσπερ ἂν εἴ τις εἴποι δίχαιον, καὶ ὁ δικαστὴς διχαστής.

---

7 ζητοῦσι δικαστὴν μέσον] Cf. Thucyd. IV. 83: Ἀρραβαῖος ἐπεκηρυκεύετο, ἑτοῖμος ὢν Βρασίδᾳ μέσῳ δικαστῇ ἐπιτρέπειν. Ar. *Pol.* IV. xii. 5: πανταχοῦ δὲ πιστότατος ὁ διαιτητής, διαιτητὴς δ' ὁ μέσος.

μεσιδίους] Used in rather a different sense, *Pol.* V. vi. 13: ἐν δὲ τῇ εἰρήνῃ διὰ τὴν ἀπιστίαν τὴν πρὸς ἀλλήλους ἐγχειρίζουσι τὴν φυλακὴν στρατιώταις καὶ ἄρχοντι μεσιδίῳ.

9 διὰ τοῦτο—διχαστής] 'Hence, too, justice gets its name, because it is a dividing in twain (δίχα), as though it were written not δίκαιον, but δίχαιον, and the judge is one who divides in twain.' This etymology, though ingenious, is false. The earlier notion connected with δίκη seems not to have been one of decision, arbitration, or justice, but rather of 'showing,' 'instruction,' 'rule,' 'manner.' The word is derived from a root δικ-, which appears in δείκνυμι, and the Latin *indico, index, judex* (the law-shower), &c. Plato, in the *Cratylus*, p. 412 D, gives a sportive etymology of δίκαιον, in accordance with the spirit of the work. Justice is there said to be the 'permeating,' τὸ διὰ ἰόν, with a κ added for euphony. Ἐπεὶ ἐπιτροπεύει τὰ ἄλλα πάντα διιόν, τοῦτο τὸ ὄνομα ἐκλήθη ὀρθῶς δίκαιον, εὐστομίας ἕνεκα τὴν τοῦ κ δύναμιν προσλαβόν.

ἐὰν γὰρ δύο ἴσων ἀφαιρεθῇ ἀπὸ θατέρου, πρὸς θάτερον δὲ 10
προστεθῇ, δυσὶ τούτοις ὑπερέχει θάτερον· εἰ γὰρ ἀφῃρέθη
μέν, μὴ προσετέθη δέ, ἑνὶ ἂν μόνον ὑπερεῖχεν. τοῦ μέσου
ἄρα ἑνί, καὶ τὸ μέσον, ἀφ' οὗ ἀφῃρέθη, ἑνί. τούτῳ ἄρα 11
γνωριοῦμεν τί τε ἀφελεῖν δεῖ ἀπὸ τοῦ πλέον ἔχοντος, καὶ
τί προσθεῖναι τῷ ἔλαττον ἔχοντι· ᾧ μὲν γὰρ τὸ μέσον
ὑπερέχει, τοῦτο προσθεῖναι δεῖ τῷ ἔλαττον ἔχοντι, ᾧ δ'
ὑπερέχεται, ἀφελεῖν ἀπὸ τοῦ μεγίστου. ἴσαι αἱ ἐφ' ὧν 12
ΑΑ ΒΒ ΓΓ ἀλλήλαις· ἀπὸ τῆς ΑΑ ἀφῃρήσθω τὸ ΑΕ,
καὶ προσκείσθω τῇ ΓΓ τὸ ἐφ' ὧν ΓΔ, ὥστε ὅλη ἡ ΔΓΓ
τῆς ΕΑ ὑπερέχει τῷ ΓΔ καὶ τῷ ΓΖ. τῆς ἄρα ΒΒ τῷ
ΓΔ. †ἔστι δὲ καὶ ἐπὶ τῶν ἄλλων τεχνῶν τοῦτο· ἀνῃροῦντο γὰρ ἄν, εἰ μὴ ἐποίει τὸ ποιοῦν καὶ ὅσον καὶ οἷον,
καὶ τὸ πάσχον ἔπασχε τοῦτο καὶ τοσοῦτον καὶ τοιοῦτον.
ἐλήλυθε δὲ τὰ ὀνόματα ταῦτα, ἥ τε ζημία καὶ τὸ κέρδος, 13
ἐκ τῆς ἑκουσίου ἀλλαγῆς· τὸ μὲν γὰρ πλέον ἔχειν ἢ τὰ

10—12 ἐὰν γὰρ—ΓΔ] 'For, of two equal lines, if a part be taken from the one and added to the other, that other will exceed the first by twice this part; for if it had been subtracted only from the one and not added to the other, that other would have exceeded the first by only once this part. Therefore the line which is added to exceeds the mean by once the part added, and the mean exceeds the line subtracted from by once the part added. By this we learn what we must take from the term which has more, and what we must add to that which has less. We must add to that which has less the amount by which the mean exceeds it, and we must take from the largest term the amount by which the mean is exceeded. Let AA, BB, and CC be equal to one another; from AA take AE, and add CD to CC; then the whole DCC exceeds EA by CD and CZ; and therefore it exceeds BB by CD.' The figure required is as follows:

E
A .... ———— A
B — ... ———— B
Z
C ———— C .... D

†ἔστι δὲ—τοιοῦτον] This clause exists in all the MSS. The Paraphrast explains it here to signify that the same principles of corrective justice are applicable to the arts and commerce, &c. But when the clause is repeated with a different context in the next chapter, the Paraphrast, no doubt feeling a difficulty about the repetition, does not again touch it. In its present position the clause has no meaning, in the next chapter it is an important remark. All we can say about its appearance here is that it is an evidence of the same want of completeness of writing which shows itself in chapter xi., and also in sundry other parts of the *Eudemian Ethics*.

13—14 ἐλήλυθε δὲ—θατέρου] 'Now these names, "loss and gain," have

ἑαυτοῦ κερδαίνειν λέγεται, τὸ δ' ἔλαττον τῶν ἐξ ἀρχῆς
ζημιοῦσθαι, οἷον ἐν τῷ ὠνεῖσθαι καὶ πωλεῖν καὶ ἐν ὅσοις
14 ἄλλοις ἄδειαν ἔδωκεν ὁ νόμος. ὅταν δὲ μήτε πλέον μήτ'
ἔλαττον ἀλλ' αὐτὰ δι' αὐτῶν γένηται, τὰ αὑτῶν φασὶν
ἔχειν καὶ οὔτε ζημιοῦσθαι οὔτε κερδαίνειν· ὥστε κέρδους
τινὸς καὶ ζημίας μέσον τὸ δίκαιόν ἐστι τῶν παρὰ τὸ ἑκούσιον, τὸ ἴσον ἔχειν καὶ πρότερον καὶ ὕστερον.

5 Δοκεῖ δέ τισι καὶ τὸ ἀντιπεπονθὸς εἶναι ἁπλῶς δίκαιον,
ὥσπερ οἱ Πυθαγόρειοι ἔφασαν· ὡρίζοντο γὰρ ἁπλῶς τὸ
1 δίκαιον τὸ ἀντιπεπονθὸς ἄλλῳ. τὸ δ' ἀντιπεπονθὸς οὐκ

---

come from voluntary exchange. For having more than one's own is called "gaining," and having less than at the commencement is called "losing," as, for instance, in buying and selling, and all the other things in which the law gives one immunity. But when the things are neither more nor less, but on a level (*αὐτὰ δι' αὐτῶν*), then men say they have their own, and neither lose nor gain. Thus justice is a mean between a sort of gain and loss in involuntary things, it is the having the same afterwards as before.'

ἐν ὅσοις ἄδειαν] In commerce of all kinds, the law allows one to gain as much as one can. In involuntary transactions, the law allows no gain to be made, but brings things always back to their level. This non-interference of the law with bargains becomes, if carried out, the principle of free-trade.

ἀλλ' αὐτὰ δι' αὐτῶν γένηται] This has puzzled the commentators. Felicianus interprets it 'sed sua cuique per se ipsa evaserint;' Argyropulus, 'sed sua per se ipsa sunt facta;' Lambinus, 'sed paria paribus respondent.' What the phrase *must* mean is plain, whether grammatically it *can* mean this is another question. It *must* mean 'neither more nor less, but equal to itself.' Perhaps it may be construed 'but result in being themselves by means of reciprocity,' *i.e.* by mutual giving and taking, *ἑαυτῶν* being equivalent to *ἀλλήλων*.

V. This chapter, commencing with a critical notice of the Pythagorean definition of justice, that 'justice is retaliation,' shows it to be inadequate, and then goes off into an interesting discussion upon the law of retaliation as it exists in the state. Proportionate retaliation, or an interchange of services, is said to be the bond of society. The law of proportion regulates exchange, and settles the value of the most diverse products. Money measures and expresses value, and turns mere barter into commerce. The chapter concludes with some general remarks on the relation of justice as a quality to the just as a principle.

1 *Δοκεῖ δὲ—ἄλλῳ*] 'Now some think that retaliation without further qualifying (*ἁπλῶς*) is justice, as the Pythagoreans said, for they defined justice simply as retaliation on one's neighbour.' On the rude and inadequate attempts at definition made by the Pythagoreans, cf. Ar. *Metaph.* I. v. 16: *ὡρίζοντό τε γὰρ ἐπιπολαίως, καὶ ᾧ πρώτῳ ὑπάρξειεν ὁ λεχθεὶς ὅρος, τοῦτ' εἶναι τὴν οὐσίαν τοῦ πράγματος*

ἐφαρμόττει οὔτ' ἐπὶ τὸ διανεμητικὸν δίκαιον οὔτ' ἐπὶ τὸ διορθωτικόν· καίτοι βούλονταί γε τοῦτο λέγειν καὶ τὸ 3
Ῥαδαμάνθυος δίκαιον·

εἴ κε πάθοι τά κ' ἔρεξε, δίκη κ' ἰθεῖα γίνοιτο.

πολλαχοῦ γὰρ διαφωνεῖ· οἷον εἰ ἀρχὴν ἔχων ἐπάταξεν, 4
οὐ δεῖ ἀντιπληγῆναι, καὶ εἰ ἄρχοντα ἐπάταξεν, οὐ πληγῆναι μόνον δεῖ ἀλλὰ καὶ κολασθῆναι. ἔτι τὸ ἑκούσιον 5
καὶ τὸ ἀκούσιον διαφέρει πολύ. ἀλλ' ἐν μὲν ταῖς κοινωνίαις 6
ταῖς ἀλλακτικαῖς συνέχει τὸ τοιοῦτον δίκαιον τὸ ἀντιπεπονθός, κατ' ἀναλογίαν καὶ μὴ κατ' ἰσότητα· τῷ ἀντιποιεῖν γὰρ ἀνάλογον συμμένει ἡ πόλις. ἢ γὰρ τὸ κακῶς ζητοῦσιν· εἰ δὲ μή, δουλεία δοκεῖ εἶναι, εἰ μὴ ἀντιποιήσει· ἢ τὸ εὖ· εἰ δὲ μή, μετάδοσις οὐ γίνεται, τῇ μεταδόσει δὲ

ἐνόμιζον, ὥσπερ εἴ τις οἴοιτο ταὐτὸν εἶναι ἐκβάλλειν καὶ τὴν [illegible]*, διότι πρῶτον ὑπάρχει τοῖς ἄλλοις τὸ ἐκβάλλειν.* Their inadequate account of justice was doubtless owing not only to an imperfect logical method, but also to the immature political and social ideas of the day. Demosthenes mentions a law of retaliation given by Zaleucus to the Locrians (*Timocr.* p. 744): *ὄντος γὰρ αὐτόθι νόμου, ἐάν τις ὀφθαλμὸν ἐκκόψῃ, ἀντεκκόψαι παρασχεῖν τὸν ἑαυτοῦ.* In the Mosaic code the same rude principle appears, *Exod.* xxi. 24, *Levit.* xxiv. 20, *Deuteron.* xix. 21.

2 It is obvious that simple retaliation cannot be the principle of distributive justice; the state does not win battles for its generals, &c. Nor is it that of corrective justice: (1) because the same treatment is different to different individuals; (2) because an involuntary harm must not be requited like a voluntary one.

3 *τὸ Ῥαδαμάνθυος*] Necessarily a primitive idea of justice.

εἴ κε πάθοι] Of uncertain authorship, attributed to Hesiod.

4 *οἷον εἰ ἀρχὴν ἔχων*] Cf. ch. iv. § 3. note. Rank is here looked at as a kind of property. It is not a question of individual goodness or badness, but an officer being struck loses more than a common soldier being struck in return, so that retaliation is in that case not justice.

6 *ἀλλ' ἐν μὲν—συμμένουσιν*] 'But in commercial intercourse, at all events, this kind of justice, namely, retaliation, is the bond of union—on principles, not of equality, but proportion, for by proportionate requital the state is held together. Men seek to requite either evil or good; to omit the one were slavery, to omit the second were to fail in that mutual interchange by which men are held together.' On mutual need as the basis for civil society, cf. Plato, *Repub.* p. 369 B: *γίγνεται τοίνυν πόλις, ἐπειδὴ τυγχάνει ἡμῶν ἕκαστος οὐκ αὐτάρκης, ἀλλὰ πολλῶν ἐνδεής.* A recognition of this principle might be called the first dawning of political economy; from it several deductions are made in the text above as to the nature of value, price, and money. These, though rudimentary, are able

7 συμμένουσιν. διὸ καὶ Χαρίτων ἱερὸν ἐμποδὼν ποιοῦνται, ἵν' ἀνταπόδοσις ᾖ· τοῦτο γὰρ ἴδιον χάριτος· ἀνθυπηρετῆσαί τε γὰρ δεῖ τῷ χαρισαμένῳ, καὶ πάλιν αὐτὸν ἄρξαι
8 χαριζόμενον. ποιεῖ δὲ τὴν ἀντίδοσιν τὴν κατ' ἀναλογίαν ἡ κατὰ διάμετρον σύζευξις, οἷον οἰκοδόμος ἐφ' ᾧ Α, σκυτοτόμος ἐφ' ᾧ Β, οἰκία ἐφ' ᾧ Γ, ὑπόδημα ἐφ' ᾧ Δ. δεῖ οὖν λαμβάνειν τὸν οἰκοδόμον παρὰ τοῦ σκυτοτόμου τοῦ ἐκείνου ἔργου, καὶ αὐτὸν ἐκείνῳ μεταδιδόναι τὸ αὑτοῦ. ἐὰν οὖν πρῶτον ᾖ τὸ κατὰ τὴν ἀναλογίαν ἴσον, εἶτα τὸ ἀντιπεπονθὸς γένηται, ἔσται τὸ λεγόμενον. εἰ δὲ μή, οὐκ ἴσον, οὐδὲ συμμένει· οὐθὲν γὰρ κωλύει κρεῖττον εἶναι τὸ θατέρου

---

and interesting, but the relation of the law of value (τὸ δίκαιον ἐν ταῖς κοιν. ταῖς ἀλλ.) to the other kinds of justice is not stated.

τὸ ἀντιπεπονθός, κατ' ἀναλογίαν καὶ μὴ κατ' ἰσότητα] This seems to be written as if in correction of Ar. *Pol.* II. ii. 4. Διόπερ τὸ ἴσον τὸ ἀντιπεπονθὸς σώζει τὰς πόλεις, ὥσπερ ἐν τοῖς ἠθικοῖς εἴρηται πρότερον. On which see Vol. I. Essay I. pp. 51, 52.

7 διὸ—χαριζόμενον] 'Hence, too, it is that men build a temple of the Graces in their streets, that there may be reciprocity. For this is the property of grace, one must serve in return one who has done a favour, and again be in turn the first to confer favours.' Seneca (*Benef.* i. 3) mentions with some disdain the various symbolical meanings which were supposed to be expressed by the figures of the Graces, and on which Chrysippus appears to have written an elaborate treatise. Of course no English word will exactly answer to χάρις.

8 ποιεῖ δὲ—σύζευξις] 'Now the joining of the diagonal of a square gives us proportionate return.' The diagram supposed to be drawn is as follows:

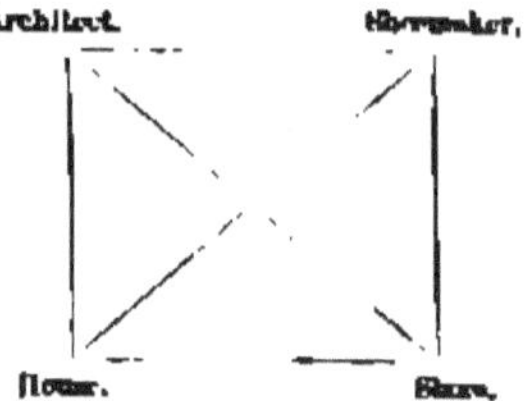
Architect.
Shoemaker.
House.
Shoe.

The joining of the diagonal gives each producer some of the other's work, and thus an exchange is made, but the respective value of the commodities must be first adjusted, else there can be no fair exchange. What, then, is the law of value? It is enunciated a little later (§ 10). δεῖ τοίνυν—τροφήν. 'As an architect (or a farmer it may be) is to a shoemaker, so many shoes must there be to a house or to corn.' That is, the value of the product is determined by the quality of the labour spent upon it. The sort of comparison here made between the quality of farmer and shoemaker seems connected with a Greek notion of personal dignity and a dislike of βαναυσία. But in the following section a view more in accordance with Political Economy is taken,—for it is said that all products must be measured against one

ἔργον ἢ τὸ θατέρου, δεῖ οὖν ταῦτα ἰσασθῆναι. ἔστι δὲ 9
τοῦτο καὶ ἐπὶ τῶν ἄλλων τεχνῶν· ἀνῃροῦντο γὰρ ἄν, εἰ
μὴ ἐποίει τὸ ποιοῦν καὶ ὅσον καὶ οἷον, καὶ τὸ πάσχον
ἔπασχε τοῦτο καὶ τοσοῦτον καὶ τοιοῦτον. οὐ γὰρ ἐκ δύο
ἰατρῶν γίνεται κοινωνία, ἀλλ' ἐξ ἰατροῦ καὶ γεωργοῦ καὶ
ὅλως ἑτέρων καὶ οὐκ ἴσων· ἀλλὰ τούτους δεῖ ἰσασθῆναι.
διὸ πάντα συμβλητὰ δεῖ πως εἶναι, ὧν ἐστὶν ἀλλαγή. 10
ἐφ' ὃ τὸ νόμισμ' ἐλήλυθε, καὶ γίνεταί πως μέσον· πάντα
γὰρ μετρεῖ, ὥστε καὶ τὴν ὑπεροχὴν καὶ τὴν ἔλλειψιν, πόσα
ἄττα δὴ ὑποδήματ' ἴσον οἰκίᾳ ἢ τροφῇ. δεῖ τοίνυν ὅπερ
οἰκοδόμος πρὸς σκυτοτόμον, τοσαδὶ ὑποδήματα πρὸς οἰκίαν
ἢ τροφήν. εἰ γὰρ μὴ τοῦτο, οὐκ ἔσται ἀλλαγὴ οὐδὲ κοινωνία. τοῦτο δ', εἰ μὴ ἴσα εἴη πως, οὐκ ἔσται. δεῖ ἄρα 11
ἑνί τινι πάντα μετρεῖσθαι, ὥσπερ ἐλέχθη πρότερον. τοῦτο
δ' ἐστὶ τῇ μὲν ἀληθείᾳ ἡ χρεία, ἣ πάντα συνέχει· εἰ γὰρ
μηθὲν δέοιντο ἢ μὴ ὁμοίως, ἢ οὐκ ἔσται ἀλλαγὴ ἢ οὐχ ἡ
αὐτή. οἷον δ' ὑπάλλαγμα τῆς χρείας τὸ νόμισμα γέγονε

---

standard, and that this is in reality 'demand' (χρεία). It is demand, then, or in other words the higgling of the market, which determines how many shoes are to be given for a house. But the result ought to be such (§ 12) that the architect + the number of shoes that he will receive (or the equivalent of these in money) will be to the shoemaker + a house, as the architect was to the shoemaker, originally. That is, each producer will have got his deserts.

9 ἔστι δὲ τοῦτο—ἰσασθῆναι] Cf. ch. iv. § 12, note. 'Now this is the case with the other arts also (*i.e.* beside those of the architect and shoemaker), for they would have been destroyed if there had not been the producer producing so much, and of a certain kind, and the consumer (τὸ πάσχον) consuming just the same quantity and quality. For out of two physicians no commerce arises, but out of a physician and a farmer it does, and, in short, out of persons who are different from one another, and not equal; these, then, require to be brought to an equality.' The division of labour, the mutual dependence of the arts, and the correspondence of supply and demand, are here well stated. The terms ποιοῦν and πάσχον may probably have some reference to the ἀντιπεπονθός, which is the subject of the chapter.

11 οἷον δ' ὑπάλλαγμα τῆς χρείας τὸ νόμισμα γέγονε κατὰ συνθήκην] 'Now money is a sort of representative of demand conventionally established.' This excellent definition was not altogether new; Plato had already said (*Repub.* p. 371 B): ἀγορὰ δὴ ἡμῖν καὶ νόμισμα ξύμβολον τῆς ἀλλαγῆς ἕνεκα γενήσεται ἐκ τούτου. The present chapter is disfigured by repetitions. Thus cf. § 15: τοῦτο δ' ἐξ ὑποθέσεως· διὸ νόμισμα καλεῖται. The saying (§ 10) τὸ νόμισμ' ἐλήλυθε καὶ γίνεταί πως μέσον, is repeated

κατὰ συνθήκην· καὶ διὰ τοῦτο τοὔνομα ἔχει νόμισμα, ὅτι οὐ φύσει ἀλλὰ νόμῳ ἐστί, καὶ ἐφ' ἡμῖν μεταβαλεῖν
12 καὶ ποιῆσαι ἄχρηστον. ἔσται δὴ ἀντιπεπονθός, ὅταν ἰσασθῇ, ὥστε ὅπερ γεωργὸς πρὸς σκυτοτόμον, τὸ ἔργον τὸ τοῦ σκυτοτόμου πρὸς τὸ τοῦ γεωργοῦ. εἰς σχῆμα δ' ἀναλογίας οὐ δεῖ ἄγειν, ὅταν ἀλλάξωνται, εἰ δὲ μή, ἀμφοτέρας ἕξει τὰς ὑπεροχὰς τὸ ἕτερον ἄκρον, ἀλλ' ὅταν ἔχωσι τὰ αὑτῶν. οὕτως ἴσοι καὶ κοινωνοί, ὅτι αὕτη ἡ ἰσότης δύναται ἐπ' αὐτῶν γίνεσθαι. γεωργὸς Α, τροφὴ Γ, σκυτοτόμος

---

§ 14: τὸ δὴ νόμισμα ὥσπερ μέτρον σύμμετρα ποιῆσαν ἰσάζει. The law of value is given twice, § 10 and § 12, &c.

12 ἔσται δὴ ἀντιπεπονθὸς—γίνεσθαι] 'Retaliation, then, will take place when the terms have been equalised, and the production of the shoemaker has been made to bear the same relation to that of the farmer, as a farmer himself does to a shoemaker. We must not, however, bring the parties to a diagram of proportion after exchange has taken place, else the one extremity of the figure will have both superiorities assigned to it, but at a moment when the parties still retain their own products. They are thus equal and capable of trading, for proportionate equality can be established between them.' This vexed passage appears to describe the steps in a commercial transaction. There being a mutual need between producers of a different kind, their products require to be equalised. This is done by reducing the goods to a standard of inverse proportion. As a farmer to a shoemaker, so shoes to corn; thus, if a farmer's labour be 5 times better than a shoemaker's, then 5 pair of shoes = a quarter of corn; or if a pair of shoes = 10 shillings, then a quarter of corn = 50 shillings. When this process of equalisation has been effected (ὅταν ἰσασθῇ),—which is done by 'demand' or the higgling of the market,—then simple retaliation, or 'tit for tat,' begins. After an exchange has been made, or, in short, after the price of an article has once been expressed in money, it is no longer the time to talk of 'the quality of labour,' or for either side to claim an advantage on this account. If he did he would have 'both superiorities' reckoned to him, *i.e.* his own superiority over the other producer, and the superiority of his product over that of the other (see § 8, οὐθὲν κωλύει κρεῖττον εἶναι τὸ θατέρου ἔργον). Having enjoyed the superiority of price already, in which the quality of labour was an element, he would now proceed to claim the superiority of labour by itself, which would thus be reckoned to him twice over. Ὅταν ἀλλάξωνται can mean nothing else than 'when they *have* exchanged,' ὅταν with the aorist implying a completed act. It seems unnecessary to say that the value of a thing is not to be settled after it is sold. Rather it is after the goods have come to market, and had a market price put upon them, that considerations of their production must cease. The expression, therefore, is not clear, but the above interpretation seems the most natural that

Β, τὸ ἔργον αὐτοῦ τὸ ἰσασμένον Δ. εἰ δ' οὕτω μὴ ἦν
ἀντιπεπονθέναι, οὐκ ἂν ἦν κοινωνία. ὅτι δ' ἡ χρεία συνέ- 13
χει ὥσπερ ἕν τι ὄν, δηλοῖ ὅτι ὅταν μὴ ἐν χρείᾳ ὦσιν
ἀλλήλων, ἢ ἀμφότεροι ἢ ἅτερος, οὐκ ἀλλάττονται, ὥσπερ
ὅταν οὗ ἔχει αὐτὸς δέηταί τις, οἷον οἴνου, διδόντες σίτου
ἐξαγωγῆς. δεῖ ἄρα τοῦτο ἰσασθῆναι. ὑπὲρ δὲ τῆς μελ- 14
λούσης ἀλλαγῆς, εἰ νῦν μηδὲν δεῖται, ὅτι ἔσται ἐὰν δεηθῇ,
τὸ νόμισμα οἷον ἐγγυητής ἐσθ' ἡμῖν· δεῖ γὰρ τοῦτο φέροντι
εἶναι λαβεῖν. πάσχει μὲν οὖν καὶ τοῦτο τὸ αὐτό· οὐ
γὰρ ἀεὶ ἴσον δύναται· ὅμως δὲ βούλεται μένειν μᾶλλον.
διὸ δεῖ πάντα τετιμῆσθαι· οὕτω γὰρ ἀεὶ ἔσται ἀλλαγή.
εἰ δὲ τοῦτο, κοινωνία. τὸ δὴ νόμισμα ὥσπερ μέτρον σύμμετρα ποιῆσαν ἰσάζει· οὔτε γὰρ ἂν μὴ οὔσης ἀλλαγῆς
κοινωνία ἦν, οὔτ' ἀλλαγὴ ἰσότητος μὴ οὔσης, οὔτ' ἰσότης
μὴ οὔσης συμμετρίας. τῇ μὲν οὖν ἀληθείᾳ ἀδύνατον τὰ 15
τοσοῦτον διαφέροντα σύμμετρα γενέσθαι, πρὸς δὲ τὴν
χρείαν ἐνδέχεται ἱκανῶς· ἓν δή τι δεῖ εἶναι, τοῦτο δ' ἐξ

---

can be given of the passage. The words ἀλλ' ὅταν ἔχωσι τὰ αὑτῶν are opposed to ὅταν ἀλλάξωνται. The punctuation therefore has been altered above, in concurrence with Fritzsche and with the learned paper by Mr. H. Jackson in the *Journal of Philology* (vol. iv. p. 316), the other conclusions of which are not accepted. Ἄκρον above seems to mean 'one of the extremities of the figure' (ἐφ' ᾧ Α, κ.τ.λ.). 'Both the superiorities' must be those named or implied in § 8—10, the superiority of the one product over the other, and the superiority of the one producer over the other.

13 ὅτι δ' ἡ χρεία—ἰσασθῆναι] 'And that mutual want like a principle of unity binds men together, this fact demonstrates, namely, that when men are not in want of each other, whether both parties or one be thus independent, they do not exchange; whereas, when some one else wants the commodity that a man has (they effect an exchange), one party wanting, for instance, wine, and the other being willing to give it for an export of corn: and then an equality has to be brought about.' Some MSS., and the Paraphrast, read ἐξαγωγήν, 'and giving for it an export of corn.' Διδόναι ἐξαγωγήν, 'to grant an exportation,' occurs in Theophrast. *Char.* xx.: δεδομένης ἑαυτῷ ἐξαγωγῆς ξύλων ἀτελοῦς.

14 ὑπὲρ δὲ—μᾶλλον] 'But with a view to future exchange, supposing one does not want an article at present, money is a security that one will be able to get the article when one wants it, for with money in his hand a man must be entitled to take whatever he wishes. It is true that money is under the same law as other commodities; for its value fluctuates, but still its tendency is to remain more fixed than other things.' On these excellent remarks nothing farther need be said. The term ἐγγυητὴς is quoted from the sophist Lycophron by Aristotle, *Pol.* III. ix. 8, in application to the law.

15 τοῦτο δ' ἐξ ὑποθέσεως] 'Conventionally' opposed to ἁπλῶς, cf. *Eth.*

ὑποθέσεως· διὸ νόμισμα καλεῖται. τοῦτο γὰρ πάντα ποιεῖ σύμμετρα· μετρεῖται γὰρ πάντα νομίσματι. οἰκία Α, μναῖ δέκα Β, κλίνη Γ. τὸ δὴ Α τοῦ Β ἥμισυ, εἰ πέντε μνῶν ἀξία ἡ οἰκία, ἢ ἴσον· ἡ δὲ κλίνη δέκατον μέρος τὸ Γ τοῦ Β· δῆλον τοίνυν πόσαι κλῖναι ἴσον οἰκίᾳ, ὅτι
16 πέντε. ὅτι δ' οὕτως ἡ ἀλλαγὴ ἦν πρὶν τὸ νόμισμα εἶναι, δῆλον· διαφέρει γὰρ οὐδὲν ἢ κλῖναι πέντε ἀντὶ οἰκίας, ἢ ὅσου αἱ πέντε κλῖναι.

17 Τί μὲν οὖν τὸ ἄδικον καὶ τί τὸ δίκαιόν ἐστιν, εἴρηται. διωρισμένων δὲ τούτων δῆλον ὅτι ἡ δικαιοπραγία μέσον ἐστὶ τοῦ ἀδικεῖν καὶ ἀδικεῖσθαι· τὸ μὲν γὰρ πλέον ἔχειν τὸ δ' ἔλαττόν ἐστιν. ἡ δὲ δικαιοσύνη μεσότης ἐστὶν οὐ

---

iv. ix. 7. The merely conventional character of money is strongly stated by Aristotle, *Pol.* I. ix. 11: Ὁτὲ δὲ πάλιν λῆρος εἶναι δοκεῖ τὸ νόμισμα καὶ νόμος παντάπασι, φύσει δ' οὐθέν, ὅτι μεταθεμένων τε τῶν χρωμένων οὐθενὸς ἄξιον οὐδὲ χρήσιμον, κ.τ.λ.

16 ὅτι δ' οὕτως ἡ ἀλλαγή] The origin of commerce seems taken from this place by Paulus, cf. *Digest.* I. *De Contr. Empt.*: 'Origo emendi vendendique a permutationibus coepit; olim enim non ita erat nummus, neque aliud merx aliud pretium vocabatur, sed unusquisque secundum necessitatem rerum ac temporum utilibus inutilia permutabat, quando plerumque evenit ut quod alteri superest alteri desit; sed quia non semper nec facile concurrebat ut, quum tu haberes quae ego desiderarem, invicem ego haberem quod tu accipere velles, electa materia est cujus publica ac perpetua aestimatio difficultatibus permutationum aequalitate quantitatis subveniret.'

17 τί μὲν οὖν—εἴρηται] 'We have now stated what is the nature of the unjust and the just abstractedly.' A fresh division of the book commences here; after discussing the various kinds of justice objectively, that is, as principles which manifest themselves in society, the writer proceeds to consider justice subjectively, that is, as manifested in the character of individuals.

ἡ δικαιοπραγία—ἀδικεῖσθαι] 'Just treatment is plainly a mean between injuring and being injured.' Δικαιοπραγία is formed on the analogy of εὐπραγία, and as εὖ πράττειν is used ambiguously to denote both 'doing' and 'faring well' (cf. *Eth.* I. iv. 2), so δικαιοπραγία includes both the doing and the receiving justice.

ἡ δὲ δικαιοσύνη μεσότης κ.τ.λ.] Justice is a mean state or balance in a different sense from the other virtues. It is not a balance in the mind, but rather the will to comply with what society and circumstances pronounce to be fair (τοῦ μέσου ἐστίν). Justice, according to this view, is compliance with an external standard. While in courage, temperance, and the like, there is a blooming of the individual character, each man being a law to himself, in justice there is an abnegation of individuality, in obedience to a standard which is one and the same for all. It must be remembered that the account of ἐπιείκεια in this book supplements that of justice and takes off from its otherwise over-legal character.

τὸν αὐτὸν τρόπον ταῖς πρότερον ἀρεταῖς, ἀλλ' ὅτι μέσου
ἐστίν· ἡ δ' ἀδικία τῶν ἄκρων. καὶ ἡ μὲν δικαιοσύνη ἐστὶ
καθ' ἣν ὁ δίκαιος λέγεται πρακτικὸς κατὰ προαίρεσιν τοῦ
δικαίου, καὶ διανεμητικὸς καὶ αὑτῷ πρὸς ἄλλον καὶ ἑτέρῳ
πρὸς ἕτερον, οὐχ οὕτως ὥστε τοῦ μὲν αἱρετοῦ πλέον αὑτῷ
ἔλαττον δὲ τῷ πλησίον, τοῦ βλαβεροῦ δ' ἀνάπαλιν, ἀλλὰ
τοῦ ἴσου τοῦ κατ' ἀναλογίαν, ὁμοίως δὲ καὶ ἄλλῳ πρὸς
ἄλλον. ἡ δ' ἀδικία τοὐναντίον τοῦ ἀδίκου. τοῦτο δ' ἐστὶν 18
ὑπερβολὴ καὶ ἔλλειψις τοῦ ὠφελίμου ἢ βλαβεροῦ παρὰ
τὸ ἀνάλογον. διὸ ὑπερβολὴ καὶ ἔλλειψις ἡ ἀδικία, ὅτι
ὑπερβολῆς καὶ ἐλλείψεώς ἐστιν, ἐφ' αὑτοῦ μὲν ὑπερβολῆς
μὲν τοῦ ἁπλῶς ὠφελίμου, ἐλλείψεως δὲ τοῦ βλαβεροῦ· ἐπὶ
δὲ τῶν ἄλλων τὸ μὲν ὅλον ὁμοίως, τὸ δὲ παρὰ τὸ ἀνάλογον, ὁποτέρως ἔτυχεν. τοῦ δὲ ἀδικήματος τὸ μὲν ἔλαττον
τὸ ἀδικεῖσθαί ἐστι, τὸ δὲ μεῖζον τὸ ἀδικεῖν. περὶ μὲν οὖν 19
δικαιοσύνης καὶ ἀδικίας, τίς ἑκατέρας ἐστὶν ἡ φύσις,
εἰρήσθω τοῦτον τὸν τρόπον, ὁμοίως δὲ καὶ περὶ τοῦ δικαίου
καὶ ἀδίκου καθόλου.

Ἐπεὶ δ' ἔστιν ἀδικοῦντα μήπω ἄδικον εἶναι, ὁ ποῖα 6
ἀδικήματα ἀδικῶν ἤδη ἄδικός ἐστιν ἑκάστην ἀδικίαν, οἷον
κλέπτης ἢ μοιχὸς ἢ λῃστής; ἢ οὕτω μὲν οὐδὲν διοίσει; καὶ

18 διὸ ὑπερβολὴ—ὁποτέρως ἔτυχεν] 'Hence, too, injustice is an excess and a defect, because it is a principle that aims at excess and defect, in one's own case the excess of what is beneficial absolutely, and the defect of what is hurtful; but in the case of others, while the general result will be similar, it will not matter in which of these two ways proportion is violated.' That is, an unjust award may be made by giving a person too much good as well as too little, and too little evil as well as too much. Injustice is here said to be an extreme ὅτι ὑπερβολῆς ἐστίν, just in the same way as justice was before said to be a mean state ὅτι μέσου ἐστίν.

VI. This chapter, which is written confusedly after the manner of Eudemus, apparently has for its object to restrict the term justice yet more definitely than has hitherto been done. We are now entering on the second division of the book, and the question is, what will constitute an individual unjust? This question tends to elucidate the nature of justice and injustice as individual qualities. But before answering it, there is a digression. It must be remembered, says the writer, that we are treating of justice in the plain sense of the word, that is, civil justice, not that metaphorical justice which might be spoken of as existing in families. On the nature of this justice, proper or civil justice, and on the metaphorical kinds, some remarks are given.

γὰρ ἂν συγγένοιτο γυναικὶ εἰδὼς τὸ ᾗ, ἀλλ' οὐ διὰ προαι-
2 ρέσεως ἀρχὴν ἀλλὰ διὰ πάθος. ἀδικεῖ μὲν οὖν, ἄδικος δ'
οὐκ ἔστιν, οἷον οὐδὲ κλέπτης, ἔκλεψε δέ, οὐδὲ μοιχός,
3 ἐμοίχευσε δέ· ὁμοίως δὲ καὶ ἐπὶ τῶν ἄλλων. πῶς μὲν οὖν
ἔχει τὸ ἀντιπεπονθὸς πρὸς τὸ δίκαιον, εἴρηται πρότερον·
4 δεῖ δὲ μὴ λανθάνειν ὅτι τὸ ζητούμενόν ἐστι καὶ τὸ ἁπλῶς
δίκαιον καὶ το πολιτικὸν δίκαιον. τοῦτο δέ ἐστιν ἐπὶ κοινωνῶν βίου πρὸς τὸ εἶναι αὐτάρκειαν, ἐλευθέρων καὶ ἴσων ἢ
κατ' ἀναλογίαν ἢ κατ' ἀριθμόν· ὥστε ὅσοις μή ἐστι τοῦτο, οὐκ ἔστι τούτοις πρὸς ἀλλήλους τὸ πολιτικὸν δίκαιον,
ἀλλά τι δίκαιον καὶ καθ' ὁμοιότητα. ἔστι γὰρ δίκαιον,
οἷς καὶ νόμος πρὸς αὐτούς· νόμος δ', ἐν οἷς ἀδικία· ἡ γὰρ

---

3 *πῶς μὲν οὖν—πρότερον*] The allusion is to ch. v. § 4—6, and the meaning appears to be simply, in the variety of cases that may occur, punishment by simple retaliation will not do. The sentence however appears irrelevant.

4 *δεῖ δὲ μὴ—κατ' ἀριθμόν*] 'Now we must not forget that the object of our inquiry is at once justice in the plain sense of the word (*ἁπλῶς*) and justice as existing in the state. But this exists amongst those who live in common, with a view to the supply of their mutual wants, free and equal, either proportionately or literally.' *Τὸ ἁπλῶς δίκαιον* is opposed to *καθ' ὁμοιότητα*. It is not meant here to separate *τὸ ἁπ. δίκ.* from *τὸ πολ. δίκ.*, rather it is implied that they are both the same. The only justice that can be called so without a figure of speech is that between fellow citizens, who have mutual rights and same sort of equality, cf. Ar. *Pol.* III. vi. 11, where it is said that all constitutions that aim at the common advantage *ὀρθαὶ τυγχάνουσιν οὖσαι κατὰ τὸ ἁπλῶς δίκαιον*. Proportionate equality belongs to aristocracies and constitutional governments, numerical or exact equality to democracies. Cf. Ar. *Pol.* VI. II. 2.

4—5 *ἔστι γὰρ δίκαιον—τύραννος*] 'For what is just exists among those who live under a common law, and law is where there is injustice, (for legal judgment is a decision between the just and the unjust). Now wherever there is injustice there is wrong dealing, but it does not follow that where there is wrong dealing there is injustice. Wrong dealing consists in allotting oneself too much absolute good and too little absolute evil; and hence it is that we do not suffer a man to rule, but the impersonal reason, for a man does this for himself (i.e. rules, cf. *ἑαυτῷ ποιεῖ* below), and becomes a tyrant.' This passage does not give the origin of justice, but the signs by which you may know it. Justice could not be said to depend on law (especially as law is said to depend on injustice, for we should thus argue in a circle), but where law exists you may know that justice exists. The argument then is that justice exists between citizens who have a law with each other, and not between father and children between whom there is no law. Law implies justice because it springs out of cases where a sense of wrong has been felt.

δίκη κρίσις τοῦ δικαίου καὶ τοῦ ἀδίκου. ἐν οἷς δ' ἀδικία,
καὶ τὸ ἀδικεῖν ἐν τούτοις, ἐν οἷς δὲ τὸ ἀδικεῖν, οὐ πᾶσιν
ἀδικία· τοῦτο δ' ἐστὶ τὸ πλέον αὑτῷ νέμειν τῶν ἁπλῶς
ἀγαθῶν, ἔλαττον δὲ τῶν ἁπλῶς κακῶν· διὸ οὐκ ἐῶμεν 5
ἄρχειν ἄνθρωπον, ἀλλὰ τὸν λόγον, ὅτι ἑαυτῷ τοῦτο ποιεῖ
καὶ γίνεται τύραννος. ἔστι δ' ὁ ἄρχων φύλαξ τοῦ δικαίου,
εἰ δὲ τοῦ δικαίου, καὶ τοῦ ἴσου. ἐπεὶ δ' οὐθὲν αὑτῷ πλέον 6
εἶναι δοκεῖ, εἴπερ δίκαιος· οὐ γὰρ νέμει πλέον τοῦ ἁπλῶς
ἀγαθοῦ αὑτῷ, εἰ μὴ πρὸς αὑτὸν ἀνάλογόν ἐστιν· διὸ ἑτέρῳ
ποιεῖ· καὶ διὰ τοῦτο ἀλλότριον εἶναί φασιν ἀγαθὸν τὴν
δικαιοσύνην, καθάπερ ἐλέχθη καὶ πρότερον. μισθὸς ἄρα 7
τις δοτέος, τοῦτο δὲ τιμὴ καὶ γέρας· ὅτῳ δὲ μὴ ἱκανὰ
τὰ τοιαῦτα, οὗτοι γίνονται τύραννοι. τὸ δὲ δεσποτικὸν 8
δίκαιον καὶ τὸ πατρικὸν οὐ ταὐτὸν τούτοις ἀλλ' ὅμοιον·
οὐ γάρ ἐστιν ἀδικία πρὸς τὰ αὑτοῦ ἁπλῶς, τὸ δὲ κτῆμα
καὶ τὸ τέκνον, ἕως ἂν ᾖ πηλίκον καὶ μὴ χωρισθῇ, ὥσπερ
μέρος αὑτοῦ, αὑτὸν δ' οὐθεὶς προαιρεῖται βλάπτειν· διὸ 9
οὐκ ἔστιν ἀδικία πρὸς αὑτόν. οὐδ' ἄρα ἄδικον οὐδὲ δίκαιον

ἐν οἷς δ' ἀδικία κ.τ.λ.] This seems to mean that law has not arisen merely from the *fact* of unequal dealings (ἀδικεῖν), but from a sense of the violation of a principle (ἀδικία). Thus the principle of justice is prior to all law and not created out of it. Τοῦτο δ', *i.e.* τὸ ἀδικεῖν. Following up this conception of the *à priori* character of justice, the writer says we must be governed not by a man, who may act selfishly, but by an impersonal standard of the right. That selfish rule is tyranny. Aristotle asserts in *Pol.* III. vii. 5: *ἡ μὲν γὰρ τυραννίς ἐστι μοναρχία πρὸς τὸ συμφέρον τὸ τοῦ μοναρχοῦντος.* Cf. also *Pol.* III. xvi. 3: *τὸν ἄρα νόμον ἄρχειν αἱρετώτερον μᾶλλον ἢ τῶν πολιτῶν ἕνα τινά—ὁ μὲν οὖν τὸν νοῦν κελεύων ἄρχειν δοκεῖ κελεύειν ἄρχειν τὸν θεὸν καὶ τοὺς νόμους, ὁ δ' ἄνθρωπον κελεύων προστίθησι καὶ θηρίον. ἥ τε γὰρ ἐπιθυμία τοιοῦτον, καὶ ὁ θυμὸς ἄρχοντας διαστρέφει καὶ τοὺς ἀρίστους ἄνδρας. διόπερ ἄνευ ὀρέξεως νοῦς ὁ νόμος ἐστίν.*

6 *ἐπεὶ δ' οὐθὲν—γέρας*] The apodosis to ἐπεὶ is μισθὸς ἄρα. From οὐ γὰρ to πρότερον is parenthetical. 'But since he does not seem to gain at all, if he is a just man (for he does not allot to himself more of the absolutely good than to others, unless it be proportional to his own merits, and hence he acts for others, and justice thus is said to be the good of others), we must give him some reward, and this comes in the shape of honour and reverence.'

καθάπερ ἐλέχθη τὸ πρότερον] The reference is to ch. I. § 17.

8 *τὸ δὲ—ὅμοιον.* 'Now the justice of masters and parents is not identical with what we have gone through (τούτοις i.e. ἁπλ. καὶ πολιτ. δικ.), but is only analogous to it.'

9 *διὸ—ἄρχεσθαι*] 'Hence a man cannot have a spirit of wrong towards

τὸ πολιτικόν· κατὰ νόμον γὰρ ἦν, καὶ ἐν οἷς ἐπεφύκει εἶναι νόμος· οὗτοι δ' ἦσαν οἷς ὑπάρχει ἰσότης τοῦ ἄρχειν καὶ ἄρχεσθαι. διὸ μᾶλλον πρὸς γυναῖκά ἐστι δίκαιον ἢ πρὸς τέκνα καὶ κτήματα· τοῦτο γάρ ἐστι τὸ οἰκονομικὸν δίκαιον· ἕτερον δὲ καὶ τοῦτο τοῦ πολιτικοῦ.

7 Τοῦ δὲ πολιτικοῦ δικαίου τὸ μὲν φυσικόν ἐστι τὸ δὲ νομικόν, φυσικὸν μὲν τὸ πανταχοῦ τὴν αὐτὴν ἔχον δύναμιν, καὶ οὐ τῷ δοκεῖν ἢ μή, νομικὸν δὲ ὃ ἐξ ἀρχῆς μὲν οὐδὲν διαφέρει οὕτως ἢ ἄλλως, ὅταν δὲ θῶνται, διαφέρει, οἷον τὸ

---

himself; nor civil justice or injustice; for this is, as we have said (ἦν), according to law and among those who can naturally have law; namely, those, as we said (ἦσαν), who have an equality of ruling and being ruled.'

VII. Continues the discussion as to the nature of civil justice, in which there are two elements, the natural (φυσικόν) and the conventional (νομικόν). They are distinguished, and arguments are brought against the sophistical position that all justice is merely conventional. The chapter as above is not conveniently divided. We need not have had a fresh commencement with § 1. τοῦ δὲ πολιτικοῦ, which is a carrying on of the same digression before made; and we might well have had the end of a chapter at § 5. κατὰ φύσιν ἢ ἀρίστη, after which there is a return to the main question as to justice and injustice in the acts and the characters of individuals. In his later edition Bekker makes one undivided chapter including Chaps. VI., VII., VIII., of the present edition.

1 τοῦ δὲ πολιτικοῦ—διαφέρει] 'Now in civil justice there is a natural element and a conventional element; that is natural which has the same force everywhere, and does not depend on being adopted or not adopted (τῷ δοκεῖν ἢ μή); while that is conventional which at the outset does not matter whether it be so or differently, but when men have instituted it, then matters.' The distinction here drawn is like that between ἴδιος and κοινὸς νόμος in Aristotle's *Rhetoric*, I. xiii., and also that between moral and positive laws in modern treatises. Natural justice is law because it is right, conventional justice is right because it is law. Τὸ νομικὸν is not to be confused with τὸ νόμιμον (cf. ch. i. § 8), which is justice expressed in the law, and which is nearly equivalent to πολιτικὸν δίκαιον, containing therefore both the natural and conventional elements. In the early stages of society all law is regarded with equal reverence. Afterwards, in the sceptical period, the merely conventional character of many institutions is felt, and doubt is thrown on the validity of the whole fabric. Afterwards the proper distinction is made, and the existence of something above all mere convention is recognised. The idea of 'nature' as forming the basis of law, which was started in the school of Aristotle, was afterwards developed by the Stoics, and still further drawn out by Cicero and the Roman jurists. It became a leading formula in the Roman law, and hence has influenced the modern school of continental jurists, until a reaction was made against it by Bentham.

μνᾶς λυτροῦσθαι, ἢ τὸ αἶγα θύειν ἀλλὰ μὴ δύο πρόβατα, ἔτι ὅσα ἐπὶ τῶν καθ' ἕκαστα νομοθετοῦσιν, οἷον τὸ θύειν Βρασίδᾳ, καὶ τὰ ψηφισματώδη. δοκεῖ δ' ἐνίοις εἶναι 2
πάντα τοιαῦτα, ὅτι τὸ μὲν φύσει ἀκίνητον καὶ πανταχοῦ τὴν αὐτὴν ἔχει δύναμιν, ὥσπερ τὸ πῦρ καὶ ἐνθάδε καὶ ἐν Πέρσαις καίει, τὰ δὲ δίκαια κινούμενα ὁρῶσιν. τοῦτο δ' 3

τὸ μνᾶς λυτροῦσθαι] Herod. (VI. 79) speaks of *two* minae as the ransom, *ἄποινά ἐστι Πελοποννησίοισι δύο μνέαι τεταγμέναι κατ' ἄνδρα αἰχμάλωτον ἐκτίνειν.*

τὸ αἶγα θύειν] Cf. Herod. II. 42: *ὅσοι μὲν δὴ Διὸς Θηβαιέος ἵδρυνται ἱρὸν ἢ νομοῦ Θηβαίου εἰσί, οὗτοι μέν νυν πάντες ὀίων ἀπεχόμενοι αἶγας θύουσι.*

τὸ θύειν Βρασίδᾳ] *i.e.* in Amphipolis, cf. Thucyd. v. xi.: *καὶ τὸ λοιπὸν οἱ Ἀμφιπολῖται περιέρξαντες αὐτοῦ τὸ μνημεῖον, ὡς ἥρωί τε ἐντέμνουσι καὶ τιμὰς δεδώκασιν ἀγῶνας καὶ ἐτησίους θυσίας νομίσαντες τὸν Βρασίδαν σωτῆρα σφῶν γεγενῆσθαι.*

2 δοκεῖ δὲ—ὁρῶσιν] 'Now some think that all institutions are of this character, because, while the natural is fixed and has everywhere the same force (as fire burns equally here and in Persia), they see the rules of justice altered.' Καὶ ἐνθάδε καὶ ἐν τοῖς Πέρσαις. This appears to have been a common formula, cf. Plato, *Minos*, p. 315 E: *ἐγὼ μὲν (νομίζω) τά τε δίκαια δίκαια καὶ τὰ ἄδικα ἄδικα. οὐκοῦν καὶ παρὰ πᾶσιν οὕτως ὡς ἐνθάδε νομίζεται;—ναί.—οὐκοῦν καὶ ἐν Πέρσαις;—καὶ ἐν Πέρσαις.* In the same dialogue, p. 315, are given specimens of the different laws and customs in different times and places (D): *Μυρία δ' ἄν τις ἔχοι τοιαῦτα εἰπεῖν. πολλὴ γὰρ εὐρυχωρία τῆς ἀποδείξεως, ὡς οὔτε ἡμεῖς ἡμῖν αὐτοῖς ἀεὶ κατὰ ταὐτὰ νομίζομεν οὔτε ἀλλήλοις οἱ ἄνθρωποι.* The variety of customs and ideas is brought forward by Locke and Paley to disprove the existence of an innate 'moral sense.' This variety is generally overstated, and the list of aberrations is mainly obtained from the usages of barbarous tribes. On the origin of the opposition between 'nature' and 'convention,' and on the use made of this by the Sophists, see Vol. I. Essay II. p. 149.

3 τοῦτο δ'—οὐ φύσει] 'But this is not the case (*i.e.* that justice is mutable), though it is so to a certain extent. May be among the gods justice is immutable; but with us, although there is somewhat that exists by nature, yet all is mutable. Though this does not do away with the distinction between what is by nature and what is not by nature.' The writing here is very compressed, ἀλλ' ἔστιν ἔν, *i.e.* τὰ δίκαια κινούμενα, to which also *οὐδαμῶς* afterwards must be referred. The answer given to the sophistical argument against justice consists in denying the premise that 'what is by nature is immutable.' This might be the case, it is answered, in an ideal world (*παρά γε τοῖς θεοῖς*), but in our world laws are interrupted, and the manifestation of them is less perfect (*κινητὸν μέντοι πᾶν*). Again, 'nature' must be taken to mean not only a law but a tendency (see note on *Eth.* II. i. 3), as, for instance, the right hand is 'naturally,' but not always, stronger than the left, while merely conventional institutions exhibit no natural law (*οὐ φύσει ἀλλὰ*

οὐκ ἔστιν οὕτως ἔχον, ἀλλ' ἔστιν ὥς. καίτοι παρά γε
τοῖς θεοῖς ἴσως οὐδαμῶς· παρ' ἡμῖν δ' ἐστὶ μέν τι καὶ
φύσει, κινητὸν μέντοι πᾶν. ἀλλ' ὅμως ἐστὶ τὸ μὲν φύσει
4 τὸ δ' οὐ φύσει. ποῖον δὲ φύσει τῶν ἐνδεχομένων καὶ
ἄλλως ἔχειν, καὶ ποῖον οὐ ἀλλὰ νομικὸν καὶ συνθήκῃ,
εἴπερ ἄμφω κινητὰ ὁμοίως, δῆλον. καὶ ἐπὶ τῶν ἄλλων ὁ
αὐτὸς ἁρμόσει διορισμός· φύσει γὰρ ἡ δεξιὰ κρείττων,
5 καίτοι ἐνδέχεταί τινας ἀμφιδεξίους γενέσθαι. τὰ δὲ
κατὰ συνθήκην καὶ τὸ συμφέρον τῶν δικαίων ὅμοιά ἐστι
τοῖς μέτροις· οὐ γὰρ πανταχοῦ ἴσα τὰ οἰνηρὰ καὶ σιτηρὰ
μέτρα, ἀλλ' οὗ μὲν ὠνοῦνται, μείζω, οὗ δὲ πωλοῦσιν,
ἐλάττω. ὁμοίως δὲ καὶ τὰ μὴ φυσικὰ ἀλλ' ἀνθρώπινα
δίκαια οὐ ταὐτὰ πανταχοῦ, ἐπεὶ οὐδ' αἱ πολιτεῖαι, ἀλλὰ
6 μία μόνον πανταχοῦ κατὰ φύσιν ἡ ἀρίστη. τῶν δὲ δικαίων
καὶ νομίμων ἕκαστον ὡς τὰ καθόλου πρὸς τὰ καθ' ἕκαστα
ἔχει· τὰ μὲν γὰρ πραττόμενα πολλά, ἐκείνων δ' ἕκαστον
ἕν· καθόλου γάρ. διαφέρει δὲ τὸ ἀδίκημα καὶ τὸ ἄδικον

συνθήκῃ), and are like weights and measures, which entirely depend on the convenience of men.

παρά γε τοῖς θεοῖς] Of course there is nothing theological in this allusion. In *Eth.* x. viii. 7, the notion of attributing justice to the gods is ridiculed. The present mention of the gods is not meant to convey anything about their nature, it merely contrasts a divine or ideal state with the human and actual. An exactly similar mention of the gods is made below, ch. ix. § 17.

4 *ἐνδέχεταί τινας*] Bekker reads *τινας*, Zell and Cardwell *πάντας*, all without mentioning any variation in their MSS. The latter of the two readings is supported by the Paraphrast and also by the author of the *Magna Moralia* (I. xxxiv. 21): *λέγω δ' οἷον εἰ τῇ ἀριστερᾷ μελετῷμεν πάντες ἀεὶ βάλλειν, γινοίμεθ' ἂν ἀμφιδέξιοι.* In either case, the sense is nearly the same, *πάντας* implying 'any one out of all,' as above, *κινητὸν μέντοι πᾶν*.

5 *ὅμοια τοῖς μέτροις*] The meaning appears to be, that measures differ in size in the producing (*οὗ μὲν ὠνοῦνται*) and the consuming (*οὗ δὲ πωλοῦσιν*) countries.

ὁμοίως δὲ—ἀρίστη] 'So, too, those institutions which are not based on nature, but on human will, are not the same in all places, for not even are forms of government the same, though there is one alone which for all places is naturally the best.' From the primary difference in governments will follow manifold other differences in conventional usages. For the Aristotelian idea of the one best government, see *Politics* III. vii., III. xv., &c.

6 *τῶν δὲ δικαίων—καθόλου γάρ*] 'Now every just and lawful rule stands like the universal in relation to the particulars, for while actions are manifold, the rule is one, being universal.'

καὶ τὸ δικαίωμα καὶ τὸ δίκαιον. ἄδικον μὲν γάρ ἐστι τῇ φύσει ἢ τάξει. τὸ αὐτὸ δὲ τοῦτο, ὅταν πραχθῇ, ἀδίκημά ἐστι, πρὶν δὲ πραχθῆναι, οὔπω, ἀλλ' ἄδικον. ὁμοίως δὲ καὶ δικαίωμα. καλεῖται δὲ μᾶλλον δικαιοπράγημα τὸ κοινόν, δικαίωμα δὲ τὸ ἐπανόρθωμα τοῦ ἀδικήματος. καθ' ἕκαστον δὲ αὐτῶν, ποῖά τε εἴδη καὶ πόσα καὶ περὶ ποῖα τυγχάνει ὄντα, ὕστερον ἐπισκεπτέον.

Ὄντων δὲ τῶν δικαίων καὶ ἀδίκων τῶν εἰρημένων, ἀδικεῖ 8
μὲν καὶ δικαιοπραγεῖ, ὅταν ἑκών τις αὐτὰ πράττῃ· ὅταν
δ' ἄκων, οὔτ' ἀδικεῖ οὔτε δικαιοπραγεῖ ἀλλ' ἢ κατὰ συμ-
βεβηκός· οἷς γὰρ συμβέβηκε δικαίοις εἶναι ἢ ἀδίκοις,
πράττουσιν. ἀδίκημα δὲ καὶ δικαιοπράγημα ὥρισται τῷ 2
ἑκουσίῳ καὶ ἀκουσίῳ· ὅταν γὰρ ἑκούσιον ᾖ, ψέγεται,
ἅμα δὲ καὶ ἀδίκημα τότ' ἐστίν· ὥστ' ἔσται τι ἄδικον μέν,
ἀδίκημα δ' οὔπω, ἐὰν μὴ τὸ ἑκούσιον προσῇ. λέγω δ' 3
ἑκούσιον μέν, ὥσπερ καὶ πρότερον εἴρηται, ὃ ἄν τις τῶν

We have a transition of subject now, a return from the digression on civil justice, to inquire into individual responsibility, &c. The transition is made by saying that the principles of justice and injustice (τὸ δίκαιον and τὸ ἄδικον) are universals and differ from just and unjust acts. At first the writer makes δικαίωμα stand to δίκαιον, as ἀδίκημα to ἄδικον. Afterwards he substitutes δικαιοπράγημα as a more correct word, inasmuch as δικαίωμα had another special meaning to denote the setting right of injustice—legal satisfaction. It is not improbable that Eudemus here is correcting phraseology of Aristotle, who at all events in his *Rhetoric*, I. xiii. 1, uses δικαίωμα as the opposite of ἀδίκημα, merely to denote a just action. Τὰ δ' ἀδικήματα πάντα καὶ τὰ δικαιώματα διέλωμεν, κ.τ.λ.

VIII. The general principles of justice having now been defined, the question is what constitutes justice and injustice in the individual? In one word the will. This chapter adds some needless remarks on the nature of the voluntary, and distinguishes between the different degrees of a wrong done, according to the amount of purpose which accompanied it. The same act externally might be a misfortune, if happening beyond calculation; a mistake, if through carelessness; a wrong, if through temptation; the act of an unjust man, if through deliberate villany (§§ 6—8). This distinction is illustrated by the legal view with regard to acts done in anger (§§ 9—10). All voluntary just acts are just. Some involuntary acts are still unpardonable.

3 λέγω δ' ἑκούσιον μέν, ὥσπερ καὶ πρότερον εἴρηται] The reference is to the *Eudemian Ethics* II. ix. 2: Ὅσα μὲν οὖν ἐφ' ἑαυτῷ ὂν μὴ πράττειν πράττει μὴ ἀγνοῶν καὶ δι' αὑτόν, ἑκούσια ταῦτ' ἀνάγκη εἶναι, καὶ τὸ ἑκούσιον τοῦτ' ἐστίν· ὅσα δ' ἀγνοῶν καὶ διὰ τὸ ἀγνοεῖν, ἄκων.

ἐφ' αὐτῷ ὄντων εἰδὼς καὶ μὴ ἀγνοῶν πράττῃ μήτε ὃν μήτε ᾧ μήτε οὗ ἕνεκα, οἷον τίνα τύπτει καὶ τίνι καὶ τίνος ἕνεκα, κἀκείνων ἕκαστον μὴ κατὰ συμβεβηκὸς μηδὲ βίᾳ, ὥσπερ εἴ τις λαβὼν τὴν χεῖρα αὐτοῦ τύπτοι ἕτερον, οὐχ ἑκών· οὐ γὰρ ἐπ' αὐτῷ. ἐνδέχεται δὲ τὸν τυπτόμενον πατέρα εἶναι, τὸν δ' ὅτι μὲν ἄνθρωπος ἢ τῶν παρόντων τις γινώσκειν, ὅτι δὲ πατὴρ ἀγνοεῖν. ὁμοίως δὲ τὸ τοιοῦτον διωρίσθω καὶ ἐπὶ τοῦ οὗ ἕνεκα, καὶ περὶ τὴν πρᾶξιν ὅλην. τὸ δὴ ἀγνοούμενον, ἢ μὴ ἀγνοούμενον μὲν μὴ ἐπ' αὐτῷ δ' ὄν, ἢ βίᾳ, ἀκούσιον· πολλὰ γὰρ καὶ τῶν φύσει ὑπαρχόντων εἰδότες καὶ πράττομεν καὶ πάσχομεν, ὧν οὐθὲν οὔθ' ἑκούσιον οὔτ' ἀκούσιόν ἐστιν, οἷον τὸ γηρᾶν ἢ ἀποθνήσκειν.
4 ἔστι δ' ὁμοίως ἐπὶ τῶν ἀδίκων καὶ τῶν δικαίων καὶ τὸ κατὰ συμβεβηκός· καὶ γὰρ ἂν τὴν παρακαταθήκην ἀποδοίη τις ἄκων καὶ διὰ φόβον, ὃν οὔτε δίκαια πράττειν οὔτε δικαιοπραγεῖν φατέον ἀλλ' ἢ κατὰ συμβεβηκός. ὁμοίως δὲ καὶ τὸν ἀναγκαζόμενον καὶ ἄκοντα τὴν παρακαταθήκην μὴ ἀποδιδόντα κατὰ συμβεβηκὸς φατέον ἀδικεῖν καὶ τὰ
5 ἄδικα πράττειν. τῶν δὲ ἑκουσίων τὰ μὲν προελόμενοι πράττομεν τὰ δ' οὐ προελόμενοι, προελόμενοι μὲν ὅσα προ-
6 βουλευσάμενοι, ἀπροαίρετα δὲ ὅσα ἀπροβούλευτα. τριῶν δὴ οὐσῶν βλαβῶν τῶν ἐν ταῖς κοινωνίαις, τὰ μὲν μετ'

ὥσπερ εἴ τις λαβὼν τὴν χεῖρα κ.τ.λ.] The same illustration is given in the *Eudemian Ethics* II. viii. 10, where the discussion has a great affinity to the present chapter.

ἐπὶ τοῦ οὗ ἕνεκα] See the note on *Eth.* III. i. 18.

πολλὰ γὰρ—ἀποθνήσκειν] 'Since we knowingly both do and suffer many of those things that happen to us by nature, none of which are either voluntary or involuntary, as for instance growing old or dying.' To constitute voluntariness we must do knowingly things that are within the sphere of the will (ἐφ' ἡμῖν). Physical things are not within this sphere. It would have been more accurate to say that we do not *do* them. It is characteristic of Eudemus to turn to the consideration of physiological facts; see the notes below, on *Eth.* VII. ch. xiv.

6 τριῶν δὴ οὐσῶν βλαβῶν τῶν ἐν ταῖς κοινωνίαις] 'Therefore there being three kinds of harm that may be done in the intercourse of men,' &c. Really four kinds are specified, but the last (διὰ μοχθηρίαν) seems to be an addition to the old list, consisting of the misfortune, the error, and the wrong, which division is to be found in Aristotle's *Rhetoric*, I. ch. xiii. The present discussion is promised in *Eth. Eud.* II. x. 19: ἅμα δ' ἐκ τούτων φανερὸν καὶ ὅτι καλῶς διορίζονται οἱ τῶν παθημάτων τὰ μὲν ἑκούσια τὰ δ' ἀκούσια τὰ δ' ἐκ προνοίας

ἀγνοίας ἁμαρτήματά ἐστιν, ὅταν μήτε ὃν μήτε ὃ μήτε ᾧ μήτε οὗ ἕνεκα ὑπέλαβε πράξῃ· ἢ γὰρ οὐ βαλεῖν ἢ οὐ τούτῳ ἢ οὐ τοῦτον ἢ οὐ τούτου ἕνεκα ᾠήθη, ἀλλὰ συνέβη οὐχ οὗ ἕνεκα ᾠήθη, οἷον οὐχ ἵνα τρώσῃ ἀλλ' ἵνα κεντήσῃ, ἢ οὐχ ὅν, ἢ οὐχ ὥς. ὅταν μὲν οὖν παραλόγως ἡ βλάβη 7
γένηται, ἀτύχημα, ὅταν δὲ μὴ παραλόγως, ἄνευ δὲ κακίας, ἁμάρτημα· ἁμαρτάνει μὲν γὰρ ὅταν ἡ ἀρχὴ ἐν αὐτῷ ᾖ τῆς αἰτίας, ἀτυχεῖ δ' ὅταν ἔξωθεν. ὅταν δὲ εἰδὼς μὲν μὴ 8
προβουλεύσας δέ, ἀδίκημα, οἷον ὅσα τε διὰ θυμὸν καὶ ἄλλα πάθη, ὅσα ἀναγκαῖα ἢ φυσικά, συμβαίνει τοῖς ἀνθρώποις· ταῦτα γὰρ βλάπτοντες καὶ ἁμαρτάνοντες ἀδικοῦσι μέν, καὶ ἀδικήματά ἐστιν, οὐ μέντοι πω ἄδικοι διὰ ταῦτα οὐδὲ πονηροί· οὐ γὰρ διὰ μοχθηρίαν ἡ βλάβη· ὅταν 9
δ' ἐκ προαιρέσεως, ἄδικος καὶ μοχθηρός. διὸ καλῶς τὰ ἐκ θυμοῦ οὐκ ἐκ προνοίας κρίνεται· οὐ γὰρ ἄρχει ὁ θυμῷ ποιῶν, ἀλλ' ὁ ὀργίσας. ἔτι δὲ οὐδὲ περὶ τοῦ γενέσθαι ἢ 10
μὴ ἀμφισβητεῖται, ἀλλὰ περὶ τοῦ δικαίου· ἐπὶ φαινομένῃ γὰρ ἀδικίᾳ ἡ ὀργή ἐστιν. οὐ γὰρ ὥσπερ ἐν τοῖς συναλλάγμασι περὶ τοῦ γενέσθαι ἀμφισβητοῦσιν, ὧν ἀνάγκη τὸν ἕτερον εἶναι μοχθηρόν, ἂν μὴ διὰ λήθην αὐτὸ δρῶσιν· ἀλλ' ὁμολογοῦντες περὶ τοῦ πράγματος, περὶ τοῦ ποτέρως δίκαιον ἀμφισβητοῦσιν. ὁ δ' ἐπιβουλεύσας οὐκ ἀγνοεῖ, ὥστε ὁ μὲν οἴεται ἀδικεῖσθαι, ὁ δ' οὔ. ἂν δ' ἐκ προαιρέσεως βλάψῃ, ἀδικεῖ. καὶ κατὰ ταῦτ' ἤδη τὰ ἀδικήματα ὁ 11

[illegible]τοῦσιν· εἰ γὰρ καὶ μὴ διαμφισβητοῦσιν, ἀλλ' ἔνεστί γέ τι τῆς ἀληθείας· ἀλλὰ περὶ μὲν τούτων ἐροῦμεν ἐν τῇ περὶ τῶν δικαίων ἐπισκέψει.

9—10 διὸ καλῶς—ἀδικεῖ] 'Hence too acts done from anger are well judged not to proceed from purpose, for not he who acts in anger, but he who provoked the anger is the beginner. Again, the question is not about the act having taken place or not, but about the justice of it; for anger arises on the appearance of injustice. It is not as in contracts, where men dispute about the thing having been done, and where (if the thing has been done) one of the parties must be a villain, unless they have done it in forgetfulness. But (in the present case) agreeing about the fact, they dispute on which side justice is. Now he that has laid a plot against another cannot plead ignorance (in mitigation of the charge of injustice against him), so that B (the party who commits an act of wrathful retaliation on A, whom he alleges to have plotted against him) maintains that he has been injured, while the other party, A, denies it. But if A has purposely hurt B, he is certainly

ἀδικῶν ἄδικος, ὅταν παρὰ τὸ ἀνάλογον ᾖ ἢ παρὰ τὸ ἴσον. ὁμοίως δὲ καὶ δίκαιος, ὅταν προελόμενος δικαιοπραγῇ.
12 δικαιοπραγεῖ δέ, ἂν μόνον ἑκὼν πράττῃ. τῶν δ' ἀκουσίων τὰ μέν ἐστι συγγνωμονικὰ τὰ δ' οὐ συγγνωμονικά· ὅσα μὲν γὰρ μὴ μόνον ἀγνοοῦντες ἀλλὰ καὶ δι' ἄγνοιαν ἁμαρ-

guilty of injustice towards him.' Owing to the obscurity of expression, this passage has given great trouble to the commentators. The context is a carrying on of the distinction between ἁμάρτημα, ἀδίκημα, and ἀδικία. What distinguishes these is the amount of purpose they contain. This, says the writer, is illustrated by the way in which acts of anger are treated legally. In violations of civil contract the question is merely as to fact,—did the contract exist, and has it been consciously violated? But in cases of assault, &c., committed in anger, the fact is admitted, but justification is pleaded in respect of some act of injustice which provoked the acts complained of. Thus the question is moved off from the acts themselves, and is entirely concerned with their antecedents. Was it a real injustice that gave rise to them? That this is what the writer means, is shown by the words of the text (§ 10) ἀμφισβητεῖται—περὶ τοῦ δικαίου· ἐπὶ φαινομένῃ γὰρ ἀδικίᾳ ἡ ὀργή ἐστιν. According to the text, when an act of wrathful retaliation has been committed, the question is, was the act that provoked this retaliation an act of injustice or not? And this turns very much on the question whether it was a harm done knowingly and on purpose? (ὁ ἐπιβουλεύσας οὐκ ἀγνοεῖ—ἂν δ' ἐκ προαιρέσεως βλάψῃ, ἀδικεῖ.) We thus return to the general proposition (§ 11) that injustice of act requires only voluntariness, but injustice of character deliberate purpose. The reference here is to the point of view of the law-courts, and may have been suggested, like so much else in this book, by the discussions in the *Politics* of Aristotle. *Cf. Pol.* iv. xvi. 1–5, where the different kinds of law-courts are specified, and it is mentioned as one of the cases that fall to be treated of in a criminal court,—where homicide is admitted, but its justification is pleaded: φονικοῦ μὲν οὖν εἴδη, ἄν τ' ἐν τοῖς αὐτοῖς δικασταῖς ἄν τ' ἐν ἄλλοις, περί τε τῶν ἐκ προνοίας καὶ περὶ τῶν ἀκουσίων, καὶ ὅσα ὁμολογεῖται μέν, ἀμφισβητεῖται δὲ περὶ τοῦ δικαίου, κ.τ.λ.

ἐπὶ φαινομένῃ γὰρ ἀδικίᾳ] This is a reasonable deduction from Aristotle's definition of anger, *Rhet.* ii. ii. 1, ὄρεξις μετὰ λύπης τιμωρίας φαινομένης διὰ φαινομένην ὀλιγωρίαν, κ.τ.λ. If anger arises from a sense of wounded *amour propre*, the idea of injustice and wrong must certainly be counted among the most common causes of its being excited.

12 ἀγνοοῦντες μὲν διὰ πάθος δὲ μήτε φυσικὸν μήτ' ἀνθρώπινον] This would seem to imply a state in which moral insensibility and temporary mental obscuration have been caused by an access of brutality (θηριότης) as described in *Eth.* vii. v. 3. αὗται μὲν θηριώδεις, αἱ δὲ διὰ τε νόσους γίνονται καὶ μανίας ἐνίοις, ὥσπερ ὁ τὴν μητέρα καθιερεύσας καὶ φαγών, καὶ ὁ τοῦ συνδούλου τὸ ἧπαρ. The police courts afford frequent instances of the infliction of brutal injuries, which are 'not forgivable,' though the perpetrators seem hardly responsible beings.

τάνουσι, συγγνωμονικά, ὅσα δὲ μὴ δι' ἄγνοιαν, ἀλλ' ἀγνοοῦντες μὲν διὰ πάθος δὲ μήτε φυσικὸν μήτ' ἀνθρώπινον, οὐ συγγνωμονικά.

Ἀπορήσειε δ' ἄν τις, εἰ ἱκανῶς διώρισται περὶ τοῦ 9
ἀδικεῖσθαι καὶ ἀδικεῖν, πρῶτον μὲν εἰ ἔστιν ὥσπερ Εὐριπίδης εἴρηκε, λέγων ἀτόπως

μητέρα κατέκτα τὴν ἐμήν, βραχὺς λόγος,
ἑκὼν ἑκοῦσαν, ἢ θέλουσαν οὐχ ἑκών.

IX. This chapter, by means of mooting and answering certain difficulties and objections with regard to the nature of justice and injustice, completes and deepens the conception of them that has hitherto been given. These questions are as follows: (1) Can one be injured voluntarily? §§ 1—2. (2) Is the recipient of an injury always injured? §§ 3—8. The latter question is first generally answered, and then, §§ 9—13, it is re-stated in the form of two other questions, namely, Is the distributor of an unjust distribution, or he that gains by it, unjust? and, Can a man injure himself? By mooting these points it is at once shown that justice implies a relationship of two wills, and that an act of injustice implies a collision of two wills: a loss on one side and a gain on the other. The chapter ends with some remarks correcting popular errors, and deepening the conception of justice. (1) Justice is no easy thing consisting in an external act. It consists in an internal spirit, § 14. (2) To know it is not like knowing a set of facts. It implies a knowledge of principles, § 15. (3) The just man could not at will act unjustly. The character of the act depends on the state of mind, § 16. (4) Justice is limited to a human sphere, § 17.

1 *Ἀπορήσειε δ' ἄν—ἀδικεῖν*] 'Now one might doubt whether we have adequately defined being injured and injuring; in the first place, whether it be as Euripides says, in his strange language, A. "I killed my mother, and there's an end of it." B. "Was it with the will of both, or was she willing while you were unwilling?" In short, is it as a matter of fact possible that one should be voluntarily injured, or, on the contrary, is that always involuntary, just as all injuring is voluntary? And is all injustice, like all injuring, to be summed up under the one category or the other, or is it sometimes voluntary and sometimes involuntary? The same may be said about being justly treated, for all just doing is voluntary, so that it might be supposed that being injured and being justly treated would be opposed to each other as to being voluntary or involuntary correspondingly to the two active terms ([illegible] [illegible]). But it would be absurd to say of being justly treated that it is always voluntary, for some are treated justly against their will.'

εἰ ἱκανῶς διώρισται] This shows the purpose of the chapter, to complete the definition of justice and injustice by looking at them on the passive side.

ὥσπερ Εὐριπίδης] Wagner (*Eur. Fragm.* p. 40) says the lines come from the *Alcmaeon* of Euripides. The Scholiast refers them to the

πότερον γὰρ ὡς ἀληθῶς ἔστιν ἑκόντα ἀδικεῖσθαι, ἢ οὔ ἀλλ' ἀκούσιον ἅπαν, ὥσπερ καὶ τὸ ἀδικεῖν πᾶν ἑκούσιον. καὶ ἆρα πᾶν οὕτως ἢ ἐκείνως, ὥσπερ καὶ τὸ ἀδικεῖν πᾶν ἑκού-
2 σιον, ἢ τὸ μὲν ἑκούσιον τὸ δ' ἀκούσιον. ὁμοίως δὲ καὶ ἐπὶ τοῦ δικαιοῦσθαι· τὸ γὰρ δικαιοπραγεῖν πᾶν ἑκούσιον, ὥστ' εὔλογον ἀντικεῖσθαι ὁμοίως καθ' ἑκάτερον τό τ' ἀδικεῖσθαι καὶ τὸ δικαιοῦσθαι ἢ ἑκούσιον ἢ ἀκούσιον εἶναι. ἄτοπον δ' ἂν δόξειε καὶ ἐπὶ τοῦ δικαιοῦσθαι, εἰ πᾶν ἑκούσιον· ἔνιοι γὰρ
3 δικαιοῦνται οὐχ ἑκόντες. ἐπεὶ καὶ τόδε διαπορήσειεν ἄν τις, πότερον ὁ τὸ ἄδικον πεπονθὼς ἀδικεῖται πᾶς ἢ ὥσπερ καὶ ἐπὶ τοῦ πράττειν, καὶ ἐπὶ τοῦ πάσχειν ἐστίν· κατὰ συμβεβηκὸς γὰρ ἐνδέχεται ἐπ' ἀμφοτέρων μεταλαμβάνειν τῶν δικαίων. ὁμοίως δὲ δῆλον ὅτι καὶ ἐπὶ τῶν ἀδίκων· οὐ γὰρ ταὐτὸν τὸ τἄδικα πράττειν τῷ ἀδικεῖν οὐδὲ τὸ ἄδικα πάσχειν τῷ ἀδικεῖσθαι. ὁμοίως δὲ καὶ ἐπὶ τοῦ δικαιοπραγεῖν καὶ δικαιοῦσθαι· ἀδύνατον γὰρ ἀδικεῖσθαι μὴ ἀδικοῦντος ἢ
4 δικαιοῦσθαι μὴ δικαιοπραγοῦντος. εἰ δ' ἔστιν ἁπλῶς τὸ

Bellerophon. Wagner writes them as a dialogue, supposing the persons to be Alcmaeon and Phegeus. He conjectures *κατέκταν*, which appears more probable than the usual reading *κατέκτα*, and which accordingly has been adopted in the above translation.

2 The passive terms are not opposed to each other in respect of voluntariness in the way that might be expected from the opposition between the active terms under which they stand.

ἀδικεῖν · *δικαιοπραγεῖν*
ἀδικεῖσθαι — *δικαιοῦσθαι*.

For *ἀδικεῖσθαι* is always involuntary, but *δικαιοῦσθαι* is not always voluntary. A man may be 'treated justly' by being hanged.

3 Not every one who suffers what is unjust is injured, for injury implies intention on the part of the injuror. Cf. Aristotle, *Rhet.* I. xiii. 5: ἔστι δὴ τὸ ἀδικεῖσθαι τὸ ὑπὸ ἑκόντος τὰ ἄδικα πάσχειν.

4—6 *εἰ δ' ἔστιν—πράττει*] 'Now if to injure is simply defined "to hurt any one willingly," and "willingly" means "knowing the person, and the instrument, and the manner," and the incontinent man hurts himself willingly, then it follows that one can be willingly injured, and it will be possible to injure oneself. But this was one of the points in question, whether it is possible to injure oneself. Again, one might from incontinence be hurt willingly by another who was acting willingly, so that in that way it would be possible to be injured willingly. But shall we not rather say that the definition is not correct, but that we must add to the formula "hurt any one willingly, knowing person, instrument, and manner," the terms "against that person's wish?" It is true one is hurt and one suffers injustice willingly, but no

ἀδικεῖν τὸ βλάπτειν ἑκόντα τινά, τὸ δ' ἑκόντα εἰδότα καὶ
ὃν καὶ ᾧ καὶ ὥς, ὁ δ' ἀκρατὴς ἑκὼν βλάπτει αὐτὸς αὑτόν,
ἑκών τ' ἂν ἀδικοῖτο καὶ ἐνδέχοιτο αὐτὸν αὑτὸν ἀδικεῖν.
ἔστι δὲ καὶ τοῦτο ἕν τι τῶν ἀπορουμένων, εἰ ἐνδέχεται
αὐτὸν αὑτὸν ἀδικεῖν. ἔτι ἑκὼν ἄν τις δι' ἀκρασίαν ὑπ' 5
ἄλλου βλάπτοιτο ἑκόντος, ὥστ' εἴη ἂν ἑκόντ' ἀδικεῖσθαι. ἢ
οὐκ ὀρθὸς ὁ διορισμός, ἀλλὰ προσθετέον τῷ βλάπτειν
εἰδότα καὶ ὃν καὶ ᾧ καὶ ὥς τὸ παρὰ τὴν ἐκείνου βούλησιν;
βλάπτεται μὲν οὖν τις ἑκὼν καὶ τἄδικα πάσχει, ἀδικεῖται 6
δ' οὐθεὶς ἑκών· οὐθεὶς γὰρ βούλεται, οὐδ' ὁ ἀκρατής, ἀλλὰ
παρὰ τὴν βούλησιν πράττει· οὔτε γὰρ βούλεται οὐθεὶς ὃ
μὴ οἴεται εἶναι σπουδαῖον, ὅ τε ἀκρατὴς οὐχ ἃ οἴεται δεῖν
πράττειν πράττει. ὁ δὲ τὰ αὑτοῦ διδούς, ὥσπερ Ὅμηρός 7
φησι δοῦναι τὸν Γλαῦκον τῷ Διομήδει

χρύσεα χαλκείων, ἑκατόμβοι' ἐννεαβοίων,

---

one is injured willingly. For no one wishes (harm), nor does the incontinent man, but he acts against his wish. For no one wishes for what he does not think to be good, and the incontinent man does not do what he thinks to be good.'

4 ἑκών] is opposed to κατὰ πρόθεσιν as implied in προσθετέον. Cf. VII. iv. 2—3.

τὸ βλάπτειν] Harm does not constitute injustice without a violation of the will. Cf. Ar. *Rhet.* I. xiii. 6: ἀνάγκη τὸν ἀδικούμενον βλάπτεσθαι, καὶ ἀκουσίως βλάπτεσθαι.

ὁ δ' ἀκρατὴς] The incontinent man may harm himself, or be led into ruin by others. The phenomena of incontinence appear to have constantly occupied the attention of Eudemus. They not only form the main subject of *Eth.* Book VII. (*Eth. Eud.* VI.), but they are also mixed up with the discussion on the voluntary, *Eth. Eud.* II. viii.

6 οὔτε γὰρ βούλεται κ.τ.λ.] In his inmost self every one wishes for what he thinks good. Thus the incontinent man, following his desire, acts against his own real wish. This is the same point of view as is taken in the *Gorgias* of Plato (p. 466 sqq.). It is rather different from that in *Eth.* III. ch. iv. (on which see notes), though the word οἴεται prevents an absolute collision. The terms παρὰ τὴν βούλησιν are rather awkwardly introduced in the text, for it is said they are necessary to turn mere harm into injustice, but with regard to the incontinent man, while acting voluntarily he receives 'harm—against his wish.' Yet he is not injured voluntarily, because the terms 'against his wish' constitute him an involuntary agent. In short, in this case παρὰ τὴν βούλησιν is made to qualify, not the harm, but the voluntariness of the recipient. There is a slight confusion in the expression, but on the whole the tendency here is to attribute a less degree of voluntariness to weak and foolish acts than was done by Aristotle in his discussions on the voluntary; *Eth.* III. i. 14, &c.

οὐκ ἀδικεῖται· ἐπ' αὐτῷ γάρ ἐστι τὸ διδόναι, τὸ δ' ἀδικεῖσθαι οὐκ ἐπ' αὐτῷ, ἀλλὰ τὸν ἀδικοῦντα δεῖ ὑπάρχειν.
8 περὶ μὲν οὖν τοῦ ἀδικεῖσθαι, ὅτι οὐχ ἑκούσιον, δῆλον.
Ἔτι δ' ὧν προειλόμεθα δύ' ἔστιν εἰπεῖν, πότερόν ποτ'
ἀδικεῖ ὁ νείμας παρὰ τὴν ἀξίαν τὸ πλεῖον ἢ ὁ ἔχων, καὶ εἰ
9 ἔστιν αὐτὸν αὑτὸν ἀδικεῖν· εἰ γὰρ ἐνδέχεται τὸ πρότερον
λεχθὲν καὶ ὁ διανέμων ἀδικεῖ ἀλλ' οὐχ ὁ ἔχων τὸ πλέον, εἴ
τις πλέον ἑτέρῳ ἢ αὑτῷ νέμει εἰδὼς καὶ ἑκών, οὗτος αὐτὸς
αὑτὸν ἀδικεῖ. ὅπερ δοκοῦσιν οἱ μέτριοι ποιεῖν· ὁ γὰρ
ἐπιεικὴς ἐλαττωτικός ἐστιν. ἢ οὐδὲ τοῦτο ἁπλοῦν; ἑτέρου
γὰρ ἀγαθοῦ, εἰ ἔτυχεν, ἐπλεονέκτει, οἷον δόξης ἢ τοῦ ἁπλῶς
καλοῦ. ἔτι λύεται καὶ κατὰ τὸν διορισμὸν τοῦ ἀδικεῖν·
οὐδὲν γὰρ παρὰ τὴν αὑτοῦ πάσχει βούλησιν, ὥστε οὐκ
ἀδικεῖται διά γε τοῦτο, ἀλλ' εἴπερ, βλάπτεται μόνον.
10 φανερὸν δὲ καὶ ὅτι ὁ διανέμων ἀδικεῖ, ἀλλ' οὐχ ὁ τὸ πλέον
ἔχων ἀεί· οὐ γὰρ ᾧ τὸ ἄδικον ὑπάρχει ἀδικεῖ, ἀλλ' ᾧ τὸ
ἑκόντα τοῦτο ποιεῖν· τοῦτο δ' ὅθεν ἡ ἀρχὴ τῆς πράξεως, ἥ
11 ἐστιν ἐν τῷ διανέμοντι ἀλλ' οὐκ ἐν τῷ λαμβάνοντι. ἔτι
ἐπεὶ πολλαχῶς τὸ ποιεῖν λέγεται, καὶ ἔστιν ὡς τὰ ἄψυχα
κτείνει καὶ ἡ χεὶρ καὶ ὁ οἰκέτης ἐπιτάξαντος, οὐκ ἀδικεῖ
12 μέν, ποιεῖ δὲ τὰ ἄδικα. ἔτι εἰ μὲν ἀγνοῶν ἔκρινεν, οὐκ
ἀδικεῖ κατὰ τὸ νομικὸν δίκαιον οὐδ' ἄδικος ἡ κρίσις ἐστίν,
ἔστι δ' ὡς ἄδικος· ἕτερον γὰρ τὸ νομικὸν δίκαιον καὶ τὸ
πρῶτον· εἰ δὲ γινώσκων ἔκρινεν ἀδίκως, πλεονεκτεῖ καὶ

8—13 *ἔτι δ' ὧν προειλόμεθα δύ' ἔστιν εἰπεῖν*] 'But of the questions which we determined on there remain two to discuss,' namely, (1) whether the distributor of an unjust distribution does the wrong, or he who gains by it? (2) Can a man injure himself, as for instance by taking less than his share? These questions are as good as answered already; it is already clear that no one can injure himself. Again the act belongs to the distributor and not to the receiver. If the distributor acts from corrupt motives he is unjust, if unconsciously and by accident he is not unjust, though justice may have been violated by his decision.

11—12 *ἔτι ἐπεὶ—πρῶτον*] 'Again, as the word *doing* is used in more senses than one, and there is a sense in which inanimate things kill—or one's hand—or the slave who does his master's bidding—so the distributor may be the instrument of doing injustice, without himself injuring. Again, if he decided in ignorance, in the eye of the law he is not guilty of injuring, nor is his decision unjust, though from another point of view it is unjust, for justice according to law is distinct from abstract justice.' The

αὐτὸς ἢ χάριτος ἢ τιμωρίας. ὥσπερ οὖν κἂν εἴ τις μερί- 13
σαιτο τοῦ ἀδικήματος, καὶ ὁ διὰ ταῦτα κρίνας ἀδίκως
πλέον ἔχει· καὶ γὰρ ἐπ' ἐκείνων ὁ τὸν ἀγρὸν κρίνας οὐκ
ἀγρὸν ἀλλ' ἀργύριον ἔλαβεν. οἱ δ' ἄνθρωποι ἐφ' ἑαυτοῖς 14
οἴονται εἶναι τὸ ἀδικεῖν, διὸ καὶ τὸ δίκαιον εἶναι ῥᾴδιον.
τὸ δ' οὐκ ἔστιν· συγγενέσθαι μὲν γὰρ τῇ τοῦ γείτονος καὶ
πατάξαι τὸν πλησίον καὶ δοῦναι τῇ χειρὶ τὸ ἀργύριον
ῥᾴδιον καὶ ἐπ' αὐτοῖς, ἀλλὰ τὸ ὡδὶ ἔχοντας ταῦτα ποιεῖν
οὔτε ῥᾴδιον οὔτ' ἐπ' αὐτοῖς. ὁμοίως δὲ καὶ τὸ γνῶναι τὰ 15
δίκαια καὶ τὰ ἄδικα οὐδὲν οἴονται σοφὸν εἶναι, ὅτι περὶ ὧν
οἱ νόμοι λέγουσιν οὐ χαλεπὸν συνιέναι. ἀλλ' οὐ ταῦτ'
ἐστὶ τὰ δίκαια ἀλλ' ἢ κατὰ συμβεβηκός, ἀλλὰ πῶς πραττόμενα καὶ πῶς νεμόμενα δίκαια· τοῦτο δὲ πλέον ἔργον ἢ
τὰ ὑγιεινὰ εἰδέναι, ἐπεὶ κἀκεῖ μέλι καὶ οἶνον καὶ ἐλλέβορον
καὶ καῦσιν καὶ τομὴν εἰδέναι ῥᾴδιον, ἀλλὰ πῶς δεῖ νεῖμαι
πρὸς ὑγίειαν καὶ τίνι καὶ πότε, τοσοῦτον ἔργον ὅσον ἰατρὸν
εἶναι. δι' αὐτὸ δὲ τοῦτο καὶ τοῦ δικαίου οἴονται εἶναι οὐθὲν 16
ἧττον τὸ ἀδικεῖν, ὅτι οὐθὲν ἧττον ὁ δίκαιος ἀλλὰ καὶ μᾶλλον
δύναιτ' ἂν ἕκαστον πρᾶξαι τούτων· καὶ γὰρ συγγενέσθαι

---

first case supposes the distributor to act as the instrument of others, the second that he makes a mistake through ignorance. In the latter case abstract justice (τὸ πρῶτον δίκαιον) is violated, and yet legally (κατὰ τὸ νομικόν) no injustice can be complained of. πρῶτον here appears used analogously to πρώτη φιλοσοφία, πρώτη ὕλη, &c., to denote that which is most real and necessary, and also most abstract as being most removed from individual modifications. The Paraphrast and many of the commentators understand § 11 to refer to the receiver, not to the distributor. It might also be taken in a quite general sense, as applying to all such subservient acts. But it seems simplest to refer it to the distributor.

14—17 These sections contain remarks concluding the subject of justice. As they correct popular errors regarding its nature, they may be considered a continuation of the ἀπορίαι, with which the chapter commenced. The views which are here combated are, (1) a shallow and external notion about justice and injustice as if they merely consisted in outward acts; (2) a sophistical opinion that to know justice merely consists in knowing the details of the laws, cf. *Eth.* x. ix. 20; (3) an opinion that justice implies its contrary, as if it were an art (δύναμις); see above ch. i. § 4. This opinion would be a consequence of the Socratic doctrine that justice is knowledge. Plato saw what this doctrine led to and drew out the paradoxical conclusion, *Repub.* p. 334 A, *Hipp. Min.* pp. 375—6. The Aristotelian theory that justice is a moral state (ἕξις) set the difficulty at rest.

γυναικὶ καὶ πατάξαι, καὶ ὁ ἀνδρεῖος τὴν ἀσπίδα ἀφεῖναι καὶ στραφεὶς ἐφ' ὁποτεραοῦν τρέχειν. ἀλλὰ τὸ δειλαίνειν καὶ τὸ ἀδικεῖν οὐ τὸ ταῦτα ποιεῖν ἐστί, πλὴν κατὰ συμβεβηκός, ἀλλὰ τὸ ὡδὶ ἔχοντα ταῦτα ποιεῖν, ὥσπερ καὶ τὸ ἰατρεύειν καὶ τὸ ὑγιάζειν οὐ τὸ τέμνειν ἢ μὴ τέμνειν ἢ
17 φαρμακεύειν ἢ μὴ φαρμακεύειν ἐστίν, ἀλλὰ τὸ ὡδί. ἔστι δὲ τὰ δίκαια ἐν τούτοις οἷς μέτεστι τῶν ἁπλῶς ἀγαθῶν, ἔχουσι δ' ὑπερβολὴν ἐν τούτοις καὶ ἔλλειψιν· τοῖς μὲν γὰρ οὐκ ἔστιν ὑπερβολὴ αὐτῶν, οἷον ἴσως τοῖς θεοῖς, τοῖς δ' οὐθὲν μόριον ὠφέλιμον, τοῖς ἀνιάτως κακοῖς, ἀλλὰ πάντα βλάπτει, τοῖς δὲ μέχρι του· διὰ τοῦτ' ἀνθρώπινόν ἐστιν.

10 Περὶ δὲ ἐπιεικείας καὶ τοῦ ἐπιεικοῦς, πῶς ἔχει ἡ μὲν ἐπιείκεια πρὸς δικαιοσύνην τὸ δ' ἐπιεικὲς πρὸς τὸ δίκαιον,

---

17 *ἔστι δὲ — ἐστιν*] 'Now the relations of justice exist between those who share in what are commonly called goods, but with regard to them can have both too much and too little. For some cannot have too much, as perhaps the gods; and to others again no portion is advantageous, but all is hurtful—I mean the utterly bad; while there is a class who can receive goods up to a certain point. Hence justice is human.' Two ideal states, one of the absolutely good, the other of the absolutely bad, are here depicted in contrast to the condition of human society. The idea of property cannot of course be connected with God (cf. *Eth.* x. viii. 7), who has and is all good (cf. *Eth.* i. vi. 3, ix. iv. 4); nor again with those who are so degraded that they could not receive any benefit at all from what are called goods (cf. ch. i. § 9). The passage is a curious one, and may remind us of the position assigned by Aristotle (cf. *Pol.* i. ii. 14) to man in his social condition, as something between the beast and the god.

X. Some account of equity (*ἐπιείκεια*) forms a suitable complement to the theory of justice, and we find the subject so treated in Aristotle's *Rhetoric*, i. xiii., from which it is not improbable that the present chapter may be partly borrowed. Professor Spengel is mistaken in saying that this chapter is out of place, being introduced into the midst of the *ἀπορίαι* on justice. Evidently it is chapter xi., and not chapter x., that is out of place. Spengel thinks that the words *περὶ δὲ ἐπιεικείας* would come in well after the words *τίνα μὲν οὖν ἔχει τὸ ἀντιπεπονθὸς πρὸς τὸ δίκαιον, εἴρηται πρότερον* (which occur ch. vi. § 3), as if first retaliation and then equity should be discussed in relation to justice. But it is evident that they stand on a different footing, as treated in this book. Retaliation is a principle existing *in* justice and with certain modifications constituting it; equity is something outside justice and correcting it.

Ἐπιείκεια has a close connexion with what is called *γνώμη* (consideration), *Eth.* vi. xi. 1, cf. *Rhet.* i. xiii. And thus it is treated of by the author of the *Magna Moralia* amongst the intel-

ἐχόμενόν ἐστιν εἰπεῖν· οὔτε γὰρ ὡς ταὐτὸν ἁπλῶς οὔθ' ὡς ἕτερον τῷ γένει φαίνεται σκοπουμένοις, καὶ ὁτὲ μὲν τὸ ἐπιεικὲς ἐπαινοῦμεν καὶ ἄνδρα τὸν τοιοῦτον, ὥστε καὶ ἐπὶ τὰ ἄλλα ἐπαινοῦντες μεταφέρομεν ἀντὶ τοῦ ἀγαθοῦ, τὸ ἐπιεικέστερον ὅτι βέλτιον δηλοῦντες· ὁτὲ δὲ τῷ λόγῳ ἀκολουθοῦσι φαίνεται ἄτοπον εἰ τὸ ἐπιεικὲς παρὰ τὸ δίκαιόν τι ὂν ἐπαινετόν ἐστιν· ἢ γὰρ τὸ δίκαιον οὐ σπουδαῖον, ἢ τὸ ἐπιεικὲς οὐ δίκαιον, εἰ ἄλλο· ἢ εἰ ἄμφω σπουδαῖα, ταὐτόν ἐστιν. ἡ μὲν οὖν ἀπορία σχεδὸν συμβαίνει 2
διὰ ταῦτα περὶ τὸ ἐπιεικές, ἔχει δ' ἅπαντα τρόπον τινὰ ὀρθῶς καὶ οὐθὲν ὑπεναντίον ἑαυτοῖς· τό τε γὰρ ἐπιεικὲς

---

lectual qualities, and is coupled with what he calls *εὐγνωμοσύνη*, *Magna Moralia*, II. i. 1, sqq.

To us the contents of this chapter appear natural and easy to apprehend. The idea of equity as the complement of law and justice is to us perfectly familiar, but the writer saw a difficulty in saying how logically (*τῷ λόγῳ ἀκολουθοῦσι*) equity could be praised if it contradicted justice. The answer is well given above, that equity is a higher and finer kind of justice coming in where the law was too coarse and general. The best illustration of this conception is to be found in the beautiful description given in *Rhet.* I. xiii. 'It is equity to pardon human failings, and to look to the lawgiver and not to the law; to the spirit and not to the letter; to the intention and not to the action; to the whole and not to the part; to the character of the actor in the long run and not in the present moment; to remember good rather than evil, and good that one has received, rather than good that one has done; to bear being injured (*τὸ ἀνέχεσθαι ἀδικούμενον*); to wish to settle a matter by words rather than by deeds; lastly, to prefer arbitration to judgment, for the arbitrator sees what is equitable, but the judge only the law, and for this an arbitrator was first appointed, in order that equity might flourish.'

1 *ὁτὲ μὲν—ἀγαθοῦ*] 'Sometimes we praise what is equitable and the equitable character in such a way, that we transfer the term and use it instead of the term good in praising people for all other qualities besides.' The word *ἐπιεικής* is constantly used merely in the sense of 'good,' cf. *Eth.* IV. ix. 7, *ἐξ ὑποθέσεως ἐπιεικές*, and above, ch. iv. § 3, &c., but it is a mistake to consider this the *later* sense of the word, as if 'equitable' were the primary sense. 'Ἐπιεικής (from εἰκός) first means 'customary,' as in Homer; then 'seemly,' then 'good' in general; afterwards it is probable that an association of *εἴκω*, 'to yield,' became connected with the word, and hence the notion of moderation and of waiving one's rights arose, and *τὸ ἐπιεικές* was constantly contrasted with *τὸ δίκαιον*. Thus in Herod. III. 53: *πολλοὶ τῶν δικαίων τὰ ἐπιεικέστερα προτιθεῖσι*. Cf. Plato, *Laws*, p. 757 D: *τὸ γὰρ ἐπιεικὲς καὶ ξύγγνωμον τοῦ τελέου καὶ ἀκριβοῦς παρὰ δίκην τὴν ὀρθήν ἐστι παρατεθραυσμένον*, &c. Out of this contrast the idea of equity was developed.

δικαίου τινὸς ὂν βέλτιόν ἐστι δίκαιον, καὶ οὐχ ὡς ἄλλο τι γένος ὂν βέλτιόν ἐστι τοῦ δικαίου. ταὐτὸν ἄρα δίκαιον καὶ ἐπιεικές, καὶ ἀμφοῖν σπουδαίοιν ὄντοιν κρεῖττον τὸ ἐπιεικές.
3 ποιεῖ δὲ τὴν ἀπορίαν ὅτι τὸ ἐπιεικὲς δίκαιον μέν ἐστιν, οὐ τὸ κατὰ νόμον δέ, ἀλλ' ἐπανόρθωμα νομίμου δικαίου.
4 αἴτιον δ' ὅτι ὁ μὲν νόμος καθόλου πᾶς, περὶ ἐνίων δ' οὐχ οἷόν τε ὀρθῶς εἰπεῖν καθόλου. ἐν οἷς οὖν ἀνάγκη μὲν εἰπεῖν καθόλου, μὴ οἷόν τε δὲ ὀρθῶς, τὸ ὡς ἐπὶ τὸ πλέον λαμβάνει ὁ νόμος, οὐκ ἀγνοῶν τὸ ἁμαρτανόμενον· καὶ ἔστιν οὐδὲν ἧττον ὀρθῶς· τὸ γὰρ ἁμάρτημα οὐκ ἐν τῷ νόμῳ οὐδ' ἐν τῷ νομοθέτῃ ἀλλ' ἐν τῇ φύσει τοῦ πράγματός
5 ἐστιν· εὐθὺς γὰρ τοιαύτη ἡ τῶν πρακτῶν ὕλη ἐστίν. ὅταν οὖν λέγῃ μὲν ὁ νόμος καθόλου, συμβῇ δ' ἐπὶ τούτου παρὰ τὸ καθόλου, τότε ὀρθῶς ἔχει, ᾗ παραλείπει ὁ νομοθέτης καὶ ἥμαρτεν ἁπλῶς εἰπών, ἐπανορθοῦν τὸ ἐλλειφθέν, ὃ κἂν ὁ νομοθέτης αὐτὸς οὕτως ἂν εἴποι ἐκεῖ παρών, καὶ εἰ ᾔδει,
6 ἐνομοθέτησεν ἄν. διὸ δίκαιον μέν ἐστι, καὶ βέλτιόν τινος δικαίου, οὐ τοῦ ἁπλῶς δὲ ἀλλὰ τοῦ διὰ τὸ ἁπλῶς ἁμαρτήματος. καὶ ἔστιν αὕτη ἡ φύσις ἡ τοῦ ἐπιεικοῦς, ἐπανόρθωμα νόμου, ᾗ ἐλλείπει διὰ τὸ καθόλου. τοῦτο γὰρ αἴτιον καὶ τοῦ μὴ πάντα κατὰ νόμον εἶναι, ὅτι περὶ ἐνίων
7 ἀδύνατον θέσθαι νόμον, ὥστε ψηφίσματος δεῖ. τοῦ γὰρ ἀορίστου ἀόριστος καὶ ὁ κανών ἐστιν, ὥσπερ καὶ τῆς Λεσβίας οἰκοδομῆς ὁ μολίβδινος κανών· πρὸς γὰρ τὸ σχῆμα τοῦ λίθου μετακινεῖται καὶ οὐ μένει ὁ κανών, καὶ τὸ ψή-
8 φισμα πρὸς τὰ πράγματα. τί μὲν οὖν ἐστὶ τὸ ἐπιεικές,

4 περὶ ἐνίων δ' οὐχ οἷόν τε κ.τ.λ.] That law is necessarily imperfect and unable to cope with details, Aristotle constantly admits, cf. *Polit.* III. xi. 19: περὶ ὅσων ἐξαδυνατοῦσιν οἱ νόμοι λέγειν ἀκριβῶς διὰ τὸ μὴ ῥᾴδιον εἶναι καθόλου περὶ πάντων. *Pol.* II. viii. 23: ἐατέον ἐνίας ἁμαρτίας καὶ τῶν νομοθετῶν. *Pol.* III. xv. 9: μηθὲν παρὰ τὸν νόμον πράττοντες, ἀλλ' ἢ περὶ ὧν ἐκλείπειν ἀναγκαῖον αὐτόν.

6 ὥστε ψηφίσματος δεῖ] 'There are some cases for which it is impossible to legislate, you require a special decree to meet them.' The ψήφισμα, like the exercise of equity, was a remedy to make up the insufficiency of laws. On its special character, cf ch. vii. § 1, and *Eth.* VI. viii. 2, see also Arnold on Thucyd. III. 36.

7 τοῦ γὰρ—πράγματα] 'For the rule for what is indefinite must be itself indefinite, like the leaden rule in the Lesbian architecture—the rule is not fixed, but shifts itself according to the shape of the stone, and so does

καὶ ὅτι δίκαιον, καὶ τίνος βέλτιον δικαίου, δῆλον. Φανερὸν δ' ἐκ τούτου καὶ ὁ ἐπιεικὴς τίς ἐστιν· ὁ γὰρ τῶν τοιούτων προαιρετικὸς καὶ πρακτικός, καὶ ὁ μὴ ἀκριβοδίκαιος ἐπὶ τὸ χεῖρον ἀλλ' ἐλαττωτικός, καίπερ ἔχων τὸν νόμον βοηθόν, ἐπιεικής ἐστι, καὶ ἡ ἕξις αὕτη ἐπιείκεια, δικαιοσύνη τις οὖσα καὶ οὐχ ἑτέρα τις ἕξις.

Πότερον δ' ἐνδέχεται ἑαυτὸν ἀδικεῖν ἢ οὔ, φανερὸν ἐκ 11
τῶν εἰρημένων· τὰ μὲν γάρ ἐστι τῶν δικαίων τὰ κατὰ
πᾶσαν ἀρετὴν ὑπὸ τοῦ νόμου τεταγμένα, οἷον οὐ κελεύει
ἀποκτιννύναι ἑαυτὸν ὁ νόμος, ἃ δὲ μὴ κελεύει, ἀπαγορεύει·
ἔτι ὅταν παρὰ τὸν νόμον βλάπτῃ μὴ ἀντιβλάπτων, ἑκὼν 2
ἀδικεῖ, ἑκὼν δὲ ὁ εἰδὼς καὶ ὃν καὶ ᾧ. ὁ δὲ δι' ὀργὴν ἑαυτὸν
σφάττων ἑκὼν τοῦτο δρᾷ παρὰ τὸν ὀρθὸν λόγον, ὃ οὐκ ἐᾷ ὁ
νόμος· ἀδικεῖ ἄρα. ἀλλὰ τίνα; ἢ τὴν πόλιν, αὑτὸν δ' οὔ; 3
ἑκὼν γὰρ πάσχει, ἀδικεῖται δ' οὐδεὶς ἑκών. διὸ καὶ ἡ
πόλις ζημιοῖ, καί τις ἀτιμία πρόσεστι τῷ ἑαυτὸν διαφθείραντι ὡς τὴν πόλιν ἀδικοῦντι. ἔτι καθ' ὃ ἄδικος, ὁ μόνον 4

---

the decree according to the nature of the case.' 'Lesbian architecture' appears to have been a kind of Cyclopian masonry, which may have remained in Lesbos from the early Pelasgian occupiers of the island. Polygon stones were used in it, which could not be measured by a straight rule, cf. *Æsch. Fragm.* 70,

ἀλλ' ὁ μέν τις Λέσβιος
κῦμ' ἐν τριγώνοις ἐκπεραινέτω ῥυθμοῖς,

where κῦμα means a waved moulding.

XI. This chapter, which is merely an instance of Eudemian mal-arrangement, starts by discussing an already settled question, Can a man injure himself? Amidst the somewhat feeble reasonings and the repetitions which it presents, it is not quite without interest in the view that is taken of suicide, §§ 2, 3, and in the saying that it is a mere metaphor to speak of justice between the higher and lower parts of a man.

1 ἐκ τῶν εἰρημένων] i.e. ch. i. §§ 12—20. The question is complicated by introducing a mention of universal justice (τὰ κατὰ πᾶσαν ἀρετήν), and the extraordinary assertion is made that 'whatever the law does not command it forbids.' We might well ask, Did the Athenian law command its citizens to breathe, to eat, to sleep, &c.?

2—3 The suicide sins against the state, not against himself. This is proved by the fact that the state affixes infamy to the dead. In *Æschines, Ctesiph.* p. 636, § 64, it is mentioned that the hand of a suicide was buried apart from himself. And in Plato's *Laws*, IX. p. 873 c. sqq., regulations are laid down for the burial of suicides. In the words ἀδικεῖ ἄρα, ἀλλὰ τίνα; there is a change of meaning from the intransitive ἀδικεῖν, to 'do wrong,' to the transitive verb to 'injure.'

ἀδικῶν καὶ μὴ ὅλως φαῦλος, οὐκ ἔστιν ἀδικῆσαι ἑαυτόν. τοῦτο γὰρ ἄλλο ἐκείνου. ἔστι γάρ πως ὁ ἄδικος οὕτω πονηρὸς ὥσπερ ὁ δειλός, οὐχ ὡς ὅλην ἔχων τὴν πονηρίαν, ὥστ᾽ οὐδὲ κατὰ ταύτην ἀδικεῖ· ἅμα γὰρ ἂν τῷ αὐτῷ εἴη ἀφῃρῆσθαι καὶ προσκεῖσθαι τὸ αὐτό· τοῦτο δὲ ἀδύνατον, ἀλλ᾽ ἀεὶ ἐν πλείοσιν ἀνάγκη εἶναι τὸ δίκαιον καὶ τὸ ἄδικον.
5 ἔτι δὲ ἑκούσιόν τε καὶ ἐκ προαιρέσεως καὶ πρότερον. ὁ γὰρ διότι ἔπαθε, καὶ τὸ αὐτὸ ἀντιποιῶν οὐ δοκεῖ ἀδικεῖν· αὐτὸς
6 δ᾽ ἑαυτόν, τὰ αὐτὰ ἅμα καὶ πάσχει καὶ ποιεῖ. ἔτι εἴη ἂν ἑκόντα ἀδικεῖσθαι. πρὸς δὲ τούτοις, ἄνευ τῶν κατὰ μέρος ἀδικημάτων οὐθεὶς ἀδικεῖ, μοιχεύει δ᾽ οὐδεὶς τὴν ἑαυτοῦ οὐδὲ τοιχωρυχεῖ τὸν ἑαυτοῦ τοῖχον οὐδὲ κλέπτει τὰ ἑαυτοῦ. ὅλως δὲ λύεται τὸ ἑαυτὸν ἀδικεῖν κατὰ τὸν διορισμὸν τὸν
7 περὶ τοῦ ἑκουσίως ἀδικεῖσθαι. φανερὸν δὲ καὶ ὅτι ἄμφω μὲν φαῦλα, καὶ τὸ ἀδικεῖσθαι καὶ τὸ ἀδικεῖν· τὸ μὲν γὰρ ἔλαττον τὸ δὲ πλέον ἔχειν ἐστὶ τοῦ μέσου καὶ ὥσπερ ὑγιεινὸν μὲν ἐν ἰατρικῇ, εὐεκτικὸν δὲ ἐν γυμναστικῇ· ἀλλ᾽ ὅμως χεῖρον τὸ ἀδικεῖν· τὸ μὲν γὰρ ἀδικεῖν μετὰ κακίας

---

4 ἅμα γὰρ— ἄδικον] 'For it would be thus possible for the same thing to be gained and lost by the same person; but this is not possible, justice and injustice must always take place between more persons than one,' cf. ch. iii. § 4.

6 ὅλως δὲ λύεται κ.τ.λ.] A verbal repetition of what was said above, ch. ix. § 9.

7—9 The chapter ends by touching upon two points which have an apparent reference to Plato, (1) the assertion that to injure is worse than to be injured, which the writer here qualifies with a consideration; (2) the conception of justice existing between the different parts in the mind of an individual, which is here pronounced to be a metaphor.

καὶ ὥσπερ—γυμναστικῇ] This sentence is parenthetical and elliptic. The train of thought appears to be: 'Injuring and being injured are both bad, they are both departures from the mean, and it is (with justice) as with health in medicine and good condition in training,' namely, it is a state of balance between excess and defect, cf. *Eth.* II. ii. 6.

ἀλλ᾽ ὅμως χεῖρον τὸ ἀδικεῖν] This is exactly the point which is urged by Socrates in the *Gorgias* of Plato (p. 473 A. 509 C), and seems to his hearers a paradox. It is qualified above by the admission that being injured might be in its consequences (*κατὰ συμβεβηκός*) a worse evil than injuring; just as a stumble might cause a man's death, and so be accidentally worse than a pleurisy. Is it then worse to be ruined by the cheating of others, or to cheat some one of a sixpence? The writer above acknowledges that moral science will maintain the severity of its verdict, and say cheating is the worse (*ἀλλ᾽ οὐδὲν μέλει τῇ τέχνῃ κ.τ.λ.*). Of

καὶ ψεκτόν, καὶ κακίας ἢ τῆς τελείας καὶ ἁπλῶς ἢ ἐγγύς
(οὐ γὰρ ἅπαν τὸ ἑκούσιον μετὰ ἀδικίας), τὸ δ᾽ ἀδικεῖσθαι
ἄνευ κακίας καὶ ἀδικίας. καθ᾽ αὑτὸ μὲν οὖν τὸ ἀδικεῖσθαι 8
ἧττον φαῦλον, κατὰ συμβεβηκὸς δ᾽ οὐθὲν κωλύει μεῖζον
εἶναι κακόν. ἀλλ᾽ οὐδὲν μέλει τῇ τέχνῃ, ἀλλὰ πλευρῖτιν
λέγει μείζω νόσον προσπταίσματος· καίτοι γένοιτ᾽ ἄν
ποτε θάτερον κατὰ συμβεβηκός, εἰ προσπταίσαντα διὰ τὸ
πεσεῖν συμβαίη ὑπὸ τῶν πολεμίων ληφθῆναι καὶ ἀποθανεῖν.
κατὰ μεταφορὰν δὲ καὶ ὁμοιότητά ἐστιν οὐκ αὐτῷ πρὸς 9
αὑτὸν δίκαιον ἀλλὰ τῶν αὐτοῦ τισίν, οὐ πᾶν δὲ δίκαιον
ἀλλὰ τὸ δεσποτικὸν ἢ τὸ οἰκονομικόν· ἐν τούτοις γὰρ τοῖς
λόγοις διέστηκε τὸ λόγον ἔχον μέρος τῆς ψυχῆς πρὸς τὸ
ἄλογον. εἰς ἃ δὴ βλέπουσι καὶ δοκεῖ εἶναι ἀδικία πρὸς
αὑτόν, ὅτι ἐν τούτοις ἔστι πάσχειν τι παρὰ τὰς ἑαυτῶν
ὀρέξεις· ὥσπερ οὖν ἄρχοντι καὶ ἀρχομένῳ εἶναι πρὸς ἄλληλα δίκαιόν τι καὶ τούτοις. περὶ μὲν οὖν δικαιοσύνης καὶ 10
τῶν ἄλλων τῶν ἠθικῶν ἀρετῶν διωρίσθω τὸν τρόπον
τοῦτον.

---

course being depraved in mind is the worst of all evils. It is not this (*ἄδικον εἶναι*), but a single act of wrong (*τὸ ἀδικεῖν*), that will bear comparison with the evil of being injured.

9 *κατὰ μεταφορὰν δὲ—τούτοις*] 'Now metaphorically and by analogy one is capable of justice, not towards one's own self, but towards certain parts of oneself, not every kind of justice, but despotic or household justice. For in the theories alluded to there is a separation made between the reasonable and unreasonable part of man's nature. Regarding this, people consider that one can have injustice towards oneself, because these separate parts may be made to suffer a contradiction of their respective inclinations; so then, like ruler and ruled, they have a sort of justice among each other.'

ἐν τούτοις γὰρ τοῖς λόγοις] It can hardly be doubted that there is a reference here to Plato, *Repub.* p. 441 A, 443 D, 432 A, &c. To deny the appropriateness of the term 'justice' to express a harmony between the different parts of man's nature is unlike the point of view taken *Eth.* IX. c. iv., where the friendship which the good man has with himself is described at length. Eudemus, however, was much busied with problems as to the unity of the will, and probably advanced to some extent the Peripatetic psychology.

PLAN OF BOOK VI.

TURNING to the contents of this Sixth Book, we see at once that it includes two subjects, and that the intermixture of these two has given rise to some little confusion. The questions are (1) What is the moral standard? (2) What are the intellectual ἀρεταί?

Commencing with the former question, the writer goes off into the latter. And thus Thought (φρόνησις) is treated of at some length as a perfection of the moral intellect, but is hardly touched upon with regard to its operation as the moral standard.

After the two above-mentioned questions have been proposed, without any statement of their connexion, the discussion of the intellectual ἀρεταί commences by a division of the reason into scientific and calculative. Ch. I.

Truth is the object of both, but truth is divided into practical and speculative. The former enters into and becomes an element in the decisions of the will. Ch. II.

Truth of whatever kind is attained by only five organs of the mind—Science, Art, Thought, Reason, and Philosophy. These then are severally discussed; and Philosophy, after being treated independently, has Thought brought in again in contrast to itself. Ch. III.—VII.

The relation of Thought to Economy and Politics is then discussed. Ch. VIII.

Prudence (εὐβουλία), Apprehension (σύνεσις), and Considerateness (γνώμη), as being component elements of Thought, are severally treated of, and some remarks are added on the natural and intuitive character of these practical qualities. Ch. IX.—XI.

The book ends by the statement and solution of difficulties with regard to Thought and Philosophy, their respective *use*, and their relation to each other in point of superiority.

With regard to the *use* of Thought some important though not very clear remarks are made on its inseparable connexion with Virtue. Though inseparable, it is not, however, identical with Virtue, as Socrates wrongly asserted. In relation to Philosophy, Thought is concerned with the means, while Philosophy is concerned with the end. Ch. XII.—XIII.

The upshot of the book, then, is, that it treats of the intellectual *ἀρεταί*. There are two—not *five*, as some would say, reckoning as such the five organs of truth, nor again an indefinite number, as Aristotle would seem to say, admitting 'Apprehension,' &c. (*Eth.* I. xiii. 20); but two essentially, Philosophy and Thought. These are contrasted with each other, but in such a way that Thought, though the least excellent, is brought into prominence, and is the real theme of the book. With all the discrepancies of statement which are apparent between different passages in this book, 'Thought' comes out in its general outlines as the perfection of the practical reason combined with the will; as inseparable, if distinguishable, from Virtue itself. The picture of this quality and of its growth in the mind is made the occasion of many interesting remarks; but the question how the mind acts in determining the mean, and what is the nature of the moral standard, is left still unanswered.

For the term φρόνησις, as used in this book, it is not possible to find an exact equivalent in English. 'Prudence,' which is generally employed for this purpose, is not suitable; for φρόνησις, according to Platonic views, included the contemplation of absolute existence (see Vol. I. Essay III. p. 193). 'Thought' is the equivalent for φρόνησις in its general Greek sense, and it has been thought better, in the following notes, to take 'Thought' in a peculiar and technical sense to represent the peculiar and technical application of φρόνησις, which here occurs.

ΗΘΙΚΩΝ [ΕΥΔΗΜΙΩΝ] VI.

Ἐπεὶ δὲ τυγχάνομεν πρότερον εἰρηκότες ὅτι δεῖ τὸ μέσον αἱρεῖσθαι καὶ μὴ τὴν ὑπερβολὴν μηδὲ τὴν ἔλλειψιν, τὸ δὲ μέσον ἐστὶν ὡς ὁ λόγος ὁ ὀρθὸς λέγει, τοῦτο διέλωμεν. ἐν πάσαις γὰρ ταῖς εἰρημέναις ἕξεσι, καθάπερ καὶ ἐπὶ τῶν ἄλλων, ἔστι τις σκοπὸς πρὸς ὃν ἀποβλέπων ὁ τὸν λόγον ἔχων ἐπιτείνει καὶ ἀνίησιν, καί τις

I. This chapter states, though somewhat indefinitely, the question which is to be answered in the ensuing book. Referring back to a previous mention of 'the mean,' it proposes now to discuss 'the right law' by which the mean is determined. For only to know that action must be 'in the mean, and according to the right law,' is a mere blank formula which requires filling up (ἀληθὲς μέν, οὐθὲν δὲ σαφές). What then is the right law, and what is the standard of it (τίς τ' ἐστὶν ὁ ὀρθὸς λόγος καὶ τούτου τίς ὅρος)? In answering this question, the procedure must be to discuss the most perfect developments of the intellectual faculties, for by so doing we shall learn the proper function of each (ληπτέον ἄρ' ἑκατέρου τούτων τίς ἡ βελτίστη ἕξις· αὕτη γὰρ ἀρετὴ ἑκατέρου, ἡ δ' ἀρετὴ πρὸς τὸ ἔργον τὸ οἰκεῖον). As the inner nature of man was before divided into two parts, the rational and irrational, so we may now subdivide the rational part into two elements, the scientific and the calculative, in accordance with the two classes of objects which are presented to the mind, and which we may conclude are dealt with by separate faculties, namely, the permanent, which is dealt with by the scientific element in us, and the contingent, which is the object of calculation or deliberation.

1 ἐπεὶ δὲ τυγχάνομεν πρότερον εἰρηκότες] The reference is to *Eth. Eud.* II. v. 1: ἐπεὶ δ' ὑπόκειται ἀρετὴ εἶναι ἡ τοιαύτη ἕξις ἀφ' ἧς πρακτικοὶ τῶν βελτίστων καὶ καθ' ἣν ἄριστα διάκεινται περὶ τὸ βέλτιστον, βέλτιστον δὲ καὶ ἄριστον τὸ κατὰ τὸν ὀρθὸν λόγον, τοῦτο δ' ἐστὶ τὸ μέσον ὑπερβολῆς καὶ ἐλλείψεως τῆς πρὸς ἡμᾶς κ.τ.λ.

ἐν πάσαις γὰρ—λόγον] 'For in all the states of mind which we have described, as also in all others, there is a certain mark to which he who is in possession of "the law" (ὁ τὸν λόγον ἔχων) looks, and tightens or relaxes (the strings) accordingly, and there is a certain standard of those mean states which we say are between

ἐστὶν ὅρος τῶν μεσοτήτων, ἅς μεταξύ φαμεν εἶναι τῆς ὑπερβολῆς καὶ τῆς ἐλλείψεως, οὔσας κατὰ τὸν ὀρθὸν λόγον. ἔστι δὲ τὸ μὲν εἰπεῖν οὕτως ἀληθὲς μέν, οὐθὲν δὲ 2
σαφές· καὶ γὰρ ἐν ταῖς ἄλλαις ἐπιμελείαις, περὶ ὅσας ἐστὶν ἐπιστήμη, τοῦτ' ἀληθὲς μὲν εἰπεῖν, ὅτι οὔτε πλείω οὔτε ἐλάττω δεῖ πονεῖν οὐδὲ ῥᾳθυμεῖν, ἀλλὰ τὰ μέσα καὶ ὡς ὁ ὀρθὸς λόγος· τοῦτο δὲ μόνον ἔχων ἄν τις οὐθὲν ἂν εἰδείη πλέον, οἷον ποῖα δεῖ προσφέρεσθαι πρὸς τὸ σῶμα,

---

excess and deficiency, being in accordance with the right law.' Ἐπιτεῖναι καὶ ἀνεῖναι is a metaphor from tuning the strings of a lyre. Cf. Plato, *Lysis*, p. 209 B: καὶ ἐπειδάν, ὡς ἐγᾦμαι, τὴν λύραν λάβῃς, οὐ διακωλύουσί σε οὔθ' ὁ πατὴρ οὔθ' ἡ μήτηρ ἐπιτεῖναί τε καὶ ἀνεῖναι ἣν ἂν βούλῃ τῶν χορδῶν. *Phaedo*, p. 98 C: καὶ τὰ μὲν ὀστᾶ ἐστὶ στερεά, καὶ διαφυὰς ἔχει χωρὶς ἀπ' ἀλλήλων, τὰ δὲ νεῦρα οἷα ἐπιτείνεσθαι καὶ ἀνίεσθαι. This metaphor is not quite in accordance with that other metaphor of 'looking to the mark,' but in fact the term σκοπός seems to have become so regular a formula with Eudemus as to have lost its metaphorical association. By Aristotle σκοπός was used as a pure metaphor, the application of which was borrowed from Plato (cf. *Eth.* I. ii. 2, note). But in the writing of Eudemus it seems used as a scientific term equivalent to τέλος; cf. *Eth. Eud.* II. x. 20: ἐπεὶ δὲ βουλεύεται ἀεὶ ὁ βουλευόμενος ἕνεκά τινος, καὶ ἔστι σκοπός τις ἀεὶ τῷ βουλευομένῳ πρὸς ὃν σκοπεῖ τὸ συμφέρον, περὶ μὲν τοῦ τέλους οὐθεὶς βουλεύεται. *Ib.* II. xi. 2: λέγομεν δὲ προανακρούσαντες. Ἔστι γὰρ τὸν μὲν σκοπὸν ὀρθὸν εἶναι, ἐν δὲ τοῖς πρὸς τὸν σκοπὸν διαμαρτάνειν· ἔστι δὲ τὸν μὲν σκοπὸν ἡμαρτῆσθαι, τὰ δὲ πρὸς ἐκεῖνον περαίνοντα ὀρθῶς ἔχειν, καὶ μηδέτερον. The similar use of ὅρος by Eudemus is not found in *Eth. Nic.*, but appears borrowed from the mode of writing in the *Politics* of Aristotle (see Vol. I. Essay I. pp. 60—61). Cf. *Eth. Eud.* II. v. 8 (which is especially referred to in the present passage), τίς δ' ὁ ὀρθὸς λόγος καὶ πρὸς τίνα δεῖ ὅρον ἀποβλέποντας λέγειν τὸ μέσον, ὕστερον ἐπισκεπτέον. *Ib.* VIII. iii. 12: δεῖ τινὰ εἶναι ὅρον καὶ τῆς ἕξεως καὶ τῆς αἱρέσεως καὶ περὶ φυγῆς χρημάτων πλήθους καὶ ὀλιγότητος καὶ τῶν εὐτυχημάτων. *Ib.* VIII. iii. 15.

2 ἔστι δὲ σαφές] 'Now to say this is to say what is true enough, but not explicit.' This same expression, with the same illustration of the medical art, is repeated *Eth. Eud.* VIII. iii. 13: ἐν μὲν τοῖς πρότερον ἐλέχθη τὸ ὡς ὁ λόγος· τοῦτο δ' ἐστὶν ὥσπερ ἂν εἴ τις ἐν τοῖς περὶ τὴν τροφὴν εἴπειεν ὡς ἡ ἰατρικὴ καὶ ὁ λόγος ταύτης. τοῦτο δ' ἀληθὲς μέν, οὐ σαφὲς δέ. Cf. *Ib.* I. vi. 2: ἐκ γὰρ τῶν ἀληθῶς μὲν λεγομένων οὐ σαφῶς δὲ προϊοῦσιν ἔσται καὶ τὸ σαφῶς. In the present place there is an apparent protest against the indefiniteness and relativity of Aristotle's moral theory of 'the mean' and 'the law.' Eudemus does not seem (according to the statement here) content to give greater explicitness to the idea of the 'law' by the development of the idea of the wise man who is its impersonation. But he asks (separating σκοπός and ὅρος from the λόγος), 'What is the mark to which one possessing the law must

εἴ τις εἴπειεν ὅτι ὅσα ἡ ἰατρικὴ κελεύει καὶ ὡς ὁ ταύτην
3 ἔχων. διὸ δεῖ καὶ περὶ τὰς τῆς ψυχῆς ἕξεις μὴ μόνον
ἀληθὲς εἶναι τοῦτ' εἰρημένον, ἀλλὰ καὶ διωρισμένον τίς τ'
ἐστὶν ὁ ὀρθὸς λόγος καὶ τούτου τίς ὅρος.

4 Τὰς δὴ τῆς ψυχῆς ἀρετὰς διελόμενοι τὰς μὲν εἶναι τοῦ
ἤθους ἔφαμεν τὰς δὲ τῆς διανοίας. περὶ μὲν οὖν τῶν
ἠθικῶν διεληλύθαμεν, περὶ δὲ τῶν λοιπῶν, περὶ ψυχῆς
5 πρῶτον εἰπόντες, λέγωμεν οὕτως. πρότερον μὲν οὖν ἐλέχθη
δύ' εἶναι μέρη τῆς ψυχῆς, τό τε λόγον ἔχον καὶ τὸ ἄλογον·
νῦν δὲ περὶ τοῦ λόγον ἔχοντος τὸν αὐτὸν τρόπον διαιρετέον.
καὶ ὑποκείσθω δύο τὰ λόγον ἔχοντα, ἓν μὲν ᾧ θεωροῦμεν
τὰ τοιαῦτα τῶν ὄντων ὅσων αἱ ἀρχαὶ μὴ ἐνδέχονται ἄλλως

---

look?' What is the standard of the law? In reality these questions get no answer. They only cloud the subject by introducing a confusion of formulæ.

4 τὰς μὲν εἶναι τοῦ ἤθους ἔφαμεν] Cf. *Eth. Eud.* II. i. 18: ἀρετῆς δ' εἴδη δύο, ἡ μὲν ἠθικὴ ἡ δὲ διανοητική· ἐπαινοῦμεν γὰρ οὐ μόνον τοὺς δικαίους, ἀλλὰ καὶ τοὺς συνετοὺς καὶ τοὺς σοφούς.

5 πρότερον μὲν οὖν ἐλέχθη δύ' εἶναι] Cf. *Eth. Eud.* II. iv. 1: Εἰλημμένων δὲ τούτων, μετὰ ταῦτα λεκτέον ὅτι ἐπειδὴ δύο μέρη τῆς ψυχῆς καὶ αἱ ἀρεταὶ κατὰ ταῦτα διῄρηνται, καὶ αἱ μὲν τοῦ λόγον ἔχοντος διανοητικαί, ὧν ἔργον ἀλήθεια, ἢ περὶ τοῦ πῶς ἔχει ἢ περὶ γενέσεως, αἱ δὲ τοῦ ἀλόγου, ἔχοντος δ' ὄρεξιν.

καὶ ὑποκείσθω—αὐτοῖς] 'And let us suppose that the parts possessing reason are two, one by which we apprehend such existences as depend on necessary principles, and one by which we apprehend contingent matter, for to objects differing in genus there must be different members of the mind severally adapted, if it be true that these members obtain their knowledge by reason of a certain resemblance to and affinity with the object of knowledge.' We have here a division of the mind in accordance with a division of the objects of which the mind is cognizant. And as a justification of this we have the assumption that knowledge implies a resemblance and affinity between object and subject. With regard to this, Aristotle (*De Animâ*, I. ii. 10) says that 'those philosophers who wished to account for knowledge and perception identified the ψυχή with the principles of things, because like is known by like.' Ὅσοι δ' ἐπὶ τὸ γινώσκειν καὶ τὸ αἰσθάνεσθαι τῶν ὄντων (ἀποβλέπουσιν), οὗτοι δὲ λέγουσι τὴν ψυχὴν τὰς ἀρχάς, οἱ μὲν πλείους ποιοῦντες, οἱ δὲ μίαν ταύτην, ὥσπερ Ἐμπεδοκλῆς μὲν ἐκ τῶν στοιχείων πάντων, εἶναι δὲ καὶ ἕκαστον ψυχὴν τούτων, λέγων οὕτω

γαίῃ μὲν γὰρ γαῖαν ὀπώπαμεν, ὕδατι δ' ὕδωρ,
αἰθέρι δ' αἰθέρα δῖαν, ἀτὰρ πυρὶ πῦρ ἀΐδηλον,
στοργῇ δὲ στοργήν, νεῖκος δέ τε νείκεϊ λυγρῷ.

ἔχειν, ἐν δὲ ᾧ τὰ ἐνδεχόμενα· πρὸς γὰρ τὰ τῷ γένει ἕτερα καὶ τῶν τῆς ψυχῆς μορίων ἕτερον τῷ γένει τὸ πρὸς ἑκάτερον πεφυκός, εἴπερ καθ' ὁμοιότητά τινα καὶ οἰκειότητα ἡ γνῶσις ὑπάρχει αὐτοῖς. λεγέσθω δὲ τούτων τὸ 6 μὲν ἐπιστημονικὸν τὸ δὲ λογιστικόν· τὸ γὰρ βουλεύεσθαι καὶ λογίζεσθαι ταὐτόν, οὐθεὶς δὲ βουλεύεται περὶ τῶν μὴ

τὸν αὐτὸν δὲ τρόπον καὶ Πλάτων ἐν τῷ Τιμαίῳ τὴν ψυχὴν ἐκ τῶν στοιχείων ποιεῖ· γινώσκεσθαι γὰρ τῷ ὁμοίῳ τὸ ὅμοιον, τὰ δὲ πράγματα ἐκ τῶν ἀρχῶν εἶναι. Sir W. Hamilton says (*Discussions on Philosophy*, p. 60): 'Some philosophers (as Anaxagoras, Heraclitus, Alcmæon) maintained that knowledge implied even a *contrariety* of subject and object. But since the time of Empedocles, no opinion has been more universally admitted than that the *relation of knowledge* inferred the *analogy of existence*. This analogy may be supposed in two potences. What knows and what is known are either, first, *similar*, or second, the *same*; and if the general principle be true, the latter is the more philosophical.' The fact is, that every act of knowledge is a unity of contradictions. It would be absurd to deny that the subject is contrary to the object, and it would be equally absurd to deny that the subject is the same as the object. As Empedocles says, the mind only knows fire by being fire, but, on the other hand, if, in knowing fire, the mind only *were* fire, and were not contrary to fire, then to know fire would only be to add fire to fire. But it is *qua* 'knowing' that the mind is contrary to its object, not *qua* knowing any particular object. Thus from the diversity of objects we are justified in concluding a diversity in the mind. But we must be sure that objects are really different from one another in genus (τῷ γένει ἕτερα), before we conclude the existence of different parts, faculties, or elements corresponding to them, else we may attribute to different principles in the mind phenomena that were only modifications of each other, and not by any means implying a diversity of principle.

6 λεγέσθω δὲ—ἔχοντος] 'Of these let one be called the "scientific," the other the "calculative" part, for deliberating and calculating are the same, and no one deliberates about necessary matter. The calculative part, then, is one division of the rational.' The psychology here is an advance in dogmatic clearness of statement beyond what we find in the writings of Aristotle. The terms τὸ ἐπιστημονικὸν and τὸ λογιστικὸν are not opposed to each other in the *De Animâ*. λογιστικὸν has not there taken the definite meaning which it wears in the present book. Rather it is used in a general sense to denote 'rational.' Thus in asking how the ψυχὴ is to be divided, Aristotle says (*De An.* III. ix. 2): ἔχει δ' ἀπορίαν εὐθὺς πῶς τε δεῖ μόρια λέγειν τῆς ψυχῆς καὶ πόσα. τρόπον γάρ τινα ἄπειρα φαίνεται καὶ οὐ μόνον ἅ τινες λέγουσι διορίζοντες, λογιστικὸν καὶ θυμικὸν καὶ ἐπιθυμητικόν (*i.e.* Plato, *Repub.* pp. 436–441). οἱ δὲ τὸ λόγον ἔχον καὶ τὸ ἄλογον. Cf. *Ib.* III. ix. 5: ἐν τῷ λογιστικῷ γὰρ ἡ βούλησις γίνεται. *Ib.* III. x. 10: φαντασία δὲ πᾶσα ἢ λογιστικὴ ἢ αἰσθητική. Cf. *Topics*,

ἐνδεχομένων ἄλλως ἔχειν. ὥστε τὸ λογιστικόν ἐστιν ἕν τι
7 μέρος τοῦ λόγον ἔχοντος. ληπτέον ἄρ' ἑκατέρου τούτων
τίς ἡ βελτίστη ἕξις· αὕτη γὰρ ἀρετὴ ἑκατέρου, ἡ δ'
ἀρετὴ πρὸς τὸ ἔργον τὸ οἰκεῖον.

2 Τρία δ' ἐστὶν ἐν τῇ ψυχῇ τὰ κύρια πράξεως καὶ

---

v. v. 4, where in stating the various ways in which the logical *property* may be predicated of a substance, it is said, ἢ ἁπλῶς καθάπερ ζῴου τὸ ζῆν, ἢ κατ' ἄλλο, καθάπερ ψυχῆς τὸ φρόνιμον, ἢ ὡς τὸ πρῶτον, καθάπερ λογιστικοῦ τὸ φρόνιμον (φρόνιμον and λογιστικὸν being here both used most probably in a general sense for 'thought' and 'reason'). Again, τὸ ἐπιστημονικὸν is used, not as here opposed to τὸ λογιστ., but generally. *De Anim.* III. xi. 3: τὸ δ' ἐπιστημονικὸν οὐ κινεῖται ἀλλὰ μένει. However, the distinction here given is already prepared in the *De Animâ*, and is even stated (though less dogmatically) in a place which was probably borrowed by the present writer. *Ib.* III. x. 2: νοῦς δὲ ὁ ἕνεκά του λογιζόμενος καὶ ὁ πρακτικός· διαφέρει δὲ τοῦ θεωρητικοῦ τῷ τέλει.

οὐδεὶς δὲ βουλεύεται, κ.τ.λ.] Cf. *Eth. Eud.* II. x. 9: περὶ ὧν οὐδεὶς ἂν οὐδ' ἐγχειρήσειε βουλεύεσθαι μὴ ἀγνοῶν. Περὶ ὧν δ' ἐνδέχεται μὴ μόνον τὸ εἶναι καὶ μή, ἀλλὰ καὶ τὸ βουλεύσασθαι τοῖς ἀνθρώποις. We before observed (cf. *Eth.* III. iii. 3, note) that Aristotle, in the parallel passage, did not use the terms τὰ ἐνδεχόμενα and τὰ μὴ ἐνδεχόμενα. To combine logical with psychological formulæ is the characteristic of Eudemus.

II. The last chapter having divided the reason into scientific and calculative, the present chapter proceeds to bridge over the interval between the intellect and moral action. This is done by assuming three principles in man—sensation, reason, and desire. Sensation merges into the other two, and then it is shown that in purpose, the cause of action, there is the meeting point of desire and reason, not of the pure or speculative reason (answering to the 'scientific part' of the last chapter), but the practical reason aiming at an end (which answers to the 'calculative part' in the former division). Thus there are two kinds of truth, one pure, the other having a relation to the will, and 'agreeing with right desire.' This distinction is a great step towards answering the question with which the present book is concerned. Truth having been divided into pure and practical, it only remains to see the forms under which the mind deals with these two kinds, and the highest developments of the mind will be disclosed, arranged under a twofold head.

1 τρία δ' ἐστὶν] Cf. Ar. *De Animâ*, III. x. 1: φαίνεται δέ γε δύο ταῦτα κινοῦντα, ἢ ὄρεξις ἢ νοῦς, εἴ τις τὴν φαντασίαν τιθείη ὡς νόησίν τινα· .... ἄμφω ἄρα ταῦτα κινητικὰ κατὰ τόπον, νοῦς καὶ ὄρεξις. Νοῦς δὲ ὁ ἕνεκά του λογιζόμενος καὶ ὁ πρακτικός· διαφέρει δὲ τοῦ θεωρητικοῦ τῷ τέλει. .... Καὶ ἡ φαντασία δὲ ὅταν κινῇ οὐ κινεῖ ἄνευ ὀρέξεως. It is highly probable that Eudemus had this passage before his eyes. The only alteration he has made is to substitute αἴσθησις for φαντασία, and to speak of the deter-

ἀληθείας, αἴσθησις νοῦς ὄρεξις. τούτων δ' ἡ αἴσθησις 2
οὐδεμιᾶς ἀρχὴ πράξεως· δῆλον δὲ τῷ τὰ θηρία αἴσθησιν μὲν ἔχειν, πράξεως δὲ μὴ κοινωνεῖν. ἔστι δ' ὅπερ ἐν διανοίᾳ κατάφασις καὶ ἀπόφασις, τοῦτ' ἐν ὀρέξει δίωξις καὶ φυγή· ὥστ' ἐπειδὴ ἡ ἠθικὴ ἀρετὴ ἕξις προαιρετική, ἡ δὲ προαίρεσις ὄρεξις βουλευτική, δεῖ διὰ ταῦτα τόν τε λόγον ἀληθῆ εἶναι καὶ τὴν ὄρεξιν ὀρθήν, εἴπερ ἡ προαίρεσις σπουδαία, καὶ τὰ αὐτὰ τὸν μὲν φάναι τὴν δὲ διώκειν. αὕτη μὲν οὖν ἡ
διάνοια καὶ ἡ ἀλήθεια πρακτική. τῆς δὲ θεωρητικῆς 3
διανοίας καὶ μὴ πρακτικῆς μηδὲ ποιητικῆς τὸ εὖ καὶ κακῶς τἀληθές ἐστι καὶ ψεῦδος· τοῦτο γάρ ἐστι παντὸς διανοητικοῦ ἔργον, τοῦ δὲ πρακτικοῦ καὶ διανοητικοῦ ἡ ἀλήθεια
ὁμολόγως ἔχουσα τῇ ὀρέξει τῇ ὀρθῇ. πράξεως μὲν οὖν 4
ἀρχὴ προαίρεσις, ὅθεν ἡ κίνησις ἀλλ' οὐχ οὗ ἕνεκα, προαι-

---

minators of truth and action as three, with one merged in the other two, instead of calling them two with a third implied. *Τούτων δ' ἡ αἴσθησις κ.τ.λ.* answers to *καὶ ἡ φαντασία κ.τ.λ.*

2 *δῆλον δὲ τῷ τὰ θηρία—πράξεως μὴ κοινωνεῖν*] The definite meaning of *πράττειν* and *πρᾶξις* to denote 'moral action' appears perhaps rather more strongly in Eudemus than in Aristotle. Cf. *Eth. Eud.* II. vi. 2: *πρὸς δὲ τούτοις ὅ γ' ἄνθρωπος καὶ πράξεών τινών ἐστιν ἀρχὴ μόνον τῶν ζῴων· τῶν γὰρ ἄλλων οὐδὲν εἴποιμεν ἂν πράττειν.* *Ib.* II. viii. 6: *οὐ γὰρ φαμὲν τὸ παιδίον πράττειν, οὐδὲ τὸ θηρίον, ἀλλ' ὅταν ἤδη διὰ λογισμὸν πράττοντα.*

ὅπερ ἐν διανοίᾳ κ.τ.λ.] All this is a compressed result of Aristotle's discussions, *De Animâ*, III. x.—xi.

ἐπειδὴ ἡ ἠθικὴ ἀρετὴ] Cf. *Eth. Eud.* II. x. 28: *ἀνάγκη τοίνυν—τὴν ἀρετὴν εἶναι τὴν ἠθικὴν ἕξιν προαιρετικὴν μεσότητος τῆς πρὸς ἡμᾶς ἐν ἡδέσι καὶ λυπηροῖς.*

ἡ δὲ προαίρεσις] Cf. *Eth. Eud.* II. x. 14: *δῆλον ὅτι ἡ προαίρεσις μέν ἐστιν ὄρεξις τῶν ἐφ' αὐτῷ βουλευτική.*

τόν τε λόγον ἀληθῆ εἶναι καὶ τὴν ὄρεξιν ὀρθήν] 'The decision of the reason must be true, and the desire must be right.' The terminology here used is rather more accurate than that of Aristotle, *De An.* III. x. 4: *νοῦς μὲν οὖν πᾶς ὀρθός· ὄρεξις δὲ καὶ φαντασία καὶ ὀρθὴ καὶ οὐκ ὀρθή.* Cf. *Eth.* III. ii. 13, where it is said that *ὀρθὸς* is the proper epithet for purpose (*i.e.* as a function of the will), *ἀληθὴς* for the functions of the intellect.

4–5 *πράξεως μὲν οὖν—ἄνθρωπος*] 'Now of moral action purpose is the cause (I mean the efficient cause, not the final), and the efficient cause of purpose is desire, and reasoning on the end to be aimed at. Hence purpose can neither be separated from reason and intellect, nor from a particular state of the moral nature. Well-doing and its contrary imply intellect and moral character. Now intellect by itself moves nothing, only intellect aiming at an end, that is, practical intellect. This controls

ρέσεως δὲ ὄρεξις καὶ λόγος ὁ ἕνεκά τινος· διὸ οὔτ' ἄνευ
νοῦ καὶ διανοίας οὔτ' ἄνευ ἠθικῆς ἐστὶν ἕξεως ἡ προαίρεσις·
εὐπραξία γὰρ καὶ τὸ ἐναντίον ἐν πράξει ἄνευ διανοίας καὶ
ἤθους οὐκ ἔστιν. διάνοια δ' αὐτὴ οὐθὲν κινεῖ, ἀλλ' ἡ ἕνεκά
του καὶ πρακτική· αὕτη γὰρ καὶ τῆς ποιητικῆς ἄρχει·
ἕνεκα γάρ του ποιεῖ πᾶς ὁ ποιῶν, καὶ οὐ τέλος ἁπλῶς ἀλλὰ
πρός τι καὶ τινὸς τὸ ποιητόν. ἀλλὰ τὸ πρακτόν· ἡ γὰρ
εὐπραξία τέλος, ἡ δ' ὄρεξις τούτου· διὸ ἢ ὀρεκτικὸς νοῦς
ἡ προαίρεσις ἢ ὄρεξις διανοητική, καὶ ἡ τοιαύτη ἀρχὴ
6 ἄνθρωπος. οὐκ ἔστι δὲ προαιρετὸν οὐθὲν γεγονός, οἷον

---

the productive intellect as well, since he that produces, produces for the sake of some end, and the thing produced is not an end in and for itself, but is only an end relatively and for a particular individual. But the thing done is an End-in-itself, since well-doing is an end, and this is what we desire. Hence purpose may be defined as desiring reason, or as rational desire, and such a principle as this is man.' We have here a *resumé* of Aristotle's views in *De Animâ*, *l. c.* Another division of the intellect, however, is introduced, that into practical, productive, and speculative, which is to be found implied in *Eth.* I. i. 1, and is stated *Metaphys.* V. i. 5: *ὥστε εἰ πᾶσα διάνοια ἢ πρακτικὴ ἢ ποιητικὴ ἢ θεωρητική κ.τ.λ.* It is here shown that the productive faculties of man are subordinate to the practical thought, since no artist produces anything purely and solely for its own sake; however much he may seem to do so, still his art as a part of his life falls under the control of his will and reason.

διάνοια δ' αὐτὴ οὐθὲν κινεῖ, ἀλλ' ἡ ἕνεκά του] There is a slight confusion here. Aristotle had said (*De An.* III. ix. 10, III. x. 2, III. x. 4), that the reason dealing with ends differed from the speculative reason, that reason neither speculative nor practical was the moving cause of action (III. ix. 10: *ἀλλὰ μὴν οὐδὲ τὸ λογιστικὸν καὶ ὁ καλούμενος νοῦς ἐστὶν ὁ κινῶν· ὁ μὲν γὰρ θεωρητικὸς οὐθὲν νοεῖ πρακτόν—οὐδ' ὅταν θεωρῇ τι τοιοῦτον κ.τ.λ.*), and that intellect could not move anything without desire conjoined (III. x. 4: *νῦν δὲ ὁ μὲν νοῦς οὐ φαίνεται κινῶν ἄνευ ὀρέξεως*), but Eudemus mixes up these points. He says that 'intellect by itself moves nothing,' and then as if in opposition to intellect by itself he puts 'but practical intellect does.' He should have said 'practical intellect *plus* desire.'

καὶ πρακτική] Καὶ is used here denoting identity. Cf. *Eth.* V. vi. 4: *τὸ ἁπλῶς δίκαιον καὶ τὸ πολιτικὸν δίκαιον.* Ar. *De An.* III. x. 2; *νοῦς δὲ ὁ ἕνεκά του λογιζόμενος καὶ ὁ πρακτικός.*

εὐπραξία] On the ambiguity of this term, cf. *Eth.* I. iv. 2, note.

6 *οὐκ ἔστι δὲ προαιρετὸν οὐθὲν γεγονός*] 'Now nothing that is past is ever the object of purpose.' This assertion, with the quotation from Agathon to illustrate it, appears certainly to be a digression. The nature of purpose had been quite sufficiently

οὐθεὶς προαιρεῖται Ἴλιον πεπορθηκέναι· οὐδὲ γὰρ βουλεύεται περὶ τοῦ γεγονότος ἀλλὰ περὶ τοῦ ἐσομένου καὶ ἐνδεχομένου, τὸ δὲ γεγονὸς οὐκ ἐνδέχεται μὴ γενέσθαι· διὸ ὀρθῶς Ἀγάθων

> μόνου γὰρ αὐτοῦ καὶ θεὸς στερίσκεται,
> ἀγένητα ποιεῖν ἅσσ' ἂν ᾖ πεπραγμένα.

ἀμφοτέρων δὴ τῶν νοητικῶν μορίων ἀλήθεια τὸ ἔργον. καθ' ἃς οὖν μάλιστα ἕξεις ἀληθεύσει ἑκάτερον, αὗται ἀρεταὶ ἀμφοῖν.

Ἀρξάμενοι οὖν ἄνωθεν περὶ αὐτῶν πάλιν λέγωμεν. 3
ἔστω δὴ οἷς ἀληθεύει ἡ ψυχὴ τῷ καταφάναι ἢ ἀποφάναι, πέντε τὸν ἀριθμόν· ταῦτα δ' ἐστὶ τέχνη ἐπιστήμη

---

explained already, especially in reference to the present context. However, to exclude the past, and circumstances which though contingent have become historical, from the sphere of deliberation, is an addition to Aristotle's list of exclusions (*Eth.* III. iii. 1—10), and on this account probably Eudemus was glad to introduce the above remarks.

III. This chapter proposes to consider the two parts of the reason (scientific and calculative) from a fresh point of view (ἀρξάμενοι—πάλιν). It accordingly gives a list of five modes under which the mind attains truth; namely, art, science, thought, philosophy, and reason. It then proceeds to give some account of science. This account will be found to be a mere *cento* of remarks from the logical writings of Aristotle. The chief points specified are as follows. Science deals only with necessary matter. It is demonstrative, starting from truths already known, and proceeding by means of induction or syllogism. Its premises are obtained by induction, but they must be more certain than the conclusion, else the knowledge of the conclusion will be not scientific, but merely accidental.

1 πέντε τὸν ἀριθμόν] It seems in the highest degree probable that this list was suggested by a passage in Aristotle's *Post. Analytics* (I. xxxiii. 8), where, after a discussion on the difference between science and opinion, it is said: τὰ δὲ λοιπὰ πῶς δεῖ διανεῖμαι ἐπί τε διανοίας καὶ νοῦ καὶ ἐπιστήμης καὶ τέχνης καὶ φρονήσεως καὶ σοφίας, τὰ μὲν φυσικῆς τὰ δὲ ἠθικῆς θεωρίας μᾶλλον ἐστιν. It will be observed that Aristotle in this passage does not propose six terms to be distinguished from each other, but three pairs of terms which are to be separately discussed, part of them (*i.e.* probably the two first pairs) by psychology (φυσικῆς θεωρίας), and part of them (*i.e.* σοφία and φρόνησις) by ethics. Eudemus, taking up the whole list, has omitted διάνοια, which he does not distinguish from νοῦς, and has given the rest as an exhaustive division of the modes by which the mind apprehends truth. By so doing

φρόνησις σοφία νοῦς· ὑπολήψει γὰρ καὶ δόξῃ ἐνδέχεται διαψεύδεσθαι. ἐπιστήμη μὲν οὖν τί ἐστιν, ἐντεῦθεν φανερόν, εἰ δεῖ ἀκριβολογεῖσθαι καὶ μὴ ἀκολουθεῖν ταῖς ὁμοιότησιν. πάντες γὰρ ὑπολαμβάνομεν, ὃ ἐπιστάμεθα, μὴ ἐνδέχεσθαι ἄλλως ἔχειν· τὰ δ' ἐνδεχόμενα ἄλλως, ὅταν ἔξω τοῦ θεωρεῖν γένηται, λανθάνει εἰ ἔστιν ἢ μή. ἐξ ἀνάγκης ἄρα ἐστὶ τὸ ἐπιστητόν. ἀΐδιον ἄρα· τὰ γὰρ ἐξ ἀνάγκης ὄντα ἁπλῶς πάντα ἀΐδια, τὰ δ' ἀΐδια, ἀγένητα
3 καὶ ἄφθαρτα. ἔτι διδακτὴ πᾶσα ἐπιστήμη δοκεῖ εἶναι,
καὶ τὸ ἐπιστητὸν μαθητόν. ἐκ προγινωσκομένων δὲ πᾶσα

---

he has made a cross division, for *σοφία* does not stand apart from *νοῦς* and *ἐπιστήμη*, but includes them, and surely so complex an idea as 'philosophy' ought not to be placed on the same level with the intuitions of the reason, the simplest and deepest forms of the mind. In ch. vi. § 2, however, the logical exhaustiveness of the division is made the only ground for proving that the principles of science are apprehended by reason.

ὑπολήψει γὰρ—διαψεύδεσθαι] 'For conception and opinion may be false.' This is suggested probably by Ar. *Post. Anal.* II. xix. 7: Ἐπεὶ δὲ τῶν περὶ τὴν διάνοιαν ἕξεων, αἷς ἀληθεύομεν, αἱ μὲν ἀεὶ ἀληθεῖς εἰσιν, αἱ δὲ ἐπιδέχονται τὸ ψεῦδος, οἷον δόξα καὶ λογισμός, ἀληθῆ δ' ἀεὶ ἐπιστήμη καὶ νοῦς, κ.τ.λ. In Ar. *De An.* III. iii. 7, ὑπόληψις is used in so general a sense for the apprehensions of the mind as to include ἐπιστήμη, δόξα, and φρόνησις. If opposed (as here) to scientific certainty, it comes to very much the same as δόξα.

2 *ἐπιστήμη μὲν—ἐπιστητόν*] 'Now what science is, will be clear from the following considerations, if we wish to speak exactly and not be misled by resemblances. We all conceive that what we *know* is necessarily what it is—if it be so only contingently, as soon as it is out of our ken, we cannot tell whether it be so or not. Therefore the object of science is necessary matter.'

ταῖς ὁμοιότησιν] i.e., the various analogical and inaccurate uses of the word 'knowledge.' Ἐπιστήμη is to be defined ἁπλῶς and not καθ' ὁμοιότητα, cf. *Eth.* v. vi. 4. The present passage is taken from *Post. Anal.* I. ii. 1: Ἐπίστασθαι δὲ οἰόμεθ' ἕκαστον ἁπλῶς—ὅταν τήν τ' αἰτίαν οἰώμεθα γινώσκειν δι' ἣν τὸ πρᾶγμά ἐστιν, ὅτι ἐκείνου αἰτία ἐστί, καὶ μὴ ἐνδέχεσθαι τοῦτ' ἄλλως ἔχειν.—ὥστε οὗ ἁπλῶς ἐστιν ἐπιστήμη, τοῦτ' ἀδύνατον ἄλλως ἔχειν.

ἔξω τοῦ θεωρεῖν] 'Out of the reach of our observation.' Θεωρ. here retains more of its original sense of 'seeing' than generally; cf. *e.g.* ch. i. § 5: ἐν μὲν ᾧ θεωροῦμεν τὰ τοιαῦτα κ.τ.λ. *Eth.* I. vii. 21. In the following chapter, § 4, θεωρεῖν is used for to 'consider,' or 'speculate,' though not in the special sense of philosophical speculation.

τὰ δ' ἀΐδια κ.τ.λ.] For a specimen of 'things eternal' cf. *Eth.* III. iii. 3, and see note.

3 *ἔτι διδακτὴ—συλλογισμῷ*] 'Again all science appears capable of being imparted by demonstration, and the matter of science appears capable of

διδασκαλία, ὥσπερ καὶ ἐν τοῖς ἀναλυτικοῖς λέγομεν· ἡ μὲν γὰρ δι' ἐπαγωγῆς, ἡ δὲ συλλογισμῷ. ἡ μὲν δὴ ἐπαγωγὴ ἀρχή ἐστι καὶ τοῦ καθόλου, ὁ δὲ συλλογισμὸς ἐκ τῶν καθόλου. εἰσὶν ἄρα ἀρχαὶ ἐξ ὧν ὁ συλλογισμός, ὧν οὐκ ἔστι συλλογισμός· ἐπαγωγὴ ἄρα. ἡ μὲν ἄρα ἐπιστήμη 4
ἐστὶν ἕξις ἀποδεικτική, καὶ ὅσα ἄλλα προσδιοριζόμεθα ἐν τοῖς ἀναλυτικοῖς· ὅταν γάρ πως πιστεύῃ καὶ γνώριμοι

---

being so apprehended. But all demonstration depends on pre-existent knowledge (as we say in analytics also), for it proceeds either by induction or syllogism.'

ὥσπερ λέγομεν] This is a general mode of expression, not a particular reference; some MSS. however read *ἐλέγομεν*. Eudemus, as we know, wrote a book on analytics (cf. Vol. I. Essay I. p. 31). In his *Ethics*, II. vi. 5, he speaks, as here, *generally* of analytics, *δῆλον δ' ὃ ἐπιχειροῦμεν ὅτι ἀναγκαῖον, ἐκ τῶν ἀναλυτικῶν*. In the present passage he is borrowing, not quoting, from the opening of Aristotle's *Post. Anal.* *Πᾶσα διδασκαλία καὶ πᾶσα μάθησις διανοητικὴ ἐκ προϋπαρχούσης γίνεται γνώσεως*. It is the first proof of knowing a thing, to be able to impart it, cf. *Metaphys.* I. i. 12: *ὅλως τε σημεῖον τοῦ εἰδότος τὸ δύνασθαι διδάσκειν ἐστίν*. Hence, by association with the idea of science, *διδασκαλία* comes to be almost identical with demonstration, cf. *Sophist. Elench.* ii. 1: *Ἔστι δὴ τῶν ἐν τῷ διαλέγεσθαι λόγων τέτταρα γένη, διδασκαλικοὶ καὶ διαλεκτικοὶ καὶ πειραστικοὶ καὶ ἐριστικοί, διδασκαλικοὶ μὲν οἱ ἐκ τῶν οἰκείων ἀρχῶν ἑκάστου μαθήματος καὶ οὐκ ἐκ τῶν τοῦ ἀποκρινομένου δοξῶν συλλογιζόμενοι, δεῖ γὰρ πιστεύειν τὸν μανθάνοντα.* Cf. ib. x. 11.

ἡ μὲν γὰρ δι' ἐπαγωγῆς κ.τ.λ.] This is taken from *Post. Anal.* I. i. 2: where Aristotle, having said that all demonstration depends on previous knowledge, adds that this is true with regard to the mathematics, and also in dialectical arguments, *ὁμοίως δὲ καὶ περὶ τοὺς λόγους οἵ τε διὰ συλλογισμῶν καὶ οἱ δι' ἐπαγωγῆς· ἀμφότεροι γὰρ διὰ προγινωσκομένων ποιοῦνται τὴν διδασκαλίαν, οἱ μὲν λαμβάνοντες ὡς παρὰ ξυνιέντων, οἱ δὲ δεικνύντες τὸ καθόλου διὰ τοῦ δῆλον εἶναι τὸ καθ' ἕκαστον.* What Aristotle had said of dialectical arguments, Eudemus applies to science, which he accordingly asserts to be sometimes inductive. His further assertion that the principles of deductive science are obtained by induction is inconsistent with the conclusion of ch. vi., though it agrees with Ar. *Post. Anal.* II. xix. 6. In fact *ἐπαγωγή* seems to be used by Aristotle in the *Post. Anal.* as equivalent to that amount of experience which is the *condition*, not the *cause*, of necessary truths. Cf. ib. I. i. 4.

4 *ἡ μὲν—ἀναλυτικοῖς*] 'Science, then, is a demonstrative state of mind, with all the other qualifications which we add in analytics.' Cf. Ar. *Post. Anal.* I. ii. 2: *Ἀνάγκη καὶ τὴν ἀποδεικτικὴν ἐπιστήμην ἐξ ἀληθῶν τ' εἶναι καὶ πρώτων καὶ ἀμέσων καὶ γνωριμωτέρων καὶ προτέρων καὶ αἰτίων τοῦ συμπεράσματος.* Aristotle, in his account of science, represents it from its objective side as a deduction of ideas rather than as a state of mind.

ὅταν γὰρ—ἐπιστήμην] 'For a man *knows* when he is convinced, and is

αὐτῷ ὦσιν αἱ ἀρχαί, ἐπίσταται, εἰ γὰρ μὴ μᾶλλον τοῦ συμπεράσματος, κατὰ συμβεβηκὸς ἕξει τὴν ἐπιστήμην. περὶ μὲν οὖν ἐπιστήμης διωρίσθω τὸν τρόπον τοῦτον.

4 Τοῦ δ' ἐνδεχομένου ἄλλως ἔχειν ἔστι τι καὶ ποιητὸν καὶ
2 πρακτόν, ἕτερον δ' ἐστὶ ποίησις καὶ πρᾶξις· πιστεύομεν δὲ περὶ αὐτῶν καὶ τοῖς ἐξωτερικοῖς λόγοις. ὥστε καὶ ἡ μετὰ λόγου ἕξις πρακτικὴ ἕτερόν ἐστι τῆς μετὰ λόγου ποιητικῆς ἕξεως. διὸ οὐδὲ περιέχονται ὑπ' ἀλλήλων· οὔτε γὰρ
3 ἡ πρᾶξις ποίησις οὔτε ἡ ποίησις πρᾶξίς ἐστιν. ἐπεὶ δ' ἡ οἰκοδομικὴ τέχνη τις ἐστὶ καὶ ὅπερ ἕξις τις μετὰ λόγου ποιητική, καὶ οὐδεμία οὔτε τέχνη ἐστὶν ἥτις οὐ μετὰ λόγου ποιητικὴ ἕξις ἐστίν, οὔτε τοιαύτη ἣ οὐ τέχνη, ταὐτὸν ἂν

---

sure of the premises; since if he is not more sure of them than of the conclusion, the knowledge which he has will be only accidental.' Taken from *Post. Anal.* I. ii. 1: *Ἐπίστασθαι δὲ οἰόμεθ' ἕκαστον ἁπλῶς, ἀλλὰ μὴ τὸν σοφιστικὸν τρόπον τὸν κατὰ συμβεβηκός*, κ.τ.λ. To know results without the proofs Aristotle called 'accidental' knowledge, and this mode of knowledge he attributed to the Sophists; cf. *Metaphys.* v. ii. &c.

πιστεύῃ] Cf. *Sophist. Elench.* ii. 1 (*l.c.*): *δεῖ γὰρ πιστεύειν τὸν μανθάνοντα*. *Infra*, ch. viii. § 6: *τὰ μὲν οὐ πιστεύουσιν οἱ νέοι, ἀλλὰ λέγουσιν*.

IV. Eudemus altered the list of mental operations given by Aristotle (*Post. Anal. l.c.*) only by the position of *νοῦς*, which in first stating his list Eudemus places at the end, probably because, having separated it from *διάνοια*, he was uncertain about its admission; afterwards he discusses it before *σοφία*, as being prior to it in order of time. The list then appears in Aristotle, *διάνοια νοῦς, ἐπιστήμη τέχνη, φρόνησις σοφία*; in Eudemus, *ἐπιστήμη, τέχνη, φρόνησις, σοφία, νοῦς* (afterwards *νοῦς, σοφία*). This chapter, in treating of art, gives but a scanty account, apparently borrowed from different passages in the *Metaphysics* of Aristotle. Art, like action, belongs to the sphere of the contingent, but its difference from action is universally recognised (*πιστεύομεν καὶ τοῖς ἐξ. λόγ.*). As shown by an instance, it consists in 'a productive state of mind in harmony with a true law.' It has to do with producing and contriving the production of things that fall neither under the law of nature nor necessity. Rather art deals with the same objects as chance, by which it is often assisted.

1—2 *τοῦ δ' ἐνδεχομένου—λόγοις*] 'Now contingent matter includes the objects both of production and action, but production and action are different. On this point even popular notions sufficiently bear us out.' With regard to *ἐξωτερικοὶ λόγοι*, cf. *Eth.* I. xiii. 9, and see Vol. I. Essays, Appendix B.

3 *ἐπεὶ δ'—ποιητική*] 'But since architecture is an art, and may be defined as (*ὅπερ*) a certain state of mind rationally (*μετὰ λόγου*) productive, and there is no art which is not a rationally productive state of

εἴη τέχνη καὶ ἕξις μετὰ λόγου ἀληθοῦς ποιητική. ἔστι δὲ 4
τέχνη πᾶσα περὶ γένεσιν, καὶ τὸ τεχνάζειν, καὶ θεωρεῖν
ὅπως ἂν γένηταί τι τῶν ἐνδεχομένων καὶ εἶναι καὶ μὴ εἶναι,
καὶ ὧν ἡ ἀρχὴ ἐν τῷ ποιοῦντι ἀλλὰ μὴ ἐν τῷ ποιουμένῳ·
οὔτε γὰρ τῶν ἐξ ἀνάγκης ὄντων ἢ γινομένων ἡ τέχνη ἐστίν,
οὔτε τῶν κατὰ φύσιν· ἐν αὑτοῖς γὰρ ἔχουσι ταῦτα τὴν
ἀρχήν. ἐπεὶ δὲ ποίησις καὶ πρᾶξις ἕτερον, ἀνάγκη τὴν
τέχνην ποιήσεως ἀλλ' οὐ πράξεως εἶναι. καὶ τρόπον τινα 5

---

mind, nor again any such state which is not an art: art must be the same as "productive state of mind rightly directed."' The procedure here is to take a species of art, and, abstracting what is peculiar, to leave the generic conception remaining, which thus is taken as the definition of the genus.

ὅπερ] A logical formula implying identity, convertibility of terms, cf. *Eth.* vii. xiii. 1: *οὐ γὰρ ἂν φαίη ὅπερ κακόν τι εἶναι τὴν ἡδονήν.*

οὔτε τοιαύτη ἣ οὐ τέχνη] This is a slight discrepancy from Aristotle, who speaks of three modes of production, art, faculty, and intellect, without, however, specifying the difference between them, *Metaphys.* vi. vii. 3: *πᾶσαι δ' εἰσὶν αἱ ποιήσεις ἢ ἀπὸ τέχνης ἢ ἀπὸ δυνάμεως ἢ ἀπὸ διανοίας.* *Ib.* x. vii. 3: *ποιητικῆς μὲν γὰρ ἐν τῷ ποιοῦντι καὶ οὐ τῷ ποιουμένῳ τῆς κινήσεως ἡ ἀρχή, καὶ τοῦτ' ἐστὶν εἴτε τέχνη τις εἴτ' ἄλλη τις δύναμις.*

4 *ἔστι δὲ—ποιουμένῳ*] 'Now all art is about creation, and the contriving and considering how something may be created of those things whose existence is contingent, and whose efficient cause exists in the producer and not in the thing produced.' There is not any distinction intended between *τεχνάζειν* and *θεωρεῖν*. The absence of the article before *θεωρεῖν* shows that these belong to the same idea; they are both only an expansion of the term *γένεσιν*, and are not to be separated from it, as if the writer was describing different stages in the process of art. We find *τεχνάζειν* used by Aristotle simply in the sense of 'contriving,' *Pol.* i. xi. 12: *ἀμφότεροι γὰρ ἑαυτοῖς ἐτέχνασαν γενέσθαι μονοπωλίαν.* *Ib.* vi. v. 8: *τεχναστέον οὖν ὅπως ἂν εὐπορία γένοιτο χρόνιος.*

ὧν ἡ ἀρχὴ κ.τ.λ.] Taken from Aristotle, *Metaphys.* x. vii. 3 (*l.c.*). Cf. v. i. 5: *τῶν μὲν ποιητικῶν ἐν τῷ ποιοῦντι ἡ ἀρχὴ ἢ νοῦς ἢ τέχνη ἢ δύναμίς τις, τῶν δὲ πρακτικῶν ἐν τῷ πράττοντι ἡ προαίρεσις.* There is the same classification of causes here as in *Eth.* iii. iii. 7, into nature, necessity, chance, and the human intellect. On Aristotle's conception of nature, see Vol. I. Essay V.

5 *καὶ τρόπον τινὰ—τέχνη*] 'And in a way chance and art are concerned with the same objects.' Eudemus, taking this observation from Aristotle, illustrates it, after his own fashion, with a quotation from Agathon. Cf. *Metaphys.* vi. vii. 4: *ταὐτὸν (ποιήσεων) δέ τινες γίγνονται καὶ ἀπὸ ταὐτομάτου καὶ ἀπὸ τύχης παραπλησίως ὥσπερ ἐν τοῖς ἀπὸ φύσεως γιγνομένοις.* Cf. *Ib.* vi. ix. 1, where the following question is started: *ἀπορήσειε δ' ἄν τις διὰ τί τὰ μὲν γίγνεται καὶ τέχνῃ καὶ ἀπὸ ταὐτομάτου, οἷον ὑγίεια, τὰ δ' οὔ, οἷον οἰκία.* The answer is, that there is a

περὶ τὰ αὐτά ἐστιν ἡ τύχη καὶ ἡ τέχνη, καθάπερ καὶ Ἀγάθων φησὶ

τέχνη τύχην ἔστερξε καὶ τύχη τέχνην.

6 ἡ μὲν οὖν τέχνη, ὥσπερ εἴρηται, ἕξις τις μετὰ λόγου ἀληθοῦς ποιητική ἐστιν, ἡ δ' ἀτεχνία τοὐναντίον μετὰ λόγου ψευδοῦς ποιητικὴ ἕξις, περὶ τὸ ἐνδεχόμενον ἄλλως ἔχειν.

5 Περὶ δὲ φρονήσεως οὕτως ἂν λάβοιμεν, θεωρήσαντες

---

principle of self-movement in the matter to be operated on in the one case, but not in the other. That the devices of art are often suggested, and its results assisted, by chance, need not be confirmed by examples; but while art is thus assisted by chance, on the other hand, it is the main object of art to eliminate chance. Cf. *Metaphys.* I. i. 5: ἡ μὲν γὰρ ἐμπειρία τέχνην ἐποίησεν, ὡς φησὶ Πῶλος, ὀρθῶς λέγων, ἡ δ' ἀπειρία τύχην. The theory of art is but meagre in the writings of Aristotle. His great defect with regard to the subject is, his not having entered into the philosophy of the imagination. Yet still he gives us remarks of far greater interest than what is contained in the brief *résumé* of Eudemus, cf. especially the saying, *Metaphys.* VI. vii. 4, that 'all things are done by art, of which the idea exists in the mind,' ἀπὸ τέχνης δὲ γίγνεται ὅσων τὸ εἶδος ἐν τῇ ψυχῇ, and add *Post. Anal.* II. xix. 4: ἐκ δ' ἐμπειρίας ἢ ἐκ παντὸς ἠρεμήσαντος τοῦ καθόλου ἐν τῇ ψυχῇ, τοῦ ἑνὸς παρὰ τὰ πολλά, ὃ ἂν ἐν ἅπασιν ἓν ἐνῇ ἐκείνοις τὸ αὐτό, τέχνης ἀρχὴ καὶ ἐπιστήμης, ἐὰν μὲν περὶ γένεσιν, τέχνης, ἐὰν δὲ περὶ τὸ ὄν, ἐπιστήμης.

V. Thought (φρόνησις) is next discussed. Its nature we learn from the use of the word 'thoughtful' (φρόνιμος) to denote those who take good counsel with regard to the general ordering of life. This subject admits of no scientific demonstration; again, it is different from art. We see the quality of 'thought' exemplified in such men as Pericles, who know what is good for themselves and others. This knowledge and insight is preserved by temperance, which hence gets its name (σωφροσύνη). Art admits of degrees of excellence, but 'thought' does not. Voluntary error in art is better than non-voluntary, but the reverse in 'thought,' which thus is shown to be more than a mere quality of the intellect,—it becomes part of ourselves (φρονήσεως οὐκ ἔστι λήθη).

1 περὶ δὲ φρονήσεως] From Socrates to Eudemus we may trace a distinct progress with regard to the doctrine of φρόνησις. Socrates said 'virtue is knowledge' (ἐπιστήμη). Plato first 'virtue is,' afterwards 'virtue *implies* thought' (φρόνησις). Cf. *Meno*, p. 98 D: διδακτὸν ἔδοξεν εἶναι, εἰ φρόνησις ἡ ἀρετή. *Theaet.* p. 176 B: ὁμοίωσις δὲ (τῷ θεῷ) δίκαιον καὶ ὅσιον μετὰ φρονήσεως γενέσθαι. *Phaedo*, p. 69 A: ἐκεῖνο μόνον τὸ νόμισμα ὀρθόν, ἀντ' οὗ δεῖ ἅπαντα ταῦτα καταλλάττεσθαι, φρόνησις, καὶ τούτου μὲν πάντα καὶ μετὰ τούτου ὠνούμενά τε καὶ πιπρασκόμενα τῷ ὄντι ᾖ, καὶ ἀνδρεία καὶ σωφροσύνη καὶ δικαιοσύνη, καὶ ξυλλήβδην ἀληθὴς ἀρετὴ ᾖ μετὰ φρονήσεως, καὶ προσγιγνομένων καὶ ἀπογιγνομένων

τίνας λέγομεν τοὺς φρονίμους. δοκεῖ δὴ φρονίμου εἶναι τὸ δύνασθαι καλῶς βουλεύσασθαι περὶ τὰ αὑτῷ ἀγαθὰ καὶ συμφέροντα, οὐ κατὰ μέρος, οἷον ποῖα πρὸς ὑγίειαν ἢ ἰσχύν, ἀλλὰ ποῖα πρὸς τὸ εὖ ζῆν. σημεῖον δ' ὅτι καὶ 2
τοὺς περί τι φρονίμους λέγομεν, ὅταν πρὸς τέλος τι σπουδαῖον εὖ λογίσωνται, ὧν μή ἐστι τέχνη. ὥστε καὶ ὅλως ἂν εἴη φρόνιμος ὁ βουλευτικός. βουλεύεται δ' οὐθεὶς περὶ 3

καὶ ἡδονῶν καὶ φόβων καὶ τῶν ἄλλων πάντων τῶν τοιούτων· χωριζόμενα δὲ φρονήσεως καὶ ἀλλαττόμενα ἀντὶ ἀλλήλων, μὴ σκιαγραφία τις ᾖ ἡ τοιαύτη ἀρετὴ καὶ τῷ ὄντι ἀνδραποδώδης. This 'thought,' however, he defined as the contemplation of the absolute (*Phædo*, p. 79 D), and thus identified the moral consciousness with philosophy (see Vol. I. Essay III. p. 193). Aristotle, as we have already seen (*Post. Anal.* I. xxxiii. 8, quoted on ch. iii. 1), proposed as a subject for discussion the distinction between φρόνησις and σοφία. With him φρόνησις was gradually coming to assume its distinctive meaning as practical wisdom; but this was not always clearly marked. Cf. *Topics*, v. vi. 10, where it is said to be the essential property of φρόνησις to be the highest condition of the reasoning faculty (τὸ λογιστικόν), just as it is of temperance to be the highest condition of the appetitive part. In another place of the *Topics* (IV. ii. 2) it is incidentally mentioned that some think φρόνησις to be both a virtue and also a science, but that it is not universally conceded to be a science. δοκεῖ γὰρ ἐνίοις ἡ φρόνησις ἀρετή τε καὶ ἐπιστήμη εἶναι, καὶ οὐδέτερον τῶν γενῶν ὑπ' οὐδετέρου περιέχεσθαι· οὐ μὴν ὑπὸ πάντων γε συγχωρεῖται τὴν φρόνησιν ἐπιστήμην εἶναι. In the *Politics*, III. iv. 17, it is said to be the only virtue properly belonging to a ruler. Ἡ δὲ φρόνησις ἄρχοντος ἴδιος ἀρετὴ μόνη· τὰς γὰρ ἄλλας ἔοικεν ἀναγκαῖον εἶναι κοινὰς καὶ τῶν ἀρχομένων καὶ τῶν ἀρχόντων. Ἀρχομένου δέ γε οὐκ ἔστιν ἀρετὴ φρόνησις, ἀλλὰ δόξα ἀληθής. Thus it is used for practical wisdom, but in a broad general sense, with reference to state affairs rather than to individual life, implying, however, an absolute consciousness as opposed to ἀληθὴς δόξα. Frequently Aristotle uses φρόνησις simply to denote 'thought' or 'wisdom,' without reference to its sphere. Cf. *Eth.* I. vi. 11, I. viii. 6, &c. Finally, it appears in its distinctive sense, *De An.* I. ii. 9. 'Anaxagoras says that all animals possess νοῦς, they certainly do not all possess equally the reason that gives what we call "thought."' οὐ φαίνεται δ' ὅ γε κατὰ φρόνησιν λεγόμενος νοῦς πᾶσιν ὁμοίως ὑπάρχειν. *Rhet.* I. ix. 13: φρόνησις δ' ἐστὶν ἀρετὴ διανοίας, καθ' ἣν εὖ βουλεύεσθαι δύνανται περὶ ἀγαθῶν καὶ κακῶν τῶν εἰρημένων εἰς εὐδαιμονίαν. *Eth.* X. viii. 3, where there is a contrast between the life of contemplation and of practical virtue, φρόνησις is spoken of as inseparably connected with the latter, while the happiness of contemplation by the pure reason is something apart. In the present book we have the Eudemian exposition and development of Aristotle's theory, which entirely contrasts φρόνησις with σοφία, and limits the former to the regulation of individual life.

3 βουλεύεται δ' οὐθεὶς] A verbal

τῶν ἀδυνάτων ἄλλως ἔχειν, οὐδὲ τῶν μὴ ἐνδεχομένων αὐτῷ πρᾶξαι· ὥστ' εἴπερ ἐπιστήμη μὲν μετ' ἀποδείξεως, ὧν δ' αἱ ἀρχαὶ ἐνδέχονται ἄλλως ἔχειν, τούτων μή ἐστιν ἀπόδειξις (πάντα γὰρ ἐνδέχεται καὶ ἄλλως ἔχειν, καὶ οὐκ ἔστι βουλεύσασθαι περὶ τῶν ἐξ ἀνάγκης ὄντων), οὐκ ἂν εἴη ἡ φρόνησις ἐπιστήμη οὐδὲ τέχνη, ἐπιστήμη μὲν ὅτι ἐνδέχεται τὸ πρακτὸν ἄλλως ἔχειν, τέχνη δ' ὅτι ἄλλο τὸ γένος
4 πράξεως καὶ ποιήσεως. λείπεται ἄρα αὐτὴν εἶναι ἕξιν ἀληθῆ μετὰ λόγου πρακτικὴν περὶ τὰ ἀνθρώπῳ ἀγαθὰ καὶ κακά· τῆς μὲν γὰρ ποιήσεως ἕτερον τὸ τέλος, τῆς δὲ
5 πράξεως οὐκ ἂν εἴη· ἔστι γὰρ αὐτὴ ἡ εὐπραξία τέλος. διὰ τοῦτο Περικλέα καὶ τοὺς τοιούτους φρονίμους οἰόμεθα εἶναι, ὅτι τὰ αὑτοῖς ἀγαθὰ καὶ τὰ τοῖς ἀνθρώποις δύνανται θεωρεῖν· εἶναι δὲ τοιούτους ἡγούμεθα τοὺς οἰκονομικοὺς καὶ τοὺς πολιτικούς. ἔνθεν καὶ τὴν σωφροσύνην τούτῳ προσα-
6 γορεύομεν τῷ ὀνόματι, ὡς σώζουσαν τὴν φρόνησιν. σώζει δὲ τὴν τοιαύτην ὑπόληψιν. οὐ γὰρ ἅπασαν ὑπόληψιν

---

repetition of ch. i. § 6. Cf. *Eth. Eud.* ii. x. 9 (*l.c.*).

4 τῆς μὲν γὰρ] A repetition of ch. ii. § 5.

5 διὰ τοῦτο—πολιτικούς] 'Hence we consider such men as Pericles "thoughtful," because they have a faculty of perceiving what is good for themselves and good for men in general. And we attribute the same character to those who have a turn for the management of households and of state affairs.' On φρόνησις as a quality for the ruler of a state, cf. Ar. *Pol.* iii. iv. 17 (*l.c.*), and on the connexion established by Eudemus between thought for the individual, for the family, and for the state, see below, ch. viii. § 1, note.

ἔνθεν—ὑπόληψιν] 'Hence it is that we call temperance by its present name (σωφροσύνη) as preserving one's thought (σώζουσαν τὴν φρόνησιν), and this is the kind of conception which it preserves,' i.e. a moral conception (περὶ τὸ πρακτόν) about the right and wrong, or, as it is here put, about 'the end' (τὸ οὗ ἕνεκα) of actions. The false etymology here given comes from Plato's *Cratylus*, p. 411 D, where, after a sportive derivation of φρόνησις, that of σωφροσύνη is added: Ἡ φρόνησις· φορᾶς γάρ ἐστι καὶ ῥοῦ νόησις. Εἴη δ' ἂν καὶ ὄνησιν ὑπολαβεῖν φορᾶς· ἀλλ' οὖν περί γε τὸ φέρεσθαί ἐστιν. εἰ δὲ βούλει, ἡ γνώμη παντάπασι δηλοῖ γονῆς σκέψιν καὶ νώμησιν· τὸ γὰρ νωμᾶν καὶ τὸ σκοπεῖν ταὐτόν. εἰ δὲ βούλει, αὐτὸ ἡ νόησις τοῦ νέου ἐστὶν ἕσις· τὸ δὲ νέα εἶναι τὰ ὄντα σημαίνει γιγνόμενα ἀεὶ εἶναι· τούτου οὖν ἐφίεσθαι τὴν ψυχὴν μηνύει τὸ ὄνομα ὁ θέμενος τὴν νεόεσιν. οὐ γὰρ νόησις τὸ ἀρχαῖον ἐκαλεῖτο, ἀλλ' ἀντὶ τοῦ η εἶ ἔδει λέγειν δύο, νοέεσιν. σωφροσύνη δὲ σωτηρία οὗ νῦν δὴ ἐσκέμμεθα, φρονήσεως. Of course σωφροσύνη merely means 'sound-mindedness.' But the whole conception of the relation of Temperance to 'Thought' here given agrees with Plato, *Repub.* 518, c—e.

διαφθείρει οὐδὲ διαστρέφει τὸ ἡδὺ καὶ τὸ λυπηρόν, οἷον
ὅτι τὸ τρίγωνον δυσὶν ὀρθαῖς ἴσας ἔχει ἢ οὐκ ἔχει, ἀλλὰ
τὰς περὶ τὸ πρακτόν. αἱ μὲν γὰρ ἀρχαὶ τῶν πρακτῶν τὸ
οὗ ἕνεκα τὰ πρακτά· τῷ δὲ διεφθαρμένῳ δι' ἡδονὴν ἢ λύπην
εὐθὺς οὐ φαίνεται ἡ ἀρχή, οὐδὲ δεῖν τούτου ἕνεκεν οὐδὲ διὰ
ταῦθ' αἱρεῖσθαι πάντα καὶ πράττειν· ἔστι γὰρ ἡ κακία
φθαρτικὴ ἀρχῆς· ὥστ' ἀνάγκη τὴν φρόνησιν ἕξιν εἶναι
μετὰ λόγου ἀληθῆ, περὶ τὰ ἀνθρώπινα ἀγαθὰ πρακτικήν.
ἀλλὰ μὴν τέχνης μὲν ἐστὶν ἀρετή, φρονήσεως δ' οὐκ ἔστιν· 7
καὶ ἐν μὲν τέχνῃ ὁ ἑκὼν ἁμαρτάνων αἱρετώτερος, περὶ δὲ
φρόνησιν ἧττον, ὥσπερ καὶ περὶ τὰς ἀρετάς. δῆλον οὖν
ὅτι ἀρετή τίς ἐστι καὶ οὐ τέχνη. δυοῖν δ' ὄντοιν μεροῖν 8

---

7 ἀλλὰ μὴν—τέχνη] 'It must be added, that while in art there are degrees of excellence, there are none in thought; and while in art he that errs voluntarily is the better, he that does so in wisdom is the worse, as is the case with the virtues also. Therefore it is plain that thought is a sort of virtue, and not an art.' Ἧττον, as contrasted with *αἱρετώτερος*, stands for *ἧττον αἱρετός*. The phrase *ἀρετὴ τέχνης* occurs again ch. vii. § 1. The present passage probably has reference to *Topics*, IV. ii. 2 (*l.c.*), *δοκεῖ γὰρ ἐνίοις ἡ φρόνησις ἀρετή τε καὶ ἐπιστήμη εἶναι*, where *ἐπιστήμη* answers to *τέχνη* in the place before us. To say that there are no degrees of excellence in 'thought' gives it an absolute character, just as it is said that there are degrees in the understanding, but not in the reason. Common language would admit of degrees in thoughtfulness. Cf. Ar. *Metaphys.* I. i. 2: *διὰ τοῦτο ταῦτα φρονιμώτερα καὶ μαθητικώτερα τῶν μὴ δυναμένων μνημονεύειν ἐστίν*. *De An.* I. ii. 9, *l.c.* But here 'thought' is considered as something ideal, just as afterwards, ch. xiii. § 6, it is said to imply all the virtues.

ὁ ἑκὼν ἁμαρτάνων] Eudemus seems often inclined to betake himself to a small antagonism against Platonic doctrines; whether in detail this was original, or borrowed from oral remarks or lost writings of Aristotle, we cannot tell. Cf. *Eth.* V. ix. 16, V. xi. 9, VI. xiii. 3, &c. Here there seems to be an allusion to the Socratico-Platonic paradox which forms the subject of the *Hippias Minor*, that to do injustice voluntarily was better than doing it involuntarily (see Vol. I. Essay II. p. 168). Here the contrary is assumed with regard to 'thought,' and the conclusion drawn is, that 'thought' is not an art, in other words (as is said more distinctly afterwards), not merely intellectual. If 'thought' were merely intellectual, then voluntary error in action would not be error at all, because knowledge would remain behind unimpaired; but if 'thought' is a state of the will as well as of the intellect, then voluntary error, as implying a defect of the will, is the worst kind of error. The worst kind of error, morally, is considered to be sinning against knowledge, knowing the right and doing the wrong, which some philosophers deny to be possible. See below, Book VII. ch. iii.

8 δυοῖν δ'—ἐστιν] 'And as there

τῆς ψυχῆς τῶν λόγον ἐχόντων, θατέρου ἂν εἴη ἀρετή, τοῦ δοξαστικοῦ· ἥ τε γὰρ δόξα περὶ τὸ ἐνδεχόμενον ἄλλως ἔχειν καὶ ἡ φρόνησις. ἀλλὰ μὴν οὐδ' ἕξις μετὰ λόγου μόνον· σημεῖον δ' ὅτι λήθη τῆς μὲν τοιαύτης ἕξεώς ἐστι, φρονήσεως δ' οὐκ ἔστιν.

6 Ἐπεὶ δ' ἡ ἐπιστήμη περὶ τῶν καθόλου ἐστὶν ὑπόληψις

---

are two parts of man's nature which possess reason, thought will be the highest state of one of these, namely, the opiniative part, for opinion and thought both deal with the contingent. We must add that it is not merely an intellectual state (ἕξις μετὰ λόγου), the proof of which is that while such states admit forgetfulness, thought does not.' Τὸ δοξαστικὸν answers to τὸ λογιστικόν, ch. i. § 6. That opinion deals with contingent matter, we are told, Ar. *Post. Anal.* I. xxxiii. 2: λείπεται δόξαν εἶναι περὶ τὸ ἀληθὲς μὲν ἢ ψεῦδος, ἐνδεχόμενον δὲ καὶ ἄλλως ἔχειν. After associating opinion with thought, the writer separates them just as Aristotle separates προαίρεσις from δόξα, *Eth.* III. ii. 11. In the present passage there is a great want of clearness. We are told that thought is an excellence, or highest state, of a part of the intellect. Hence we should naturally conclude that it was λόγος τις (cf. ch. xiii. § 5), but the formula throughout used is, that thought is ἕξις μετὰ λόγου. This formula, in the sense of 'accompanied by inference,' 'able to give an account of itself,'—is applied by Aristotle to ἐπιστήμη (see note on the next page); and so too Plato, *Theaetetus*, 201 D: τὴν μετὰ λόγου ἀληθῆ δόξαν ἐπιστήμην εἶναι. Cf. *Eth. Eud.* VIII. ii. 3: οὐ γὰρ ἄλογος ἡ φρόνησις, ἀλλ' ἔχει λόγον διὰ τί οὕτω πράττει. Thought then is first defined to be 'a reasoning state of mind;' afterwards we are told that thought is not simply a ἕξις μετὰ λόγου, by which the writer evidently means to say, that thought is not a mere state of the intellect. It may be indeed true that the moral intellect cannot be separated from the will and personality (cf. ch. xii. § 10), but what is to be complained of is, that the formulæ used for expressing all the truths connected with this subject are so very imperfect.

σημεῖον δ' ὅτι λήθη] Cf. *Eth.* I. x. 10: where it is said that 'the moments of virtuous consciousness in the mind are more abiding than the sciences,' and see note. To φρόνησις in the Platonic and general sense, of course forgetfulness might attach. Cf. *Laws*, p. 732 B: ἀνάμνησις δ' ἐστὶν ἐπιρροὴ φρονήσεως ἀπολειπούσης.

VI. This chapter treats of reason, but goes no further into the subject than as follows,—science implies principles, and we cannot apprehend these principles by science itself nor by three out of the other four modes of mind which give us truth. It therefore remains, on the grounds of exhaustive division, that reason must be the organ by which we apprehend first principles.

On examination it will be found that the contents of the chapter are borrowed almost *verbatim* from Aristotle's *Post. Analyt.* II. xix. 7: Ἐπεὶ δὲ τῶν περὶ τὴν διάνοιαν ἕξεων, αἷς ἀληθεύομεν, αἱ μὲν ἀεὶ ἀληθεῖς εἰσιν, αἱ δὲ ἐπιδέχονται τὸ ψεῦδος, οἷον δόξα καὶ λογισμός,

καὶ τῶν ἐξ ἀνάγκης ὄντων, εἰσὶ δ' ἀρχαὶ τῶν ἀποδεικτῶν καὶ πάσης ἐπιστήμης (μετὰ λόγου γὰρ ἡ ἐπιστήμη), τῆς ἀρχῆς τοῦ ἐπιστητοῦ οὔτ' ἂν ἐπιστήμη εἴη οὔτε τέχνη οὔτε φρόνησις· τὸ μὲν γὰρ ἐπιστητὸν ἀποδεικτόν, αἱ δὲ τυγχάνουσιν οὖσαι περὶ τὰ ἐνδεχόμενα ἄλλως ἔχειν. οὐδὲ δὴ σοφία τούτων ἐστίν· τοῦ γὰρ σοφοῦ περὶ ἐνίων ἔχειν ἀπόδειξίν ἐστιν. εἰ δὴ οἷς ἀληθεύομεν καὶ μηδέποτε διαψευ- 3
δόμεθα περὶ τὰ μὴ ἐνδεχόμενα ἢ καὶ ἐνδεχόμενα ἄλλως ἔχειν, ἐπιστήμη καὶ φρόνησίς ἐστι καὶ σοφία καὶ νοῦς, τούτων δὲ τῶν τριῶν μηδὲν ἐνδέχεται εἶναι (λέγω δὲ τρία φρόνησιν ἐπιστήμην σοφίαν), λείπεται νοῦν εἶναι τῶν ἀρχῶν.

Τὴν δὲ σοφίαν ἔν τε ταῖς τέχναις τοῖς ἀκριβεστάτοις 7

ἀληθῆ δ' ἀεὶ ἐπιστήμη καὶ νοῦς, καὶ οὐδὲν ἐπιστήμης ἀκριβέστερον ἄλλο γένος ἢ νοῦς, αἱ δ' ἀρχαὶ τῶν ἀποδείξεων γνωριμώτεραι, ἐπιστήμη δ' ἅπασα μετὰ λόγου ἐστί, τῶν ἀρχῶν ἐπιστήμη μὲν οὐκ ἂν εἴη, ἐπεὶ δ' οὐδὲν ἀληθέστερον ἐνδέχεται εἶναι ἐπιστήμης ἢ νοῦν, νοῦς ἂν εἴη τῶν ἀρχῶν, ἔκ τε τούτων σκοποῦσι καὶ ὅτι ἀποδείξεως ἀρχὴ οὐκ ἀπόδειξις, ὥστ' οὐδ' ἐπιστήμης ἐπιστήμη. Εἰ οὖν μηδὲν ἄλλο παρ' ἐπιστήμην γένος ἔχομεν ἀληθές, νοῦς ἂν εἴη ἐπιστήμης ἀρχή. Aristotle argues that principles must be apprehended either by science or reason; they cannot be apprehended by science, therefore they must be by reason. Eudemus, it will be observed, follows this mode of arguing, only he applies it to all the five organs of truth, which he had before arbitrarily laid down as an exhaustive list. In following implicitly the passage above cited, he has ignored for the time the earlier part of the same chapter, in which Aristotle attributes the origin of universals rather to induction; *ib.* § 6: δῆλον δὴ ὅτι ἡμῖν τὰ πρῶτα ἐπαγωγῇ γνωρίζειν ἀναγκαῖον, καὶ γὰρ καὶ αἴσθησις οὕτω τὸ καθόλου ἐμποιεῖ. Also he is at variance with his own statement above, ch. iii. § 3.

μετὰ λόγου γὰρ ἡ ἐπιστήμη] 'For science implies inference.' This is evidently the meaning of the present sentence, taken as it is from *Post. Anal. l.c.* *Λόγος* is frequently used to denote 'inference.' Cf. ch. viii. § 9: ὁ μὲν γὰρ νοῦς τῶν ὅρων, ὧν οὐκ ἔστι λόγος: xi. 4. τῶν ἐσχάτων νοῦς ἐστὶ καὶ οὐ λόγος, &c.

οὐδὲ δὴ—ἐστιν] 'Nor of course does philosophy apprehend these principles, for it is the part of the philosopher to possess demonstration about some things.' It need hardly be said that this is a very poor ground for establishing the point in question.

VII. What 'philosophy' is may be learnt from the use of the word *σοφός*, as applied to the arts. It denotes 'nicety,' 'subtlety,' 'exactness.' Philosophy, then, is the most subtle of the sciences. It embraces not only deductions, but also principles. It is 'a science of the highest objects with the head on.' It is above both practical thought and science. It is one and permanent, while they

τὰς τέχνας ἀποδίδομεν, οἷον Φειδίαν λιθουργὸν σοφὸν καὶ
Πολύκλειτον ἀνδριαντοποιόν, ἐνταῦθα μὲν οὖν οὐθὲν ἄλλο
2 σημαίνοντες τὴν σοφίαν ἢ ὅτι ἀρετὴ τέχνης ἐστίν· εἶναι δέ
τινας σοφοὺς οἰόμεθα ὅλως οὐ κατὰ μέρος οὐδ᾽ ἄλλο τι
σοφούς, ὥσπερ Ὅμηρός φησιν ἐν τῷ Μαργίτῃ·

> τὸν δ᾽ οὔτ᾽ ἂρ σκαπτῆρα θεοὶ θέσαν οὔτ᾽ ἀροτῆρα
> οὔτ᾽ ἄλλως τι σοφόν.

ὥστε δῆλον ὅτι ἡ ἀκριβεστάτη ἂν τῶν ἐπιστημῶν εἴη ἡ
3 σοφία. δεῖ ἄρα τὸν σοφὸν μὴ μόνον τὰ ἐκ τῶν ἀρχῶν
εἰδέναι, ἀλλὰ καὶ περὶ τὰς ἀρχὰς ἀληθεύειν. ὥστ᾽ εἴη ἂν
ἡ σοφία νοῦς καὶ ἐπιστήμη, ὥσπερ κεφαλὴν ἔχουσα ἐπιστήμη τῶν τιμιωτάτων. ἄτοπον γὰρ εἴ τις τὴν πολιτικὴν

---

are manifold, relative, and changeable. It is higher, as the cosmos is higher than man. Philosophy and not practical thought was the reputed property of men like Thales and Anaxagoras, who were thought to know strange and out-of-the-way, but useless things. On the other hand, 'thought' (φρόνησις) is good counsel about human things. It implies knowledge of particulars as well as of universals. Indeed, the knowledge of the particular gained by experience is its most important element, though it includes the universal also, and in its own sphere, namely, that of action, it is supreme and paramount (ἀρχιτεκτονική).

1—2 τὴν δὲ σοφίαν—σοφία] 'The term σοφία we apply in the arts to those who are the most finished artists, as, for instance, we call Phidias a consummate (σοφός) sculptor, and Polycletus a consummate statuary, and in this application we mean nothing else by σοφία than the highest excellence in art. But we conceive that some men possess the quality in a general and not a particular way,—"nor in aught else accomplished," as Homer says in the *Margites*—

'"Not skilled to dig or plough the gods have made him,
Nor in aught else accomplished."

We may argue, then, that σοφία, in the sense of philosophy, is the most consummate of the sciences.' On the meaning of ἀκρίβεια as applied to the arts, and on the transition of meaning when it is applied to philosophy, see *Eth.* I. vii. 18, note, and II. vi. 9, note.

3 ὥστ᾽ εἴη—τιμιωτάτων] 'So that philosophy must be the union of reason and science, as it were a science of the highest objects with its head on.' This excellent definition does not appear to have anything in Aristotle exactly answering to it. There are two chief places where Aristotle treats of σοφία, namely, *Metaphysics*, Book I. i.—ii., and *ib.* Book X. ch. i.—vii. *Metaphys.* Book I. opens by showing an ascending scale in knowledge,—perception, experience, art, and the theoretic sciences, or philosophy. Of philosophy we are told that it is the science of first causes, it is most universal, most exact, and most entirely sought for its own sake, &c.

ἢ τὴν φρόνησιν σπουδαιοτάτην οἴεται εἶναι, εἰ μὴ τὸ
ἄριστον τῶν ἐν τῷ κόσμῳ ἄνθρωπός ἐστιν. εἰ δὴ ὑγιεινὸν 4
μὲν καὶ ἀγαθὸν ἕτερον ἀνθρώποις καὶ ἰχθύσι, τὸ δὲ λευκὸν
καὶ εὐθὺ ταὐτὸν ἀεί, καὶ τὸ σοφὸν ταὐτὸν πάντες ἂν
εἴποιεν, φρόνιμον δὲ ἕτερον· τὸ γὰρ περὶ αὑτὸ ἕκαστα εὖ

(*Met.* I. ii. 2–6). Philosophy begins in wonder, wonder at first about things near at hand, afterwards about the sun, moon, and stars, and the creation of the universe (*Ib.* § 9). It ends in certainty and a sense of the necessity of certain truths (*Ib.* § 16). We may see that this account is perfectly general—it does not distinguish in philosophy between mathematics, physics, and metaphysics. It even attributes a practical scope to philosophy, saying that philosophy, by taking cognisance of the good, determines the object of the other sciences (*Ib.* § 7). *ἀρχικωτάτη δὲ τῶν ἐπιστημῶν, καὶ μᾶλλον ἀρχικὴ τῆς ὑπηρετούσης, ἡ γνωρίζουσα τίνος ἕνεκέν ἐστι πρακτέον ἕκαστον· τοῦτο δ' ἐστὶ τἀγαθὸν ἐν ἑκάστοις, ὅλως δὲ τὸ ἄριστον ἐν τῇ φύσει πάσῃ.* From a certain immaturity thus shown, it would be difficult to believe that the account in *Metaphys.* Book I. was written after that in the present chapter of the *Ethics.* In *Metaphys.* Book X. the subject is taken up anew, and treated much more fully. Physics, practical science, and mathematics, are now separated from philosophy proper. *Ib.* i. 4: *οὐδὲ περὶ τὰς ἐν τοῖς φυσικοῖς εἰρημένας αἰτίας τὴν ζητουμένην ἐπιστήμην θετέον. Οὔτε γὰρ περὶ τὸ οὗ ἕνεκεν· τοιοῦτον γὰρ τἀγαθόν, τοῦτο δ' ἐν τοῖς πρακτοῖς ὑπάρχει καὶ τοῖς οὖσιν ἐν κινήσει.* *Ib.* i. 7: *οὐδὲ μὴν περὶ τὰ μαθηματικά—χωριστὸν γὰρ αὐτῶν οὐθέν.* These, however, are branches of philosophy. *Ib.* iv. 3: *διὸ καὶ ταύτην (τὴν φυσικὴν) καὶ τὴν μαθηματικὴν ἐπιστήμην μέρη τῆς σοφίας εἶναι θετέον.* Cf. *Met.* III. iii. 4: *ἔστι δὲ σοφία τις καὶ ἡ φυσική, ἀλλ' οὐ πρώτη.* Hence we get the famous division of speculative sciences, *Met.* X. vii. 9: *δῆλον τοίνυν ὅτι τρία γένη τῶν θεωρητικῶν ἐπιστημῶν ἐστί, φυσική, μαθηματική, θεολογική. Βέλτιστον μὲν οὖν τὸ τῶν θεωρητικῶν ἐπιστημῶν γένος, τούτων δ' αὐτῶν ἡ τελευταία λεχθεῖσα· περὶ τὸ τιμιώτατον γάρ ἐστι τῶν ὄντων, βελτίων δὲ καὶ χείρων ἑκάστη λέγεται κατὰ τὸ οἰκεῖον ἐπιστητόν.* Philosophy, then, in the highest sense, may be called theology, or the science of the divine, that is, of pure, transcendental (*χωριστή*), immutable being. It is the science of being *quâ* being (*τοῦ ὄντος ᾗ ὂν ἐπιστήμη*). Eudemus,* following in the wake of this discussion, has adopted as much of its results as suited his purpose. He speaks of philosophy as having the highest objects (*τῶν τιμιωτάτων*, cf. *Met.* X. vii. 9, *l.c.*), but he does not distinguish its different branches. He includes in it both physical and mathematical ideas (§ 4, *τὸ δὲ λευκὸν καὶ εὐθὺ ταὐτὸν ἀεί*; *ib. ἐξ ὧν ὁ κόσμος συνέστηκεν*), though he uses *σοφὸς* once in its special sense to denote a metaphysical, as opposed to mathematical or physical, philosopher. Ch. viii. § 6: *μαθηματικὸς μὲν παῖς γένοιτ' ἄν, σοφὸς δ' ἢ φυσικὸς οὔ.* In short, his object is rather to contrast philosophy with practical thought than exactly to define it. His attributing to it a union of intuition with reasoning seems however a happy result of his present method of discussion. (See Vol. I. Essay I. p. 52, sq.)

θηριοῦν φαῖεν ἂν εἶναι φρόνιμον, καὶ τούτῳ ἐπιτρέψειαν αὐτά. διὸ καὶ τῶν θηρίων ἔνια φρόνιμά φασιν εἶναι, ὅσα περὶ τὸν αὑτῶν βίον ἔχοντα φαίνεται δύναμιν προνοητικήν. φανερὸν δὲ καὶ ὅτι οὐκ ἂν εἴη ἡ σοφία καὶ ἡ πολιτικὴ ἡ αὐτή· εἰ γὰρ τὴν περὶ τὰ ὠφέλιμα τὰ αὑτοῖς ἐροῦσι σοφίαν, πολλαὶ ἔσονται σοφίαι· οὐ γὰρ μία περὶ τὸ ἁπάντων ἀγαθὸν τῶν ζῴων, ἀλλ' ἑτέρα περὶ ἕκαστον, εἰ μὴ καὶ ἰατρικὴ μία περὶ πάντων τῶν ὄντων. εἰ δ' ὅτι βέλτιστον ἄνθρωπος τῶν ἄλλων ζῴων, οὐδὲν διαφέρει· καὶ γὰρ ἀνθρώπου ἄλλα πολὺ θειότερα τὴν φύσιν, οἷον φανερώτατά γε ἐξ ὧν ὁ κόσμος συνέστηκεν. ἐκ δὴ τῶν εἰρημένων δῆλον ὅτι ἡ σοφία ἐστὶ καὶ ἐπιστήμη καὶ νοῦς τῶν τιμιωτάτων τῇ φύσει. διὸ Ἀναξαγόραν καὶ Θαλῆν καὶ τοὺς τοιούτους σοφοὺς μὲν φρονίμους δ' οὔ φασιν εἶναι, ὅταν ἴδωσιν ἀγνοοῦντας τὰ συμφέρονθ' ἑαυτοῖς, καὶ περιττὰ μὲν καὶ

---

4 εἰ δ' ὅτι βέλτιστον—συνέστηκεν] 'And if it be said that man is the best of the animals, this will make no difference, for there are besides other things far diviner in their nature than man, such as, to quote the most obvious instance, the parts out of which the symmetry of the heavens is composed.' On the Aristotelian view of man's position in the scale of dignity in the universe, see Vol. I. Essay V. p. 286. On Aristotle's doctrine of the divine nature of the stars, &c., cf. *De Cœlo*, i. ii. 9: *Ἔκ τε δὴ τούτων φανερὸν ὅτι πέφυκέ τις οὐσία σώματος ἄλλη παρὰ τὰς ἐνταῦθα συστάσεις, θειοτέρα καὶ προτέρα τούτων ἁπάντων* (this has given rise to the notion of the 'quintessence'). *Ib.* i. ii. 11, which repeats the same. *Ib.* ii. iii. 2: *Ἕκαστόν ἐστιν, ὧν ἐστιν ἔργον, ἕνεκα τοῦ ἔργου. Θεοῦ δ' ἐνέργεια ἀθανασία· τοῦτο δ' ἐστὶ ζωὴ ἀΐδιος. Ὥστ' ἀνάγκη τῷ θείῳ κίνησιν ἀΐδιον ὑπάρχειν. Ἐπεὶ δ' ὁ οὐρανὸς τοιοῦτος (σῶμα γάρ τι θεῖον) διὰ τοῦτο ἔχει τὸ ἐγκύκλιον σῶμα, ὃ φύσει κινεῖται κύκλῳ ἀεί.* Cf. *Metaphys.* xi. viii. 5: *Ἥ τε γὰρ τῶν ἄστρων φύσις ἀΐδιος οὐσία τις.* *Ib.* x. vi. 6: *Ὅλως δ' ἄτοπον ἐκ τοῦ φαίνεσθαι τὰ δεῦρο μεταβάλλοντα καὶ μηδέποτε διαμένοντα ἐν τοῖς αὐτοῖς, ἐκ τούτων περὶ τῆς ἀληθείας τὴν κρίσιν ποιεῖσθαι. Δεῖ γὰρ ἐκ τῶν ἀεὶ κατὰ ταὐτὰ ἐχόντων καὶ μηδεμίαν μεταβολὴν ποιουμένων τἀληθὲς θηρεύειν. τοιαῦτα δ' ἐστὶ τὰ κατὰ τὸν κόσμον.*

5 διὸ Ἀναξαγόραν καὶ Θαλῆν] Cf. *Eth.* x. viii. 11; Plato, *Theætetus*, p. 174 A: *Ὥσπερ καὶ Θαλῆν ἀστρονομοῦντα, ὦ Θεόδωρε, καὶ ἄνω βλέποντα, πεσόντα εἰς φρέαρ, Θρᾷττά τις ἐμμελὴς καὶ χαρίεσσα θεραπαινὶς ἀποσκῶψαι λέγεται, ὡς τὰ μὲν ἐν οὐρανῷ προθυμοῖτο εἰδέναι, τὰ δ' ἔμπροσθεν αὐτοῦ καὶ παρὰ πόδας λανθάνοι αὐτόν. Ταὐτὸν δὲ ἀρκεῖ σκῶμμα ἐπὶ πάντας ὅσοι ἐν φιλοσοφίᾳ διάγουσι.* On the other hand, Aristotle (*Politics*, i. xi. 9) tells a story of Thales turning his philosophy to practical account, foreseeing by astronomical observations that there would be a good crop of olives, buying up the crop in Miletus

θαυμαστὰ καὶ χαλεπὰ καὶ δαιμόνια εἰδέναι αὐτούς φασιν, ἄχρηστα δ', ὅτι οὐ τὰ ἀνθρώπινα ἀγαθὰ ζητοῦσιν. ἡ δὲ 6 φρόνησις περὶ τὰ ἀνθρώπινα καὶ περὶ ὧν ἔστι βουλεύσασθαι· τοῦ γὰρ φρονίμου μάλιστα τοῦτ' ἔργον εἶναί φαμεν, τὸ εὖ βουλεύεσθαι, βουλεύεται δ' οὐθεὶς περὶ τῶν ἀδυνάτων ἄλλως ἔχειν, οὐδ' ὅσων μὴ τέλος τί ἐστι, καὶ τοῦτο πρακτὸν ἀγαθόν. ὁ δ' ἁπλῶς εὔβουλος ὁ τοῦ ἀρίστου ἀνθρώπῳ τῶν πρακτῶν στοχαστικὸς κατὰ τὸν λογισμόν. οὐδ' ἐστὶν ἡ φρόνησις τῶν καθόλου μόνον, ἀλλὰ δεῖ καὶ τὰ 7 καθ' ἕκαστα γνωρίζειν· πρακτικὴ γάρ, ἡ δὲ πρᾶξις περὶ τὰ καθ' ἕκαστα. διὸ καὶ ἔνιοι οὐκ εἰδότες ἑτέρων εἰδότων πρακτικώτεροι, καὶ ἐν τοῖς ἄλλοις οἱ ἔμπειροι· εἰ γὰρ εἰδείη ὅτι τὰ κοῦφα εὔπεπτα κρέα καὶ ὑγιεινά, ποῖα δὲ κοῦφα ἀγνοοῖ, οὐ ποιήσει ὑγίειαν, ἀλλ' ὁ εἰδὼς ὅτι τὰ ὀρνίθεια κοῦφα καὶ ὑγιεινὰ ποιήσει μᾶλλον. ἡ δὲ φρόνησις πρακτική. ὥστε δεῖ ἄμφω ἔχειν, ἢ ταύτην μᾶλλον. εἴη δ' ἄν τις καὶ ἐνταῦθα ἀρχιτεκτονική.

Ἔστι δὲ καὶ ἡ πολιτικὴ καὶ ἡ φρόνησις ἡ αὐτὴ μὲν 8

---

beforehand, and having sold at his own price, πολλὰ χρήματα συλλέξαντα ἐπιδεῖξαι ὅτι ῥᾴδιόν ἐστι πλουτεῖν τοῖς φιλοσόφοις, ἂν βούλωνται, ἀλλ' οὐ τοῦτ' ἐστὶ περὶ ὃ σπουδάζουσιν.

6 *βουλεύεται δ' οὐθεὶς*] A repetition for the third time of the same remark, cf. ch. i. § 6, ch. v. § 3.

7 Owing to its practical character, 'thought' (φρόνησις) necessarily implies a knowledge of particulars. The particular, indeed, would seem for action the more important element, as appears also in other things, if we compare science with empirical knowledge.

διὸ καὶ ἔνιοι οὐκ εἰδότες] Cf. Ar. *Met.* I. i. 7—8 (whence this passage may probably be borrowed), πρὸς μὲν οὖν τὸ πράττειν ἐμπειρία τέχνης οὐδὲν δοκεῖ διαφέρειν, ἀλλὰ καὶ μᾶλλον ἐπιτυγχάνοντας ὁρῶμεν τοὺς ἐμπείρους τῶν ἄνευ τῆς ἐμπειρίας λόγον ἐχόντων. αἴτιον δ' ὅτι ἡ μὲν ἐμπειρία τῶν καθ' ἕκαστόν ἐστι γνῶσις, ἡ δὲ τέχνη τῶν καθόλου, αἱ δὲ πράξεις καὶ αἱ γενέσεις πᾶσαι περὶ τὸ καθ' ἕκαστόν εἰσιν.

VIII. This chapter fulfils a promise made before in the *Eudemian Ethics* (I. viii. 18), by distinguishing 'thought' from other modifications of the same practical quality, namely, economy and the various forms of politics. This distinction would at first sight tend to reduce 'thought' to mere egotism (§ 3. δοκεῖ μάλιστ' εἶναι ἡ περὶ αὐτὸν καὶ ἕνα. § 4: τὸ αὑτῷ εἰδέναι), and thus to isolate the individual within himself. In order to obviate this, the writer brings forward arguments to show that the welfare of the individual is bound up with that of the family and the state (§ 4). He urges the difficulty of knowing one's own interest, hence concluding that 'thought' is no mere instinct of selfishness. 'Thought' implies a wide experience, on which account boys

2 ἕξις, τὸ μέντοι εἶναι οὐ ταὐτὸν αὐταῖς. τῆς δὲ περὶ πόλιν ἡ μὲν ὡς ἀρχιτεκτονικὴ φρόνησις νομοθετική, ἡ δὲ ὡς τὰ καθ' ἕκαστα τὸ κοινὸν ἔχει ὄνομα, πολιτική· αὕτη δὲ πρακτικὴ καὶ βουλευτική· τὸ γὰρ ψήφισμα πρακτὸν ὡς τὸ ἔσχατον. διὸ πολιτεύεσθαι τούτους μόνους λέγουσιν· μόνοι

---

cannot attain to it, no more than they can to philosophy, though they are often clever in mathematics (§§ 5—6). 'Thought' is a sort of deduction with a universal and a particular element (§ 7), and yet we must distinguish it from science on this very account, that it deals with particulars (§ 8). It is the opposite to reason, which is of first principles, while thought is rather an intuition of particular facts (analogous to apprehending a mathematical figure). At all events, *one* form of thought is of this character.

1—3 ἔστι δὲ—δικαστική] 'Now politics and "thought" are really the same faculty of mind, though they would be defined differently. Thought dealing with the state is divided into—first, legislation, which is the master-spirit as it were; and secondly, politics in detail, which is practical as being deliberative (for a "measure" is like the practical application of a general principle) and which usurps the common name of politics; hence too they who are concerned with particular measures alone get the name of politicians, for these alone *act*, like workmen under a master. Just so that appears to be especially "thought" which is concerned with the individual self. And this kind usurps the common name of "thought," while the other kinds I have alluded to may be specified as—first, economy; second, legislation; and third, politics (in the restricted sense), which may be subdivided into the deliberative and the judicial.' This distinction was promised before, *Eth. Eud.* I. viii. 8 Ὥστε τοῦτ' ἂν εἴη αὐτὸ τὸ ἀγαθὸν τὸ τέλος τῶν ἀνθρώπῳ πρακτῶν. Τοῦτο δ' ἐστὶ τὸ ὑπὸ τὴν κυρίαν πασῶν. Αὕτη δ' ἐστὶ πολιτικὴ καὶ οἰκονομικὴ καὶ φρόνησις. Διαφέρουσι γὰρ αὗται αἱ ἕξεις πρὸς τὰς ἄλλας τῷ τοιαῦται εἶναι· πρὸς δ' ἀλλήλας εἴ τι διαφέρουσιν, ὕστερον λεκτέον. It would appear that Eudemus by a sort of afterthought united the conception of φρόνησις, which was developed later, to that of πολιτική to which Aristotle had assigned the apprehension of the chief good for man (cf. *Eth.* I. ii. 5). But in so doing he had to bring together two different things; for φρόνησις was a psychological term expressing a faculty of the mind, but πολιτική was merely one of the divisions of the sciences. In order to make them commensurate, Eudemus alters the signification of πολιτική. He treats it as a state of mind (ἕξις), as a mode of φρόνησις, dealing with the state either universally or in details. From the same later point of view he adds also οἰκονομική; cf. Ar. *Pol.* I. iii. 1: Ἐπεὶ δὲ φανερὸν ἐξ ὧν μορίων ἡ πόλις συνέστηκεν, ἀναγκαῖον περὶ οἰκονομίας εἰπεῖν πρότερον, &c.

2 ὡς τὸ ἔσχατον] The ψήφισμα or particular measure is here compared to the minor term in a syllogism, *i.e.* it constitutes the application of a general principle. Cf. *Eth.* v. x. 6. On the use of ἔσχατον in this purely technical and logical sense, cf. §§ 8—9: Ar. *Met.* x. i. 9: νῦν γὰρ λόγοι καὶ ταῦτα ἐσχάτων τῶν καθόλου

γὰρ πράττουσιν οὗτοι ὥσπερ οἱ χειροτέχναι· δοκεῖ δὲ καὶ 3
φρόνησις μάλιστ' εἶναι ἡ περὶ αὐτὸν καὶ ἕνα. καὶ ἔχει
αὕτη τὸ κοινὸν ὄνομα, φρόνησις· ἐκείνων δὲ ἡ μὲν οἰκονομία
ἡ δὲ νομοθεσία ἡ δὲ πολιτική, καὶ ταύτης ἡ μὲν βουλευτικὴ
ἡ δὲ δικαστική. εἶδος μὲν οὖν τι ἂν εἴη γνώσεως τὸ αὑτῷ 4
εἰδέναι· ἀλλ' ἔχει διαφορὰν πολλήν· καὶ δοκεῖ ὁ τὰ περὶ

καὶ οὐ τῶν ἐσχάτων. *Post. Anal.* I. i. 4: οὐ διὰ τὸ μέσον τὸ ἔσχατον γνωρίζεται.

3 The classification here intended is as follows,—φρόνησις or thought being first a general term and including politics with the other faculties mentioned, and secondly a special kind contrasted with the other faculties—

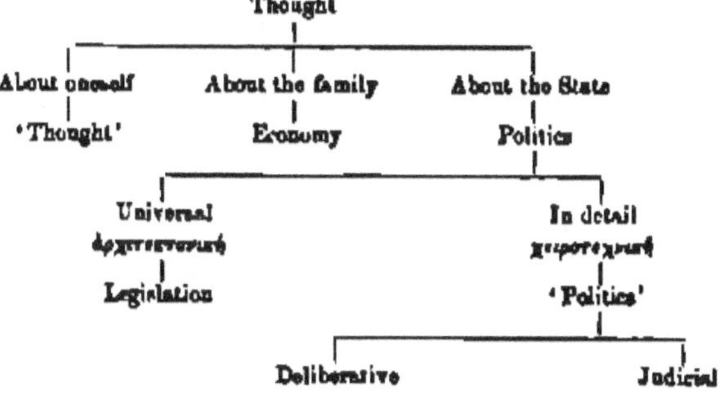
Thought
About oneself
About the family
About the State
'Thought'
Economy
Politics
Universal
ἀρχιτεκτονική
Legislation
In detail
χειροτεχνική
'Politics'
Deliberative
Judicial

4 εἶδος μὲν οὖν—πολιτείας] 'Now it must be considered a species of knowledge to know one's own interest, but this opens matter for controversy. The man who knows his own concerns and occupies himself with these is commonly considered thoughtful, while politicians are called busybodies, and hence Euripides wrote:—

Small wisdom were it in me to aspire,
When well I might, mixed with the common herd,
Enjoy a lot full equal with the best.
But ah! how full of vanity is man!
The restless meddling spirits in the state
Are gaped at still and made the country's gods.

Men with these selfish principles seek their own advantage, and this, they consider, is what they have to do. From this notion the idea has grown that *they* are the thoughtful. And yet, perhaps, the welfare of the individual is inseparable from the regulation of the household and from the existence of a state.'

τὸ αὑτῷ εἰδέναι] Fritzsche reads τὸ τὰ αὑτῷ with the authority of two MSS., adding 'Ceterum in hâc quoque præfractâ orationis brevitate qui multum Eudemi Moralia diurnâ nocturnâque manu volutavit Eudemi stilum agnoscat necesse est.'

αὐτὸν εἰδὼς καὶ διατρίβων φρόνιμος εἶναι, οἱ δὲ πολιτικοὶ πολυπράγμονες· διὸ Εὐριπίδης

> πῶς δ' ἂν φρονοίην, ᾧ παρῆν ἀπραγμόνως
> ἐν τοῖσι πολλοῖς ἠριθμημένῳ στρατοῦ
> ἴσον μετασχεῖν;
> τοὺς γὰρ περισσοὺς καί τι πράσσοντας πλέον. . .

ζητοῦσι γὰρ τὸ αὑτοῖς ἀγαθόν, καὶ οἴονται τοῦτο δεῖν
πράττειν. ἐκ ταύτης οὖν τῆς δόξης ἐλήλυθε τὸ τούτους
φρονίμους εἶναι· καίτοι ἴσως οὐκ ἔστι τὸ αὑτοῦ εὖ ἄνευ
οἰκονομίας οὐδ' ἄνευ πολιτείας· ἔτι δὲ τὰ αὑτοῦ πῶς δεῖ
5 διοικεῖν, ἄδηλον καὶ σκεπτέον. σημεῖον δ' ἐστὶ τοῦ εἰρη-
μένου καὶ διότι γεωμετρικοὶ μὲν νέοι καὶ μαθηματικοὶ
γίνονται καὶ σοφοὶ τὰ τοιαῦτα, φρόνιμος δ' οὐ δοκεῖ γίνεσθαι. αἴτιον δ' ὅτι τῶν καθ' ἕκαστά ἐστιν ἡ φρόνησις, ἃ
γίνεται γνώριμα ἐξ ἐμπειρίας, νέος δ' ἔμπειρος οὐκ ἔστιν·
6 πλῆθος γὰρ χρόνου ποιεῖ τὴν ἐμπειρίαν· ἐπεὶ καὶ τοῦτ' ἄν
τις σκέψαιτο, διὰ τί δὴ μαθηματικὸς μὲν παῖς γένοιτ' ἄν,
σοφὸς δ' ἢ φυσικὸς οὔ. ἢ ὅτι τὰ μὲν δι' ἀφαιρέσεώς

πολυπράγμονες] This is often opposed to τὰ αὑτοῦ πράττειν. Cf. Plato, *Gorgias*, p. 526 C: φιλοσόφου τὰ αὑτοῦ πράξαντος καὶ οὐ πολυπραγμονήσαντος ἐν τῷ βίῳ. *Repub.* p. 433 A: τὸ τὰ αὑτοῦ πράττειν καὶ μὴ πολυπραγμονεῖν.

Εὐριπίδης] In the *Philoctetes*; the later lines are thus filled up by Wagner, *Fragm. Eur.* p. 401:—

> ἴσον μετασχεῖν τῷ σοφωτάτῳ τύχης;
> οὐδὲν γὰρ οὕτω γαῦρον ὡς ἀνὴρ ἔφυ.
> τοὺς μὲν περισσοὺς καί τι πράσσοντας πλέον
> τιμῶμεν ἄνδρας τ' ἐν πόλει νομίζομεν.

The Scholiast and Paraphrast both conjecture Ζεὺς μισεῖ to govern περισσούς. This would give no metre, and only a very inferior sense.

4—5 ἔτι—γίνεσθαι] 'Moreover the directing one's own affairs is by no means simple, it is a subject for much consideration. In proof whereof we may allege that while boys learn geometry and mathematics, and become clever in such things, no boy seems to attain to "thoughtfulness."' The writer is arguing against the identification of 'thought' with an instinct of selfishness. If it were so simple, why should not boys possess it? διότι is for ὅτι, as in *Eth. Eud.* VII. x. 20: Αἴτιον δὲ τοῦ μάχεσθαι, διότι καλλίων μὲν ἡ ἠθικὴ φιλία, ἀναγκαιοτέρα δὲ ἡ χρησίμη. Cf. Ar. *Meteor.* III. iii. 5: Σημεῖον δὲ τούτου διότι ἐντεῦθεν γίγνεται ὁ ἄνεμος ὅθεν ἂν ἡ κυρία γίγνηται διάστασις. *Ib.* I. xiii. 23: Τό τε ὑπὸ τοῖς ὄρεσιν ἔχειν τὰς πηγὰς μαρτυρεῖ διότι τῷ συρρεῖν ἐπ' ὀλίγον καὶ κατὰ μικρὸν ἐκ πολλῶν νοτίδων διαδίδωσιν ὁ τόπος καὶ γίγνονται οὕτως αἱ πηγαὶ τῶν ποταμῶν.

6 σοφὸς δ' ἢ φυσικὸς οὔ] 'But not a metaphysician or physical philosopher.' Σοφὸς is here used in a distinctive sense, 'philosopher,' *par excellence*, with a science above physics

ἐστιν, τῶν δ' αἱ ἀρχαὶ ἐξ ἐμπειρίας· καὶ τὰ μὲν οὐ
πιστεύουσιν οἱ νέοι ἀλλὰ λέγουσιν, τῶν δὲ τὸ τί ἐστιν οὐκ
ἄδηλον; ἔτι ἡ ἁμαρτία ἢ περὶ τὸ καθόλου ἐν τῷ βουλεύσασθαι ἢ περὶ τὸ καθ' ἕκαστον· ἢ γὰρ ὅτι πάντα τὰ 7
βαρύσταθμα ὕδατα φαῦλα, ἢ ὅτι τοδὶ βαρύσταθμον. ὅτι
δ' ἡ φρόνησις οὐκ ἐπιστήμη, φανερόν· τοῦ γὰρ ἐσχάτου 8
ἐστίν, ὥσπερ εἴρηται· τὸ γὰρ πρακτὸν τοιοῦτον. ἀντίκειται μὲν δὴ τῷ νῷ. ὁ μὲν γὰρ νοῦς τῶν ὅρων, ὧν οὐκ ἔστι 9

---

and mathematics, cf. ch. vii. § 3. note.

ἢ ὅτι—ἄδηλον] 'The reason surely is that the former matters (i.e. mathematics) are abstract, while the principles of the latter (physics and philosophy) are got by experience; thus boys repeat truths of the latter kind, without being really convinced of them; while the nature of the other subjects is easy to comprehend.'

δι' ἀφαιρέσεως] The form in Aristotle is either ἐν ἀφαιρέσει or ἐξ ἀφαιρέσεως. He constantly applies these terms to denote the mathematics. The *locus classicus* on this subject is *Metaphys.* x. iii. 7: Καθάπερ δ' ὁ μαθηματικὸς περὶ τὰ ἐξ ἀφαιρέσεως τὴν θεωρίαν ποιεῖται, περιελὼν γὰρ πάντα τὰ αἰσθητὰ θεωρεῖ, οἷον βάρος καὶ κουφότητα καὶ σκληρότητα καὶ τοὐναντίον, ἔτι δὲ καὶ θερμότητα καὶ ψυχρότητα καὶ τὰς ἄλλας τὰς αἰσθητὰς ἐναντιώσεις, μόνον δὲ καταλείπει τὸ ποσὸν καὶ συνεχές, κ.τ.λ. Cf. *De Cœlo*, III. i. 11: διὰ τὸ τὰ μὲν ἐξ ἀφαιρέσεως λέγεσθαι τὰ μαθηματικά, τὰ δὲ φυσικὰ ἐκ προσθέσεως. *De Anim.*, III. vii. 10: οὕτω τὰ μαθηματικὰ οὐ κεχωρισμένα ὡς κεχωρισμένα νοεῖ, ὅταν νοῇ ἐκεῖνα.

πιστεύουσι] Cf. ch. iii. § 4, note, and *Eth.* VII. iii. 8: οἱ πρῶτον μαθόντες συνείρουσι μὲν τοὺς λόγους, ἴσασι δ' οὔπω.

7 Another argument to prove the complex and difficult character of 'thought' is that it implies a kind of syllogism, wherein both the major premiss and the minor equally admit of error.

τὰ βαρύσταθμα ὕδατα φαῦλα] This was probably a medical notion of the day. Cf. *Problems*, I. xiii. where a similar superstition is maintained: Διὰ τί τὸ τὰ ὕδατα μεταβάλλειν νοσώδεις φασὶν εἶναι, τὸ δὲ τὸν ἀέρα οὔ;—ὕδατος μὲν πολλὰ εἴδη ἐστὶ καὶ διάφορα καθ' αὑτά, ἀέρος δὲ οὔ, ὥστε καὶ τοῦτο αἴτιον.

8 ὅτι δ'—τοιοῦτον] 'But (though implying a syllogism) it is plain that "thought" is not science, for it deals with the particular, as we have said, the action being of this kind.'

9 ἀντίκειται—εἶδος] 'To reason, indeed, it forms the opposite pole; for while reason deals with those terms which are above all inference, "thought" on the other hand deals with the particular, which is below demonstration, and is apprehended by perception; not the perception of the separate senses, but analogous to that faculty by which we perceive that the immediate object presented to us in mathematics is a triangle. For on this side also demonstration must cease. However it is rather this particular mode of thought which is a perception, the other presents a different form.'

ἀντίκειται μὲν δὴ τῷ νῷ] Having

λόγος, ἡ δὲ τοῦ ἐσχάτου, οὗ οὐκ ἔστιν ἐπιστήμη ἀλλ' αἴσθησις, οὐχ ἡ τῶν ἰδίων, ἀλλ' οἵᾳ αἰσθανόμεθα ὅτι τὸ ἐν τοῖς μαθηματικοῖς ἔσχατον τρίγωνον· στήσεται γὰρ κἀκεῖ.

---

alluded to the syllogistic nature of 'thought,' the writer seems to have been reminded to distinguish it from science; and thus, having before (ch. v. § 8: ch. vii. § 6) contrasted it with art and philosophy, he is led on to finish the round by placing it in contrast with reason.

οὐχ ἡ τῶν ἰδίων, ἀλλ' οἵᾳ αἰσθανόμεθα] This is the same as Aristotle's famous distinction between the 'separate senses' and the 'common sense.' His own words are clear on the point, cf. *De Animâ*, II. vi. 2: *λέγω δ' ἴδιον μὲν (αἰσθητὸν) ὃ μὴ ἐνδέχεται ἑτέρᾳ αἰσθήσει αἰσθάνεσθαι, καὶ περὶ ὃ μὴ ἐνδέχεται ἀπατηθῆναι, οἷον ὄψις χρώματος καὶ ἀκοὴ ψόφου καὶ γεῦσις χυμοῦ.—Τὰ μὲν οὖν τοιαῦτα λέγεται ἴδια ἑκάστου, κοινὰ δὲ κίνησις, ἠρεμία, ἀριθμός, σχῆμα, μέγεθος· τὰ γὰρ τοιαῦτα οὐδεμιᾶς ἐστὶν ἴδια, ἀλλὰ κοινὰ πάσαις· καὶ γὰρ ἁφῇ κίνησίς τίς ἐστιν αἰσθητὴ καὶ ὄψει.* It will be seen that figure (*σχῆμα*) is one of the objects of the 'common sense;' the text gives as an instance of this the perception of a triangle. In *De An.* III. i. 6, Aristotle adds 'unity' to the list of 'common sensibles,' but he reduces them all to modifications of the perception of motion: *ταῦτα γὰρ πάντα κινήσει αἰσθανόμεθα, οἷον μέγεθος κινήσει. Ὥστε καὶ σχῆμα· μέγεθος γάρ τι τὸ σχῆμα. Τὸ δ' ἠρεμοῦν τῷ μὴ κινεῖσθαι· ὁ δ' ἀριθμὸς τῇ ἀποφάσει τοῦ συνεχοῦς, κ.τ.λ.* He admits (*De An.* II. vi. 4) that 'common sensibles' can scarcely be said to be apprehended by sense at all, *τῶν δὲ καθ' αὑτὰ αἰσθητῶν τὰ ἴδια κυρίως ἐστὶν αἰσθητά*, cf. *Ib.* III. i. 6, where it is said these are apprehended *accidentally* or concomitantly by the senses. This is surely the true view; we see in the apprehension of number, figure, and the like, not an operation of sense, but the mind putting its own forms and categories, *i.e.* itself, on the external object. It would follow then that the senses cannot really be separated from the mind; the senses and the mind each contribute an element to every knowledge. Aristotle's doctrine of *κοινὴ αἴσθησις* would go far, if carried out, to modify his doctrine of the simple and innate character of the senses, *e.g.* sight (cf. *Eth.* II. i. 4), and would prevent its absolute collision with Berkeley's *Theory of Vision.* On the general subject of *κοιν. αἰσθ.* see Sir W. Hamilton, *Reid's Works*, pp. 828—830.

ὅτι τὸ ἐν τοῖς μαθηματικοῖς ἔσχατον τρίγωνον] This has been frequently understood to mean that 'the ultimate or simplest possible figure is a triangle.' But the Paraphrast does not so explain it; his words are *τοῦτον δὲ τὸν τρόπον καὶ οἱ μαθηματικοὶ τὸ αἰσθητὸν γινώσκουσι τρίγωνον, κ.τ.λ.* And referring to Ar. *Post. Analyt.* I. i. 4, we find exactly this instance given of a *particular* knowledge, the result of observation, *ὅτι μὲν γὰρ πᾶν τρίγωνον ἔχει δυσὶν ὀρθαῖς ἴσας, προῄδει· ὅτι δὲ τόδε τὸ ἐν τῷ ἡμικυκλίῳ τρίγωνόν ἐστιν ἅμα ἐπαγόμενος ἐγνώρισεν.* The term *ἔσχατον* is used in the very next line: *ἐνίων γὰρ τοῦτον τὸν τρόπον ἡ μάθησίς ἐστι, καὶ οὐ διὰ τοῦ μέσου τὸ ἔσχατον γνωρίζεται.* It is true that in different places Aristotle uses *ἔσχατον* in different senses, as denoting with various applications

ἀλλ' αὕτη μᾶλλον αἴσθησις † ἡ φρόνησις, ἐκείνης δ' ἄλλο εἶδος.

Τὸ ζητεῖν δὲ καὶ τὸ βουλεύεσθαι διαφέρει· τὸ γὰρ βου- 9
λεύεσθαι ζητεῖν τι ἐστίν. δεῖ δὲ λαβεῖν καὶ περὶ εὐβουλίας
τί ἐστι, πότερον ἐπιστήμη τις ἢ δόξα ἢ εὐστοχία ἢ ἄλλο
τι γένος. ἐπιστήμη μὲν δὴ οὐκ ἔστιν· οὐ γὰρ ζητοῦσι 2
περὶ ὧν ἴσασιν, ἡ δ' εὐβουλία βουλή τις, ὁ δὲ βουλευόμενος

---

the end of a series, thus cf. *De An.* III. x. 2, where it means 'final cause,' *Eth.* III. iii. 11, 'the last step in analysis;' *Metaph.* VI. iij. 6, 'matter,' &c. But in the place before us τὸ ἔσχατον has been already appropriated to the logical meaning of 'particular,' 'minor term,' 'immediate truth,' cf. § 2 and § 8.

στήσεται γὰρ κἀκεῖ] 'For on that side too (*i.e.* in dealing with an object of the sense as well as an intuition of reason) demonstration must stop.' Ἵστασθαι is a common logical form, it is opposed to προϊέναι εἰς ἄπειρον, and is frequently impersonal, cf. *Post. Anal.* I. iii. 1: ἀδύνατον γὰρ τὰ ἄπειρα διελθεῖν. Εἴ τε ἵσταται καὶ εἰσὶν ἀρχαί, κ.τ.λ. *Met.* II. iv, 22, &c.

ἀλλ' αὕτη μᾶλλον αἴσθησις † ἡ φρόνησις] Three of Bekker's MSS. read ἢ φρόνησις, and this seems most natural, and to give the best sense (though ἡ is supported by the Paraphrast). What the writer means is apparently to add that only one kind of thought can be called analogous to the apprehension of a triangle; αὕτη refers to ἡ καθ' ἕκαστα φρόνησις, mentioned above, ch. vii. § 7: δεῖ ἄμφω ἔχειν ἢ ταύτην μᾶλλον. There is another kind (ἐκείνης), namely, the possession of universal ideas (τῶν καθόλου) (*l.c.*), which is of a different nature.

IX. This chapter commences the examination of a set of faculties cognate to 'Thought,' or forming part of it. The first of these is good counsel (εὐβουλία). This, says the writer, is to be distinguished from science, which does not deliberate; from guessing (εὐστοχία), which is too quick; from sagacity (ἀγχίνοια), which is a kind of guessing; and from opinion, which is too definite. It consists, then, in a certain 'rightness,' it chooses the right means to a good end. The conception of this end 'Thought' itself must supply. There is a great assumption here of the manner of Aristotle. The chapter seems formed after *Eth.* III. ii.; § 6 reminds us of many similar passages in Book IV., and § 7 is after the manner of *Eth.* I. iii. 5. There is an advance upon Aristotle's account of deliberation (*Eth.* III. iii.) in two points, (1) the process is illustrated here by the logical formula of the syllogism, (2) there is a mention here of the faculty whereby ends are apprehended, which Aristotle had left unnoticed. See *Eth.* III. iii. 1, note.

1 It is an abrupt, awkward commencement of the chapter to say, 'enquiring and deliberating are different, for deliberating is a species of enquiring.' But what is meant apparently is, to bring 'good counsel' under the head of enquiring, which separates it at once from both science and opinion.

ζητεῖ καὶ λογίζεται. ἀλλὰ μὴν οὐδ' εὐστοχία. ἄνευ τε γὰρ λόγου καὶ ταχύ τι ἡ εὐστοχία, βουλεύονται δὲ πολὺν χρόνον, καὶ φασὶ πράττειν μὲν δεῖν ταχὺ τὰ βουλευθέντα,
3 βουλεύεσθαι δὲ βραδέως. ἔτι ἡ ἀγχίνοια ἕτερον καὶ ἡ εὐβουλία· ἔστι δ' εὐστοχία τις ἡ ἀγχίνοια. οὐδὲ δὴ δόξα ἡ εὐβουλία οὐδεμία. ἀλλ' ἐπεὶ ὁ μὲν κακῶς βουλευόμενος ἁμαρτάνει, ὁ δ' εὖ ὀρθῶς βουλεύεται, δῆλον ὅτι ὀρθότης τις ἡ εὐβουλία ἐστίν, οὔτ' ἐπιστήμης δὲ οὔτε δόξης· ἐπιστήμης μὲν γὰρ οὐκ ἔστιν ὀρθότης (οὐδὲ γὰρ ἁμαρτία), δόξης δ' ὀρθότης ἀλήθεια· ἅμα δὲ καὶ ὥρισται ἤδη πᾶν οὗ δόξα ἐστίν. ἀλλὰ μὴν οὐδ' ἄνευ λόγου ἡ εὐβουλία. διανοίας ἄρα λείπεται· αὕτη γὰρ οὔπω φάσις· καὶ γὰρ ἡ δόξα οὐ

---

2 φασὶ πράττειν μὲν δεῖν ταχὺ κ.τ.λ.] Fritzsche quotes Isocr. *Demon.* p. 9, c. § 35: *Βουλεύου μὲν βραδέως, ἐπιτέλει δὲ ταχέως τὰ δόξαντα.* Herod. vii. 49: *ἀνὴρ δὴ οὕτω ἂν εἴη ἄριστος, εἰ βουλευόμενος μὲν ἀρρωδέοι, πᾶν ἐπιλεγόμενος πείσεσθαι χρῆμα, ἐν δὲ τῷ ἔργῳ θρασὺς εἴη.*

3 ἔστι δ' εὐστοχία τις ἡ ἀγχίνοια] This is announced by Aristotle, *Post. Anal.* i. xxxiv. 1, in the very next line to that passage on the distinction of the organs of truth, which apparently suggested so much of the subjects of the present book, *ἡ δ' ἀγχίνοιά ἐστιν εὐστοχία τις ἐν ἀσκέπτῳ χρόνῳ τοῦ μέσου.* In more general terms ἀγχίνοια is defined by Plato, *Charmides*, p. 160 A, as ὀξύτης τις τῆς ψυχῆς.

ἐπιστήμης μὲν—λογίζεται]. 'Now in science there is no such thing as "rightness," for there is no such thing as wrongness. In opinion, on the other hand, rightness is truth (and not good counsel). And besides, whatever we have an opinion about is already decided. But good counsel is not by any means beyond questioning (ἄνευ λόγου). Therefore it must be a kind of operation of the reason (διανοίας ἄρα λείπεται), for this does not amount to decision. Opinion is not an inquiry, but is already a kind of decision. On the other hand, he that deliberates, whether well or ill, is inquiring after something and calculating.'

ἐπιστήμης] This is said here just as it was before said, ch. v. § 7, that there were no degrees of excellence in Thought.

δόξης δ'] Cf. *Eth.* iii. ii. 13, and above, ch. ii. § 2, note.

διανοίας ἄρα] Plato, *Repub.* p. 511 D, proposed to confine the term διάνοια to the discursive understanding as opposed to νοῦς, the intuitive and speculative reason, *διάνοιαν δὲ καλεῖν μοι δοκεῖς τὴν τῶν γεωμετρικῶν τε καὶ τὴν τῶν τοιούτων ἕξιν ἀλλ' οὐ νοῦν, ὡς μεταξύ τι δόξης τε καὶ νοῦ τὴν διάνοιαν οὖσαν.* Aristotle probably had the same distinction in view, *Post. Anal.* i. xxxiii. 9 (*l.c.*), πῶς δεῖ διανεῖμαι ἐπί τε διανοίας καὶ νοῦ. But he did not maintain the distinction in his works, and certainly it is not observed by Eudemus in the present book, where both νοῦς πρακτικὸς and διάνοια θεωρητικὴ are spoken of. In the place before us διάνοια apparently means the exercise of the reason.

ζήτησις ἀλλὰ φάσις τις ἤδη, ὁ δὲ βουλευόμενος, ἐάν τε εὖ
ἐάν τε κακῶς βουλεύηται, ζητεῖ τι καὶ λογίζεται. ἀλλ' 4
ὀρθότης τίς ἐστιν ἡ εὐβουλία βουλῆς· διὸ ἡ βουλὴ ζητητέα
πρῶτον τί καὶ περὶ τί. ἐπεὶ δ' ἡ ὀρθότης πλεοναχῶς,
δῆλον ὅτι οὐ πᾶσα· ὁ γὰρ ἀκρατὴς καὶ ὁ φαῦλος ὃ προτίθεται †ἰδεῖν ἐκ τοῦ λογισμοῦ τεύξεται, ὥστε ὀρθῶς ἔσται
βεβουλευμένος, κακὸν δὲ μέγα εἰληφώς. δοκεῖ δ' ἀγαθόν
τι εἶναι τὸ εὖ βεβουλεῦσθαι· ἡ γὰρ τοιαύτη ὀρθότης βουλῆς
εὐβουλία, ἡ ἀγαθοῦ τευκτική. ἀλλ' ἔστι καὶ τούτου 5
ψευδεῖ συλλογισμῷ τυχεῖν, καὶ ὃ μὲν δεῖ ποιῆσαι τυχεῖν,
δι' οὗ δ' οὔ, ἀλλὰ ψευδῆ τὸν μέσον ὅρον εἶναι· ὥστ' οὐδ'
αὕτη πω εὐβουλία, καθ' ἣν οὗ δεῖ μὲν τυγχάνει, οὐ μέντοι

---

4 ἐπεὶ δ'—βεβουλεῦσθαι] 'But since the term "rightness" is used in more senses than one, it is plain that "good counsel" does not answer to all the senses. For the incontinent or bad man will obtain, by his calculation, what he proposes to himself as necessary, so that he will have deliberated rightly, yet secured a great evil. Whereas, to have deliberated well is generally thought (δοκεῖ) to be a good.'

πλεοναχῶς] *i.e.* Rightness of means, either respective, or irrespective, of rightness in the end; or, again, rightness of end (§ 5), whatever may have been the means.

ὁ γὰρ ἀκρατής] It would seem rather the abandoned man (ἀκόλαστος) who by calculation attains bad ends. The incontinent man would not generally have deliberation attributed to him, cf. *Eth.* VII. ii. 2. But the characters cannot be kept very distinct.

†ἰδεῖν] Madvig and Mr. Jackson propose to read δεῖν for ἰδεῖν, quoting Plato, *Sophist.* 221 A, ὅπερ ἄρτι προὐθέμεθα δεῖν ἐξευρεῖν. The emendation seems probable, and has been adopted in the above translation.

δοκεῖ δ' ἀγαθόν] Fritzsche quotes Herod. VII. 10: τὸ γὰρ εὖ βουλεύεσθαι κέρδος μέγιστον εὑρίσκω ἐόν. Sophocles, *Antig.* 1050: κράτιστον κτημάτων εὐβουλία. Isocr. *Demon.* p. 9. c. § 35: ἡγοῦ κράτιστον εἶναι παρὰ μὲν τῶν θεῶν εὐτυχίαν, παρὰ δὲ ἡμῶν αὐτῶν εὐβουλίαν.

5 ἀλλ' ἔστι—εἶναι] 'But, farther, it is possible to obtain what is good by a false syllogism, and to hit on doing what one ought, not however by the right means, but with a false middle term.' It is an inaccuracy to speak of a 'false middle term.' Falsehood or truth is the attribute of a proposition not a term, cf. *De Interpret.* I. 3: περὶ γὰρ σύνθεσιν καὶ διαίρεσίν ἐστι τὸ ψεῦδος καὶ τὸ ἀληθές. If the conception of the end be right and yet the syllogism wrong, it follows that the minor premiss must be false, thus:

Preservation of health is good:
Abstinence from intellectual labour is
preservation of health:

the result of which syllogism will be the preservation of health, but by the sacrifice of mental culture.

6 δι' οὗ ἔδει. ἔτι ἔστι πολὺν χρόνον βουλευόμενον τυχεῖν,
τὸν δὲ ταχύ. οὐκοῦν οὐδ' ἐκείνη πω εὐβουλία, ἀλλ' ὀρθότης
7 ἡ κατὰ τὸ ὠφέλιμον, καὶ οὗ δεῖ καὶ ὡς καὶ ὅτε. ἔτι ἔστι
καὶ ἁπλῶς εὖ βεβουλεῦσθαι καὶ πρός τι τέλος. ἡ μὲν δὴ
ἁπλῶς ἡ πρὸς τὸ τέλος τὸ ἁπλῶς κατορθοῦσα, ἡ δέ τις ἡ
πρός τι τέλος. εἰ δὴ τῶν φρονίμων τὸ εὖ βεβουλεῦσθαι,
ἡ εὐβουλία εἴη ἂν ὀρθότης ἡ κατὰ τὸ συμφέρον πρός τι
τέλος, οὗ ἡ φρόνησις ἀληθὴς ὑπόληψίς ἐστιν.

10 Ἔστι δὲ καὶ ἡ σύνεσις καὶ ἡ ἀσυνεσία, καθ' ἃς λέγομεν συνετοὺς καὶ ἀσυνέτους, οὐθ' ὅλως τὸ αὐτὸ ἐπιστήμῃ ἢ δόξῃ

6—7 The writer first raises good counsel to the rank of one of the virtues, by the mention of all the qualifications necessary; afterwards he seems to modify this by saying that, besides the absolute good counsel which aims at the absolute end, there is also such a thing as relative good counsel aiming at relative ends.

One might have thought that it was unnecessary to give so separate a psychological existence to excellence in deliberation. However, the quality here described answers more nearly than φρόνησις to what we call 'prudence.' Φρόνησις, we are here told, is the conception of ends, and afterwards (ch. xii. § 9) it is shown to be the faculty of means. In truth, it is both, according to the Aristotelian views (as far as we can discern them); it implies both prudence (εὐβουλία), and also a certain moral condition (ἀρετή), and it is implied by both of them. As compared with the one it is of ends, and as compared with the other it is of means.

X. This chapter treats of another faculty which forms an element in wisdom, and yet may be distinguished from it, namely, apprehension (σύνεσις). Apprehension is not mere opinion (else all would possess it), nor is it a science, for it deals with no separate class of objects whether necessary or contingent (οὔτε γὰρ περὶ τῶν ἀεὶ ὄντων καὶ ἀκινήτων ἡ σύνεσίς ἐστιν, οὔτε περὶ τῶν γιγνομένων ὁτουοῦν). It deals with all that can be matter of human deliberation, in short, with the same objects as Thought. But Thought *commands*, it is concerned with right action, in short, it belongs to the will as well as to reason. But apprehension only *judges*, it is merely intellectual. It is neither the having nor the getting Thought, but rather it is the application of one's knowledge to give a meaning to the *dicta* of wisdom. It is 'understanding,' as its name implies, or 'putting things together' (συνιέναι) when another person speaks.

Aristotle had spoken of σύνεσις as one of the intellectual excellencies, *Eth.* I. xiii. 20: σοφίαν μὲν καὶ σύνεσιν καὶ φρόνησιν διανοητικάς. Eudemus does not apply the term ἀρετή to this, or to any of the other intellectual qualities which he treats of, except Thought and Philosophy. He gives here a psychological account of σύνεσις, the operation of which he confines to intellectual insight with regard to moral subjects, apprehension of

(πάντες γὰρ ἂν ἦσαν συνετοί) οὔτε τις μία τῶν κατὰ μέρος
ἐπιστημῶν, οἷον ἰατρικὴ περὶ ὑγιεινῶν ἢ γεωμετρία περὶ
μεγέθους· οὔτε γὰρ περὶ τῶν ἀεὶ ὄντων καὶ ἀκινήτων ἡ
σύνεσίς ἐστιν οὔτε περὶ τῶν γιγνομένων ὁτουοῦν, ἀλλὰ
περὶ ὧν ἀπορήσειεν ἄν τις καὶ βουλεύσαιτο. διὸ περὶ τὰ
αὐτὰ μὲν τῇ φρονήσει ἐστίν, οὐκ ἔστι δὲ ταὐτὸν σύνεσις
καὶ φρόνησις· ἡ μὲν γὰρ φρόνησις ἐπιτακτική ἐστιν· τί 2
γὰρ δεῖ πράττειν ἢ μή, τὸ τέλος αὐτῆς ἐστίν· ἡ δὲ σύνεσις
κριτικὴ μόνον· ταὐτὸν γὰρ σύνεσις καὶ εὐσυνεσία καὶ συνετοὶ καὶ εὐσύνετοι. ἔστι δ᾽ οὔτε τὸ ἔχειν τὴν φρόνησιν 3
οὔτε τὸ λαμβάνειν ἡ σύνεσις· ἀλλ᾽ ὥσπερ τὸ μανθάνειν
λέγεται συνιέναι, ὅταν χρῆται τῇ ἐπιστήμῃ, οὕτως ἐν τῷ
χρῆσθαι τῇ δόξῃ ἐπὶ τὸ κρίνειν περὶ τούτων περὶ ὧν ἡ
φρόνησίς ἐστιν, ἄλλου λέγοντος, καὶ κρίνειν καλῶς· τὸ
γὰρ εὖ τῷ καλῶς ταὐτόν. καὶ ἐντεῦθεν ἐλήλυθε τοὔνομα ἡ 4

---

the meaning of moral dicta and critical judgment thereon. That there is such a faculty of apprehension, and of sympathetic or critical understanding, quite distinct from moral goodness in people, the experience of life seems to show.

The author of the *Magna Moralia* gives a much inferior account of σύνεσις (I. xxxv. 17), making its characteristic to be that it deals with *small* matters, περὶ μικρῶν τε καὶ ἐν μικροῖς ἡ κρίσις.

1 διὸ περὶ τὰ αὐτὰ μὲν τῇ φρονήσει] It is used nearly equivalently to φρόνησις by Thucyd. I. 140: Δικαιῶ τοῖς κοινῇ δόξασιν, ἢν ἄρα τι καὶ σφαλλώμεθα, βοηθεῖν, ἢ μηδὲ κατορθοῦντας τῆς ξυνέσεως μεταποιεῖσθαι.

2 ἡ μὲν γὰρ φρόνησις ἐπιτακτική ἐστιν—ἡ δὲ σύνεσις κριτικὴ μόνον] The opposition of these terms is taken from Plato, *Politicus*, p. 259 E—260 C, where it is argued that the arithmetician (λογιστής) is content with a knowledge and judgment about numbers, whereas the architect (ἀρχιτέκτων) must go on to apply his knowledge by directing the workmen—thus that all science may be divided under the two heads of critical and mandatory. (260 A) Οὐκοῦν γνωστικαὶ μὲν αἵ τε τοιαῦται ξύμπασαι καὶ ὁπόσαι ξυντέτακται τῇ λογιστικῇ, κρίσει δὲ καὶ ἐπιτάξει διαφέρετον ἀλλήλοιν τούτω τὼ γένει;—Φαίνεσθον. Ἆρ᾽ οὖν συμπάσης τῆς γνωστικῆς εἰ τὸ μὲν ἐπιτακτικὸν μέρος, τὸ δὲ κριτικὸν διαιρούμενοι προσείποιμεν, ἐμμελῶς ἂν φαῖμεν διῃρῆσθαι; κατά γε τὴν ἐμὴν δόξαν.

3 ἀλλ᾽ ὥσπερ τὸ μανθάνειν λέγεται συνιέναι ὅταν χρῆται τῇ ἐπιστήμῃ] The word μανθάνειν was ambiguous in Greek, it meant either to 'learn' or to 'understand.' The Sophists used to play on this ambiguity, arguing that one could 'learn what one knew already.' Cf. Ar. *Soph. Elench.* iv. 1, 2, which illustrates the present passage: Εἰσὶ δὲ παρὰ μὲν τὴν ὁμωνυμίαν οἱ τοιοίδε τῶν λόγων, οἷον ὅτι μανθάνουσιν οἱ ἐπιστάμενοι· τὰ γὰρ ἀποστοματιζόμενα μανθάνουσιν οἱ γραμματικοί. Τὸ γὰρ μανθάνειν ὁμώνυμον, τό τε ξυνιέναι χρώμενον τῇ ἐπιστήμῃ καὶ τὸ λαμβάνειν ἐπιστήμην.

σύνεσις, καθ' ἣν εὐσύνετοι, ἐκ τῆς ἐν τῷ μανθάνειν· λέγομεν γὰρ τὸ μανθάνειν συνιέναι πολλάκις.

11 Ἡ δὲ καλουμένη γνώμη, καθ' ἣν εὐγνώμονας καὶ ἔχειν φαμὲν γνώμην, ἡ τοῦ ἐπιεικοῦς ἐστὶ κρίσις ὀρθή. σημεῖον δέ· τὸν γὰρ ἐπιεικῆ μάλιστά φαμεν εἶναι συγγνωμονικόν, καὶ ἐπιεικὲς τὸ ἔχειν περὶ ἔνια συγγνώμην. ἡ δὲ συγγνώμη γνώμη ἐστὶ κριτικὴ τοῦ ἐπιεικοῦς ὀρθή. ὀρθὴ δ' ἡ τοῦ ἀληθοῦς.

2 Εἰσὶ δὲ πᾶσαι αἱ ἕξεις εὐλόγως εἰς ταὐτὸ τείνουσαι· λέγομεν γὰρ γνώμην καὶ σύνεσιν καὶ φρόνησιν καὶ νοῦν ἐπὶ τοὺς αὐτοὺς ἐπιφέροντες γνώμην ἔχειν καὶ νοῦν ἤδη καὶ φρονίμους καὶ συνετούς· πᾶσαι γὰρ αἱ δυνάμεις αὗται τῶν ἐσχάτων εἰσὶ καὶ τῶν καθ' ἕκαστον, καὶ ἐν μὲν τῷ κριτικὸς

XI. This chapter (which is not conveniently divided as it stands) opens with a mention of the quality of considerateness (γνώμη), and proceeds to point out how various qualities unite in wisdom, and what are the natural and intuitive elements which it contains.

1 ἡ δὲ καλουμένη γνώμη] By the progress of psychology, this term came to bear the special meaning of 'considerateness.' At first it meant knowledge in general, cf. Theognis, vv. 895 sq.

Γνώμης δ' οὐδὲν ἄμεινον ἀνὴρ ἔχει αὐτὸς ἐν αὑτῷ,
Οὐδ' ἀγνωμοσύνης, Κύρν', ὀδυνηρότερον.

In Thucydides it bore a variety of significations, especially when used in the plural, standing for almost anything mental, 'minds' as opposed to bodies, 'thoughts' as opposed to deeds; 'feelings,' 'principles,' 'maxims,' &c. In Aristotle's *Rhetoric*, II. xxi. 2–15, γνώμη is used for a moral maxim (such as those of the so-called Gnomic Poets); so also, for all popular sayings, *Soph. El.* xvii. 17. It was probably from the association of συγγνώμη that γνώμη came to have its distinctive meaning. The author of the *Magna Moralia* calls it εὐγνωμοσύνη, and makes it a sort of passive form of ἐπιείκεια (II. ii. 1): ἔστι μὲν οὖν οὐκ ἄνευ ἐπιεικείας ἡ εὐγνωμοσύνη· τὸ μὲν γὰρ κρῖναι τοῦ εὐγνώμονος, τὸ δὲ δὴ πράττειν κατὰ τὴν κρίσιν τοῦ ἐπιεικοῦς.

In the text above, it is said that 'considerateness is a right judgment of the equitable man.' 'Pardon is a right critical considerateness of the equitable man.'

ὀρθὴ δ' ἡ τοῦ ἀληθοῦς] 'Now by a *right* considerateness is meant a *true* one.' This must be the import of the sentence, but the writor says not ἀληθής, but τοῦ ἀληθοῦς—probably 'by attraction' to τοῦ ἐπιεικοῦς. But it is an inaccuracy of language to speak of 'a true man' in the sense of 'a man whose judgment is true.' Stahr translates τοῦ ἐπιεικοῦς as if it were neuter. But 'the equitable man' here apparently gives the standard for γνώμη, as the φρόνιμοι for virtue, *Eth.* II. vi. 15.

2 εἰσὶ δὲ—ἄλλον] 'Now all the (above-mentioned) conditions of mind

εἶναι περὶ ὧν ὁ φρόνιμος, συνετὸς καὶ εὐγνώμων ἢ συγγνώ-
μων· τὰ γὰρ ἐπιεικῆ κοινὰ τῶν ἀγαθῶν ἁπάντων ἐστὶν ἐν
τῷ πρὸς ἄλλον. ἔστι δὲ τῶν καθ' ἕκαστα καὶ τῶν ἐσχά- 3
των πάντα τὰ πρακτά· καὶ γὰρ τὸν φρόνιμον δεῖ γινώσκειν
αὐτά, καὶ ἡ σύνεσις καὶ ἡ γνώμη περὶ τὰ πρακτά, ταῦτα
δ' ἔσχατα. καὶ ὁ νοῦς τῶν ἐσχάτων ἐπ' ἀμφότερα· καὶ 4
γὰρ τῶν πρώτων ὅρων καὶ τῶν ἐσχάτων νοῦς ἐστὶ καὶ οὐ
λόγος, καὶ ὁ μὲν κατὰ τὰς ἀποδείξεις τῶν ἀκινήτων ὅρων

---

naturally tend to the same point; we apply (ἐπιφέροντες) the terms considerateness, apprehension, thought, and reason to the same persons, and say (λέγομεν) that they have considerateness, that they have attained to (ἤδη) reason—that they are thoughtful—that they are apprehensive. For all these faculties deal with ultimate truths (τῶν ἐσχάτων) and particulars; and it is by being able to judge of those matters with which the thoughtful man is concerned, that a man is apprehensive, considerate, or forgiving. Equity extends itself over all the forms of good which consist in a relation to one's neighbour.'

νοῦν ἤδη] What this means is not quite clear. It may refer to what is said in § 6, ἥδε ἡ ἡλικία νοῦν ἔχει. Thus it might be nearly equivalent to our saying of a person that he had 'attained to years of discretion.' Or again, it may refer to the moment of action, and ἤδη would be thus equivalent to the French *voilà*. 'There is reason exhibited.' Ἤδη is used similarly to denote the present moment, *Eth. Eud.* II. viii. 11: Καὶ γὰρ ὁ ἐγκρατευόμενος λυπεῖται παρὰ τὴν ἐπιθυμίαν πράττων ἤδη, καὶ χαίρει τὴν ἀπ' ἐλπίδος ἡδονήν, ὅτι ὕστερον ὠφεληθήσεται, ἢ καὶ ἤδη ὠφελεῖται ὑγιαίνων.

τὰ γὰρ ἐπιεικῆ] This is said because γνώμη and συγγνώμη are acts of equity. Cf. *Eth.* v. x. 1, note.

4—5 καὶ ὁ νοῦς τῶν ἐσχάτων—νοῦς] 'And reason is of the ultimates at both ends of the series. Both the first and the last terms are apprehended, not by inference, but by reason. On the one hand, the scientific and demonstrative reason (ὁ μὲν κατὰ τὰς ἀποδείξεις) apprehends those terms which are immutable and primary. And on the other hand, the practical reason (ὁ ἐν ταῖς πρακτικαῖς) apprehends the ultimate (ἐσχάτου) and contingent truth, and the minor premiss. For these constitute the sources of our idea of the end, the universal being developed out of the particulars. Of these particulars, then, one must have perception, and this perception is reason.' The writer having before (in § 3) connected the faculties of 'apprehension,' &c., with 'Thought,' on the ground of their all being concerned with ultimate truths, proceeds to include reason (νοῦς) under the same category, and says that this apprehends ἔσχατα at both ends of the series. But now comes in a piece of confusion which is thoroughly Eudemian, for he goes on to say that the scientific reason apprehends first truths or principles (cf. ch. vi.), while the practical reason apprehends *last* terms or particulars. To mix up considerations of the scientific reason with the present discussion is to introduce what is entirely irrelevant. We are

καὶ πρώτων, ὁ δ' ἐν ταῖς πρακτικαῖς τοῦ ἐσχάτου καὶ ἐνδεχομένου καὶ τῆς ἑτέρας προτάσεως· ἀρχαὶ γὰρ τοῦ οὗ
5 ἕνεκα αὗται· ἐκ τῶν καθ' ἕκαστα γὰρ τὸ καθόλου. τούτων οὖν ἔχειν δεῖ αἴσθησιν, αὕτη δ' ἐστὶ νοῦς. διὸ καὶ φυσικὰ δοκεῖ εἶναι ταῦτα, καὶ φύσει σοφὸς μὲν οὐδείς, γνώμην δ'
6 ἔχειν καὶ σύνεσιν καὶ νοῦν. σημεῖον δ' ὅτι καὶ ταῖς ἡλικίαις οἰόμεθα ἀκολουθεῖν, καὶ ἥδε ἡ ἡλικία νοῦν ἔχει καὶ γνώμην, ὡς τῆς φύσεως αἰτίας οὔσης. διὸ καὶ ἀρχὴ καὶ

---

here a bringing together of two things which were before placed in contrast with each other (ch. viii. § 9), namely, the reason which apprehends first principles, and thought apprehending particular facts (ἐσχάτων). In the present passage, what was before called thought (φρόνησις) is called reason (νοῦς), and it is said that reason is the faculty which perceives or apprehends the particular in moral subjects (ἐν ταῖς πρακτικαῖς). This, then, is the main purport of the present remarks. Setting aside as irrelevant what is said of the scientific reason, we learn that the moral judgment is intuitive, that moral intuitions are to be attributed to the reason, and that out of these particular intuitions the moral universal grows up. When stripped of its ambiguities of statement, the sense of the passage becomes unexceptional. We may compare it with the incidental observations of Aristotle, *Eth.* I. iv. 7: Ἀρχὴ γὰρ τὸ ὅτι· καὶ εἰ τοῦτο φαίνοιτο ἀρκούντως, οὐδὲν προσδεήσει τοῦ διότι. ὁ δὲ τοιοῦτος ἢ ἔχει ἢ λάβοι ἂν ἀρχὰς ῥᾳδίως. *Ib.* vii. 20: ἱκανὸν ἔν τισι τὸ ὅτι δειχθῆναι καλῶς, οἷον καὶ περὶ τὰς ἀρχάς· τὸ δ' ὅτι πρῶτον καὶ ἀρχή. The expression of Eudemus is not so strong as that of Aristotle. Eudemus says ἐκ τῶν καθ' ἕκαστα τὸ καθόλου, while Aristotle said ἀρχὴ τὸ ὅτι. The latter must be true if reason be the organ by which the fact is apprehended, for reason is in itself universal, and whatever it apprehends must be of the nature of the universal.

ἀρχαὶ γὰρ τοῦ οὗ ἕνεκα αὗται] This is similar in form of expression to ch. iii. § 3: ἡ μὲν δὴ ἐπαγωγὴ ἀρχή ἐστι καὶ τοῦ καθόλου. On οὗ ἕνεκα see below, ch. xii. § 10, note.

αὕτη δ' ἐστὶ νοῦς] To say that 'reason is a perception of particulars' is only the counterpart of Aristotle's saying that we can have 'a perception of universals,' *Eth.* I. vii. 20: τῶν ἀρχῶν αἱ μὲν αἰσθήσει θεωροῦνται. Aristotle expresses the intuitive character of reason by saying that it 'touches' its object. Cf. *Metaphys.* VIII. x. 5, τὸ μὲν θιγεῖν καὶ φάναι ἀληθές . . . . τὸ δ' ἀγνοεῖν μὴ θιγγάνειν. *Ib.* XI. vii. 8, αὑτὸν δὲ νοεῖ ὁ νοῦς κατὰ μετάληψιν τοῦ νοητοῦ· νοητὸς γὰρ γίγνεται θιγγάνων καὶ νοῶν, ὥστε ταὐτὸν νοῦς καὶ νοητόν. That reason, while it is on the one hand intuitive, is on the other hand developed by experience, we learn from the discussions in *Post. Anal.* II. ch. xix. The same is expressed above in the saying that 'reason is the beginning and the end.'

5—6 διὸ καὶ φυσικὰ—ὀρθῶς] 'Hence it is that these faculties are thought to come naturally, and that although no one without conscious effort (φύσει) gets to be a philosopher, men do get naturally to have considerateness, and apprehension, and

τέλος νοῦς· ἐκ τούτων γὰρ αἱ ἀποδείξεις καὶ περὶ τούτων.
ὥστε δεῖ προσέχειν τῶν ἐμπείρων καὶ πρεσβυτέρων ἢ φρονίμων ταῖς ἀναποδείκτοις φάσεσι καὶ δόξαις οὐχ ἧττον τῶν
ἀποδείξεων· διὰ γὰρ τὸ ἔχειν ἐκ τῆς ἐμπειρίας ὄμμα ὁρῶσιν ὀρθῶς. τί μὲν οὖν ἐστὶν ἡ φρόνησις καὶ ἡ σοφία, καὶ 7
περὶ τίνα ἑκατέρα τυγχάνει οὖσα, καὶ ὅτι ἄλλου τῆς
ψυχῆς μορίου ἀρετὴ ἑκατέρα, εἴρηται.

Διαπορήσειε δ' ἄν τις περὶ αὐτῶν τί χρήσιμοί εἰσιν. 12
ἡ μὲν γὰρ σοφία οὐδὲν θεωρεῖ ἐξ ὧν ἔσται εὐδαίμων ἄνθρω-

---

reason. A proof of this is, that we think they ought successively to appear as age advances, and (we say that) such and such an age possesses reason and considerateness, as if these things came from nature. Hence reason is the beginning and the end, the matter of premises and conclusions is the same. Thus we must pay regard to the unproved assertions and opinions of the elderly and experienced, or of the thoughtful, no less than to demonstrations. For, from having obtained the eye of "old experience," they see aright.' In these excellent remarks the subject is brought round again to the contrast between Philosophy and Thought. The former never comes naturally, but the latter does. The nature of reason, and its growth in the mind, is illustrated by the common fact of the respect paid to age.

ἐκ τούτων—καὶ περὶ τούτων] Cf. *Eth.* I. iii. 4: *περὶ τοιούτων καὶ ἐκ τοιούτων λέγοντας.* The 'subject' of the demonstration is the conclusion, cf. *Eth.* I. viii. 1, *Σκεπτέον ... οὐ μόνον ἐκ τοῦ συμπεράσματος καὶ ἐξ ὧν ὁ λόγος.*

ὄμμα] Cf. *Eth.* I. vi. 12, *ὡς γὰρ ἐν σώματι ὄψις, ἐν ψυχῇ νοῦς.* Plato, *Repub.* p. 533 D, *ἐν βορβόρῳ βαρβαρικῷ τινι τὸ τῆς ψυχῆς ὄμμα κατορωρυγμένον ἠρέμα ἕλκει καὶ ἀνάγει ἄνω.*

XII. In this and the following chapter, by mooting the question, of what use are Thought and Philosophy? the writer shows the relation of the two qualities to each other, and the inseparable connexion existing between thought and virtue. The following difficulties are first stated. (1) Philosophy is not practical, it does not consider at all the means to happiness, how then can it be useful? (2) Thought, on the other hand, though it treats of happiness, might be said to be mere knowledge. It might be said that a man no more *acts* well from having this knowledge of the good, than he *is* well from having a knowledge of medicine. (3) Or again, if thought be useful for telling us *how* to be good, why not get this advice from others? Why should it be necessary to *have* thought, any more than it is to learn medicine, when one can go to a doctor? (4) If philosophy be better than thought, how is it that the latter controls the former? The answer to question (1) is, that both philosophy and thought are good in themselves, and desirable as being perfections of our nature, even though they were not useful as means to anything beyond. But they are not without results. Philosophy, if it does not serve as an instrument to happiness, is identical with happi-

πος (οὐδεμιᾶς γάρ ἐστι γενέσεως), ἡ δὲ φρόνησις τοῦτο μὲν ἔχει, ἀλλὰ τίνος ἕνεκα δεῖ αὐτῆς, εἴπερ ἡ μὲν φρόνησίς ἐστιν ἡ περὶ τὰ δίκαια καὶ καλὰ καὶ ἀγαθὰ ἀνθρώπῳ, ταῦτα δ' ἐστὶν ἃ τοῦ ἀγαθοῦ ἐστὶν ἀνδρὸς πράττειν, οὐδὲν δὲ πρακτικώτεροι τῷ εἰδέναι αὐτά ἐσμεν, εἴπερ ἕξεις αἱ ἀρεταί εἰσιν, ὥσπερ οὐδὲ τὰ ὑγιεινὰ οὐδὲ τὰ εὐεκτικά, ὅσα μὴ τῷ ποιεῖν ἀλλὰ τῷ ἀπὸ τῆς ἕξεως εἶναι λέγεται· οὐθὲν γὰρ πρακτικώτεροι τῷ ἔχειν τὴν ἰατρικὴν καὶ γυμναστικήν
2 ἐσμεν. εἰ δὲ μὴ τούτων χάριν φρόνιμον θετέον ἀλλὰ τοῦ
γίνεσθαι, τοῖς οὖσι σπουδαίοις οὐθὲν ἂν εἴη χρήσιμος, ἔτι δ' οὐδὲ τοῖς μὴ ἔχουσιν· οὐθὲν γὰρ διοίσει αὐτοὺς ἔχειν ἢ ἄλλοις ἔχουσι πείθεσθαι, ἱκανῶς τ' ἔχοι ἂν ἡμῖν ὥσπερ καὶ

---

ence itself. Questions (2) and (3) are answered by showing the relation of thought to virtue. Virtue gives the right aim, and thought the right means. They are inseparable from one another. Thought without virtue would be mere cleverness apt to degenerate into cunning, and virtue without wisdom would be a mere gift of nature, a generous instinct capable of perversion. While thus inseparable from virtue, thought is not to be identified with it. In this respect an advance has been made beyond the crude formula of Socrates. Wisdom accompanies the virtues, and is a sort of centre-point to them all (ἅμα τῇ φρονήσει μιᾷ οὔσῃ πᾶσαι ὑπάρξουσιν, xiii. 6). Question (4) is easily answered, since wisdom rather ministers to philosophy than thinks of controlling it.

1 οὐδεμιᾶς γάρ ἐστι γενέσεως] Suggested perhaps by *Eth.* x. vii. 5, where it is said of the θεωρητικὴ ἐνέργεια—οὐδὲν γὰρ ἀπ' αὐτῆς γίνεται παρὰ τὸ θεωρῆσαι. *Ib.* § 7: δοκεῖ . . . παρ' αὐτὴν οὐδενὸς ἐφίεσθαι τέλους.

εἴπερ ἡ μὲν φρόνησίς ἐστιν ἡ περὶ τὰ δίκαια καὶ καλὰ καὶ ἀγαθὰ ἀνθρώπῳ] 'If thought be that which is concerned with things just and beautiful and good for man.' 'Ἡ is indefinite, being probably feminine on account of the preceding φρόνησις. This passage is the first that asserts strongly the moral nature of 'thought.' We are told here that it takes cognisance of the just and the beautiful; before it was only said to be concerned with what was *good* (περὶ τὰ ἀνθρώπινα ἀγαθά, ch. v. § 6). These concluding discussions about φρόνησις show the inadequacy of the term 'prudence,' by which it has been so often translated, really to represent it.

οὐδὲν δὲ πρακτικώτεροι τῷ εἰδέναι αὐτά] The answer to this objection has virtually been already given, ch. v. § 8: where φρόνησιν was said *not* to be a merely intellectual quality.

2 εἰ δὲ μὴ—πείθεσθαι] 'But suppose we assume that a man is thoughtful not for this object (*i.e.* mere knowledge of virtue), but with a view to becoming (virtuous), we must then concede that to those who *are* virtuous thought will not be useful,—nor any more so to those who have not got (virtue), for there will be no difference whether they have (thought) themselves, or follow the advice of

περὶ τὴν ὑγίειαν· βουλόμενοι γὰρ ὑγιαίνειν ὅμως οὐ μανθάνομεν ἰατρικήν. πρὸς δὲ τούτοις ἄτοπον ἂν εἶναι δόξειεν, 3
εἰ χείρων τῆς σοφίας οὖσα κυριωτέρα αὐτῆς ἔσται· ἡ γὰρ
ποιοῦσα ἄρχει καὶ ἐπιτάττει περὶ ἕκαστον. περὶ δὴ
τούτων λεκτέον· νῦν μὲν γὰρ ἠπόρηται περὶ αὐτῶν μόνον.
πρῶτον μὲν οὖν λέγομεν ὅτι καθ' αὑτὰς ἀναγκαῖον αἱρετὰς 4
αὐτὰς εἶναι, ἀρετάς γ' οὔσας ἑκατέραν ἑκατέρου τοῦ μορίου,
καὶ εἰ μὴ ποιοῦσι μηδὲν μηδετέρα αὐτῶν. ἔπειτα καὶ 5
ποιοῦσι μέν, οὐχ ὡς ἰατρικὴ δὲ ὑγίειαν, ἀλλ' ὡς ἡ ὑγίεια,
οὕτως ἡ σοφία εὐδαιμονίαν· μέρος γὰρ οὖσα τῆς ὅλης
ἀρετῆς τῷ ἔχεσθαι ποιεῖ καὶ τῷ ἐνεργεῖν εὐδαίμονα. ἔτι 6

---

others possessing it.' The compression used here is quite in the style of Eudemus, and so is the confusion caused by the careless writing in τοῖς μὴ ἔχουσιν· οὐδὲν γὰρ διοίσει αὐτοὺς ἔχειν, where ἔχουσιν and ἔχειν appear to refer to two different things.

3 εἰ χείρων τῆς σοφίας οὖσα κυριωτέρα αὐτῆς ἔσται] This difficulty may have been partly suggested by the prominent position assigned to Thought in the present book (cf. ch. vii. § 7: εἴη δ' ἄν τις καὶ ἐνταῦθα ἀρχιτεκτονική), partly by the authoritative character attributed to politics by Aristotle, *Eth.* I. ii. 4–6: δόξειε δ' ἂν τῆς κυριωτάτης καὶ μάλιστα ἀρχιτεκτονικῆς· τοιαύτη δ' ἡ πολιτικὴ φαίνεται κ.τ.λ. Cf. Plato on the *βασιλικὴ τέχνη*, *Euthydem.* p. 291 B, quoted Vol. I. Essay III. p. 190.

4 Thought and Philosophy cannot be otherwise than desirable, as they are the best state of the human mind. And the mind must necessarily (ἀναγκαῖον) desire its own best state.

5 ἔπειτα — εὐδαίμονα] 'Furthermore they *do* produce happiness—philosophy produces it, not in the way that medicine produces health, but rather it operates like health itself. Being a part of the entire well-being (τῆς ὅλης ἀρετῆς) of man, it makes one happy by the consciousness of possessing it.'

τῆς ὅλης ἀρετῆς] This phrase, which never occurs in the writings of Aristotle, is frequent in those of Eudemus. Cf. *Eth. Eud.* II. i. 9: καὶ ἔστι ζωὴ καὶ τελέα καὶ ἀτελής, καὶ ἀρετὴ ὡσαύτως (ἡ μὲν γὰρ ὅλη, ἡ δὲ μόριον). *Ib.* § 14: διὸ καὶ ἄλλο εἴ τι μόριόν ἐστι ψυχῆς, οἷον τὸ θρεπτικόν, ἡ τούτου ἀρετὴ οὐκ ἔστι μόριον τῆς ὅλης ἀρετῆς. *Eth. Eud.* IV. (*Nic.* V.) ii. 7: ὅτι μὲν οὖν εἰσὶ δικαιοσύναι πλείους, καὶ ὅτι ἔστι τις καὶ ἑτέρα παρὰ τὴν ὅλην ἀρετήν, δῆλον. *Ib.* § 10: ἡ μὲν οὖν κατὰ τὴν ὅλην ἀρετὴν τεταγμένη δικαιοσύνη. This conception Eudemus came to identify with καλοκἀγαθία, *Eth. Eud.* VIII. iii. 1: κατὰ μέρος μὲν οὖν περὶ ἑκάστης ἀρετῆς εἴρηται πρότερον· ἐπεὶ δὲ χωρὶς διείλομεν τὴν δύναμιν αὐτῶν, καὶ περὶ τῆς ἀρετῆς διαρθρωτέον τῆς ἐκ τούτων, ἣν ἐκαλοῦμεν ἤδη καλοκἀγαθίαν.

τῷ ἔχεσθαι καὶ ἐνεργεῖν] Ἐνεργεῖν added on to ἔχεσθαι expresses the fruition, as well as the possession, of philosophy. It implies that philosophy exists not only *in*, but *for*, the mind. See Vol. I. Essay IV. pp. 242, sq.

6 ἔτι—τούτων] 'Again, man's proper function is discharged by an

τὸ ἔργον ἀποτελεῖται κατὰ τὴν φρόνησιν καὶ τὴν ἠθικὴν ἀρετήν· ἡ μὲν γὰρ ἀρετὴ τὸν σκοπὸν ποιεῖ ὀρθόν, ἡ δὲ φρόνησις τὰ πρὸς τοῦτον. τοῦ δὲ τετάρτου μορίου τῆς ψυχῆς οὐκ ἔστιν ἀρετὴ τοιαύτη, τοῦ θρεπτικοῦ· οὐθὲν γὰρ
7 ἐπ' αὐτῷ πράττειν ἢ μὴ πράττειν. περὶ δὲ τοῦ μηθὲν εἶναι πρακτικωτέρους διὰ τὴν φρόνησιν τῶν καλῶν καὶ δικαίων, μικρὸν ἄνωθεν ἀρκτέον, λαβόντας ἀρχὴν ταύτην. ὥσπερ γὰρ καὶ τὰ δίκαια λέγομεν πράττοντάς τινας οὔπω δικαίους εἶναι, οἷον τοὺς τὰ ὑπὸ τῶν νόμων τεταγμένα ποιοῦντας ἢ ἄκοντας ἢ δι' ἄγνοιαν ἢ δι' ἕτερόν τι καὶ μὴ δι' αὐτά (καίτοι πράττουσί γε ἃ δεῖ καὶ ὅσα χρὴ τὸν σπουδαῖον), οὕτως, ὡς ἔοικεν, ἔστι τὸ πῶς ἔχοντα πράττειν ἕκαστα ὥστ' εἶναι ἀγαθόν, λέγω δ' οἷον διὰ προαίρεσιν
8 καὶ αὐτῶν ἕνεκα τῶν πραττομένων. τὴν μὲν οὖν προαίρεσιν ὀρθὴν ποιεῖ ἡ ἀρετή, τὸ δ' ὅσα ἐκείνης ἕνεκα πέφυκε πράτ-

---

accordance with thought and moral virtue. For virtue makes the aim right, and thought the means to the attainment of this.' The conception of τὸ ἔργον is taken from Ar. *Eth.* I. vii. 10. The rest of the psychology here is different from that of Aristotle (see *Eth.* III. v. 1. note), but is identical with that adopted by Eudemus in his earlier books. Cf. *Eth. Eud.* II. xi. 1: τούτων δὲ διωρισμένων λέγωμεν πότερον ἡ ἀρετὴ ἀναμάρτητον ποιεῖ τὴν προαίρεσιν καὶ τὸ τέλος ὀρθόν, οὕτως ὥστε οὗ ἕνεκα δεῖ προαιρεῖσθαι, ἢ ὥσπερ δοκεῖ τισί, τὸν λόγον. Ἔστι δὲ τοῦτο ἐγκράτεια· αὕτη γὰρ οὐ διαφθείρει τὸν λόγον. Ἔστι δ' ἀρετὴ καὶ ἐγκράτεια ἕτερον. Λεκτέον δ' ὕστερον περὶ αὐτῶν (this refers to ch. v. § 6, where, however, σωφροσύνη is substituted for ἐγκράτεια). *Ib.* § 3: πότερον δ' ἡ ἀρετὴ ποιεῖ τὸν σκοπὸν ἢ τὰ πρὸς τὸν σκοπόν; τιθέμεθα δὴ ὅτι τὸν σκοπόν, διότι τούτου οὐκ ἔστι συλλογισμὸς οὐδὲ λόγος. *Ib.* § 6, quoted below.

τοῦ δὲ τετάρτου κ.τ.λ.] The parts are, (1) the scientific reason, (2) the practical reason, (3) the moral nature (λόγου μετέχον), (4) the vegetative element,—'Ἀρετὴ τοιαύτη, *i.e.* 'moral virtue.' The vegetative soul has its own ἀρετὴ or 'excellence,' in a general sense.

7 The first step to prove the use and practical necessity of thought, is to show that moral action implies consciousness and a conscious purpose.

8 τὴν μὲν—δυνάμεως] 'Now virtue makes the purpose right, but the means to this (ὅσα ἐκείνης ἕνεκα πέφυκε πράττεσθαι) do not belong to virtue, but to another faculty.' There is some confusion here in speaking of the means to a purpose, προαίρεσις itself being in the Aristotelian psychology a faculty of means; but cf. *Eth. Eud.* II. xi. 5—6, where προαίρεσις is said to imply both end and means, and whence the present passage is repeated almost *verbatim*. Ἔστι γὰρ πᾶσα προαίρεσις τινὸς καὶ ἕνεκά τινος. Οὗ μὲν οὖν ἕνεκα τὸ μέσον ἐστίν, οὗ αἰτία ἡ ἀρετὴ τὸ (τῷ, Fritzsche, e conj.) προαιρεῖσθαι οὗ ἕνεκα. Ἔστι μέντοι ἡ προαίρεσις οὐ τούτου, ἀλλὰ

τεσθαι οὐκ ἔστι τῆς ἀρετῆς ἀλλ' ἑτέρας δυνάμεως. λεκτέον
δ' ἐπιστήσασι σαφέστερον περὶ αὐτῶν. ἔστι δή τις δύνα- 9
μις ἣν καλοῦσι δεινότητα· αὕτη δ' ἐστὶ τοιαύτη ὥστε τὰ
πρὸς τὸν ὑποτεθέντα σκοπὸν συντείνοντα δύνασθαι ταῦτα
πράττειν καὶ τυγχάνειν αὐτῶν. ἂν μὲν οὖν ὁ σκοπὸς ᾖ
καλός, ἐπαινετή ἐστιν, ἂν δὲ φαῦλος, πανουργία· διὸ καὶ
τοὺς φρονίμους δεινοὺς καὶ πανούργους φαμὲν εἶναι. ἔστι 10
δ' ἡ φρόνησις οὐχ ἡ δεινότης, ἀλλ' οὐκ ἄνευ τῆς δυνάμεως
ταύτης. ἡ δ' ἕξις τῷ ὄμματι τούτῳ γίνεται τῆς ψυχῆς
οὐκ ἄνευ ἀρετῆς, ὡς εἴρηταί τε καὶ ἔστι δῆλον· οἱ γὰρ συλλογισμοὶ τῶν πρακτῶν ἀρχὴν ἔχοντές εἰσιν, ἐπειδὴ τοιόνδε

τῶν τούτου ἕνεκα. Τὸ μὲν οὖν τυγχάνειν τούτων ἄλλῃ δυνάμει, ὅσα ἕνεκα τοῦ τέλους δεῖ πράττειν· τοῦ δὲ τὸ τέλος ὀρθὸν εἶναι τῆς προαιρέσεως, οὗ ἡ ἀρετὴ αἰτία.

8—10 λεκτέον δ'—ἀγαθόν] 'But we must speak on the point with a more exact attention. There is a certain faculty which is called "cleverness," this is of a nature to perform and to hit upon the means that conduce to any given aim. Now if the aim be good, this faculty is praiseworthy, but if bad, it turns to cunning. Hence both thoughtful men and cunning men got the name of "clever." Now thought is not cleverness, but it is not without a faculty of the kind. But this eye of the mind attains its full condition not without virtue, as we have already stated, and as is clear, for the syllogisms of action have as their major premiss—"Since such and such is the end and the best"—(being whatever it is,—something for the sake of argument, it matters not what). But this (major premiss) cannot be apprehended except by the good man; for vice distorts (the mind), and makes it false with regard to the principles of action. Hence it is evident that one cannot possess "thought" unless he be good.'

καὶ τοὺς φρονίμους δεινοὺς καὶ πανούργους φαμὲν εἶναι] We should have expected τοὺς πανούργους. That want of clearness of mind which is characteristic of Eudemus shows itself in his use of the article, cf. ch. xi. § 6: τῶν ἐμπείρων καὶ πρεσβυτέρων ἢ φρονίμων, where one would have expected τῶν φρονίμων.

Fritzsche quotes Plato, *Theaet.* p. 177 A: ἂν μὴ ἀπαλλαγῶσι τῆς δεινότητος—ταῦτα δὴ καὶ παντάπασιν ὡς δεινοὶ καὶ πανοῦργοι ἀνοήτων τινῶν ἀκούσονται. Demosth. *Ol.* 1. p. 9: πανοῦργος ὢν καὶ δεινὸς ἄνθρωπος πράγμασι χρήσασθαι.

10 ἡ δ' ἕξις τῷ ὄμματι τούτῳ] The whole conception of reason, 'the eye of the soul,' being capable of being perverted into worldly cunning or of being kept pure by good moral habits, comes, originally, no doubt, from Plato, *Repub.* 518 E: ἡ δὲ τοῦ φρονῆσαι παντὸς μᾶλλον θειοτέρου τινὸς τυγχάνει, ὡς ἔοικεν, οὖσα, ὃ τὴν μὲν δύναμιν οὐδέποτε ἀπόλλυσιν, ὑπὸ δὲ τῆς περιαγωγῆς χρήσιμόν τε καὶ ὠφέλιμον καὶ ἄχρηστον αὖ καὶ βλαβερὸν γίγνεται. ἢ οὔπω ἐννενόηκας, τῶν λεγομένων πονηρῶν μέν, σοφῶν δέ, ὡς δριμὺ μὲν βλέπει τὸ ψυχάριον καὶ ὀξέως διορᾷ ταῦτα ἐφ'

τὸ τέλος καὶ τὸ ἄριστον, ὁτιδήποτε ὄν. ἔστω γὰρ λόγου χάριν τὸ τυχόν. τοῦτο δ' εἰ μὴ τῷ ἀγαθῷ, οὐ φαίνεται· διαστρέφει γὰρ ἡ μοχθηρία καὶ διαψεύδεσθαι ποιεῖ περὶ τὰς πρακτικὰς ἀρχάς. ὥστε φανερὸν ὅτι ἀδύνατον φρόνιμον εἶναι μὴ ὄντα ἀγαθόν.

13 Σκεπτέον δὴ πάλιν καὶ περὶ ἀρετῆς· καὶ γὰρ ἡ ἀρετὴ παραπλησίως ἔχει ὡς ἡ φρόνησις πρὸς τὴν δεινότητα· οὐ ταὐτὸν μέν, ὅμοιον δέ· οὕτω καὶ ἡ φυσικὴ ἀρετὴ πρὸς τὴν κυρίαν. πᾶσι γὰρ δοκεῖ ἕκαστα τῶν ἠθῶν ὑπάρχειν φύσει πως· καὶ γὰρ δίκαιοι καὶ σωφρονικοὶ καὶ ἀνδρεῖοι καὶ

ᾗ τέτρωνται, ἐν τῷ φαύλην ἔχον τὴν ὄψιν, κακίᾳ δ' ἠναγκασμένον ὑπηρετεῖν, ὥστε ὅσῳ ἂν ὀξύτερον βλέπῃ, τοσούτῳ πλείω κακὰ ἐργαζόμενον;

ὡς εἴρηταί τε] Ch. ii. § 4: διὸ οὔτ' ἄνευ νοῦ καὶ διανοίας, οὔτ' ἄνευ ἠθικῆς ἐστὶν ἕξεως ἡ προαίρεσις. *Eth. Eud.* II. xi. 5: διὰ τὴν ἀρετὴν ἂν ὀρθὸν εἴη τὸ τέλος κ.τ.λ.

οἱ γὰρ συλλογισμοὶ τῶν πρακτῶν] The form of the practical syllogism is similarly given, *Eth. Eud.* II. xi. 4: ὥσπερ γὰρ ταῖς θεωρητικαῖς αἱ ὑποθέσεις ἀρχαί, οὕτω καὶ ταῖς ποιητικαῖς τὸ τέλος ἀρχὴ καὶ ὑπόθεσις· 'ἐπειδὴ δεῖ τόδε ὑγιαίνειν, ἀνάγκη τοδὶ ὑπάρξαι, εἰ ἔσται ἐκεῖνο,' ὥσπερ ἐκεῖ, 'εἰ ἔστι τὸ τρίγωνον δύο ὀρθαί, ἀνάγκη τοδὶ εἶναι.' On the doctrine of the practical syllogism, see Vol. I. Essay IV. pp. 262, sq.

XIII. Σκεπτέον δὴ—κυρίαν] 'We must consider then, over again, the nature of virtue. For there is a relation in virtue analogous to that borne by thought to cleverness. Cleverness, though not the same as wisdom, is similar to it, and this is the way in which natural virtue stands related to virtue proper.' The doctrine of the natural element in virtue was clearly given by Aristotle, cf. *Eth.* x. ix. 6–8: Γίνεσθαι δ' ἀγαθοὺς οἴονται, οἱ μὲν φύσει, οἱ δ' ἔθει, οἱ δὲ διδαχῇ. Τὸ μὲν οὖν τῆς φύσεως δῆλον ὡς οὐκ ἐφ' ἡμῖν ὑπάρχει, ἀλλὰ διά τινας θείας αἰτίας τοῖς ὡς ἀληθῶς εὐτυχέσιν ὑπάρχει—Δεῖ δὴ τὸ ἦθος προϋπάρχειν πως οἰκεῖον τῆς ἀρετῆς, στέργον τὸ καλὸν καὶ δυσχεραῖνον τὸ αἰσχρόν. In the present passage, the analogy between the development of the reason and of the moral will is well drawn out. At first, there is the intellectual faculty, cleverness, undetermined as yet for good or bad, but requiring a right direction to be given to its aims. This the moral feelings can alone supply. On the other side, there is the generous instinct, the impulse to bravery, justice, and the like, but this is deficient in consciousness and in the idea of a law, which reason can alone supply. The joint development of these two sides gives, on the one hand, 'thought,' on the other hand, virtue, in its complete and proper form. What there is difficult or strange in the doctrine is, that virtue has apparently assigned to it the intellectual function of apprehending the end of action. This appears an inversion. Ἀρετή seems now to have changed places with λόγος. But, at all events, the point is clearly established that an intellectual side and a moral side are entirely inseparable.

τἆλλα ἔχομεν εὐθὺς ἐκ γενετῆς· ἀλλ' ὅμως ζητοῦμεν ἕτερόν τι τὸ κυρίως ἀγαθὸν καὶ τὰ τοιαῦτα ἄλλον τρόπον ὑπάρχειν· καὶ γὰρ παισὶ καὶ θηρίοις αἱ φυσικαὶ ὑπάρχουσιν ἕξεις, ἀλλ' ἄνευ νοῦ βλαβεραὶ φαίνονται οὖσαι. πλὴν τοσοῦτον ἔοικεν ὁρᾶσθαι, ὅτι ὥσπερ σώματι ἰσχυρῷ ἄνευ ὄψεως κινουμένῳ συμβαίνει σφάλλεσθαι ἰσχυρῶς διὰ τὸ μὴ ἔχειν ὄψιν, οὕτω καὶ ἐνταῦθα· ἐὰν δὲ λάβῃ νοῦν, ἐν 2
τῷ πράττειν διαφέρει. ἡ δ' ἕξις ὁμοία οὖσα τότ' ἔσται κυρίως ἀρετή. ὥστε καθάπερ ἐπὶ τοῦ δοξαστικοῦ δύο ἐστὶν εἴδη, δεινότης καὶ φρόνησις, οὕτω καὶ ἐπὶ τοῦ ἠθικοῦ δύο ἐστί, τὸ μὲν ἀρετὴ φυσικὴ τὸ δ' ἡ κυρία, καὶ τούτων ἡ κυρία οὐ γίνεται ἄνευ φρονήσεως. διόπερ τινές φασι 3
πάσας τὰς ἀρετὰς φρονήσεις εἶναι, καὶ Σωκράτης τῇ μὲν

καὶ γὰρ παισὶ—ἀρετή] 'For the natural dispositions belong both to children and beasts, but without reason they appear harmful. At least this seems evident, that as a strong body, if moved without sight, comes into violent collisions because it has not sight to guide it, so is it in mental things (ἐνταῦθα). If the natural qualifications have reason added to them, they then excel in action, and the state, which (before) was a semblance of virtue, now becomes virtue in the true sense of the term.' Φυσικαὶ ἕξεις is used inaccurately for φυσικαὶ διαθέσεις, cf. *Eth.* II. vii. 6, note. On the moral qualities of brutes Aristotle often speaks; cf. *Hist. An.* I. i.; IX. i. &c. The 'courage' of brutes, being undirected, is no doubt harmful, so the generosity, &c., of boys. That fine natures are capable of the worst perversion, is an opinion to be found stated in Plato's *Republic*, p. 491 E: Οὐκοῦν, ἦν δ' ἐγώ, ὦ Ἀδείμαντε, καὶ τὰς ψυχὰς οὕτω φῶμεν τὰς εὐφυεστάτας κακῆς παιδαγωγίας τυχούσας διαφερόντως κακὰς γίγνεσθαι; ἢ οἴει τὰ μεγάλα ἀδικήματα καὶ τὴν ἄκρατον πονηρίαν ἐκ νεανικῆς φύσεως τροφῇ διολομένης γίγνεσθαι, ἀσθενῆ δὲ φύσιν μεγάλων οὔτε ἀγαθῶν οὔτε κακῶν αἰτίαν ποτὲ ἔσεσθαι;

3—5 διόπερ—μετὰ λόγου] 'Hence it is that some say that all the virtues are manifestations of thought; and thus Socrates was partly right and partly wrong in his investigations. He was wrong in considering the virtues manifestations of thought, but perfectly right in holding that they were inseparable from thought. The same point is testified to by the fact that, at present, persons, when they wish to define virtue, add the terms "state (specifying the particular object), according to the right law." And *that* law is right which is in accordance with thought. All men therefore seem to have a presentiment that a particular state in accordance with thought is virtue. But a little alteration is necessary. Not merely the state *according* to the right law, but that which is *conscious of* (μετὰ) the right law constitutes virtue. Now in such matters thought is right law. Socrates then considered that the

ὀρθῶς ἐζήτει τῇ δ' ἡμάρτανεν· ὅτι μὲν γὰρ φρονήσεις
ᾤετο εἶναι πάσας τὰς ἀρετάς, ἡμάρτανεν, ὅτι δ' οὐκ ἄνευ
4 φρονήσεως, καλῶς ἔλεγεν. σημεῖον δέ· καὶ γὰρ νῦν
πάντες, ὅταν ὁρίζωνται τὴν ἀρετήν, προστιθέασι τὴν ἕξιν,
εἰπόντες καὶ πρὸς ἅ ἐστι, τὴν κατὰ τὸν ὀρθὸν λόγον·
ὀρθὸς δ' ὁ κατὰ τὴν φρόνησιν. ἐοίκασι δὴ μαντεύεσθαί
πως ἅπαντες ὅτι ἡ τοιαύτη ἕξις ἀρετή ἐστιν ἡ κατὰ τὴν
5 φρόνησιν. δεῖ δὲ μικρὸν μεταβῆναι· οὐ γὰρ μόνον ἡ
κατὰ τὸν ὀρθὸν λόγον, ἀλλ' ἡ μετὰ τοῦ ὀρθοῦ λόγου ἕξις
ἀρετή ἐστιν. ὀρθὸς δὲ λόγος περὶ τῶν τοιούτων ἡ φρόνησίς
ἐστιν. Σωκράτης μὲν οὖν λόγους τὰς ἀρετὰς ᾤετο εἶναι
6 (ἐπιστήμας γὰρ εἶναι πάσας), ἡμεῖς δὲ μετὰ λόγου. δῆλον
οὖν ἐκ τῶν εἰρημένων ὅτι οὐχ οἷόν τε ἀγαθὸν εἶναι κυρίως
ἄνευ φρονήσεως, οὐδὲ φρόνιμον ἄνευ τῆς ἠθικῆς ἀρετῆς.
ἀλλὰ καὶ ὁ λόγος ταύτῃ λύοιτ' ἄν, ᾧ διαλεχθείη τις ἂν
ὅτι χωρίζονται ἀλλήλων αἱ ἀρεταί· οὐ γὰρ ὁ αὐτὸς εὐφυέ-

---

virtues were laws (for he defined them all as sciences), but we consider that they are conscious of a law.'

καὶ Σωκράτης] On the doctrine of Socrates that 'virtue is science,' see Vol. I. Essay II. pp. 164, sq. In *Eth.* III. viii. 6, the phrase is ὅθεν καὶ ὁ Σωκράτης, on which Bishop Fitzgerald remarks that by prefixing the article Aristotle appears to have indicated the Socrates of Plato's dialogues, the dramatic, and not the historical, philosopher. Thus speaking similarly of *characters* in books, Aristotle says, *Eth.* III. viii. 2, τὸν Διομήδην καὶ τὸν Ἕκτορα. *Ib.* II. ix. 3, ἡ Καλυψώ. II. ix. 6, πρὸς τὴν Ἑλένην. And contrariwise of real persons he speaks without the article. *Eth.* I. iv. 5. Εὖ γὰρ καὶ Πλάτων ἠπόρει. *Ib.* I. v. 3, ὁμοιοπαθεῖν Σαρδαναπάλλῳ. I. vi. 8, οἷς δὴ καὶ Σπεύσιππος. I. x. 1, κατὰ Σόλωνα. All through the first book of the *Metaphysics*, when writing the history of philosophy, Aristotle speaks of the different philosophers without the article, and so too elsewhere in contrasting Socrates with Plato, &c. The only exceptions to this rule are the cases of *renewed mention*. Cf. *Met.* XII. iv. 5: Δύο γάρ ἐστιν ἅ τις ἂν ἀποδοίη Σωκράτει δικαίως—Ἀλλ' ὁ μὲν Σωκράτης κ.τ.λ. But in discussing Plato's *Republic* and *Laws* (*Pol.* II. i.—vi.), Aristotle invariably speaks of ὁ Σωκράτης, οἱ τοῦ Σωκράτους λόγοι, &c., as referring not to a real but to a represented personage. Assuming that Eudemus has followed the same rule, we may conclude that here and in *Eth.* VII. ii. 1, Σωκράτης μὲν γὰρ ὅλως ἐμάχετο, *Ib.* VII. iii. 14, ὃ ἐζήτει Σωκράτης,—the actual and historical Socrates is designated.

καὶ γὰρ νῦν πάντες] i.e. since the establishment of the Peripatetic doctrine. Eudemus refines upon the usual Peripatetic formula, substituting μετὰ λόγου for κατὰ λόγον. On the meaning of this alteration see *Eth.* I. vii. 14, note.

6 ἀλλὰ καὶ ὁ λόγος—[illegible]]

στατος πρὸς ἁπάσας, ὥστε τὴν μὲν ἤδη τὴν δ' οὔπω εἰληφὼς ἔσται· τοῦτο γὰρ κατὰ μὲν τὰς φυσικὰς ἀρετὰς ἐνδέχεται, καθ' ἃς δὲ ἁπλῶς λέγεται ἀγαθός, οὐκ ἐνδέχεται· ἅμα γὰρ τῇ φρονήσει μιᾷ οὔσῃ πᾶσαι ὑπάρξουσιν. δῆλον 7 δέ, κἂν εἰ μὴ πρακτικὴ ἦν, ὅτι ἔδει ἂν αὐτῆς διὰ τὸ τοῦ μορίου ἀρετὴν εἶναι, καὶ ὅτι οὐκ ἔσται ἡ προαίρεσις ὀρθὴ ἄνευ φρονήσεως οὐδ' ἄνευ ἀρετῆς· ἡ μὲν γὰρ τὸ τέλος ἡ δὲ τὰ πρὸς τὸ τέλος ποιεῖ πράττειν. ἀλλὰ μὴν οὐδὲ κυρία 8 γ' ἐστὶ τῆς σοφίας οὐδὲ τοῦ βελτίονος μορίου, ὥσπερ οὐδὲ τῆς ὑγιείας ἡ ἰατρική· οὐ γὰρ χρῆται αὐτῇ, ἀλλ' ὁρᾷ ὅπως γένηται· ἐκείνης οὖν ἕνεκα ἐπιτάττει, ἀλλ' οὐκ ἐκείνῃ. ἔτι ὅμοιον κἂν εἴ τις τὴν πολιτικὴν φαίη ἄρχειν τῶν θεῶν, ὅτι ἐπιτάττει περὶ πάντα τὰ ἐν τῇ πόλει.

'Thus the opinion is refuted of him who would argue that the virtues are separated from one another, that the same man is not equally gifted by nature for all the virtues, so that he will acquire one now and another later. This is possible with regard to natural good qualities, but not so with regard to those which constitute a good man absolutely; for together with Thought, which is one, all the virtues will be in his possession.' The same perfect character is attributed to Thought below, *Eth.* VII. ii. 5: *πρακτικός γε ὁ φρόνιμος· τῶν γὰρ ἐσχάτων τις καὶ τὰς ἄλλας ἔχων ἀρετάς.* The theory is, that he who has thought can do no wrong. It will be seen how nearly this approaches to the Stoical idea of the 'wise man.'

7 This section is a mere repetition, in Eudemian fashion, of what has gone before, ch. xii. §§ 4, 10; *Eth. Eud.* II. xi. 6 (*l.c.*). Cf. also ch. ii. § 4: *διὸ οὔτ' ἄνευ νοῦ καὶ διανοίας οὔτ' ἄνευ ἠθικῆς ἐστὶν ἕξεως ἡ προαίρεσις.*

8 The relation of thought to Philosophy is clearly stated by the author of the *Magna Moralia*, who paraphrases the present passage (*M. M.* I. xxxv. 32), *ἡ φρόνησις ὥσπερ ἐπίτροπός τις ἐστι τῆς σοφίας, καὶ παρασκευάζει ταύτῃ σχολὴν καὶ τὸ ποιεῖν τὸ αὑτῆς ἔργον, κατέχουσα τὰ πάθη καὶ ταῦτα σωφρονίζουσα.*

PLAN OF BOOK VII.

THIS last of the Nicomacho-Eudemian Books consists of two parts, of which the one is a necessary complement to Aristotle's ethical system; the other superfluous, being little more than a modification of Aristotle's (far superior) treatise on Pleasure.

Part I. having enumerated the moral states which are above, below, and between virtue and vice, mentions six ordinary opinions on these states (Ch. I.), points out the difficult questions to which those opinions give rise (Ch. II.), and proceeds to elucidate them.

In Ch. III. the question is discussed, How is Incontinence compatible with a knowledge of the right?

In Ch. IV. the question, Whether Incontinence is confined to any definite object-matter?

Chs. V. and VI., pursuing the same inquiry, treat of certain morbid and unnatural kinds of Incontinence, and of Incontinence (analogously so called) in the matter of anger.

Ch. VII. compares generally Incontinence with Intemperance, treats of the subordinate forms of the intermediate moral states (endurance, softness, &c.), and traces Incontinence to two separate sources in the character.

Ch. VIII. continues the comparison between Intemperance and Incontinence, reverts to two questions before mooted, namely:—(1) Is Intemperance more curable than Incontinence? (2) Is Incontinence to be regarded as absolutely bad? and gives a negative answer to both.

Ch. IX. §§ 1—4 discusses the question mooted in Ch. II., Does Continence consist in sticking to an opinion or purpose, right or wrong? In answering this question, a good distinction is drawn between Obstinacy and Continence.

Ch. IX. § 5—Ch. X. winds up the previous discussions, and

formally settles the remaining questions of Ch. II. Is Intemperance the same as Incontinence? Can the thoughtful man be incontinent?

These chapters form, as we have said, a necessary complement to the Aristotelian ethical system, taking a more practical point of view (ἄλλην ἀρχήν) than that which would divide mankind simply into the virtuous and the vicious. Moral systems in general have perhaps too much neglected this field of the intermediate states; and general language has not definitely adopted the distinction between the 'Intemperate' and the 'Incontinent,' as the use of these English words at once testifies, for we are evidently obliged to give a certain special and technical meaning to the word 'Intemperate' in order to make it stand as the representative of ἀκόλαστος.[1] A subtle, but not always clear, psychology is employed to explain the phenomena of moral weakness, and it is observable that physical and medical considerations are prominently appealed to throughout this book. The remarks on bestiality, cretinism, or morbid depravity (θηριότης) here made have attracted the notice of modern writers on the psychology of insanity (as for instance Dr. Thomas Mayo).[2] And the interesting allusions here made to the

---

1 The attributes assigned (c. vii. § 2) to the Intemperate man, who 'of deliberate purpose pursues excessive pleasures, for their own sake, and never repents of doing so, and thus is incurable,'—make this a sort of ideally vicious character. A similar conception of ideal vice in its extremest form, with the element of cruelty added, is to be found in Shelley's portrait of Count Cenci: see *The Cenci*, Act i. sc. i.

As to my character for what men call
crime,
Seeing I please my senses as I list,
And vindicate that right with force
or guile,
It is a public matter, and I care not
If I discuss it with you.
All men delight in sensual luxury,
All men enjoy revenge; and most
exult
Over the tortures they can never feel;
But I delight in nothing else. I love
The sight of agony, and the sense of
joy,
When this shall be another's and that
mine.
And I have no remorse, and little fear,
Which are, I think, the checks of
other men, &c.

2 'Now according to this view of the subject, we have a class of persons, differing from the majority of mankind in their incapacity for moral distinction, differing from the insane, in not labouring under any suspension of the power of will. On the first of these grounds, they have a right to a place in our system of mental pathology. On the last, they must constitute a distinct head from insanity. I am not at present considering this class generally; I exclude indeed that

melancholic, or billious, temperament might be illustrated, not only from Aristotle's *Problems*, but also from Burton's Anatomy of Melancholy. The chief thing that we have to complain of in this book is the too vague way in which incontinence is treated. For the sake of forming a more definite notion of the standard of Greek morality, we could have wished a graphic portrait of the continent man, in the style of Aristotle's fourth Book. As it is, we must be content to know that the continent man yields to temptation less, and the incontinent man more, than people in general.

Part II. consists of that superfluous treatise on Pleasure, the authorship of which has been so much disputed. While professing to treat of pleasure as falling under the philosophy of human life, the writer seems to confine himself almost entirely to a refutation of three positions maintained by the Platonic school: 1st. That pleasure is in no sense a good. 2nd. That most pleasures (*i.e.* physical pleasures) are bad. 3rd. That no pleasure can be the chief good.

The first and third of these positions are refuted in Chs. XII. and XIII., and the second in Ch. XIV. The subject is treated in this book under a more physiological and practical aspect than in the tenth book of the Nicomachean work.

---

section of persons, in whom the absence of principle is obviated by the harmlessness of their tendencies. I am speaking of persons destitute of the moral faculty, and *also* vicious in their propensities. For these I have borrowed the designation given to them by Aristotle: and I call them *brutal*.' —Mayo, *Elements of the Pathology of the Human Mind*, p. 127.

ΗΘΙΚΩΝ [ΕΥΔΗΜΙΩΝ] VII.

ΜΕΤΑ δὲ ταῦτα λεκτέον, ἄλλην ποιησαμένους ἀρχήν, ὅτι τῶν περὶ τὰ ἤθη φευκτῶν τρία ἐστὶν εἴδη, κακία ἀκρασία θηριότης. τὰ δ' ἐναντία τοῖς μὲν δυσὶ δῆλα· τὸ μὲν γὰρ ἀρετὴν τὸ δ' ἐγκράτειαν καλοῦμεν· πρὸς δὲ τὴν θηριότητα μάλιστ' ἂν ἁρμόττοι λέγειν τὴν ὑπὲρ ἡμᾶς ἀρετήν, ἡρωϊκήν τινα καὶ θείαν, ὥσπερ Ὅμηρος περὶ Ἕκτορος πεποίηκε λέγοντα τὸν Πρίαμον ὅτι σφόδρα ἦν ἀγαθός.

I. This chapter proposes a new field of inquiry (ἄλλην ἀρχήν) in Ethics, namely to consider those intermediate states, continence and incontinence, together with their subordinate forms (softness, luxury, and endurance), which are 'neither identical with virtue and vice, nor yet wholly distinct from them.' After an enumeration of the moral states above, below, and between, virtue and vice, the writer announces that his method of inquiry will be, as elsewhere, to collect current opinions on the subject, to raise doubts and objections to them, and by a process of sifting to reject such existing opinions as are untenable, and to leave a residue of 'sufficiently demonstrated' theory. He accordingly mentions six common notions about the states in question.

1 τὰ δ' ἐναντία κ.τ.λ.] A scale of the moral states is here drawn out, which stands as follows: 1. Divine virtue, or pure reason. 2. Virtue (afterwards called temperance, σωφροσύνη), or the perfect harmony of passion subjugated to reason. 3. Continence, or the mastery of reason over passion after a struggle. 4. Incontinence, or the mastery of passion over reason, after a struggle. 5. Vice (afterwards called ἀκολασία, intemperance), or the perfect harmony of reason subjugated to passion. 6. Bestiality, or pure passion. It is remarkable that the terms σωφροσύνη and ἀκολασία, which in this book certainly supply the place of ἀρετή and κακία, are actually introduced extremely late. Cf. ch. v. § 8.

ἡρωϊκήν τινα] Cf. Arist. *Pol.* vii. xiv. 2, where the gods and heroes are mentioned as excelling men. Dr. Hampden, in his *Bampton Lectures*, mentions that, in the canonisation of a Roman Catholic Saint, it was customary to declare that he had graduated 'in heroico gradu virtutis.'

οὐδὲ ἐῴκει
ἀνδρός γε θνητοῦ πάϊς ἔμμεναι ἀλλὰ θεοῖο.

2 ὥστ' εἰ, καθάπερ φασίν, ἐξ ἀνθρώπων γίνονται θεοὶ δι'
ἀρετῆς ὑπερβολήν, τοιαύτη τις ἂν εἴη δῆλον ὅτι ἡ τῇ θηριώδει ἀντιτιθεμένη ἕξις· καὶ γὰρ ὥσπερ οὐδὲ θηρίου ἐστὶ
κακία οὐδ' ἀρετή, οὕτως οὐδὲ θεοῦ, ἀλλ' ἡ μὲν τιμιώτερον
3 ἀρετῆς, ἡ δ' ἕτερόν τι γένος κακίας. ἐπεὶ δὲ σπάνιον καὶ
τὸ θεῖον ἄνδρα εἶναι, καθάπερ οἱ Λάκωνες εἰώθασι προσαγορεύειν, ὅταν ἀγασθῶσι σφόδρα του (σεῖος ἀνήρ φασιν),
οὕτω καὶ ὁ θηριώδης ἐν τοῖς ἀνθρώποις σπάνιος. μάλιστα
δ' ἐν τοῖς βαρβάροις ἐστίν, γίνεται δ' ἔνια καὶ διὰ νόσους
καὶ πηρώσεις· καὶ τοὺς διὰ κακίαν δὲ τῶν ἀνθρώπων
4 ὑπερβάλλοντας οὕτως ἐπιδυσφημοῦμεν. ἀλλὰ περὶ μὲν
τῆς τοιαύτης διαθέσεως ὕστερον ποιητέον τινὰ μνείαν, περὶ
δὲ κακίας εἴρηται πρότερον· περὶ δὲ ἀκρασίας καὶ μαλακίας
καὶ τρυφῆς λεκτέον, καὶ περὶ ἐγκρατείας καὶ καρτερίας·
οὔτε γὰρ ὡς περὶ τῶν αὐτῶν ἕξεων τῇ ἀρετῇ καὶ τῇ μοχθη-
5 ρίᾳ ἑκατέραν αὐτῶν ὑποληπτέον, οὔθ' ὡς ἕτερον γένος. δεῖ

οὐδὲ ἐῴκει] *Il.* xxiv. 258.

3 οἱ Λάκωνες] Apparently taken from the *Meno* of Plato, p. 99 D.

4 ὕστερον] i.e. in chapter v.

πρότερον εἴρηται] Cf. *Eth. Eud.* II. ii. 28, &c.

5 δεῖ δ' ὥσπερ ἐπὶ τῶν ἄλλων—ἱκανῶς] 'Our course must be, as elsewhere, to state existing ideas (τὰ φαινόμενα), and, having gone through the doubts (which these ideas suggest), to establish thus if possible all, but if not all, anyhow the greater number and the most important of the ideas which are generally admitted (ἔνδοξα) about these conditions of mind. For if the difficulties be resolved and at the same time the generally admitted ideas be suffered to stand, the thing will be established sufficiently.' This passage is obscure, chiefly on account of the ambiguity in the words ἐὰν γὰρ λύηταί τε τὰ δυσχερῆ καὶ καταλείπηται τὰ ἔνδοξα. Two meanings might be attributed to λύηται τὰ δυσχερῆ, which might either refer (1) to the *rejection* of ideas that involved a difficulty; or (2) to the *clearing up* of difficulties attaching to any of the popular ideas. The former interpretation would seem best to suit the context, and to be justified by the actual procedure of subsequent chapters, and accordingly the following is the way in which the passage is rendered by the Paraphrast. λέγωμεν δὴ περὶ αὐτῶν κατὰ τὸν τρόπον καθ' ὃν καὶ περὶ τῶν ἄλλων εἴπομεν· ἐκθησόμεθα γὰρ τοὺς δοκοῦντας περὶ αὐτῶν λόγους, ἂν τοὺς μὴ συμβαίνοντας τῇ ἀληθείᾳ ἐλέγξαντες, τοὺς μάλιστα ἐνδόξους καταλείψαντες βεβαιώσομεν· καὶ οὕτως ἔσται φανερὸς ὁ περὶ αὐτῶν λόγος. But on looking below we find a sentence answering to, and in fact repeating, the present one in such a way that we cannot help taking it as a decisive guide as to what is here meant. After a statement of the

δ', ὥσπερ ἐπὶ τῶν ἄλλων, τιθέντας τὰ φαινόμενα καὶ πρῶτον διαπορήσαντας οὕτω δεικνύναι μάλιστα μὲν πάντα τὰ ἔνδοξα περὶ ταῦτα τὰ πάθη, εἰ δὲ μή, τὰ πλεῖστα καὶ κυριώτατα· ἐὰν γὰρ λύηταί τε τὰ δυσχερῆ καὶ καταλείπηται τὰ ἔνδοξα, δεδειγμένον ἂν εἴη ἱκανῶς.

Δοκεῖ δὴ ἥ τε ἐγκράτεια καὶ καρτερία τῶν σπουδαίων 6
καὶ τῶν ἐπαινετῶν εἶναι, ἡ δ' ἀκρασία τε καὶ μαλακία τῶν φαύλων τε καὶ ψεκτῶν, καὶ ὁ αὐτὸς ἐγκρατὴς καὶ ἐμμενετικὸς τῷ λογισμῷ καὶ ἀκρατὴς καὶ ἐκστατικὸς τοῦ λογισμοῦ. καὶ ὁ μὲν ἀκρατὴς εἰδὼς ὅτι φαῦλα πράττει διὰ πάθος, ὁ δ' ἐγκρατὴς εἰδὼς ὅτι φαῦλαι αἱ ἐπιθυμίαι οὐκ ἀκολουθεῖ διὰ τὸν λόγον. καὶ τὸν σώφρονα μὲν ἐγκρατῆ καὶ καρτερικόν, τὸν δὲ τοιοῦτον οἱ μὲν πάντα σώφρονα οἱ

---

various ideas, and of the difficulties which they suggest, the writer adds *εἰ μὲν οὖν ἀπορίαι τοιαῦταί τινες συμβαίνουσιν, τούτων δὲ τὰ μὲν ἀνελεῖν δεῖ, τὰ δὲ καταλιπεῖν· ἡ γὰρ λύσις τῆς ἀπορίας εὕρεσίς ἐστιν* (ii. 12). The words before us, *λύηται τὰ δυσχερῆ*, correspond with *τὰ μὲν ἀνελεῖν* (*τῶν ἀποριῶν*) and with *ἡ λύσις τῆς ἀπορίας*. It is to be observed, however, that *καταλείπειν* is used in the one place to refer to the popular ideas, and in the other to the objections (*ἀπορίαι*) urged against those ideas. *τὰ φαινόμενα*, as shown by what follows, is here equivalent to *τὰ λεγόμενα* in § 7, the common sayings and ideas of men. It is used in the same sense, *Eth. Eud.* I. vi. 1: *πειρατέον δὲ περὶ τούτων πάντων ζητεῖν τὴν πίστιν διὰ τῶν λόγων, μαρτυρίοις καὶ παραδείγμασι χρώμενον τοῖς φαινομένοις.*

6—7 The common ideas are now enumerated. They are six in number:

(1) 'That continence and endurance are morally good, while incontinence and softness are morally bad.'

(2) 'That the continent man is he who sticks to his opinion, while the incontinent man is he who departs from his opinion.'

(3) 'That the incontinent man errs through his peculiar state, knowing all the while that he is doing wrong;' while owing to this knowledge the continent man abstains.'

(4) 'That temperance is the same as continence, and in like manner incontinence is sometimes confused with intemperance.'

(5) 'It is occasionally maintained that "thoughtful" and clever men may be incontinent.'

(6) 'That there is such a thing as incontinence of other things beside pleasure, *e.g.* of anger, of honour, and of gain.'

6 *δοκεῖ δὴ κ.τ.λ.*] Cf. Xenophon, *Memorab.* I. v. 4—5, where it is said that Socrates considered *ἐγκράτεια* the foundation of the virtues. (Cf. *Ib.* IV. v. 1, IV. v. 3—7, 11.)

καὶ τὸν σώφρονα μὲν ἐγκρατῆ καὶ καρτερικόν] The distinction between *σωφροσύνη*, *ἐγκράτεια*, and *καρτερία*, was not accurately maintained either by Xenophon or Plato; cf. *Memorab.* IV. v. 7, II. i. 1, &c. Plato, *Gorgias*, p. 491 D: *πῶς ἑαυτοῦ ἄρχοντα λέγεις; οὐδὲν ποικίλον, ἀλλ' ὥσπερ οἱ πολλοί, σώφρονα ὄντα καὶ ἐγκρατῆ αὐτὸν ἑαυτοῦ, τῶν ἡδονῶν καὶ ἐπιθυμιῶν ἄρχοντα τῶν ἐν ἑαυτῷ.* *Rep.* p. 430 E: *κόσμος πού*

ὁ δ' οὔ, καὶ τὸν ἀκόλαστον ἀκρατῆ καὶ τὸν ἀκρατῆ ἀκόλα-
7 στον συγκεχυμένως, οἱ δ' ἑτέρους εἶναί φασιν. τὸν δὲ φρόνιμον ὁτὲ μὲν οὔ φασιν ἐνδέχεσθαι εἶναι ἀκρατῆ, ὁτὲ δ' ἐνίους φρονίμους ὄντας καὶ δεινοὺς ἀκρατεῖς εἶναι. ἔτι ἀκρατεῖς λέγονται καὶ θυμοῦ καὶ τιμῆς καὶ κέρδους. τὰ μὲν οὖν λεγόμενα ταῦτ' ἐστίν.

2 Ἀπορήσειε δ' ἄν τις πῶς ὑπολαμβάνων ὀρθῶς ἀκρατεύεταί τις. ἐπιστάμενον μὲν οὖν οὔ φασί τινες οἷόν τε εἶναι·

---

vii . . . ἡ σωφροσύνη ἐστὶ καὶ ἡδονῶν τινων καὶ ἐπιθυμιῶν ἐγκράτεια.

τὸν ἀκόλαστον ἀκρατῆ] Fritzsche refers to Xen. *Mem.* iv. v. 6 sqq., and for the opposite comparison to Xen. *Mem.* ii. i. 1: ἐδόκει προτρέπειν τοὺς συνόντας ἀσκεῖν ἐγκράτειαν βρωτοῦ καὶ ποτοῦ καὶ λαγνείας καὶ ὕπνου καὶ ῥίγους καὶ θάλπους καὶ πόνου. γνοὺς γάρ τινα τῶν συνόντων ἀκολαστοτέρως ἔχοντα πρὸς τὰ τοιαῦτα, κ.τ.λ.

7 ἀκρατεῖς λέγονται καὶ θυμοῦ καὶ τιμῆς καὶ κέρδους] Cf. Plato, *Legg.* ix. p. 869 A. Isocr. *Demon.* p. 6: ἐφ' οἷς κρατεῖσθαι τὴν ψυχὴν αἰσχρόν, τούτων ἐγκράτειαν ἄσκει πάντων, κέρδους, ὀργῆς, ἡδονῆς, λύπης.

II. This chapter contains a statement of the objections and difficulties which may be raised against the abovementioned ideas.

1—4 state the difficulties which attach to the third-mentioned idea—that the incontinent man sins against knowledge. How is this possible? how can one know the best and not do it? Socrates denied the possibility of incontinence altogether, making it convertible with ignorance; but with what kind of ignorance remains to be asked. Others confess that it is not knowledge which is perverted in the mind of the incontinent, but only opinion, *i.e.* a vague and weak conviction.

5 Continuing the same subject, introduces also an objection to idea (5)—that the thoughtful man may be incontinent. Some fancy that Thought (though not knowledge in the scientific sense) may coexist with incontinence. But this shows a misconception of the nature of 'thought.' The thoughtful man can do no wrong.

6 Contains an objection to idea (4). How can continence be the same as temperance, since the former implies evil desires to be controlled, but the latter is a harmonious state of the moral nature?

7—10 Shows the difficulties and absurdities which attach to idea (2), that continence consists in sticking to your opinion. If so it must be bad sometimes; Neoptolemus was incontinent; folly and incontinence combined will produce right actions; the abandoned man will be a more hopeful character than the incontinent, &c.

11 Urges against the sixth of the ideas, that the term 'incontinence' cannot be indiscriminately relative to wealth, honour, &c. There must be some absolute conception of incontinence, independent of these qualifications.

1 Ἀπορήσειε δ'—ἀκρατεύεται] 'Now one might raise the question, how it is that a person with right conceptions comes to act incontinently. That a man who had absolute *knowledge* should do so, some say would be impossible, for it would be a strange

δεινὸν γὰρ ἐπιστήμης ἐνούσης, ὡς ᾤετο Σωκράτης, ἄλλο τι κρατεῖν καὶ περιέλκειν αὐτὸν ὥσπερ ἀνδράποδον. Σωκράτης μὲν γὰρ ὅλως ἐμάχετο πρὸς τὸν λόγον ὡς οὐκ οὔσης ἀκρασίας· οὐθένα γὰρ ὑπολαμβάνοντα πράττειν παρὰ τὸ βέλτιστον, ἀλλὰ δι' ἄγνοιαν. Οὗτος μὲν οὖν ὁ λόγος ἀμ- 2
φισβητεῖ τοῖς φαινομένοις ἐναργῶς, καὶ δέον ζητεῖν περὶ τὸ πάθος, εἰ δι' ἄγνοιαν, τίς ὁ τρόπος γίνεται τῆς ἀγνοίας. ὅτι γὰρ οὐκ οἴεταί γε ὁ ἀκρατευόμενος πρὶν ἐν τῷ πάθει γενέσθαι, φανερόν. εἰσὶ δέ τινες οἳ τὰ μὲν συγχωροῦσι τὰ 3

---

thing, as Socrates thought, if knowledge were in a man, that anything else should master him and twist him about like a slave. Socrates in short was totally opposed to the idea, (arguing) as if incontinence did not exist at all, for he said no one with a conception of what was best could act differently from that best, but he could only so act through ignorance.' On this doctrine of Socrates, and on its connection with the rest of his ethical views, see Vol. I. Essay II. p. 165. The omission of the article before Σωκράτης seems to show that the real man, and not the personage of Plato's dialogues, is referred to, (see above, note on *Eth.* VI. xiii. 3), but yet the words of the passage before us have obvious reference to Plato's *Protagoras*, p. 352 B: δοκεῖ δὲ τοῖς πολλοῖς περὶ ἐπιστήμης τοιοῦτόν τι, οὐκ ἰσχυρὸν οὐδ' ἡγεμονικὸν οὐδ' ἀρχικὸν εἶναι· οὐδὲ ὡς περὶ τοιούτου αὐτοῦ ὄντος διανοοῦνται, ἀλλ' ἐνούσης πολλάκις ἀνθρώπῳ ἐπιστήμης, οὐ τὴν ἐπιστήμην αὐτοῦ ἄρχειν, ἀλλ' ἄλλο τι, τοτὲ μὲν θυμόν, τοτὲ δὲ ἡδονήν, τοτὲ δὲ λύπην, ἐνίοτε δὲ ἔρωτα, πολλάκις δὲ φόβον, ἀτεχνῶς διανοούμενοι περὶ τῆς ἐπιστήμης, ὥσπερ περὶ ἀνδραπόδου, περιελκομένης ὑπὸ τῶν ἄλλων ἁπάντων.

ὅλως ἐμάχετο] This is repeated in strong terms by the author of the *Magna Moralia*, II. vi. 2: Σωκράτης μὲν οὖν ὁ πρεσβύτης ἀνῄρει ὅλως καὶ οὐκ ἔφη ἀκρασίαν εἶναι, λέγων ὅτι οὐθεὶς εἰδὼς τὰ κακὰ ὅτι κακά εἰσιν ἕλοιτ' ἄν. Cf. Plato, *Protag.* p. 357 E: ἡ δὲ ἐξαμαρτανομένη πρᾶξις ἄνευ ἐπιστήμης ἴστε που καὶ αὐτοὶ ὅτι ἀμαθίᾳ πράττεται, &c.

2 οὗτος μὲν οὖν—φανερόν] 'Now this reasoning is manifestly at variance with experience, and we require to ask with regard to the state, supposing it to arise from ignorance, what manner of ignorance it is that takes place, for it is plain that the person who acts incontinently does not at all events think (that he must so act) before he gets into the particular state.' φαινομένοις here refers no doubt to the actual facts of life, and accordingly the rendering of the Paraphrast is, οὗτος δὲ ὁ λόγος ἐναντίος ἐστὶ τοῖς φανεροῖς. And yet there is probably some allusion also to the φαινόμενα mentioned above (i. 5); we may represent the double allusion of the word by translating it 'experience,' comparing with it also the use of τὰ ὑπάρχοντα, *Eth.* I. viii. 1.

οὐκ οἴεταί γε] There seems to be an ellipsis of δεῖν πράττειν ἃ πράττει. Cf. below, iii. 2: ὁ δ' οὐκ οἴεται μέν, διώκει δέ. The writer argues that if incontinence be ignorance, it is a peculiar kind of ignorance, an ignorance that comes on (γίνεται), not a consistent ignorance; for the incontinent person does not think ignorantly, *i.e.* wrongly, before the time of temptation. On

δ' οὔ· τὸ μὲν γὰρ ἐπιστήμης μηθὲν εἶναι κρεῖττον ὁμολογοῦσι, τὸ δὲ μηθένα πράττειν παρὰ τὸ δόξαν βέλτιον οὐχ
ὁμολογοῦσι, καὶ διὰ τοῦτο τὸν ἀκρατῆ φασὶν οὐκ ἐπιστήμην
4 ἔχοντα κρατεῖσθαι ὑπὸ τῶν ἡδονῶν ἀλλὰ δόξαν. ἀλλὰ
μὴν εἴγε δόξα καὶ μὴ ἐπιστήμη, μηδ' ἰσχυρὰ ὑπόληψις ἡ
ἀντιτείνουσα ἀλλ' ἠρεμαία, καθάπερ ἐν τοῖς διστάζουσι,
συγγνώμη τῷ μὴ μένειν ἐν αὐταῖς πρὸς ἐπιθυμίας ἰσχυράς·
τῇ δὲ μοχθηρίᾳ οὐ συγγνώμη, οὐδὲ τῶν ἄλλων οὐδενὶ τῶν
5 ψεκτῶν. φρονήσεως ἄρα ἀντιτεινούσης· αὕτη γὰρ ἰσχυρότατον. ἀλλ' ἄτοπον· ἔσται γὰρ ὁ αὐτὸς ἅμα φρόνιμος
καὶ ἀκρατής, φήσειε δ' οὐδ' ἂν εἷς φρονίμου εἶναι τὸ πράττειν ἑκόντα τὰ φαυλότατα. πρὸς δὲ τούτοις δέδεικται πρότερον ὅτι πρακτικός γε ὁ φρόνιμος· τῶν γὰρ ἐσχάτων τις
6 καὶ τὰς ἄλλας ἔχων ἀρετάς. ἔτι εἰ μὲν ἐν τῷ ἐπιθυμίας
ἔχειν ἰσχυρὰς καὶ φαύλας ὁ ἐγκρατής, οὐκ ἔσται ὁ σώφρων
ἐγκρατὴς οὐδ' ὁ ἐγκρατὴς σώφρων· οὔτε γὰρ τὸ ἄγαν σώφρονος οὔτε τὸ φαύλας ἔχειν. ἀλλὰ μὴν δεῖ γε· εἰ μὲν
γὰρ χρησταὶ αἱ ἐπιθυμίαι, φαύλη ἡ κωλύουσα ἕξις μὴ ἀκολουθεῖν, ὥσθ' ἡ ἐγκράτεια οὐ πᾶσα σπουδαία· εἰ δ' ἀσθενεῖς καὶ μὴ φαῦλαι, οὐθὲν σεμνόν, οὐδ' εἰ φαῦλαι καὶ ἀσθε-
7 νεῖς, οὐθὲν μέγα. ἔτι εἰ πάσῃ δόξῃ ἐμμενετικὸν ποιεῖ ἡ
ἐγκράτεια, φαύλη, οἷον εἰ καὶ τῇ ψευδεῖ. καὶ εἰ πάσης δόξης

Plato's conception of moral ignorance, see Vol. I. Essay III. p. 186.

3 *ἐπιστήμης μηθὲν εἶναι κρεῖττον*] Cf. *Eth. Eud.* VIII. i. 10: *καὶ ὀρθῶς τὸ Σωκρατικόν, ὅτι οὐδὲν ἰσχυρότερον φρονήσεως, ἀλλ' ὅτι ἐπιστήμην ἔφη, οὐκ ὀρθόν.* Plato, *Protag.* p. 352 D: *αἰσχρόν ἐστι -σοφίαν καὶ ἐπιστήμην μὴ οὐχὶ πάντων κράτιστον φάναι εἶναι τῶν ἀνθρωπείων πραγμάτων.*

5 *πρὸς δὲ τούτοις—ἀρετάς*] 'And besides, it has been previously demonstrated that the thoughtful man is emphatically (*γε*) one who acts, for his province is to deal with particulars, and he possesses also all the virtues.' *πρότερον*, cf. *Eth.* VI. vii. 7, VI. viii. 8; *τῶν ἐσχάτων* is here the genitive of the object, as, in the place just quoted, *τοῦ γὰρ ἐσχάτου ἐστὶν* (*ἡ φρόνησις*).

καὶ τὰς ἄλλας ἔχων ἀρετάς] Cf. *Eth.* VI. xiii. 6; *καὶ τὰς ἄλλας* is equivalent to *καὶ αὖ πάσας*. See the note on *Eth.* II. i. 4.

7 The rough and hasty conception of continence which would confound it with obstinacy is here refuted by showing that absurdities would follow from it. Continence would be sometimes an evil, and incontinence sometimes a good. From this point of view, the conduct of Neoptolemus (who first promised to deceive Philoctetes, and afterwards abandoned the design as unworthy) must be called incontinent and at the same time right. The al-

ἡ ἀκρασία ἐνστατικόν, ἔσται τις σπουδαία ἀκρασία, οἷον ὁ Σοφοκλέους Νεοπτόλεμος ἐν τῷ Φιλοκτήτῃ· ἐπαινετὸς γὰρ οὐκ ἐμμένων οἷς ἐπείσθη ὑπὸ τοῦ Ὀδυσσέως διὰ τὸ λυπεῖσθαι ψευδόμενος. ἔτι ὁ σοφιστικὸς λόγος ψευδόμενος ἀπο- 8
ρία· διὰ γὰρ τὸ παράδοξα βούλεσθαι ἐλέγχειν, ἵνα δεινοὶ ὦσιν ὅταν ἐπιτύχωσιν, ὁ γενόμενος συλλογισμὸς ἀπορία

---

lusion is repeated below, c. ix. § 4. For the sake of observing more accurately the 'noble incontinence' of Neoptolemus, it is worth while to quote at length the passage referred to (Soph. *Phil.* 895—916).

ΝΕ. παπαῖ· τί δῆτ' ἂν δρῷμ' ἐγὼ τοὐνθένδε γε;
ΦΙ. τί δ' ἔστιν, ὦ παῖ; ποῖ ποτ' ἐξέβης λόγῳ;
ΝΕ. οὐκ οἶδ' ὅποι χρὴ τἄπορον τρέπειν ἔπος.
ΦΙ. ἀπορεῖς δὲ τοῦ σύ; μὴ λέγ', ὦ τέκνον, τάδε.
ΝΕ. ἀλλ' ἐνθάδ' ἤδη τοῦδε τοῦ πάθους κυρῶ.
ΦΙ. οὐ δή σε δυσχέρεια τοῦ νοσήματος ἔπεισεν ὥστε μή μ' ἄγειν ναύτην ἔτι;
ΝΕ. ἅπαντα δυσχέρεια, τὴν αὑτοῦ φύσιν ὅταν λιπών τις δρᾷ τὰ μὴ προσεικότα.
ΦΙ. ἀλλ' οὐδὲν ἔξω τοῦ φυτεύσαντος σύ γε δρᾷς οὐδὲ φωνεῖς, ἐσθλὸν ἄνδρ' ἐπωφελῶν.
ΝΕ. αἰσχρὸς φανοῦμαι· τοῦτ' ἀνιῶμαι πάλαι.
ΦΙ. οὔκουν ἐν οἷς γε δρᾷς· ἐν οἷς δ' αὐδᾷς ὀκνῶ.
ΝΕ. ὦ Ζεῦ, τί δράσω; δεύτερον ληφθῶ κακός,
κρύπτων θ' ἃ μὴ δεῖ καὶ λέγων αἴσχιστ' ἐπῶν;
ΦΙ. ἀνὴρ ὅδ', εἰ μὴ 'γὼ κακὸς γνώμην ἔφυ,
προδούς μ' ἔοικε κἀκλιπὼν τὸν πλοῦν στελεῖν.
ΝΕ. λιπὼν μὲν οὐκ ἔγωγε· λυπηρῶς δὲ μὴ πέμπω σε μᾶλλον, τοῦτ' ἀνιῶμαι πάλαι.
ΦΙ. τί ποτε λέγεις, ὦ τέκνον; ὡς οὐ μανθάνω.
ΝΕ. οὐδέν σε κρύψω. δεῖ γὰρ ἐς Τροίαν σε πλεῖν
πρὸς τοὺς Ἀχαιοὺς καὶ τὸν Ἀτρειδῶν στόλον.

8—9 ἔτι ὁ σοφιστικὸς—κακὰ πράξει] 'Again (if we accept the above-mentioned definition of continence) the sophistical argument [though lying] will cause us perplexity. For from the sophists wishing to confute, and at the same time astonish (παράδοξα ἐλέγχειν), in order that on succeeding they may establish a reputation for ability,—they construct a piece of reasoning which perplexes, since the intellect is fettered, on the one hand not wishing to abide by a conclusion which does not please, and, on the other hand, being unable to get loose, from having no means of breaking the chain of argument. Now from one of their reasonings it ensues that folly together with incontinence will make up virtue; for (he who possesses those qualities) does the reverse of what he conceives (he ought) by reason of his incontinence, but he conceives good to be bad and that he ought not to do it, and thus he will do what is good and not what is bad.' In the Oxford edition of Bekker (1837) there is a misprint of μένειν μὲν δή. The Berlin edition of Bekker, like all other editions, reads μένειν μὲν μή. The MSS. appear to vary with regard to μὲν (which by some of them is omitted), but not with regard to μή.

γίνεται· δέδεται γὰρ ἡ διάνοια, ὅταν μένειν μὲν μὴ βού-
λητται διὰ τὸ μὴ ἀρέσκειν τὸ συμπερανθέν, προϊέναι δὲ μὴ
9 δύνηται διὰ τὸ λῦσαι μὴ ἔχειν τὸν λόγον. συμβαίνει δ' ἔκ
τινος λόγου ἡ ἀφροσύνη μετὰ ἀκρασίας ἀρετή. τἀναντία γὰρ
πράττει ὧν ὑπολαμβάνει διὰ τὴν ἀκρασίαν, ὑπολαμβάνει δὲ
τἀγαθὰ κακὰ εἶναι καὶ οὐ δεῖν πράττειν, ὥστε τἀγαθὰ καὶ

The great difficulty in the passage before us is caused by the word *ψευδόμενος*. This is explained either to be (1) an additional adjective to *ὁ σοφιστικὸς λόγος*, in which position it has an awkward appearance, or (2) to refer to the well-known puzzle of Eubulides the Megarian, which was called *ὁ ψευδόμενος*, and in logic books 'Mentiens' or 'the liar.' The puzzle was as follows: '*If a man says that he lies, does he lie or speak the truth?*' to which of course no simple answer can be given. He may lie, and yet speak the truth in saying that he lies; for if he lies in saying that he lies, then he speaks the truth. This was a specimen of the 'eristic' of the Megarians, which consisted to a great extent in drawing out the difficulties that beset the common forms of language. Chrysippus wrote six books on the puzzle of 'the Liar;' and Philetas of Cos is said to have died of vexation from failing to solve it. Hegel (*Geschichte der Philos.* ii. 117) compares it to the squaring of the circle. But clearly this puzzle has nothing to do with the subject under discussion in the text. Indeed one might almost fancy that the word *ψευδόμενος* was an interpolation which had crept in owing to the recurrence of the words *διὰ τὸ λύεσθαι ψευδόμενοι* in the line before. The acquaintance of the copyist with the fallacy 'Mentiens' might have tended to shroud the mistake. Evidently the words *συμβαίνει δ' ἔκ τινος λόγου* are an explanation of *ὁ σοφιστικὸς λόγος*, and the Paraphrast, seeing this, ignores the word *ψευδόμενος* altogether. Supposing, however, that it be allowed to stand, we must interpret it in a logical sense, not as if it had anything to do with the fallacy of Eubulides. The explanation of it is to be found in the *Sophist. Elench.* of Aristotle, iii. 1–2, where it is said that the aims of the Sophists and Eristics are five in number, *ἔλεγχος καὶ ψεῦδος καὶ παράδοξον καὶ σολοικισμὸς* (making one talk bad grammar) *καὶ πέμπτον τὸ ποιῆσαι ἀδολεσχῆσαι* (making one repeat the same thing over and over) . . . *μάλιστα μὲν γὰρ προαιροῦνται φαίνεσθαι ἐλέγχοντες, δεύτερον δὲ ψευδόμενόν τι δεικνύναι, τρίτον εἰς παράδοξον ἄγειν*, κ.τ.λ. In the above passage we see that the writer has brought together two of these separate terms, speaking of *παράδοξα ἐλέγχειν*. It is possible that he may also have qualified the 'sophistical reasoning' with another of these logical formulæ. The above-mentioned fallacy is an instance of the Sophists' way of tampering with moral notions in order to be thought clever.

δέδεται ἡ διάνοια] Cf. Ar. *Metaph.* ii. 1. 2: *λύειν δ' οὐκ ἔστιν ἀγνοοῦντας τὸν δεσμόν· ἀλλ' ἡ τῆς διανοίας ἀπορία δηλοῖ τοῦτο περὶ τοῦ πράγματος· ᾗ γὰρ ἀπορεῖ, ταύτῃ παραπλήσιον πέπονθε τοῖς δεδεμένοις· ἀδύνατον γὰρ ἀμφοτέρως προελθεῖν εἰς τὸ ἔμπροσθεν.* If we grant the premiss that continence is sticking to an opinion of whatever kind, we cannot 'get loose' from the conclusion forced upon us by the Sophists.

οὐ τὰ κακὰ πράξει. ἔτι ὁ τῷ πεπεῖσθαι πράττων καὶ διώ- 10
κων τὰ ἡδέα καὶ προαιρούμενος βελτίων ἂν δόξειεν τοῦ μὴ
διὰ λογισμὸν ἀλλὰ δι' ἀκρασίαν· εὐϊατότερος γὰρ διὰ τὸ
μεταπεισθῆναι ἄν. ὁ δ' ἀκρατὴς ἔνοχος τῇ παροιμίᾳ ἐν ᾗ
φαμὲν "ὅταν τὸ ὕδωρ πνίγῃ, τί δεῖ ἐπιπίνειν;" εἰ μὲν
γὰρ μὴ ἐπέπειστο ἃ πράττει, μεταπεισθεὶς ἂν ἐπαύσατο·
νῦν δὲ πεπεισμένος οὐδὲν ἧττον ἄλλα πράττει. ἔτι εἰ 11
περὶ πάντα ἀκρασία ἐστὶ καὶ ἐγκράτεια, τίς ὁ ἁπλῶς
ἀκρατής; οὐθεὶς γὰρ ἁπάσας ἔχει τὰς ἀκρασίας, φαμὲν
δ' εἶναί τινας ἁπλῶς. αἱ μὲν οὖν ἀπορίαι τοιαῦταί τινες
συμβαίνουσιν, τούτων δὲ τὰ μὲν ἀνελεῖν δεῖ τὰ δὲ 12
καταλιπεῖν· ἡ γὰρ λύσις τῆς ἀπορίας εὕρεσίς ἐστιν.

Πρῶτον μὲν οὖν σκεπτέον πότερον εἰδότες ἢ οὔ, καὶ πῶς 3
εἰδότες, εἶτα περὶ ποῖα τὸν ἀκρατῆ καὶ τὸν ἐγκρατῆ

---

10 *ἔτι ὁ τῷ—ἄλλα πράττει*] 'Again he who on conviction and with full purpose acts and pursues pleasure would seem to be in a better state than he who does so not from reasoning, but from incontinence; for (the former) is more curable, since there is a possibility of changing his convictions, whereas the incontinent man is open to the saying "When water chokes, what must one take to wash it down?" Had he not been convinced before with regard to his actions, there might have been a hope of his mind being enlightened and his ceasing so to act; but as it is, with all the conviction in the world, he still acts contrary to it.' This is a *reductio ad absurdum* of the saying that incontinence means never acting on your conviction, and that continence means sticking to your conviction. If it were so, intemperance (*ἀκολασία*) would seem to be a sort of continence, and, on the other hand, incontinence would seem incurable. The reverse, however, of all this is true. See below ch. viii.

εἰ μὲν γὰρ μὴ ἐπέπειστο] Some MSS. omit *μή*, which is not to be wondered at, as there is a transition of meaning in the use of *ἐπέπειστο*: (1) the intemperate man is said to act *τῷ πεπεῖσθαι*, i.e. with a wrong conviction, thinking bad to be good; (2) the incontinent man acts *οὐ τῷ πεπεῖσθαι*, not by reason of a conviction that he ought to do as he does; (3) the incontinent man *πέπεισται ἃ πράττει*, has a full conviction with regard to what he does (*i.e.* that it is wrong), but does not abide by that conviction.

12 *αἱ μὲν οὖν—ἐστιν*] 'This then is the kind of difficulties which arise; part of them we must explain away (*ἀνελεῖν*), while we leave part unanswered, for resolving a difficulty is finding something out.' Cf. Ar. *Metaphys.* II. i. 2: *ἔστι δὲ τοῖς εὐπορῆσαι βουλομένοις προὔργου τὸ διαπορῆσαι καλῶς· ἡ γὰρ ὕστερον εὐπορία λύσις τῶν πρότερον ἀπορουμένων ἐστί, λύειν δ' οὐκ ἔστιν ἀγνοοῦντας τὸν δεσμόν.* See above, ch. i. 5, note.

III. This chapter discusses that which is really the most important and interesting question with regard

θετέον, λέγω δὲ πότερον περὶ πᾶσαν ἡδονὴν καὶ λύπην ἢ περί τινας ἀφωρισμένας, καὶ τὸν ἐγκρατῆ καὶ τὸν καρτερικόν, πότερον ὁ αὐτὸς ἢ ἕτερός ἐστιν· ὁμοίως δὲ καὶ περὶ τῶν ἄλλων ὅσα συγγενῆ τῆς θεωρίας ἐστὶ ταύτης.
2 ἔστι δ' ἀρχὴ τῆς σκέψεως, πότερον ὁ ἐγκρατὴς καὶ ὁ ἀκρατής εἰσι τῷ περὶ ἃ ἢ τῷ πῶς ἔχοντες τὴν διαφοράν, λέγω δὲ πότερον τῷ περὶ ταδὶ εἶναι μόνον ἀκρατὴς ὁ ἀκρατής, ἢ οὒ ἀλλὰ τῷ ὥς, ἢ οὒ ἀλλ' ἐξ ἀμφοῖν· ἔπειτ' εἰ περὶ πάντ' ἐστὶν ἡ ἀκρασία καὶ ἡ ἐγκράτεια ἢ οὔ· οὔτε γὰρ περὶ πάντ' ἐστὶν ὁ ἁπλῶς ἀκρατής, ἀλλὰ περὶ ἅπερ ὁ ἀκόλαστος, οὔτε τῷ πρὸς ταῦτα ἁπλῶς ἔχειν (ταὐτὸν γὰρ ἂν ἦν τῇ ἀκολασίᾳ), ἀλλὰ τῷ ὡδὶ ἔχειν. ὁ μὲν γὰρ ἄγεται προαιρούμενος, νομίζων ἀεὶ δεῖν τὸ παρὸν ἡδὺ διώκειν· ὁ δ'

---

to incontinence and the whole nature of the moral will, namely, how is it possible to know the right and yet do the wrong? It treats of the third of the popular opinions mentioned above (ch. i. § 6), and the difficulties arising out of the same (ch. ii. §§ 1—4). The commencement of the chapter is rather confused, as it touches on, without discussing, the nature of the object-matter of continence and incontinence, &c. With § 3 the main question is opened, namely the relation of knowledge to incontinence, and a preliminary step is taken by the assertion that it makes no difference whether it be right *opinion* or *knowledge* which the incontinent man possesses, since opinion may be held quite as *strongly* as knowledge.

In §§ 5—8 it is shown that the real point to be ascertained is, what is meant by *knowing* or *having knowledge*. A man may have knowledge which is in abeyance, either because he does not apply a minor premise to his general principle, or because he is under the influence of sleep, wine, madness, or the like.

9—14 A more intimate examination tells us that there may be two syllogisms in the mind, the one leading to continence and the other to incontinence. The former is not drawn out, but remains in want of a minor premise; the latter through the instincts of sense and desire becomes realised and is acted on. However, the former knowledge cannot be said to have been present in a complete form to the mind, and therefore Socrates was not wrong in denying that knowledge of the right could exist, and yet be overborne.

1—2 There is something awkward in the way in which the questions to be discussed in succeeding chapters are here propounded. The writer might have made it his ἀρχὴ τῆς σκέψεως to consider what is the exact point of difference between continence and incontinence, but as a matter of fact he has not done so. There is a want of art in the sudden announcement (ὁ μὲν γὰρ ἄγεται, κ.τ.λ.) of the distinction between intemperance and incontinence. The same want of art, proceeding from whatever cause, marks

οὐκ οἴεται μέν, διώκει δέ. περὶ μὲν οὖν τοῦ δόξαν ἀληθῆ 3
ἀλλὰ μὴ ἐπιστήμην εἶναι παρ' ἣν ἀκρατεύονται, οὐθὲν διαφέρει πρὸς τὸν λόγον· ἔνιοι γὰρ τῶν δοξαζόντων οὐ διστάζουσιν, ἀλλ' οἴονται ἀκριβῶς εἰδέναι. εἰ οὖν διὰ τὸ ἠρέμα 4
πιστεύειν οἱ δοξάζοντες μᾶλλον τῶν ἐπισταμένων παρὰ τὴν ὑπόληψιν πράξουσιν, οὐθὲν διοίσει ἐπιστήμη δόξης· ἔνιοι γὰρ πιστεύουσιν οὐδὲν ἧττον οἷς δοξάζουσιν ἢ ἕτεροι οἷς ἐπίστανται· δηλοῖ δ' Ἡράκλειτος. ἀλλ' ἐπεὶ διχῶς λέγομεν 5
τὸ ἐπίστασθαι (καὶ γὰρ ὁ ἔχων μὲν οὐ χρώμενος δὲ τῇ ἐπιστήμῃ καὶ ὁ χρώμενος λέγεται ἐπίστασθαι), διοίσει τὸ ἔχοντα μὲν μὴ θεωροῦντα δὲ ἃ μὴ δεῖ πράττειν τοῦ ἔχοντα καὶ θεωροῦντα· τοῦτο γὰρ δοκεῖ δεινόν, ἀλλ' οὐκ εἰ

---

the whole of these two sections, and the main business of the chapter only commences with section 3.

3—4 *περὶ μὲν οὖν τοῦ δόξαν ἀληθῆ κ.τ.λ.*] Cf. above ch. ii. §§ 3—4. We must dismiss any idea that the phenomena of incontinence can be explained by saying that the incontinent man has only moral *opinions*, and that opinions are weak. 'Heraclitus shows' that opinions may be as strongly held as scientific certainties. Of course neither Aristotle nor his school would wish to do away with the distinction which Plato had established between δόξα and *ἐπιστήμη*. It is only as connected with the will, and as forming a ground for action, that opinion can be considered as strong as science.

δηλοῖ δ' Ἡράκλειτος] Heraclitus had a reputation with the ancients for pride and dogmatism; cf. Diog. Laert. IX. i. 5: *ἤκουσέ τε οὐδενὸς ἀλλ' αὑτὸν ἔφη διζήσασθαι καὶ μαθεῖν πάντα παρ' ἑαυτοῦ*. *Ib.* IX. i. 1: *μεγαλόφρων δὲ γέγονε παρ' ὁντιναοῦν καὶ ὑπερόπτης, ὡς καὶ ἐκ τοῦ συγγράμματος αὐτοῦ δῆλον ἐν ᾧ φησι· πολυμαθίη νόον οὐ διδάσκει· Ἡσίοδον γὰρ ἂν ἐδίδαξε καὶ Πυθαγόρην, αὖθίς τε Ξενοφάνεά τε καὶ Ἑκαταῖον. εἶναι γὰρ ἓν τὸ σοφόν, ἐπίστασθαι γνώμην ἥτε οἱ ἐγκυβερνήσει πάντα διὰ πάντων.*

5 *ἀλλ' ἐπεὶ διχῶς—θεωρεῖν*] 'But since we use the term "knowing" in two senses, both to denote the man who possesses without applying, and the man who applies knowledge, there will be a difference between doing what is wrong, when you have the knowledge but do not attend to it, and doing the same when you have the knowledge and pay attention to it. The latter case seems strange, but not so if you act without attending.' This distinction between the possession and the application of knowledge, which is of the utmost importance for explaining moral weakness, was perhaps first started by Plato in the *Theaetetus*, pp. 197—198, where he introduces his famous image of the pigeon-house. Every knowledge once acquired by the mind is like a bird caught and placed in a pigeon-house; it is possessed, but not available, till it be chased within the enclosure and captured anew.

μὴ θεωροῦντα] *θεωρεῖν* is used to express 'direct observation,' just as in *Eth.* VI. iii. 2: *ὅταν ἔξω τοῦ θεωρεῖν γένηται.*

6 μὴ θεωρῶν. ἔτι ἐπεὶ δύο τρόποι τῶν προτάσεων, ἔχοντα
μὲν ἀμφοτέρας οὐδὲν κωλύει πράττειν παρὰ τὴν ἐπιστήμην, χρώμενον μέντοι τῇ καθόλου ἀλλὰ μὴ τῇ κατὰ
μέρος· πρακτὰ γὰρ τὰ καθ' ἕκαστα. διαφέρει δὲ καὶ τὸ
καθόλου· τὸ μὲν γὰρ ἐφ' ἑαυτοῦ τὸ δ' ἐπὶ τοῦ πράγματός
ἐστιν, οἷον ὅτι παντὶ ἀνθρώπῳ συμφέρει τὰ ξηρά, καὶ ὅτι
οὗτος ἄνθρωπος ἢ ὅτι ξηρὸν τὸ τοιόνδε· ἀλλ' εἰ τόδε τοιόνδε, ἢ οὐκ ἔχει ἢ οὐκ ἐνεργεῖ. κατά τε δὴ τούτους διοίσει
τοὺς τρόπους ἀμήχανον ὅσον, ὥστε δοκεῖν οὕτω μὲν εἰδέναι
7 μηθὲν ἄτοπον, ἄλλως δὲ θαυμαστόν. ἔτι τὸ ἔχειν τὴν
ἐπιστήμην ἄλλον τρόπον τῶν νῦν ῥηθέντων ὑπάρχει τοῖς
ἀνθρώποις· ἐν τῷ γὰρ ἔχειν μὲν μὴ χρῆσθαι δὲ διαφέρουσαν ὁρῶμεν τὴν ἕξιν, ὥστε καὶ ἔχειν πως καὶ μὴ
ἔχειν, οἷον τὸν καθεύδοντα καὶ μαινόμενον καὶ οἰνωμένον.
ἀλλὰ μὴν οὕτω διατίθενται οἱ ἐν τοῖς πάθεσιν ὄντες·
θυμοὶ γὰρ καὶ ἐπιθυμίαι ἀφροδισίων καὶ ἔνια τῶν τοιούτων ἐπιδήλως καὶ τὸ σῶμα μεθιστᾶσιν, ἐνίοις δὲ

---

6 *ἔτι ἐπεὶ—θαυμαστόν*] 'Again since the premisses (in a syllogism) are of two modes, nothing hinders a man acting against knowledge, although he possesses both these, if he apply only the universal premiss, but not the particular, for it is particulars which are the objects of action. Moreover there is a distinction which may be made in the universal itself; part of it applies to the subject (*ἐφ' ἑαυτοῦ*), and part to the object (*ἐπὶ τοῦ πράγματος*), for instance (you may have the universal) "dry things are good for all men," and (the minor premiss) "this is a man," or "such and such is dry;" but (the farther knowledge) that "this object is such and such," the person either has not or it is not realised. According then to these different modes of the premisses there will be an immense difference (in the way one knows), so that there is nothing paradoxical in (the incontinent man) "knowing" in the way I have specified, but that he should know otherwise would be marvellous.' This section well points out the number of particular applications which have to be made before a general moral principle can be realised and acted on. Else it remains in abeyance, and the man who possesses it may yet act against it.

7 *ἐν τῷ γὰρ ἔχειν—οἰνωμένον*] 'For in the case of having and not using we see that the having (*τὴν ἕξιν*) becomes quite a different thing, so that in such cases a man has (knowledge) after a manner, and has it not, as for instance in sleep, in madness, and in drunkenness.' *Ἕξις* is used here simply as the active verbal noun of *ἔχω*, as it is in a passage of Plato, already alluded to, which the writer possibly had before his mind, *Theaetetus*, p. 197 A: *ἀκήκοας οὖν ὃ νῦν λέγουσι τὸ ἐπίστασθαι;—Ἴσως· οὐ μέντοι ἔν γε τῷ παρόντι μνημονεύω.—Ἐπιστήμης που [illegible] φασὶ αὐτὸ εἶναι.*

καὶ μανίας ποιοῦσιν. δῆλον οὖν ὅτι ὁμοίως ἔχειν λεκτέον τοὺς ἀκρατεῖς τούτοις. τὸ δὲ λέγειν τοὺς λόγους τοὺς ἀπὸ 8
τῆς ἐπιστήμης οὐδὲν σημεῖον· καὶ γὰρ οἱ ἐν τοῖς πάθεσι τούτοις ὄντες ἀποδείξεις καὶ ἔπη λέγουσιν Ἐμπεδοκλέους, καὶ οἱ πρῶτον μαθόντες συνείρουσι μὲν τοὺς λόγους, ἴσασι δ' οὔπω· δεῖ γὰρ συμφῦναι, τούτῳ δὲ χρόνου δεῖ· ὥστε καθάπερ τοὺς ὑποκρινομένους, οὕτως ὑποληπτέον λέγειν καὶ τοὺς ἀκρατευομένους. ἔτι καὶ ὧδε φυσικῶς ἄν τις ἐπι- 9

---

8 *τὸ δὲ λέγειν—ἀκρατευομένους*] 'Now repeating the words which belong to knowledge is no sign, for those also who are in the states I have mentioned repeat demonstrations and verses of Empedocles, and those who are beginning to learn string the words together without yet understanding them; for (to be understood) a thing must be assimilated, and for this time is required. So in short we must suppose that men in a state of incontinence speak just like actors.' This is an extremely subtle observation. The writer having said that passion is like sleep or madness, which make one know and yet not know at the same time, proceeds to remark that men acting incontinently will often speak as if they were fully aware of the nature of their acts. They will say at the very moment of yielding to temptation, 'I know I ought not to do this.' But such words are no sign that the knowledge is really felt and realised; they are only like the verses of Empedocles which a man might mutter in his sleep; they are like the repetition of a schoolboy's task; they are hollow like the ranting of an actor.

ἀπὸ τῆς ἐπιστήμης] 'That are caused by, are the results of, science.' Cf. *Met.* I. iv. 4: *ἀλλ' οὔτε ἐκεῖνοι ἀπὸ ἐπιστήμης*, 'they do it not because of science,' and see below, IX. ix. 6.

οἱ πρῶτον μαθόντες] Cf. *Eth.* VI. viii. 6.

9—11 *ἔτι καὶ ὧδε—μορίων*] 'Again in the following manner one might psychologically consider the cause. There is first a general belief, and secondly a particular belief, which is no longer under the domain of reason, but under that of sense. Now when out of these two a third is created, it is a necessity that the mind should on the one hand assert the conclusion, and in the sphere of practice should straightway carry it out. As for instance, if (there be the general proposition) "one ought to taste all that is sweet," and the particular one "this thing is sweet," it is a necessity that he who is able, and is not hindered, should at once proceed to act upon the knowledge. When therefore there is in the mind one universal which forbids tasting, but another which says, "all that is sweet is pleasant," (having a minor) "this thing is sweet," and thus the second universal is realised,—and supposing that desire happen to be there; (in this case) the first universal says, "avoid this," but desire leads us on (to take it), from the power which it has of setting in motion every one of our organs. Thus the result is that one is incontinent under the sanction as it were of reason and belief, and a belief too which is opposed not directly but only acciden-

βλέψειε τὴν αἰτίαν. ἡ μὲν γὰρ καθόλου δόξα, ἡ δ' ἑτέρα περὶ τῶν καθ' ἕκαστά ἐστιν, ὧν αἴσθησις ἤδη κυρία· ὅταν δὲ μία γένηται ἐξ αὐτῶν, ἀνάγκη τὸ συμπερανθὲν ἔνθα μὲν φάναι τὴν ψυχήν, ἐν δὲ ταῖς ποιητικαῖς πράττειν εὐθύς, οἷον, εἰ παντὸς γλυκέος γεύεσθαι δεῖ, τουτὶ δὲ γλυκὺ ὡς ἕν τι τῶν καθ' ἕκαστον, ἀνάγκη τὸν δυνάμενον καὶ μὴ κωλυόμενον ἅμα τοῦτο καὶ πράττειν. ὅταν οὖν ἡ μὲν καθόλου ἐνῇ κωλύουσα γεύεσθαι, ἡ δέ, ὅτι πᾶν τὸ γλυκὺ ἡδύ, τουτὶ δὲ γλυκύ (αὕτη δὲ ἐνεργεῖ), τύχῃ δ' ἐπιθυμία ἐνοῦσα, ἡ μὲν λέγει φεύγειν τοῦτο, ἡ δ' ἐπιθυμία ἄγει· κινεῖν γὰρ ἕκαστον δύναται τῶν μορίων· ὥστε συμβαίνει ὑπὸ λόγου

---

tally (to the true knowledge). For it is desire, and not the intellectual belief, which is opposed to the right law. And this consideration leads us to see why it is that brutes are not incontinent, namely, because they have no conception of universals, but only an image and a memory of particulars.'

This passage gives an admirable explanation of the way in which a man under temptation may ignore his moral principles. Action (as the writer implies) always depends on a syllogism in the mind, and, if a minor premiss were applied to the right moral principle, wrong action could never take place. But it is equally true that the man who acts wrongly does so under some sort of shadow of reason. The story of the temptation of Eve is typical of all similar cases of yielding. There are always arguments and considerations on which the mind, self-deceived and blinded by desire, may form a syllogism. And, as the writer observes, the misleading principle thus applied is not directly false or contrary to what is right. The saying 'sweet things are pleasant' is not in itself contrary to the principle 'intemperance is to be avoided.' Accidentally and in their effects the two propositions are brought into collision, though not originally opposed.

φυσικῶς] Perhaps 'psychologically' is the most representative translation which we can give of this word in the present passage. Psychology, up to a certain extent, was considered as a branch of physics by Aristotle, see Vol. I. Essay V. p. 294, and cf. *Eth.* IX. iii. 7.

φάναι] A circumlocution is necessary to express what was probably here meant by this word. Cf. *Eth.* VI. xi. 2.

ἔνθα μὲν] i.e. in the sphere of the reason, to which *ἐν δὲ ταῖς ποιητικαῖς* is opposed. For the latter phrase we should have expected to find *ταῖς πρακτικαῖς*, a formula which occurs *Eth.* VI. xi. 4. But in the *Eudemian Ethics*, II. xi. 4, exactly the same usage is found: *ὥσπερ γὰρ ταῖς θεωρητικαῖς αἱ ὑποθέσεις ἀρχαί, οὕτω καὶ ταῖς ποιητικαῖς τὸ τέλος ἀρχὴ καὶ ὑπόθεσις*. It is not easy to say what substantive is understood. Perhaps *αἱ πρακτικαὶ* (or *ποιητικαὶ*) *ἐπιστῆμαι* was the original phrase.

ἀνάγκη — πράττειν εὐθύς] On the doctrine of the practical syllogism, see Vol. I. Essay IV. pp. 262—269.

τῶν μορίων] i.e. 'the parts of the body.' This is mixing up a physical explanation with the account of mental phenomena. The same thing is done

πως καὶ δόξης ἀκρατεύεσθαι, οὐκ ἐναντίας δὲ καθ' αὑτήν,
ἀλλὰ κατὰ συμβεβηκός. ἡ γὰρ ἐπιθυμία ἐναντία, ἀλλ' 11
οὐχ ἡ δόξα, τῷ ὀρθῷ λόγῳ· ὥστε καὶ διὰ τοῦτο τὰ θηρία
οὐκ ἀκρατῆ, ὅτι οὐκ ἔχει τῶν καθόλου ὑπόληψιν, ἀλλὰ τῶν
καθ' ἕκαστα φαντασίαν καὶ μνήμην. πῶς δὲ λύεται ἡ 12
ἄγνοια καὶ πάλιν γίνεται ἐπιστήμων ὁ ἀκρατής, ὁ αὐτὸς
λόγος καὶ περὶ οἰνωμένου καὶ καθεύδοντος καὶ οὐκ ἴδιος
τούτου τοῦ πάθους, ὃν δεῖ παρὰ τῶν φυσιολόγων ἀκούειν.
ἐπεὶ δ' ἡ τελευταία πρότασις δόξα τε αἰσθητοῦ καὶ 13
κυρία τῶν πράξεων, ταύτην ἢ οὐκ ἔχει ὁ ἐν τῷ πάθει ὤν,

---

in the Peripatetic treatise *De Motu Animalium*; cf. especially with the present passage *Ib.* viii. 5: διὰ τοῦτο δ' ἅμα ὡς εἰπεῖν νοεῖ ὅτι πορευτέον καὶ πορεύεται, ἂν μή τι ἐμποδίζῃ ἕτερον. τὰ μὲν γὰρ ὀργανικὰ μέρη παρασκευάζει ἐπιτηδείως τὰ πάθη, ἡ δ' ὄρεξις τὰ πάθη, τὴν δ' ὄρεξιν ἡ φαντασία· αὕτη δὲ γίνεται ἢ διὰ νοήσεως ἢ δι' αἰσθήσεως.

11 The mere intellectual knowledge that a thing is pleasant is not opposed to the moral law. It is only when this knowledge has become desire, *i.e.* part of the will, which implies acting, that an opposition is felt. Brutes act on desire, but their intellectual apprehension being entirely of particulars, there is a harmony between desire and the *data* of perception which prevents our attributing incontinence to brutes.—It might be said that there are dawnings of the moral faculty, traces of a sense of right and wrong, in some animals, for instance, dogs; but the writer here does not enter upon the subject. On the meaning given by Aristotle to φαντασία, see note on *Eth.* III. v. 17.

12 'Now to explain how the oblivion (ἄγνοια) of the incontinent man is stopped, and how he comes again to the use of his knowledge, requires no special account peculiar to this condition, but the same account as is to be given about (the recovery of) the intoxicated man or the sleeper, for which we must inquire of the physiologists.' The most interesting relic of the speculations of the old physiologists upon the above question which has come down to us, is the account given by Sextus Empiricus (*Adv. Math.* VII. 129) of the opinion of Heraclitus, who thought that our rationality depended upon our communion through the senses with the universal reason that surrounds us; in sleep we become foolish because cut off from all communication with this, except through the act of breathing alone, but on awaking we are again replenished. Τοῦτον δὴ τὸν θεῖον λόγον καθ' Ἡράκλειτον δι' ἀναπνοῆς σπάσαντες νοεροὶ γινόμεθα, καὶ ἐν ὕπνοις ληθαῖοι, κατὰ δὲ ἔγερσιν πάλιν ἔμφρονες. ἐν γὰρ τοῖς ὕπνοις μυσάντων τῶν αἰσθητικῶν πόρων, χωρίζεται τῆς πρὸς τὸ περιέχον συμφυΐας ὁ ἐν ἡμῖν νοῦς, μόνης τῆς κατὰ ἀναπνοὴν προσφύσεως σωζομένης, οἱονεί τινος ῥίζης· χωρισθείς τε ἀποβάλλει ἣν πρότερον εἶχε μνημονικὴν δύναμιν. ἐν δὲ ἐγρηγορόσι πάλιν διὰ τῶν αἰσθητικῶν πόρων, ὥσπερ διά τινων θυρίδων προκύψας καὶ τῷ περιέχοντι συμβάλλων λογικὴν ἐνδύεται δύναμιν.

13—14 ἐπεὶ δ'—αἰσθητικῆς] 'But the minor premiss being a belief with regard to perception of the senses

ἢ οὕτως ἔχει ὡς οὐκ ἦν τὸ ἔχειν ἐπίστασθαι ἀλλὰ λέγειν ὥσπερ ὁ οἰνωμένος τὰ Ἐμπεδοκλέους, καὶ διὰ τὸ μὴ καθόλου μηδ᾽ ἐπιστημονικὸν ὁμοίως εἶναι δοκεῖν τῷ καθόλου τὸν ἔσχατον ὅρον. καὶ ἔοικεν ὃ ἐζήτει Σωκράτης συμ-
14 βαίνειν· οὐ γὰρ τῆς κυρίως ἐπιστήμης εἶναι δοκούσης παρούσης γίνεται τὸ πάθος, οὐδ᾽ αὕτη περιέλκεται διὰ τὸ πάθος, ἀλλὰ τῆς αἰσθητικῆς. περὶ μὲν οὖν τοῦ εἰδότα καὶ μή, καὶ πῶς εἰδότα ἐνδέχεται ἀκρατεύεσθαι, τοσαῦτα εἰρήσθω.

---

and being what determines action,—this is either not possessed by a man in the condition we have been describing, or he possesses it in a way in which, as we said (ὡς οὐκ ἦν), possession is not knowledge, but is only a form of words, like the drunken man spouting Empedocles. And since the minor term is not universal and has not the same scientific character as the universal, the question raised by Socrates seems really (καὶ) to be substantiated. For it is not knowledge properly so called that is present when the condition arises, nor is it this which is twisted about by the condition of mind that comes on,—but only perceptional knowledge.' This section winds up the discussion of the compatibility of knowledge with incontinence. The first sentence is clear enough, but there is some little obscurity in the saying that perceptional knowledge is present in incontinence, and is overborne by passion. What is meant apparently is, that passion prevents that perception which would cause the moral principle existent in the mind to be realised. Hence, in short, there is a moral oblivion, and it is quite true that Socrates was justified in saying that incontinence could not take place if knowledge of the right were really present to the consciousness of the actor.

καὶ διὰ τὸ μὴ καθόλου] Lambinus, followed by Fritzsche, places a full stop before these words, and connects them with καὶ ἔοικεν ὁ Σωκράτης. This punctuation has been adopted in the above translation as making far better sense. It must be confessed, however, that the Paraphrast favours the punctuation of Bekker. The occurrence of καὶ before ἔοικεν would naturally lead to a full stop being placed after ὅρον, but καὶ is rather to be explained as giving emphasis to ἔοικε συμβαίνειν, cf. ch. ii. 2: διὸ καὶ δοκοῦσιν ἐνίοτε κ.τ.λ. *Eth.* III. viii. 6: ὅθεν καὶ ὁ Σωκράτης. *Ib.* § 10, ὅθεν καὶ Ὅμηρος.

ἡ τελευταία πρότασις] This phrase is equivalent to ἡ ἑτέρα πρότασις, *Eth.* VI. xi. 4. The minor premiss is so called as containing the ἔσχατος ὅρος, or minor term, which is mentioned shortly after.

ὡς οὐκ ἦν] With this use of the past tense cf. *Eth.* V. vi. 9: κατὰ νόμον γὰρ ἦν, 'for this is, as we have said, according to law.'

ὃ ἐζήτει] This is sometimes translated 'what Socrates meant,' for which the Greek would have been ὃ ἤθελε or ἐβούλετο λέγειν. ὃ ἐζήτει must mean 'the questionings' or 'doubts' of Socrates, i.e. as to the possibility of acting against knowledge. Cf. *Eth.* I. iv. 5: Εὖ γὰρ καὶ Πλάτων ἠπόρει τοῦτο καὶ ἐζήτει.

τῆς αἰσθητικῆς] The phrase αἰσθητικὴ ἐπιστήμη would to some philosophers

Πότερον δ' ἐστί τις ἁπλῶς ἀκρατὴς ἢ πάντες κατὰ μέ- 4
ρος, καὶ εἰ ἔστι, περὶ ποῖά ἐστι, λεκτέον ἐφεξῆς. ὅτι μὲν οὖν
περὶ ἡδονὰς καὶ λύπας εἰσὶν οἵ τ' ἐγκρατεῖς καὶ καρτερικοὶ
καὶ οἱ ἀκρατεῖς καὶ μαλακοί, φανερόν. ἐπεὶ δ' ἐστὶ τὰ 2
μὲν ἀναγκαῖα τῶν ποιούντων ἡδονήν, τὰ δ' αἱρετὰ μὲν καθ'
αὑτὰ ἔχοντα δ' ὑπερβολήν, ἀναγκαῖα μὲν τὰ σωματικά.
λέγω δὲ τὰ τοιαῦτα, τά τε περὶ τὴν τροφὴν καὶ τὴν τῶν
ἀφροδισίων χρείαν, καὶ τὰ τοιαῦτα τῶν σωματικῶν περὶ
ἃ τὴν ἀκολασίαν ἔθεμεν καὶ τὴν σωφροσύνην. τὰ δ' ἀναγκαῖα μὲν οὔ, αἱρετὰ δὲ καθ' αὑτά. λέγω δ' οἷον νίκην τιμὴν πλοῦτον καὶ τὰ τοιαῦτα τῶν ἀγαθῶν καὶ ἡδέων. τοὺς
μὲν οὖν πρὸς ταῦτα παρὰ τὸν ὀρθὸν λόγον ὑπερβάλλοντας

---

be a contradiction in terms, as they would hold that sensible things cannot be known. A doctrine was attributed to Speusippus, of which we may be here reminded, viz. that besides science there is 'scientific perception.' Cf. Sextus Empiricus *adv. Math.* VII. 145: Σπεύσιππος δέ, ἐπεὶ τῶν πραγμάτων τὰ μὲν αἰσθητὰ τὰ δὲ νοητά, τῶν μὲν νοητῶν κριτήριον ἔλεξεν εἶναι τὸν ἐπιστημονικὸν λόγον, τῶν δὲ αἰσθητῶν τὴν ἐπιστημονικὴν αἴσθησιν, ἐπιστημονικὴν δὲ αἴσθησιν ὑπείληφε καθεστάναι τὴν μεταλαμβάνουσαν τῆς κατὰ τὸν λόγον ἀληθείας.

IV. This chapter discusses the question mooted above (ch. i. § 7. ch. ii. § 11), as to whether incontinence is an absolute term, having a definite object-matter, or is merely relative. The answer is very simple. Pleasure is divided into necessary and desirable (§ 2), or into good, bad, and indifferent (§ 5). Incontinence, in an absolute sense, applies only to the necessary or bodily pleasures. It has then the same range of objects as were before assigned to Temperance and Intemperance, and differs from Intemperance chiefly in that it goes against the reason and the will, instead of carrying them on its side. Having thus laid down a definite notion of Incontinence as something absolute and positive, it is easy to see that the idea and the term may be applied in a sort of analogous sense to mean an ill-control of the desires for other kinds of pleasures also, beside the bodily pleasures, *e.g.* wealth or honour. In such applications we must recollect that the use of the word Incontinence is metaphorical.

2 περὶ ἃ τὴν ἀκολασίαν ἔθεμεν καὶ τὴν σωφροσύνην] Cf. *Eth. Eud.* III. ii. 5: Ἐπεὶ δ' ὁ σώφρων ἐστὶ περὶ ἡδονάς, ἀνάγκη καὶ περὶ ἐπιθυμίας τινὰς αὐτὸν εἶναι. Δεῖ δὴ λαβεῖν περὶ τίνας. Οὐ γὰρ περὶ πάσας οὐδὲ περὶ ἅπαντα τὰ ἡδέα ὁ σώφρων ἐστίν, ἀλλὰ τῇ μὲν δόξῃ περὶ δύο τῶν αἰσθητῶν, περί τε τὸ γευστὸν καὶ τὸ ἁπτόν, τῇ δ' ἀληθείᾳ περὶ τὸ ἁπτόν, κ.τ.λ. This is of course taken from *Eth. Nic.* III. x. 3–8.

τοὺς μὲν οὖν) Here commences the apodosis to ἐπεὶ δ' ἐστί, which is a complicated sentence with two parentheses (λέγω δὲ τὰ τοιαῦτα—σωφροσύνην) and (λέγω δ' οἷον—ἡδέων).

τοὺς μὲν ἑτέρους ἦν] 'Those then who with regard to these latter objects

τὸν ἐν αὑτοῖς ἁπλῶς μὲν οὐ λέγομεν ἀκρατεῖς, προστιθέντες δὲ τὸ χρημάτων ἀκρατεῖς καὶ κέρδους καὶ τιμῆς καὶ θυμοῦ, ἁπλῶς δ' οὔ ὡς ἑτέρους καὶ καθ' ὁμοιότητα λεγομένους, ὥσπερ ἄνθρωπος ὁ τὰ Ὀλύμπια νενικηκώς· ἐκείνῳ γὰρ ὁ κοινὸς λόγος τοῦ ἰδίου μικρῷ διέφερεν ἀλλ' ὅμως ἕτερος ἦν. σημεῖον δέ· ἡ μὲν γὰρ ἀκρασία ψέγεται οὐχ ὡς ἁμαρτία μόνον ἀλλὰ καὶ ὡς κακία τις ἢ ἁπλῶς οὖσα ἢ κατά τι
3 μέρος, τούτων δ' οὐθείς. τῶν δὲ περὶ τὰς σωματικὰς ἀπολαύσεις, περὶ ἃς λέγομεν τὸν σώφρονα καὶ ἀκόλαστον, ὁ μὴ τῷ προαιρεῖσθαι τῶν τε ἡδέων διώκων τὰς ὑπερβολὰς καὶ τῶν λυπηρῶν φεύγων, πείνης καὶ δίψης καὶ ἀλέας καὶ ψύχους καὶ πάντων τῶν περὶ ἁφὴν καὶ γεῦσιν, ἀλλὰ

(*i.e.* good pleasures) transgress that right law which they have within themselves, we do not call simply "incontinent," but we add a qualifying term (*προστιθέντες*) and speak of them as incontinent of wealth, gain, honour, rage,—not as absolutely incontinent, because they are different from this and are only called incontinent by analogy, as in the phrase "Man that has been victor at Olympia;" there the general conception (of man) differed but little from the special conception of the individual in question, and yet still it was different.' The meaning of this passage is clear, not so however that of the illustration which closes it. It is plain that the word *ἀκρατής* when spoken of in relation to anger, money, &c., has a somewhat different sense from the unqualified term *ἀκρατής*, which implies a certain moral weakness with regard to bodily indulgence. But what is meant by saying that *ἄνθρωπος ὁ τὰ Ὀλύμπια νενικηκώς* is different from the general conception Man? There appear to be only two explanations possible: (1) that supported by the Scholiast on this place and also the Scholiast on *Eth.* v. i.,—by Alexander Aphrod. *ad Topica* 1. xvi., by Suidas, and by Eustathius on *Iliad*, λ. p. 847: namely, that there was a certain Olympionices whose name was Ἄνθρωπος. It might be said that this name Ἄνθρωπος was not more distinct from the general term 'Man,' than the term *ἀκρατής* in the phrase *ἀκρατὴς θυμοῦ* is from the general conception of incontinence. The historical tenses *διέφερεν* and *ἕτερος ἦν* are in favour of this interpretation. (2) It might be argued that these very tenses had given rise to a conjectural fiction about a person called Ἄνθρωπος. The Paraphrast takes no notice of the tradition, and treats the illustration as a logical one, which would come merely to this, 'the conception of an individual implies a certain diversity from the conception of the genus.' If this be accepted, the past tenses of the verbs must be understood to mean a reference to some previous logical discourse with which the school was familiar. In short the passage must be considered to bear traces of being a scrap from some oral lecture—a hypothesis not to be entirely set aside with regard to parts of the *Ethics* of Aristotle.

παρὰ τὴν προαίρεσιν καὶ τὴν διάνοιαν, ἀκρατὴς λέγεται,
οὐ κατὰ πρόσθεσιν, ὅτι περὶ τάδε, καθάπερ ὀργῆς, ἀλλ'
ἁπλῶς μόνον. σημεῖον δέ· καὶ γὰρ μαλακοὶ λέγονται περὶ 4
ταύτας, περὶ ἐκείνων δ' οὐδεμίαν. καὶ διὰ τοῦτ' εἰς ταὐτὸν
τὸν ἀκρατῆ καὶ τὸν ἀκόλαστον τίθεμεν καὶ ἐγκρατῆ καὶ
σώφρονα, ἀλλ' οὐκ ἐκείνων οὐδένα, διὰ τὸ περὶ τὰς αὐτάς
πως ἡδονὰς καὶ λύπας εἶναι· οἱ δ' εἰσὶ μὲν περὶ ταὐτά,
ἀλλ' οὐχ ὡσαύτως εἰσίν, ἀλλ' οἱ μὲν προαιροῦνται οἱ δ' οὐ
προαιροῦνται. διὸ μᾶλλον ἀκόλαστον ἂν εἴποιμεν, ὅστις
μὴ ἐπιθυμῶν ἢ ἠρέμα διώκει τὰς ὑπερβολὰς καὶ φεύγει
μετρίας λύπας, ἢ τοῦτον ὅστις διὰ τὸ ἐπιθυμεῖν σφόδρα· τί
γὰρ ἂν ἐκεῖνος ποιήσειεν, εἰ προσγένοιτο ἐπιθυμία νεανικὴ
καὶ περὶ τὰς τῶν ἀναγκαίων ἐνδείας λύπη ἰσχυρά; ἐπεὶ δὲ 5
τῶν ἐπιθυμιῶν καὶ τῶν ἡδονῶν αἱ μέν εἰσι τῷ γένει καλῶν
καὶ σπουδαίων· τῶν γὰρ ἡδέων ἔνια φύσει αἱρετά, τὰ δ'
ἐναντία τούτων, τὰ δὲ μεταξύ, καθάπερ διείλομεν πρότερον,
οἷον χρήματα καὶ κέρδος καὶ νίκη καὶ τιμή· πρὸς ἅπαντα
δὲ καὶ τὰ τοιαῦτα καὶ τὰ μεταξὺ οὐ τῷ πάσχειν καὶ
ἐπιθυμεῖν καὶ φιλεῖν ψέγονται, ἀλλὰ τῷ πως ὑπερβάλλειν.

---

3 *κατὰ πρόσθεσιν*] See note on *Eth.* II. iii. 5.

καθάπερ ὀργῆς] Fritzsche quotes Thucyd. III. 84: *ἡ ἀνθρωπεία φύσις— ἀκρατὴς μὲν ὀργῆς οὖσα κρείσσων δὲ τοῦ δικαίου.*

4 *ἀλλ' οὐκ ἐκείνων οὐδένα*] i.e. not one of those mentioned in § 2, who are immoderate in giving way to a fondness for riches, honour, &c.

διὸ μᾶλλον ἀκόλαστον κ.τ.λ.] It is more intemperate to pursue luxury, &c., in cold blood, than to do so under the influence of passion. It shows that luxury has become more a part of the mind itself.

5—6 The remainder of this chapter is little more than a repetition of what has gone before. Indulgence in the good pleasures is no harm, except it be to excess; even excess in them is rather folly than vice, and is not to be called by the name of incontinence, except as a sort of metaphor.

ἐπεὶ δὲ—ὑπερβάλλειν] 'Now since some desires and pleasures are in their kind beautiful and good—according to our former division of pleasures into the naturally desirable, the naturally detestable, and the intermediate—as for instance wealth, gain, victory, and honour (are good); with regard then to all such, and the intermediate pleasures, men are not blamed for feeling, desiring, and loving them, but for some sort of excess in them.' The present division of pleasures can hardly be said to have been made 'before,' though it can be harmonized with that given above in § 2. The *φύσει αἱρετά* (of which wealth and honour are specimens) answer to the *αἱρετὰ μὲν καθ' αὑτὰ ἔχοντα δ' ὑπερβολήν*; while *τὰ μεταξὺ*

διὸ ὅσοι μὲν παρὰ τὸν λόγον ἢ κρατοῦνται ἢ διώκουσι τῶν φύσει τι καλῶν καὶ ἀγαθῶν, οἷον οἱ περὶ τιμὴν μᾶλλον ἢ δεῖ σπουδάζοντες ἢ περὶ τέκνα καὶ γονεῖς· καὶ γὰρ ταῦτα τῶν ἀγαθῶν, καὶ ἐπαινοῦνται οἱ περὶ ταῦτα σπουδάζοντες· ἀλλ' ὅμως ἔστι τις ὑπερβολὴ καὶ ἐν τούτοις, εἴ τις ὥσπερ ἡ Νιόβη μάχοιτο καὶ πρὸς τοὺς θεούς, ἢ ὥσπερ Σάτυρος ὁ φιλοπάτωρ ἐπικαλούμενος περὶ τὸν πατέρα· λίαν γὰρ ἐδόκει μωραίνειν. μοχθηρία μὲν οὖν οὐδεμία περὶ ταῦτ' ἐστὶ διὰ τὸ εἰρημένον, ὅτι φύσει τῶν αἱρετῶν ἕκαστόν ἐστι δι' αὑτό· φαῦλαι δὲ καὶ φευκταὶ αὐτῶν εἰσὶν αἱ ὑπερβολαί.
6 ὁμοίως δὲ οὐδ' ἀκρασία· ἡ γὰρ ἀκρασία οὐ μόνον φευκτὸν ἀλλὰ καὶ τῶν ψεκτῶν ἐστίν. δι' ὁμοιότητα δὲ τοῦ πάθους προσεπιτιθέντες τὴν ἀκρασίαν περὶ ἑκάστου λέγουσιν, οἷον κακὸν ἰατρὸν καὶ κακὸν ὑποκριτήν, ὃν ἁπλῶς οὐκ ἂν εἴποιεν κακόν· ὥσπερ οὖν οὐδ' ἐνταῦθα, διὰ τὸ μὴ κακίαν εἶναι ἑκάστην αὐτῶν, ἀλλὰ τῷ ἀνάλογον ὁμοίαν, οὕτω δῆλον ὅτι κἀκεῖ ὑποληπτέον μόνην ἀκρασίαν καὶ ἐγκράτειαν εἶναι ἥτις ἐστὶ περὶ ταὐτὰ τῇ σωφροσύνῃ καὶ τῇ ἀκολασίᾳ, περὶ δὲ θυμὸν καθ' ὁμοιότητα λέγομεν· διὸ καὶ προστιθέντες ἀκρατῆ θυμοῦ ὥσπερ τιμῆς καὶ κέρδους φαμέν.

5 Ἐπεὶ δ' ἐστὶν ἔνια μὲν ἡδέα φύσει, καὶ τούτων τὰ μὲν

---

here correspond with the 'necessary or bodily pleasures' of the former passage. The writer has here introduced a mention of pleasures 'naturally detestable,' by which must be meant the bestial pleasures which are discussed in the following chapter. The formula τὰ δ' ἐναντία, τὰ δὲ μεταξύ, is used by Eudemus in *Eth. Eud.* ii. 3. 24: ἀλλὰ μὴν ἑκάστου γε φθορὰ καὶ ἀναστροφὴ οὐκ εἰς τὸ τυχόν, ἀλλ' εἰς τὰ ἐναντία καὶ τὰ μεταξύ. Later in the present book (ch. xiv. § 2) there is a mention made of pleasures which are not only good in themselves, but do not admit of excess.

Σάτυρος ὁ φιλοπάτωρ] Of this personage nothing is known. The story given by the Scholiast is, as Fritzsche observes, not worth repeating.

μοχθηρία μὲν οὖν] This is an anacoluthon. The sentence ought to form an apodosis and supply a verb to διὸ ὅσοι μὲν κ.τ.λ. We therefore require μοχθηροὶ μὲν οὐκ εἰσί, &c.

6 δι' ὁμοιότητα δὲ] The writer seems here to make a mistake about the history of the word ἀκρατής, just as before (*Eth.* v. 2. 1) about the history of the word ἄνισος. Ἀκρατὴς in a limited and special sense, to denote want of control over a particular set of desires, is certainly later than the general use of the word, as in the phrase ἀκρατὴς ὀργῆς, &c. Hence the latter is not to be regarded (historically) as a metaphorical extension of the former.

V. This chapter discusses those

ἁπλῶς τὰ δὲ κατὰ γένη καὶ ζῴων καὶ ἀνθρώπων, τὰ δ' οὐκ ἔστιν ἀλλὰ τὰ μὲν διὰ πηρώσεις τὰ δὲ δι' ἔθη γίνεται, τὰ δὲ διὰ μοχθηρὰς φύσεις, ἔστι καὶ περὶ τούτων ἕκαστα παραπλησίας ἰδεῖν ἕξεις. λέγω δὲ τὰς θηριώδεις, οἷον 2
τὴν ἄνθρωπον ἣν λέγουσι τὰς κυούσας ἀνασχίζουσαν τὰ παιδία κατεσθίειν, ἢ οἵοις χαίρειν φασὶν ἐνίους τῶν ἀπηγριωμένων περὶ τὸν Πόντον, τοὺς μὲν ὠμοῖς τοὺς δὲ ἀνθρώπων κρέασιν, τοὺς δὲ τὰ παιδία δανείζειν ἀλλήλοις εἰς εὐωχίαν, ἢ τὸ περὶ Φάλαριν λεγόμενον. αὗται μὲν θη- 3
ριώδεις, αἱ δὲ διά τε νόσους γίνονται καὶ μανίαν ἐνίοις,

---

kinds of incontinence which are something more than incontinence, being morbid or bestial. Certain pleasures are specified which imply a depravity either of nature or habits. A sort of classification of these is suggested, but the whole style of the chapter is careless and inaccurate.

1 ἐπεὶ δ'—ἕξεις] 'Now while some things are natural pleasures, either absolutely so, or relatively to the different races of animals and men, other pleasures are not natural, but depend on physical defects or habits or depravity of the nature; and we may see moral conditions corresponding to each of these latter kinds.' The apodosis to ἐπεὶ is ἔστι καὶ περὶ τούτων. The things which are 'pleasures absolutely' are for instance life and consciousness; while it depends on the constitution of the race whether it be pleasant to live on land or water, &c. In this passage φύσις is used in two senses, (1) φύσει = in accordance with the entire constitution of things, not only what is, but what ought to be. (This corresponds with head V. in the note on *Eth.* II. i. 3.) (2) φύσεις means individual natures, not as they ought to be, but as they are. (See the same note, head IV.)

2 τὰς θηριώδεις] i.e. ἕξεις.

τὴν ἄνθρωπον] 'The female.' The word ἄνθρωπος (in the feminine) was applied contemptuously, as for instance to female slaves. Here it denotes the monstrous nature of the person in question, who was not to be called 'a woman.' Perhaps for the same reason it was applied by Herodotus to the gigantic Phya. Book I. ch. 60: καὶ ἐν τῷ ἄστεϊ πειθόμενοι τὴν γυναῖκα εἶναι αὐτὴν τὴν θεὸν προσεκύνεόν τε τὴν ἄνθρωπον καὶ ἐδέκοντο τὸν Πεισίστρατον. Cf. *Mag. Mor.* I. xv. 2: Οἷόν φασι κατά τινα γυναῖκα φίλτρον τινὶ δοῦναι πιεῖν εἶτα τὸν ἄνθρωπον ἀποθανεῖν ὑπὸ τοῦ φίλτρου, τὴν δ' ἄνθρωπον ἐν Ἀρείῳ πάγῳ ἀποφυγεῖν.

τοὺς δὲ τὰ παιδία δανείζειν ἀλλήλους εἰς εὐωχίαν] 'And others (they say) lend their children to each other (in turn) to be served up as a banquet.' Cf. 2 Kings vi. 26—29, where the same horrible arrangement is said to have been made under the compulsion of famine. The shores of the Black Sea seem to have had a character for cannibalism. Cf. Ar. *Pol.* VIII. iv. 3: πολλὰ δ' ἐστὶ τῶν ἐθνῶν ἃ πρὸς τὸ κτείνειν καὶ πρὸς τὴν ἀνθρωποφαγίαν εὐχερῶς ἔχει, καθάπερ τῶν περὶ τὸν Πόντον Ἀχαιοί τε καὶ Ἡνίοχοι.

τὸ περὶ Φάλαριν λεγόμενον] Some story now lost, which is apparently referred to again in § 7.

3 αἱ δὲ διά τε νόσους—αἱ δὲ νοση-

ὥσπερ ὁ τὴν μητέρα καθιερεύσας καὶ φαγών, καὶ ὁ τοῦ
συνδούλου τὸ ἧπαρ. αἱ δὲ νοσηματώδεις ἢ ἐξ ἔθους, οἷον
τριχῶν τίλσεις καὶ ὀνύχων τρώξεις, ἔτι δ' ἀνθράκων καὶ
γῆς, πρὸς δὲ τούτοις ἡ τῶν ἀφροδισίων τοῖς ἄρρεσιν· τοῖς
μὲν γὰρ φύσει τοῖς δ' ἐξ ἔθους συμβαίνουσιν, οἷον τοῖς ὑβρι-
4 ζομένοις ἐκ παίδων. ὅσοις μὲν οὖν φύσις αἰτία, τούτους
μὲν οὐδεὶς ἂν εἴπειεν ἀκρατεῖς, ὥσπερ οὐδὲ τὰς γυναῖκας,
ὅτι οὐκ ὀπυίουσιν ἀλλ' ὀπυίονται· ὡσαύτως δὲ καὶ τοῖς
5 νοσηματωδῶς ἔχουσι δι' ἔθος. τὸ μὲν οὖν ἔχειν ἕκαστα
τούτων ἔξω τῶν ὅρων ἐστὶ τῆς κακίας, καθάπερ καὶ ἡ θη-
ριότης· τὸ δ' ἔχοντα κρατεῖν ἢ κρατεῖσθαι οὐχ ἡ ἁπλῆ
ἀκρασία ἀλλ' ἡ καθ' ὁμοιότητα, καθάπερ καὶ τὸν περὶ τοὺς
θυμοὺς ἔχοντα τοῦτον τὸν τρόπον τοῦ πάθους, ἀκρατῆ δ' οὐ
λεκτέον. πᾶσα γὰρ ὑπερβάλλουσα καὶ ἀφροσύνη καὶ δειλία καὶ ἀκολασία καὶ χαλεπότης αἱ μὲν θηριώδεις αἱ δὲ
6 νοσηματώδεις εἰσίν· ὁ μὲν γὰρ φύσει τοιοῦτος οἷος δεδιέναι πάντα, κἂν ψοφήσῃ μῦς, θηριώδη δειλίαν δειλός, ὁ

ματώδεις] These clauses are a repetition of each other, the style is unfinished.

ἡ τῶν ἀφροδισίων τοῖς ἄρρεσιν] It is important to observe here the strong terms in which the unnatural character of these practices is denounced. An equally strong and more explicit passage occurs in the *Laws* of Plato, p. 636 B, where the advantages and disadvantages of the gymnasia and syssitia are discussed: Καὶ δὴ καὶ παλαιὸν νόμιμον δοκεῖ τοῦτο τὸ ἐπιτήδευμα κατὰ φύσιν τὰς περὶ τὰ ἀφροδίσια ἡδονὰς οὐ μόνον ἀνθρώπων ἀλλὰ καὶ θηρίων διεφθαρκέναι. Καὶ τούτων τὰς ὑμετέρας πόλεις (Sparta and Crete) πρώτας ἄν τις αἰτιῷτο καὶ ὅσαι τῶν ἄλλων μάλιστα ἅπτονται τῶν γυμνασίων· καὶ εἴτε παίζοντα εἴτε σπουδάζοντα ἐννοεῖν δεῖ τὰ τοιαῦτα, ἐννοητέον ὅτι τῇ θηλείᾳ καὶ τῇ τῶν ἀρρένων φύσει εἰς κοινωνίαν ἰούσῃ τῆς γεννήσεως ἡ περὶ ταῦτα ἡδονὴ κατὰ φύσιν ἀποδεδόσθαι δοκεῖ, ἀρρένων δὲ πρὸς ἄρρενας ἢ θηλειῶν πρὸς θηλείας παρὰ φύσιν καὶ τῶν πρώτων τὸ τόλμημα εἶναι δι' ἀκράτειαν ἡδονῆς.

4—5 ὅσοις μὲν οὖν—λεκτέον] 'Where nature is the cause, one cannot call people incontinent, just as no one would find fault with women for being not male but female; and it is the same with those who by habit have superinduced a morbid condition. To possess, indeed, any of these tendencies is beyond the pale of vice, just as bestiality is; and if a person possesses them, his subduing them or being subdued by them is a matter not of simple incontinence (or continence), but is the "analogous" kind, exactly as a man who is in this condition with regard to his angry passions may be called (incontinent of anger), but not simply incontinent.' What the writer here implies is quite true, that morality requires for its sphere certain natural conditions of body and mind. In states that are entirely morbid, whether originally so or from the

δὲ τὴν γαλῆν ἐδεδίει διὰ νόσον· καὶ τῶν ἀφρόνων οἱ μὲν ἐκ
φύσεως ἀλόγιστοι καὶ μόνον τῇ αἰσθήσει ζῶντες θηριώδεις,
ὥσπερ ἔνια γένη τῶν πόρρω βαρβάρων, οἱ δὲ διὰ νόσους,
οἷον τὰς ἐπιληπτικάς, ἢ μανίας νοσηματώδεις. τούτων 7
δ' ἔστι μὲν ἔχειν τινὰ ἐνίοτε μόνον, μὴ κρατεῖσθαι δέ, λέγω
δὲ οἷον εἰ Φάλαρις κατεῖχεν ἐπιθυμῶν παιδίου φαγεῖν ἢ
πρὸς ἀφροδισίων ἄτοπον ἡδονήν· ἔστι δὲ καὶ κρατεῖσθαι,
μὴ μόνον ἔχειν. ὥσπερ οὖν καὶ μοχθηρία ἡ μὲν κατ' 8
ἄνθρωπον ἁπλῶς λέγεται μοχθηρία, ἡ δὲ κατὰ πρόσθεσιν,
ὅτι θηριώδης ἢ νοσηματώδης, ἁπλῶς δ' οὔ, τὸν αὐτὸν
τρόπον δῆλον ὅτι καὶ ἀκρασία ἐστὶν ἡ μὲν θηριώδης ἡ δὲ
νοσηματώδης, ἁπλῶς δὲ ἡ κατὰ τὴν ἀνθρωπίνην ἀκολασίαν
μόνη. ὅτι μὲν οὖν ἀκρασία καὶ ἐγκράτειά ἐστι μόνον
περὶ ἅπερ ἀκολασία καὶ σωφροσύνη, καὶ ὅτι περὶ τὰ 9
ἄλλα ἐστὶν ἄλλο εἶδος ἀκρασίας, λεγόμενον κατὰ μεταφορὰν καὶ οὐχ ἁπλῶς, δῆλον·

Ὅτι δὲ καὶ ἧττον αἰσχρὰ ἀκρασία ἡ τοῦ θυμοῦ ἢ ἡ 6
τῶν ἐπιθυμιῶν, θεωρήσωμεν. ἔοικε γὰρ ὁ θυμὸς ἀκούειν μέν τι τοῦ λόγου, παρακούειν δέ, καθάπερ οἱ ταχεῖς τῶν διακόνων, οἳ πρὶν ἀκοῦσαι πᾶν τὸ λεγόμενον ἐκθέουσιν, εἶτα ἁμαρτάνουσι τῆς προστάξεως, καὶ οἱ κύνες, πρὶν σκέψασθαι εἰ φίλος, ἂν μόνον ψοφήσῃ, ὑλακτοῦσιν· οὕτως ὁ θυμὸς διὰ θερμότητα καὶ ταχυτῆτα τῆς φύσεως ἀκούσας μέν, οὐκ ἐπίταγμα δ' ἀκούσας, ὁρμᾷ πρὸς τὴν

---

effects of an ill-regulated life, the distinctions of right and wrong are no longer applicable. Cf. ch. vii. 7.

7 εἰ Φάλαρις κατεῖχεν] 'Had Phalaris refrained.' With this use of κατέχω, cf. Aristoph. *Peace*, 944, where it is applied to a wind lulling:

> ἐπείγετε νῦν ἐν ὅσῳ
> σοβαρὰ θεόθεν κατέχει
> πολέμου μετάτροπος αὔρα.

And Soph. *Œd. Rex*, 782:

> κἀγὼ βαρυνθεὶς τὴν μὲν οὖσαν ἡμέραν
> μόλις κατέσχον.

VI. It having been repeatedly laid down that there are some kinds of incontinence not simply to be called so without a qualification, there now follows a comparison of some of these kinds, from a moral point of view, with incontinence proper. Incontinence of anger is not so bad as incontinence of lust, (1) because there is more semblance of reason in anger; (2) because anger is more a matter of constitution; (3) it admits of less deliberate purpose; (4) because anger is exercised under a sort of pain, and not in wantonness. As to the rest, incontinence which exceeds the pale of human weakness is more horrible, but at the same time is rarer, and less mischievous, than vice.

τιμωρίαν. ὁ μὲν γὰρ λόγος ἢ ἡ φαντασία ὅτι ὕβρις ἢ ὀλιγωρία ἐδήλωσεν, ὁ δ' ὥσπερ συλλογισάμενος ὅτι δεῖ τῷ τοιούτῳ πολεμεῖν χαλεπαίνει δὴ εὐθύς· ἡ δ' ἐπιθυμία, ἐὰν μόνον εἴπῃ, ὅτι ἡδὺ ὁ λόγος ἢ ἡ αἴσθησις, ὁρμᾷ πρὸς τὴν ἀπόλαυσιν. ὥσθ' ὁ μὲν θυμὸς ἀκολουθεῖ τῷ λόγῳ πως, ἡ δ' ἐπιθυμία οὔ. αἰσχίων οὖν. ὁ μὲν γὰρ τοῦ θυμοῦ ἀκρατὴς τοῦ λόγου πως ἡττᾶται, ὁ δὲ τῆς ἐπιθυμίας καὶ οὐ τοῦ

2 λόγου. ἔτι ταῖς φυσικαῖς μᾶλλον συγγνώμη ἀκολουθεῖν

---

1 ὁ μὲν γὰρ λόγος—οὔ] 'For first (μὲν) reason or fancy tells that there is insult or slight, and then (anger) drawing a sort of conclusion, "I must fight with such and such," forthwith rages accordingly. But desire, if reason or sense merely assert that a thing is pleasant, rushes to the enjoyment of it; so that anger in a way follows reason, but desire does not.' φαντασία here seems nearly to correspond to our word 'fancy,' which has of course grown out of the Greek term, though it has come to imply widely different associations. We are told in Ar. *De An.* III. iii. 15 that φαντασία may be mistaken. See the note on *Eth.* III. v. 17.

The present passage might seem discrepant from ch. iii. § 10, *ὥστε συμβαίνει ὑπὸ λόγου πως καὶ δόξης ἀκρατεύεσθαι*, where incontinence is said to have some sort of reasoning in what it does. And if the comparison were exactly carried out, it would probably appear that incontinent anger had no more reason in it than incontinent desire. But it is true that anger is fundamentally based on an idea of justice, however wild that idea may be. Hence there is a peculiar force in *συλλογισάμενος ὅτι δεῖ*. And hence too anger is a less immediately selfish passion than desire. It is less debasing in the long run to the character. On anger, cf. *Eth.* v. viii. 10: *οὐδὲ περὶ τοῦ γενέσθαι ἢ μὴ ἀμφισβητεῖται, ἀλλὰ περὶ τοῦ δικαίου· ἐπὶ φαινομένῃ γὰρ ἀδικίᾳ ἡ ὀργή ἐστιν*: and Ar. *Rhet.* II. ii. 1: *Ἔστω δὴ ὀργὴ ὄρεξις μετὰ λύπης τιμωρίας φαινομένης διὰ φαινομένην ὀλιγωρίαν*. The illustrations in the text comparing anger to an over-hasty servant who runs off before he has heard half the message, or to a dog who barks without waiting to see who it is, are most admirable.

2 The next plea urged in favour of anger is that it is more natural (or, we might say, constitutional) than desire: in support of which two humorous stories are told in the text (see Vol. I. Essay III. p. 216). The argument appears somewhat contradictory to *Eth.* II. iii. 10: *ἔτι δὲ χαλεπώτερον ἡδονῇ μάχεσθαι ἢ θυμῷ, καθάπερ φησὶν Ἡράκλειτος*. However, when we look closely at the text, we find that it is 'excessive and unnecessary desire' with which anger is here compared (*τῶν ἐπιθυμιῶν τῶν τῆς ὑπερβολῆς καὶ τῶν μὴ ἀναγκαίων*). This no doubt makes the above assertion true, but it gives a new conception of incontinence, as compared with the mention of *ἀναγκαῖα ἡδέα*, c. iv. § 2. It sets incontinence too much in the light of *θηριότης*. But indeed the vagueness of the term *ἀκρασία*, and the uncertainty as to what it exactly implies, must be felt throughout the present discussions.

With regard to anger, it is true that hot temper is frequently consti-

ὀρέξεσιν, ἐπεὶ καὶ ἐπιθυμίαις ταῖς τοιαύταις μᾶλλον ὅσαι κοιναὶ πᾶσι, καὶ ἐφ' ὅσον κοιναί· ὁ δὲ θυμὸς φυσικώτερον καὶ ἡ χαλεπότης τῶν ἐπιθυμιῶν τῶν τῆς ὑπερβολῆς καὶ τῶν μὴ ἀναγκαίων, ὥσπερ ὁ ἀπολογούμενος ὅτι τὸν πατέρα τύπτοι. 'καὶ γὰρ οὗτος' ἔφη 'τὸν ἑαυτοῦ κἀκεῖνος τὸν ἄνωθεν,' καὶ τὸ παιδίον δείξας 'καὶ οὗτος ἐμέ' ἔφη, 'ὅταν ἀνὴρ γένηται· συγγενὲς γὰρ ἡμῖν.' καὶ ὁ ἑλκόμενος ὑπὸ τοῦ υἱοῦ παύεσθαι ἐκέλευε πρὸς ταῖς θύραις· καὶ γὰρ αὐτὸς ἑλκύσαι τὸν πατέρα μέχρις ἐνταῦθα. ἔτι ἀδικώτεροι οἱ 3
ἐπιβουλότεροι. ὁ μὲν οὖν θυμώδης οὐκ ἐπίβουλος, οὐδ' ὁ θυμός, ἀλλὰ φανερός· ἡ δ' ἐπιθυμία, καθάπερ τὴν Ἀφροδίτην φασί·

δολοπλόκου γὰρ κυπρογενοῦς·

καὶ τὸν κεστὸν ἱμάντα Ὅμηρος·

πάρφασις, ἥ τ' ἔκλεψε νόον πύκα περ φρονέοντος.

ὥστ' εἴπερ ἀδικωτέρα καὶ αἰσχίων ἡ ἀκρασία αὕτη τῆς περὶ τὸν θυμόν ἐστι, καὶ ἁπλῶς ἀκρασία καὶ κακία πως. ἔτι οὐδεὶς ὑβρίζει λυπούμενος, ὁ δ' ὀργῇ ποιῶν πᾶς ποιεῖ 4

---

tutional. It appears more difficult to tame down and eradicate, even with the help of time, than other passions. The Stoics gave peculiar attention to its control.

3 ἔτι ἀδικώτεροι—κακία πως] 'Again there is more wrong where there is more craft. The angry man and anger are not crafty, but open; while lust is crafty, as they say Aphrodite is,

"The wily Cyprian goddess."

And Homer sings of her embroidered girdle (that on it is wrought)

"Allurement which can steal the wise man's sense."

So that if this kind of incontinence is more wrongful than incontinence of anger, it is also worse, and thus deserves to be called by the simple name "incontinence," and amounts to a sort of vice.'

δολοπλόκου] From some lyric poet. Muretus compares the fragment of Sappho:

Ποικιλόθρον' ἀθάνατ' Ἀφροδίτα,
Παῖ Διὸς δολόπλοκε, λίσσομαί σε.

τὸν κεστὸν ἱμάντα Ὅμηρος] *Iliad*, xiv. 214—217:—

Ἦ, καὶ ἀπὸ στήθεσφιν ἐλύσατο κεστὸν ἱμάντα,
Ποικίλον· ἔνθα δέ οἱ θελκτήρια πάντα τέτυκτο·
Ἔνθ' ἔνι μὲν φιλότης, ἐν δ' ἵμερος, ἐν δ' ὀαριστὺς
Πάρφασις, ἥ τ' ἔκλεψε νόον πύκα περ φρονεόντων.

4 Incontinence of desire is full of wantonness and exultation, while anger implies pain and suffering. This argument is similar to that used, *Eth.* III. xii. 2, to prove that intemperance is more voluntary than cowardice.

λυπούμενος, ὁ δ' ὑβρίζων μεθ' ἡδονῆς. εἰ οὖν οἷς ὀργίζεσθαι
μάλιστα δίκαιον, ταῦτα ἀδικώτερα, καὶ ἡ ἀκρασία ἡ
5 δι' ἐπιθυμίαν· οὐ γάρ ἐστιν ἐν θυμῷ ὕβρις. ὡς μὲν τοίνυν
αἰσχίων ἡ περὶ ἐπιθυμίας ἀκρασία τῆς περὶ τὸν θυμόν, καὶ
ὅτι ἐστὶν ἡ ἐγκράτεια καὶ ἡ ἀκρασία περὶ ἐπιθυμίας καὶ
6 ἡδονὰς σωματικάς, δῆλον, αὐτῶν δὲ τούτων τὰς διαφορὰς
ληπτέον. ὥσπερ γὰρ εἴρηται κατ' ἀρχάς, αἱ μὲν ἀνθρωπικαί εἰσι καὶ φυσικαί, καὶ τῷ γένει καὶ τῷ μεγέθει, αἱ δὲ
θηριώδεις, αἱ δὲ διὰ πηρώσεις καὶ νοσήματα. τούτων δὲ
περὶ τὰς πρώτας σωφροσύνη καὶ ἀκολασία μόνον ἐστίν· διὸ
καὶ τὰ θηρία οὔτε σώφρονα οὔτ' ἀκόλαστα λέγομεν ἀλλ'
ἢ κατὰ μεταφορὰν καὶ εἴ τινι ὅλως ἄλλο πρὸς ἄλλο διαφέρει γένος τῶν ζῴων ὕβρει καὶ σιναμωρίᾳ καὶ τῷ παμφάγον εἶναι· οὐ γὰρ ἔχει προαίρεσιν οὐδὲ λογισμόν, ἀλλ'
ἐξέστηκε τῆς φύσεως, ὥσπερ οἱ μαινόμενοι τῶν ἀνθρώπων.
7 ἔλαττον δὲ θηριότης κακίας, φοβερώτερον δέ· οὐ γὰρ διέ-

ὁ δ' ὑβρίζων μεθ' ἡδονῆς] 'While he who wantons acts with pleasure.' There seems to be a double meaning in this passage to the word ὑβρίζει, exactly as there might be to our word 'wantonness.' It first means 'to act insolently' or 'wantonly' in a general sense, and secondly, it means to 'act wantonly' in a particular sense, *i.e.* lasciviously.

6 αὐτῶν δὲ τούτων τὰς διαφορὰς ληπτέον] *i.e.* the difference between continence and incontinence, which with other things is treated of in the next chapter. There is a want of method about the sequence of different parts in this book. The reference which follows, ὥσπερ εἴρηται κατ' ἀρχάς only goes back to ch. v. 1, and gives colour to a suspicion that the book may have been put together out of separate pieces, and perhaps lectures, one of which may have commenced with the fifth chapter.

διὸ καὶ τὰ θηρία—ἀνθρώπων] 'Hence we do not call brutes either temperate or intemperate, except by a metaphor, and where it happens that one whole race of animals in comparison with another is remarkable for wantonness it may be (τινι), or lechery, or voracity; for (animals) have no purpose or reasoning, but are beside themselves like madmen.' Different races of animals have good or bad moral characteristics ascribed to them. The goat, the ass, and the monkey have a bad reputation for wantonness, and the shark, &c., for voracity. It is not quite clear what is meant by ἐξέστηκε τῆς φύσεως. Perhaps it may best be taken to imply not that animals transgress their own nature, but simply that they get into a state of ecstasy, like madmen, and have no sense nor any principle which would justify their being called either temperate or intemperate.

7 ἔλαττον δὲ—θηρίον] 'Now brutality is a less evil than vice, though it is more fearful, for in it the good principle is not corrupted, as in a man, but does not exist. Therefore (comparing

φθαρται τὸ βέλτιστον, ὥσπερ ἐν τῷ ἀνθρώπῳ, ἀλλ' οὐκ ἔχει. ὅμοιον οὖν ὥσπερ ἄψυχον συμβάλλειν πρὸς ἔμψυχον, πότερον κάκιον· ἀσινεστέρα γὰρ ἡ φαυλότης ἀεὶ ἡ τοῦ μὴ ἔχοντος ἀρχήν, ὁ δὲ νοῦς ἀρχή. παραπλήσιον οὖν τὸ συμβάλλειν ἀδικίαν πρὸς ἄνθρωπον ἄδικον· ἔστι γὰρ ὡς ἑκάτερον κάκιον· μυριοπλάσια γὰρ ἂν κακὰ ποιήσειεν ἄνθρωπος κακὸς θηρίου.

Περὶ δὲ τὰς δι' ἁφῆς καὶ γεύσεως ἡδονὰς καὶ λύπας καὶ 7
ἐπιθυμίας καὶ φυγάς, περὶ ἃς ἥ τε ἀκολασία καὶ ἡ σωφροσύνη διωρίσθη πρότερον, ἔστι μὲν οὕτως ἔχειν ὥστε ἡττᾶσθαι καὶ ὧν οἱ πολλοὶ κρείττους, ἔστι δὲ κρατεῖν καὶ ὧν οἱ πολλοὶ ἥττους· τούτων δ' ὁ μὲν περὶ ἡδονὰς ἀκρατὴς ὁ δ' ἐγκρατής, ὁ δὲ περὶ λύπας μαλακὸς ὁ δὲ καρτερικός. μεταξὺ δ' ἡ τῶν πλείστων ἕξις, κἂν εἰ ῥέπουσι μᾶλλον

---

brutality with vice) is like comparing what is inanimate with a living thing, and asking which is worse. Evil is always less harmful when it has no guiding principle, and reason is the guiding principle. So it is just like comparing injustice with an unjust man; each is in a different sense worse. A bad man will do ten thousandfold more evil than a beast.'

ἔχει] sc. τὸ θηρίον. The whole passage is briefly expressed, but perhaps requires no further comment.

VII. This chapter, after a general comparison between intemperance and incontinence (§ 1—3), makes some remarks on endurance, softness, and childishness (§ 4—7); and ends by distinguishing two kinds of incontinence, of which the one proceeds from impetuosity, the other from weakness of character.

1 πρότερον] *Eth. Eud.* III. ii. 6. Cf. above ch. iv. § 2.

ἔστι μὲν—χείρους] 'It is possible to be in such a state as to yield to things that most men are superior to, and again it is possible to overcome things that most men yield to. Of those who possess these opposite dispositions, with regard to *pleasures*, the first is an incontinent man, and the second a continent man; with regard to *pains*, the first is soft and the second enduring. But the state of the majority of mankind lies between these opposites, albeit men verge rather to the side of the worse.' Moral designations may be fixed either in relation to the standard of what is, or of what ought to be. Cf. *Eth.* III. xi. 4: τῶν γὰρ φιλοτοιούτων λεγομένων ἢ τῷ χαίρειν οἷς μὴ δεῖ, ἢ τῷ μᾶλλον ἢ οἱ πολλοί. *Ib.* IV. iv. 4: ἐπαινοῦντες μὲν ἐπὶ τὸ μᾶλλον ἢ οἱ πολλοί, ψέγοντες δ' ἐπὶ τὸ μᾶλλον ἢ δεῖ. The above passage fixes the terms 'continent' and 'incontinent' relatively to what *is*, as implying more or less continence than people in general have. And yet there is evidently some reference beside to the standard of what ought to be, else it could not be said that people in general verge rather to the worse side. To represent the majority of mankind as possessing a mediocre moral character, neither eminently

2 πρὸς τὰς χείρους. ἐπεὶ δ' ἔνιαι τῶν ἡδονῶν ἀναγκαῖαί εἰσιν αἱ δ' οὔ, καὶ μέχρι τινός, αἱ δ' ὑπερβολαὶ οὔ, οὐδ' αἱ ἐλλείψεις, ὁμοίως δὲ καὶ περὶ ἐπιθυμίας ἔχει καὶ λύπας, ὁ μὲν τὰς ὑπερβολὰς διώκων τῶν ἡδέων ἢ καθ' ὑπερβολὰς † ἢ διὰ προαίρεσιν, δι' αὐτὰς καὶ μηδὲν δι' ἕτερον ἀποβαῖνον, ἀκόλαστος· ἀνάγκη γὰρ τοῦτον μὴ εἶναι μεταμελητικόν, ὥστ' ἀνίατος· ὁ γὰρ ἀμεταμέλητος ἀνίατος. ὁ δ' ἐλλείπων ὁ ἀντικείμενος, ὁ δὲ μέσος σώφρων. ὁμοίως δὲ καὶ ὁ φεύγων τὰς σωματικὰς λύπας μὴ δι' ἧτταν ἀλλὰ διὰ προαί-
3 ρεσιν. τῶν δὲ μὴ προαιρουμένων ὁ μὲν ἄγεται διὰ τὴν ἡδονήν, ὁ δὲ διὰ τὸ φεύγειν τὴν λύπην τὴν ἀπὸ τῆς ἐπιθυ-

---

good nor bad, but inclining to weakness, was in accordance with the Greek point of view. Widely different from this was what may be called the Semitic point of view, which, regarding man with greater religious earnestness, attributed to him 'desperate wickedness.' The latter feeling was not confined to the Jews and to the pages of the Bible, but in some degree made itself known to the world in the Stoical philosophy. See Essay VI. p. 356, &c.

2 *ἐπεὶ δ' ἔνιαι—ἀνίατος*] 'Now as some pleasures are necessary, but others are not to be called so, as being (*καὶ*) only necessary in certain degrees, while their excesses or deficiencies are not necessary (and the same division holds with regard to desires and pains), he who pursues excessive pleasures, or who pursues pleasures not in themselves excessive in an excessive way, and does so from deliberate purpose, with no ulterior aim beyond the pleasures themselves, is abandoned (*ἀκόλαστος*), (and he may well be called so), for it stands to reason (*ἀνάγκη*) that he is not likely to repent, and so he is incurable; for without repentance there is no cure.'

οὐδ' αἱ ἐλλείψεις] This might seem superfluous. But what is meant is, that in some pleasures the *μέσον* is good and necessary. Cf. below, *ὁ δ' ἐλλείπων ὁ ἀντικείμενος*.

ἢ καθ' ὑπερβολὰς † ἢ διὰ προαίρεσιν] The Paraphrast well expresses the meaning of this passage as follows: *ὁ μὲν τὰς ὑπερβολὰς διώκων τῶν ἡδονῶν, καὶ ἢ τὰς φύσει μεγάλας ἀεὶ ζητῶν ἡδονάς, ἢ τὰς φύσει μετρίας ὑπερβαλλόντως ζητῶν, οὐχ ἡττώμενος βιαίως ὑπ' αὐτῶν, ἀλλὰ μετὰ προαιρέσεως ἐπ' αὐτὰς τρέχων, οὐ δι' ἄλλο τι, δόξαν, φέρε εἰπεῖν, ἢ κέρδος, ἀλλὰ αὐτὰς δι' ἑαυτάς, ἀκόλαστος.* It is plain that *ἢ* before *διὰ προαίρεσιν* in the text must be a mistake. One of Bekker's MSS. reads *καὶ*—which would be very easily changed into *ἢ*, especially with the clause *ἢ καθ' ὑπερβολὰς* preceding. It would answer also to the expansion of the Paraphrast, *οὐχ ἡττώμενος κ.τ.λ.*

ἀνάγκη γὰρ] If a man with deliberate purpose pursues pleasure for its own sake, he is not likely to repent of his course, therefore he is *ἀκόλαστος*. This is the first intimation we have had that an unrepenting character belongs to 'intemperance'; it is an irregular argument, unless we regard it as laying some stress on the etymology of the word *ἀκόλαστος*. Cf. *Eth.* III. xii. 5—7, IV. i. 5.

μίας, ὥστε διαφέρουσιν ἀλλήλων. παντὶ δ' ἂν δόξειε χείρων εἶναι, εἴ τις μὴ ἐπιθυμῶν ἢ ἠρέμα πράττοι τι αἰσχρόν, ἢ εἰ σφόδρα ἐπιθυμῶν, καὶ εἰ μὴ ὀργιζόμενος τύπτοι ἢ εἰ ὀργιζόμενος· τί γὰρ ἂν ἐποίει ἐν πάθει ὤν; διὸ ὁ ἀκόλαστος χείρων τοῦ ἀκρατοῦς. τῶν δὴ λεχθέντων τὸ μὲν μαλακίας εἶδος μᾶλλον, ὁ δ' ἀκόλαστος. ἀντίκειται δὲ τῷ 4
μὲν ἀκρατεῖ ὁ ἐγκρατής, τῷ δὲ μαλακῷ ὁ καρτερικός· τὸ μὲν γὰρ καρτερεῖν ἐστὶν ἐν τῷ ἀντέχειν, ἡ δ' ἐγκράτεια ἐν τῷ κρατεῖν, ἕτερον δὲ τὸ ἀντέχειν καὶ κρατεῖν, ὥσπερ καὶ τὸ μὴ ἡττᾶσθαι τοῦ νικᾶν· διὸ καὶ αἱρετώτερον ἐγκράτεια καρτερίας ἐστίν. ὁ δ' ἐλλείπων πρὸς ἃ οἱ πολλοὶ καὶ 5
ἀντιτείνουσι καὶ δύνανται, οὗτος μαλακὸς καὶ τρυφῶν· καὶ γὰρ ἡ τρυφὴ μαλακία τίς ἐστιν· ὃς ἕλκει τὸ ἱμάτιον, ἵνα μὴ πονήσῃ τὴν ἀπὸ τοῦ αἴρειν λύπην, καὶ μιμούμενος τὸν κάμνοντα οὐκ οἴεται ἄθλιος εἶναι, ἀθλίῳ ὅμοιος ὤν. ὁμοίως 6

---

3 ὥστε διαφέρουσιν ἀλλήλων] 'So that they are distinct from one another,' i.e. on the one hand the reprobate (ἀκόλαστον), in his two forms of systematically seeking pleasure, and of systematically avoiding pain; and on the other hand the morally weak, whether in the form of yielding to the allurements of pleasure (ἀκρατής), or flying from the pressure of pain (μαλακός). The comparison is not between the two forms of the μὴ προαιρούμενοι, but these are together contrasted with ἀκολασία.

παντὶ δ' ἂν δόξειε] A repetition of ch. iv. § 4, on which see note.

τῶν δὴ λεχθέντων τὸ μὲν μαλακίας εἶδος μᾶλλον, ὁ δ' ἀκόλαστος] The temptation is great to refer τῶν δὴ λεχθέντων to τῶν μὴ προαιρουμένων, and to read ἀκρατὴς for ἀκόλαστος, taking the sentence in connection with what follows. But when we consider (1) the unanimity of MSS.; (2) that μαλακία has been already distinguished from ἀκρασία, in § 1; (3) the import of μᾶλλον (cf. Eth. vi. viii. 9, αὕτη μᾶλλον αἴσθησις ἢ φρόνησις, ἐκείνης δ' ἄλλο εἶδος), we shall be led to see that the sentence comes in, though rather in a disjointed way, to wind up the comparison here made generally between incontinence and intemperance (cf. ch. vi. § 5, and above, § 1). Incontinence may be said to be more like a kind of softness, while determinate vice is something different. Μαλακία, according to this interpretation, is used here in a general sense, in the next section with a special and limited import.

4 Continence, it is argued, is finer than endurance, just as victory is finer than holding out. This argument is not sound, since continence is in reality nothing more than holding out against temptation. To noble natures continence would doubtless cause a greater struggle than mere endurance of pains, and in this sense it might be called finer.

5 ὁ δ' ἐλλείπων—ὅμοιος ὤν] 'Now he who faints before things against which most men hold out and are strong,—he is soft and luxurious (for luxury, it may be added, is a kind of

δ' ἔχει καὶ περὶ ἐγκράτειαν καὶ ἀκρασίαν· οὐ γὰρ εἴ τις ἰσχυρῶν καὶ ὑπερβαλλουσῶν ἡδονῶν ἡττᾶται ἢ λυπῶν, θαυμαστόν, ἀλλὰ συγγνωμονικόν, εἰ ἀντιτείνων, ὥσπερ ὁ Θεοδέκτου Φιλοκτήτης ὑπὸ τοῦ ἔχεως πεπληγμένος ἢ ὁ Καρκίνου ἐν τῇ Ἀλόπῃ Κερκύων, καὶ ὥσπερ οἱ κατέχειν πειρώμενοι τὸν γέλωτα ἀθρόον ἐκκαγχάζουσιν, οἷον συνέπεσε Ξενοφάντῳ, ἀλλ' εἴ τις πρὸς ἃς οἱ πολλοὶ δύνανται ἀντέχειν, τούτων ἡττᾶται καὶ μὴ δύναται ἀντιτείνειν, μὴ διὰ φύσιν τοῦ γένους ἢ διὰ νόσον, οἷον ἐν τοῖς Σκυθῶν βασιλεῦσιν ἡ μαλακία διὰ τὸ γένος, καὶ ὡς τὸ θῆλυ πρὸς τὸ
7 ἄρρεν διέστηκεν. δοκεῖ δὲ καὶ ὁ παιδιώδης ἀκόλαστος εἶναι, ἔστι δὲ μαλακός· ἡ γὰρ παιδιὰ ἄνεσίς ἐστιν, εἴπερ ἀνάπαυσις· τῶν δὲ πρὸς ταύτην ὑπερβαλλόντων ὁ παιδιώδης
8 ἐστίν. ἀκρασίας δὲ τὸ μὲν προπέτεια τὸ δ' ἀσθένεια· οἱ μὲν γὰρ βουλευσάμενοι οὐκ ἐμμένουσιν οἷς ἐβουλεύσαντο διὰ τὸ

---

softness), he for instance who trails his cloak, rather than have the trouble of lifting it, and who imitates the languor of an invalid, without seeing that it is miserable to be like one who is miserable.' This passage is somewhat in the style of the *Characters* of Theophrastus. To illustrate the affectation of weakness described above, Cary quotes from Athenaeus a story of the Sybarites, one of whom said that he had been in the fields, and that 'to see the men digging had given him a rupture.' To which his friend replied, that 'the very mention of it gave him a pain in his side.'

6 *ὁ Θεοδέκτου Φιλοκτήτης*] A play by Theodectes the rhetorician, a friend of Aristotle's. Fritzsche quotes Cicero *Tusc.* II. vii. 19: Adspice Philoctetam, cui concedendum est gementi: ipsum enim Herculem viderat in Œta magnitudine dolorum ejulantem, &c.

Καρκίνου] Of this tragic poet nothing appears to be known.

Ξενοφάντῳ] Giphanius finds in Seneca, *De Ira*, II. 2, a mention of Xenophantus as a musician of Alexander the Great.

οἷον ἐν τοῖς Σκυθῶν βασιλεῦσιν ἡ μαλακία διὰ τὸ γένος] Aspasius for Σκυθῶν reads Περσῶν. But the commentators refer us to Herodotus I. 105: *τοῖσι δὲ τῶν Σκυθέων συλήσασι τὸ ἱρὸν τὸ ἐν Ἀσκάλωνι καὶ τοῖσι τούτων αἰεὶ ἐκγόνοισι ἐνέσκηψε ἡ θεὸς θήλεαν νοῦσον· ὥστε ἅμα λέγουσί τε οἱ Σκύθαι διὰ τοῦτό σφεας νοσέειν.* Hippocrates gives a description of this malady, which appears to have been a kind of impotence (*De Aer. Aq. et Loc.* VI. 108): *εὐνουχίαι γίνονται καὶ γυναικεῖα ἐργάζονται καὶ ὡς αἱ γυναῖκες διαλέγονταί τε ὁμοίως, καλεῦνταί τε οἱ τοιοῦτοι ἀνανδριεῖς.* 'This impotency Hippocrates ascribes to venesection, but he mentions that the natives believed it to be a judgment from the gods. It is said that traces of the disease are still found among the inhabitants of Southern Russia.'—Mr. Rawlinson's *Herodotus*, Vol. I. p. 248.

καὶ ὡς τὸ θῆλυ] Cf. c. v. § 4.

8 *ἀκρασίας δὲ—φαντασίᾳ*] 'Now incontinence is sometimes impetuosity

πάθος, οἱ δὲ διὰ τὸ μὴ βουλεύσασθαι ἄγονται ὑπὸ τοῦ πάθους· ἔνιοι γάρ, ὥσπερ προγαργαλίσαντες οὐ γαργαλίζονται, οὕτω καὶ προαισθόμενοι καὶ προϊδόντες καὶ προεγείραντες ἑαυτοὺς καὶ τὸν λογισμὸν οὐχ ἡττῶνται ὑπὸ τοῦ πάθους, οὔτ' ἂν ἡδὺ ᾖ οὔτ' ἂν λυπηρόν. μάλιστα δ' οἱ ὀξεῖς καὶ μελαγχολικοὶ τὴν προπετῆ ἀκρασίαν εἰσὶν ἀκρατεῖς· οἱ μὲν γὰρ διὰ τὴν ταχυτῆτα, οἱ δὲ διὰ τὴν σφοδρότητα οὐκ ἀναμένουσι τὸν λόγον, διὰ τὸ ἀκολουθητικοὶ εἶναι τῇ φαντασίᾳ.

---

and sometimes weakness. Some men, when they have deliberated, do not abide by their deliberations, owing to the state into which they are thrown, (and this is weakness): while others, from never having deliberated, are carried away by their feelings. Some on the contrary, like the beginners in a tickling match, who cannot be tickled,—having prescience, and foresight, and having roused up themselves and their reason beforehand, are not overcome by their feelings, whether pleasant or painful. It is especially persons of a quick or bilious temperament who are subject to the impetuous kind of incontinence, for the one through the rapidity, and the other through the intensity, of their nature, do not wait to see what is the law of right, because they are apt to follow impressions.'

ὥσπερ οἱ προγαργαλίσαντες] The Paraphrast understands *ἑαυτούς*, rendering the passage *ὥσπερ τὰ προτριβέντα καὶ προγαργαλισθέντα μάλα οὐ γαργαλίζονται*. And two of Bekker's MSS. read *οἱ προγαργαλισθέντες*. It might be possible by previous tickling to exhaust the irritability of the cuticle, but this would not be a usual process, and in one of the *Problems* attributed to Aristotle (XXXV. vi.) it is discussed, 'Why cannot a man tickle himself?' To which the answer is, 'For the same reason that he can hardly be tickled by anybody else if he knows that it is going to happen. For laughter implies a sudden revulsion and a surprise.' Surely this is exactly what is meant in the text.

οἱ ὀξεῖς καὶ μελαγχολικοί] An account which seems at first sight the opposite of this is given by the author of the *Magna Moralia* (II. vi. 43): Ἐκείνη μὲν οὖν (the impetuous kind of incontinence) *οὐδ' ἂν λίαν δόξειεν εἶναι ψεκτή· καὶ γὰρ ἐν τοῖς σπουδαίοις ἡ τοιαύτη ἐγγίνεται, ἐν τοῖς θερμοῖς καὶ εὐφυέσιν· ἡ δὲ* (the weak kind) *ἐν τοῖς ψυχροῖς καὶ μελαγχολικοῖς, οἱ δὲ τοιοῦτοι ψεκτοί*. If however we consult the curious disquisition on *μελαγχολικοί* and the *μέλαινα χολή* in Ar. *Problems*, XXX. i., we shall see that both passionate impetuosity and cold sluggishness were considered by the ancient physiologist to be different manifestations of the same strange temperament. *Pr.* XXX. i. 18: *Ὅσοις δὲ ἐν τῇ φύσει συνέστη κρᾶσις τοιαύτη, εὐθὺς οὗτοι τὰ ἤθη γίνονται παντοδαποί, ἄλλος κατ' ἄλλην κρᾶσιν· οἷον ὅσοις μὲν πολλὴ καὶ ψυχρὰ ἐνυπάρχει, νωθροὶ καὶ μωροί, ὅσοις δὲ λίαν πολλὴ καὶ θερμή, μανικοὶ καὶ εὐφυεῖς καὶ ἐρωτικοὶ καὶ εὐκίνητοι πρὸς τοὺς θυμοὺς καὶ τὰς ἐπιθυμίας, ἔνιοι δὲ καὶ λάλοι μᾶλλον.* With the moderns the term 'melancholy' is restricted to the cold and dejected mood; while the ancients much more commonly applied the term *μελαγχολικός* to denote

8 Ἔστι δ' ὁ μὲν ἀκόλαστος, ὥσπερ ἐλέχθη, οὐ μεταμελη-
τικός· ἐμμένει γὰρ τῇ προαιρέσει· ὁ δ' ἀκρατὴς μεταμελητικὸς πᾶς. διὸ οὐχ ὥσπερ ἠπορήσαμεν, οὕτω καὶ ἔχει,
ἀλλ' ὁ μὲν ἀνίατος, ὁ δ' ἰατός· ἔοικε γὰρ ἡ μὲν μοχθηρία τῶν νοσημάτων οἷον ὑδέρῳ καὶ φθίσει, ἡ δ' ἀκρασία
τοῖς ἐπιληπτικοῖς· ἡ μὲν γὰρ συνεχής, ἡ δ' οὐ συνεχὴς πονηρία. καὶ ὅλως δ' ἕτερον τὸ γένος ἀκρασίας καὶ κα-
κίας· ἡ μὲν γὰρ κακία λανθάνει, ἡ δ' ἀκρασία οὐ λανθάνει.
2 αὐτῶν δὲ τούτων βελτίους οἱ ἐκστατικοὶ ἢ οἱ τὸν λόγον
ἔχοντες μέν, μὴ ἐμμένοντες δέ· ὑπ' ἐλάττονος γὰρ πάθους

---

warmth, passion, and eccentricity of genius. Cf. Plato, *Repub.* 573 c: Τυραννικὸς δέ, ἦν δ' ἐγώ, ὦ δαιμόνιε, ἀνὴρ ἀκριβῶς γίγνεται, ὅταν ἢ φύσει ἢ ἐπιτηδεύμασιν ἢ ἀμφοτέροις μεθυστικός τε καὶ ἐρωτικὸς καὶ μελαγχολικὸς γένηται. Cf. also Ar. *Probl.* xi. xxxviii: τὸ τῇ φαντασίᾳ ἀκολουθεῖν ταχέως τὸ μελαγχολικὸν εἶναι ἐστίν. In the language of our own day, 'The passionate heart of the poet is whirl'd into folly and vice.' For more remarks on μέλαινα χολή, see below.

VIII. This chapter is not separated by any marked logical boundary from the preceding one. Rather it is a continuation of the same subject, as it goes on comparing incontinence with intemperance. Two previously mooted questions are now discussed, namely, is intemperance more curable than incontinence? (which is answered in the negative), and, is incontinence to be regarded as absolutely bad? (See above ch. i. § 6.) This is also answered in the negative.

1 Ἔστι δ' ὁ μὲν ἀκόλαστος, ὥσπερ ἐλέχθη, οὐ μεταμελητικός] Cf. c. vii. § 2. The continuity of the subject is preserved, if we consider that the writer, having mentioned the various ways in which incontinent people submit to temptation, next reflects that, after yielding, these are all repentant (μεταμελητικὸς πᾶς), while the intemperate man forms a contrast to them, and is unrepentant.

διὸ οὐχ ὥσπερ ἠπορήσαμεν] Cf. ch. ii. § 10. Intemperance, which is a corruption of the will, is like a chronic disorder, while incontinence, which is a temporary derangement of the will, is like an epileptic seizure.

ἡ γὰρ κακία λανθάνει] As being a false sort of harmony in the mind, in which no struggle is felt.

2 αὐτῶν δὲ—ἐμμένοντες δέ] 'Now looking at incontinence itself and the two kinds of it which I have mentioned, those people who are carried away are better than the sort who are in possession of "the law" but do not abide by it.' As said before, the thread of reasoning goes on continuously from the end of the preceding chapter (according to Bekker's division), and so there is nothing remarkable in the writer's now reverting to the two kinds of incontinence, as if he had never digressed from discussing them. Οἱ ἐκστατικοὶ here answers to the ὀξεῖς καὶ μελαγχολικοὶ (οἱ) τὴν προπετῆ ἀκρασίαν εἰσὶν ἀκρατεῖς. The words ἐκστάσεις, ἐκστῆναι, and ἐκστατικός, are frequently used in the *Problems*, (l.c.) in connection with the μελαγχολικοί. Cf. *Ib.* xxx. i. 3:

ἡττῶνται, καὶ οὐκ ἀπροβούλευτοι ὥσπερ ἕτεροι· ὅμοιος γὰρ ὁ ἀκρατής ἐστι τοῖς ταχὺ μεθυσκομένοις καὶ ὑπ' ὀλίγου οἴνου καὶ ἐλάττονος ἢ ὡς οἱ πολλοί. ὅτι μὲν οὖν κακία ἡ 3
ἀκρασία οὐκ ἔστι, φανερόν. ἀλλά πῃ ἴσως· τὸ μὲν γὰρ παρὰ προαίρεσιν τὸ δὲ κατὰ προαίρεσίν ἐστιν. οὐ μὴν ἀλλ' ὅμοιόν γε κατὰ τὰς πράξεις ὥσπερ τὸ Δημοδόκου εἰς Μιλησίους 'Μιλήσιοι ἀξύνετοι μὲν οὐκ εἰσίν, δρῶσι δ' οἷάπερ οἱ ἀξύνετοι.' καὶ οἱ ἀκρατεῖς ἄδικοι μὲν οὐκ εἰσίν, ἀδικοῦσι δέ. ἐπεὶ δ' ὁ μὲν τοιοῦτος οἷος μὴ διὰ τὸ πε- 4
πεῖσθαι διώκειν τὰς καθ' ὑπερβολὴν καὶ παρὰ τὸν ὀρθὸν λόγον σωματικὰς ἡδονάς, ὁ δὲ πέπεισται διὰ τὸ τοιοῦτος εἶναι οἷος διώκειν αὐτάς, ἐκεῖνος μὲν οὖν εὐμετάπειστος, ὁ δ' οὔ· ἡ γὰρ ἀρετὴ καὶ ἡ μοχθηρία τὴν ἀρχὴν ἡ μὲν φθεί-

---

where it is said of Ajax, ἐκστατικὸς ἐγένετο παντελῶς (i.e. mad). Cf. above ch. vi. § 6. Ἐκστατικὸς is used presently (§ 5) in a different sense to express 'departing from' a purpose, as also before, ch. i. § 6, and ii. § 7.

οἱ τὸν λόγον ἔχοντες] On this phrase see *Eth.* vi. i. 1, and note.

ὅμοιος γὰρ—οἱ πολλοί] 'For the man who is weakly incontinent is like those who are soon intoxicated, and by a small quantity of wine, less than intoxicates people in general.' Ὁ ἀκρατὴς seems used in this sentence as if specially applicable to the weak kind of incontinence. It is in contrast to ἐκστατικός. Weakness is worse than being carried away by passion, for it is acting against warning, and with less temptation.

3 Incontinence is not vice, though it resembles vice in what it does (κατὰ τὰς πράξεις), but it goes against the will, while vice goes with the will. It is like the saying of Demodocus against the Milesians: 'The Milesians are not fools, but they act just as if they were fools.' The incontinent are not bad, but they do wrong.

Δημοδόκου] This was an epigrammatist of the island of Leros, not far from Miletus. Some of his epigrams against different cities are preserved in the *Anthology*. A slight change in the reading shows the above to be in verse:

Μιλήσιοι ἀξύνετοι μὲν
Οὐκ εἰσίν, δρῶσιν δ' οἷάπερ ἀξύνετοι.

4 ἡ γὰρ ἀρετὴ—ἐναντίος] 'For virtue on the one hand preserves, while vice destroys, the major premiss. Now the end is in action just what the hypotheses are in mathematics, namely, a major premiss on which everything depends; hence, neither in the one case nor in the other is it the chain of inference (ὁ λόγος) that demonstrates the major premiss, but in the case of action (ἐνταῦθα) it is virtue, either natural or acquired, to which a right opinion with regard to the major premiss is due. He who possesses this is temperate, while the contrary person is intemperate.' This passage comes in as a final argument against the notion that incontinence is more curable than intemperance. In the latter the fountain-head of action (the ἀρχή) is destroyed. While the temperate man has in himself the source of all good action, the intemperate man is the direct opposite, and the

ρει ἡ δὲ σώζει, ἐν δὲ ταῖς πράξεσι τὸ οὗ ἕνεκα ἀρχή, ὥσπερ ἐν τοῖς μαθηματικοῖς αἱ ὑποθέσεις· οὔτε δὴ ἐκεῖ ὁ λόγος διδασκαλικὸς τῶν ἀρχῶν οὔτε ἐνταῦθα, ἀλλ' ἀρετὴ ἢ φυσικὴ ἢ ἐθιστὴ τοῦ ὀρθοδοξεῖν περὶ τὴν ἀρχήν. Σώφρων μὲν οὖν ὁ τοιοῦτος, ἀκόλαστος δ' ὁ ἐναντίος. ἔστι δέ τις διὰ πάθος ἐκστατικὸς παρὰ τὸν ὀρθὸν λόγον, ὃν ὥστε μὲν μὴ πράττειν κατὰ τὸν ὀρθὸν λόγον κρατεῖ τὸ πάθος, ὥστε δ' εἶναι τοιοῦτον οἷον πεπεῖσθαι διώκειν ἀνέδην δεῖν τὰς τοιαύτας ἡδονὰς οὐ κρατεῖ· οὗτός ἐστιν ὁ ἀκρατής, βελτίων τοῦ

---

incontinent man is something intermediate.

ἡ δὲ σώζει] cf. *Eth.* vi. v. 6, where almost all the ideas which occur above are given, even the reference to mathematical axioms. *Ib.* ch. xii. § 10: where a still more explicit statement is made of the relation of virtue to the practical syllogism.

αἱ ὑποθέσεις] This term is used precisely in the same way in the *Eudemian Ethics*, ii. x. 20: *περὶ μὲν τοῦ τέλους οὐθεὶς βουλεύεται, ἀλλὰ τοῦτ' ἐστὶν ἀρχὴ καὶ ὑπόθεσις, ὥσπερ ἐν ταῖς θεωρητικαῖς ἐπιστήμαις ὑποθέσεις· εἴρηται δὲ περὶ αὐτῶν ἐν μὲν τοῖς ἐν ἀρχῇ βραχέως, ἐν δὲ τοῖς ἀναλυτικοῖς δι' ἀκριβείας* (i.e. the *Analytics* of Eudemus). Cf. *Ib.* ch. xi. § 4: *ὥσπερ γὰρ ταῖς θεωρητικαῖς αἱ ὑποθέσεις ἀρχαί, οὕτω καὶ ταῖς ποιητικαῖς τὸ τέλος ἀρχὴ καὶ ὑπόθεσις.* In *Eth. Eud.* vii. ii. 4, *ὑπόθεσις* is used as equivalent to *ἀρχή*.—(§ 3) *περὶ τούτων . . . πειρατέον διορίσαι, λαβοῦσιν ἀρχὴν τήνδε . . . τούτου δὲ διωρισμένου ληπτέον ὑπόθεσιν ἑτέραν.* Plato, *Repub.* p. 510—511, reproaches mathematics with always resting on hypotheses of which they can give no account. P. 510 c: *οἶμαι γάρ σε εἰδέναι ὅτι οἱ περὶ τὰς γεωμετρίας τε καὶ λογισμοὺς καὶ τὰ τοιαῦτα πραγματευόμενοι, ὑποθέμενοι τό τε περιττὸν καὶ τὸ ἄρτιον καὶ τὰ σχήματα καὶ γωνιῶν τριττὰ εἴδη καὶ ἄλλα τούτων ἀδελφὰ καθ' ἑκάστην μέθοδον, ταῦτα μὲν ὡς εἰδότες, ποιησάμενοι ὑποθέσεις αὐτά, οὐδένα λόγον οὔτε αὑτοῖς οὔτε ἄλλοις ἔτι ἀξιοῦσι περὶ αὐτῶν διδόναι ὡς παντὶ φανερῶν, ἐκ τούτων δ' ἀρχόμενοι τὰ λοιπὰ ἤδη διεξιόντες τελευτῶσιν ὁμολογουμένως ἐπὶ τοῦτο, οὗ ἂν ἐπὶ σκέψιν ὁρμήσωσιν.*

Aristotle, *Post. Analyt.* i. ii. 7, defines thesis or assumption as an immediate syllogistic principle, indemonstrable, but not (as the axioms are) a necessary antecedent to all reasoning. He divides these into hypotheses and definitions, which differ in that the former assert existence or non-existence, while the latter do not. The hypothesis then is a peculiar principle (*οἰκεία ἀρχή*), and differs from an axiom, (1) in that it varies in the different sciences; (2) in that it is wanting in recognisable necessity. (Cf. *Post. Anal.* i. x. 6: *οὐκ ἔστι δ' ὑπόθεσις . . . ὃ ἀνάγκη εἶναι δι' αὑτὸ καὶ δοκεῖν ἀνάγκη*). The Aristotelian hypothesis is however widely different from the hypothesis of the moderns, which means in short little more than a conjecture. For more particulars on this subject see Mr. Poste's *Logic of Science* (Oxford, 1850), p. 139—143.

τοῦ ὀρθοδοξεῖν] By what the grammarians call *zeugma*, this genitive goes with *τῶν ἀρχῶν*, as governed by *διδασκαλικός*. One would have expected *αἴτιος*.

ἀκολάστου, οὐδὲ φαῦλος ἁπλῶς· σώζεται γὰρ τὸ βέλτιστον, ἡ ἀρχή. ἄλλος δ' ἐναντίος, ὁ ἐμμενετικὸς καὶ οὐκ ἐκστατικὸς διά γε τὸ πάθος. φανερὸν δὴ ἐκ τούτων ὅτι ἡ μὲν σπουδαία ἕξις, ἡ δὲ φαύλη.

Πότερον οὖν ἐγκρατής ἐστιν ὁ ὁποιῳοῦν λόγῳ καὶ ὁποι- 9
ᾳοῦν προαιρέσει ἐμμένων ἢ ὁ τῇ ὀρθῇ, καὶ ἀκρατὴς δὲ ὁ ὁποιᾳοῦν μὴ ἐμμένων προαιρέσει καὶ ὁποιῳοῦν λόγῳ ἢ ὁ τῷ ψευδεῖ λόγῳ καὶ τῇ προαιρέσει τῇ μὴ ὀρθῇ, ὥσπερ ἠπορήθη πρότερον; ἢ κατὰ μὲν συμβεβηκὸς ὁποιᾳοῦν,

---

5 ἄλλος δ' ἐναντίος κ.τ.λ.] Incontinence having been shown to be an intermediate state not so bad as intemperance, it is here added, that the true opposite to the incontinent man is he

'Who, through the heat of conflict, keeps the law
In calmness made, and sees what he foresaw;'

i.e. not the temperate but the continent. And though incontinence is not absolutely bad, yet relatively, if you compare it with its opposite, you must call one bad and the other good.

IX. The first part of this chapter (§§ 1—4) takes up again the question before started (ch. i. § 6, ch. ii. § 7—10), Does continence consist in sticking to any opinion and purpose, whether wrong or right? After some refinements, which are perhaps unnecessary, as to the continent man 'accidentally' or 'non-essentially' maintaining a wrong opinion, a good distinction is given between obstinacy and continence. Obstinate people (ἰσχυρογνώμονες), if not mere dullards (οἱ ἀμαθεῖς καὶ οἱ ἄγροικοι), are self-opinionated, which state of mind is rather incontinence than continence, for it is a yielding to the desire for victory and self-assertion. The continent man on the other hand is not at all deaf to the voice of persuasion, it is only the voice of passion when opposed to reason which he resists. Nor is a man to be called incontinent if he deserts a resolution, even for the sake of pleasure. Since Neoptolemus deserted his resolution to deceive, in order to obtain the noble pleasure of preserving his honour.

1 ἢ ὁ τῷ ψευδεῖ λόγῳ καὶ τῇ προαιρέσει τῇ μὴ ὀρθῇ] Various solutions have been proposed for the difficulty involved in this sentence. (1) Aspasius, followed by Argyropulus, Fritzsche, &c., think that ἐμμένων is to be understood as carried on from μὴ ἐμμένων in the line before. But this will not do. The ἀκρατής cannot be said to 'abide by a false opinion.' (2) Some understand the clause as applying to cases like those of Neoptolemus. 'Is a man incontinent who does not stick to a false opinion?' But all this is implied in ὁ ὁποιᾳοῦν κ.τ.λ. And moreover this interpretation would give a new sense to ἢ, making it a particle of apposition instead of a particle of contrast, which is required for the sake of correspondence with the opening sentence. (3) One of Bekker's MSS. reads τῷ μὴ ψευδεῖ λόγῳ καὶ τῇ προαιρέσει τῇ ὀρθῇ. This is a very natural correction to make, and it seems followed by

καθ' αὑτὸ δὲ τῷ ἀληθεῖ λόγῳ καὶ τῇ ὀρθῇ προαιρέσει
ὁ μὲν ἐμμένει ὁ δ' οὐκ ἐμμένει· εἰ γάρ τις τοδὶ διὰ τοδὶ
αἱρεῖται ἢ διώκει, καθ' αὑτὸ μὲν τοῦτο διώκει καὶ αἱρεῖται,
κατὰ συμβεβηκὸς δὲ τὸ πρότερον. ἁπλῶς δὲ λέγομεν τὸ
καθ' αὑτό, ὥστε ἔστι μὲν ὡς ὁποιᾳοῦν δόξῃ ὁ μὲν ἐμμένει
2 ὁ δ' ἐξίσταται, ἁπλῶς δὲ ὁ τῇ ἀληθεῖ. εἰσὶ δέ τινες καὶ
ἐμμενετικοὶ τῇ δόξῃ, οὓς καλοῦσιν ἰσχυρογνώμονας, οἷον
δύσπειστοι καὶ οὐκ εὐμετάπειστοι· οἳ ὅμοιον μέν τι ἔχουσι
τῷ ἐγκρατεῖ, ὥσπερ ὁ ἄσωτος τῷ ἐλευθερίῳ καὶ ὁ θρασὺς
τῷ θαρραλέῳ, εἰσὶ δ' ἕτεροι κατὰ πολλά. ὁ μὲν γὰρ διὰ
πάθος καὶ ἐπιθυμίαν οὐ μεταβάλλει, ὁ ἐγκρατής, ἐπεὶ
εὔπειστος, ὅταν τύχῃ, ἔσται ὁ ἐγκρατής· ὁ δὲ οὐχ ὑπὸ
λόγου, ἐπεὶ ἐπιθυμίας γε λαμβάνουσι, καὶ ἄγονται πολλοὶ
3 ὑπὸ τῶν ἡδονῶν. εἰσὶ δὲ ἰσχυρογνώμονες οἱ ἰδιογνώμονες
καὶ οἱ ἀμαθεῖς καὶ οἱ ἄγροικοι, οἱ μὲν ἰδιογνώμονες δι' ἡδονὴν καὶ λύπην· χαίρουσι γὰρ νικῶντες, ἐὰν μὴ μεταπεί-
θωνται, καὶ λυποῦνται, ἐὰν ἄκυρα τὰ αὐτῶν ᾖ ὥσπερ
ψηφίσματα· ὥστε μᾶλλον τῷ ἀκρατεῖ ἐοίκασιν ἢ τῷ
4 ἐγκρατεῖ. εἰσὶ δέ τινες οἳ τοῖς δόξασιν οὐκ ἐμμένουσιν οὐ
δι' ἀκρασίαν, οἷον ἐν τῷ Φιλοκτήτῃ τῷ Σοφοκλέους ὁ

---

the Paraphrast, who has *ὁ μὴ ἐμμένων τῇ ὀρθῇ*. But since the correction is so natural, why should such a preponderance of MSS. have failed to adopt it? Though the sense absolutely requires some such reading, it seems better to conclude that there is some original confusion in the text. The author may have carelessly written as above, from a mistaken antithesis to *ἢ ὁ τῇ ὀρθῇ* in the former sentence.

κατὰ συμβεβηκὸς δὲ τὸ πρότερον] One chooses the means 'accidentally.' This is a mere illustration of the import of *καθ' αὑτό* and *συμβεβηκός*. The whole paragraph seems perfectly irrelevant. It may be compared with *Eth.* v. xi. 8: *καθ' αὑτὸ μὲν οὖν τὸ ἀδικεῖσθαι ἧττον φαῦλον, κατὰ συμβεβηκὸς δ' οὐθὲν κωλύει μεῖζον εἶναι κακόν*, which is a weak qualification of the moral principle, that to injure is worse than to be injured.

2 *ὥσπερ ὁ ἄσωτος κ.τ.λ.*] The same illustrations are coupled together in the *Eudemian Ethics* III. vii. 14: *τὸ ὁμοιότερον ἧττον ἐναντίον φαίνεται, οἷον πέπονθε τὸ θράσος πρὸς τὸ θάρσος καὶ ἀσωτία πρὸς ἐλευθεριότητα.*

ὁ δὲ οὐχ —ἡδονῶν] 'But the obstinate man (is immovable) not from the influence of reason, for such men assuredly admit desires, and many of them are carried away by the allurement of pleasures.' The curious phrase *ἐπιθυμίας λαμβάνουσι* occurs in the *Eudemian Ethics*, III. ii. 13: *πάντες γὰρ τούτοις φύσει τε χαίρουσι, καὶ ἐπιθυμίας λαμβάνουσι.*

4 *οἷον ἐν τῷ Φιλοκτήτῃ*] See above ch. ii. § 7, note.

Νεοπτόλεμος. καίτοι δι' ἡδονὴν οὐκ ἐνέμεινεν, ἀλλὰ καλήν· τὸ γὰρ ἀληθεύειν αὐτῷ καλὸν ἦν, ἐπείσθη δ' ὑπὸ τοῦ Ὀδυσσέως ψεύδεσθαι. Οὐ γὰρ πᾶς ὁ δι' ἡδονήν τι πράττων οὔτ' ἀκόλαστος οὔτε φαῦλος οὔτ' ἀκρατής, ἀλλ' ὁ δι' αἰσχράν.

Ἐπεὶ δ' ἐστί τις καὶ τοιοῦτος οἷος ἧττον ἢ δεῖ τοῖς σω- 5
ματικοῖς χαίρων, καὶ οὐκ ἐμμένων τῷ λόγῳ ἡ τοιοῦτος,
τούτου καὶ τοῦ ἀκρατοῦς μέσος ὁ ἐγκρατής· ὁ μὲν γὰρ
ἀκρατὴς οὐκ ἐμμένει τῷ λόγῳ διὰ τὸ μᾶλλόν τι, οὗτος δὲ
διὰ τὸ ἧττόν τι· ὁ δ' ἐγκρατὴς ἐμμένει καὶ οὐδὲ δι' ἕτερον
μεταβάλλει. Δεῖ δέ, εἴπερ ἡ ἐγκράτεια σπουδαῖον, ἀμφοτέρας τὰς ἐναντίας ἕξεις φαύλας εἶναι, ὥσπερ καὶ φαί-
νονται· ἀλλὰ διὰ τὸ τὴν ἑτέραν ἐν ὀλίγοις καὶ ὀλιγάκις
εἶναι φανεράν, ὥσπερ ἡ σωφροσύνη τῇ ἀκολασίᾳ δοκεῖ
ἐναντίον εἶναι μόνον, οὕτω καὶ ἡ ἐγκράτεια τῇ ἀκρασίᾳ.
ἐπεὶ δὲ καθ' ὁμοιότητα πολλὰ λέγεται, καὶ ἡ ἐγκράτεια ἡ 6

5—ch. x. § 5. In his later edition Bekker makes this portion of the text into a separate chapter, which seems a better arrangement. We have now a winding up of the previous discussions. Continence is not only the contrary of incontinence, but is also a sort of mean. It bears an analogy to temperance, but must not be identical with it. Neither must incontinence and intemperance be confounded (see above ch. i. § 6). Nor must it be thought possible that the 'thoughtful' man can be incontinent, though the clever man may (see ch. i. § 7). Incontinence is like sleep or drunkenness, not a state of wakeful knowledge (see ch. iii. §§ 6—8). Its acts are voluntary, but yet it is not absolutely wicked, since it implies no deliberate purpose. The incontinent man is like a state which has good laws, but does not act upon them. The bad man like a state with a bad code, which she carries out. Both the terms incontinence and continence are used comparatively, as implying more firmness than is common, or less. Of the two kinds of incontinence, that which is caused by passion is more curable than that caused by weakness, that which proceeds from habit is more curable than that which is natural.

5 *καὶ οὐδὲ δι' ἕτερον μεταβάλλει*] This is an Atticism for *καὶ δι' οὐδέτερον*. The attempt to make continence into 'a mean' can hardly be called successful. It can only be done by assuming the same *ἔλλειψις* for this quality as for temperance. You will have one set of terms, *ἀκολασία*, *σωφροσύνη*, *ἀναισθησία*, and another set *ἀκρασία*, *ἐγκράτεια*, *ἀναισθησία*. It is plain that *ἐγκράτεια* is not a mean, in the sense of being a balance, or harmony of the mind. It is only imperfect temperance, it is temperance in the act of forming.

6 *ἡ ἐγκράτεια ἡ τοῦ σώφρονος καθ' ὁμοιότητα ἠκολούθηκεν*] 'The "continence" of the temperate man has come to be called so derivatively (*ἠκολούθηκεν*) and by analogy.'

τοῦ σώφρονος καθ' ὁμοιότητα ἠκολούθηκεν· ὅ τε γὰρ
ἐγκρατὴς οἷος μηδὲν παρὰ τὸν λόγον διὰ τὰς σωματικὰς
ἡδονὰς ποιεῖν καὶ ὁ σώφρων, ἀλλ' ὁ μὲν ἔχων ὁ δ' οὐκ ἔχων
φαύλας ἐπιθυμίας, καὶ ὁ μὲν τοιοῦτος οἷος μὴ ἥδεσθαι
παρὰ τὸν λόγον, ὁ δ' οἷος ἥδεσθαι ἀλλὰ μὴ ἄγεσθαι.
7 ὅμοιοι δὲ καὶ ὁ ἀκρατὴς καὶ ὁ ἀκόλαστος, ἕτεροι μὲν
ὄντες, ἀμφότεροι δὲ τὰ σωματικὰ ἡδέα διώκουσιν, ἀλλ' ὁ
μὲν καὶ οἰόμενος δεῖν, ὁ δ' οὐκ οἰόμενος.

10 Οὐδ' ἅμα φρόνιμον καὶ ἀκρατῆ ἐνδέχεται εἶναι τὸν
αὐτόν· ἅμα γὰρ φρόνιμος καὶ σπουδαῖος τὸ ἦθος
2 δέδεικται ὤν. ἔτι οὐ τῷ εἰδέναι μόνον φρόνιμος ἀλλὰ
καὶ τῷ πρακτικός· ὁ δ' ἀκρατὴς οὐ πρακτικός. τὸν
δὲ δεινὸν οὐδὲν κωλύει ἀκρατῆ εἶναι· διὸ καὶ δοκοῦσιν
ἐνίοτε φρόνιμοι μὲν εἶναί τινες ἀκρατεῖς δέ, διὰ τὸ τὴν
δεινότητα διαφέρειν τῆς φρονήσεως τὸν εἰρημένον τρόπον
ἐν τοῖς πρώτοις λόγοις, καὶ κατὰ μὲν τὸν λόγον ἐγγὺς
3 εἶναι, διαφέρειν δὲ κατὰ τὴν προαίρεσιν. οὐδὲ δὴ ὡς
ὁ εἰδὼς καὶ θεωρῶν, ἀλλ' ὡς ὁ καθεύδων ἢ οἰνωμένος. καὶ ἑκὼν μὲν (τρόπον γάρ τινα εἰδὼς καὶ ὃ ποιεῖ
καὶ οὗ ἕνεκα), πονηρὸς δ' οὔ· ἡ γὰρ προαίρεσις ἐπιεικής·
ὥσθ' ἡμιπόνηρος. καὶ οὐκ ἄδικος· οὐ γὰρ ἐπίβουλος· ὁ

X. 1 ἅμα γὰρ φρόνιμος καὶ σπουδαῖος τὸ ἦθος δέδεικται ὤν] Cf. ch. ii. § 5. *Eth.* vi. xiii. 6.

2 τὸν εἰρημένον τρόπον ἐν τοῖς πρώτοις λόγοις] Cf. *Eth.* vi. xii. 8—9. The phrase ἐν τοῖς πρώτοις is used by Aristotle, *Eth.* iv. iv. 1, 4, in reference to the Second Book of *Ethics*. It must mean something more than πρότερον, one would think. It seems to point to a sort of interval between the later passage and that referred to. Cf. ch. i. § 1: ἄλλην ποιησαμένους ἀρχήν.

3 καὶ ἑκὼν μὲν] Cf. *Eth.* v. ix. 4—6, where the question is discussed, Does the incontinent man voluntarily do wrong and injury to himself as well as harm?

ἡ γὰρ προαίρεσις ἐπιεικής] Προαίρεσις here must mean the general state of the will. It is only one form of incontinence, which errs against a definitely formed purpose. Incontinence is always παρὰ τὴν βούλησιν (cf. *Eth.* v. ix. 6); in passionate natures it is ἄνευ προαιρέσεως. The Aristotelian psychology seems however to have admitted the formation of προαιρέσεις which are not carried out into action, and the question thus arises, Are purposes or actions most decisive as constituting virtue? See *Eth.* iii. ii. 1, note, and *Eth.* x. viii. 5.

ὥσθ' ἡμιπόνηρος] 'So that he is only half depraved.' This epithet occurs in Ar. *Pol.* v. xi. 34: ἔτι δ' αὐτὸν (the monarch) διακεῖσθαι (ἀναγκαῖον) κατὰ τὸ ἦθος ἤτοι καλῶς πρὸς ἀρετὴν ἢ ἡμίχρηστον ὄντα, καὶ μὴ πονηρὸν ἀλλ'

μὲν γὰρ αὐτῶν οὐκ ἐμμενετικὸς οἷς ἂν βουλεύσηται, ὁ δὲ μελαγχολικὸς οὐδὲ βουλευτικὸς ὅλως. καὶ ἔοικε δὴ ὁ ἀκρατὴς πόλει ἣ ψηφίζεται μὲν ἅπαντα τὰ δέοντα καὶ νόμους ἔχει σπουδαίους, χρῆται δὲ οὐδέν, ὥσπερ Ἀναξανδρίδης ἔσκωψεν

ἡ πόλις ἐβούλεθ', ᾗ νόμων οὐδὲν μέλει·

ὁ δὲ πονηρὸς χρωμένῃ μὲν τοῖς νόμοις, πονηροῖς δὲ χρωμένῃ. 4
ἔστι δ' ἀκρασία καὶ ἐγκράτεια περὶ τὸ ὑπερβάλλον τῆς τῶν πολλῶν ἕξεως· ὁ μὲν γὰρ ἐμμένει* μᾶλλον ὁ δ' ἧττον τῆς τῶν πλείστων δυνάμεως. εὐϊατοτέρα δὲ τῶν ἀκρασιῶν, ἣν οἱ μελαγχολικοὶ ἀκρατεύονται, τῶν βουλευομένων μὲν μὴ ἐμμενόντων δέ, καὶ οἱ δι' ἐθισμοῦ ἀκρατεῖς τῶν φυσικῶν· ῥᾷον γὰρ ἔθος μετακινῆσαι φύσεως· διὰ γὰρ τοῦτο καὶ τὸ ἔθος χαλεπόν, ὅτι τῇ φύσει ἔοικεν, ὥσπερ καὶ Εὔηνος λέγει

φημὶ πολυχρόνιον μελέτην ἔμεναι, φίλε, καὶ δὴ
ταύτην ἀνθρώποισι τελευτῶσαν φύσιν εἶναι.

τί μὲν οὖν ἐστιν ἐγκράτεια καὶ τί ἀκρασία καὶ τί καρτερία 5
καὶ τί μαλακία, καὶ πῶς ἔχουσιν αἱ ἕξεις αὗται πρὸς ἀλλήλας, εἴρηται.

ἡμιπόνηρος. In Plato, *Repub.* p. 352 c, the term ἡμιμόχθηροι is used, in proving that there must be honour even among thieves.

οὐ γὰρ ἐπίβουλος] Though just as compared with anger is called ἐπίβουλος (cf. ch. vi. § 3), yet it is true on the other hand that the incontinent man is not a designing character.

ὁ δὲ μελαγχολικὸς] Cf. above ch. vii. § 8, ch. viii. § 2.

ὥσπερ Ἀναξανδρίδης] A Rhodian comic poet, who is said to have satirized the Athenians. Aristotle mentions one of his plays, the Γεροντομανία (*Rhet.* III. xii. 3). Also a famous saying of his (*Ib.* III. xi. 8), Ἀναξανδρίδου τὸ ἐπαινούμενον—

καλόν γ' ἀποθανεῖν πρὶν θανάτου δρᾶν ἄξιον.

And another witticism (*Ib.* III. x. 7). Cf. Athenaeus, *Deipnos.* ix. 16.

4 τῆς τῶν πλείστων δυνάμεως] Cf. ch. vii. 1. note.

ὥσπερ καὶ Εὔηνος] An elegiac and gnomic poet of Paros, who appears to have been a contemporary and friend of Socrates.

φημὶ πολυχρόνιον κ.τ.λ.]

'Habit sticketh long and fast,
Second nature 'tis at last.'

μελέτην] 'That which is acquired by culture and habit.' That habit is 'second nature,' we are told by Aristotle, *De Mem.* ii. 16: ὥσπερ γὰρ φύσις ἤδη τὸ ἔθος, διὸ ἃ πολλάκις ἐννοοῦμεν ταχὺ ἀναμιμνησκόμεθα· ὥσπερ γὰρ φύσει τόδε μετὰ τόδε ἐστίν, οὕτω καὶ ἐνεργείᾳ· τὸ δὲ πολλάκις φύσιν ποιεῖ.

11 Περὶ δὲ ἡδονῆς καὶ λύπης θεωρῆσαι τοῦ τὴν πολιτικὴν φιλοσοφοῦντος· οὗτος γὰρ τοῦ τέλους ἀρχιτέκτων, πρὸς ὃ βλέποντες ἕκαστον τὸ μὲν κακὸν τὸ δ' ἀγαθὸν ἁπλῶς
2 λέγομεν. ἔτι δὲ καὶ τῶν ἀναγκαίων ἐπισκέψασθαι περὶ

XI. We now come to a treatise upon the nature of Pleasure. With regard to the authorship and character of this treatise see the remarks in Vol. I. Essay I. pp. 63 64, and Essay III. p. 249. A notable scholium, discovered by Professor Brandis in the Vatican, and quoted by Spengel and Fritzsche, attributes it to Eudemus, though in a merely conjectural way; see below ch. xiii. § 2, note. In the outset of the *Eudemian Ethics*, a discussion on Pleasure is promised in terms which correspond both to the contents and the position of the present chapters. (*Eth. Eud.* I. v. 11.) τούτων δ' (*i.e.* with regard to the three kinds of life) ἡ μὲν περὶ τὰ σώματα καὶ τὰς ἀπολαύσεις ἡδονή, καὶ τίς καὶ ποία τις γίνεται καὶ διὰ τίνων, οὐκ ἄδηλον, ὥστ' οὐ τίνες εἰσὶ δεῖ ζητεῖν αὐτάς, ἀλλ' εἰ συντείνουσί τι πρὸς εὐδαιμονίαν ἢ μή, καὶ πῶς συντείνουσι, καὶ πότερον εἰ δεῖ προσάπτειν τῷ ζῆν καλῶς ἡδονάς τινας, ταύτας δεῖ προσάπτειν, ἢ τούτων μὲν ἄλλον τινὰ τρόπον ἀνάγκη κοινωνεῖν, ἕτεραι δ' εἰσὶν ἡδοναὶ δι' ἃς εὐλόγως οἴονται τὸν εὐδαίμονα ζῆν ἡδέως καὶ μὴ μόνον ἀλύπως. ἀλλὰ περὶ μὲν τούτων ὕστερον ἐπισκεπτέον, περὶ δ' ἀρετῆς καὶ φρονήσεως πρῶτον θεωρήσωμεν. It is quite in agreement with the *terms* of this programme that the present treatise is prominently concerned with the discussion of *bodily* pleasure (ἡ περὶ τὰ σώματα καὶ τὰς ἀπολαύσεις ἡδονή). At the close of the *Eudemian Ethics* there is also a reference backward to these chapters (*Eth. Eud.* VIII. iii. 11): καὶ περὶ ἡδονῆς δ' εἴρηται ποῖόν τι καὶ πῶς ἀγαθόν, καὶ ὅτι τά τε ἁπλῶς ἡδέα καὶ καλά, καὶ τά (γε) ἁπλῶς ἀγαθὰ ἡδέα. οὐ γίνεται δὲ ἡδονὴ μὴ ἐν πράξει· διὰ τοῦτο ὁ ἀληθῶς εὐδαίμων καὶ ἥδιστα ζήσει, καὶ τοῦτο οὐ μάτην οἱ ἄνθρωποι ἀξιοῦσιν. (Cf. this Book, ch. xii. § 3, and § 7; ch. xiii. § 2.)

1—2 περὶ δὲ ἡδονῆς—χαίρειν] 'Pleasure and pain are subjects which come within the scope of him who makes politics a philosophy, for he has to frame the idea of that supreme end, in reference to which we call things absolutely good and bad. Also these are quite necessary for us to consider, since we have laid down the principle that moral virtue and vice are concerned with pains and pleasures, and since people in general hold that pleasure is involved in happiness, whence they have given the happy man his name (μακάριος from χαίρειν).'

There are three reasons given here for discussing pleasure: (1) Because it has claims to be 'the end.' (Cf. *Eth. Eud.* II. i. 1, where as a reason for discussing psychology it is said, φρονήσεις γὰρ καὶ ἀρετὴ καὶ ἡδονὴ ἐν ψυχῇ, ὧν ἔνια ἢ πάντα τέλος εἶναι δοκεῖ πᾶσιν). (2) From the connection before shown to exist between pleasure and morality, cf. *Eth. Eud.* II. iv. 2—4. (3) Because the idea of pleasure is involved in the common idea of happiness, as shown by the etymology (a false one) of μακάριος.

ἀρχιτέκτων τοῦ τέλους] *i.e.* to conceive in a grand and liberal way, independently of details, that supreme human good at which a state should aim. Cf. *Eth.* I. xiii. 1—3, and I. i. 4, note.

ἁπλῶς λέγομεν] There is some con-

αὐτῶν· τήν τε γὰρ ἀρετὴν καὶ τὴν κακίαν τὴν ἠθικὴν περὶ λύπας καὶ ἡδονὰς ἔθεμεν, καὶ τὴν εὐδαιμονίαν οἱ πλεῖστοι μεθ' ἡδονῆς εἶναί φασιν, διὸ καὶ τὸν μακάριον ὠνομάκασιν
ἀπὸ τοῦ χαίρειν. τοῖς μὲν οὖν δοκεῖ οὐδεμία ἡδονὴ εἶναι 3
ἀγαθόν, οὔτε καθ' αὑτὸ οὔτε κατὰ συμβεβηκός· οὐ γὰρ εἶναι ταὐτὸν ἀγαθὸν καὶ ἡδονήν· τοῖς δ' ἔνιαι μὲν εἶναι αἱ δὲ πολλαὶ φαῦλαι. ἔτι δὲ τούτων τρίτον, εἰ καὶ πᾶσαι ἀγαθόν, ὅμως μὴ ἐνδέχεσθαι εἶναι τὸ ἄριστον ἡδονήν.
ὅλως μὲν οὐκ ἀγαθόν, ὅτι πᾶσα ἡδονὴ γένεσίς ἐστιν εἰς 4
φύσιν αἰσθητή, οὐδεμία δὲ γένεσις συγγενὴς τοῖς τέλεσιν, οἷον οὐδεμία οἰκοδόμησις οἰκίᾳ. ἔτι ὁ σώφρων φεύγει τὰς ἡδονάς. ἔτι ὁ φρόνιμος τὸ ἄλυπον διώκει, οὐ τὸ ἡδύ. ἔτι ἐμπόδιον τῷ φρονεῖν αἱ ἡδοναί, καὶ ὅσῳ μᾶλλον χαίρει, μᾶλλον, οἷον τὴν τῶν ἀφροδισίων· οὐδένα γὰρ ἂν δύνασθαι νοῆσαί τι ἐν αὐτῇ. ἔτι τέχνη οὐδεμία ἡδονῆς· καίτοι πᾶν ἀγαθὸν τέχνης ἔργον. ἔτι παιδία καὶ θηρία διώκει τὰς
ἡδονάς. τοῦ δὲ μὴ πάσας σπουδαίας, ὅτι εἰσὶ καὶ 5

---

fusion in this expression, for though things are called good in reference to the supreme end, yet they are not called so *absolutely*. All such goods are merely means, and therefore goods relatively. What is here meant is more definitely expressed in *Eth. Eud.* I. viii. 18, ὅτι δ' αἴτιον τὸ τέλος τῶν ὑφ' αὑτό, δηλοῖ ἡ διδασκαλία. ὁρισάμενοι γὰρ τὸ τέλος τἆλλα δεικνύουσιν, ὅτι ἕκαστον αὐτῶν ἀγαθόν· αἴτιον γὰρ τὸ οὗ ἕνεκα. On ἁπλῶς ἀγαθὰ as a Eudemian formula, see Vol. I. Essay I. p. 62.

μεθ' ἡδονῆς] The first sentence of the *Eudemian Ethics* asserts that happiness is not only most good and beautiful, but also most pleasurable; this is taken, of course, from *Eth. Nic.* I. viii. 4.

3—5 The writer now mentions three existing opinions with regard to pleasure, and the arguments by which they are supported.

1 That pleasure is in no sense a good.
 (α) because it is a state of becoming (γένεσις);
 (β) because the temperate man avoids pleasures;
 (γ) because the thoughtful man aims not at pleasure, but at a painless condition;
 (δ) because pleasure hinders thought;
 (ε) because there is no art of pleasure;
 (ζ) because children and brutes follow pleasure.

2 That some pleasures may be good but that most are bad; supported by instances of morbid and hurtful pleasures.

3 That pleasure is at all events not the chief good; because it is not an end-in-itself, but a state of becoming.

τοῖς μὲν οὖν δοκεῖ] The opinions stated here are negative. The writer

αἰσχραὶ καὶ ὀνειδιζόμεναι, καὶ ἔτι βλαβεραί· νοσώδη γὰρ ἔνια τῶν ἡδέων. ὅτι δ' οὐκ ἄριστον ἡ ἡδονή, ὅτι οὐ τέλος ἀλλὰ γένεσις. τὰ μὲν οὖν λεγόμενα σχεδὸν ταῦτ' ἐστίν.

12 *Ὅτι δ' οὐ συμβαίνει διὰ ταῦτα μὴ εἶναι ἀγαθὸν μηδὲ τὸ ἄριστον, ἐκ τῶνδε δῆλον. πρῶτον μέν, ἐπεὶ τὸ ἀγαθὸν*

---

in all probability had before him Aristotle's treatise on Pleasure (*Eth.* x. i.—v.) He deviates from it slightly, and exhibits that kind of differences which might be expected under the circumstances. He does not, like Aristotle, state the positive view (held by Eudoxus) that pleasure is the chief good, but commences with the opinions of the objectors to this view (*i.e.* Speusippus and the Platonists of his school). The principal argument which he attributes to them (that pleasure is a *γένεσις*) is given, though not in such a definite form, *Eth.* x. iii. 4. Argument (ζ) appears to be implied in the objection against Eudoxus which is mentioned *Eth.* x. ii. 4. Argument (ε) may be the same perhaps as that given *Eth.* x. iii. 2 (that pleasure is *ἄπειρον*). The other arguments are not taken from Aristotle; they may perhaps have been derived from the books of Speusippus on this subject (*περὶ ἡδονῆς α'*, *Ἀρίστιππος α'*. See Vol. I. Essay III. p. 217).

The second view belongs probably to a more moderate section of the Older Academy. It still however requires qualification, and to this effect the writer argues below, in ch. xii.

The third view,—that pleasure, however good, cannot be the chief good,—was held by both Plato and Aristotle (though the argument by which it is supported, *ὅτι οὐ τέλος ἀλλὰ γένεσις*, was Plato's alone, cf. *Philebus* p. 53 c, 54 A. &c. *Eth.* x. ii. 3, x. iii. 8—13). Eudemus, identifying pleasure with happiness, denies this, ch. xii. § 1, ch. xiii. § 2.

XII. The arguments used in this chapter are as follows: (1) Before deciding on the goodness or badness of pleasure, a distinction has to be made between absolute and relative goodness or badness, and then various degrees have to be admitted among the relative kinds of goodness, § 1. (2) We must allow that real pleasure consists in life itself (*ἐνέργεια*), not what merely produces life (*γένεσις*). Hence all the arguments founded on defining pleasure to be a *γένεσις* fall to the ground. Those processes which restore nature are only pleasures in a subsidiary and accidental way. And even in them what is pleasant is the life (*ἐνέργεια*) which accompanies them, §§ 2—3. (3) Some pleasures may be morbid or they may hinder thought; but this only proves that *from one point of view* they are not good: but again the pleasures of thought are an assistance to thought, §§ 4—5. (4) There is no art of pleasure, because art is of conditions, not of functions, not of life itself, § 6. (5) The arguments about the thoughtful man, the temperate man, and the child (ch. xi. § 4), all apply merely to the inferior and subsidiary, that is the bodily, pleasures, § 7.

The course of procedure here is like that in *Eth.* x. ii.—iii., where the objections of the school of Speusippus are answered before Aristotle gives his own theory of the nature of pleasure. The arguments above are rather confused in statement. Those in § 1

διχῶς (τὸ μὲν γὰρ ἁπλῶς τὸ δὲ τινί), καὶ αἱ φύσεις καὶ αἱ ἕξεις ἀκολουθήσουσιν, ὥστε καὶ αἱ κινήσεις καὶ αἱ γενέσεις, καὶ αἱ φαῦλαι δοκοῦσαι εἶναι αἱ μὲν ἁπλῶς φαῦλαι τινὶ δ' οὒ ἀλλ' αἱρεταὶ τῷδε, ἔνιαι δ' οὐδὲ τῷδε ἀλλὰ ποτὲ καὶ ὀλίγον χρόνον, αἱρεταὶ δ' οὔ· αἱ δ' οὐδ' ἡδοναί, ἀλλὰ φαίνονται, ὅσαι μετὰ λύπης καὶ ἰατρείας ἕνεκεν, οἷον αἱ τῶν καμνόντων. ἔτι ἐπεὶ τοῦ ἀγαθοῦ τὸ 2

---

are apparently meant to answer the assertion that no pleasure is good, *οὔτε καθ' αὑτὸ οὔτε κατὰ συμβεβηκός.* The writer wishes first to urge that pleasure may be relatively good, if not absolutely so; he afterwards goes on to maintain that it is absolutely good.

Other passages of Eudemus bear a similarity to this, cf. *Eth. Eud.* III. i. 7: ἀλλ' ἴσως τὸ φοβερὸν λέγεται, ὥσπερ καὶ τὸ ἡδὺ καὶ τἀγαθόν, διχῶς. τὰ μὲν γὰρ ἁπλῶς, τὰ δὲ τινὶ μὲν καὶ ἡδέα καὶ ἀγαθά ἐστιν, ἁπλῶς δ' οὔ, ἀλλὰ τοὐναντίον φαῦλα καὶ οὐχ ἡδέα, ὅσα τοῖς πονηροῖς ὠφέλιμα, καὶ ὅσα ἡδέα τοῖς παιδίοις ᾗ παιδία. VII. ii. 4—7, &c.

1 ὅτι δ' οὐ συμβαίνει—καμνόντων] 'But that it does not follow from these arguments that (pleasure) is not a good, nor even that it is not the chief good, will be seen from the following considerations. First, the term "good" has a double import, it means either the absolute or the relative good; in accordance with this distinction, different constitutions and states will be either absolutely or relatively good, and so too the processes of change and transition (which produce them). Thus some of these processes which appear bad may be so in the abstract (ἁπλῶς), while they are not so relatively (τινί), but are desirable for the particular individual. Others again cannot be called desirable even *for* the particular individual, except on occasion and for a short time; others are not pleasures at all, but only seem so, being accompanied by pain and being (merely) for the sake of relief, as for instance the pleasures of the sick.'

2 ἔτι ἐπεὶ—ἀπὸ τούτων] 'Secondly, "good" may be either a state or the operation of a state, and so the processes which restore any one to his normal state (φυσικὴν ἕξιν) are pleasurable (not in themselves, but) accidentally (and by association). In fact there is an operation or vital action in desire, namely that of the powers in us which remain unimpaired (τῆς ὑπολοίπου ἕξεως καὶ φύσεως). (And it may be proved that pleasure depends not on want and desire, but on vital action), because there are pleasures which do not imply want and desire, as for instance the pleasures of thought, which take place when the nature is in no respect deficient. A proof (that the processes before-mentioned are only accidentally pleasurable) is to be found in the fact that men do not find delight in the same pleasure while their nature is being recruited (ἀναπληρουμένης) and when it is in a settled condition, but when it is settled they delight in things which are absolutely pleasant, and during the other process in things that are even quite the reverse; as in sharp and bitter things, which are not naturally nor abstractedly pleasant. Nor is the enjoyment of them natural, for as pleasant things, regarded objectively (τὰ ἡδέα), are to one another, so are the subjective feelings which these excite (ἡδοναί).'

μὲν ἐνέργεια τὸ δ' ἕξις, κατὰ συμβεβηκὸς αἱ καθιστᾶσαι εἰς τὴν φυσικὴν ἕξιν ἡδεῖαί εἰσιν. ἔστι δ' ἡ ἐνέργεια ἐν ταῖς ἐπιθυμίαις τῆς ὑπολοίπου ἕξεως καὶ φύσεως, ἐπεὶ καὶ ἄνευ λύπης καὶ ἐπιθυμίας εἰσὶν ἡδοναί, οἷον αἱ τοῦ θεωρεῖν ἐνέργειαι, τῆς φύσεως οὐκ ἐνδεοῦς οὔσης. σημεῖον δ' ὅτι οὐ τῷ αὐτῷ χαίρουσιν ἡδεῖ ἀναπληρουμένης τε τῆς φύσεως καὶ καθεστηκυίας, ἀλλὰ καθεστηκυίας μὲν τοῖς ἁπλῶς ἡδέσιν, ἀναπληρουμένης δὲ καὶ τοῖς ἐναντίοις· καὶ γὰρ ὀξέσι καὶ πικροῖς χαίρουσιν, ὧν οὐδὲν οὔτε φύσει ἡδὺ οὔθ' ἁπλῶς ἡδύ. ὥστ' οὐδ' ἡδοναί· ὡς γὰρ τὰ ἡδέα πρὸς ἄλληλα συνέστηκεν, οὕτω καὶ αἱ ἡδοναὶ αἱ ἀπὸ τούτων.
3 ἔτι οὐκ ἀνάγκη ἕτερόν τι εἶναι βέλτιον τῆς ἡδονῆς, ὥσπερ

This passage is expressed so elliptically as to require several links of thought to be supplied. In the above translation this has been attempted. A bare rendering of the sentences into English would leave them utterly unintelligible.

αἱ καθιστᾶσαι] i.e. αἱ κινήσεις καὶ αἱ γενέσεις, carried on from the previous section. The argument is that it is only life and the vital action (φυσικὴ ἕξις καὶ ταύτης ἐνέργεια) which is good and pleasant; the restorative processes are only secondarily, non-essentially, and by a sort of inference, pleasant. The words καθιστᾶσαι and καθεστηκυίας correspond with the term κατάστασις, which is used of pleasure in Ar. *Rhetoric*, I. xi. 1: κατάστασιν ἀθρόαν καὶ αἰσθητὴν εἰς τὴν ὑπάρχουσαν φύσιν.

τῆς ὑπολοίπου ἕξεως] The argument goes on to add that even in these restorative processes there is vital action (ἐνέργεια), namely of those organs that remain unimpaired. The Paraphrast and others understand ὑπολοίπου to mean 'deficient,' and as being equivalent to ἐνδεοῦς in the next line. But the above translation is not only more suitable to the doctrine of the Peripatetics (see Vol. I. Essay IV. pp. 246—249), but it is borne out by c. xiv. § 7: λέγω δὲ κατὰ συμβεβηκὸς ἡδέα τὰ ἰατρεύοντα· ὅτι γὰρ συμβαίνει ἰατρεύεσθαι τοῦ ὑπομένοντος ὑγιοῦς πράττοντός τι, διὰ τοῦτο ἡδὺ δοκεῖ εἶναι. Cf. *Eth.* x. iii. 6.

ὀξέσι καὶ πικροῖς] Mentioned as an instance of things only pleasant during a morbid condition of the body. Cf. *Eth.* x. iii. 8.

3 ἔτι οὐκ ἀνάγκη—ἔστι δ' ἕτερον] 'Moreover it does not follow that there must be something better than pleasure, as some argue, in the same way that the end is better than the process which leads to it. For all pleasures are not transition-states nor the accompaniments of such, but they are rather life itself and the end itself. They do not result from our coming to our powers (γινομένων), but from our using those powers (χρωμένων); and it is not true that *all* pleasures have an end separate from them; this is only true of such as are felt by persons in the process of being restored to their normal condition. Hence it is not right to define pleasure as a "sensible transition," but rather we should call it "a vital action of one's natural state," and

τινές φασι τὸ τέλος τῆς γενέσεως· οὐ γὰρ γενέσεις εἰσὶν οὐδὲ μετὰ γενέσεως πᾶσαι, ἀλλ' ἐνέργειαι καὶ τέλος· οὐδὲ γινομένων συμβαίνουσιν, ἀλλὰ χρωμένων· καὶ τέλος οὐ πασῶν ἕτερόν τι, ἀλλὰ τῶν εἰς τὴν τελέωσιν ἀγομένων τῆς φύσεως. διὸ καὶ οὐ καλῶς ἔχει τὸ αἰσθητὴν γένεσιν φάναι εἶναι τὴν ἡδονήν, ἀλλὰ μᾶλλον λεκτέον ἐνέργειαν τῆς κατὰ φύσιν ἕξεως, ἀντὶ δὲ τοῦ αἰσθητὴν ἀνεμπόδιστον. δοκεῖ δὲ γένεσίς τις εἶναι, ὅτι κυρίως ἀγαθόν· τὴν

---

instead of "sensible," "unimpeded." Now pleasure appears to people to be a transition-process from its being good in the full sense of the term, for people confound the ideas of process and action, whereas they are distinct.'

ὥσπερ τινές φασι] In all probability the school, and perhaps the actual writings of Speusippus, are here alluded to. Nowhere in Plato do the exact words of this definition of pleasure occur (*γένεσις εἰς φύσιν αἰσθητή*), but they represent his views, though perhaps carried rather farther. The present section places in opposition to each other the theories of the Platonic and the Aristotelian school, of whom the one considered pleasure to be a relief from pain, a return from depression, an addition to the vital powers; the other considered it to be the play of life itself, the flow of life outward rather than anything received. On these two divergent theories see Vol. I. Essay IV. pp. 216—219. The same subject may be found worked out at greater length, and with interesting notices of the opinions held by later philosophers, in Sir W. Hamilton's *Lectures on Metaphysics*, vol. II. lect. xliii. pp. 441—475.

ἀλλὰ μᾶλλον λεκτέον ἐνέργειαν] Aristotle when writing accurately distinguishes pleasure from the moments of life and consciousness (*ἐνέργειαι*), from which it is inseparable. Cf. *Eth.* x. v. 6: *αἱ δὲ* (ἡδοναὶ) *σύνεγγυς ταῖς ἐνεργείαις, καὶ ἀδιόριστοι οὕτως ὥστ' ἔχειν ἀμφισβήτησιν εἰ ταὐτόν ἐστιν ἡ ἐνέργεια τῇ ἡδονῇ. οὐ μὴν ἔοικέ γε ἡ ἡδονὴ διάνοια εἶναι οὐδ' αἴσθησις· ἄτοπον γάρ· ἀλλὰ διὰ τὸ μὴ χωρίζεσθαι φαίνεταί τισι ταὐτόν.* He however does not more specifically define it than as *ἐπιγιγνόμενόν τι τέλος* (*τῇ ἐνεργείᾳ*), *Eth.* x. iv. 8, &c. Eudemus does not preserve the distinction, but simply says that pleasure should be defined as 'the unimpeded play of life.' Aristotle himself occasionally writes in this way; cf. *Metaphys.* xi. vii. 7: *ἐπεὶ καὶ ἡ ἡδονὴ ἐνέργεια τούτου.*

ἀνεμπόδιστον] This word is borrowed from Aristotle's *Politics*, iv. xi. 3. See Vol. I. Essay I. pp. 54—55.

δοκεῖ δὲ γένεσίς τις εἶναι, ὅτι κυρίως ἀγαθόν] 'At first sight there appears to be a contradiction in saying that pleasure is thought not to be a good, because it is a *γένεσις* (ch. xi. § 4); and that it is thought to be a *γένεσις* because it is a good. The explanation is that the latter clause refers not to the Platonists, but to the Cyrenaics. The Cyrenaics, who considered pleasure the chief good, defined it as an equable process in the soul.' Plato accepted this definition, and turned it against them, arguing that by the very terms used the Cyrenaics had proved pleasure not to be the chief good. The Platonists then were originally

4 γὰρ ἐνέργειαν γένεσιν οἴονται εἶναι, ἔστι δ' ἕτερον. τὸ δ'
εἶναι φαύλας ὅτι νοσώδη ἔνια ἡδέα, τὸ αὐτὸ καὶ ὅτι
ὑγιεινὰ ἔνια φαῦλα πρὸς χρηματισμόν. ταύτῃ οὖν φαῦλα
ἄμφω, ἀλλ' οὐ φαῦλα κατά γε τοῦτο, ἐπεὶ καὶ τὸ θεωρεῖν
5 ποτὲ βλάπτει πρὸς ὑγίειαν, ἐμποδίζει δὲ οὔτε φρονήσει
οὔθ' ἕξει οὐδεμιᾷ ἡ ἀφ' ἑκάστης ἡδονή, ἀλλ' αἱ ἀλλότριαι,
ἐπεὶ αἱ ἀπὸ τοῦ θεωρεῖν καὶ μανθάνειν μᾶλλον ποιήσουσι
6 θεωρεῖν καὶ μανθάνειν. τὸ δὲ τέχνης μὴ εἶναι ἔργον
ἡδονὴν μηδεμίαν εὐλόγως συμβέβηκεν· οὐδὲ γὰρ ἄλλης
ἐνεργείας οὐδεμιᾶς τέχνη ἐστίν, ἀλλὰ τῆς δυνάμεως·
καίτοι καὶ ἡ μυρεψικὴ τέχνη καὶ ἡ ὀψοποιητικὴ δοκεῖ
7 ἡδονῆς εἶναι. τὸ δὲ τὸν σώφρονα φεύγειν καὶ τὸν φρόνιμον διώκειν τὸν ἄλυπον βίον, καὶ τὸ τὰ παιδία καὶ τὰ

---

indebted for their definition of pleasure (*αἰσθητὴ γένεσις*) to the Cyrenaics. See Vol. I. Essay II. pp. 175—176.

3—5 *τὸ δ' εἶναι φαύλας—μανθάνειν*] 'To say that pleasures are bad because some pleasant things are unhealthy is like saying (health is bad) because some healthy things are bad for money making. From that point of view it is true they are both bad, but they are not on account of this incidental badness bad *simpliciter*; since even thinking is sometimes injurious to health; but neither thought nor any other state of mind is impeded by its own pleasure, but only by foreign pleasures; for the pleasures of thinking and learning will make one think and learn more.' The argument here is that a thing good in itself may be relatively bad, *e.g.* health, and thought itself. One good may clash with another, and be from that point of view (*ταύτῃ*) bad. The writing is elliptical; we might have expected ἁπλῶς to be added to φαῦλα. The last clause in section 5, which asserts that a mental function is rather assisted than impaired by its own proper pleasure, is taken from *Ar. Eth.* x. v. 2—3. Νοσώδη seems to mean 'producing disease,' cf. ch. xi. § 5: as *νοσηματώδης* before (ch. v. § 3, &c.) means 'produced by disease.' Φρονήσει is evidently used above as the verbal noun of *φρονεῖν*, in the general sense of 'thought,' and not in the restricted sense which is given to it in Book vi. Cf. *Eth.* i. vi. 11; *Eth. Eud.* ii. i. 1 (quoted above).

6 *τὸ δὲ τέχνης κ.τ.λ.*] Cf. ch. xi. § 6. An answer is now given to an argument probably occurring in the works of Speusippus. This argument, if fairly represented here, must have had a false major premiss, namely, 'All that is good is the subject of art.' The answer consists of two different pleas; (1) pleasure, like life, is above art, which can only deal with the conditions tending to these things. (2) In another sense there *are* arts of pleasure, *e.g.* the cook's or the perfumer's art.

7 Most of the arguments against pleasure ignore the distinction between different kinds of pleasures, the one kind being of the nature of life, and the end, and therefore good in themselves (§ 3): the other kind being

θηρία διώκειν, τῷ αὐτῷ λύεται πάντα. ἐπεὶ γὰρ εἴρηται πῶς ἀγαθαὶ ἁπλῶς καὶ πῶς οὐκ ἀγαθαὶ πᾶσαι αἱ ἡδοναί, τὰς τοιαύτας τὰ θηρία καὶ τὰ παιδία διώκει, καὶ τὴν τούτων ἀλυπίαν ὁ φρόνιμος, τὰς μετ' ἐπιθυμίας καὶ λύπης καὶ τὰς σωματικάς (τοιαῦται γὰρ αὗται) καὶ τὰς τούτων ὑπερβολάς, καθ' ἃς ὁ ἀκόλαστος ἀκόλαστος. διὸ ὁ σώφρων φεύγει ταύτας, ἐπεὶ εἰσὶν ἡδοναὶ καὶ σώφρονος.

Ἀλλὰ μὴν ὅτι καὶ ἡ λύπη κακὸν ὁμολογεῖται, καὶ 13
φευκτόν· ἡ μὲν γὰρ ἁπλῶς κακόν, ἡ δὲ τῷ πῇ ἐμποδι-

---

connected with inferior conditions of our nature, with pain, want, &c., and being therefore only secondarily and accidentally good (§ 2). This latter kind of pleasures, and excess in them, are made the ground of reproaches against pleasure in general.

XIII. In this chapter, after refuting (§ 1) the objection of Speusippus (that pleasure may be the opposite of pain without being a good), Eudemus urges the claims of pleasure, of the highest kind, to be considered the chief good, because from the terms of its definition it is inseparable from and indeed identical with happiness (§ 2). It is a mere paradox to talk of a man being happy in torture, &c. Happiness requires prosperity, that an 'unimpeded function' may be obtained, i.e. pleasure, though there must not be too much prosperity, else happiness is 'impeded' in another way (§§ 3—4). The instinct of all creatures testifies to pleasure being the chief good (§ 5); and it is a mistake to think that bodily pleasure is the only kind that exists (§ 6). In short that pleasure is necessary for happiness proves that it is a good (§ 7).

1 ἀλλὰ μὴν—ἡδονήν] 'But we may go further—it is universally agreed that pain is an evil, and detestable—for it is either absolutely an evil, or is so relatively as impeding the individual in some way or other.—But that which is contrary to the detestable in that very point which makes it detestable and evil, is good. Therefore it follows that pleasure must be a good. For the answer of Speusippus to this argument does not hold, that "(pleasure is contrary to pain and to the absence of pain) in the same way that the greater is contrary to the less, and also to the equal." For no one could ever say that pleasure is identical with any form of evil.' That pleasure is a good because it is the contrary of pain, is an argument attributed to Eudoxus, *Eth.* x. ii. 2. Aristotle there (*Ib.* § 5) mentions the answer to it, and refutes that answer as above. Eudemus, in accordance with his usual style, adds the name of Speusippus. Aulus Gellius, IX. 5, mentions this doctrine: 'Speusippus vetusque omnis Academia voluptatem et dolorem duo mala esse dicunt opposita inter sese: bonum autem esse quod utriusque medium foret.' Accordingly, the neutral state between pain and pleasure would have to be regarded as good. Aristotle and Eudemus reply that the point of contrariety between pain and pleasure is that the one is φευκτόν, and the other αἱρετόν, therefore the one must be considered an evil, the other a good.

στικῆ. τῷ δὲ φευκτῷ τὸ ἐναντίον ᾗ φευκτόν τι καὶ κακόν, ἀγαθόν. ἀνάγκη οὖν τὴν ἡδονὴν ἀγαθόν τι εἶναι. ὡς γὰρ Σπεύσιππος ἔλυεν, οὐ συμβαίνει ἡ λύσις, ὥσπερ τὸ μεῖζον τῷ ἐλάττονι καὶ τῷ ἴσῳ ἐναντίον· οὐ γὰρ ἂν φαίη
2 ὅπερ κακόν τι εἶναι τὴν ἡδονήν. ἄριστόν τ' οὐδὲν κωλύει ἡδονήν τινα εἶναι, εἰ ἔνιαι φαῦλαι ἡδοναί, ὥσπερ καὶ ἐπιστήμην τινὰ ἐνίων φαύλων οὐσῶν. ἴσως δὲ καὶ ἀναγκαῖον, εἴπερ ἑκάστης ἕξεώς εἰσιν ἐνέργειαι ἀνεμπόδιστοι, εἴθ' ἡ πασῶν ἐνέργειά ἐστιν εὐδαιμονία εἴτε ἡ τινὸς αὐτῶν,

---

ὅπερ κακόν τι] Cf. *Eth.* vi. iv. 3, note. We are probably to understand τι, with the Paraphrast and Scholiast. Speusippus would have said that pleasure *is* an evil. Cf. *Eth.* x. ii. 5.

2 ἄριστόν τ' οὐδὲν κωλύει] This admission is directly contrary to the conclusions of Aristotle (cf. *Eth.* x. iii. 13). It is to be explained as an after development of the system of Aristotle, and an attempt to bring different parts of that system into harmony with each other. Aristotle having used the same formula (*ἐνέργεια*) to express both pleasure and happiness, Eudemus from the force of the terms identifies them. In this he is quite justified, for it is impossible to distinguish the highest kind of pleasure or joy from happiness, especially if we consider peace (*ἐνέργεια τῆς ἀοχλησίας*) to be a mode of joy. It is in accordance with the rest of the *Eudemian Ethics* to speak in this way of pleasure as being an essential element in, and as inseparable from, happiness. Cf. *Eth. Eud.* i. i. 6—7, i. v. 11—12 (quoted above), viii. iii. 11, &c.

The Vatican scholium on this passage speaks of it as being merely dialectical (but this is from an unwillingness to recognise the discrepancy between Books vii. and x.). It proceeds to attribute the present treatise conjecturally to Eudemus. διὰ μὲν οὖν τούτων δοκεῖ ταὐτὸν ἀποφαίνεσθαι τἀγαθὸν καὶ τὴν ἡδονήν· οὐ μὴν οὕτως ἔχει, ἀλλὰ πρὸς τοὺς λέγοντας γένεσιν εἶναι ἢ φαύλας τινὰς τῶν ἡδονῶν, ὡς καὶ δι' αὐτὸ τὸ μὴ εἶναι αὐτὴν τὸ ἀγαθὸν ἐπιχειρεῖ ἐνδόξως ὡς ἐνὸν αὐτὴν τὸ ἄριστον λέγειν, ἐπεὶ ἔν γε τοῖς Νικομαχείοις ὕστερον διείλεκται καὶ περὶ ἡδονῆς Ἀριστοτέλης σαφῶς εἴρηκεν αὐτὴν μὴ ταὐτὸν εἶναι τῇ εὐδαιμονίᾳ, ἀλλὰ παρακολουθεῖν ὥσπερ τοῖς ἀκμαίοις τὴν ὥραν. σημεῖον δὲ τοῦ μὴ εἶναι ταῦτ' Ἀριστοτέλους ἀλλ' Εὐδήμου τὸ ἐν τῷ κ' (Book X.) λέγειν περὶ ἡδονῆς ὡς οὐδέπω περὶ αὐτῆς διειλεγμένου. πλὴν εἴτε Εὐδήμου ταῦτά ἐστιν εἴτ' Ἀριστοτέλους, ἐνδόξως εἴρηται. διὰ τοῦτο λέγεται τὸ ἄριστον ἡδονή, ὅτι σὺν τῷ ἀρίστῳ καὶ ἀχώριστον αὐτοῦ. τούτῳ δ' ὁμολογεῖ καὶ τὰ ἑξῆς. This which is a remarkably favourable specimen of the Scholia, may serve to show the wavering and unprofitable character of the commentaries.

ὥσπερ καὶ ἐπιστήμην] This must not be taken very strictly, since pleasure and knowledge cannot *both* be the chief good. Both however may be considered as forms of the absolute good. Cf. *Eth.* i. vii. 5. The article is omitted at first with ἄριστον, but is added below. Knowledge is good, though some things it is better not to know.

ἂν ᾖ ἀνεμπόδιστος, αἱρετωτάτην εἶναι· τοῦτο δ' ἐστὶν ἡδονή. ὥστε εἴη ἄν τις ἡδονὴ τὸ ἄριστον, τῶν πολλῶν ἡδονῶν φαύλων οὐσῶν, εἰ ἔτυχεν, ἁπλῶς. καὶ διὰ τοῦτο πάντες τὸν εὐδαίμονα ἡδὺν οἴονται βίον εἶναι, καὶ ἐμπλέκουσι τὴν ἡδονὴν εἰς τὴν εὐδαιμονίαν, εὐλόγως· οὐδεμία γὰρ ἐνέργεια τέλειος ἐμποδιζομένη, ἡ δ' εὐδαιμονία τῶν τελείων· διὸ προσδεῖται ὁ εὐδαίμων τῶν ἐν σώματι ἀγαθῶν καὶ τῶν ἐκτὸς καὶ τῆς τύχης, ὅπως μὴ ἐμποδίζηται
ταῦτα. οἱ δὲ τὸν τροχιζόμενον καὶ τὸν δυστυχίαις με- 3
γάλαις περιπίπτοντα εὐδαίμονα φάσκοντες εἶναι, ἐὰν ᾖ
ἀγαθός, ἢ ἑκόντες ἢ ἄκοντες οὐδὲν λέγουσιν. διὰ δὲ τὸ 4
προσδεῖσθαι τῆς τύχης δοκεῖ τισὶ ταὐτὸν εἶναι ἡ εὐτυχία τῇ εὐδαιμονίᾳ, οὐκ οὖσα, ἐπεὶ καὶ αὐτὴ ὑπερβάλλουσα ἐμπόδιός ἐστιν, καὶ ἴσως οὐκέτι εὐτυχίαν καλεῖν δίκαιον·

καὶ ἐμπλέκουσι τὴν ἡδονὴν εἰς τὴν εὐδαιμονίαν, εὐλόγως] Cf. *Eth. Eud.* I. v. 11 (which passage is here referred to): *ἕτεραι δ' εἰσὶν ἡδοναὶ δι' ἃς εὐλόγως οἴονται τὸν εὐδαίμονα ζῆν ἡδέως καὶ μὴ μόνον ἀλύπως.*

τῶν ἐν σώματι ἀγαθῶν καὶ τῶν ἐκτὸς καὶ τῆς τύχης] This is the principle with regard to happiness which is laid down in *Eth. Nic.* I. viii. 15—17. It was afterwards considered characteristic of the Peripatetic School. Cf. Cicero, *De Fin.* II. vi. 19: 'Aristoteles virtutis usum cum vitae perfectae prosperitate conjunxit.'

3 *οἱ δὲ—λέγουσιν*] 'But they who allege that he who is being racked on the wheel, or he that is plunged in great calamities, is happy, provided he be virtuous, talk nonsense, whether intentionally or not.' Cf. *Eth. Nic.* I. v. 6. The words *ἑκόντες οὐδὲν λέγουσιν* answer to *εἰ μὴ θέσιν διαφυλάττων* in that place. The paradox alluded to was maintained by the Cynics, and afterwards by the Stoics (who denied that pain was an evil). Cf. Cicero, *Tusc.* v. ix. 24: 'Theophrastus quum statuisset verbera, tormenta, cruciatus, patriae eversiones, exsilia, orbitates, magnam vim habere ad male misereque vivendum, non est ausus elate et ample loqui, quum humiliter demisseque sentiret.—Vexatur autem ab omnibus primum in eo libro quem scripsit de vita beata, in quo multa disputat, quamobrem is, qui torquentur, qui crucietur, beatus esse non possit: in eo etiam putatur dicere in rotam beatam vitam non escendere' (quoted by Fritzsche). Cf. also Cicero, *Paradoxa*, ii.

4 *ταὐτὸν εἶναι ἡ εὐτυχία*] Cf. *Eth. Eud.* I. i. 4: *ἢ διὰ τύχην· πολλοὶ γὰρ ταὐτόν φασιν εἶναι τὴν εὐδαιμονίαν καὶ τὴν εὐτυχίαν.* This, together with the present passage, is taken from *Eth. Nic.* I. viii. 17.

αὐτὴ ὑπερβάλλουσα ἐμπόδιός ἐστιν] A more forcible expression of what is said *Eth.* x. viii. 9: *οὐ γὰρ ἐν τῇ ὑπερβολῇ τὸ αὔταρκες κ.τ.λ.*

καὶ ἴσως—αὐτῆς] 'And perhaps (when it is overweening), we should no longer call it prosperity; for the standard of prosperity consists in its being conducive to happiness.' Cf. *Eth. Eud.* VIII. iii. 12: *τῶν φύσει μὲν*

5 πρὸς γὰρ τὴν εὐδαιμονίαν ὁ ὅρος αὐτῆς. καὶ τὸ διώκειν δ' ἅπαντα καὶ θηρία καὶ ἀνθρώπους τὴν ἡδονὴν σημεῖόν τι τοῦ εἶναί πως τὸ ἄριστον αὐτήν.

> Φήμη δ' οὔ τί γε πάμπαν ἀπόλλυται, ἥν τινα λαοὶ
> πολλοί . . .

6 ἀλλ' ἐπεὶ οὐχ ἡ αὐτὴ οὔτε φύσις οὔθ' ἕξις ἡ ἀρίστη οὔτ' ἔστιν οὔτε δοκεῖ, οὐδ' ἡδονὴν διώκουσι τὴν αὐτὴν πάντες, ἡδονὴν μέντοι πάντες. ἴσως δὲ καὶ διώκουσιν οὐχ ἣν οἴονται οὐδ' ἣν ἂν φαῖεν, ἀλλὰ τὴν αὐτήν· πάντα γὰρ φύσει ἔχει τι θεῖον. ἀλλ' εἰλήφασι τὴν τοῦ ὀνόματος κληρονομίαν αἱ σωματικαὶ ἡδοναὶ διὰ τὸ πλειστάκις τε

ἀγαθῶν οἷον ἐπιεικεστέραν δὲ δεῖ τινὰ εἶναι ὅρον καὶ ἕξεως καὶ τῆς αἱρέσεως, καὶ περὶ φυγῆς χρημάτων πλήθους καὶ ὀλιγότητος καὶ τῶν εὐτυχημάτων· and Vol. I. Essay I. p. 60.

5 *καὶ τὸ διώκειν δ'—θεῖον*] 'In short that all things pursue pleasure, both beasts and men, is a proof that it is in some sort the chief good,—

> "For mankind's universal voice cannot
> Be wholly vain and false."

Since however there is no one nature or state which is, or is thought to be, the best for all, so neither do they all pursue the same pleasure, but still they all pursue pleasure. Nay, perhaps unconsciously they are pursuing, not what they think, or would declare, but (in reality) the same; for all things have within them by nature a divine instinct.' This is said, *Eth.* x. ii. 1, to have been the argument of Eudoxus: Εὔδοξος μὲν οὖν τὴν ἡδονὴν τἀγαθὸν ᾤετο εἶναι διὰ τὸ πάνθ' ὁρᾶν ἐφιέμενα αὐτῆς καὶ ἔλλογα καὶ ἄλογα. *Ib.* § 4. Aristotle justifies the argument against objectors in much the same terms as those adopted in the text.

ἥν τινα λαοὶ πολλοί] sc. φημίζουσι. Hesiod, *Works and Days*, v. 761. Cf. *Eth.* x. ii. 4: ὃ γὰρ πᾶσι δοκεῖ, τοῦτ' εἶναί φαμεν.

ἴσως δὲ καὶ] Perhaps by a mysterious instinct all creatures, in seeking life and joy, seek under different manifestations one and the same principle of good. Cf. the dream-images in Goethe's Faust:

> 'Einige glimmen
> Ueber die Höhen,
> Andere schwimmen
> Ueber die Seen,
> Andere schweben,
> Alle zum Leben;
> Alle zur Ferne
> Liebender Sterne,
> Seliger Huld.'

Aristotle, *Eth.* x. ii. 4 (which is the source of the above passage), does not go so far as to make all creatures aim at the same good, ἴσως δὲ καὶ ἐν τοῖς φαύλοις ἐστί τι φυσικὸν ἀγαθὸν κρεῖττον ἢ καθ' αὑτά, ὃ ἐφίεται τοῦ οἰκείου ἀγαθοῦ.

ἀλλ' εἰλήφασι—οἴονται εἶναι] 'But bodily pleasures have usurped the possession of the name of pleasure, from men's most often resorting to them, and from all men partaking of them; hence because these are the only pleasures they know of, they think they are the only ones which exist.' *παραβάλλειν* appears to mean 'lay themselves alongside,' 'apply themselves to.'

παραβάλλειν εἰς αὐτὰς καὶ πάντας μετέχειν αὐτῶν· διὰ τὸ μόνας οὖν γνωρίμους εἶναι ταύτας μόνας οἴονται εἶναι.

Φανερὸν δὲ καὶ ὅτι, εἰ μὴ ἡδονὴ ἀγαθὸν καὶ ἡ ἐνέργεια, 7
οὐκ ἔσται ζῆν ἡδέως τὸν εὐδαίμονα· τίνος γὰρ ἕνεκα δέοι ἂν αὐτῆς, εἴπερ μὴ ἀγαθόν, ἀλλὰ καὶ λυπηρῶς ἐνδέχεται ζῆν; οὔτε κακὸν γὰρ οὔτ' ἀγαθὸν ἡ λύπη, εἴπερ μηδ' ἡδονή· ὥστε διὰ τί ἂν φεύγοι; οὐδὲ δὴ ἥδιον ὁ βίος ὁ τοῦ σπουδαίου, εἰ μὴ καὶ αἱ ἐνέργειαι αὐτοῦ.

Περὶ δὲ δὴ τῶν σωματικῶν ἡδονῶν ἐπισκεπτέον τοῖς 14
λέγουσιν ὅτι ἔνιαί γε ἡδοναὶ αἱρεταὶ σφόδρα, οἷον αἱ

---

7 φανερὸν δὲ—αὐτοῦ] 'Finally it is plain that unless pleasure and the action of life are a good, the happy man cannot live pleasurably. For why should he need pleasure, if it be not a good, and if it be possible for him to live painfully? (and it will be possible), for pain will be neither evil nor good, unless pleasure is; so why should he avoid it? and hence it will follow that the life of the good man will not be more pleasurable than that of the bad man, if his moments of action are not more pleasurable.' This is a *reductio ad absurdum* of the position that pleasure is not a good. We shall be reduced to think (1) that the happy man may live devoid of pleasure: for nothing that is not good can form part of happiness—or even he may live a life of pain, which is the contrary of pleasure; (2) that the good man will have no more pleasure than the bad man, unless pleasure attaches to good acts, in which case it will be part of the good.

XIV. Hitherto Eudemus has followed the lead of Aristotle, only in one respect making a slight development of his conclusions. He now discusses a subject untouched by Aristotle, but which he had proposed to himself in his first book; cf. *Eth. Eud.* i. v. 11: *πότερον, εἰ δεῖ προσάπτειν τῷ ζῆν καλῶς ἡδονάς τινας, ταύτας* (i.e. *τὰς σωματικάς*) *δεῖ προσάπτειν, ἢ τούτων μὲν ἄλλον τινὰ τρόπον ἀνάγκη κοινωνεῖν—ἀλλὰ περὶ μὲν τούτων ὕστερον ἐπισκεπτέον.* Assuming that there are higher pleasures, and that pleasure in the highest form is identical with happiness and the chief good, what is to be said of bodily pleasure? is it an evil or a good? and why is it that men indulge in it so much? To this twofold problem the answers are, Bodily pleasure is in itself a good, as being the contrary of pain; but it is only good under certain limits, as it admits of excess, and the excess is bad (§ 2). There are various reasons why bodily pleasure recommends itself to human nature. (1) It expels the sense of pain, and hence as an anodyne is universally desired from a physical law, for life is full of labour, and the ordinary functions of the senses are laborious acts, only mitigated by custom, §§ 4, 5. (2) The period of youth especially craves after physical pleasure. (3) There are special cases where it is in a way necessary, namely, where peculiarities of temperament render men constitutionally depressed and in want of a sort of relief, §§ 4, 6. (4) From the mixture of the material with the

καλαί, ἀλλ' οὐχ αἱ σωματικαὶ καὶ περὶ ἃς ὁ ἀκόλαστος.
2 διὰ τί οὖν αἱ ἐναντίαι λῦπαι μοχθηραί; κακῷ γὰρ ἀγαθὸν ἐναντίον. ἢ οὕτως ἀγαθαὶ αἱ ἀναγκαῖαι, ὅτι καὶ τὸ μὴ κακὸν ἀγαθόν ἐστιν; ἢ μέχρι του ἀγαθαί; τῶν μὲν γὰρ ἕξεων καὶ κινήσεων ὅσων μή ἐστι τοῦ βελτίονος ὑπερβολή, οὐδὲ τῆς ἡδονῆς· ὅσων δ' ἐστί, καὶ τῆς ἡδονῆς ἐστίν. τῶν δὲ σωματικῶν ἀγαθῶν ἐστὶν ὑπερβολή, καὶ ὁ φαῦλος τῷ διώκειν τὴν ὑπερβολήν ἐστιν, ἀλλ' οὐ τὰς ἀναγκαίας· πάντες γὰρ χαίρουσί πως καὶ ὄψοις καὶ οἴνοις καὶ ἀφροδισίοις, ἀλλ' οὐχ ὡς δεῖ. ἐναντίως δ' ἐπὶ τῆς λύπης· οὐ γὰρ τὴν ὑπερβολὴν φεύγει, ἀλλ' ὅλως· οὐ γάρ ἐστι τῇ ὑπερβολῇ λύπη ἐναντία ἀλλ' ἢ τῷ διώκοντι τὴν ὑπερβολήν.

3 Ἐπεὶ δ' οὐ μόνον δεῖ τἀληθὲς εἰπεῖν ἀλλὰ καὶ τὸ αἴτιον τοῦ ψεύδους· τοῦτο γὰρ συμβάλλεται πρὸς τὴν πίστιν· ὅταν γὰρ εὔλογον φανῇ τὸ διὰ τί φαίνεται ἀληθὲς οὐκ ὂν

---

spiritual in us, we are unable to continue perpetually delighting in one pure pleasure, that is, the pleasure of thought. God alone is capable of this; to us, through a fault in our nature (οὐ γὰρ ἁπλῆ οὐδ' ἐπιεικής), change appears sweet, because lower and contradictory elements in us require to be allowed their due action, § 8.

1 τοῖς λέγουσιν] i.e. that section of the Platonists referred to above, ch. xi. § 3: τοῖς δ' ἐνίας μὲν εἶναι, αἱ δὲ πολλαὶ φαῦλαι.

2 τῶν δὲ σωματικῶν—ὑπερβολήν] 'But right bodily pleasures admit of excess, and the bad man (is bad) in that he seeks that excess, instead of seeking such pleasures as are necessary. All men find delight in meat, and wine, and love, though not all according to the proper law. And reversely all men avoid pain (ἐναντίως δ' ἐπὶ τῆς λύπης). A man does not avoid the excess of pain, but pain in general. Pain is not contrary to the excess of pleasure, except to him who pursues the excess of pleasure.' This argument goes to prove that bodily pleasure is in itself good; only when in excess is it evil. On the other hand all pain is evil. Pleasure and pain then are opposite terms, the one being good and the other evil. To make the doctrine of Speusippus (ch. xiii. 1) hold good, it would be necessary to make pain and the excess of pleasure opposite terms. But they are not so, except perhaps in the mind of the intemperate man, who thinks that the only alternative is between excessive pleasure and a painful sensation.

3 This section is not logically continuous with what immediately precedes. It no longer deals with the opinion of the Platonists that bodily pleasure is an evil, but takes up another question already partly anticipated, ch. xiii. § 6; namely, How is the vulgar error to be accounted for, which gives so much prominence to physical pleasure in the scale of pleasures?

ἀληθές, πιστεύειν ποιεῖ τῷ ἀληθεῖ μᾶλλον· ὥστε λεκτέον διὰ τί φαίνονται αἱ σωματικαὶ ἡδοναὶ αἱρετώτεραι.
πρῶτον μὲν οὖν δὴ ὅτι ἐκκρούει τὴν λύπην· καὶ διὰ τὰς 4
ὑπερβολὰς τῆς λύπης, ὡς οὔσης ἰατρείας, τὴν ἡδονὴν διώκουσι τὴν ὑπερβάλλουσαν καὶ ὅλως τὴν σωματικήν. σφοδραὶ δὲ γίνονται αἱ ἰατρεῖαι, διὸ καὶ διώκονται, διὰ τὸ παρὰ τὸ ἐναντίον φαίνεσθαι. καὶ οὐ σπουδαῖον δὴ δοκεῖ ἡ ἡδονὴ διὰ δύο ταῦτα, ὥσπερ εἴρηται, ὅτι αἱ μὲν φαύλης φύσεώς εἰσι πράξεις, ἢ ἐκ γενετῆς, ὥσπερ θηρίου, ἢ δι' ἔθος, οἷον αἱ τῶν φαύλων ἀνθρώπων. αἱ δ' ἰατρεῖαι, ὅτι ἐνδεοῦς, καὶ ἔχειν βέλτιον ἢ γίνεσθαι. αἱ δὲ συμβαίνουσι τελεουμένων· κατὰ συμβεβηκὸς οὖν σπουδαῖαι. ἔτι διώ- 5
κονται διὰ τὸ σφοδραὶ εἶναι ὑπὸ τῶν ἄλλαις μὴ δυναμέ-

---

4 πρῶτον—φαίνεσθαι] 'The first reason is that it drives out pain. When overwhelmed with pain, as a remedy men seek excessive pleasure, and in short bodily pleasure. Now remedies are naturally violent, and they are adopted because they seem to match (παρά) their opposites.' On the opinion that remedies are the opposites of the diseases to be cured, cf. *Eth.* II. iii. 4.

καὶ οὐ σπουδαῖον δὴ—σπουδαῖαι] 'It is on account of these two causes, then, that pleasure is thought not to be a good; first, that some pleasures, as we have said before (ch. v. 1.), are the actions of a depraved nature, whether congenital, like that of a beast, or acquired, like that of depraved men; secondly, that other pleasures are remedies, implying imperfection, since a normal condition (ἔχειν) is better than the process of arriving at that condition, and some pleasures take place while we are arriving at a complete state of being, hence they are only inferentially and not directly (κατὰ συμβεβηκὸς) good.' This paragraph reverts parenthetically to the opinion of the Platonists.

5—6 ἔτι διώκονται—γίνονται] The argument is now resumed from the sentence ending φαίνεσθαι. 'Another reason why physical pleasure is sought, is its comparatively coarse and violent character, which suits those who require strong excitement. And indeed such men even create in themselves certain artificial thirsts for pleasure. If this does not hurt their health, it is no harm. Such men are incapable of enjoying the purer and simpler pleasures, and a neutral state of the sensations is to many painful by a law of nature. For the living creature ever travails, as the physiological books testify, telling us that the acts of seeing and hearing are laborious, only that we are accustomed to them (so they say). So also the young, in the first place, owing to the principle of growth in them, are like those who are intoxicated, and youth is full of pleasure. And again those of bilious nature are ever in need of an anodyne. Their body is continually fretted by reason of their temperament, and they are ever in vehement desire. Now pleasure, be it the opposite of a given pain, or be it what it may, provided it be strong

νων χαίρειν· αὐτοὶ γοῦν αὑτοῖς δίψας τινὰς παρασκευάζουσιν. ὅταν μὲν οὖν ἀβλαβεῖς, ἀνεπιτίμητον, ὅταν δὲ βλαβεράς, φαῦλον· οὔτε γὰρ ἔχουσιν ἕτερα ἐφ' οἷς χαίρουσιν, τό τε μηδέτερον πολλοῖς λυπηρὸν διὰ τὴν φύσιν· ἀεὶ γὰρ πονεῖ τὸ ζῷον, ὥσπερ καὶ οἱ φυσικοὶ λόγοι μαρτυροῦσι, τὸ ὁρᾶν καὶ τὸ ἀκούειν φάσκοντες εἶναι λυπηρόν· ἀλλ' ἤδη συνήθεις ἐσμέν, ὡς φασίν.
6 ὁμοίως δ' ἐν μὲν τῇ νεότητι διὰ τὴν αὔξησιν ὥσπερ οἱ οἰνωμένοι διάκεινται, καὶ ἡδὺ ἡ νεότης. οἱ δὲ μελαγχολικοὶ τὴν φύσιν ἀεὶ δέονται ἰατρείας· καὶ γὰρ τὸ σῶμα δακνόμενον διατελεῖ διὰ τὴν κρᾶσιν, καὶ ἀεὶ ἐν ὀρέξει σφοδρᾷ εἰσίν. ἐξελαύνει δὲ ἡδονὴ λύπην ἥ τ' ἐναντία καὶ ἡ τυχοῦσα, ἐὰν ᾖ ἰσχυρά· καὶ διὰ ταῦτα ἀκόλαστοι καὶ
7 φαῦλοι γίνονται. αἱ δ' ἄνευ λυπῶν οὐκ ἔχουσιν ὑπερ-

---

enough, drives out that pain. And hence persons of the bilious temperament become intemperate and vicious.' This passage gives two reasons to explain why a neutral state of the sensations is distasteful, first a general reason: that the laborious action of the human faculties calls for alleviation; second, a special reason: that certain periods of life and certain temperaments produce a craving after physical indulgence.

δίψας τινὰς] Fritzsche, after the Scholiast, understands this literally, that some men make themselves thirsty to enjoy the pleasure of drinking. But the use of the plural seems to indicate that we should rather follow the Paraphrast, and the majority of the commentators, in understanding it generally of artificial desires for pleasure, *ἐπισκευαστὰς ἐπιθυμίας*, as the Paraphrast calls them.

ὁμοίως δ' ἐν μὲν κ. τ. λ.] The best commentary on this passage will be found in Aristotle's *Problems*, bk. xxx. ch. i., where a frequent comparison is made between the effects of wine, youth, and the melancholy or (bilious) temperament, in producing desire. Cf. § 5: *ὁ γὰρ οἶνος ὁ πολὺς μάλιστα φαίνεται παρασκευάζειν τοιούτους οἵους λέγομεν τοὺς μελαγχολικοὺς εἶναι.* § 10: *καὶ ὁ οἶνος δὲ πνευματώδης τὴν δύναμιν. διὸ δή ἐστι τὴν φύσιν ὅμοια ὅ τε οἶνος καὶ ἡ κρᾶσις, κ.τ.λ.* Cf. *Prob.* iv. xxx.: *διὰ τί ἀφροδισιαστικοὶ οἱ μελαγχολικοί; ἢ ὅτι πνευματώδεις, κ.τ.λ.* The Scholiast gives a vapid explanation of the words *ὥσπερ οἱ οἰνωμένοι* in the passage before us. Evidently, all that is meant is to compare the *desires* of youth with those of drunkenness, and of the melancholy temperament. We may compare the lines of Goethe:

'Trunken müssen wir alle sein;
Jugend ist Trunkenheit ohne Wein.'

The principle of *αὔξησις* in youth is represented as producing the same results as the humours (*χυμὸς ὁ μελαγχολικός—ἡ τῆς μελαίνης χολῆς κρᾶσις*) in the bilious temperament.

7—8 *αἱ δ' ἄνευ λυπῶν—ἐπιεικεῖς*] 'The pleasures unpreceded by pain do not admit of excess, they are essentially and not accidentally pleasures.

βολήν. αὗται δὲ αἱ τῶν φύσει ἡδέων καὶ μὴ κατὰ συμβεβηκός. λέγω δὲ κατὰ συμβεβηκὸς ἡδέα τὰ ἰατρεύοντα· ὅτι γὰρ συμβαίνει ἰατρεύεσθαι τοῦ ὑπομένοντος ὑγιοῦς πράττοντός τι, διὰ τοῦτο ἡδὺ δοκεῖ εἶναι· φύσει δ' ἡδέα, ἃ ποιεῖ πρᾶξιν τῆς τοιᾶσδε φύσεως. οὐκ ἀεὶ δ' οὐθὲν ἡδὺ 8
τὸ αὐτὸ διὰ τὸ μὴ ἁπλῆν ἡμῶν εἶναι τὴν φύσιν, ἀλλ' ἐνεῖναί τι καὶ ἕτερον, καθὸ φθαρτά, ὥστε ἄν τι θάτερον πράττῃ, τοῦτο τῇ ἑτέρᾳ φύσει παρὰ φύσιν, ὅταν δ' ἰσάζῃ, οὔτε λυπηρὸν δοκεῖ οὔθ' ἡδὺ τὸ πραττόμενον. ἐπεὶ εἴ του ἡ φύσις ἁπλῆ εἴη, ἀεὶ ἡ αὐτὴ πρᾶξις ἡδίστη ἔσται. διὸ ὁ θεὸς ἀεὶ μίαν καὶ ἁπλῆν χαίρει ἡδονήν· οὐ γὰρ μόνον κινήσεώς ἐστιν ἐνέργεια ἀλλὰ καὶ ἀκινησίας, καὶ ἡδονὴ μᾶλλον ἐν ἠρεμίᾳ ἐστὶν ἢ ἐν κινήσει. μεταβολὴ δὲ πάντων γλυκύτατον, κατὰ τὸν ποιητήν, διὰ πονηρίαν τινά· ὥσπερ γὰρ ἄνθρωπος εὐμετάβολος ὁ πονηρός, καὶ ἡ φύσις ἡ δεομένη μεταβολῆς· οὐ γὰρ ἁπλῆ οὐδ' ἐπιεικής.

Περὶ μὲν οὖν ἐγκρατείας καὶ ἀκρασίας καὶ περὶ ἡδονῆς 9

By the accidental pleasures, I mean such as are of the nature of a remedy. Because, when it happens that we are relieved, owing to some operation of that part in us which continues sound, the result is a sensation of pleasure. By the natural pleasures, I mean those which produce the action of any given nature. The same thing is never continuously pleasant to us, because our nature is not simple, but there is in us a second element, by reason of which we are destructible. Thus, when the one element is in action, it thwarts the tendencies of the second element. And when the two elements are balanced, the result appears neither painful nor pleasant. If there is any being whose nature is simple, the same mode of action will be continuously and in the highest degree pleasurable to him. Hence God enjoys everlastingly one pure pleasure. For there is a function not only of motion, but of rest; and pleasure consists rather in tranquillity than in motion. "Change," as the poet says, "is the sweetest of all things," on account of a certain fault in our nature. The bad man is fond of change, and of the same character is the nature which requires change; it is not simple or good.' In the above passage we see a reproduction, and to some extent a carrying out, of Aristotle's doctrines in the tenth Book of the *Ethics*, cf. especially ch. iv. 9: *πῶς οὖν οὐδεὶς συνεχῶς ἥδεται; ἢ κάμνει; πάντα γὰρ τὰ ἀνθρώπεια ἀδυνατεῖ συνεχῶς ἐνεργεῖν.* On the comparison between the compound nature of man and the purely divine nature of God, *cf.* ch. vii. 8: *ὁ δὲ τοιοῦτος ἂν εἴη βίος κρείττων ἢ κατ' ἄνθρωπον· οὐ γὰρ ᾗ ἄνθρωπός ἐστιν οὕτω βιώσεται, ἀλλ' ᾗ θεῖόν τι ἐν αὐτῷ ὑπάρχει· ὅσῳ δὲ διαφέρει τοῦτο τοῦ συνθέτου, τοσούτῳ καὶ ἡ ἐνέργεια τῆς κατὰ τὴν ἄλλην ἀρετήν.*

καὶ λύπης εἴρηται, καὶ τί ἕκαστον καὶ πῶς τὰ μὲν ἀγαθὰ αὐτῶν ἐστὶ τὰ δὲ κακά· λοιπὸν δὲ καὶ περὶ φιλίας ἐροῦμεν.

It is to be remarked that the present Book, which commences with a mention of *θεία ἀρετή*, or the operation of reason unalloyed by passion, ends with a mention of *θεία ἡδονή*, which is the consciousness of the same.

λοιπὸν—ἐροῦμεν] These words which are perfectly suitable to the *Eudemian Ethics*, to which this book originally belonged, have caused, by their occurrence here, an obvious literary confusion in the *Nicomachean* treatise. See Vol. I. Essay I. p. 58.

PLAN OF BOOKS VIII.—IX.

ARISTOTLE'S treatise on Friendship, here contained, is quite continuous. The division of it into two books is merely artificial. There is really no break between the end of Book VIII. and the beginning of Book IX. The words περὶ μὲν οὖν τούτων ἐπὶ τοσοῦτον εἰρήσθω (VIII. xiv. 4) have been introduced, whether by the Author's, or by an Editor's, hand, to create a division and to constitute two books conformable in length to the other books of the *Ethics*.

The use of the phrase ἐν ἀρχῇ (VIII. ix. 1, VIII. xiii. 1, IX. iii. 1), in reference to the earlier chapters of Book VIII., has led some persons to suppose that this was originally an independent treatise. But nothing is more clear than that it was written to form a part of Aristotle's work on Ethics. Besides general expressions of the author's purpose to confine himself to an ethical point of view (see VIII. i. 7, IX. ii. 2), we find direct quotations of, or references to, the first books of the *Nicomachean Ethics*. (Compare IX. ix. 5 with *Eth. Nic.* I. vii. 14; and I. viii. 13, and IX. iv. 2, with *Eth. Nic.* III. iv. 5.)

The present treatise has a close connection with the first three books of the *Nicomachean Ethics*. But it is remarkable that it has no connection with Books V., VI., VII. Friendship is here treated in relation to Happiness and in relation to Justice. What is said of Happiness forms the complement to *Eth. Nic.* Book I., but what is said of Justice has no reference to *Eth. Nic.* Book V.; rather it appears written tentatively, probably before the *Politics* of Aristotle, from which the theories of *Eth. Nic.* Book V. seem to have been derived. (See VIII. vi. 6, VIII. vii. 2—3, VIII. ix., x., IX. i. 1—2.)

Again, it is equally striking that there is no reference to Book VII. in the parts of this treatise where the phenomena of vice are discussed (see IX. iv. 8—9, IX. viii. 6). Indeed the views taken here are inconsistent with those of Book VII., which contain a more rigid analysis. (Compare IX. iv. 8 with VII. viii. 1.)

The style of these two Books is certainly unlike that of Books V., VI., VII., while it bears a close similarity with that of *Eth. Nic.* I. and X. Not one of the 'Eudemian' forms of expression is to be found here.

The treatise on Friendship may be roughly divided into three parts:—

I. On the different kinds of Friendship, and on the nature of the highest and truest type, VIII. i.—viii.

II. On the connection of Friendship with Justice, (1) as arising (with certain exceptions, see c. xii.) out of political relationships, or coinciding with them; (2) as implying obligations to be repaid. VIII. ix.—IX. iii.

III. On other questions connected with the nature of Friendship, and especially on its relation to Happiness. IX. iv.—xii.

Though the treatise is continuous, yet it is easy to see that the writer's views became deeper and more definite as he advanced. (Thus compare IX. vi. with VIII. i. 4; IX. x. with VIII. i. 5; and VIII. vi. 2—3, VIII. viii. 7 with VIII. i. 6.)

At the same time we see what a powerful instrument was the Aristotelian analysis for producing clearness of view. By an analysis of the objects of liking (*τὸ φιλητόν*, VIII. ii. 1), Aristotle clears away all the vagueness which the *Lysis* of Plato had left around the nature of Friendship. By an application of his own philosophical form *ἐνέργεια* (IX. vii. 4—6, IX. ix. 5—6, IX. xii. 1), he obtains a profound theory of the operation of the highest kind of Friendship in relation to human happiness.

In these Books there is no allusion to the sentimental relationship, in vogue among the Dorians from the earliest ages, between a warrior and his squire (the *εἰσπνήλης* and *ἀΐτης*, or 'inbreather' and 'listener'). All here is broadly human. And yet the idea of 'Friendship' is purely Greek. The Romans imitated it. But in modern times it has been much superseded by the idea of sympathetic marriage. Christianity ignores Friendship; and theoretically it now exists only as a temporary advantage for the young.

ΗΘΙΚΩΝ ΝΙΚΟΜΑΧΕΙΩΝ VIII.

ΜΕΤΑ δὲ ταῦτα περὶ φιλίας ἕποιτ' ἂν διελθεῖν· ἔστι
γὰρ ἀρετή τις ἢ μετ' ἀρετῆς, ἔτι δ' ἀναγκαιότατον
εἰς τὸν βίον· ἄνευ γὰρ φίλων οὐδεὶς ἕλοιτ' ἂν ζῆν, ἔχων τὰ
λοιπὰ ἀγαθὰ πάντα· καὶ γὰρ πλουτοῦσι καὶ ἀρχὰς καὶ
δυναστείας κεκτημένοις δοκεῖ φίλων μάλιστ' εἶναι χρεία·
τί γὰρ ὄφελος τῆς τοιαύτης εὐετηρίας ἀφαιρεθείσης εὐεργεσίας, ἣ γίγνεται μάλιστα καὶ ἐπαινετωτάτη πρὸς
φίλους; ἢ πῶς ἂν τηρηθείη καὶ σῴζοιτ' ἄνευ φίλων;
ὅσῳ γὰρ πλείων, τοσούτῳ ἐπισφαλεστέρα. ἐν πενίᾳ τε 2
καὶ ταῖς λοιπαῖς δυστυχίαις μόνην οἴονται καταφυγὴν
εἶναι τοὺς φίλους. καὶ νέοις δὲ πρὸς τὸ ἀναμάρτητον καὶ
πρεσβυτέροις πρὸς θεραπείαν καὶ τὸ ἐλλεῖπον τῆς πράξεως
δι' ἀσθένειαν βοηθεῖ, τοῖς τ' ἐν ἀκμῇ πρὸς τὰς καλὰς
πράξεις·

σύν τε δύ' ἐρχομένω·

I. The discussion of Friendship is justified here (analogously to the way in which the discussion of the voluntary is justified, *Eth.* III. i. 1—2) *first*, on the ground of its connection with virtue, *secondly*, on the ground that it is a means to happiness (*ἀναγκαιότατον*) in all conditions of life. As a commencement of the discussion, Aristotle mentions the difficulties raised on the subject in the *Lysis* of Plato: Does friendship depend on similarity or on contrast? Can bad men be friends to each other? and he adds another: Is there only one species of friendship, or are there more? Aristotle by his own analysis of the likeable (τὸ φιλητόν) immediately cuts straight through these difficulties.

1 *ἀρετή τις ἢ μετ' ἀρετῆς*] We have here no reference to that harmonious manner in society, the mean between flattery and moroseness, which is included in the list of the virtues (*Eth.* II. vii. 13) under the name of φιλία, but is afterwards said to be nameless (*Eth.* IV. vi. 4) and to be devoid of the feeling of affection.

τί γὰρ ὄφελος—φίλους] 'For what is the use of that sort of abundance, if one is deprived of the power of doing good, which is exercised most especially, and in its most praiseworthy form, towards friends?'

2 *σύν τε δύ' ἐρχομένω*] The saying of Diomede when about to penetrate the Trojan camp, *Il.* x. 224:

3 καὶ γὰρ νοῆσαι καὶ πρᾶξαι δυνατώτεροι. φύσει τ' ἐνυπάρχειν ἔοικε πρὸς τὸ γεγεννημένον τῷ γεννήσαντι καὶ πρὸς τὸ γεννῆσαν τῷ γεννηθέντι, οὐ μόνον ἐν ἀνθρώποις ἀλλὰ καὶ ἐν ὄρνισι καὶ τοῖς πλείστοις τῶν ζῴων, καὶ τοῖς ὁμοεθνέσι πρὸς ἄλληλα, καὶ μάλιστα τοῖς ἀνθρώποις, ὅθεν τοὺς φιλανθρώπους ἐπαινοῦμεν. ἴδοι δ' ἄν τις καὶ ἐν ταῖς πλάναις ὡς οἰκεῖον ἅπας ἄνθρωπος ἀνθρώπῳ καὶ
4 φίλον. ἔοικε δὲ καὶ τὰς πόλεις συνέχειν ἡ φιλία, καὶ οἱ νομοθέται μᾶλλον περὶ αὐτὴν σπουδάζειν ἢ τὴν δικαιοσύνην· ἡ γὰρ ὁμόνοια ὅμοιόν τι τῇ φιλίᾳ ἔοικεν εἶναι, ταύτης δὲ μάλιστ' ἐφίενται καὶ τὴν στάσιν ἔχθραν οὖσαν μάλιστα ἐξελαύνουσιν. καὶ φίλων μὲν ὄντων οὐδὲν δεῖ δικαιοσύνης, δίκαιοι δ' ὄντες προσδέονται φιλίας, καὶ τῶν δικαίων τὸ
5 μάλιστα φιλικὸν εἶναι δοκεῖ. οὐ μόνον δ' ἀναγκαῖόν ἐστιν ἀλλὰ καὶ καλόν· τοὺς γὰρ φιλοφίλους ἐπαινοῦμεν, ἥ τε πολυφιλία δοκεῖ τῶν καλῶν ἕν τι εἶναι, καὶ ἔνιοι τοὺς αὐτοὺς οἴονται ἄνδρας ἀγαθοὺς εἶναι καὶ φίλους.

6 Διαμφισβητεῖται δὲ περὶ αὐτῆς οὐκ ὀλίγα. οἱ μὲν

σύν τε δύ' ἐρχομένω, καί τε πρὸ ὃ τοῦ ἐνόησεν,
ὅππως κέρδος ἔῃ· μοῦνος δ' εἴπερ τε νοήσῃ,
ἀλλά τέ οἱ βράσσων τε νόος, λεπτὴ δέ τε μῆτις.

The words here quoted had become proverbial. Cf. Plato, *Alcib.* II. 140 A; *Protag.* 348 C.

3 τοῖς ὁμοεθνέσι] This word is applied here to brutes as well as men. In the same sense ὁμογενέσιν is used, *Eth. Eud.* VII. v. 3, and συγγενῆ, Ar. *Rhet.* I. xi. 25.

ἴδοι δ' ἄν τις φίλον] 'And in travelling too one may see how near and dear every man is to man,' *i.e.* one may see this both as a matter of general observation, and as oneself meeting with kindness and hospitality.

4 καὶ οἱ νομοθέται] Cf. the speech of Lysias in Plato's *Phædrus.*

καὶ τῶν δικαίων—δοκεῖ] 'And the height of justice appears to be of the nature of friendship.' Under the words τῶν δικαίων τὸ μάλιστα equity (τὸ ἐπιεικές) appears to be meant. Cf. *Eth.* V. x. 6—8.

5 ἀλλὰ καὶ καλόν] This is repeating in other words that friendship is ἀρετή τις. The distinction between ἀναγκαῖον and καλόν is common in Aristotle, and the one term suggests the other. Cf. *Eth.* IX. xi. 1.

ἥ τε πολυφιλία δοκεῖ] 'To have many friends is commonly thought to be something beautiful.' This popular opinion is considerably qualified on further examination; cf. *Eth.* IX. x. 6.

καὶ ἔνιοι—φίλους] 'And some think that the term "good friend" is convertible with that of "good man."' Cf. a similar form of expression, *Eth.* V. ii. 11: οὐ γὰρ ἴσως ταὐτὸν ἀνδρί τ' ἀγαθῷ εἶναι καὶ πολίτῃ παντί.

6 διαμφισβητεῖται] The questions mentioned here are raised in the *Lysis*

γὰρ ὁμοιότητά τινα τιθέασιν αὐτὴν καὶ τοὺς ὁμοίους φίλους, ὅθεν τὸν ὅμοιόν φασιν ὡς τὸν ὅμοιον, καὶ κολοιὸν ποτὶ κολοιόν, καὶ ὅσα τοιαῦτα· οἱ δ' ἐξ ἐναντίας κεραμεῖς πάντας τοὺς τοιούτους ἀλλήλοις φασὶν εἶναι. καὶ περὶ αὐτῶν τούτων ἀνώτερον ἐπιζητοῦσι καὶ φυσικώτερον, Εὐριπίδης μὲν φάσκων ἐρᾶν μὲν ὄμβρου γαῖαν ξηρανθεῖσαν, ἐρᾶν δὲ σεμνὸν οὐρανὸν πληρούμενον ὄμβρου πεσεῖν ἐς γαῖαν, καὶ Ἡράκλειτος τὸ ἀντίξουν συμφέρον καὶ ἐκ τῶν διαφερόντων καλλίστην ἁρμονίαν καὶ πάντα κατ' ἔριν γίνεσθαι· ἐξ ἐναντίας δὲ τούτοις ἄλλοι τε καὶ Ἐμπεδοκλῆς· τὸ γὰρ ὅμοιον τοῦ ὁμοίου ἐφίεσθαι. τὰ μὲν οὖν 7
φυσικὰ τῶν ἀπορημάτων ἀφείσθω (οὐ γὰρ οἰκεῖα τῆς παρούσης σκέψεως)· ὅσα δ' ἐστὶν ἀνθρωπικὰ καὶ ἀνήκει εἰς τὰ ἤθη καὶ τὰ πάθη, ταῦτ' ἐπισκεψώμεθα, οἷον πότερον ἐν πᾶσι γίνεται φιλία ἢ οὐχ οἷόν τε μοχθηροὺς

---

of Plato, pp. 214–215. (214 A) λέγουσι δέ (οἱ ποιηταί) πως ταῦτα, ὡς ἐγᾦμαι, ὡδί·

αἰεί τοι τὸν ὁμοῖον ἄγει θεὸς ὡς τὸν ὁμοῖον

καὶ ποιεῖ γνώριμον . . . οὐκοῦν καὶ τοῖς τῶν σοφωτάτων συγγράμμασιν ἐντετύχηκας ταῦτ' αὐτὰ λέγουσιν, ὅτι τὸ ὅμοιον τῷ ὁμοίῳ ἀνάγκη ἀεὶ φίλον εἶναι; εἰσὶ δέ που οὗτοι οἱ περὶ φύσεώς τε καὶ τοῦ ὅλου διαλεγόμενοι καὶ γράφοντες. ἀληθῆ, ἔφη, λέγεις . . . (215 C) Ἤδη ποτέ του ἤκουσα λέγοντος, καὶ ἄρτι ἀναμιμνήσκομαι, ὅτι τὸ μὲν ὅμοιον τῷ ὁμοίῳ καὶ οἱ ἀγαθοὶ τοῖς ἀγαθοῖς πολεμιώτατοι εἶεν· καὶ δὴ καὶ τὸν Ἡσίοδον ἐπήγετο μάρτυρα, λέγων ὡς ἄρα

καὶ κεραμεὺς κεραμεῖ κοτέει καὶ ἀοιδὸς ἀοιδῷ
καὶ πτωχὸς πτωχῷ.

καὶ τἆλλα δὴ πάντα οὕτως ἔφη ἀναγκαῖον εἶναι μάλιστα τὰ ὁμοιότατα πρὸς ἄλληλα φθόνου τε καὶ φιλονεικίας καὶ ἔχθρας ἐμπίπλασθαι, τὰ δ' ἀνομοιότατα φιλίας . . . τὸ γὰρ ἐναντιώτατον τῷ ἐναντιωτάτῳ εἶναι μάλιστα φίλον. ἐπιθυμεῖν γὰρ τοῦ τοιούτου ἕκαστον, ἀλλ' οὐ τοῦ ὁμοίου· τὸ μὲν γὰρ ξηρὸν ὑγροῦ, τὸ δὲ ψυχρὸν θερμοῦ, τὸ δὲ πικρὸν γλυκέος, τὸ δὲ ὀξὺ ἀμβλέος, τὸ δὲ κενὸν πληρώσεως, καὶ τὸ πλῆρες δὲ κενώσεως. Which of the two views is true, is not decided in the *Lysis*, where however it is laid down that friendship cannot consist in pure contrariety.

καὶ περὶ αὐτῶν—φυσικώτερον] 'And about these very questions some inquire more deeply and physically,' *i.e.* not limiting their view to the phenomena of friendship itself, but bringing in the analogies of the whole of nature. Aristotle sets aside such speculations as not belonging to ethics; he remarks parenthetically below (*Eth.* VIII. viii. 7), that the contrary in nature does not desire its extreme contrary, but the mean.

Εὐριπίδης] The verses occur in a fragment of an uncertain play, which is preserved by Athenæus, XIII. p. 599.

τὸ ἀντίξουν συμφέρον] 'The opposing conduces,' a play on words characteristic of the oracular style of Heraclitus.

ἢ οὐχ οἷόν τε μοχθηροὺς ὄντας]

ὄντας φίλους εἶναι, καὶ πότερον ἓν εἶδος τῆς φιλίας ἐστὶν
ἢ πλείω. οἱ μὲν γὰρ ἓν οἰόμενοι, ὅτι ἐπιδέχεται τὸ
μᾶλλον καὶ τὸ ἧττον, οὐχ ἱκανῷ πεπιστεύκασι σημείῳ·
δέχεται γὰρ τὸ μᾶλλον καὶ τὸ ἧττον καὶ τὰ ἕτερα τῷ
εἴδει. †εἴρηται δ' ὑπὲρ αὐτῶν ἔμπροσθεν.

2 Τάχα δ' ἂν γένοιτο περὶ αὐτῶν φανερὸν γνωρισθέντος
τοῦ φιλητοῦ· δοκεῖ γὰρ οὐ πᾶν φιλεῖσθαι ἀλλὰ τὸ φιλητόν, τοῦτο δ' εἶναι ἀγαθὸν ἢ ἡδὺ ἢ χρήσιμον. δόξειε δ' ἂν
χρήσιμον εἶναι δι' οὗ γίνεται ἀγαθόν τι ἢ ἡδονή, ὥστε
2 φιλητὰ ἂν εἴη τἀγαθόν τε καὶ τὸ ἡδὺ ὡς τέλη. πότερον
οὖν τἀγαθὸν φιλοῦσιν ἢ τὸ αὐτοῖς ἀγαθόν; διαφωνεῖ γὰρ
ἐνίοτε ταῦτα. ὁμοίως δὲ καὶ περὶ τὸ ἡδύ. δοκεῖ δὲ τὸ
αὑτῷ ἀγαθὸν φιλεῖν ἕκαστος, καὶ εἶναι ἁπλῶς μὲν τἀγαθὸν φιλητόν, ἑκάστῳ δὲ τὸ ἑκάστῳ. φιλεῖ δ' ἕκαστος οὐ
τὸ ὂν αὑτῷ ἀγαθὸν ἀλλὰ τὸ φαινόμενον. διοίσει δ' οὐδέν·
3 ἔσται γὰρ τὸ φιλητὸν φαινόμενον. τριῶν δ' ὄντων δι' ἃ

This question is started in the *Lysis*, p. 214 D: *τοῦτο τοίνυν αἰνίττονται, ὡς ἐμοὶ δοκοῦσιν, ὦ ἑταῖρε, οἱ τὸ ὅμοιον τῷ ὁμοίῳ φίλον λέγοντες, ὡς ὁ ἀγαθὸς τῷ ἀγαθῷ μόνος μόνῳ φίλος, ὁ δὲ κακὸς οὔτ' ἀγαθῷ οὔτε κακῷ οὐδέποτε εἰς ἀληθῆ φιλίαν ἔρχεται.*

οἱ μὲν γὰρ ἓν οἰόμενοι κ.τ.λ.] 'For they who think that there is only one species of friendship, because it admits of degrees, trust to an insufficient proof. For things also that differ in species admit of degrees. But we have spoken about them before.' Aristotle immediately proceeds to show that there are three distinct species of friendship, in accordance with the three objects of liking. He also says that the friendships for pleasure or profit are *less* friendships than that for the good (*ἧττόν εἰσιν*, VIII. vi. 7). All three kinds admit of the idea (*λόγος*) of friendship, thus they agree in genus and are comparable in point of degree. Cf. Ar. *Categ.* viii. 36: *ἁπλῶς δέ, ἐὰν μὴ ἐπιδέχηται ἀμφότερα τὸν τοῦ προσκειμένου λόγον, οὐ ῥηθήσεται τὸ ἕτερον τοῦ ἑτέρου μᾶλλον.* As there is no place in the *Ethics* where Aristotle has discussed this logical question before, a Scholiast says with regard to the last words of the paragraph: *ἔοικε δὲ εἰρῆσθαι ἐν τοῖς ἐκπεπτωκόσι τῶν Νικομαχείων.* But most probably the words *εἴρηται δ' ὑπὲρ αὐτῶν* are the interpolation of a copyist, who was perhaps thinking vaguely of *Eth.* II. viii. 5, to which the commentators generally refer. These words spoil the grammar of the sentence, as *περὶ αὐτῶν* is used in the next line with a different reference.

II. 2 *πότερον οὖν—αὐτοῖς ἀγαθόν*] Aristotle here guards himself against the appearance of having admitted the Platonic theory, that the absolute good is always the object of human desire. Cf. *Eth.* III. iv. 1, and note.

ἔσται γὰρ—φαινόμενον] 'For in that case the object of liking will be an apparent and not an absolute object.'

φιλοῦσιν, ἐπὶ μὲν τῇ τῶν ἀψύχων φιλήσει οὐ λέγεται φιλία· οὐ γάρ ἐστιν ἀντιφίλησις, οὐδὲ βούλησις ἐκείνων ἀγαθοῦ· γελοῖον γὰρ ἴσως τῷ οἴνῳ βούλεσθαι τἀγαθά· ἀλλ' εἴπερ, σώζεσθαι βούλεται αὐτόν, ἵνα αὐτὸς ἔχῃ. τῷ δὲ φίλῳ φασὶ δεῖν βούλεσθαι τἀγαθὰ ἐκείνου ἕνεκα. τοὺς δὲ βουλομένους οὕτω τἀγαθὰ εὔνους λέγουσιν, ἐὰν μὴ ταὐτὸ καὶ παρ' ἐκείνου γίγνηται· εὔνοιαν γὰρ ἐν ἀντιπεπονθόσι φιλίαν εἶναι. ἢ προσθετέον μὴ λανθάνουσαν· 4
πολλοὶ γάρ εἰσιν εὖνοι οἷς οὐχ ἑωράκασιν, ὑπολαμβάνουσι δὲ ἐπιεικεῖς εἶναι ἢ χρησίμους· τοῦτο δὲ ταὐτὸν κἂν ἐκείνων τις πάθοι πρὸς τοῦτον. εὖνοι μὲν οὖν οὗτοι φαίνονται ἀλλήλοις· φίλους δὲ πῶς ἄν τις εἴποι λανθάνοντας ὡς ἔχουσιν ἑαυτοῖς; δεῖ ἄρα εὐνοεῖν ἀλλήλοις καὶ βούλεσθαι τἀγαθὰ μὴ λανθάνοντας δι' ἕν τι τῶν εἰρημένων.

Διαφέρει δὲ ταῦτα ἀλλήλων εἴδει· καὶ αἱ φιλήσεις ἄρα 3
καὶ αἱ φιλίαι. τρία δὴ τὰ τῆς φιλίας εἴδη, ἰσάριθμα τοῖς φιλητοῖς· καθ' ἕκαστον γάρ ἐστιν ἀντιφίλησις οὐ λανθάνουσα. οἱ δὲ φιλοῦντες ἀλλήλους βούλονται τἀγαθὰ ἀλλήλοις ταύτῃ ᾗ φιλοῦσιν. οἱ μὲν οὖν διὰ τὸ χρήσιμον φιλοῦντες ἀλλήλους οὐ καθ' αὑτοὺς φιλοῦσιν, ἀλλ' ᾗ γίγνεταί τι αὐτοῖς παρ' ἀλλήλων ἀγαθόν. ὁμοίως δὲ καὶ οἱ δι' ἡδονήν· οὐ γὰρ τῷ ποιούς τινας εἶναι ἀγαπῶσι τοὺς εὐτραπέλους, ἀλλ' ὅτι ἡδεῖς αὐτοῖς. οἵ τε δὴ διὰ τὸ χρήσιμον 2
φιλοῦντες διὰ τὸ αὐτοῖς ἀγαθὸν στέργουσι, καὶ οἱ δι' ἡδονὴν

---

3 *τῇ τῶν ἀψύχων*] Suggested by the *Lysis* of Plato, p. 212 D, where οἶνος is mentioned as an object of liking: *οὐδ' ἄρα φίλιπποί εἰσιν, οὓς ἂν οἱ ἵπποι μὴ ἀντιφιλῶσιν, οὐδὲ φιλόρτυγες, οὐδ' αὖ φιλόκυνές γε καὶ φίλοινοι κ.τ.λ.*

4 *ἢ—τοῦτον*] 'Or must we add the proviso that (this good feeling) must not be unknown? For many are kindly disposed to men whom they have never seen, but whom they suppose to be good or useful, and one of these latter might reciprocate the same feeling.' *τοῦτον*, being substituted for the plural *πολλοί*, gives definiteness. Cf. IX. i. 4: *τούτοις καὶ προσέχει, κἀκείνου γε χάριν ταῦτα δώσει.*

III. 1 *ταύτῃ ᾗ φιλοῦσιν*] 'According to the particular mode of their friendship.' The differences of mode are specified afterwards.

οὐ καθ' αὑτοὺς φιλοῦσιν] 'Do not love each other for their very selves.' This phrase *καθ' αὑτοὺς* is rather a logical formula than an ordinary grammatical combination. It seems to have arisen from *καθ' αὑτό*, 'the absolute.' Cf. VIII. iii. 7, and the use of *δι' αὑτούς*, VIII. iv. 6, IX. i. 7.

διὰ τὸ αὑτοῖς ἡδύ, καὶ οὐχ ᾗ ὁ φιλούμενός ἐστιν, ἀλλ' ᾗ χρήσιμος ἢ ἡδύς. κατὰ συμβεβηκός τε δὴ αἱ φιλίαι αὗταί εἰσιν· οὐ γὰρ ᾗ ἐστὶν ὅσπερ ἐστὶν ὁ φιλούμενος, ταύτῃ φιλεῖται, ἀλλ' ᾗ πορίζουσιν οἱ μὲν ἀγαθόν τι οἱ δ' ἡδονήν.
3 εὐδιάλυτοι δὴ αἱ τοιαῦταί εἰσι, μὴ διαμενόντων αὐτῶν ὁμοίων· ἐὰν γὰρ μηκέτι ἡδεῖς ἢ χρήσιμοι ὦσι, παύονται φιλοῦντες. τὸ δὲ χρήσιμον οὐ διαμένει, ἀλλ' ἄλλοτε ἄλλο γίγνεται. ἀπολυθέντος οὖν δι' ὃ φίλοι ἦσαν, διαλύεται
4 καὶ ἡ φιλία, ὡς οὔσης τῆς φιλίας πρὸς ἐκεῖνα. μάλιστα δ' ἐν τοῖς πρεσβύταις ἡ τοιαύτη δοκεῖ φιλία γίνεσθαι (οὐ γὰρ τὸ ἡδὺ οἱ τηλικοῦτοι διώκουσιν ἀλλὰ τὸ ὠφέλιμον), καὶ τῶν ἐν ἀκμῇ καὶ νέων ὅσοι τὸ συμφέρον διώκουσιν. οὐ πάνυ δ' οἱ τοιοῦτοι οὐδὲ συζῶσι μετ' ἀλλήλων· ἐνίοτε γὰρ οὐδ' εἰσὶν ἡδεῖς· οὐδὲ δὴ προσδέονται τῆς τοιαύτης ὁμιλίας, ἐὰν μὴ ὠφέλιμοι ὦσιν· ἐπὶ τοσοῦτον γάρ εἰσιν ἡδεῖς ἐφ' ὅσον ἐλπίδας ἔχουσιν ἀγαθοῦ. εἰς ταύτας δὲ καὶ τὴν ξενικὴν
5 τιθέασιν. ἡ δὲ τῶν νέων φιλία δι' ἡδονὴν εἶναι δοκεῖ· κατὰ πάθος γὰρ οὗτοι ζῶσι, καὶ μάλιστα διώκουσι τὸ ἡδὺ αὑτοῖς καὶ τὸ παρόν· τῆς ἡλικίας δὲ μεταπιπτούσης καὶ τὰ ἡδέα γίνεται ἕτερα. διὸ ταχέως γίγνονται φίλοι καὶ παύονται· ἅμα γὰρ τῷ ἡδεῖ ἡ φιλία μεταπίπτει, τῆς δὲ τοιαύτης ἡδονῆς ταχεῖα ἡ μεταβολή. καὶ ἐρωτικοὶ δ' οἱ νέοι· κατὰ πάθος γὰρ καὶ δι' ἡδονὴν τὸ πολὺ τῆς ἐρωτικῆς· διόπερ φιλοῦσι καὶ ταχέως παύονται, πολλάκις τῆς αὐτῆς ἡμέρας μεταπίπτοντες. συνημερεύειν δὲ καὶ συζῆν οὗτοι βούλονται· γίνεται γὰρ αὐτοῖς τὸ κατὰ φιλίαν οὕτως.

6 Τελεία δ' ἐστὶν ἡ τῶν ἀγαθῶν φιλία καὶ κατ' ἀρετὴν ὁμοίων· οὗτοι γὰρ τἀγαθὰ ὁμοίως βούλονται ἀλλήλοις ᾗ ἀγαθοί· ἀγαθοὶ δ' εἰσὶ καθ' αὑτούς. οἱ δὲ βουλόμενοι τἀγαθὰ τοῖς φίλοις ἐκείνων ἕνεκα μάλιστα φίλοι· δι' αὑτοὺς γὰρ οὕτως ἔχουσι, καὶ οὐ κατὰ συμβεβηκός·

---

2 καὶ οὐχ ᾗ ὁ φιλούμενός ἐστιν, ἀλλ' ᾗ χρήσιμος ἢ ἡδύς] The reading surely should be ὁ φιλούμενος ἔστιν, 'not by reason of the existence of the person who is loved, but by reason of his being useful or pleasant.' The personal existence of the friend is, according to Aristotle, the chief blessing of friendship. Cf. IX. ix. 10: εἰ δὴ τῷ μακαρίῳ τὸ εἶναι αἱρετόν ἐστι καθ' αὑτό, ἀγαθὸν τῇ φύσει ὂν καὶ ἡδύ, παραπλήσιον δὲ καὶ τὸ τοῦ φίλου ἐστίν, καὶ ὁ φίλος τῶν αἱρετῶν ἂν εἴη.

διαμένει οὖν ἡ τούτων φιλία ἕως ἂν ἀγαθοὶ ὦσιν, ἡ δ' ἀρετὴ μόνιμον. καὶ ἔστιν ἑκάτερος ἁπλῶς ἀγαθὸς καὶ τῷ φίλῳ· οἱ γὰρ ἀγαθοὶ καὶ ἁπλῶς ἀγαθοὶ καὶ ἀλλήλοις ὠφέλιμοι. ὁμοίως δὲ καὶ ἡδεῖς· καὶ γὰρ ἁπλῶς οἱ ἀγαθοὶ ἡδεῖς καὶ ἀλλήλοις· ἑκάστῳ γὰρ καθ' ἡδονήν εἰσιν αἱ οἰκεῖαι πράξεις καὶ αἱ τοιαῦται, τῶν ἀγαθῶν δὲ αἱ αὐταὶ ἢ ὅμοιαι. ἡ τοιαύτη δὲ φιλία μόνιμος εὐλόγως
ἐστίν· συνάπτει γὰρ ἐν αὐτῇ πάνθ' ὅσα τοῖς φίλοις δεῖ 7
ὑπάρχειν. πᾶσα γὰρ φιλία δι' ἀγαθόν ἐστιν ἢ δι' ἡδονήν, ἢ ἁπλῶς ἢ τῷ φιλοῦντι, καὶ καθ' ὁμοιότητά τινα· ταύτῃ δὲ πάνθ' ὑπάρχει τὰ εἰρημένα καθ' αὑτούς· ταύτῃ γὰρ ὅμοια καὶ τὰ λοιπά, τό τε ἁπλῶς ἀγαθὸν καὶ ἡδὺ ἁπλῶς ἐστίν, μάλιστα δὲ ταῦτα φιλητά, καὶ τὸ φιλεῖν δὲ καὶ ἡ φιλία
ἐν τούτοις μάλιστα καὶ ἀρίστη. σπανίας δ' εἰκὸς τὰς 8
τοιαύτας εἶναι· ὀλίγοι γὰρ οἱ τοιοῦτοι. ἔτι δὲ προσδεῖται χρόνου καὶ συνηθείας· κατὰ τὴν παροιμίαν γὰρ οὐκ ἔστιν

---

6 ἑκάστῳ γὰρ—ὅμοιαι] 'For to every man his own actions and those similar to them are pleasurable, and the actions of the good are (to the good) identical (with their own actions) or similar.' The friend being *alter ego*, the delight of friendship is that it gives an increased sense of existence.

7 συνάπτει] Neuter, as in VIII. iv. 5: *οὐ πάνυ δ' αὗται συνάπτουσιν.*

πᾶσα γὰρ—τινα] 'For every friendship is for good or for pleasure; either absolute, or else relative to him who feels the friendship, and only bearing a certain resemblance to the absolutely good or pleasurable.' The comma should surely be omitted after τῷ φιλοῦντι. Aristotle is not here saying (as the commentators fancy) that every friendship implies similarity, but that every friendship, whether the genuine type or one of the secondary and reflected species, aims at either good or pleasure. This is made clear by the next chapter, § 4: πρώτως μὲν καὶ κυρίως τὴν τῶν ἀγαθῶν ᾗ ἀγαθοί, τὰς δὲ λοιπὰς καθ' ὁμοιότητα.

ταύτῃ δὲ—τὰ λοιπά] 'But this friendship has all the specified qualities essentially belonging to the persons who feel it (καθ' αὑτούς)—(I say essentially) for even the other kinds of friendship are resemblances of this (the perfect kind).' This passage has vexed the commentators. Zell thinks that ὅμοια may be referred to καθ' ὁμοιότητά τινα in the previous sentence (which he mistakes), and explains, 'In this kind of friendship there is similarity and all the other requisite qualities.' But we surely then should have expected τὰ ὅμοια. Cardwell, following Giphanius, Zwinger, and the Scholiast, reads ταύτῃ γὰρ ὅμοιοι καὶ τὰ λοιπά. 'In this kind of friendship, men are similar, *et cetera*.' Stahr doubts the genuineness of the entire section. The common reading, as above explained, seems borne out by the opening of the next chapter, ἡ δὲ διὰ τὸ ἡδὺ ὁμοίωμα ταύτης ἔχει. Cf. VIII. vi. 7. Ὅμοια here is in opposition to ταύτῃ—καθ' αὑτούς.

εἰδῆσαι ἀλλήλους πρὶν τοὺς λεγομένους ἅλας συναναλῶσαι· οὐδ' ἀποδέξασθαι δὴ πρότερον οὐδ' εἶναι φίλους, πρὶν ἂν
9 ἑκάτερος ἑκατέρῳ φανῇ φιλητὸς καὶ πιστευθῇ. οἱ δὲ ταχέως τὰ φιλικὰ πρὸς ἀλλήλους ποιοῦντες βούλονται μὲν φίλοι εἶναι, οὐκ εἰσὶ δέ, εἰ μὴ καὶ φιλητοί, καὶ τοῦτ' ἴσασιν· βούλησις μὲν γὰρ ταχεῖα φιλίας γίνεται, φιλία δ' οὔ. αὕτη μὲν οὖν καὶ κατὰ τὸν χρόνον καὶ κατὰ τὰ λοιπὰ τελεία ἐστί, καὶ κατὰ πάντα ταὐτὰ γίνεται καὶ ὅμοια ἑκατέρῳ παρ' ἑκατέρου, ὅπερ δεῖ τοῖς φίλοις ὑπάρχειν·

4 Ἡ δὲ διὰ τὸ ἡδὺ ὁμοίωμα ταύτης ἔχει· καὶ γὰρ οἱ ἀγαθοὶ ἡδεῖς ἀλλήλοις. ὁμοίως δὲ καὶ ἡ διὰ τὸ χρήσιμον· καὶ γὰρ τοιοῦτοι ἀλλήλοις οἱ ἀγαθοί. μάλιστα δὲ καὶ ἐν τούτοις αἱ φιλίαι διαμένουσιν, ὅταν τὸ αὐτὸ γίγνηται παρ' ἀλλήλων, οἷον ἡδονή, καὶ μὴ μόνον οὕτως ἀλλὰ καὶ ἀπὸ τοῦ αὐτοῦ, οἷον τοῖς εὐτραπέλοις, καὶ μὴ ὡς ἐραστῇ καὶ ἐρωμένῳ· οὐ γὰρ ἐπὶ τοῖς αὐτοῖς ἥδονται οὗτοι, ἀλλ' ὁ μὲν ὁρῶν ἐκεῖνον, ὁ δὲ θεραπευόμενος ὑπὸ τοῦ ἐραστοῦ· ληγούσης δὲ τῆς ὥρας ἐνίοτε καὶ ἡ φιλία λήγει· τῷ μὲν γὰρ οὐκ ἔστιν ἡδεῖα ἡ ὄψις, τῷ δ' οὐ γίνεται ἡ θεραπεία. πολλοὶ δ' αὖ διαμένουσιν, ἐὰν ἐκ τῆς συνηθείας τὰ ἤθη στέρ-
2 ξωσιν, ὁμοήθεις ὄντες. οἱ δὲ μὴ τὸ ἡδὺ ἀντικαταλλαττόμενοι ἀλλὰ τὸ χρήσιμον ἐν τοῖς ἐρωτικοῖς καὶ εἰσὶν ἧττον φίλοι καὶ διαμένουσιν. οἱ δὲ διὰ τὸ χρήσιμον ὄντες φίλοι ἅμα τῷ συμφέροντι διαλύονται· οὐ γὰρ ἀλλήλων ἦσαν φίλοι ἀλλὰ τοῦ λυσιτελοῦς. δι' ἡδονὴν μὲν οὖν καὶ διὰ τὸ χρήσιμον καὶ φαύλους ἐνδέχεται φίλους εἶναι ἀλλήλοις, καὶ ἐπιεικεῖς φαύλοις καὶ μηδέτερον ὁποιονοῦν, δι' αὑτοὺς

---

8 τοὺς λεγομένους ἅλας] 'The salt of the proverb,' cf. *Eth. Eud.* vii. ii. 35: διὸ εἰς παροιμίαν ἐλήλυθεν ὁ μέδιμνος τῶν ἁλῶν. Cicero, *Lælius*, ch. xix.: Verumque illud est quod dicitur, multos modios salis simul edendos esse, ut amicitiæ munus expletum sit.

οὐδ' ἀποδέξασθαι δὴ φίλους] 'Nor indeed can they be satisfied that they are friends at all.' Cf. viii. v. 3: οἱ δ' ἀποδεχόμενοι ἀλλήλους. ix. iii. 3: ἐὰν δ' ἀποδέχηται ὡς ἀγαθόν. Xen. *Mem.* iv. i. 1: ἀποδέχεσθαι Σωκράτην.

9 εἰ μὴ—ἴσασιν] 'Unless they are likeable (by one another), and are assured of this.'

IV. 2 καὶ εἰσὶν ἧττον—διαμένουσιν] 'Are both friends in a less degree and are (less) abiding.'

καὶ μηδέτερον ὁποιονοῦν] 'And he who is neither good nor bad may be a friend

δὲ δῆλον ὅτι μόνους τοὺς ἀγαθούς· οἱ γὰρ κακοὶ οὐ χαίρουσιν
ἑαυτοῖς, εἰ μή τις ὠφέλεια γίγνοιτο. καὶ μόνη δὲ ἡ τῶν 3
ἀγαθῶν φιλία ἀδιάβλητός ἐστιν· οὐ γὰρ ῥᾴδιον οὐδενὶ
πιστεῦσαι περὶ τοῦ ἐν πολλῷ χρόνῳ ὑπ' αὐτῶν δεδοκι-
μασμένου. καὶ τὸ πιστεύειν ἐν τούτοις, καὶ τὸ μηδέποτ' ἂν
ἀδικῆσαι, καὶ ὅσα ἄλλα ἐν τῇ ὡς ἀληθῶς φιλίᾳ ἀξιοῦται.
ἐν δὲ ταῖς ἑτέραις οὐδὲν κωλύει τὰ τοιαῦτα γίνεσθαι.
ἐπεὶ γὰρ οἱ ἄνθρωποι λέγουσι φίλους καὶ τοὺς διὰ τὸ χρή- 4
σιμον, ὥσπερ αἱ πόλεις (δοκοῦσι γὰρ αἱ συμμαχίαι ταῖς
πόλεσι γίνεσθαι ἕνεκα τοῦ συμφέροντος), καὶ τοὺς δι' ἡδονὴν
ἀλλήλους στέργοντας, ὥσπερ οἱ παῖδες, ἴσως λέγειν μὲν
δεῖ καὶ ἡμᾶς φίλους τοὺς τοιούτους, εἴδη δὲ τῆς φιλίας
πλείω, καὶ πρώτως μὲν καὶ κυρίως τὴν τῶν ἀγαθῶν ᾗ
ἀγαθοί, τὰς δὲ λοιπὰς καθ' ὁμοιότητα· ᾗ γὰρ ἀγαθόν τι
καὶ ὅμοιον, ταύτῃ φίλοι· καὶ γὰρ τὸ ἡδὺ ἀγαθὸν τοῖς
φιληδέσιν. οὐ πάνυ δ' αὗται συνάπτουσιν, οὐδὲ γίνονται 5
οἱ αὐτοὶ φίλοι διὰ τὸ χρήσιμον καὶ διὰ τὸ ἡδύ· οὐ γὰρ
πάνυ συνδυάζεται τὰ κατὰ συμβεβηκός. εἰς ταῦτα δὲ
τὰ εἴδη τῆς φιλίας νενεμημένης οἱ μὲν φαῦλοι ἔσονται 6

---

either to the good or to the bad, or to him who is neither one nor the other.' For the word *μηδέτερος* to express a neutral or intermediate state, cf. *Eth.* VII. xiv. § 1 τὸ μηδέτερον, 'that which is neither pleasure, nor pain.'

3 *καὶ μόνη δὲ—γίνεσθαι*] 'And in short the friendship of the good is alone incapable of being disturbed by accusations. For it is not easy (for the good) to believe any person about a man whom they have long proved. And the sayings about "having faith," and that (the friend) "never could wrong one," and all the other points which are demanded in ideal friendship, are realised in the friendship of the good. But in the other kinds nothing prevents disturbances from accusations (τὰ τοιαῦτα) arising.' *Διαβάλλειν* is 'to set two people by the ears.' Cf. Plato, *Repub.* p. 498 C: *μὴ διάβαλλε ἐμὲ καὶ Θρασύμαχον ἄρτι φίλους γεγονότας.*

4 *ᾗ γὰρ ἀγαθόν τι καὶ ὅμοιον, ταύτῃ φίλοι*] 'For so far as (these kinds of friendship exhibit) something good and resembling the good, so far (those who exercise them) are friends.' The commentators are again deceived by the word ὅμοιον, taking it to mean 'similarity of character.' See above ch. iii. § 7, note.

5 *οὐ πάνυ—συμβεβηκός*] 'But the above-mentioned kinds of friendship do not always coincide. Nor do the same men become friends for the sake of the useful, as for the sake of the pleasant. For things only accidentally connected are not always found together.' On συμβεβηκός, cf. Ar. *Met.* IV. xxx. 1: *συμβεβηκὸς λέγεται ὃ ὑπάρχει μέν τινι καὶ ἀληθὲς εἰπεῖν, οὐ μέντοι οὔτ' ἐξ ἀνάγκης οὔτ' ἐπὶ τὸ πολύ.* See also below, § 6.

φίλοι δι' ἡδονὴν ἢ τὸ χρήσιμον, ταύτῃ ὅμοιοι ὄντες, οἱ δ' ἀγαθοὶ δι' αὑτούς φίλοι· ᾗ γὰρ ἀγαθοί. οὗτοι μὲν οὖν ἁπλῶς φίλοι, ἐκεῖνοι δὲ κατὰ συμβεβηκὸς καὶ τῷ ὡμοιῶσθαι τούτοις.

5 Ὥσπερ δ' ἐπὶ τῶν ἀρετῶν οἱ μὲν καθ' ἕξιν οἱ δὲ κατ' ἐνέργειαν ἀγαθοὶ λέγονται, οὕτω καὶ ἐπὶ τῆς φιλίας· οἱ μὲν γὰρ συζῶντες χαίρουσιν ἀλλήλοις καὶ πορίζουσι τἀγαθά, οἱ δὲ καθεύδοντες ἢ κεχωρισμένοι τοῖς τόποις οὐκ ἐνεργοῦσι μέν, οὕτω δ' ἔχουσιν ὥστ' ἐνεργεῖν φιλικῶς· οἱ γὰρ τόποι οὐ διαλύουσι τὴν φιλίαν ἁπλῶς, ἀλλὰ τὴν ἐνέργειαν. ἐὰν δὲ χρόνιος ἡ ἀπουσία γίνηται, καὶ τῆς φιλίας δοκεῖ λήθην ποιεῖν· ὅθεν εἴρηται

πολλὰς δὴ φιλίας ἀπροσηγορία διέλυσεν.

2 οὐ φαίνονται δ' οὔθ' οἱ πρεσβῦται οὔθ' οἱ στρυφνοὶ φιλικοὶ
εἶναι· βραχὺ γὰρ ἐν αὐτοῖς τὸ τῆς ἡδονῆς, οὐδεὶς δὲ δύναται
συνημερεύειν τῷ λυπηρῷ οὐδὲ τῷ μὴ ἡδεῖ· μάλιστα γὰρ ἡ
φύσις φαίνεται τὸ μὲν λυπηρὸν φεύγειν, ἐφίεσθαι δὲ τοῦ
3 ἡδέος. οἱ δ' ἀποδεχόμενοι ἀλλήλους, μὴ συζῶντες δέ, εὔνοις
ἐοίκασι μᾶλλον ἢ φίλοις. οὐδὲν γὰρ οὕτως ἐστὶ φίλων
ὡς τὸ συζῆν· ὠφελείας μὲν γὰρ οἱ ἐνδεεῖς ὀρέγονται, συνημερεύειν δὲ καὶ οἱ μακάριοι· μονώταις μὲν γὰρ εἶναι τούτοις ἥκιστα προσήκει. συνδιάγειν δὲ μετ' ἀλλήλων οὐκ ἔστι μὴ ἡδεῖς ὄντας μηδὲ χαίροντας τοῖς αὐτοῖς, ὅπερ ἡ ἑταιρικὴ δοκεῖ ἔχειν.

4 Μάλιστα μὲν οὖν ἐστὶ φιλία ἡ τῶν ἀγαθῶν, καθάπερ πολλάκις εἴρηται· δοκεῖ γὰρ φιλητὸν μὲν καὶ αἱρετὸν τὸ ἁπλῶς ἀγαθὸν ἢ ἡδύ, ἑκάστῳ δὲ τὸ αὑτῷ τοιοῦτον· ὁ δ'

---

6 ταύτῃ ὅμοιοι ὄντες] 'In this respect (i.e. as affording and seeking pleasure or utility) being like (the good).'

V. 1 οἱ δὲ καθεύδοντες—ἐνέργειαν] 'But those who are asleep, or who are separated by the intervals of space, do not exercise friendship, though they have all the disposition to exercise it. For the intervals of space do not destroy friendship, but only its exercise.' This is of course a most inadequate translation of ἐνεργεῖν and ἔχουσιν. These words must be understood by a study of Aristotle's forms of thought. See Vol. I. Essay IV. On the ἐνέργεια of friendship, cf. *Eth.* ix. ix.

3 οἱ ἀποδεχόμενοι ἀλλήλους] 'They who are satisfied with one another.' Cf. above, viii. iii. 3.

ὅπερ ἡ ἑταιρικὴ δοκεῖ ἔχειν] 'And this (i.e. pleasure and sympathy) seems the property of companionship.'

4 ὁ δ' ἀγαθὸς τῷ ἀγαθῷ δι' ἄμφω ταῦτα] 'Now the good man (is a

ἀγαθὸς τῷ ἀγαθῷ δι' ἄμφω ταῦτα. ἔοικε δ' ἡ μὲν φί- 5
λησις πάθει, ἡ δὲ φιλία ἕξει· ἡ γὰρ φίλησις οὐχ ἧττον
πρὸς τὰ ἄψυχά ἐστιν, ἀντιφιλοῦσι δὲ μετὰ προαιρέσεως,
ἡ δὲ προαίρεσις ἀφ' ἕξεως. καὶ τἀγαθὰ βούλονται τοῖς
φιλουμένοις ἐκείνων ἕνεκα, οὐ κατὰ πάθος ἀλλὰ καθ' ἕξιν.
καὶ φιλοῦντες τὸν φίλον τὸ αὑτοῖς ἀγαθὸν φιλοῦσιν· ὁ γὰρ
ἀγαθὸς φίλος γινόμενος ἀγαθὸν γίνεται ᾧ φίλος. ἑκάτερος οὖν φιλεῖ τε τὸ αὑτῷ ἀγαθόν, καὶ τὸ ἴσον ἀνταποδίδωσι
τῇ βουλήσει καὶ τῷ ἡδεῖ· λέγεται γὰρ φιλότης ἡ ἰσότης.
Μάλιστα δὴ τῇ τῶν ἀγαθῶν ταῦθ' ὑπάρχει. ἐν δὲ 6
τοῖς στρυφνοῖς καὶ πρεσβυτικοῖς ἧττον γίνεται ἡ φιλία,
ὅσῳ δυσκολώτεροί εἰσι καὶ ἧττον ταῖς ὁμιλίαις χαίρουσιν.
ταῦτα γὰρ δοκεῖ μάλιστ' εἶναι φιλικὰ καὶ ποιητικὰ φιλίας.
διὸ νέοι μὲν γίνονται φίλοι ταχύ, πρεσβῦται δ' οὔ· οὐ γὰρ
γίγνονται φίλοι οἷς ἂν μὴ χαίρωσιν· ὁμοίως δ' οὐδ' οἱ στρυ-

---

friend) to the good man for the sake of both these things' (*i.e.* the absolutely good and the absolutely pleasant).

5 *ἔοικε δ'—ἕξει*] 'Loving is like an emotion, but friendship like a settled disposition of the mind. For loving exists just as well towards inanimate objects; but when men reciprocate friendship it implies purpose, and purpose proceeds from a settled disposition of the mind.' In *Eth.* IV. vi. 5 (cf. II. v. 2), Aristotle makes friendship to be an emotion, or characterized by emotion. The present passage does not in the least contradict this, as ἕξις, or a settled disposition of mind, is merely the result of regulated emotions, and the tendency to reproduce them.

ἡ δὲ προαίρεσις, κ.τ.λ.] In *Eth.* III. ii. 1, Aristotle speaks of 'purpose' as the test of character; *ib.* § 11, as constituting character; *ib.* § 2, as not acting suddenly; *ib.* § 17, as implying reason and forethought.

ἑκάτερος—ἡδεῖ] 'Each of the two then loves that which is a personal good to himself, and he makes an equal return both in wishing good and in (actual) pleasure.' Zell, following two MSS., reads εἴδει. But Bekker's reading (ἡδεῖ) appears preferable: (1) because ἴσον εἴδει would not be a natural expression; it confounds *degree* with *kind*; we should expect ταὐτὸ εἴδει: (2) because ἡδεῖ gives very good sense, since it is one thing to reciprocate the motives or feelings of friendship, and another to give your friend the same amount of pleasure as he gives you.

λέγεται—ἰσότης] 'For equality is said to constitute friendship.' A Pythagorean saying, connecting moral ideas with the ideas of number. Cf. Diog. Laert. VIII. i. 8: *εἶπέ τε πρῶτος (ὥς φησι Τίμαιος) κοινὰ τὰ φίλων εἶναι· καὶ φιλίαν ἰσότητα.*

VI. 1. This section is an awkward repetition of what has been said before, ch. v. § 2. This, however, merely shows that we have probably the uncorrected draft of Aristotle's treatise on Friendship.

φυοί. ἀλλ' οἱ τοιοῦτοι εὔνοι μέν εἰσιν ἀλλήλοις· βούλονται γὰρ τἀγαθὰ καὶ ἀπαντῶσιν εἰς τὰς χρείας· φίλοι δ' οὐ
πάνυ εἰσὶ διὰ τὸ μὴ συνημερεύειν μηδὲ χαίρειν ἀλλήλοις, ἃ
2 δὴ μάλιστ' εἶναι δοκεῖ φιλικά. πολλοῖς δ' εἶναι φίλον κατὰ
τὴν τελείαν φιλίαν οὐκ ἐνδέχεται, ὥσπερ οὐδ' ἐρᾶν πολλῶν
ἅμα· ἔοικε γὰρ ὑπερβολῇ, τὸ τοιοῦτο δὲ πρὸς ἕνα πέφυκε
γίνεσθαι, πολλοὺς δ' ἅμα τῷ αὐτῷ ἀρέσκειν σφόδρα οὐ
3 ῥᾴδιον, ἴσως δ' οὐδ' ἀγαθοὺς εἶναι. δεῖ δὲ καὶ ἐμπειρίαν
λαβεῖν καὶ ἐν συνηθείᾳ γενέσθαι, ὃ παγχάλεπον. διὰ τὸ
χρήσιμον δὲ καὶ τὸ ἡδὺ πολλοῖς ἀρέσκειν ἐνδέχεται· πολλοὶ
4 γὰρ οἱ τοιοῦτοι, καὶ ἐν ὀλίγῳ χρόνῳ αἱ ὑπηρεσίαι. τούτων
δὲ μᾶλλον ἔοικε φιλίᾳ ἡ διὰ τὸ ἡδύ, ὅταν ταὐτὰ ὑπ' ἀμφοῖν γίγνηται καὶ χαίρωσιν ἀλλήλοις ἢ τοῖς αὐτοῖς, οἷαι
τῶν νέων εἰσὶν αἱ φιλίαι· μᾶλλον γὰρ ἐν ταύταις τὸ ἐλευθέριον. ἡ δὲ διὰ τὸ χρήσιμον ἀγοραίων. καὶ οἱ μακάριοι δὲ χρησίμων μὲν οὐδὲν δέονται, ἡδέων δέ· συζῆν μὲν
γὰρ βούλονταί τισι, τὸ δὲ λυπηρὸν ὀλίγον μὲν χρόνον φέ-
ρουσιν, συνεχῶς δ' οὐθεὶς ἂν ὑπομείναι, οὐδ' αὐτὸ τὸ ἀγα-

2 πολλοῖς—εἶναι] 'It is not possible to be a friend to many men on the footing of the perfect kind of friendship, just as one cannot be in love with many at the same time. For (the perfect friendship) is a sort of excess of feeling, which naturally arises towards one person alone; again, it is not easy for many persons to be intensely pleasing to the same individual, and perhaps not easy that many should be good.' ὑπερβολή here would be nearly represented by the French word *abandon*; it implies the throwing away of limits and restraints, a giving up of one's whole self. Cf. IX. iv. 6: ἡ ὑπερβολὴ τῆς φιλίας τῇ πρὸς αὑτὸν ὁμοιοῦται. Of course there is an association of Aristotelian ideas (μεσότης, ἔλλειψις, &c.) in the term. It is repeated *Eth.* IX. x. 5, where the question of the plurality of friendships is carefully gone into.

3 πολλοῖς ἀρέσκειν ἐνδέχεται] We should have expected πολλοὺς ἡμῖν ἀρέσκειν, on the analogy of the last sentence, πολλοὺς τῷ αὐτῷ ἀρέσκειν, but the writing seems careless and the expression is inverted.

οἱ τοιοῦτοι] *i.e.* the useful and the pleasant. Cf. § 6, where τοιοῦτοι again takes its sense from the context.

4 ἀγοραίων] 'Of mercenary persons.' Cf. Ar. *Pol.* IV. iv. 10: λέγω δ' ἀγοραῖον (πλῆθος) τὸ περὶ τὰς πράσεις καὶ τὰς ὠνὰς καὶ τὰς ἐμπορίας καὶ καπηλείας διατρῖβον. *Ib.* VI. iv. 12: ὁ γὰρ βίος φαῦλος, καὶ οὐθὲν ἔργον μετ' ἀρετῆς ὧν μεταχειρίζεται τὸ πλῆθος τό τε τῶν βαναύσων καὶ τὸ τῶν ἀγοραίων ἀνθρώπων καὶ τὸ θητικόν.

χρησίμων μὲν οὐδὲν δέονται] *i.e.* Happiness by its definition implies a sufficiency of external means, *Eth.* I. viii. 15.

οὐδ' αὐτὸ τὸ ἀγαθόν, εἰ λυπηρὸν] If Aristotle had been capable of a

θόν, εἰ λυπηρὸν αὐτῷ εἴη· διὸ τοὺς φίλους ἡδεῖς ζητοῦσιν.
δεῖ δ' ἴσως καὶ ἀγαθοὺς τοιούτους ὄντας, καὶ ἔτι αὐτοῖς·
οὕτω γὰρ ὑπάρξει αὐτοῖς ὅσα δεῖ τοῖς φίλοις. οἱ δ' ἐν 5
ταῖς ἐξουσίαις διηρημένοις φαίνονται χρῆσθαι τοῖς φίλοις·
ἄλλοι γὰρ αὐτοῖς εἰσὶ χρήσιμοι καὶ ἕτεροι ἡδεῖς, ἄμφω δ'
οἱ αὐτοὶ οὐ πάνυ· οὔτε γὰρ ἡδεῖς μετ' ἀρετῆς ζητοῦσιν οὔτε
χρησίμους εἰς τὰ καλά, ἀλλὰ τοὺς μὲν εὐτραπέλους τοῦ
ἡδέος ἐφιέμενοι, τοὺς δὲ δεινοὺς πρᾶξαι τὸ ἐπιταχθέν· ταῦτα
δ' οὐ πάνυ γίνεται ἐν τῷ αὐτῷ· ἡδὺς δὲ καὶ χρήσιμος 6
ἅμα εἴρηται ὅτι ὁ σπουδαῖος· ἀλλ' ὑπερέχοντι οὐ γίνεται ὁ
τοιοῦτος φίλος, ἂν μὴ καὶ τῇ ἀρετῇ ὑπερέχηται· εἰ δὲ μή,
οὐκ ἰσάζει ἀνάλογον ὑπερεχόμενος. οὐ πάνυ δ' εἰώθασι
τοιοῦτοι γίνεσθαι.

Εἰσὶ δ' οὖν αἱ εἰρημέναι φιλίαι ἐν ἰσότητι· τὰ γὰρ αὐτὰ 7
γίγνεται ἀπ' ἀμφοῖν καὶ βούλονται ἀλλήλοις, ἢ ἕτερον

---

joke, we must have considered this to be meant as such. It is a contradiction in terms to speak of the Absolute Good as painful. But the argument is given in a merely matter-of-fact way. See Vol. I. Essay III. p. 215.

δεῖ δ' ἴσως—αὐτοῖς] 'And perhaps (in seeking friends) one ought (to require) that even good men should have this qualification (*i.e.* pleasantness), and moreover not in a merely universal way, but relatively to oneself.'

5 οἱ δ' ἐν ταῖς—φίλοις] 'Great potentates' (cf. *Eth.* I. v. 3) 'however seem to make use of their friends separately;' *i.e.* they keep two sets of friends, one for profit or business, and another for pleasure.

6 ἡδὺς δὲ—γίνεσθαι] 'Now we have already said that the good man is both pleasant and useful at once. But such a man does not become a friend to his superior (in rank), unless he be surpassed (by that superior) in virtue also. Else, he does not find himself in that position of equality which is produced by superiority in proportion to merit. Such persons, however (as potentates who surpass the good in virtue), are not produced every day.' The commentators have strangely interpreted this passage, making ὑπερέχηται take for its nominative ὁ ὑπερέχων, as though Aristotle had said that a good man would not be a friend to a potentate, if that potentate had superior moral qualities; and as though 'equality' were produced by one man having all the merit and another all the power. On the contrary, Aristotle would have said that 'proportionate equality' is produced, according to the principles of distributive justice, by each man having in proportion to his merits, cf. *Eth.* v. iii. 6, *Pol.* III. ix. 15. There is no sense of inequality produced by the position of a man socially exalted, if he be also exalted in intellect and character; inequality is felt when a fool or a villain occupies a high social position. Cf. *Pol.* III. ix. 15:

ἀνθ' ἑτέρου ἀντικαταλλάττονται, οἷον ἡδονὴν ἀντ' ὠφελείας. ὅτι δ' ἧττόν εἰσιν αὗται αἱ φιλίαι καὶ μένουσιν, εἴρηται. δοκοῦσι δὲ καὶ δι' ὁμοιότητα καὶ ἀνομοιότητα ταὐτοῦ εἶναί τε καὶ οὐκ εἶναι φιλίαι· καθ' ὁμοιότητα γὰρ τῆς κατ' ἀρετὴν φαίνονται φιλίαι (ἡ μὲν γὰρ τὸ ἡδὺ ἔχει ἡ δὲ τὸ χρήσιμον, ταῦτα δ' ὑπάρχει κἀκείνῃ), τῷ δὲ τὴν μὲν ἀδιάβλητον καὶ μόνιμον εἶναι, ταύτας δὲ ταχέως μεταπίπτειν ἄλλοις τε διαφέρειν πολλοῖς, οὐ φαίνονται φιλίαι δι' ἀνομοιότητα ἐκείνης.

7 Ἕτερον δ' ἐστὶ φιλίας εἶδος τὸ καθ' ὑπεροχήν, οἷον πατρὶ πρὸς υἱὸν καὶ ὅλως πρεσβυτέρῳ πρὸς νεώτερον, ἀνδρὶ πρὸς γυναῖκα καὶ παντὶ ἄρχοντι πρὸς ἀρχόμενον. διαφέρουσι δ' αὗται καὶ ἀλλήλων· οὐ γὰρ ἡ αὐτὴ γονεῦσι πρὸς τέκνα καὶ ἄρχουσι πρὸς ἀρχομένους, ἀλλ' οὐδὲ πατρὶ πρὸς υἱὸν καὶ υἱῷ πρὸς πατέρα, οὐδ' ἀνδρὶ πρὸς γυναῖκα καὶ γυναικὶ πρὸς ἄνδρα. ἑτέρα γὰρ ἑκάστῳ τούτων ἀρετὴ καὶ τὸ ἔργον, ἕτερα δὲ καὶ δι' ἃ φιλοῦσιν·
2 ἕτεραι οὖν καὶ αἱ φιλήσεις καὶ αἱ φιλίαι. ταὐτὰ μὲν δὴ οὔτε γίγνεται ἑκατέρῳ παρὰ θατέρου οὔτε δεῖ ζητεῖν· ὅταν δὲ γονεῦσι μὲν τέκνα ἀπονέμῃ ἃ δεῖ τοῖς γεννήσασι, γονεῖς δὲ υἱέσιν ἃ δεῖ τοῖς τέκνοις, μόνιμος ἡ τῶν τοιούτων καὶ ἐπιεικὴς ἔσται φιλία. ἀνάλογον δ' ἐν πάσαις ταῖς καθ' ὑπεροχὴν οὔσαις φιλίαις καὶ τὴν φίλησιν δεῖ γίνεσθαι, οἷον τὸν ἀμείνω μᾶλλον φιλεῖσθαι ἢ φιλεῖν, καὶ τὸν ὠφελιμώτερον, καὶ τῶν ἄλλων ἕκαστον ὁμοίως· ὅταν γὰρ κατ' ἀξίαν ἡ φίλησις γίγνηται, τότε γίγνεταί πως ἰσότης ὃ δὴ τῆς φιλίας εἶναι δοκεῖ.

3 Οὐχ ὁμοίως δὲ τὸ ἴσον ἔν τε τοῖς δικαίοις καὶ ἐν τῇ φιλίᾳ φαίνεται ἔχειν· ἔστι γὰρ ἐν μὲν τοῖς δικαίοις ἴσον πρώτως τὸ κατ' ἀξίαν, τὸ δὲ κατὰ ποσὸν δευτέρως, ἐν δὲ τῇ φιλίᾳ τὸ μὲν κατὰ ποσὸν πρώτως, τὸ δὲ κατ' ἀξίαν δευ-

ὥσπερ τούτοις τῆς πόλεως μέτεστι πλεῖον—ἢ τοῖς κατὰ πλοῦτον ὑπερέχουσι, κατ' ἀρετὴν δ' ὑπερεχομένοις.

7 εἴρηται] Cf. VIII. iii. 2—3.

VII. 2 ἀνάλογον δ'] The same principle of distributive justice, maintained above in § 6 of the last chapter is again appealed to. Where friends are not equal, their friendship must be regulated by proportion.

3 οὐχ ὁμοίως—δευτέρως] 'But equality seems to stand differently in justice and in friendship. In justice

τέρως. δῆλον δ', ἐὰν πολὺ διάστημα γίγνηται ἀρετῆς ἢ κακίας ἢ εὐπορίας ἤ τινος ἄλλου· οὐ γὰρ ἔτι φίλοι εἰσίν, ἀλλ' οὐδ' ἀξιοῦσιν. ἐμφανέστατον δὲ τοῦτ' ἐπὶ τῶν θεῶν· πλεῖστον γὰρ οὗτοι πᾶσι τοῖς ἀγαθοῖς ὑπερέχουσιν. δῆλον δὲ καὶ ἐπὶ τῶν βασιλέων· οὐδὲ γὰρ τούτοις ἀξιοῦσιν εἶναι φίλοι οἱ πολὺ καταδεέστεροι, οὐδὲ τοῖς ἀρίστοις ἢ σοφωτάτοις οἱ μηδενὸς ἄξιοι. ἀκριβὴς μὲν οὖν ἐν τοῖς τοιούτοις 5
οὐκ ἔστιν ὁρισμός, ἕως τίνος οἱ φίλοι· πολλῶν γὰρ ἀφαιρουμένων ἔτι μένει, πολὺ δὲ χωρισθέντος, οἷον τοῦ θεοῦ,
οὐκέτι. ὅθεν καὶ ἀπορεῖται, μή ποτ' οὐ βούλονται οἱ φίλοι 6
τοῖς φίλοις τὰ μέγιστα τῶν ἀγαθῶν, οἷον θεοὺς εἶναι· οὐδὲ γὰρ ἔτι φίλοι ἔσονται αὐτοῖς, οὐδὲ δὴ ἀγαθά· οἱ γὰρ φίλοι ἀγαθά. εἰ δὴ καλῶς εἴρηται ὅτι ὁ φίλος τῷ φίλῳ βούλεται τἀγαθὰ ἐκείνου ἕνεκα, μένειν ἂν δέοι οἷός ποτ' ἐστὶν ἐκεῖνος· ἀνθρώπῳ δὲ ὄντι βουλήσεται τὰ μέγιστα ἀγαθά. ἴσως δ' οὐ πάντα· αὐτῷ γὰρ μάλισθ' ἕκαστος βούλεται τἀγαθά.

---

proportionate equality is primary, and quantitative equality secondary; in friendship, quantitative equality is the first, and proportionate equality the second consideration.' Distributive justice begins by presupposing inequalities between man and man, and by proportionate assignments it equalizes these. Justice, however, cares little about bringing men to quantitative or exact equality. The latter kind of equality at all events is aimed at only in democracies, while the proportionate equality belongs to aristocracies and constitutional governments, cf. Ar. *Pol.* VI. ii. 2. Friendship on the other hand begins by presupposing equality between the parties, and though a certain amount of inequality may be made up by proportionate assignment of affection, &c., yet a wide interval of inequality will render friendship altogether impossible.

4 πλεῖστον γὰρ οὗτοι] The reading πλείστων in the Oxford reprint of Bekker's edition (1837) is a misprint. The original Berlin edition has πλεῖστον.

5 ἀκριβὴς—οὐκέτι] 'In such cases there is no exact definition up to what point friendship is possible; for though many (advantages) be taken away (from the one side), friendship still abides; but when (the one friend) is far removed from the other, as, for instance, God is from man, there is no friendship any longer.'

6 ὅθεν καὶ—τἀγαθά] 'From this the question has arisen whether friends wish for their friends the greatest of all goods, as for instance to be gods. For having attained this, they would no longer at all be friends to those who formed the wish, and therefore no advantage to them, for friends are an advantage. If then it has been rightly stated that the friend wishes all that is good to his friend for that friend's sake, it will be necessary for that friend to remain as he is, and then he will wish for him, being a man, the greatest goods.

8 Οἱ πολλοὶ δὲ δοκοῦσι διὰ φιλοτιμίαν βούλεσθαι φιλεῖσθαι
μᾶλλον ἢ φιλεῖν, διὸ φιλοκόλακες οἱ πολλοί· ὑπερεχόμενος γὰρ φίλος ὁ κόλαξ, ἢ προσποιεῖται τοιοῦτος εἶναι καὶ
μᾶλλον φιλεῖν ἢ φιλεῖσθαι. τὸ δὲ φιλεῖσθαι ἐγγὺς εἶναι
2 δοκεῖ τοῦ τιμᾶσθαι, οὗ δὴ οἱ πολλοὶ ἐφίενται. οὐ δι' αὑτὸ
δ' ἐοίκασιν αἱρεῖσθαι τὴν τιμήν, ἀλλὰ κατὰ συμβεβηκός· χαίρουσι γὰρ οἱ μὲν πολλοὶ ὑπὸ τῶν ἐν ταῖς ἐξουσίαις τιμώμενοι διὰ τὴν ἐλπίδα· οἴονται γὰρ τεύξεσθαι παρ' αὐτῶν, ἄν του δέωνται· ὡς δὴ σημείῳ τῆς εὐπαθείας χαίρουσι τῇ τιμῇ. οἱ δ' ὑπὸ τῶν ἐπιεικῶν καὶ εἰδότων ὀρεγόμενοι τιμῆς βεβαιῶσαι τὴν οἰκείαν δόξαν ἐφίενται περὶ αὑτῶν· χαίρουσι δὴ ὅτι εἰσὶν ἀγαθοί, πιστεύοντες τῇ τῶν λεγόντων κρίσει. τῷ φιλεῖσθαι δὲ καθ' αὑτὸ χαίρουσιν· διὸ δόξειεν ἂν κρεῖττον εἶναι τοῦ τιμᾶσθαι, καὶ ἡ φιλία
3 καθ' αὑτὴν αἱρετὴ εἶναι. δοκεῖ δ' ἐν τῷ φιλεῖν μᾶλλον ἢ
ἐν τῷ φιλεῖσθαι εἶναι. σημεῖον δ' αἱ μητέρες τῷ φιλεῖν χαίρουσαι· ἔνιαι γὰρ διδόασι τὰ ἑαυτῶν τρέφεσθαι, καὶ φιλοῦσι μὲν εἰδυῖαι, ἀντιφιλεῖσθαι δ' οὐ ζητοῦσιν, ἐὰν ἀμφότερα μὴ ἐνδέχηται, ἀλλ' ἱκανὸν αὐταῖς ἔοικεν εἶναι, ἐὰν ὁρῶσιν εὖ πράττοντας, καὶ αὐταὶ φιλοῦσιν αὐτούς, κἂν

After all, perhaps he will not wish him to have everything. For every one especially wishes for himself what is good.' Under the words ἀπορεῖται μή ποτ' οὐ is included a question both as to fact and cause. Οὐδὲ γὰρ denies the fact and states the cause, which is that if we wished our friend to become a god, we should wish him to be in a position where he can no longer be our friend. The last sentence (ἴσως δ' οὐ πάντα) qualifies the previous statement, and guards against the notion that any human friendship can be utterly disinterested and selfless. The same topic is fully discussed in the eighth chapter of Book IX.

VIII. 1—2 Though the essence of friendship consists rather in loving than in being loved, the mass of men prefer the latter, as ministering to their vanity. Being loved is akin to being honoured. Parenthetically it may be observed, that honour is sought not for itself but on account of things variously associated with it (κατὰ συμβεβηκός). (1) To be honoured by the great affords a hope of promotion. (2) To be honoured by the wise and good is an evidence to men of their own merits. Thus honour is desired as a means to the consciousness of virtue. Cf. *Eth.* I. v. 5: ἐοίκασι τὴν τιμὴν διώκειν ἵνα πιστεύωσιν ἑαυτοὺς ἀγαθοὺς εἶναι· ζητοῦσι γοῦν ὑπὸ τῶν φρονίμων τιμᾶσθαι, καὶ παρ' οἷς γιγνώσκονται, καὶ ἐπ' ἀρετῇ.

3 The active spirit of love, as opposed to the passive gratification of being loved, is exemplified by the case of mothers, who give their children

ἐκεῖνοι μηδὲν ὧν μητρὶ προσήκει ἀπονέμωσι διὰ τὴν ἄγνοι- 4
αν. μᾶλλον δὲ τῆς φιλίας οὔσης ἐν τῷ φιλεῖν, καὶ τῶν φιλοφίλων ἐπαινουμένων, φίλων ἀρετὴ τὸ φιλεῖν ἔοικεν, ὥστ'
ἐν οἷς τοῦτο γίνεται κατ' ἀξίαν, οὗτοι μόνιμοι φίλοι καὶ ἡ
τούτων φιλία. οὕτω δ' ἂν καὶ οἱ ἄνισοι μάλιστ' εἶεν φίλοι· 5
ἰσάζοιντο γὰρ ἄν. ἡ δ' ἰσότης καὶ ὁμοιότης φιλότης, καὶ
μάλιστα μὲν ἡ τῶν κατ' ἀρετὴν ὁμοιότης· μόνιμοι γὰρ ὄντες
καθ' αὐτοὺς καὶ πρὸς ἀλλήλους μένουσι, καὶ οὔτε δέονται
φαύλων οὔθ' ὑπηρετοῦσι τοιαῦτα, ἀλλ' ὡς εἰπεῖν καὶ δια-
κωλύουσι· τῶν ἀγαθῶν γὰρ μήτ' αὐτοὺς ἁμαρτάνειν μήτε
τοῖς φίλοις ἐπιτρέπειν. οἱ δὲ μοχθηροὶ τὸ μὲν βέβαιον οὐκ
ἔχουσιν· οὐδὲ γὰρ αὐτοῖς διαμένουσιν ὅμοιοι ὄντες· ἐπ'
ὀλίγον δὲ χρόνον γίγνονται φίλοι, χαίροντες τῇ ἀλλήλων
μοχθηρίᾳ. οἱ χρήσιμοι δὲ καὶ ἡδεῖς ἐπὶ πλεῖον διαμένου- 6
σιν· ἕως γὰρ ἂν πορίζωσιν ἡδονὰς ἢ ὠφελείας ἀλλήλοις.
ἐξ ἐναντίων δὲ μάλιστα μὲν δοκεῖ ἡ διὰ τὸ χρήσιμον γίγνεσθαι φιλία, οἷον πένης πλουσίῳ, ἀμαθὴς εἰδότι· οὗ γὰρ
τυγχάνει τις ἐνδεὴς ὤν, τούτου ἐφιέμενος ἀντιδωρεῖται ἄλλο.
ἐνταῦθα δ' ἄν τις ἕλκοι καὶ ἐραστὴν καὶ ἐρώμενον, καὶ
καλὸν καὶ αἰσχρόν. διὸ φαίνονται καὶ οἱ ἐρασταὶ γελοῖοι
ἐνίοτε, ἀξιοῦντες φιλεῖσθαι ὡς φιλοῦσιν· ὁμοίως δὴ φιλη-
τοὺς ὄντας ἴσως ἀξιωτέον, μηδὲν δὲ τοιοῦτον ἔχοντας
γελοῖον. ἴσως δὲ οὐδ' ἐφίεται τὸ ἐναντίον τοῦ ἐναντίου καθ' 7
αὐτό, ἀλλὰ κατὰ συμβεβηκός. ἡ δ' ὄρεξις τοῦ μέσου ἐστίν·

to be brought up by other persons, and go on loving them, though not even recognised by them.

4—5 It is this active spirit of love which constitutes the virtue of friendship, and which causes us to praise those who are of a friendly disposition. This then explains what was above stated merely as a fact, *Eth.* VIII. i. 5. The same spirit serves as the equalising principle in unequal friendships, greater merit being met by greater love.

5—7 Friendship is based on equality and similarity, especially the friendship of the good. Friendships for the sake of pleasure or profit seem rather based on contrariety, as for instance on the contrariety of riches and poverty. But, after all, one would say not that the contrary seeks its contrary, but that the contrary seeks the mean.

5 *μάλιστα μὲν ἡ τῶν κατ' ἀρετὴν ὁμοιότης*] Cf. the *Lysis* of Plato, p. 214, quoted above upon ch. i. 6.

τῶν ἀγαθῶν—ἐπιτρέπειν] 'For the good will neither do wrong themselves, nor permit their friends to do it.'

7 *ὄρεξις τοῦ μέσου*] This phrase is in accordance with the pantheistic side of Aristotle's philosophy, attri-

τοῦτο γὰρ ἀγαθόν, οἷον τῷ ξηρῷ οὐχ ὑγρῷ γενέσθαι ἀλλ'
ἐπὶ τὸ μέσον ἐλθεῖν, καὶ τῷ θερμῷ καὶ τοῖς ἄλλοις ὁμοίως.
ταῦτα μὲν οὖν ἀφείσθω· καὶ γάρ ἐστιν ἀλλοτριώτερα.

9 Ἔοικε δέ, καθάπερ ἐν ἀρχῇ εἴρηται, περὶ ταὐτὰ καὶ ἐν
τοῖς αὐτοῖς εἶναι ἥ τε φιλία καὶ τὸ δίκαιον· ἐν ἁπάσῃ γὰρ
κοινωνίᾳ δοκεῖ τι δίκαιον εἶναι, καὶ φιλία δέ· προσαγορεύουσι γοῦν ὡς φίλους τοὺς σύμπλους καὶ συστρατιώτας, ὁμοίως δὲ καὶ τοὺς ἐν ταῖς ἄλλαις κοινωνίαις·
καθ' ὅσον δὲ κοινωνοῦσιν, ἐπὶ τοσοῦτόν ἐστι φιλία· καὶ
γὰρ τὸ δίκαιον. καὶ ἡ παροιμία 'κοινὰ τὰ φίλων,'
2 ὀρθῶς· ἐν κοινωνίᾳ γὰρ ἡ φιλία. ἔστι δ' ἀδελφοῖς μὲν
καὶ ἑταίροις πάντα κοινά, τοῖς δ' ἄλλοις ἀφωρισμένα, καὶ
τοῖς μὲν πλείω τοῖς δ' ἐλάττω· καὶ γὰρ τῶν φιλιῶν αἱ
μὲν μᾶλλον αἱ δ' ἧττον. διαφέρει δὲ καὶ τὰ δίκαια· οὐ
γὰρ ταὐτὰ γονεῦσι πρὸς τέκνα καὶ ἀδελφοῖς πρὸς ἀλλήλους,
οὐδ' ἑταίροις καὶ πολίταις, ὁμοίως δὲ καὶ ἐπὶ τῶν ἄλλων
3 φιλιῶν. ἕτερα δὴ καὶ τὰ ἄδικα πρὸς ἑκάστους τούτων,
καὶ αὔξησιν λαμβάνει τῷ μᾶλλον πρὸς φίλους εἶναι,
οἷον χρήματα ἀποστερῆσαι ἑταῖρον δεινότερον ἢ πολίτην,
καὶ μὴ βοηθῆσαι ἀδελφῷ ἢ ὀθνείῳ, καὶ πατάξαι πατέρα
ἢ ὁντινοῦν ἄλλον. αὔξεσθαι δὲ πέφυκεν ἅμα τῇ φιλίᾳ
καὶ τὸ δίκαιον, ὡς ἐν τοῖς αὐτοῖς ὄντα καὶ ἐπ' ἴσον
4 διήκοντα. αἱ δὲ κοινωνίαι πᾶσαι μορίοις ἐοίκασι τῆς
πολιτικῆς· συμπορεύονται γὰρ ἐπί τινι συμφέροντι, καὶ
πορίζομενοί τι τῶν εἰς τὸν βίον· καὶ ἡ πολιτικὴ δὲ

---

buting in nature a desire for the good. Cf. *De Anima*, II. iv. 3: πάντα γὰρ ἐκείνου (τοῦ θείου) ὀρέγεται, κἀκείνου ἕνεκα πράττει ὅσα πράττει κατὰ φύσιν. *Eth.* X. ii. 4: ἴσως δὲ καὶ ἐν τοῖς φαύλοις ἐστί τι φυσικὸν ἀγαθὸν κρεῖττον ἢ καθ' αὑτά, ὃ ἐφίεται τοῦ οἰκείου ἀγαθοῦ.

IX. 1 *ἐν ἀρχῇ*] *Eth.* VIII. i. 4.

περὶ ταὐτὰ καὶ ἐν τοῖς αὐτοῖς] 'About the same things, and in the same persons.' Cf. *Eth.* V. iii. 5: οἷς τε γὰρ δίκαιον τυγχάνει ὄν, δύο ἐστί, καὶ ἐν οἷς τὰ πράγματα, δύο. *Pol.* III. ix. 3: τὴν μὲν τοῦ πράγματος ἰσότητα ὁμολογοῦσι, τὴν δὲ οἷς ἀμφισβητοῦσι.

3 *Αὔξεσθαι δὲ—διήκοντα*] 'Justice of necessity becomes more binding as friendship becomes closer, for they exist in the same subjects, and are coextensive in their application.'

4 *αἱ δὲ κοινωνίαι—βίον*] 'All communities are like parts of the political community; for (the members of them) unite with a view to some advantage, and to providing some of the conveniences of life.'

κοινωνία τοῦ συμφέροντος χάριν δοκεῖ καὶ ἐξ ἀρχῆς συνελθεῖν καὶ διαμένειν· τούτου γὰρ καὶ οἱ νομοθέται στοχάζονται, καὶ δίκαιόν φασιν εἶναι τὸ κοινῇ συμφέρον. αἱ μὲν 5
οὖν ἄλλαι κοινωνίαι κατὰ μέρη τοῦ συμφέροντος ἐφίενται,
οἷον πλωτῆρες μὲν τοῦ κατὰ τὸν πλοῦν πρὸς ἐργασίαν
χρημάτων ἤ τι τοιοῦτον, συστρατιῶται δὲ τοῦ κατὰ τὸν
πόλεμον, εἴτε χρημάτων εἴτε νίκης ἢ πόλεως ὀρεγόμενοι,
ὁμοίως δὲ καὶ φυλέται καὶ δημόται. ἔνιαι δὲ τῶν
κοινωνιῶν δι' ἡδονὴν δοκοῦσι γίγνεσθαι, θιασωτῶν καὶ
ἐρανιστῶν· αὗται γὰρ θυσίας ἕνεκα καὶ συνουσίας. πᾶσαι
δ' αὗται ὑπὸ τὴν πολιτικὴν ἐοίκασιν εἶναι· οὐ γὰρ τοῦ
παρόντος συμφέροντος ἡ πολιτικὴ ἐφίεται, ἀλλ' εἰς ἅπαντα
τὸν βίον, θυσίας τε ποιοῦντες καὶ περὶ ταύτας συνόδους,
τιμὰς ἀπονέμοντες τοῖς θεοῖς, καὶ αὑτοῖς ἀναπαύσεις
πορίζοντες μεθ' ἡδονῆς. αἱ γὰρ ἀρχαῖαι θυσίαι καὶ
σύνοδοι φαίνονται γίνεσθαι μετὰ τὰς τῶν καρπῶν συγκομιδὰς οἷον ἀπαρχαί· μάλιστα γὰρ ἐν τούτοις ἐσχόλαζον
τοῖς καιροῖς. πᾶσαι δὴ φαίνονται αἱ κοινωνίαι μόρια τῆς 6
πολιτικῆς εἶναι· ἀκολουθήσουσι δὲ αἱ τοιαῦται φιλίαι
ταῖς τοιαύταις κοινωνίαις.

Πολιτείας δ' ἐστὶν εἴδη τρία, ἴσαι δὲ καὶ παρεκβάσεις, 10
οἷον φθοραὶ τούτων. εἰσὶ δ' αἱ μὲν πολιτεῖαι βασιλεία

---

5 *θιασωτῶν καὶ ἐρανιστῶν*] Cardwell refers for illustration of these terms to Demosthenes, pp. 313, 23; 403, 19; 1355, 3; 1217, 14.

By omitting, with Fritzsche, Bekker's full stop after *συνουσίας*, and by placing the words *οὐ γὰρ—τὸν βίον* in a parenthesis, we see that the participles *ποιοῦντες*, *ἀπονέμοντες*, *πορίζοντες* are to be referred to *κοινωνίαι*, as implied in *κοινωνιῶν* above. The passage which speaks of men 'awarding honour to the gods, while providing recreation and pleasure for themselves,' is highly characteristic of the Greek religion. This sort of thing can perhaps be best understood in the present day by those who have seen the religious festivals of the Hindoos. Cf. Plato's *Republic*, p. 364 E: *θυσίαις τε καὶ παιδιαῖς—μεθ' ἡδονῶν τε καὶ ἑορτῶν*.

X. This chapter, containing a classification of forms of government and of the perversions to which they are exposed, can hardly have been written after the *Politics* of Aristotle. It has rather the appearance of a first essay, the conclusions of which were afterwards worked out into detail, and partly modified. Thus Aristotle in the *Politics* by no means concedes the position that monarchy is the best form of government. He argues, *Pol.* III. xv. 4—16, that it is better for a

τε καὶ ἀριστοκρατία, τρίτη δ' ἡ ἀπὸ τιμημάτων, ἣν τιμοκρατικὴν λέγειν οἰκεῖον φαίνεται, πολιτείαν δ' αὐτὴν
2 εἰώθασιν οἱ πλεῖστοι καλεῖν. τούτων δὲ βελτίστη μὲν ἡ βασιλεία, χειρίστη δ' ἡ τιμοκρατία. παρέκβασις δὲ βασιλείας μὲν τυραννίς· ἄμφω γὰρ μοναρχίαι, διαφέρουσι δὲ πλεῖστον· ὁ μὲν γὰρ τύραννος τὸ ἑαυτῷ συμφέρον σκοπεῖ, ὁ δὲ βασιλεὺς τὸ τῶν ἀρχομένων. οὐ γάρ ἐστι βασιλεὺς ὁ μὴ αὐτάρκης καὶ πᾶσι τοῖς ἀγαθοῖς ὑπερέχων· ὁ δὲ τοιοῦτος οὐδενὸς προσδεῖται· τὰ ὠφέλιμα οὖν αὐτῷ μὲν οὐκ ἂν σκοποίη, τοῖς δ' ἀρχομένοις· ὁ γὰρ μὴ τοιοῦτος

---

state to be governed by good laws than by the best individual will; further on, *Pol.* III. xvii., he qualifies this by admitting that for some peoples monarchy is better suited.

1 παρεκβάσεις] 'Perversions' or 'abnormal growths'; cf. *Pol.* III. vi. 11, where a form of government is pronounced to be normal as long as it aims at the public good, abnormal when its end is private interest: φανερὸν τοίνυν ὡς ὅσαι μὲν πολιτεῖαι τὸ κοινῇ συμφέρον σκοποῦσιν, αὗται μὲν ὀρθαὶ τυγχάνουσιν οὖσαι κατὰ τὸ ἁπλῶς δίκαιον, ὅσαι δὲ τὸ σφέτερον μόνον τῶν ἀρχόντων, ἡμαρτημέναι πᾶσαι καὶ παρεκβάσεις τῶν ὀρθῶν πολιτειῶν· δεσποτικαὶ γάρ, ἡ δὲ πόλις κοινωνία τῶν ἐλευθέρων ἐστίν.

πολιτείαν δ' αὐτὴν εἰώθασιν οἱ πλεῖστοι καλεῖν] 'But most people are accustomed to term it "a constitution."' The word πολιτεία was used by the Greeks in a restricted sense, just as the word 'constitution' is in English, to denote a balanced form of government. Cf. Ar. *Pol.* III. vii. 3: ὅταν δὲ τὸ πλῆθος πρὸς τὸ κοινὸν πολιτεύηται συμφέρον, καλεῖται τὸ κοινὸν ὄνομα πασῶν τῶν πολιτειῶν, πολιτεία. Aristotle does not use the word in the *Politics* to denote a timocracy. In the ninth chapter of Book IV. he uses it to denote a mixed form between oligarchy and democracy. He also uses it to express his own ideal of a state, which was far from being a timocracy.

2 ὁ γὰρ μὴ τοιοῦτος κληρωτὸς ἄν τις εἴη βασιλεύς] 'For he who had not these qualifications would be a sort of ballot-box king.' It is difficult to express the word κληρωτός, which as coupled with βασιλεύς is certainly meant to be contemptuous. Aristotle does not appear to mean any definite form of monarchy, so we learn nothing from *Pol.* III. xiv., to which the commentators refer us. Aristotle here says that the genuine king must be independent in property and position, and above all his subjects in this respect. Externally wanting nothing for himself, he will administer the state for the good of his subjects. If this is not the case, he will be no genuine king, but a *parvenu*, κληρωτός τις, like a person who had been raised to the throne by the contingency of lot, and therefore insecure in his position, with perhaps only a temporary tenure of office. The word ἀμίσθους is coupled with μὴ κληρωτάς, (as an epithet of πενταρχίας), *Pol.* II. xi. 7. It is possible that in the present passage a notion of 'paid services' may be implied. If so, 'hireling monarch' would express the terms under notice.

κληρωτὸς ἄν τις εἴη βασιλεύς. ἡ δὲ τυραννὶς ἐξ ἐναντίας
ταύτῃ· τὸ γὰρ ἑαυτῷ ἀγαθὸν διώκει. καὶ φανερώτερον
ἐπὶ ταύτης ὅτι χειρίστη· κάκιστον δὲ τὸ ἐναντίον τῷ 3
βελτίστῳ. μεταβαίνει δ' ἐκ βασιλείας εἰς τυραννίδα·
φαυλότης γάρ ἐστι μοναρχίας ἡ τυραννίς· ὁ δὴ μοχθηρὸς
βασιλεὺς τύραννος γίνεται. ἐξ ἀριστοκρατίας δὲ εἰς
ὀλιγαρχίαν κακίᾳ τῶν ἀρχόντων, οἳ νέμουσι τὰ τῆς
πόλεως παρὰ τὴν ἀξίαν, καὶ πάντα ἢ τὰ πλεῖστα τῶν
ἀγαθῶν ἑαυτοῖς, καὶ τὰς ἀρχὰς ἀεὶ τοῖς αὐτοῖς, περὶ
πλείστου ποιούμενοι τὸ πλουτεῖν· ὀλίγοι δὴ ἄρχουσι καὶ
μοχθηροὶ ἀντὶ τῶν ἐπιεικεστάτων. ἐκ δὲ δὴ τιμοκρατίας
εἰς δημοκρατίαν· σύνοροι γάρ εἰσιν αὗται· πλήθους γὰρ
βούλεται καὶ ἡ τιμοκρατία εἶναι, καὶ ἴσοι πάντες οἱ ἐν τῷ
τιμήματι. ἥκιστα δὲ μοχθηρόν ἐστιν ἡ δημοκρατία· ἐπὶ
μικρὸν γὰρ παρεκβαίνει τὸ τῆς πολιτείας εἶδος. μεταβάλλουσι μὲν οὖν μάλισθ' οὕτως αἱ πολιτεῖαι· ἐλάχιστον
γὰρ οὕτω καὶ ῥᾷστα μεταβαίνουσιν. ὁμοιώματα δ' αὐτῶν 4
καὶ οἷον παραδείγματα λάβοι τις ἂν καὶ ἐν ταῖς οἰκίαις.
ἡ μὲν γὰρ πατρὸς πρὸς υἱεῖς κοινωνία βασιλείας ἔχει
σχῆμα· τῶν τέκνων γὰρ τῷ πατρὶ μέλει. ἐντεῦθεν δὲ
καὶ Ὅμηρος τὸν Δία πατέρα προσαγορεύει· πατρικὴ γὰρ
ἀρχὴ βούλεται ἡ βασιλεία εἶναι. ἐν Πέρσαις δ' ἡ τοῦ
πατρὸς τυραννική· χρῶνται γὰρ ὡς δούλοις τοῖς υἱέσιν.
τυραννικὴ δὲ καὶ ἡ δεσπότου πρὸς δούλους· τὸ γὰρ τοῦ
δεσπότου συμφέρον ἐν αὐτῇ πράττεται. αὕτη μὲν οὖν ὀρθὴ
φαίνεται, ἡ Περσικὴ δ' ἡμαρτημένη· τῶν διαφερόντων
γὰρ αἱ ἀρχαὶ διάφοροι. ἀνδρὸς δὲ καὶ γυναικὸς ἀριστο- 5
κρατικὴ φαίνεται· κατ' ἀξίαν γὰρ ὁ ἀνὴρ ἄρχει, καὶ περὶ
ταῦτα ἃ δεῖ τὸν ἄνδρα· ὅσα δὲ γυναικὶ ἁρμόζει, ἐκείνῃ
ἀποδίδωσιν. ἁπάντων δὲ κυριεύων ὁ ἀνὴρ εἰς ὀλιγαρχίαν
μεθίστησιν· παρὰ τὴν ἀξίαν γὰρ αὐτὸ ποιεῖ, καὶ οὐχ ᾗ
ἀμείνων. ἐνίοτε δὲ ἄρχουσιν αἱ γυναῖκες ἐπίκληροι οὖσαι·

---

4 τῶν διαφερόντων—διάφοροι] 'For those who differ should be governed differently.' And therefore the Persian system is wrong, which governs children as if they were the same as slaves.

5 γυναῖκες ἐπίκληροι οὖσαι] The Greek feeling about 'heiresses' is strongly expressed in a fragment of Menander (l.c.):

ὅστις γυναῖκ' ἐπίκληρον ἐπιθυμεῖ λαβεῖν
πλουτοῦσαν, ἤτοι μῆνιν ἐκτίνει θεῶν,
ἢ βούλετ' ἀτυχεῖν, μακάριος καλούμενος.

οὐ δὴ γίνονται κατ' ἀρετὴν αἱ ἀρχαί, ἀλλὰ διὰ πλοῦτον
6 καὶ δύναμιν, καθάπερ ἐν ταῖς ὀλιγαρχίαις. τιμοκρατικῇ δ' ἔοικεν ἡ τῶν ἀδελφῶν· ἴσοι γάρ, πλὴν ἐφ' ὅσον ταῖς ἡλικίαις διαλλάττουσιν· διόπερ ἂν πολὺ ταῖς ἡλικίαις διαφέρωσιν, οὐκέτι ἀδελφικὴ γίνεται ἡ φιλία. δημοκρατία δὲ μάλιστα μὲν ἐν ταῖς ἀδεσπότοις τῶν οἰκήσεων (ἐνταῦθα γὰρ πάντες ἐξ ἴσου), καὶ ἐν αἷς ἀσθενὴς ὁ ἄρχων καὶ ἑκάστῳ ἐξουσία.

11 Καθ' ἑκάστην δὲ τῶν πολιτειῶν φιλία φαίνεται, ἐφ' ὅσον καὶ τὸ δίκαιον, βασιλεῖ μὲν πρὸς τοὺς βασιλευομένους ἐν ὑπεροχῇ εὐεργεσίας· εὖ γὰρ ποιεῖ τοὺς βασιλευομένους, εἴπερ ἀγαθὸς ὢν ἐπιμελεῖται αὐτῶν, ἵν' εὖ πράττωσιν, ὥσπερ νομεὺς προβάτων· ὅθεν καὶ Ὅμηρος τὸν Ἀγα-
2 μέμνονα ποιμένα λαῶν εἶπεν. τοιαύτη δὲ καὶ ἡ πατρική, διαφέρει δὲ τῷ μεγέθει τῶν εὐεργετημάτων· αἴτιος γὰρ τοῦ εἶναι δοκοῦντος μεγίστου, καὶ τροφῆς καὶ παιδείας· καὶ τοῖς προγόνοις δὲ ταῦτα ἀπονέμεται· φύσει τε ἀρχικὸν πατὴρ υἱῶν καὶ πρόγονοι ἐκγόνων καὶ βασιλεὺς βασι-
3 λευομένων. ἐν ὑπεροχῇ δὲ αἱ φιλίαι αὗται, διὸ καὶ τιμῶνται οἱ γονεῖς. καὶ τὸ δίκαιον δὴ ἐν τούτοις οὐ ταὐτὸ
4 ἀλλὰ τὸ κατ' ἀξίαν· οὕτω γὰρ καὶ ἡ φιλία. καὶ ἀνδρὸς δὲ πρὸς γυναῖκα ἡ αὐτὴ φιλία καὶ ἐν ἀριστοκρατίᾳ· κατ' ἀρετὴν γάρ, καὶ τῷ ἀμείνονι πλέον ἀγαθόν, καὶ τὸ ἁρμόζον
5 ἑκάστῳ· οὕτω δὲ καὶ τὸ δίκαιον. ἡ δὲ τῶν ἀδελφῶν τῇ ἑταιρικῇ ἔοικεν· ἴσοι γὰρ καὶ ἡλικιῶται, οἱ τοιοῦτοι δ' ὁμοπαθεῖς καὶ ὁμοήθεις ὡς ἐπὶ τὸ πολύ. ἔοικε δὴ ταύτῃ καὶ ἡ κατὰ τὴν τιμοκρατικήν· ἴσοι γὰρ οἱ πολῖται βούλονται καὶ ἐπιεικεῖς εἶναι· ἐν μέρει δὴ τὸ ἄρχειν, καὶ
6 ἐξ ἴσου· οὕτω δὴ καὶ ἡ φιλία. ἐν δὲ ταῖς παρεκβάσεσιν, ὥσπερ καὶ τὸ δίκαιον ἐπὶ μικρόν ἐστιν, οὕτω καὶ ἡ φιλία.

XI. 3 ἐν ὑπεροχῇ—γονεῖς] 'All these friendships imply superiority on the one side, and hence it is that parents are honoured,' i.e. because superiority demands honour, as well as love.

5 ἴσοι γὰρ—εἶναι] 'For it is the part of the citizens (in a timocracy) to live equally and equitably with one another.' To understand the full meaning of ἐπιεικεῖς, see the fine passage from *Rhet.* I. xiii., translated in the note on *Eth.* v. x. 1., and cf. iv. x. 6. βούλονται expresses a natural tendency, cf. viii. x. 3: πλήθους γὰρ βούλεται καὶ ἡ τιμοκρατία εἶναι.

ἐστί, καὶ ἥκιστα ἐν τῇ χειρίστῃ· ἐν τυραννίδι γὰρ οὐδὲν ἢ μικρὸν φιλίας. ἐν οἷς γὰρ μηδὲν κοινόν ἐστι τῷ ἄρχοντι καὶ τῷ ἀρχομένῳ, οὐδὲ φιλία· οὐδὲ γὰρ δίκαιον· ἀλλ' οἷον τεχνίτῃ πρὸς ὄργανον καὶ ψυχῇ πρὸς σῶμα καὶ δεσπότῃ πρὸς δοῦλον· ὠφελεῖται μὲν γὰρ πάντα ταῦτα ὑπὸ τῶν χρωμένων, φιλία δ' οὐκ ἔστι πρὸς τὰ ἄψυχα οὐδὲ δίκαιον. ἀλλ' οὐδὲ πρὸς ἵππον ἢ βοῦν, οὐδὲ πρὸς δοῦλον ᾗ δοῦλος. οὐδὲν γὰρ κοινόν ἐστιν· ὁ γὰρ δοῦλος
ἔμψυχον ὄργανον, τὸ δ' ὄργανον ἄψυχος δοῦλος. ᾗ μὲν 7
οὖν δοῦλος, οὐκ ἔστι φιλία πρὸς αὐτόν, ᾗ δ' ἄνθρωπος· δοκεῖ γὰρ εἶναί τι δίκαιον παντὶ ἀνθρώπῳ πρὸς πάντα τὸν δυνάμενον κοινωνῆσαι νόμου καὶ συνθήκης· καὶ φιλίας δή,
καθ' ὅσον ἄνθρωπος. ἐπὶ μικρὸν δὴ καὶ ἐν ταῖς τυραννίσιν 8
αἱ φιλίαι καὶ τὸ δίκαιον, ἐν δὲ ταῖς δημοκρατίαις ἐπὶ πλεῖστον· πολλὰ γὰρ τὰ κοινὰ ἴσοις οὖσιν.

Ἐν κοινωνίᾳ μὲν οὖν πᾶσα φιλία ἐστίν, καθάπερ εἴρηται· 12
ἀφορίσειε δ' ἄν τις τήν τε συγγενικὴν καὶ τὴν ἑταιρικήν. αἱ δὲ πολιτικαὶ καὶ φυλετικαὶ καὶ συμπλοϊκαί, καὶ ὅσαι τοιαῦται, κοινωνικαῖς ἐοίκασι μᾶλλον· οἷον γὰρ καθ' ὁμολογίαν τινὰ φαίνονται εἶναι. εἰς ταύτας δὲ τάξειεν ἄν
τις καὶ τὴν ξενικήν. καὶ ἡ συγγενικὴ δὲ φαίνεται πολυ- 2
ειδὴς εἶναι, ἠρτῆσθαι δὲ πᾶσα ἐκ τῆς πατρικῆς· οἱ γονεῖς μὲν γὰρ στέργουσι τὰ τέκνα ὡς ἑαυτῶν τι ὄντα, τὰ δὲ τέκνα τοὺς γονεῖς ὡς ἀπ' ἐκείνων τι ὄντα. μᾶλλον δ' ἴσασιν οἱ γονεῖς τὰ ἐξ αὐτῶν ἢ τὰ γεννηθέντα ὅτι ἐκ τού-

---

6 ὠφελεῖται—δίκαιον] 'For though all these things receive benefit from those who make use of them, yet neither friendship nor justice is possible toward inanimate objects.' The corresponding passage in the *Eudemian Ethics* serves as a commentary on this: *Eth. Eud.* VII. x. 4: *συμβαίνει δὲ καὶ αὐτὸ τὸ* [e conj. Bonitz] *ὄργανον ἐπιμελείας τυγχάνειν, ἧς δίκαιον πρὸς τὸ ἔργον, ἐκείνου γὰρ ἕνεκέν ἐστι.* The instrument receives just so much care from its master, as will keep it in proper condition for the exercise of its functions. The slave, who is treated not as a person but as a thing, receives the same kind of attention. Friendship and justice imply the recognition of personality, they imply treating men not as instruments, but as ends in themselves. On the slavery of the body to the soul, cf. Ar. *Pol.* I. v. 6—8.

XII. 1 *ἀφορίσειε δ' ἄν τις*] In saying that all friendships imply community of interests, an exception is to be made of the friendships of relations

των, καὶ μᾶλλον συνῳκείωται τὸ ἀφ᾽ οὗ τῷ γεννηθέντι ἢ
τὸ γενόμενον τῷ ποιήσαντι· τὸ γὰρ ἐξ αὐτοῦ οἰκεῖον τῷ
ἀφ᾽ οὗ, οἷον ὀδοὺς ἢ θρὶξ ἢ ὁτιοῦν τῷ ἔχοντι· ἐκείνῳ δ᾽ οὐθὲν
τὸ ἀφ᾽ οὗ, ἢ ἧττον. καὶ τῷ πλήθει δὲ τοῦ χρόνου· οἱ
μὲν γὰρ εὐθὺς γενόμενα στέργουσιν, τὰ δὲ προελθόντα
τοῖς χρόνοις τοὺς γονεῖς, σύνεσιν ἢ αἴσθησιν λαβόντα. ἐκ
τούτων δὲ δῆλον καὶ δι᾽ ἃ φιλοῦσι μᾶλλον αἱ μητέρες.
3 γονεῖς μὲν οὖν τέκνα φιλοῦσιν ὡς ἑαυτούς (τὰ γὰρ ἐξ αὐτῶν οἷον ἕτεροι αὐτοὶ τῷ κεχωρίσθαι), τέκνα δὲ γονεῖς ὡς
ἀπ᾽ ἐκείνων πεφυκότα, ἀδελφοὶ δ᾽ ἀλλήλους τῷ ἐκ τῶν
αὐτῶν πεφυκέναι· ἡ γὰρ πρὸς ἐκεῖνα ταὐτότης ἀλλήλοις
ταὐτοποιεῖ· ὅθεν φασὶ ταὐτὸν αἷμα καὶ ῥίζαν καὶ τὰ τοι-
4 αῦτα. εἰσὶ δὴ ταὐτό πως καὶ ἐν διῃρημένοις. μέγα δὲ πρὸς
φιλίαν καὶ τὸ σύντροφον καὶ τὸ καθ᾽ ἡλικίαν· ἧλιξ γὰρ
ἥλικα, καὶ οἱ συνήθεις ἑταῖροι· διὸ καὶ ἡ ἀδελφικὴ τῇ ἑταιρικῇ ὁμοιοῦται. ἀνεψιοὶ δὲ καὶ οἱ λοιποὶ συγγενεῖς ἐκ
τούτων συνῳκείωνται. τῷ γὰρ ἀπὸ τῶν αὐτῶν εἶναι. γίγνονται δ᾽ οἱ μὲν οἰκειότεροι οἱ δ᾽ ἀλλοτριώτεροι τῷ σύνεγ-
5 γυς ἢ πόρρω τὸν ἀρχηγὸν εἶναι. ἔστι δ᾽ ἡ μὲν πρὸς γονεῖς
φιλία τέκνοις, καὶ ἀνθρώποις πρὸς θεούς, ὡς πρὸς ἀγαθὸν
καὶ ὑπερέχον· εὖ γὰρ πεποιήκασι τὰ μέγιστα· τοῦ γὰρ
εἶναι καὶ τραφῆναι αἴτιοι, καὶ γενομένοις τοῦ παιδευθῆναι.
6 ἔχει δὲ καὶ τὸ ἡδὺ καὶ τὸ χρήσιμον ἡ τοιαύτη φιλία μᾶλλον τῶν ὀθνείων, ὅσῳ καὶ κοινότερος ὁ βίος αὐτοῖς ἐστίν.
ἔστι δὲ καὶ ἐν τῇ ἀδελφικῇ ἅπερ καὶ ἐν τῇ ἑταιρικῇ, καὶ
μᾶλλον ἐν τοῖς ἐπιεικέσι, καὶ ὅλως ἐν τοῖς ὁμοίοις, ὅσῳ
οἰκειότεροι καὶ ἐκ γενετῆς ὑπάρχουσι στέργοντες ἀλλήλους, καὶ ὅσῳ ὁμοηθέστεροι οἱ ἐκ τῶν αὐτῶν καὶ σύντροφοι

---

and companions, which depend on feeling rather than on any sort of compact.

3 ἡ γὰρ πρὸς ἐκεῖνα ταὐτότης ἀλλήλοις ταὐτοποιεῖ] 'For their identity with the parents identifies them with one another.' *ἐκεῖνα* is in the neuter gender on account of the words *ἐκ τῶν αὐτῶν* to which it immediately refers.

4 ἀνεψιοὶ δὲ—εἶναι] 'But cousins and all other relations get their bond of unity from them (*i.e.* the brothers); for (it depends) on their coming from the same stock. Relations are more or less closely united to one another, in proportion as their common ancestor is more or less near.'

5 πρὸς θεοὺς ὡς πρὸς ἀγαθὸν καὶ ὑπερέχον] Cf. *Eth.* VIII. vii. 4. IX. i. 7.

καὶ παιδευθέντες ὁμοίως· καὶ ἡ κατὰ τὸν χρόνον δοκιμασία πλείστη καὶ βεβαιοτάτη. ἀνάλογον δὲ καὶ ἐν τοῖς λοι- 7
ποῖς τῶν συγγενῶν τὰ φιλικά. ἀνδρὶ δὲ καὶ γυναικὶ φιλία δοκεῖ κατὰ φύσιν ὑπάρχειν· ἄνθρωπος γὰρ τῇ φύσει συνδυαστικὸν μᾶλλον ἢ πολιτικόν, ὅσῳ πρότερον καὶ ἀναγκαιότερον οἰκία πόλεως, καὶ τεκνοποιία κοινότερον τοῖς ζῴοις. τοῖς μὲν οὖν ἄλλοις ἐπὶ τοσοῦτον ἡ κοινωνία ἐστίν, οἱ δ' ἄνθρωποι οὐ μόνον τῆς τεκνοποιίας χάριν συνοικοῦσιν, ἀλλὰ καὶ τῶν εἰς τὸν βίον· εὐθὺς γὰρ διῄρηται τὰ ἔργα, καὶ ἔστιν ἕτερα ἀνδρὸς καὶ γυναικός· ἐπαρκοῦσιν οὖν ἀλλήλοις, εἰς τὸ κοινὸν τιθέντες τὰ ἴδια. διὰ ταῦτα δὲ καὶ τὸ χρήσιμον εἶναι δοκεῖ καὶ τὸ ἡδὺ ἐν ταύτῃ τῇ φιλίᾳ. εἴη δ' ἂν καὶ δι' ἀρετήν, εἰ ἐπιεικεῖς εἶεν· ἔστι γὰρ ἑκατέρου ἀρετή, καὶ χαίροιεν ἂν τῷ τοιούτῳ. σύνδεσμος δὲ τὰ τέκνα δοκεῖ εἶναι· διὸ θᾶττον οἱ ἄτεκνοι διαλύονται· τὰ γὰρ τέκνα κοινὸν ἀγαθὸν ἀμφοῖν, συνέχει δὲ τὸ κοινόν. τὸ δὲ πῶς 8
συμβιωτέον ἀνδρὶ πρὸς γυναῖκα καὶ ὅλως φίλῳ πρὸς φίλον, οὐδὲν ἕτερον φαίνεται ζητεῖσθαι ἢ πῶς δίκαιον· οὐ γὰρ ταὐτὸν φαίνεται τῷ φίλῳ πρὸς τὸν φίλον καὶ τὸν ὀθνεῖον καὶ τὸν ἑταῖρον καὶ τὸν συμφοιτητήν.

Τριττῶν δ' οὐσῶν φιλιῶν, καθάπερ ἐν ἀρχῇ εἴρηται, 13
καὶ καθ' ἑκάστην τῶν μὲν ἐν ἰσότητι φίλων ὄντων τῶν δὲ καθ' ὑπεροχήν (καὶ γὰρ ὁμοίως ἀγαθοὶ φίλοι γίνονται καὶ

&c. Aristotle throughout these books speaks of 'the gods' from the point of view of the popular religion.

7 πρότερον καὶ ἀναγκαιότερον οἰκία πόλεως] In point of time the family is prior to the state, but in point of idea (λόγῳ) and essentially (φύσει) the state is prior. Cf. Ar. *Pol.* I. ii. 12: καὶ πρότερον δὴ τῇ φύσει πόλις ἢ οἰκία καὶ ἕκαστος ἡμῶν ἐστιν. Τὸ γὰρ ὅλον πρότερον ἀναγκαῖον εἶναι τοῦ μέρους· ἀναιρουμένου γὰρ τοῦ ὅλου οὐκ ἔσται ποὺς οὐδὲ χείρ, εἰ μὴ ὁμωνύμως. Aristotle argues that, without the idea of the 'state,' the terms 'man' and 'family' would lose their meaning. Thus the idea of family presupposes that of the state, which will accordingly be prior. In the same way, the family is more necessary as a means, the state as an end.

ἐπαρκοῦσιν οὖν—ἴδια] 'They help one another therefore, bringing what they each have separately into the common stock.' Fritzsche quotes the saying of Ischomachus to his wife in the *Œconomics* of Xenophon (vii. 13): νῦν δὲ οἶκος ἡμῖν ὅδε κοινός ἐστιν. Ἐγώ τε γάρ, ὅσα μοί ἐστιν, ἅπαντα εἰς τὸ κοινὸν ἀποφαίνω, σύ τε ὅσα ἠνέγκω, πάντα εἰς τὸ κοινὸν κατέθηκας.

XIII. 1 ἐν ἀρχῇ] *Eth.* VIII. iii. 1.

ἀμείνων χείρονι, ὁμοίως δὲ καὶ ἡδεῖς, καὶ διὰ τὸ χρήσιμον
ἰσάζοντες ταῖς ὠφελείαις καὶ διαφέροντες), τοὺς ἴσους μὲν
κατ' ἰσότητα δεῖ τῷ φιλεῖν καὶ τοῖς λοιποῖς ἰσάζειν, τοὺς
2 δ' ἀνίσους τῷ ἀνάλογον ταῖς ὑπεροχαῖς ἀποδιδόναι. γίγνεται δὲ τὰ ἐγκλήματα καὶ αἱ μέμψεις ἐν τῇ κατὰ τὸ
χρήσιμον φιλίᾳ ἢ μόνῃ ἢ μάλιστα εὐλόγως. οἱ μὲν γὰρ
δι' ἀρετὴν φίλοι ὄντες εὖ δρᾶν ἀλλήλους προθυμοῦνται·
τοῦτο γὰρ ἀρετῆς καὶ φιλίας. πρὸς τοῦτο δ' ἁμιλλωμένων οὐκ ἔστιν ἐγκλήματα οὐδὲ μάχαι· τὸν γὰρ φιλοῦντα
καὶ εὖ ποιοῦντα οὐδεὶς δυσχεραίνει, ἀλλ' ἐὰν ᾖ χαρίεις,
ἀμύνεται εὖ δρῶν. ὁ δ' ὑπερβάλλων, τυγχάνων οὗ ἐφίεται,
οὐκ ἂν ἐγκαλοίη τῷ φίλῳ· ἑκάτερος γὰρ τοῦ ἀγαθοῦ
3 ἐφίεται. οὐ πάνυ δ' οὐδ' ἐν τοῖς δι' ἡδονήν· ἅμα γὰρ
ἀμφοῖν γίνεται οὗ ὀρέγονται, εἰ τῷ συνδιάγειν χαίρουσιν.
γελοῖος δ' ἂν φαίνοιτο καὶ ὁ ἐγκαλῶν τῷ μὴ τέρποντι,
4 ἐξὸν μὴ συνδημερεύειν· ἡ δὲ διὰ τὸ χρήσιμον ἐγκληματική·
ἐπ' ὠφελείᾳ γὰρ χρώμενοι ἀλλήλοις ἀεὶ τοῦ πλείονος δέονται, καὶ ἔλαττον ἔχειν οἴονται τοῦ προσήκοντος, καὶ μέμφονται ὅτι οὐχ ὅσων δέονται τοσούτων τυγχάνουσιν ἄξιοι ὄν-
τες· οἱ δ' εὖ ποιοῦντες οὐ δύνανται ἐπαρκεῖν τοσαῦτα ὅσων οἱ
5 πάσχοντες δέονται. ἔοικε δέ, καθάπερ τὸ δίκαιόν ἐστι διτ-
τόν, τὸ μὲν ἄγραφον τὸ δὲ κατὰ νόμον, καὶ τῆς κατὰ τὸ

---

2 τὸν γὰρ—εὖ δρῶν] 'No one takes it ill that one loves and benefits him, but, if he be of gentle mind, pays his benefactor back in good deeds.' The subject to ἀμύνεται is implied in οὐδείς. Fritzsche quotes Horace, *Sat.* I. i. 1.

> *Nemo* quam sibi sortem
> Seu ratio dederit, seu fors objecerit, illâ
> Contentus vivat, *laudet* diversa sequentes.

χαρίεις has nothing to do with 'gratitude.' It means much the same as is conveyed in the word 'gentleman.' Cf. *Eth.* I. v. 4: οἱ δὲ χαρίεντες καὶ πρακτικοί. IV. viii. 9: χαρίεις καὶ ἐλευθέριος.

5 ἔοικε—διαλύωνται] 'Now as justice is twofold, the one unwritten, the other according to law, so also of utilitarian friendship there appear to be two branches, the one moral, and the other legal. The complaints then (which arise) chiefly take place when men do not conclude their connection in the same branch in which they commenced it.' συναλλάττειν is to make a contract, διαλύεσθαι to wind up a contract by the mutual performance of the terms. Men who consider that they have entered upon a so-called friendship with a fixed stipulation (νομική) of certain advantages to be received, will complain if the final stipulation is denied, and only a general moral obligation (ἠθική) to render services is admitted.

χρήσιμον φιλίας ἡ μὲν ἠθικὴ ἡ δὲ νομικὴ εἶναι. γίγνεται
οὖν τὰ ἐγκλήματα μάλισθ' ὅταν μὴ κατὰ τὴν αὐτὴν
συναλλάξωσι καὶ διαλύωνται. ἔστι δὴ νομικὴ μὲν ἡ ἐπὶ 6
ῥητοῖς, ἡ μὲν πάμπαν ἀγοραία ἐκ χειρὸς εἰς χεῖρα, ἡ δὲ
ἐλευθεριωτέρα εἰς χρόνον, καθ' ὁμολογίαν δὲ τί ἀντὶ τίνος.
δῆλον δ' ἐν ταύτῃ τὸ ὀφείλημα κοὐκ ἀμφίλογον, φιλικὸν
δὲ τὴν ἀναβολὴν ἔχει· διὸ παρ' ἐνίοις οὐκ εἰσὶ τούτων
δίκαι, ἀλλ' οἴονται δεῖν στέργειν τοὺς κατὰ πίστιν συν-
αλλάξαντας. ἡ δ' ἠθικὴ οὐκ ἐπὶ ῥητοῖς, ἀλλ' ὡς φίλῳ 7
δωρεῖται ἢ ὁτιδήποτε ἄλλο. κομίζεσθαι δὲ ἀξιοῖ τὸ ἴσον
ἢ πλέον, ὡς οὐ δεδωκὼς ἀλλὰ χρήσας. οὐχ ὁμοίως δὲ 8
συναλλάξας καὶ διαλυόμενος ἐγκαλέσει. τοῦτο δὲ συμβαίνει διὰ τὸ βούλεσθαι μὲν πάντας ἢ τοὺς πλείστους τὰ
καλά, προαιρεῖσθαι δὲ τὰ ὠφέλιμα. καλὸν δὲ τὸ εὖ ποιεῖν
μὴ ἵνα ἀντιπάθῃ, ὠφέλιμον δὲ τὸ εὐεργετεῖσθαι. δυναμένῳ 9

---

6 ἔστι—συναλλάξαντας] 'That which is on statal conditions then is legal (utilitarian friendship). One sort of it is wholly commercial, implying payment on the spot (ἐκ χειρὸς εἰς χεῖρα); another is more liberal, allowing time (εἰς χρόνον), but still on the understanding of a specified return. In this then the debt is plain and undoubted, but the delay which it admits of is friendly. Hence in some states no suits are allowed in cases of this kind, but men think that those who have contracted on faith should abide (by the issue).' ἀναβολή in commerce answers to 'credit,' cf. Plato's *Laws*, XI. p. 915 D: μηδ' ἐπὶ ἀναβολῇ πρᾶσιν μηδὲ ὠνὴν ποιεῖσθαι. Or it may answer to buying or selling for future delivery. φιλικόν ('of the nature of friendship') stands here as a predicate. Cf. *Eth.* VIII. i. 4: τῶν δικαίων τὸ μάλιστα φιλικὸν εἶναι δοκεῖ.

7—8 ἡ δ' ἠθικὴ—εὐεργετεῖσθαι] 'On the other hand the moral (branch of utilitarian friendship) is not on statal conditions, but the gift, or whatever else it be, is made as if to a friend. Yet (the giver) claims to get as much, or more, as though he had not given but lent. And if he does not come off in the connection as well as he commenced, he will complain. Now this (sort of disappointment) takes place because all or most men *wish* that which is noble, but *practically choose* that which is expedient. It is noble to do good not with a view to receive it back, but it is expedient to be benefited.' This passage discriminately exposes a sort of vacillation between disinterestedness and self-interest, which occurs in utilitarian friendships. A man at one moment thinks vaguely (βούλεται) of aiming at the noble, and makes a gift as if he expected no return. But presently the more definite bent of his mind (προαίρεσις) reverts to the profitable, and he claims to get back as good as he gave. On the distinction between βούλεσθαι and προαιρεῖσθαι cf. *Eth.* III. iv. 1, v. ix. 6, and the notes.

9 δυναμένῳ δὴ—ἢ μή] 'If one is able, then one ought to pay back the full value of what one has received;

δὴ ἀνταποδοτέον τὴν ἀξίαν ὧν ἔπαθεν, † καὶ ἑκόντι· ἄκοντα γὰρ φίλον οὐ ποιητέον. ὡς δὴ διαμαρτόντα ἐν τῇ ἀρχῇ καὶ εὖ παθόντα ὑφ' οὗ οὐκ ἔδει· οὐ γὰρ ὑπὸ φίλου, οὐδὲ δι' αὐτὸ τοῦτο δρῶντος· καθάπερ οὖν ἐπὶ ῥητοῖς εὐεργετηθέντα διαλυτέον. καὶ ὁμολογήσαι δ' ἂν δυνάμενος ἀποδώσειν· ἀδυνατοῦντα δ' οὐδ' ὁ δοὺς ἠξίωσεν ἄν· ὥστ' εἰ δυνατός, ἀποδοτέον. ἐν ἀρχῇ δ' ἐπισκεπτέον ὑφ' οὗ εὐεργετεῖται καὶ
10 ἐπὶ τίνι, ὅπως ἐπὶ τούτοις ὑπομένῃ ἢ μή. ἀμφισβήτησιν δ' ἔχει πότερα δεῖ τῇ τοῦ παθόντος ὠφελείᾳ μετρεῖν καὶ πρὸς ταύτην ποιεῖσθαι τὴν ἀνταπόδοσιν, ἢ τῇ τοῦ δράσαντος εὐεργεσίᾳ. οἱ μὲν γὰρ παθόντες τοιαῦτά φασι λαβεῖν παρὰ τῶν εὐεργετῶν ἃ μικρὰ ἦν ἐκείνοις καὶ ἐξῆν παρ' ἑτέρων λαβεῖν, κατασμικρίζοντες· οἱ δ' ἀνάπαλιν τὰ μέγιστα τῶν παρ' αὑτοῖς, καὶ ἃ παρ' ἄλλων οὐκ ἦν, καὶ ἐν
11 κινδύνοις ἢ τοιαύταις χρείαις. ἆρ' οὖν διὰ μὲν τὸ χρήσιμον τῆς φιλίας οὔσης ἡ τοῦ παθόντος ὠφέλεια μέτρον ἐστίν; οὗτος γὰρ ὁ δεόμενος, καὶ ἐπαρκεῖ αὐτῷ ὡς κομιούμενος τὴν ἴσην· τοσαύτη οὖν γεγένηται ἡ ἐπικουρία ὅσον οὗτος ὠφέληται, καὶ ἀποδοτέον δὴ αὐτῷ ὅσον ἐπηύρατο, ἢ καὶ πλέον· κάλλιον γάρ. ἐν δὲ ταῖς κατ' ἀρετὴν

for one must not make a man a friend against his will (*i.e.* treat him as if he were disinterested, when he did not really mean to be so). (One must act) as if one had made a mistake at the outset, and had received a benefit from one whom one ought not to have received it from, that is to say not from a friend, or from some one doing a friendly action; one must conclude the business therefore as if one had been benefited on stated conditions. And (in this case) one would stipulate to repay to the best of one's ability;—if one were unable, not even the giver could demand it; so in short, if one is able, one should repay. But one ought to consider at the outset by whom one is benefited, and on what terms, so that one may agree to accept those terms, or not.' The words καὶ ἑκόντι are omitted in the above translation. They are left out by two of the MSS., and while they merely interrupt the sense of the passage, they may easily be conceived to have arisen out of the following words ἄκοντα γάρ. The passage prescribes the mode of dealing with a person who having conferred a benefit (as described in the last section) expects a return for it. The accusative case διαμαρτόντα is governed by the verbal adjective διαλυτέον which follows, cf. *Eth.* VII. i. 1: λυτέον ἄλλην ποιησαμένους ἀρχήν. Some editions read ὁμολογῆσαι δ' ἄν, which the commentators explain to be governed by δεῖ, as implied in the verbal adjectives ἀνταποδοτέον, διαλυτέον.

11 ἆρ' οὖν—πλέον] 'Surely, as the friendship is for the sake of utility,

ἐγκλήματα μὲν οὐκ ἔστιν, μέτρῳ δ' ἔοικεν ἡ τοῦ δράσαντος
προαίρεσις· τῆς ἀρετῆς γὰρ καὶ τοῦ ἤθους ἐν τῇ προαιρέσει
τὸ κύριον.

Διαφέρονται δὲ καὶ ἐν ταῖς καθ' ὑπεροχὴν φιλίαις· ἀξιοῖ 14
γὰρ ἑκάτερος πλέον ἔχειν, ὅταν δὲ τοῦτο γίγνηται, διαλύεται ἡ φιλία. οἴεται γὰρ ὅ τε βελτίων προσήκειν αὐτῷ
πλέον ἔχειν· τῷ γὰρ ἀγαθῷ νέμεσθαι πλέον· ὁμοίως δὲ καὶ
ὁ ὠφελιμώτερος· ἀχρεῖον γὰρ ὄντα οὔ φασι δεῖν ἴσον
ἔχειν· λειτουργίαν τε γὰρ γίνεσθαι καὶ οὐ φιλίαν, εἰ μὴ
κατ' ἀξίαν τῶν ἔργων ἔσται τὰ ἐκ τῆς φιλίας· οἴονται
γάρ, καθάπερ ἐν χρημάτων κοινωνίᾳ πλεῖον λαμβάνουσιν
οἱ συμβαλλόμενοι πλεῖον, οὕτω δεῖν καὶ ἐν τῇ φιλίᾳ. ὁ δ'
ἐνδεὴς καὶ ὁ χείρων ἀνάπαλιν· φίλου γὰρ ἀγαθοῦ εἶναι τὸ
ἐπαρκεῖν τοῖς ἐνδεέσιν· τί γάρ, φασίν, ὄφελος σπουδαίῳ ἢ
δυνάστῃ φίλον εἶναι, μηθέν γε μέλλοντα ἀπολαύειν; ἔοικε 2
δὲ ἑκάτερος ὀρθῶς ἀξιοῦν, καὶ δεῖν ἑκατέρῳ πλέον νέμειν
ἐκ τῆς φιλίας, οὐ τοῦ αὐτοῦ δέ, ἀλλὰ τῷ μὲν ὑπερέχοντι
τιμῆς, τῷ δ' ἐνδεεῖ κέρδους· τῆς μὲν γὰρ ἀρετῆς καὶ τῆς
εὐεργεσίας ἡ τιμὴ γέρας, τῆς δ' ἐνδείας ἐπικουρία τὸ κέρδος.
οὕτω δ' ἔχειν τοῦτο καὶ ἐν ταῖς πολιτείαις φαίνεται· οὐ 3
γὰρ τιμᾶται ὁ μηδὲν ἀγαθὸν τῷ κοινῷ πορίζων· τὸ κοινὸν
γὰρ δίδοται τῷ τὸ κοινὸν εὐεργετοῦντι, ἡ τιμὴ δὲ κοινόν. οὐ
γὰρ ἔστιν ἅμα χρηματίζεσθαι ἀπὸ τῶν κοινῶν καὶ τιμᾶ-
σθαι· ἐν πᾶσι γὰρ τὸ ἔλαττον οὐδεὶς ὑπομένει. τῷ δὴ

---

the benefit accruing to the recipient is the gauge (of what is to be repaid). For he (the recipient) is the asking party, and (the other) assists him on the understanding that he will receive the same value. The assistance rendered then is exactly so much as the recipient has been benefited; and he ought therefore to repay as much as he has reaped, or even more.'

XIV. 1 *διαφέρονται*] 'Men have differences' in those friendships which are contracted between a superior and an inferior. Aristotle says that these differences ought to be settled by both parties respectively getting more than each other; the one receiving more money or good, the other receiving more honour.

3 *οὐ γὰρ ἔστιν—ὑπομένει*] 'For it is not allowable that a man should at once gain money and honour out of the public, for no one endures to have the inferior position in all points.' This notion, that the state-officers should have *either* pay or honour, but not both, is expressed before, *Eth.* v. vi. 6, 7. It is drawn from the Athenian ideas of liberty and equality, but is hardly in accordance with the practice of the modern world.

περὶ χρήματα ἐλαττουμένῳ τιμὴν ἀπονέμουσι καὶ τῷ δωροδόκῳ χρήματα· τὸ κατ' ἀξίαν γὰρ ἐπανισοῖ καὶ σῴζει
τὴν φιλίαν, καθάπερ εἴρηται. οὕτω δὴ καὶ τοῖς ἀνίσοις
ὁμιλητέον, καὶ τῷ εἰς χρήματα ὠφελουμένῳ ἢ εἰς ἀρετὴν
4 τιμὴν ἀνταποδοτέον, ἀνταποδιδόντα τὸ ἐνδεχόμενον. τὸ δυνατὸν γὰρ ἡ φιλία ἐπιζητεῖ, οὐ τὸ κατ' ἀξίαν· οὐδὲ γὰρ
ἔστιν ἐν πᾶσι, καθάπερ ἐν ταῖς πρὸς τοὺς θεοὺς τιμαῖς καὶ
τοὺς γονεῖς· οὐδεὶς γὰρ ἄν ποτε τὴν ἀξίαν ἀποδοίη, εἰς
δύναμιν δὲ ὁ θεραπεύων ἐπιεικὴς εἶναι δοκεῖ. διὸ κἂν δόξειεν οὐκ ἐξεῖναι υἱῷ πατέρα ἀπείπασθαι, πατρὶ δ' υἱόν·
ὀφείλοντα γὰρ ἀποδοτέον, οὐθὲν δὲ ποιήσας ἄξιον τῶν
ὑπηργμένων δέδρακεν, ὥστ' ἀεὶ ὀφείλει. οἷς δ' ὀφείλεται,
ἐξουσία ἀφεῖναι· καὶ τῷ πατρὶ δή. ἅμα δ' ἴσως οὐθείς
ποτ' ἂν ἀποστῆναι δοκεῖ μὴ ὑπερβάλλοντος μοχθηρίᾳ· χωρὶς γὰρ τῆς φυσικῆς φιλίας τὴν ἐπικουρίαν ἀνθρωπικὸν μὴ
διωθεῖσθαι. τῷ δὲ φευκτὸν ἢ οὐ σπουδαστὸν τὸ ἐπαρκεῖν, μοχθηρῷ ὄντι· εὖ πάσχειν γὰρ οἱ πολλοὶ βούλονται,
τὸ δὲ ποιεῖν φεύγουσιν ὡς ἀλυσιτελές. περὶ μὲν οὖν τούτων
ἐπὶ τοσοῦτον εἰρήσθω.

---

4 ἀπείπασθαι] 'To disown.' Cardwell quotes Herodotus I. 59: εἴ τίς οἱ τυγχάνει ἐὼν παῖς, τοῦτον ἀπείπασθαι. Demosthenes 1006. 21: (ὁ νόμος) τοὺς γονέας ποιεῖ κυρίους οὐ μόνον θέσθαι τοὔνομα ἐξ ἀρχῆς, ἀλλὰ καὶ πάλιν ἐξαλεῖψαι ἐὰν βούλωνται, καὶ ἀποκηρύξαι.

χωρὶς γὰρ—διωθεῖσθαι] 'For independently of natural affection, it is a human instinct not to reject the assistance (which he might derive from his son).' διωθεῖσθαι is used in the same sense, *Eth.* IX. xi. 6.

περὶ μὲν οὖν τούτων ἐπὶ τοσοῦτον εἰρήσθω] These words may have been written by Aristotle himself, with the view of dividing his treatise on Friendship into two books, of the same length as the books into which all his various writings are divided. Or, on the other hand, they may have been added, for the same purpose, by an editor.

ΗΘΙΚΩΝ ΝΙΚΟΜΑΧΕΙΩΝ IX.

ἘΝ ΠΑΣΑΙΣ δὲ ταῖς ἀνομοιοειδέσι φιλίαις τὸ ἀνάλογον
ἰσάζει καὶ σώζει τὴν φιλίαν, καθάπερ εἴρηται, οἷον
καὶ ἐν τῇ πολιτικῇ τῷ σκυτοτόμῳ ἀντὶ τῶν ὑποδημάτων
ἀμοιβὴ γίνεται κατ' ἀξίαν, καὶ τῷ ὑφάντῃ καὶ τοῖς λοιποῖς.
ἐνταῦθα μὲν οὖν πεπόρισται κοινὸν μέτρον τὸ νόμισμα, καὶ 2
πρὸς τοῦτο δὴ πάντα ἀναφέρεται, καὶ τούτῳ μετρεῖται· ἐν
δὲ τῇ ἐρωτικῇ ἐνίοτε μὲν ὁ ἐραστὴς ἐγκαλεῖ ὅτι ὑπερφιλῶν
οὐκ ἀντιφιλεῖται, οὐθὲν ἔχων φιλητόν, εἰ οὕτως ἔτυχεν,
πολλάκις δ' ὁ ἐρώμενος ὅτι πρότερον ἐπαγγελλόμενος
πάντα νῦν οὐθὲν ἐπιτελεῖ. συμβαίνει δὲ τὰ τοιαῦτα, ἐπειδὰν 3
ὁ μὲν δι' ἡδονὴν τὸν ἐρώμενον φιλῇ, ὁ δὲ διὰ τὸ χρήσιμον
τὸν ἐραστήν, ταῦτα δὲ μὴ ἀμφοῖν ὑπάρχῃ. διὰ ταῦτα
γὰρ τῆς φιλίας οὔσης διάλυσις γίνεται, ἐπειδὰν μὴ γίνηται
ὧν ἕνεκα ἐφίλουν· οὐ γὰρ αὐτοὺς ἔστεργον ἀλλὰ τὰ ὑπάρχοντα, οὐ μόνιμα ὄντα· διὸ τοιαῦται καὶ αἱ φιλίαι. ἡ δὲ
τῶν ἠθῶν καθ' αὑτὴν οὖσα μένει, καθάπερ εἴρηται. διαφέ- 4

I. In heterogeneous friendships, equality is to be obtained by the rule of proportion. The same rule holds good in political economy, where the most heterogeneous products are equalized against one another. In political economy there is the convenience of a common standard, money, by which products may be measured. In friendship there is, unfortunately, no such standard.

1 *ἀνομοιοειδέσι*] This is not quite the same as *ταῖς καθ' ὑπεροχὴν φιλίαις*. It implies relationships in which the two parties have respectively different objects in view, as for instance, in the case of the employer and the employed, the *ἐρώμενος* and the *ἐραστής*, &c.

καθάπερ εἴρηται] Cf. *Eth.* VIII. xiii. 1.

ἐν τῇ πολιτικῇ] By the modern division of sciences, Political Economy has been raised into separate existence, so as in its method to be entirely independent of, and in its results subordinate to, Politics. On the Aristotelian theory of the law of value in exchange, see *Eth.* V. v. 8, and note.

3 *ἡ δὲ τῶν ἠθῶν*] 'Moral friendship' or 'friendship based on character,' the same as *ἡ κατ' ἀρετὴν φιλία*. Cf. *Eth.* VIII. xiii. 11: *ἐν δὲ ταῖς κατ' ἀρετὴν—τῆς ἀρετῆς γὰρ καὶ τοῦ ἤθους,*

ρονται δὲ καὶ ὅταν ἕτερα γίγνηται αὐτοῖς καὶ μὴ ὧν ὀρέγονται· ὅμοιον γὰρ τῷ μηθὲν γίγνεσθαι, ὅταν οὗ ἐφίεται μὴ τυγχάνῃ, οἷον καὶ τῷ κιθαρῳδῷ ὁ ἐπαγγελλόμενος, καὶ ὅσῳ ἄμεινον ᾄσειεν, τοσούτῳ πλείω· εἰς ἕω δ᾽ ἀπαιτοῦντι τὰς ὑποσχέσεις ἀνθ᾽ ἡδονῆς ἡδονὴν ἀποδεδωκέναι ἔφη. εἰ μὲν οὖν ἑκάτερος τοῦτο ἐβούλετο, ἱκανῶς ἂν εἶχεν· εἰ δ᾽ ὁ μὲν τέρψιν ὁ δὲ κέρδος, καὶ ὁ μὲν ἔχει ὁ δὲ μή, οὐκ ἂν εἴη τὸ κατὰ τὴν κοινωνίαν καλῶς· ὧν γὰρ δεόμενος τυγχάνει, τούτοις καὶ προσέχει, κἀκείνου γε χάριν ταῦτα δώσει.
5 τὴν ἀξίαν δὲ ποτέρου τάξαι ἐστί, τοῦ προϊεμένου ἢ τοῦ προλαβόντος; ὁ γὰρ προϊέμενος ἔοικ᾽ ἐπιτρέπειν ἐκείνῳ. ὅπερ φασὶ καὶ Πρωταγόραν ποιεῖν· ὅτε γὰρ διδάξειεν ἁδήποτε, τιμῆσαι τὸν μαθόντα ἐκέλευεν ὅσου δοκεῖ ἄξια ἐπί-

---

κ.τ.λ. Of course the above terms have nothing to do with the 'moral' branch of utilitarian friendship, mentioned *Eth.* VIII. xiii. 5. 7.

4 οἷον—ἔφη] 'As in the case of him who promises (a reward) to the harper, and "the better he sang, the more he should have," but when the man next morning demands the fulfilment of his promises, said that "he had paid pleasure for pleasure,"' (*i.e.* the pleasure of hope, for the pleasure of hearing music). The present tenses ἐπαγγελλόμενος, ἀπαιτοῦντι, seem to imply an oft-repeated and current story. The story itself is repeated by Plutarch (*De Alexandri Fortunâ*, II. 1), where the trick is attributed to Dionysius. Διονύσιος γοῦν ὁ τύραννος, ὥς φασι, κιθαρῳδοῦ τινος εὐδοκιμοῦντος ἀκούων ἐπηγγείλατο δωρεὰν αὐτῷ τάλαντον· τῇ δ᾽ ὑστεραίᾳ τοῦ ἀνθρώπου τὴν ὑπόσχεσιν ἀπαιτοῦντος· χθές, εἶπεν, εὐφραινόμενος ὑπὸ σοῦ παρ᾽ ὃν ᾖδες χρόνον, εὔφραινον κἀγώ σε ταῖς ἐλπίσιν· ὥστε τὸν μισθὸν ὧν ἔτερπες ἀπελάμβανες εὐθύς, ἀντιτερπόμενος.

ὧν γὰρ δεόμενος—δώσει] 'For a man sets his mind on the things he happens to want, and for the sake of that he will give what he himself possesses.' The beginning of the sentence (ὧν γὰρ δεόμενος) is a general statement, the words κἀκείνου γε contain an application of the general statement to a particular case.

5 τὴν ἀξίαν δὲ—τοσοῦτον] 'But whose part is it to settle the value (of a benefit),—is it the part of the giver in the first instance, or of the recipient? (One would say it was the part of him who was the recipient in the first instance), for the giver seems to leave it to the other. Which they mention Protagoras as doing, for whenever he taught anything he used to bid the learner estimate "how much worth he thinks he has learnt," and he used to take exactly so much.' ὁ προϊέμενος is used in a peculiar sense here to denote 'qui prior donum dedit,' in opposition to ὁ προλαβών (or ὁ προέχων, § 8), 'qui prior ab altero accepit.' Protagoras was said to be the first philosopher who taught for money. He probably found it not disadvantageous to assume a high and liberal attitude towards his pupils. On the wealth which he amassed by teaching, see Plato's *Meno*, p. 91 D, and above, Vol. I. Essay II. p. 118.

στασθαι, καὶ ἐλάμβανε τοσοῦτον. ἐν τοῖς τοιούτοις δ' 6
ἐνίοις ἀρέσκει τὸ 'μισθὸς δ' ἀνδρί.' οἱ δὲ προλαβόντες
τὸ ἀργύριον, εἶτα μηθὲν ποιοῦντες ὧν ἔφασαν, διὰ τὰς
ὑπερβολὰς τῶν ἐπαγγελιῶν, εἰκότως ἐν ἐγκλήμασι γίνον-
ται· οὐ γὰρ ἐπιτελοῦσιν ἃ ὡμολόγησαν. τοῦτο δ' ἴσως 7
ποιεῖν οἱ σοφισταὶ ἀναγκάζονται διὰ τὸ μηθένα ἂν δοῦναι
ἀργύριον ὧν ἐπίστανται. οὗτοι μὲν οὖν ὧν ἔλαβον τὸν
μισθὸν μὴ ποιοῦντες, εἰκότως ἐν ἐγκλήμασίν εἰσιν· ἐν οἷς
δὲ μὴ γίγνεται διομολογία τῆς ὑπουργίας, οἱ μὲν δι'
αὑτοὺς προϊέμενοι εἴρηται ὅτι ἀνέγκλητοι· τοιαύτη γὰρ ἡ
κατ' ἀρετὴν φιλία. τὴν ἀμοιβήν τε ποιητέον κατὰ τὴν
προαίρεσιν· αὕτη γὰρ τοῦ φίλου καὶ τῆς ἀρετῆς. οὕτω δ'
ἔοικε καὶ τοῖς φιλοσοφίας κοινωνήσασιν· οὐ γὰρ πρὸς χρή-
μαθ' ἡ ἀξία μετρεῖται, τιμή τ' ἰσόρροπος οὐκ ἂν γένοιτο,

6—7 *ἐν τοῖς τοιούτοις—ἐπίστανται*] 'In such matters some like the principle of "a stated wage." Those, however, who take the money beforehand, and then do nothing of what they promised, are naturally blamed in consequence of their excessive promises, for they do not fulfil what they agreed. But this course the Sophists are perhaps obliged to adopt, because no one would be likely to give money for the things which they know.' Protagoras had no fixed price for his teaching, he left it to the pupil. But some people prefer having terms settled beforehand, *μισθὸς εἰρημένος*, as it is called in the line of Hesiod (*Works and Days*, v. 368): *Μισθὸς δ' ἀνδρὶ φίλῳ εἰρημένος ἄρκιος ἔστω*. It is the perversion of this when men take the money beforehand, and then fail in performing that which was paid for. The Sophists (says Aristotle with severe irony) are perhaps *obliged* to insist on payment beforehand, on account of the utter worthlessness of their teaching. Aristotle contrasts the conduct of Protagoras (of whom he speaks honourably) with that of 'the Sophists' after the profession had become regularly settled.

7 *ἐν οἷς δὲ—φιλία*] 'But supposing there is no agreement with regard to the service rendered—then, in the first place (*οἱ μὲν*), with regard to those who give purely for personal reasons, we have said that *they* are free from all chance of complaint; for this is the mode of virtuous friendship.' *δι' αὑτοὺς* is more of a logical than a grammatical formula, and would be represented by *per se* in Latin. This phrase and *καθ' αὑτοὺς* are frequently used by Aristotle to characterise the highest kind of friendship, which is an 'absolute' feeling. *Eth.* VIII. iii. 1: *οἱ μὲν οὖν διὰ τὸ χρήσιμον φιλοῦντες ἀλλήλους οὐ καθ' αὑτοὺς φιλοῦσιν*. In the following section, *ἐπί τινι*, 'for some external object,' is contrasted with *δι' αὑτούς*, 'that which looks to the personal character alone.' Cf. IX. x. 6: *δι' ἀρετὴν δὲ καὶ δι' αὑτοὺς (φιλία) οὐκ ἔστι πρὸς πολλούς*.

οὕτω δ' ἔοικε—ἐνδεχόμενον] 'And thus it seems that they ought to act who are made partakers in philosophy (*i.e.* they should measure the benefit

ἀλλ' ἴσως ἱκανόν, καθάπερ καὶ πρὸς θεοὺς καὶ πρὸς γονεῖς,
8 τὸ ἐνδεχόμενον. μὴ τοιαύτης δ' οὔσης τῆς δόσεως ἀλλ' ἐπί τινι, μάλιστα μὲν ἴσως δεῖ τὴν ἀνταπόδοσιν γίγνεσθαι δοκοῦσαν ἀμφοῖν κατ' ἀξίαν εἶναι, εἰ δὲ τοῦτο μὴ συμβαίνοι, οὐ μόνον ἀναγκαῖον δόξειεν ἂν τὸν προέχοντα τάττειν, ἀλλὰ καὶ δίκαιον· ὅσον γὰρ οὗτος ὠφελήθη ἢ ἀνθ' ὅσου τὴν ἡδονὴν εἵλετ' ἄν, τοσοῦτον ἀντιλαβὼν ἕξει τὴν παρὰ τούτου ἀξίαν· καὶ γὰρ ἐν τοῖς ὠνίοις οὕτω φαίνεται γινόμε-
9 νον, ἐνιαχοῦ τ' εἰσὶ νόμοι τῶν ἑκουσίων συμβολαίων δίκας μὴ εἶναι ὡς δέον, ᾧ ἐπίστευσε, διαλυθῆναι πρὸς τοῦτον καθάπερ ἐκοινώνησεν. ᾧ γὰρ ἐπετράφθη, τοῦτον οἴεται δικαιότερον εἶναι τάξαι τοῦ ἐπιτρέψαντος. τὰ πολλὰ γὰρ οὐ τοῦ ἴσου τιμῶσιν οἱ ἔχοντες καὶ οἱ βουλόμενοι λαβεῖν· τὰ γὰρ οἰκεῖα καὶ ἃ διδόασιν ἑκάστοις φαίνεται πολλοῦ ἄξια. ἀλλ' ὅμως ἡ ἀμοιβὴ γίνεται πρὸς τοσοῦτον ὅσον ἂν τάττωσιν οἱ λαβόντες. δεῖ δ' ἴσως οὐ τοσούτου τιμᾶν ὅσου ἔχοντι φαίνεται ἄξιον, ἀλλ' ὅσου πρὶν ἔχειν ἐτίμα.

2 Ἀπορίαν δ' ἔχει καὶ τὰ τοιάδε, οἷον πότερα δεῖ πάντα τῷ πατρὶ ἀπονέμειν καὶ πείθεσθαι, ἢ κάμνοντα μὲν ἰατρῷ πειστέον, στρατηγὸν δὲ χειροτονητέον τὸν πολεμικόν· ὁμοίως δὲ φίλῳ μᾶλλον ἢ σπουδαίῳ ὑπηρετητέον, καὶ εὐεργέτῃ ἀνταποδοτέον χάριν μᾶλλον ἢ ἑταίρῳ δοτέον, ἐὰν
2 ἀμφοῖν μὴ ἐνδέχηται. ἆρ' οὖν πάντα τὰ τοιαῦτα ἀκριβῶς μὲν διορίσαι οὐ ῥᾴδιον; πολλὰς γὰρ καὶ παντοίας ἔχει διαφορὰς καὶ μεγέθει καὶ μικρότητι καὶ τῷ καλῷ

---

received by the intention of their teacher), for the worth of philosophy is not measured against money, and no amount of honour can balance it. But, perhaps, as also towards the gods and one's parents, it is enough if one gives what one can.' Aristotle, perhaps mindful of the twenty years which he passed in the school of Plato, places very highly the spiritual dignity of teaching in philosophy. After ἴσως, ποιητέον εἶναι is to understood.

8 μὴ τοιαύτης δ' οὔσης] 'In the second place, when the gift is not of this kind,' *i.e.* not δι' αὐτούς.

τὸν προέχοντα] 'The first recipient, see above § 5.

8—9 καὶ γὰρ ἐν—ἐκοινώνησεν] 'For this is what is done in the market (*i.e.* the buyer, who is the recipient, settles the price); and in some places it is the law that there must be no actions on voluntary contracts, it being right that one should conclude with a person whom one has trusted on the same terms as those on which one entered on the contract with him.' Cf. *Eth.* VIII. xiii. 6: κοινωνεῖν here is used in the same sense as συναλλάττειν there.

καὶ ἀναγκαίῳ. ὅτι δ' οὐ πάντα τῷ αὐτῷ ἀποδοτέον, οὐκ 3
ἄδηλον. καὶ τὰς μὲν εὐεργεσίας ἀνταποδοτέον ὡς ἐπὶ τὸ
πολὺ μᾶλλον ἢ χαριστέον ἑταίροις, καὶ ὥσπερ δάνειον, ᾧ
ὀφείλει ἀποδοτέον μᾶλλον ἢ ἑταίρῳ δοτέον. ἴσως δ' οὐδὲ 4
τοῦτ' ἀεί, οἷον τῷ λυτρωθέντι παρὰ λῃστῶν πότερον τὸν
λυσάμενον ἀντιλυτρωτέον, κἂν ὁστισοῦν ᾖ, ἢ καὶ μὴ
ἑαλωκότι ἀπαιτοῦντι δὲ ἀποδοτέον, ἢ τὸν πατέρα λυτρωτέον; δόξειε γὰρ ἂν καὶ ἑαυτοῦ μᾶλλον τὸν πατέρα.
ὅπερ οὖν εἴρηται, καθόλου μὲν τὸ ὀφείλημα ἀποδοτέον, ἐὰν 5
δ' ὑπερτείνῃ ἡ δόσις τῷ καλῷ ἢ τῷ ἀναγκαίῳ, πρὸς ταῦτ'
ἀποκλιτέον· ἐνίοτε γὰρ οὐδ' ἐστὶν ἴσον τὸ τὴν προϋπαρχὴν
ἀμείψασθαι, ἐπειδὰν ὁ μὲν σπουδαῖον εἰδὼς εὖ ποιήσῃ, τῷ
δὲ ἡ ἀνταπόδοσις γίγνηται, ὃν οἴεται μοχθηρὸν εἶναι. οὐδὲ
γὰρ τῷ δανείσαντι ἐνίοτε ἀντιδανειστέον· ὁ μὲν γὰρ
οἰόμενος κομιεῖσθαι ἐδάνεισεν ἐπιεικεῖ ὄντι, ὁ δ' οὐκ ἐλπίζει
κομιεῖσθαι παρὰ πονηροῦ. εἴτε τοίνυν τῇ ἀληθείᾳ οὕτως
ἔχει, οὐκ ἴσον τὸ ἀξίωμα· εἴτ' ἔχει μὲν μὴ οὕτως οἴονται
δέ, οὐκ ἂν δόξαιεν ἄτοπα ποιεῖν. ὅπερ οὖν πολλάκις 6
εἴρηται, οἱ περὶ τὰ πάθη καὶ τὰς πράξεις λόγοι ὁμοίως
ἔχουσι τὸ ὡρισμένον τοῖς περὶ ἅ εἰσιν. ὅτι μὲν οὖν οὐ
ταὐτὰ πᾶσιν ἀποδοτέον, οὐδὲ τῷ πατρὶ πάντα, καθάπερ

---

5 ὅπερ οὖν εἴρηται—ποιεῖν] 'As I have said then, as a general rule the debt should be repaid, but if the giving (to some one else) preponderates in moral glory, or in the urgency of the case (over repaying), one must incline to this; for sometimes it is not even an equal thing to requite the former favour, (namely) when the one man knowing the other to be good has benefited him, but on the other hand, the repayment has to be made to one whom one thinks to be a scoundrel. For sometimes a man ought not even to lend money in return to one who has lent money to him. For *he* lent it to one who is good, thinking to get it back again, but the other does not hope to get it back again from a villain. If this be the real state of the case, the claim is of course not equal: and even if it be not, but the parties only think so, such conduct does not seem unreasonable.' This and the other casuistical questions here discussed have very little interest.

εἴρηται] vide § 3.

προϋπαρχὴν] 'that which was pre-existing,' here 'primary obligation.' Cf. *Eth.* viii. xiv. 4: οὐθὲν ποιήσας ἄξιον τῶν ὑπηργμένων. *Eth.* iv. ii. 14: οἷς τὰ τοιαῦτα προϋπάρχει.

ὁ μὲν—τῷ δὲ] These words, by carelessness of writing, refer to the same subject.

εἴτε τοίνυν—εἴτ' ἔχει μὲν μὴ] This double protasis, instead of having as usual only one, has a double apodosis.

6 ὅπερ οὖν πολλάκις εἴρηται] Cf. *Eth.* i. iii. 1; ii. ii. 3, and above § 2.

7 οὐδὲ τῷ Διὶ θύεται, οὐκ ἄδηλον· ἐπεὶ δ' ἕτερα γονεῦσι καὶ ἀδελφοῖς καὶ ἑταίροις καὶ εὐεργέταις, ἑκάστοις τὰ οἰκεῖα καὶ τὰ ἁρμόττοντα ἀπονεμητέον. οὕτω δὲ καὶ ποιεῖν φαίνονται· εἰς γάμους μὲν γὰρ καλοῦσι τοὺς συγγενεῖς· τούτοις γὰρ κοινὸν τὸ γένος καὶ αἱ περὶ τοῦτο δὴ πράξεις· καὶ εἰς τὰ κήδη δὲ μάλιστ' οἴονται δεῖν τοὺς συγγενεῖς
8 ἀπαντᾶν διὰ ταὐτό. δόξειε δ' ἂν τροφῆς μὲν γονεῦσι δεῖν μάλιστ' ἐπαρκεῖν, ὡς ὀφείλοντας, καὶ τοῖς αἰτίοις τοῦ εἶναι κάλλιον ὂν ἢ ἑαυτοῖς εἰς ταῦτ' ἐπαρκεῖν. καὶ τιμὴν δὲ γονεῦσι καθάπερ θεοῖς, οὐ πᾶσαν δέ· οὐδὲ γὰρ τὴν αὐτὴν πατρὶ καὶ μητρί· οὐδ' αὖ τὴν τοῦ σοφοῦ ἢ τοῦ στρατηγοῦ, ἀλλὰ τὴν πατρικήν, ὁμοίως δὲ καὶ τὴν μητ-
9 ρικήν. καὶ παντὶ δὲ τῷ πρεσβυτέρῳ τιμὴν τὴν καθ' ἡλικίαν, ὑπαναστάσει καὶ κατακλίσει καὶ τοῖς τοιούτοις. πρὸς ἑταίρους δ' αὖ καὶ ἀδελφοὺς παρρησίαν καὶ ἁπάντων κοινότητα. καὶ συγγενέσι δὴ καὶ φυλέταις καὶ πολίταις καὶ τοῖς λοιποῖς ἅπασιν ἀεὶ πειρατέον τὸ οἰκεῖον ἀπονέμειν, καὶ συγκρίνειν τὰ ἑκάστοις ὑπάρχοντα κατ' οἰκειότητα
10 καὶ ἀρετὴν ἢ χρῆσιν. τῶν μὲν οὖν ὁμογενῶν ῥᾴων ἡ κρίσις, τῶν δὲ διαφερόντων ἐργωδεστέρα. οὐ μὴν διά γε τοῦτο ἀποστατέον, ἀλλ' ὡς ἂν ἐνδέχηται, οὕτω διοριστέον.

3 Ἔχει δ' ἀπορίαν καὶ περὶ τοῦ διαλύεσθαι τὰς φιλίας ἢ μὴ πρὸς τοὺς μὴ διαμένοντας. ἢ πρὸς μὲν τοὺς διὰ τὸ

οὐδὲ τῷ Διὶ θύεται] 'Not even to Zeus are all things indiscriminately sacrificed.' It is given as an illustration of conventional right, *Eth.* v. vii. 1, that goats and not sheep are sacrificed to Zeus.

7 καὶ εἰς τὰ κήδη—διὰ ταὐτό] 'And for the same reason men think that relations ought especially to meet at funeral ceremonies.'

8 τροφῆς ἐπαρκεῖν] 'To furnish subsistence.' Fritzsche quotes Xenophon, *Memor.* II. vi. 23: δύνανται δὲ καὶ χρημάτων οὐ μόνον—κοινωνεῖν, ἀλλὰ καὶ ἐπαρκεῖν ἀλλήλοις.

9 ὑπαναστάσει καὶ κατακλίσει] 'Rising up to greet them, and conducting them to the seat of honour.' Cf. Plato *Repub.* p. 425 A: σιγάς τε τῶν νεωτέρων παρὰ πρεσβυτέροις, ἃς πρέπει, καὶ κατακλίσεις καὶ ὑπαναστάσεις.

10 τῶν μὲν οὖν ὁμογενῶν ῥᾴων ἡ κρίσις] i.e. It is easy to compare a relation with a relation, a tribesman with a tribesman, &c., but to compare a tribesman with a relation would be more troublesome.

III. 1 πρὸς τοὺς μὴ διαμένοντας] 'Who do not continue the same.' Cf. *Eth.* x. iii. 3: ἀλλ' ἀνειμένη διαμένει ἕως τινός.

ἐγκαλέσειε δ'—ἦθος] 'But one might complain, if a man who liked one for

χρήσιμον ἢ τὸ ἡδὺ φίλους ὄντας, ὅταν μηκέτι ταῦτ'
ἔχωσιν, οὐδὲν ἄτοπον διαλύεσθαι; ἐκείνων γὰρ ἦσαν φίλοι·
ὧν ἀπολιπόντων εὔλογον τὸ μὴ φιλεῖν. ἐγκαλέσειε δ' ἄν
τις, εἰ διὰ τὸ χρήσιμον ἢ τὸ ἡδὺ ἀγαπῶν προσεποιεῖτο διὰ
τὸ ἦθος· ὅπερ γὰρ ἐν ἀρχῇ εἴπομεν, πλεῖσται διαφοραὶ
γίγνονται τοῖς φίλοις, ὅταν μὴ ὁμοίως οἴωνται καὶ ὦσι
φίλοι. ὅταν μὲν οὖν διαψευσθῇ τις καὶ ὑπολάβῃ φι- 2
λεῖσθαι διὰ τὸ ἦθος, μηθὲν τοιοῦτον ἐκείνου πράττοντος,
ἑαυτὸν αἰτιῷτ' ἄν· ὅταν δ' ὑπὸ τῆς ἐκείνου προσποιήσεως
ἀπατηθῇ, δίκαιον ἐγκαλεῖν τῷ ἀπατήσαντι, καὶ μᾶλλον ἢ
τοῖς τὸ νόμισμα κιβδηλεύουσιν, ὅσῳ περὶ τιμιώτερον ἡ
κακουργία. ἐὰν δ' ἀποδέχηται ὡς ἀγαθόν, γένηται δὲ 3
μοχθηρὸς καὶ δοκῇ, ἆρ' ἔτι φιλητέον; ἢ οὐ δυνατόν, εἴπερ
μὴ πᾶν φιλητὸν ἀλλὰ τἀγαθόν; οὔτε δὲ φιλητέον πονηρὸν
οὔτε δεῖ· φιλοπόνηρον γὰρ οὐ χρὴ εἶναι, οὐδ' ὁμοιοῦσθαι
φαύλῳ· εἴρηται δ' ὅτι τὸ ὅμοιον τῷ ὁμοίῳ φίλον. ἆρ'
οὖν εὐθὺς διαλυτέον; ἢ οὐ πᾶσιν, ἀλλὰ τοῖς ἀνιάτοις κατὰ
τὴν μοχθηρίαν; ἐπανόρθωσιν δ' ἔχουσι μᾶλλον βοηθητέον
εἰς τὸ ἦθος ἢ τὴν οὐσίαν, ὅσῳ βέλτιον καὶ τῆς φιλίας
οἰκειότερον. δόξειε δ' ἂν ὁ διαλυόμενος οὐδὲν ἄτοπον ποιεῖν·
οὐ γὰρ τῷ τοιούτῳ φίλος ἦν· ἀλλοιωθέντα οὖν ἀδυνατῶν
ἀνασῶσαι ἀφίσταται. εἰ δ' ὁ μὲν διαμένοι ὁ δ' ἐπιεικέσ- 4
τερος γένοιτο καὶ πολὺ διαλλάττοι τῇ ἀρετῇ, ἆρα χρηστέον
φίλῳ, ἢ οὐκ ἐνδέχεται; ἐν μεγάλῃ δὲ διαστάσει μάλιστα

---

profit, or pleasure, pretended to like one for his character.'

ὅπερ γὰρ ἐν ἀρχῇ] This observation, that 'differences arise, when men are not really friends to each other in the way they think,' has never been exactly made before. The commentators variously refer us to *Eth.* VIII. iii. 3, VIII. iv. 1, and IX. i. 4, none of which passages correspond.

2 *ὅταν μὲν οὖν διαψευσθῇ τις*] 'Whenever one is mistaken,' *i.e.* by his own misconception. Cf. Ar. *Metaph.* III. iii. 7: *βεβαιοτάτη δ' ἀρχὴ πασῶν περὶ ἣν διαψευσθῆναι ἀδύνατον.* The word *διαψευσθῇ* answers to *διαμαρτόντα* in *Eth.* VIII. xiii. 9.

κιβδηλεύουσιν] To counterfeit friendship, says Aristotle, is worse than counterfeiting the coinage. The commentators quote Theognis, vv. 119 sqq., where the same maxim occurs.

3 *οὔτε δὲ φιλητέον πονηρὸν οὔτε δεῖ*] The MSS. vary extremely about the reading of this passage, in which there is evidently something wrong. *οὔτε δεῖ* is at all events an interpolation. Fritzsche thinks that the whole is a double gloss upon *φιλοπόνηρον*.

ἐπανόρθωσιν δ' ἔχουσι] 'To those who are capable of restoration.'

δῆλον γίνεται, οἷον ἐν ταῖς παιδικαῖς φιλίαις· εἰ γὰρ ὁ μὲν διαμένοι τὴν διάνοιαν παῖς ὁ δ' ἀνὴρ εἴη οἷος κράτιστος, πῶς ἂν εἶεν φίλοι μήτ' ἀρεσκόμενοι τοῖς αὐτοῖς μήτε χαίροντες καὶ λυπούμενοι; οὐδὲ γὰρ περὶ ἀλλήλους ταῦθ' ὑπάρξει αὐτοῖς, ἄνευ δὲ τούτων οὐκ ἦν φίλους εἶναι·
5 συμβιοῦν γὰρ οὐχ οἷόν τε. εἴρηται δὲ περὶ τούτων. ἆρ' οὖν οὐθὲν ἀλλοιότερον πρὸς αὐτὸν ἑκτέον ἢ εἰ μὴ ἐγεγόνει φίλος μηδέποτε; ἢ δεῖ μνείαν ἔχειν τῆς γενομένης συνηθείας, καὶ καθάπερ φίλοις μᾶλλον ἢ ὀθνείοις οἰόμεθα δεῖν χαρίζεσθαι, οὕτω καὶ τοῖς γενομένοις ἀπονεμητέον τι διὰ τὴν προγεγενημένην φιλίαν, ὅταν μὴ δι' ὑπερβολὴν μοχθηρίας ἡ διάλυσις γένηται.

4 Τὰ φιλικὰ δὲ τὰ πρὸς τοὺς φίλους, καὶ οἷς αἱ φιλίαι ὁρίζονται, ἔοικεν ἐκ τῶν πρὸς ἑαυτὸν ἐληλυθέναι. τιθέασι γὰρ φίλον τὸν βουλόμενον καὶ πράττοντα τἀγαθὰ ἢ τὰ φαινόμενα ἐκείνου ἕνεκα, ἢ τὸν βουλόμενον εἶναι καὶ ζῆν τὸν φίλον αὐτοῦ χάριν· ὅπερ αἱ μητέρες πρὸς τὰ τέκνα πεπόνθασι, καὶ τῶν φίλων οἱ προσκεκρουκότες. οἱ δὲ τὸν συνδιάγοντα καὶ ταὐτὰ αἱρούμενον, ἢ τὸν συναλγοῦντα καὶ συγχαίροντα τῷ φίλῳ· μάλιστα δὲ καὶ τοῦτο περὶ τὰς μητέρας συμβαίνει. τούτων δέ τινι καὶ τὴν φιλίαν
2 ὁρίζονται. πρὸς ἑαυτὸν δὲ τούτων ἕκαστον τῷ ἐπιεικεῖ

---

4 ἄνευ δὲ τούτων οὐκ ἦν φίλους εἶναι] 'But without these things it is not possible, as we said, that they should be friends.' On this use of the past tense ἦν in reference to what has been previously said by the writer, cf. *Metaph.* XI. vi. 1: ἐπεὶ δ' ἦσαν τρεῖς οὐσίαι, *Eth.* III. v. 3: τοῦτο δ' ἦν τὸ ἀγαθοῖς καὶ κακοῖς εἶναι. V. i. 12: ἐπεὶ δ' ὁ παράνομος ἄδικος ἦν, &c. Aristotle is here referring to *Eth.* VIII. iii. 9; VIII. v. 3.

IV. 1 ὅπερ αἱ μητέρες—προσκεκρουκότες] 'Which mothers feel towards their children, and which friends who have had a rupture (feel towards each other),' *i.e.* they quite disinterestedly, since in the latter case intercourse is precluded, wish each other to live. On the disinterested feeling of mothers, cf. *Eth.* VIII. viii. 3. On the use of προσκεκρουκότες, cf. *Politics*, II. v. 4: αἱ πλεῖσται διαφερόμεναι ἐκ τῶν ἐν ποσὶ καὶ ἐκ μικρῶν προσκρούοντες ἀλλήλοις. ἔτι δὲ τῶν θεραπόντων τούτοις μάλιστα προσκρούομεν, οἷς πλεῖστα προσχρώμεθα πρὸς τὰς διακονίας τὰς ἐγκυκλίους.

2 πρὸς ἑαυτὸν—εἶναι] 'The good man has every one of these feelings towards himself, and other men have them in so far as they set up to be good;' (*i.e.* wherever they fall short in these feelings, they fall short also in their attempt to be good). 'For, as we have said, virtue and the good man are the standard for everything.' Cf. *Eth.* III. iv. 5; X. v. 10.

ὑπάρχει, τοῖς δὲ λοιποῖς, ᾗ τοιοῦτοι ὑπολαμβάνουσιν εἶναι. ἔοικε γάρ, καθάπερ εἴρηται, μέτρον ἑκάστῳ ἡ ἀρετὴ καὶ ὁ σπουδαῖος εἶναι. οὗτος γὰρ ὁμογνωμονεῖ ἑαυτῷ, καὶ τῶν 3
αὐτῶν ὀρέγεται κατὰ πᾶσαν τὴν ψυχήν, καὶ βούλεται δὴ ἑαυτῷ τἀγαθὰ καὶ τὰ φαινόμενα καὶ πράττει (τοῦ γὰρ ἀγαθοῦ τἀγαθὸν διαπονεῖν) καὶ ἑαυτοῦ ἕνεκα· τοῦ γὰρ διανοητικοῦ χάριν, ὅπερ ἕκαστος εἶναι δοκεῖ. καὶ ζῆν δὲ βούλεται ἑαυτὸν καὶ σώζεσθαι, καὶ μάλιστα τοῦτο ᾧ φρονεῖ· ἀγαθὸν γὰρ τῷ σπουδαίῳ τὸ εἶναι. ἕκαστος δ' 4
ἑαυτῷ βούλεται τἀγαθά, γενόμενος δ' ἄλλος οὐδεὶς αἱρεῖται πάντ' ἔχειν ἐκεῖνο τὸ γενόμενον, (ἔχει γὰρ καὶ νῦν ὁ θεὸς τἀγαθόν), ἀλλ' ὢν ὅ τι ποτ' ἐστίν. δόξειε δ' ἂν τὸ νοοῦν ἕκαστος εἶναι, ἢ μάλιστα. συνδιάγειν τε ὁ τοιοῦτος ἑαυτῷ 5
βούλεται· ἡδέως γὰρ αὐτὸ ποιεῖ· τῶν τε γὰρ πεπραγμένων ἐπιτερπεῖς αἱ μνῆμαι, καὶ τῶν μελλόντων ἐλπίδες ἀγαθαί· αἱ τοιαῦται δ' ἡδεῖαι. καὶ θεωρημάτων δ' εὐπορεῖ τῇ διανοίᾳ, συναλγεῖ τε καὶ συνήδεται μάλισθ' ἑαυτῷ· πάντοτε γάρ ἐστι τὸ αὐτὸ λυπηρόν τε καὶ ἡδύ, καὶ οὐκ ἄλλοτ' ἄλλο· ἀμεταμέλητος γὰρ ὡς εἰπεῖν. τῷ δὴ πρὸς αὐτὸν μὲν ἕκαστα τούτων ὑπάρχειν τῷ ἐπιεικεῖ, πρὸς δὲ τὸν φίλον ἔχειν ὥσπερ πρὸς ἑαυτόν (ἔστι γὰρ ὁ φίλος ἄλλος αὐτός), καὶ ἡ φιλία τούτων εἶναί τι δοκεῖ, καὶ φίλοι οἷς

4 ἕκαστος δ' ἑαυτῷ βούλεται—μάλιστα] 'But every man wishes what is good *for himself*. No one, on condition of becoming another man, chooses that that new thing, which he should become, should possess everything, (for God has now all good); but (every man desires to possess what is good) remaining his present self. And the thinking faculty would appear to be each man's proper self, or more so than anything else.' The usual punctuation of this passage has been altered to obtain the above translation, which has been suggested to the annotator, and which seems to give a more natural explanation of the text than has been arrived at by the commentators, who universally explain ἀλλ' ὢν ὅ τι ποτ' ἐστὶν to refer to the unchangeableness or to the personality of God. If the passage be read as above, it will be seen that the words ὢν ὅ τι ποτ' ἐστὶν are in opposition to γενόμενος δ' ἄλλος. Aristotle says that to every man his personality is what is dear to him, he would not relinquish this to gain all the world, for by relinquishing it *he* would not gain anything. With a changed personality, *he* would no more possess any good thing, than he now possesses it because God possesses all good. All his wishes are made on the basis of being still what he is. The good man, who fosters his thinking faculty, most of all takes care of his proper self.

6 ταῦθ' ὑπάρχει. πρὸς αὑτὸν δὲ πότερόν ἐστιν ἢ οὐκ ἔστι
φιλία, ἀφείσθω ἐπὶ τοῦ παρόντος· δόξειε δ' ἂν ταύτῃ
εἶναι φιλία, ᾗ ἐστὶ δύο ἢ πλείω ἐκ τῶν εἰρημένων, καὶ ὅτι
7 ἡ ὑπερβολὴ τῆς φιλίας τῇ πρὸς αὑτὸν ὁμοιοῦται. φαίνεται
δὲ τὰ εἰρημένα καὶ τοῖς πολλοῖς ὑπάρχειν, καίπερ οὖσι
φαύλοις. ἆρ' οὖν ᾗ ἀρέσκουσιν ἑαυτοῖς καὶ ὑπολαμβάνουσιν ἐπιεικεῖς εἶναι, ταύτῃ μετέχουσιν αὐτῶν; ἐπεὶ τῶν
γε κομιδῇ φαύλων καὶ ἀνοσιουργῶν οὐθενὶ ταῦθ' ὑπάρχει,
8 ἀλλ' οὐδὲ φαίνεται. σχεδὸν δὲ οὐδὲ τοῖς φαύλοις· διαφέρονται γὰρ ἑαυτοῖς, καὶ ἑτέρων μὲν ἐπιθυμοῦσιν ἄλλα
δὲ βούλονται, οἷον οἱ ἀκρατεῖς· αἱροῦνται γὰρ ἀντὶ τῶν

---

6 *πρὸς αὑτὸν δὲ—ὁμοιοῦται*] 'But whether friendship towards oneself is, or is not, possible, we may leave undecided for the present. It would seem to be possible in so far as two or more of the above mentioned conditions exist, and because the extreme of friendship resembles one's feelings towards oneself.' Several commentators explain *ᾗ ἐστὶ δύο ἢ πλείω* to mean 'in so far as man consists of two or more parts,' and *ἐκ τῶν εἰρημένων* they would translate 'in accordance with what we have before said,' referring to *Eth.* I. xiii. 9. In this sense the passage would be a parallel one to *Eth.* v. xi. 9. But it is clear from the next section that *ἐκ τῶν εἰρημένων* refers to the definitions of friendship, given in § 1 of this chapter. *ἀφείσθω* is used as in *Eth.* VIII. i. 7, VIII. viii. 7. We are not here referred to the subsequent discussion in *Eth.* IX. viii., where by no means the same subject is renewed.

8 *Σχεδὸν δὲ οὐδὲ τοῖς φαύλοις—ἑαυτούς*] 'But one might almost say that these things do not appertain to the bad at all. For they are at variance with themselves, and desire one set of things while they wish another, just like the incontinent; instead of what seems to them to be good they choose the pleasant though it is hurtful; and others through cowardice and want of spirit abstain from doing what they think to be best for themselves; and they who through wickedness have committed many crimes hate their life, and fly from it, and put an end to themselves.' The 'desire' of the wicked, as being of the particular and subject to the domination of the senses (*Eth.* VII. iii. 9), is at variance with their 'wish,' which is of the universal and implies a conception of the good. Cf. *Eth.* v. ix. 6, VIII. xiii. 8. The description of bad men given here ignores and is at variance with the conclusions of Book VII. In that book the strength, and here the weakness, of vice is represented. Thus in *Eth.* VII. viii. the bad man is described as unrepentant, abiding by his purpose (§ 1), having the major premiss of his mind corrupted (§ 4), and therefore having no wish for the good, even in the universal. The account in Book VII., which makes *ἀκολασία* or abandoned vice free from all weakness, is more theoretical and less drawn from nature than the above description. All that is said here has a close relation to, and was probably suggested by, the words in the *Lysis* of Plato, p. 214 C: *τοὺς δὲ κακούς, ὥσπερ καὶ λέγεται*

δοκούντων ἑαυτοῖς ἀγαθῶν εἶναι τὰ ἡδέα βλαβερὰ ὄντα·
οἱ δ' αὖ διὰ δειλίαν καὶ ἀργίαν ἀφίστανται τοῦ πράττειν ἃ οἴονται ἑαυτοῖς βέλτιστα εἶναι· οἷς δὲ πολλὰ καὶ
δεινὰ πέπρακται διὰ τὴν μοχθηρίαν, μισοῦσί τε καὶ
φεύγουσι τὸ ζῆν καὶ ἀναιροῦσιν ἑαυτούς. ζητοῦσί τε οἱ 9
μοχθηροὶ μεθ' ὧν συνδιημερεύσουσιν, ἑαυτοὺς δὲ φεύγουσιν·
ἀναμιμνήσκονται γὰρ πολλῶν καὶ δυσχερῶν, καὶ τοιαῦθ'
ἕτερα ἐλπίζουσι, καθ' ἑαυτοὺς ὄντες, μεθ' ἑτέρων δ' ὄντες
ἐπιλανθάνονται. οὐθέν τε φιλητὸν ἔχοντες οὐθὲν φιλικὸν
πάσχουσι πρὸς ἑαυτούς. οὐδὲ δὴ συγχαίρουσιν οὐδὲ
συναλγοῦσιν οἱ τοιοῦτοι ἑαυτοῖς· στασιάζει γὰρ αὐτῶν ἡ
ψυχή, καὶ τὸ μὲν διὰ μοχθηρίαν ἀλγεῖ ἀπεχόμενόν τινων,
τὸ δ' ἥδεται, καὶ τὸ μὲν δεῦρο τὸ δ' ἐκεῖσε ἕλκει ὥσπερ
διασπῶντα. εἰ δὲ μὴ οἷόν τε ἅμα λυπεῖσθαι καὶ ἥδεσθαι, 10
ἀλλὰ μετὰ μικρόν γε λυπεῖται ὅτι ἥσθη, καὶ οὐκ ἂν
ἐβούλετο ἡδέα ταῦτα γενέσθαι αὐτῷ· μεταμελείας γὰρ οἱ
φαῦλοι γέμουσιν. οὐ δὴ φαίνεται ὁ φαῦλος οὐδὲ πρὸς
ἑαυτὸν φιλικῶς διακεῖσθαι διὰ τὸ μηδὲν ἔχειν φιλητόν.
εἰ δὴ τὸ οὕτως ἔχειν λίαν ἐστὶν ἄθλιον, φευκτέον τὴν
μοχθηρίαν διατεταμένως καὶ πειρατέον ἐπιεικῆ εἶναι· οὕτω
γὰρ καὶ πρὸς ἑαυτὸν φιλικῶς ἂν ἔχοι καὶ ἑτέρῳ φίλος
γένοιτο.

Ἡ δ' εὔνοια φιλίᾳ μὲν ἔοικεν, οὐ μὴν ἐστί γε φιλία· 5
γίνεται γὰρ εὔνοια καὶ πρὸς ἀγνῶτας καὶ λανθάνουσα,

περὶ αὐτῶν, μηδέποτε ὁμοίους μηθ' αὐτοὺς εἶναι, ἀλλ' ἐμπλήκτους τε καὶ ἀσταθμήτους.

9—10 στασιάζει—γέμουσιν] 'For their soul is in tumult, the one part of it, through viciousness, grieves at abstaining from certain things, but the other part is pleased (at this abstinence), and the one pulls this way, the other that way, as though tearing (the man) in pieces. If it is not possible to feel pain and pleasure at the same moment, at all events after a little while (the bad man) is pained that he felt pleasure, and he "could have wished that those pleasures had not happened to him;" for the wicked are full of repentance.' This picture of the mental struggles of the bad does not recall either the phraseology or the doctrines of Book VII., where μοχθηρία is contrasted with, and opposed to, ἀκρασία (cf. VII. VIII. 1). The metaphor στασιάζει occurs repeatedly in Plato's *Republic*, cf. I. p. 352 A: (ἡ ἀδικία) ἐν ἑνὶ—ἐνοῦσα—πρῶτον μὲν ἀδύνατον αὐτὸν πράττειν ποιήσει στασιάζοντα καὶ οὐχ ὁμονοοῦντα αὐτὸν ἑαυτῷ, ἔπειτα ἐχθρὸν καὶ ἑαυτῷ καὶ τοῖς δικαίοις. Cf. *Eth.* I. xiii. 15.

V. Ἡ δ' εὔνοια—ἀκολουθεῖ] 'Now

φιλία δ' οὔ. καὶ πρότερον δὲ ταῦτ' εἴρηται. ἀλλ' οὐδὲ φίλησίς ἐστιν· οὐ γὰρ ἔχει διάτασιν οὐδ' ὄρεξιν, τῇ
2 φιλήσει δὲ ταῦτ' ἀκολουθεῖ. καὶ ἡ μὲν φίλησις μετὰ συνηθείας, ἡ δ' εὔνοια καὶ ἐκ προσπαίου, οἷον καὶ περὶ τοὺς ἀγωνιστὰς συμβαίνει· εὖνοι γὰρ αὐτοῖς γίνονται καὶ συνθέλουσιν, συμπράξαιεν δ' ἂν οὐδέν· ὅπερ γὰρ εἴπομεν, προσπαίως εὖνοι γίνονται καὶ ἐπιπολαίως στέργουσιν.
3 ἔοικε δὴ ἀρχὴ φιλίας εἶναι, ὥσπερ τοῦ ἐρᾶν ἡ διὰ τῆς ὄψεως ἡδονή· μὴ γὰρ προησθεὶς τῇ ἰδέᾳ οὐθεὶς ἐρᾷ, ὁ δὲ χαίρων τῷ εἴδει οὐθὲν μᾶλλον ἐρᾷ, ἀλλ' ὅταν καὶ ἀπόντα

---

good-will is like friendship, but yet it is not friendship, for good-will is exercised both towards unknown persons, and when its own existence is unknown (to the object), which is not the case with friendship. But all this has been said already. It is not even the same as loving; for it exhibits neither violence nor longing, which are the accompaniments of loving.' The Saxon word 'Good-will,' and not the Latin 'Benevolence,' which is too abstract and general, is the representative of εὔνοια. Good-will, says Aristotle, is engendered by the appearance of noble qualities, it is rapidly conceived, but is passive in its character, and is only the prelude of friendship. There being no correspondent adjective to the substantive 'Good-will,' we must express εὖνοι by 'Well-disposed.' Just as in *Eth.* III. the cognate faculties to Purpose, and in *Eth.* VI. the cognate qualities to Thought are discussed, so Aristotle here introduces a discussion of the feelings which are cognate to Friendship.

καὶ πρότερον δὲ] VIII. ii. 3—4.

διάτασιν] 'Intensity,' 'straining,' 'violence.' In the previous section διατεταμένως means 'strenuously.' Cf. Ar. *Polit.* VII. xvii. 6: τὰς διατάσεις τῶν παίδων καὶ κλαυθμούς, 'the violent passions and cryings of children.'

2 ἡ δ' εὔνοια—συμβαίνει] While loving implies acquaintance and familiarity, good-will is conceived instantaneously; thus men conceive good-will towards particular competitors in the games from their appearance, and are inclined to wish them success.

3 Good-will, says Aristotle, is the prelude of Friendship, just as the pleasure of the eye is the prelude of love. This however does not constitute love. The test of love is longing for a person in absence. Cf. Ar. *Rhet.* I. xi. 11: where the same test is given. In accordance with the unhappy notions of the Greeks, ἀπόντα is here put in the masculine gender.

ἡ διὰ τῆς ὄψεως] In Plato's *Cratylus*, p. 420 A. it is suggested that Ἔρως is derived from εἰσρεῖν.—Ἔρως ὅτι εἰσρεῖ ἔξωθεν καὶ οὐκ οἰκεία ἐστὶν ἡ ῥοὴ αὕτη τῷ ἔχοντι, ἀλλ' ἐπείσακτος διὰ τῶν ὀμμάτων, διὰ ταῦτα ἀπὸ τοῦ εἰσρεῖν ἔσρος τό γε παλαιὸν ἐκαλεῖτο. Cf. Shakspeare, *Merchant of Venice*, Act. III. Sc. ii.

'It is engendered in the eyes,
By gazing fed.'

And *Romeo and Juliet*, Act I. Sc. iii.
'I'll look to like, if looking liking move.'

οὐ τὴν διὰ τὸ χρήσιμον] 'Good-will' is essentially disinterested in its character.

ποθῇ καὶ τῆς παρουσίας ἐπιθυμῇ. οὕτω δὴ καὶ φίλους οὐχ οἷόν τ' εἶναι μὴ εὔνους γενομένους, οἱ δ' εὖνοι οὐθὲν μᾶλλον φιλοῦσιν· βούλονται γὰρ μόνον τἀγαθὰ οἷς εἰσὶν εὖνοι, συμπράξαιεν δ' ἂν οὐθέν, οὐδ' ὀχληθεῖεν ὑπὲρ αὐτῶν. διὸ μεταφέρων φαίη τις ἂν αὐτὴν ἀργὴν εἶναι φιλίαν, χρονιζομένην δὲ καὶ εἰς συνήθειαν ἀφικνουμένην γίνεσθαι φιλίαν, οὐ τὴν διὰ τὸ χρήσιμον οὐδὲ τὴν διὰ τὸ ἡδύ· οὐδὲ γὰρ εὔνοια ἐπὶ τούτοις γίνεται. ὁ μὲν γὰρ εὐεργετηθεὶς ἀνθ' ὧν πέπονθεν ἀπονέμει τὴν εὔνοιαν, τὰ δίκαια δρῶν· ὁ δὲ βουλόμενός τιν' εὐπραγεῖν, ἐλπίδα ἔχων εὐπορίας δι' ἐκείνου, οὐκ ἔοικ' εὔνους ἐκείνῳ εἶναι, ἀλλὰ μᾶλλον ἑαυτῷ,
καθάπερ οὐδὲ φίλος, εἰ θεραπεύει αὐτὸν διά τινα χρῆσιν. 4
ὅλως δ' ἡ εὔνοια δι' ἀρετὴν καὶ ἐπιείκειάν τινα γίνεται, ὅταν τῳ φανῇ καλός τις ἢ ἀνδρεῖος ἤ τι τοιοῦτον, καθάπερ καὶ ἐπὶ τῶν ἀγωνιστῶν εἴπομεν.

Φιλικὸν δὲ καὶ ἡ ὁμόνοια φαίνεται· διόπερ οὐκ ἔστιν 6
ὁμοδοξία· τοῦτο μὲν γὰρ καὶ ἀγνοοῦσιν ἀλλήλους ὑπάρξειεν ἄν. οὐδὲ τοὺς περὶ ὁτουοῦν ὁμογνωμονοῦντας ὁμονοεῖν φασίν, οἷον τοὺς περὶ τῶν οὐρανίων (οὐ γὰρ φιλικὸν τὸ περὶ τούτων ὁμονοεῖν), ἀλλὰ τὰς πόλεις ὁμονοεῖν φασίν, ὅταν περὶ τῶν συμφερόντων ὁμογνωμονῶσι καὶ ταὐτὰ
προαιρῶνται καὶ πράττωσι τὰ κοινῇ δόξαντα. περὶ τὰ 2
πρακτὰ δὴ ὁμονοοῦσιν, καὶ τούτων περὶ τὰ ἐν μεγέθει καὶ τὰ ἐνδεχόμενα ἀμφοῖν ὑπάρχειν ἢ πᾶσιν, οἷον αἱ πόλεις, ὅταν πᾶσι δοκῇ τὰς ἀρχὰς αἱρετὰς εἶναι, ἢ συμμαχεῖν Λακεδαιμονίοις, ἢ ἄρχειν Πιττακόν, ὅτε καὶ αὐτὸς ἤθελεν.

VI. 1 φιλικὸν δὲ—ὁμοδοξία] 'Unanimity also appears to be of the nature of friendship; therefore it is not the same as agreement of opinion.' On φιλικόν, cf. *Eth.* VIII. i. 4; VIII. xiii. 6.

οἷον τοὺς περὶ τῶν οὐρανίων] Cf. *Eth.* III. iii. 3: περὶ δὲ τῶν ἀιδίων οὐδεὶς βουλεύεται, οἷον περὶ τοῦ κόσμου. Aristotle arrives at his definition of ὁμόνοια inductively, saying that we do not find the name applied to agreement of opinion in general, nor again to agreement of opinion about every particular subject, but we do find it used of states whose citizens are unanimous on the measures to be adopted for the common weal. Hence we get the idea that unanimity is 'political friendship.' Cf. *Eth.* VIII. i. 4, where ὁμόνοια is used as the opposite of στάσις.

2 ἢ ἄρχειν Πιττακόν, ὅτε καὶ αὐτὸς ἤθελεν] 'Or (if all agree) that Pittacus shall rule, (supposing this to be) during the period when he himself was willing to rule.' Pittacus, having held his

ὅταν δ' ἑκάτερος ἑαυτὸν βούληται, ὥσπερ οἱ ἐν ταῖς Φοινίσσαις, στασιάζουσιν· οὐ γάρ ἐσθ' ὁμονοεῖν τὸ αὐτὸ ἑκάτερον ἐννοεῖν ὁδήποτε, ἀλλὰ τὸ ἐν τῷ αὐτῷ, οἷον ὅταν καὶ ὁ δῆμος καὶ οἱ ἐπιεικεῖς τοὺς ἀρίστους ἄρχειν. οὕτω γὰρ πᾶσι γίγνεται οὗ ἐφίενται. πολιτικὴ δὲ φιλία φαίνεται ἡ ὁμόνοια, καθάπερ καὶ λέγεται· περὶ τὰ συμφέροντα γάρ
3 ἐστι καὶ τὰ εἰς τὸν βίον ἀνήκοντα. ἔστι δ' ἡ τοιαύτη ὁμόνοια ἐν τοῖς ἐπιεικέσιν· οὗτοι γὰρ καὶ ἑαυτοῖς ὁμονοοῦσι καὶ ἀλλήλοις, ἐπὶ τῶν αὐτῶν ὄντες ὡς εἰπεῖν· τῶν τοιούτων γὰρ μένει τὰ βουλήματα καὶ οὐ μεταρρεῖ ὥσπερ εὔριπος, βούλονταί τε τὰ δίκαια καὶ τὰ συμφέροντα,
4 τούτων δὲ καὶ κοινῇ ἐφίενται. τοὺς δὲ φαύλους οὐχ οἷόν τε ὁμονοεῖν πλὴν ἐπὶ μικρόν, καθάπερ καὶ φίλους εἶναι, πλεονεξίας ἐφιεμένους ἐν τοῖς ὠφελίμοις, ἐν δὲ τοῖς πόνοις καὶ ταῖς λειτουργίαις ἐλλείποντας· ἑαυτῷ δ' ἕκαστος βουλόμενος ταῦτα τὸν πέλας ἐξετάζει καὶ κωλύει· μὴ γὰρ τηρούντων τὸ κοινὸν ἀπόλλυται. συμβαίνει οὖν αὐτοῖς στασιάζειν, ἀλλήλους μὲν ἐπαναγκάζοντας, αὐτοὺς δὲ μὴ βουλομένους τὰ δίκαια ποιεῖν.

7 Οἱ δ' εὐεργέται τοὺς εὐεργετηθέντας δοκοῦσι μᾶλλον φιλεῖν ἢ οἱ εὖ παθόντες τοὺς δράσαντας, καὶ ὡς παρὰ

---

elective monarchy for ten years, resigned. Had the citizens *after* this period wished him to reign, his own will would have been wanting to make unanimity in the state.

οἱ ἐν ταῖς Φοινίσσαις] Eteocles and Polynices. Cf. Eurip. *Phœnissæ*, vv. 588, sqq.

τὸ αὐτὸ ἑκάτερον ἐννοεῖν ὁδήποτε] The commentators illustrate this by the joke of the man who said 'that he and his wife had always perfectly agreed—in wishing to govern the house.'

3 *ἐπὶ τῶν αὐτῶν ὄντες, ὡς εἰπεῖν*] 'Being on the same moorings, as it were,' as opposed to the ebbings and flowings of a Euripus. Cf. Demosthenes, *De Corona*, p. 319, § 281, *οὐκ ἐπὶ τῆς αὐτῆς ὁρμεῖ τοῖς πολλοῖς*, sc. *ἀγκύρας*.

4 This is a picture of the discord produced by evil passions, where every one grasping at the larger share in good things, and shirking his part in labours and services, watches (*ἐξετάζει*) his neighbour to prevent him encroaching. Thus men force each other to do what is right, while unwilling to do it themselves.

VII. Aristotle says, it is noticed as something extraordinary (*ὡς παρὰ λόγον ἐπιζητεῖται*) that benefactors seem to love those, to whom they have done a kindness, more than the benefited persons love them. The common explanation of the paradox

λόγον γινόμενον ἐπιζητεῖται. τοῖς μὲν οὖν πλείστοις φαίνεται, ὅτι οἱ μὲν ὀφείλουσι τοῖς δὲ ὀφείλεται· καθάπερ οὖν ἐπὶ τῶν δανείων οἱ μὲν ὀφείλοντες βούλονται μὴ εἶναι οἷς ὀφείλουσιν, οἱ δὲ δανείσαντες καὶ ἐπιμέλονται τῆς τῶν ὀφειλόντων σωτηρίας, οὕτω καὶ τοὺς εὐεργετήσαντας βούλεσθαι εἶναι τοὺς παθόντας ὡς κομιουμένους τὰς χάριτας, τοῖς δ' οὐκ εἶναι ἐπιμελὲς τὸ ἀνταποδοῦναι. Ἐπίχαρμος μὲν οὖν τάχ' ἂν φαίη ταῦτα λέγειν αὐτοὺς ἐκ πονηροῦ θεωμένους, ἔοικε δ' ἀνθρωπικῷ· ἀμνήμονες γὰρ οἱ πολλοί, καὶ μᾶλλον εὖ πάσχειν ἢ ποιεῖν ἐφίενται. δόξειε 2
δ' ἂν φυσικώτερον εἶναι τὸ αἴτιον, καὶ οὐχ ὅμοιον τῷ περὶ τοὺς δανείσαντας· οὐ γάρ ἐστι φίλησις περὶ ἐκείνους, ἀλλὰ τοῦ σώζεσθαι βούλησις τῆς κομιδῆς ἕνεκα· οἱ δ' εὖ πεποιηκότες φιλοῦσι καὶ ἀγαπῶσι τοὺς πεπονθότας, κἂν μηδὲν ὦσι χρήσιμοι μηδ' εἰς ὕστερον γένοιντ' ἄν. ὅπερ 3
καὶ ἐπὶ τῶν τεχνιτῶν συμβέβηκεν· πᾶς γὰρ τὸ οἰκεῖον ἔργον ἀγαπᾷ μᾶλλον ἢ ἀγαπηθείη ἂν ὑπὸ τοῦ ἔργου ἐμψύχου γενομένου. μάλιστα δ' ἴσως τοῦτο περὶ τοὺς ποιητὰς συμβαίνει· ὑπεραγαπῶσι γὰρ οὗτοι τὰ οἰκεῖα

---

is, that benefactors look forward to obtaining a return for their kindness, they thus cherish the persons of those who are indebted to them. This selfish theory views mankind on the dark side (ἐκ πονηροῦ θεωμένους), but is not altogether devoid of truth. A deeper (φυσικώτερον) reason however may be assigned for the phenomenon in question, namely, that as we can only be said to exist when we are conscious of our vital powers (ἐσμὲν ἐνεργείᾳ), so anything which gives or increases the sense of those powers is dear to us. The benefited person stands to the benefactor in the relation of a work to the artist, he is an exponent of the benefactor's self, and is thus regarded with feelings of affection, as being associated by the benefactor with the sense of his own existence (στέργει δὴ τὸ ἔργον, διότι καὶ τὸ εἶναι). These feelings of course cannot be reciprocated by the benefited person. Again, the benefactor associates an idea of the beautiful (τὸ καλόν) with the recipient of his good deeds; the other associates with *him* only an idea of the profitable, and this is a less loveable idea, especially when viewed in the past, and become a matter of memory. Again, the active part taken by the benefactor has more affinity to the active principle of loving.

τοῖς μὲν οὖν πλείστοις] This explanation is put by Thucydides (II. 40) into the mouth of Pericles: βεβαιότερος δὲ ὁ δράσας τὴν χάριν ὥστε ὀφειλομένην δι' εὐνοίας ᾧ δέδωκε σῴζειν, ὁ δ' ἀντοφείλων ἀμβλύτερος, εἰδὼς οὐκ ἐς χάριν, ἀλλ' εἰς ὀφείλημα τὴν ἀρετὴν ἀποδώσων.

Ἐπίχαρμος] The words ἐκ πονηροῦ θεωμένους seem to have been taken

4 ποιήματα, στέργοντες ὥσπερ τέκνα. τοιούτῳ δὴ ἔοικε καὶ τὸ τῶν εὐεργετῶν· τὸ γὰρ εὖ πεπονθὸς ἔργον ἐστὶν αὐτῶν· τοῦτο δὴ ἀγαπῶσι μᾶλλον ἢ τὸ ἔργον τὸν ποιήσαντα. τούτου δ' αἴτιον ὅτι τὸ εἶναι πᾶσιν αἱρετὸν καὶ φιλητόν, ἐσμὲν δ' ἐνεργείᾳ· τῷ ζῆν γὰρ καὶ πράττειν. ἐνεργείᾳ δὴ ὁ ποιήσας τὸ ἔργον ἔστι πως· στέργει δὴ τὸ ἔργον, διότι καὶ τὸ εἶναι. τοῦτο δὲ φυσικόν· ὃ γάρ ἐστι
5 δυνάμει, τοῦτο ἐνεργείᾳ τὸ ἔργον μηνύει. ἅμα δὲ καὶ τῷ μὲν εὐεργέτῃ καλὸν τὸ κατὰ τὴν πρᾶξιν, ὥστε χαίρειν ἐν ᾧ τοῦτο, τῷ δὲ παθόντι οὐθὲν καλὸν ἐν τῷ δράσαντι, ἀλλ'
6 εἴπερ, συμφέρον· τοῦτο δ' ἧττον ἡδὺ καὶ φιλητόν. ἡδεῖα δ' ἐστὶ τοῦ μὲν παρόντος ἡ ἐνέργεια, τοῦ δὲ μέλλοντος ἡ ἐλπίς, τοῦ δὲ γεγενημένου ἡ μνήμη. ἥδιστον δὲ τὸ κατὰ

---

out of some iambic or trochaic verse of the Sicilian poet, but the verse itself has not been preserved.

4 τοιούτῳ δὴ—μηνύει] 'The case of benefactors seems then something of the same kind. For the object benefited is their "work;" they love this therefore more than the work loves him who made it. The cause of this is that existence is desired and loved by all, but we exist by consciousness, that is to say, by living and acting. Thus he who has made the work in question exists consciously, and therefore he loves the work, because he loves his existence. And this is a principle of nature; for that which exists potentially, the work proves to exist actually.' On this mode of paraphrasing ἐνέργεια, see Vol. I. Essay IV. Any work of art, or creation of the mind, or moral achievement, is here said to shew us externally to ourselves. It causes us to exist ἐνεργείᾳ, that is, not only in ourselves, but *for* ourselves. It thus becomes a union of the objective and the subjective. And this philosophical principle explains a whole class of homogeneous facts, not only the feelings of benefactors towards the benefited, but of poets towards their poems, of parents, and especially mothers, towards their children; and of those who have made fortunes towards their property. These facts were brought together, without being analysed, by Plato, cf. *Republic*, p. 330 B–C. Cf. *Eth.* iv. i. 20.

ἐνεργείᾳ δὴ—πως] Many commentators understand these words to mean, 'Therefore by means of conscious activity the maker is in a sense his work,' in which they are supported by Eustratius and the Paraphrast. This would not materially alter the general drift of the passage.

6 ἡδεῖα δ' ἐστὶ—μνήμη] 'Now of the present the living reality is sweet, of the future the hope, of the past the memory.' In two clauses of this sentence subjective words are used (ἐλπίς and μνήμη), but ἐνέργεια in the remaining clause hovers between the objective and the subjective. Cf. Ar. *De Memoria*, i. 4. where αἴσθησις is used in an analogous sentence: τοῦ μὲν παρόντος (ἐστὶν) αἴσθησις, τοῦ δὲ μέλλοντος ἐλπίς, τοῦ δὲ γεγενημένου μνήμη.

τὴν ἐνέργειαν, καὶ φιλητὸν ὁμοίως. τῷ μὲν οὖν πεποιηκότι μένει τὸ ἔργον (τὸ καλὸν γὰρ πολυχρόνιον), τῷ δὲ
παθόντι τὸ χρήσιμον παροίχεται. ἥ τε μνήμη τῶν μὲν
καλῶν ἡδεῖα, τῶν δὲ χρησίμων οὐ πάνυ ἢ ἧττον· ἡ προσδοκία δ' ἀνάπαλιν ἔχειν ἔοικεν. καὶ ἡ μὲν φίλησις
ποιήσει ἔοικεν, τὸ φιλεῖσθαι δὲ τῷ πάσχειν. τοῖς ὑπερέχουσι δὴ περὶ τὴν πρᾶξιν ἕπεται τὸ φιλεῖν καὶ τὰ
φιλικά. ἔτι δὲ τὰ ἐπιπόνως γινόμενα πάντες μᾶλλον 7
στέργουσιν, οἷον καὶ τὰ χρήματα οἱ κτησάμενοι τῶν
παραλαβόντων· δοκεῖ δὴ τὸ μὲν εὖ πάσχειν ἄπονον εἶναι,
τὸ δ' εὖ ποιεῖν ἐργῶδες. διὰ ταῦτα δὲ καὶ αἱ μητέρες
φιλοτεκνότεραι· ἐπιπονωτέρα γὰρ ἡ γέννησις, καὶ μᾶλλον
ἴσασιν ὅτι αὐτῶν. δόξειε δ' ἂν τοῦτο καὶ τοῖς εὐεργέταις
οἰκεῖον εἶναι.

Ἀπορεῖται δὲ καὶ πότερον δεῖ φιλεῖν ἑαυτὸν μάλιστα 8
ἢ ἄλλον τινά· ἐπιτιμῶσι γὰρ τοῖς ἑαυτοὺς μάλιστα ἀγαπῶσι, καὶ ὡς ἐν αἰσχρῷ φιλαύτους ἀποκαλοῦσι, δοκεῖ
τε ὁ μὲν φαῦλος ἑαυτοῦ χάριν πάντα πράττειν, καὶ ὅσῳ
ἂν μοχθηρότερος ᾖ, τοσούτῳ μᾶλλον· ἐγκαλοῦσι δὴ αὐτῷ
ὅτι οὐδὲν ἀφ' ἑαυτοῦ πράττει· ὁ δ' ἐπιεικὴς διὰ τὸ καλόν,
καὶ ὅσῳ ἂν βελτίων ᾖ, μᾶλλον διὰ τὸ καλόν, καὶ φίλου
ἕνεκα· τὸ δ' αὑτοῦ παρίησιν. τοῖς λόγοις δὲ τούτοις τὰ 2

VIII. In this interesting chapter, Aristotle discusses the difficulty as to 'whether one ought to love oneself especially, or some one else.' On the one hand, 'self-loving' is used as a term of reproach; on the other hand, one's feelings towards oneself are made the standard for one's feelings towards friends. These two points of view require reconciliation, which may be effected by a distinction of terms. For the word 'self' has two senses—the lower and the higher self, the one consisting in appetites and passions, the other in the intellect and the higher moral faculties. He that gratifies his lower self at the expense of others is 'self-loving' in the bad sense of the term. He that ministers to his higher self promotes at the same time the good of others, and is worthy of all praise. Such self-love as this may lead a man even to die for his friends or for his country. A man, grasping at the noble, may give up honour, power, life itself; and thus the greatest self-sacrifice will be identical with the greatest self-love. These considerations show in what sense one ought, and in what sense one ought not, to 'love oneself.'

1 *ὡς ἐν αἰσχρῷ*] 'As a term of reproach.'

οὐδὲν ἀφ' ἑαυτοῦ πράττει] 'He does nothing apart from himself.' 'Nihil a suis rationibus alienum.'

2 *τοῖς λόγοις δὲ—οὐκ ἀλόγως*] 'With these theories men's actions, not un-

ἔργα διαφωνεῖ, οὐκ ἀλόγως. φασὶ γὰρ δεῖν φιλεῖν μάλιστα τὸν μάλιστα φίλον, φίλος δὲ μάλιστα ὁ βουλόμενος ᾧ βούλεται τἀγαθὰ ἐκείνου ἕνεκα, καὶ εἰ μηδεὶς εἴσεται. ταῦτα δ' ὑπάρχει μάλιστ' αὐτῷ πρὸς αὑτόν, καὶ τὰ λοιπὰ δὴ πάνθ' οἷς ὁ φίλος ὁρίζεται· εἴρηται γὰρ ὅτι ἀπ' αὐτοῦ πάντα τὰ φιλικὰ καὶ πρὸς τοὺς ἄλλους διήκει. καὶ αἱ παροιμίαι δὲ πᾶσαι ὁμογνωμονοῦσιν, οἷον τὸ 'μία ψυχή' καὶ 'κοινὰ τὰ φίλων' καὶ 'ἰσότης φιλότης' καὶ 'γόνυ κνήμης ἔγγιον.' πάντα γὰρ ταῦτα πρὸς αὑτὸν μάλισθ' ὑπάρχει· μάλιστα γὰρ φίλος αὑτῷ, καὶ φιλητέον δὴ μάλισθ' ἑαυτόν. ἀπορεῖται δ' εἰκότως ποτέροις χρεὼν ἕπεσθαι, ἀμφοῖν ἐχόντοιν τὸ πιστόν.

3 ἴσως οὖν τοὺς τοιούτους δεῖ τῶν λόγων διαιρεῖν καὶ διορίζειν ἐφ' ὅσον ἑκάτεροι καὶ πῇ ἀληθεύουσιν. εἰ δὴ λάβοιμεν τὸ φίλαυτον πῶς ἑκάτεροι λέγουσιν, τάχ' ἂν

4 γένοιτο δῆλον. οἱ μὲν οὖν εἰς ὄνειδος ἄγοντες αὐτὸ φιλαύτους καλοῦσι τοὺς ἑαυτοῖς ἀπονέμοντας τὸ πλεῖον ἐν χρήμασι καὶ τιμαῖς καὶ ἡδοναῖς ταῖς σωματικαῖς· τούτων γὰρ οἱ πολλοὶ ὀρέγονται, καὶ ἐσπουδάκασι περὶ αὐτὰ ὡς ἄριστα ὄντα, διὸ καὶ περιμάχητά ἐστιν. οἱ δὴ περὶ ταῦτα πλεονέκται χαρίζονται ταῖς ἐπιθυμίαις καὶ ὅλως τοῖς πάθεσι καὶ τῷ ἀλόγῳ τῆς ψυχῆς. τοιοῦτοι δ' εἰσὶν οἱ πολλοί· διὸ καὶ ἡ προσηγορία γεγένηται ἀπὸ τοῦ πολλοῦ φαύλου ὄντος. δικαίως δὴ τοῖς οὕτω φιλαύτοις ὀνειδί-

5 ζεται. ὅτι δὲ τοὺς τὰ τοιαῦθ' αὑτοῖς ἀπονέμοντας εἰώθασι λέγειν οἱ πολλοὶ φιλαύτους, οὐκ ἄδηλον· εἰ γάρ τις ἀεὶ σπουδάζοι τὰ δίκαια πράττειν αὐτὸς μάλιστα πάντων ἢ τὰ σώφρονα ἢ ὁποιαοῦν ἄλλα τῶν κατὰ τὰς ἀρετάς, καὶ ὅλως ἀεὶ τὸ καλὸν ἑαυτῷ περιποιοῖτο, οὐθεὶς ἐρεῖ τοῦτον

6 φίλαυτον οὐδὲ ψέξει. δόξειε δ' ἂν ὁ τοιοῦτος μᾶλλον εἶναι φίλαυτος· ἀπονέμει γοῦν ἑαυτῷ τὰ κάλλιστα καὶ μάλιστ' ἀγαθά, καὶ χαρίζεται ἑαυτοῦ τῷ κυριωτάτῳ, καὶ πάντα

---

reasonably, are at variance.' To the list of the meanings of the word *ἔργον* given in the note on *Eth.* I. vii. 11, we must add the above use of τὰ ἔργα to mean 'actions' as opposed to theory. Cf. *Eth.* X. i. 3: οἱ γὰρ περὶ τῶν ἐν τοῖς πάθεσι καὶ ταῖς πράξεσι λόγοι ἧττόν εἰσι πιστοὶ τῶν ἔργων. X. viii. 12: τὸ δ' ἀληθὲς ἐν τοῖς πρακτοῖς ἐκ τῶν ἔργων καὶ τοῦ βίου κρίνεται. Aristotle says that men do not 'act' as if they considered self-love to be wholly bad, and he proves this by quoting popular proverbs, which support the contrary view.

τούτῳ κεῖται· ὥσπερ δὲ καὶ πόλις τὸ κυριώτατον
μάλιστ' εἶναι δοκεῖ καὶ πᾶν ἄλλο σύστημα, οὕτω καὶ
ἄνθρωπος· καὶ φίλαυτος δὴ μάλιστα ὁ τοῦτο ἀγαπῶν καὶ
τούτῳ χαριζόμενος. καὶ ἐγκρατὴς δὲ καὶ ἀκρατὴς λέγεται τῷ κρατεῖν τὸν νοῦν ἢ μή, ὡς τούτου ἑκάστου ὄντος·
καὶ πεπραχέναι δοκοῦσιν αὐτοὶ καὶ ἑκουσίως τὰ μετὰ
λόγου μάλιστα. ὅτι μὲν οὖν τοῦθ' ἕκαστός ἐστιν ἢ μάλιστα, οὐκ ἄδηλον, καὶ ὅτι ὁ ἐπιεικὴς μάλιστα τοῦτ'
ἀγαπᾷ. διὸ φίλαυτος μάλιστ' ἂν εἴη, καθ' ἕτερον εἶδος
τοῦ ὀνειδιζομένου, καὶ διαφέρων τοσοῦτον ὅσον τὸ κατὰ
λόγον ζῆν τοῦ κατὰ πάθος, καὶ ὀρέγεσθαι τοῦ καλοῦ ἢ τοῦ
δοκοῦντος συμφέρειν. τοὺς μὲν οὖν περὶ τὰς καλὰς 7
πράξεις διαφερόντως σπουδάζοντας πάντες ἀποδέχονται
καὶ ἐπαινοῦσιν· πάντων δὲ ἁμιλλωμένων πρὸς τὸ καλὸν
καὶ διατεινομένων τὰ κάλλιστα πράττειν κοινῇ τ' ἂν
πάντ' εἴη τὰ δέοντα καὶ ἰδίᾳ ἑκάστῳ τὰ μέγιστα τῶν
ἀγαθῶν, εἴπερ ἡ ἀρετὴ τοιοῦτόν ἐστιν. ὥστε τὸν μὲν
ἀγαθὸν δεῖ φίλαυτον εἶναι· καὶ γὰρ αὐτὸς ὀνήσεται τὰ
καλὰ πράττων καὶ τοὺς ἄλλους ὠφελήσει· τὸν δὲ μοχθηρὸν οὐ δεῖ· βλάψει γὰρ καὶ ἑαυτὸν καὶ τοὺς πέλας,
φαύλοις πάθεσιν ἑπόμενος. τῷ μοχθηρῷ μὲν οὖν διαφωνεῖ 8
ἃ δεῖ πράττειν καὶ ἃ πράττει· ὁ δ' ἐπιεικής, ἃ δεῖ, ταῦτα
καὶ πράττει· πᾶς γὰρ νοῦς αἱρεῖται τὸ βέλτιστον ἑαυτῷ,
ὁ δ' ἐπιεικὴς πειθαρχεῖ τῷ νῷ. ἀληθὲς δὲ περὶ τοῦ 9
σπουδαίου καὶ τὸ τῶν φίλων ἕνεκα πολλὰ πράττειν καὶ
τῆς πατρίδος, κἂν δέῃ ὑπεραποθνήσκειν· προήσεται γὰρ
καὶ χρήματα καὶ τιμὰς καὶ ὅλως τὰ περιμάχητα ἀγαθά,

---

6 ὥσπερ δὲ καὶ πόλις—ἄνθρωπος] 'But as the predominant part (in a state) seems before all things to *be* the state, and as the predominant part in every other system seems to *be* that system, so (the predominant part in man seems, above all things, to *be*) man.' Cf. *Eth.* x. vii. 9: δόξειε δ' ἂν καὶ εἶναι ἕκαστος τοῦτο, εἴπερ τὸ κύριον καὶ ἄμεινον. On the uses of the word κύριος cf. note on *Eth.* i. ii. 4, in the above passage τὸ κυριώτατον means the 'most absolute,' the 'ruling' part. Cf. Ar. *Politics*, iii. vii. 2: πολίτευμα δ' ἐστὶ τὸ κύριον τῶν πόλεων, ἀνάγκη δ' εἶναι κύριον ἢ ἕνα ἢ ὀλίγους ἢ τοὺς πολλούς.

7 εἴπερ ἡ ἀρετὴ τοιοῦτόν ἐστιν] 'If virtue is one of the greatest of goods.'

8—10 The sentiments expressed in these sections may be compared with the elevated description of the self-sacrifice of the brave man, in *Eth.* iii.

περιποιούμενος ἑαυτῷ τὸ καλόν· ὀλίγον γὰρ χρόνον ἡσθῆναι σφόδρα μᾶλλον ἕλοιτ' ἂν ἢ πολὺν ἠρέμα, καὶ
βιῶσαι καλῶς ἐνιαυτὸν ἢ πόλλ' ἔτη τυχόντως, καὶ μίαν
πρᾶξιν καλὴν καὶ μεγάλην ἢ πολλὰς καὶ μικράς. τοῖς
δ' ὑπεραποθνήσκουσι τοῦτ' ἴσως συμβαίνει· αἱροῦνται δὴ
μέγα καλὸν ἑαυτοῖς. καὶ χρήματα προοῖντ' ἂν ἐφ' ᾧ
πλείονα λήψονται οἱ φίλοι· γίγνεται γὰρ τῷ μὲν φίλῳ
χρήματα, αὐτῷ δὲ τὸ καλόν· τὸ δὴ μεῖζον ἀγαθὸν ἑαυτῷ
10 ἀπονέμει. καὶ περὶ τιμὰς δὲ καὶ ἀρχὰς ὁ αὐτὸς τρόπος·
πάντα γὰρ τῷ φίλῳ ταῦτα προήσεται· καλὸν γὰρ αὐτῷ
τοῦτο καὶ ἐπαινετόν. εἰκότως δὴ δοκεῖ σπουδαῖος εἶναι,
ἀντὶ πάντων αἱρούμενος τὸ καλόν. ἐνδέχεται δὲ καὶ
πράξεις τῷ φίλῳ προΐεσθαι, καὶ εἶναι κάλλιον τοῦ αὐτὸν
11 πρᾶξαι τὸ αἴτιον τῷ φίλῳ γενέσθαι. ἐν πᾶσι δὴ τοῖς
ἐπαινετοῖς ὁ σπουδαῖος φαίνεται ἑαυτῷ τοῦ καλοῦ πλέον
νέμων. οὕτω μὲν οὖν φίλαυτον εἶναι δεῖ, καθάπερ
εἴρηται· ὡς δ' οἱ πολλοί, οὐ χρή.

9 Ἀμφισβητεῖται δὲ καὶ περὶ τὸν εὐδαίμονα, εἰ δεήσεται φίλων ἢ μή. οὐθὲν γάρ φασι δεῖν φίλων τοῖς μακαρίοις

---

ix. 4—5. But we may particularly note here the delicacy of thought which suggests that the good man may on occasion give up to his friend the doing of noble acts, and thus acquire to himself a still greater nobility. A comparison is sometimes instituted between the φιλαυτία of Aristotle and the 'self-love' of Bishop Butler. But the 'self-love' described by Butler is a creeping quality, it deals with means rather than with ends, and considers the 'interest' of man in this world or the next. Aristotle's φιλαυτία is simply a devotion to what is great and noble.

IX. Does the happy man, who is all-sufficient in himself, need friends, or not? To prove the affirmative of this question, Aristotle uses the following arguments.

1 *A priori*, we might assume that, as happiness is the sum of all human goods, the possession of friends, one of the greatest of external goods, would necessarily be included (§ 2).

2 Friends will be required by the happy man, not so much as the givers, but rather as the recipients, of kindness.

3 We might assume also that the happy man should neither be condemned to be a solitary, nor to live with strangers and chance people (§ 3).

4 Those who take the negative side in the question have an unworthy conception of friends, as persons affording profit or pleasure. The happy man is almost independent of such (§ 4), but yet he may want friends in a higher sense. Happiness consists in the play of life (*ἐνέργεια*), and he that sees before his eyes the virtuous

καὶ αὐτάρκεσιν· ὑπάρχειν γὰρ αὐτοῖς τἀγαθά· αὐτάρκεις οὖν ὄντας οὐδενὸς προσδεῖσθαι, τὸν δὲ φίλον, ἕτερον αὐτὸν ὄντα, πορίζειν ἃ δι' αὐτοῦ ἀδυνατεῖ· ὅθεν τὸ

ὅταν ὁ δαίμων εὖ διδῷ, τί δεῖ φίλων;

ἔοικε δ' ἀτόπῳ τὸ πάντ' ἀπονέμοντας τἀγαθὰ τῷ εὐδαί- 2
μονι φίλους μὴ ἀποδιδόναι, ὃ δοκεῖ τῶν ἐκτὸς ἀγαθῶν μέγιστον εἶναι. εἴ τε φίλου μᾶλλόν ἐστι τὸ εὖ ποιεῖν ἢ πάσχειν, καὶ ἔστι τοῦ ἀγαθοῦ καὶ τῆς ἀρετῆς τὸ εὐεργετεῖν, κάλλιον δ' εὖ ποιεῖν φίλους ὀθνείων, τῶν εὖ πεισομένων δεήσεται ὁ σπουδαῖος. διὸ καὶ ἐπιζητεῖται πότερον ἐν εὐτυχίαις μᾶλλον δεῖ φίλων ἢ ἐν ἀτυχίαις, ὡς καὶ τοῦ ἀτυχοῦντος δεομένου τῶν εὐεργετησόντων καὶ τῶν εὐτυχούντων οὓς εὖ ποιήσουσιν. ἄτοπον δ' ἴσως καὶ τὸ μονώτην ποιεῖν τὸν μακάριον· οὐθεὶς γὰρ ἕλοιτ' ἂν καθ' αὑτὸν 3
τὰ πάντ' ἔχειν ἀγαθά· πολιτικὸν γὰρ ὁ ἄνθρωπος καὶ συζῆν πεφυκός. καὶ τῷ εὐδαίμονι δὴ τοῦθ' ὑπάρχει· τὰ γὰρ τῇ φύσει ἀγαθὰ ἔχει. δῆλον δ' ὡς μετὰ φίλων καὶ ἐπιεικῶν κρεῖττον ἢ μετ' ὀθνείων καὶ τῶν τυχόντων

---

acts of a friend has a delightful sense of the play of life, seeing harmonious action and identifying it with himself (ἐπιεικεῖς καὶ οἰκείας, § 5).

5 Again, the sympathy and excitement of friends enables a man to prolong that vivid action and glow of the mind which is the essence of happiness (§§ 5—6).

6 It also confirms him in the practice of virtue (§§ 6—7).

7 Finally, a deeper reason may be assigned for the necessity of friends to the happy man; it depends on our love of life. That sympathetic consciousness (συναισθάνεσθαι) which we have of a friend's existence, by means of intercourse with him, is, only in a secondary degree (παραπλήσιον), the same as the sense of our own existence.

1 αὐτάρκεσιν] The quality αὐτάρκεια is claimed for happiness, *Eth.* I. vii. 6, where Aristotle guards himself against the supposition that it implies a lonely life, and where he promises to return to the subject. τὸ γὰρ τέλειον ἀγαθὸν αὔταρκες εἶναι δοκεῖ. τὸ δ' αὔταρκες λέγομεν οὐκ αὐτῷ μόνῳ τῷ ζῶντι βίον μονώτην, κ.τ.λ. Ἀλλὰ τοῦτο μὲν εἰσαῦθις ἐπισκεπτέον.

ὅταν ὁ δαίμων] from the *Orestes* of Euripides, 665, sqq:

τοὺς φίλους
ἐν τοῖς κακοῖς χρὴ τοῖς φίλοισιν ὠφελεῖν·
ὅταν δ' ὁ δαίμων εὖ διδῷ, τί δεῖ φίλων;
ἀρκεῖ γὰρ αὐτὸς ὁ θεὸς ὠφελεῖν θέλων.

2 ἀπονέμοντας] 'Us who allot,' cf. *Eth.* I. viii. 8, where happiness is said to be τέλειόν τι καὶ αὔταρκες. The form of expression here used is similar to that in *Eth.* I. x. 2: Ἢ τοῦτό γε παντελῶς ἄτοπον, ἄλλως τε καὶ τοῖς λέγουσιν ἡμῖν ἐνέργειάν τινα τὴν εὐδαιμονίαν;

4 συνημερεύειν· δεῖ ἄρα τῷ εὐδαίμονι φίλων. τί οὖν λέγουσιν οἱ πρῶτοι, καὶ πῇ ἀληθεύουσιν; ἢ ὅτι οἱ πολλοὶ φίλους οἴονται τοὺς χρησίμους εἶναι; τῶν τοιούτων μὲν οὖν οὐθὲν δεήσεται ὁ μακάριος, ἐπειδὴ τἀγαθὰ ὑπάρχει αὐτῷ. οὐδὲ δὴ τῶν διὰ τὸ ἡδύ, ἢ ἐπὶ μικρόν· ἡδὺς γὰρ ὁ βίος ὢν οὐθὲν δεῖται ἐπεισάκτου ἡδονῆς. οὐ δεόμενος δὲ τῶν τοιούτων
5 φίλων οὐ δοκεῖ δεῖσθαι φίλων. τὸ δ' οὐκ ἔστιν ἴσως ἀληθές· ἐν ἀρχῇ γὰρ εἴρηται ὅτι ἡ εὐδαιμονία ἐνέργειά τίς ἐστιν, ἡ δ' ἐνέργεια δῆλον ὅτι γίνεται καὶ οὐχ ὑπάρχει ὥσπερ κτῆμά τι. εἰ δὲ τὸ εὐδαιμονεῖν ἐστὶν ἐν τῷ ζῆν καὶ ἐνεργεῖν, τοῦ δ' ἀγαθοῦ ἡ ἐνέργεια σπουδαία καὶ ἡδεῖα καθ' αὑτήν, καθάπερ ἐν ἀρχῇ εἴρηται, ἔστι δὲ καὶ τὸ οἰκεῖον τῶν ἡδέων, θεωρεῖν δὲ μᾶλλον τοὺς πέλας δυνάμεθα ἢ ἑαυτοὺς καὶ τὰς ἐκείνων πράξεις ἢ τὰς οἰκείας, αἱ τῶν σπουδαίων δὴ πράξεις φίλων ὄντων ἡδεῖαι τοῖς ἀγαθοῖς· ἄμφω γὰρ ἔχουσι τὰ τῇ φύσει ἡδέα. ὁ μακάριος δὴ

4 *ἐπεισάκτου ἡδονῆς*] 'Adventitious pleasure,' 'pleasure introduced from without,' cf. *Eth.* I. viii. 12: *οὐδὲν δὴ προσδεῖται τῆς ἡδονῆς ὁ βίος αὐτῶν ὥσπερ περιάπτου τινός, ἀλλ' ἔχει τὴν ἡδονὴν ἐν ἑαυτῷ*. Cf. *Eth.* x. vii. 3. The word *ἐπείσακτος* occurs in Plato's *Cratylus*, p. 420 B, quoted above in the note on IX. v. 3.

5 *ἐν ἀρχῇ—βίος*] 'For we said at the outset (*Eth.* I. vii. 14) that happiness is a kind of vital action, and it is plain that this arises in us, and does not exist in us like a possession. But if being happy consists in the play of life, and the actions of the good man are good and essentially pleasurable, as we said before (*Eth.* I. viii. 13), and also the sense of a thing being identified with oneself is one of the sources of pleasure, but we are able to contemplate our neighbours better than ourselves, and their actions better than our own, then the actions of good men being their friends are pleasurable to the good; for (such actions) contain both the two elements that are essentially pleasurable. The supremely happy man then will require friends of this character, if he wishes to contemplate actions which are good and also identified with himself: and such are the actions of the good man being his friend. Again, men think that the happy man ought to live pleasurably, whereas life is painful to the solitary man, for by oneself it is difficult to maintain long a vivid state of the mind, but with others and in relation to others this is easier.'

The first part of this sentence contains a complex protasis, to which the apodosis is *αἱ τῶν σπουδαίων δή*, κ.τ.λ.

τοῦ δ' ἀγαθοῦ ἡ ἐνέργεια] In the passage referred to (*Eth.* I. viii. 13) the words are *αἱ κατ' ἀρετὴν πράξεις*, which may justify the above translation.

ἄμφω γὰρ ἔχουσι] Some of the commentators take *ἄμφω* as though it were the nominative case to *ἔχουσι*, and meant 'both the good man and his friend.' But it would be irrelevant

φίλων τοιούτων δεήσεται, εἴπερ θεωρεῖν προαιρεῖται πράξεις ἐπιεικεῖς καὶ οἰκείας· τοιαῦται δ' αἱ τοῦ ἀγαθοῦ
φίλου ὄντος. οἴονταί τε δεῖν ἡδέως ζῆν τὸν εὐδαίμονα·
μονώτῃ μὲν οὖν χαλεπὸς ὁ βίος· οὐ γὰρ ῥᾴδιον καθ' αὑτὸν
ἐνεργεῖν συνεχῶς, μεθ' ἑτέρων δὲ καὶ πρὸς ἄλλους ῥᾷον.
ἔσται οὖν ἡ ἐνέργεια συνεχεστέρα, ἡδεῖα οὖσα καθ' αὑτήν, 6
ὃ δεῖ περὶ τὸν μακάριον εἶναι· ὁ γὰρ σπουδαῖος, ᾗ σπουδαῖος, ταῖς κατ' ἀρετὴν πράξεσι χαίρει, ταῖς δ' ἀπὸ κακίας
δυσχεραίνει, καθάπερ ὁ μουσικὸς τοῖς καλοῖς μέλεσιν ἥδεται, ἐπὶ δὲ τοῖς φαύλοις λυπεῖται. γίνοιτο δ' ἂν καὶ 7
ἄσκησίς τις τῆς ἀρετῆς ἐκ τοῦ συζῆν τοῖς ἀγαθοῖς, καθάπερ καὶ Θέογνίς φησιν. φυσικώτερον δ' ἐπισκοποῦσιν
ἔοικεν ὁ σπουδαῖος φίλος τῷ σπουδαίῳ τῇ φύσει αἱρετὸς
εἶναι· τὸ γὰρ τῇ φύσει ἀγαθὸν εἴρηται ὅτι τῷ σπουδαίῳ
ἀγαθὸν καὶ ἡδύ ἐστι καθ' αὑτό· τὸ δὲ ζῆν ὁρίζονται τοῖς
ζῴοις δυνάμει αἰσθήσεως, ἀνθρώποις δ' αἰσθήσεως ἢ νοήσεως·

---

to speak of the feelings of the friend. The question is, what advantage does the happy man get out of having friends? ἄμφω here evidently applies to τὰ τῇ φύσει ἡδέα, as is further proved by the words ἐπιεικεῖς καὶ οἰκείας in the next sentence; it refers to what has gone before, τοῦ δ' ἀγαθοῦ—οἰκείων τῶν ἡδέων.

6—7 ὁ γὰρ σπουδαῖος—φησιν] The good man, feeling the same sort of pleasure in the moral acts reciprocated between himself and his friend which the musical man feels in good music, will prolong and enjoy that reciprocation, and as Theognis says 'will learn what is good by associating with the good.' The advantage here attributed to friendship is that, by adding the element of pleasure to the best functions of our nature, it assists and developes them. Cf. *Eth.* x. v. 2: συναύξει γὰρ τὴν ἐνέργειαν ἡ οἰκεία ἡδονή—ὁμοίως δὲ καὶ οἱ φιλόμουσοι καὶ φιλοικοδόμοι καὶ τῶν ἄλλων ἕκαστοι ἐπιδιδόασιν εἰς τὸ οἰκεῖον ἔργον χαίροντες αὐτῷ.

καθάπερ ὁ μουσικὸς] On the 'moral sense' in its analogy to the 'musical ear,' cf. *Eth.* x. iii. 10.

7 τὸ δὲ ζῆν—νοεῖν] 'People define "living" in the case of animals by the power of sensation, in the case of men by the power of sensation or thought. But the word "power" has its whole meaning in reference to the exercise of that power, and the distinctive part of the conception lies in the "exercise." Thus the act of living appears distinctively to be an act of perceiving or thinking.' The train of reasoning in this latter part of the chapter is, that life consists in consciousness; life is good and sweet; consciousness is intensified, and life therefore is made better and sweeter, by intercourse with friends.

τοῖς ζῴοις] On the ascending scale of life from the plant to the man, cf. *De Anim.* ii. iii. 1—9. *Eth.* i. vii. 12, and Vol. I. Essay V. p. 294.

ἡ δὲ δύναμις εἰς τὴν ἐνέργειαν ἀνάγεται. τὸ δὲ κύριον ἐν τῇ ἐνεργείᾳ· ἔοικε δὴ τὸ ζῆν εἶναι κυρίως τὸ αἰσθάνεσθαι ἢ νοεῖν. τὸ δὲ ζῆν τῶν καθ' αὑτὸ ἀγαθῶν καὶ ἡδέων· ὡρισμένον γάρ, τὸ δ' ὡρισμένον τῆς τἀγαθοῦ φύσεως. τὸ δὲ τῇ φύσει ἀγαθὸν καὶ τῷ ἐπιεικεῖ· διόπερ ἔοικε πᾶσιν ἡδὺ
8 εἶναι. οὐ δεῖ δὲ λαμβάνειν μοχθηρὰν ζωὴν καὶ διεφθαρμένην, οὐδ' ἐν λύπαις· ἀόριστος γὰρ ἡ τοιαύτη, καθάπερ τὰ ὑπάρχοντα αὐτῇ. ἐν τοῖς ἐχομένοις δὲ περὶ τῆς λύπης
9 ἔσται φανερώτερον. εἰ δ' αὐτὸ τὸ ζῆν ἀγαθὸν καὶ ἡδύ (ἔοικε δὲ καὶ ἐκ τοῦ πάντας ὀρέγεσθαι αὐτοῦ, καὶ μάλιστα τοὺς ἐπιεικεῖς καὶ μακαρίους· τούτοις γὰρ ὁ βίος αἱρετώτατος, καὶ ἡ τούτων μακαριωτάτη ζωή), ὁ δ' ὁρῶν ὅτι ὁρᾷ αἰσθάνεται καὶ ὁ ἀκούων ὅτι ἀκούει καὶ ὁ βαδίζων ὅτι βαδίζει, καὶ ἐπὶ τῶν ἄλλων ὁμοίως ἔστι τι τὸ αἰσθανό-

---

ἡ δὲ δύναμις εἰς τὴν ἐνέργειαν ἀνάγεται] Cf. *Metaphysics*, VIII. ix. 5: *φανερὸν ὅτι τὰ δυνάμει ὄντα εἰς ἐνέργειαν ἀναγόμενα εὑρίσκεται.*

διόπερ ἔοικε πᾶσιν ἡδὺ εἶναι] 'Wherefore it appears to be sweet to all,' *i.e.* of course ordinary individuals love life, in which there is a certain physical sweetness, cf. Ar. *Politics*, III. vi. 5: *Δῆλον δ' ὡς καρτεροῦσι πολλὴν κακοπάθειαν οἱ πολλοὶ τῶν ἀνθρώπων γλιχόμενοι τοῦ ζῆν, ὡς ἐνούσης τινὸς εὐημερίας ἐν αὐτῷ καὶ γλυκύτητος φυσικῆς.* This Greek view of the sweetness of life contrasts with the philosophy of the Hindoos, which represents life as a burden, and individuality as a curse.

8 *Οὐ δεῖ δὲ—φανερώτερον*] 'But one must not take (as an instance) a vicious and corrupt life, nor one in pain; for such a life is unharmonised, like its characteristics. In the following discourse the nature of pain will be made more clear.'

ἀόριστος] 'Unlimited;' 'without law, balance, order, harmony.' On the use made by Aristotle of this Pythagorean formula, see *Eth.* II. vi. 14, and Vol. I. Essay IV. pp. 251—256.

Ἐν τοῖς ἐχομένοις] We have here an unfulfilled promise, for in 'the following book' there is nothing on the 'unlimited' or 'unharmonised' nature of pain. The sentence may possibly be an interpolation.

9 *Εἰ δ' αὐτὸ τὸ ζῆν ἀγαθὸν*] This is the beginning of a complex protasis, which goes on prolonging itself, *ὁ δ' ὁρῶν—τὸ δ' ὅτι αἰσθανόμεθα*, &c., till at last it finds its apodosis in § 10: *καθάπερ οὖν τὸ αὐτὸν εἶναι αἱρετόν ἐστιν ἑκάστῳ, οὕτω καὶ τὸ τὸν φίλον, ἢ παραπλησίως.*

καὶ ἐπὶ τῶν ἄλλων—νοεῖν] 'And with respect to all the other functions, in like manner there is something which perceives that we are exercising them, so then we can perceive that we perceive, and think that we think. But this (perceiving) that we perceive or think, is perceiving that we exist; for existing, as we said (§ 7), consists in perceiving or thinking.' *ἐνεργοῦμεν* is here used in a purely objective sense; the *ἐνέργεια* is here distinguished from the consciousness which necessarily accompanies it, and with

μενον ὅτι ἐνεργοῦμεν, ὥστε αἰσθανοίμεθ' ἂν ὅτι αἰσθανόμεθα καὶ νοοῖμεν ὅτι νοοῦμεν. τὸ δ' ὅτι αἰσθανόμεθα ἢ νοοῦμεν, ὅτι ἐσμέν· τὸ γὰρ εἶναι ἦν αἰσθάνεσθαι ἢ νοεῖν. τὸ δ' αἰσθάνεσθαι ὅτι ζῇ, τῶν ἡδέων καθ' αὑτό· φύσει γὰρ ἀγαθὸν ζωή, τὸ δ' ἀγαθὸν ὑπάρχον ἐν ἑαυτῷ αἰσθάνεσθαι ἡδύ. αἱρετὸν δὲ τὸ ζῆν καὶ μάλιστα τοῖς ἀγαθοῖς, ὅτι τὸ εἶναι ἀγαθόν ἐστιν αὐτοῖς καὶ ἡδύ· συναισθανόμενοι γὰρ τοῦ καθ' αὑτὸ ἀγαθοῦ ἥδονται. ὡς δὲ πρὸς ἑαυτὸν ἔχει ὁ 10
σπουδαῖος, καὶ πρὸς τὸν φίλον· ἕτερος γὰρ αὐτὸς ὁ φίλος ἐστίν. καθάπερ οὖν τὸ αὐτὸν εἶναι αἱρετόν ἐστιν ἑκάστῳ, οὕτω καὶ τὸ τὸν φίλον, ἢ παραπλησίως. τὸ δ' εἶναι ἦν αἱρετὸν διὰ τὸ αἰσθάνεσθαι αὑτοῦ ἀγαθοῦ ὄντος. ἡ δὲ τοιαύτη αἴσθησις ἡδεῖα καθ' ἑαυτήν. συναισθάνεσθαι ἄρα δεῖ καὶ τοῦ φίλου ὅτι ἔστιν, τοῦτο δὲ γίνοιτ' ἂν ἐν τῷ συζῆν καὶ κοινωνεῖν λόγων καὶ διανοίας· οὕτω γὰρ ἂν δόξειε τὸ συζῆν ἐπὶ τῶν ἀνθρώπων λέγεσθαι, καὶ οὐχ ὥσπερ ἐπὶ τῶν βοσκημάτων τὸ ἐν τῷ αὐτῷ νέμεσθαι. εἰ δὴ τῷ μακαρίῳ τὸ εἶναι αἱρετόν ἐστι καθ' αὑτό, ἀγαθὸν τῇ φύσει ὂν καὶ ἡδύ, παραπλήσιον δὲ καὶ τὸ τοῦ φίλου ἐστίν, καὶ ὁ φίλος τῶν αἱρετῶν ἂν εἴη. ὃ δ' ἐστὶν αὐτῷ αἱρετόν, τοῦτο δεῖ ὑπάρχειν αὐτῷ, ἢ ταύτῃ ἐνδεὴς ἔσται. δεήσει ἄρα τῷ εὐδαιμονήσοντι φίλων σπουδαίων.

Ἆρ' οὖν ὡς πλείστους φίλους ποιητέον, ἢ καθάπερ ἐπὶ 10
τῆς ξενίας ἐμμελῶς εἰρῆσθαι δοκεῖ

μήτε πολύξεινος μήτ' ἄξεινος,

---

which it is frequently identified. See Vol. I. Essay IV. The absolute unity of existence with thought here laid down anticipates the 'cogito ergo sum' of Descartes.

10 Συναισθάνεσθαι—νέμεσθαι] 'Therefore we ought to have a sympathetic consciousness of the existence of our friend, and this can arise by means of living together with him, and sharing words and thought with him, which is the true meaning of "living together" in the case of men; it does not mean, as with cattle, simply herding in the same spot.' This view of the importance of 'intercourse,' and of the advantages to be derived from it, is repeated and summarized in ch. xii., and forms the conclusion of the treatise.

X. The question of the plurality of friends is brought under analysis in this chapter. The number of one's friends for use or for pleasure is shown to be limited by convenience. The

καὶ ἐπὶ τῆς φιλίας ἁρμόσει μήτ' ἄφιλον εἶναι μήτ' αὖ
2 πολύφιλον καθ' ὑπερβολήν; τοῖς μὲν δὴ πρὸς χρῆσιν καὶ
πάνυ δόξειεν ἂν ἁρμόζειν τὸ λεχθέν· πολλοῖς γὰρ ἀνθυπηρετεῖν ἐπίπονον, καὶ οὐχ ἱκανὸς ὁ βίος αὐτοῖς τοῦτο πράττειν. οἱ πλείους δὴ τῶν πρὸς τὸν οἰκεῖον βίον ἱκανῶς
περίεργοι καὶ ἐμπόδιοι πρὸς τὸ καλῶς ζῆν· οὐθὲν οὖν δεῖ
αὐτῶν. καὶ οἱ πρὸς ἡδονὴν δὲ ἀρκοῦσιν ὀλίγοι, καθάπερ ἐν
3 τῇ τροφῇ τὸ ἥδυσμα. τοὺς δὲ σπουδαίους πότερον πλείστους κατ' ἀριθμόν, ἢ ἔστι τι μέτρον καὶ φιλικοῦ πλήθους,
ὥσπερ πόλεως; οὔτε γὰρ ἐκ δέκα ἀνθρώπων γένοιτ'
ἂν πόλις, οὔτ' ἐκ δέκα μυριάδων ἔτι πόλις ἐστίν. τὸ δὲ
ποσὸν οὐκ ἔστιν ἴσως ἕν τι, ἀλλὰ πᾶν τὸ μεταξύ τινων
ὡρισμένων. καὶ φίλων δή ἐστι πλῆθος ὡρισμένον, καὶ
ἴσως οἱ πλεῖστοι, μεθ' ὧν ἂν δύναιτό τις συζῆν· τοῦτο
4 γὰρ ἐδόκει φιλικώτατον εἶναι, ὅτι δ' οὐχ οἷόν τε πολλοῖς συζῆν καὶ διανέμειν αὑτόν, οὐκ ἄδηλον. ἔτι δὲ

---

number of one's friends, properly so called, is shown to be limited by one's incapacity to feel the highest kind of affection (ὑπερβολή τις φιλίας) for many individuals, and by the practical difficulties which would attend a close intercourse (συζῆν) with many persons at once, who would also have to associate harmoniously with each other. On the whole the question is answered in the negative.

1 *ἐμμελῶς εἰρῆσθαι*] 'Neatly expressed.'

μήτε πολύξεινον] From Hesiod, *Works and Days*, 713:

μηδὲ πολύξεινον μηδ' ἄξεινον καλέεσθαι.

The line is untranslateable into English, as we have no word (like the German *Gastfreund*) to express both 'host,' and 'guest,' as *ξένος* does.

2 This section may be said to retract, upon further consideration, what was admitted, *Eth.* VIII. vi. 3: *διὰ τὸ χρήσιμον δὲ καὶ τὸ ἡδὺ πολλοῖς ἀρέσκειν ἐνδέχεται· πολλοὶ γὰρ οἱ τοιοῦτοι, καὶ ἐν ὀλίγῳ χρόνῳ αἱ ὑπηρεσίαι.*

ἱκανῶς] This reading, adopted by Bekker from a majority of MSS., is surprising; *ἱκανοὶ περίεργοι* would not be a natural phrase, whereas the context really requires *οἱ πλείους δὴ τῶν πρὸς τὸν οἰκεῖον βίον ἱκανῶν.*

3 *οὔτε γὰρ—πόλις ἐστίν*] 'For a state could not consist of ten men, nor again if consisting of a hundred thousand does it still continue to be a state.' This extremely limited idea of the size of a state is based on the Greek notion that each citizen must personally take part in the administration of affairs. On this hypothesis, a state consisting of a hundred thousand citizens might easily appear unwieldy. Aristotle in the *Politics*, VII. iv. 9, represents the state as an organism of limited size: *ἔστι τι καὶ πόλεσι μεγέθους μέτρον, ὥσπερ καὶ τῶν ἄλλων πάντων, ζῴων, φυτῶν, ὀργάνων· καὶ γὰρ τούτων ἕκαστον οὔτε λίαν μικρὸν οὔτε κατὰ μέγεθος ὑπερβάλλον ἕξει τὴν αὑτοῦ δύναμιν, κ.τ.λ.*

κἀκείνους δεῖ ἀλλήλοις φίλους εἶναι, εἰ μέλλουσι πάντες
μετ' ἀλλήλων συνημερεύειν· τοῦτο δ' ἐργῶδες ἐν πολλοῖς
ὑπάρχειν. χαλεπὸν δὲ γίνεται καὶ τὸ συγχαίρειν καὶ 5
τὸ συναλγεῖν οἰκείως πολλοῖς· εἰκὸς γὰρ συμπίπτειν ἅμα
τῷ μὲν συνήδεσθαι τῷ δὲ συνάχθεσθαι. ἴσως οὖν εὖ ἔχει
μὴ ζητεῖν ὡς πολυφιλώτατον εἶναι, ἀλλὰ τοσούτους ὅσοι
εἰς τὸ συζῆν ἱκανοί· οὐδὲ γὰρ ἐνδέχεσθαι δόξειεν ἂν
πολλοῖς εἶναι φίλον σφόδρα. διόπερ οὐδ' ἐρᾶν πλειόνων·
ὑπερβολὴ γάρ τις εἶναι βούλεται φιλίας, τοῦτο δὲ πρὸς
ἕνα· καὶ τὸ σφόδρα δὴ πρὸς ὀλίγους. οὕτω δ' ἔχειν 6
ἔοικε καὶ ἐπὶ τῶν πραγμάτων· οὐ γίγνονται γὰρ φίλοι
πολλοὶ κατὰ τὴν ἑταιρικὴν φιλίαν, αἱ δ' ὑμνούμεναι ἐν
δυσὶ λέγονται. οἱ δὲ πολύφιλοι καὶ πᾶσιν οἰκείως
ἐντυγχάνοντες οὐδενὶ δοκοῦσιν εἶναι φίλοι, πλὴν πολιτικῶς, οὓς καὶ καλοῦσιν ἀρέσκους. πολιτικῶς μὲν οὖν

διόπερ οὐδ' ἐρᾶν πλειόνων] This is almost a *verbatim* repetition of *Eth.* viii. vi. 2, which passage contains the germ of the present chapter.

6 *οὕτω δ'—τοσούτους*] 'And this seems to be practically the case; for we do not find that people have many friends (together) on the footing of companionship. And the classical friendships of story are recorded to have been between pairs. But they who have many friends, and who associate familiarly with all, seem to be friends to none, except in a civil way, and men call them "over-complaisant." In a civil way indeed it is possible to be a friend to many without being over-complaisant, but being really kind; but on a moral and personal footing this is not possible in relation to many; one must be content to find even a few worthy of this.'

ἐπὶ τῶν πραγμάτων] Opposed to τοῖς λόγοις implied in τὸ λεχθὲν above. Cf. the use of τὰ ἔργα, *Eth.* ix. viii. 2.

ἑταιρικὴν] Cf. *Eth.* viii. xii. 1—6, and viii. v. 3. 'Companionship,' which Aristotle compares to the feeling between brothers, is much more akin to the perfect and ideal friendship than it is to either of the lower forms of friendship (for gain or for pleasure). It is essentially based on personal considerations (δι' αὐτούς), though not necessarily on moral considerations (δι' ἀρετήν).

αἱ δ' ὑμνούμεναι] Fritzsche quotes Plutarch, *De Am. Mult.* 2: *τὸν μακρὸν καὶ παλαιὸν αἰῶνα μάρτυρα ἅμα τοῦ λόγου καὶ σύμβουλον λάβωμεν, ἐν ᾧ κατὰ ζεῦγος φιλίας λέγονται Θησεὺς καὶ Πειρίθους, Ἀχιλλεὺς καὶ Πάτροκλος, Ὀρέστης καὶ Πυλάδης, Φιντίας καὶ Δάμων, Ἐπαμινώνδας καὶ Πελοπίδας.*

οἱ δὲ πολύφιλοι—οὐδενὶ δοκοῦσιν εἶναι φίλοι] Cf. *Eudemian Ethics*, vii. xii. 17: *τὸ ζητεῖν ἡμῖν καὶ εὔχεσθαι πολλοὺς φίλους, ἅμα δὲ λέγειν ὅτι οὐθεὶς φίλος ᾧ πολλοὶ φίλοι, ἄμφω λέγεται ὀρθῶς*, which sentence reconciles the above passage with *Eth.* viii. i. 5. In an external way (πολιτικῶς) a man should have many friends, personally (δι' αὐτούς) a few.

ἀρέσκους] Cf. *Eth.* ii. vii. 13. iv. vi. 9.

ἔστι πολλοῖς εἶναι φίλον καὶ μὴ ἄρεσκον ὄντα, ἀλλ' ὡς
ἀληθῶς ἐπιεικῆ· δι' ἀρετὴν δὲ καὶ δι' αὐτοὺς οὐκ ἔστι
πρὸς πολλούς, ἀγαπητὸν δὲ καὶ ὀλίγους εὑρεῖν τοιούτους.

11 Πότερον δ' ἐν εὐτυχίαις μᾶλλον φίλων δεῖ ἢ ἐν δυστυχίαις; ἐν ἀμφοῖν γὰρ ἐπιζητοῦνται· οἵ τε γὰρ ἀτυχοῦντες δέονται ἐπικουρίας, οἵ τ' εὐτυχοῦντες συμβίων καὶ
οὓς εὖ ποιήσουσιν· βούλονται γὰρ εὖ δρᾶν. ἀναγκαιότερον μὲν δὴ ἐν ταῖς ἀτυχίαις, διὸ τῶν χρησίμων
ἐνταῦθα δεῖ, κάλλιον δ' ἐν ταῖς εὐτυχίαις, διὸ καὶ τοὺς
ἐπιεικεῖς ζητοῦσιν· τούτους γὰρ αἱρετώτερον εὐεργετεῖν
2 καὶ μετὰ τούτων διάγειν. ἔστι γὰρ καὶ ἡ παρουσία
αὐτὴ τῶν φίλων ἡδεῖα καὶ ἐν ταῖς δυστυχίαις· κουφίζονται γὰρ οἱ λυπούμενοι συναλγούντων τῶν φίλων. διὸ
κἂν ἀπορήσειέν τις πότερον ὥσπερ βάρους μεταλαμβά-
νουσιν, ἢ τοῦτο μὲν οὔ, ἡ παρουσία δ' αὐτῶν ἡδεῖα οὖσα
καὶ ἡ ἔννοια τοῦ συναλγεῖν ἐλάττω τὴν λύπην ποιεῖ. εἰ
μὲν οὖν διὰ ταῦτα ἢ δι' ἄλλο τι κουφίζονται, ἀφείσθω·
3 συμβαίνειν δ' οὖν φαίνεται τὸ λεχθέν. ἔοικε δ' ἡ παρουσία
μικτή τις αὐτῶν εἶναι. αὐτὸ μὲν γὰρ τὸ ὁρᾶν τοὺς φίλους
ἡδύ, ἄλλως τε καὶ ἀτυχοῦντι, καὶ γίνεταί τις ἐπικουρία
πρὸς τὸ μὴ λυπεῖσθαι· παραμυθητικὸν γὰρ ὁ φίλος καὶ
τῇ ὄψει καὶ τῷ λόγῳ, ἐὰν ᾖ ἐπιδέξιος· οἶδε γὰρ τὸ ἦθος
4 καὶ ἐφ' οἷς ἥδεται καὶ λυπεῖται. τὸ δὲ λυπούμενον
αἰσθάνεσθαι ἐπὶ ταῖς αὐτοῦ ἀτυχίαις λυπηρόν· πᾶς γὰρ
φεύγει λύπης αἴτιος εἶναι τοῖς φίλοις. διόπερ οἱ μὲν

δι' αὐτούς] Cf. *Eth.* ix. i. 7, and note.

τοιούτους] *i.e.* capable of being made personal friends.

XI. The question whether friends are most needed in adversity or prosperity is here answered by saying, that in adversity friendship is more necessary, and in prosperity more beautiful. Some remarks are added on the exact operation of friendship in alleviating sorrow, and some practical rules are deduced.

2 ὥσπερ βάρους μεταλαμβάνουσιν] 'Whether they take part of the burden, as it were.' This is the ordinary metaphor. Cf. Xenophon, *Memor.* ii. vii. 1. (Σωκράτης) Ἀρίσταρχόν ποτε ὁρῶν σκυθρωπῶς ἔχοντα· Ἔοικας, ἔφη, ὦ Ἀρίσταρχε, βαρέως φέρειν τι· χρὴ δὲ τοῦ βάρους μεταδιδόναι τοῖς φίλοις. ἴσως γὰρ ἄν τί σε καὶ ἡμεῖς κουφίσαιμεν. Aristotle hints at, without fully giving, a more psychological account of the operation of friendship in adversity.

3 μικτή τις] Cf. *Eth.* iii. i. 6, iv. ix. 8.

ἀνδρώδεις τὴν φύσιν εὐλαβοῦνται συλλυπεῖν τοὺς φίλους αὐτοῖς, κἂν μὴ ὑπερτείνῃ τῇ ἀλυπίᾳ, τὴν ἐκείνοις γινομένην λύπην οὐχ ὑπομένει, ὅλως τε συνθρήνους οὐ προσίεται διὰ τὸ μηδ' αὐτὸς εἶναι θρηνητικός· γύναια δὲ καὶ οἱ τοιοῦτοι ἄνδρες τοῖς συστένουσι χαίρουσι, καὶ φιλοῦσιν ὡς φίλους καὶ συναλγοῦντας. μιμεῖσθαι δ' ἐν ἅπασι δεῖ δῆλον ὅτι τὸν βελτίω. ἡ δ' ἐν ταῖς εὐτυχίαις τῶν φίλων παρουσία τήν τε διαγωγὴν ἡδεῖαν ἔχει καὶ τὴν ἔννοιαν ὅτι ἥδονται ἐπὶ τοῖς αὐτοῦ ἀγαθοῖς. διὸ δόξειεν ἂν δεῖν εἰς μὲν τὰς εὐτυχίας καλεῖν τοὺς φίλους προθύμως· εὐεργετητικὸν γὰρ εἶναι καλόν· εἰς δὲ τὰς ἀτυχίας ὀκνοῦντα· μεταδιδόναι γὰρ ὡς ἥκιστα δεῖ τῶν κακῶν, ὅθεν τὸ

ἅλις ἐγὼ δυστυχῶν.

μάλιστα δὲ παρακλητέον, ὅταν μέλλωσιν ὀλίγα ὀχληθέντες μεγάλ' αὐτὸν ὠφελήσειν. ἰέναι δ' ἀνάπαλιν ἴσως ἁρμόζει πρὸς μὲν τοὺς ἀτυχοῦντας ἄκλητον καὶ προθύμως (φίλου γὰρ εὖ ποιεῖν, καὶ μάλιστα τοὺς ἐν χρείᾳ καὶ τὸ μὴ ἀξιώσαντας· ἀμφοῖν γὰρ κάλλιον καὶ ἥδιον), εἰς δὲ τὰς εὐτυχίας συνεργοῦντα μὲν προθύμως (καὶ γὰρ εἰς ταῦτα χρεία φίλων), πρὸς εὐπάθειαν δὲ σχολαίως· οὐ

---

4 κἂν μὴ ὑπερτείνῃ τῇ ἀλυπίᾳ—θρηνητικός] 'And (such a one), unless he be excessively impassive, cannot endure the pain which is brought upon them; and altogether he does not like sympathetic wailers, not being given to wailing himself.' The words κἂν μὴ κ.τ.λ. have troubled the commentators. The Paraphrast explains them as if meaning:—'And unless (the sympathetic presence of friends) be exceedingly painless to them.' But evidently the clause is brought in in reference to οἱ ἀνδρώδεις. 'Manly natures' are not at all unlikely to be somewhat blunt and callous, and deficient in sensibility for the feelings of others. One might almost fancy that Aristotle was thinking of the *Ajax* of Sophocles, vv. 319, 320:

πρὸς γὰρ κακοῦ τε καὶ βαρυψύχου γόους τοιούσδ' ἀεί ποτ' ἀνδρὸς ἐξηγεῖτ' ἔχειν.

5 ἅλις ἐγὼ δυστυχῶν] These words are not to be found in any extant play or fragment. The nearest approach to them is in Sophocles, *Œd. Tyr.* 1061: ἅλις νοσοῦσ' ἐγώ.

6 φίλου γὰρ—ἥδιον] 'For it behoves a friend to benefit (his friends), and especially those who are in need, and to (benefit) them when they have not asked. For this is nobler and sweeter for both parties.' With καὶ τὸ, εὖ ποιεῖν is to be repeated. Some editions, against the MSS., read καὶ τούς.

γὰρ καλὸν τὸ προθυμεῖσθαι ὠφελεῖσθαι. δόξαν δ' ἀηδίας ἐν τῷ διωθεῖσθαι ἴσως εὐλαβητέον· ἐνίοτε γὰρ συμβαίνει. ἡ παρουσία δὴ τῶν φίλων ἐν ἅπασιν αἱρετὴ φαίνεται.

12 Ἆρ' οὖν, ὥσπερ τοῖς ἐρῶσι τὸ ὁρᾶν ἀγαπητότατόν ἐστι καὶ μᾶλλον αἱροῦνται ταύτην τὴν αἴσθησιν ἢ τὰς λοιπάς, ὡς κατὰ ταύτην μάλιστα τοῦ ἔρωτος ὄντος καὶ γινομένου, οὕτω καὶ τοῖς φίλοις αἱρετώτατόν ἐστι τὸ συζῆν; κοινωνία γὰρ ἡ φιλία. καὶ ὡς πρὸς ἑαυτὸν ἔχει, οὕτω καὶ πρὸς τὸν φίλον. περὶ αὑτὸν δ' ἡ αἴσθησις ὅτι ἔστιν αἱρετή· καὶ περὶ τὸν φίλον δή. ἡ δ' ἐνέργεια γίνεται αὐτοῖς ἐν τῷ συζῆν, ὥστ' εἰκότως τούτου ἐφίενται.
2 καὶ ὅ τί ποτ' ἐστὶν ἑκάστοις τὸ εἶναι ἢ οὗ χάριν αἱροῦνται
τὸ ζῆν, ἐν τούτῳ μετὰ τῶν φίλων βούλονται διάγειν·
διόπερ οἱ μὲν συμπίνουσιν, οἱ δὲ συγκυβεύουσιν, ἄλλοι δὲ
συγγυμνάζονται καὶ συγκυνηγοῦσιν ἢ συμφιλοσοφοῦσιν,
ἕκαστοι ἐν τούτῳ συνημερεύοντες ὅ τί περ μάλιστα ἀγαπῶσι τῶν ἐν τῷ βίῳ· συζῆν γὰρ βουλόμενοι μετὰ τῶν
φίλων, ταῦτα ποιοῦσι καὶ τούτων κοινωνοῦσιν οἷς οἴονται
3 συζῆν. γίνεται οὖν ἡ μὲν τῶν φαύλων φιλία μοχθηρά·
κοινωνοῦσι γὰρ φαύλων ἀβέβαιοι ὄντες, καὶ μοχθηροὶ δὲ

δόξαν δ'—συμβαίνει] 'But one should beware perhaps of getting the reputation of churlishness in rejecting (benefits); for this sometimes happens.' ἀηδία answers to the 'insuavis, acerbus' of Horace, *Sat.* I. iii. 85.

XII. In conclusion, the best thing in friendship is—intercourse. This gives vividness to the pursuits of life; and when good men have intercourse with each other, they mutually strengthen and increase the good that is in them.

1 ἡ δ' ἐνέργεια γίνεται αὐτοῖς ἐν τῷ συζῆν] 'But it is by living together that they attain the fulness of life.' The word ἐνέργεια here has evident reference to ἡ αἴσθησις ὅτι ἔστιν in the preceding sentence. Zell and Cardwell follow some of the MSS. in reading αὐτῆς, *i.e.* τῆς αἰσθήσεως. But ἡ ἐνέργεια stands naturally alone (cf. *Eth.* IX. ix. 6), meaning 'the vivid sense of life.' And a similar collocation occurs *Eth.* VIII. iii. 5: γίνεται γὰρ αὐτοῖς τὸ κατὰ φιλίαν οὕτως.

3 κοινωνοῦσι γὰρ—ἀλλήλοις] 'For, being of an unstable nature, they have fellowship in evil, and become bad by assimilation to each other.' Cf. *Eth.* IX. i. 7: τοῖς φιλοσοφίας κοινωνήσασιν. The word ἀβέβαιοι here is not connected with the use of βέβαιον in *Eth.* VIII. viii. 5: Οἱ δὲ μοχθηροὶ τὸ μὲν βέβαιον οὐκ ἔχουσιν. Aristotle is not talking here of the instability of the friendship between bad men, but of its evil results mutually. Throughout the treatise on Friendship

γίνονται ὁμοιούμενοι ἀλλήλοις· ἡ δὲ τῶν ἐπιεικῶν ἐπιεικής, συναυξανομένη ταῖς ὁμιλίαις· δοκοῦσι δὲ καὶ βελτίους γίνεσθαι ἐνεργοῦντες καὶ διορθοῦντες ἀλλήλους· ἀπομάττονται γὰρ παρ' ἀλλήλων οἷς ἀρέσκονται, ὅθεν

ἐσθλῶν μὲν γὰρ ἄπ' ἐσθλά.

†περὶ μὲν οὖν φιλίας ἐπὶ τοσοῦτον εἰρήσθω· ἑπόμενον δ' ἂν εἴη διελθεῖν περὶ ἡδονῆς. 4

---

he speaks of the *weakness* of vice (cf. note on ix. iv. 9), and here he says that bad men, from the weakness and instability of their natures, imbibe evil example.

ἀπομάττονται — ἀρέσκονται] 'For they take the stamp of one another in those things which they like.' Cf. Aristophanes, *Ranæ*, v. 1040:

ὅθεν ἡ 'μὴ φρὴν ἀπομαξαμένη πολλὰς
ἀρετὰς ἐποίησεν.

ἐσθλῶν μὲν γὰρ] On this passage of Theognis, which is referred to above, *Eth.* ix. ix. 7, see Vol. I. Essay II. p. 92. It is after Aristotle's manner to end a treatise with a line of poetry; cf. *Metaphysics*, xi. x. 14, where the book ends with the verse

Οὐκ ἀγαθὸν πολυκοιρανίη· εἷς κοίρανος
ἔστω.

Accordingly the unnecessary paragraph περὶ μὲν οὖν φιλίας κ.τ.λ. is probably the interpolation of an editor.

PLAN OF BOOK X.

THIS Book,—beginning with a treatise on Pleasure, (which subject is introduced (1) because of its connection with Morals; (2) because of the controversies about it), and rising from the critical examination of extreme views to Aristotle's own theory of Pleasure, namely, that it is the sense of the Vital Functions, or in other words, of the harmonious action of some one faculty;—proceeds, almost without transition, to declare that Happiness in the truest sense of the term must consist in the action of the highest faculty, and that, this highest faculty being Reason, Philosophy must, beyond all comparison with anything else, whether idle amusement or even the exercise of the moral virtues, constitute Happiness, or that practical Chief Good which is the end of Man, and the province of the ethical branch of Politics.

Thus far this branch of Science, having obtained a definite conception, might be thought to be complete. But it still remains, says Aristotle, to ask whether something cannot be added towards its practical realization, and, as habits of life are clearly necessary for the attainment of human excellence, on which the Chief Good depends, it follows that we shall require such domestic institutions as may be favourable to the cultivation of human excellence. These institutions, whether of public or private ordinance, can only be rightly conceived after a scientific study of the principles of Legislation, *i.e.* of Politics in its highest form. To this then Aristotle proposes to address himself, considering it to be a branch of science which has hitherto been neglected. He roughly sketches out the plan of his work on Politics, with a transition to which the ethical treatise concludes.

This tenth book then shows us the *Ethics* as a rounded whole. It is written in close connection with Book I. (cf. X. vi. 1), and it sums up referentially the contents of Books I. II. III. IV. VIII. IX. But while the *Ethics* are thus rounded off in their beginning and end, and as to part of their contents, it is clear on the other hand that they contain a *lacuna* which has been artificially filled up.

It is very significant that the present book makes no reference to the contents of Books V. VI. VII.; and it seems impossible to avoid thinking that Aristotle wrote the conclusion to his ethical treatise at a time when he had not as yet composed certain parts which were meant to be introduced into it. Whether he afterwards ever composed those parts in literary form, or whether he merely gave materials for them in his oral discourses, we have now no means of knowing. That Books V. VI. and VII. were not actually composed by Aristotle we have seen many reasons for believing.

ΗΘΙΚΩΝ ΝΙΚΟΜΑΧΕΙΩΝ Χ.

ΜΕΤΑ δὲ ταῦτα περὶ ἡδονῆς ἴσως ἕπεται διελθεῖν· μάλιστα γὰρ δοκεῖ συνῳκειῶσθαι τῷ γένει ἡμῶν· διὸ
παιδεύουσι τοὺς νέους οἰακίζοντες ἡδονῇ καὶ λύπῃ. δοκεῖ
δὲ καὶ πρὸς τὴν τοῦ ἤθους ἀρετὴν μέγιστον εἶναι τὸ χαίρειν
οἷς δεῖ καὶ μισεῖν ἃ δεῖ· διατείνει γὰρ ταῦτα διὰ παντὸς
τοῦ βίου, ῥοπὴν ἔχοντα καὶ δύναμιν πρὸς ἀρετήν τε καὶ
τὸν εὐδαίμονα βίον· τὰ μὲν γὰρ ἡδέα προαιροῦνται, τὰ δὲ
2 λυπηρὰ φεύγουσιν. ὑπὲρ δὲ τῶν τοιούτων ἥκιστ' ἂν
δόξειε παρετέον εἶναι, ἄλλως τε καὶ πολλὴν ἐχόντων
ἀμφισβήτησιν. οἱ μὲν γὰρ τἀγαθὸν ἡδονὴν λέγουσιν, οἱ
δ' ἐξ ἐναντίας κομιδῇ φαῦλον, οἱ μὲν ἴσως πεπεισμένοι
οὕτω καὶ ἔχειν, οἱ δὲ οἰόμενοι βέλτιον εἶναι πρὸς τὸν βίον
ἡμῶν ἀποφαίνειν τὴν ἡδονὴν τῶν φαύλων, καὶ εἰ μὴ ἐστίν·
ῥέπειν γὰρ τοὺς πολλοὺς πρὸς αὐτὴν καὶ δουλεύειν ταῖς
ἡδοναῖς, διὸ δεῖν εἰς τοὐναντίον ἄγειν· ἐλθεῖν γὰρ ἂν οὕτως

I. The treatise on Pleasure opens analogously to that on the Voluntary (*Eth.* III. i. 1), and that on Friendship (VIII. i. 1, 6), justifying the introduction of the subject, (1) as connected with Ethics, (2) as having been made matter of controversy.

1 *μάλιστα γὰρ—ἡμῶν*] 'For it seems to be most intimately connected with the human race.' *Omni sed non soli*, see below v. 8.

διὸ παιδεύουσι κ.τ.λ.] This is all taken from Plato's *Laws*, II. p. 653. See note on *Eth.* II. iii. 2, where the passage is quoted.

πρὸς τὴν τοῦ ἤθους ἀρετήν] Some MSS. read ἀρχήν, which it is strange that the commentators should have thought a natural reading, supported by *αἱ μὲν τῆς φρονήσεως ἀρχαί* (below, viii. 3). Because *φρόνησις* is regarded by Aristotle as a syllogism, or set of syllogisms, having ἀρχαί or major premises,—it does not follow that the phrase ἡ τοῦ ἤθους ἀρχή is admissible.

2 *οἱ μὲν γὰρ—μένοι*] 'For some call pleasure the chief good, others on the contrary call it exceedingly evil, (of these latter) some perhaps believing it to be so, but others thinking it for the interests of morality to declare pleasure to be an evil, even if it be not so, because most men incline to-

ἐπὶ τὸ μέσον. μή ποτε δὲ οὐ καλῶς τοῦτο λέγεται. οἱ 3
γὰρ περὶ τῶν ἐν τοῖς πάθεσι καὶ ταῖς πράξεσι λόγοι ἧττόν εἰσι πιστοὶ τῶν ἔργων· ὅταν οὖν διαφωνῶσι τοῖς κατὰ τὴν αἴσθησιν, καταφρονούμενοι καὶ τἀληθὲς προσαναιροῦσιν· ὁ γὰρ ψέγων τὴν ἡδονήν, ὀφθείς ποτ' ἐφιέμενος, ἀποκλίνειν δοκεῖ πρὸς αὐτὴν ὡς τοιαύτην οὖσαν ἅπασαν· τὸ διορίζειν γὰρ οὐκ ἔστι τῶν πολλῶν. ἐοίκασιν οὖν οἱ ἀλη- 4
θεῖς τῶν λόγων οὐ μόνον πρὸς τὸ εἰδέναι χρησιμώτατοι εἶναι, ἀλλὰ καὶ πρὸς τὸν βίον· συνῳδοὶ γὰρ ὄντες τοῖς ἔργοις πιστεύονται, διὸ προτρέπονται τοὺς ξυνιέντας ζῆν κατ' αὐτούς. τῶν μὲν οὖν τοιούτων ἅλις, τὰ δ' εἰρημένα περὶ τῆς ἡδονῆς ἐπέλθωμεν.

---

wards it, and are enslaved to pleasures, and so one ought to lead men in the opposite direction, for thus they will arrive at the mean.'

In all probability Aristotle here alludes immediately to two sections of the Platonists, (1) the party represented by Eudoxus, whose arguments are quoted; (2) that headed by Speusippus, whose anti-hedonistic arguments were contained in two books mentioned by Diogenes Laertius, under the titles Περὶ ἡδονῆς α΄· Ἀρίστιππος α΄, and which are now passed under review. Under the class of those who 'call pleasure the chief good,' Aristotle less directly refers to Aristippus, who, though he belonged to a bygone era, still lived in the pages of Plato's Philebus, and in the book of Speusippus bearing his name.

ἐλθεῖν γὰρ—μέσον] Cf. *Eth.* ii. ix. 5, where it is said that by going counter to one's natural bias one may attain the mean. Aristotle does not approve of this being done by means of a sacrifice of truth.

3 μή ποτε—λέγεται] 'But perhaps this is not rightly said.' Cf. Plato, *Meno*, p. 89 c: ἀλλὰ μὴ τοῦτο οὐ καλῶς ὡμολογήσαμεν. This use of μήποτε became very common in the later Greek.

ὁ γὰρ ψέγων—πολλῶν] 'For he who blames pleasure (unreservedly), and yet is seen occasionally desiring it, is thought to incline towards it as being altogether good; for ordinary persons cannot discriminate.' τοιαύτην here, as τοιοῦτος does frequently in Aristotle, takes its sense from the context. Cf. *Eth.* viii. vi. 6. x. ii. 4, &c. From what is above stated we learn that, the decline of philosophy having commenced, some of the Platonists enunciated theories which were meant to be practically useful, rather than true. Thus they overstated what they believed to be the truth about pleasure, in order to counteract men's universal tendency towards it. Aristotle 'doubts whether this is good policy.' Their whole theory is likely to be upset by their occasionally indulging in the higher kinds of pleasure.

τοὺς ξυνιέντας] 'Those who comprehend them,' *i.e.* appreciating the truth of the theories, as shown by their agreement with men's actions. Cf. *Eth.* vi. x. 1, note. On τοῖς ἔργοις cf. ix. viii. 2.

2 Εὔδοξος μὲν οὖν τὴν ἡδονὴν τἀγαθὸν ᾤετ' εἶναι διὰ τὸ πάνθ' ὁρᾶν ἐφιέμενα αὐτῆς, καὶ ἔλλογα καὶ ἄλογα· ἐν πᾶσι δ' εἶναι τὸ αἱρετὸν ἐπιεικές, καὶ τὸ μάλιστα κράτιστον· τὸ δὴ πάντ' ἐπὶ ταὐτὸ φέρεσθαι μηνύειν ὡς πᾶσι τοῦτο ἄριστον· ἕκαστον γὰρ τὸ αὑτῷ ἀγαθὸν εὑρίσκειν, ὥσπερ καὶ τροφήν· τὸ δὴ πᾶσιν ἀγαθόν, καὶ οὗ πάντ' ἐφίεται, τἀγαθὸν εἶναι. ἐπιστεύοντο δ' οἱ λόγοι διὰ τὴν τοῦ ἤθους ἀρετὴν μᾶλλον ἢ δι' αὑτούς· διαφερόντως γὰρ

II. This chapter contains the grounds on which Eudoxus 'used to think that pleasure is the chief good'; and an examination of three objections, which had been started to these reasonings. The arguments of Eudoxus are, (1) that all things seek pleasure, (2) that pain is essentially (*καθ' αὑτό*) an object of aversion, and therefore pleasure, its contrary, must be essentially an object of desire, (3) that pleasure is always desired as an end-in-itself, and not as a means to anything, (4) that pleasure when added to any other good, makes it more desirable. The objections to these arguments are, (1) the opinion of Plato (which serves as an objection to argument 4th), that the chief good must be incapable of being added to any other good, and so made better. This objection Aristotle allows as valid. (2) An objection to the 1st argument, probably suggested by Plato's *Philebus*, p. 67, and repeated by Speusippus,—that the testimony of irrational creatures is of no value. This objection is disallowed. (3) The counter-argument of Speusippus to the 2nd argument of Eudoxus,—that not pleasure, but the neutral state, is the true contrary to pain. This is refuted.

1 *τὸ αἱρετὸν ἐπιεικές*] We have here a quotation of the very words of Eudoxus. In § 4 Aristotle generally approves of the present argument. His whole conclusion is to be found *Eth.* x. iii. 13:—that Eudoxus was more right than his opponents, but wrong in not discriminating between the different kinds of pleasure, and in going so far as to say that pleasure is the chief good. The term *τὸ αἱρετόν*, in opposition to *τὸ φευκτόν*, seems to have played a great part in the reasonings of Eudoxus. It is admitted by Plato, *Philebus*, p. 20, as a necessary attribute of the chief good, and so also by Aristotle, *Eth.* i. vii. 8; x. ii. 4. Here it is implied in the word *ἐφιέμενα*. It appears simply to mean 'that which is a reasonable object of desire,' cf. *Eth.* viii. viii. 2: *ἡ φιλία καθ' αὑτὴν αἱρετή*, and x. iii. 13, *ἡδονὴ οὐ πᾶσα αἱρετή*. As implying will and choice, it is applicable in a relative, as well as an absolute sense, to means as well as to ends. Book iii. of the *Topics* contains hints on the method of dealing with this term, and throws light on its use, which fluctuates between a reference to the good, the useful, and the pleasant (cf. *Top.* iii. iii. 7).

ἐπιστεύοντο δ' οἱ λόγοι] This is a pleasing allusion to the personal character of Eudoxus of Cnidus, who lived about 366 B.C., and who enjoyed great fame as an astronomer. He appears to have introduced the sphere from Egypt into Greece. The poem of Aratus is a versification of his *φαινόμενα*. Certain stories in Diogenes would leave the impression that, being Plato's pupil, he quarreled with his

ἐδόκει σώφρων εἶναι· οὐ δὴ ὡς φίλος τῆς ἡδονῆς ἐδόκει ταῦτα λέγειν, ἀλλ' οὕτως ἔχειν κατ' ἀλήθειαν. οὐχ ἧττον 2
δ' ᾤετ' εἶναι φανερὸν ἐκ τοῦ ἐναντίου· τὴν γὰρ λύπην καθ' αὑτὸ πᾶσι φευκτὸν εἶναι, ὁμοίως δὴ τοὐναντίον αἱρετόν. μάλιστα δ' εἶναι αἱρετὸν ὃ μὴ δι' ἕτερον μηδ' ἑτέρου χάριν αἱρούμεθα· τοιοῦτον δ' ὁμολογουμένως εἶναι τὴν ἡδονήν· οὐδένα γὰρ ἐπερωτᾶν τίνος ἕνεκα ἥδεται, ὡς καθ' αὑτὴν οὖσαν αἱρετὴν τὴν ἡδονήν. προστιθεμένην τε ὁτῳοῦν τῶν ἀγαθῶν αἱρετώτερον ποιεῖν, οἷον τῷ δικαιοπραγεῖν καὶ σωφρονεῖν· καὶ αὔξεσθαι δὴ τὸ ἀγαθὸν αὐτὸ αὑτῷ.
ἔοικε δὴ οὗτός γε ὁ λόγος τῶν ἀγαθῶν αὐτὴν ἀποφαίνειν, 3
καὶ οὐδὲν μᾶλλον ἑτέρου· πᾶν γὰρ μεθ' ἑτέρου ἀγαθοῦ αἱρετώτερον ἢ μονούμενον. τοιούτῳ δὴ λόγῳ καὶ Πλάτων ἀναιρεῖ ὅτι οὐκ ἔστιν ἡδονὴ τἀγαθόν· αἱρετώτερον γὰρ εἶναι τὸν ἡδὺν βίον μετὰ φρονήσεως ἢ χωρίς, εἰ δὲ τὸ μικτὸν κρεῖττον, οὐκ εἶναι τὴν ἡδονὴν τἀγαθόν· οὐδενὸς γὰρ προστεθέντος αὐτὸ τἀγαθὸν αἱρετώτερον γίνεσθαι. δῆλον δ' ὡς οὐδ' ἄλλο οὐδὲν τἀγαθὸν ἂν εἴη, ὃ μετά τινος

---

master. Aristotle (or, as Diogenes says, 'Nicomachus') is the only authority for his ethical opinions.

2 ὃ μὴ δι' ἕτερον] The end is better than the means, but this does not prove anything as to the comparative superiority of pleasure to the rest of the whole class of ends. Thus the argument of Eudoxus overshot the mark. A similar argument of his is mentioned with careless approbation, *Eth.* I. xii. 5: δοκεῖ καλῶς συνηγορῆσαι, says Aristotle, 'Eudoxus is thought to have pleaded well' in favour of pleasure being the chief good, because it is never praised. This argument would only prove that it belongs to the class of τὰ τίμια.

προστιθεμένην] It is suggested as a commonplace of reasoning, *Topics*, III. ii. 2, that you may say 'Justice and courage are better *with* pleasure than *without*.'

3 πᾶν γὰρ—χωρίς] 'For that "every good is better in combination with another good than alone." This is indeed the very argument by which Plato proves pleasure *not* to be the highest good. For the pleasant life is more desirable with wisdom than without.' Cf. *Philebus*, pp. 21—22: where however the proposition οὐδενὸς προστεθέντος—γίνεσθαι is not to be found. Plato only argued that, as the highest conception of human good implied a combination of both pleasure and knowledge, pleasure separately could not be the chief good. It is a deduction of Aristotle's from the terms ἱκανὸν καὶ τέλεον, used by Plato, that the chief good is incapable of addition or improvement. Cf. *Topics*, III. ii. 2: where it is said that the end *plus* the means cannot be called more desirable than the end by itself, cf. *Eth.* I. vii. 8, where the same

4 τῶν καθ' αὑτὸ ἀγαθῶν αἱρετώτερον γίνεται. τί οὖν ἐστὶ
τοιοῦτον, οὗ καὶ ἡμεῖς κοινωνοῦμεν; τοιοῦτον γὰρ ἐπιζητεῖται. οἱ δ' ἐνιστάμενοι ὡς οὐκ ἀγαθὸν οὗ πάντ' ἐφίεται,
μὴ οὐθὲν λέγωσιν· ὃ γὰρ πᾶσι δοκεῖ, τοῦτ' εἶναί φαμεν.
ὁ δ' ἀναιρῶν ταύτην τὴν πίστιν οὐ πάνυ πιστότερα ἐρεῖ·
εἰ μὲν γὰρ τὰ ἀνόητα ὠρέγετο αὐτῶν, ἦν ἄν τι τὸ λεγόμενον, εἰ δὲ καὶ τὰ φρόνιμα, πῶς λέγοιεν ἄν τι; ἴσως δὲ
καὶ ἐν τοῖς φαύλοις ἐστί τι φυσικὸν ἀγαθὸν κρεῖττον ἢ
5 καθ' αὑτά, ὃ ἐφίεται τοῦ οἰκείου ἀγαθοῦ. οὐκ ἔοικε δὲ
οὐδὲ περὶ τοῦ ἐναντίου καλῶς λέγεσθαι. οὐ γάρ φασιν, εἰ
ἡ λύπη κακόν ἐστι, τὴν ἡδονὴν ἀγαθὸν εἶναι· ἀντικεῖσθαι
γὰρ καὶ κακὸν κακῷ καὶ ἄμφω τῷ μηδετέρῳ, λέγοντες
ταῦτα οὐ κακῶς, οὐ μὴν ἐπί γε τῶν εἰρημένων ἀληθεύοντες.
ἀμφοῖν μὲν γὰρ ὄντων κακῶν καὶ φευκτὰ ἔδει ἄμφω εἶναι,
τῶν μηδετέρων δὲ μηδέτερον ἢ ὁμοίως· νῦν δὲ φαίνονται τὴν
μὲν φεύγοντες ὡς κακόν, τὴν δ' αἱρούμενοι ὡς ἀγαθόν·
οὕτω δὴ καὶ ἀντίκειται.

3 Οὐ μὴν οὐδ' εἰ μὴ τῶν ποιοτήτων ἐστὶν ἡ ἡδονή, διὰ
τοῦτ' οὐδὲ τῶν ἀγαθῶν· οὐδὲ γὰρ αἱ τῆς ἀρετῆς ἐνέργειαι

---

opinion seems to be conveyed, though that interpretation of the passage has been disputed.

4 *τί οὖν—ἐπιζητεῖται*] 'What is there then which has these characteristics (*i.e.* supreme goodness without the capability of addition) which we men can partake of? For such is the very object of our enquiries.' That is, not a transcendental good, but something to be practically realised. Cf. *Eth.* I. vi. 13.

ὃ γὰρ πᾶσι δοκεῖ] This acceptance of the testimony of instinct occurs also in the Eudemian book, *Eth.* VII. xiii. 5.

ὁ δ' ἀναιρῶν] Probably Speusippus, taking up a suggestion from Plato, *Philebus*, p. 67.

τοῖς φαύλοις] In the neuter gender, 'the lower creatures;'—alluding to the θηρία mentioned by Plato, *Philebus*, l. c.

5 *οὐ γάρ φασιν*] As we learn from the Eudemian book, *Eth.* VII. xiii. 1, Speusippus was the author of this objection.

III. Aristotle investigates remaining arguments used by the Platonists to prove that pleasure is not a good; (1) that it is 'not a quality.' This argument would prove too much, as it would be equally decisive against happiness, or the actions of virtue; (2) that it is 'unlimited.' But (*a*) in one sense this will apply to virtue also, (*b*) in another sense it is only applicable to the 'mixed pleasures,' which are analogous to health, *i.e.* a proportion variable according to circumstances; (3) that it is 'not final'

ποιότητές εἰσιν, οὐδ᾽ ἡ εὐδαιμονία. λέγουσι δὲ τὸ μὲν 2
ἀγαθὸν ὡρίσθαι, τὴν δ᾽ ἡδονὴν ἀόριστον εἶναι, ὅτι δέχεται τὸ μᾶλλον καὶ τὸ ἧττον. εἰ μὲν οὖν ἐκ τοῦ ἥδεσθαι τοῦτο κρίνουσι, καὶ περὶ τὴν δικαιοσύνην καὶ τὰς ἄλλας ἀρετάς, καθ᾽ ἃς ἐναργῶς φασὶ μᾶλλον καὶ ἧττον τοὺς ποιοὺς ὑπάρχειν κατὰ τὰς ἀρετάς, ἔσται τὸ αὐτό· δίκαιοι γάρ εἰσι μᾶλλον καὶ ἀνδρεῖοι, ἔστι δὲ καὶ δικαιοπραγεῖν καὶ σωφρονεῖν μᾶλλον καὶ ἧττον. εἰ δ᾽ ἐν ταῖς ἡδοναῖς, μή ποτ᾽ οὐ λέγουσι τὸ αἴτιον, ἂν ὦσιν

---

or perfect, but in some sort 'a transition.' Against which Aristotle argues, (*a*) that it cannot be a *motion* because not admitting the idea of speed, (*b*) that it cannot be a *creation*, because not capable of being resolved into its component parts, (*c*) that it cannot be a *filling up*, for this is merely corporeal, and even in the case of bodily pleasure it is not the body that feels; (*d*) that there are many disgraceful pleasures. To which it may be answered, that pleasures differ in kind, and even if some be bad, others may be absolutely good.

1 *εἰ μὴ τῶν ποιοτήτων*] This seems to be the only record of an argument, probably occurring in the works of Speusippus, that 'pleasure is not a good, because it is not a quality.' It points to the moralising tendency, above noticed, of this school of Platonists, as if they said that nothing could be called 'good' which did not form part of man's moral character.

2 *εἰ μὲν οὖν ἐκ τοῦ ἥδεσθαι*] Pleasure may be said to admit of degrees: first, in reference to men's different capacities of feeling it, but in this respect it will stand on the same footing as courage and justice.

εἰ δ᾽ ἐν ταῖς ἡδοναῖς—μικταί] 'In the second place, if (they predicate this attribute of "unlimited" as existing, not in the recipients of pleasure, but) in the pleasures themselves, perhaps they omit to state the reason of the fact, namely, that while some pleasures are unmixed, others are mixed.' Plato in the *Philebus* divides pleasures into mixed and unmixed. Of each he makes three classes. Mixed pleasures are (1) bodily pleasures, the restoration of harmony in the animal frame, where the bodily pain of want or desire is mixed up with the bodily pleasure of gratification; (2) the pleasure of expecting this restoration, where the bodily pain of want is mixed up with the mental pleasure of the idea of relief; (3) the pleasure which we feel in the ludicrous, where the mental pain of seeing the un-beautiful is mixed with the mental pleasure of laughing at it. The unmixed pleasures, *i.e.* in which no pain is implied, are (1) those of smell; (2) those of sight and hearing; (3) those that belong to the intellect. Of these two classes Plato confines the attribute of *ἀμετρία*, 'want of measure,' to the first class. The unmixed or pure pleasures necessarily possess *ἐμμετρία*, cf. *Phileb.* p. 52 c. The same doctrine is given *Eth.* VII. xiv. 6: *αἱ δ᾽ ἄνευ λυπῶν (ἡδοναὶ) οὐκ ἔχουσιν ὑπερβολήν.* Speusippus, forgetful of this distinction, appears to have made *ἀμετρία* (*ἀόριστον εἶναι*) a universal predicate of pleasure.

3 αἱ μὲν ἀμιγεῖς αἱ δὲ μικταί. τί γὰρ κωλύει, καθάπερ
ὑγίεια ὡρισμένη οὖσα δέχεται τὸ μᾶλλον καὶ τὸ ἧττον,
οὕτω καὶ τὴν ἡδονήν; οὐ γὰρ ἡ αὐτὴ συμμετρία ἐν
πᾶσίν ἐστιν, οὐδ' ἐν τῷ αὐτῷ μία τις ἀεί, ἀλλ' ἀνιεμένη
διαμένει ἕως τινός, καὶ διαφέρει τῷ μᾶλλον καὶ ἧττον.
τοιοῦτον δὴ καὶ τὸ περὶ τὴν ἡδονὴν ἐνδέχεται εἶναι.
4 τέλειόν τε τἀγαθὸν τιθέντες, τὰς δὲ κινήσεις καὶ τὰς
γενέσεις ἀτελεῖς, τὴν ἡδονὴν κίνησιν καὶ γένεσιν ἀποφαίνειν
πειρῶνται. οὐ καλῶς δ' ἐοίκασι λέγειν οὐδ' εἶναι κίνη-
σιν· πάσῃ γὰρ οἰκεῖον εἶναι δοκεῖ τάχος καὶ βραδυτής,
καὶ εἰ μὴ καθ' αὑτήν, οἷον τῇ τοῦ κόσμου, πρὸς ἄλλο·

---

3 *τί γὰρ κωλύει κ.τ.λ.*] Even the mixed pleasures, says Aristotle, admit the idea of proportion (*συμμετρία*), just as health is a proportion, though a relative and variable one, of the elements in the human body. In the *Topics*, vi. ii. 1. the words *ἡ ὑγίεια συμμετρία θερμῶν καὶ ψυχρῶν* are given as an instance of an ambiguous definition, *συμμετρία* being used in more senses than one.

οὐ γὰρ—ἧττον] 'Health is not the same proportion of elements in all men, nor even in the same man always, but with a certain laxity of variation it still remains health, though admitting of difference in the degrees (according to which the elements are compounded).'

4 *τέλειόν τε τἀγαθὸν τιθέντες κ.τ.λ.*] Plato, in the *Philebus*, p. 53 c, accepted the doctrine of the Cyrenaics, *ὅτι ἀεὶ γένεσίς ἐστιν* (*ἡ ἡδονή*), and then, by the contrast of means and end, *γένεσις* and *οὐσία*, he proved that pleasure could not be the chief good. As said above, Vol. I. Essay IV. p. 248, Plato seems to have recognised a class of pleasures above those which were mere states of transition, but to have had no formula to express them. Speusippus probably applied the argument drawn from the Cyrenaic definition not merely *ad hominem*, as Plato had done, but as if absolutely valid.

οἷον τῇ τοῦ κόσμου] i.e. *οὐκ ἔστι τάχος καὶ βραδυτὴς καθ' αὑτήν*. 'All motion has speed and slowness properly belonging to it, if not relatively to itself, as for instance the motion of the universe has no speed or slowness in itself (because it moves equably),—at all events in relation to other things.' Aristotle argues that though it is possible 'to be pleased' (*ἡσθῆναι—μεταβάλλειν εἰς ἡδονήν*) more or less quickly, it is not possible to 'feel pleasure' (*ἥδεσθαι*) either quickly or slowly. This argument seems a verbal one, like some of those in *Eth.* i. vi. against Plato's doctrine of ideas. If pleasure be *identified* with *κίνησις*, the argument holds good. But if it only be held to have the same relation to *κίνησις* as Aristotle himself makes it have to *ἐνέργεια*, *Eth.* x. viii. 4. the argument falls to the ground. This argument and the one in § 6 really only apply to the want of a sufficiently subjective formula to express pleasure. If pleasure were defined as 'the consciousness of a transition,' there might then be degrees of speed in the transition, though not in the consciousness of it.

τῇ δ' ἡδονῇ τούτων οὐδέτερον ὑπάρχει· ἡσθῆναι μὲν γὰρ ἔστι ταχέως ὥσπερ ὀργισθῆναι, ἥδεσθαι δ' οὔ, οὐδὲ πρὸς ἕτερον, βαδίζειν δὲ καὶ αὔξεσθαι καὶ πάντα τὰ τοιαῦτα. μεταβάλλειν μὲν οὖν εἰς τὴν ἡδονὴν ταχέως καὶ βραδέως ἔστιν, ἐνεργεῖν δὲ κατ' αὐτὴν οὐκ ἔστι ταχέως, λέγω δ'
ἥδεσθαι. γένεσίς τε πῶς ἂν εἴη; δοκεῖ γὰρ οὐκ ἐκ τοῦ 5
τυχόντος τὸ τυχὸν γίγνεσθαι, ἀλλ' ἐξ οὗ γίγνεται, εἰς τοῦτο διαλύεσθαι. καὶ οὗ γένεσις ἡ ἡδονή, τούτου ἡ λύπη
φθορά. καὶ λέγουσι δὲ τὴν μὲν λύπην ἔνδειαν τοῦ κατὰ 6
φύσιν εἶναι, τὴν δ' ἡδονὴν ἀναπλήρωσιν. ταῦτα δὲ σωματικά ἐστι τὰ πάθη. εἰ δή ἐστι τοῦ κατὰ φύσιν ἀναπλήρωσις ἡ ἡδονή, ἐν ᾧ ἀναπλήρωσις, τοῦτ' ἂν καὶ ἥδοιτο· τὸ σῶμα ἄρα· οὐ δοκεῖ δέ· οὐδ' ἔστιν ἄρα ἀναπλήρωσις ἡ ἡδονή, ἀλλὰ γινομένης μὲν ἀναπληρώσεως ἥδοιτ' ἄν τις, καὶ τεμνόμενος λυποῖτο. ἡ δόξα δ' αὕτη

Aristotle's real objection to the term *κίνησιν* lies deeper than these mere dialectical skirmishings, and has been explained, Vol. I. Essay IV. pp. 246—9.

5 *γένεσίς τε—φθορά*] 'And how can it be a creation? For it does not seem to be the case that *anything* can be created out of *anything*; a thing is resolved into that out of which it is created. And (as the Platonists say) pain is the destruction of that of which pleasure is the creation.' This elliptical argument seems to require for its conclusion, 'Where then are the elements out of which our perfect nature (*οὐσία*) is created by the process called pleasure, and into which it is resolved by the destructive process called pain?' We find pain called a destruction in the *Philebus*, p. 31 E: *δίψος δ' αὖ φθορὰ καὶ λύπη καὶ λύσις, ἡ δὲ τοῦ ὑγροῦ πάλιν τὸ ξηρανθὲν πληροῦσα δύναμις ἡδονή*. Aristotle, arguing polemically, says, 'Where then are the elements with which the creative and the destructive process must begin and end?' He afterwards reasonably substitutes *ἐνέργεια* for *γένεσις* as a better formula, but the above polemic seems not to have much value.

6 *οὐδ' ἔστιν ἄρα—λυποῖτο*] 'Neither is pleasure therefore a replenishment, though one may feel pleasure while replenishment is taking place, just as one may feel pain while one is being cut.' Pleasure, says Aristotle, may be synchronous with replenishment, but cannot be identical with it, for pleasure is a state of the mind, and not of the body, cf. *Eth.* I. viii. 10: *τὸ μὲν γὰρ ἥδεσθαι τῶν ψυχικῶν*. All that is proved here is that a more subjective formula than *ἀναπλήρωσις* is required to express the nature of pleasure. Plato had used the formula *πλήρωσις*, *Philebus*, p. 31 E, and Speusippus probably repeated it.

τεμνόμενος] The words *τομαὶ καὶ καύσεις* were commonly used by Plato, as instances of bodily pain. Cf. *Timaeus*, p. 65 B: *ταῦτα δ' αὖ περὶ τὰς καύσεις καὶ τομὰς τοῦ σώματος γιγνόμενά ἐστι κατάδηλα*.

δοκεῖ γεγενῆσθαι ἐκ τῶν περὶ τὴν τροφὴν λυπῶν καὶ
ἡδονῶν· ἐνδεεῖς γὰρ γινομένους καὶ προλυπηθέντας ἥδεσθαι
7 τῇ ἀναπληρώσει. τοῦτο δ' οὐ περὶ πάσας συμβαίνει τὰς
ἡδονάς· ἄλυποι γάρ εἰσιν αἵ τε μαθηματικαὶ καὶ τῶν
κατὰ τὰς αἰσθήσεις αἱ διὰ τῆς ὀσφρήσεως, καὶ ἀκροάματα δὲ καὶ ὁράματα πολλὰ καὶ μνῆμαι καὶ ἐλπίδες.
τίνος οὖν αὗται γενέσεις ἔσονται; οὐδενὸς γὰρ ἔνδεια
8 γεγένηται, οὗ γένοιτ' ἂν ἀναπλήρωσις. πρὸς δὲ τοὺς
προφέροντας τὰς ἐπονειδίστους τῶν ἡδονῶν λέγοι τις ἂν
ὅτι οὐκ ἔστι ταῦθ' ἡδέα· οὐ γὰρ εἰ τοῖς κακῶς διακειμένοις ἡδέα ἐστίν, οἰητέον αὐτὰ καὶ ἡδέα εἶναι πλὴν
τούτοις, καθάπερ οὐδὲ τὰ τοῖς κάμνουσιν ὑγιεινὰ ἢ
γλυκέα ἢ πικρά, οὐδ' αὖ λευκὰ τὰ φαινόμενα τοῖς
9 ὀφθαλμιῶσιν. ἢ οὕτω λέγοιτ' ἄν, ὅτι αἱ μὲν ἡδοναὶ
αἱρεταί εἰσιν, οὐ μὴν ἀπό γε τούτων, ὥσπερ καὶ τὸ
πλουτεῖν, προδόντι δ' οὔ, καὶ τὸ ὑγιαίνειν, οὐ μὴν ὁτιοῦν
10 φαγόντι. ἢ τῷ εἴδει διαφέρουσιν αἱ ἡδοναί· ἕτεραι γὰρ
αἱ ἀπὸ τῶν καλῶν τῶν ἀπὸ τῶν αἰσχρῶν, καὶ οὐκ ἔστιν
ἡσθῆναι τὴν τοῦ δικαίου μὴ ὄντα δίκαιον οὐδὲ τὴν τοῦ
μουσικοῦ μὴ ὄντα μουσικόν, ὁμοίως δὲ καὶ ἐπὶ τῶν ἄλλων.
11 ἐμφανίζειν δὲ δοκεῖ καὶ ὁ φίλος, ἕτερος ὢν τοῦ κόλακος,
οὐκ οὖσαν ἀγαθὸν τὴν ἡδονὴν ἢ διαφόρους εἴδει· ὁ μὲν γὰρ
πρὸς τἀγαθὸν ὁμιλεῖν δοκεῖ, ὁ δὲ πρὸς ἡδονήν, καὶ τῷ μὲν

---

7 *ἄλυποι γάρ εἰσιν αἵ τε μαθηματικαὶ κ.τ.λ.*] This is all admitted in so many words by Plato, *Phileb.* p. 52 A: *ἔτι δὴ τοίνυν ταύταις* (i.e. to the pleasures of smell, sight and hearing) *προσθῶμεν τὰς περὶ τὰ μαθήματα ἡδονάς, εἰ ἄρα δοκοῦσιν ἡμῖν αὗται πείνας μὲν μὴ ἔχειν τοῦ μανθάνειν μηδὲ διὰ μαθημάτων πείνης ἀλγηδόνας ἐξ ἀρχῆς γενομένας.*

8 *πρὸς δὲ τοὺς προφέροντας κ.τ.λ.*] This argument of the Platonists is quoted *Eth.* vii. xi. 5.

10 *τὴν τοῦ μουσικοῦ*] Cf. *Eth.* ix. ix. 6; x. iv. 10. The arguments here given to prove that pleasures differ in kind are (*a*) that some men are incapable of feeling certain pleasures; (*b*) that the flatterer is different from the friend; (*c*) that the pleasures of childhood differ from those of maturity. The whole reasoning is repeated in better form in chap. V.

11 *ἐμφανίζειν δὲ δοκεῖ καὶ ὁ φίλος*] The term 'friend' is used here in a distinctive sense to denote 'the true friend,' just as it is in *Eth.* viii. xiii. 9: *ἄκοντα γὰρ φίλον οὐ ποιητέον.* Common language, which contrasts the flatterer, who ministers pleasure, from the friend, who ministers good, testifies to the non identity of pleasure (in all forms) with good.

ὀνειδίζεται, τὸν δ' ἐπαινοῦσιν ὡς πρὸς ἕτερα ὁμιλοῦντα.
οὐδείς τ' ἂν ἕλοιτο ζῆν παιδίου διάνοιαν ἔχων διὰ βίου, 12
ἡδόμενος ἐφ' οἷς τὰ παιδία ὡς οἷόν τε μάλιστα, οὐδὲ
χαίρειν ποιῶν τι τῶν αἰσχίστων, μηδέποτε μέλλων
λυπηθῆναι. περὶ πολλά τε σπουδὴν ποιησαίμεθ' ἂν καὶ
εἰ μηδεμίαν ἐπιφέροι ἡδονήν, οἷον ὁρᾶν, μνημονεύειν, εἰδέναι,
τὰς ἀρετὰς ἔχειν. εἰ δ' ἐξ ἀνάγκης ἕπονται τούτοις
ἡδοναί, οὐδὲν διαφέρει· ἑλοίμεθα γὰρ ἂν ταῦτα καὶ εἰ μὴ
γίνοιτ' ἀπ' αὐτῶν ἡδονή. ὅτι μὲν οὖν οὔτε τἀγαθὸν ἡ 13
ἡδονὴ οὔτε πᾶσα αἱρετή, δῆλον ἔοικεν εἶναι, καὶ ὅτι εἰσί
τινες αἱρεταὶ καθ' αὑτὰς διαφέρουσαι τῷ εἴδει ἢ ἀφ' ὧν.
τὰ μὲν οὖν λεγόμενα περὶ τῆς ἡδονῆς καὶ λύπης ἱκανῶς
εἰρήσθω.

Τί δ' ἐστὶν ἢ ποῖόν τι, καταφανέστερον γένοιτ' ἂν ἀπ' 4
ἀρχῆς ἀναλαβοῦσιν. δοκεῖ γὰρ ἡ μὲν ὅρασις καθ' ὁντι-

---

12 περὶ πολλά τε] If pleasure, according to Eudoxus, were the chief good, all pursuits would be prized in proportion to their affording pleasure, but this Aristotle shows not to be the case.

IV. Having finished his critical remarks on existing theories (τὰ λεγόμενα) about pleasure, Aristotle proceeds synthetically to state his own views, as follows: (1) Pleasure is, like sight, something whole and entire, not gradually arrived at, but a moment of consciousness, at once perfect, independent of the conditions of time, §§ 1—4. (2) It arises from any faculty obtaining its proper object, but is better in proportion to the excellence of the faculty exercised, §§ 5-7. (3) It is thus the perfection of our functions, but is distinct from the functions themselves, § 8. (4) It cannot be continuously maintained, owing to the weakness of our powers, our functions being soon blunted by fatigue, § 9. (5) Pleasure, in short, results from the sense of life, and is inseparably connected with the idea of life, §§ 10—11.

1 τί δ' ἐστὶν ἢ ποῖόν τι] Cf. *Eth.* II. v. 1: *μετὰ δὲ ταῦτα τί ἐστιν ἡ ἀρετὴ σκεπτέον. Ib.* vi. 1: *δεῖ δὲ μὴ μόνον οὕτως εἰπεῖν, ὅτι ἕξις, ἀλλὰ καὶ ποία τις.* The genus (τί ἐστι) of pleasure here given is that it is ὅλον τι, one of those moments of consciousness which are complete in themselves; the differentia (ποῖόν τι) is that it results from the exercise of any faculty upon its proper object. It may be said that this definition would leave pleasure undefined; but in fact it is a simple sensation, not admitting of entire explication.

ἡ μὲν ὅρασις] Modern researches in optics would tend to modify this view of the entirely *simple* nature of an act of sight. But it may be conceded that any 'process' which takes place in sight is too swift to be noticed by the mind. Cf. Locke, *Essay on the Human Understanding*, book II. c. xiv. § 10. 'Such a part of duration as this, wherein we perceive no succession, is that which we may call an instant, and is that which takes up

νοῦν χρόνον τελεία εἶναι· οὐ γάρ ἐστιν ἐνδεὴς οὐδενός, ὃ εἰς ὕστερον γενόμενον τελειώσει αὐτῆς τὸ εἶδος. τοιούτῳ δ' ἔοικε καὶ ἡ ἡδονή· ὅλον γάρ τι ἐστι, καὶ κατ' οὐδένα χρόνον λάβοι τις ἂν ἡδονὴν ἧς ἐπὶ πλείω χρόνον
2 γινομένης τελειωθήσεται τὸ εἶδος. διόπερ οὐδὲ κίνησίς ἐστιν· ἐν χρόνῳ γὰρ πᾶσα κίνησις καὶ τέλους τινός, οἷον ἡ οἰκοδομικὴ τελεία, ὅταν ποιήσῃ οὗ ἐφίεται. ἢ ἐν ἅπαντι δὴ τῷ χρόνῳ †ἢ τούτῳ. ἐν δὲ τοῖς μέρεσι τοῦ χρόνου πᾶσαι ἀτελεῖς, καὶ ἕτεραι τῷ εἴδει τῆς ὅλης καὶ ἀλλήλων· ἡ γὰρ τῶν λίθων σύνθεσις ἑτέρα τῆς τοῦ κίονος ῥαβδώσεως, καὶ αὗται τῆς τοῦ ναοῦ ποιήσεως. καὶ ἡ μὲν τοῦ ναοῦ τελεία· οὐδενὸς γὰρ ἐνδεὴς πρὸς τὸ προκείμενον· ἡ δὲ τῆς κρηπῖδος καὶ τοῦ τριγλύφου ἀτελής· μέρους γὰρ ἑκατέρα. τῷ εἴδει οὖν διαφέρουσι, καὶ οὐκ ἔστιν ἐν ὁτῳοῦν χρόνῳ λαβεῖν κίνησιν τελείαν τῷ εἴδει,
3 ἀλλ' εἴπερ, ἐν τῷ ἅπαντι. ὁμοίως δὲ καὶ ἐπὶ βαδίσεως καὶ τῶν λοιπῶν· εἰ γάρ ἐστιν ἡ φορὰ κίνησις πόθεν ποῖ, καὶ ταύτης διαφοραὶ κατ' εἴδη, πτῆσις βάδισις ἅλσις καὶ

---

the time of only one idea in our minds without the succession of another, wherein therefore we perceive no succession at all.'

2 διόπερ—ἅπαντι] 'Therefore it is not a process; for every process is under conditions of time and aims at some end, as for instance, the (process of) architecture is perfect, when it has effected what it aims at. May we not say (ἢ) then that it is perfect in the particular (τούτῳ) time viewed as a whole? But in the separate parts of the time occupied all processes are imperfect, and are different in species, both from the whole process, and from each other. For the collection of the stones is different from the fluting of the pillars, and both from the making of the temple. And the making the temple is a perfect process, for it wants nothing towards its proposed object; but that of the basement and the triglyph are imperfect, for they are each the making of a part. Therefore they differ in species, and it is not possible to find a process perfect in species in any time whatsoever, unless it be in the time occupied viewed as a whole.' With Michelet, who follows two MSS., ἢ has been omitted above before τούτῳ. The reading ἢ τούτῳ makes no sense, unless one which would be opposed to what is said afterwards (οὐκ ἔστιν ἐν ὁτῳοῦν κ. τ. λ.)

ἢ ἐν ἅπαντι] The form ἢ with a question, used for conveying Aristotle's opinion on any subject, occurs again in § 9 of this chapter, ἢ κάμνει; In the illustration given, two of the processes mentioned are merely preparatory, the collection of the stones for building, and the fluting of the pillars before they are set up; two others are substantive parts of the building, the laying of the foundation (the first act), and the adding the triglyph, which was a

τὰ τοιαῦτα. οὐ μόνον δ' οὕτως, ἀλλὰ καὶ ἐν αὐτῇ τῇ
βαδίσει· τὸ γὰρ πόθεν ποῖ οὐ ταὐτὸν ἐν τῷ σταδίῳ καὶ
ἐν τῷ μέρει, καὶ ἐν ἑτέρῳ μέρει καὶ ἑτέρῳ, οὐδὲ τὸ διεξιέναι
τὴν γραμμὴν τήνδε κἀκείνην· οὐ μόνον γὰρ γραμμὴν διαπορεύεται, ἀλλὰ καὶ ἐν τόπῳ οὖσαν, ἐν ἑτέρῳ δ' αὕτη
ἐκείνης. δι' ἀκριβείας μὲν οὖν περὶ κινήσεως ἐν ἄλλοις
†εἴρηται, ἔοικε δ' οὐκ ἐν ἅπαντι χρόνῳ τελεία εἶναι, ἀλλ' αἱ
πολλαὶ ἀτελεῖς καὶ διαφέρουσαι τῷ εἴδει, εἴπερ τὸ πόθεν
ποῖ εἰδοποιόν. τῆς ἡδονῆς δ' ἐν ὁτῳοῦν χρόνῳ τέλειον τὸ 4
εἶδος. δῆλον οὖν ὡς ἕτεραί τ' ἂν εἶεν ἀλλήλων, καὶ τῶν
ὅλων τι καὶ τελείων ἡ ἡδονή. δόξειε δ' ἂν τοῦτο καὶ ἐκ
τοῦ μὴ ἐνδέχεσθαι κινεῖσθαι μὴ ἐν χρόνῳ, ἥδεσθαι δέ· τὸ
γὰρ ἐν τῷ νῦν ὅλον τι. ἐκ τούτων δὲ δῆλον καὶ ὅτι οὐ
καλῶς λέγουσι κίνησιν ἢ γένεσιν εἶναι τὴν ἡδονήν. οὐ
γὰρ πάντων ταῦτα λέγεται, ἀλλὰ τῶν μεριστῶν καὶ μὴ

---

fluted tablet added as an ornament to the frieze (perhaps the last act in the creation of the temple). The creation of the temple as a whole, regarded in the whole time which it occupies, is alone to be regarded as a perfect process.

3—4 ὁμοίως δὲ—εἴδει] 'So too in the case of walking, and all other processes. For if passage be a process from place to place, even of this there are different species, flying, walking, jumping, and the like. And not only this, but even in walking itself (there are different species), for the whence and the whither are not the same in the whole course and in the part of the course, and in one part and the other part; nor is it the same thing to cross this line and that. For a person not only passes a line, but a line in space, and this line is in different space from that line. We shall treat exactly of process elsewhere, but it seems not to be perfect in every time, but the majority of processes seem imperfect and differing in species, if the whence and the whither constitute a differentia. But pleasure seems perfect in kind in any time (of its existence) whatsoever.' Every process is under conditions of time, and its parts being under a law of succession are essentially different from each other: the θάτερον from the πρότερον, the beginning, middle, and end, from one another. In pleasure nothing of the kind is to be found. One moment of pleasure does not lead up, as a preparative, to another more advanced moment. Pleasure, when felt, is, *ipso facto*, complete.

ἐν ἄλλοις † εἴρηται] Cf. *Physics*, IV. and V. But as the *Physics* were probably a later work, εἴρηται may be here a mis-reading for εἰρήσεται, as in the instance given, Vol. I. Essay I. page 68, note.

οὐκ ἐν ἅπαντι] 'Non in quolibet tempore:' this is of course different from ἐν ἅπαντι τῷ χρόνῳ τούτῳ, and ἐν τῷ ἅπαντι, in the preceding section.

ἐν ὁτῳοῦν] 'In quolibet,' but above, οὐκ ἔστιν ἐν ὁτῳοῦν means 'in nullo potest.'

4 δῆλον οὖν—ἡδονή] 'It is clear

ὅλων· οὐδὲ γὰρ ὁράσεώς ἐστι γένεσις οὐδὲ στιγμῆς οὐδὲ
μονάδος, οὐδὲ τούτων οὐθὲν κίνησις οὐδὲ γένεσις· οὐδὲ δὴ
5 ἡδονῆς· ὅλον γάρ τι. αἰσθήσεως δὲ πάσης πρὸς τὸ αἰσθητὸν ἐνεργούσης, τελείως δὲ τῆς εὖ διακειμένης πρὸς τὸ κάλλιστον τῶν ὑπὸ τὴν αἴσθησιν· τοιοῦτον γὰρ μάλιστ'
εἶναι δοκεῖ ἡ τελεία ἐνέργεια· αὐτὴν δὲ λέγειν ἐνεργεῖν, ἢ
ἐν ᾧ ἐστί, μηθὲν διαφερέτω· καθ' ἕκαστον δὲ βελτίστη
ἐστὶν ἡ ἐνέργεια τοῦ ἄριστα διακειμένου πρὸς τὸ κράτιστον τῶν ὑφ' αὐτήν. αὕτη δ' ἂν τελειοτάτη εἴη καὶ
ἡδίστη· κατὰ πᾶσαν γὰρ αἴσθησίν ἐστιν ἡδονή, ὁμοίως δὲ
καὶ διάνοιαν καὶ θεωρίαν, ἡδίστη δ' ἡ τελειοτάτη, τελειοτάτη δ' ἡ τοῦ εὖ ἔχοντος πρὸς τὸ σπουδαιότατον τῶν
6 ὑφ' αὐτήν. τελειοῖ δὲ τὴν ἐνέργειαν ἡ ἡδονή. οὐ τὸν
αὐτὸν δὲ τρόπον ἥ τε ἡδονὴ τελειοῖ καὶ τὸ αἰσθητόν τε
καὶ ἡ αἴσθησις, σπουδαῖα ὄντα, ὥσπερ οὐδ' ἡ ὑγίεια καὶ
7 ὁ ἰατρὸς ὁμοίως αἰτιά ἐστι τοῦ ὑγιαίνειν. καθ' ἑκάστην
δ' αἴσθησιν ὅτι γίνεται ἡδονή, δῆλον· φαμὲν γὰρ ὁράματα καὶ ἀκούσματα εἶναι ἡδέα. δῆλον δὲ καὶ ὅτι
μάλιστα, ἐπειδὰν ἥ τε αἴσθησις ᾖ κρατίστη καὶ πρὸς
τοιοῦτον ἐνεργῇ· τοιούτων δ' ὄντων τοῦ τε αἰσθητοῦ καὶ
τοῦ αἰσθανομένου, ἀεὶ ἔσται ἡδονὴ ὑπάρχοντός γε τοῦ
8 ποιήσοντος καὶ τοῦ πεισομένου. τελειοῖ δὲ τὴν ἐνέργειαν ἡ ἡδονὴ οὐχ ὡς ἡ ἕξις ἐνυπάρχουσα, ἀλλ' ὡς ἐπιγιγνόμενόν τι τέλος, οἷον τοῖς ἀκμαίοις ἡ ὥρα· ἕως ἂν
οὖν τό τε νοητὸν ἢ αἰσθητὸν ᾖ οἷον δεῖ καὶ τὸ κρῖνον

then that (process and pleasure) must be different from one another, and that pleasure belongs to the class of things whole and perfect.'

6 τελειοῖ δὲ—ὑγιαίνειν] 'Pleasure renders the exercise of a faculty perfect, but not in the same way in which the goodness of the faculty itself and of its object does so, just as health and the physician are in different ways the cause of one's being well;' *i.e.* pleasure is the formal, and not the efficient, cause of a perfect function. 'Cause' in this Aristotelian usage becomes equivalent to 'result.' The illustration used here is given also, with a slight confusion of terms, in the Eudemian book, *Eth.* vi. xii. 5, Ἔπειτα καὶ ποιοῦσι μέν, οὐχ ὡς ἰατρικὴ δὲ ὑγίειαν, ἀλλ' ὡς ἡ ὑγίεια.

7 τοιούτων δ' ὄντων—πεισομένου] 'But if the object and the percipient be in this (highest) condition, there always will be pleasure, as long as subject and object remain.' The relative terms τὸ ποιοῦν and τὸ πάσχον take their meaning from the way in which they are applied. Thus, *Eth.* v. v. 9, they are used for 'producer and consumer.' Here τὸ ποιοῦν is used

ἢ θεωροῦν, ἔσται ἐν τῇ ἐνεργείᾳ ἡ ἡδονή· ὁμοίων γὰρ
ὄντων καὶ πρὸς ἄλληλα τὸν αὐτὸν τρόπον ἐχόντων τοῦ τε
παθητικοῦ καὶ τοῦ ποιητικοῦ ταὐτὸ πέφυκε γίνεσθαι.
πῶς οὖν οὐδεὶς συνεχῶς ἥδεται; ἢ κάμνει; πάντα γὰρ 9
τὰ ἀνθρώπεια ἀδυνατεῖ συνεχῶς ἐνεργεῖν. οὐ γίνεται
οὖν οὐδ' ἡδονή· ἕπεται γὰρ τῇ ἐνεργείᾳ. ἔνια δὲ τέρπει
καινὰ ὄντα, ὕστερον δὲ οὐχ ὁμοίως διὰ ταὐτό· τὸ μὲν
γὰρ πρῶτον παρακέκληται ἡ διάνοια καὶ διατεταμένως
περὶ αὐτὰ ἐνεργεῖ, ὥσπερ κατὰ τὴν ὄψιν οἱ ἐμβλέποντες,
μετέπειτα δ' οὐ τοιαύτη ἡ ἐνέργεια ἀλλὰ παρημελημένη·
διὸ καὶ ἡ ἡδονὴ ἀμαυροῦται. ὀρέγεσθαι δὲ τῆς ἡδονῆς 10
οἰηθείη τις ἂν ἅπαντας, ὅτι καὶ τοῦ ζῆν ἅπαντες ἐφίενται·
ἡ δὲ ζωὴ ἐνέργειά τίς ἐστι, καὶ ἕκαστος περὶ ταῦτα καὶ
τούτοις ἐνεργεῖ ἃ καὶ μάλιστ' ἀγαπᾷ, οἷον ὁ μὲν μουσικὸς
τῇ ἀκοῇ περὶ τὰ μέλη, ὁ δὲ φιλομαθὴς τῇ διανοίᾳ περὶ
τὰ θεωρήματα, οὕτω δὲ καὶ τῶν λοιπῶν ἕκαστος. ἡ δ'
ἡδονὴ τελειοῖ τὰς ἐνεργείας, καὶ τὸ ζῆν δέ, οὗ ὀρέγονται.
εὐλόγως οὖν καὶ τῆς ἡδονῆς ἐφίενται· τελειοῖ γὰρ ἑκάστῳ
τὸ ζῆν, αἱρετὸν ὄν. πότερον δὲ διὰ τὴν ἡδονὴν τὸ ζῆν 11
αἱρούμεθα ἢ διὰ τὸ ζῆν τὴν ἡδονήν, ἀφείσθω ἐν τῷ

---

for the percipient, τὸ πάσχον for the object perceived.

8 ὁμοίων γὰρ ὄντων—γίνεσθαι] 'For from similar pairs of relatives, bearing the same relation to one another, *i.e.* the active and passive, the same result is naturally produced.' This appears to be an abstract and *à priori* way of stating the universality of pleasure attendant on the harmony between a faculty and its proper object.

9 πῶς οὖν—ἀμαυροῦται] 'How is it then that no one is continuously in a state of pleasure? The reason must be that one grows weary. For all human things are incapable of continuous activity. Pleasure therefore ceases to be produced, for it depends on the activity of the faculties. It is on this same account that some things please us while they are new, but afterwards not in the same way. For at first the intellect is excited and acts strenuously on the objects in question (as in the case of sight, when one first fixes one's glance) but afterwards the action is not equally vivid, but relaxed, and so one's pleasure also fades.' On this doctrine, cf. Vol. I. Essay IV. and Ar. *Metaph.* VIII. viii. 18, there quoted, p. 250.

10 It is natural to say that all desire pleasure, from its inseparable connection with the sense of life, and with each of the vital functions. Thus far Eudoxus was right, but he was wrong in not recognising a difference in kind between different pleasures, and this point is demonstrated in the ensuing chapter.

παρόντι. συνεζεῦχθαι μὲν γὰρ ταῦτα φαίνεται καὶ χωρισμὸν οὐ δέχεσθαι· ἄνευ τε γὰρ ἐνεργείας οὐ γίνεται ἡδονή, πᾶσάν τε ἐνέργειαν τελειοῖ ἡ ἡδονή.

5 Ὅθεν δοκοῦσι καὶ τῷ εἴδει διαφέρειν· τὰ γὰρ ἕτερα τῷ εἴδει ὑφ' ἑτέρων οἰόμεθα τελειοῦσθαι. οὕτω γὰρ φαίνεται καὶ τὰ φυσικὰ καὶ τὰ ὑπὸ τέχνης, οἷον ζῷα καὶ δένδρα καὶ γραφὴ καὶ ἀγάλματα καὶ οἰκία καὶ σκεῦος. ὁμοίως δὲ καὶ τὰς ἐνεργείας τὰς διαφερούσας τῷ εἴδει ὑπὸ
2 διαφερόντων εἴδει τελειοῦσθαι. διαφέρουσι δ' αἱ τῆς διανοίας τῶν κατὰ τὰς αἰσθήσεις καὶ αὗται ἀλλήλων κατ' εἶδος· καὶ αἱ τελειοῦσαι δὴ ἡδοναί. φανείη δ' ἂν τοῦτο καὶ ἐκ τοῦ συνῳκειῶσθαι τῶν ἡδονῶν ἑκάστην τῇ ἐνεργείᾳ ἣν τελειοῖ. συναύξει γὰρ τὴν ἐνέργειαν ἡ οἰκεία ἡδονή·

V. Pleasures may be thought to differ in kind, (1) because our several functions (mental and others) differ from each other in kind, and things different in kind are perfected by things different in kind, §§ 1—2. (2) Because while its *own* pleasure promotes any particular exercise of the faculties, an *alien* pleasure impedes it, §§ 2—5. (3) Because the human functions differ from each other in a moral point of view, and the pleasures therefore which are so closely connected with them as almost to be identical must differ in the same way from each other, §§ 6—7. (4) Creatures different in kind must have, and by common consent do have, different pleasures, § 8. (5) The pleasures of man when in a morbid state must differ from the pleasures of man when in a healthy state. As a corollary to the last argument it may be added, that reasonings against pleasure from a reference to the morbid pleasures have no weight. The answer to them would be, that such are not pleasures at all.

1 *καὶ τὰ φυσικὰ καὶ τὰ ὑπὸ τέχνης*] The *ἐνέργειαι* mentioned in this section must be those of the rational faculty. Thus we have the classification of things capable of being made perfect, into nature, art, and the moral and intellectual life of man. Cf. *Eth.* III. iii. 7: *αἴτια γὰρ δοκοῦσιν εἶναι φύσις καὶ ἀνάγκη καὶ τύχη, ἔτι δὲ νοῦς καὶ πᾶν τὸ δι' ἀνθρώπου.*

2 *φανείη δ'—τελειοῖ*] 'This would also seem to be shown by the intimate connection existing between each pleasure and the function which it perfects.' Cf. *Eth.* X. i. 1: *μάλιστα γὰρ δοκεῖ συνῳκειῶσθαι τῷ γένει ἡμῶν.* Pleasure, generally speaking, is proper to the human race; from another point of view, each function has its own proper pleasure, and the pleasure 'proper' to one function is 'alien' to other functions. This distinction of *οἰκεία* and *ἀλλοτρία ἡδονή* was perhaps suggested by a passage in the *Republic* of Plato, IX 587 A, where these terms are used, though not with quite the same application. It is there said that in the philosopher each part of his soul does its proper work and attains its proper pleasure; but when some lower passion has the predominance, that passion, causing

μᾶλλον γὰρ ἕκαστα κρίνουσι καὶ ἐξακριβοῦσιν οἱ μεθ' ἡδονῆς ἐνεργοῦντες, οἷον γεωμετρικοὶ γίνονται οἱ χαίροντες τῷ γεωμετρεῖν, καὶ κατανοοῦσιν ἕκαστα μᾶλλον, ὁμοίως δὲ καὶ οἱ φιλόμουσοι καὶ φιλοικοδόμοι καὶ τῶν ἄλλων ἕκαστοι ἐπιδιδόασιν εἰς τὸ οἰκεῖον ἔργον χαίροντες αὐτῷ. συναύξουσι δὲ αἱ ἡδοναί, τὰ δὲ συναύξοντα οἰκεῖα. τοῖς ἑτέροις δὲ τῷ εἴδει καὶ τὰ οἰκεῖα ἕτερα τῷ εἴδει. ἔτι δὲ 3
μᾶλλον τοῦτ' ἂν φανείη ἐκ τοῦ τὰς ἀφ' ἑτέρων ἡδονὰς ἐμποδίους ταῖς ἐνεργείαις εἶναι· οἱ γὰρ φίλαυλοι ἀδυνατοῦσι τοῖς λόγοις προσέχειν, ἐὰν κατακούσωσιν αὐλοῦντος, μᾶλλον χαίροντες αὐλητικῇ τῆς παρούσης ἐνεργείας· ἡ κατὰ τὴν αὐλητικὴν οὖν ἡδονὴ τὴν περὶ τὸν λόγον ἐνέργειαν φθείρει. ὁμοίως δὲ τοῦτο καὶ ἐπὶ τῶν ἄλλων 4
συμβαίνει, ὅταν ἅμα περὶ δύο ἐνεργῇ· ἡ γὰρ ἡδίων τὴν ἑτέραν ἐκκρούει, κἂν πολὺ διαφέρῃ κατὰ τὴν ἡδονήν, μᾶλλον, ὥστε μηδ' ἐνεργεῖν κατὰ τὴν ἑτέραν. διὸ χαίροντες ὁτῳοῦν σφόδρα οὐ πάνυ δρῶμεν ἕτερον, καὶ ἄλλα ποιοῦμεν ἄλλοις ἠρέμα ἀρεσκόμενοι, καὶ ἐν τοῖς θεάτροις οἱ τραγηματίζοντες, ὅταν φαῦλοι οἱ ἀγωνιζόμενοι ὦσι, τότε μάλιστ' αὐτὸ δρῶσιν. ἐπεὶ δ' ἡ μὲν οἰκεία 5
ἡδονὴ ἐξακριβοῖ τὰς ἐνεργείας καὶ χρονιωτέρας καὶ βελτίους ποιεῖ, αἱ δ' ἀλλότριαι λυμαίνονται, δῆλον ὡς πολὺ διεστᾶσιν· σχεδὸν γὰρ αἱ ἀλλότριαι ἡδοναὶ ποιοῦσιν ὅπερ αἱ οἰκεῖαι λῦπαι· φθείρουσι γὰρ τὰς ἐνεργείας αἱ οἰκεῖαι λῦπαι, οἷον εἴ τῳ τὸ γράφειν ἀηδὲς καὶ ἐπίλυπον ἢ τὸ λογίζεσθαι· ὁ μὲν γὰρ οὐ γράφει, ὁ δ' οὐ λογίζεται, λυπηρᾶς οὔσης τῆς ἐνεργείας. συμβαίνει δὴ περὶ τὰς

---

disturbance, does not itself attain its own pleasure, and compels the other faculties to pursue a pleasure which is alien to them: ὅταν δὲ ἅμα τῶν ἑτέρων τι κρατήσῃ, ὑπάρχει αὐτῷ μήτε τὴν ἑαυτοῦ ἡδονὴν ἐξακριβοῦν τά τε ἄλλα ἀναγκάζειν ἀλλοτρίαν καὶ μὴ ἀληθῆ ἡδονὴν διώκειν.

ἐξακριβοῦσιν] 'They work out.' Cf. note on *Eth.* I. vii. 18. The word ἐξακριβοῦν is used transitively *Eth.* I. xiii. 7, and below, X. v. 5, where from the analogy of the arts it means to 'give the last finish to.' It is used intransitively *Eth.* I. vi. 13: ἐξακριβοῦν ὑπὲρ τούτων, 'to refine.'

4 καὶ ἐν τοῖς θεάτροις — δρῶσιν] 'And those who munch sweetmeats in the theatres do so especially when the actors are bad.' This is one of those illustrations from common life, which are richly strewed about the writings of Aristotle.

ἐνεργείας τοὐναντίον ἀπὸ τῶν οἰκείων ἡδονῶν τε καὶ λυπῶν· οἰκεῖαι δ' εἰσὶν αἱ ἐπὶ τῇ ἐνεργείᾳ καθ' αὑτὴν γινόμεναι. αἱ δ' ἀλλότριαι ἡδοναὶ εἴρηται ὅτι παραπλήσιόν τι τῇ λύπῃ ποιοῦσιν· φθείρουσι γάρ, πλὴν οὐχ ὁμοίως.
6 διαφερουσῶν δὲ τῶν ἐνεργειῶν ἐπιεικείᾳ καὶ φαυλότητι, καὶ τῶν μὲν αἱρετῶν οὐσῶν τῶν δὲ φευκτῶν τῶν δ' οὐδετέρων, ὁμοίως ἔχουσι καὶ αἱ ἡδοναί· καθ' ἑκάστην γὰρ ἐνέργειαν οἰκεία ἡδονή ἐστιν. ἡ μὲν οὖν τῇ σπουδαίᾳ οἰκεία ἐπιεικής, ἡ δὲ τῇ φαύλῃ μοχθηρά· καὶ γὰρ αἱ ἐπιθυμίαι τῶν μὲν καλῶν ἐπαινεταί, τῶν δ' αἰσχρῶν ψεκταί. οἰκειότεραι δὲ ταῖς ἐνεργείαις αἱ ἐν αὐταῖς ἡδοναὶ τῶν ὀρέξεων· αἱ μὲν γὰρ διωρισμέναι εἰσὶ καὶ τοῖς χρόνοις καὶ τῇ φύσει, αἱ δὲ σύνεγγυς ταῖς ἐνεργείαις, καὶ ἀδιόριστοι οὕτως ὥστ' ἔχειν
7 ἀμφισβήτησιν εἰ ταὐτόν ἐστιν ἡ ἐνέργεια τῇ ἡδονῇ. οὐ μὴν ἔοικέ γε ἡ ἡδονὴ διάνοια εἶναι οὐδ' αἴσθησις· ἄτοπον γάρ· ἀλλὰ διὰ τὸ μὴ χωρίζεσθαι φαίνεταί τισι ταὐτόν. ὥσπερ οὖν αἱ ἐνέργειαι ἕτεραι, καὶ αἱ ἡδοναί. διαφέρει δὲ ἡ ὄψις ἁφῆς καθαριότητι, καὶ ἀκοὴ καὶ ὄσφρησις γεύσεως· ὁμοίως δὴ διαφέρουσι καὶ αἱ ἡδοναί, καὶ τούτων αἱ περὶ
8 τὴν διάνοιαν, καὶ ἑκάτεραι ἀλλήλων. δοκεῖ δ' εἶναι ἑκάστῳ ζῴῳ καὶ ἡδονὴ οἰκεία, ὥσπερ καὶ ἔργον· ἡ γὰρ κατὰ τὴν ἐνέργειαν. καὶ ἐφ' ἑκάστῳ δὲ θεωροῦντι τοῦτ' ἂν φανείη· ἑτέρα γὰρ ἵππου ἡδονὴ καὶ κυνὸς καὶ ἀνθρώπου, καθάπερ Ἡράκλειτός φησιν ὄνον σύρματ' ἂν ἑλέσθαι μᾶλλον ἢ χρυσόν· ἥδιον γὰρ χρυσοῦ τροφὴ ὄνοις. αἱ μὲν

6—7 καὶ ἀδιόριστοι—ταὐτόν] 'And they are so indivisible as to raise a doubt whether the function is not identical with the pleasure attached to it. And yet pleasure can hardly be thought or perception, this would be absurd; but through their not being separated, some persons fancy them to be identical.' To 'divide' and to 'distinguish' are, as Coleridge tells us, two different things. Pleasure, though not divided, should be distinguished from the vital functions. The author of the Eudemian books, however, *Eth.* VII. xii. 3. identified them, and we might well ask Aristotle why happiness, any more than pleasure, should be identified with ἐνέργεια.

7 καθαριότητι] On the superior purity of sight, hearing, and smell over taste, cf. Plato, *Philebus*, p. 51. and *Eth.* III. x. 3—11.

8 ὥσπερ καὶ ἔργον] Cf. Plato, *Republic*, p. 352 E: Ἆρ' οὖν τοῦτο ἂν θείης καὶ ἵππου καὶ ἄλλου ὁτουοῦν ἔργον, ὃ ἂν ἢ μόνῳ ἐκείνῳ ποιῇ τις ἢ ἄριστα;

καθάπερ Ἡράκλειτος—χρυσόν] 'As

οὖν τῶν ἑτέρων τῷ εἴδει διαφέρουσιν εἴδει, τὰς δὲ τῶν αὐτῶν ἀδιαφόρους εὔλογον εἶναι. διαλλάττουσι δ' οὐ 9
μικρὸν ἐπί γε τῶν ἀνθρώπων· τὰ γὰρ αὐτὰ τοὺς μὲν τέρπει τοὺς δὲ λυπεῖ, καὶ τοῖς μὲν λυπηρὰ καὶ μισητά ἐστι τοῖς δὲ ἡδέα καὶ φιλητά. καὶ ἐπὶ γλυκέων δὲ τοῦτο συμβαίνει· οὐ γὰρ τὰ αὐτὰ δοκεῖ τῷ πυρέττοντι καὶ τῷ ὑγιαίνοντι, οὐδὲ θερμὸν εἶναι τῷ ἀσθενεῖ καὶ τῷ εὐεκτικῷ. ὁμοίως δὲ τοῦτο καὶ ἐφ' ἑτέρων συμβαίνει. δοκεῖ δ' ἐν 10
ἅπασι τοῖς τοιούτοις εἶναι τὸ φαινόμενον τῷ σπουδαίῳ. εἰ δὲ τοῦτο καλῶς λέγεται, καθάπερ δοκεῖ, καὶ ἔστιν ἑκάστου μέτρον ἡ ἀρετὴ καὶ ὁ ἀγαθός, ᾗ τοιοῦτος, καὶ ἡδοναὶ εἶεν ἂν αἱ τούτῳ φαινόμεναι καὶ ἡδέα οἷς οὗτος χαίρει. τὰ δὲ τούτῳ δυσχερῆ εἴ τῳ φαίνεται ἡδέα, οὐδὲν θαυμαστόν· πολλαὶ γὰρ φθοραὶ καὶ λῦμαι ἀνθρώπων γίνονται· ἡδέα δ' οὐκ ἔστιν, ἀλλὰ τούτοις καὶ οὕτω διακειμένοις. τὰς μὲν οὖν ὁμολογουμένως αἰσχρὰς δῆλον ὡς οὐ 11
φατέον ἡδονὰς εἶναι, πλὴν τοῖς διεφθαρμένοις· τῶν δ' ἐπιεικῶν εἶναι δοκουσῶν ποίαν ἢ τίνα φατέον τοῦ ἀνθρώπου εἶναι; ἢ ἐκ τῶν ἐνεργειῶν δῆλον; ταύταις γὰρ ἕπονται αἱ ἡδοναί. εἴτ' οὖν μία ἐστὶν εἴτε πλείους αἱ τοῦ τελείου καὶ μακαρίου ἀνδρός, αἱ ταύτας τελειοῦσαι ἡδοναὶ κυρίως

Heraclitus says that "an ass would prefer hay to gold,"—the reason being that he is an *ass*. This saying of Heraclitus, which reminds us of the Æsopic fable of the Cock and the Jewel, was probably meant to satirise the low desires of the human race. It forms the *pendant* to that other saying, 'Zeus looks on the wisest man as we look on an ape.'

10 *ἔστιν ἑκάστου μέτρον ἡ ἀρετὴ καὶ ὁ ἀγαθός*] That there is a definite standard of pleasure and of taste, as of other apparently variable things, is most clearly laid down in Aristotle's discussion upon the saying of Protagoras, that 'man is the measure of all things.' Cf. *Metaphysics*, x. vi. 6: *φανερὸν δὲ ταῦτ' ἐκ τῶν γιγνομένων κατὰ τὴν αἴσθησιν· οὐδέποτε γὰρ τὸ αὐτὸ φαίνεται τοῖς μὲν γλυκύ, τοῖς δὲ τοὐναντίον, μὴ διεφθαρμένων καὶ λελωβημένων τῶν ἑτέρων τὸ αἰσθητήριον καὶ κριτήριον τῶν λεχθέντων χυμῶν. τούτου δ' ὄντος τοιούτου τοὺς ἑτέρους μὲν ὑποληπτέον μέτρον εἶναι, τοὺς δ' ἑτέρους οὐχ ὑποληπτέον. ὁμοίως δὲ τοῦτο λέγω καὶ ἐπὶ ἀγαθοῦ καὶ κακοῦ, καὶ καλοῦ καὶ αἰσχροῦ, καὶ τῶν ἄλλων τῶν τοιούτων.* Those who are vicious and corrupt are to be pronounced not to be right judges of what is good or pleasant. Their pleasures are to be pronounced not pleasures at all. Cf. Plato, *Philebus*, p. 40 c: *ψευδέσιν ἄρα ἡδοναῖς τὰ πολλὰ οἱ πονηροὶ χαίρουσιν, οἱ δ' ἀγαθοὶ τῶν ἀνθρώπων ἀληθέσιν.*

λέγοιντ' ἂν ἀνθρώπου ἡδοναὶ εἶναι, αἱ δὲ λοιπαὶ δευτέρως καὶ πολλοστῶς, ὥσπερ αἱ ἐνέργειαι.

6 Εἰρημένων δὲ τῶν περὶ τὰς ἀρετάς τε καὶ φιλίας καὶ
ἡδονάς, λοιπὸν περὶ εὐδαιμονίας τύπῳ διελθεῖν, ἐπειδὴ
τέλος αὐτὴν τίθεμεν τῶν ἀνθρωπίνων. ἀναλαβοῦσι δὴ τὰ
2 προειρημένα συντομώτερος ἂν εἴη ὁ λόγος. εἴπομεν
δ' ὅτι οὐκ ἔστιν ἕξις· καὶ γὰρ τῷ καθεύδοντι διὰ βίου
ὑπάρχοι ἄν, φυτῶν ζῶντι βίον, καὶ τῷ δυστυχοῦντι
τὰ μέγιστα. εἰ δὴ ταῦτα μὴ ἀρέσκει, ἀλλὰ μᾶλλον
εἰς ἐνέργειάν τινα θετέον, καθάπερ ἐν τοῖς πρότερον εἴρηται, τῶν δ' ἐνεργειῶν αἱ μέν εἰσιν ἀναγκαῖαι καὶ δι' ἕτερα
αἱρεταί, αἱ δὲ καθ' αὑτάς, δῆλον ὅτι τὴν εὐδαιμονίαν τῶν
καθ' αὑτὰς αἱρετῶν τινὰ θετέον καὶ οὐ τῶν δι' ἄλλο· οὐδενὸς
3 γὰρ ἐνδεὴς ἡ εὐδαιμονία ἀλλ' αὐτάρκης. καθ' αὑτὰς δ'
εἰσὶν αἱρεταί, ἀφ' ὧν μηδὲν ἐπιζητεῖται παρὰ τὴν ἐνέργειαν.
τοιαῦται δ' εἶναι δοκοῦσιν αἱ κατ' ἀρετὴν πράξεις· τὰ
γὰρ καλὰ καὶ σπουδαῖα πράττειν τῶν δι' αὑτὰ αἱρετῶν.
καὶ τῶν παιδιῶν δὲ αἱ ἡδεῖαι· οὐ γὰρ δι' ἕτερα αὐτὰς
αἱροῦνται· βλάπτονται γὰρ ἀπ' αὐτῶν μᾶλλον ἢ ὠφελοῦνται, ἀμελοῦντες τῶν σωμάτων καὶ τῆς κτήσεως. καταφεύγουσι δ' ἐπὶ τὰς τοιαύτας διαγωγὰς τῶν εὐδαιμονι-

VI. Aristotle having concluded his treatise upon the nature of pleasure reverts now to the general question of the nature of happiness, or the chief good for man. He takes up from the first book the following fundamental propositions: (1) that happiness must be an action (*ἐνέργεια*) and not a state (*ἕξις*) of the faculties; (2) that it must be final and satisfying; (3) that it must consist in some development of the faculties sought for its own sake. The remainder of the chapter is occupied with excluding games and amusements from the above definition. Though exercises of the faculties sought for their own sake, these are (*a*) patronised by unworthy judges,—tyrants, children, and the like; (*b*) after all, they are rather the means to working, than ends in themselves; (*c*) they do not represent the higher faculties in man.

1 *εἰρημένων δὲ τῶν περὶ τὰς ἀρετάς τε καὶ φιλίας καὶ ἡδονάς*] Cf. *Eth.* x. xiii. 1, where the analysis of ἀρετή, or human excellence (the most important part of the conception of happiness, *Eth.* I. x. 9) is introduced; *Eth.* VIII. i. 1, where the discussion of friendship, partly as connected with virtue and partly as an external blessing, is justified; *Eth.* x. i. 1, where a treatise on pleasure is added on account of the human interest of the topic, and the controversies which have been raised about it.

2 *εἴπομεν δ' ὅτι κ.τ.λ.*] Cf. *Eth.* I. vii. 13; I. v. 6.

3 *τῶν εὐδαιμονιζομένων*] 'Of those

ζομένων οἱ πολλοί, διὸ παρὰ τοῖς τυράννοις εὐδοκιμοῦσιν οἱ ἐν ταῖς τοιαύταις διαγωγαῖς εὐτράπελοι· ὧν γὰρ ἐφίενται, ἐν τούτοις παρέχουσι σφᾶς αὐτοὺς ἡδεῖς· δέονται δὲ τοιούτων. δοκεῖ μὲν οὖν εὐδαιμονικὰ ταῦτα εἶναι διὰ τὸ τοὺς ἐν δυναστείαις ἐν τούτοις ἀποσχολάζειν, οὐδὲν δὲ ἴσως 4
σημεῖον οἱ τοιοῦτοί εἰσιν· οὐ γὰρ ἐν τῷ δυναστεύειν ἡ ἀρετὴ οὐδ' ὁ νοῦς, ἀφ' ὧν αἱ σπουδαῖαι ἐνέργειαι· οὐδ' εἰ ἄγευστοι οὗτοι ὄντες ἡδονῆς εἰλικρινοῦς καὶ ἐλευθερίου ἐπὶ τὰς σωματικὰς καταφεύγουσιν, διὰ τοῦτο ταύτας οἰητέον αἱρετωτέρας εἶναι· καὶ γὰρ οἱ παῖδες τὰ παρ' αὐτοῖς τιμώμενα κράτιστα οἴονται εἶναι. εὔλογον δή, ὥσπερ παισὶ καὶ ἀνδράσιν ἕτερα φαίνεται τίμια, οὕτω καὶ φαύλοις καὶ ἐπιεικέσιν. καθάπερ οὖν πολλάκις εἴρηται, 5
καὶ τίμια καὶ ἡδέα ἐστὶ τὰ τῷ σπουδαίῳ τοιαῦτα ὄντα· ἑκάστῳ δὲ ἡ κατὰ τὴν οἰκείαν ἕξιν αἱρετωτάτη ἐνέργεια, καὶ τῷ σπουδαίῳ δὴ ἡ κατὰ τὴν ἀρετήν. οὐκ ἐν παιδιᾷ 6
ἄρα ἡ εὐδαιμονία· καὶ γὰρ ἄτοπον τὸ τέλος εἶναι παιδιάν, καὶ πραγματεύεσθαι καὶ κακοπαθεῖν τὸν βίον ἅπαντα τοῦ παίζειν χάριν. ἅπαντα γὰρ ὡς εἰπεῖν ἑτέρου ἕνεκα αἱρούμεθα πλὴν τῆς εὐδαιμονίας· τέλος γὰρ αὕτη. σπουδάζειν δὲ καὶ πονεῖν παιδιᾶς χάριν ἠλίθιον φαίνεται καὶ λίαν παιδικόν· παίζειν δ' ὅπως σπουδάζῃ, κατ' Ἀνάχαρσιν, ὀρθῶς ἔχειν δοκεῖ· ἀναπαύσει γὰρ ἔοικεν ἡ παιδιά, ἀδυνατοῦντες δὲ συνεχῶς πονεῖν ἀναπαύσεως δέονται. οὐ

who are called happy,' cf. *Eth.* I. ix. 11: τελευτήσαντα ἀθλίως οὐδεὶς εὐδαιμονίζει.

3—4 δοκεῖ μὲν οὖν — ἐνέργειαι] 'These things are *fancied* to be constitutive of happiness because monarchs spend their leisure in them. But perhaps after all monarchs are no evidence, for neither virtue nor reason, on which the higher functions of man depend, are involved in kingly power.' Cf. *Eth.* I. v. 3, where it is said that brutish pleasures 'obtain consideration' owing to potentates, who have everything at their command, devoting themselves to such.

4 ἄγευστοι] This reminds one of the saying about greedy and corrupt kings, in Hesiod, *Works and Days*, vv. 40, 41:

νήπιοι· οὐδὲ ἴσασιν ὅσῳ πλέον ἥμισυ παντός,
οὐδ' ὅσον ἐν μαλάχῃ τε καὶ ἀσφοδέλῳ μέγ' ὄνειαρ.

6 οὐκ ἐν παιδιᾷ ἄρα ἡ εὐδαιμονία] With the whole of the present chapter we may compare the interesting discussion in Ar. *Politics*, VIII. v. 12—14. On the relation of amusements to happiness, see Vol. I. Essay IV. p. 225.

δὴ τέλος ἡ ἀνάπαυσις· γίνεται γὰρ ἕνεκα τῆς ἐνεργείας. δοκεῖ δ' ὁ εὐδαίμων βίος κατ' ἀρετὴν εἶναι· οὗτος δὲ μετὰ
7 σπουδῆς, ἀλλ' οὐκ ἐν παιδιᾷ. βελτίω τε λέγομεν τὰ σπουδαῖα τῶν γελοίων καὶ τῶν μετὰ παιδιᾶς, καὶ τοῦ βελτίονος ἀεὶ καὶ μορίου καὶ ἀνθρώπου σπουδαιοτέραν τὴν ἐνέργειαν· ἡ δὲ τοῦ βελτίονος κρείττων καὶ εὐδαιμονικω-
8 τέρα ἤδη. ἀπολαύσειέ τ' ἂν τῶν σωματικῶν ἡδονῶν ὁ τυχὼν καὶ ἀνδράποδον οὐχ ἧττον τοῦ ἀρίστου. εὐδαιμονίας δ' οὐδεὶς ἀνδραπόδῳ μεταδίδωσιν, εἰ μὴ καὶ βίου· οὐ γὰρ ἐν ταῖς τοιαύταις διαγωγαῖς ἡ εὐδαιμονία, ἀλλ' ἐν ταῖς κατ' ἀρετὴν ἐνεργείαις, καθάπερ καὶ πρότερον εἴρηται.

7 Εἰ δ' ἐστὶν ἡ εὐδαιμονία κατ' ἀρετὴν ἐνέργεια, εὔλογον κατὰ τὴν κρατίστην· αὕτη δ' ἂν εἴη τοῦ ἀρίστου. εἴτε δὴ νοῦς τοῦτο εἴτε ἄλλο τι ὃ δὴ κατὰ φύσιν δοκεῖ ἄρχειν καὶ ἡγεῖσθαι καὶ ἔννοιαν ἔχειν περὶ καλῶν καὶ θείων, εἴτε θεῖον ὂν καὶ αὐτὸ εἴτε τῶν ἐν ἡμῖν τὸ θειότατον, ἡ τούτου ἐνέργεια κατὰ τὴν οἰκείαν ἀρετὴν εἴη ἂν ἡ τελεία εὐδαι-
2 μονία. ὅτι δ' ἐστὶ θεωρητική, εἴρηται. ὁμολογούμενον δὲ

---

8 *εὐδαιμονίας δ' οὐδεὶς—βίου*] 'For no one allows a slave to share in happiness, any more than in the social life of a citizen.' In *Politics*, I. xiii. 13, it is said that the slave, as distinguished from the artisan, is *κοινωνὸς ζωῆς*, i.e. he 'lives with the family,' but he is not *κοινωνὸς βίου*, he does not share in the career of his master.

VII. Aristotle's argument now culminates in the declaration that happiness, in the highest sense, consists in philosophy; (1) because this is the function of the most excellent part of our nature; (2) because it most admits of continuance; (3) because it affords most pure and solid pleasure; (4) because it has pre-eminently the character of being self-sufficient; (5) because it is above all things an end in itself, and not a means to ulterior results; (6) because it is a sort of repose, and as it were the fruit of our exertions. It is indeed something higher than man regarded as a composite being, and is only attainable by him through virtue of a divine element which is in him. But we must not listen to those who would preach down our divine aspirations. On the contrary we should encourage them, and endeavour to live in harmony with our noblest part, which is in fact our proper self.

1 *εἴτε θεῖον—θειότατον*] 'Whether it be, itself too, absolutely divine, or relatively speaking the divinest thing in our nature.' Philosophy is said in the *Metaphysics*, I. ii. 14, to be most divine in two ways, first, as being kindred to the thought of God; second, as being knowledge of things divine. *τοιαύτη δὲ διχῶς ἂν εἴη μόνον· ἥν τε γὰρ μάλιστ' ἂν ὁ θεὸς ἔχοι, θεία τῶν ἐπιστημῶν ἐστί, κἂν εἴ τις τῶν θείων εἴη.* Cf. the note on *Eth.* I. ii. 8.

τοῦτ' ἂν δόξειεν εἶναι καὶ τοῖς πρότερον καὶ τῷ ἀληθεῖ. κρατίστη τε γὰρ αὕτη ἐστὶν ἡ ἐνέργεια· καὶ γὰρ ὁ νοῦς τῶν ἐν ἡμῖν, καὶ τῶν γνωστῶν, περὶ ἃ ὁ νοῦς. ἔτι δὲ συνεχεστάτη· θεωρεῖν τε γὰρ δυνάμεθα συνεχῶς μᾶλλον
ἢ πράττειν ὁτιοῦν, οἰόμεθά τε δεῖν ἡδονὴν παραμεμῖχθαι 3
τῇ εὐδαιμονίᾳ, ἡδίστη δὲ τῶν κατ' ἀρετὴν ἐνεργειῶν ἡ κατὰ τὴν σοφίαν ὁμολογουμένως ἐστίν· δοκεῖ γοῦν ἡ φιλοσοφία θαυμαστὰς ἡδονὰς ἔχειν καθαριότητι καὶ τῷ βεβαίῳ, εὔλογον δὲ τοῖς εἰδόσι τῶν ζητούντων ἡδίω τὴν
διαγωγὴν εἶναι. ἥ τε λεγομένη αὐτάρκεια περὶ τὴν θεω- 4
ρητικὴν μάλιστ' ἂν εἴη· τῶν μὲν γὰρ πρὸς τὸ ζῆν ἀναγκαίων καὶ σοφὸς καὶ δίκαιος καὶ οἱ λοιποὶ δέονται, τοῖς δὲ τοιούτοις ἱκανῶς κεχορηγημένων ὁ μὲν δίκαιος δεῖται

2 ὅτι δ' ἐστὶ θεωρητική, εἴρηται] It is difficult to point out a precise passage corresponding to this reference (cf. *Eth.* IX. iii. 1, where a similar vague reference occurs). But perhaps it partly is meant to recal *Eth.* I. xiii. 20: διορίζεται δὲ καὶ ἡ ἀρετὴ κατὰ τὴν διαφορὰν ταύτην· λέγομεν γὰρ αὐτῶν τὰς μὲν διανοητικὰς τὰς δὲ ἠθικάς, partly *Eth.* I. v. 7: τρίτος δ' ἐστὶν ὁ θεωρητικός, περὶ οὗ τὴν ἐπίσκεψιν ἐν τοῖς ἑπομένοις ποιησόμεθα. There is nothing in Book VI. which corresponds.

3 εὔλογον δὲ—εἶναι] 'And it is reasonable to suppose that those who *know* pass their time more pleasantly than those who are enquiring.' This is opposed to the often repeated saying that 'the search for truth is more precious than truth itself.' Thus Bishop Butler says, 'Knowledge is not our proper happiness. Whoever will in the least attend to the thing will see, that it is the gaining, not the having of it, which is the entertainment of the mind. Indeed, if the proper happiness of man consisted in knowledge considered as a possession or treasure, men who are possessed of the largest share would have a very ill time of it; as they would be infinitely more sensible than others of their poverty in this respect. Thus *he who increases knowledge* would eminently *increase sorrow*.' (*Sermon* XV.) In one respect these two views are reconcileable; for Aristotle never meant to say that the ἕξις or κτῆσις τῆς σοφίας constitutes happiness, but the ἐνέργεια κατὰ τὴν σοφίαν, 'the play of the mind under the guidance of philosophy.' He contrasts the peace and repose of conviction with the restlessness of doubt. In the same spirit Bacon said (Essay I.), 'Certainly, it is heaven upon earth to have a man's mind move in charity, rest in providence, and turn upon the poles of truth.' But in another respect the views of Aristotle are irreconcileable with those above quoted from Butler. The one over-states, nearly as much as the other understates, the blessings of knowledge. And Aristotle strangely leaves out of account that sense of ignorance which the wisest man will always retain. His statement is chargeable with philosophic pride, from which Socrates and Plato were free. (See Vol. I. Essay III. p. 215.)

πρὸς οὓς δικαιοπραγήσει καὶ μεθ' ὧν, ὁμοίως δὲ καὶ ὁ
σώφρων καὶ ὁ ἀνδρεῖος καὶ τῶν ἄλλων ἕκαστος, ὁ δὲ
σοφὸς καὶ καθ' αὑτὸν ὢν δύναται θεωρεῖν, καὶ ὅσῳ ἂν
σοφώτερος ᾖ μᾶλλον· βέλτιον δ' ἴσως συνεργοὺς ἔχων,
5 ἀλλ' ὅμως αὐταρκέστατος. δόξαι τ' ἂν αὐτὴ μόνη δι'
αὑτὴν ἀγαπᾶσθαι· οὐδὲν γὰρ ἀπ' αὐτῆς γίνεται παρὰ τὸ
θεωρῆσαι, ἀπὸ δὲ τῶν πρακτῶν ἢ πλεῖον ἢ ἔλαττον περι-
6 ποιούμεθα παρὰ τὴν πρᾶξιν. δοκεῖ τε ἡ εὐδαιμονία ἐν τῇ
σχολῇ εἶναι· ἀσχολούμεθα γὰρ ἵνα σχολάζωμεν, καὶ
πολεμοῦμεν ἵν' εἰρήνην ἄγωμεν. τῶν μὲν οὖν πρακτικῶν
ἀρετῶν ἐν τοῖς πολιτικοῖς ἢ ἐν τοῖς πολεμικοῖς ἡ ἐνέργεια·
αἱ δὲ περὶ ταῦτα πράξεις δοκοῦσιν ἄσχολοι εἶναι, αἱ μὲν
πολεμικαὶ καὶ παντελῶς· οὐδεὶς γὰρ αἱρεῖται τὸ πολεμεῖν
τοῦ πολεμεῖν ἕνεκα, οὐδὲ παρασκευάζει πόλεμον· δόξαι
γὰρ ἂν παντελῶς μιαιφόνος τις εἶναι, εἰ τοὺς φίλους πολεμίους ποιοῖτο, ἵνα μάχαι καὶ φόνοι γίγνοιντο. ἔστι δὲ
καὶ ἡ τοῦ πολιτικοῦ ἄσχολος, καὶ παρ' αὐτὸ τὸ πολιτεύεσθαι περιποιουμένη δυναστείας καὶ τιμὰς ἢ τήν γε εὐδαιμονίαν αὑτῷ καὶ τοῖς πολίταις, ἑτέραν οὖσαν τῆς πολι-
7 τικῆς, ἣν καὶ ζητοῦμεν δῆλον ὡς ἑτέραν οὖσαν. εἰ δὴ
τῶν μὲν κατὰ τὰς ἀρετὰς πράξεων αἱ πολιτικαὶ καὶ
πολεμικαὶ κάλλει καὶ μεγέθει προέχουσιν, αὗται δ'
ἄσχολοι καὶ τέλους τινὸς ἐφίενται καὶ οὐ δι' αὑτὰς
αἱρεταί εἰσιν, ἡ δὲ τοῦ νοῦ ἐνέργεια σπουδῇ τε διαφέρειν
δοκεῖ θεωρητικὴ οὖσα, καὶ παρ' αὑτὴν οὐδενὸς ἐφίεσθαι
τέλους, ἔχειν τε ἡδονὴν οἰκείαν, αὕτη δὲ συναύξει τὴν
ἐνέργειαν, καὶ τὸ αὔταρκες δὴ καὶ σχολαστικὸν καὶ
ἄτρυτον ὡς ἀνθρώπῳ, καὶ ὅσα ἄλλα τῷ μακαρίῳ ἀπονέμεται, κατὰ ταύτην τὴν ἐνέργειαν φαίνεται ὄντα. ἡ
τελεία δὴ εὐδαιμονία αὕτη ἂν εἴη ἀνθρώπου, λαβοῦσα

---

6 *ἔστι δὲ καὶ ἡ τοῦ πολιτικοῦ—ἑτέραν οὖσαν*] 'But moreover the (function) of the politician also is restless, and beyond mere administration it aims at power and distinctions, or, if happiness for the man himself and his citizens, at all events a happiness which is something distinct from the exercise of the political art; nay, we are in search of this happiness—plainly as something distinct.' *σοφία*, while producing happiness, is identical with it; but *πολιτικὴ* is to happiness as means to end. Cf. *Eth.* vi. xii. 5: *οὐχ ὡς ἰατρικὴ ὑγίειαν, ἀλλ' ὡς ἡ ὑγίεια, οὕτως ἡ σοφία (ποιεῖ) εὐδαιμονίαν*. The

μῆκος βίου τέλειον· οὐδὲν γὰρ ἀτελές ἐστι τῶν τῆς εὐδαιμονίας. ὁ δὲ τοιοῦτος ἂν εἴη βίος κρείττων ἢ κατ' 8
ἄνθρωπον· οὐ γὰρ ᾗ ἄνθρωπός ἐστιν οὕτω βιώσεται, ἀλλ'
ᾗ θεῖόν τι ἐν αὐτῷ ὑπάρχει· ὅσῳ δὲ διαφέρει τοῦτο τοῦ
συνθέτου, τοσούτῳ καὶ ἡ ἐνέργεια τῆς κατὰ τὴν ἄλλην ἀρετήν. εἰ δὴ θεῖον ὁ νοῦς πρὸς τὸν ἄνθρωπον, καὶ ὁ κατὰ
τοῦτον βίος θεῖος πρὸς τὸν ἀνθρώπινον βίον. οὐ χρὴ δὲ
κατὰ τοὺς παραινοῦντας ἀνθρώπινα φρονεῖν ἄνθρωπον ὄντα
οὐδὲ θνητὰ τὸν θνητόν, ἀλλ' ἐφ' ὅσον ἐνδέχεται ἀθανατίζειν
καὶ πάντα ποιεῖν πρὸς τὸ ζῆν κατὰ τὸ κράτιστον τῶν ἐν
αὐτῷ· εἰ γὰρ καὶ τῷ ὄγκῳ μικρόν ἐστι, δυνάμει καὶ τιμιότητι πολὺ μᾶλλον πάντων ὑπερέχει. δόξειε δ' ἂν καὶ εἶναι 9
ἕκαστος τοῦτο, εἴπερ τὸ κύριον καὶ ἄμεινον· ἄτοπον οὖν
γίνοιτ' ἄν, εἰ μὴ τὸν αὑτοῦ βίον αἱροῖτο ἀλλά τινος ἄλλου.

---

words ἣν καὶ ζητοῦμεν may be referred to *Eth.* I. ii. 9: ἡ μὲν οὖν μέθοδος τούτων ἐφίεται, πολιτική τις οὖσα.

8 κατὰ τοὺς παραινοῦντας] The moralists, says Aristotle, take a shallow view in bidding us tame down our aspirations to our mortal condition. Cf. *Rhet.* II. xxi. 6, where the gnome, θνατὰ χρὴ τὸν θνατὸν φρονεῖν, is quoted from Epicharmus. Isocrates (*Ad Dem.* p. 9 b) gives a sort of reconciliation of the views: ἀθάνατα μὲν φρόνει τῷ μεγαλόψυχος εἶναι· θνητὰ δὲ τῷ συμμέτρως τῶν ὑπαρχόντων ἀπολαύειν, which reminds one of George Herbert's quaint lines:—

'Pitch thy behaviour low, thy projects high:
So shalt thou humble and magnanimous be:
Sink not in spirit: who aimeth at the sky
Shoots higher much than he that means a tree.
A grain of glorie mixt with humblenesse
Cures both a fever and lethargicknesse.'

εἰ γὰρ καὶ τῷ ὄγκῳ—ὑπερέχει] 'For though (this noblest part) be small in proportionate bulk, yet in power and dignity it far surpasses all the other parts of our nature.' Aristotle here signifies that the divine particle (νοῦς) bears a small proportion to the whole of our composite nature. And in accordance with this he elsewhere intimates that only at short and rare intervals can man enjoy the fruition of his diviner nature. Cf. *Metaph.* XI. vii. 9: εἰ οὖν οὕτως εὖ ἔχει, ὡς ἡμεῖς ποτέ, ὁ θεὸς ἀεί, θαυμαστόν. *Pol.* VIII. v. 12: ἐν μὲν τῷ τέλει συμβαίνει τοῖς ἀνθρώποις ὀλιγάκις γίγνεσθαι. With which we may compare the saying of Spinoza (*De Intellectus Emendatione*, II.), that at first he found himself only able to rest in the idea of 'the truly good' for short intervals, yet that these intervals became longer and more frequent as he went on. 'Et quamvis in initio haec intervalla essent rara et per admodum exiguum temporis durarent, postquam tamen Verum Bonum magis ac magis mihi innotuit, intervalla ista frequentiora et longiora fuerunt.' Aristotle idealises these moments of the philosopher, suppos-

τὸ λεχθέν τε πρότερον ἁρμόσει καὶ νῦν· τὸ γὰρ οἰκεῖον ἑκάστῳ τῇ φύσει κράτιστον καὶ ἥδιστόν ἐστιν ἑκάστῳ. καὶ τῷ ἀνθρώπῳ δὴ ὁ κατὰ τὸν νοῦν βίος, εἴπερ τοῦτο μάλιστα ἄνθρωπος. οὗτος ἄρα καὶ εὐδαιμονέστατος.

8 Δευτέρως δ' ὁ κατὰ τὴν ἄλλην ἀρετήν· αἱ γὰρ κατ' αὐτὴν ἐνέργειαι ἀνθρωπικαί· δίκαια γὰρ καὶ ἀνδρεῖα καὶ ἄλλα τὰ κατὰ τὰς ἀρετὰς πρὸς ἀλλήλους πράττομεν ἐν συναλλάγμασι καὶ χρείαις καὶ πράξεσι παντοίαις ἔν τε τοῖς πάθεσι διατηροῦντες τὸ πρέπον ἑκάστῳ. ταῦτα δ'
2 εἶναι φαίνεται πάντα ἀνθρωπικά. ἔνια δὲ καὶ συμβαίνειν ἀπὸ τοῦ σώματος δοκεῖ, καὶ πολλὰ συνῳκειῶσθαι
3 τοῖς πάθεσιν ἡ τοῦ ἤθους ἀρετή. συνέζευκται δὲ καὶ ἡ φρόνησις τῇ τοῦ ἤθους ἀρετῇ, καὶ αὕτη τῇ φρονήσει, εἴπερ αἱ μὲν τῆς φρονήσεως ἀρχαὶ κατὰ τὰς ἠθικάς εἰσιν ἀρετάς, τὸ δ' ὀρθὸν τῶν ἠθικῶν κατὰ τὴν φρόνησιν. συ-

---

ing them to extend throughout life, ἡ τελεία δὴ εὐδαιμονία αὕτη ἂν εἴη ἀνθρώπου, λαβοῦσα μῆκος βίου τέλειον.

VIII. Aristotle, pursuing this theme, declares further the paramount excellence of the philosophic life, by showing that the life of practical morality holds a merely secondary place, (1) because it is bound up with man's composite nature, that is, with the passions; (2) because it is more dependent on external circumstances; (3) because such a life cannot possibly be attributed to the gods. He adds that though the philosopher will certainly require a degree of external prosperity, this will only be a very moderate degree, as the sayings of ancient sages testify. And if there be any providence of the gods watching over men, it may be presumed that this will especially watch over the philosopher, who loves and honours that which is divine.

3 συνέζευκται δὲ — ἀνθρωπικά] 'Thought moreover seems inseparably connected with excellence of the moral nature, and this with thought, since the major premisses of thought are in accordance with the moral virtues, and "the right" in morals is that which is in accordance with thought. But as thought and moral virtue are bound up with the passions, they must be concerned with our composite nature; and the virtues of the composite nature must be purely human.' And therefore secondary to philosophy, which is more than human. This passage appears to contain the germ of much that is expanded in the Eudemian books, cf. *Eth.* vi. xii. 9—10; xiii. 4. But we may observe, 1st, that thought (φρόνησις) is here as if for the first time coming *forward* in opposition to philosophy (σοφία), and not in that recognised opposition which would have been the case, had Book VI. been previously written; 2nd, that there is no reference to any previous discussions on the moral syllogism.

συνέζευκται] 'Thought' and moral virtue are here said to be reciprocally connected, just as it is said of pleasure

νηρτημέναι δ' αὗται καὶ τοῖς πάθεσι περὶ τὸ σύνθετον ἂν εἶεν· αἱ δὲ τοῦ συνθέτου ἀρεταὶ ἀνθρωπικαί. καὶ ὁ βίος δὴ ὁ κατ' αὐτὰς καὶ ἡ εὐδαιμονία. ἡ δὲ τοῦ νοῦ κεχωρισμένη· τοσοῦτον γὰρ περὶ αὐτῆς εἰρήσθω· διακριβῶσαι γὰρ μεῖζον τοῦ προκειμένου ἐστίν. δόξειε δ' ἂν καὶ τῆς ἐκτὸς 4
χορηγίας ἐπὶ μικρὸν ἢ ἐπ' ἔλαττον δεῖσθαι τῆς ἠθικῆς· τῶν μὲν γὰρ ἀναγκαίων ἀμφοῖν χρεία καὶ ἐξ ἴσου ἔστω, εἰ καὶ μᾶλλον διαπονεῖ περὶ τὸ σῶμα ὁ πολιτικός, καὶ ὅσα τοιαῦτα· μικρὸν γὰρ ἄν τι διαφέροι· πρὸς δὲ τὰς ἐνεργείας πολὺ διοίσει. τῷ μὲν γὰρ ἐλευθερίῳ δεήσει χρημάτων πρὸς τὸ πράττειν τὰ ἐλευθέρια, καὶ τῷ δικαίῳ δὴ εἰς τὰς ἀνταποδόσεις (αἱ γὰρ βουλήσεις ἄδηλοι, προσποιοῦνται δὲ καὶ οἱ μὴ δίκαιοι βούλεσθαι δικαιοπραγεῖν), τῷ ἀνδρείῳ δὲ δυνάμεως, εἴπερ ἐπιτελεῖ τι τῶν κατὰ τὴν ἀρετήν, καὶ τῷ σώφρονι ἐξουσίας· πῶς γὰρ δῆλος ἔσται ἢ οὗτος ἢ τῶν ἄλλων τις; ἀμφισβητεῖται δὲ πότερον 5
κυριώτερον τῆς ἀρετῆς ἡ προαίρεσις ἢ αἱ πράξεις, ὡς ἐν ἀμφοῖν οὔσης. τὸ δὴ τέλειον δῆλον ὡς ἐν ἀμφοῖν ἂν εἴη. πρὸς δὲ τὰς πράξεις πολλῶν δεῖται, καὶ ὅσῳ ἂν μείζους ὦσι καὶ καλλίους, πλειόνων. τῷ δὲ θεωροῦντι οὐδενὸς 6

---

and life, chap. iv. 11: συνεζεῦχθαι μὲν γὰρ ταῦτα φαίνεται καὶ χωρισμὸν οὐ δέχεσθαι.

τὸ σύνθετον] Cf. chap. vii. 8. The term occurs repeatedly in the *Phaedo* of Plato, cf. p. 86 A: αὐτὴ δ' ἡ λύρα καὶ αἱ χορδαὶ σώματά τε καὶ σωματοειδῆ καὶ ξύνθετα καὶ γεώδη ἐστὶ καὶ τοῦ θνητοῦ ξυγγενῆ. Cf. *Eth.* vii. xiv. 3.

4 τῶν μὲν γὰρ ἀναγκαίων—διοίσει] 'For though on the one hand both (the philosopher and the practical man) will have an equal need of the ordinary means of life, even if the practical man takes more trouble about the concerns of the body and such like—for there will be but little difference in this respect—on the other hand there will be a wide difference with regard to the discharge of their respective functions.' The term ὁ πολιτικός here appears to be used in opposition to ὁ σοφός (§ 13), not as distinctively indicating 'the politician,' but as representing the whole class of the active virtues, which are subsequently analysed. Thus, *Eth.* i. v. 4, we find οἱ χαρίεντες καὶ πρακτικοὶ given as equivalents for οἱ πολιτικοί.

τῷ ἀνδρείῳ δὲ δυνάμεως] δύναμις here seems used in a sense exactly corresponding to 'physical power.' In modern warfare, a weak body may often be accompanied by the highest personal courage, but in the ancient mode of fighting this would have been impossible or useless.

τῷ σώφρονι ἐξουσίας] 'The temperate man will require full liberty of gratification.' Cf. *Eth.* i. v. 3: διὰ τὸ πολλοὺς τῶν ἐν ταῖς ἐξουσίαις ὁμοιοπαθεῖν Σαρδαναπάλλῳ. viii. vi. 5: οἱ δ' ἐν ταῖς

τῶν τοιούτων πρός γε τὴν ἐνέργειαν χρεία, ἀλλ' ὡς εἰπεῖν καὶ ἐμπόδιά ἐστι πρός γε τὴν θεωρίαν· ᾗ δ' ἄνθρωπός ἐστι καὶ πλείοσι συζῇ, αἱρεῖται τὰ κατ' ἀρετὴν πράττειν·
7 δεήσεται οὖν τῶν τοιούτων πρὸς τὸ ἀνθρωπεύεσθαι. ἡ δὲ τελεία εὐδαιμονία ὅτι θεωρητική τίς ἐστιν ἐνέργεια, καὶ ἐντεῦθεν ἂν φανείη. τοὺς θεοὺς γὰρ μάλιστα ὑπειλήφαμεν μακαρίους καὶ εὐδαίμονας εἶναι· πράξεις δὲ ποίας ἀπονεῖμαι χρεὼν αὐτοῖς; πότερα τὰς δικαίας; ἢ γελοῖοι φανοῦνται συναλλάττοντες καὶ παρακαταθήκας ἀποδιδόντες καὶ ὅσα τοιαῦτα; ἀλλὰ τὰς ἀνδρείους, ὑπομένοντας τὰ φοβερὰ καὶ κινδυνεύοντας, ὅτι καλόν; ἢ τὰς ἐλευθερίους; τίνι δὲ δώσουσιν; ἄτοπον δ' εἰ καὶ ἔσται αὐτοῖς νόμισμα ἤ τι τοιοῦτον. αἱ δὲ σώφρονες τί ἂν εἶεν; ἢ φορτικὸς ὁ ἔπαινος, ὅτι οὐκ ἔχουσι φαύλας ἐπιθυμίας; διεξιοῦσι δὲ πάντα φαίνοιτ' ἂν τὰ περὶ τὰς πράξεις μικρὰ καὶ ἀνάξια θεῶν. ἀλλὰ μὴν ζῆν τε πάντες ὑπειλήφασιν αὐτοὺς καὶ ἐνεργεῖν ἄρα· οὐ γὰρ δὴ καθεύδειν ὥσπερ τὸν Ἐνδυμίωνα. τῷ δὴ ζῶντι τοῦ πράττειν ἀφαιρουμένου, ἔτι δὲ μᾶλλον τοῦ ποιεῖν, τί λείπεται πλὴν θεωρία; ὥστε ἡ τοῦ θεοῦ ἐνέργεια, μακαριότητι διαφέρουσα, θεωρητικὴ ἂν εἴη. καὶ τῶν ἀνθρωπίνων δὴ ἡ ταύτῃ συγγενεστάτη εὐδαιμονικωτάτη. σημεῖον δὲ καὶ τὸ μὴ μετέχειν τὰ λοιπὰ ζῷα εὐδαιμονίας, τῆς τοιαύτης ἐνεργείας ἐστερημένα τελείως. τοῖς μὲν γὰρ θεοῖς ἅπας ὁ βίος μακάριος, τοῖς δ' ἀνθρώποις, ἐφ' ὅσον ὁμοίωμά τι τῆς τοιαύτης ἐνεργείας

ἐξουσίαις. The use of the article, and of the plural number, makes a slight difference in signification.

7 *διεξιοῦσι δὲ—θεῶν*] 'And if we went through all the virtues, we should see that whatever relates to moral action is petty and unworthy of the gods.' Aristotle argues here that we cannot attribute morality to the Deity without falling into mere anthropomorphism; but it might be replied that there is the same difficulty in conceiving of God as engaged in philosophic thought. Aristotle himself felt this difficulty, and elsewhere defined the thought of God as 'the thinking upon thought' (*Metaph.* xi. ix. 4), which would not only deprive the Deity of all those fatherly and tender functions, which the human race is prone to attribute to Him; but would also remove Him from the conditions of all human thinking. If it be conceded that the life of God is only *analogous* to that of the philosopher; we might then ask, why not also analogous to the life of the good man? Plato, by placing the 'idea of justice' in the supra-sensible world, allowed a more than mortal interest to morality.

ὑπάρχει· τῶν δ' ἄλλων ζῴων οὐδὲν εὐδαιμονεῖ, ἐπειδὴ
οὐδαμῇ κοινωνεῖ θεωρίας. ἐφ' ὅσον δὴ διατείνει ἡ θεωρία,
καὶ ἡ εὐδαιμονία, καὶ οἷς μᾶλλον ὑπάρχει τὸ θεωρεῖν, καὶ
εὐδαιμονεῖν, οὐ κατὰ συμβεβηκὸς ἀλλὰ κατὰ τὴν θεωρίαν·
αὐτὴ γὰρ καθ' αὑτὴν τιμία. ὥστ' εἴη ἂν ἡ εὐδαιμονία
θεωρία τις. δεήσει δὲ καὶ τῆς ἐκτὸς εὐημερίας ἀνθρώπῳ 9
ὄντι· οὐ γὰρ αὐτάρκης ἡ φύσις πρὸς τὸ θεωρεῖν, ἀλλὰ δεῖ
καὶ τὸ σῶμα ὑγιαίνειν καὶ τροφὴν καὶ τὴν λοιπὴν θεραπείαν ὑπάρχειν. οὐ μὴν οἰητέον γε πολλῶν καὶ μεγάλων
δεήσεσθαι τὸν εὐδαιμονήσοντα, εἰ μὴ ἐνδέχεται ἄνευ
τῶν ἐκτὸς ἀγαθῶν μακάριον εἶναι· οὐ γὰρ ἐν τῇ ὑπερβολῇ τὸ αὔταρκες οὐδ' ἡ πρᾶξις, δυνατὸν δὲ καὶ μὴ
ἄρχοντα γῆς καὶ θαλάττης πράττειν τὰ καλά· καὶ γὰρ 10
ἀπὸ μετρίων δύναιτ' ἄν τις πράττειν κατὰ τὴν ἀρετήν. τοῦτο δ' ἔστιν ἰδεῖν ἐναργῶς· οἱ γὰρ ἰδιῶται τῶν
δυναστῶν οὐχ ἧττον δοκοῦσι τὰ ἐπιεικῆ πράττειν, ἀλλὰ
καὶ μᾶλλον. ἱκανὸν δὲ τοσαῦθ' ὑπάρχειν· ἔσται γὰρ ὁ
βίος εὐδαίμων τοῦ κατὰ τὴν ἀρετὴν ἐνεργοῦντος. καὶ Σό- 11
λων δὲ τοὺς εὐδαίμονας ἴσως ἀπεφαίνετο καλῶς, εἰπὼν
μετρίως τοῖς ἐκτὸς κεχορηγημένους, πεπραγότας δὲ τὰ
κάλλισθ', ὡς ᾤετο, καὶ βεβιωκότας σωφρόνως· ἐνδέχεται
γὰρ μέτρια κεκτημένους πράττειν ἃ δεῖ. ἔοικε δὲ καὶ

And he speaks of the just man, by the practice of virtue, being 'made like to God.' *Rep.* 613 A, quoted below.

10 Aristotle seems to lose no opportunity of expressing his contempt for great potentates. 'Reason is not implied in kingly power,' *Eth.* x. vi. 4. 'One may do noble deeds without ruling over land and sea,' &c. We may again refer to George Herbert, who in his verses on Church Musick says,

'Now I in you without a bodie move,
Rising and falling with your wings;
We both together sweetly live and love,
Yet say sometimes, *God help poore kings.*'

ἱκανὸν δὲ τοσαῦθ' ὑπάρχειν] i.e. τὰ μέτρια, referring to ἀπὸ τῶν μετρίων above.

κατὰ τὴν ἀρετήν] i.e. whether philosophic or moral excellence.

11 καὶ Σόλων δὲ] Referring to the well-known story in Herodotus, I. c. 30 sq., where Solon pronounces Tellus, the Athenian citizen, to have been the happiest man he had ever known.

ἔοικε δὲ καὶ Ἀναξαγόρας—μόνον] 'Anaxagoras moreover seems not to have conceived of "the happy man" as a rich man or a potentate, when he said that he should not be surprised if (his "happy man") appeared a strange person to the crowd, for they judge by externals, having no sense

Ἀναξαγόρας οὐ πλούσιον οὐδὲ δυναστὴν ὑπολαβεῖν τὸν εὐδαίμονα, εἰπὼν ὅτι οὐκ ἂν θαυμάσειεν εἴ τις ἄτοπος φανείη τοῖς πολλοῖς· οὗτοι γὰρ κρίνουσι τοῖς ἐκτός, τούτων
12 αἰσθανόμενοι μόνον. συμφωνεῖν δὴ τοῖς λόγοις ἐοίκασιν αἱ τῶν σοφῶν δόξαι. πίστιν μὲν οὖν καὶ τὰ τοιαῦτα ἔχει τινά, τὸ δ' ἀληθὲς ἐν τοῖς πρακτοῖς ἐκ τῶν ἔργων καὶ τοῦ βίου κρίνεται· ἐν τούτοις γὰρ τὸ κύριον. σκοπεῖν δὴ τὰ προειρημένα χρὴ ἐπὶ τὰ ἔργα καὶ τὸν βίον ἐπιφέροντας, καὶ συνᾳδόντων μὲν τοῖς ἔργοις ἀποδεκτέον, διαφωνούντων
13 δὲ λόγους ὑποληπτέον. ὁ δὲ κατὰ νοῦν ἐνεργῶν καὶ τοῦτον θεραπεύων καὶ διακείμενος ἄριστα καὶ θεοφιλέστατος ἔοικεν εἶναι· εἰ γάρ τις ἐπιμέλεια τῶν ἀνθρωπίνων ὑπὸ θεῶν γίνεται, ὥσπερ δοκεῖ, καὶ εἴη ἂν εὔλογον χαίρειν

---

of aught beside.' Anaxagoras, being asked to define 'the happy man,' said that his opinion, if he declared it, would be thought paradoxical.

12 *συμφωνεῖν δὴ—ὑποληπτέον*] 'The opinions of the philosophers appear then to coincide with our arguments. Authority of this kind affords a certain ground of belief. But truth in practical matters is settled by an appeal to facts and human life, for in them rests the decision. We ought then to consider previous sayings with a reference to facts and life: if those sayings agree with facts, we should accept them, if they differ, we must account them mere theories.' Cf. *Eth.* I. viii. 1.

13 *θεοφιλέστατος ἔοικεν εἶναι*] The term *θεοφιλής* occurs repeatedly in Plato; cf. especially the interesting passage in *Republic*, p. 613 A: where it is said that 'all things work together' for the good of those whom the gods love. *οὕτως ἄρα ὑποληπτέον περὶ τοῦ δικαίου ἀνδρός, ἐάν τ' ἐν πενίᾳ γίγνηται ἐάν τ' ἐν νόσοις ἤ τινι ἄλλῳ τῶν δοκούντων κακῶν, ὡς τούτῳ ταῦτα εἰς ἀγαθόν τι τελευτήσει ζῶντι ἢ καὶ ἀποθανόντι· οὐ γὰρ δὴ ὑπό γε θεῶν ποτε ἀμελεῖται ὃς ἂν προθυμεῖσθαι ἐθέλῃ δίκαιος γίγνεσθαι καὶ ἐπιτηδεύων ἀρετὴν εἰς ὅσον δυνατὸν ἀνθρώπῳ ὁμοιοῦσθαι θεῷ.*

εἰ γάρ τις—ὥσπερ δοκεῖ] 'For if there be any care of human affairs by the gods, as men think there is.' We may compare Shakespeare's

'If powers divine
Behold our human actions, as they do.'

Aristotle expresses here no opinion, one way or the other, as to the reality of a Divine Providence. *Δοκεῖ* merely indicates that an opinion is held; the word is frequently used to indicate a false opinion or fancy. Cf. *Eth.* VII. xii. 3: *δοκεῖ δὲ γένεσίς τις εἶναι, ὅτι κυρίως ἀγαθόν*. X. vi. 3: *δοκεῖ μὲν οὖν εὐδαιμονικὰ ταῦτα εἶναι, ὅτι κ.τ.λ.* Plato had said that moral virtue (see the last note) placed men peculiarly under the care of the gods. Aristotle, differing from Plato in his conception of the Deity, says, If there be any care of men by the gods, it must surely be extended in an especial degree not to the just man, but to the philosopher, since philosophy is most akin to the life of the Deity Himself.

τε αὐτοὺς τῷ ἀρίστῳ καὶ τῷ συγγενεστάτῳ (τοῦτο δ' ἂν εἴη ὁ νοῦς) καὶ τοὺς ἀγαπῶντας μάλιστα τοῦτο καὶ τιμῶντας ἀντευποιεῖν ὡς τῶν φίλων αὐτοῖς ἐπιμελουμένους καὶ ὀρθῶς τε καὶ καλῶς πράττοντας. ὅτι δὲ πάντα ταῦτα τῷ σοφῷ μάλισθ' ὑπάρχει, οὐκ ἄδηλον. θεοφιλέστατος ἄρα. τὸν αὐτὸν δ' εἰκὸς καὶ εὐδαιμονέστατον· ὥστε κἂν οὕτως εἴη ὁ σοφὸς μάλιστ' εὐδαίμων.

Ἆρ' οὖν εἰ περὶ τούτων καὶ τῶν ἀρετῶν, ἔτι δὲ καὶ 9
φιλίας καὶ ἡδονῆς ἱκανῶς εἴρηται τοῖς τύποις, τέλος ἔχειν οἰητέον τὴν προαίρεσιν, ἢ καθάπερ λέγεται, οὐκ ἔστιν ἐν τοῖς πρακτοῖς τέλος τὸ θεωρῆσαι ἕκαστα καὶ γνῶναι, ἀλλὰ μᾶλλον τὸ πράττειν αὐτά; οὐδὲ δὴ περὶ 2

κἂν οὕτως] 'Even on this supposition.' It seems probable that Aristotle had in his mind the very words of Plato, above quoted.

IX. The theory of human life now being complete, Aristotle asks if anything more is wanting? The answer is Yes, since theory is not by itself enough to make men good. For virtue three things are required, nature, teaching, and custom. The first is beyond man's control; the second may be identified with theory, which we have now supplied; the third requires institutions for the regulation of life, which may either be (1) of public, or (2) of private ordinance. As a fact, the state too much neglects (§ 14) the arrangement of daily life, and therefore private individuals must address themselves to the task, in a scientific spirit, and must first learn the principles of legislation. Whence are these principles to be learnt? On the one hand we find that practical politicians neither write nor speak on the principles of their art. On the other hand the Sophists, who profess to teach politics, are far from understanding even what they are, and their mode of teaching is merely empirical. So far from imparting principles, they go to work in an eclectic way, collecting laws, which are mere results, lying, as it were, on the surface. Legislation, as a science, has in short been neglected hitherto, and must now be essayed. We must enter at once upon the whole theory of the state, examining former speculations, and existing constitutions, and developing a conception of the best form of government.

According to the sequence of ideas in this chapter, it would appear that the connecting link between ethics and politics is to be found in the word ἔθος, custom, or mode of life. As custom has great influence upon men's power of attaining virtue and the chief good, and on the other hand as the institutions of individual life have a close connection with those of the state, it follows that politics are the complement of ethics.

1 ἀλλὰ μᾶλλον τὸ πράττειν αὐτά] Under the head of 'doing' are of course included the functions of thought, which, as we have just been told, are the highest forms of action in man. Cf. *Pol.* VII. iii. 8: ἀλλὰ τὸν πρακτικὸν οὐκ ἀναγκαῖον εἶναι πρὸς

ἀρετῆς ἱκανὸν τὸ εἰδέναι, ἀλλ' ἔχειν καὶ χρῆσθαι πει-
3 ρατέον, ἢ εἴ πως ἄλλως ἀγαθοὶ γινόμεθα. εἰ μὲν οὖν ἦσαν οἱ λόγοι αὐτάρκεις πρὸς τὸ ποιῆσαι ἐπιεικεῖς, πολλοὺς ἂν μισθοὺς καὶ μεγάλους δικαίως ἔφερον κατὰ τὸν Θέογνιν, καὶ ἔδει ἂν τούτους πορίσασθαι. νῦν δὲ φαίνονται προτρέψασθαι μὲν καὶ παρορμῆσαι τῶν νέων τοὺς ἐλευθερίους ἰσχύειν, ἦθός τ' εὐγενὲς καὶ ὡς ἀληθῶς φιλόκαλον ποιῆσαι ἂν κατοκώχιμον ἐκ τῆς ἀρετῆς, τοὺς δὲ
4 πολλοὺς ἀδυνατεῖν πρὸς καλοκαγαθίαν προτρέψασθαι· οὐ γὰρ πεφύκασιν αἰδοῖ πειθαρχεῖν ἀλλὰ φόβῳ, οὐδ' ἀπέχεσθαι τῶν φαύλων διὰ τὸ αἰσχρὸν ἀλλὰ διὰ τὰς τιμωρίας· πάθει γὰρ ζῶντες τὰς οἰκείας ἡδονὰς διώκουσι καὶ δι' ὧν αὗται ἔσονται, φεύγουσι δὲ τὰς ἀντικειμένας λύπας, τοῦ δὲ καλοῦ καὶ ὡς ἀληθῶς ἡδέος οὐδ' ἔννοιαν ἔχουσιν, ἄγευ-
5 στοι ὄντες. τοὺς δὴ τοιούτους τίς ἂν λόγος μεταρρυθμίσαι; οὐ γὰρ οἷόν τε ἢ οὐ ῥᾴδιον τὰ ἐκ παλαιοῦ τοῖς ἤθεσι κατειλημμένα λόγῳ μεταστῆσαι. ἀγαπητὸν δ' ἴσως ἐστὶν εἰ πάντων ὑπαρχόντων, δι' ὧν ἐπιεικεῖς
6 δοκοῦμεν γίνεσθαι, μεταλάβοιμεν τῆς ἀρετῆς. γίνεσθαι δ' ἀγαθοὺς οἴονται οἱ μὲν φύσει, οἱ δ' ἔθει, οἱ δὲ διδαχῇ. τὸ μὲν οὖν τῆς φύσεως δῆλον ὡς οὐκ ἐφ' ἡμῖν ὑπάρχει, ἀλλὰ διά τινας θείας αἰτίας τοῖς ὡς ἀληθῶς εὐτυχέσιν

ἑτέρους, καθάπερ οἴονταί τινες, οὐδὲ τὰς διανοίας εἶναι μόνας ταύτας πρακτικὰς τὰς τῶν ἀποβαινόντων χάριν γιγνομένας ἐκ τοῦ πράττειν, ἀλλὰ πολὺ μᾶλλον τὰς αὐτοτελεῖς καὶ τὰς αὑτῶν ἕνεκεν θεωρίας καὶ διανοήσεις. So too under ἀρετή, σοφία is included in its highest form.

3 πολλοὺς ἂν μισθοὺς] The saying of Theognis (v. 432) was that the Asclepiadae would have deserved great reward had they known how to heal the *minds* of men.

> Εἰ δ' Ἀσκληπιάδαις τοῦτο ἔδωκε θεός,
> Ἰᾶσθαι κακότητα καὶ ἀτηρὰς φρένας ἀνδρῶν,
> Πολλοὺς ἂν μισθοὺς καὶ μεγάλους ἔφερον.

The last line is quoted in the *Meno* of Plato, p. 95 E, to indicate that Theognis held teaching inefficacious to produce virtue. Aristotle borrows the application. On Theognis see Vol. I. Essay II. p. 91 sqq.

κατοκώχιμον ἐκ τῆς ἀρετῆς] 'Under the influence of virtue.' This word, which is also written κατακώχιμον, seems derived from κατέχειν, with a reduplication. In Ar. *Pol.* II. ix. 8, we find κατακώχιμοι τινές, and *ib.* VIII. vii. 4. κατακώχιμοι ὑπό.

5 τὰ ἐκ παλαιοῦ τοῖς ἤθεσι κατειλημμένα] 'What has long been ingrained in the character.'

6 τοῖς ὡς ἀληθῶς εὐτυχέσιν] 'To those who are in the most ideal sense of the term to be called fortunate.' Cf. *Eth.* III. v. 17: καὶ τὸ εὖ καὶ τὸ

ὑπάρχει· ὁ δὲ λόγος καὶ ἡ διδαχὴ μή ποτ' οὐκ ἐν ἅπασιν ἰσχύῃ, ἀλλὰ δέῃ προδιειργάσθαι τοῖς ἔθεσι τὴν τοῦ ἀκροατοῦ ψυχὴν πρὸς τὸ καλῶς χαίρειν καὶ μισεῖν, ὥσπερ γῆν τὴν θρέψουσαν τὸ σπέρμα. οὐ γὰρ ἂν ἀκούσειε λόγου 7
ἀποτρέποντος οὐδ' αὖ συνείη ὁ κατὰ πάθος ζῶν· τὸν δ' οὕτως ἔχοντα πῶς οἷόν τε μεταπεῖσαι; ὅλως τ' οὐ δοκεῖ λόγῳ ὑπείκειν τὸ πάθος ἀλλὰ βίᾳ. δεῖ δὴ τὸ ἦθος προϋ- 8
πάρχειν πως οἰκεῖον τῆς ἀρετῆς, στέργον τὸ καλὸν καὶ δυσχεραῖνον τὸ αἰσχρόν. ἐκ νέου δ' ἀγωγῆς ὀρθῆς τυχεῖν πρὸς ἀρετὴν χαλεπὸν μὴ ὑπὸ τοιούτοις τραφέντα νόμοις· τὸ γὰρ σωφρόνως καὶ καρτερικῶς ζῆν οὐχ ἡδὺ τοῖς πολλοῖς, ἄλλως τε καὶ νέοις. διὸ νόμοις δεῖ τετάχθαι τὴν τροφὴν καὶ τὰ ἐπιτηδεύματα· οὐκ ἔσται γὰρ λυπηρὰ συνήθη γινόμενα. οὐχ ἱκανὸν δ' ἴσως νέους ὄντας τροφῆς 9
καὶ ἐπιμελείας τυχεῖν ὀρθῆς, ἀλλ' ἐπειδὴ καὶ ἀνδρωθέντας δεῖ ἐπιτηδεύειν αὐτὰ καὶ ἐθίζεσθαι, καὶ περὶ ταῦτα δεοίμεθ' ἂν νόμων, καὶ ὅλως δὴ περὶ πάντα τὸν βίον· οἱ γὰρ πολλοὶ ἀνάγκῃ μᾶλλον ἢ λόγῳ πειθαρχοῦσι καὶ ζημίαις ἢ τῷ καλῷ. διόπερ οἴονταί τινες τοὺς νομοθετοῦντας δεῖν 10
μὲν παρακαλεῖν ἐπὶ τὴν ἀρετὴν καὶ προτρέπεσθαι τοῦ καλοῦ χάριν, ὡς ὑπακουσομένων τῶν ἐπιεικῶς τοῖς ἔθεσι προηγμένων, ἀπειθοῦσι δὲ καὶ ἀφυεστέροις οὖσι κολάσεις

καλὸν τοῦτο πεφυκέναι ἡ τελεία καὶ ἀληθινὴ ἂν εἴη εὐφυΐα.

9 οὐχ ἱκανὸν δ'—τὸν βίον] 'It is not enough perhaps that, while young, people should meet with right nurture and superintendence, but, as when grown up they must practise the things in question, and accustom themselves to them, so we shall need laws about these things, and in general about the whole of life.' In a spirit the very opposite of this remark, Pericles is reported (Thucyd. II. 37) to have boasted of the freedom enjoyed by the Athenians from all vexatious interference with the daily conduct of individuals: ἐλευθέρως δὲ τά τε πρὸς τὸ κοινὸν πολιτεύομεν καὶ ἐς τὴν πρὸς ἀλλήλους τῶν καθ' ἡμέραν ἐπιτηδευμάτων ὑποψίαν, οὐ δι' ὀργῆς τὸν πέλας, εἰ καθ' ἡδονήν τι δρᾷ, ἔχοντες, οὐδὲ ἀζημίους μὲν λυπηρὰς δὲ τῇ ὄψει ἀχθηδόνας προστιθέμενοι. On the one hand Thucydides praised the free system of Athens; on the other hand Aristotle praised the organised and educational system of Sparta; see below, § 13, and cf. *Eth.* I. xiii. 3, and note. He was probably led into this political mistake, partly by the state of society in Athens itself, partly by the influence of Plato, from whom he imbibed one of the essential ideas of communism,—namely, that the state should arrange as much as possible, instead of as little as possible.

τε καὶ τιμωρίας ἐπιτιθέναι, τοὺς δ' ἀνιάτους ὅλως ἐξορίζειν· τὸν μὲν γὰρ ἐπιεικῆ καὶ πρὸς τὸ καλὸν ζῶντα τῷ λόγῳ πειθαρχήσειν, τὸν δὲ φαῦλον ἡδονῆς ὀρεγόμενον λύπῃ κολάζεσθαι ὥσπερ ὑποζύγιον. διὸ καί φασι δεῖν τοιαύτας γίνεσθαι τὰς λύπας αἳ μάλιστ' ἐναντιοῦνται

11 ταῖς ἀγαπωμέναις ἡδοναῖς. εἰ δ' οὖν, καθάπερ εἴρηται, τὸν ἐσόμενον ἀγαθὸν τραφῆναι καλῶς δεῖ καὶ ἐθισθῆναι, εἶθ' οὕτως ἐν ἐπιτηδεύμασιν ἐπιεικέσι ζῆν καὶ μήτ' ἄκοντα μήθ' ἑκόντα πράττειν τὰ φαῦλα, ταῦτα δὲ γίγνοιτ' ἂν βιουμένοις κατά τινα νοῦν καὶ τάξιν ὀρθήν, ἔχουσαν ἰσχύν.

12 ἡ μὲν οὖν πατρικὴ πρόσταξις οὐκ ἔχει τὸ ἰσχυρὸν οὐδὲ τὸ ἀναγκαῖον, οὐδὲ δὴ ὅλως ἡ ἑνὸς ἀνδρός, μὴ βασιλέως ὄντος ἤ τινος τοιούτου· ὁ δὲ νόμος ἀναγκαστικὴν ἔχει δύναμιν, λόγος ὢν ἀπό τινος φρονήσεως καὶ νοῦ. καὶ τῶν μὲν ἀνθρώπων ἐχθαίρουσι τοὺς ἐναντιουμένους ταῖς ὁρμαῖς, κἂν ὀρθῶς αὐτὸ δρῶσιν· ὁ δὲ νόμος οὐκ ἔστιν ἐπαχθὴς

13 τάττων τὸ ἐπιεικές. ἐν μόνῃ δὲ τῇ Λακεδαιμονίων πόλει μετ' ὀλίγων ὁ νομοθέτης ἐπιμέλειαν δοκεῖ πεποιῆσθαι τροφῆς τε καὶ ἐπιτηδευμάτων· ἐν δὲ ταῖς πλείσταις τῶν πόλεων ἐξημέληται περὶ τῶν τοιούτων, καὶ ζῇ ἕκαστος ὡς βούλεται, κυκλωπικῶς θεμιστεύων παίδων ἠδ' ἀλόχου.

14 κράτιστον μὲν οὖν τὸ γίγνεσθαι κοινὴν ἐπιμέλειαν καὶ ὀρθὴν καὶ δρᾶν αὐτὸ δύνασθαι· κοινῇ δ' ἐξαμελουμένων ἑκάστῳ δόξειεν ἂν προσήκειν τοῖς σφετέροις τέκνοις καὶ φίλοις εἰς ἀρετὴν συμβάλλεσθαι, ἢ προαιρεῖσθαί γε. μάλιστα δ' ἂν τοῦτο δύνασθαι δόξειεν ἐκ τῶν εἰρημένων νομοθετικὸς γενόμενος· αἱ μὲν γὰρ κοιναὶ ἐπιμέλειαι

---

13 κυκλωπικῶς] Referring to Homer, *Odyss.* ix. 114:

> θεμιστεύει δὲ ἕκαστος
> παίδων ἠδ' ἀλόχων, οὐδ' ἀλλήλων
> ἀλέγουσιν.

Aristotle considers that any people among whom the state does not settle by law the customs of daily life is unworthy to be called a society at all. He ignores that element called 'public opinion,' which in so many respects, and more naturally, supplies the place of legislation.

14 καὶ δρᾶν αὐτὸ δύνασθαι] 'And that it should have power to effect the object in question.' This apparently refers to § 12: ἡ μὲν οὖν πατρικὴ πρόσταξις οὐκ ἔχει τὸ ἰσχυρὸν κ.τ.λ.

μάλιστα δ'—γενόμενος] 'But from what we have said it would appear that a person would best be able to

δῆλον ὅτι διὰ νόμων γίγνονται, ἐπιεικεῖς δ' αἱ διὰ τῶν
σπουδαίων. γεγραμμένων δ' ἢ ἀγράφων, οὐδὲν ἂν δόξειε
διαφέρειν, οὐδὲ δι' ὧν εἷς ἢ πολλοὶ παιδευθήσονται, ὥσπερ
οὐδ' ἐπὶ μουσικῆς καὶ γυμναστικῆς καὶ τῶν ἄλλων ἐπιτηδευμάτων. ὥσπερ γὰρ ἐν ταῖς πόλεσιν ἐνισχύει τὰ
νόμιμα καὶ τὰ ἔθη, οὕτω καὶ ἐν οἰκίαις οἱ πατρικοὶ
λόγοι καὶ τὰ ἔθη, καὶ ἔτι μᾶλλον διὰ τὴν συγγένειαν καὶ
τὰς εὐεργεσίας· προϋπάρχουσι γὰρ στέργοντες καὶ εὐπειθεῖς τῇ φύσει. ἔτι δὲ καὶ διαφέρουσιν αἱ καθ' ἕκαστον 15
παιδεῖαι τῶν κοινῶν, ὥσπερ ἐπὶ ἰατρικῆς· καθόλου μὲν
γὰρ τῷ πυρέττοντι συμφέρει ἡσυχία καὶ ἀσιτία, τινὶ
δ' ἴσως οὔ, ὅ τε πυκτικὸς ἴσως οὐ πᾶσι τὴν αὐτὴν μάχην
περιτίθησιν. ἐξακριβοῦσθαι δὴ δόξειεν ἂν μᾶλλον τὸ καθ'
ἕκαστον ἰδίας τῆς ἐπιμελείας γινομένης· μᾶλλον γὰρ τοῦ
προσφόρου τυγχάνει ἕκαστος. ἀλλ' ἐπιμεληθείη μὲν
ἄριστα καθ' ἓν καὶ ἰατρὸς καὶ γυμναστὴς καὶ πᾶς ἄλλος
ὁ τὸ καθόλου εἰδὼς ὅτι πᾶσιν ἢ τοῖς τοιοῖσδε· τοῦ κοινοῦ
γὰρ αἱ ἐπιστῆμαι λέγονταί τε καὶ εἰσίν. οὐ μὴν ἀλλὰ 16
καὶ ἑνός τινος οὐδὲν ἴσως κωλύει καλῶς ἐπιμεληθῆναι καὶ
ἀνεπιστήμονα ὄντα, τεθεαμένον δ' ἀκριβῶς τὰ συμβαίνοντα ἐφ' ἑκάστῳ δι' ἐμπειρίαν, καθάπερ καὶ ἰατροὶ ἔνιοι
δοκοῦσιν ἑαυτῶν ἄριστοι εἶναι, ἑτέρῳ οὐδὲν ἂν δυνάμενοι
ἐπαρκέσαι. οὐδὲν δ' ἧττον ἴσως τῷ γε βουλομένῳ τεχνικῷ γενέσθαι καὶ θεωρητικῷ ἐπὶ τὸ καθόλου βαδιστέον
εἶναι δόξειεν ἄν, κἀκεῖνο γνωριστέον ὡς ἐνδέχεται· εἴρηται
γὰρ ὅτι περὶ τοῦθ' αἱ ἐπιστῆμαι. τάχα δὲ καὶ τῷ 17

---

do this (*i.e.* to help his children and friends towards virtue) after learning the principles of legislation.' As we find from *Eth.* vi. viii. 2. legislation was considered by Aristotle to be the superior (ἀρχιτεκτονική) form of political thought. A person possessing the general principles of scientific legislation (see below, § 16) would be best able to deduce rules for the guidance of his family, and at the same time to allow of such exceptions as individual peculiarities might call for. That the family is a deduction from the state, which is prior in point of idea, we know to have been Aristotle's opinion, *Pol.* i. ii. 12.

16 οὐ μὴν ἀλλὰ—ἐμπειρίαν] 'And yet perhaps nothing hinders a man even without scientific knowledge treating well some particular case, from an accurate observation, empirically, of what results on each thing being tried.' Cf. *Metaph.* i. i. 7: πρὸς μὲν οὖν τὸ πράττειν ἐμπειρία τέχνης οὐδὲν δοκεῖ διαφέρειν, ἀλλὰ καὶ

βουλομένῳ δι' ἐπιμελείας βελτίους ποιεῖν, εἴτε πολλοὺς εἴτ' ὀλίγους, νομοθετικῷ πειρατέον γενέσθαι, εἰ διὰ νόμων ἀγαθοὶ γενοίμεθ' ἄν. ὅντινα γὰρ οὖν καὶ τὸν προτεθέντα διαθεῖναι καλῶς οὐκ ἔστι τοῦ τυχόντος, ἀλλ' εἴπερ τινός, τοῦ εἰδότος, ὥσπερ ἐπ' ἰατρικῆς καὶ τῶν λοιπῶν ὧν
18 ἐστὶν ἐπιμέλειά τις καὶ φρόνησις. ἆρ' οὖν μετὰ τοῦτο ἐπισκεπτέον πόθεν ἢ πῶς νομοθετικὸς γένοιτ' ἄν τις, ἢ καθάπερ ἐπὶ τῶν ἄλλων, παρὰ τῶν πολιτικῶν; μόριον γὰρ ἐδόκει τῆς πολιτικῆς εἶναι. ἢ οὐχ ὅμοιον φαίνεται ἐπὶ τῆς πολιτικῆς καὶ τῶν λοιπῶν ἐπιστημῶν τε καὶ δυνάμεων; ἐν μὲν γὰρ τοῖς ἄλλοις οἱ αὐτοὶ φαίνονται τάς τε δυνάμεις παραδιδόντες καὶ ἐνεργοῦντες ἀπ' αὐτῶν, οἷον ἰατροὶ καὶ γραφεῖς· τὰ δὲ πολιτικὰ ἐπαγγέλλονται μὲν διδάσκειν οἱ σοφισταί, πράττει δ' αὐτῶν οὐδείς, ἀλλ' οἱ πολιτευόμενοι, οἳ δόξαιεν ἂν δυνάμει τινὶ τοῦτο πράττειν καὶ ἐμπειρίᾳ μᾶλλον ἢ διανοίᾳ· οὔτε γὰρ γράφοντες οὔτε λέγοντες περὶ τῶν τοιούτων φαίνονται (καίτοι κάλλιον ἦν ἴσως ἢ λόγους δικανικούς τε καὶ δημηγορικούς), οὐδ' αὖ πολιτικοὺς πεποιηκότες τοὺς σφετέρους υἱεῖς ἤ τινας
19 ἄλλους τῶν φίλων. εὔλογον δ' ἦν, εἴπερ ἐδύναντο· οὔτε γὰρ ταῖς πόλεσιν ἄμεινον οὐδὲν κατέλιπον ἄν, οὔθ' αὑτοῖς ὑπάρξαι προέλοιντ' ἂν μᾶλλον τῆς τοιαύτης δυνάμεως, οὐδὲ δὴ τοῖς φιλτάτοις. οὐ μὴν μικρόν γε ἔοικεν ἡ ἐμπειρία συμβάλλεσθαι· οὐδὲ γὰρ ἐγίγνοντ' ἂν διὰ τῆς πολιτικῆς συνηθείας πολιτικοί· διὸ τοῖς ἐφιεμένοις
20 περὶ πολιτικῆς εἰδέναι προσδεῖν ἔοικεν ἐμπειρίας. τῶν δὲ

μᾶλλον ἐπιτυγχάνοντας ὁρῶμεν τοὺς ἐμπείρους τῶν ἄνευ τῆς ἐμπειρίας λόγον ἐχόντων.

17 *ὅντινα γὰρ οὖν καὶ τὸν προτεθέντα*] 'Any one you like to propose.' Cf. *Eth.* i. iii. 8: *τί προτιθέμεθα*, 'what we propose to ourselves.'

18 *μόριον γὰρ ἐδόκει τῆς πολιτικῆς εἶναι*] 'For, as we said, legislation is generally considered to be a branch of politics.' This probably refers to *Eth.* i. ii. 7: *χρωμένης δὲ ταύτης ταῖς λοιπαῖς πρακτικαῖς τῶν ἐπιστημῶν, ἔτι δὲ νομοθετούσης τί δεῖ πράττειν καὶ τίνων ἀπέχεσθαι.*

ἐπαγγέλλονται μὲν διδάσκειν οἱ σοφισταί] Cf. Plato, *Meno*, p. 95 B: *οἱ σοφισταί σοι οὗτοι, οἵπερ μόνοι ἐπαγγέλλονται, δοκοῦσι διδάσκαλοι εἶναι ἀρετῆς;* The whole of the present discussion on the teaching of political science is evidently suggested by that on the teaching of virtue in the *Meno*, where it was shown that the great statesmen do not attempt to teach their sons virtue, and that the Sophists, who

σοφιστῶν οἱ ἐπαγγελλόμενοι λίαν φαίνονται πόρρω εἶναι τοῦ διδάξαι· ὅλως γὰρ οὐδὲ ποῖόν τί ἐστιν ἢ περὶ ποῖα ἴσασιν· οὐ γὰρ ἂν τὴν αὐτὴν τῇ ῥητορικῇ οὐδὲ χείρω ἐτίθεσαν, οὐδ' ἂν ᾤοντο ῥᾴδιον εἶναι τὸ νομοθετῆσαι συναγαγόντι τοὺς εὐδοκιμοῦντας τῶν νόμων· ἐκλέξασθαι γὰρ εἶναι τοὺς ἀρίστους, ὥσπερ οὐδὲ τὴν ἐκλογὴν οὖσαν συνέσεως καὶ τὸ κρῖναι ὀρθῶς μέγιστον, ὥσπερ ἐν τοῖς κατὰ μουσικήν· οἱ γὰρ ἔμπειροι περὶ ἕκαστα κρίνουσιν ὀρθῶς τὰ ἔργα, καὶ δι' ὧν ἢ πῶς ἐπιτελεῖται συνιᾶσιν, καὶ ποῖα ποίοις συνᾴδει· τοῖς δ' ἀπείροις ἀγαπητὸν τὸ μὴ διαλανθάνειν εἰ εὖ ἢ κακῶς πεποίηται τὸ ἔργον, ὥσπερ ἐπὶ γραφικῆς. οἱ δὲ νόμοι τῆς πολιτικῆς ἔργοις ἐοίκασιν· πῶς οὖν ἐκ τούτων νομοθετικὸς γένοιτ' ἄν τις,
ἢ τοὺς ἀρίστους κρίναι; οὐ γὰρ φαίνονται οὐδ' ἰατρικοὶ 21
ἐκ τῶν συγγραμμάτων γίνεσθαι. καίτοι πειρῶνταί γε λέγειν οὐ μόνον τὰ θεραπεύματα, ἀλλὰ καὶ ὡς ἰαθεῖεν ἂν καὶ ὡς δεῖ θεραπεύειν ἑκάστους, διελόμενοι τὰς ἕξεις.

---

profess to teach it, are doubtful instructors.

20 οἱ δὲ νόμοι—ἐοίκασιν] 'But laws are as it were the results of political science.' Aristotle's account of the Sophists' method of teaching politics is precisely analogous to his account of the way in which they taught dialectic. He here speaks of their taking a shallow view of politics, and making it an inferior branch of rhetoric; and he adds that they adopted a superficial eclecticism, making collections of laws without touching upon the principles from which legislation must depend. They thus imparted mere results, which to those who are uninstructed in principles are wholly useless. In the same way (*Soph. Elench.* xxxiii. 16) he says they gave various specimens of argument to be learnt by heart, and that this was no more use than if a person who undertook to teach shoemaking were to provide his pupils with an assortment of shoes. λόγους γὰρ οἱ μὲν ῥητορικοὺς οἱ δὲ ἐρωτητικοὺς ἐδίδοσαν ἐκμανθάνειν, εἰς οὓς πλειστάκις ἐμπίπτειν ᾠήθησαν ἑκάτεροι τοὺς ἀλλήλων λόγους. Διόπερ ταχεῖα μὲν ἄτεχνος δ' ἦν ἡ διδασκαλία τοῖς μανθάνουσι παρ' αὐτῶν· οὐ γὰρ τέχνην ἀλλὰ τὰ ἀπὸ τῆς τέχνης διδόντες παιδεύειν ὑπελάμβανον, ὥσπερ ἂν εἴ τις ἐπιστήμην φάσκων παραδώσειν ἐπὶ τὸ μηδὲν πονεῖν τοὺς πόδας, εἶτα σκυτοτομικὴν μὲν μὴ διδάσκοι, μηδ' ὅθεν δυνήσεται πορίζεσθαι τὰ τοιαῦτα, δοίη δὲ πολλὰ γένη παντοδαπῶν ὑποδημάτων.

21 οὐ γὰρ φαίνονται—ἕξεις] 'For men do not appear to learn the physician's art from treatises, though (they who write such treatises) aim at stating not only modes of treatment, but how people can be cured, and how each person is to be treated, according to a classification of habits (of body).' συγγραμμάτων here is frequently translated 'prescriptions,' but, from what Aristotle says about them, clearly something more is meant. In the *Minos*

ταῦτα δὲ τοῖς μὲν ἐμπείροις ὠφέλιμα εἶναι δοκεῖ, τοῖς δ' ἀνεπιστήμοσιν ἀχρεῖα. ἴσως οὖν καὶ τῶν νόμων καὶ τῶν πολιτειῶν αἱ συναγωγαὶ τοῖς μὲν δυναμένοις θεωρῆσαι καὶ κρῖναι τί καλῶς ἢ τοὐναντίον καὶ ποῖα ποίοις ἁρμόττει, εὔχρηστ' ἂν εἴη· τοῖς δ' ἄνευ ἕξεως τὰ τοιαῦτα διεξιοῦσι τὸ μὲν κρίνειν καλῶς οὐκ ἂν ὑπάρχοι, εἰ μὴ ἄρα αὐτόματον, εὐσυνετώτεροι δ' εἰς ταῦτα τάχ' ἂν γίνοιντο.
22 παραλιπόντων οὖν τῶν προτέρων ἀνερεύνητον τὸ περὶ τῆς νομοθεσίας, αὐτοὺς ἐπισκέψασθαι μᾶλλον βέλτιον ἴσως, καὶ ὅλως δὴ περὶ πολιτείας, ὅπως εἰς δύναμιν ἡ περὶ τὰ
23 ἀνθρώπινα φιλοσοφία τελειωθῇ. πρῶτον μὲν οὖν εἴ τι κατὰ μέρος εἴρηται καλῶς ὑπὸ τῶν προγενεστέρων πειραθῶμεν ἐπελθεῖν, εἶτα ἐκ τῶν συνηγμένων πολιτειῶν θεω-

---

which bears Plato's name we find *συγγράμματα* used as a generic word, of which several species, *ἰατρικά*, *γεωργικά*, *μαγειρικά*, &c., are mentioned, and are compared (as here) with 'laws.' Cf. *Minos*, p. 316 c sqq.: *ἤδη ποτὲ ἐνέτυχες συγγράμματι περὶ ὑγιείας τῶν καμνόντων; Ἔγωγε.—Ἰατρικὰ ἄρα καὶ ἰατρικοὶ νόμοι ταῦτα τὰ συγγράμματα ἐστὶ τὰ τῶν ἰατρῶν; Ἰατρικὰ μέντοι.—Ἆρ' οὖν καὶ τὰ γεωργικὰ συγγράμματα γεωργικοὶ νόμοι εἰσίν;* κ. τ. λ. The *συγγράμματα* here mentioned were perhaps 'reports of cases,' or monographs on particular diseases.

τοῖς δ' ἄνευ—γίνοιντο] 'But those who without proper training study such things would not be able to judge of them correctly (except by mere accident), though they might gain an appreciative faculty with regard to the subject.' *ἕξις* here denotes the state of mind formed by scientific training. Such a training especially produces 'judgment' (*τὸ κρίνειν καλῶς*). Cf. *Pol.* III. xi. 14: *ἔσται γὰρ ἕκαστος μὲν χείρων κριτὴς τῶν εἰδότων*. *Eth.* I. iii. 5, and note. This kind of judgment, as being deep and original, is distinguished above from *σύνεσις*, the power of appreciation, but in *Eth.* VI. x. 2, *σύνεσις* is called *κριτική*, in a lower sense, and as contrasted with wisdom, which is *ἐπιτακτική*.

22 *παραλιπόντων οὖν*] One must be struck with the disdainful way in which Aristotle here quite sets aside the *Republic* and *Laws* of Plato, by which he had been himself so much influenced, as if they were not to be reckoned as even attempts at founding the science of politics. Below, he alludes to them as 'perhaps on some particular points having made good remarks.'

πρῶτον μὲν οὖν] A rough outline of the *Politics* is here given, as Aristotle conceived it before writing it. The sketch is so very general that it omits the subject of Book I., and yet critics have thought that this passage may be taken as evidence of what the order of books in Aristotle's *Politics* should be.

ἐκ τῶν συνηγμένων πολιτειῶν] 'From my collection of constitutions.' Cf. Cicero, *De Finibus*, v. iv.: 'Omnium fere civitatum, non Graeciae solum, sed etiam barbariae, ab Aristotele mores,

ρῆσαι τὰ ποῖα σώζει καὶ φθείρει τὰς πόλεις καὶ τὰ ποῖα ἑκάστας τῶν πολιτειῶν, καὶ διὰ τίνας αἰτίας αἱ μὲν καλῶς αἱ δὲ τοὐναντίον πολιτεύονται· θεωρηθέντων γὰρ τούτων τάχ' ἂν μᾶλλον συνίδοιμεν καὶ ποία πολιτεία ἀρίστη, καὶ πῶς ἑκάστη ταχθεῖσα, καὶ τίσι νόμοις καὶ ἔθεσι χρωμένη. λέγωμεν οὖν ἀρξάμενοι.

---

instituta, disciplinas; a Theophrasto leges etiam cognovimus.' Diogenes Laertius, in his list of the works of Aristotle, mentions (v. i. 12): πολιτεῖαι πόλεων δυοῖν δεούσαιν ἑξήκοντα καὶ ἑκατόν, καὶ ἰδίᾳ δημοκρατικαί, ὀλιγαρχικαί, ἀριστοκρατικαί, καὶ τυραννικαί. The fragments of this work have been collected by C. F. Neumann, and may be found in the Oxford reprint of Bekker's edition of Aristotle.

INDEX VERBORUM.

A

ἈΒΕΒΑΙΟΙ IX. xii. 3.

ἀβλαβεῖς VII. xiv. 5.

ἀγαθὸν I. iii. 5. vii. 17. viii. 12. x. 11. xiii. 12. II. iii. 7. 10. iv. 5. vi. 3. IV. iii. 15, 20. V. ii. 11. VI. xiii. 6. VII. i. 1. xiii. 3. VIII. iii. 6. v. 4. 5. xi. 1. X. v. 10. ἀγαθὴ II. i. 5. ἀγαθὸν I. ii. 1, 7. iv. 1. v. 1, 8. vi. 2, 5, 6, 11, 13. vii. 1, 6, 15, 17. viii. 9. x. 3, 13. xi. 5. xii. 2. xiii. 5. II. vi. 2, 14. III. iv. 2, 3, 5, 6. v. 17. vi. 6. ix. 6. IV. iii. 14. V. i. 10, 17. iii. 17. vi. 6. VI. vii. 4, 6. viii. 4. ix. 4. xii. 7, 10. xiii. 1, 6. VII. xi. 1, 3, 4. xii. 1, 3. xiii. 1, 7. xiv. 2. VIII. ii. 1, 2. iii. 1, 2, 7. iv. 4. v. 4, 5. vi. 4. viii. 7. x. 2. xi 4. xii. 5, 7. xiv. 3. IX. iii. 3. iv. 3. viii. 7, 9. ix. 7, 8, 9, 10. X. ii. 1, 2, 4, 5. iii. 2, 11. ix. 11. ἀγαθοῦ I. i. 1. iv. 1. vi. 8, 15. xi. 5. III. iv. 1. v. 17. V. i. 10. iii. 14, 15. iv. 6. vi. 6. ix. 9. x. 1. VI. ix. 4. xii. 1. VII. xii. 2. VIII. iii. 4. xiii. 2. xiv. 1. IX. iv. 3. ix. 1, 5, 7, 9, 10. X. ii. 3, 4. ἀγαθῷ III. ii. 10. v. 18. IV. iii. 19. V. ii. 11. VI. xii. 10. VIII. v. 4. xiv. 1. ἀγαθοὶ I. viii. 16. II. i. 6, 7. ii. 1. v. 5. vi. 9. VIII. iii. 6. iv. 1, 4, 5. v. 1. viii. 2. xiii. 1. IX. ix. 9. X. ix. 1, 17. ἀγαθαὶ I. viii. 13. VII. xii. 7. xiv. 2. IX. iv. 8. ἀγαθὰ I. iv. 4. vi. 11, 14. viii. 2. III. ii. 13. IV. iii. 10, 20, 21. V. i. 9. VI. v. 1. 4, 5, 6. vii. 5. xii. 1. xiv. 9. VIII. i. 1. v. 5. vii. 7. IX. viii. 6, 9. ix. 3. ἀγαθῶν I. vi. 4, 7, 10, 14. vii. 8. viii. 2, 3, 15. ix. 7. xii. 4, 5. IV. iii. 10, 35. V. vi. 4. ix. 17. xi. 2. VII. iv. 2, 5. xiii. 2. xiv. 2. VIII. iii. 6. iv. 3, 4. v. 4. 5. vii. 6. viii. 5. x. 2. IX. iv. 8. viii. 7. ix. 1, 7. X. ii. 2, 3. iii. 1. viii. 9. ἀγαθοὺς I. v. 5. ix. 8. x. 4. xiii. 2. II. i. 5. VIII. i. 5. iv. 2. vi. 2, 4. ἀγαθοῖς I. x. 15. III. v. 3. IV. iii. 15. VIII. vii. 4. x. 2. IX. ix. 5, 7. xi. 5.

Ἀγάθων VI. ii. 6. iv. 5.

ἄγαλμα X. v. 1.

ἀγαλματοποιῷ I. vii. 10.

Ἀγαμέμνονα VIII. xi. 1.

ἄγαν VII. ii. 6.

ἀγαπᾷ III. xi. 8. IX. vii. 3. viii. 6. X. iv. 10. ἀγαπῶσι I. v. 2. IV. i. 20. VIII. iii. 1. vii. 2. viii. 1. IX. xii. 2. ἀγαπῴη III. x. 11. ἀγαπῶν IX. iii. 1. viii. 6. ἀγαπῶντες X. viii. 13. ἀγαπηθείη IX. vii. 3. ἀγαπᾶται I. v. 8. ἀγαπᾶσθαι X. vii. 5. ἀγαπώμενα I. vi. 8. ἀγαπωμένους X. ix. 10.

ἀγαπητὸν I. iii. 4. IX. x. 6. X. ix. 5, 20.

ἀγαπητότατον IX. xii. 2.

ἀγασθῶσι VII. i. 3.

ἀγέννητα VI. ii. 6. ἀγέννητα VI. iii. 2.

ἀγεννοῦς IV. i. 31. ἀγεννὴς IV. iii. 26.

ἄγευστοι X. vi. 4. ix. 4.

ἀγνοεῖ III. i. 14, 15. V. viii. 10. ἀγνοοῦσι IX. vi. 1. ἀγνοεῖ VI. vii. 7. ἀγνοήσειε III. i. 17. ἀγνοῶν I. vi. 15. III. v. 8, 9. IV. iii. 35. V. viii. 3. ἀγνοῶν III. i. 14, 16. v. 12. V. viii. 3. ix. 12. x. 3. ἀγνοοῦντες III. viii. 16. IV. iii. 36. V. viii. 12. ἀγνοοῦντας III. i. 14. v. 8. VI. iii. 5. ἀγνοήσας III. i. 18. ἀγνοούμενον V. viii. 3.

ἄγνοια III. i. 15. VII. iii. 12. ἀγνοίας III. i. 18. v. 8. V. viii. 6. VII. ii. 2. ἄγνοιαν I. iv. 3. III. i. 3, 13, 14, 19, 20. v. 7, 17. V. viii. 12. xii. 7. VII. ii. 1, 2. VIII. viii. 3.

ἀγνῶτας IV. iv. 5. IX. v. 1.

ἀγοραία VIII. xiii. 6. ἀγοραίων VIII. vi. 4.

ἀγορεύων III. viii. 2. ἀγορεύουσι V. i. 13.
ἄγραφα VIII. xiii. 5. ἀγράφων X. ix. 14.
ἄγριοι IV. viii. 10. ἄγριον III. x. 7. ἄγριοι IV. viii. 3.
ἀγροικία II. vii. 13.
ἄγροικος II. vii. 13. ἄγροικοι II. ii. 7. VII. ix. 3.
ἀγρὸν V. ix. 3.
ἀγυμνασίαν III. v. 15. ἀγχίνοια VI. ix. 3.
ἄγει VII. iii. 10. ἄγειν V. v. 12. X. i. 2. ἄγωμεν X. vii. 6. ἄγοντες IX. viii. 4. ἄγουσα II. vi. 9. ἄγεται III. xi. 6. VII. iii. 2. vii. 3. ἄγοντα VII. vii. 8. ix. 2. ἀγομένων VII. xii. 3. ἦχθαι I. iv. 6. II. iii. 8. ἄγεσθαι III. xi. 3. VII. ix. 6.
ἀγωγῆς X. ix. 8. ἀγωγὴν X. vii. 3.
ἀγῶσι III. viii. 8.
ἀγωνίαν III. v. 11.
ἀγωνιζόμενοι I. viii. 9. X. v. 4.
ἀγωνισταὶ IX. v. 2. ἀγωνιστῶν IX. v. 4.
ἀδαὴς III. vi. 10.
ἄδειαν V. iv. 13.
ἀδέκαστοι II. ix. 6.
ἀδελφικὴ VIII. x. 6. xii. 4. ἀδελφικῇ VIII. xii. 6.
ἀδελφῷ VIII. ix. 3. ἀδελφοὶ VIII. xii. 3. ἀδελφὸν VIII. x. 6. xi. 5. ἀδελφοῖς VIII. ix. 2. IX. ii. 7. ἀδελφοὺς IX. ii. 9.
ἀδεσπότοις VIII. x. 6.
ἄδηλον IV. i. 8. vi. 3. VI. viii. 4, 6. IX. ii. 3, 6. viii. 5, 6. x. 4. X. viii. 13. ἄδηλοι X. viii. 4. ἀδήλους III. iii. 10.
ἀδιάβλητος VIII. iv. 3. ἀδιάβλητον VIII. vi. 7.
ἀδιαφόρους X. v. 8.
ἀδικεῖν II. vi. 19. IV. iii. 15. V. v. 17, 18. vi. 4. viii. 4. ix. 1, 3, 4, 8, 9, 14, 16. xi. 1, 5, 6, 7. ἀδικεῖ V. ii. 2. iv. 3. vi. 2. viii. 1, 11. ix. 8, 9, 10, 11, 12. xi. 2, 4, 6. ἀδικήσαι V. xi. 4. VIII. iv. 3. ἀδικοῦσι V. i. 3. viii. 8. VII. viii. 3. ἀδικῶν V. iii. 14. vi. 1. viii. 11. xi. 4. ἀδικοῦντος V. ix. 3. ἀδικοῦντι V. xi. 3. ἀδικοῦντα III. v. 13. V. vi. 1. ix. 7. ἀδικεῖται V. v. 3. ix. 3, 6, 7, 9. xi. 3. ἀδικοῖτο V. ix. 4. ἀδικεῖσθαι IV. i. 26. V. v. 17, 18. viii. 10. ix. 1, 3, 5, 7, 8. xi. 5, 6, 7, 8. ἀδικούμενος V. v. 14.
ἀδίκημα V. vii. 7. viii. 2, 8. ἀδικήματος V. v. 18. vii. 7. ix. 13. ἀδικήματα V. ii. 5. vi. 1. viii. 8, 11. ἀδικημάτων V. xi. 6.
ἀδικία V. i. 7, 19. ii. 3, 6, 8, 9, 10. v. 17, 18. vi. 4, 8, 9. xi. 9. ἀδικίας V. i. 1, 3. ii. 1, 9. v. 19. xi. 7. ἀδικίαν IV. vii. 7. V. ii. 2, 5. vi. 1. VII. vii. 7. ἀδικίᾳ V. viii. 10.
ἄδικος III. v. 13, 14. V. i. 8, 9, 10, 12. ii. 4. iii. 1. vi. 1, 2. viii. 8, 11. ix. 12. xi. 4. VII. x. 3. ἄδικον III. v. 13. V. i. 7, 8. ii. 3, 8, 9, 10. iii. 1, 3, 14. iv. 2, 3, 4. v. 17. vi. 1, 9. vii. 7. viii. 2. ix. 3, 10. xi. 4. VII. vi. 7. ἀδίκου V. ii. 3, 9. v. 18, 19. vi. 4. ἀδίκῳ III. v. 14. ἄδικοι II. i, 7. III. i. 14. V. viii. 8. VII. viii. 3. ἀδίκων V. viii. 1, 4. ix. 3. ἀδίκοις V. viii. 1. ἄδικα V. i, 3. viii. 4. ix. 3, 6, 11, 15. VIII. ix. 3. ἀδίκους III. v. 10. IV. i. 42. ἀδικωτέρα VII. vi. 3, 4. ἀδίκως V. ix. 12, 13.
ἀδιορίστου III. iii. 10. X. v. 6.
ἀδολέσχας III. x. 2.
ἀδοξίας IV. ix. 1. ἀδοξίαν III. vi. 3.
ἀδυναμία IV. i. 37.
ἀδυνατεῖ IX. ix. 1. X. iv. 9. ἀδυνατοῦσι V. i. 15. X. v. 3. ἀδυνατεῖν X. x. 3. ἀδυνατοῦντα VIII. xiii. 9. ἀδυνατοῦντες X. vi. 6.
ἀδύνατον I. viii. 15. V. v. 15. ix. 3. x. 6. xi. 4. VI. xii. 10. ἀδυνάτῳ III. iii. 13. ἀδύνατα III. ii. 10. ἀδυνάτων III. ii. 7. VI. v. 3. vii. 6.
ἀεὶ I. vii. 8, 11. II. ii. 23. vi. 18. III. iii. 4, 8, 16. IV. iii. 14. iv. 4. V. i. 10. ii. 5. iv. 2. v. 14. ix. 10. xi. 4. VI. vii. 4. x. 1. VII. iii. 2. vii. 7. xiv. 5, 6. VIII. x. 3. xiii. 4. xiv. 4. IX. ii. 4, 9. viii. 5. X. iii. 3. iv. 7. vi. 7.
ᾄσειε IX. i. 4.
ἀηδὴς II. vii. 13. ἀηδεῖς X. v. 5. ἀηδίας IX. xi. 6. ἀηδῶς IV. iii. 25.
ἀθανασίας III. ii. 7.
ἀθανατίζειν X. vii. 8.
Ἀθηναίους IV. iii. 25.
ἀθλητὴν III. ii. 8. ἀθληταὶ III. viii. 8.
ἄθλιος I. x. 4. 13. 14. VII. vii. 5. ἀθλίῳ VII. vii. 5. ἄθλιον I. x. 8. IX. iv. 10. ἀθλίων I. xiii. 12. ἀθλίως I. ix. 14.
ἀθλοθετῶν I. iv. 5.
ἆθλον I. ix. 3. IV. iii. 10, 15.
ἀθρόον VII. vii. 6.
αἶγα III. x. 7. V. vii. 1.

αἰδεῖσθαι IV. ix. 7. αἰδούμενοι II. vii. 14.

αἰδήμων II. vii. 14. III. vi. 3. αἰδήμονα IV. ix. 3.

ἀΐδιον I. v. 6. VI. iii. 2. ἀΐδια III. ii. 10. VI. iii. 2. ἀϊδίων III. iii. 3.

αἰδὼς II. vii. 14. IV. ix. 6, 7. αἰδοῦς IV. ix. 1, 3. αἰδοῖ X. ix. 4. αἰδῶ III. viii. 3, 4.

αἰκία V. ii. 13.

αἷμα III. viii. 10. VIII. xii. 3.

αἱρεῖν II. iii. 7. αἱρέσεις II. iii. 7.

αἱρετὸς IX. ix. 7. αἱρετὴ VIII. viii. 2. IX. xi. 6. xii. 1. X. iii. 13. αἱρετὸν I. vii. 4, 8. III. ii. 17. xii. 1. V. iii. 16. VIII. v. 4. IX. vii. 4. ix. 9, 10. X. ii. 1, 2. iv. 10. αἱρετοῦ V. v. 17. αἱρετῷ X. ii. 2. αἱρεταὶ III. i. 6. VII. xii. 1. xiv. 1. X. iii. 9. 13. vi. 2, 3. vii. 7. αἱρετὰ III. i. 10. IV. iii. 18. VII. iv. 2, 5. αἱρετῶν I. vii. 4. VII. iv. 5. IX. ix. 10. X. v. 6. vi. 2, 3. αἱρετὰς VI. xii. 4. IX. vi. 2. αἱρετώτερος III. viii. 9. VI. v. 7. αἱρετώτερον I. vii. 8. VII. vii. 4. IX. xi. 1. X. ii. 2, 3. αἱρετωτέραν I. vii. 8. αἱρετώτεραι VII. xiv. 3. αἱρετωτέρα I. i. 4. αἱρετωτέρας X. vi. 4. αἱρετώτατος IX. ix. 9. αἱρετωτάτη X. vi. 5. αἱρετώτατον IX. xii. 1. αἱρετωτάτην I. vii. 8. VII. xiii. 2.

αἱρεῖται I. vii. 5. II. vi. 8. III. vii. 13. ix. 4. V. i. 10. VII. ix. 1. IX. iv. 4. viii. 8. X. vii. 6. αἱροῦνται III. iv. 6. IX. iv. 8. viii. 9. xii. 1, 2. X. vi. 3. αἱροῖτο X. vii. 9. αἱρούμεθα I. ii. 1. vii. 3, 5. X. ii. 2. iv. 11. vi. 6. ἑλοίμεθα I. vii. 5. X. iii. 12. ἕλοιτο III. i. 6. IV. i. 14. VIII. i. 1. IX. viii. 9. ix. 3. X. iii. 12. ἑλέσθαι X. v. 8. αἱρεῖσθαι II. vii. 16. III. ii. 13. xi. 6. V. i. 9. VI. i. 1. v. 6. VIII. viii. 2. αἱρούμενος III. iv. 2. IV. vi. 8. IX. viii. 10. αἱρούμενον IX. iv. 1. αἱρούμενοι X. ii. 5. αἱρήσεται III. v. 17. αἱρετέον III. i. 9, 10.

αἴρειν VII. vii. 5.

αἰσθάνεται IX. ix. 9. αἰσθανόμεθα VI. viii. 9. IX. ix. 9. αἰσθάνεσθαι IV. v. 6. IX. ix. 7, 9, 10. xi. 4. αἰσθανομένῳ I. x. 3. αἰσθανόμενον IX. ix. 9. αἰσθανόμενοι X. viii. 11. ᾔσθετο III. x. 7.

αἴσθησις VI. ii. 1, 2. viii. 9. VII. iii. 9. vi. 1. IX. ix. 10. X. iv. 6, 7. v. 7. αἰσθήσεων III. iii. 16. IX. ix. 7. X. iv. 5. αἰσθήσει IV. v. 13. VII. v. 6. αἴσθησιν III. x. 4. VI. ii. 2. xi. 4. VIII. xii. 2. IX. xii. 1. X. i. 3. iv. 5. 7. αἰσθήσεις X. iii. 7. v. 2. αἰσθήσεων II. i. 4. III. x. 10.

αἰσθητικὴ I. vii. 12. αἰσθητικῆς VII. iii. 13.

αἰσθητὴ VII. xi. 4. αἰσθητὸν X. iv. 5, 6, 8. αἰσθητοῦ, VII. iii. 13. X. iv. 7. αἰσθητὴν VII. xii. 3.

αἰσχροκέρδεια IV. i. 41.

αἰσχροκερδεῖς IV. i. 43.

αἰσχρολογία IV. viii. 5.

αἰσχροπραγεῖν IV. i. 8.

αἰσχρὸν III. i. 4, 7. v. 2. vi. 3. vii. 13. viii. 4. 9, 14. ix. 4. IV. i. 39. vii. 7. VII. vii. 3. VIII. vii. 6. X. ix. 4, 8. αἰσχρὰ III. i. 9. 23. v. 3. IV. i. 7. iii. 15. ix. 5, 7. VII. vi. 1. αἰσχραὶ VII. xi. 5. αἰσχροῦ II. iii. 7. III. viii. 3, 9. αἰσχρῷ IX. viii. 1. αἰσχρὰν VII. ix. 4. αἰσχρὰς X. v. 11. αἴσχιον VII. vi. 1, 3. 5. αἴσχιστα III. i. 7. αἰσχίστων X. iii. 12. αἰσχρῶν III. i. 11. xii. 6. IV. i. 39. ix. 5. X. iii. 10. v. 6. αἰσχροῖς III. v. 15.

Αἰσχύλος III. i. 17.

αἰσχύνη IV. ix. 4.

αἰσχύνεται IV. iii. 24. αἰσχύνοιτο IV. ix. 7. αἰσχύνεσθαι IV. ix. 6, 7. αἰσχυνόμενοι IV. ix. 2. αἰσχυντέον IV. ix. 5.

αἰσχυντηλὸς IV. ix. 3.

αἰτητικὸς IV. i. 16.

αἰτία II. viii. 8. III. i. 10, 15. VII. v. 4. X. iv. 6. αἰτίας II. viii. 7. V. viii. 7. VI. xi. 6. X. ix. 6, 23. αἰτίαν I. vii. 20. ix. 6, 10. II. vii. 9. III. iii. 4. IV. i. 14. VII. iii. 9. αἰτίαι III. iii. 7.

αἴτιος III. v. 8, 17. VII. xi. 2. IX. xi. 4. αἰτίου III. i. 23. αἰτίῳ I. x. 10. αἴτιον I. iv. 4. xii. 8. xiii. 11. III. iii. 11. v. 8. V. x. 4, 6. VI. viii. 5. VII. xiv. 3. IX. vii. 2, 4. viii. 10. X. iii. 2. αἰτίοις IX. ii. 8. αἴτιοι III. v. 7, 10. VIII. xii. 5.

αἰτιᾶσθαι III. i. 11. αἰτιῷτο IX. iii. 2.

αἰφνιδίοις III. viii. 15.

ἄκαρπα IV. iii. 33.

ἀκίνδυνοι III. xii. 2.

ἀκινησίας VII. xiv. 8.

ἀκίνητον V. vii. 2. ἀκινήτων VI. x. 1, 4.

ἄκλητον IX. xi. 6.

ἀκμῇ VIII. i. 2. iii. 4.

ἀκμαίους X. iv. 8.

ἀκμάζων III. xi. 1.

ἀκοὴ X. v. 7. **ἀκοῇ** X. iv. 10. **ἀκοὴν** III. x. 4.

ἀκολασία II. vii. 3. viii. 6, 8. III. x. 1, 8, 10. xi. 5. xii. 1. VII. v. 5, 9. vi. 6. vii. 1. **ἀκολασίας** III. v. 15. xii. 5. IV. i. 35. **ἀκολασίᾳ** VII. iii. 2. iv. 6. ix. 5. **ἀκολασίαν** II. viii. 8. IV. i. 3. V. ii. 5. VII. iv. 2. v. 8.

ἀκολασταίνειν II. vi. 19. **ἀκολασταίνοντα** III. v. 13.

ἀκόλαστος II. ii. 7. iii. 1. viii. 2. III. xi. 5, 6. xii. 4. V. ii. 4. VII. iii, 2. vii. 2, 3, 7. viii. 1. ix. 4, 7. xii. 7. xiv. 1. **ἀκολάστου** III. x. 6. VII. viii. 5. **ἀκολάστῳ** III. v. 14. xii. 4. **ἀκόλαστον** II. viii. 2. III. v. 13. VII. i. 6. iv. 3. 4. **ἀκόλαστοι** II. i. 7. III. x. 2, 3, 5. 9. xi. 4. IV. i. 35. VII. xiv. 6. **ἀκόλαστα** VII. vi. 6. **ἀκολάστους** III. v. 10. x. 2, 4, 5.

ἀκολουθεῖ III. vii. 10. V. i. 6. VII. i. 6. vi. 1. IX. v. 1. **ἀκολουθοῦσι** II. i. 8. V. x. 1. **ἠκολούθησε** VII. ix. 6. **ἀκολουθήσουσι** VII. xii. 1. VIII. ix. 6. **ἀκολουθεῖν** VI. iii. 2. xi. 6. VII. ii. 6. vi. 2.

ἀκολουθητικὸς I. iii. 6. **ἀκολουθητικοὶ** VII. vii. 8.

ἀκόλουθον IV. ii. 1.

ἀκούσιον III. i. 1, 6, 13. 15. V. v. 5. viii. 3. ix. 1, 2. **ἀκουσίου** III. i. 15, 19. 20. ii. 1. **ἀκουσίῳ** V. viii. 2. **ἀκούσια** III. i. 3, 6, 10, 21, 24. 25. 26, 27. V. ii. 13. **ἀκουσίων** V. ii. 13. viii. 12. **ἀκουσίους** III. i. 1. V. iv. 1. **ἀκουσίοις** III. i. 16, 23.

ἀκούσματα X. iv. 7.

ἀκούει IV. iii. 25. IX. ix. 9. **ἀκούουσι** II. iv. 6. **ἀκούων** I. iv. 7. IV. viii. 8. IX. ix. 9. **ἀκούοντα** IV. viii. 7. **ἀκούειν** IV. viii. 1, 5. VII. iii. 12. vi. 1. xiv. 5. **ἀκουσάτω** I. iv. 7. **ἀκοῦσαι** II. i. 4. IV. viii. 10. VII. vi. 1. **ἀκούσας** VII. vi. 1. **ἀκούσειε** X. ix. 7. **ἀκούσονται** I. iii. 6. IV. viii. 8. **ἀκουσόμενον** I. iv. 6. **ἀκουστικὸν** I. xiii. 9.

ἀκρασία VII. i. 1, 6. ii. 7, 11. iii. 2. iv. 2. 6. v. 5. 8, 9. vi. 1, 3. 4. 5. viii 1, 3. x. 4. 5. **ἀκρασίας** VII. i. 4. ii. 1, 9. 11. v. 9. vii. 8. viii. 1. xiv. 9. **ἀκρασίᾳ** VII. ix. 5. **ἀκρασίαν** V. ix. 5. VII. ii. 9. 10. iv. 6. vii. 6, 8. ix. 4. **ἀκρασιῶν** VII. x. 4.

ἀκρατεύεται VII. ii. 1. **ἀκρατεύονται** VII. iii. 3. x. 4. **ἀκρατεύεσθαι** VII. iii. 10, 14. **ἀκρατευόμενοι** VII. ii. 2. **ἀκρατευσαμένους** VII. iii. 8.

ἀκρατὴς III. ii. 4. V. ix. 4, 6. VI. ix. 4. VII. i. 6. ii. 5. 10, 11. iii. 1, 2. 12. iv. 1, 3. vi. 1. vii. 1, 8. viii. 1, 2, 5. ix. 1. 4. 5, 7. x. 2, 3. IX. viii. 6. **ἀκρατοῦς** I. xiii. 15. VII. vii. 3. ix. 5. **ἀκρατεῖ** VII. vii. 4. ix. 3. **ἀκρατῆ** VII. i. 6. ii. 3. iii. 11. iv. 4, 6. v. 5. x. 1, 2. **ἀκρατεῖς** IV. i. 3. VII. i. 7. iii. 7. iv. 2. v. 4. viii. 3. x. 2, 4. IX. iv. 8. **ἀκρατῶν** I. xiii. 15. **ἀκρατέσι** I. iii. 7.

ἀκράτων III. v. 14.

ἀκριβὴς VIII. vii. 5. **ἀκριβὲς** I. iii. 1. 4. II. ii. 4. **ἀκριβοῦς** III. iii. 8. **ἀκριβέστερον** II. vii. 5. **ἀκριβεστέρα** II. vi. 9. **ἀκριβεστάτη** VI. vii. 2. **ἀκριβεστάτοις** VI. vii. 1.

ἀκρίβειαν I. vii. 18. **ἀκρίβειας** X. iv. 3.

ἀκριβοδίκαιος V. x. 8.

ἀκριβολογία IV. ii. 8. **ἀκριβολογεῖσθαι** VI. iii. 2.

ἀκριβῶς II. ii. 3. VII. iii. 3. IX. ii. 2. X. ix. 16.

ἀκροάματα X. iii. 7.

ἀκροατὴς I. iii. 5. **ἀκροατοῦ** I. iii. 8. X. ix. 6.

ἄκρος IV. iii. 8. **ἄκρων** II. vi. 20. viii. 7. V. v. 12. **ἄκρα** II. vii. 8. viii. 3. IV. iv. 6. **ἄκραι** II. viii. 1. **ἄκρον** II. vi. 5. vii. 10, ix. 3. IV. v. 1. V. v. 17. **ἄκρα** II. vii. 11. IV. iv. 4. vi. 9. **ἄκροις** II. viii. 4. 5. **ἄκρους** II. viii. 1. **ἀκρότατον** I. iv. 1.

ἀκρότης II. vi. 17.

ἄκρως II. ix. 4.

ἀκροχειριζόμενοι III. i. 17.

ἀκρόχολοι IV. v. 9.

ἄκυρα VII. ix. 3.

ἀλαζονεία II. vii. 12. IV. vii. 15. **ἀλαζονείας** IV. vii. 1.

ἀλαζονευόμενοι IV. vii. 13. **ἀλαζονεύονται** IV. vii. 13.

ἀλαζονικὸν IV. vii. 15.

ἀλαζὼν II. vii. 12. III. vii. 8. IV. vii. 2. 6, 11. 12, 17.

ἅλας VIII. iii. 8.

ἀλγεῖν III. v. 7. **ἀλγεῖ** IX. iv. 9. **ἀλγοῦσι** III. viii. 12.

ἀλγεινὸν III. ix. 3.

ἀλγηδόνος III. viii. 11, 12.

ἀλέας VII. iv. 3.

ἀλείπτης II. vi. 7.

ἀλήθεια II. vii. 12. VI. ii. 2, 3, 6. ix. 3. ἀληθείας I. vi. 1. IV. iii. 28. VI. ii. 1. ἀληθείᾳ IV. iii. 16. V. v. 11, 15. IX. ii. 5. ἀλήθειαν I. vi. 1. xiii. 2. III. iv. 4. v. 17. IV. iii. 20. viii. 12. ix. 5. X. ii. 1.

ἀληθεύει IV. vii. 7. VI. iii. 1. ἀληθεύομεν VI. vi. 2. ἀληθεύουσι IX. viii. 3. ix. 4. ἀληθεύειν VI. vii. 3. VII. ix. 4. ἀληθεύων IV. vii. 8. ἀληθεύοντος IV. vii. 7. ἀληθεύοντας X. ii. 5. ἀληθευόντων IV. vii. 1. ἀληθεύσει IV. vii. 8. VI. ii. 6.

ἀληθευτικὸς IV. vii. 1. ἀληθευτικῷ IV. vii. 17. ἀληθευτικοῦ IV. vii. 6.

ἀληθὴς II. vii. 13. ix. 7. ἀληθὲς II. vii. 11, 12. IV. vii. 6. VI. i. 2. VII. xiv. 3. IX. viii. 9. ix. 5. X. viii. 12. ἀληθεῖς X. i. 2. ἀληθοῦς IV. vii. 9. VI. iv. 3, 6. xi. 1. ἀληθεῖ VII. ix. 1. xiv. 2. X. vii. 2. ἀληθῆ III. v. 17. VI. ii. 2. v. 6. VII. iii. 3.

ἀληθινὴ III. v. 17. ἀληθινώτερον II. vii. 1.

ἀληθῶς IV. iii. 14, 22. V. ix. 1. VI. i. 3. VIII. iv. 3. IX. x. 6. X. ix. 3, 4, 6.

ἀλήτῃ IV. iii. 3.

ἄλις I. v. 6. xiii. 14. IX. xi. 5. X. i. 4.

ἁλίσκω. ἁλισκόντι IX. ii. 4.

ἀλκὴ III. vi. 12.

'Αλκμαίωνα III. i. 8.

ἀλλὰ καὶ I. vii. 6. viii. 8. xiii. 6. II. ii. 8. iv. 3, 4. vi. 1. vii. 1. III. vi. 11. VI. xiii. 6. VII. iv. 2. x. 2. xiii. 7. xiv. 3, 8. VIII. i. 3, 5. iv. 1. xii. 7. IX. i. 8. X. i. 4. iv. 3. viii. 8. ix. 21.

ἀλλὰ μὲν VI. xiii. 8.

ἀλλὰ μὴν I. vi. 6. viii. 13. III. ii. 7. V. ii. 2. VI. v. 7, 8. ix. 2, 3. VII. ii. 4, 6. iii. 7. xiii. 1. X. viii. 7.

ἀλλὰ μὴ III. i. 11.

ἀλλ' ἢ IV. iii. 27, 29. V. ii. 5. viii. 1, 4. ix. 15. VII. vi. 6.

ἀλλαγὴ V. v. 10, 11, 14. 15. 16. ἀλλαγῆς V. iv. 13. v. 14, 15.

ἀλλακτικαῖς V. v. 6.

ἀλλάττονται V. v. 13. ἀλλάξονται V. v. 13.

ἀλλήλων II. vii. 11. viii. 4, 5. V. v. 11. VI. iv. 2. xiii. 6. VII. vii. 3. VIII. iii. 1, 4. iv. 1, 2. v. 3. vii. 1. viii. 5. x. 4. IX. xii. 3. X. iv. 2, 4. v. 2. 7. ἀλλήλοις II. viii. 4. VII. v. 2. VIII. i. 6. ii. 4. iii. 1, 6. iv. 1, 4. v. 1. vi. 1, 4. 7. viii. 6. ix. 2. xii. 3. 7. xiii. 4. IX. vi. 3. x. 4. xii. 3. ἀλλήλαις II. viii. 1. V. iv. 12. ἀλλήλους V. vi. 4. VIII. iii. 1. 9. iv. 2, 3. viii. 5. xii. 3, 6. xiii. 2. IX. iii. 4. vi. 1, 4. xii. 3. X. viii. 1. ἀλλήλας II. vii. 11. VII. x. 5. ἄλληλα II. viii. 4. V. iv. 2. xi. 9. VII. xii. 2. VIII. i. 3. X. iv. 8.

ἄλλος I. vi. 8. IV. i. 14. VII. viii. 5. IX. iv. 4, 5. X. ix. 15. ἄλλη I. xiii. 15. V. ii. 3, 6. ἄλλο I. i. 5. iv. 3. vi. 10, 12. vii. 2, 4, 5. ix. 2, 9. xi. 6. xiii. 15. II. i. 2. ix. 8. III. iv. 3. v. 7. ix. 6. IV. vi. 9. viii. 7. V. iv. 2. x. 1, 2. xi. 4. VI. v. 3. vii. 1, 2, 9. ix. 1. VII. ii. 1. v. 9. vi. 6. VIII. iii. 3. viii. 6. xiii. 7. IX. iv. 5. viii. 6. xi. 2. X. ii. 3. iii. 4. vi. 2. vii. 1. ἄλλου I. iv. 7. v. 8. II. iv. 2. V. ix. 5. VI. x. 3. xi. 7. VIII. vii. 4. X. vii. 9. ἄλλῳ I. vi. 13. ix. 3. III. v. 15. IV. vii. 7. VII. xii. 6. ἄλλῳ I. vi. 12. vii. 1. III. iv. 3. IV. viii. 7. V. i. 17. v. 1, 18. ἄλλῃ I. vii. 2. ἄλλον I. vi. 8. x. 1. IV. iii. 29. viii. 12. V. i. 13. ii. 10. v. 17, 18. xi. 2. VI. xiii. 1. VII. iii. 7. VIII. ix. 3. IX. viii. 1. ἄλλων I. xiii. 11. III. iii. 4. IV. i. 13. 35. VII. i. 1. X. vii. 8. viii. 1. ἄλλοι I. iv. 3. II. ix. 4. III. viii. 6. IV. iii. 28, 31. VIII. i. 6. vi. 5. IX. xii. 2. ἄλλαι I. i. 4. vii. 21. II. ii. 1. vii. 6, 11. VIII. ix. 5. ἄλλα I. ii. 1. xii. 5. II. iii. 5. iv. 3. v. 2. ix. 4. III. ii. 2. xii. 3. IV. i. 22. V. viii. 8. x. 1. VI. iii. 4. vii. 4. VII. ii. 10. VIII. iv. 3. IX. iv. 8. x. v. 4. vii. 7. viii. 1. ἄλλην I. ii. 7. viii. 12. xii. 2. II. i. 4. ii. 7, 8. vii. 11. viii. 3. III. iii. 15. iv. 4. v. 16. xi. 6, 8. IV. i. 21. iii. 21. viii. 10. V. ii. 12. iv. 12. v. 9. 18. vi. 2. vii. 4. VI. i. 1. vii. 4. VII. i. 5. ii. 4. iii. 1. VIII. vii. 2. ix. 2. xiii. 10. IX. 9. X. iii. 10. v. 2, 4. vii. 4. viii. 4, 8. ix. 18. ἄλλοις I. vii. 19. viii. 6. III. v. 9. viii. 6. x. 7. V. v. 13. VI. vii. 7. xii. 2. VIII. vi. 7. viii. 7. ix. 2. xii. 7. X. iv. 3. v. 4. ἄλλαις VIII. ix. 1. X. ix. 18. ἄλλους I. x. 13. III. x. 6. IX. viii. 7. ix. 5. X. ix. 18. ἄλλας II. ii. 2. iv. 3. III. v. 6. x. 2. IV. iv. 6. V. i. 14. ii. 1. VI. i. 2. VII. ii. 5. xiv. 5. X. iii. 2.

ἄλλως I. vii. 21. viii. 9. ix. 1. II. ii. 2.

iii. 5. IV. i. 31. V. vii. 1, 4. VI. i. 5. 6. iii. 2. iv. 1, 6. v. 3. 8. vi. 1, 2. vii. 2, 6. VII. ii. 6. X. ix. 2.
ἄλλως τε καὶ I. vi. 1. x. 2. IV. iii. 30. IX. xi. 3. X. i. 2. ix. 8.
ἄλλοθι II. vii. 16.
ἄλλοτε III. iii. 5. VIII. iii. 3. IX. iv. 5.
ἀλλοιωθέντα IX. iii. 3.
ἀλλοιότερον IX. iii. 5.
ἀλλότριαι VII. xii. 5. X. v. 5. ἀλλότριον I. xiii. 14. IV. i. 9. 17. V. vi. 6. ἀλλοτρίων IV. i. 39. ἀλλοτριώτερα VIII. viii. 7. ἀλλοτριώτεραι VIII. xii. 4.
ἀλόγιστοι VII. v. 6.
ἄλογον I. xiii. 9. 18. III. v. 13. V. xi. 9. VI. i. 5. ἀλόγου I. xiii. 11. ἀλόγῳ IX. viii. 4. ἄλογα III. i. 27. X. ii. 1. ἀλόγων III. ii. 3. x. 1. ἀλόγως IV. i. 21. IX. viii. 2.
Ἀλόπῃ VII. vii. 6.
ἀλόχου X. ix. 13.
ἄλσει X. iv. 3.
ἀλυπίᾳ IX. xi. 4. ἀλυπίαν VII. xii. 7.
ἄλυπος III. xii. 3. ἄλυπον IV. i. 13. VII. xii. 4, 7. ἄλυποι IV. vi. 1. X. iii. 7.
ἀλύπως IV. i. 13.
ἀλυσιτελὲς VIII. xiv. 4.
ἅμα III. v. 23. vi. 12. IV. i. 3, 24. 34. V. viii. 2. xi. 4, 5. VI. ix. 3. xiii. 6. VII. iii. 9. x. 1. VIII. iii. 5. iv. 2. vi. 2, 6. ix. 3. xiii. 3. xiv. 3, 4. IX. iv. 10. vii. 5. x. 5. X. v. 4.
ἀμαθὴς VIII. viii. 6. ἀμαθεῖς VII. ix. 3.
ἁμαρτάνουσι II. i. 5. III. xi. 3. 4. IV. i. 44. V. viii. 12. VII. vi. 1. ἁμαρτάνοντες V. viii. 8. ἁμαρτάνων VI. v. 7. ἡμάρτανεν VI. xiii. 3. ἥμαρτεν V. x. 5. ἁμαρτάνειν II. vi. 14, 18. ix. 5. IV. v. 4. ix. 3. VIII. viii. 5. ἁμαρτάνεται II. vi. 12, 20. ἁμαρτανόμενον V. x. 4. ἁμαρτησόμεθα II. ix. 6. ἁμαρτηθέντα III. i. 26. ἁμαρτάνει IV. v. 13. V. viii. 7. VI. ix. 3. ἡμαρτημένοι IV. iii. 35. ἡμαρτημένη VIII. x. 4.
ἁμάρτημα V. viii. 7. x. 4. ἁμαρτήματος V. x. 6. ἁμαρτήματα V. viii. 6.
ἁμαρτητικὸς II. iii. 7.
ἁμαρτία VI. viii. 7. ix. 3. VII. iv. 2. ἁμαρτίας III. xii. 5. ἁμαρτίαν III. i. 14. ἁμαρτιῶν III. vii. 4.
ἀμαυροῦται X. iv. 9.
ἀμείψασθαι IX. ii. 5.
ἀμείνων II. vi. 9. VIII. x. 5. xiii. 1. ἄμεινον III. ii. 14. IX. x. 4. X. vii. 9. ix. 19. ἀμείνους VIII. xi. 4. ἀμείνω VIII. vii. 2.
ἀμέλειαν III. v. 15.
ἀμελήσει IV. i. 17. ἀμελοῦντες X. vi. 3.
ἀμετακίνητος II. iv. 3.
ἀμεταμέλητος VII. vii. 2. IX. iv. 5.
ἀμήχανον VII. iii. 7.
ἀμιγεῖς X. iii. 2.
ἁμιλλωμένων VIII. xiii. 2. IX. viii. 7.
ἀμνήμονες IX. vii. 1.
ἀμοιβὴ IX. i. 1, 9. ἀμοιβὴν IX. i. 7.
ἀμύνεται VIII. xiii. 2.
ἀμυντικὸς IV. v. 6.
ἀμφιδεξίους V. vii. 4.
ἀμφίλογον VIII. xiii. 6.
ἀμφισβητεῖ VII. ii. 2. ἀμφισβητοῦσιν I. iv. 2. ἀμφισβητῶσιν V. iv. 7. ἀμφισβητεῖν IV. iv. 4. ἀμφισβητεῖται V. viii. 9. IX. ix. 1. X. viii. 5. ἀμφισβητητέον III. v. 5.
ἀμφισβήτησις I. vi. 8. ἀμφισβήτησιν I. x. 3. III. i. 4. V. viii. 10. VIII. xiii. 10. X. i. 2. v. 6.
ἀμφότεροι IV. i. 43. vii. 6. V. v. 13. VII. ix. 7. ἀμφότερα II. vi. 10. IV. i. 24. iv. 5. ix. 2. VI. xi. 4. VIII. viii. 3. ἀμφοτέροις V. v. 12. VII. iii. 6. ix. 5. ἀμφοτέρων V. ix. 3. VI. ii. 6.
ἄμφω II. vi. 13. viii. 4. III. i. 26. viii. 13. ix. 2. IV. i. 24. iii. 20. iv. 1. V. ii. 6. vii. 4. x. 1. xi. 7. VI. vii. 7. VII. xii. 4. VIII. v. 4. vi. 5. x. 2. IX. ii. 1. ix. 5. X. ii. 5. ἀμφοῖν I. vi. 1. V. x. 2. VI. ii. 6. VII. iii. 2. VIII. vi. 4, 7. xii. 7. IX. i. 3, 8. vi. 2. viii. 2. xi. 1, 6. X. ii. 5. viii. 4, 5.
ἂν cum infin. III. ii. 8. cum indic. V. xi. 4.
ἂν pro ἐὰν III. viii. 11. V. viii. 2, 10. 11. VI. xii. 9. VII. vi. 1. VIII. ii. 3. viii. 2.
ἀνὰ III. viii. 10.
ἀναβολὴν VIII. xiii. 6.
ἀναγκάζειν III. i. 11. ἀναγκάζουσι III. viii. 4. ἀναγκαζόμενον V. viii. 4. ἀναγκαζομένους III. viii. 4. ἀναγκάζονται III. i. 9. IV. i. 34. IX. i. 7. ἀναγκάσαντα III. i. 8. ἀναγκασθῶσι IV. i. 39. ἀναγκασθῆναι III. i. 8. ἀναγκασθέντας III. i. 9.

ἀναγκαστικὴν X. ix. 12.
ἀναγκαῖον I. ix. 7. II. ii. 1. iii. 9. III. i. 1. IV. i. 17. ii. 10. iii. 28. xii. 4. VII. vi. 2. xi. 2. xiii. 2. VIII. i. 5. IX. i. 8. X. ix. 12. ἀναγκαίῳ IX. ii. 2, 5. ἀναγκαῖαι VII. vii. 2. xiv. 2. X. vi. 2. ἀναγκαίας VII. xiv. 2. ἀναγκαία IV. viii. 1. V. viii. 8. VII. iv. 2. ἀναγκαίων IV. iii. 32. VII. iv. 4. X. vii. 4. viii. 4. ἀναγκαιότερον VIII. xii. 7. IX. xi. 1. ἀναγκαιότατον VIII. i. 1.
ἀνάγκη III. iii. 7. V. i. 5. iii. 4. viii. 10. x. 3. xi. 4. VI. iv. 6. v. 6. VII. iii. 9. vii. 2. xii. 3. xiii. 1. ἀνάγκης I. viii. 9. III. iii. 4. VI. iii. 2. iv. 4. v. 3. vi. 1. X. iii. 12. ἀνάγκῃ V. iii. 5. X. ix. 6. ἀνάγκην III. viii. 5.
ἀναγράψαι I. vii. 17.
ἀνάγεται IX. ix. 7. ἀναγάγῃ III. iii. 17. ἀναγαγεῖν III. v. 6.
ἀναθήματα IV. ii. 11. ἀναθήμασι IV. ii. 15.
ἀναιρεῖν I. vi. 1. ἀναιρεῖ X. ii. 3. ἀναιροῦσι IX. iv. 8. ἀναιρῶν X. ii. 4. ἀνελεῖν VII. ii. 12. ἀνῃροῦντο V. iv. 12. v. 9.
ἀναισθησία II. viii. 6. III. xi. 8.
ἀναίσθητος II. ii. 7. vii. 3. viii. 2. ἀναισθήτου III. v. 12. ἀναίσθητον II. viii. 2.
ἀναισχυντία II. vi. 18. IV. ix. 7.
ἀναίσχυντος II. vii. 14. III. vi. 3.
ἀνακυκλεῖσθαι I. x. 7.
ἀναλαβόντες I. iv. 1. III. v. 23. ἀναλαβοῦσι X. iv. 1. vi. 1. ἀναλαβεῖν III. v. 14.
ἀναλγησίαν I. x. 12.
ἀνάλγητος III. vii. 7.
ἀναλίσκει IV. ii. 20. ἀναλίσκειν IV. i. 22, 25, 34. ii. 20. ἀναλίσκοντες IV. i. 35. ἀνάλωσι IV. i. 27. ἀναλώσαι IV. ii. 21. ἀναλῶσαι IV. ii. 20. ἀναλώσας IV. i. 22. ii. 21.
ἀναλογία V. iii. 8, 14. ἀναλογίας V. v. 12. ἀναλογίαν I. vi. 12. V. iii. 13. iv. 2, 3, 9. v. 6, 8, 18. vi. 4.
ἀνάλογον II. i. 6. viii. 3. V. iii. 8, 12, 14. iv. 2. v. 6, 18. vi. 6. viii. 11. VII. iv. 6. VIII. vi. 6. vii. 2. xii. 7. IX. i. 1. ἀνάλογα V. iii. 9.
ἀναλύειν III. iii. 11.
ἀναλύσει III. iii. 12.
ἀναλυτικοῖς VI. iii. 3, 4.
ἀναμάρτητον VIII. i. 2.
ἀναμένουσι VII. vii. 8.
ἀναμιμνήσκονται IX. iv. 9.
ἀνάμνησις III. x. 5.
Ἀναξαγόρας X. viii. 11. Ἀναξαγόραν VI. vii. 5.
Ἀναξανδρίδης VII. x. 3.
ἀνάξιον IV. iii. 6. ἀνάξιοι IV. iii. 35. ἀνάξια X. viii. 7.
ἀναξίως II. vii. 15.
ἀνάπαλιν I. iv. 5. III. i. 7. IV. vii. 3. V. iii. 15. v. 17. VIII. xiii. 10. xiv. 1. IX. vii. 6. xi. 6.
ἀνάπαυσις IV. viii. 11. VII. vii. 7. X. vii. 6. ἀναπαύσεως IV. viii. 1. X. vii. 6. ἀναπαύσει X. vi. 6. ἀναπαύσεις VIII. ix. 5.
ἀναπλήρωσις III. xi. 3. X. iii. 6, 7. ἀναπληρώσεως X. iii. 6. ἀναπληρώσει X. iii. 6. ἀναπλήρωσιν X. iii. 6.
ἀναπληρουμένης VII. xii. 2.
ἀναποδείκτοις VI. xi. 6.
ἀναστρέφεσθαι II. i. 7.
ἀνασχίζουσαν VII. v. 2.
ἀνασῶσαι IX. iii. 3.
ἀναθήσει III. viii. 2.
ἀνατολῶν III. iii. 4.
ἀναφέρων IV. vi. 6. ἀναφέροντες III. v. 18. ἀναφέρεσθαι I. xii. 5. ἀναφέρεται IV. ii. 12. IX. i. 2. ἀναφερόμενοι I. xii. 3.
ἀναφορᾶς I. xii. 3.
Ἀνάχαρσιν X. vi. 6.
ἀναχωροῦσι X. viii. 5.
ἀνδράποδον VII. ii. 1. X. vi. 8. ἀνδραπόδῳ X. vi. 8.
ἀνδραποδῶδες IV. v. 6. ἀνδραποδώδους IV. viii. 5. ἀνδραποδώδεις I. v. 3. III. x. 8. xi. 3.
ἀνδρεία II. ii. 7. vii. 2. III. vii. 6, 13. viii. 6, 11, 12. ix. 1, 2. ἀνδρείας II. ii. 7, 9. vi. 20. III. v. 23. vii. 8. ix. 7. xi. 5. ἀνδρείᾳ II. viii. 6, 7. ἀνδρείαν I. iii. 3. II. viii. 5. III. vii. 6. viii. 6, 10. ix. 3, 4.
ἀνδρεῖος II. iii. 1. viii. 2. III. vi. vii. viii. 9. ix. 1, 4. V. ix. 16. IX. v. 4. X. vii. 4. ἀνδρείου I. xiii. 17. III. vii. 13. viii. 14. V. i. 14. ἀνδρείῳ III. vi. 3. vii. 6. ix. 4. X. viii. 4. ἀνδρεῖον I. xii. 2. II. viii. 3. III. viii. 5. ἀνδρεῖοι II. i. 4, 7. ii. 9. III. vii. 12. viii. 1, 6, 10, 11, 12, 13, 16, 17. ix. 2. VI. xiii. 1. X. iii. 2. ἀνδρεῖα II. i. 4. III. viii. 12. X. viii. 1. ἀνδρείους III. ix. 6. X. viii. 7. ἀν-

δρειοτέρων III. viii. 15. ἀνδρειότατοι III. viii. 1, 8.
ἀνδριαντοποιὸν VI. vii. 1.
ἀνδρίζονται III. vi. 12.
ἀνδροφονία II. vi. 18.
ἀνδρώδη IV. iv. 4. ἀνδρώδεις II. ix. 7. IV. v. 13. IX. xi. 4.
ἀνδρωθέντας X. ix. 9.
ἀνέγκλητοι IX. i. 7.
ἀνέδην VII. viii. 5.
ἀνέκπληκτος III. vii. 2.
ἀνελευθερία II. vii. 4. IV. i. 3, 29, 37, 44. ἀνελευθερίας IV. i. 38. ἀνελευθερίαν IV. i. 3. V. ii. 2.
ἀνελεύθερος II. vii. 4. viii. 2. ἀνελευθέρου IV. i. 31, 32. ἀνελεύθερον IV. ii. 18. ἀνελεύθεροι IV. i. 31. 43. ἀνελευθέρων IV. i. 43. ἀνελευθέρους IV. i. 37. 40, 42.
ἀνεμπόδιστοι VII. xiii. 2. ἀνεμπόδιστον VII. xii. 3. xiii. 2.
ἀνεπιστήμονα X. ix. 16. ἀνεπιστήμονι X. ix. 21.
ἀνεπιτίμητον VII. xiv. 5.
ἀνερεύνητον X. ix. 22.
ἄνευ I. vii. 14. viii. 6. x. 11. II. v. 4. IV. iii. 11, 16, 20. v. 11. vi. 5. V. iii. 3. viii. 7. xi. 6, 7. VI. ii. 4. viii. 4. ix. 2, 3. xii. 10. xiii. 1. 2, 3, 6, 7. VII. xii. 2. xiv. 7. VIII. i. 1. IX. iii. 4. X. iv. 11. viii. 9. ix. 21.
ἀνέχεσθαι IV. v. 6.
ἀνεψιοὶ VIII. xii. 4.
ἀνήγγελλον III. iii. 18.
ἀνήκει VIII. i. 7. ἀνήκοντα IX. vi. 2.
ἀνὴρ I. iv. 7. V. ii. 11. VII. i. 3. vi. 2. VIII. x. 5. IX. iii. 4. ἀνδρὸς I. vii. 14. VI. xii. 1. VII. i. 1. VIII. x. 5. xi. 4. X. v. 11. ix. 12. ἀνδρὶ V. ii. 11. VIII. vii. 1. xii. 7, 8. IX. i. 6. ἄνδρα V. x. 1. VII. i. 3. VIII. vii. 1. x. 5. ἄνδρες I. viii. 7. IX. xi. 4. ἀνδρῶν I. xii. 4. ἀνδράσι X. vi. 4. ἄνδρας I. vi. 1. VIII. i. 5.
ἀνθεκτέον IV. v. 14.
ἀνθράκων VII. v. 3.
ἀνθρώπεια X. iv. 9. ix. 22.
ἀνθρωπεύεσθαι X. viii. 6.
ἀνθρωπικὸν V. viii. 12. VIII. xiv. 4. ἀνθρωπικὴ III. xi. 7. ἀνθρωπικῷ IX. vii. 1. ἀνθρωπικῆς I. xiii. 14. ἀνθρωπικαὶ X. viii. 1, 3. ἀνθρωπικὰ III. i. 27. X. viii. 1. ἀνθρωπικῶν III. iii. 6. ἀνθρωπικώτερον IV. v. 12.
ἀνθρώπειος I. ix. 9. ἀνθρώπειον I. ii. 7. vii. 15. xiii. 5. V. ix. 17. X. vii. 8. ἀνθρωπίνης I. xiii. 5. ἀνθρωπίνῃ I. xiii. 12. ἀνθρωπίνην I. xiii. 5, 6. III. i. 7. VII. v. 8. ἀνθρωπίνων I. ix. 2. x. 10. X. vi. 1. viii. 7. ἀνθρώπινα V. vii. 5. VI. v. 6. vii. 5, 6. X. vii. 8. ἀνθρώπιναι VII. vi. 6.
ἀνθρωπολόγος IV. iii. 30.
ἄνθρωπος I. vi. 5. vii. 6. II. vi. 3. III. iii. 15. vii. 2. xi. 7. V. viii. 3. VI. ii. 5. vii. 3, 4. xii. 1. VII. iii. 6. iv. 2. vii. 7. xiv. 8. VIII. i. 3. xi. 7. xii. 7. IX. viii. 6. ix. 3. X. vii. 8, 9. viii. 6. ἀνθρώπου I. vi. 5, 16. vii. 10, 11, 14. II. vi. 3. III. i. 27. iii. 7. VI. vii. 4. X. v. 8, 11. vi. 7. vii. 7. ἀνθρώπῳ I. vi. 5, 13. vii. 10. III. viii. 14. VI. v. 4. vii. 6. xii. 1. VII. iii. 6. vii. 7. VIII. i. 3. vii. 6. xi. 7. IX. ix. 7. X. vii. 7, 9. viii. 8. ἄνθρωπον I. x. 3. III. v. 5. vii. 1. V. vi. 5. VII. v. 2, 6. vii. 7. X. vii. 8. ἄνθρωποι III. i. 3. viii. 12. x. 10. V. i. 9. ix. 14. VIII. iv. 4. xii. 7. ἀνθρώπων I. x. 1. III. iii. 7. VII. i. 2, 3. v. 1, 2. vi. 6. xiv. 4. IX. ix. 10. x. 3. X. v. 9, 10. viii. 13. ix. 12. ἀνθρώποις I. ix. 2. IV. i. 37. ii. 16. V. viii. 8. VI. vii. 4. VII. i. 3. iii. 7. VIII. i. 3. xii. 5. X. viii. 8. ἀνθρώποισι VII. x. 4. ἀνθρώπους I. x. 16. II. i. 7. VII. xiii. 5.
ἀνθυπηρετεῖν IX. x. 2. ἀνθυπηρετῆσαι V. v. 7.
ἀνίατος IV. i. 37. VII. vii. 2. viii. 1. ἀνιάτοις IX. iii. 3. ἀνιάτους X. ix. 10.
ἀνιάτως V. ix. 17.
ἀνίησι VI. i. 1. ἀνιωμένη X. iii. 3. ἀνιωμένως II. v. 2.
ἄνισος V. i. 11. iii. 1. ἀνίσου V. iii. 1, 3. ἄνισον V. i. 8. ii. 8, 9, 12. iii. 1. iv. 1, 3, 4. ἄνισοι VIII. viii. 5. ἄνισα V. iv. 4. 8. ἀνίσοις VIII. xiv. 3. ἀνίσων VIII. xiii. 1.
ἀνόητοι IV. iii. 3. ἀνοήτῳ III. xii. 7. ἀνόητα X. ii. 4.
ἀνομοιοειδέσι IX. i. 1.
ἀνομοιότερον II. viii. 7.
ἀνομοιότης II. viii. 5. ἀνομοιότητα VIII. vi. 7.
ἀνόνητος I. iii. 7.
ἀνόπλους III. viii. 8.
ἀνοργησία II. vii. 10.
ἀόργητος II. vii. 10.

ἀντανισουργῶν IX. iv. 7.
ἀνταποδιδῷ IV. v. 10. ἀνταποδίδωσι VIII. v. 5. ἀνταποδοῦναι IX. vii. 1. ἀνταποδοτέον VIII. xiii. 9. xiv. 3. IX. ii. 1, 3, 5.
ἀνταπόδοσις V. v. 7. IX. ii. 5. ἀνταπόδοσιν VIII. xiii. 10. IX. i. 8. ἀνταποδόσεις X. viii. 4.
ἀντευεργετικὸν IV. iii. 24.
ἀντευποιεῖν X. viii. 13.
ἀντέχειν VII. vii. 4, 6.
ἀντὶ III. i. 7, 9, 10. ix. 4. xi. 6. IV. 5. 10. V. v. 16. x. 1. ἀνθ' ὧν IX. v. 3.
ἀντιβαῖνον I. xiii. 16.
ἀντιβλάπτων V. xi. 2.
ἀντιδανειστέον IX. ii. 5.
ἀντίδοσις V. v. 8.
ἀντιδωρεῖται VIII. viii. 6.
ἀντικαταλλάττονται VIII. vi. 7. ἀντικαταλλαττόμενοι VIII. iv. 2.
ἀντίκειται II. viii. 6. VI. viii. 9. VII. vii. 4. X. ii. 5. ἀντίκεινται II. viii. 1. ἀντικεῖσθαι IV. iv. 6. vi. 9. vii. 17. ix. 2. X. ii. 5. ἀντικείμενοι VII. vii. 2. ἀντικειμένας X. ix. 5. ἀντικειμένων IV. i. 45. V. iv. 3.
ἀντιλαβὼν IX. i. 8.
ἀντίξουν VIII. i. 6.
ἀντιπάθῃ VIII. xiii. 8. ἀντιπεπονθὸς V. v. 1, 2, 6, 8, 12. vi. 3. ἀντιπεπονθέναι V. v. 12. ἀντιπεπονθόσι VIII. ii. 3.
ἀντιπληγῆναι V. iv. 4.
ἀντιποιεῖν V. v. 6. ἀντιποίησις V. v. 6.
ἀντιποιῶν V. xi. 5.
ἀντιτείνει I. xiii. 15. ἀντιτείνουσι VII. ii. 4. ἀντιτεινούσης VII. ii. 5. ἀντιτείνουσι VII. vii. 5. ἀντιτείνων VII. vii. 6. ἀντιτείνειν VII. vii. 6. ἀντιτείνοντες IV. vi. 1, 2.
ἀντιτίθεμεν II. viii. 7. IV. v. 12. ἀντιτίθεται IV. iii. 37. ἀντιτεθειμένη VII. i. 2.
ἀντιφιλεῖν VIII. v. 5. ἀντιφιλεῖται IX. i. 2. ἀντιφιλεῖσθαι VIII. viii. 3.
ἀντιφίλησις VIII. ii. 3. iii. 1.
ἄνω II. i. 2. ἀνώνυμον VIII. i. 6. ἄνωθεν VI. iii. 1. xii. 7. VII. vi. 2.
ἀνώνυμος II. vii. 2, 8. III. vii. 7. IV. iv. 5. vii. 1. ἀνώνυμα II. vii. 2, 11. III. vii. 7. ἀνωνύμου IV. iv. 4. v. 1. ἀνώνυμον IV. v. 1. vi. 9. ἀνώνυμοι II. vii. 8. ἀνωνύμων II. vii. 10.
ἀνωφελὴς I. iii. 6.
ἄξενος IX. x. 1.
ἀξία IV. i. 2. ii. 12. iii. 10, 17. V. v. 15. IX. i. 5, 7, 9. ἀξίας III. xi. 8. ἀξίαν I. x. 4. IV. ii. 3, 13, 19. iii. 3, 8, 11, 35. V. iii. 7. iv. 8. VIII. vii. 2, 3. viii. 4. x. 3, 5. xi. 3. xiii. 9. xiv. 3, 4. IX. i. 1, 5, 8.
ἄξιος IV. iii. 3, 4, 6, 7, 9, 14, 15, 17, 35. ἄξιον III. ix. 4. IV. ii. 6, 10, 23. VIII. xiv. 4. IX. i. 9. ἄξιοι IV. i. 21. iii. 36. VIII. vii. 4. xiii. 4.
ἀξιοῖ IV. iii. 7, 8, 9. VIII. xiii. 7. xiv. 1. ἀξιοῦντες VIII. viii. 6. ἀξιοῦν II. vi. 19. IV. iii. 35. VIII. xiv. 2. ἠξίωσε VIII. xiii. 9. ἀξιώσαντας IX. xi. 6. ἀξιοῦσι IV. iii. 11. VIII. vii. 4. ἀξιοῦται IV. iii. 20. VIII. iv. 3. ἀξιοῦνται IV. iii. 19. ἀξιῶν IV. iii. 3, 4, 6. ἀξιωτέον VIII. viii. 6.
ἀξίωμα III. viii. 16. IV. ii. 14. iii. 12. IX. ii. 5. ἀξιώματα IV. ii. 15. ἀξιώματι IV. iii. 10, 26. vi. 8.
ἀξύνετοι VII. viii. 3.
ἀοργησία IV. v. 5.
ἀόριστος V. x. 7. IX. ix. 8. ἀορίστου V. x. 7. ἀόριστον IV. viii. 7. X. iii. 2.
ἀπαγορεύει V. xi. 1. ἀπαγορεύων V. i. 14.
ἀπαγριοῦν, ἀπηγριωμένων VII. v. 2.
ἀπάγοντες II. ix. 5.
ἀπαθείας II. iii. 5.
ἀπαιδαγώγητος IV. i. 36.
ἀπαιδεύτων IV. viii. 5.
ἀπαιτοῦντι IX. i. 4. ii. 4. ἀπαιτητέον I. vii. 20. ἀπαιτητέοι II. ii. 3.
ἀπάνευθε III. viii. 4.
ἀπαντῶσι VIII. vi. 1. ἀπαντᾷν IX. ii. 7.
ἀπαρνοῦνται IV. vii. 14.
ἀπαρχαὶ VIII. ix. 5.
ἀπατήσαντι IX. iii. 2. ἀπατηθῇ IX. iii. 2. ἠπατημένοι III. viii. 16.
ἀπάτη III. iv. 5.
ἀπειθῶν III. v. 14. ἀπειθοῦσι X. ix. 10.
ἀπείπασθαι VIII. xiv. 4.
ἀπειροκαλία II. vii. 6. IV. ii. 4.
ἄπειρος I. iii. 5. ἄπειρον I. ii. 1. vii. 7. III. iii. 16. ἀπείρων II. vi. 14. ἀπείρου IV. i. 20.
ἀπέραντος I. xi. 2.
ἀπέχων II. vi. 5. ἀπέχοντα II. viii. 5, 7. ἀπέχονται IV. i. 39. ἀπέχεσθαι I. ii. 7. III. ix. 4. ἀπεχόμεθα II. iii. 1. ἀπεχόμενος II. ii. 7. iii. 1. IV. viii. 10. ἀπεχόμενον IX. iv. 9.
ἀπιστοῦντες III. iii. 10.
ἄπληστος III. xii. 7.

ἁπλῇ VII. v. 5. xiv. 8. ἁπλοῦν V. ix. 9. ἁπλῆν VII. xiv. 8.
ἁπλῶς I. iii. 5. iv. 5. vii. 4, 14. xi. 5. II. iii. 5. v. 3, 5. vi. 14, 18. vii. 16. III. i. 5, 6, 10. vi. 2. V. i. 9, 10, 15, 20. ii. 11. iv. 5. v. 1, 18. vi. 4, 6, 8. ix. 4, 9, 17. x. 1, 5, 6. xi. 4, 7. VI. ii. 5. iii. 2. vii. 6. x. 7. xiii. 6. VII. ii. 11. iii. 2. iv. 1, 2, 3, 6. v. 1, 8, 9. vi. 3. viii. 5. ix. 1, 2, 5. xii. 1, 7. xiii. 1, 2. VIII. ii. 2. iii. 6, 7. iv. 5. v. 1, 4.
ἀπό. ἀφ' αὑτοῦ IX. viii. 1.
ἀποβαίνουσι IV. vi. 8. ἀποβαίνειν VII. vii. 2. ἀποβαίνοντος I. vii. 5. ἀποβήσεται III. iii. 10.
ἀποβάλλεται III. i. 5.
ἀποβλέπων VI. i. 1.
ἀποβολὴν III. vi. 4.
ἀπογιγνώσκω. ἀπογνῶναι III. vi. 11.
ἀπογόνους I. vii. 7. ἀπογόνων I. x. 3. xi. 1.
ἀποδεικτικὴ VI. iii. 4.
ἀποδεικτὸν VI. vi. 1. ἀποδεικτῶν VI. vi. 1.
ἀπόδειξις VI. v. 3. ἀποδείξεως VI. v. 3. ἀπόδειξιν VI. vi. 1. ἀποδείξεις I. iii. 4. VI. xi. 4, 6. VII. iii. 8. ἀποδείξεων VI. xi. 6.
ἀποδέχεσθαι I. iii. 4. ἀποδέχεται IV. vi. 5. ἀποδεχόμενοι VIII. v. 3. ἀποδέχονται IX. viii. 7. ἀποδέχηται IX. iii. 3. ἀποδέξεται IV. iii. 17. vi. 3, 7. ἀποδέξασθαι VIII. iii. 8. ἀποδεκτέον I. iii. 8. iv. 8. X. viii. 12.
ἀποδίδομεν II. i. 4. VI. vii. 1. ἀποδίδωσι II. vi. 2. VIII. x. 5. ἀποδιδόασι I. iv. 2. IV. v. 8. ἀποδιδόντα V. viii. 4. VIII. xiv. 3. ἀποδιδόντας X. viii. 7. ἀποδιδόναι II. i. 8. IX. ix. 1. ἀποδόντες II. vi. 3. ἀποδώσειν VIII. xiii. 9. ἀποδοίη V. viii. 4. VIII. xiv. 4. ἀποδοῦναι III. i. 10. IV. v. 13. ἀποδεδωκέναι IX. i. 4. ἀποδοτέον VIII. xiii. 9, 11. xiv. 4. IX. ii. 3, 4, 5, 6. ἀποδίδοται IV. vi. 4.
ἀποθανετέον III. i. 8.
ἀποθνήσκοιεν III. i. 4. ἀποθάνῃ I. x. 2. V. iv. 4. ἀποθανεῖν III. vi. 2. V. xi. 8. ἀποθνήσκειν III. vii. 13. V. viii. 2. ἀποθνήσκει III. viii. 9.
ἀποκαλοῦσι IX. viii. 1. ἀποκαλοῦντες II. ix. 7.
ἀποκλίνει IV. vii. 19. ἀποκλίνουσι IV. i. 35. ἀποκλίνοντας IV. v. 1. ἀποκλίνειν II. ix. 9. X. i. 3. ἀποκλιτέον IX. ii. 5.
ἀποκτεῖναι III. i. 17. ἀποκτιννύναι V. xi. 1.
ἀπόλαυσις IV. vii. 13. ἀπολαύσεις III. ix. 9. ἀπόλαυσιν VII. vi. 1. ἀπολαύσεις VII. iv. 3.
ἀπολαυστικὸν I. v. 2.
ἀπολαύειν VIII. xiv. 1. ἀπολαύων II. ii. 7. ἀπολαύουσι X. vi. 8.
ἀπολειπόντων IX. iii. 1.
ἀπόλλυσι IV. v. 7. ἀπολεῖ IV. ii. 21. ἀπώλοντο I. iii. 3. ἀπόλλυται VII. xiii. 5. ἀπολλύμενοι IV. i. 5.
ἀπολογούμενος VII. vi. 2.
ἀπολυθέντος VIII. iii. 3.
ἀπομάττονται IX. xii. 3.
ἀπομνημονεύειν IV. iii. 30.
ἀπονέμει IX. v. 3. viii. 6, 9. ἀπονέμομεν IV. iii. 10. ἀπονέμουσι VIII. xiv. 3. ἀπονέμῃ VIII. vii. 2. ἀπονέμουσι VIII. viii. 3. ἀπονέμειν IV. iii. 17. IX. ii. 1, 9. ἀπονέμων IV. vi. 8. ἀπονέμοντος VIII. ix. 5. ἀπονέμονται IX. viii. 5. ix. 2. ἀπονεῖμαι X. viii. 7. ἀπονέμεται IV. iii. 15. VIII. xi. 2. X. vii. 7. ἀπονεμητέον IX. ii. 7. iii. 5.
ἄπονον IX. vii. 7.
ἀπόντα IX. v. 3. ἀπόντων III. xi. 8.
ἀποπαύονται IV. v. 8.
ἀποπεμπόμενοι II. ix. 6.
ἀπορεῖται I. ix. 1. VIII. vii. 6. IX. viii. 1, 2. ἀπορουμένων V. ix. 4. ἠπόρει I. iv. 5. ἀπορήσειε I. vi. 5. II. iv. 1. V. ix. 1. VII. ii. 1. IX. xi. 2. ἀπορηθὲν I. x. 6. ἠπορήθη VII. ix. 1. ἠπόρηται VI. xii. 3. ἠπορήσαμεν VII. viii. 2.
ἀπορημάτων VIII. i. 7.
ἀπορία V. x. 2. VII. ii. 8. ἀπορίας IV. i. 31. VII. ii. 12. ἀπορίαν I. x. 4. V. x. 3. IX. ii. 1. iii. 1. ἀπορίαι VII. ii. 12.
ἄπορον I. vi. 16.
ἀπόῤῥητα III. i. 17.
ἀποστατέον IX. ii. 10.
ἀποστερεῖται III. ix. 4. ἀποστερῆσαι VIII. ix. 3. ἀποστέρησιν V. iv. 3. VI. x. 1. ἀποστερεῖ IV. iii. 35.
ἀποστήματι I. x. 4.
ἀποστολὰς IV. ii. 15.
ἀπεσχεδιασμένοι V. i. 14.
ἀποσχολάζειν X. vi. 3.
ἀποτελεῖ II. vi. 2. ἀποτελεῖν I. viii. 9. ἀποτελεῖται IV. ix. 2. VI. xii. 6.

ἀποτρέψοντος X. ix. 7.
ἀποτρίψασθαι II. iii. 8.
ἀποτυγχάνων III. xi. 6. ἀποτυχεῖν II. vi. 14.
ἀπουσία III. xi. 5. VIII. v. 1.
ἀποφαίνειν X. i. 2. ii. 3. iii. 4. ἀποφαίνονται I. x. 8. ἀπεφαίνετο X. viii. 11. ἀπεφήναντο I. i. 1.
ἀπόφασις VI. ii. 2.
ἀποφάναι VI. iii. 1.
ἀποχωρεῖν II. ix. 3.
ἀπραγμόνως VI. viii. 4.
ἀπρακτεῖν I. v. 6.
ἀπρεπῆ IV. viii. 7.
ἀπροαίρετα V. viii. 5. ἀπροαιρέτως II. v. 4.
ἀπροβούλευτα V. viii. 5. ἀπροβούλευτοι VII. viii. 2.
ἀπροσηγορία VIII. v. 1.
ἀπωθοῦνται II. viii. 3.
ἆρ VI. vii. 2.
ἄρα I. iii. 5. vi. 11, 12. vii. 12. viii. 14. II. i. 3. iii. 6. vi. 13. 15. ix. 10. IV. iii. 14. V. i. 8. ii. 3. 4. iii. 5. 8, 11, 12, 14. iv. 7, 10, 11, 12. v. 11, 13. vi. 7. 9. ix. 1. x. 2. xi. 2. VI. i. 7. iii. 2, 3. 4. v. 4. vii. 3. ix. 3. VII. ii. 5. VIII. ii. 4. iii. 1. IX. ix. 3, 10. X. iii. 6. vi. 6. vii. 9. viii. 7, 13. ix. 23.
ἆρα III. iv. 4. IX. iii. 3, 4.
ἆρά γε I. x. 2. III. ii. 17.
ἄρ' οὖν I. ii. 2. VIII. xiii. 11. IX. ii. 2. iii. 3. iv. 7. x. 1. xii. 1. X. ix. 1, 18.
Ἀργεῖοι III. viii. 16.
ἀργία I. xiii. 13. ἀργίαν IX. iv. 8.
ἀργὸν I. vii. 11. IV. iii. 27. ἀργὸν IX. v. 3.
ἀργύριον II. ix. 9. IV. vii. 11. V. ix. 13. 14. IX. i. 6, 7. ἀργυρίου IV. vii. 11.
ἄρεσκος II. vii. 13. IV. vii. 9. ἄρεσκον IX. x. 6. ἄρεσκοι IV. vi. 1. ἀρέσκουσι IX. x. 6.
ἀρέσκει III. iv. 4. IV. i. 39. IX. i. 6. X. vi. 2. ἀρέσκουσι IX. iv. 7. ἀρέσκονται IX. xii. 3. ἀρεσκόμενος IV. i. 27. ἀρεσκόμενοι IX. iii. 4. X. v. 4. ἀρέσκειν VII. ii. 8. VIII. vi. 2, 3.
ἀρετὴ I. v. 5. viii. 6. xiii. 12, 20. II. i. 6. ii. 1. iii. 1, 3. 6, 10, 11. v. 1, 6. vii. 14. ix. 1. III. v. 1, 17, 19. IV. ii. 1, 10. iv. 1. ix. 8. V. i. 15. 18, 20. VI. i. 7. ii. 2. v. 7, 8. vii. 1. xi. 7. xii. 6, 8. xiii. 1, 2, 4, 5. VII. i. 2. viii. 4. VIII. i. 1. iii. 6, vii. 1. viii. 4. xii. 7. IX. iv. 2. viii. 7. X. v. 10. vi. 4. viii. 2. ἀρετῆς I. ix. 3, 10. xii. 6. xiii. 1, 5, 14. II. i. 1. vi. 11, 12, 14. viii. 1. III. i. 1. IV. i. 7, 24, 25. iii. 15, 17, 21. vii. 7. ix. 1. V. i. 15, 19. ii. 1, 10, 11. VI. xii. 5, 8, 10. xiii. 1, 6, 7. VII. i. 2. VIII. i. 1. vi. 5. vii. 4. xiii. 2, 11. xiv. 2. IX. i. 7. ix. 2. 7. X. iii. 1, viii. 5. ix. 1, 3. 5. 8. ἀρετῇ I. v. 5. II. iii. 10. IV. iii. 14. V. i. 15, 18. VII. i. 4. VIII. vi. 6. IX. iii. 4. X. viii. 3. ἀρετὴν I. v. 6. vii. 5, 14. 15. viii. 8, 10, 11, 13. 17. ix. 3. 4. 7. x. 9, 10, 11, 15. xii. 2. xiii. 1, 6. II. vi. 16. III. viii. 3. ix. 4. IV. i. 6, 12, 13. ii. 13. iii. 3, 21. V. ii. 7, 10. iii. 7. xi. 1. xii. 6. VI. xiii. 4, 7. VII. i. 1. xi. 2. VIII. iii. 6. viii. 5. x. 5. xi. 4. xii. 7. xiii. 2, 11. xiv. 3. IX. i. 7, 9. v. 4. ix. 6. x. 6. X. i. 1. ii. 1, 3. vi. 5, 8. vii. 1, 3. 8. viii. 1, 4, 6, 10. ix. 8, 14. ἀρεταὶ I. vi. 3. vii. 15. II. i. 3. iii. 3. v. 3. 4, 6. III. v. 20. x. 1. VI. ii. 6. xii. 1. xiii. 6. X. viii. 3. ἀρετῶν II. i. 2, 7. ii. 7, 9. iv. 3. vii. 16. III. v. 1, 21. IV. iii. 16. V. i. 15, 17. xi. 10. VIII. v. 1. X. vii. 6. ix. 1. ἀρεταῖς III. ix. 5. IV. ii. 7. V. v. 17. ἀρετὰς I. xiii. 20. II. i. 4. ii. 2. iii. 5. iv. 3. v. 3, 4. IV. iv. 6. vii. 1. ix. 7. V. i. 14. VI. i. 4. v. 7. xii. 4. xiii. 3, 5, 6. VII. ii. 5. IX. viii. 6. X. iii. 2, 12. vi. 1. vii. 7. viii. 1.
ἀριθμέω, ἠριθμημένων VI. viii. 4.
ἀριθμητικὴν II. vi. 7. V. iv. 3. 9.
ἀριθμοῦ V. iii. 8. ἀριθμῷ V. iii. 14. ἀριθμὸν V. vi. 4. VI. iii. 1. IX. x. 3. ἀριθμῶν I. vi. 2.
ἀριστείων I. xii. 5.
ἀριστερὰ I. xiii. 15.
ἄριστος IV. iii. 14. V. i. 18. ἀρίστη V. vii. 6. VII. xiii. 6. VIII. iii. 7. ἄριστον I. ii. 1. vii. 3. 9. viii. 9, 14. ix. 3, 8. II. vi. 11, 17. III. v. 17. VI. vii. 3. xii. 10. VII. xi. 3, 5. xii. 1. xiii. 2, 5. X. ii. 1. ἀρίστου VI. vii. 6. X. vi. 8. vii. 1. ἀρίστῳ X. viii. 13. ἀρίστην I. vii. 15. viii. 14. ix. 6. ἄριστοι X. ix. 16. ἀρίστων I. xii. 4. ἀρίστοις V. i. 13. VIII. vii. 4. ἀρίσταις I. viii. 14. ἀρίστους IX. vi. 2. X. ix. 20. ἄριστα III. ii. 14. iii. 6. viii. 8. IV. i. 6. IX. viii. 4. X. iv. 5. viii. 13. ix. 15.

ἀριστοκρατία VIII. x. 1. ἀριστοκρατίας VIII. x. 3. ἀριστοκρατίᾳ VIII. xi. 4.
ἀριστοκρατικὴ VIII. x. 4. ἀριστοκρατικοὶ V. iii. 7.
ἀρκεῖ II. iv. 3. ἀρκοῦσι IX. x. 2. ἀρκούμενοι II. vii. 5.
ἀρκούντως I. iv. 7. xiii. 9.
ἄρτιον III. viii. 4.
ἁρμόζει III. ii. 9. IV. ii. 16. vi. 5. ix. 3. VIII. x. 5. IX. xi. 6. ἁρμόζοι IV. iii. 15. ἁρμόζον VIII. xi. 4. ἁρμόζειν IX. x. 2. ἁρμόσει V. vii. 4. IX. x. 1. X. vii. 9.
ἁρμονίαν VIII. i. 6.
ἁρμόττει IV. viii. 5. X. ix. 21. ἁρμόττοι VII. i. 1. ἁρμόττοντα IX. ii. 7.
ἀρνεῖσθαι IV. vii. 3.
ἀροτῆρα VI. vii. 2.
ἁρπαγὴ V. ii. 13.
ἄῤῥεν VII. vii. 6. ἄῤῥεσι VII. v. 3.
ἀῤῥωστιῶν III. v. 22.
ἀρτάομαι. ἠρτῆσθαι VIII. xii. 2.
ἄρτος III. iii. 16.
ἀρτύοντες III. x. 9.
ἀρχαίαι VIII. ix. 5. ἀρχαίων III. iii. 18.
ἀρχὴ I. iv. 7. vii. 20, 23. III. i. 3, 6, 10, 12, 20. iii. 13, 15. v. 8, 14. V. i. 16. ii. 13. viii. 7. ix. 10. VI. ii. 2, 4. iii. 3. iv. 4. v. 6. xi. 6. VII. iii. 2. vii. 7. viii. 4, 5. VIII. x. 4. IX. v. 3. ἀρχῆς I. xiii. 4. III. v. 14, 22. viii. 9. V. iv. 13. vii. 1. v. 6. vi. 1. VIII. ix. 4. X. iv. 1. ἀρχῇ I. ix. 8. IV. ii. 6. VIII. ix. 1. xiii. 1, 9. IX. iii. 1. ix. 5. ἀρχὴν I. xii. 8. III. iii. 17. v. 5. V. v. 4. vi. 1. VI. iv. 4. xii. 7, 10. VII. i. 1. vi. 7. viii. 4. X. i. 1. ἀρχαὶ III. v. 6. VI. i. 5. iii. 3, 4. v. 6. vi. 1. viii 5. xi. 4. VIII. x. 4, 5. X. viii. 3. ἀρχῶν I. iv. 5. vii. 21. VI. vi. 2. vii. 3. viii. 4. ἀρχὰς I. iv. 5, 6. vii. 20. II. ii. 3. III. v. 6. VI. vii. 3. xi. 6. xii. 10. VII. vi. 6. VIII. i. 1. x. 3. IX. vi. 2. viii. 10.
ἀρχηγὸν VIII. xii. 4.
ἀρχιθεώρων IV. ii. 2.
ἀρχικὸν VIII. xi. 2.
ἀρχιτεκτονικὴ VI. vii. 7. viii. 2. ἀρχιτεκτονικῆς I. ii. 4. ἀρχιτεκτονικῶν I. i. 4.
ἀρχιτέκτων VII. xi. 1.
ἄρχουσι VIII. vii. 1. x. 3, 5. ἄρξαι V. v. 7. ἄρχει V. viii. 9. VI. ii. 5. xii. 3. VIII. x. 5. ἄρχειν IV. v. 13. V. vi. 5, 9. VI. xiii. 8. VIII. xi. 5. IX. vi. 2. X. vii. 1. ἄρχεσθαι V. vi. 9.
ἄρχων V. i. 16. vi. 5. VIII. x. 6. ἄρχοντι V. i. 17. xi. 9. VIII. vii. 1. xi. 6. ἄρχοντα V. v. 4. ἄρχον III. xii. 7. ἀρξάντων III. viii. 4. VIII. x. 3. ἄρχονται X. viii. 10. ἀρκτέον I. iv. 5. VI. xii. 7. ἀρξάμενοι VI. iii. 1. X. ix. 23. ἀρχόμενον VIII. vii. 1. ἀρχομένῳ II. vi. 7. V. xi. 9. VIII. xi. 5. ἀρχομένων VIII. x. 2. ἀρχομένοις VIII. x. 2. ἀρχομένους VIII. vii. 1.
ἀσεβεῖν IV. i. 42.
ἀσθένεια VII. vii. 8. ἀσθενείας III. v. 15. VIII. i. 2.
ἀσθενὴς VIII. x. 6. ἀσθενεῖ X. v. 9. ἀσθενεῖν IV. iii. 26. VII. ii. 6.
ἀσινεστέρα VII. vi. 7.
ἀσιτία X. ix. 15.
ἀσκήσεις IX. ix. 7. ἄσκησιν I. ix. 3.
ἀσκητὸν I. ix. 1.
ἀσπίδα V. ii. 2. ix. 16.
ἄσσα VI. ii. 6.
ἀστεῖος IV. iii. 5.
ἀσύμμετροι III. iii. 3.
ἀσυνεσία VI. x. 1.
ἀσύνετοι VI. x. 1.
ἀσυνήθεις IV. vi. 5.
ἀσφαλῶς I. x. 3.
ἀσχημονεῖν III. xii. 3.
ἀσχημοσύνην IV. vi. 7.
ἀσχήμονες IV. ii. 22. ἀσχημονέστεροι IV. vii. 11.
ἄσχολος X. vii. 6. ἄσχολοι X. vii. 6, 7.
ἀσχολούμεθα X. vii. 6.
ἀσωτία II. vii. 4. IV. i. 3, 29. ἀσωτίας IV. i. 30, 37, 44. ἀσωτίᾳ II. viii. 5. ἀσωτίαν IV. i. 35, 44.
ἄσωτος II. vii. 4. viii. 2. IV. i. 5, 23, 28, 32, 36. VII. ix. 2. ἄσωτον II. viii. 2. ἄσωτοι IV. i. 30. ἀσώτου IV. i. 33. ἀσώτους IV. i. 13, 23.
ἀτάραχος III. ix. 1. IV. v. 3. ἀτάραχον III. viii. 15.
ἄτεκνος I. viii. 16. ἄτεκνοι VIII. xii. 7.
ἀτελὴς X. iv. 2. ἀτελὲς X. vii. 7. ἀτελεῖς X. iii. 4. iv. 2, 3. ἀτελεστέρα I. v. 6.
ἅτερος V. v. 13. ἅτεροι VII. viii. 2.
ἀτεχνία VI. iv. 6.
ἀτεχνῶς I. xiii. 15.
ἀτιμία V. xi. 3. ἀτιμίας IV. iii. 10, 17. ἀτιμίαι I. x. 3.
ἄτιμοι III. viii. 1.
ἄτοπος X. viii. 11. ἄτοπον I. x. 2, 5, 7. III. i. 24, 27. IV. ix. 6. V. ix. 2. x. 1.

VI. vii. 3. xii. 3. VII. ii. 5. iii. 6. v. 7. IX. iii. 1, 3. ix. 3. X. v. 7. vi. 6. vii. 9. viii. 7. ἀτόπῳ IX. ix. 2. ἄτοπα IX. ii. 5.
ἀτόνως V. ix. 1.
ἄτρυτον X. vii. 7.
ἄττα V. v. 10.
ἀτυχεῖ V. viii. 7. ἀτυχῶν IV. iii. 18. ἀτυχοῦντος IX. ix. 2. ἀτυχοῦντι IX. xi. 3. ἀτυχοῦντες IX. xi. 1. ἀτυχοῦντας IX. xi. 6.
ἀτύχημα V. viii. 7. ἀτυχημάτων I. x. 14.
ἀτυχίᾳ V. i. 9. ἀτυχίαν IV. iii. 18. ἀτυχίας I. x. 12. IX. xi. 5. ἀτυχίαις IX. ix. 2. xi. 1, 4.
αὖ I. iv. 7. III. i. 13. iv. 3. IV. i. 1, 39. 40. iii. 31. vi. 5. IX. ii. 8, 9. iv. 8.
αὐθαίρετα III. v. 17.
αὐθέκαστος IV. vii. 4.
αὐλοῦντος X. v. 3.
αὐλητῇ I. vii. 10.
αὐλητικῇ X. v. 3. αὐλητικὴν X. v. 3.
αὐλοῖς I. vii. 3.
αὔξει II. ii. 6. αὔξεσθαι I. xiii. 11. VIII. ix. 3. X. ii. 2. iii. 4. αὔξεται II. iii. 11.
αὔξησιν II. i. 1. VII. xiv. 6. VIII. ix. 3.
αὐξήσεις II. ii. 8.
αὐξητικὴν I. vii. 12.
αὐτάρκεια X. vii. 4. αὐταρκείας I. vii. 6. αὐτάρκειαν V. vi. 4.
αὐτάρκης VIII. x. 2. X. vi. 2. viii. 9. αὔταρκες I. vii. 6, 7, 8. X. vii. 7. viii. 9. αὐτάρκους IV. iii. 33. αὐτάρκεις III. iii. 8. IX. ix. 1. αὐτάρκεσι IX. ix. 1. αὐταρκέστατος X. vii. 4.
αὖτε I. iv. 7.
αὐτοανθρώπῳ I. vi. 5.
αὐτοέκαστον I. vi. 5.
αὐτόματον X. ix. 21.
αὐχένα V. i. 7.
αὐχμῶν III. iii. 5.
ἀφαιρέσεως VI. viii. 6.
ἀφαιρῶν V. iv. 4. ἀφεῖλε V. iv. 8. ἀφελεῖν II. vi. 9. V. iv. 11. ἀφαιρουμένων VIII. vii. 5. ἀφαιρεθείσης VIII. i. 1. ἀφαιρεθῇ V. iv. 10. ἀφῃρέθη V. iv. 10. ἀφῄρηται V. iv. 12. ἀφῃρῆσθαι V. xi. 4. ἀφῃρημένῳ X. viii. 7. ἀφαιρεῖσθαι I. xi. 5. ἀφῄρηνται III. x. 11.
ἀφανὲς I. x. 15. ἀφανῶν II. ii. 6. ἀφανίζεσθαι III. ix. 3.
ἀφειδὴς IV. iii. 23.
ἀφεκτέον III. i. 14.
ἀφέλκειν II. ix. 5.
ἀφὴ III. x. 8. ἀφῆς III. x. 9, 11. VII. vii. 1. X. v. 7. ἀφῇ III. x. 8. ἀφὴν VII. iv. 3.
ἄφθαρτα VI. iii. 2.
ἀφιέναι VIII. xiv. 4. ἀφεῖναι III. i. 17. V. ix. 16. ἀφέντι III. v. 14. ἀφεῖσθαι I. v. 8. V. ii. 10. VIII. i. 7. viii. 7. IX. iv. 6. xi. 2. X. iv. 11. ἀφετέον I. vi. 13.
ἀφικνουμένῳ IX. v. 3. ἀφίκετο IV. i. 36. ἀφῖκται I. vii. 2.
ἀφιλίαν III. vi. 3.
ἄφιλον I. xi. 1. IX. x. 1.
ἀφιλοτιμία IV. iv. 5. ἀφιλοτιμίαν IV. iv. 5.
ἀφιλότιμος II. vii. 8. ἀφιλότιμον IV. iv. 3, 4.
ἀφίσταται IX. iii. 3. ἀφίστανται III. iii. 13. vii. 12. viii. 11. IV. iii. 35. IX. iv. 8. ἀφιστᾶσι IV. iv. 1. ἀποστῆναι VIII. xiv. 4. ἀφίστησιν II. viii. 5.
ἀφοβίᾳ II. vii. 2.
ἄφοβος III. vi. 3, 4. ἄφοβον III. viii. 15.
ἀφόρητον IV. v. 7.
ἀφορίσαι II. ix. 8. ἀφωρισμένον III. iii. 17. ἀφορίσωμεν III. x. 1. ἀφωρισμένα VIII. ix. 2. ἀφοριστέον I. vii. 12. ἀφορίσειε VIII. xii. 1. ἀφωρισμέναι VII. iii. 1.
ἀφροδισίοις III. x. 9. VII. xiv. 2. ἀφροδισίων VII. iii. 7. iv. 2. v. 3, 7. xii. 4.
Ἀφροδίτην VII. vi. 3.
ἀφροσύνη VII. ii. 2. v. 5.
ἀφρόνων VII. v. 6.
ἀφυεστέρους X. ix. 10.
ἀχθόμενος II. iii. 1. IV. i. 17.
ἀχορήγητον I. viii. 15.
ἀχρεῖος IV. viii. 10. ἀχρεῖον VIII. xiv. 1. ἀχρεῖα X. ix. 21.
ἀχρήϊος I. iv. 7.
ἀχώριστα I. xiii. 10.
ἄψυχον VIII. xi. 6. ἀψύχου VII. vii. 7. ἄψυχα V. ix. 12. VIII. v. 5. xi. 6. ἀψύχων VIII. ii. 3.

B.

βαδίζει IX. ix. 9. βαδίζων II. ii. 8. IX. ix. 9. βαδίζειν V. i. 4. X. iii. 4. βαδίζῃ V. i. 4. βαδιστέον X. ix. 16.
βάδισις X. iv. 3. βαδίσεως X. iv. 3. βαδίσει X. iv. 3.
βάλληται I. iv. 7. βαλεῖν III. v. 14. V. viii. 6.

βάναυσοι IV. ii. 20. βαναυσία II. vii. 6. IV. ii. 4.

βαρβάρων VII. v. 6. βαρβάροις VII. i. 3.

βάρος IV. v. 10. βάρους IX. xi. 2.

βαρεῖα IV. iii. 34. βαρέα III. iv. 4.

βαρύσταθμον VI. viii. 7. βαρύσταθμα VI. viii. 7.

βασιλεία VIII. x. 1, 2, 4. βασιλείας VIII. x. 2, 3. 4.

βασιλεὺς VIII. x. 2, 3. xi. 2. βασιλέως X. ix. 12. βασιλεῖ VIII. xi. 1. βασιλεῖς III. iii. 18. βασιλέων VIII. vii. 4. βασιλεῦσι VII. vii. 6.

βασιλευομένων VIII. xi. 2. βασιλευομένους VIII. xi. 1.

βαυκοπανοῦργοι IV. vii. 15.

βέβαιον VIII. viii. 5. βεβαίῳ X. vii. 3. βεβαιοτάτη VIII. xii. 6.

βεβαιότης I. x. 10.

βεβαιῶσαι VIII. viii. 2.

βεβαίως II. iv. 3.

βελτίων I. xiii. 7. II. iii. 5. IV. i. 31, 32. iii. 14. VII. ii. 10. viii. 5. IX. viii. 1. βελτίονος VI. xiii. 8. X. iv. 7. βελτίω I. i. 2. xiii. 3. IX. xi. 4. X. vi. 7. βέλτιον I. vi. 1, 14. ix. 5. xii. 4. xiii. 1. II. iii. 10. III. i. 13. V. x. 1, 2, 6, 8. VII. ii. 3. xii. 3. xiv. 4. VIII. xiv. 1. IX. iii. 3. X. ix. 1, 22. βελτίους VII. viii. 2. IX. xii. 3. X. v. 5. ix. 17.

βέλτιστον I. ix. 2. IV. v. 10. VI. vii. 4. VII. ii. 1. viii. 5. IX. viii. 8. βελτίστη VI. i. 7. VIII. 10. 2. X. iv. 5. βελτίστῳ VIII. x. 2. βέλτιστα I. xiii. 15. IX. iv. 8. βελτίστων II. iii. 6.

βίᾳ III. i. 3, 11, 20. v. 7. V. viii. 3. X. ix. 8.

βιασθέντος III. i. 12.

βίαιος I. v. 6. βίαια III. i. 10, 11. V. ii. 13. βίαιον III. i. 3, 12.

βίος I. viii. 10, 12. x. 9. VII. xiii. 7. VIII. xii. 6. IX. ix. 4, 5, 9. x. 2. X. vi. 6. vii. 8, 9. viii. 3, 8, 10. βίον I. v. 4, 6. ix. 10. x. 4, 11. xiii. 12. IV. iii. 23. V. vi. 4. X. i. 1. iii. 12. vi. 2, 8. vii. 7. viii. 12. βίῳ I. vii. 16. viii. 9. II. iii. 8. vii. 13. III. xii. 2. IV. vii. 4. 7. viii. 1, 11, 12. IX. xii. 2. βίου I. ii. 2. iii. 5. v. 2. 3. vii. 6, 7. ix. 11. x. 12. 15. xi. 3. II. vii. 11. III. ix. 6. VI. vii. 4. VII. xii. 7. xiii. 2. VIII. i. 1. ix. 4, 5. xii. 7. IX. vi. 2. x. 2. X. i. 1, 2, 4. ii. 3. vi. 2, 6. vii. 8, 9. viii. 12. ix. 9. βίων I. v. 1.

βιωτέον III. v. 14.

βεβιωκότι I. x. 4. βεβιωκότας X. viii. 11. βιῶσαι IX. viii. 9. βιωσομένους X. ix. 11. βιώσεται X. vii. 8. βιωσόμενον I. x. 15.

βλαβερὸν IV. vi. 7. βλαβεροῦ V. v. 18. βλαβερὰ IV. ii. 22. VI. xiii. 1. VII. xi. 5. βλαβερᾷ IX. v. 8. βλαβερὸς VII. xiv. 5.

βλαβὴ V. viii. 7, 8. βλαβὴν IV. vi. 7. βλαβῶν V. viii. 6. βλαβὰς I. iii. 3.

βλάβους V. iv. 3.

βλάπτει V. ix. 4. 17. VII. xii. 4. βλάπτειν V. vi. 8. ix. 4, 5. ἔβλαψε V. iv. 3. βλάψῃ V. viii. 11. βλάπτοντες V. viii. 8. βλάψει IX. viii. 7. βλάπτῃ V. xi. 2. βλάπτεται V. ix. 6, 9. βλάπτονται X. vi. 3. βλάπτοιτο V. ix. 5. βέβλαπται V. iv. 3.

βλέπει V. iv. 3. βλέπουσι V. xi. 9. βλέπειν IV. i. 18. βλέπουσα II. vi. 9. βλέποντες II. vi. 9. VII. xi. 1.

βοηθείας VIII. i. 2.

βοηθεῖν II. ii. 5. βοηθῆσαι V. ii. 2. βοηθῆσαι VIII. ix. 3. βοηθητέον IX. iii. 3.

βοήθημα I. vi. 15.

βοηθῶν V. x. 8.

βορὰν III. x. 7.

βοσκημάτων I. v. 3. IX. ix. 10.

βουλεύονται III. iii. 1, 7. VI. ix. 2. βουλεύσαιτο III. iii. 2. VI. ii. 1. βουλεύεται III. iii. 3, 6, 11. VI. i. 6. ii. 6. v. 3. vii. 6. ix. 3. βουλευόμεθα III. iii. 7, 8, 11. βουλεύεσθαι III. iii. 10. VI. i. 6. v. 1. vii. 6. viii. 7. ix. 1, 2, 4, 7. βουλεύσεται III. iii. 16. βουλευόμενος III. iii. 11. VI. ix. 2, 3. βουλεύσασθαι III. iii. 19. VI. v. 3. vii. 6. VII. vii. 8. βουλευθέντα VI. ix. 2. βουλεύηται VI. ix. 3. βεβουλευμένοι VI. ix. 4. βουλευόμενον VI. ix. 6. βεβουλεῦσθαι VI. ix. 7. βουλευσάμενοι VII. vii. 8. ἐβουλεύσαντο VII. vii. 8. βουλεύσηται VII. x. 3. βουλευσαμένου VII. x. 4.

βούλευσις III. iii. 12. βούλευσιν III. iii. 19.

βουλευτικὸς VI. v. 2. VII. x. 3. βουλευτικὴ III. iii. 19. VI. ii. 2. viii. 2. 3.

βουλευτὸν III. iii. 1, 2, 16, 17. βουλευτοῦ III. iii. 19. βουλευτῶν III. v. 1.

βουλὴ III. iii. 1, 8, 15. VI. ix. 2, 4. βουλὴν III. iii. 17. VI. ix. 4.
βούλημα II. i. 5. βουλήματα IX. vi. 3.
βούλησις III. ii. 7, 8. iv. 1. VIII. ii. 3. iii. 9. IX. vii. 2. βούλησιν III. ii. 3. V. ix. 5, 6, 9. βουλήσει VIII. v. 5. βουλήσεις X. viii. 4.
βουλητὸν III. iv. 2, 3, 4. βουλητοῦ III. v. 1.
βούλεται I. x. 3. xiii. 2. III. i. 15. iv. 2. vii. 8. IV. i. 5. iii. 25. v. 3. V. iv. 7. v. 14. ix. 6. VIII. ii. 3. vii. 6. x. 3, 4. IX. iv. 3, 4, 5. viii. 2. x. 5. X. ix. 13. βουλόμεθα I. ii. 1. III. iii. 9. IV. vi. 4. βούλονται I. vi. 5. IV. iii. 18, 36. V. i. 3. v. 3. VIII. iii. 1, 5. 6, 9. v. 5. vi. 1, 4. 7. vii. 6. xi. 5. xiv. 4. IX. iv. 8. v. 3. vi. 3. vii. 1. xi. 1. xii. 2. βούλεσθαι I. x. 7. III. v. 13. IV. i. 34. VII. ii. 8. VIII. ii. 3. 4. viii. 1. xiii. 8. IX. vii. 1. X. viii. 4. βουλόμενος III. i. 17. IV. i. 17. IX. v. 3. vi. 4. viii. 2. βουλόμενοι III. vii. 12. IV. i. 43. VI. xii. 2. VIII. iii. 6. IX. i. 9. xii. 2. βούληται III. v. 14. VII. ii. 8. IX. vi. 2. βουλομένους V. i. 3. VIII. ii. 3. IX. vi. 4. ἐβούλετο VII. x. 3. IX. i. 4. iv. 10. βουλήσονται VIII. vii. 6. βουλόμενον IX. iv. 1. βουλομένῳ X. ix. 16, 17.
βοὴν III. x. 7. βοῒ I. vii. 12. βοῦν I. ix. 9. VIII. xi. 6.
βραδέως VI. ix. 2. X. iii. 4.
βραδεῖα IV. iii. 34.
βραδυτῆς X. iii. 4.
Βρασίδᾳ V. vii. 1.
βραχὺν V. ix. 1. βραχὺ VIII. v. 2.
βρῖθος I. xi. 3.
βρώματα III. xi. 7. βρωμάτων III. x. 6.
βρώσει III. x. 7.
βωμολοχία II. vii. 13.
βωμολόχος II. vii. 13. IV. viii. 10. βωμολόχοι IV. viii. 3, 4.

Γ.

γαῖαν VIII. i. 6.
γαλῆν VII. v. 6.
γαμικοῖς IV. ii. 20.
γάμοις IV. ii. 15. γάμους IX. ii. 7.
γαργαλιζόμενοι VII. vii. 8.
γαστρίμαργοι III. xi. 3.
γείτονος V. ix. 14.
γελοῖον IV. iii. 15. VIII. xiii. 3. γελοῖον III. i. 11, 24. IV. viii. 3, 6. VIII. ii. 3. viii. 6. γελοίου IV. viii. 3, 4, 10. γελοίῳ IV. viii. 3. γελοίων I. xii. 3. VIII. viii. 6. X. viii. 7. γελοῖον X. viii. 7. γελοῖα III. i. 8.
γέλωτα IV. viii. 3, 10. VII. vii. 6.
γέμουσι IX. iv. 10.
γένεσις VII. xi. 4, 5. xii. 3. X. iii. 5. iv. 4. γενέσεως VI. xii. 1. VII. xii. 3. γενέσει III. iii. 12. γένεσιν II. i. 1. VI. iv. 4. VII. xii. 3. X. iii. 4. iv. 4. γενέσεις II. ii. 8. VII. xii. 1, 3. X. iii. 4, 7.
γενετῆς VI. xiii. 1. VII. x. 4. VIII. xii. 6.
γεννάδας I. x. 12.
γεννήσαντι VIII. i. 3. γεγεννημένον VIII. i. 3. γεννήσασι VIII. vii. 2. γεννηθέντα VIII. xii. 2. γεννηθέντι VIII. xii. 2. γεννώμενον VIII. xii. 2.
γέννησις IX. vii. 7.
γεννητικὸν III. v. 5.
γένος I. iii. 4. III. v. 21. V. x. 2. VI. v. 3. ix. 1. VII. i. 3, 5. vi. 7. vii. 6. viii. 1. IX. ii. 7. γένους VII. vii. 6. γένει I. vii. 14. II. vii. 6. IV. ii. 17, 19. V. ii. 6. x. 1. VI. i. 5. VII. iv. 5. X. i. 1. γένη VII. v. 1, 6. vi. 5.
γευμάτων III. x. 10.
γέρας V. vi. 7. VIII. xiv. 2.
γεῦσις III. x. 8. γεύσεως III. x. 9. VII. vii. 1. X. v. 7. γεύσει III. x. 9. γεῦσιν VII. iv. 3.
γεύεσθαι VII. iii. 9, 10.
γεωμετρεῖν X. v. 2.
γεωμέτρης I. vii. 19.
γεωμετρία VI. x. 1.
γεωμετρικὴν V. iii. 13. γεωμετρικοὶ VI. viii. 5. X. v. 2. γεωμετρικῇ V. iii. 13.
γεωργὸς V. 12. γεωργοῦ V. v. 9, 12.
γῆς VII. v. 3. γῆν X. ix. 6.
γῆρας IV. i. 37. γήρως I. ix. 11.
γραφὴν V. viii. 3.
γίνεται I. i. 3. iii. 7. vii. 8, 15. viii. 3. x. 12. xiii. 13. II. i. 6. ii. 7, 8. iii. 10, 11. iv. 5. vi. 3. viii. 8. III. i. 7. iii. 8. vii. 4. viii. 3. ix. 3. x. 5. IV. ii. 15. iii. 16, 37. v. 7, 10. ix. 4. V. i. 5. ii. 5. iii. 14, 15. iv. 1. v. 6, 9, 10. vi. 5. viii. 5. VI. xii. 10. xiii. 2. VII. i. 3. ii. 2, 8. iii. 12, 13. v. 1. VIII. i. 1, 7. ii. 1. iii. 1, 5, 9. iv. 1. v. 5. vi. 1, 5, 6, 7. vii. 2. viii. 4. x. 3.

xiii. 2, 3, 5. IX. i. 1, 3, 7, 9. iii. 4. v. 1, 3, 4. vi. 2. viii. 10. ix. 5. x. 5. xi. 3. xii. 1, 3. X. ii. 3. iii. 5. iv. 7, 9, 11. vi. 6. vii. 6. viii. 13. γινομένης I. vi. 1. II. ix. 4. X. iii. 6. iv. 1. ix. 15. γένοιτο I. vii. 10. x. 13, 14. xiii. 4. II. iii. 7. III. iii. 6, 13. IV. iii. 17. V. v. 3. IX. iii. 4. viii. 3. X. iii. 7, 12. iv. 1. ix. 18, 20. γενόμενοι I. vii. 17. γίνηται I. vii. 19. IV. iii. 18. vi. 9. V. iv. 2. VIII. ii. 3. iv. 1. v. 1. vi. 4. vii. 2, 4. xiv. 1. IX. i. 3, 4. ii. 5. γίνεσθαι I. vii. 23. x. 4. xii. 8. II. iii. 4, 5. iv. 1. III. iii. 11. iv. 5. xi. 7. VI. viii. 5. xii. 2. VII. xiv. 4. VIII. i. 6. iii. 4. iv. 3, 4. vi. 2, 5. vii. 2. viii. 6. ix. 5. xiv. 1. IX. i. 4, 8. v. 3. xii. 3. X. ii. 3. iii. 5. iv. 8. x. 5, 6, 14, 21. γινομένων IV. v. 10. IX. xii. 1. γίνονται I. viii. 9. ix. 11. II. i. 4, 6, 7. ii. 8. iii. 5. vii. 3. III. i. 9, 14. v. 12, 21. viii. 9, 14. xi. 3, 7. IV. i. 24. iii. 21. V. vi. 7. VI. viii. 5. VII. i. 2. v. 3. xiv. 3, 6. VIII. iii. 5. iv. 5. vi. 1. viii. 5. x. 5. xii. 4. xiii. 1. IX. i. 6. v. 2. x. 6. xii. 3. X. v. 2, 10. ix. 14. γίνεται I. x. 4. VIII. iv. 2. IX. ix. 7, 10. X. vii. 9. ix. 11. γένηται V. iv. 14. v. 8. viii. 7. VI. iii. 2. iv. 4. xiii. 8. IX. i. 3. iii. 3, 5. γεγένηται I. xiii. 3. X. iii. 7. γέγονε V. v. 11. γεγονὸς VI. ii. 6. γενόμενος I. x. 14. IV. i. 36. VII. ii. 8. IX. iv. 4. X. ix. 14. γινόμεθα II. i. 4, 7. ii. 9. v. 5. X. ix. 2. γινόμενον II. i. 5. IX. i. 8. vii. 1. X. iv. 1. ἐγίνοντο II. i. 7. X. ix. 19. γενόμεθα II. ii. 1. γενέσθαι II. ii. 1. iv. 3, 5. III. ii. 8. v. 10, 14. x. 10. V. v. 12, 15. vii. 4. viii. 10. VI. i. 6. VII. ii. 2. VIII. vi. 3. viii. 7. IX. iv. 10. viii. 10. X. ix. 16, 17. γινόμενα I. x. 12. II. ii. 6. iv. 3. v. 1. III. i. 3. γενόμενοι II. ii. 9. γινόμενοι II. ii. 9. γινόμεναι II. iii. 4. III. x. 11. IV. v. 14. X. v. 5. γινομένων I. x. 12. II. iii. 11. III. i. 1. iii. 4. VI. iv. 4. x. 1. VII. xii. 3. γινομένους X. iii. 6. ἐγένετο II. iii. 11. γινομέναις II. vii. 15 IV. vi. 7. γινομένοις III. v. 14. VIII. xii. 5. IX. iii. 5. γενόμενα VIII. xii. 2. IX. vii. 7. X. ix. 8. γινομένην IX. xi. 4. γένοιντο IX. vii. 2. X. ix. 21.

γεγονότος VI. ii. 6. γενόμενος VIII. v. 5. γενομένης IX. iii. 5. γενόμενον IX. iv. 4. γενομένου IX. vii. 3. γένοιντο X. vii. 6. γενοίμεθα X. ix. 17. γεγενῆσθαι X. iii. 6. γεγενημένου IX. vii. 6. γεγένηται VIII. xiii. 11. IX. viii. 4. ἐγεγόνει IX. iii. 5. γενομένους IX. v. 3.

γινώσκειν V. viii. 3. VI. xi. 3. γινώσκει I. iii. 5. γινώσκονται I. v. 5. γινώσκων V. ix. 12. γνόντες III. iii. 9. γνῶναι V. ix. 15. X. ix. 1. γνωσθεῖσι III. i. 9.

Γλαύκον V. ix. 12.

γλισχροὶ IV. i. 39.

γλιχόμενοι IV. viii. 3.

γλυκὺ VII. iii. 9, 10. γλυκέος VII. iii. 9. γλυκέα III. iv. 4. X. iii. 8. γλυκείων X. v. 9. γλυκύτατον VII. xiv. 8.

γνώμη VI. xi. 1, 3. γνώμην VI. xi. 1, 2, 6.

γνωρίζειν I. vi. 4. VI. vii. 7. γνωρίζεται V. i. 5. γνωρίσωμεν V. iv. 11. γνωρισθέντος VIII. ii. 1. γνωριστέον X. ix. 16.

γνώριμοι III. v. 22. γνώριμον II. ix. 5. γνωρίμων I. iv. 5. γνωρίμους IV. vi. 5. VII. xiii. 6. γνώριμοι VI. iii. 4. γνώριμα VI. viii. 5. γνωρίμοις IV. vi. 8.

γνῶσις I. ii. 2. iii. 6, 7. iv. 1. VI. i. 5. γνῶσιν I. vi. 15. xiii. 7. III. vii. 16. γνώσεως VI. viii. 4.

γνωστῶν X. vii. 2.

γονεῖς I. vii. 7. x. 4. IV. i. 20. VII. iv. 5. VIII. vii. 2. xi. 3. xii. 2, 3, 5. xiv. 4. IX. i. 7. γονεῦσι I. vii. 6. x. 5. VIII. vii. 1, 2. ix. 2. IX. ii. 7, 8. γονέων III. i. 4.

γόνυ IX. viii. 2.

γοῦν I. v. 5. xiii. 17. IV. iii. 18. iv. 5. VII. xiv. 5. VIII. ix. 1. IX. viii. 6. X. vii. 3.

γραμμάτων III. iii. 8.

γραμματικὴν II. iv. 2.

γραμματικὸς II. iv. 2. γραμματικὸν ibid. γραμματικοί, γραμματικά II. iv. 1.

γραμματικῶν II. iv. 2.

γραμμῆς V. iv. 8. γραμμὴν X. iv. 3.

γραφεῖς X. ix. 18.

γραφὴ X. v. 1. γραφῇ III. x. 3.

γραφικῆς X. ix. 20.

γράφει X. v. 5. γράφειν ibid. γράφοντες X. ix. 18. γεγραμμένων X. ix. 14.

γραπτέον X. iii. 8.

γυμνάσια II. ii. 16. γυμνασίων II. vi. 7. γυμνασίοις III. x. 11.

γυμναστὴς X. ix. 15.

γυμναστικὴ I. vi. 4. γυμναστικῆς X. ix. 14. γυμναστικῇ V. xi. 7. γυμναστικὴν III. iii. 8. VI. xii. 1.

γυμνικοῖς III. ix. 9.

γόνατα IX. xi. 4.

γυναικὸς VIII. x. 5. xii. 7. γυναικὶ I. vii. 6. V. vi. 1. ix. 16. VIII. vii. 1. x. 5. xii. 7. γυναῖκα III. vi. 5. V. vi. 9. VIII. vii. 1. xi. 4. xii. 8. γυναῖκες VIII. x. 5. γυναῖκας VII. v. 4.

Δ.

δαιμόνια VI. vii. 5. δαιμόνιον IV. ii. 11.

δαίμων IX. ix. 1.

δαπανώμενον VII. xiv. 6.

δανείζειν VII. v. 2. δανείσαντι IX. ii. 5. ἐδάνεισε IX. ii. 5. δανείσαντες IX. vii. 1. δανείσαντας IX. vii. 2.

δάνειον IX. ii. 3. δανείων IX. vii. 1.

δανειστὴν V. ii. 13.

δαπανᾶν IV. ii. 16. δαπανῶν IV. i. 23. ii. 3, 20. δαπανήσεται II. ix. 2. IV. ii. 5. δαπανήσεις IV. i. 24. ii. 7, 10, 13.

δαπάνη IV. i. 7. ii. 1. δαπάνης IV. ii. 6, 10. δαπάνην IV. i. 29. ii. 6. δαπάναι IV. ii. 6. δαπάναις IV. i. 23.

δαπάνημα IV. ii. 6. δαπανήματος IV. ii. 19. δαπανήματι IV. ii. 18. δαπανημάτων IV. ii. 11, 16, 20. δαπανήμασι IV. ii. 15.

δαπανηρὸν IV. ii. 15. δαπανηροὶ IV. i. 35. δαπανηροὺς IV. i. 3. δαπανηρὰς IV. ii. 1.

δεῖ I. ii. 7. iv. 6. vii. 17. ix. 10. x. 7. xiii. 7. II. i. 4, 8. ii. 4, 6. iii. 1, 2. 5. iv. 1. vi. 1, 11, 18. vii. 1, 8, 13. ix. 3. 4. 5, 6, 9. III. i. 7, 14, 19, 24. ii. 13. 14. iii. 13. 16. v. 8, 17. vi. 3. 4. vii. 2, 4. 5. 10, 12. viii. 5. ix. 1. x. 3. 4. xi. 4. 5. 7. 8. xii. 6, 7, 8, 9. IV. i. 3. 7. 12. 13. 15. 17. 22, 23. 24. 25. 28, 31. 33. 35. 40, 42, 43. ii. 4. 6, 10, 12, 20, 21. iii. 8, 10, 14. iv. 1, 2, 3, 4. 5. v. 3. 5. 7. 8, 10, 14. vi. 3. 5. 6. viii. 4. V. i. 9. iv. 11. v. 4. 7. 8, 9, 10, 11, 12, 13. 14. 15. vi. 4. ix. 7, 15. x. 6. VI. i. 1, 2, 3. ii. 2. iii. 2. vii. 3, 7. ix. 1, 5. 6. x. 2. xi. 3. 4. 6. xii. 1, 7. xiii. 5. VII. i. 5. ii. 6, 10, 12. iii. 5, 9, 12. iv. 5. vi. 1. vii. 3. ix. 5. xiv. 2, 3. VIII. iii. 4. 7, 9. iv. 4. vi. 3. 4. vii. 2. x. 5. xiii. 1, 10. IX. i. 8, 9. ii. 1. iii. 5. viii. 1, 2, 3. 7. 8, 11. ix. 2, 3. 6, 8, 10. x. 1, 2, 4. xi. 1, 4. 5. X. i. 1. iv. 7. viii. 9. 11. ix. 8, 9, 11, 21. δεῖν I. vi. 1. IV. ii. 11. vi. 1. ix. 3. 4. V. iii. 7. ix 6. VI. v. 6. viii. 4. ix. 2. VII. ii. 9. iii. 2. viii. 5. ix. 7. VIII. ii. 3. xiii. 6. xiv. 1, 2. IX. ii. 7, 8. viii. 2. ix. 1, 5. xi. 5. X. i. 2. vii. 3. ix. 10. δεήσει I. vi. 11. IX. ix. 10. X. viii. 4, 9. ἔδει II. i. 7. IV. viii. 9. VI. ix. 5. xiii. 7, 9. X. ii. 5. ix. 3. δέοι VII. xiii. 7. VIII. vii. 6. δέῃ IX. viii. 9. X. ix. 6. δεήσονται IX. ix. 1, 2. 4. 5. X. viii. 6. δέηται V. v. 13. δεηθῇ V. v. 14. δεῖται II. i. 1. V. v. 14. IX. ix. 4. X. vii. 4. viii. 5. δεῖσθαι IV. iii. 26. IX. ix. 4. X. viii. 4. δέονται VII. xiv. 6. VIII. vi. 4. viii. 5. xiii. 4. IX. ix. 1. X. vi. 3, 6. vii. 4. δέοιντο V. v. 11. δέωνται VIII. viii. 2. δεήσεσθαι X. viii. 9. δεοίμεθα X. ix. 9. δεόμενος VIII. xiii. 11. IX. i. 4. ix. 4. δεομένη VII. xiv. 8. δεομένων IX. ix. 2.

δεητικὸν IV. iii. 32.

δεδιέναι VII. v. 6. ἐδεδίει VII. v. 6.

δεικνύναι VII. i. 5. δείξει V. i. 16. δεῖξαι X. i. 17. δείξας VII. vi. 2. δεδειγμένον VII. i. 5. δέδεικται VII. ii. 5. x. 1. δειχθήσεται I. vii. 20. δειχθήσονται IV. ix. 8.

δειλαίνειν II. vi. 19. V. ix. 16.

δειλία II. viii. 6, 7. III. xii. 3. VII. v. 5. δειλίας III. xii. 1. δειλίαν V. ii. 2, 5. VII. v. 6. IX. iv. 8.

δειλὸς II. ii. 7. iii. 1. vii. 2. viii. 2, 3. III. vi. 5. vii. 10, 11, 12. V. xi. 4. VII. v. 6. δειλοῦ III. vii. 13. δειλὸν II. viii. 2, 3. δειλοὶ II. i. 7. III. vi. 4. viii. 1, 9.

δεινὸν VII. ii. 1. iii. 5. x. 2. δεινοὶ VII. ii. 8. δεινὰ I. xi. 4. II. iii. 1. IV. ix. 2. IX. iv. 8. δεινῶν III. vi. 6. viii. 11. δεινοῖς II. i. 7. δεινὸς VI. xii. 9. VII. i. 7. VIII. vi 5.

δεινότερον VIII. ix. 3. δεινότατα III. i. 8.

δεινότης VI. xiii. 2. δεινότητα VI. xii. 9. xiii. 1. VII. x. 2.

δέκα II. vi. 6, 7. V. v. 15. IX. x. 3.

δέκατον V. v. 15.

δένδρα X. v. 1.
δεξιὰ I. xiii. 15. V. vii. 4.
δέον II. vii. 1. III. xi. 3. IV. i. 25, 27, 36. ii. 13, 20. VII. ii. 2. IX. i. 9. iii. 5. δέοντος I. ii. 2. II. vii. 16. δέοντα VII. x. 2. IX. viii. 4.
δεσμὸς V. ii. 13.
δεσπότῃ VIII. xi. 6. δεσπότου VIII. x. 4.
δεσποτικὸν V. vi. 8. xi. 9.
δεῦρο IX. iv. 9.
δεύτερον II. ix. 4. V. iii. 9. δευτέρου V. iii. 9. δευτέρως VIII. vii. 3. X. v. 11. viii. 1.
δέχεται VIII. i. 7. X. iii. 2, 3. δέχεσθαι X. iv. 11. δέξασθαι II. i. 3.
δέδεκται VII. ii. 8.
δὴ I. ii. 1. vi. 7, 12. vii. 2, 5, 8, 10, 12, 14, 19. viii. 1, 2, 12. x. 2, 4, 7, 11, 14. xi. 3, 5. xii. 2. xiii. 8, 15, 18. II. i. 7, 8. vi. 3, 4, 8, 9. III. i. 1, 6, 10, 11, 12, 13, 16, 18, 19, 27. ii. 2, 10, 16. iii. 15, 16. iv. 4. v. 1, 16, 17, 19, 23. vi. 5, 10. vii. 6, 11. viii. 6, 11, 12, 13, 17. ix. 2, 4, 5. x. 7, 8, 9, 10, 11. IV. i. 4, 5, 6, 19, 31, 43. ii. 2, 6, 7, 10. iii. 8, 9, 10, 18. iv. 5. v. 13. vii. 1, 2. viii. 8, 10. ix. 2. V. i. 3, 8. v. 10, 12, 14, 15, 16. viii. 3. xi. 9. VI. i. 4. ii. 6. iii. 1, 3. v. 1. vi. 1, 2. vii. 4, 5. ix. 3, 7. xii. 3, 9. xiii. 1, 4. VII. iii. 6. iv. 5. viii. 4. ix. 1. x. 3. xiii. 7. xiv. 1, 3. VIII. iii. 1, 2, 3, 4, 8. v. 1. vi. 1. vii. 2, 6. viii. 1, 2, 6. ix. 3, 6. x. 3. xi. 3, 5, 6, 7, 8. xii. 3. xiii. 1, 9, 11. xiv. 3, 4. IX. ii. 7. iii. 3. iv. 3, 5, 9, 10. v. 3. vi. 2. vii. 4, 7. viii. 1, 2, 3, 4, 6, 9, 10, 11. ix. 3, 4, 5, 10. x. 2, 3, 5. xi. 1, 6. X. ii. 1, 2, 3, 5. iii. 3, 6. iv. 2, 4, 9. v. 2, 5, 7. vi. 1, 2, 4, 6. vii. 1, 7, 8, 9. viii. 3, 5, 7, 8, 12. ix. 2, 5, 8, 9, 12, 15, 19, 22.
Δηλιακὸν I. viii. 14.
δῆλος X. viii. 4. δηλῇ V. i. 7. δῆλον I. ii. 1. v. 5, 8. vi. 3, 9, 13. vii. 3, 8. x. 4, 8, 12. xii. 1, 3, 4, 7. xiii. 4, 7. II. i. 2, 4. III. i. 17. iii. 18. v. 11, 23. xi. 5. xii. 5. IV. i. 24. iv. 4. v. 13, 14. viii. 1, 4. V. i. 8, 12, 20. ii. 2, 7. iii. 1, 7, 9. v. 15, 16, 17. vii. 4. ix. 3, 8. x. 8. VI. ii. 2. v. 7. vii. 2, 5. ix. 3, 4. xii. 10. xiii. 6, 7. VII. iii. 7. vi. 5. xii. 1. VIII. iv. 2. vii. 4. xii. 2. xiii. 6. IX. iii. 4. viii. 3. ix. 3, 5. X. ii. 3. iii. 13. iv. 4, 7. v. 5, 11. vi. 2. vii. 6. viii. 5. ix. 6. δῆλα VII. i. 1.
δηλοῦσι I. xiii. 5. III. vi. 2. VII. i. 2. iv. 6. v. 8, 9. IX. xi. 4. X. ix. 14.
δηλοῖ II. ix. 9. V. v. 13. VII. iii. 4. δηλοῦντες V. x. 1. δεδήλωται VII. vi. 1.
δημηγορικοὺς X. ix. 18.
δημιουργουμένοις I. iii. 1.
δημηγοροῦντες II. ix. 6.
Δημοδόκου VII. viii. 3.
δημοκρατία VIII. x. 3. δημοκρατίαν VIII. x. 1. δημοκρατίαι VIII. x. 6. δημοκρατίαις VIII. xi. 8.
δημοκρατικοὶ V. iii. 7.
δῆμος IX. vi. 2. δήμῳ III. iii. 18.
δημόται VIII. ix. 5.
δήποτε VI. xii. 10. VIII. xiii. 7. IX. i. 5. vi. 2.
διαγνῶναι III. iii. 10.
διάγραμμα III. iii. 11.
διαγραφῆς II. vii. 1.
διάγειν IX. xi. 1. xii. 2. διάγοντες III. v. 10.
διαγωγῆς IV. viii. 1. διαγωγὴν IX. xi. 5. διαγωγαὶ X. vi. 3. διαγωγαῖς X. vi. 3, 8.
διάδηλα I. xiii. 12.
διάθεσις II. vii. 13. διαθέσεις VII. i. 4. διαθέσεις II. vii. 6, 8. διαθέσεων II. viii. 1.
διαιρεῖν I. xi. 2. IX. viii. 3. διαιρεῖται III. ii. 10. διελόμενοι II. vii. 6. VI. i. 4. X. ix. 21. διείλομεν VII. iv. 5. διείλομεν VI. i. 1. διῄρηνται V. iii. 10. διῄρηται V. iv. 4. VIII. xii. 7. διῃρημένη V. iii. 9. διῃρημένοις VIII. vi. 5. xii. 3. διαιρεθῇ V. iv. 8. διῃρήσθωσαν III. x. 2. διαιρετέον VI. i. 5.
διαιρετῷ II. vi. 4.
δίαιτα I. vi. 3.
διακεῖσθαι II. v. 4. IX. iv. 10. διάκεινται VII. xiv. 6. διακείμενος X. viii. 13. διακειμένου X. iv. 5. διακειμένῳ X. iv. 5. διακειμένοις III. iv. 4. X. iii. 8. v. 11.
διακόνους VII. vi. 1.
διηκρίβωται III. iii. 8. διακριβῶσαι X. viii. 3.
διακρίνει III. xi. 7.
διακωλύουσι VIII. viii. 5.
διαλάμπει I. x. 12.
διαλανθάνειν X. ix. 20. διαλανθάνει IV. vii. 13.
διαλεχθείη VI. xiii. 6.
διαλλάττουσι VIII. x. 6. X. v. 9. διαλ-

λάττοι IX. iii. 4. διαλλαττομένους IV. v. 11.
διαλύει VIII. v. 1. διαλύονται VIII. iv. 2. xii. 7. διαλύωνται VIII. xiii. 5. διαλυόμενοι VIII. xiii. 8. IX. iii. 3. διαλύεσθαι IX. iii. 1. X. iii. 5. διαλυθῆναι IX. i. 8. διαλύονται VIII. iii. 3. xiv. 1. διαλυτέον VIII. xiii. 9. IX. iii. 3.
διάλυσις IX. i. 3. iii. 5.
διαμαρτάνει IV. i. 28. διαμαρτάνειν I. viii. 7. διαμαρτόντα VIII. xiii. 9.
διαμένει VIII. iii. 3, 6. ix. 4. X. iii. 3. διαμένει IX. iii. 4. διαμένουσι VIII. iv. 1, 2. viii. 5, 6. διαμενόντων VIII. iii. 3. διαμένοντας IX. ii. 1.
διαμέτρου III. iii. 3. διάμετρον V. v. 8.
διαμφισβητεῖται VIII. i. 6.
διανεμητικὸς V. v. 17. διανεμητικὸν V. iv. 2. v. 2.
διανέμειν IX. x. 4. διανέμων V. ix. 9, 10. διανέμοντι V. ix. 10.
διανοούμενον I. vii. 13.
διανοητική II. i. 1. VI. ii. 5. διανοητικῆς II. i. 1. διανοητικοῦ VI. ii. 3. VIII. iv. 3. διανοητικὰς I. xiii. 20.
διάνοια VI. ii. 2, 5. VII. ii. 8. X. iv. 9. v. 7. διανοίας III. ii. 17. x. 2. VI. i. 4. ii. 3, 4. ix. 3. IX. ix. 3. X. v. 2. διανοίᾳ VI. ii. 2. IX. iv. 5. X. iv. 10. ix. 18. διάνοιαν VII. iv. 3. IX. iii. 4. X. iii. 12. iv. 5. v. 7.
διανομή V. iv. 2. διανομῆς V. iii. 12. διανομαῖς V. ii. 12. iii. 7.
διαπονεῖ X. viii. 4. διαπονεῖν IX. iv. 3.
διαπορῆσαι I. vi. 1. διαπορήσειε V. ix. 3. VI. xii. 1. διαπορήσαντας VII. i. 5. διαπορηθὲν I. x. 10. διαπορεῖσθαι I. xi. 5.
διαπορεύεται X. iv. 3.
διαρθρῶσαι I. vii. 17.
διασαφῆσαι I. vii. 2. διασαφηθείη I. iii. 1.
διασώζοντα IX. iv. 9.
διασπᾶται IX. iii. 4.
διάστημα VIII. vii. 4.
διαστρέφει VI. v. 6. xii. 10. διεστραμμένα II. ix. 5.
διάστασιν IX. v. 1.
διατάσσει I. ii. 6.
διατείνει IV. i. 38. ii. 1. III. i. 1. X. viii. 8. διατεινομένων IX. viii. 7.
διατεταμένοι IX. iv. 10. X. iv. 9.
διατελεῖ VII. xiv. 6. διατελοῦσι III. v. 11.
διατηροῦντες X. viii. 1.
διατιθέασι IV. iv. 1. διατίθενται VII. iii. 7. διαθεῖναι X. ix. 18.
διατρίβων VI. viii. 4.
διαφέρει I. i. 5. iii. 7. viii. 9. xi. 4. xiii. 10, 16. II. i. 5, 8. vii. 6. III. i. 13. 26. ii. 15. iv. 5. vii. 1. xi. 7. xii. 5. IV. i. 34. ii. 18. iii. 2. vi. 5. vii. 8. viii. 5, 6. ix. 5. V. i. 20. iv. 3. v. 5, 16. vii. 1, 7. VI. vii. 4. ix. 1. xiii. 1. VII. iii. 3, 6. vi. 6. VIII. iii. 1. ix. 2. xi. 2. X. iii. 3, 12. v. 7. vii. 8. διαφέρουσι I. iv. 5. II. vii. 6, 11. IV. viii. 4, 12. VII. iii. 7. vii. 3. VIII. vii. 1. x. 2. X. iii. 10. iv. 2. v. 2, 7, 8. ix. 15. διαφέρῃ X. v. 4. διαφέρον X. viii. 4. διαφέρειν I. xiii. 12. VII. x. 2. VIII. vi. 7. X. v. 1. vii. 7. ix. 14. διέφερε VII. iv. 2. διαφερέτω X. iv. 5. διοίσει IV. viii. 1. V. vi. 1. VI. xii. 2. VII. iii. 4, 5, 6. VIII. ii. 2. X. viii. 4. διαφέρουσι VIII. x. 6. διαφέρονται VIII. xiv. 1. IX. i. 4. iv. 8. διοίσουσι I. vi. 5. διαφέρων IX. viii. 6. διαφέρουσα X. viii. 7. διαφέροντος IV. vii. 7. διαφέρουσαν II. vii. 8. διαφέροντα IV. v. 2. V. v. 15. διαφέροντες I. vi. 11. VIII. xiii. 1. διαφέρουσαι X. iii. 13. διαφερόντων I. x. 12. VIII. i. 6. x. 4. IX. ii. 10. X. v. 1. διαφερουσῶν X. v. 6. διαφερούσας X. v. 1.
διαφερόντως I. vii. 19. IV. vi. 7. IX. viii. 7. X. ii. 1.
διαφθείρει VI. v. 9. διαφθείραντι V. xi. 3. διέφθαρται VII. vi. 7. διεφθαρμένῳ VI. v. 6. διεφθαρμένης IX. ix. 8. διεφθαρμένοις X. v. 11.
διαφορὰ I. i. 2. διαφορὰν I. iii. 2. xi. 5. xiii. 20. V. iv. 3. VI. viii. 4. VII. iii. 2. διαφορὰς I. xi. 2. II. i. 8. IV. vi. 8. VII. vi. 6. IX. ii. 2. διαφορᾷ III. i. 10. IX. iii. 1. X. iv. 3.
διάφοροι VIII. x. 4. διαφόρους X. iii. 10.
διαφόρως III. vii. 12. IV. vi. 8.
διαφυλάττειν I. v. 6.
διαφωνεῖ I. viii. 1. V. v. 4. VIII. ii. 2. IX. viii. 2, 8. διαφωνεῖν I. vi. 15. διαφωνοῦσι X. i. 3. διαφωνούντων X. viii. 12.
διαψεύδεσθαι VI. iii. 1. xii. 10. διαψευδόμεθα VI. vi. 2. διαψευσθῇ IX. iii. 3.
διδασκαλία VI. iii. 3. διδασκαλίας II. i. 1.
διδασκαλικὸς VII. viii. 4.

διδάσκειν X. ix. 18. διδάξειν IX. i. 5. διδάξαι X. ix. 20. διδάξοντες II. i. 7. διδακτὴ VI. iii. 3.

διδαχὴ X. ix. 6. διδαχῇ X. ix. 6.

διδόναι IV. i. 7, 17. 29. 30. 31. 39. 43. V. ix. 7. δοῦναι II. ix. 2. IV. i. 9. 39. V. ix. 7, 14. IX. i. 7. δίδοται VIII. xiv. 3. δώσουσι X. viii. 7. δόντες V. v. 13. διδόασι VIII. viii. 3. IX. i. 9 δεδωκὼς VIII. xiii. 7. δοὺς VIII. xiii. 9. διδόντες IV. i. 10. δώσει IV. i. 12, 17, 22, 24, 31. IX. i. 4. διδοὺς IV. i. 14. V. ix. 7. διδομένων IV. i. 19. διδόντος ibid. δίδωσι IV. i. 19, 31. διδόντα IV. i. 19, 31. διδῷ IV. i. 19. IX. ix. 1. διδόντας IV. i. 30. δοῖεν IV. i. 35. δόσεων IV. ii. 3. δέδωκεν V. iv. 13. δοθέντων I. x. 13.

διεξιέναι X. iv. 3. διεξιοῦσι X. viii. 7. ix. 21.

διελθεῖν III. ii. 1. IV. ii. 1. VIII. i. 1. IX. xii. 4. X. i. 1. vi. 1. διελθόντες IV. vii. 1. διεληλύθαμεν VI. i. 4.

διηγητικοὺς III. x. 2.

διήκει IX. viii. 2. διήκοντα VIII. ix. 3.

διικνεῖται I. xi. 5. διικνοῦνται I. xiii. 13.

διίστησι V. xi. 9. VII. vii. 7. διιστᾶσι X. v. 5.

δικαιοπραγεῖ V. viii. 1, 11. δικαιοπραγῇ V. viii. 11. δικαιοπραγήσει X. vii. 4. δικαιοπραγεῖν X. ii. 2. iii. 2. viii. 4. I. viii. 12. V. viii. 4. ix. 2, 3. δικαιοπραγοῦντος V. ix. 3. δικαιοπραγοῦσι V. i. 3.

δικαιοπράγημα V. vii. 7. viii. 2.

δικαιοπραγία V. v. 17.

δίκαιος II. iv. 4, 5. III. v. 15. V. i. 8, 12. v. 17. vii. 6. viii. 11 ix. 16. X. vii. 4. δίκαιον I. viii. 12. xii. 2. 4. V. i. 1, 8, 12. ii. 8, 10. iii. 3, 7, 8, 10, 11, 12, 14. iv. 2, 3, 6, 7, 14. v. 1, 2, 3, 6, 17. vi. 3, 4. 8, 9. viii. 10. ix. 12, 14. x. 1, 2, 3, 6, 8. xi. 4, 9. VII. vi. 4. xiii. 4. VIII. ix. 1, 3, 4. xi. 1, 3, 4, 6, 7, 8. xii. 8. xiii. 5. IX. i. 8. iii. 2. X. iii. 10. δικαίου V. ii. 9. iii. 17. iv. 7. v. 17. 19. vi. 4, 5. vii. 1. viii. 10. ix. 16. x. 2, 3, 6, 8. X. iii. 10. δικαίῳ V. iv. 2. X. viii. 4. δίκαιοι II. i. 4. 7. iv. 4. VI. xiii. 1. VIII. i. 4. X. iii. 2. δίκαια I. iii. 2. viii. 10. II. i. 4. iv. 1, 3. 4. 5. V. i. 3. 12. vii. 2, 5. viii. 4. ix. 15, 17. VI. xii. 1, 7. VIII. ix. 2. IX. v. 3. vi. 3, 4. viii. 5. X. viii. 1. δικαίων I. iv. 6. V. i. 3. vii. 5. 6. viii. 1, 4. ix. 3. xi. 1. VI. xii. 7. VIII. i. 4. δικαίους II. iv. 1. VI. xii. 7. δικαίοις V. viii. 1. VIII. vii. 3. δικαίας X. viii. 7. δικαιότερον IX. i. 9. δικαιότατον I. viii. 14.

δικαιοσύνη V. i. 1, 15, 17, 19, 20. ii. 9. 10. v. 17. x. 8. δικαιοσύνης II. vii. 16. IV. ix. 8. V. i. 1. ii. 9, 12. v. 19. xi. 10. VIII. i. 4. δικαιοσύνῃ V. i. 15. δικαιοσύνην IV. i. 10. vii. 7. V. i. 2. ii. 1. vi. 6. x. 1. VIII. i. 4. X. iii. 2. δικαιοσύναι V. ii. 7.

δικαιοῦσθαι V. ix. 2, 3. δικαιοῦνται V. ix. 2.

δικαίωμα V. vii. 7.

δικανικοὺς X. ix. 18.

δικαστὴς V. iv. 4, 7, 8, δικαστὴν V. iv. 7.

δικαστικὴ VI. viii. 3.

δίκη V. iv. 3. vi. 4. δίκαι VIII. xiii. 6. δίκας IX. i. 9.

διὸ I. i. 1. iii. 5. iv. 6. v. 2, 8. II. i. 8. iii. 2, 5, 8. vi. 14, 17. viii. 3, 8. ix. 2, 3. III. v. 14. vi. 2. vii. 9. viii. 15. 16. ix. 2. x. 10. xi. 2, 3, 6. xii. 2, 3, 7. 9. IV. i. 4. 7, 21, 23, 31, 35. ii. 13. iii. 18, 19, 25. 29. V. i. 3. iv. 7. v. 7, 10, 14, 15, 18. vi. 5, 6, 9. viii. 9. ix. 14. x. 6. xi. 2. VI. i. 3. ii. 5, 6. vii. 4, 5, 7. viii. 2, 4. ix. 4. xi. 5, 6. xii. 9. VII. iv. 4, 5, 6. vi. 6. vii. 3, 4. viii. 3. x. 2. xi. 3. xii. 3. xiii. 2. xiv. 4, 8. VIII. iii. 5. vi. 1. viii. 1, 2. 6. xi. 3. xii. 4, 7. xiii. 6. xiv. 4. IX. v. 3. viii. 4, 6. ix. 2. xi. 1, 5. X. i. 1, 2, 4. v. 4. vi. 3. ix. 8, 10, 19.

διοικεῖν VI. viii. 4.

Διομήδης III. viii. 2. Διομήδει V. ix. 7. Διομήδην III. viii. 2.

διομολογία IX. i. 7.

διόπερ I. vi. 2. II. i. 1. ix. 2. IV. i. 34. iii. 31. VI. xiii. 3. VIII. iii. 5. x. 6. IX. vi. 1. ix. 7. x. 5. xi. 4. xii. 2. X. iv. 2. ix. 10.

διορθοῦντες IX. xii. 3.

διορθωτικὸν V. ii. 12. iv. 1. v. 2.

διορίζειν IX. viii. 3. X. i. 3. διωρίσθω I. x. 16. V. viii. 3. ix. 10. VI. iii. 4. διορίζεται I. xiii. 20. II. iii. 5. διορισθήσεται II. vii. 5. διορίσαι II. ix. 7. III. i. 1, 16. IV. v. 13. IX. ii. 2. διώρισται I. viii. 14. V. ii. 8. ix. 1. διωρίσθη VII. vii. 1. διορισθῶσι I. vii.

23. διωρισμέναι X. v. 6. διωρισμένον VI. i. 3. διωρισμένων I. xii. 1. III. ii. 1. V. v. 17. διωριστέον V. ii. 10, 11. IX. ii. 10.
διορισμὸς V. vii. 4. ix. 5. διορισμὸν V. ix. 9. xi. 6.
διώκει I. iv. 7. V. xi. 5. VI. viii. 5. IX. vii. 4.
διπλῆ III. v. 8.
δὶς V. iii. 9.
διστάζομεν III. iii. 8, 9. διστάζουσι VII. ii. 4. iii. 3.
διττὸν I. xiii. 18, 19. VIII. xiii. 5. διττῆς II. i. 1.
διττῶν I. iv. 5. vi. 9. vii. 13.
δίχα V. iv. 8, 9.
διχαῖον V. iv. 9.
διχαστὴς ibid.
διχῶς VII. iii. 3. xii. 1.
δίψην VII. iv. 3. δίψας VII. xiv. 5.
διωθεῖσθαι VIII. xiv. 4. IX. xi. 6.
διώκειν I. iii. 7. v. 14. II. iii. 5. VI. ii. 2. VII. iii. 2. viii. 4. 5. xii. 7. xiii. 5. xiv. 2. διώκουσι V. i. 9. VIII. iv. 5. ix. 7. xiii. 6. xiv. 4. VIII. iii. 4. 5. X. ix. 4. διώκομεν I. vi. 10. διώκει VII. iii. 2. iv. 4. ix. 1. xi. 4. xii. 7. VIII. x. 3. διώκεται I. i. 4. vi. 10. διώκων VII. ii. 10. iv. 3. vii. 2. διώκοντι VII. xiv. 2. διώκονται VII. xiv. 4. 5. διωκόμενα I. vi. 8. διωκτὸν I. vii. 4.
δίωξις VI. ii. 2.
δοκεῖ I. i. 1. v. 4. 6. vi. 7. vii. 5, 6, 10, 13. 23. viii. 6. x. 3. xii. 5. xiii. 2, 12. II. viii. 7. III. i. 3, 13, 14, 18, 25, 27. ii. 1, 6, 10. iv. 1. vi. 3, 6. vii. 8. viii. 6, 15. xii. 3. IV. i. 1, 5, 7. 23. 31, 32, 37. ii. 1. iii. 3, 19. 34. 35. v. 4. vii. 2. viii. 1, 8, 11. ix. 2. V. i. 4, 8, 10, 15, 16, 17. iii. 3. v. 1, 6. vi. 6. vii. 2. xi. 5, 9. VI. iii. 3. v. 1. viii. 3, 5. ix. 4. xi. 5. xiii. 1. VII. i. 6. iii. 5, 6. vii. 7. ix. 5. xi. 3. xii. 3, 6. xiii. 4. 6. xiv. 3. 8. VIII. i. 1, 4, 5. ii. 1, 2. iii. 4. v. 1, 3. 4. vi. 1. vii. 2. viii. 1, 3. 6. ix. 1, 4. xi. 7. xii. 7. xiv. 4. IX. i. 5. iii. 3. iv. 3, 5. vii. 7. viii. 1, 6, 10. ix. 2, 4. x. 1. X. i. 1, 3. ii. 4. iii. 4. 5, 6, 12. iv. 5. v. 8, 9. 10. vi. 3, 6. vii. 1, 3. 6, 7. viii. 2, 13. ix. 7, 13, 21.
δόξειε I. ii. 4. vi. 1, 14. vii. 10, 17. III. i. 20. vi. 7. ix. 3. x. 3. 10. xii. 3. IV. i. 31. ii. 1. iii. 7, 14. iv. 1. vii. 8. ix. 2. VI. xii. 3. VII. ii. 10. vii. 3. VIII. ii. 1. viii. 2. xiv. 4. IX. i. 8. ii. 4. iii. 3. iv. 4. 6. vii. 2, 7. viii. 6. ix. 10. x. 2. 5. xi. 5. X. i. 2. iv. 4. vii. 2, 5, 9. viii. 4. ix. 14. 15. 16. ἔδοξε VII. iv. 5. IX. x. 3. X. ii. 1. ix. 18. δοκεῖν I. iii. 2. V. vi. 1. VII. iii. 13. δοκοῦσι I. x. 10. III. ii. 14. iii. 7. v. 9. viii. 1, 10. x. 1. xi. 1. IV. i. 4, 20, 30, 38, 39. iii. 18, 25, 35. v. 5. vi. 1, 7. vii. 14. viii. 3. ix. 9. VI. viii. 4. VII. x. 2. VIII. iv. 4. viii. 1. ix. 5. IX. vii. 1. viii. 6. x. 6. xii. 3. X. v. 1. vi. 3. vii. 6. viii. 10. ix. 16. δοκοίη III. ii. 7. δοκοῦν III. iv. 3. δοκῇ III. v. 8. IX. vi. 2. δόξει V. ii. 4. δόξαιεν IX. ii. 5. X. ix. 18. δόξασι VII. ix. 4. δοκοῦσαι I. iv. 4. δοκοῦντες III. viii. 17. δοκοῦσιν VII. iii. 13. δοκοῦντος VIII. xi. 2. IX. viii. 6. δοκούντων X. v. 11. δοκοῦσαι VII. xii. 1. δοκοῦσαν IX. i. 8. δοκούντων IX. iv. 8. δόξαντα IX. vi. 1.
δοκιμάζοντες III. x. 9. δεδοκιμασμέναι VIII. iv. 3.
δοκιμασία VIII. xii. 6.
δολοπλάνου VII. vi. 3.
δολοφονία V. ii. 13.
δόξας I. iv. 4. δόξαν I. vii. 2. viii. 2. III. ii. 3. IV. ix. 5. VII. ii. 3. iii. 3. IX. xi. 6. δόξαις I. xi. 1. VI. xi. 6. δόξα III. ii. 10, 13, 15. IV. iii. 35. VI. v. 8. ix. 1, 3. VII. ii. 4. iii. 9, 11, 13. X. iv. 6. δόξῃ III. ii. 11, 15. VI. iii. 1. x. 1, 3. VII. ii. 7. ix. 1, 2. δόξαι X. vii. 6. viii. 12. δόξης IV. iii. 28. vii. 12, 13. V. ix. 9. VI. viii. 4. ix. 3. VII. ii. 7. iii. 4, 10.
δοξάζειν III. ii. 11. 14. δοξάζουσι VII. iii. 4. δοξάζομεν III. ii. 12, 13. δοξάζει IV. iii. 22. δοξάζοντες VII. iii. 4. δοξαζόντων VII. iii. 3.
δοξαστικοῦ VI. v. 8. xiii. 2.
δόρυ III. i. 17.
δόσις IV. i. 7. IX. ii. 5. δόσεως IV. i. 20, 38. IX. i. 8. δόσει IV. i. 1, 8, 11. 12, 18, 24. 29. 38. 39. iv. 2. δόσιν II. vii. 4. IV. i. 1, 24. 29. δόσεις IV. i. 35. δόσεσι IV. i. 23.
δοτέος V. vi. 7. δοτέον IX. ii. 1, 3.
δοτικοί IV. i. 37.
δουλαπατία V. ii. 13.
δουλεία V. v. 6.
δουλεύειν X. i. 2.

δουλικὸν IV. iii. 29.
δοῦλος VIII. xi. 6, 7. δούλους VIII. x. 4. δούλοις ibid.
δρᾶν VIII. xiii. 2. IX. xi. 1. X. ix. 14. δρῶν VIII. xiii. 2. IX. v. 3. δρῶμεν X. v. 4. δρῶντας III. v. 7. VIII. xiii. 9. δράσαντος VIII. xiii. 10, 11. δράσαντι IX. vii. 5. δράσαντας IX. vii. 1. δρᾷ V. xi. 2. δρῶσι III. viii. 4. 5. 11. IV. iii. 21. V. viii. 10. VII. viii. 4. X. v. 4. ix. 12. δέδρακεν VIII. xiv. 4.
δρομικὸν I. xii. 2.
δρόμου II. vi. 7.
δριμὺ III. viii. 10.
δυνάμεθα II. ii. 9. IX. ix. 5. X. vii. 2. δύνανται II. ii. 8. iv. 4. III. vii. 8. IV. i. 26, 31. ii. 5. V. i. 15. v. 12, 14. VII. iii. 10. vii. 6. VIII. v. 2. X. vii. 4. δυνησόμεθα II. ii. 9. ix. 7. δύνασθαι III. viii. 7. IV. iii. 21. V. i. 15. VI. v. 5. VII. vii. 5, 6. VIII. xiii. 4. δύνασθαι II. v. 5. IV. iii. 29. VI. v. 1. xii. 9. VII. xi. 4. X. ix. 14. δυνάμενοι III. viii. 7, 21. X. ix. 16. ἐδύναντο X. ix. 19. δυνάμενος VIII. xiii. 9. δυναμένῳ ibid. δυναμένου VII. xiv. 5. δυνάμενον VII. iii. 9. VIII. xi. 7. δύνηται VII. ii. 8. δύναιτο IV. v. 7. V. ix. 16. IX. x. 3. X. viii. 10. δυναμένους IV. v. 13. δυναμένοις X. ix. 21.
δύναμις I. xiii. 12. V. i. 4. ii. 6. VI. xii. 9, 10. IX. 9, 7. δυνάμεως I. viii. 15. VI. xii. 8, 10. VII. x. 4. xii. 6. X. viii. 4. ix. 19. δυνάμει IV. vii. 12. IX. vii. 4. ix. 7. X. ix. 18. δύναμιν I. xiii. 11. V. vii. 1, 2. VI. vii. 4. VIII. x. 5. xiv. 4. X. i. 1. ix. 12, 22. δυνάμεις II. i. 4. v. 1, 2, 5, 6. VI. xi. 2. X. ix. 18. δυνάμεων I. ii. 3. 6. xii. 1. V. i. 4. X. ix. 18.
δυναστείαν IV. iii. 18. δυναστείας VIII. i. 1. X. vii. 6. δυναστεῖαι IV. iii. 18. δυναστείαις X. vi. 3.
δυναστεύων X. vi. 4. δυναστεύοντες IV. iii. 19.
δυνάστης VIII. xiv. 1. δυνάσταις X. viii. 8. δυναστῶν X. viii. 10.
δυνατὸν I. ix. 4. III. iii. 13. v. 14. VIII. xiii. 9. xiv. 3. IX. iii. 3. X. viii. 10. δυνατοὶ II. v. 2, 3. δυνατώτεροι VIII. i. 2. δυνατὰ III. iii. 13.
δύο I. xiii. 10. II. vi. 6, 7, 15. viii. 1. 7. ix. 2. V. ii. 13. iii. 5. iv. 10. v. 9. vii. 1. ix. 8. VI. i. 5. xiii. 2. VII. iii. 6. xiv. 3. VIII. i. 2. IX. iv. 6. X. v. 4. δυοῖν V. iii. 5. VI. v. 8. δυσὶ IV. i. 29, 38. V. iii. 4. 9. iv. 10. VI. v. 6. VII. i. 1. IX. x. 6.
δυσαφαίρετον I. v. 4.
δυσγενὴς I. viii. 16.
δυσάλωτοι IV. v. 10.
δύσελπις III. vii. 11.
δύσερις II. vii. 13. IV. vi. 9. δυσέριδες IV. vi. 2.
δύσκολος II. vii. 13. IV. vi. 9. δύσκολοι IV. 6, 2. δυσκολώτεροι VIII. vi. 1.
δύσπειστοι VII. ix. 2.
δυσπραξίαι I. xi. 6.
δυστυχῶν IX. xi. 5. δυστυχοῦντι X. vi. 2.
δυστυχημάτων I. x. 3.
δυστυχίαι I. x. 3. δυστυχίαις VII. xiii. 3. VIII. i. 2. IX. xi. 1, 2.
δυσχεραίνει III. xi. 8. IV. viii. 10. VIII. xiii. 2. IX. ix. 6. δυσχεραίνουσι III. vi. 11. δυσχεραίνων III. i. 13. IV. vi. 9. δυσχεραίνοντες IV. viii. 3. δυσχεραίνειν X. ix. 10. δυσχερανεῖ IV. vi. 3. 7.
δυσχερῆ VII. i. 5. X. v. 10. δυσχερῶν IX. iv. 9.
δωρεὰς IV. ii. 15.
δωρεῖται VIII. xiii. 7.
δώρημα I. ix. 2.
δωροδόκῳ VIII. xiv. 4.
δώρων IV. ii. 18. δῶρα IV. ii. 15.

E.

ἐὰν II. v. 2, 3. vi. 4. III. iii. 13. v. 8. viii. 16. IV. i. 19, 25. iii. 7. vi. 8. vii. 5. V. i. 5, 6. iii. 9. iv. 2, 7. v. 8. viii. 11. ix. 3. VII. i. 5. vi. 1. ix. 3. xiii. 3. xiv. 6. VIII. iii. 3. 4. iv. 1. v. 1. vi. 6. vii. 4. viii. 3. xiii. 2. IX. ii. 1. 5. iii. 3. viii. 9. xi. 3. X. iii. 2. v. 3. 4.
ἐάν γε III. v. 14.
ἔαρ I. vii. 16.
ἑαυτὸν I. xiii. 14.
ἐᾷ V. xi. 2. ἐῶμεν V. vi. 5.
ἐγγίνονται II. i. 3. ἐγγίνεται II. i. 2.
ἐγγένῃ V. ii. 3.
ἐγγυητὴς V. v. 14.
ἐγγὺς III. x. 7. V. xi. 7. VII. vii. 2. VIII. viii. 1. ἔγγιον IX. viii. 2. ἐγγύτερον II. viii. 7.

ἐγείρῃ III. viii. 10.

ἐγερτέον III. viii. 10.

ἐγκαλεῖ IX. i. 2. ἐγκαλοῦσι IX. viii. 1. ἐγκαλέσαι VIII. xiii. 8. ἐγκαλέσει IX. iii. 1. ἐγκαλοίη VIII. xiii. 2. ἐγκαλεῖν IX. iii. 2. ἐγκαλῶν VIII. xiii. 3. ἐγκαλεῖται IV. i. 21.

ἐγκλήματα V. iii. 6. VIII. xiii. 2, 5. 11. ἐγκλήμασι IX. i, 6, 7.

ἐγκληματική VIII. xiii. 4.

ἐγκατέλιπε V. ii. 5.

ἐγκράτεια IV. ix. 8. VII. i. 6. ii. 6, 7, 11. iii. 2. v. 9. vi. 5. vii. 4. ix. 5, 6. x. 3, 5. ἐγκρατείας VII. i. 4. xiv. 9. ἐγκράτειαν VII. i. 1. iv. 6. vii. 6.

ἐγκρατής III. ii. 4. VI. i. 6. ii. 6. iii. 2. vii. 4. ix. 1, 2, 5. 6. IX. viii. 6. ἐγκρατοῦς I. xiii. 15. 17. ἐγκρατεῖ VII. ix. 1, 2, 3. ἐγκρατῆ VII. i. 6. iii. 1. iv. 4. ἐγκρατεῖς VII. iv. 1. vii. 1.

ἐγκυκλίοις I. v. 6.

ἐγκώμια I. xii. 6, 7.

ἐγχειροῦσι III. iii. 13.

ἐγκεχρονισμένον II. iii. 8.

ἔγωγε IX. xi. 5.

ἐδωδῇ III. x. 7.

ἐθέλει IX. vi. 2.

ἐθίζονται II. i. 2. ἐθισθείη II. i. 2. IV. i. 31. ἐθίζῃ II. i. 2. ἐθίζοντες II. i. 5. ἐθιζόμενοι II. i. 7. ii. 9. ἐθίζεσθαι II. i. 8. X. ix. 9. ἐθισθῆναι III. xii. 2. X. ix. 11. ἐθιζομένους VII. v. 3.

ἐθισμοῦ VII. x. 4. ἐθισμῷ I. vii. 21. ἐθισμοί III. xii. 2.

ἔθνει I. ii. 8.

ἔθος VII. v. 4. xiv. 4. ἔθους II. i. 1, 3. VII. v. 3. x. 4. ἔθει X. ix. 6. ἔθη VII. v. 1. ἔθεσι I. iv. 6. X. x. 6, 10, 23.

εἰώθασι II. vi. 9. VII. i. 3. VIII. vi. 6. x. 1. IX. viii. 5.

εἰ V. v. 6. ix. 2. VI. iii. 2. VII. iii. 2, 9. vi. 1.

εἰ δὲ μή VII. i. 5.

εἰ μή VI. vii. 4. xiii. 7. VII. xiii. 7. VIII. iii. 9. iv. 2. xiv. 1. X. iii. 4, 12. vi. 8. viii. 9.

εἴγε VII. ii. 4.

εἰδοποιόν X. iv. 3.

εἶδος I. vi. 8, 10. V. ii. 12. iii. 17. iv. 2. VI. viii. 4, 9. VII. v. 9. vii. 3. VIII. i. 7. vii. 1. x. 3. IX. viii. 6. X. iv. 1, 2, 4. v. 2. εἴδει VIII. i. 7. iii. 1. v. 5. IX. v. 3. X. iii. 10, 11, 13. iv. 3. v. 1. 2, 8. εἴδη I. vi. 1. VI. xiii. 2. VII. i. 1. VIII. iii. 1. iv. 4, 6. x. 1. X. iv. 3.

εἰδῶμεν I. vi. 4. II. ii. 1. εἰδὼς I. vi. 16. II. iv. 3. III. i. 14. ix. 4. V. vi. 1. vii. 7. viii. 3, 8. ix. 9. xi. 2. VI. vii. 7. viii. 4. VII. i. 6. x. 3. IX. ii. 5. X. ix. 15. εἴσεται IX. viii. 2. ἰδεῖν II. i. 4. VI. ix. 4. VII. v. 1. X. viii. 10. ἴδοι III. i. 13. V. x. 5. εἰδείη VI. i. 2. vii. 7. ἴδωσι VI. vii. 5. εἰδότες II. ix. 2. X. ix. 17. εἰδότι III. i. 20. VIII. viii. 6. εἰδότα V. ix. 4, 6. VII. iii. 14. εἰδόσι X. vii. 3. εἰδότων VI. vii. 7. VIII. viii. 2. οἶδε IX. xi. 3. εἰδῆσαι VIII. iii. 8. εἰδῶσι VIII. viii. 3. εἰδείημεν IV. vii. 1. εἰδέναι I. iii. 7. xiii. 7. II. iv. 3. III. i. 17. V. ix. 15. VI. vii. 3, 5. viii. 4. xii. 2. VII. iii. 3. x. 2. X. i. 4. iii. 12. ix. 1, 19. εἰδότες III. v. 22. V. viii. 3. VI. vii. 7. VII. iii. 1. ἴδοι III. x. 6. IV. viii. 6. VIII. i. 31. ἰδεῖν III. x. 7. εἰσόμεθα I. vi. 14.

εἶεν V. v. 3.

εἰκάζειν II. vi. 14.

εἰκὸς VIII. iii. 8. IX. x. 4. Q. viii. 13.

εἰκότως I. ix. 9. xiii. 13. IV. i. 44. IX. i. 6, 7. viii. 2, 10. xii. 1.

ἔοικε I. vii. 2. 12, 15. viii. 17. x. 10. xi. 3. 5. xii. 8. xiii. 11, 15. III. i. 10, 12, 14. ii. 9. 17. iii. 11, 15. iv. 5. v. 4. 7. viii. 1, 10, 12. xi. 6. xii. 1, 6. IV. ii. 5. iii. 1, 16, 35. iv. 1, 4, 6. vi. 4. 7. vii. 10. ix. 1. VI. xii. 7. xiii. 1. VII. iii. 13. vi. 1. x. 3. 4. VIII. i. 3. 5. v. 5. vi. 2, 4. viii. 3, 4. ix. 1. x. 6. xi. 5. xiii. 5, 11. xiv. 2. IX. i. 5, 7. iv. 1, 2. v. 1, 3. vii. 1, 4, 6. ix. 2, 7, 9. x. 6. xi. 3. X. ii. 2, 5. iii. 13. iv. 1. 3. v. 7. vi. 6. viii. 11, 13. ix. 19. ἐοίκασι I. v. 1, 5. vi. 7. III. i. 6. VI. xiii. 4. VII. ix. 3. VIII. v. 3. viii. 2. ix. 4. 5. xii. 1. X. i. 4. iii. 4. viii. 12. ix. 20. ἐῴκει VII. i. 1.

εἰλικρινοῦς X. vi. 4.

εἶναι VI. viii. 1. IX. xii. 2. ἐσμὲν IX. vii. 4. ix. 9. ἔσται VI. i. 5. ἐσόμενον VI. ii. 6. ἔσται VI. iii. 1. ἔσονται VI. vii. 4. ἐσόμενον X. ix. 11. ἔμεναι VII. x. 4.

εἴπερ I. vi. 5, 6. vii. 10. viii. 13. ix. 5. x. 3, 14. III. ix. 3. IV. iii. 14. ix. 4. V. iv. 7. vi. 6. vii. 4. ix. 9. VI,

i. 5. ii. 2. v. 3. xii. 1. VII. vi. 3. vii. 7. ix. 5. xiii. 2. 7. VIII. ii 3. xi. 1. IX. viii. 7. ix. 5. X. iv. 3. vii. 9. viii. 3. 4. ix 17, 19.

εἰρήνην X. vii. 6.

εἴρων II. vii. 12. IV. vii. 3. *εἴρωνες* IV. vii. 14.

εἰρωνεία II. vii. 12. IV. iii. 28. *εἰρωνείᾳ* IV. vii. 16. *εἰρωνείαν* IV. iii. 28.

εἰρωνευόμενοι IV. vii. 16.

εἷς I. vi. 5. V. iii. 14. VII. ii. 5. v. 4. IX. iii. 3. vii. 5. X. ix. 14. *ἓν* I. vi. 3. 7, 8, 12, 13. vii. 3. viii. 7. II. vi. 5. III. xi. 3. IV. i. 5. iii. 9. V. ii. 12. iii. 17. iv. 1. v. 13. 15. vii. 6. ix. 4. VI. i. 5, 6. VII. iii. 9. VIII. i. 5. 7. ii. 4. IX. x. 3. X. ix. 15. *μία* I. vi. 4. vi. 16. II. i. 2. viii. 8. V. vii. 5. VI. vii. 4. VII. iii. 9. X. iii. 3. v. 11. *ἑνὸς* I. vi. 12. X. ix. 12, 16. *μιᾶς* II. viii. 1. *μιᾷ* I. vi. 3. VI. xiii. 6. *ἑνὶ* I. ii. 8. II. i. 7. V. ii. 6. iii. 9. iv. 10. v. 11. *ἕνα* IV. i. 32. V. i. 13. VI. vii. 3. VIII. vi. 2. IX. x. 5. *μίαν* I. i. 4. vi. 4. 9, 11. viii. 14. II. viii. 7. VII. xiv. 8. IX. viii. 9.

εἰσδύναξ IV. ii. 15.

εἰσαῦθις I. vii. 7. IV. vi. 8.

εἰσφέρων IV. ii. 20. *εἰσενεχθέντα* V. iv. 2.

εἶτα I. vii. 17. III. i. 23. viii. 7. IV. iii. 36. v. 8. V. v. 8. VII. ii. 1. vi. 1. xiii. 2. IX. i. 6. ii. 5. X. ix. 23.

εἴτε III. iii. 4. v. 19. IV. viii. 10. VIII. ix. 5. X. v. 11. vii. 1. ix. 11, 17.

εἴτις VII. iv. 5. *εἴτι* X. ix. 23. *εἴτῳ* X. v. 5, 10.

ἕκαστος I. iii. 5. III. iii. 17. v. 17. vii. 5. VIII. ii. 2. vii. 6. xiii. 2. IX. iv. 3. 4. vi. 4. viii. 6. X. iv. 10. vii. 9. ix. 13, 15. *ἑκάστη* X. ix. 23. *ἕκαστον* I. iii. 4, 5. vi. 16. vii. 5, 15. viii. 13. x. 7. xi. 2, 4. xii. 2. II. ix. 7. III. vii. 6. xii. 3. IV. i. 6, 17. vii. 1. V. i. 12. ii. 11. vii. 6, 7. ix. 16. VI. vii. 4. viii. 7. xi. 2. xii. 3. VII. iii. 9, 10. iv. 5, 6. xi. 1. xiv. 9. VIII. iii. 1. vii. 2. IX. iv. 2. X. ii. 1. ix. 15. *ἑκάστου* I. vii. 11. IX. viii. 6. X. v. 10. ix. 21. *ἑκάστης* I. vii. 1. III. v. 23. VII. xii. 5. xiii. 2. *ἑκάστῃ* IV. iii. 14. *ἑκάστην* III. iv. 5. V. ii. 10. vi. 1. VII. iv. 6. VIII. xi. 1. xiii. 1. X. iv. 7. v. 2, 6. *ἕκαστοι* III. iii. 7. IV. iii. 35. IX. xii. 2. X. v. 2. *ἑκάστῳ* I. viii. 10. II. ix. 2. III. iv. 3, 4. v. 19. IV. i. 6. VIII. ii. 2. iii. 6. v 4. vii. 1. x. 6. xi. 4. IX. ix. 10. X. iv. 10. v. 8. vi. 5. vii. 9. viii. 1. ix. 14, 16. *ἕκαστα* I. iii. 4. 7. II. ii. 4. vii. 1. ix. 8. III. i. 10, 15. 20. iii. 16. iv. 4. v. 10. 12, 22. viii. 6. xii. 4. IV. iii. 15. v. 13. vi. 5. vii. 5. V. vii. 1, 6. VI. vii. 4. 7. viii. 2, 5. xi. 3. 4. xii. 7. xiii. 1. VII. iii. 6, 9. 11. v. 1. vi. 5. IX. iv. 5. X. v. 2. ix. 1, 20. *ἑκάστων* III. v. 7. IX. iv. 2. *ἑκάστους* I. vii. 18. III. iv. 4. 5. IV. ii. 16. vi. 5, 8. IX. i. 9. ii. 7, 9. xii. 2. *ἑκάστοις* I. ii. 6. VIII. ix. 3. *ἑκάστας* I. vii. 22. X. ix. 23.

ἑκάτεροι II. viii. 3. III. x. 2. VIII. iii. 6, 8. v. 5. xiv. 1, 2. IX. vi. 2. *ἑκατέρων* II. viii. 3. V. iii. 13. viii. 3. ix. 2. VI. i. 5, 6. VII. vi. 7. IX. vi. 2. *ἑκατέρας* II. vii. 16. V. v. 19. *ἑκατέρου* II. vi. 5. IV. vii. 6. VI. i. 6. xii. 4. VIII. iii. 9. xii. 7. *ἑκάτεραι* X. v. 7. *ἑκάτερα* VI. xi. 7. X. iv. 2. *ἑκατέραν* VII. i. 4. *ἑκατέρῳ* VIII. iii. 8, 9. vii. 2. xiv. 2. *ἑκάτερον* IX. viii. 3.

ἑκατόμβαια V. ix. 7.

ἐκβαλὰς III. i. 5.

ἐκγόνων I. x. 5. VIII. xi. 2. *ἐκγόνους* I. x. 4.

ἐκδεχόμενα IV. i. 5.

ἐκεῖ V. x. 5. VII. viii. 4. *ἐκεῖσε* IX. iv. 9.

ἐκεῖνος I. iv. 7. III. vii. 8. V. ii. 4. VII. iv. 4 viii. 4. VIII. vii. 6. *ἐκείνῳ* II. ii. 3. III. iii. 11. IX. iv. 4. *ἐκείνου* I. x. 6. V. v. 8. ix. 6. xi. 4. VIII. ii. 3 vii. 6. IX. iii. 2. iv. 1. v. 3. viii. 2. *ἐκείνης* VI. viii. 9. ix. 6. xii. 8. xiii. 8. VIII. vi. 7. X. iv. 3. *ἐκείνῃ* V. v. 8. ix. 13. VII. iv. 2. VIII. xii. 2. IX. i. 5. v. 3. *ἐκείνη* VI. xiii. 8. VIII. x. 5. *ἐκεῖνον* VIII. iv. 1. *ἐκεῖνα* III. viii. 16. VIII. iv. 6. viii. 3. *ἐκείνων* II. ix. 6. IV. iii. 16, 21. V. ii. 9. vii. 6. VI. viii. 3. VII. iv. 4 VIII. ii. 3, 4. 6. v. 5. xii. 2, 3. IX. iii. 1. ix. 5. *ἐκείνους* I. xi. 5. IV. iii. 26. VIII. xiii. 10. IX. xi. 4. *ἐκείνοις* IX. vii. 2. *ἐκεῖνο* I. v. 8. V. iii. 6. VIII. iii. 3. xii. 3. *ἐκείνην* V. iv. 3. *κἀκεῖνο* V. iii. 6.

ἐκθέμενος VII. vi. 1.

ἐκκαγχάζουσι VII. vii. 6.
ἐκκρούουσι III. xii. 7. ἐκκρούει VII. xiv. 4. X. v. 4.
ἐκλέξασθαι X. ix. 20.
ἐκλογὴν X. ix. 20.
ἑκούσιος V. ii. 13. ἑκούσιον III. i. 6, 13, 20. ii. 2, 16. v. 4. 17. 19. xii. 2, 3. V. iv. 14. v. 5. viii. 2, 3. ix. 1, 2, 8. xi. 5, 7. ἑκουσίου III. ii. 1, 2. V. iv. 13. ἑκουσίῳ III. xii. 1. V. viii. 2. ἑκουσία III. i. 4, 6, 10. ii. 2. v. 6, 7. xii. 4. V. ii. 13. ἑκούσιαι III. v. 1, 15, 20, 21, 22. ἑκουσίαν V. viii. 5. IX. i. 9. ἑκουσίοις III. i. 1, 6, 10. IV. ix. 6. V. iv. 1. ἑκουσίους III. i. 22, 23. v. 19. V. xi. 6. IX. viii. 6.
ἐκπεσεῖν III. i. 17.
ἐκστατικὸς VII. i. 6. viii. 5. ἐκστατικὸν VII. ii. 7. ἐκστατικοὶ VII. viii. 2.
ἐκτὸς I. viii. 2, 3, 6, 15. x. 3. 15. II. ix. 3. III. i. 10, 11. IV. iii. 10, 35. VII. xiii. 2. X. viii. 4, 11.
Ἕκτωρ III. viii. 2, 4. Ἕκτορι VII. i. 1. Ἕκτορα III. viii. 2.
ἑκὼν III. i. 5, 6, 13. v. 4, 13, 14. IV. ix. 6. V. viii. 1, 3, 11. ix. 1, 4, 5, 6, 9. xi. 2, 3. VI. v. 7. VII. x. 3. ἑκόντες III. v. 14. V. ix. 2. VII. xiii. 3. ἑκόντι VIII. xiii. 9. ἑκοῦσαν V. ix. 2. ἑκόντος V. ix. 5. ἑκόντα V. ix. 1, 4, 5, 10. xi. 3. VII. ii. 5. X. ix. 11.
ἐλάττων IV. iii. 25. ἔλαττον II. vi. 4. vii. 12. viii. 2. IV. vii. 9, 14. V. i. 10. iii. 1, 4, 14, 15. 16. iv. 6, 11, 13, 14. v. 17, 18. vi. 4. xi. 7. VIII. xiii. 4. xiv. 3. X. vii. 5. viii. 4. ἐλάττονος V. iv. 6, 9. VII. viii. 2. ἐλάττονι V. iv. 8. VII. xiii. 1. ἐλάττω II. ii. 6. IV. i. 18. 19. vii. 3, 4. V. vii. 5. VI. i. 2. VIII. ix. 2. IX. xi. 2. ἐλαττόνων IV. i. 19. iii. 7, 17.
ἐλαττουμένῳ VIII. xiv. 3.
ἐλαττωτικὸς V. ix. 9. x. 8.
ἔλαφον III. x. 7.
ἐλαφροτέροις I. xi. 3.
ἐλάχιστον IV. ii. 21. VIII. x. 3. ἐλαχίστου I. vii. 8 IV. ii. 9. ἐλάχιστα II. ix. 4. ἐλαχίστοις V. iii. 4, 5, 8, 10.
ἐλεγχθεὶς III. viii. 2.
ἐλέγχειν VII. ii. 8.
Ἑλένην II. ix. 6.
ἐλεῆσαι II. v. 2. vi. 10. III. v. 15.
ἔλεος III. i. 16. ἐλέου III. i. 1. ἔλεον II. v. 2.
ἐλεεῖ III. viii. 11.
ἐλευθερία X. viii. 4. ἐλευθερίαν V. iii. 7.
ἐλευθέριος II. viii. 2. IV. i. 1, 6, 12, 14, 23, 24, 26, 31. ii. 3, 10. ἐλευθερίου II. vii. 6. IV. i. 7, 14, 18. viii. 5. X. vi. 4. ἐλευθερίῳ IV. viii. 5, 7. VII. ix. 2. X. viii. 4. ἐλευθέριον I. viii. 12. IV. i. 19, 20. ii. 10. V. vi. 4. VIII. vi. 4. ἐλευθέριοι III. vi. 4. IV. i. 10, 11, 35. ἐλευθερίους I. viii. 12. ἐλευθερίοις X. viii. 7. ix. 3. ἐλευθεριωτέρα VIII. xiii. 6. ἐλευθεριώτερον IV. i. 19. ἐλευθεριώτεροι IV. i. 20. ἐλευθεριώτατοι III. x. 11.
ἐλευθεριότης II. vii. 4. IV. i. 18. ii. 1. iv. 1. ἐλευθεριότητος IV. i. 1, 24, 25. ii. 1, 10. ἐλευθεριότητι IV. i. 44. ἐλευθεριότητα I. xiii. 20. II. vii. 8. viii. 5. IV. i. 10, 22.
ἕλκει VII. vii. 5. IX. iv. 9. ἕλκοι VIII. viii. 6. ἑλκόμενος VII. vi. 2.
ἑλκῦσαι VII. vi. 2.
ἐλλέβορον V. ix. 15.
ἐλλείπειν II. vi. 16. ἐλλείπει II. vi. 5. vii. 4, 15. III. vii. 10. IV. i. 29. iii. 12. V. x. 6. ἐλλεῖπον II. vii. 2, 8, 10, 13, 14. IV. iii. 35. VII. vii. 2, 5. ἐλλείποντες II. vii. 3. III. xi. 7. ἐλλεῖπον I. vii. 17. VIII. i. 2. ἐλλείποντα II. ii. 6. ἐλλείπουσι II. vii. 4. viii. 2. III. vii. 12. IV. i. 38, 39. iii. 8. ἐλλείποντας II. ix. 7. IV. v. 13. IX. vi. 4. ἐλλειφθὲν V. x. 5.
ἔλλειψις I. iii. 7. II. vi. 10, 12, 14, 20. vii. 4, 6, 7, 10. viii. 6. IV. ii. 4. iv. 2. 4. v. 5. vii. 15. viii. 2. V. v. 18. ἐλλείψεως II. ii. 7. vi. 4, 9. 19, 20. V. v. 18. VI. i. 1. ἐλλείψει IV. i. 38. ii. 21. ἔλλειψιν II. vi. 8, 15, 19. viii. 1. ix. 1, 9. III. x. 3. IV. v. 3. 4. V. v. 10. ix. 17. VI. i. 1. ἐλλείψεις II. vi. 18 viii. 2. IV. i. 3, 29. v. 14. VII. vii. 2.
ἔλλογα X. ii. 1.
ἐλπίζει IX. ii. 5. ἐλπίζουσι IX. iv. 9.
ἐλπίδα I. ix. 10. VIII. viii. 2. IX. v. 3. ἐλπίδας IX. iv. 5. X. iii. 7. ἐλπίδας VIII. iii. 4.
ἔμβαλε III. viii. x.
ἐμβλέποντες X. iv. 9.
ἐμβρύοις I. xiii. 11.
ἐμμελὴς IV. viii. 1. ἐμμελέστερον IV. vii. 9.

ἐμμελῶς I. x. 11. IV. iii. 21. viii. 3. IX. x. 1.

ἐμμενετικὸς VII. i. 6. viii. 5. x. 3. ἐμμενετικὸν VII. ii. 7. ἐμμενετικοὶ VII. ix. 2.

ἐμμένει VII. viii. 1. ix. 1, 5. x. 4. ἐμμένων VII. ii. 7, ix. 1, 5. ἐμμένουσι XII. vii. 8. ix. 4. ἐμμεῖναι III. i. 10. ἐνέμεινεν VII. ix. 4. ἐμμενόντων VII. x. 4.

Ἐμπεδοκλῆς VIII. i. 6. Ἐμπεδοκλέους VII. iii. 8, 13.

ἐμπειρία III. viii. 6. X. ix. 19. ἐμπειρίας II. i. 1. III. viii. 7. VI. viii. 5, 6. xi. 6. X. ix. 19. ἐμπειρίαν III. vi. 11. VI. viii. 5. VIII. vi. 3. X. ix. 16. ἐμπειρίᾳ X. ix. 18.

ἔμπειρος VI. viii. 5. ἔμπειροι VI. vii. 7. X. ix. 20. ἐμπείρων VI. xi. 6. ἐμπείροις X. ix. 21.

ἐμποδίζει I. x. 12. VII. xi. 5. ἐμποδίζηται VII. xiii. 2. ἐμποδιζομένη VII. xiii. 2.

ἐμποδιστικὴ VII. xiii. 2.

ἐμπόδια VII. xiii. 4. ἐμπόδιον VII. xi. 4. ἐμπόδιοι IX. x. 2. ἐμποδίους X. v. 3. ἐμπόδια X. viii. 5. ἐμποδίων III. xi. 8.

ἐμποδὼν IV. vii. 16. V. v. 7.

ἐμποιοῦσι IV. v. 10. ἐμποιοῦντα IV. v. 2.

ἐμπορευθὲν VIII. i. 7.

ἐμφαίνεσθαι I. vi. 11.

ἐμφανέστατον VIII. vii. 4.

ἐμφανίζειν X. iii. 11.

ἔμφρονα I. x. 13.

ἐμψύχου IX. vii. 3. ἔμψυχον V. iv. 7. vi. 7. VIII. xi. 6.

ἐναλλὰξ V. iii. 11.

ἐναντίος III. vii. 11. VII. viii. 4, 5. ἐναντία I. xiii. 15. II. viii. 5, 8. III. iv. 3. IV. i. 24. V. i. 4, 5, 19. VII. i. 1, iii. 10. iv. 5. xiv. 2, 6. ἐναντίον I. x. 9. II. ix. 3. VIII. viii. 7. X. ii. 2, 5. ἐναντίας I. x. 4. IV. vi. 2. V. i. 5. VII. iii. 10. ix. 5. VIII. i. 6. x. 2. X. i. 2. ἐναντίων I. xi. 5. xiii. 15. II. iii. 6. viii. 7. ix. 5. IV. i. 44. V. iv. 6. VI. ii. 4. VII. ix. 5. xiii. 1. xiv. 2, 4. VIII. viii. 7. x. 2. X. ii. 2. ἐναντίαι I. x. 9. II. viii. 1. IV. i. 24. VII. xiv. 2. ἐναντίοις I. vi. 8. II. iii. 7. III. iii. 4. V. i. 4. VIII. viii. 6. ἐναντιώτερα II. viii. 7, 8. ἐναντίους VII. xii. 2.

ἐναντιότης II. viii. 4.

ἐναντιοῦται III. ii. 5. ἐναντιοῦσθαι III. xii. 7. ἐναντιοῦνται X. ix. 10. ἐναντιουμένους X. ix. 12. ἐναντιούμενον I. xiii. 16.

ἐναντίως II. vii. 4. V. iv. 6. VII. xiv. 2.

ἐναντίωσις IV. vi. 7.

ἐναργῶν I. iv. 3. ἐναργέστερον I. vii. 9.

ἐναργῶς VII. ii. 2. X. iii. 2. viii. 10.

ἐνδεὴς III. xi. 1. VIII. viii. 6, xiv. 1. IX. ix. 10. X. iv. 1, 2. vi. 2. ἐνδεεῖς I. vi. 15. ἐνδεοῦς VII. xiv. 4. ἐνδεεῖ I. vii. 7. ἐνδεεῖς VIII. v. 3. X. iii. 6. ἐνδεέσι VIII. xiv. 1. ἐνδεεῖ VIII. xiv. 2.

ἔνδεια II. viii. 6. ἐνδείας II. ii. 6. III. xi. 3. IV. i. 20. VII. iv. 4. VIII. xiv. 2. ἐνδείᾳ X. iii. 7. ἔνδειαν X. iii. 6.

ἐνδείκνυσθαι I. iii. 4.

ἐνδέχεται I. viii. 9. ix. 11. x. 4. II. iv. 2. V. v. 15. vii. 4. viii. 3. ix. 3, 4, 9. xi. 1. VI. ii. 6. iii. 1. v. 3. vi. 2. xii. 6. VII. iii. 14. x. 1: xiii. 7. VIII. iv. 2. vi. 2, 3. IX. iii. 4. viii. 10. X. iii. 4. vii. 8. viii. 9. 11. ix. 6. ἐνδέχοιτο V. ix. 4. ἐνδέχονται VI. i. 5. v. 3. ἐνδέχεσθαι I. v. 6. VI. iii. 2. VII. i. 7. xi. 3. IX. x. 5. X. iv. 4. ἐνδέχηται VIII. viii. 3. IX. xi. 1, 10. ἐνδεχόμενον IX. i. 7. ἐνδεχόμενα VI. i. 5. iii. 1. vi. 1, 2. VIII. xiv. 3. IX. vi. 2. ἐνδεχομένου VII. ii. 6. iv. 1, 6. v. 8. xi. 4. ἐνδεχομένων V. vii. 4. VI. i. 6. iv. 4. v. 3.

ἐνδοιάσειεν VII. xii. 2.

ἔνδοξοι I. viii. 7. ἐνδόξους IV. ii. 14. ἐνδόξων IV. vii. 2. ἔνδοξα IV. vii. 14. VII. i. 5.

ἐνεῖναι VII. xiv. 18. ἐνῇ VII. iii. 10. ἐνοῦσα VII. iii. 10. ἐνούσης VII. ii. 1.

Ἐνδυμίωνα X. viii. 7.

ἕνεκα I. vii. 1. II. ii. 2. vi. 1. vii. 13. ix. 2. III. i. 16, 18. iii. 15. vii. 2, 5, 6. viii. 12. ix. 3. IV. i. 12. 14, 20, 35, 40, 43. ii. 6, 20. iii. 15. vi. 8. vii. 5, 10, 11, 14. V. ii. 4. viii. 3, 6. VI. ii. 4. 5. v. 6. xi. 4. xii. 1, 7, 8. xiii. 8. VII. viii. 4. x. 3. xiii. 7. VIII. ii. 3. 6. iv. 4. v. 5. vii. 6. ix. 5. IX. i. 3. iv. 1, 3. vii. 2. viii. 1, 2, 9. X. ii. 2. vi. 6. vii. 6.

ἕνεκεν VII. xii. 1.

ἐνέργεια I. vii. 14, 15. viii. 8. ix. 7. xiii. 1. III. xii. 7. VII. xii. 2, 3.

xiii. 2, 7. X. xiv. 8. IX. vii. 6. ix. 5, 6. xii. 1. X. iv. 5, 9. v. 6. vi. 5. vii. 1, 2, 7, 8. viii. 7. ἐνεργείας I. i. 5. viii. 2. ix. 9. x. 10. II. i. 4. 8. III. vii. 6. VII. xii. 6. X. iv. 10, 11. v. 1, 3. 5. vi. 6. viii. 4. 5, 8. ἐνεργείᾳ I. viii. 9. IX. vii. 4. ix. 7. X. iv. 8, 9. v. 2, 5. ἐνέργειαν I. vii. 13, 14. viii. 9. x. 2. xiii. 6. VII. xii. 3. VIII. v. 1. IX. vii. 6. ix. 7. X. iv. 6, 8, 11. v. 2, 3, 6, 8. vi. 2, 3, 7. vii. 7. ἐνέργειαι I. i. 2. viii. 3. x. 9, 13. II. ii. 8. III. v. 1, 10. VII. xii. 2. xiii. 2, 7. III. iii. 1. v. 7, 11. vi. 4. vii. 6. viii. 1. ἐνεργειῶν I. i. 2. II. i. 7. X. v. 6, 11. vi. 2. vii. 3. ἐνεργείαις I. viii. 14. x. 12. IV. ii. 6. X. v. 3, 6. vi. 8.
ἐνεργεῖ II. iii. 3. VII. iii. 6, 10. X. iv. 9, 10. ἐνεργῇ X. iv. 7. v. 4. ἐνεργεῖν I. xiii. 12. III. v. 12. ix. 5. VI. xii. 5. VIII. v. 1. IX. ix. 5. X. iii. 4. iv. 5, 9. v. 4. viii. 7. ἐνεργοῦντα I. x. 15. ἐνεργῶν V. ii. 2. X. viii. 13. ἐνεργοῦντες III. v. 11. IX. xii. 3. X. v. 2. viii. 10. ix. 18. ἐνεργοῦμεν IX. ix. 9. ἐνεργοῦσαι X. iv. 5. ἐνεργήσαντες II. i. 4.
ἔνθα VII. iii. 9.
ἐνθάδε V. vii. 2.
ἔνθεν VI. v. 5.
ἐνιαυτὸν IX. viii. 9
ἐνιαχοῦ IX. i. 8.
ἔνιοι I. iv. 3. viii. 17. III. ii. 14. vi. 4. IV. i. 39. II. iv. 7. ix. 2. VI. vii. 7. VII. iii. 3, 4. vii. 8. VIII. i. 5. X. ix. 16. ἔνιαι VII. vii. 2. xi. 3. xii. 1. xiii. 2. VIII. viii. 3. ix. 5. ἐνίων I. viii. 16. III. iii. 1. V. x. 4. VI. vi. 1. VII. xiii. 2. ἐνίοις II. viii. 5. III. i. 7. v. 15. xi. 4. V. vii. 2. VII. iii. 7. v. 3. VIII. xiii. 6. IX. i. 6. ἔνια I. xiii. 9. II. vi. 18. III. i. 8. vi. 3. xi. 2. IV. viii. 9, 10. VI. vii. 4. xi. 1. VII. i. 3. iii. 7. iv. 5. v. 1, 6. xi. 5. xii. 4. X. iv. 9. viii. 2.
ἐνίοτε III. i. 1, 7, 9, 16. IV. i. 3, 35. 38. v. 13. vii. 15. VII. v. 7. x. 2. VIII. ii. 2, 4. iv. 1. viii. 6. x. 5. IX. i. 2, 5. xi. 6.
ἐνιστάμεναι X. ii. 4.
ἐνισχύει X. ix. 14.
ἐννεαβοίων V. ix. 7.
ἐννοεῖν IX. vi. 2.
ἔννοια IX. xi. 2. ἔννοιαν IX. xi. 5. X. vii. 1. ix. 4.
ἔνοχοι VII. ii. 10.
ἐνταῦθα IV. ii. 17. iv. 6. viii. 1. VI. vii. i. 7. xiii. 1. VII. iv. 6. vi. 2. viii. 4. VIII. viii. 6. x. 6. IX. i. 2. xi. 1.
ἐντεῦθεν V. iii. 6. VI. iii. 2. x. 4. VIII. x. 4. X. viii. 7.
ἔντιμοι III. viii. 1. ἔντιμα IV. iii. 27. ἐντίμους IV. iii. 36. ἐντιμότερον IV. iii. 19. ἐντιμοτέρας I. ii. 6. ἐντιμότατα IV. ii. 15.
ἐντυγχάνουσι IV. vi. 1. ἐντυγχάνοντες IX. x. 6. ἐντύχωσι III. iii. 13.
ἐνυπάρχειν VIII. i. 3. ἐνυπάρχοντα X. iv. 8.
ἐξ II. vi. 6, 7.
ἐξαγωγῆς V. v. 13.
ἐξαίφνης III. ii. 2. viii. 15.
ἐξακριβοῖ X. v. 5. ἐξακριβοῦν I. vi. 13. xii. 7. xiii. 8. ἐξακριβοῦσι X. v. 2.
ἐξακριβοῦσθαι X. ix. 15.
ἐξαμελουμένων X. ix. 14. ἐξημέληται X. ix. 13.
ἐξηρτηκότι I. viii. 9.
ἐξεῖναι VIII. xiv. 4. ἐξῆν III. v. 14. VIII. xiii. 10.
ἐξελαύνει VII. xiv. 6. ἐξελαύνουσι VIII. i. 4. ἐξελαυνόμενα III. viii. 12.
ἐξελέγχονται IV. iii. 36.
ἐξετάζει IX. vi. 4. ἐξετάζειν I. iv. 4.
ἐξῆς II. vii. 9. IV. i. 1.
ἕξιν II. iii. 5. vi. 1, 3, 15. vii. 13. ix. 9. IV. ii. 6. iv. 5. v. 1, 4. vii. 12. V. i. 4, 5, 20. x. 8. VI. i. 6. ii. 2, 6. iii. 4. iv. 2, 3, 6. v. 8. viii. 1. xii. 10. xiii. 2, 4. 5. VII. i. 2. ii. 6. viii. 5. xii. 2. xiii. 6. X. iv. 8. vi. 2. ἕξεων III. v. 17. viii. 15. IV. ii. 4. v. 14. ix. 2. VI. ii. 4. iv. 2. v. 8. xii. 1. VII. x. 4. xii. 2, 3. xiii. 2. VIII. v. 5. X. ix. 21. ἕξει I. viii. 9. IV. i. 19. viii. 5. ix. 1. VIII. v. 5. ἕξις I. viii. 9. xiii. 20. III. iv. 4. vii. 6. viii. 15. IV. iii. 2. vi. 4. vii. 7. V. i. 3. VI. v. 4. 6. xiii. 3. VII. iii. 7. xii. 2. VIII. v. 1, 5. vi. 5. ἕξεις II. i. 7, 8. ii. 2. v. 1, 2, 6. viii. 2. III. v. 12, 21, 22. IV. ii. 22. v. 15. vi. 3. V. i. 5. VI. i. 3. xi. 2. xii. 1. xiii. 1. VII. v. 1. vii. 1. ix. 5. x. 5. xii. 1. X. ix. 21. ἕξεσι I. xiii. 20. II. iii. 1. III. v. 20, 22. V. i. 4. VII. i. 4. xiv. 2.
ἐξίστησι III. xii. 2, 3. ἐξίστανται VII. ix. 1. ἐξίστησι VII. vi. 6.
ἐξὸν VIII. xiii. 3.

ἐξορίζειν X. ix. 18.
ἐξουσία VIII. x. 6. xiv. 4. ἐξουσίαις I. v. 3. VIII. vi. 5. viii. 2. ἐξουσίας X. viii. 4.
ἔξω III. i. 11. VI. iii. 2. v. 5.
ἔξωθεν III. i. 3. 12. V. viii. 7.
ἐξωτερικοῖς I. xiii. 9. VI. iv. 2.
ἐπαγγελιῶν IX. i. 6.
ἐπάγγελλει X. ix. 20. ἐπαγγέλλονται X. ix. 18. ἐπαγγελλόμενοι IX. i. 2, 4.
ἐπαγωγὴ VI. iii. 3. ἐπαγωγῆς VI. iii. 3. ἐπαγωγῇ I. vii. 21.
ἐπαινετικὸς IV. iii. 31.
ἐπαινετὸς IV. vii. 6, 8. VII. ii. 7. ἐπαινετή II. ix. 9. IV. v. 14. vi. 3. VI. xii. 9. ἐπαινετὸν I. xii. 2. II. vii. 11. ix. 2. IV. vii. 6. V. x. 1. IX. viii. 10. ἐπαινεταί X. v. 6. ἐπαινετοῖς IX. viii. 11. ἐπαινετῶν I. xii. 1, 5. VII. i. 6. ἐπαινετὰς I. xiii. 20. ἐπαινετά II. vii. 11. ἐπαινετωτάτη VIII. i. 1.
ἐπαινεῖ I. xii. 4. ἐπαινοῦσι IX. viii. 7. X. iii. 11. ἐπαινοῦμεν I. xii. 2. xiii. 15. 20. II. vii. 8. ix. 7. IV. iv. 4. v. 13. ix. 2. V. x. 1. VIII. i. 3, 5. ἐπαινοῦντες IV. iv. 4. vi. 1. V. x. 1. VII. iv. 5. ἐπαινῆται IV. iii. 31. ἐπαινεῖσθαι I. xii. 2. 5. ἐπαινούμεθα II. v. 3. 5. ἐπαινοῦνται II. v. 3. vi. 12. vii. 14. III. ii. 13. ix. 2. IV. i. 1. iv. 5. v. 3. ἐπαινοῦνται III. i. 7. IV. i. 10. ἐπαινουμένων VIII. viii. 4. ἐπαινέσειε IV. ix. 3.
ἔπαινος I. xii. 4. 6. IV. i. 8. vii. 13. X. viii. 7. ἔπαινοι III. i. 9. ἐπαίνων I. xii. 3. III. i. 1. ἐπαίνους I. xii. 3.
ἐπακολουθεῖν I. x. 9. ἐπακολουθῆσαι I. vi. 7.
ἐπακουσομένων X. ix. 10.
ἐπὰν V. iv. 10.
ἐπαναγκάζοντες IX. vi. 4.
ἐπαναφορὰ V. ii. v.
ἐπανέλθωμεν I. vii. 1.
ἐπανισοῖ V. iv. 8. VIII. xiv. 3.
ἐπανιτέον I. x. 6.
ἐπανόρθωμα V. vii. 7. x. 3, 6.
ἐπανόρθωσιν IX. iii. 3.
ἐπανορθωτικὸν V. iv. 6.
ἐπανορθοῦν V. x. 5.
ἐπαρκεῖ VIII. xiii. 11. ἐπαρκοῦσι VIII. xii. 7. ἐπαρκέσαι X. ix. 16. ἐπαρκεῖν IV. i. 17. VIII. xiii. 4. xiv. 1, 4. IX. ii. 8.
ἐπαχθὴς X. ix. 12.
ἐπεὶ I. vi. 3. 4. vii. 3. xiii. 1. II. ii. 1. v. 1. vii. 16. ix. 4. III. i. 13. viii. 11. IV. i. 31. V. i. 9. 12. ii. 9. iii. 1, 3. vi. 1, 6. vii. 5. ix. 3. 11, 15. VI. i. 1. iv. 3, 5. vi. 1. viii. 6. ix. 3, 4. VII. i. 3. iii. 5, 6, 13. iv. 2, 5. v. 1. vi. 2. vii. 2. viii. 4. ix. 2, 5. 6. xii. 1, 2. 4. 5, 7. xiii. 3. 6. xiv. 3. 8. VIII. iv. 4. IX. ii. 7. iv. 7. X. v. 5.
ἐπειδὰν I. x. 2, 12. IX. i. 3. 5. X. iv. 7.
ἐπειδὴ I. iii. 6. iv. 1. vii. 6. x. 15. xiii. 14. III. ii. 16. VI. ii. 2. xii. 10. IX. ix. 4. X. vi. 1. ix. 9.
ἐπεισάκτου IX. ix. 5.
ἔπειτα II. iv. 3. VI. xii. 5. VII. iii. 2.
ἐπεκτείνονται I. vii. 7.
ἐπελθεῖν IV. vii. 1. X. ix. 23. ἐπέλθωμεν X. i. 4.
ἐπερωτῶν X. ii. 2.
ἐπήβολος I. x. 14. ἐπήβολοι I. viii. 9.
ἐπηύρατο VIII. xii. 11.
ἐφ' ὧν V. iv. 12. ἐφ' ᾧ V. v. 8. IX. viii. 9.
ἐπιβάτην II. vi. 2.
ἐπιβλέψαι VII. iii. 9.
ἐπιβούλευτος V. viii. 10.
ἐπίβουλος VII. vi. 3. x. 3. ἐπιβουλότεροι VII. vi. 3.
ἐπιγινομένων X. iv. 8. ἐπιγινομένῃ II. iii. 1.
ἐπίγραμμα I. viii. 14.
ἐπιδεικνύμενοι IV. ii. 20.
ἐπιδέξιος IV. viii. 10. IX. xi. 3. ἐπιδεξίου IV. viii. 5.
ἐπιδεξιότης IV. viii. 5.
ἐπιδέχεται I. iii. 4. VIII. i. 7.
ἐπιδῆλοι VII. iii. 7.
ἐπιδιδόασι X. v. 2.
ἐπιδιάζονται II. vii. 8.
ἐπίδοσιν II. viii. 8. ἐπιδόσεις I. vii. 17.
ἐπιδιορθωσαίμεν VII. i. 3.
ἐπιείκεια V. x. 1, 8. ἐπιεικείας V. x. 1. ἐπιεικείᾳ X. v. 6. ἐπιείκειαν IV. i. 39. IX. v. 4.
ἐπιεικὴς III. vi. 3. vii. 8. IV. ix. 6. V. iv. 3. ix. 9. x. 8. VII. x. 3. xiv. 8. VIII. vii. 2. xiv. 4. IX. viii. 1, 6, 8. xii. 3. X. v. 6. ἐπιεικοῦς IV. ix. 4. V. x. 1, 6. VI. xi. 1. ἐπιεικεῖς IV. ix. 7. V. x. 1, 2. 3. 8. xi. 1. X. ii. 1. ix. 12. ἐπιεικεῖ IV. i. 24. viii. 5. IX. ii. 5. iv. 2, 5. ix. 7. ἐπιεικῆ IV. vi. 4. ix. 6. V. iv. 3. VI. xi. 1, 2. IX. iv. 10. x. 6. X. viii. 10. ix. 11.
ἐπιεικέσι VIII. ii. 4. iv. 2. xi. 5. xii.

7. IX. iv. 7. vi. 2. ix. 5. xi. 1. X. ix. 3. 5. 14. ἐπιεικῶν I. xiii. 13. VIII. viii. 2. IX. ix. 3. xii. 3. X. v. 11. ix. 10. ἐπιεικέσι III. v. 3. VIII. xii. 6. IX. vi. 3. X. vi. 4. ix. 11. ἐπιεικέστερος IX. iii. 4. ἐπιεικέστερον V. x. 1. ἐπιεικεστάτων VIII. x. 3.
ἐπιζητεῖ VIII. xiv. 4. ἐπιζητεῖν I. iii. 4. vi. 15. vii. 18. ἐπιζητοῦσι I. vi. 15. ἐπιζητοῦντι I. vii. 19. VIII. i. 6. ἐπιζητεῖται IX. vii. 1. ix. 2. X. ii. 4. vi. 3. ἐπιζητούμενον I. x. 6. ἐπιζητοῦνται IX. xi. 1. ἐπιζητητέον I. iii. 1.
ἐπίθεται III. xi. 1.
ἐπιθυμεῖ III. xi. 1. xii. 9. ἐπιθυμεῖν III. i. 24. VII. iv. 4, 5. ἐπιθυμῆσαι II. vi. 10. ἐπιθυμῇ IX. v. 3. ἐπιθυμοῦσι IV. i. 34. IX. iv. 8. ἐπιθυμῶν III. ii. 4. xi. 6. VII. iv. 4. v. 7. vii. 3. ἐπιθυμοῦντι III. xii. 4.
ἐπιθυμήματα III. x. 6. ἐπιθυμημάτων III. x. 5.
ἐπιθυμητικὸν I. xiii. 8. III. xii. 8, 9.
ἐπιθυμία III. ii. 3, 5. xi. 3, 6. xii. 6. VII. iii. 10, 11. iv. 4. vi. 1, 3. ἐπιθυμίας II. i. 7. VII. ii. 4. 6. vi. 1, 5. vii. 1, 3. ix. 2, 6. xii. 2, 7. X. viii. 7. ἐπιθυμίαν II. v. 2. III. i. 21, 23. 25. ii. 3. viii. 11. xii. 6. V. ii. 4. VII. vi. 4. vii. 2. ix. 2. ἐπιθυμίᾳ III. ii. 3. ἐπιθυμίαι VII. i. 6. ii. 6. iii. 7. X. v. 6. ἐπιθυμίαις III. xi. 3. VII. vi. 2. xii. 2. IX. viii. 4.
ἐπικαλούμενος VII. iv. 5.
ἐπίκληροι VIII. x. 5.
ἐπικουρία VIII. xiii. 11. xiv. 2. 4. IX. xi. 3. ἐπικουρίας IX. xi. 1.
ἐπιλανθάνονται IX. iv. 9.
ἐπιλέγειν II. vi. 9.
ἐπιλείπει IV. i. 30, 34.
ἐπιληπτικοῖς VII. viii. 1. ἐπιληπτικὸς VII. v. 6.
ἐπίλυπον III. i. 13. ix. 2. X. v. 5. ἐπιλύπου III. ii. 5.
ἐπιμέλεια X. viii. 13. ix. 17. ἐπιμελείας I. ix. 4. IV. i. 36. X. ix. 9, 15. 17. ἐπιμέλειαν I. ix. 8. X. ix. 13. 14. ἐπιμέλειαι X. ix. 14. ἐπιμελείαις VI. i. 2.
ἐπιμελεῖται VIII. xi. 1. ἐπιμελουμένους X. viii. 13. ἐπιμεληθείη X. ix. 16. ἐπιμεληθῆναι III. v. 9. X. ix. 16. ἐπιμελούμενον IV. i. 21. ἐπιμελοῦνται IX. vii. 1.
ἐπιμελὲς IX. vii. 1.
ἐπιμελῶς II. iv. 6.
ἐπιπόνους III. iv. 4.
ἐπιπαθὴς I. vii. 13.
ἐπιπίνειν VII. ii. 10.
ἐπιπολάζοντος IV. viii. 4. ἐπιπολαζούσας I. iv. 4.
ἐπιπολαιότερον I. v. 4.
ἐπιπολαίως IX. v. 2.
ἐπιπολὺ III. iii. 10. IV. i. 37.
ἐπίπονον IX. x. 2. ἐπίπονα III. vi. 13. ἐπιπονώτερα IX. vii. 7.
ἐπιπόνως IX. vii. 7.
ἐπισκεπτέον I. vii. 7. xiii. 1, 5. V. vii. 7. VII. xiv. 1. VIII. xiii. 9. X. ix. 18.
ἐπισκεψόμεθα I. xii. 1. VIII. i. 7. ἐπισκέψασθαι I. vi. 1. VII. xi. 2. X. ix. 22.
ἐπίσκεψιν I. v. 7.
ἐπισκοπεῖν I. vi. 16. ἐπισκοποῦντι IV. iii. 15. ἐπισκοποῦσι III. i. 1. iii. 11. IX. ix. 7.
ἐπιστάμεθα VI. iii. 2. ἐπίστασθαι III. v. 8. VII. iii. 5, 13. IX. i. 5. ἐπίστανται VII. iii. 4. IX. i. 7. ἐπιστάμενον VII. ii. 1. iii. 4. ἐπιστήσαντι VI. xii. 8. ἐπίσταται VI. iii. 4.
ἐπιστήμη I. vi. 4. II. vi. 9. V. i. 4. VI. i. 2. iii. 1, 2, 3, 4. v. 3. vi. 1, 2. vii. 3, 9. ix. 1, 2. VII. ii. 4. iii. 4. ἐπιστήμης VI. iii. 4. vii. 1. ix. 3. VII. ii. 1, 3. iii. 8, 14. ἐπιστήμῃ VI. x. 1, 3. VII. iii. 5. ἐπιστήμην III. viii. 6. VI. iii. 4. vi. 2. VII. ii. 3. iii. 3, 6, 7. xiii. 2. ἐπιστῆμαι X. ix. 15, 16. ἐπιστημῶν I. i. 3, 5. ii. 3. 6, 7. x. 9. III. iii. 8. V. i. 4. VI. vii. 2. x. 1. X. ix. 18. ἐπιστήμαις I. vi. 15. ἐπιστήμας III. iii. 9. VI. xiii. 5.
ἐπιστημονικὸν VI. i. 6. VII. iii. 13.
ἐπιστήμων II. vi. 8. VII. iii. 12. ἐπιστήμοσι IV. ii. 5.
ἐπιστητὸν VI. iii. 2, 3. vi. 1. ἐπιστητοῦ VI. vi. 1.
ἐπισφαλέστερα VIII. i. 1.
ἐπίταγμα VII. vi. 1.
ἐπιτακτικὴ VI. x. 2.
ἐπιτάττει VI. xii. 3. xiii. 8. ἐπιτάξαντος V. ix. 11. ἐπιταχθὲν VIII. vi. 5.
ἐπιτείνει VI. i. 1.
ἐπιτελεῖ II. vi. 9. IX. i. 2. X. viii. 4. ἐπιτελοῦσι IX. i. 6. ἐπιτελεῖται X. ix. 20. ἐπιτελουμένου III. iii. 11.
ἐπιτερπεῖς IX. iv. 5.
ἐπιτηδεύειν X. ix. 9.
ἐπιτηδεύματα X. ix. 8. ἐπιτηδευμάτων

IV. iii. 35. X. ix. 13, 14. ἐπιτηδεύ-μασι X. ix. 11.
ἐπιτιθέναι X. ix. 10.
ἐπιτιμᾷ III. v. 15. ἐπιτιμᾶσθαι III. v. 15. ἐπιτιμῶσι IX. viii. 1. ἐπιτιμῶνται III. v. 16. ἐπιτιμώμενα ibid. ἐπιτιμῶμεν III. v. 15.
ἐπιτίμησιν I. xiii. 18.
ἐπιτίμια III. v. 8. viii. 1.
ἐπιτοπολὺ V. i. 6. VIII. xi. 5. IX. ii. 3. ἐπιτοπλεῖον V. x. 4.
ἐπιτρέπειν VIII. viii. 5. IX. i. 5. ἐπι-τρέψαι I. ix. 6. ἐπιτρέψειαν VI. vii. 4. ἐπιτρέψαντος IX. i. 9. ἐπετρέφθη IX. i. 9.
ἐπιτυχεῖν II. vi. 14. ἐπιτύχωσιν VII. ii. 8. ἐπιτευξόμεθα I. vi. 4.
ἐπιφανής IV. v. 1.
ἐπιφανῶς IV. iii. 36.
ἐπιφέρει I. x. 12. III. vi. 10. ἐπιφέρει X. iii. 2. ἐπιφέρουσι IV. ii. 22. ἐπι-φέρομεν IV. i. 3. ἐπιφέροντες VI. xi. 2.
ἐπιφανέστερον VIII. xiv. 4.
ἐπιχαιρεκακία II. vi. 18. ἐπιχαιρεκακίας II. vii. 15.
ἐπιχαιρέκακος II. vii. 15.
Ἐπίχαρμος IX. vii. 1.
ἐπιχειρῶν IV. ii. 13. ἐπιχειροῦσι IV. iii. 36.
ἕπεται II. iii. 3. v. 2. III. ii. 1. IV. i. 8, 12, 24. IX. vii. 7. X. i. 1. iii. 12. iv. 9. ἕποιτο VIII. i. 1. ἕπον-ται X. v. 11. ἕπεσθαι IX. viii. 2. ἑπόμενος IX. viii. 7. ἑπόμενον IX. xii. 4. ἑπόμεναι IV. i. 24. ἑπομένους I. v. 7. ἑπομένη I. vii. 12. ἑπόμενα I. viii. 23.
ἐπονείδιστος III. x. 10. ἐπονείδιστον III. xii. 2. ἐπονειδίστους X. iii. 8.
ἔπη VII. iii. 8.
εἶπε VIII. xi. 1. εἴπῃ VII. vi. 1. εἴπω-μεν VII. iv. 4. εἴποι I. viii. 12. IV. viii. 10. V. iv. 9. x. 5. VI. i. 2. VII. v. 4. VIII. ii. 4. εἴπομεν I. viii. 13, 15, 17. ix. 9. x. 9, 13. xii. 3. xiii. 17. II. ii. 3. iii. 5. v. 5. IV. ii. 6. iv. 4. IX. iii. 1. v. 2, 4. X. vi. 2. εἰπεῖν V. iv. 5. ix. 8. x. 1, 4. VI. i. 2. VII. xiv. 3. VIII. viii. 5. IX. iv. 5. vi. 3. X. vi. 6. viii. 5. εἴπωμεν III. v. 23. IV. vii. 1, 6. ix. 8. εἴπαμεν VI. vii. 4. VII. iv. 6. εἶπον V. ii. 2. x. 5. X. viii. 11. εἰπόντι I. iv. 7. εἰπόντες IV. viii. 3. VI. i. 4. xiii. 3.
ἐρανιστῶν VIII. ix. 6. ἐρανιστὰς IV. ii. 20.
ἐραστὴς IX. i. 2. ἐραστοῦ VIII. iv. 1. ἐραστῇ ibid. ἐραστὴν VIII. viii. 6. IX. i. 3. ἐρασταὶ VIII. viii. 6.
ἐρᾷ I. viii. 14. IX. v. 3. ἐρᾶν VIII. i. 6. vi. 2. IX. v. 3. x. 5. ἐρώμενον IX. i. 2. ἐρωμένῳ VIII. iv. 1. ἐρώ-μενον VIII. viii. 6. IX. i. 3. ἐρῶσι IX. xii. 1.
ἐργάζεται II. vi. 10. ἐργαζόμενοι IV. i. 40.
ἐργασίαν VIII. ix. 5. ἐργασίας IV. i. 40.
ἔργον I. vii. 10, 11, 14, 19. II. vi. 2, 3, 9. ix. 2. IV. ii. 6, 10. iii. 27. V. i. 18. v. 8, 12. ix. 15. VI. i. 6. ii. 3. 6. vii. 6. xii. 6. VII. xi. 4. xii. 6. VIII. vii. 1. IX. vii. 3, 4, 6. X. v. 2, 8. ix. 20. ἔργου III. v. 17. IV. ii. 6, 10. IX. vii. 3. ἔργῳ I. vii. 10. IV. ii. 6, 12, 18. ἔργα I. i. 2. vii. 11. xii. 2. II. vi. 9. IV. i. 20. ii. 6. V. i. 14. v. 8. VIII. xii. 7. IX. viii. 2. X. viii. 12. ix. 20. ἔργων I. vii. 19. xii. 6. IV. ii. 16. V. iii. 14. VIII. xiv. 1. X. i. 3. viii. 12. ἔργοις II. iii. 1. vi. 9. III. vii. 12. X. i. 4. viii. 12. ix. 20.
ἐργῶδες IX. vii. 7. x. 4. ἐργωδέστερον I. xiii. 8. ἐργωδέστερα IX. ii. 10.
ἐρεῖ IV. iii. 31. IX. viii. 6. X. ii. 4. ἐροῦσι VI. vii. 4. ἐροῦμεν I. x. 8, 16. II. vii. 16. IV. ii. 4. VII. xiv. 9.
εἴρηται I. v. 6. viii. 4. ix. 7. II. v. 6. ix. 1. III. iii. 15. iv. 1. v. 21. vii. 7, 13. ix. 2. IV. i. 23, 29, 33. ii. 12, 15, 20. iii. 18, 37. v. 13. vi. 6, 9. V. iii. 9. v. 7. vi. 3. vii. 3. VI. iv. 6. viii. 8. xi. 7. xii. 10. VII. i. 4. vi. 5. x. 5. xii. 7. xiv. 4, 9. VIII. i. 7. v. 1. 4. vi. 6, 7. vii. 6. ix. 1. xii. 1. xiii. 1. xiv. 3. IX. i. 1, 3, 7. ii. 5, 6. iii. 3, 4. iv. 2. v. 1. viii. 2, 11. ix. 5, 7. X. iv. 3. v. 3. vi. 2, 5, 8. vii. 1. ix. 1, 11, 16, 23. εἰρῆσθαι IX. x. 1. εἰρήσθω I. vi. 6. II. iii. 11. III. iii. 20. IV. i. 45. V. v. 19 VII. iii. 14. VIII. xiv. 4. IX. xii. 4. X. iii. 13. viii. 3. εἰρή-σθωσαν IV. v. 15. εἴρηνται III. viii. 17. IV. vii. 1. εἴρηκε V. ix. 1. εἰρήκαμεν II. ii. 1. vi. 3. εἰρη-μένας VI. i. 1. εἰρημένοις I. v. 2. IV. iii. 3. εἰρημένων VI. i. 3. VII.

iv. 5. x. 2. εἰρημένῃ III. viii. 8. V. ii. 8. εἰρημένων VI. viii. 5. εἰρημένα IV. i. 32. vii. 13. VIII. iii. 7. IX. iv. 7. X. i. 4. εἰρημένον I. xii. 7. III. i. 14. ii. 16. ix. 7. IV. viii. 4. V. i. 20. viii. 1. xi. 1. VI. vii. 5. xiii. 6. VIII. ii. 4. IX. iv. 6. X. iii. 1. vi. 1. ix. 14. εἰρημέναις VI. i. 1. εἰρημένοις I. viii. 12. III. v. 5. εἰρη-μένοις IV. vi. 3. viii. 12. VIII. vi. 7. εἰρημένην V. v. 2.
ἐρήμοις IV. iv. 4.
ἐρᾶν VIII. i. 6.
Ἑρμαίῳ III. viii. 9.
ἐρυθραίνονται IV. ix. 2.
Ἐρύξιος III. x. 10.
ἐλθεῖν IV. i. 31. VIII. viii. 7. ἔλθωσι III. iii. 11. ἐλήλυθε V. iv. 13. v. 10. VI. viii. 4. x. 4. ἐληλυθέναι IX. iv. 1.
ἐσθὴς IV. vii. 15. ἐσθῆτι IV. iii. 36.
ἐσθίειν III. xi. 3.
ἐσθλὸς I. iv. 7. ἐσθλὰ IX. xii. 3. ἐσθ-λῶν ibid. ἐσθλοὶ II. vi. 14.
Ἕσπερος V. i. 15.
ἑστιᾶν IV. ii. 11. ἑστιῶν IV. ii. 20.
ἔσχατον III. iii. 11, 12. VI. viii. 2, 9. VII. iii. 13. ἐσχάτου VI. viii. 8, 9. xi. 4. ἔσχατα VI. xi. 3. ἐσχάτων VI. xi. 2, 3, 4. VII. ii. 5.
ἑταιρικὴ VIII. v. 3. ἑταιρικῇ VIII. xi. 5. xii. 4, 6. ἑταιρικὴν VIII. xii. 1. IX. x. 6.
ἑταῖρον VIII. ix. 3. xii. 8. ἑταίρῳ IX. ii. 1, 3. ἑταῖροι VIII. xii. 4. ἑταί-ροις VIII. xii. 2. IX. ii. 3, 7. ἑταί-ρους IX. ii. 9.
ἕτερος III. i. 13. VII. iii. 1. iv. 2. IX. ix. 10. X. iii. 11. ἑτέρου III. v. 17. xi. 7. IV. iii. 31. V. iii. 12. ix. 9. VIII. vi. 7. X. ii. 2, 3. vi. 6. ἕτερα I. vi. 3. vii. 3. III. iv. 4. xi. 2. V. ii. 9. VI. i. 5. VII. xiv. 5. VIII. i. 7. iii. 5. vii. 1. ix. 3. xii. 7. IX. i. 4. ii. 7. iv. 9. X. iii. 11. iv. 4. v. 1, 2. vi. 2. 3, 4. ἕτερον I. ii. 1. iv. 3. vii. 4. xiii. 16. II. viii. 7. III. i. 14. vi. 12. viii. 16. xi. 7. V. i. 20. ii. 9, 12. v. 12, 17. vi. 9. viii. 3, 10. ix. 12. x. 1. VI. i. 5. iv. 1, 2. 5. v. 4. vii. 4. ix. 3. xii. 7. xiii. 1. VII. i. 2, 4. vii. 2, 4. viii. 1. ix. 5. xii. 3. xiv. 8. VIII. vi. 7. vii. 1. xii. 8. IX. viii. 6. ix. 1. X. ii. 2. iii. 4. ἑτέρας I. i. 4. V. ii. 11. VI. xi. 4. xii. 8. ἑτέρα II. viii. 8. V. ii. 7. x. 8. VI. vii. 4. xii. 4. VII. iii. 9. VIII. vii. 1. X. iv. 2. v. 8. ἑτέρῳ V. v. 17. vi. 6. ix. 9. X. iv. 3. ix. 15. 16. ἑτέρᾳ VII. xiv. 8. ἑτέρων VII. ix. 5. X. v. 4. vii. 6. ἕτεροι I. iii. 3. vi. 11. viii. 6. xiii. 3. VII. iii. 4. ix. 2, 7. VIII. vi. 5. xii. 3. ἕτεραι III. viii. 1. VIII. vii. 1. X. iii. 10. iv. 2. v. 7. ἑτέραν III. ii. 7. IV. i. 39. V. v. 9. VIII. xiii. 10. IX. iv. 8, 9, 10. ix. 5. X. v. 1, 3. 8, 9. ἑτέροις III. xi. 2. X. v. 2. ἑτέ-ροις VIII. iv. 3. ἑτέρους IV. i. 39. VII. i. 6. iv. 2.
ἑτέρωθεν IV. i. 34.
ἔτι I. ii. 7. iii. 6. v. 5. vi. 3, 4. vii. 2, 8, 9. 16. viii. 16. xiii. 17. II. i. 4, 6. ii. 4. iii. 3, 5. 7, 8, 10. iv. 3. v. 4. 5. vi. 4. 14, 16. viii. 5. ix. 2. III. i. 9, 19, 26. IV. i. 22. ii. 8. iii. 7. iv. 4. vii. 8. V. ii. 4, 5. iii. 7. v. 5. vi. 1. viii. 10. ix. 5. 8, 9. 11. 12. xi. 2. 4, 5. VI. iii. 3. viii. 4. 7. ix. 3. 7. xii. 6. xiii. 8. VII. i. 7. ii. 6, 7, 8, 10, 11. iii. 6, 7. 9. v. 3. vi. 2, 3. 4. x. 2. xi. 2, 3. 4. xii. 3. xiii. 4. xiv. 5. VIII. i. 1. 5. iii. 8. vi. 4. vii. 4. 5, 6. IX. iii. 3. vii. 7. x. 3. X. v. 3. vii. 2. viii. 7. ix. 14. 15.
ἔτη IX. viii. 9.
ἕτοιμος III. ix. 6.
εὖ I. iv. 2, 5, 7. vii. 10, 14. 15. viii. 4. 9. x. 9. 12. II. i. 5, 6. iii. 5, 9, 10. iv. 3, 5, 6. v. 2, 3. vi. 2, 9. 10, 17, 18. vii. 15. ix. 2, 8, 9. III. iv. 4. v. 17. IV. i. 6, 7, 8, 16, 31. iii. 24. 25. viii. 7. V. i. 16. v. 6. VI. ii. 3. v. 1, 2. vii. 4, 6. viii. 4. ix. 3. 4. 7. x. 3. VIII. viii. 3. 4. xi. 1. xii. 5. xiii. 2, 4, 8, 9. xiv. 4. IX. ii. 5. vii. 1, 2, 7. ix. 2. x. 5. xi. 1, 6. X. iv. 5. ix. 20.
εὐβουλία VI. ix. 2, 3. 4, 5, 6, 7. εὐβου-λίας VI. ix. 1.
εὔβουλος VI. vii. 6.
εὐγενείας I. viii. 16. εὐγένειαν V. iii. 7.
εὐγενὲς X. ix. 3. εὐγενοῦς IV. iii. 19. εὐγενεῖς IV. ii. 14.
εὐγνώμων VI. xi. 2. εὐγνώμονας VI. xi. 1.
εὐδαιμονεῖν I. iv. 2. ix. 5. III. ii. 9. IX. ix. 5. X. viii. 8. εὐδαιμονήσειν I. vii. 5. εὐδαιμονεῖ X. viii. 8. εὐδαι-μονήσοντα X. viii. 9. εὐδαιμονήσοντι IX. ix. 10.

εὐδαιμονία I. vii. 5. 8. viii. 14. xii. 7. xiii. 1. VII. xiii. 2. IX. ix. 5. X. iii. 1. vi. 2, 6, 8. vii. 1, 6, 7. viii. 3, 7, 8. εὐδαιμονίας I. iv. 2. vii. 5. x. 9, 14. xii. 1. xiii. 1. V. i. 13. X. vi. 1, 6, 8. vii. 7. viii. 8. εὐδαιμονίᾳ I. viii. 17. VII. xiii. 3. X. vii. 3. εὐδαιμονίαν I. iv. 2. v. 1. vii. 5, 7, 9. viii. 5, 14. ix. 2. x. 2, 7, 15. xii. 4. xiii. 5, 6. VI. xii. 5. VII. xi. 2. xiii. 2, 4. X. vi. 2. vii. 6.

εὐδαιμονίζειν I. x. 7. εὐδαιμονίσειε I. v. 6. εὐδαιμονίζει I. ix. 11. εὐδαιμονίζομεν I. xii. 4. εὐδαιμονιζόμενον X. vi. 3. εὐδαιμονιστέον I. x. 1.

εὐδαιμονικὸς I. viii. 16. εὐδαιμονικὰ X. vi. 3. εὐδαιμονικωτέρα X. vi. 7. εὐδαιμονικωτάτη X. viii. 7.

εὐδαιμονισμὸς IV. vii. 13.

εὐδαίμων I. ix. 19. x. 2. 4, 14. VI. xii. 1. VII. xiii. 2. X. vi. 6. viii. 10, 13. εὐδαίμονα I. ix. 9. εὐδαίμονι I. x. 11. IX. ix. 2, 3. εὐδαίμονος I. vii. 16. viii. 4. x. 3, 8, 15. VI. xii. 5. VII. xiii. 2, 3, 7. IX. ix. 1, 5. X. i. 1. viii. 11. εὐδαίμονες I. xi. 5. 6. xiii. 12. X. viii. 7, 11. εὐδαιμονέστατος X. vii. 9. εὐδαιμονέστατον X. viii. 13. εὐδαιμονέστερος III. ix. 4.

εὐδιάλυτοι VIII. iii. 3.

εὐδαιμονεῖν X. vi. 3. εὐδαιμονοῦντας X. ix. 20.

Εὔδοξος I. xii. 3. X. ii. 1.

εὐεκτικῷ X. v. 9. εὐεκτικὸν V. i. 5. xi. 7. εὐεκτικὰ V. i. 5. VI. xii. 1. εὐεκτικῶν V. i. 5.

εὐέλπιδος III. vii. 11. εὐέλπιδες III. vi. 11. viii. 13, 14. εὐελπίδων III. viii. 16.

εὐεξία V. i. 5. εὐεξίαν III. xi. 8.

εὐεργεσίας IV. iii. 25. VIII. i. 1. xi. 1. xiv. 2. IX. ii. 3. X. ix. 14. εὐεργεσίᾳ VIII. xiii. 10.

εὐεργετεῖν IX. ix. 2. xi. 1. εὐεργετοῦντι VIII. xiv. 3. εὐεργετεῖσθαι IV. i. 16. VIII. xiii. 8. εὐεργετεῖται VIII. xiii. 9. εὐεργετήσαντας IX. vii. 1. εὐεργετησόντων IX. ix. 2. εὐεργετούμενος IV. iii. 24. εὐεργετηθεὶς IX. v. 3. εὐεργετηθέντα VIII. xiii. 9. εὐεργετηθέντας IX. vii. 1.

εὐεργετημάτων VIII. xi. 2.

εὐεργέται IX. vii. 1. εὐεργετῶν VIII. xiii. 10. IX. vii. 4. εὐεργέτῃ IX. ii. 1. vii. 5. εὐεργέταις IX. ii. 7. vii. 7.

εὐεργετητικὸν IX. xi. 5.

εὐετηρίας VIII. i. 1. εὐετηρίαν I. viii. 6.

εὐζωΐα I. viii. 4.

εὐημερέστερον I. xiii. 17.

εὐημερίας I. viii. 17. X. viii. 9.

Εὔηνος VII. x. 4.

εὐθαρσὴς III. vi. 4.

εὐθήρατον III. i. 11.

εὐθὺς II. i. 8. iii. 2. vi. 18. V. x. 4. VI. v. 6. xiii. 1. VII. iii. 9. vi. 1. VIII. xii. 2, 7. IX. iii. 3.

εὐθὺ VI. vii. 4.

εὐίατος IV. i. 31. εὐιατότερος VII. ii. 10. εὐιατοτέρα VII. x. 4.

εὐκατάφοροι II. viii. 8.

εὐκαταφρόνητοι IV. vii. 15.

εὐκοινώνητος IV. i. 26.

εὐάθλους I. x. 12.

εὐλάβειαν IV. i. 39.

εὐλαβεῖται IV. vii. 8. εὐλαβούμενος IV. iv. 8. εὐλαβοῦνται IX. xi. 4. εὐλαβήσεται IV. vii. 8. εὐλαβητέον IX. xi. 6.

εὔλογον I. vi. 15. viii. 7. ix. 2, 5. V. ix. 2. VII. xiv. 3. IX. iii. 1. X. v. 8. vi. 4. vii. 1, 3. viii. 13. ix. 19. εὐλογώτερον I. xiii. 11.

εὐλόγως VI. xi. 2. VII. xii. 6. VIII. iii. 7. xiii. 2. X. iv. 10.

εὐμετάβολον I. x. 14. VII. xiv. 8. εὐμετάβολος I. x. 7.

εὐμετάπειστοι VII. ix. 2. εὐμετάπειστος VII. viii. 4.

εὐνῆς III. xi. 1.

εὐνοεῖν VIII. ii. 4.

εὔνοια IX. v. 1, 2, 3, 4. εὔνοιαν VIII. ii. 3. IX. v. 3.

εὐνομίας III. iii. 11.

εὔνοι VIII. ii. 4. vi. 1. IX. v. 2, 3. εὔνους VIII. v. 3. εὔνους VIII. ii. 3. IX. v. 3.

εὐπαθείας VIII. viii. 1. εὐπαθείαν IX. xi. 6.

εὐπαρακολούθητον II. vii. 11.

εὐπειθὲς III. xii. 7, 8. εὐπειθεῖς X. ix. 14.

εὔπειστοι VII. ix. 2.

εὔπορα VI. vii. 7.

εὐπορεῖ IX. iv. 7.

εὐπορίας VIII. vii. 4. IX. v. 3.

εὐπραξία I. viii. 4. VI. ii. 4, 5. v. 4. εὐπραξίαι I. x. 3. xi. 6.

εὕρεσις VII. ii. 12. εὑρήσεως III. iii. 5. εὑρήσει III. iii. 11.

εὑρετὴς I. vii. 17.

Εὐριπίδης V. ix. 1. VI. viii. 4. VIII. i. 6. Εὐριπίδου III. i. 8.
Εὔριπος, IX. vi. 3.
εὑρίσκειν II. vi. 16. X. ii. 1. εὑρὼν III. x. 7. εὑρεῖν IX. x. 6.
εὐσθενοῦντα I. ix. 11.
εὐστοχία VI. ix. 1, 2.
εὐσυνεσία VI. x. 2.
εὐσύνετοι VI. x. 2, 4. εὐσυνετώτεροι X. ix. 21.
εὐσχημόνως I. x. 13.
εὐσχημονέστερον IV. viii. 6.
εὐσχήμονα IV. viii. 3.
εὐτεκνίας I. viii. 16.
εὐτραπελία II. vii. 13.
εὐτράπελος II. vii. 13. IV. viii. 19. εὐτράπελοι IV. viii. 3, 4. X. vi. 3. εὐτραπέλους VIII. iv. 1. εὐτραπέλοις VIII. iii. 1. vi. 5.
εὔτροποι IV. viii. 3.
εὐτυχεῖν IV. iii. 18. εὐτυχοῦντες IX. xi. 1. εὐτυχούντων IX. ix. 2.
εὐτυχήματα IV. iii. 19, 21, 36. εὐτυχημάτων I. x. 12.
εὐτυχέσιν X. ix. 6.
εὐτυχία V. i. 9. VII. xiii. 3. εὐτυχίας IX. xi. 5, 6. εὐτυχίαν I. viii. 17. IV. iii. 18. VII. xiii. 4. εὐτυχίαις IV. iii. 26. IX. ix. 2. xi. 1, 2, 5.
εὐυπέρβλητον IV. ii. 19.
εὐφιλοτίμητα IV. ii. 11.
εὐφυὴς III. v. 17. εὐφυέστατος VI. xiii. 6.
εὐφυΐα III. v. 17.
εὐχερῶς IV. i. 16, 34, 35.
εὔχεσθαι V. i. 9. εὔχονται V. i. 9. ηὔξατο III. x. 10.
εὔχρηστα X. ix. 21.
εὐωχίαν VII. v. 2.
ἐφάπτεται III. ix. 5.
ἐφαρμόττει V. iv. 2. ἐφαρμόττειν II. vii. 1.
ἐφεξῆς VII. iv. 1.
ἔφεσις III. v. 17.
ἐφημέρων I. vi. 6.
ἐφίεται VIII. viii. 7. ix. 5. xiii. 2. IX. i. 4. X. ii. 1, 4. iv. 2. ἐφίενται III. v. 17. IV. i. 39. iii. 10, 35. VIII. i. 4. viii. 1, 2. ix. 5. IX. vi. 2, 3. vii. 1. xii. 1. X. iv. 10. vi. 3. vii. 7. ἐφίεσθαι I. i. 1. iv. 1. VIII. i. 6. v. 2. X. vii. 7. ἐφιέμενος VIII. viii. 6. X. i. 3. ἐφιεμένων IV. iv. 3. ἐφιέμενοι VIII. vi. 5. ἐφιέμεναι I. vi. 15. ἐφιέμενα X. ii. 1. ἐφιεμένους IX. vi. 4. ἐφιεμένοις X. ix. 19.
ἐχθαίρειν IV. vi. 5. ἐχθαίρουσι X. ix. 12.
ἐχθρὸν VIII. i. 4. ἐχθρῶν IV. iii. 31.
ἔχεων VII. vii. 6.
ἔχομεν I. xiii. 3. II. v. 2. III. v. 6. VI. xiii. 1. ἔχει I. ii. 2. iii. 2, 3. iv. 7. vi. 15. viii. 12. x. 3. xi. 3. xiii. 7, 8. II. i. 1, 7. ii. 2, 3, 4, 7, 8. iii. 5. iv. 2, 3. vi. 3. vii. 8. III. i. 4. vi. 3. vii. 8, 12. IV. i. 31. ii. 14, 15, 18. iii. 18. V. i. 4. iii. 6, 14. v. 11, 12. vi. 3. vii. 2, 6. ix. 13. x. 1, 2, 5. VI. v. 6. viii. 2, 3, 4. xi. 6. xii. 1. xiii. 1. VII. ii. 11. iii. 6, 11, 13. vi. 6. vii. 2, 6. viii. 1. x. 3. xii. 3. VIII. iv. 1. vi. 7. x. 4. xii. 6. xiii. 6. IX. i. 4. ii. 1, 2, 5. iii. 1. iv. 4. ix. 3, 10. x. 5. xi. 5. xii. 1. X. viii. 12. ix. 12. ἔχουσι V. iii. 6. v. 12. IX. iii. 1. ἕξει III. v. 17. x. 7. IV. iii. 18. viii. 10. V. v. 12. VI. iii. 4. VII. xii. 5. IX. i. 8. ἔχονται III. ix. 6. V. ix. 14. VIII. viii. 6. ἔχοντες I. ii. 2. vi. 14. II. i. 4. III. i. 5. viii. 7, 8. IV. iii. 18, 20, 21. VI. xii. 10. VII. iii. 2. viii. 2. IX. i. 9. iv. 9. ἔχειν I. iv. 4. ix. 5. x. 4. xii. 2, 8. xiii. 18, 19. II. iv. 3. vii. 8. III. i. 13. ix. 3. IV. i. 21. iii. 17, 32, 35. iv. 1. ix. 6. V. i. 16. ii. 12. iv. 8, 13. 14. vii. 4. xi. 7. VI. i. 5, 6. ii. 2. iii. 2. iv. 1, 6. v. 3, 8. vi. 1, 2. vii. 6, 7. x. 3. xi. 1, 2, 5, 6. xii. 1. xiii. 1. VII. ii. 6, 8. iii. 2, 7, 13. v. 5, 7. vi. 7. vii. 1. xiv. 4. VIII. v. 3. vii. 3. xiii. 4, 10. xiv. 1, 3. IX. i. 9. iii. 5. iv. 4, 5, 10. vii. 6. ix. 3. x. 6. X. i. 2. ii. 1. iii. 12. v. 6. vi. 6. vii. 1, 3, 7. ix. 1, 2. ἔχοντα I. v. 6. vii. 17. II. iv. 3. III. v. 17. V. ix. 16. VI. i. 5. vii. 4. xii. 7. VII. ii. 3. iii. 5, 6. iv. 2. v. 5. X. i. 1. ix. 7. ἔχοντος I. vii. 13. III. xii. 2. V. iv. 11. VI. i. 5, 6. VII. vi. 7. X. iv. 5. ἔχον I. vii. 13. xiii. 9, 10, 19. IV. i. 25. ii. 19. vii. 1. V. vii. 1, 2. xi. 9. VI. i. 5. ἔχουσι I. vii. 23. II. vi. 9. III. vi. 4. vii. 12. viii. 12. xii. 5. IV. i. 4. v. 8, 10. V. ii. 6. iv. 2. ix. 17. VI. iv. 4. VII. ix. 2. x. 5. xiv. 5, 7. VIII. iii. 4, 6. v. 1. viii. 5. IX. ii. 6. iii. 3. ix. 5. X. v. 6. viii. 7. ix. 4. ἐχόντων I. xi. 2. VI. v. 8. X. i. 2. iv. 8. ἔχοι I. xi. 2. IV. i. 22. IX. iv. 10. ἔσχηκε II. i. 1. ἔσχομεν II. i. 4. εἶχεν II. i. 7. IX. i. 4. ἔχῃ II. iv. 3. III. ix. 4. IV. i.

17, 21. VIII. ii. 3. ἔχων II. iv. 3. vii. 12, 13. III. iii. 1. ix. 1. xi. 8. IV. i. 5, 6. V. i. 15. iv. 5. ix. 9, 10. x. 8. xi. 4. III. xi. 8. VI. i. 2. VII. ii. 5. iii. 5. ix. 6. x. 3. VIII. i. 1. IX. i. 2. v. 3. X. iii. 12. vii. 4. ἕξουσι II. iv. 6. V. iii. 6. VII. v. 4. ἔχονται II. vii. 11. ἔχοντι III. vii. 1. V. iv. 11. VIII. xii. 2. IX. i. 9. ἔχομεν V. ii. 6. ἐχόμενον V. x. 1. ἔχουσα VI. ii. 3. vii. 3. ἔχεσθαι VI. xii. 5. ἑκτέον IX. iii. 5. ἐχόντων IX. viii. 2. ἐχομένης IX. ix. 8. ἔχουσαν X. ix. 11.
Εῷ IX. i. 4.
Ἑῷοι V. i. 15.
ἕως I. x. 1. III. iii. 11. xi. 3. V. vi. 8. VIII. iii. 6. vii. 5. viii. 6. X. iii. 3. iv. 8.

Z.

Ζεὺς VI. viii. 4. Διὶ IV. iii. 25. IX. ii. 6. Δία VIII. x. 4.
ἔζεσεν III. viii. 10.
ζῆλον II. v. 2.
ζημία V. iv. 5, 6. ζημίας V. iv. 6, 14. ζημίᾳ V. iv. 4, 13. ζημίαις X. ix. 9.
ζημιοῖ V. xi. 3. ζημιούμενος V. ii. 4. ζημιοῦσθαι V. iv. 13, 14.
ζῆν I. iii. 7. iv. 2. vii. 12. viii. 4. III. ix. 4. xii. 8. IV. i. 5, 35. iii. 23, 39. V. ii. 10. VI. v. 1. VII. xiii. 7. VIII. i. 1. IX. iv. 1, 3, 8. vii. 4. viii. 6. ix. 5, 7, 9. x. 2. xii. 2. X. i. 4. iii. 12. iv. 10, 11. vii. 4, 8. viii. 7. ix. 8, 11. ζῶντα I. v. 6. X. ix. 10. ζῶντι I. vii. 6. x. 3. X. vi. 2. viii. 7. ζῇ I. x. 1. IV. vii. 5. IX. ix. 9. X. ix. 13. ζώντων I. x. 13. ζῶντες III. v. 10. VII. v. 6. X. ix. 4. ζῶσι III. xii. 7. VIII. iii. 5. ζῶν X. ix. 7. ζῶντας I. x. 7. xi. 4. IV. ix. 3.
ζητεῖ II. vi. 8. VI. ix. 2, 3. ζητεῖν III. iii. 11. VI. ix. 1. VII. ii. 2. VIII. vii. 2. IX. x. 5. ζητῶν III. iii. 17. ζητοῦμεν V. ii. 1. VI. xiii. 1. X. vii. 6. ζητούντων X. vii. 8. ζητεῖσθαι VIII. xii. 7. ζητοῦσι I. v. 5. V. iv. 7. v. 6. VI. vii. 5. viii. 4. ix. 2. VIII. vi. 4, 5. viii. 3. IX. iv. 9. xi. 1. ἐζήτει I. iv. 5. VI. xiii. 3. VII. iii. 13. ζητουμένου I. v. 4. ζητούμενον I. v. 8. vii. 1, 3. ix. 7. x. 11. V. vi. 4. ζητεῖται I. vi. 13. vii. 12. III. iii. 14. ζητουμένων I. vii. 23. ἐζητοῦμεν I. xiii. 5. ζητούμενα I. xiii. 8.
ζήτησιν I. xiii. 4. III. iii. 12. VI. ix. 3. ζητήσεων I. vi. 1.
ζητητέα VI. ix. 4.
ζωὴ IX. ix. 9. X. iv. 10. ζωῆς I. x. 12, 13. ζωὴν I. vii. 12, 14. IX. ix. 8.
ζῷον VII. xiv. 5. ζῴῳ I. vii. 12. X. v. 8. ζῷα III. ii. 2. x. 8, 10. xi. 7. X. v. 1. viii. 8. ζῴων I. ix. 9. III. i. 22. VI. vii. 4. VII. v. 1. vi. 6. VIII. i. 3. X. viii. 8. ζῴοις II. iii. 7. VIII. xii. 7. IX. ix. 7.

H.

ἢ V. i. 20. x. 5, 6. VIII. iii. 1, 6. iv. 6. x. 5. X. v. 10.
ἡγεῖσθαι X. vii. 1. ἡγούμενον III. iii. 17. ἡγούμεθα VI. v. 5.
ἤδη I. iii. 3. x. 3. II. iv. 1. vi. 3. III. iii. 17. vi. 1. V. i. 16. vi. 1. viii. 11. ix. 3. xi. 2. xiii. 6. VII. iii. 9. xiv. 4. X. vi. 7.
ἥδεται III. xi. 8. IV. i. 28. IX. iv. 9. ix. 6. xi. 3. X. ii. 2. iv. 9. ἥδεσθαι I. viii. 10. IV. i. 25. VII. ix. 6. IX. iv. 10. X. iii. 2, 4, 6. iv. 4. ἡσθῆναι II. vi. 10. IX. viii. 9. X. iii. 4, 10. ἥδονται III. viii. 12. VIII. iv. 1. IX. ix. 9. xi. 5. ἡσθῇ IX. iv. 10. ἡσθήσονται IV. iii. 17. ἡδόμενος III. x. 10. X. iii. 12.
ἡδονὴ II. iii. 2. v. 2. III. x. 7. xi. 5. xii. 2. VII. xi. 3, 4, 5. xii. 5. xiii. 2, 7. xiv. 4, 6, 8. VIII. ii. 1. iv. 1. IX. v. 3. X. ii. 3. iii. 1, 5, 6, 12, 13. iv. 1, 4, 5, 6, 7, 8, 9, 10, 11. v. 2, 3, 5, 7, 8. ἡδονῆς I. vi. 11. viii. 6, 12. II. ii. 7. ix. 4. III. i. 11. IV. vi. 8. VII. vi. 4. xi. 1, 2, 4. xii. 3, 6. xiv. 2, 9. VIII. iii. 5. v. 2. ix. 5. IX. i. 4. ix. 4. xii. 4. X. i. 4. ii. 1. iii. 13. iv. 4, 10. v. 2. vi. 4. ix. 1, 10. ἡδονῇ I. xii. 5. II. iii. 8, 10. X. i. 1. iii. 4. v. 6. ἡδονὴν I. iv. 3. v. 2. vii. 5. viii. 12. II. iii. 1, 7. vii. 15. ix. 6. III. v. 5. xi. 6. xii. 2. IV. i. 35. v. 10. vi. 1. vii. 1. viii. 12. V. ii. 6. VI. v. 6. VII. iii. 1, v. 7. ix. 3, 4. xi. 3. xii. 3, 6. xiii. 1, 2, 5, 6. xiv. 8. VIII. iii. 1, 2, 5, 6, 7. iv. 2, 4, 6. vi. 7. ix. 5. xiii. 3. IX. i. 3, 4, 8. x. 2. X. i. 2, 3. ii. 1, 2, 3, 5. iii. 2, 3, 4, 6. 11, 12. iv. 1, 4. 11. v. 4. vii. 3, 8.

ἡδοναὶ I. vi. 10. VII. xi. 4. xii. 1, 2, 7. xiii. 2, 6. xiv. 1, 3. X. iii. 9, 10, 12. v. 2, 5. 6, 7, 10, 11. ἡδονῶν II. ii. 9. iii. 1. III. x. 1, 11. xi. 4. VII. ii. 3. iv. 2, 5. vii. 2, 3, 6. ix. 2. xiii. 2. xiv. 1. X. iii. 6, 8. v. 2. vi. 8. ἡδοναῖς IX. viii. 4. X. i. 2. iii. 2. ix. 10. ἡδονὰς II. iii. 1, 3. 5. 6, 10, 11. vii. 3. viii. 8. III. x. 1, 2, 8. xi. 5, 7. 8. IV. i. 35. vi. 7. VII. iv. 1, 4. vi. 5. vii. 1. viii. 4, 5. ix. 6. xi. 2, 4. VIII. viii. 6. X. iii. 7. v. 3, 11. vi. 1. vii. 3. ix. 4.

ἡδέως III. ix. 5. IV. i. 13. 24. ii. 8. iii. 25. xiii. 7. IX. iv. 5. ix. 5.

ἡδὺς I. viii. 9. II. vii. 13. IV. vi. 9. VIII. iii. 2. vi. 6. IX. ix. 4. ἡδεῖα VIII. iv. 1. IX. vii. 6. ix. 5, 6, 10. xi. 2. ἡδὺ I. viii. 10. II. iii. 7. vii. 11, 13. ix. 6. III. i. 11. iv. 6. ix. 3. xi. 7. IV. i. 13. viii. 7, 12. VI. v. 6. VII. iii. 2, 10. vi. 1. vii. 8. xi. 4. xii. 2. xiv. 6, 7, 8. VIII. ii. 1, 2. iii. 2, 4. 5, 7. iv. 1, 2, 4, 5. v. 2, 4. vi. 3, 4. 7. xii. 6, 7. IX. iii. 1. iv. 5. v. 3. vii. 5. ix. 4, 7, 9, 10. xi. 3. X. ix. 8. ἡδέος II. iii. 7. III. ii. 8. xi. 5. xii. 6, 7. VIII. v. 2. vi. 5. X. ix. 4. ἡδεῖ VII. xii. 1. VIII. iii. 5. v. 2. ἡδὺν VII. xiii. 2. X. ii. 3. ἡδεῖαν IX. xi. 5. ἡδεῖς VIII. iii. 1, 3. 4, 6. iv. 1. v. 3. vi. 4. 5. vii. 6. xiii. 1. X. vi. 3. ἡδέα I. viii. 11. III. i. 11, 25. iv. 4. xi. 2, 8. VII. ii. 10. v. 1. ix. 7. xii. 2, 4. xiv. 7. VIII. iii. 5. iv. 8, 10. IX. ix. 5. X. i. 1. iii. 8. iv. 7. v. 9, 10. vi. 5. ἡδεῖαι I. viii. 2, 13. VII. xii. 2. IX. iv. 5. ix. 5. X. vi. 3. ἡδίων III. ix. 2. xi. 5, 6, 8. VII. iv. 2, 3, 5. vii. 2. xi. 5. xiv. 7. VIII. vi. 4. IX. ix. 5, 7, 9. ἡδίον VII. xii. 2. ἡδίων VII. xiii. 7. X. v. 4. ἥδιον IX. xi. 6. X. v. 8. ἡδίστη VII. xiv. 8. X. iv. 5. vii. 3. ἥδιστον I. viii. 14. IX. vii. 6. X. vii. 9. ἡδίω III. xi. 2. X. vii. 3.

ἥδυσμα IX. x. 2.

ἠθικὰς I. xiii. 20. X. viii. 3. ἠθικῆς II. i. 1. VI. ii. 4. xiii. 6. X. viii. 4. ἠθικὴ II. i. 1. iii. 1. ix. 1. VI. ii. 2. VII. viii. 4. VIII. xiii. 5, 7. ἠθικῶν II. i. 2. V. xi. 10. VI. i. 4. X. viii. 3. ἠθικὴν II. vi. 2. VI. xii. 6. VII. xi. 2. ἠθικοῦ VI. xiii. 2.

ἦθος I. iii. 7. IV. i. 31. vii. 1. VII. x. 1. IX. iii. 1, 2. 3. xi. 3. X. ix. 1, 8. ἤθους I. xiii. 20. IV. viii. 3. VI. i. 4. ii. 4. VIII. xiii. 11. X. i. 1. ii. 1. viii. 2, 3. ἤθη III. ii. 1. IV. i. 35. vii. 14. viii. 3. VII. i. 1. VIII. i. 7. iv. 1. X. ix. 14. ἠθῶν VI. xiii. 1. IX. i. 3. ἤθεσι X. ix. 5.

ἥκιστα I. xiii. 12. III. ii. 6. IV. i. 13. 21. iii. 32. VIII. v. 3. x. 3. xi. 6. IX. xi. 5. X. i. 2.

ἥκει III. iii. 16. xii. 17. ἥκομεν II. ix. 5.

ἠλίθιος III. ii. 7. iii. 2. IV. ii. 13. iii. 3. ἠλιθίου IV. i. 31. ἠλίθιον X. vi. 6. ἠλίθιοι IV. iii. 35, 36. v. 5.

ἡλικίαν I. iii. 7. VIII. xii. 4. IX. ii. 9. ἡλικίας IV. i. 31. VIII. iii. 5. ἡλικία VI. xi. 6. ἡλικίᾳ IV. ix. 3. ἡλικίαις VI. xi. 6. VIII. x. 6.

ἡλικιῶται VIII. xi. 5.

ἧλιξ, ἥλικα VIII. xii. 4.

ἡμέρα I. vii. 16. ἡμέρας III. x. 2. VIII. iii. 5.

ἡμέτερον III. xi. 2.

ἡμιπόνηροι VII. x. 3.

ἡμισείας V. iv. 8.

ἥμισυ I. vii. 23. xiii. 12. V. v. 15.

Ἡράκλειτος II. iii. 10. VII. iii. 4. VIII. i. 6. X. v. 8.

ἠρέμα III. i. 16. IV. v. 14. VII. iii. 4. vii. 3. IX. viii. 9. X. v. 4.

ἠρεμία VII. ii. 4.

ἠρεμίας II. iii. 5. ἠρεμίᾳ VII. xiv. 8.

ἠρεμεῖν VII. i. 1.

Ἡσιόδου I. iv. 7.

ἡσυχία X. ix. 15.

ἡσύχιοι III. vii. 12.

ἧττων VII. vii. 2.

ἡττᾶσθαι VII. vii. 1, 4. ἡττῶνται VII. vii. 8. viii. 2.

ἧττον I. viii. 16. xi. 2. xiii. 16. II. iii. 8. vi. 10. vii. 3, 8. ix. 3. 6, 8. III. i. 27. ii. 6, 10. iii. 8. v. 7. 19. vii. 1, 3. viii. 15. ix. 4. 6. x. 1. xi. 7. xii. 4. IV. i. 9, 10. iv. 2, 5. v. 13. vi. 8. V. ix. 16. x. 4. xi. 8. VI. v. 7. xi. 6. VII. ii. 10. iii. 4. vi. 1. ix. 5. x. 4. VIII. i. 7. iv. 2. v. 5. vi. 1, 7. ix. 2. IX. vii. 5, 6. X. i. 3. ii. 2. iii. 2, 3. vi. 8. viii. 10. ix. 16.

ἥττω IV. viii. 10. ἥττους VII. vii. 1

Θ.

θαλάττῃ III. vi. 8, 11. θαλάττης X. viii. 10.

θαλάττιοι III. iv. 11.
Θαλῆν VI. vii. 5.
θάνατος III. vi. 6. viii. 9. ix. 4. V. ii. 13. θάνατον III. vi. 3. 7. 10, 11. viii. 9. IV. ix. 2. θανάτῳ III. ix. 4.
θαρραλέα III. vii. 1, 4. 13. ix. 1.
θαρραλέοι III. viii. 13. θαρραλέῳ VII. ix. 2.
θαρρεῖ III. vi. 5. θαρροῦσι III. viii. 13. θαρρῶν III. vii. 5. θαρρεῖν II. i. 8. vii. 2. III. vii. 7, 10. 11. θαρρῆσαι II. vi. 10.
θάρρη II. vi. 2. III. vi. 1. ix. 1.
θάρσος II. v. 2.
θάτερον V. iv. 10. xi. 8. VII. xiv. 8. θατέρου V. iv. 10. v. 8. VI. v. 8. VIII. vii. 2. θάτερα V. i. 6.
θᾶττον IV. v. 7. VIII. xii. 7.
θαυμάζουσι I. iv. 3. θαυμάσειεν X. viii. 11. θαυμάζεσθαι IV. ii. 20.
θαυμαστικὸς IV. iii. 30.
θαυμαστὸς V. i. 15. θαυμαστὴ IV. ii. 10. θαυμαστὸν IV. ii. 10. VII. iii. 6. vii. 6. X. v. 11. θαυμαστὰς X. vii. 3. θαυμαστὰ VI. vii. 5.
θέαμα I. viii. 10.
θεατὴς I. vii. 19.
θεάτροις X. v. 4.
θεωμένους IX. vii. 1. τεθεάμενος I. vi. 16.
θεῖον X. vii. 8. θειότερα VI. vii. 4. θείαν I. ix. 1. VII. i. 1. θειότερον I. ii. 8. xii. 4. θείας X. ix. 6. θειότατον X. vii. 1. θεῖον X. vii. 1. θειοτάτου I. ix. 3. θεῖον I. ix. 3. xii. 8. VII. i. 3. xiii. 6. X. vii. 1, 8. θειοτάτους I. xii. 4.
θέλουσαν V. ix. 1.
θεμιστεύων X. ix. 13.
Θέογνις IX. ix. 7. Θέογνιν X. ix. 3.
Θεοδέκτου VII. vii. 6.
θεόπεμπτος I. ix. 3.
θεὸς I. vi. 3. VI. ii. 6. VII. xiv. 8. IX. iv. 4. θεοῦ VII. i. 2. VIII. vii. 5. X. viii. 7. θεοῖο VII. i. 1. θεὸν I. xii. 5. θεοὶ VI. vii. 2. VII. i. 2. θεῶν I. ix. 2. VI. xiii. 8. X. viii. 7, 13. θεοὺς I. xii. 3, 4. IV. ii. 11. VII. iv. 5. VIII. vii. 6. xii. 5. xiv. 4. IX. i. 7. X. viii. 7. θεοῖς IV. ii. 16. iii. 10. V. vii. 3. ix. 17. VIII. ix. 5. IX. ii. 8. X. viii. 8.
θεόσδοτον I. ix. 2.
θεοφιλέστατος, θεοφιλέστατον X. viii. 13.
θεραπεία VIII. iv. 1. θεραπείας VIII. i. 2. X. viii. 9.
θεραπεύματα X. ix. 21.
θεραπεύει IX. v. 3. θεραπεύειν X. ix. 21. θεραπεύων VIII. xiv. 4. X. viii. 13. θεραπεύοντα I. xiii. 7. III. iv. 6. θεραπευόμενοι VIII. iv. 1.
θερμαίνεσθαι III. v. 7.
θερμασίας III. x. 11.
θερμὸν X. v. 9. θερμῷ VIII. viii. 7. θερμὰ III. iv. 4.
θερμότητα VII. vi. 1.
θέσιν I. v. 6.
θετέον I. vii. 13. x. 2. X. vi. 2.
Θέτιν IV. iii. 25.
θεωρεῖ VI. xi. 1. θεωροῦνται I. vii. 21. θεωρηθείη I. x. 6. θεωρήσει I. x. 11. θεωρήσαμεν I. xiii. 1. θεωρητέον I. xiii. 8. II. ii. 6. θεωρήσωμεν III. vi. 4. VII. vi. 1. θεωροῦντι X. v. 8. viii. 6. θεωροῦν X. iv. 8. θεωρῆσαι IV. ii. 5. VII. xi. 1. X. vii. 5. ix. 1, 21, 23. θεωροῦμεν VI. i. 5. θεωρεῖν VI. iii. 2. iv. 4. v. 5. vii. 4. VII. xii. 2, 5. IX. ix. 5. X. vii. 2, 4. viii. 8, 9. θεωρῶν VII. iii. 5. x. 3. θεωρηθέντων X. ix. 23. θεωρήσαντες VI. v. 1. θεωροῦντα VII. iii. 5.
θεωρήματα X. iv. 10. θεωρημάτων IX. iv. 5.
θεωρητικὴ X. vii. 1, 7. viii. 7. θεωρητικῆς VI. ii. 3. θεωρητικῷ X. ix. 16. θεωρητικὴν X. vii. 4. θεωρητικὸς I. v. 2, 7.
θεωρία IV. ii. 10. X. viii. 7, 8. θεωρίαν X. iv. 5. viii. 8. θεωρίας II. ii. 1. VII. iii. 1. X. viii. 8.
θῆλυ VII. vii. 6.
θηρίου VII. i. 2. vi. 7. xiv. 4. θηρίοις VI. xiii. 1. θηρίων VI. vii. 4. θηρία III. viii. 10, 11. VI. ii. 2. VII. iii. 11. vi. 6. xi. 4. xii. 7. xiii. 5.
θηριότης VII. i. 1. v. 5. vi. 7. θηριότητα VII. i. 1.
θηριώδης VII. i. 3. v. 8. θηριώδεις III. x. 11. θηριώδεις III. x. 8. VII. v. 2, 3. 5. 6. vi. 6. θηριώδει VII. i. 2. θηριώδη VII. v. 6.
θησαυροῦ III. iii. 5.
θητικοὶ IV. iii. 29.
θιασωτῶν VIII. ix. 5.
θλίβει I. x. 12.
θνήσκω. τεθνᾶσι I. viii. 16. τεθνεὼς I. x. 6. τεθνεῶτι I. x. 3. III. vi. 6. τεθνεῶτα I. x. 3.
θνητὸν X. vii. 8. θνητοῦ VII. i. 1. θνητὰ X. vii. 8.

θρασύδειλοι III. vii. 9.
θρασυνόμενοι III. vii. 9.
θρασὺς II. ii. 8. vii. 2. viii. 2. 3. III. vii. 7, 8, 12. VII. ix. 2. θρασὺν II. viii. 2, 3. θρασεῖς III. vii. 12.
θρασύτης II. viii. 6, 7. θρασύτητι II. viii. 5.
θρεπτικὴν I. vii. 12. θρεπτικοῦ VI. xii. 6. θρεπτικὸν I. xiii. 14.
θρηνητικὸς IX. xi. 4.
θρὶξ VIII. xii. 2. τριχῶν VII. v. 3.
θυμιαμάτων III. x. 5.
θυμοειδεῖς III. viii. 10.
θυμὸς III. ii. 3, 6. viii. 10, 11. VII. vi. 2, 3. θυμοῦ III. viii. 10, 11. 12. V. viii. 9. VII. i. 7. iv. 2, 6. vi. 1. θυμῷ I. iv. 7. II. iii. 10. III. viii. 10. V. viii. 9. VII. vi. 4. θυμὸν III. i. 21, 23. 26. ii. 3, 6. viii. 10, 12. IV. v. 10. V. viii. 8. VII. vi. 3, 5. θυμοὶ VII. iii. 7. θυμοὺς VII. v. 5.
θυμώδης VII. vi. 3.
θύραν V. i. 7. θύραις VII. vi. 2.
θυσίας IV. ii. 11. VIII. ix. 5. θυσίας VIII. ix. 5.
θύειν V. vii. 1. θύεται IX. ii. 6.

I.

ἰατὸς VII. viii. 1. ἰατοὶ X. ix. 21.
ἰατρείας VII. xii. 1. xiv. 4, 6. ἰατρεῖαι II. iii. 4. VII. xiv. 4.
ἰατρεύει I. vi. 16. ἰατρεύοντα VII. xiv. 7. ἰατρεύειν V. ix. 16. ἰατρεύεσθαι VII. xiv. 7.
ἰατρικὴ I. vi. 4. VI. i. 1. vii. 4. x. 1. xii. 5. xiii. 8. ἰατρικῆς I. i. 3. xiii. 7. II. ii. 4. X. ix. 15, 17. ἰατρικῇ I. vii. 1. V. xi. 7. ἰατρικὴν III. iii. 8. VI. xii. 1, 2.
ἰατρικώτερον I. vi. 16.
ἰατρὸς I. vi. 16. III. iii. 11. X. iv. 6. ix. 15. ἰατροῦ V. v. 9. ἰατρῷ IX. ii. 1. ἰατρὸν IV. vii. 13. V. ix. 15. VII. iv. 6. ἰατρῶν I. xiii. 7. II. iv. 6. V. v. 9. ἰατροῖς III. v. 14. ἰατροὶ X. ix. 16 18.
ἰδέα I. vi. 3. ἰδέας I. vi. 2, 10, 13. ἰδέᾳ IX. v. 3. ἰδέαν I. vi. 2. 4. 9, 11, 16. viii. 12. V. i. 7.
ἰδιογνώμονες VII. ix. 3.
ἴδιοι VII. iii. 12. ἰδίαν IV. i. 17. ii. 15. VI. viii. 9. ἰδία III. iv. 5. VIII. xii. 7. ἰδίᾳ III. v. 7. ἴδιον I. vii. 12. III. i. 1 . V. iii. 8. v. 7. ἴδιαι III. xi. 1. ἰδίας III. xi. 4. X. ix. 15. ἰδίου VII. iv. 2.
ἰδιῶται X. viii. 10. ἰδιώταις III. viii. 8. ἰδιώτας IV. i. 30.
ἱδρύμενον I. x. 8.
ἰέναι IV. iii. 27. V. iv. 7. IX. xi. 6.
ἱερῶν V. v. 7. ἱερῷ IV. ii. 17. ἱερὰ IV. i. 42.
ἰθεῖα V. v. 3.
ἱκανὸς IX. x. 2. ἱκανοὶ IX. x. 5. ἱκανῷ VIII. i. 7. ἱκανὸν I. iv. 4. vii. 20. VIII. viii. 3. IX. i. 7. X. viii. 10. ix. 2, 9. ἱκανοῖς III. iii. 19. ἱκανὰ V. vi. 7. ἱκανῶν IX. x. 2.
ἱκανῶς I. iii. 1. iv. 6. v. 6. x. 15. xi. 2. xii. 8. II. ix. 1. V. v. 15. x. 1. VI. xii. 2. VII. i. 5. IX. i. 4. X. iii. 13. vii. 4. ix. 1.
Ἴλιον VI. ii. 6.
ἱμάντα VII. vi. 3.
ἱμάτιον VII. vii. 5.
ἵνα I. v. 5. II. vii. 11. IV. iii. 31. V. v. 7. viii. 6. VII. ii. 8. VIII. ii. 3. xi. 1. viii. 8. X. vii. 6.
ἱππικὴν I. i. 4. ἱππικῶν I. i. 4.
ἵππος I. viii. 10. ἵππου II. vi. 2. X. v. 8. ἵππῳ I. vii. 13. ἵππον I. ix. 9. II. vi. 2. VIII. xi. 6.
ἰσάζει V. v. 14. VIII. vi. 6. IX. i. 1. ἰσάζειν V. iv. 4. VIII. xiii. 1. ἰσάζῃ VII. xiv. 8. ἰσασθῆναι V. v. 8, 9, 13 ἰσασθῇ V. v. 12. ἰσασμένον V. v. 12 ἰσάζοντο VIII. viii. 5. ἰσάζοντες VIII. xiii. 1.
ἰσάριθμα VIII. iii. 1.
ἰσαχῶς I. vi. 3.
ἴσασι VI. ix. 2.
ἰσάζοντος IX. i. 7.
ἴσον V. i. 8. ἴσου II. vii. 4. V. v. 18. vi. 5. VIII. x. 6. xi. 5. IX. i. 9. X. viii. 4. ἴσης IV. ii. 10. ἴσῳ VII. xiii. 1. ἴσον II. vi. 4, 5. viii. 2. V. i. 8. ii. 8, 12. iii. 2, 3. iv. 3, 6, 8, 9, 14. v. 8, 10, 14, 15. viii. 11. VI. viii. 4. VIII. v. 5. vii. 3. ix. 3. xiii. 7. xiv. 1. IX. ii. 5. ἴσοι V. iii. 6. v. 12. VIII. x. 3, 6. xi. 5. ἴσαι V. iv. 12. VIII. x. 1. ἴσα V. iii. 6. v. 10. vii. 5. ἴσων V. iv. 10. v. 9. vi. 4. ἴσοις V. iv. 3. ἴσας VI. v. 6. ἴσους VIII. xiii. 1. ἴσην VIII. xiii. 11.
ἰσότης V. iii. 6, 8. v. 12. 14. vi. 9. VIII. v. 5. vii. 2. viii. 5. IX. viii. 2. ἰσότητος V. v. 14. ἰσότητι VIII. xiii. 1. ἰσότητα V. v. 6. VIII. vi. 7. xiii. 1.

Ἵστημι. ἱστηκὸς II. ii. 3. στήσεται VI. viii. 9.
ἰσχυρίζεσθαι IV. iii. 27.
ἰσχυρογνώμονες VII. ix. 3. ἰσχυρογνώμονας VII. ix. 2.
ἰσχυρὸς II. ii. 8. ἰσχυρῷ VI. xiii. 1. ἰσχυρὸν I. xii. 2. X. ix. 12. ἰσχυρὰ VII. ii. 4. iv. 4. xiv. 6. ἰσχυρὰς VII. ii. 4, 6. ἰσχυρῶν VII. vii. 6. ἰσχυρότατοι I. viii. 9. ἰσχυρότατον VII. ii. 5.
ἰσχυρῶς VI. xiii. 1.
ἰσχὺν II. ii. 6. VI. v. 1. V. ix. 11. ἴσχυον II. ii. 6, 8.
ἰσχύει II. iv. 4. ἰσχύῃ X. ix. 6. ἰσχύειν X. ix. 3. ἰσχύοντες III. viii. 8.
ἴσως I. iv. 4, 5. vi. 1, 13, 16. vii. 9, 17. viii. 9. 16. ix. 3. xi. 5. xii. 7. xiii. 8, 16, 17. II. vi. 7. ix. 7. III. i. 1, 6, 8, 16, 21, 24. ii. 11. iii. 1. iv. 5. v. 10. ix. 5, 6. IV. viii. 9. V. ii. 11. vii. 4. ix. 17. VI. viii. 4. VII. viii. 3. xiii. 2, 4. 6. VIII. ii. 3. iv. 4. vi. 2, 4. vii. 6. viii. 6, 7. xiv. 4. IX. i. 7, 8. ii. 4. vii. 3. viii. 3, 9. ix. 3, 5. x. 3, 5. xi. 6. X. i. 1, 2. ii. 4. vi. 4. vii. 4. viii. 11. ix. 5, 9, 15, 16, 18, 21, 22.
ἱππικώτατον III. viii. 10.
ἰχθύσι VI. vii. 4.

K.

καθάπερ I. i. 4. 5. ii. 2. iii. 7. vi. 11. vii. 11. viii. 15, 17. ix. 11. x. 9, 13. xi. 3. xii. 4. xiii. 10, 15. II. ii. 1. iii. 10. ix. 3. III. iii. 15. vii. 7, 13. IV. i. 33. ii. 1. iv. 1. V. vi. 6. VI. i. 1. iv. 5. xiii. 2. VII. i. 2, 3. ii. 4. iii. 8. iv. 3, 5. v. 5. vi. 1, 3. VIII. v. 4. ix. 1. x. 5. xii. 1. xiii. 1, 5, 9. xiv. 1, 3. 4. IX. i. 1, 3, 7, 9. ii. 6, 8. iii. 5. iv. 2. v. 3, 4. vi. 2. 4. vii. 1. viii. 11. ix. 5, 6, 7, 8, 10. x. 1. X. iii. 3, 8. v. 10. vi. 2, 5, 8. ix. 1, 11, 16, 18.
καθαριότητι X. v. 7. vii. 3.
καθεύδειν I. v. 6. X. viii. 7. καθεύδων VII. x. 3. καθεύδοντας VII. iii. 12. καθεύδοντα VII. iii. 7. καθεύδοντι I. viii. 9. X. vi. 2. καθεύδοντες VIII. v. 1.
καθιερεύσας VII. v. 3.
καθεστᾶσαι VII. xii. 2. καθεστηκυίας. VII. xii. 2.
καθὸ VII. xiv. 8.
καθόλου I. vi. 1, 3. xi. 2. II. ii. 4. vii. 1. III. i. 15. IV. vi. 6. v. 19. V. vii. 6. x. 4, 5, 6. VI. iii. 3. vi. 1. vii. 7. viii. 7. xi. 4. VII. iii. 6. 9. 10, 11, 13. IX. ii. 5. X. ix. 15. 16.
καὶ γὰρ VII. vi. 2. VIII. ix. 1.
καὶ δὴ VII. x. 4.
καινὰ X. iv. 9. καινῶν IV. viii. 6.
καίπερ I. vi. 1. II. ii. 5. III. ii. 7. V. x. 8. IX. iv. 7.
καίτοι I. vi. 15. III. v. 7. x. 3. V. v. 3. vii. 1, 4. X. ix. 18.
καιρὸς I. vi. 3. II. vii. 16. καιροῦ I. vi. 4. καιρὸν II. ii. 4. III. i. 6. καιροὺς VIII. ix. 5.
καίει V. vii. 2.
κἀκεῖ V. ix. 15. VI. viii. 9. VII. iv. 6.
κἀκεῖνοι VII. vi. 2. κἀκεῖνο X. ix. 16. κἀκείνῃ VIII. vi. 7. κἀκείνου IX. i. 4. κἀκείνην X. iv. 3. κἀκείνων IX. x. 4.
κακηγορεῖν V. i. 14.
κακηγορία V. ii. 13.
κακία II. iii. 6. vii. 10. III. v. 2. 19. V. i. 19. VI. v. 6. VII. i. 1, 2. iv. 2. v. 5. vi. 4. viii. 1, 3. κακίας II. v. 3, 4. vi. 14. III. v. 17. vi. 4. IV. i. 3. V. i. 19. ii. 10. viii. 7. xi. 7. VII. i. 2. 4. v. 5. vi. 7. viii. 1. VIII. vii. 4. IX. ix. 6. κακίᾳ VIII. x. 3. κακίαν III. ii. 14. VII. i. 3. iv. 6. xi. 2. κακίαι II. v. 3. III. v. 15, 20. IV. ii. 22. κακιῶν II. vi. 15. viii. 1. ix. 1. III. v. 16. IV. i. 45.
κακολόγοι IV. iii. 31.
κακοπαθεῖν I. v. 6. X. vi. 6.
κακοποιεῖν III. v. 17.
κακοποιοὶ IV. iii. 35.
κακὸς I. xiii. 12. II. iii. 7, 10. IV. vii. 10. VII. vi. 7. κακοῦ III. vi. 2. V. iii. 15. iv. 6. κακῷ III. ii. 10. v. 18, 19. VII. xiv. 2. X. ii. 5. κακὸν I. x. 3. II. vi. 14. III. iv. 2, 6. vi. 6. vii. 13. IV. i. 5, 44. iii. 35. v. 7. V. i. 10. iii. 15. xi. 8. VI. ix. 4. VII. iv. 6. xi. 1. xiii. 1, 7. xiv. 2. X. ii. 5. κακοὶ II. i. 6, 7. v. 5. vi. 14. III. i. 14. IV. iii. 35. VIII. iv. 2. κακῶν I. ix. 3. II. ix. 4. III. i. 4. V. i. 10. vi. 4. IX. xi. 5. X. ii. 5. κακοῖς III. v. 3. V. ix. 17. κακὰ III. ii. 11. vi. 2, 3. IV. iii. 30. VI. v. 4. VII. ii. 9. vi. 7. xiv. 9. κάκιον VII. vi. 7. κάκιστος V. i. 18. κάκιστον VIII. x. 2.
κακουργοῦντες III. v. 10.

κακουργία IX. iii. 2.
κακῶς I. x. 9. II. i. 6. iii. 9, 10. v. 2. III. xii. 6. IV. i. 6. V. ii. 2. v. 6. VI. ii. 3. ix. 3. X. ii. 5. iii. 8. ix. 20.
καλεῖν VII. xiii. 4. VIII. x. 2. IX. xi. 5. καλοῦμεν IV. i. 3. VII. i. 1. καλέσωμεν II. vii. 10. καλοῦσι II. viii. 3. V. iii. 13. iv. 7. VI. xii. 9. VII. ix. 2. IX. ii. 7. viii. 4. x. 6. καλεῖται III. xii. 5. IV. ii. 4. V. i. 7. iv. 6. v. 15. vii. 7. καλοῦνται IV. vi. 1. καλουμένη VI. xi. 1.
κάλλος IV. iii. 5. κάλλους I. viii. 16. κάλλει X. vii. 7.
καλοκἀγαθίας IV. iii. 16. καλοκἀγαθίαν X. ix. 3.
καλὸς VI. xii. 9. IX. v. 4. καλὴ I. x. 13. καλὸν I. x. 12. II. iii. 7. ix. 2. III. i. 4. v. 2. vi. 3, 10, 12. vii. 6, 13. viii. 5, 11, 12. 14. ix. 4. xi. 8. xii. 9. IV. i. 17, 35. ii. 21. vi. 6, 7. vii. 6. ix. 4. VIII. i. 5. viii. 6. xiii. 8. IX. vii. 5, 6. viii. 1, 5, 7, 9, 10. xi. 5, 6. X. viii. 9. ix. 8, 10. καλοῦ II. iii. 7. III. vii. 2, 6. viii. 3. IV. i. 12, 14. 34. ii. 7, 20. V. ix. 9. IX. viii. 6, 11. X. ix. 4, 10. καλῷ III. i. 7. IV. vi. 8. IX. ii. 5. X. ix. 9. καλῆς IV. i. 14. καλοὶ IV. iii. 5. καλαὶ I. viii. 13. IV. i. 12, 35. VII. xiv. 1. καλῶν I. iv. 6. viii. 9. ix. 8. x. 14. xii. 6. II. iii. 1. III. i. 7, 11. IV. iii. 35. VI. xii. 7. VII. iv. 5. VIII. i. 5. IX. vii. 6. X. iii. 10. v. 6. vii. 1. καλοῖς IV. iv. 3. VI. xiii. 3. IX. ix. 6. καλὴν VII. ix. 4. IX. viii. 9. καλαῖς I. viii. 18. καλὰ I. iii. 4. viii. 15. III. i. 11, 23. iv. 4. v. 3, 7. IV. i. 7, 8. iii. 33. VI. xii. 1. VIII. vi. 7. xiii. 8. IX. viii. 7. X. vi. 3. viii. 10. καλὰς VIII. i. 2. IX. viii. 7. κάλλιον I. ii. 8. VIII. xiii. 1. IX. ii. 8. viii. 10. ix. 2. xi. 1, 6. X. ix. 18. καλλίους X. vii. 7. κάλλισται I. viii. 9. καλλίστη IV. ii. 18. καλλίστην VIII. i. 6. κάλλιστον I. viii. 14. ix. 6. x. 13. III. v. 17. IV. ii. 9. X. iv. 5. κάλλιστα I. ix. 5. x. 11, 13. III. iii. 11. IV. ii. 16. IX. viii. 6, 7. X. viii. 11. καλλίστοις III. vi. 8. IV. iii. 10.
Καλυψὼ II. ix. 3.
καλῶς I. i. 1. iii. 5. iv. 6. vii. 14, 17, 20, 22. viii. 2. 13. xii. 5. III. i. 21. v. 17. IV. i. 25. V. viii. 9. VI. v. 1. x. 3. xii. 3. VIII. vii. 6. IX. i. 4. viii. 9. x. 2. X. i. 3. ii. 5. iii. 4. iv. 4. v. 10. viii. 11, 13. ix. 6, 11, 17, 21, 23.
κάμνει X. iv. 9. κάμνοντα VII. vii. 5. IX. ii. 1. καμνόντων VII. xii. 1. κάμνουσι II. iv. 6. X. iii. 8. κεκμηκόσι I. xi. 5. κεκμηκότας I. xi. 5.
κἂν IV. v. 7. vi. 7. V. ix. 4. x. 5. VI. xiii. 7, 8. IX. xi. 2. X. viii. 13. ix. 12.
κανονίζομεν II. iii. 8.
κανὼν III. iv. 5. V. x. 7.
καπνοῦ II. ix. 3.
Καρκίνου VII. vii. 6.
καρπίμων IV. iii. 33.
καρπῶν VIII. ix. 5.
καρτερεῖν VII. v. 5. vii. 4.
καρτερία VII. i. 6. x. 5. καρτερίας VII. i. 4. vii. 4.
καρτερικὸς VII. vii. 1, 4. καρτερικὸν VII. i. 6. iii. 1. καρτερικοὶ VII. iv. 2.
καρτερικῶς X. ix. 8.
καταβέβληνται I. v. 8.
καταδεέστεροι VIII. vii. 4.
καταζῆν I. x. 10.
κατακλίσει IX. ii. 9.
κατακούσωσι X. v. 3.
κατέκτα V. ix. 1.
κατακώχιμον X. ix. 3.
κατειλημμένα X. ix. 5.
καταλείπειν IV. i. 18. κατέλιπον X. ix. 19. καταλιπεῖν VII. ii. 12. καταλείπηται VII. i. 5.
καταλλάττονται III. ix. 6.
κατανοοῦσι X. v. 1.
καταπέλτην III. i. 17.
καταπλὴξ II. vii. 14.
κατεσκεύαζον I. vi. 2. κατασκευάσασθαι IV. ii. 16.
κατασκευαὶ IV. ii. 11.
κατασμικρίζοντες VIII. xiii. 10.
κατατρίβοντας III. x. 2.
καταφανὴς III. vii. 10. καταφανέστερον X. iv. 1.
κατάφασις VI. ii. 2.
καταφεύγοντες II. iv. 6. καταφεύγουσι V. iv. 7. X. vi. 3, 4.
καταφάναι VI. iii. 1.
καταφρονεῖ IV. iii. 22. καταφρονοῦσι IV. iii. 21. καταφρονεῖν II. ii. 9. καταφρονούμενοι X. i. 3.
καταφρονητικὸς IV. iii. 28.
καταφυγὴν VIII. i. 2.
κατίδωμεν II. vii. 11.

κατεσθίειν VII. v. 2.
κατέχουσι IV. v. 8, 10. κατεῖχε VII. v. 7. κατέχειν VII. vii. 6.
κατηγορούμενον I. vi. 13.
κατηγορίαν I. vi. 4. κατηγορίαις I. vi. 3.
κατήκοον I. xiii. 18.
κατορθοῦν I. viii. 7. II. vi. 14, 18. κατορθοῦσα VI. ix. 6. κατορθοῦται II. vi. 12.
κατορθωτικὸς II. iii. 7.
κάτω II. i. 2.
καῦσιν V. ix. 15.
καχεξία V. i. 5. καχεξίαν V. i. 5.
κεῖται III. v. 18. κείμενος V. i. 14.
κελεύει V. xi. 1. VI. i. 2. κελεύων V. i. 14. ἐκέλευε VII. vi. 2. IX. i. 5.
Κελτοὺς III. vii. 7.
κενὴν I. ii. 1.
κεραμεῖς VIII. i. 6.
κερδαίνειν IV. i. 43. V. ii. 4. iv. 13, 14. κερδαίνουσι IV. i. 43. ἐκέρδανεν V. ii. 5.
κέρδος V. iv. 5, 6, 13. VII. iv. 5. VIII. xiv. 2. IX. i. 4. κέρδους IV. i. 41, 43. vii. 12, 13, 14. V. ii. 6. iv. 4, 6, 14. VII. i. 7. iv. 2, 6. κέρδη III. ix. 6.
Κερκύων VII. vii. 6.
κεστὸν VII. vi. 3.
κεφαλαίου II. vii. 5. κεφαλαίῳ II. ix. 7.
κεφαλὴν VI. vii. 3.
κῆδη IX. ii. 7.
κιβδηλεύουσι IX. iii. 2.
κιθαρίζειν I. vii. 14. II. i. 6. κιθαρίζοντες II. i. 4.
κιθαριστοῦ I. vii. 14. κιθαρισταὶ II. i. 4. 6.
κιθαρῳδῷ IX. i. 4.
κίμβικες IV. i. 39.
κινδυνεύειν IV. iii. 23. κινδυνεύοντας X. viii. 7. ἐκινδύνευσαν III. viii. 9.
κίνδυνοι III. viii. 9. κινδύνῳ III. vi. 8. κίνδυνον III. viii. 11, 12. κινδύνων III. vii. 12. κινδύνοις III. viii. 13. VIII. xiii. 10. κινδύνους III. viii. 1, 10. ix. 6.
κινεῖ VI. ii. 5. κινεῖν III. i. 6. VII. iii. 10. κινῆσαι I. xiii. 15. κινηθήσεται I. x. 14. κινεῖσθαι II. v. 4. X. i. 4. κινούμενα V. vii. 1. κινουμένῳ VI. xiii. 1.
κίνησις IV. iii. 34. VI. ii. 4. X. iv. 23. κινήσεως VII. xiv. 8. X. iv. 3. κινήσει III. iii. 4. VII. xiv. 8. κίνησιν X. iii. 4. iv. 2, 4. κινήσεις IV. viii. 3. VII. xii. 1. X. iii. 4. κινήσεων I. xiii. 13. IV. viii. 3. VII. xiv. 2.
κινητὸν V. vii. 4. κινητὰ V. vii. 4.
κίονος X. iv. 2.
κίσσηριν III. i. 17.
κλεὶν V. i. 7.
κλείουσι V. i. 7.
κλέπτης V. vi. 1, 2.
κλέπτει V. xi. 6. ἔκλεψε V. vi. 2. VII. vi. 3.
κληρονομίαν VII. xiii. 6.
κληρωτὸς VIII. x. 2.
κλίνη V. v. 15. κλινῶν V. v. 15, 16.
κλοπὴ II. vi. 18. V. ii. 13.
κνήμας IX. viii. 2.
κοῖλον I. xiii. 10.
κοινὸς VII. iv. 2. κοινὴ I. vi. 2. vii. 12. xiii. 12. II. iii. 7. IX. viii. 7. κοινὸν I. vi. 3, 11. vii. 12. II. ii. 7. III. ii. 3. IV. i. 41. ii. 7, 11. V. i. 11. ii. 11. vii. 7. VI. viii. 2, 3. VIII. xi. 6. xii. 7. xiv. 3. IV. i. 2. ii. 9. iii. 4. κοινοῦ X. ix. 15. κοινῷ I. xiii. 11. xiv. 3. κοινῇ I. vi. 13. III. v. 21. V. i. 13. VIII. ix. 4. IX. vi. 1, 3. X. ix. 14. κοινὴν X. ix. 14. κοιναὶ III. xi. 1. VII. vi. 2. X. ix. 14. κοινὰ IV. ii. 15. VI. xi. 2. VIII. ix. 1, 2. xi. 8. IX. viii. 2. κοινῶν V. iv. 2. VIII. xiv. 3. X. ix. 15. κοινότερος VIII. xii. 6. κοινότερον VIII. xii. 7. κοινοτέρῳ III. x. 10.
κοινότητα IX. ii. 9.
κοινωνεῖ I. xiii. 8. III. ii. 2. x. 8. X. viii. 8. κοινωνεῖν IV. vi. 1. VI. ii. 2. IX. ix. 10. κοινωνοῦσι I. xi. 5. V. ii. 12. VIII. ix. 1. IX. xii. 2, 3. κοινωνῆσαι I. ix. 9. VIII. xi. 7. ἐκοινώνησε IX. i. 9. κοινωνήσασι IX. i. 7. κοινωνοῦμεν X. ii. 4.
κοινωνία V. v. 9, 10, 12, 14. VIII. ix. 4. x. 4. xii. 7. IX. xii. 1. κοινωνίᾳ V. i. 13, 16. VIII. ix. 1. xii. 1. xiv. 2. κοινωνίαι VII. ix. 4, 5, 6. κοινωνίαις V. v. 6. viii. 6. VIII. ix. 1, 6. κοινωνίαν II. vii. 11. IV. viii. 12. IX. i. 4. κοινωνιῶν VIII. ix. 5.
κοινωνικαῖς VIII. xii. 1.
κοινωνοὶ V. v. 12. κοινωνῷ V. i. 17. κοινωνῶν V. vi. 4.
κολάζουσι III. v. 7, 8. κεκολάσθαι III. xii. 6. κολάζεσθαι X. ix. 10. κολα-

σθῆναι V. v. 4. κεκολασμένον III. xii. 8.
κόλαξ II. vii. 13. IV. vi. 9. VIII. viii. 1. κόλακος X. iii. 11. κόλακες IV. iii. 29. κόλαξιν IV. i. 35.
κολάσεις II. iii. 4. III. i. 2. X. ix. 10.
κολωνὸν VIII. i. 6.
κομιδῇ III. v. 12. IX. iv. 7. X. i. 2. κομιδῆς IX. vii. 2.
κομιζόμεθα II. i. 4. κομίσαι III. i. 3. κομίσαντες I. vi. 2. κομίζεσθαι VIII. xiii. 7. κομιζομένους IX. vii. 1. κομιούμενος VIII. xiii. 11. κομιεῖσθαι IX. ii. 5.
κομμοῦντα IV. iii. 36.
κομψότητα II. viii. 8.
κόσμος IV. ii. 16. iii. 16. VI. vii. 4. κόσμου III. iii. 3. X. iii. 4. κόσμῳ VI. vii. 3.
κουφίζονται IX. xi. 2.
κοῦφα VI. vii. 7.
κρᾶσιν VII. xiv. 6.
κρατεῖ VII. viii. 5. κρατεῖν VII. ii. 1. vii. 1, 4. IX. viii. 6. κρατεῖσθαι VII. ii. 3. v. 5, 7. κρατοῦνται VII. iv. 5.
κράτιστος IX. iii. 5. κρατίστη V. i. 15. X. iv. 7. vii. 2. κράτιστον X. ii. 1. iv. 5. vii. 8. ix. 14. κρατίστην X. vii. 1. κράτιστοι III. viii. 13. κρατίστους III. ix. 6. κράτιστα III. viii. 7. X. vi. 4.
κρέα VI. vii. 7. κρέασι VII. v. 2.
κρείττων I. v. 5. V. vii. 4. X. vi. 7. vii. 8. κρεῖττον I. xii. 5. V. v. 8. x. 2. VII. ii. 3. VIII. viii. 3. IX. ix. 3. X. ii. 3. 4. κρείττους III. viii. 9. VII. vii. 1.
κρηπῖδος X. iv. 2.
Κρητῶν I. xiii. 3.
κρίνομεν II. ix. 6. ἔκρινεν V. ix. 12. κρίνεται V. viii. 9. X. viii. 12. κρίνειν III. ii. 1. VI. x. 3. X. ix. 21. κρίναντες III. iii. 19. κρίνει I. iii. 5. viii. 13. III. iv. 4. κρῖναι X. ix. 20. κρινεῖ III. v. 17. κρῖναι X. ix. 20, 21. κρίνας V. ix. 13. κρίνουσι X. iii. 2. v. 2. viii. 11. ix. 20. κρῖνον X. iv. 8.
κρίσις II. ix. 8. III. x. 9. IV. v. 13. V. vi. 4. ix. 12. VI. xi. 1. κρίσει VIII. viii. 2. κρίσεσι IV. i. 1.
κριτὴς I. iii. 5.
κριτικὸς VI. xi. 2. κριτικὴ VI. x. 2. xi. 1.
κεκτῆσθαι IV. iii. 33. κτησάμενοι IV. i. 20. IX. vii. 7. κεκτημένους X. viii. 11. κεκτημένοις VIII. i. 1.
κτείνει V. ix. 11. κτείνῃ V. iv. 4.
κτῆμα IV. ii. 10. V. vi. 8. IX. ix. 5. κτήματα V. vi. 9. κτημάτων IV. i. 17. κτήματος IV. ii. 10.
κτῆσις IV. i. 7. κτήσεως IV. i. 23. X. vi. 3. κτήσει I. viii. 2.
κτητὸν I. vi. 13. κτητὰ I. vi. 14.
κυβερνητικῆς II. ii. 4. κυβερνητικὴν III. iii. 8.
κυβερνήτης IV. i. 43.
κύκλου II. ix. 2. κύκλῳ III. ix. 3.
Κυκλωπικῶς X. ix. 13.
κύματα III. vii. 7. κύματος II. ix. 4.
κυμινοπρίστης IV. i. 39.
Κυπρογενοῦς VII. vi. 3.
κυριεύων VIII. x. 5.
κύριος III. i. 4. v. 8. κύρια VI. ii. 1. xiii. 2, 6. VII. iii. 9, 13. κυρίαν VI. xiii. 1. κύριοι III. i. 3. v. 9, 17, 22. viii. 4. κύριαι I. ix. 13. II. ii. 1. κυρίοις V. i. 13. κυριωτέρα VI. xii. 3. κυριωτάτης I. ii. 4. κυριώτερον I. vii. 13. X. viii. 5. κυριώτατα I. viii. 2. III. i. 18. VII. i. 5. κυριωτάτους III. i. 18. κυριώτατον IX. viii. 6. κυριωτάτῳ IX. viii. 6. κυρίων VIII. xiii. 11. IX. ix. 7. X. vii. 9. viii. 12.
κυρίως I. xiii. 19. VI. xiii. 1, 2, 6. VII. iii. 13. xii. 3. VIII. iv. 4. IX. ix. 7. X. v. 11.
κυρτὸν I. xiii. 10. III. vi. 10.
κωκύσαι VII. v. 2.
κῶνος III. x. 7. VII. vi. 1. κῶνοι III. viii. 4.
κωλυτικὰ I. vi. 8.
κωλύει I. x. 15. III. ix. 6. IV. i. 19. V. ii. 10. v. 8. xi. 8. VII. iii. 6. x. 2. xiii. 2. VIII. iv. 3. IX. vi. 4. X. iii. 3. ix. 16. κωλύοντες III. v. 7. κωλύουσι IV. viii. 9. κωλύεσθαι IV. ix. 3. κωλύονται VII. ii. 6. iii. 10. κωλυόμενον VII. iii. 9.
κωμῳδῶν IV. viii. 6.
κωμῳδοῖς IV. ii. 20.

Λ.

λαγωῶν III. x. 7.
λαθραῖα V. ii. 13.
Λακεδαιμονίων I. xiii. 3. III. iii. 6. X. ix. 13. Λακεδαιμονίοις IX. vi. 2.

Λάκωσι IV. iii. 25. VII. i. 3. Λακώνων IV. vii. 15. Λάκωσι III. viii. 16.

λαμβάνειν II. ii. 8. IV. i. 7, 9. 29, 39. 40. V. v. 8. VI. x. 3. λαμβάνομεν II. i. 4. λαμβάνουσι II. vi. 6. IV. i. 9, 33. 34. 40. VII. ix. 2. VIII. xiv. 1. λαμβάνοντας IV. i. 42. ἐλάμβανε IX. i. 5. λάβωμεν IV. iii. 1. λαβεῖν I. ii. 8. II. vi. 4. ix. 2. III. ii. 12. v. 17. V. v. 14. VI. ix. 1. VIII. vi. 3. xiii. 10. IX. i. 9. X. iv. 2. λάβοι I. iv. 7. VIII. x. 4. X. iv. 1. ἐλάβομεν II. i. 4. λάβωσι V. iv. 8. λαβὼν V. viii. 3. ἔλαβεν V. ix. 13. λάβοιμεν VI. v. 1. IX. viii. 3. λαβόντας VI. xii. 7. λάβῃ VI. xiii. 2. λαβόντα VIII. xii. 2. ἔλαβον IX. i. 7. λαβοῦσα X. vii. 7. ληψομένῳ II. vi. 7. λήψεται IV. i. 15, 17. 24. 31. εἰλήφθω V. i. 8. ληφθῆναι V. xi. 8. εἰληφὼς VI. ix. 4. xiii. 6. εἰλήφασι VII. xiii. 6. λαμβάνοντι IV. i. 8. V. ix. 10. λαμβάνοντες IV. i. 10. IX. i. 9. λαμβάνοντα IV. i. 30, 31. λαμβάνει IV. i. 31. V. x. 4. VIII. ix. 3. λήψονται IX. viii. 9. ληφθείη I. vii. 10.

λαμπάδος I. vii. 7. λαμπάδα II. vi. 7. vii. 1. ix. 4. V. ii. 7. VI. i. 7. VII. vi. 6.

λαμπρύνεται IV. ii. 20. λαμπρυνόμεναι IV. ii. 4.

λαμπρῶς IV. ii. 11.

λανθάνει II. ix. 8. V. i. 7. VI. iii. 2. VII. viii. 1. λανθανέτω I. iv. 5. λανθάνουσαι VIII. ii. 4. λανθάνειν IV. iii. 28. vi. 4. λανθανόντας VIII. ii. 4. λανθάνουσα VIII. ii. 4. IX. v. 1.

λαῶν VIII. vii. 1.

λέγω I. xiii. 11. II. v. 2. vi. 5, 10. IV. vi. 8. V. viii. 3. VI. vi. 2. xii. 7. VII. iii. 1, 2. iv. 2. v. 2, 7. xiv. 7. X. iii. 4. λέγει III. ii. 11. x. 4. IV. vii. 5. V. iii. 9. xi. 9. VI. i. 1. VII. iii. 10. x. 4. λέγομεν I. iv. 1. vii. 4. 6. viii. 2. ix. 9. x. 3. xiii. 6. 20. II. iv. 1. VI. 9. vii. 5. viii. 8. III. ii. 2. vi. 4. x. 2, 5. xii. 8. IV. i. 2, 23, 42. ii. 2. v. 11. vii. 7. V. i. 3, 13. iv. 6. VI. iii. 3. v. 1, 2. x. 1, 4. xi. 2. xii. 7. VII. iii. 5. iv. 2, 3. 6. vi. 6. ix. 1. xi. 1. X. vi. 7. λέγουσι I. iv. 2. viii. 7. II. iii. 5. IV. iii. 36. V. iii. 7. ix. 15. VI. viii. 2. 6. VII. iii. 8. iv. 6. v. 2. xiii. 3. VIII. ii. 3. iv. 4. IX. viii. 3. ix. 4. X. i. 2. iii. 2. 6. iv. 4. ἐλέγομεν I. vi. 2. II. vii. 8. ix. 4. ἔλεγε VI. xiii. 3. λέγοι III. v. 7. X. iii. 8. λέγοιεν X. ii. 4. λέγῃ V. x. 5. λέγωμεν I. iv. 1. v. 1. II. vii. 9. III. x. 1. IV. i. 1. VI. i. 4. iii. 1. xii. 4. λέγωσι X. ii. 4. λέγειν I. vi. 5. 7. vii. 9. x. 15. III. ii. 3, 9. v. 4. IV. iii. 25, 28. vi. 4. vii. 14. viii. 1, 3. 5. 6. ix. 1. V. i. 3. v. 3. VII. i. 1. iii. 8, 13. VIII. iv. 4. x. 1. IX. vii. 1. viii. 5. X. ii. 1. iii. 4. iv. 5. ix. 21. λέγων IV. viii. 10. V. ix. 1. λέγοντα II. vi. 7. VII. i. 1. λέγοντος VI. i. 3. λέγοντες I. xiii. 20. II. vii. 10. III. i. 17. ii. 3. IV. vii. 14. X. ii. 5. ix. 18. λέγουσι I. viii. 8. x. 2. III. iv. 2, 3. IV. viii. 3. VII. xiv. 1. λέγοντας I. iii. 4. iv. 3. λέγεται I. vi. 1, 2, 3, 9, 12. viii. 10. xiii. 9, 13. II. iv. 4. 5. vi. 18. vii. 8, 14, 16. III. i. 21. v. 20. vi. 3. xi. 5. IV. i. 19, 44. ii. 3. iii. 10. viii. 10. V. i. 8. ii. 13. iv. 5. 13. v. 17. ix. 11. x. 3. xii. 1. xiii. 6. VII. iii. 5. iv. 3. v. 8. ix. 6. VIII. ii. 3. v. 5. IX. viii. 6. X. i. 3. iv. 4. v. 10. ix. 1. λεγόμεθα II. v. 2, 3, 4, 5. λέγονται I. viii. 3. III. viii. 1. ix. 2. x. 2, 3. xi. 3. IV. i. 10. iii. 20. vii. 14. VII. i. 7. iv. 3. VIII. v. 1. IX. x. 6. X. ix. 15. λέγοιτο I. iii. 1. vi. 9. viii. 2. III. vi. 10. IV. v. 2. X. iii. 9. λεγέσθω II. vii. 12. VI. i. 6. λέγηται V. i. 6. λεγόντων VIII. viii. 2. ἐλέγετο I. vi. 3. λέγοιντο X. v. 11. λεγομένων I. iii. 4. viii. 1, 2. III. xi. 4. IV. v. 13. λεγομένης I. vii. 13. λεγόμενα I. ix. 10. λεγομένη II. vii. 7. X. vii. 4. λεγομένου III. i. 19. IV. iv. 4. λεγομένοις III. x. 9. λεγόμενον V. v. 8. VII. v. 2, 9. vi. 1. X. ii. 4. λελεγμένα VII. i. 7. xi. 5. X. iii. 13. λεγομένους VII. iv. 2. VIII. iii. 8. λεχθεισῶν I. i. 5. λεχθέντων VII. vii. 3. λεχθέντα I. v. 8. x. 16. λεχθεῖσιν I. vi. 8. λέγεσθαι I. vi. 8. vii. 13. II. ii. 3. vii. 1. III. i. 15. V. i. 6. IX. ix. 10. X. ii. 5. λεχθῆναι I. vii. 9. λεχθέντι I. viii. 5. λεχθὲν I. xi. 2. V. ix. 9. IX. x. 2. xi. 2. X. vii. 9. λεχθεῖσαν IV. i. 44. ἐλέχθη IV. iv. 1. X. v. 11. vi. 6. VI. i. 5. VII. viii. 1. λεπτὸν III. i. 6. iii. 2. V. ii. 9. VI. xii. 3, 8. VII. i. 1, 4. iii. 7. iv. 1. v. 5. xii. 3. xiv. 3.

Λείπειν V. i. 14. Λείπεται I. vii. 13. II. v. 6. VI. v. 4. vi. 2. ix. 3. X. viii. 7. Λείπονται III. viii. 9.
Λειτουργίαν VIII. xiv. 1. Λειτουργίαις IX. vi. 4.
Λεσβίας V. x. 7.
Λευκὸν VI. vii. 4. Λευκὰ X. iii. 8. Λευκότερον I. vi. 6.
Λευκότερος I. vi. 11.
Λέων III. x. 7.
Λήγει VIII. iv. 1. Ληγούσης ibid.
Λήθη VI. v. 8. Λήθην I. x. 10. V. viii. 10. VIII. v. 1.
Λήκυθος IV. ii. 18.
Λῃστικὸν IV. i. 20. Λῃστικοὶ IV. i. 34.
Λήψει IV. i. 7, 15. 24. Λήψεις II. vii. 4. IV. i. 8, 29. 38. iv. 2. Λῆψιν II. vii. 4. IV. i. 24, 40.
Λῃσταῖς IV. i. 43. V. vi. 1. Λῃστῶν IX. ii. 4.
Λίαν I. ix. 6. xi. 1. III. xi. 3. IV. ii. 22. vii. 11, 15, 16. VII. iv. 5. IX. iv. 10. X. vi. 6. ix. 20.
Λίθοι II. i. 2. Λίθων V. x. 7. Λίθον III. i. 17. v. 14. Λίθων X. iv. 2.
Λιθουργὸν VI. vii. 1.
Λογίζεται VI. ix. 2, 3. X. v. 5. Λογίζονται VI. v. 2. Λογίζεσθαι VI. i. 6. X. v. 5.
Λογικῶν II. vii. 16.
Λογισμῷ VII. i. 6. Λογισμὸν III. i. 26. xii. 7. VI. vii. 6. VII. ii. 10. vi. 6. vii. 8. Λογισμοῦ III. viii. 15. VI. ix. 4. VII. i. 6.
Λογιστικὸν VI. i. 6.
Λόγοι I. vi. 5, 8, 16. vii. 2. viii. 1, 8. II. ii. 2, 3, 4. III. v. 21. vii. 2, 5. viii. 12. xi. 8. xii. 9. IV. v. 3. V. iii. 10. ix. 1. VI. i. 1, 2, 3. ii. 4. viii. 9. xi. 4. xii. 5, 6. VII. ii. 2, 8, 12. iv. 2. vi. 1. viii. 4. X. ii. 3. vi. 1. ix. 5, 6, 12. Λόγον I. v. 3. vii. 14. ix. 7. xiii. 15, 17, 18. II. ii. 4, 5. iii. 5. III. ii. 17. viii. 15. IV. iii. 11. V. iii. 3. 8. VI. iv. 2, 3, 6. v. 4, 6, 8. vi. I. ix. 2, 3. xii. 10. xiii. 5. VII. ii. 9. iii. 10. vi. 1. ix. 2. IX. viii. 6. X. ix. 7. Λόγῳ I. vii. 13. viii. 4. x. 10. xiii. 10, 15, 17. II. i. 7. vi. 15. ix. 8. III. xii. 7, 9. IV. v. 13. vii. 4, 7. V. iii. 15. x. 1. VII. iii. 11. ix. 1, 5. IX. xi. 3. X. ii. 3. ix. 5, 7. 9, 10. Λόγων I. iii. 7. iv. 4. vi. 11. vii. 13, 14. x. 4, 15. xiii. 9, 15, 16, 18, 19. II. ii. 2. iv. 6. vi. 17. III. xii. 8. V. iv. 2. vi. 5. xi. 2, 9. VI. i. 1, 5, 6. ii. 2. v. 8. xiii. 4, 5. VII. i. 6. ii. 1. iii. 3. iv. 2, 5. vii. 8. viii. 2, 4, 5. ix. 6. x. 2. IX. vii. 1. viii. 6. X. v. 3. Λόγοις I. iii. 6. iv. 5. v. 8. vi. 11. II. ii. 3. VII. xiv. 5. IX. ii. 6. X. i. 3. ii. 1. ix. 3. 14. Λόγου II. vii. 11. IV. vi. 1. viii. 12. IX. viii. 3. ix. 10. X. i. 4. Λόγους I. iii. 1. xiii. 9. II. vii. 1. IV. vii. 1. V. xi. 9. VI. iv. 2. VII. x. 2. IX. viii. 2. X. v. 3. viii. 12. Λόγων I. vi. 8. VI. xiii. 5. VII. iii. 8. X. viii. 12. ix. 18.
Λελογχωμένον III. i. 17.
Λοιδορεῖν IV. viii. 9.
Λοιδόρημα IV. viii. 9.
Λοιπὸν II. vii. 13. V. iv. 1. VII. xiv. 9. X. vi. 1. Λοιπαὶ X. v. 11. Λοιπὴν X. viii. 9. Λοιπαῖς I. vii. 1. VIII. i. 2. Λοιπὰ I. vii. 1. xii. 8. III. iii. 7. v. 18, 19. xi. 7. VIII. i. 1. iii. 7, 9. IX. viii. 2. X. viii. 8. Λοιπῶν I. ix. 7. II. vii. 9. III. i. 5. iii. 9, 11. VI. i. 4. X. iv. 3. 10. ix. 17, 18. Λοιποὶ II. i. 6. VIII. xii. 4. X. vii. 4. Λοιποῖς III. iii. 4. VIII. xii. 7. xiii. 1. IX. i. 1. ii. 9. iv. 2. Λοιπὰς VIII. iv. 1. IX. xii. 1.
Λυμαίνεται I. x. 12. Λυμαίνονται X. v. 5.
Λυμαὶ X. v. 10.
Λυπεῖν IV. vi. 2, 5, 6, 7. 8. viii. 3. 7. Λυπῆσαι IV. vi. 8. Λυπούμενος II. iii. 1. III. i. 13. IV. i. 27. VII. vi. 4. Λυπεῖσθαι II. iii. 2, 9. vii. 15. xi. 5, 6. IV. i. 25. v. 5. VII. ii. 7. IX. iv. 10. xi. 3. Λυπηθῆναι II. v. 2. vi. 10. X. iii. 12. Λυπεῖται II. vi. 15. III. xi. 6, 8. IV. i. 28. IX. iv. 10. ix. 7. xi. 3. Λυπήσεται III. ix. 4. IV. i. 25. Λυπουμένους III. x. 2. Λυποῦνται VII. ix. 3. Λυπούμενοι IX. iii. 4. xi. 2. Λυπούμενον IX. xi. 4. Λυποῖτο X. iii. 6. Λυπεῖ X. v. 9.
Λύπη II. iii. 3. v. 2. III. xii. 2. VII. iv. 4. xiii. 1, 7. xiv. 2. X. ii. 5. iii. 5. Λύπης II. ix. 4. III. xi. 6. IV. v. 10. VII. xi. 1. xii. 1, 2, 7. xiv. 2, 4. 9. IX. ix. 8. xi. 4. X. iii. 13. Λύπῃ II. iii. 8. X. i. 1. v. 5. ix. 10. Λύπην II. iii. 1. vii. 15. III. iv. 6. viii. 11. xi. 5. xii. 1, 3. IV. vi. 7. vii. 1. VI. v. 6. VII. iii. 1. vii. 3, 5. ix. 3. xiv. 4, 6. IX. xi. 2, 4. X. ii. 2. iii. 6. Λυπῶν VII. vii. 6. xiv. 7. X. iii. 6. v. 5. Λύπαις III. vii. 10. IX. ix. 8.

λύπαις I. x. 12. II. iii. 1, 5, 6, 10, 11. vii. 3. III. x. 1. xi. 5. IV. vi. 7. VII. iv. 1, 3. vii. 1, 2. xi. 2. X. ix. 4, 10. Λῦπαι VII. xiv. 2. X. v. 5.
λυπηροῦ II. iii. 7. III. ii. 5. λυπηρὰς X. v. 5. λυπηρῷ VIII. v. 2. λυπηρὸν III. i. 7. vii. 13. viii. 4. ix. 3, 4. IV. i. 13. VI. v. 6. vii. 8. VII. xiv. 5, 8. VIII. v. 2. vi. 4. IX. iv. 5. xi. 4. λυπηρὰν III. i. 19. λυπηρὰ III. i. 9, 25. ix. 2, 4. X. i. 2. v. 9. ix. 8. λυπηρῶν VII. iv. 3.
λύσις VII. ii. 12. xiii. 1.
λυσιτελοῖ VIII. iv. 2.
λυτροῦσθαι V. vii. 1. λυτρωθέντι IX. ii. 4.
λυτρωτέον IX. ii. 4.
λύεται V. ix. 9. xi. 6. VII. iii. 12. xii. 7. λύοιτο VI. xiii. 6. λύηται VII. i. 5. λῦσαι VII. ii. 8. λυσάμενον IX. ii. 4. ἔλυε VII. xiii. 1.
λωποδύτης IV. i. 43.
λῷστον I. viii. 14.

M.

μαθηματικὸς VI. viii. 6. μαθηματικαὶ V. iii. 13. VI. viii. 5. μαθηματικοῖς VI. viii. 9. VII. viii. 4. μαθηματικοῦ I. iii. 4. μαθηματικαῖς III. iii. 12. X. iii. 7. μαθηματικῶν I. xiii. 18.
μάθησιν I. ix. 3.
μαθητὸν I. ix. 1. VI. iii. 3.
μαινόμενος III. i. 17. iii. 2. vii. 7. μαινόμενον VII. iii. 7. μαινόμενοι VII. vi. 6.
μάκαρ III. v. 4.
μακαρίζοντες I. ix. 10. μακαρίσειεν I. x. 3. μακαρίζειν I. x. 7. μακαρίζομεν I. xii. 4. μακαρίζει I. xii. 4.
μακάριον I. vii. 16. viii. 16. ix. 3. x. 7, 12. xi. 5. VII. xi. 2. IX. ix. 3, 6. X. viii. 9. μακαρίους I. x. 10, 16. IX. ix. 9. X. viii. 7. μακαριώτερον I. x. 12. μακαρίων I. x. 13. μακάριος I. x. 14. III. v. 4. IX. ix. 5. X. viii. 8. μακάριοι VIII. v. 3. vi. 4. μακαρίοις IX. ix. 1. μακαριωτάτῃ IX. ix. 9. μακαρίῳ IX. ix. 10. X. vii. 7. μακαρίου X. v. 11.
μακαριότητι X. viii. 7.
μακαρίως I. x. 4.
μακρὸν I. xi. 2. μακρότερον III. x. 10.
μαλακία III. vii. 13. VII. i. 6. vii. 5, 6. x. 5. μαλακίας VII. i. 4. vii. 3.
μαλακὸς VII. vii. 1, 5, 7. μαλακῷ VII. vii. 4. μαλακοὶ VII. iv. 2, 3.
μάλιστα I. ii. 4. iv. 4. v. 2. vii. 5. viii. 2, 13. ix. 2, 6, 11. x. 10, 11. xiii. 2, 12. II. ii. 8, 9. iii. 7. ix. 4, 6, 7. III. i. 18. ii. 13. vi. 10. viii. 1, 3. 6. 7. 8. ix. 4. x. 11. xi. 6. 8. xii. 6. IV. i. 11, 21. ii. 15. iii. 7. 9. 10, 11, 17. 18. v. 10. vi. 4. 14. V. i. 15. VI. ii. 6. vii. 6. viii. 3. xi. 1. VII. i. 1, 3, 5. vi. 4. vii. 8. VIII. i. 1, 3. 4. iii. 4. 5, 6, 7. iv. 1. v. 2, 4. vi. 1. vii. 6. viii. 5. 6. x. 3. x. 1. xii. 2, 5. IX. i. 8. ii. 7. 8. iii. 4. iv. 1, 3. 4. 5. vii. 3. viii. 1, 2, 5, 6. ix. 9. xi. 5, 6. xii. 1, 2. X. i. 1. ii. 1, 2, 12. iv. 4. 7, 10. v. 4. vii. 4. 9. viii. 7, 13. ix. 10.
μᾶλλον I. ii. 2. v. 4. 6, 8. vi. 6, 12, 14. 16. vii. 2. xi. 2, 4. 5. xii. 1. xiii. 7. II. i. 8. ii. 4. iii. 8. vi. 10. vii. 8, 11. viii. 5, 6, 7, 8. ix. 3, 8. III. i. 7, 8, 10. ii. 1, 9, 10, 13. iii. 8. 9. v. 15, 17. vii. 1, 3, 10, 13. viii. 9, 15. ix. 1, 4. x. 2, 5. xi. 4. 5. 8. xii. 1, 2. IV. i. 1, 3. 7. 8, 9, 14. 20, 27. 37. 42, 44. ii. 3. 9. 16. iii. 20, 28, 30. 33. 35. 37. iv. 2, 3. 4. 5. v. 4. 7. 8, 10, 12, 13. 14. vi. 8. vii. 1, 6, 8, 9, 10. viii. 3, 4. 6. ix. 1, 2, 7. V. i. 7. ii. 4. iii. 16. v. 14. vi. 9. vii. 7. ix. 16. XI. iii. 4. vii. 7. viii. 9. VII. iii. 4. iv. 3. vi. 2. vii. 1, 3. ix. 3. 5. x. 4. xi. 4. xii. 3. 5. xiv. 3. VIII. i. 4. 7. v. 3. vi. 4. vii. 2. viii. 1, 3. 4. ix. 3. xii. 1, 2, 6, 7. IX. ii. 1, 3. iii. 2, 3. v. 3. vii. 1, 3, 7. viii. 1. 6, 9. ix. 2, 5. xi. 1. xii. 1. X. ii. 1. iii. 2, 3. v. 2. 3. 4. 8. vi. 2. 3. vii. 3. 4. 8. viii. 4. 7, 8, 10. ix. 1, 9. 14, 15. 18, 19. 22, 23.
μανθάνειν I. ii. 6. VI. x. 3, 4. VII. xii. 5. μαθόντας II. i. 4. μανθάνομεν II. i. 4. VI. xii. 2. μαθεῖν III. v. 7. μαθόντες VII. iii. 8.
μανίας VII. iii. 7. μανίαν VII. v. 3, 6.
μανότητα V. i. 5.
μαντευόμεθα X. v. 4.
μάντιν IV. vii. 13.
Μαργίτῃ VI. vii. 2.
μαρτυρεῖ I. x. 10. II. i. 5. μαρτυροῦντι VII. xiv. 5. μαρτυρεῖσθαι III. v. 7.
μαρτυρίοις II. ii. 6.
μαστιγοῦσθαι III. vi. 5.
μάταιος IV. vii. 10. μάταιον I. vi. 10.

ματαίαν I. ii. 1. ματαιότερον I. iv. 4.
μάταιος I. iii. 6.
μάχῃ III. viii. 4. μάχην X. ix. 15. μάχαι V. iii. 6. VIII. xiii. 2. X. vii. 6.
μάχιμοι III. viii. 12. μαχιμώτατοι III. viii. 8.
μάχεται I. viii. 11. xiii. 15. μάχοιντο VII. iv. 5. μάχονται III. viii. 8. ἐμάχετο VII. ii. 1. μάχεσθαι II. iii. 10.
μέγα I. iv. 3. II. viii. 4. IV. ii. 6, 10, 17, 18. iii. 14, 15, 30, 34. VI. ix. 4. VII. ii. 6. VIII. xii. 4. IX. viii. 9. μεγάλην I. ii. 2. vii. 23. II. vii. 8. IV. iii. 37. IX. viii. 9. μεγάλαις I. ix. 11. IV. iii. 17. VII. xiii. 3 μεγάλα I. x. 12. II. vii. 6. III. iii. 10. IV. i. 42. ii. 5. iii. 1. IX. xi. 5. μεγάλας I. x. 12. μεγάλων I. x. 14. III. i. 7. IV. iii. 3, 6, 7, 9, 20, 27. X. viii. 9. μεγάλου II. viii. 4. IV. iv. 1. μεγάλαι III. xii. 7. IV. ii. 6. μεγάλοις IV. i. 24. ii. 3. μεγάλῃ IX. iii. 4. μεγάλους X. ix. 3. μεγάλῳ IV. ii. 17. iii. 5. μεγάλοι IV. iii. 11. μεγάλη IV. iii. 27. μεγάλης IV. vi. 18. μέγιστα I. v. 6. III. vi. 6. IV. ii. 15, 21. VIII. vii. 6. xii. 5. xiii. 10. IX. viii. 7. X. vi. 2. μέγιστον I. ix. 6. III. v. 17. IV. iii. 10, 18. IX. ix. 2. III. i. 1. ix. 20. μεγίστῳ III. vi. 8. μεγίστων III. ix. 4. IV. iii. 9, 14. μεγίστου V. iv. 11. VIII. xi. 2. μεγίστους IV. i. 43. μέγαν IV. iii. 26.
μεγαλοκίνδυνος IV. iii. 23.
μεγαλοπρέπεια II. vii. 6. IV. ii. 10, 15. μεγαλοπρεπείας IV. ii. 1. μεγαλοπρέπειαν II. vii. 8. IV. ii. 18. iv. 1.
μεγαλοπρεπής II. vii. 6. IV. ii. 3, 5, 7, 13, 15, 20. μεγαλοπρεποῦς IV. ii. 6, 10, 16, 19. μεγαλοπρεπῆ IV. ii. 10. μεγαλοπρεπὲς IV. ii. 10. μεγαλοπρεπέστερον IV. ii. 10. μεγαλοπρεπέστατον IV. ii. 17.
μεγαλοπρεπῶς IV. ii. 19.
μεγαλοψυχία II. vii. 7. IV. iii. 1, 5, 16, 37. μεγαλοψυχίαν II. vii. 8. IV. iii. 19. iv. 1. μεγαλοψυχίᾳ IV. iii. 37.
μεγαλόψυχος I. x. 12. IV. iii. μεγαλόψυχοι IV. iii. 11, 20. μεγαλοψύχῳ IV. iii. 15. μεγαλοψύχου IV. iii. 12, 14, 30, 34. μεγαλόψυχον IV. iii. 13, 14, 16, 21. μεγαλοψυχοτέρους IV. iii. 19.
Μεγαρεῖς IV. ii. 20.
μέγεθος IV. ii. 1, 10, 14. μεγέθει I. x. 12. III. vii. 1. IV. ii. 1, 4, 10. iii. 5. VII. vi. 6. VIII. xi. 2. IX. ii. 2. vi. 2. X. vii. 7. μεγέθη VI. x. 1.
μεθίστησι VIII. x. 5. μεθιστᾶσι VII. iii. 7. μεταστῆσαι X. ix. 5.
μέθοδος I. i. 1. ii. 9. μέθοδον V. i. 2. μεθόδῳ I. vii. 18.
μεθυσκόμενον III. viii. 14. μεθυσκομένους VII. viii. 2.
μεθύουσι III. v. 8. μεθύων III. i. 14. μεθυσθῆναι III. v. 8.
μεῖζον I. ii. 8. vii. 8. xii. 4. II. vii. 12. viii. 2. IV. i. 44. V. iii. 15, 16. iv. 8. v. 18. xi. 8. xiii. 1. IX. viii. 9. X. viii. 3. μείζονος IV. iii. 14. V. iii. 16. iv. 9. μείζω IV. ii. 21. iii. 17. vi. 8. vii. 4, 10. V. vii. 5. xi. 8. μείζους IV. iii. 16. X. viii. 5. μειζόνων III. i. 4. IV. iii. 6. vii. 8.
μεῖον V. i. 10.
μελαγχολικοὶ VII. vii. 8. x. 4. xiv. 6. μελαγχολικὸς VII. x. 3.
μελέτην VII. x. 4.
μελετώντων III. v. 11.
μελλητὴν IV. iii. 27.
μέλλουσι IX. x. 4. μέλλωσι IX. xi. 5. μελλήσειε II. iv. 5. μέλλον III. vi. 5. IV. ii. 21. X. iii. 12. μέλλει I. x. 15. μέλλοντα VIII. xiv. 2. μέλλοντος IX. vii. 6. μελλόντων IX. iv. 5. μελλ[illegible] V. v. 14.
μέλος IV. ii. 21. μέλεσι III. x. 4. IX. ix. 7. μέλη X. iv. 10.
μέλει IV. iii. 31. V. xi. 8. VII. x. 3. VIII. x. 4. μέλειν IV. iii. 28.
μεμνῆσθαι I. vii. 18.
μέμφονται VIII. xiii. 4.
μέμψεις VIII. xiii. 2.
μένος III. viii. 10.
μένει V. x. 7. VIII. xii. 5. IX. i. 3. vi. 3, 6. μεῖναι II. vi. 2. μένουσι III. viii. 16. VIII. iv. 1. vi. 7. viii. 5. μένοντα III. viii. 9. μένειν V. v. 14. VII. ii. 4, 8. VIII. vii. 6.
μέντοι I. xiii. 15. V. iii. 7. VII. 4, 8. VI. viii. 1. VII. iii. 6.
μερίσαιτο V. ix. 13.
μεριστὸν I. xiii. 10. μεριστὰ V. ii. 12. μεριστῶν IX. iv. 4.
Μερόπη III. i. 17.
μέρος V. i. 19. ii. 1, 3, 9, 12. v. 15. vi.

8. xi. 6, 9. VI. i. 6. v. 1. vii. 2. x. 1. xii. 5. VII. iii. 6. iv. 1, 2. X. ix. 23. μέρους II. vii. 1. X. iv. 2. μέρει IV. viii. 5. V. ii. 1, 3, 6, 9. VIII. xi. 5. X. iv. 3. μέρη III. i. 6, x. 11. V. ii. 9. 13. VI. i. 5. VIII. ix. 5. μερῶν III. x. 1. μέρεσι X. iv. 2. μερῶν VI. v. 8.

μεσίδιον V. iv. 7.

μέσον II. vii. 8, 12, 13, 14. IV. iii. 8. vi. 9. vii. 4, 6. viii. 10. VII. vii. 2, ix. 5. μέσῃ II. viii. 1. ix. 9. IV. v. 14. vi. 3. μέσου II. vi. 4. vii. 10. viii. 3, 4, 5, 6. ix. 2, 5. IV. i. 31, 36. iv. 4, 6. v. 1. vi. 9. V. i. 1. iii. 1, 3, 4, 12. iv. 6, 7, 9, 10, 11, 14. v. 10, 17. VI. i. 1. ix. 5. VIII. viii. 7. X. i. 2. μέσοι II. vi. 9, 13. viii. 4, 7. ix. 1, 3, 4, 7, 9. IV. v. 1. viii. 2. V. iv. 7, 10. v. 17. xi. 7. VIII. viii. 7. μέσῳ II. viii. 7, 8. μέσης II. vii. 8. IV. v. 14. μέσῃ II. viii. 1. IV. viii. 5. μέσοις IV. vi. 4. μέσαι II. viii. 2. μέσους IV. iii. 26. μέσα II. vi. 6. VII. i. 2.

μεσότης II. vii. 13, 14, 15, 17, 19, 20. vii. ix. 1. III. vi. 1. vii. 13. x. 1. IV. i. 1. iv. 1, 5. v. 1. vii. 1. V. i. 1. v. 17. μεσότητος II. ii. 7. vi. 9, 20. viii. 1. IV. i. 24. iv. 4. μεσότητι II. vi. 15. μεσότητα II. vi. 18, 19. vii. 10. μεσότητες II. vii. 11, 14, 16. III. v. 21. IV. viii. 12. μεσοτήτων VI. i. 1. μεσότητας IV. vii. 1.

μέσως II. v. 2. III. vii. 12. xi. 8.

μεταβαίνει IV. i. 36. VIII. x. 3. μεταβαίνων I. vii. 2. μεταβαίνουσι VIII. x. 3. μεταβῆναι VI. xiii. 5.

μεταβάλλει VII. ix. 2, 5. μεταβάλλοι IV. i. 33. μεταβάλλουσι VIII. x. 3. μεταβάλλειν V. v. 11. X. iii. 4.

μεταβολὴ VII. xiv. 8. VIII. iii. 5. μεταβολαὶ I. ix. 11. μεταβολὰς I. x. 4. 15.

μεταδιδόασι X. vi. 8. μεταδιδόναι V. v. 8. IX. xi. 5.

μετάδοσις V. v. 6. μεταδόσει V. v. 6.

μετακινῆσαι VII. x. 4. μετακινεῖται V. x. 7.

μεταλαμβάνειν V. ix. 3. μεταλαμβάνουσι IX. xi. 2. μεταλάβοιμεν X. ix. 5.

μεταμελείᾳ III. i. 13, 19. μεταμελείας IX. iv. 10.

μεταμελητικὸς VII. viii. 1. μεταμελητικὸν VII. vii. 2.

μεταμελόμενος III. i. 13.

μεταξὺ VI. i. 1. VII. iv. 5. vii. 1.

μεταπεῖσαι X. ix. 7. μεταπείθονται VII. ix. 3. μεταπεισθεὶς VII. ii. 10. μεταπεισθῆναι ibid.

μεταπίπτει VIII. iii. 5. μεταπίπτειν VIII. vi. 7. μεταπίπτοντες VIII. iii. 5. μεταπιπτούσης VIII. iii. 5.

μεταῤῥεῖ IX. vi. 3.

μεταῤῥυθμίσαι X. ix. 5.

μεταφέρομεν V. x. 1. μεταφέρειν IX. v. 3. μετενηνέχθαι III. xii. 6.

μεταφορὰν III. vi. 3. V. xi. 9. VII. v. 9. vi. 6.

μέτεστι IV. ii. 14. V. ix. 17.

μετίεναι I. vii. 22.

μετέωρα X. iv. 9.

μετέχει I. xiii. 18. μετέχειν I. xiii. 17. VII. xiii. 6. X. viii. 8. μετέχουσα I. xiii. 15. μετασχεῖν VI. viii. 4. μετέχουσι IX. iv. 7.

μετρεῖ V. v. 10. μετρηθῇ V. iv. 6. μετρεῖται IV. i. 2. V. v. 15. IX. i. 2. 7. μετρεῖσθαι V. v. 11. μετρεῖν VIII. xiii. 10.

μετρίας III. xii. 8. VII. iv. 3. μέτριον I. vi. 3. IV. iii. 26. iv. 4. μετρίῳ III. i. 7. μετρίου I. vi. 4. μετρίους IV. i. 35. ii. 3. μετρίων IV. iii. 7. X. viii. 10. μέτρια IV. iv. 1. X. viii. 11. μέτριοι V. ix. 9.

μετρίως III. xi. 8. IV. i. 25. iii. 17, 18. vii. 17. X. viii. 11.

μέτρον III. iv. 4. V. v. 14. VIII. xiii. 10, 11. IX. i. 2. iv. 2. ix. 3. X. v. 10. μέτρα V. vii. 5. μέτροις V. vii. 5. μέτρῳ VIII. xiii. 11.

μέχρι I. ii. 6. IV. v. 13. V. ix. 17. VII. vi. 2. vii. 2. xiv. 2.

μηδαμόθεν IV. i. 30.

μηδαμῶς IV. x. 7.

μηδὲ VII. xiii. 7. VIII. v. 3.

μηδεὶς III. i. 7. v. 17. IX. viii. 2. μηδεμιᾶς II. ii. 7. μηδεμίαν VII. xii. 6. X. iii. 12. μηδενὸς I. vii. 5, 7. IV. iii. 25. vii. 5, 7, 10. VIII. vii. 4. μηδενὶ III. i. 7. μηδὲν I. xiii. 9. x. 5. xi. 6. II. ii. 7. III. i. 3, 10, 12, 13. viii. 13. ix. 6. xi. 7. xii. 7. IV. i. 34, 39. iii. 34. V. 5. 11, 14. VI. vi. 2. VII. ii. 3. iii. 6. vii. 2. ix. 6. VIII. viii. 3, 6. xi. 6, 8. xiv. 1, 3. IX. i. 4, 6. iii. 2. iv. 10. vii. 2. X. iv. 5. vi. 3. μηδένα VII. ii. 3. IX. i. 7.

μηδέποτε I. vii. 4. VI. vi. 2. VIII. iv. 3. IX. iii. 5. X. iii. 12.
μηδετέρᾳ VI. xii. 4. μηδετέρῳ X. ii. 5. μηδέτερον I. iv. 7. VII. xiv. 5. VIII. iv. 2. X. ii. 5. μηδετέρων X. ii. 5.
μηδοτιοῦν I. xi. 1.
μηκέτι VIII. iii. 3. IX. iii. 1.
μῆκος X. vii. 7.
μῆλον III. x. 5.
μὴν I. vi. 6. viii. 13. x. 14. III. ii. 7. v. 14. vi. 11. ix. 3. xi. 2. IV. i. 22. iii. 13, 17, 18, 35. v. 7. VI. v. 7. VIII. viii. 3.
μηνύει I. xiii. 18. IX. vii. 4. μηνύειν I. xii. 5. X. ii. 1. μηνύουσι II. iii. 4.
μήποτε VIII. vii. 6. X. i. 3. iii. 2.
μήπω V. vi. 1.
μητρικὴν IX. ii. 8.
μήτηρ VIII. viii. 3. IX. ii. 8. μητέρα V. ix. 1. VII. v. 3. μητέρες VIII. viii. 3. xii. 1. IX. iv. 1. viii. 7. μητέρας IX. iv. 1.
μητροκτονῆσαι III. i. 8.
μιαιφόνον X. vii. 6.
μικροκίνδυνος IV. iii. 23.
μικροπρέπεια II. vii. 6. IV. ii. 4.
μικροπρεπὴς IV. ii. 21. μικροπρεπεῖς IV. ii. 8.
μικροὶ IV. iii. 5. μικρὸν I. viii. 9. xi. 5. xiii. 13. II. i. 1. iii. 9. iv. 3. viii. 4. ix. 8. III. ix. 3. x. 9. IV. ii. 18. iii. 18. v. 13, 14. viii. 4, 6. VI. xii. 7. xiii. 5. VIII. x. 3. xi. 6. IX. iv. 10. vi. 4. ix. 4. X. v. 9. vii. 8. viii. 4. ix. 19. μικρὰ I. x. 12. II. vii. 6, 8. III. ix. 6. iv. 1. vi. 8. vii. 15. VIII. xiii. 10. X. viii. 7. μικρὸς IV. vi. 7. μικροῦ II. viii. 4. IV. i. 41. μικροῖς IV. i. 24, 29. ii. 3, 20. iii. 17. μικρῷ IV. i. 31. ii. 21. VII. iv. 2. μικρᾶς IX. viii. 9. μικρῶν IV. iii. 4, 7. 32.
μικρότητι I. x. 12. IX. ii. 2.
μικροψυχία II. vii. 7. IV. iii. 37.
μικρόψυχος IV. iii. 7, 12, 35.
μικτὴ IV. ix. 8. IX. xi. 3. μικτὸν X. ii. 3. μικταὶ III. i. 6. X. iii. 2.
Μιλήσιοι VII. viii. 3. Μιλησίους ibid.
Μίλωνι II. vi. 7.
μιμεῖται III. vii. 8. ἐμιμεῖτο III. iii. 18. μιμούμενος VII. vii. 5. μιμεῖσθαι IX. xi. 4. μιμοῦνται IV. iii. 21.
μισεῖν X. i. 1. ix. 6. μισεῖ VI. viii. 4. μισοῦνται IX. iv. 8.
μισητὸν IV. viii. 7. μισητὰ I. x. 13. III. xi. 4.
μισθὸς V. vi. 7. IX. i. 6. μισθὸν IX. i. 7. μισθοὺς X. ix. 3.
μίσθωσις V. ii. 13.
μναῖ II. vi. 7. V. v. 15. μνῶν V. v. 15. μνᾶς II. vi. 7. V. vii. 1.
μνείαν VII. i. 4. IX. iii. 5. μνεῖαι IX. iv. 5.
μνήμη IX. vii. 6. μνήμην VII. iii. 11. μνῆμαι X. iii. 7.
μνημονεύειν IV. iii. 25. X. iii. 12.
μνησίκακος IV. iii. 30.
μοῖραν I. ix. 1.
μοιχεία II. vi. 18. V. i. 14.
μοιχεύει V. ii. 4. xi. 6. ἐμοίχευσε V. ii. 5. iv. 3. vi. 2. μοιχεύειν II. vi. 18. V. i. 14.
μοιχὸς V. vi. 1, 2. μοιχοὶ III. viii. 11.
μολίβδινος V. x. 7.
μόλις IV. iii. 25.
μοναδικοῦ V. iii. 8.
μοναρχίαι VIII. x. 2. μοναρχίας VIII. x. 3.
μονάρχαις III. vi. 8.
μονάδος X. iv. 4.
μοναχῶς II. vi. 14.
μόνιμος VIII. iii. 7. vii. 2. μόνιμον I. x. 7. VIII. iii. 6. vi. 7. μόνιμοι VIII. viii. 4. 5. μόνιμα IX. i. 3. μονιμώτεραι I. x. 10. μονιμώταται ibid.
μόνος IV. iii. 10. μόνη V. i. 17. VII. v. 8. VIII. iv. 3. X. vii. 5. μόνον I. iii. 2. vii. 3. viii. 1. II. ii. 8. vi. 1. vii. 1. III. v. 15. IV. ii. 1, 12. V. i. 3, 15. iii. 8. iv. 3, 9. v. 4. vii. 5. viii. 11, 12. ix. 9. xi. 4. VI. i. 2, 3. v. 8. vii. 3. viii. 2. x. 2. xii. 3. xiii. 5. VII. iii. 2. iv. 2, 3, 6. v. 6, 7, 9. vi. 1, 6. ix. 5. x. 2. xiv. 3, 8. VIII. i. 3, 5. iv. 1. xii. 7. IX. i. 8. v. 3. X. i. 4. iv. 3. viii. 11. ix. 21. μόνους VIII. v. 2. μόναις VII. xiii. 6. μόνην VII. iv. 6. VIII. i. 2. μόνοι VI. viii. 2. μόνῳ I. ii. 8. vii. 6. μόνῃ I. vi. 3. VIII. xiii. 2. X. ix. 13. μόνου VI. ii. 6.
μονούμενον I. vii. 7. X. ii. 3. μονούμενα I. vi. 10.
μονώτην I. vii. 6. IX. ix. 3. μονώταις VIII. v. 3.
μόριον I. xiii. 12. V. ix. 17. X. ix. 18. μορίου VI. xi. 7. xii. 4, 5. xiii. 7, 8. X. vi. 7. μόρια I. xiii. 10, 15. VIII. ix. 6. μορίων I. vii. 11. V. i.

13. VI. i. 5. ii. 6. VII. iii. 10. μορίοις VIII. ix. 4.
μουσικὸς IX. ix. 6. X. iv. 10. μουσικοῦ X. iii. 10. μουσικὸν X. iii. 10. μουσικῆς X. ix. 14. μουσικῇ X. ix. 20.
μουσικοὶ II. iv. 1. μουσικὰ II. iv. 1.
μοχθηρία III. v. 4. VI. xii. 10. VII. iv. 5. v. 8. viii. 1, 4. μοχθηρίας III. i. 15. V. i. 14. ii. 2. IX. iii. 5. μοχθηρίᾳ V. i. 18. VII. i. 4. ii. 4. VIII. viii. 5. xiv. 4. μοχθηρίαν V. ii. 5, 10. viii. 8. IX. iii. 3. iv. 8, 9, 10.
μοχθηρὸς III. i. 14. V. viii. 9. VIII. x. 3. IX. iii. 3. μοχθηρὰ III. v. 7. IX. xii. 3. X. v. 6. μοχθηρὸν V. viii. 10. VIII. x. 3. IX. ii. 5. viii. 7. ix. 7. μοχθηροῦ IV. i. 31. μοχθηρῷ VIII. xiv. 4. IX. viii. 8. μοχθηρὰς VII. v. 1. μοχθηροὶ VII. xiv. 2. μοχθηροὺς VIII. i. 7. μοχθηροὶ VIII. viii. 5. x. 3. IX. iv. 9. xii. 3. μοχθηρότεροι IX. viii. 1.
μυθεύονται I. ix. 11.
μυρεψικὴ VII. xii. 6.
μυριάκις II. i. 2.
μυριάδων IX. x. 3.
μυριοπλάσια VII. vi. 7.
μύρον III. x. 5.
μῦς VII. v. 6.
μυστικὰ III. i. 17.
μωραίνειν VII. iv. 5.

N.

ναὶ III. v. 2.
ναοῦ X. iv. 2.
ναυπηγικῆς I. i. 3.
νῆα II. ix. 3.
νεανικὴ VII. iv. 4.
νεαρὸς I. iii. 7.
νεμεσητικὸς II. vii. 15.
νέμεσις II. vii. 15.
νέμει V. vi. 6. ix. 10. νέμουσι VIII. x. 3. νέμειν V. vi. 4. VIII. xiv. 2. IX. viii. 11. νεῖμαι V. ix. 8. νεῖμαι V. ix. 15. νέμεσθαι VIII. xiv. 1. IX. ix. 10. νέμονται V. iii. 6. νεμόμενα V. ix. 15. νενεμημένης VIII. iv. 6. νενεμημένων I. viii. 2.
Νεοπτόλεμος VII. ii. 7. ix. 4.
νέοι I. iii. 5, 7. III. xi. 1. VI. viii. 5. νέων II. i. 8. iii. 2. IV. ix. 3. VIII. iii. 4. 5. vi. 4. X. ix. 3. νέοι VI. viii. 5, 6. VIII. iii. 5. vi. 1. νέον X. ix. 8. νέους VIII. i. 2. X. ix. 8. νέους X. i. 1. ix. 9. νέῳ IV. ix. 3. νεώτερον VIII. vii. 1.
νεότης VII. xiv. 6. νεότητι ibid.
νεωρίων II. iii. 8.
νικᾷν III. ii. 8. VII. vii. 4. νενικημένοι III. viii. 13. νικῶσι I. viii. 9. νικῶντες VII. ix. 3. νενικημένος VII. iv. 2.
νίκη I. i. 3. VII. iv. 5. νίκης VIII. ix. 5. νίκην VII. iv. 2.
Νιόβη VII. iv. 5.
νοεῖν I. iv. 7. νοήσω III. viii. 4. νοήσῃ I. iv. 7. νοῆσαι VII. ix. 4. VIII. i. 2. νοεῖν IX. ix. 7, 9. νοοῦν IX. iv. 4. νοοῦμεν IX. ix. 9.
νοήσεως IX. ix. 7.
νοητικῶν VI. ii. 6.
νοητὸν X. iv. 8.
νομὴ V. iii. 11. νομῆς III. viii. 11.
νομίζων VII. iii. 2.
νομικὴ VIII. xiii. 5, 6. νομικὸν V. ix. 12.
νόμιμος V. i. 8, 12. νόμιμον V. i. 8. ii. 8. vii. 1, 4. νομίμου V. x. 3. νομίμων V. ii. 10, 11. vii. 6. νόμιμα V. i. 12. X. ix. 14.
νόμισμα V. v. 10, 11, 14. 15. 16. IX. i. 2. iii. 2. X. viii. 7.
νομιστέον I. xiii. 16.
νομοθεσία VI. viii. 3. νομοθεσίας X. ix. 22.
νομοθετοῦσι III. i. 2. V. vii. 1. νομοθετούσης I. ii. 7. ἐνομοθέτησε V. x. 5. νομοθετοῦνται X. ix. 10. νομοθετηθῆναι X. ix. 20. νενομοθέτηται V. ii. 11.
νομοθέτης V. x. 5. X. ix. 5. νομοθέτῃ V. x. 4. νομοθέται I. xiii. 3. νομοθέται II. i. 5. IV. viii. 9. VIII. i. 4. ix. 4. νομοθέτου II. i. 5. νομοθετῶν III. v. 7.
νομοθετικὸς X. ix. 14, 18, 21. νομοθετικὴ VI. viii. 2. νομοθετικῆς V. i. 12. νομοθετικῷ X. ix. 17.
νόμος IV. viii. 10. V. i. 14. ii. 10. iv. 3, 13. vi. 4, 9. x. 4. 5. xi. 2. X. ix. 12. νόμου V. x. 6. xi. 1. VIII. xi. 7. νόμῳ I. iii. 2. V. v. 11. x. 4. νόμον V. ii. 3. vi. 9. x. 3, 8. xi. 2. VI. xii. 7. VIII. xiii. 5. νόμοι V. i. 13. ix. 15. IX. i. 8. X. ix. 20. νόμων I. xiii. 2. III. viii. 1. VII. x. 3. X. ix. 9. 14. 17. 20, 21. νόμοις III. v. 8. VII. x. 4. X. ix. 8, 23. νόμους VII. x. 3.

νοσεῖ III. v. 14. νοσεῖν ibid. νοσῶν ibid. νοσήσας I. iv. 3.
νοσήματα VII. vi. 6. νοσημάτων VII. viii. 1.
νοσηματώδης VII. v. 8, νοσηματώδεις VII. v. 3, 5, 6.
νοσηματωδῶς VII. v. 4.
νόσον III. vi. 3. 4. V. xi. 8. VII. v. 6. vii. 6. νόσου III. v. 15. νόσῳ I. vi. 4. νόσοις VII. i. 3. v. 3, 6. νόσους III. vi. 8, 11.
νοσώδη VII. xi. 5. xii. 4.
νουθέτησις I. xiii. 18.
νοῦς I. xi. 3, 12. III. iii. 7. VI. i. 1. ii. 5. iii. 1. vi. 2. vii. 3, 4. viii. 9. xi. 4, 5, 6. VII. vi. 7. IX. viii. 8. X. vi. 4. vii. 1, 2. viii. 13. νοῦ X. vii. 7. viii. 3. ix. 12. νῷ VI. viii. 9. IX. viii. 8. νοῦν I. vii. 5. III. i. 5. iii. 2. vii. 1. VI. vi. 2. xi. 2, 5, 6. xiii. 2. IX. viii. 6. X. vii. 9. viii. 13. ix. 11. νόον VII. vi. 3.
νῦν I. v. 2. vi. 4, 13. x. 6, 10. II. vii. 5, 9. III. i. 10. v. 5. x. 1. xii. 5. V. v. 14. VI. i. 5. xiii. 4. VII. iii. 7. IX. i. 2. IX. iv. 4. X. ii. 5. iv. 4. vii. 9. ix. 3.

Ξ.

ξενίας IX. x. 1.
ξενικὴν VIII. iii. 4. xii. 1.
ξένων IV. ii. 15.
Ξενοφάντῳ VII. vii. 6.
ξηρανθεῖσαν VIII. i. 6.
ξηρὸν VII. iii. 6. ξηροῦ VIII. viii. 7. ξηροῖς III. xi. 1. ξηρὰ VII. iii. 6.
ξύλον II. ix. 5.
ξυνιέναι V. ix. 15. ξυνιέντας X. i. 4.

O.

ὄγκῳ X. vii. 8.
ὅδε. ἥδε VI. xi. 8. τοδὶ VI. viii. 7. ix. 1. ταδὶ VII. iii. 2.
ὁδὸς I. iv. 5.
ὁδοὺς VIII. xii. 2.
ὀδυρόμενοι IV. ii. 21.
ὅθεν I. v. 1. vii. 17. viii. 17. ix. 1. xiii. 12. II. i. 1. vi. 9. vii. 8. III. i. 9. viii. 6, 10. x. 8. IV. i. 7, 15, 17, 24, 31, 33, 40, 42, 43. iv. 2, 3. v. 9. V. ix. 10. VI. ii. 4. VIII. i. 3. 6. v. 1. vii. 6. xi. 1. xii. 3. IX. ix. 1. xi. 5. xii. 3. X. v. 1.
ὀθνεῖον VIII. xii. 8. ὀθνείῳ VIII. ix. 3. xii. 6. ὀθνείων IV. vi. 5. IV. ix. 2. 3. ὀθνείοις IX. iii. 5.
οἰακίζοντες X. i. 2.
οἰκεῖος I. iii. 5. οἰκεία X. v. 2, 6, 8. οἰκεῖον I. v. 4. vii. 18. IV. i. 9. viii. 5. V. iv. 5. VI. i. 7. VIII. i. 3. x. 1. xi. 2. IX. ii. 9. iii. 4. vii. 3, 7. ix. 5. x. 2. X. iii. 4. v. 2, 5. vii. 9. ix. 8. οἰκείου X. ii. 4. οἰκείαν I. vii. 15. VIII. viii. 2. X. vi. 5. vii. 7. οἰκείαις VIII. iii. 6. X. v. 5. οἰκείων IV. iii. 7. X. v. 5. οἰκεῖα I. vi. 1. VIII. i. 7. IX. i. 9. ii. 7. vii. 3. οἰκείους IV. v. 6. οἰκείοις V. i. 15. οἰκείας IX. ix. 5. X. ix. 4. οἰκειότερον I. vi. 13. ix. 3. xii. 7. οἰκειότεροι VIII. xii. 4, 6. οἰκειότεραι X. v. 6. οἰκειότατον III. ii. 1.
οἰκειότητα VI. i. 5. IX. ii. 9.
οἰκείως IV. i. 4. IX. x. 5, 6.
οἰκέτης V. ix. 11.
οἰκήσεων VIII. x. 6.
οἰκία I. vii. 1. V. v. 8, 15. VIII. xii. 7. V. v. 1. οἰκίας V. v. 16. οἰκίᾳ V. v. 10, 15. VII. xi. 4. οἰκίαν V. v. 10. οἰκίαις VIII. x. 4. X. ix. 14.
οἰκοδομεῖν II. i. 6. οἰκοδομοῦντες II. i. 4.
οἰκοδόμησις VII. xi. 4.
οἰκοδομίας V. x. 7.
οἰκοδομικὴ VI. iv. 3. X. iv. 2. οἰκοδομικῇ I. vii. 1.
οἰκοδόμος V. v. 8, 10. οἰκοδόμον V. v. 8. οἰκοδόμοι II. i. 4, 6.
οἰκονομία VI. viii. 3. οἰκονομίας VI. viii. 4.
οἰκονομικὸν V. vi. 9. xi. 9. οἰκονομικὴν I. ii. 6. οἰκονομικῆς I. i. 3. οἰκονομικοὺς VI. v. 5.
οἰνηρὰ V. vii. 4.
οἴνου V. v. 3. VII. viii. 2. οἶνον V. ix. 15. οἴνῳ VIII. ii. 3. οἴνοις VII. xiv. 2. οἴνους III. x. 9.
οἰνοφλυγίας III. v. 15.
οἰόμενοι VII. iii. 13. x. 3. οἰομένου VII. iii. 12. οἰόμενον VII. iii. 7. οἰόμεναι VII. xiv. 6.
οἴεσθαι III. viii. 13. IV. ix. 6. οἴονται III. ii. 8. V. viii. 10. ix. 6. VI. vii. 2. VII. ii. 2. iii. 2. vii. 5. VIII. xiv. 1. IX. i. 9. ii. 5. οἰηθείη III. i. 17. X. iv. 10. ᾠήθη III. viii. 6. V. viii. 6. οἰόμεθα I. vii. 7. x. 13. IV. ix. 3, 4. VI. v. 5. vii. 2. xi. 5. IX. iii. 5.

X. v. 1. vii. 3. ᾤετο I. xii. 5. VI. xiii. 3, 5. VII. ii. 1. X. ii. 1, 2. viii. 11. οἴονται II. iv. 6. IV. ii. 11. V. ix. 14, 15, 16. VI. viii. 4. VII. iii. 3. xii. 3. xiii. 1, 6. VIII. i. 2, 5. xiii. 2. xiii. 3, 6. xiv. 1. IX. ii. 5, 7. iv. 8. ix. 4, 5. xii. 2. X. vi. 4. ix. 6, 10. οἰόμενος III. v. 17. IV. ii. 20, 21. iii. 34. VII. ix. 7. IX. ii. 5. ᾤοντο I. iv. 3. X. ix. 20. οἴονται IX. iii. 1. οἰόμενοι IV. iii. 21. vi. 1. VIII. i. 7. X. i. 2. οἰητέον X. iii. 8. vi. 4. viii. 9. ix. 1.
οἷος IV. iii. 24, 33. vii. 5. VII. viii. 4. ix. 5, 6. VIII. vii. 6. IX. iii. 4. οἷον I. iv. 3. vi. 3, 4, 10, 14. vii. 3, 20. viii. 9, 10, 16. x. 3. xiii. 9. II. i. 2, 4. ii. 8. v. 2. vi. 2, 6, 10, 18. viii. 6, 7, 8. III. i. 3, 4, 16, 17, 24. ii. 7, 8, 9. iii. 3, 4, 5, 6, 8, 13, 16. v. 8, 17. vi. 3, 8. viii. 2. ix. 3. x. 2, 3, 11. xi. 1. IV. i. 17, 40, 42. ii. 3, 10, 11, 15, 20. iii. 16. vi. 4. vii. 13, 14, 15. viii. 3. V. i. 4, 6, 7, 14. ii. 5. iii. 9. iv. 5, 12. v. 4, 9, 11, 13. vi. 1, 2. vii. 1. viii. 3, 6, 8. ix. 9, 17. xi. 1. VI. i. 2. ii. 6. v. 1, 6. vii. 1, 4. x. 1. xii. 7. VII. ii. 7. iii. 7, 9. iv. 2, 5. v. 2, 3, 7. vii. 6. viii. 1, 5. ix. 2, 4. xi. 4. xiv. 1, 4. VIII. i. 7. iv. 1. vi. 7. vii. 1, 2, 5, 6. viii. 6. ix. 5. x. 1, 4. xi. 6. xii. 1, 2. IX. i. 1, 4. ii. 1, 4. iv. 8. v. 2. vi. 1, 2. vii. 7. viii. 1, 2. X. iii. 4, 12. iv. 2, 8, 10. v. 1, 2, 5. ix. 18. οἷα II. iv. 4. III. viii. 6. IV. ii. 11. viii. 1, 5. οἵων II. iii. 5. οἵῳ VI. viii. 9. οἷαι VIII. vi. 4.
οἱονδήποτε III. v. 19.
οἷά περ VII. viii. 3.
οἷόν τε I. viii. 9. ix. 5, 9. III. iii. 13. v. 17. IV. i. 21. iii. 16. V. x. 4. VI. xiii. 6. VII. ii. 1. VIII. i. 7. IX. iii. 4. iv. 10. v. 3. vi. 4. x. 4. X. iii. 12. ix. 5, 7.
ὀκνηροὶ IV. iii. 35.
ὀκνοῦντα IX. xi. 5.
ὀλιγάκις VII. ix. 5.
ὀλιγαρχίαν VIII. x. 3, 5. ὀλιγαρχίαις VIII. x. 5.
ὀλιγαρχικοὶ V. iii. 7.
ὀλίγος I. vii. 6. ὀλίγον II. vi. 7. VII. xii. 1. VIII. vi. 4. viii. 5. IX. viii. 9. ὀλίγοις III. xii. 7. ὀλίγα II. vi. 6. IV. ii. 20. iii. 23, 24. VIII. i. 6. IX. xi. 5. ὀλίγου I. viii. 7. III. xi. 3. VIII. iii. 8. x. 3. IX. x. 3. ὀλίγῳ I. x. 14. VIII. vi. 3. ὀλίγων VII. viii. 2. ὀλίγοις VII. ix. 5. ὀλίγους IX. x. 5, 6. X. ix. 17. ὀλίγων IV. iii. 27.
ὀλιγωρία VII. vi. 1.
ὀλιγωρήσει IV. iii. 17.
ὀλιγώρους IV. i. 34.
ὀλόκληρος IV. i. 38. ὀλόκληρον IV. v. 7.
ὅλον III. xii. 4. V. ii. 9. iii. 11, 12. iv. 8. v. 18. X. iv. 1, 4. ὅλως I. viii. 7. ὅλων V. ii. 3. ὅλη V. i. 9. iv. 12. ὅλον X. iv. 4. ὅλης V. ii. 3, 9, 10, 11. VI. xii. 5. X. iv. 2. ὅλην V. ii. 6, 7, 10. viii. 3. xi. 4. ὅλα V. ii. 9.
ὀλοφυρτικὸς IV. iii. 32.
Ὀλύμπια VII. iv. 2. Ὀλυμπίασιν I. viii. 9.
ὅλως I. iv. 6. vii. 3, 5, 6, 10, 11. viii. 10. x. 3. xii. 2. xiii. 18. II. ii. 7. v. 2. vi. 10, 20. vii. 14. III. i. 14. ii. 9, 11. vi. 4. xi. 8. V. iii. 8. v. 9. xi. 6. VI. v. 2. vii. 2. x. 1. VII. ii. 1. vi. 6. viii. 1. xii. 4. xiv. 2, 4. VIII. vii. 1. xii. 6, 8. IX. v. 4. viii. 4, 5, 9. xi. 4. X. ix. 7, 9, 10, 12, 20, 22.
ὄμβρους VIII. i. 6. ὄμβρων III. iii. 5.
Ὅμηρος III. iii. 18. viii. 2, 10. xi. 4. V. ix. 7. VI. vii. 2. VII. i. 1. vi. 3. VIII. x. 4. xi. 1.
ὁμιλεῖ IV. vi. 5. ὁμιλῆσαι IV. vi. 6, 8. ὁμιλεῖν X. iii. 11. ὁμιλοῦντα X. iii. 11. ὁμιλοῦντες IV. vii. 1. ὁμιλητικὸν VIII. xiv. 3.
ὁμιλία IV. viii. 1. ὁμιλίας IV. viii. 10. VIII. iii. 4. ὁμιλίαις IV. vi. 1, 7. VIII. vi. 1. IX. xii. 3.
ὄμμα VI. xi. 6. ὄμματι VI. xii. 10.
ὁμογενῶν IX. ii. 10.
ὁμογνωμονεῖ IX. iv. 3. ὁμογνωμονοῦσι IX. viii. 2. ὁμογνωμονοῦσι IX. vi. 1. ὁμογνωμονοῦντας IX. vi. 1.
ὁμοδοξία IX. vi. 1.
ὁμοεθνέσι VIII. i. 3.
ὁμοήθεις VIII. iv. 1. ὁμοηθέστεροι VIII. xii. 6.
ὁμοιοπαθεῖν I. v. 3.
ὅμοιος VII. vii. 5. viii. 2. ὁμοίαν VIII. i. 6. ὁμοία VI. xiii. 2. VIII. iii. 9. ὅμοιον II. iv. 3, 6, 19. vi. 19. III. vi. 3. IV. ii. 15. V. vi. 8. VI. xiii. 1, 8. VII. vi. 7. viii. 3. ix. 2. VIII. i. 4, 6. iv. 4. IX. i. 4. vi. 3. vii. 2. X.

ix. 18. ὁμοίῳ IX. iii. 3. ὁμοίαν VII. iv. 6. ὅμοιαι IV. iii. 21. VII. ix. 6. VIII. iii. 7. iv. 6. viii. 5. ὅμοιοι VIII. iii. 6. ὁμοίων II. i. 7. VIII. iii. 3, 6. X. iv. 8. ὁμοίοις VIII. xii. 6. ὁμοίους VIII. i. 6. ὅμοια V. vii. 5.
ὁμοιότροπον II. viii. 7.
ὁμοιότης II. viii. 5. VIII. viii. 5. ὁμοιότητα II. vii. 11. III. vi. 4. xii. 5. V. vi. 4. xi. 9. VI. i. 5. VII. iv. 2, 6. v. 5. ix. 6. VIII. i. 6. iii. 7. iv. 4. ὁμοιότητι VI. iii. 2.
ὁμοιοῦται VIII. xii. 4. IX. iv. 6. ὁμοιοῦσθαι IX. iii. 3. ὁμοιούμενοι IX. xii. 3. ὁμοιῶσθαι VIII. iv. 6. ὁμοίωνται III. viii. 1.
ὁμοίωμα VIII. iv. 1. X. viii. 8. ὁμοιώματα VIII. x. 4.
ὁμοίως I. i. 1. iii. 1. iv. 2. vi. 13. vii. 1, 18, 20. viii. 12. ix. 6. x. 12. xi. 3, 6. xii. 4, 6. II. i. 6, 7. ii. 6, 7, 9. v. 2. vi. 3, 7, 12. vii. 16. viii. 2. III. iii. 9, 14. iv. 4. v. 2, 3, 9, 15, 18, 19, 20, 22. vii. 1, 4, 5. ix. 1. x. 1, 2, 4, 7. xii. 3. IV. i. 24. ii. 2. iii. 17, 35. vi. 3, 5, 8. vii. 1. viii. 1. V. i. 14. iii. 10. v. 2, 18, 19. vi. 2. vii. 4, 5, 7. viii. 3, 4, 11. ix. 2, 3, 15. VII. iii. 1, 8, 13. iv. 6. vii. 2, 6. xiv. 6. VIII. ii. 2. iii. 1, 6. iv. 1. vi. 1. vii. 2, 3. viii. 6, 7. ix. 1, 5. xii. 6. xiii. 1, 8. xiv. 1. IX. ii. 1, 6, 8. iii. 1. vii. 6. ix. 9. X. ii. 2, 5. iii. 10. iv. 3, 6, 9. v. 1, 2, 4, 5, 6, 7, 9. vii. 4.
ὁμολογεῖται I. iv. 2. VII. xiii. 1. ὁμολογοῦσι VII. ii. 3. ὁμολογῶν IV. vii. 4. ὁμολογοῦντες V. viii. 10. ὡμολόγησε VIII. xiii. 9. ὡμολόγησαν IX. i. 6. ὁμολογούμενον I. vii. 9. X. vii. 2. ὁμολογουμένην I. vii. 1. ὁμολογούμενα I. ix. 8.
ὁμολογουμένως X. ii. 2. v. 2. vii. 3.
ὁμολογίαις IV. vii. 7. ὁμολογίαν VIII. xii. 1. xiii. 6.
ὁμόλογοι III. vi. 9.
ὁμολόγων VI. ii. 3.
ὁμονοεῖν IX. vi. 1, 2, 4. ὁμονοοῦσι IX. vi. 2, 3.
ὁμόνοια VIII. i. 4. IX. vi. 1, 2, 3.
ὁμοπαθεῖς VIII. xi. 5.
ὁμοφωνεῖ I. xiii. 17.
ὁμωνυμίαν V. i. 7.
ὁμωνύμοις I. vi. 12.
ὁμωνύμως V. i. 7.
ὅμως I. vi. 10. viii. 15. x. 12. III. v. 14. V. v. 14. vii. 3. xi. 7. VI. xii. 2. xiii. 1. VII. iv. 2, 5. xi. 3. IX. i. 9. X. vii. 4.
ὀνειδίζεται IX. viii. 4. X. iii. 11. ὀνειδίσειε III. v. 15. ὀνειδιζόμεναι VII. xi. 5. ὀνειδιζομένων IX. viii. 6.
ὄνειδος IX. viii. 4. ὀνείδους III. viii. 3. ὀνείδη III. viii. 1. IV. i. 41, 43. ii. 22.
ὀνήσεται IX. viii. 7.
ὄνομα II. i. 1. III. i. 13. ii. 7. xii. 5. IV. vi. 4. V. iv. 5. VI. viii. 3. ὀνόματος II. vii. 3. III. xi. 7. IV. iii. 1. VII. xiii. 6. ὀνόματι I. iv. 2. V. ii. 6. VI. v. 5. ὀνόματα V. iv. 13.
ὀνομάζεται V. iv. 9. ὀνομάζουσιν VII. xi. 2. ὠνόμασται II. vi. 8. IV. i. 39. vi. 9. ὀνομάσθαι IV. v. 6.
ὀνομαστῶν IV. iii. 27.
ὀνοματοποιεῖν II. vii. 11.
ὄνοι III. viii. 11. ὄνους X. v. 8. ὄνου ibid.
ὀνύχων VII. v. 3.
ὀξεῖς III. vii. 12. IV. v. 9. VII. vii. 8. ὀξέσι VII. xii. 2.
ὀξύτητα I. v. 8.
ὀξυφωνία IV. iii. 34.
ὁπλίζω. ὡπλισμένοι III. viii. 8.
ὅπλα III. xii. 3. V. i. 14. ὅπλοις III. viii. 7.
ὁποῖος III. v. 7. ὁποία III. viii. 7. V. vi. 1. ὁποίῳ V. iii. 2.
ὁπωσοῦν IX. viii. 5. ὁπῃοῦν VII. ix. 1. VIII. iv. 2. ὁπωσοῦν VII. ix. 1.
ὁπόταν VII. i. 40.
ὁπότε III. i. 10.
ὁποτερανοῦν V. ix. 16.
ὁποτέρως V. v. 18.
ὅπου IV. i. 17. iii. 27.
ὀπυίουσιν. ὀπυίονται VII. v. 4.
ὅπως I. vii. 19, 22. IV. i. 17, 21. iii. 18, 31. vi. 9. VI. iv. 4. xiii. 8. VII. xiii. 2. VIII. xiii. 9. X. vi. 6. ix. 22.
ὁπωσδήποτε III. v. 18.
ὁράματα X. iii. 7. iv. 7.
ὅρασις X. iv. 1. ὁράσεως X. iv. 4.
ὁρᾷ VI. xiii. 8. VIII. ix. 9. ὁρᾶν I. vi. 10. x. 1, 7. III. iv. 5. VII. xiv. 5. IX. xi. 3. xii. 1. X. ii. 1. iii. 12. ὁρῶμεν I. ii. 6. xiii. 16. II. ii. 6. vi. 2. V. i. 3. VII. iii. 7. ὁρῶσι V. vii. 2. VI. xi. 6. ὁρᾶσθαι VI. xiii. 1. ἑωράκασι VIII. ii. 4. ὁρῶν VIII. iv. 1. IX. ix. 1.
ὀργανικά III. i. 6.

ὀργανικῶς I. ix. 7.
ὄργανον VIII. xi. 6. ὀργάνῳ III. i. 16. ὄργανα I. vii. 3. III. iii. 14. ὀργάνων I. i. 4. viii. 15.
ὀργὴ IV. v. 2. V. viii. 10. ὀργῆς IV. v. 10. VII. iv. 3. ὀργὴν II. v. 2. vii. 10. IV. v. 8, 10, 15. V. ii. 5. xi. 2. ὀργῇ VII. vi. 4. ὀργὰς II. i. 7. IV. v. 1.
ὀργίσαι V. viii. 9. ὀργισθῆναι II. v. 2. vi. 10. ix. 2. X. iii. 4. ὀργιζόμενος II. v. 3. III. i. 14. IV. v. 3, 6. VII. vii. 3. ὀργιζόμεθα II. v. 4. IV. v. 14. ὀργίζεσθαι III. i. 24. VII. vi. 4. ὀργιζόμενοι III. viii. 12. IV. v. 5. ὀργίζονται IV. v. 8, 10. ὀργιστέον II. ix. 7. IV. v. 13.
ὀργίλος II. vii. 10. ὀργίλοι II. i. 7. IV. v. 8, 9.
ὀργιλότης II. vii. 10. IV. v. 2.
ὀρέγεται I. iv. 1. VIII. xiii. 2. IX. iv. 3. X. ii. 4. ὀρέγονται IV. iv. 5. VIII. v. 3. xiii. 3. IX. i. 4. viii. 4. X. iv. 10. ὀρέγεσθαι II. vii. 8. III. i. 24. IX. viii. 6. ix. 9. X. iv. 9. ὀρεγόμεθα III. iii. 19. ὀρεγομένῳ III. xii. 4. ὀρεγόμενον III. xii. 6. X. ix. 10. ὀρεγόμενα VIII. viii. 2. ix. 5. ὀρέξεται III. xi. 8. ὠρέγετο IV. iii. 35. ὀρεγόμενοι IV. vii. 12.
ὀρεκτικὸν I. xiii. 18. ὀρεκτικὸς VI. ii. 6.
ὀρεκτοῦ III. iii. 19.
ὄρεξις III. iii. 19. xii. 6, 7. VI. ii. 1, 2, 4, 5, 6. VIII. viii. 7. ὄρεξιν I. ii. 1. III. viii. 3. VI. ii. 2. IX. v. 1. ὀρέξει VI. ii. 2, 3. ὀρέξεις I. iii. 8. V. xi. 9. ὀρέξεων X. v. 6. ὀρέξεως II. vii. 8. VII. vi. 2.
ὀρθοδοξεῖν VII. viii. 4.
ὀρθὸς II. ii. 2. III. v. 21. xi. 8. V. ix. 5. VI. i. 1, 2, 3. xiii. 4, 5. ὀρθὴ II. iii. 2. VI. xi. 1. xiii. 7. VIII. x. 4. ὀρθὸν I. x. 9. II. ii. 2. V. xi. 2. VI. i. 1. xii. 6. xiii. 4, 5. VII. iv. 2. viii. 4, 5. X. viii. 8. ὀρθοῦ VI. xiii. 5. ὀρθῷ VII. iii. 10. ὀρθῆς X. ix. 8, 9. ὀρθῇ IV. i. 13. VI. ii. 3. VII. ix. 1. ὀρθὴν I. vii. 19. VI. ii. 2. xii. 8. X. ix. 11, 14. ὀρθὰ II. vii. 11. ὀρθαῖς VI. v. 6.
ὀρθότης VI. ix. 3, 4, 6, 7.
ὀρθοῦντες II. ix. 5.
ὀρθῶς I. viii. 9. xiii. 15. III. ii. 3, 13. iv. 2, 4. IV. i. 12. ii. 13. iii. 20. v. 13. V. i. 14. x. 3, 4, 5. VI. ii. 6. ix. 3, 4. xiii. 3. VII. ii. 1. VIII. ix. 1. xiv. 2. X. vi. 6. viii. 13. ix. 12, 20.
ὁρίζονται II. iii. 5. viii. 5. III. vi. 2. IX. iv. 1. ix. 7. ὁρίσειε II. vi. 15. ὡρίζοντο III. vii. 6. IV. ii. 6. ix. 1. IX. viii. 2. ὁρίζωνται VII. xiii. 4. ὡρίσθαι X. iii. 1. ὥρισται V. viii. 2. VI. ix. 3. ὡρισμένον IX. ii. 6. ix. 7. x. 3. ὡρισμένα V. i. 12. ὁρίζοντα V. v. 1. ὡρισμένων IX. x. 3. ὡρισμένῃ II. vi. 15. ὡρισμένη X. iii. 3. ὁριστέον IV. viii. 7.
ὁρισμὸς V. ii. 6. VIII. vii. 5.
ὁρμῇ VII. vi. 1. ὁρμῶν III. viii. 11.
ὁρμὴν III. viii. 10. ὁρμαὶ I. xiii. 15. ὁρμαῖς X. ix. 12.
ὀρνέοις VIII. i. 3.
ὀρνίθεια VI. vii. 7.
ὅρος I. vii. 7. V. iii. 13, 13. VI. i. 1, 3. VII. xiii. 4. ὅρου V. iii. 12. ὅρον VI. ix. 5. VII. iii. 13. ὅρων VI. viii. 9. xi. 4. VII. v. 5.
ὅσιον I. vi. 1.
[illegible] II. iii. 5.
ὀσμὴ III. x. 7. ὀσμὴν III. x. 5. ὀσμαῖς III. x. 5, 6, 7.
ὅσον I. iii. 4. vii. 18, 19. xiii. 8. II. ix. 2. III. ix. 5. IV. v. 3. V. iv. 12. v. 9. ix. 15. VII. iii. 6. xi. 2. VIII. ix. 1. x. 6. xi. 1, 7. xiii. 11. IX. i. 8, 9. viii. 3, 6. X. vii. 8. viii. 8. ὅσα I. vi. 10. II. i. 4. iii. 5. III. i. 4. ii. 8. iii. 8. v. 7, 9. vi. 4, 10. IV. i. 12, 22, 24. ii. 11, 14, 15, 16. iii. 28. vi. 9. vii. 11. V. i. 9. ii. 6, 11, 12. vii. 1. viii. 5, 8, 12. VI. iii. 4. vii. 4. xii. 1, 8. VIII. i. 6, 7. iii. 7. iv. 4. vi. 4. x. 5. IX. i. 5. X. vii. 7. viii. 4, 7. ὅσοι I. i. 4. III. x. 2. IV. ii. 4. VII. vi. 2. xii. 1. VIII. xii. 1. ὅσῳ I. ix. 2. xiii. 7. III. iii. 8. viii. 4, 16. ix. 4. VII. xi. 4. VIII. i. 1. vi. 1. xii. 6, 7. IX. i. 4. iii. 2, 3. viii. 1. X. vii. 4, 8. viii. 5. ὅσαι II. i. 5. III. v. 7. VII. iv. 5. VIII. iii. 4. IX. x. 5. ὅσων IV. i. 2. VI. i. 5. vii. 6. VII. xiv. 2. VIII. xiii. 4. ὅσους V. x. 16. IX. i. 8, 9. ὅσαις V. iv. 13. vi. 4. VII. v. 4. ὅσοις IV. vi. 7. VI. i. 2.
ὅταν II. ix. 5. III. viii. 9, 16. x. 9. IV. ix. 2. V. iii. 3, 11, 12, 14. v. 10, 12. ix. 9. VI. ii. 2. iv. 3. VII. xiii. 1. VIII. iii. 9. v. 3. IX. i. 5. ii. 5, 6. iii. 1. iv. 1, 3. v. 2. vii. 3.

X. v. 5. ὅσπερ V. iv. 2. ὅπερ VII. iii. 2. VIII. xii. 6.
ὅστις VII. iv. 4. ὅτου VI. iv. 3. VII. iv. 6. ὅτῳ V. vi. 7.
ὁστισοῦν IX. ii. 4. ὁντινοῦν VIII. ix. 3. X. iv. 1. ix. 17. ὁτιοῦν I. xi. 5. II. vi. 18. III. i. 13. v. 7. IV. xi. 2. VIII. xii. 2. X. iii. 9. vii. 2. ὁτῳοῦν X. ii. 2. iv. 2, 4. v. 4. ὁτουοῦν VI. x. 1. IX. vi. 1.
ὀσφρήσεις X. v. 7. ὀσφρήσεως X. iii. 7.
ὅταν II. iv. 4. III. i. 7. iii. 17. viii. 9, 14. x. 6. xi. 1. IV. iii. 23. v. 10. V. iv. 4, 6, 7, 8, 14. v. 12, 13. viii. 1, 2, 6, 7, 8, 9, 11. x. 5. xi. 2. VI. iii. 2, 4. v. 2. vii. 5. x. 3. xiii. 4. VII. i. 3. ii. 8, 10. iii. 9, 10. vi. 2. ix. 2. xiv. 3, 5, 8. VIII. iv. 1. vi. 4. vii. 2. xiii. 5. xiv. 1. IX. i. 4. iii. 1, 5. v. 3, 4. vi. 1, 2. ix. 1. xi. 5. X. i. 3. iv. 2. v. 6.
ὅτε I. x. 4, 7. II. iii. 5. vi. 11, 18. vii. 8. ix. 3, 7. III. i. 6. iii. 14. vii. 4, 5. xi. 1, 8. xii. 9. IV. i. 12, 22. v. 5. V. x. 1. VI. ix. 6. VII. i. 7. IX. i. 5. vi. 2.
οὗ IV. iii. 27. V. vii. 5.
οὐδαμῇ X. viii. 8.
οὐδαμοῦ I. x. 9. IV. iii. 15. V. vii. 3.
οὐδὲ IV. i. 11, 15, 16, 21. v. 10. viii. 10. ix. 8. V. i. 4. ii. 2. vii. 5. ix. 3, 6, 9. xi. 4. VI. ii. 6. iv. 2. ix. 3. xiii. 8. VII. i. 2. ii. 5. iv. 6. xii. 6. xiii. 6. xiv. 2. VIII. iii. 4. xi. 6. IX. ii. 6. iii. 4. iv. 7, 8, 10. x. 5. X. iii. 1. iv. 5, 6.
οὐδεὶς I. v. 6. vii. 5. viii. 12. ix. 11. x. 13. xii. 4. II. iv. 5. III. i. 5, 6, 17. ii. 8, 11. iii. 3, 6, 11. v. 4, 7, 15. vi. 6. x. 4. xii. 4. IV. iii. 3. v. 10. vi. 8. V. ix. 6. xi. 3, 6. VI. i. 6. v. 3. vii. 6. xi. 5. VII. ii. 11. iv. 2. vi. 4. VIII. i. 1. v. 3. xiii. 2. IX. v. 3. X. iii. 12. iv. 9. ix. 18. οὐδεμία VI. iv. 3. ix. 3. VII. iv. 5. xi. 3, 4. xiii. 2. οὐδὲν I. i. 5. iii. 7. vi. 5. vii. 11. viii. 12. ix. 9. x. 10. xiii. 10, 12, 16. II. i. 2, 7. ii. 1, 3. iv. 3, 6. ix. 8. III. i. 6, 22, 23. ii. 10, 15, 16. iii. 6. v. 7, 19. vi. 6. viii. 11, 16. ix. 3, 4, 6. x. 2, 9. xii. 2, 5. IV. i. 19, 34, 35. ii. 3. iii. 2, 15, 30. viii. 10. ix. 5. V. ii. 2. iv. 3. v. 16. vi. 1, 6. vii. 1. viii. 3. ix. 9, 15, 17. x. 2. VI. i. 2. ii. 5, 6. vii. 1. VII. ii. 6, 10. iii. 8. x. 2. xiii. 3. VIII. v. 3. xi. 6. xii. 8. IX. iii. 1, 3. X. ii. 3. iii. 12. v. 10. vi. 4. vii. 5, 7. viii. 8. ix. 14, 16.
οὐδένα I. x. 1. VII. ii. 1. iv. 4. X. ii. 2. iv. 1. οὐδεμίαν II. ii. 4. V. ii. 2, 5. VII. iv. 4. οὐδενὸς II. vii. 13. VIII. x. 2. X. iii. 7. iv. 1, 2. vi. 2. vii. 7. viii. 6. οὐδενὶ III. xi. 8. VII. ii. 4. x. 3. IX. iv. 7. x. 6. οὐδεμιᾶν VI. ii. 2. xii. 1. VII. xii. 6. οὐδεμιᾷ VII. xii. 5.
οὐδὲν μᾶλλον IX. iv. 3. X. ii. 2.
οὐδέποτε I. vii. 5. x. 13, 14. II. vi. 18. IV. ix. 6.
οὐδέτερον IV. i. 31. X. iii. 4. οὐδέτερα IV. ix. 5. οὐδετέρους I. viii. 7. οὐδετέρων X. v. 6.
οὗ ἕνεκα V. viii. 6. VI. ii. 4. v. 6. xi. 4. VII. viii. 4. x. 3.
οὐκέτι III. v. 14.
οὐκοῦν VI. ix. 6.
οὐ μὴν IX. ii. 10. v. 1. X. ii. 5. iii. 1, 9. v. 7. viii. 9. ix. 16, 19.
οὖν I. ix. 10. V. vii. 7. viii. 3, 8. VI. ix. 3. xii. 7. xiii. 6. VII. iii. 8.
οὐρανίων IX. vi. 1.
οὐρανὸν VIII. i. 6.
οὐσία I. vi. 2. IV. i. 30. οὐσίας IV. i. 5. οὐσίαν II. vi. 17. III. xi. 8. IV. i. 5, 19, 20, 23. IX. iii. 3.
οὔτε V. ix. 6.
οὕτω I. vii. 11, 15, 16. viii. 3, 9, 13. ix. 5. xi. 3. II. i. 4, 7, 9. iv. 4, 6. vi. 7, 8. ix. 6, 9. III. i. 11. v. 14. xii. 9. IV. i. 4. ii. 6. iii. 24. iv. 2. vii. 5, 6. V. iii. 6. v. 13, 14. vi. 1. xi. 4. VI. xiii. 1. VII. i. 5. iii. 6, 7, 8. iv. 6. viii. 1. xii. 3. VIII. iii. 3. vi. 4. x. 3. xi. 3. xiv. 1, 3. IX. i. 8. ii. 7. iii. 5. iv. 10. v. 3. vi. 2. vii. 1. viii. 4, 6. ix. 1, 10. x. 6. xii. 1. X. i. 2. ii. 5. iii. 3, 9. iv. 10. v. 1, 10. vi. 4.
οὕτως I. v. 6. vi. 5, 16. vii. 10, 14. ix. 5. x. 2, 10, 14, 15, 16. xii. 8. xiii. 1, 7, 15, 18. II. i. 7, 8. ii. 7, 8. iv. 2, 6. vi. 1, 2, 9, 19, 20. vii. 8. viii. 2, 4. ix. 2. III. iv. 2, 3. v. 14, 16, 21, 22. vi. 11. vii. 8. viii. 11. xi. 8. xii. 8. IV. iii. 18, 32. vii. 1, 3. ix. 6. V. iii. 11. v. 12, 16, 17. vii. 1, 2. ix. 1. VI. i. 2, 4. v. 1. x. 3. xiii. 2. VII. i. 2, 3. iii. 13. vi. 1. ix. 5. xiv. 2. VIII. iv. 1. v. 1, 3. x. 1. IX. i. 2, 7. ii. 5, 10. iv. 10. X. i. 2. ii. 1. iv. 3. v. 6. vii. 8. viii. 13. ix. 7, 11, 14.

οὕτως II. i. 7.
ὀφείλημα VIII. xiii. 6. IX. ii. 5.
ὀφείλει II. ii. 3. VIII. xiv. 4. IX. ii. 3. ὀφείλεται VIII. xiv. 4. IX. vii. 1. ὀφείλουσι IX. vii. 1. ὀφείλοντες, ὀφειλόντων ibid. ὀφείλοντας IX. ii. 8. ὀφείλοντα VIII. xiv. 4.
ὄφελος II. ii. 1. VIII. i. 1. xiv. 1.
ὀφθαλμιῶσι X. iv. 8.
ὀφθαλμοῦ I. vii. 11. II. vi. 2. ὀφθαλμὸν II. vi. 2. ὀφθαλμοὺς I. xiii. 7.
ὀχληθεῖεν IX. v. 3. ὀχληθέντες IX. xi. 5.
ὀχληρὸν IV. vii. 14. ὀχληρότατοι IV. v. 10.
ὄψει I. vi. 12. VIII. iv. 1. X. v. 7. ὄψεως III. x. 3. VI. xiii. 1. IX. v. 3. ὄψει IX. xi. 3. ὄψιν III. v. 17. VI. xiii. 1. X. iv. 9.
ὄψα III. x. 9. ὄψων III. x. 5. ὄψους VII. xiv. 2.
ὀψοποιητικὴ VII. xii. 6.
ὀψοφάγοι III. x. 9.

Π.

πάγκακοι I. viii. 16.
παγχάλεπον VIII. viii. 6.
παθήμασι II. vii. 14. viii. 2.
παθητικοῦ X. iv. 8. παθητικοὶ II. v. 2.
πάθος I. iii. 7. II. iii. 8. vi. 18. III. viii. 12. IV. v. 2. ix. 3. V. iv. 4, 6. vi. 1. viii. 12. VII. i. 6. ii. 2. iii. 13. vii. 8. viii. 5. ix. 2. VIII. iii. 5. v. 5. IX. viii. 6. X. ix. 7. πάθους IV. v. 3, 5. ix. 2. VII. iii. 12. iv. 6. v. 5. vii. 8. πάθει II. iii. 3. IV. ix. 1, 3. VII. ii. 2. iii. 13. vii. 3. VIII. v. 5. X. ix. 5. πάθη II. iii. 3. v. 6, 10, 12. vii. 14. III. i. 1, 27. V. viii. 8. VII. i. 5. VIII. i. 7. IX. ii. 6. X. iii. 6. παθῶν I. xi. 4. πάθεσι I. iii. 6. II. vi. 16. ix. 1. VII. iii. 7, 8. IX. viii. 4, 7. X. iv. 3. viii. 1, 2.
παιδαγωγοῦ III. xii. 8.
παιδεία II. iii. 2. παιδείας V. ii. 11. VIII. xi. 2. παιδείαν V. ii. 11. παιδείᾳ X. ix. 15.
παιδεύουσι X. i. 1. παιδευθέντες VIII. xii. 6. πεπαιδευμένος I. iii. 5. πεπαιδευμένου I. iii. 4. IV. viii. 4. παιδευθῆναι VIII. xii. 5. παιδευθήσονται X. ix. 14.
παιδιὰ IV. viii. 11. VII. vii. 7. X. vi. 6. παιδιᾶς IV. viii. 1, 5. X. vi. 6, 7. παιδιᾷ II. vii. 11, 13. IV. viii. 4. X. vi. 6. παιδιὰν X. vi. 6. παιδιῶν X. vi. 3. παιδιαῖς IV. viii. 12.
παιδικοῦ IV. ii. 18. παιδικαῖς IX. iii. 4. παιδικὰς III. xii. 5. παιδικὸν X. vi. 6.
παιδίον VII. vi. 2. παιδίου VII. v. 7. X. iii. 12. παιδία III. xii. 6. VII. xi. 4. xii. 7. X. iii. 12.
παιδιώδης VII. vii. 7.
παίζειν X. vi. 6. παῖσαι III. i. 17. παίζοντες IV. viii. 3.
παῖς I. ix. 10. III. xii. 6. VI. viii. 6. VII. i. 1. IX. iii. 4. παῖδες I. viii. 16. III. i. 22. ii. 2. VIII. iv. 4. X. vi. 4. παῖδας III. vi. 5. παῖδα III. xi. 8. παίδων VII. v. 3. X. ix. 13. παισὶ VI. xiii. 1. X. vi. 4.
παλαιὸν I. viii. 3. παλαιοὶ I. viii. 7. παλαιῶν IV. viii. 6. παλαιοῦ X. ix. 5.
πάλης II. vi. 7.
πάλιν I. vii. 1. x. 4, 8, 14. V. v. 7. VI. iii. 1. xiii. 1. VII. iii. 12.
πάμπαν IV. iii. 15, 17. VII. xiii. 5. VIII. xiii. 6.
πάμπολυ II. i. 8.
παμφάγον VII. vi. 6.
παναίσχης I. viii. 16.
πανάριστος I. iv. 17.
πανουργία VI. xii. 9.
πανούργους VI. xii. 9.
πανταχόθεν III. xii. 7.
πανταχοῦ V. vii. 1, 2, 5.
παντελοῦς IV. iii. 17, 20.
παντελῶς I. v. 3. x. 2. X. vii. 6.
πάντη I. x. 11, 15.
παντοδαπῶς I. x. 4.
πάντοθεν IV. i. 40.
παντοίας I. ix. 11. παντοίαις X. viii. 1. παντοῖαι I. xi. 2. IX. ii. 2.
πάντοτε IX. iv. 4.
πάντων I. x. 11, 15. IV. iii. 23. viii. 4.
πᾶν II. vii. 3. III. ii. 12, 13. x. 9. xi. 7. IV. i. 11, 30. VIII. iii. 4. iv. 5. vi. 1, 5, 6. xiii. 3. IX. vii. 6. x. 2. X. ii. 4. v. 4.
παρὰ I. i. 2, 5. V. vii. 3.
παραβάλλειν VII. xiii. 6.
παραγγελίας II. ii. 4.
παραγίνεται I. ix. 1, 3. II. i. 4. IV. i. 38.
παράδειγμα I. vi. 14. xiii. 3.
παραδείγματα VIII. x. 4.
παραδιδόντες X. ix. 18.
παράδοξα VI. ii. 8.
παραινεῖ II. x. 3. παραινοῦντας X. vii. 8.
παρακαλεῖ I. xiii. 15. παρακαλεῖν X. ix.

10. παρακέκληται X. iv. 9. παρακλητέον IX. xi. 5.
παρακαταθήκη V. ii. 3. παρακαταθήκην V. viii. 4. παρακαταθήκας X. viii. 7.
παράκλησις I. xiii. 18.
παρακολουθεῖ II. iii. 7. III. ii. 15.
παρακούειν VII. vi. 1.
παραλαμβάνομεν III. iii. 10. παραλαβόντες IV. i. 20. παραλαβόντων IX. vii. 7.
παραλείπει V. x. 5. παραλείπουσι I. vi. 15. παραλειπόντων X. ix. 12.
παραλόγως V. viii. 7.
παραλελειμμένα I. xiii. 15.
παρημελημένη X. iv. 9.
παραμεμίχθαι X. vii. 3.
παραμυθητικὸν IX. xi. 3.
παράνομος V. i. 8, 11, 12. παράνομον V. i. 8. ii. 8, 9. παράνομα I. xi. 4.
παραπλήσιον I. iii. 4. III. viii. 12. IV. ix. 2. VII. vi. 7. IX. ix. 10. X. v. 5.
παραπλησίως IV. iii. 1. VI. xiii. 1. VII. v. 1. IX. ix. 10.
παρασείσαντι IV. iii. 15.
παρασκευάζει X. vii. 6. παρασκευάζουσι VII. xiv. 5.
παρασκευὴ III. viii. 15. παρασκευαῖς III. viii. 9.
παραστάτην V. ii. 5.
παρατάττοντες III. viii. 5.
παραφέρεται I. xiii. 15. παραφερόμενον I. xiii. 16.
παραφυλάξαι I. vi. 2.
παρακλῖνον II. i. 1.
παρῆν VI. viii. 4.
παρεμβαίνουσι VIII. x. 3. παρεμβαίνων II. ix. 8. IV. v. 13. παρεζεύχθημεν I. v. 1.
παρέκβασις VIII. x. 2. παρεκβάσεις VIII. x. 1. παρεκβάσεσιν VIII. xi. 6.
πάρεργα I. vii. 19.
παρέχει I. x. 4. παρέχουσι X. vi. 3.
παρίησι IX. viii. 1. παριτέον X. i. 2.
παρελθὼν IV. ii. 20.
παροιμία VIII. ix. 1. παροιμίαν VIII. iii. 8. παροιμίᾳ VII. ii. 10. παροιμίας IX. viii. 2.
παροιμιαζόμενοι V. i. 15.
παροίχεται IX. vii. 6.
παρόμοιον III. viii. 13.
παρορᾶν IV. iii. 30.
παρορμῆσαι X. ix. 3.
παρουσία IX. xi. 2, 3, 5, 6. παρουσίας IX. v. 3.
παῤῥησίαν IX. ii. 9.
παῤῥησιαστικὸν IV. iii. 28.
πάρφασις VII. vi. 3.
πάρεισι V. x. 5. παροῦσα II. ii. 11. παρὸν I. xiii. 10. VII. iii. 2. VIII. iii. 5. παρόντος II. ii. 5. VIII. ix. 5. IX. iv. 6. vii. 6. παρούσης VII. iii. 13. VIII. i. 7. X. v. 3. παρόντι I. x. 13. X. iv. 11. παρόντων V. vii. 3.
πᾶς II. ii. 3. vi. 8. III. i. 14. v. 15. ix. 3. XI. i. 2. IV. i. 39. iii. 6. V. ix. 3. x. 4. VI. ii. 5. VII. vi. 4. ix. 4. IX. vii. 3. viii. 8. xi. 4. X. ix. 15. πᾶσα I. i. 1, 4. iv. 1. xiii. 18. II. i. 6. iii. 5, 10. vi. 2, 9, 18. III. iii. 12. x. 9. IV. ii. 15. VI. iii. 3. iv. 4. ἅπαν VIII. i. 3. X. viii. 8. πᾶν I. iii. 5. xii. 2. xiii. 7, 10. II. i. 8. iv. 3. vi. 18. III. ii. 16. iii. 1, 7. x. 11. IV. i. 40. ii. 11. iii. 19. v. 9. viii. 8. V. vii. 3. ix. 2. xi. 9. VII. iii. 10. IX. x. 3. ἅπαν III. i. 13. V. ix. 1, 2. xi. 7. παντὸς I. vi. 8. vii. 17, 23. II. i. 5. ix. 2. VI. ii. 3. VII. iii. 9. πάσης II. ii. 8. vi. 9. III. vii. 6. VI. vi. 1. παντὶ I. vii. 10, 12. II. iii. 3. vi. 4. ix. 6. III. vi. 7. vii. 1. IV. v. 9. V. ii. 11. VII. vii. 3. πᾶσῃ II. iii. 3. IV. ix. 3. ἁπάσῃ I. vii. 1. πάντα I. i. 1. ii. 1. iv. 7. vii. 3, 11. xiii. 17. II. ii. 7. iii. 7. vi. 18. vii. 14. III. i. 11, 18. ii. 10. vi. 3. vii. 10. viii. 10. xi. 4. IV. i. 2. ii. 14, 20, 21. v. 7, 14. vi. 1, 2. V. v. 10, 15. vii. 2. ix. 17. VII. i. 6. πάντες I. vii. 1. xii. 8. II. i. 6, 7. III. i. 11. v. 17. viii. 5. IV. i. 39, 40. iii. 29. VI. iii. 2. ἅπαντες III. i. 5. πᾶσαι I. vi. 15. II. vii. 11. viii. 1. IV. i. 43. viii. 12. VI. ix. 2. πάντων I. i. 4. iv. 1. vii. 8, 14. x. 11. II. vi. 3. III. iii. 1. xi. 6. IV. vii. 1. ἁπάντων I. vi. 4. πασῶν VII. vii. 3. ἁπάσας I. i. 4. III. ix. 5. ἅπασι I. iii. 1. vi. 11. vii. 18, 20. xiii. 11. IV. ii. 12. X. ix. 6. πᾶσι I. iv. 3. ix. 4. II. iii. 7, 8. vi. 5. vii. 11, 13, 15. ix. 6, 9. III. vii. 1. IV. i. 10. viii. 10. V. vi. 4. πάσαις I. vi. 3. II. viii. 1. πάσας V. i. 3. vii. 4. ἁπάσαις I. iv. 4. ἅπαντα I. vi. 12. viii. 5, 14. III. i. 17. IV. v. 7. ἅπαντας I. vi. 15. x. 13. xi. 3. πᾶσαν I. x. 13. II. ii. 7. vii. 3. III.

x. 3. IV. ii. 1. πᾶσαν I. vii. 5. ix. 6. II. iii. 9. III. ix. 4. IV. iii. 18. V. xi. 1. VI. v. 6.

πάσχει III. vii. 5. V. v. 14. ix. 6. 9. xi. 3. 5. πάσχομεν V. viii. 3. πάσχουσι IX. iv. 9. πάσχειν II. v. 5. IV. i. 7. 8. V. ix. 3. xi. 9. VII. iv. 5. VIII. xiv. 4. IX. vii. 1. 6. 7. ix. 2. πάσχων III. i. 3. πάσχοντος III. x. 2. πάσχον V. iv. 12. v. 9. ἔπασχε V. iv. 12. v. 9. πάσχοντες VIII. xiii. 4. παθεῖν II. ix. 6. III. viii. 7. 8. ἔπαθον II. ix. 6. III. viii. 16. παθόντι III. i. 8. V. iv. 5. IX. vii. 5. 6. πάθωσι IV. iii. 25. παθὼν IV. iii. 25. πάθοι V. v. 3. VIII. ii. 4. ἔπαθε V. xi. 5. VIII. xiii. 9. παθόντα VIII. xiii. 9. παθόντος VIII. xiii. 10. 11. παθόντες VIII. xiii. 10. IX. vii. 1. παθόντας IX. vii. 1. πεισόμεθα III. v. 7. πεισομένου X. iv. 7. πεισομένων IX. ix. 2. πεπονθὼς IV. iii. 24. V. ix. 3. πεπονθέναι IV. iii. 25. IX. iv. 1. πέπονθε IX. v. 3. πεπονθότας IX. vii. 2. πεπονθὸς IX. vii. 4.

πατάξαι III. viii. 7. V. ix. 14, 16. VIII. ix. 3. πατάξειεν III. i. 17. πατάξαντι V. iv. 5. ἐπάταξεν V. ii. 5. v. 4. πατάξῃ V. iv. 4.

πατέρα V. viii. 3. VII. iv. 5. vi. 2. VIII. vii. 1. ix. 3. x. 4. xiv. 4. IX. ii. 4. πατὴρ V. viii. 3. VIII. xi. 2. πατρὸς I. xiii. 18, 19. VIII. x. 4. πατρὶ VIII. vii. 1. x. 4. xiv. 4. IX. ii. 1, 6, 8.

πατρικὴ VIII. x. 4. xi. 2. X. ix. 12. πατρικὴν IX. ii. 8. πατρικῆς VIII. xii. 2. πατρικὸν V. vi. 8.

πατρίδας IX. viii. 9.

παῦλα IV. v. 10.

παύει IV. v. 10. παύεται III. iii. 12. παύεσθαι VII. vi. 2. ἐπαύσατο VII. ii. 10. παύονται IV. v. 8. VIII. iii. 3. 5. παύσεται III. v. 14.

πειθαρχεῖ I. xiii. 17. IX. viii. 8. πειθαρχεῖν X. ix. 4. πειθαρχήσειν X. ix. 10. πειθαρχοῦσι X. ix. 9.

πειθαρχικὸν I. xiii. 18.

πείσει III. iii. 11. πείθεται I. xiii. 18. IX. viii. 6. πείθεσθαι VI. xii. 2. IX. ii. 1. πεισθῆναι III. v. 7. ἐπείσθη VII. ii. 7. ix. 4. πείθηται I. iv. 7. πέπεισται VII. viii. 4. πεπεῖσθαι VII. ii. 10. viii. 4. πεπεισμένος VII. ii. 10. πεπεισμένοι X. i. 2. ἐπέπειστο VII. ii. 10.

πεινῆν III. v. 7. πεινῶντες III. viii. 11. πεινῶσι III. x. 6.

πεῖραι VII. iv. 3.

πειρᾶται V. iv. 4. πειρῶνται X. iii. 4. ix. 21. πειρασθῶμεν X. ix. 23. πειρώμεναι VII. vii. 6. πειρατέον I. ii. 3. vii. 2, 22. II. ii. 5. vii. 11. IX. ii. 9. iv. 10. X. ix. 2, 17.

πέλας II. vii. 15. IV. ii. 22. vii. 13. IX. vi. 4. viii. 7. ix. 5.

πένης IV. ii. 13. VIII. viii. 6.

πενίᾳ VIII. i. 2. πενίαν III. vi. 3. 4. vii. 13.

πένεσθαι IV. i. 35. πενόμενος I. iv. 3.

πέντε III. viii. 1. V. v. 15, 16. VI. iii. 1.

πέψαι IV. v. 10.

πέρας I. iv. 5. III. vi. 6.

πεπερασμένου II. vi. 14.

περὶ cum genitivo IV. i. 1. 45.

περὶ cum accusativo IV. i. 1, 3, 6. viii. 12. VI. iv. 4. v. 7.

περιάπτου I. viii. 12.

περιγίνεται II. iv. 3.

περιγεγράφθω I. vii. 17.

περιγραφῇ I. vii. 17.

περιέλκειν VII. ii. 1. περιέλκεται VII. iii. 13.

περίεργοι IX. x. 2.

περιέχει V. i. 11. περιέχοι I. ii. 7. περιέχεται VI. iv. 2.

Περικλέα VI. v. 5.

περιλαβεῖν I. ii. 3. III. ix. 7. V. ii. 6.

περίλυπος IV. ii. 18.

περιορᾶν IV. v. 6.

περιμάχητα IX. viii. 4, 9.

περιπίπτοντα VII. xiii. 3. περιποιεῖν I. ix. 11. περιποιοῦντες III. viii. 16. περιποιῇ I. x. 14.

περιποιοῖτο IX. viii. 5. περιποιούμεθα X. vii. 5. περιποιούμενος IX. viii. 9. περιποιουμένη X. vii. 6.

περισσοὺς VI. viii. 4. περιττὰ VI. vii. 5.

περιτίθησι X. ix. 15.

περιφερείᾳ I. xiii. 10.

περιχαρὴς IV. iii. 18.

Πέρσαις V. vii. 2. VIII. x. 4.

Περσικὴ VIII. x. 4.

πῇ I. xiii. 19. VII. viii. 3. xiii. 1. IX. viii. 3. ix. 4.

πηλίκον V. vi. 8.

πεπηρωμένοις I. ix. 4.

πήρωσις V. ii. 13. πήρωσιν III. v. 15. πηρώσεις VII. i. 3. v. 1. vi. 6.

πιθανολογοῦντος I. iii. 4.
πιθανώτερον I. vi. 7.
πιθανώτατα I. vi. 15.
πικρῶς IV. v. 10. πικρὰ III. iv. 4. X. iii. 8. πικροῖς VII. xii. 2.
πίνων III. xi. 3.
πίστεις II. ii. 4. πιστὸν V. xi. 8. VIII. i. 6.
πιστεύομεν VI. iv. 2. πιστεύουσι VI. viii. 6. VII. iii. 4. πιστεύειν VII. iii. 4. xiv. 3. VIII. iv. 3. IX. ii. 1. πιστεῦσαι VIII. iv. 3. πιστεύοντες VIII. viii. 2. ἀπιστεῦσαι IX. i. 9. πιστεύσασι I. v. 5. πιστεύσαιμι IV. vii. 1. πιστεύοιντο X. i. 4. πεπιστεύκασι VIII. i. 7. πιστευθῇ VIII. iii. 8. πιστεύω VI. iii. 4.
πιστὸν IX. viii. 2. πιστοὶ X. i. 3. πιστότερα X. ii. 4.
Πιττακὸν IX. vi. 2.
πλάνην I. iii. 2. 3. πλάνας VIII. i. 3.
Πλάτων I. iv. 5. III. iii. 2. X. ii. 3.
πλειστάκις VII. xiii. 6.
πλεονάζει II. vi. 5.
πλεοναχῶς IV. iv. 4. V. i. 6. VI. ix. 4.
πλεονεκτεῖ V. ii. 2. ix. 12. πλεονεκτῇ V. ii. 2. ἐπλεονέκτει V. ix. 9.
πλεονέκτημα V. i. 8. 9. 10. ii. 4. πλεονεκτήματα IX. viii. 4.
πλεονεξία V. i. 10. πλεονεξίας IX. vi. 4.
πλευρᾶς III. iii. 3.
πλευρῖτιν V. xi. 8.
πληγῆς III. v. 15.
πλῆθος IV. i. 21. VI. viii. 5. IX. x. 1. πλήθους VIII. x. 3. IX. x. 1. πλήθει III. xi. 3. IV. i. 19. VIII. xii. 2. πλήθεσι III. viii. 9.
πληρωθῇ III. xi. 3.
πλημμελὴς I. ix. 17.
πλὴν I. vi. 10. xiii. 13. II. iv. 14. xii. 8. III. iii. 17. ix. 5. x. 5. 7. IV. i. 29. iii. 28. vi. 5. V. ix. 16. VI. xiii. 1. VIII. x. 6. IX. vi. 4. x. 6. X. iii. 8. v. 5. 11. vi. 6. viii. 7.
πληροῦντες III. xi. 3. πληρουμένων VIII. i. 6.
πληγῇ V. iv. 4. πληγῆναι V. v. 4. καταπεπληγμένου VII. vii. 6.
πλησίον V. v. 17. ix. 14.
πλοῖον I. i. 3.
πλοῦν II. ix. 4. VIII. ix. 5.
πλουσίῳ VIII. viii. 6. πλουσίων X. viii. 11. πλουσίους IV. i. 15.
πλουτεῖν IV. i. 20. VIII. x. 3. X. iii. 9. πλουτοῦντι IV. i. 21. VIII. i. 1. πλουτοῦντες IV. iii. 19.
πλοῦτος I. i. 3. v. 8. IV. i. 6. iii. 18. πλούτου I. viii. 15. πλούτῳ IV. i. 6. 20. πλοῦτον I. iii. 3. iv. 3. vii. 1. IV. ii. 20. iii. 18. V. iii. 7. VII. iv. 2. VIII. x. 5.
πλωτῆρσι VIII. ix. 5.
πνίγῃ VII. ii. 10.
πόθεν IV. i. 34. X. iv. 3. ix. 18.
ποθοῦντα I. vii. 9. ποθῇ IX. v. 3.
πόθον II. ii. 2.
πῃ III. i. 3. X. iv. 3.
ποιεῖ I. vii. 7. 16. x. 12. II. ii. 6. vi. 2. III. viii. 2. xi. 5. xii. 2. IV. iii. 16. 19. v. 13. V. v. 11. vi. 5. ix. 11. x. 3. xi. 5. VI. ii. 5. viii. 5. xii. 5. 6. 8. 10. xiii. 7. VII. ii. 7. vi. 4. x. 3. xiv. 3. 7. VIII. x. 5. xi. 1. 3. IX. iv. 5. xi. 2. ποιουμένους I. iii. 7. πεποιήμεθα I. v. 7. ἐποίουν I. vi. 2. ποιεῖται I. ix. 8. ποιῆσαι I. ix. 8. II. iv. 2. III. viii. 7. IV. viii. 3. V. v. 11. VI. viii. 5. X. ix. 3. ποιεῖν I. x. 13. xi. 5. 6. xiii. 2. II. i. 4. ii. 8. vi. 18. IV. i. 7. 8. 34. 37. ii. 19. 21. iii. 24. 35. vii. 3. 5. xiii. 8. V. i. 14. ix. 9. 10. 11. 14. 16. VI. ii. 6. xii. 1. VII. ix. 6. VIII. v. 1. xiii. 8. xiv. 4. IX. i. 5. 7. ii. 5. 7. iii. 1. vi. 4. vii. 1. 7. ix. 2. 3. xi. 6. X. ii. 2. vii. 8. viii. 7. ix. 17. ποιοῦντες II. i. 4. iv. 6. ix. 7. VIII. iii. 9. ix. 5. xiii. 4. IX. i. 6. 7. ποιοῦσι II. i. 5. iv. 6. ix. 5. III. v. 10. viii. 14. x. 9. IV. i. 35. VI. xii. 4. 5. VII. iii. 7. IX. xii. 2. X. v. 5. ποιεῖσθαι II. iii. 1. VIII. xiii. 10. ποιήσῃ II. iv. 2. IX. ii. 5. X. iv. 2. ποιοῦμεν II. vii. 9. X. v. 4. ἐποίησε III. x. 7. ποιήσεις I. x. 12. III. iii. 11. IV. i. 24. ii. 10. 20. vi. 5. viii. 8. 10. VI. vii. 7. IX. vii. 6. ποιοῦντος IV. i. 16. ποιοῦντι IV. ii. 12. vi. 7. VI. iv. 4. ποιεῖσθε VII. i. 1. πεπραγμένοις VII. i. 1. ποιούντων VII. iv. 2. πεποίηται X. ix. 20. πεποιῆσθαι X. ix. 13. ποιῇ IV. ii. 19. 21. ποιῶν IV. iii. 3. 5. ii. 5. VII. vi. 4. X. iii. 12. ποιοῦσα VI. xii. 3. ποιοῦνται VI. xii. 7. ποιοῦν V. iv. 12. v. 9. ποιοῦνται V. v. 6. ποιήσαν V. v. 14. ποιουμένη VI. iv. 4. ποιήσαντος X. iv. 7. πεποιηκότι IX. vii. 6. πεποιηκότας IX. vii. 2. X. ix. 18. ποιοῦντα VIII. xiii. 2. ποιήσας VIII. xiv. 4. IX. vii. 4. X. v. 5. πεποιήκασι VIII. xii. 5. ποιήσαντι VIII.

xii. 2. ποιήσαντα IX. vii. 4. ποιούμενα VIII. ix. 3. ποιήσεις VII. iv. 2. vi. 7. ἐποίει IV. iii. 7. vii. 14. V. iv. 12. v. 9. vii. 3. ποιήσωσι IV. iii. 25. ποιήσαντος IV. iii. 25. ποιήσουσι VII. xii. 5. IX. ix. 2. xi. 1. ποιησαίμεθα X. iii. 12. ποιοῖτο X. vii. 6. ποιητέον I. vii. 19. VII. i. 4. VIII. xiii. 9. IX. i. 7. x. 1. ποιῆται IV. i. 20.
ποιήματα IX. vii. 3.
ποίησις VI. iv. 1, 2, 5. ποιήσεως VI. iv. 5. v. 1, 4. X. iv. 2.
ποιητὴν VII. xiv. 8. ποιηταὶ IX. vii. 3.
ποιητικὴ VI. iv. 3, 6. ποιητικοῦ X. iv. 8. ποιητικῆς VI. ii. 3, 5. iv. 2. ποιητικὸν V. i. 5. ποιητικαῖς VII. iii. 9. ποιητικὰ I. vi. 8. V. i. 13. ii. 12. VIII. vi. 1.
ποιητὸν VI. ii. 5. iv. 1.
ποικίλον I. x. 14.
ποιμένα VIII. xi. 1.
ποία V. i. 1. X. ix. 23. ποία τις I. ix. 7. II. vi. 1, 4. V. ii. 7. ποιά τις X. iv. 1. ix. 20. ποίας I. ii. 6. II. i. 8. ii. 1. III. x. 1. V. i. 1. X. viii. 7. ποίᾳ I. vi. 2, 3. ποῖα I. vi. 10. III. i. 10. iii. 20. v. 23. vi. 6. IV. iii. 1. V. vii. 7. VI. i. 2. v. 1. vii. 7. VII. iii. 1. iv. 1. X. ix. 20, 21, 23. ποῖον I. vii. 19. xii. 2. III. i. 9. ii. 16. V. vii. 4. ποιοὺς I. ix. 8. VIII. iii. 1. X. iii. 2. ποίαις II. ix. 7. IV. v. 13. X. ix. 20, 21. ποίων III. i. 9. ποίου III. i. 10. ποῖοι III. ii. 11. v. 20. viii. 17. ποίας X. v. 11.
ποιότητες, ποιοτήτων X. iii. 1.
πολεμεῖν VII. vi. 1. X. vii. 6. πολεμῶμεν X. vii. 6.
πολεμικὴ I. i. 4. πολεμικοῖς III. vi. 4. viii. 6. IV. i. 1. X. vii. 6. πολεμικώτατα I. x. 13. πολεμικὸν IX. ii. 1. πολεμικοὶ X. vii. 6, 7.
πολέμων III. i. 17. πολεμίων V. xi. 8. πολεμίους II. vi. 2. X. vii. 6.
πολέμου III. viii. 6. πολέμῳ I. vi. 4. III. vi. 8. ix. 4. πόλεμον III. vi. 10. VIII. ix. 5. X. vii. 6.
πόλις IV. ii. 15. V. v. 6. xi. 3. VII. x. 3. IX. viii. 6. x. 3. πόλεως I. ii. 8. VIII. ix. 5. x. 3. xii. 7. IX. x. 3. πόλει I. ii. 8. VI. xiii. 8. VII. x. 3. X. ix. 13. πόλιν IV. ii. 11. V. xi. 3. VI. viii. 2. πόλεις IV. i. 42. VIII. i. 4. iv. 4. IX. vi. 1, 2. X. ix. 21. πόλεων X. ix. 13. πόλεσι I. ii. 6. 8. II. i. 5. III. vi. 9. VIII. iv. 4. X. ix. 14, 19.
πολιτεία II. i. 5. X. ix. 23. πολιτείας II. i. 5. V. ii. 12. VI. viii. 4. VIII. x. 1, 3. X. ix. 22. πολιτείαν VIII. x. 1. πολιτεῖαι V. vii. 5. VIII. x. 1. πολιτείαις VIII. xiv. 3. πολιτειῶν III. iii. 18. VIII. xi. 1. X. ix. 21, 23.
πολιτεύεσθαι VI. viii. 2. X. vii. 6. πολιτεύονται X. ix. 23. πολιτεύοιντο III. iii. 6. πολιτευόμενοι X. ix. 18.
πολίτῃ V. ii. 11. πολίτην VIII. ix. 3. πολῖται III. viii. 1. VIII. xi. 5. πολίτας I. ix. 8. xiii. 2. II. i. 5. πολίταις I. vii. 6. VIII. ix. 2. IX. ii. 9. X. vii. 6.
πολιτικὸς I. v. 1. xiii. 2. III. iii. 11. X. viii. 4. πολιτικὴ I. ii. 5, 9. iii. 2. xiii. 7. III. viii. 1. VI. vii. 4. viii. 1, 2, 3. ix. 4, 5. IX. vi. 2. πολιτικῆς I. iii. 5. viii. 15. ix. 8. xiii. 4. V. ii. 12. VIII. ix. 4, 6. X. vii. 6. ix. 18, 19. πολιτικὴν I. iv. 1. VI. vii. 3. xiii. 8. VII. xi. 1. VIII. ix. 5. πολιτικῶν I. iv. 6. X. ix. 18. πολιτικοῦ I. v. 4, 6. V. vi. 9. vii. 1. X. vii. 6. πολιτικὸν I. vii. 6. xiii. 7. V. vi. 4, 9. VIII. xii. 7. IX. ix. 2. πολιτικῷ I. xiii. 8. πολιτικῇ II. iii. 10. V. i. 13. IX. i. 1. πολιτικὰ III. viii. 9. X. ix. 18. πολιτικοὺς VI. v. 5. X. ix. 18. πολιτικοὶ VI. viii. 4. X. ix. 19. πολιτικαὶ VIII. xii. 1. X. vii. 7. πολιτικοῖς X. vii. 6. ix. 20.
πολιτικῶς IX. x. 6.
πολλάκις I. iv. 3. x. 7, 8. II. i. 4. iv. 3. III. viii. 13. IV. ii. 3. V. i. 5, 15. x. 3. VIII. iii. 5. v. 4. IX. i. 2. ii. 6. X. vi. 5.
πολλαχοῦ V. v. 4.
πολλαχῶς II. vi. 14. III. xi. 4. V. ix. 11.
πολλοστὸν X. v. 11.
πολυειδὴς IV. i. 38. πολυειδεῖς VIII. xii. 2.
Πολύκλειτον VI. vii. 1.
πολύκοινον I. ix. 4.
πολύξενος IX. x. 1.
πολυπράγμονες VI. viii. 4.
πολὺ I. xi. 4. II. vi. 7. ix. 5. III. xii. 7. IV. i. 32. v. 14. V. v. 5. VI. vii. 4. VIII. iii. 5. vii. 4. x. 6. IX. iii. 4. X. v. 4, 5. vii. 8. viii. 4. πολλῶν I. i. 3. x. 12, 14. xi. 2. VII. x.

4. xiii. 2. VIII. vi. 2. vii. 5. IX. iv. 9. X. i. 3. viii. 5, 9. πολλὰ I. i. 3. vii. 23. viii. 15. x. 12. xiii. 7. II. vi. 6. vii. 2. III. vii. 7. viii. 6. 11. ix. 3. xii. 2. IV. i. 35. ii. 19, 20. v. 2. ix. 3. V. ii. 10. vii. 6. viii. 3. VII. ix. 2, 6. VIII. xi. 8. IX. i. 9. iv. 8. viii. 9. X. iii. 12. viii. 2. πολλοῖς I. iii. 3. viii. 11. III. iv. 5. VI. viii. 4. VII. xiv. 5. VIII. vi. 2, 3. 7. IX. iv. 7. x. 2, 4, 5. X. viii. 11. ix. 8. πολλοὶ I. iv. 2. v. 2, 3, 8. viii. 7. II. iv. 6. III. vii. 9. xi. 4. IV. i. 35, 37, 38. iii. 22. iv. 4. V. i. 15. VII. vii. 1, 5, 6. viii. 2. ix. 2. xiii. 5. VIII. ii. 4. iv. 1. vi. 3. viii. 1, 2. xiv. 4. IX. vii. 1. viii. 4, 5. 11. ix. 4. x. 6. X. vi. 3. ix. 9, 14. πολλοὺς I. v. 3. II. ii. 8. III. viii. 13. IV. iii. 28. VIII. vi. 2. IX. viii. 4. x. 6. X. i. 2. ix. 3, 12. πολλαὶ I. vi. 4. ix. 11. III. i. 10. VI. vii. 4. VII. xi. 3. X. iii. 7. iv. 3. v. 11. πολλὰς I. x. 4, 12. IV. iv. 3. VIII. v. 1. IX. ii. 2. viii. 9. πολλαῖς I. x. 12. πολλῷ I. x. 14. IV. i. 40. VIII. iv. 3. πολλὴν II. ii. 8. III. xii. 6. VI. viii. 4. X. i. 2. πολλὸν IV. v. 10. VI. ix. 2, 6. IX. viii. 9. πολλῶν IX. i. 9. viii. 4. πολλῇ V. i. 7. πλείω II. viii. 4. VIII. i. 1. πλεῖον I. vii. 23. xiii. 8. II. i. 1. vi. 4. viii. 5, 7. III. xi. 3. V. iii. 4. ix. 9. VIII. viii. 6. xiv. 1, 2. IX. viii. 4. X. vii. 5. πλείους I. vii. 15. V. ii. 7. IX. x. 2. X. v. 11. πλείω I. vii. 1, 3, 19. II. ii. 6. vii. 11. IV. v. 7, 11. VI. i. 2. VIII. i. 7. iv. 4. ix. 2. IX. i. 4. iv. 6. viii. 9. X. iv. 1. πλέον II. ix. 8. IV. v. 4. V. i. 10. ii. 9. iii. 2, 14. iv. 6, 11, 13, 14. v. 17. vi. 4, 6. ix. 8, 9, 10, 13, 15. xi. 7. VI. viii. 4. VIII. xi. 4. xiii. 7, 11. xiv. 1. IX. viii. 11. πλανῶνται III. iii. 11. IV. iii. 24. IX. x. 5. X. viii. 5. πλείοσι V. iv. 6. VIII. xiii. 3. πλείοσιν V. xi. 4. X viii. 6. πλείστη II. viii. 5. VIII. xii. 6 πλεῖστον II. viii. 5. III. iv. 5. VIII. vii. 4. x. 2. xi. 8. πλείστῳ I. ix. 8. πλεῖστα I. viii. 7. VII. i. 5. VIII. x. 3. πλείστων I. iv. 2. IV. viii. 4. VII. vii. 1. x. 4. πλείσταις IV. ii. 10. VIII. x. 3. πλεῖ-σται IX. iii. 1. πλείσταις X. ix. 13. πλείστους VIII. xiii. 8. IX. x. 1, 3. πλείστοις VIII. i. 1. IX. vii. 1. πλεῖ-στοι IV. vii. 13. VII. xi. 2. VIII. x. 1. IX. x. 3.

πολυφιλία VIII. i. 5.

πολύφιλον IX. x. 1. πολύφιλοι IX. x. 6. πολυφιλώτατος IX. x. 5.

πολυχρόνιον I. vi. 6. VII x. 4. IX. vii. 6. πολυχρόνια IV. ii. 14.

πολυωφελὲς I. iii. 7.

πονεῖ V. vi. 6. VII. xiv. 5. πονεῖν VI. i. 2. X. vi. 6. πονῶσιν VII. vii. 5. πεπονῆσθαι I. xiii. 2. πεπονημένοις I. xii. 7.

πονηρία VII. viii. 1. πονηρίαν V. ii. 2. xi. 4. VII. xiv. 8.

πονηρὸς III. v. 13. V. xi. 5. VII. x. 3, 4. xiv. 8. πονηροῦ IX. ii. 5. vii. 1. πονηρὸν IX. iii. 3. πονηροὶ V. viii. 8. πονηροῖς VII. x. 4. πονηροὺς IV. i. 42.

πόνος III. ix. 3. πόνοις I. vi. 4. IX. vi. 4. πόνους II. ii. 8.

Πόντον VII. v. 2.

πορθοῦντας IV. i. 42. πεπορθημέναι VI. ii. 6.

πορίζειν IV. i. 34. IX. ix. 1. πορίζουσι IV. i. 35. VIII. iii. 2. v. 1. viii. 6. πορίζοντες VIII. ix. 5. πορίζων VIII. xiv. 3. ποριζόμενοι VIII. ix. 4. πορίσασθαι X. ix. 3. πεπόρισται IX. i. 2. πορισθῆναι III. iii. 13.

πορνοβοσκοὶ IV. i. 40.

πόῤῥω III. viii. 16. xi. 7. V. i. 7. VII. v. 6. VIII. xii. 4. X. ix. 20. πορ-ῥωτέρω II. viii. 4.

πορφύρᾳ IV. ii. 20.

ποσαχῶς V. i. 8.

πόσον II. ix. 7, 8. IV. v. 13. VIII. vii. 3. IX. x. 3. πόσα III. v. 23. V. v. 15. ποσὰ III. i. 16. V. v. 10. vii. 7. ποσῷ I. vi. 3. πόσου IV. ii. 9.

ποτε VIII. iii. 2. viii. 6.

πότε V. ix. 15. VIII. xii. 1, 4.

ποτὲ I. ii. 3. vi. 5. vii. 1, 12. III. v. 17. viii. 2. IV. i. 39. v. 5. V. ix. 8. IX. iv. 4. xii. 2.

πότερον I. iv. 5. vii. 11. ix. 1. x. 1. xiii. 10. III. i. 4, 23. xii. 5. IV. viii. 7. V. ii. 11. ix. 1, 3, 8. xi. 1. VI. ix. 1. VII. iii. 1, 2. iv. 1. vi. 7. ix. 1. VIII. i. 7. ii. 2. iv. 6. viii. 1. IX. ix. 2. x. 3. xi. 1. 2. X. iv. 11. viii. 5. ποτέρου III. xii. 5. IX. i. 5. πό-τερα I. xii. 1. III. iii. 1. VIII. xiii. 10. IX. ii. 1, 4. X. viii. 7. ποτέρως IX. vii. 2.

ποτέρως V. viii. 10.

Πουλυδάμας III. viii. 2.

ποδὸς I. vii. 11.

πρᾶγμα II. vi. 4, 6. πράγματος I. iii. 4. II. vi. 5, 8. viii. 7, 8. V. viii. 10. x. 4. VII. iii. 6. πράγματα II. iv. 4. V. iii. 5. x. 7. πραγμάτων IV. vi. 1.

πραγματεία II. ii. 1. iii. 10. πραγματείαν II. iii. 9.

πραγματεύεσθαι X. vi. 6. πραγματεύονται I. xiii. 7. IV. i. 43.

πρακτέον II. ii. 1. IV. ix. 4. πρακτέα IV. ix. 5.

πρακτικὸς I. ix. 10. V. v. 17. x. 8. VII. x. 2. πρακτικοὺς I. ix. 8. πρακτικὴ I. vii. 13. II. iii. 6. VI. ii. 2, 5. iv. 2. vii. 7. viii. 2. xiii. 7. πρακτικαὶ I. v. 4. xii. 6. V. i. 3. πρακτικαὶ III. v. 21. πρακτικοῖς I. ii. 7. VI. xi. 4. πρακτικὸν IV. iii. 27. πρακτικῆς VI. ii. 3. πρακτικοῦ VI. ii. 3. πρακτικὴν VI. v. 4, 6. πρακτικὰς VI. xii. 10. πρακτικῶν X. vii. 5, 6. πρακτικοῖς X. viii. 12. πρακτικώτεροι VI. vii. 7. xii. 1. πρακτικωτέρους VI. xii. 7.

πρακτὸν I. vi. 13. vii. 1. VI. ii. 5. iv. 1. v. 3, 6. vii. 6. viii. 2, 8. πρακτὰ I. vi. 4. VI. v. 6. xi. 3. VII. iii. 6. IX. vi. 2. πρακτῶν I. ii. 1. iv. 1. vii. 1, 8. II. ii. 3. III. iii. 7, 15. V. x. 4. VI. v. 6. vii. 6. xii. 10. πρακτοῖς X. ix. 1.

πρᾶξις I. i. 1, 4. iii. 6. vii. 10. II. vi. 18. III. i. 15, 18, 20. V. iv. 4. VI. iv. 1, 2, 5. VII. xiv. 8. VI. vii. 7. X. viii. 9. πράξεως III. i. 6. IV. i. 14. V. ix. 9. VI. ii. 1, 2, 4, 5. v. 3, 4. VIII. i. 2. πράξει I. vii. 1. II. iii. 3. III. i. 13. IV. iii. 15. ix. 6. VI. ii. 4. VII. ii. 9. πρᾶξιν III. i. 10. v. 11. viii. 3. VII. xiv. 7. IX. vii. 5, 6. viii. 9. X. vii. 5. πράξεις I. i. 2. vii. 11, 14. viii. 2, 3, 11, 13. xii. 2. II. ii. 1. iii. 3, 8, 9. vi. 10, 12. vii. 1. III. i. 6, 10, 27. iii. 15. v. 1, 22. IV. i. 12. ii. 1. V. i. 1. VII. viii. 3. xiv. 4. VIII. i. 2. iii. 6. IX. ii. 6, 7. viii. 7, 10. ix. 5. X. vi. 3. vii. 6. viii. 5, 7. πράξεων I. i. 3, 5. iii. 5. II. vi. 18. vii. 11. III. ii. 1. iii. 15. v. 5, 22. IV. iii. 35. viii. 12. VII. iii. 11. X. vii. 7. πράξεσι I. viii. 12. II. ii. 3. vi. 16. viii. 2. ix. 1. III. i. 6, 7. v. 19. IV. vii. 1. VI. i. 1. VII. viii. 4. IX. ix. 6. X. i. 4. viii. 1.

πρᾶος I. xiii. 20. IV. v. 3, 4. πρᾴως II. i. 7. πρᾶον II. vii. 10. πρᾴους II. ix. 7. IV. v. 13. πρᾴων V. i. 14.

πρᾳότης IV. v. 1, 3. πρᾳότητα II. vii. 10. IV. v. 1. IX. iv. 1. πρᾳότητι IV. v. 12.

πρᾶσις V. ii. 13.

πράττει III. i. 6, 16, 17. ii. 4. v. 13, 17. vii. 5, 6. IV. vii. 5. V. i. 17. VII. i. 6. ii. 9, 10. IX. iv. 3. viii. 1, 8. X. ix. 15. πράξῃ III. i. 7. V. viii. 6. πράττειν I. ii. 7. iv. 2. viii. 4, 15. x. 13. II. ii. 2. iv. 3, 5. III. i. 6, 14. iii. 11. v. 2, 7, 19. IV. i. 7, 8. iii. 28. ix. 4, 7. V. viii. 4. ix. 3. VI. v. 6. viii. 4. ix. 2. x. 2. xii. 1, 6, 7, 9. xiii. 1, 7. VII. ii. 1, 3, 5, 9. iii. 5, 6, 9. IX. iv. 8. vii. 4. viii. 1, 5, 7, 9. x. 2. X. vi. 3. vii. 2. viii. 4, 6, 7, 10, 11. ix. 1, 11, 10. πράττουσι I. iii. 7. vii. 1. II. iv. 1, 4, 6. vii. 15. III. i. 11. v. 18. viii. 11. IV. iii. 21. V. viii. 1. VI. viii. 2. xii. 7. πράττεται I. vii. 1. viii. 15. II. iv. 3. III. i. 4. V. i. 4. VIII. x. 4. πράττοντες I. viii. 9. II. i. 4, 7. πράττεσθαι I. xi. 4. VI. xii. 8. πράττομεν I. xii. 8. II. iii. 1. III. i. 23. V. viii. 3, 5. X. viii. 1. πράττοντι III. i. 10. πράττοντας II. ii. 4. iv. 1. III. v. 7. VI. xii. 7. VIII. viii. 3. X. viii. 13. πράττων II. iv. 3, 4. III. i. 3. VII. ii. 10. ix. 4. IX. viii. 7. πράττῃ II. iv. 3. IV. vii. 5. V. viii. 1, 3, 11. VII. xiv. 8. πράξειε II. iv. 5. IV. ix. 6. πράττηται II. vi. 20. πρᾶξαι III. i. 4. IV. i. 39. ix. 7. V. ix. 16. VI. v. 3. VIII. i. 2. vi. 5. IX. viii. 10. πράξαντες III. i. 4. πράττοντας III. i. 6. πράξας III. i. 13. πέπραχε ibid. πράττοντα III. i. 17. IV. ii. 12. ix. 7. πραχθέντα III. ii. 8. πράττοι IV. i. 22. VII. vii. 3. πράξει I. viii. 9. x. 11, 13. III. i. 22. iii. 12. IV. ix. 6. V. iii. 2. πράσσοντας VI. viii. 4. πραττόμενον VII. xiv. 8. πραττόντας VII. xiv. 7. πραττομένων VI. xii. 7. πραττόμενα V. vii. 6. ix. 15. πραχθῇ V. vii. 7. πραχθῆναι ibid. πεπραγμένα VI. ii. 6. πράξωσι VII. iii. 4. πράττωσι VIII. xi. 1. IX. vi. 1. πεπραγμένων IX. iv. 5. πεπραγμένα IX. viii. 6. πεπραγέναι X. viii. 11. πράττονται IX. iii. 2. πέπρακται IX. iv. 9.

πρεπόντως IV. ii. 13, 16.

πρέπει IV. ii. 14. πρέπουσα IV. ii. 1. πρέπον IV. ii. 2, 5, 6, 17. vi. 8. X. viii. 1. πρέπουσαι IV. ii. 6. πρέποντα IV. viii. 4. πρέπειν IV. ii. 12.
πρεπωδέστατον IV. ii. 9.
πρεσβυτέρῳ VIII. vii. 1. IX. ii. 9. πρεσβύτερον IV. ix. 3. πρεσβυτέρων VI. xi. 6. πρεσβυτέροις VIII. i. 2.
πρεσβῦται VIII. vi. 1. πρεσβύταις VIII. iii. 4.
πρεσβυτικοῖς VIII. vi. 1.
Πριαμικαῖς I. x. 14.
Πριάμου I. ix. 11. Πρίαμον VII. i. 1.
πρὶν V. v. 16. vii. 7. VII. ii. 2. vi. 1. VIII. iii. 8. IX. i. 9.
πρὸ III. ii. 17. vii. 12.
προαγαγεῖν I. vii. 17. προηγμένων X. ix. 16.
προαγωγεία V. ii. 13.
προαίρεσις I. i. 1. iv. 1. III. ii. 3, 5, 7, 9, 10, 13, 17. iii. 19, 20. VI. ii. 2, 4, 6. xiii. 7. VII. x. 3. VIII. v. 5. xiii. 11. X. viii. 5. προαιρέσει I. vii. 2. III. i. 15. ii. 5. IV. vii. 12. VII. viii. 1. ix. 1. VIII. xiii. 11. προαίρεσιν I. xiii. 4. III. ii. 2, 6. V. v. 17. VI. xii. 7, 8. VII. iv. 3. vi. 7. vii. 2. viii. 3. x. 2. IX. i. 7. X. ix. 1. προαιρέσεις II. v. 4. προαιρέσεως II. v. 4. III. ii. 1, 2, 15. V. vi. 1. viii. 9, 11. xi. 5. VI. ii. 4. VIII. v. 5.
προαιρεῖται III. ii. 8. V. v. 1, 8. VI. ii. 6. IX. ix. 5. προαιρεῖσθαι III. ii. 7, 11, 14. VII. iv. 3. VIII. xiii. 8. X. ix. 14. προαιρούμενοι I. v. 3. προαιρουμένων I. xiii. 15. VII. vii. 3. προαιρούμενος II. iv. 3. III. ii. 4. VII. ii. 10. iii. 2. προαιρούμενον III. iii. 17. IV. iv. 3. προαιρούμεθα III. ii. 9, 12, 13. προαιροῦνται VII. iv. 4. X. iv. 2. προαιρῶνται IX. vi. 1. προαιρήσεται IV. vi. 7. προελόμενοι V. viii. 5. προέλοιτο III. iii. 18. X. ix. 19. προείλοντο III. viii. 15. προελόμενος V. viii. 11. προελόμεθα V. ix. 8.
προαιρετικὸς V. x. 8. προαιρετική II. vi. 15. VI. ii. 2.
προαιρετὸν III. ii. 16. iii. 17. VI. ii. 6. προαιρετοῦ III. iii. 19. προαιρετῶν III. v. 1.
προαισθόμενοι VII. vii. 8.
πρόβατα V. vii. 1. προβάτων VIII. xi. 1.
προβουλεῦσαι V. viii. 8. προβουλευσάμενα V. viii. 5. προβεβουλευμένον III. ii. 16.
προγαργαλίσαντες VII. vii. 8.
προγενεστέρων X. ix. 23.
προγίνεται III. ii. 15. προγενομένης IX. iii. 5.
προγινωσκομένων VI. iii. 3.
πρόγονοι VIII. xi. 2. προγόνων IV. ii. 14. προγόνους VIII. xi. 2.
πρ[illegible] III. viii. 15.
προδόντι X. iii. 9.
προδιαγράψασθαι X. ix. 6.
προεγείραντες VII. vii. 8.
προϊδόντες VII. vii. 8.
προΐεσθαι VII. ii. 8. πρόεισι I. ii. 1. vii. 7. προϊοῦσι IV. i. 28.
προειρημένα III. viii. 13. X. vi. 1. viii. 12. προειρημένων I. vii. 18. προειρημένοις V. i. 2.
προελθόντες VIII. xii. 2.
προέσει II. vii. 4.
προετικὸν IV. i. 20.
προετικὸς IV. ii. 8.
προέχοντα IX. i. 8. προέχουσι X. vii. 7. προέχοντες I. v. 2.
προησθεὶς IX. v. 3.
προθυμεῖσθαι IX. xi. 6. προθυμοῦνται VIII. xiii. 2.
προθύμως IV. iii. 26. IX. xi. 5, 6.
προΐενται IV. i. 9. προϊεμένῳ III. v. 14. προϊέμενοι IX. i. 7. προϊεμένων IX. i. 5. προϊέμενος ibid. προΐενται IX. viii. 9, 10. προΐεντο IX. viii. 9.
προκείμενον X. iv. 2. προκειμένου X. viii. 3. προκειμένων I. xiii. 8.
προλαβόντος IX. i. 5. προλαβόντες IX. i. 6.
προλυπηθέντας X. iii. 6.
προνοητικὴν VI. vii. 4.
προνοίας V. viii. 9.
προορῶντα III. viii. 11.
προπέτεια VII. vii. 8.
προπετὴς VII. vii. 8. προπετεῖς III. vii. 12.
προπηλακιζόμενον IV. v. 6.
προπηλακισμὸς V. ii. 13.
πρὸς IV. i. 35. iii. 10, 12. V. ii. 11, 15. v. 12, 15. vi. 4, 6. x. 7. xi. 6. VI. i. 1, 5. xii. 3. xiii. 4. VII. ii. 4. vi. 3. vii. 6. xiii. 4. VIII. iii. 3. πρὸς ἕτερον V. i. 15, 16, 17, 18. ii. 6. πρός τι VI. ii. 5. πρὸς χρήματα IX. ii. 7.
προσαγορεύουσι VIII. x. 4. προσαγορεύουσι VIII. ix. 1. προσαγορεύειν VII.

i. 3. προσαγορεύομεν VI. v. 5. προσαγορεύονται IV. i. 5. viii. 3, 4.
προσαναιρῶσι X. i. 3.
προσάντους I. vi. 1.
προσάπτομεν IV. i. 3.
προσεγίνετο VII. iv. 4.
προσδεῖν X. ix. 10. προσδεήσει I. iv. 7. προσδεῖσθαι I. viii. 17. VII. xiii. 4. προσδεομένη I. viii. 15. προσδεῖται I. viii. 12. x. 9. VII. xiii. 2. VIII. iii. 8. x. 2. προσδέονται VIII. i. 4 iii. 4.
προσδιομολογείσθω II. ii. 3.
προσδιοριζόμεθα VI. iii. 4.
προσδοκώμενα III. i. 9.
προσδοκία IX. vii. 6. προσδοκίαν III. vi. 2.
πρόσεστι V. xi. 3. προσῇ V. viii. 2.
προσεπιτεθέντος VII. iv. 6.
προσέρχονται III. viii. 11.
προσέχειν VI. xi. 6. X. v. 3.
προσηγορία IX. viii. 4. προσηγορίαις IV. i. 39.
προσήκει IV. vi. 5. ix. 1. VIII. v. 3. viii. 3. προσῆκον VIII. xiv. 1. X. ix. 14. προσήκοντες VIII. xiii. 4.
πρόσθεσις III. v. 22. πρόσθεσιν VII. iv. 3. v. 8.
προσθετέον I. x. 15. V. ix. 5. VIII. ii. 4.
προσίεται IX. xi. 4.
προσκείσθω V. iv. 12. προσκεῖσθαι V. xi. 4.
προσκεκρουκότες IX. iv. 1.
προσλαμβάνων V. ii. 4. προσλαβόντα IV. vi. 4. προσλαβοῦσα III. viii. 12.
προσοφλήσει IV. iii. 24.
προσπαῖον IX. v. 2.
προσπαῖος IX. v. 2.
προσποιεῖται VIII. viii. 1. προσποιούμενος IV. vii. 15. προσεποιεῖτο IX. iii. 1. προσποιούμενοι IV. vii. 10. προσποιοῦνται IV. vii. 13. X. viii. 4.
προσποιήματι IV. vii. 1.
προσποίησις II. vii. 12. προσποιήσεως IX. iii. 2.
προσποιητικὸς III. vii. 8. IV. vii. 2.
προσπταίσαντος V. xi. 8.
προσπταίσαντα V. xi. 8.
πρόσταγμα III. xii. 8.
πρόσταξις X. ix. 12. προστάξεως VII. vi. 1.
προστάττει V. i. 14. ii. 10. προσταττόμενα V. ii. 10. προσταττομένων II. ix. 6. προστάξει II. vi. 7. προστάττοι III. i. 4. προστάξῃ III. v. 21. προστάττοντες III. viii. 5.
προστιθεὶς V. ii. 14. προστίθεται II. iii. 5. προστιθέμενον I. vii. 8. προστιθεμένης I. vii. 14. προσθεῖναι I. vii. 17. II. vi. 9. V. iv. 11. προστιθέασι VI. xiii. 3. προστεθέντες VII. iv. 2, 6. προσέθηκεν V. iv. 8. προστεθῇ V. iv. 10. προσετέθη V. iv. 10. προστεθέντος X. ii. 3. προστιθεμένης X. ii. 3.
προσφέρεσθαι VI. i. 2.
προσφόρου X. ix. 15.
πρότασις VII. iii. 13. προτάσεως VI. xi. 4. προτάσεων VII. iii. 6.
πρότερον I. v. 8. vi. 2. x. 6, 7. II. i. 4. v. 5. III. vii. 7, 12. viii. 3. IV. v. 13. vii. 6. V. ii. 8. iv. 14. v. 11, 17. vi. 3, 6. viii. 3. ix. 9. xi. 5. VI. i. 1, 5. VII. i. 4. ii. 5. iv. 5. vii. 1. ix. 1. VIII. iii. 8. xii. 7. IX. i. 2. v. 1. X. vi. 2, 8. vii. 2, 9. προτέρων III. xii. 5. V. iv. 2. προτέρων X. ix. 22.
προτιθέμεθα I. iii. 8. προτίθεται VI. ix. 4. προτεθέντα X. ix. 17.
προτιμᾶν I. xi. 1.
προτρέπεσθαι X. ix. 10. προτρέπονται X. i. 4. προτρέπεται III. v. 7. προτρέψοντες III. v. 7. προτρέψασθαι X. ix. 3.
προϋπαρχὴν IX. ii. 5.
προϋπάρχει IV. ii. 14. προϋπάρχειν I. ix. 4. X. ix. 8. προϋπάρχουσι X. ix. 14.
προφανῆ III. viii. 15.
προφέρονται X. iii. 8.
πρώην II. iii. 5.
Πρωταγόραν IX. i. 5.
πρυτανεῦσι IV. iii. 37.
πρῶτος III. viii. 8. πρῶτον I. vii. 17, 20. II. ii. 6. iv. 3. ix. 3. III. i. 22. iii. 11, 12. v. 23. viii. 1. IV. iii. 2. V. i. 3. v. 8. ix. 1, 12. VI. i. 4. ix. 4. xii. 4. VII. i. 5. iii. 1, 8. xii. 1. xiv. 4. X. iv. 9. ix. 22. πρῶτα III. viii. 8. IX. ix. 4. πρώτοις IV. iv. 1, 4. VII. x. 2. πρώτου V. iii. 9. πρώτων VI. xi. 4. πρώτας VII. vi. 6.
πρώτως VIII. iv. 4. vii. 3.
πτήσεις X. iv. 3.
πτήσσοντα III. viii. 4.
Πυθαγόρειοι I. vi. 7. II. vi. 14. V. v. 1.
πύκα VII. vi. 3.
πυκνότης V. i. 5. πυκνότητος ibid.
πύκται III. ix. 3.

πυκτικὸς X. ix. 15.
πῦρ II. i. 2. V. vii. 2.
πυρέττουσι X. v. 9. ix. 15.
πω VI. ix. 4, 6.
πωλεῖν V. iv. 13. πωλοῦσιν V. vii. 5.
πῶς I. iii. 8. vi. 1, 12, 16. x. 7. xiii. 16. II. ii. 1, 2. iv. 1. v. 3. vi. 3. vii. 16. ix. 1, 7. III. i. 16, 17. ii. 12. iii. 6, 8. 11, 14, 17. v. 23. IV. i. 34. ii. 9, 21. v. 13. V. vi. 3. ix. 15. x. 1. VI. viii. 4. xii. 7. VII. ii. 1. iii. 1, 2, 12, 14. iv. 5. x. 5. xii. 7. xiv. 9. VIII. i. 1. ii. 4. xii. 8. IX. iii. 4. viii. 3. X. ii. 4. iii. 5. iv. 9. viii. 4. ix. 7, 18, 20, 23.
πως I. vi. 8. viii. 9. ix. 1. xii. 2. xiii. 7, 18. II. iii. 2. iv. 3. v. 4. vi. 20. viii. 1, 8. III. iii. 13. v. 17, 20. IV. iv. 5. ix. 2. V. i. 10, 12. v. 10. ix. 15. xi. 4. VI. iii. 4. xiii. 1, 4. VII. iii. 7, 10. iv. 4. vi. 1. xiii. 5. xiv. 2. VIII. vii. 1. xii. 3. IX. vii. 4. X. ix. 8.

P.

ῥαβδίσεως X. iv. 2.
Ῥαδαμάνθυος V. v. 3.
ῥᾴδιον I. viii. 15. II. vi. 14. ix. 2, 7, 8. III. i. 10. xii. 2. IV. i. 20, 23, 30, 39. iii. 21, 26. v. 13. ix. 14, 15. VIII. iv. 3. vi. 2. IX. ii. 2. ix. 5. X. ix. 5, 20.
ῥᾳδίως I. iv. 7. x. 14.
ῥᾷον IX. ii. 10. ῥᾷον IV. i. 9. VII. x. 4. IX. ix. 5.
ῥᾷστα II. ix. 9. III. iii. 11. VIII. x. 3.
ῥᾳθυμεῖν VI. i. 2.
ῥέζω. ἔρεξε V. v. 3.
ῥέπειν X. i. 2. ῥέπουσι VII. vii. 1.
ῥηθήσεται II. ii. 2. vii. 6, 9. IV. i. 14. ῥηθέντων VII. iii. 7. ῥητέον II. vi. 2. vii. 11. VI. xii. 2.
ῥητῇ X. ix. 20. ῥητοῖς VIII. xiii. 6, 7, 9.
ῥητορικὸν I. iii. 4. ῥητορικῶν I. ii. 6.
ῥήτωρ III. iii. 11.
ῥίζαν VIII. xii. 3.
ῥῖνας III. viii. 10.
ῥίπτειν III. xii. 3. V. i. 14. ῥῖψαι III. v. 14. ῥίπτων II. i. 1, 2. ῥίψας V. ii. 2.
ῥόθον III. x. 5.
ῥώμην I. ii. 2. vii. 23. x. 12. xi. 3. X. i. 1.
ῥωννύουσι I. viii. 16.

Σ.

σαθρὸν I. x. 8.
Σαρδαναπάλλῳ I. v. 4.
σάρκινοι III. ix. 3.
σαρκὸς V. i. 5. σαρκὶ ibid.
Σάτυρος VII. iv. 5.
σαφηνείας II. vii. 11.
σαφὲς VI. i. 2. σαφέστερον VI. xii. 8.
σεῖος VII. i. 3.
σεισμὸν III. vii. 7.
σεμνὸν IV. iii. 26. VII. ii. 6. VIII. i. 6.
σεμνύνεσθαι IV. iii. 26.
σημαίνειν III. viii. 10. σημαίνοντες VI. vii. 1. VII. iv. 4.
σημεῖον II. iii. 1. V. ii. 2. VI. v. 2, 8. viii. 5. xi. 1, 6. xiii. 4. VII. iii. 8. iv. 2. xii. 2. xiii. 5. VIII. viii. 3. X. vi. 4. viii. 8. σημείῳ VIII. i. 7. viii. 2.
σθένος III. viii. 10.
Σικυωνίοις III. viii. 16.
Σιμωνίδη IV. i. 27.
σιταρχίᾳ VII. vii. 6.
σιτηρὰ V. vii. 5.
σιτία II. ii. 6.
σιτίοις III. v. 9.
σίτου V. v. 13.
σκαπτῆρα VI. vii. 2.
σκεπτέον I. viii. 1. II. v. 1. V. i. 1. VI. viii. 4. xiii. 1. VII. iii. 1.
σκεπτώμεθα II. ii. 1. σκέψαιτο IV. ii. 9. VI. viii. 6. σκεψώμεθα I. vi. 9. σκέψασθαι II. ii. 1. VII. vi. 1.
σκεῦος X. v. 2.
σκέψις I. xiii. 4. V. i. 2. σκέψεως I. ix. 3. VII. iii. 2. VIII. i. 7.
σκληροὶ IV. viii. 3.
σκοπεῖν II. ii. 4. ix. 4. X. viii. 12. σκοποῦμεν III. ii. 15. σκοπῶν IV. ii. 21. σκοπεῖ VIII. x. 2. σκοποῦσι III. iii. 1. σκοπεῖται I. iii. 2. σκοπουμένοις V. x. 1. σκοπείη VIII. x. 2.
σκοπὸς III. xii. 9. VI. i. 1. xii. 9. σκοποῦ II. vi. 14. σκοπὸν I. ii. 2. VI. xii. 6, 9.
Σκύθαι III. iii. 6. Σκυθῶν VII. vii. 6.
σκυτέως I. vii. 11.
σκυτῶν I. x. 13.
σκυτοτόμος V. v. 8, 12. σκυτοτόμου ibid. σκυτοτόμῳ IX. i. 1. σκυτοτόμον I. x. 3. V. v. 10, 12.
σκῶμμα IV. viii. 9.
σκώπτειν IV. viii. 4, 9. σκώπτοντα IV. viii. 7. σκωπτόμενον IV. viii. 3.

Σόλων I. x. 3. X. viii. 11. Σόλωνα I. x. 1.
σοφία I. viii. 6. VI. iii. 1. vi. 1, 2. viii. 2, 3, 4, 5. xi. 7. X. vii. 3. σοφίᾳ VI. vii. 4. σοφίαν I. xiii. 20. VI. vi. 2. vii. 1, 4. X. vii. 3. σοφίας VI. xii. 3. xiii. 8.
σοφισταί IX. i. 7.
σοφιστικοὶ VII. ii. 8. σοφιστικοὶ X. ix. 18. σοφιστικῶν X. ix. 20.
Σοφοκλέους VII. ii. 7. x. 4.
σοφὸς I. xiii. 20. VI. viii. 6. xi. 5. X. vii. 4. viii. 13. σοφὸν I. xiii. 20. IV. vii. 13. V. ix. 15. VI. vii. 1, 2, 3, 4. σοφοῖς I. iv. 2. σοφοῦ VI. vi. 1. IX. ii. 8. σοφοὶ VI. viii. 5. σοφοὺς VI. vii. 2, 5. σοφώτεροι X. vii. 4. σοφῶν X. viii. 11. σοφῷ X. viii. 13. σοφωτάτους VIII. vii. 4.
σπάνιος VII. i. 3. σπάνιον II. ix. 2. VII. i. 3. σπανίας VIII. iii. 8.
σπέρμα X. ix. 6.
Σπεύσιππος I. vi. 7. VII. xiii. 1.
σπευστικὸς IV. iii. 34.
σπουδάζει IV. ii. 15. σπουδάζουσι IV. i. 3. σπουδάζοντες IV. iii. 32. σπουδαστέον I. vii. 22. σπουδάζῃ X. vi. 6. σπουδάζειν IV. iii. 34. σπουδάζοντες VII. iv. 5. σπουδάζειν VIII. i. 4. X. vi. 6. σπουδαστὸς VIII. xiv. 4. ἐσπουδάσαμεν IX. viii. 4. σπουδάζοι IX. viii. 5. σπουδάζοντα IX. viii. 7.
σπουδαῖος I. viii. 13. III. iv. 4, 5. V. ii. 6. VII. x. 1. VIII. vi. 6. IX. iv. 2. viii. 10, 11. ix. 2, 6, 7, 10. X. vi. 6. σπουδαία I. xiii. 13. VI. ii. 2. VII. ii. 6, 7. IX. ix. 5. σπουδαῖον I. xii. 2. II. vi. 2. ix. 2. III. v. 19. V. ix. 6. x. 1. VI. v. 2. xii. 7. VII. ix. 5. xiv. 4. IX. ii. 5. σπουδαίου I. vii. 14. VII. xiii. 7. IX. viii. 9. σπουδαῖοι II. iv. 6. v. 3. σπουδαίῳ III. iv. 4. VIII. xiv. 1. IX. ii. 1. iv. 3. ix. 7. X. v. 10. vi. 5. σπουδαίων IV. iii. 17. VII. i. 6. iv. 5. IX. ix. 5, 10. X. ix. 14. σπουδαῖαι V. x. 1. X. iv. 6. vi. 3, 7. σπουδαίας X. v. 6. σπουδαίους V. x. 2. σπουδαίαις VI. xii. 2. σπουδαίων VII. x. 5. IX. x. 3. σπουδαῖοι VII. xi. 5. σπουδαῖαι VII xiv. 4. X. vi. 4. σπουδαιοτέραν X vi. 7. σπουδαιότερον X. iv. 5. σπουδαιοτάτην VI. vii. 3.
σπουδὴν X. iii. 12. σπουδῇ X. vii. 3.
σταδίῳ I. iv. 5. X. iv. 3.
στασιάζει IX. iv. 9. στασιάζειν IX. vi. 4. στασιάζουσι IX. vi. 2.
στάσιμον IV. iii. 34.
στάσιν VIII. i. 4.
στέργει IX. vii. 4. στέργων X. ix. 8. στέργειν IV. vi. 4, 5. VIII. xiii. 6. ἔστερξε VI. iv. 5. στέργουσι VIII. iii. 2. xii. 2. IX. v. 2. vii. 7. στέρξουσι VIII. iv. 1. στέργοντας VIII. iv. 4. στέργοντες VIII. xii. 6. IX. vii. 2. X. ix. 14. ἔστεργον IX. i. 3.
ἐστερημένα X. viii. 8.
στερίσκεται VI. ii. 6.
στέφανος III. ix. 3.
στεφανοῦνται I. viii. 9.
στιγμῆς X. iv. 4.
στοχάζονται VIII. ix. 4. στοχαζόμενοι IV. viii. 3. V. i. 13. στοχαζόμενος IV. vi. 9. στοχαζόμενον II. ix. 3. στοχάσεται IV. vi. 6.
στοχαστικὸς VI. vii. 6. στοχαστικὴ II. vi. 9, 13. ix. 1.
στρατηγικὴ I. vi. 4. στρατηγικῆς I. i. 2. στρατηγικῇ I. vii. 1. στρατηγικὴν I. i. 4.
στρατηγικώτεροι I. vi. 16.
στρατηγὸν I. x. 13. IX. ii. 1. στρατηγοῦ IX. ii. 8.
στρατιῶται III. viii. 6, 9. στρατιῶται III. ix. 6.
στρατοπέδῳ I. x. 13.
στρατοῦ VI. viii. 4.
στραφεὶς V. ix. 16.
στρυφνοὶ VIII. v. 2. vi. 1.
συγγένειαν X. ix. 14.
συγγενεῖς VIII. xi. 4. συγγενῆ VII. iii. 1. συγγενεῖς III. xii. 7. VII. vi. 2. συγγενεῖς VIII. xii. 4. IX. ii. 7. συγγενῶν VIII. xii. 7. συγγενείας IX. ii. 9. συγγενεστάτη X. viii. 7. συγγενεστάτῳ X. viii. 13.
συγγενικὴ VIII. xii. 2. συγγενικὴν VIII. xii. 1.
συγγίνεσθαι V. ix. 14, 16. συγγίνονται V. vi. 1.
συγγνώμη III. i. 7, 15. VI. xi. 1. VII. ii. 4. vi. 2. συγγνώμην III. i. 1.
συγγνώμων VI. xi. 1.
συγγνωμονικὸς IV. v. 4. συγγνωμονικὸν VI. xi. 1. VII. vii. 6. συγγνωμονικὰ V. viii. 12.
συγγνώμων VI. xi. 2.
συγγραμμάτων X. ix. 21.

συγγυμνάζουσι IX. xii. 2.
συγκομιδὰς VIII. x. 5.
συγκρίνειν IX. ii. 9.
συγκυβεύουσι IX. xii. 2.
συγκυνηγοῦσι IX. xii. 2.
συγχαίρειν IX. x. 5. συγχαίρουσι IX. iv. 9. συγχαίροντα IX. iv. 1.
συγκεχυμένως VII. i. 6.
συνέζευκται X. viii. 3. συνεζεῦχθαι X. iv. 11.
σύζευξις V. iii. 12. v. 8.
συζῆν IV. vi. 1. vii. 1. VIII. iii. 5. v. 3. vi. 4. IX. ix. 3. 7. 10. x. 3. 4. 5. xii. 1. 2. συζῇ X. viii. 8. συζῶσι VIII. iii. 4. συζῶντες VIII. v. 1. 3.
συλῶντας IV. i. 42.
συνειλημμένα II. vi. 18.
συλληφθῆναι V. i. 15.
συλλογισάμενοι VII. vi. 1. συλλογιστέον I. xi. 5.
συλλογισμὸς VI. iii. 3. VII. ii. 8. συλλογισμῷ VI. iii. 3. ix. 5. συλλογισμοὶ VI. xii. 10.
συλλυπεῖν IX. xi. 4.
συμβαίνει I. xii. 3. xiii. 13. II. viii. 7. III. i. 5. iv. 2. IV. i. 21. v. 8. V. iii. 13. 14. viii. 8. x. 2. VI. xiv. 1. VII. ii. 9. iii. 10. xii. 1. xiii. 1. xiv. 7. VIII. xiii. 8. IX. i. 3. iv. 1. v. 2. vi. 4. vii. 3. viii. 9. xi. 6. X. iii. 7. v. 4. 5. 9. συμβαίνοι IX. i. 8. συμβαίνειν I. iii. 3. vii. 6. x. 4. xi. 4. VII. iii. 13. IX. xi. 2. X. viii. 2. συμβαίνοντα I. x. 12. X. ix. 16. συμβαινόντων I. xi. 2. συμβαίνουσι II. vii. 15. VII. ii. 12. v. 3. xii. 3. xiv. 4. συνέβη III. viii. 9. V. viii. 6. συμβῇ III. viii. 14. V. x. 5. συμβαίνῃ IV. i. 25. συμβέβηκε V. viii. 1. VII. xii. 6. IX. vii. 3. συμβεβηκὸς III. x. 5. 7. V. viii. 1. 3. 4. ix. 3. 15. 16. xi. 8. VI. iii. 4. VII. iii. 10. ix. 1. xi. 3. xii. 2. xiv. 4. 7. VIII. iii. 2. 6. iv. 5. 6. viii. 2. 7. X. viii. 8. συμβεβηκότι I. vi. 2. συμβαίη V. xi. 8.
συμβάλλεται VII. xiv. 3. συμβάλλεσθαι I. xi. 1. 6. IV. iii. 19. X. ix. 14. 19. συμβάλλεται III. i. 10. συμβαλλομένου III. i. 12. συμβάλλειν VII. vi. 7. συμβαλλόμενος IV. viii. 10. συμβαλλόμενοι VIII. xiv. 1.
συμβίων IX. xi. 1.
συμβιοῦν IV. v. 13. IX. iii. 4. συμβιωτέον VIII. xii. 8.
συμβλητὰ V. v. 10.
συμβολαίων IX. i. 9.
συμβούλους III. iii. 10.
συμμαχεῖν IX. vi. 2.
συμμαχίαι VIII. iv. 4.
συμμένει V. v. 6. 8. συμμένουσι V. v. 6.
συμμεταβάλλοι I. x. 4.
συμμετρία X. iii. 3. συμμετρίας V. v. 14.
σύμμετροι IV. iii. 5. σύμμετρα II. ii. 6. V. v. 14. 15.
συμπείθει IV. v. 10.
συμπεραίνεσθαι I. iii. 4. συμπερανθὲν VII. ii. 8. iii. 9.
συμπεράσματος I. viii. 1. VI. ii. 4.
συμπαραλαμβάνουσι I. viii. 6.
συμπίνουσι IX. xii. 2.
συμπίπτειν IX. x. 5. συνέπεσε VII. vii. 6.
συμπλέοντες IV. i. 3.
συμπλεῦσαι VIII. xii. 1.
σύμπλοοι VIII. ix. 1.
συμπορεύονται VIII. ix. 4.
συμπράξαιεν IX. v. 2. 3.
συμφανὲς I. ix. 7.
συμφέρει III. ii. 12. VII. iii. 6. X. ix. 15. συμφέρειν IX. viii. 6. συμφέρον II. iii. 7. IV. vi. 6. V. vii. 5. VI. ix. 7. VIII. i. 6. iii. 4. ix. 4. x. 2. 4. IX. vii. 4. συμφέροντα II. ii. 3. III. i. 15. V. i. 17. VI. v. 1. vii. 5. IX. vi. 2. 3. συμφέροντος II. iii. 7. V. i. 13. VIII. iv. 4. ix. 4. 5. συμφέροντι IV. vi. 8. VIII. iv. 2. ix. 4. συμφερόντων IX. vi. 1.
συμφιλοσοφοῦσι IX. xii. 2.
συμφοιτητὴς VIII. xii. 8.
συμφοραῖς I. ix. 11.
συμφυέστερον IV. i. 37.
συμφῦναι VII. iii. 8.
συμφωνεῖν II. vii. 1. III. xii. 9. X. viii. 12.
συναγαγόντι X. ix. 20. συνηγμένων X. ix. 21.
συναγωγαὶ X. ix. 21.
συνῆθει I. viii. 1. X. ix. 20. συνηθέντων X. viii. 12.
συναισθανόμενοι IX. ix. 9. συναισθάνεσθαι IX. ix. 10.
συναίτιοι III. v. 20.
συνακολουθείημεν I. x. 8.
συναλγεῖν IX. x. 5. xi. 2. συναλγεῖ IX. iv. 2. συναλγοῦσι IX. iv. 9. συναλγοῦντα IX. iv. 1. συναλγοῦντας IX. xi. 4. συναλγούντων IX. xi. 2.
συναλλάγμασι II. i. 7. V. ii. 12. iv. 1. 3. viii. 10. X. viii. 1. συναλλαγμάτων V. ii. 13.

συναλλάξαι VIII. xiii. 8. συναλλάξωσι VIII. xiii. 5. συναλλάξαντες VIII. xiii. 6.
συναναλῶσαι VIII. iii. 8.
συνάπτει VIII. iii. 7. συνάπτουσι VIII. iv. 5.
συναριθμεῖται II. iv. 3. συναριθμουμένης I. vii. 8.
συνηρτημέναι X. viii. 3.
συναυξανομένη IX. xii. 3.
συναύξει X. v. 2. vii. 7. συναύξουσι X. v. 2. συναύξοντα X. v. 2.
συνάχθεσθαι IX. ix. 5.
σύνδεσμος VIII. xii. 7.
συνδιάγειν VIII. v. 3. xiii. 3. IX. iv. 5. συνδιάγοντα IX. iv. 1.
συνδιάλου VII. v. 3.
συνδυάζει V. iii. 11. συνδυάζεται IV. i. 30. VIII. iv. 5.
συνδυαστικὸν VIII. xii. 7.
σύνεγγυς III. ii. 7. V. i. 7. VIII. xii. 4. X. v. 6.
συνειδότες I. iv. 3. συνίδοιμεν X. ix. 23. συνειδότες IV. vii. 1.
συνείη X. ix. 7.
συνείρουσι VII. iii. 8.
συνεπικοσμεῖν I. x. 12.
συνεπόμενος IV. vi. 8.
συνεργεῖν III. viii. 11. συνεργοῦντα IX. xi. 6.
συνεργὸς I. vii. 17. συνεργὰ I. ix. 7. συνεργοὺς X. vii. 4.
συνερχομένων VIII. i. 2. συνελθεῖν VIII. ix. 4.
σύνεσις VI. x. 1, 3, 4. xi. 3. σύνεσιν I. xiii. 20. VI. xi. 2, 5. VIII. xii. 2. συνέσεως X. ix. 20.
συνετὸς I. xiii. 2. VI. xi. 2. συνετοὶ VI. x. 1, 2. συνετοὺς VI. x. 1. xi. 2.
συνεχὴς V. iii. 9, 14. VII. viii. 2. συνεχεῖ II. vi. 5. συνεχεστέρα IX. ix. 6. συνεχέστατα I. x. 10. συνεχεστάτη X. vii. 2.
συνέχει V. v. 6, 11, 13. VIII. xii. 7. συνέχειν VIII. i. 4.
συνεχῶς VIII. vi. 4. IX. ix. 5. X. iv. 9. vi. 6. vii. 2.
συνηγορῆσαι I. xii. 5.
συνήδεται IX. iv. 5. συνήδεσθαι IX. x. 5.
συνηδύνειν IV. vi. 6, 7, 8. συνηδύνοντες IV. vi. 9.
συνηθείᾳ VIII. vi. 3. συνηθείας VIII. iii. 8. iv. 1. IX. iii. 5. v. 2. X. ix. 19. συνήθειαν IX. v. 3.
συνήθεις IV. vi. 5. VII. xiv. 5. VIII. xii. 4. συνήθων IV. vi. 5. συνήθη X. ix. 8.
συνημερεύειν VIII. iii. 5. v. 2, 3. vi. 1. xiii. 3. IX. ix. 3. x. 4. συνημερεύοντες IX. xii. 2. συνημερεύουσι IX. iv. 9.
συνθέλουσι IX. v. 2.
σύνθεσις X. iv. 2.
συνθετὸν X. viii. 3. συνθετοῦ X. vii. 8. viii. 3.
συνθήκην V. vii. 4. συνθήκης VIII. xi. 7. συνθήκην V. v. 11. vii. 5.
συνιέναι VI. x. 3, 4.
συνικνεῖσθαι I. x. 5. συνικνουμένων I. xi. 2.
συνίσασι X. ix. 20.
συνίστησιν VI. vii. 4. VII. xii. 2.
σύνοδοι, συνόδους VIII. ix. 5.
συνορᾶται VIII. xii. 2. συνορᾶσθαι X. i. 1. v. 2. viii. 2. συνορᾶται VIII. xii. 4.
συνοικοῦσι VIII. xii. 7.
συμπλέξασι III. viii. 6.
σύνοψιν VIII. x. 3.
συνουσίας VIII. ix. 5.
συντείνει IV. vii. 7. συντείνοντα VI. xii. 9.
συντελεῖν I. vi. 12.
συντεθῇ V. iii. 11.
συντομώτερον X. vi. 1.
σύντονος IV. iii. 34.
συντέθραπται II. iii. 8.
σύντροφον VIII. xii. 4. σύντροφοι VIII. xii. 6.
συνῳδοὶ X. i. 4. συνᾴδει I. viii. 8.
συνώνυμος V. ii. 6.
σύρματα X. v. 8.
συστενάζουσι IX. xi. 4.
σύστημα II. viii. 6.
συστοιχίᾳ I. vi. 7.
συστρατιῶται VIII. ix. 5. συστρατιώτας VIII. ix. 1.
σφαῖρα IV. ii. 18.
ἐσφαιρῶσθαι III. i. 17.
σφάλλεσθαι VI. xiii. 1.
σφάλλειν V. xi. 2.
σφετέροις X. ix. 14. σφετέρους X. ix. 18.
σφόδρα III. i. 16. xi. 8. IV. i. 18. v. 14. VII. i. 1, 3. iv. 4. vii. 3. xiv. 1. VIII. vi. 2. IX. viii. 9. x. 5. X. v. 4.
σφοδραὶ III. xii. 7. VII. xiv. 4, 5. σφοδρᾷ VII. xiv. 6.
σφοδρότερα VII. vii. 8.

σφοδρῶς II. v. 2.
σχεδὸν I. iv. 2. v. 4. viii. 4. II. vii. 10. IV. v. 1. vii. 1. V. ii. 10. x. 2. VII. xi. 5. IX. iv. 8. X. v. 5.
σχῆμα V. v. 12. x. 7. VIII. x. 4. σχήματι III. x. 3.
σχολάζων VIII. ix. 5. σχολάζομεν X. vii. 6.
σχολαίων IX. xi. 6.
σχολαστικὸν X. vii. 7.
σχολῇ X. vii. 6.
σώζει II. ii. 6. VI. v. 6. VII. viii. 4. VIII. xiv. 3. IX. i. 1. X. ix. 23. σώζειν I. ii. 8. σώζεται II. ii. 7. VII. vii. 5. σωζούσης II. vi. 9. σώζοιντο III. i. 4. σώζωσιν VI. v. 5. σώζεσθαι VIII. ii. 3. IX. iv. 3. vii. 2. σώζοιτο VIII. i. 1.
Σωκράτης III. viii. 6. IV. vii. 14. VI. xiii. 3, 5. VII. ii. 1. iii. 13.
σῶμα I. viii. 2. xiii. 7. II. iv. 6. III. v. 16. x. 11. VI. i. 2. VII. iii. 7. xiv. 6. VIII. xi. 6. X. iii. 6. viii. 4, 9. σώματι I. vi. 12. IV. iii. 5. VI. xiii. 1. VII. xiii. 2. σώματος I. xiii. 6, 7, 10, 15. III. v. 15. x. 2. σώμασι I. xiii. 16. σώματα III. viii. 8. IV. viii. 4. σωμάτων III. iv. 4. X. vi. 3.
σωματικαὶ III. x. 2. VII. xiii. 6. xiv. 1, 3. σωματικὴν VII. xiv. 4. σωματικῶν I. xii. 6. II. iii. 1. VII. iv. 2. xiv. 1, 2. X. vi. 8. σωματικάς III. x. 3. VII. iv. 3. vi. 5. vii. 2. viii. 4. ix. 6. xii. 7. X. vi. 4. σωματικὰ IV. ix. 2. VII. iv. 2. ix. 7. X. iii. 6. σωματικοῦ VII. ix. 5. σωματικαῖς IX. viii. 4.
σωτηρίας III. i. 16. viii. 9. IX. vii. 1. σωτηρίᾳ I. vi. 1. III. i. 5, 17. σωτηρίαν III. vi. 11. V. ii. 6.
σωφρονεῖν X. ii. 2. iii. 2.
σωφρονικοὶ VI. xiii. 1.
σωφρόνως II. iv. 3. X. viii. 11. ix. 8.
σωφροσύνη II. ii. 7. vii. 3. III. x. 1, 3, 8. VII. v. 9. vi. 6. vii. 1. ix. 5. σωφροσύνης II. ii. 7. vi. 20. III. x. 1. xii. 10. σωφροσύνην II. viii. 6, 8. VII. iv. 6. σωφρονέστερον I. xiii. 20. VI. v. 5. VII. iv. 2.
σώφρων I. xiii. 20. II. iii. 1. iv. 4, 5. viii. 2. III. ix. 5, 8. xi. 9. IV. i. 1. iii. 4. VII. ii. 6. vii. 2. viii. 4. ix. 6. xi. 4. xii. 7. X. ii. 1. vii. 4. σώφρονος I. xiii. 17. III. xii. 9. V. i. 14. VII. ii. 6. ix. 6. xii. 7. σώφρονα II. i. 4. iv. 1, 3, 4, 5. IV. iv. 4. VII. i. 6. iv. 3, 4. vi. 6. xii. 7. IX. viii. 5. σώφρονες II. i. 4, 7. ii. 9. iv. 1, 4. III. x. 2, 3. X. viii. 7. σωφρόνων II. iv. 1. III. x. 4. σώφρονι X. viii. 4.

T.

τἀγαθὸν I. i. 1. v. 4. vi. 3. vii. 1, 10. xii. 5. III. iv. 2, 4. VIII. ii. 1, 2. IX. iii. 3. iv. 3, 4. X. i. 2. ii. 1, 3. iii. 4, 13. τἀγαθοῦ I. vi. 11. III. iv. 1. τἀγαθῷ I. iii. 3. vi. 9. III. ii. 1. VII. ii. 9. VIII. ii. 3, 4. iii. 1, 6. v. 1. vii. 6. IX. iv. 1, 3, 4. v. 3. viii. 2. ix. 1, 2, 4.
τἀληθὲς I. iii. 4. viii. 1. III. iv. 4, 5. VI. ii. 3. VII. xiv. 3.
τἆλλα IV. i. 12. iii. 18. VI. xiii. 1.
τἀναντία VII. ii. 9.
τάξει V. vii. 7. τάξιν V. i. 11. X. ix. 11.
ταπεινοὶ IV. iii. 29. ταπεινοὺς IV. iii. 26.
τάττει III. xii. 9. τάττειν IX. i. 8. τάττων X. ix. 12. τάττουσι I. viii. 17. τάξαι III. viii. 4. IX. i. 5, 9. τάξῃ IV. v. 3. τάξειε VIII. xii. 1. τάττουσι IX. i. 9. ταχθεῖσα X. ix. 23. τεταγμένῃ V. ii. 10. τεταγμένα V. xi. 2. VI. xii. 7. τέτακται X. ix. 8.
ταὐτὸ VI. vii. 4. viii. 1. x. 2. xi. 2. xiii. 1. VII. iii. 2. xiii. 4. VIII. xii. 3. IX. ii. 7. X. iv. 8. v. 6, 7. ταὐτοῦ VIII. vi. 7. ταὐτὰ IV. ii. 10, 16. V. ii. 9. vii. 5. VII. iv. 4. VIII. vi. 4. ix. 1, 2. IX. ii. 6. iv. 1. ταὐτὸν III. ii. 2, 11, 15. V. ii. 9, 11. vi. 8. ix. 3, 16. x. 1, 2. VI. i. 6. ταὐτῷ VI. viii. 3. VIII. iii. 7. IX. iv. 6, 7. ix. 10.
ταὐτότης VIII. xii. 3.
τάφῳ IV. ii. 16.
τάφρον III. viii. 5.
τάχα I. v. 6. vi. 14. vii. 10. x. 6. xi. 2. xiii. 1. VIII. ii. 1. IX. vii. 1. viii. 3. X. ix. 17, 21, 23.
ταχέως IV. i. 30. v. 8. VIII. iii. 5, 9. vi. 7. X. iii. 4.
τάχος X. iii. 4.
ταχὺ I. viii. 1. IV. i. 34. VI. ix. 2, 6. VII. viii. 2. VIII. vi. 1. ταχεῖα VIII. iii. 5, 9. ταχεῖς VII. vi. 1.

ταχυτὴς IV. iii. 34. ταχύτερα VII. vi. 1. vii. 8.
τείνουσαι VI. xi. 2.
τέκνον V. vi. 8. τέκνα V. vi. 9. VII. iv. 5. VIII. vii. 1, 2. ix. 2. xii. 2, 3. τέκνων I. x. 3. III. v. 5. VIII. x. 4. τέκνοις I. vii. 6. VIII. vii. 2. xii. 5. X. ix. 14.
τεκνοποιεῖν VIII. xii. 7.
τεκνοποιΐας VIII. xii. 7.
τέκτων I. vi. 16. vii. 19. τέκτονος I. vii. 11.
τέλειος VII. xiii. 2. τελεία III. v. 17. X. iv. 1, 2, 3, 5. vii. 1, 7. viii. 7. τέλειον I. viii. 3, 4, 6, 8. x. 15. X. iii. 4. iv. 4. vii. 7. τελείων I. ix. 10. X. v. 11. τελείας I. x. 10. V. i. 15. xi. 7. τελείῳ I. vii. 16. x. 14. III. v. 19. τελείαν I. x. 15. xiii. 1. VIII. vi. 1. X. iv. 2. τέλεια I. vii. 3. V. i. 15. VIII. iii. 6, 9. τελείων I. xii. 7. VIII. xiii. 2. X. iv. 4. τελείοις I. xiii. 1. τελειότερον I. ii. 8. vii. 4. τελειότατον I. vii. 3. τελειοτάτην I. vii. 15. τελειοτάτη X. iv. 5.
τελειοῦται X. v. 2, 11. τελειώσει X. iv. 1. τελειωθήσεται X. iv. 1. τελειοῖ X. iv. 6, 8, 10, 11. v. 2. τελειοῦσθαι X. v. 1. τελειουμένων VII. xiv. 4. τελειουμένους II. i. 3. τελειωθῇ X. ix. 22.
τελείωσιν VIII. xii. 3.
τέλος I. ii. 1. iii. 6. v. 4, 6. vii. 1, 8. viii. 3. ix. 3, 8. x. 1, 7, 15. III. i. 6. ii. 9. iii. 11, 16. v. 1, 17, 18, 19, 20. vii. 2, 6. ix. 3. VI. ii. 5. v. 2, 4. vii. 6. ix. 7. x. 2. xi. 6. xii. 10. xiii. 7. VII. xi. 5. xii. 3. X. iv. 8. vi. 1, 6. ix. 1. τέλους III. ii. 9. iii. 11. iv. 1. v. 1, 17, 22. VII. xi. 1. X. iv. 2. vii. 7. τέλει III. vii. 6. τέλη I. i. 2, 3, 4, 5. v. 8. vii. 3. III. iii. 11, 16, 20. VIII. ii. 2. τελῶν I. i. 2. III. iii. 11. τέλεσι VII. xi. 4.
τελευταία VII. iii. 13.
τελευτῶσαν VII. x. 4. τελευτήσαντα I. x. 15. τελευτήσαντι I. x. 4. τελευτήσαντα I. x. 11. τελευτηκότας I. xi. 4.
τέμνειν V. ix. 16. τεμνόμενος X. iii. 6. τετμημένης V. iv. 8.
τέρπει X. iv. 9. v. 9. τέρπειν IV. viii. 7. τέρποντι VIII. xiii. 3.
τέρψιν IX. i. 4.
τετάρτου VI. xii. 6.
τετράγωνος I. x. 11.
τέτταρα V. iii. 9. τέτταρσιν V. iii. 5. 8, 9.
τεχνάζειν VI. iv. 4.
τέχνη I. i. 1. II. i. 6. iii. 10. VI. iii. 1. iv. 3, 4, 5, 6. v. 2, 3, 7. vi. 1. VII. xi. 4. xii. 6. τέχνης II. vi. 9. VI. v. 7. vii. 1. VII. xi. 4. xii. 6. X. v. 1. τέχνῃ I. vii. 1. V. xi. 8. VI. v. 7. τέχνην I. vi. 16. ix. 6. II. ii. 4. VI. iv. 5. τεχνῶν I. i. 3. vii. 17. II. i. 4. iv. 2, 3. V. iv. 12. v. 9. τέχναις VI. vii. 1. τέχναι II. iv. 3. III. iii. 9. VI. vii. 1.
τεχνικῷ X. ix. 16.
τεχνίτῃ I. vii. 10. VIII. xi. 6. τεχνῖται II. vi. 9. τεχνίτας I. vi. 15. x. 13. τεχνιτῶν IX. vii. 3.
τηλικοῦτοι VIII. iii. 4. τηλικοῦτον I. vi. 15. τηλικαῦτα I. xi. 6. τηλικούτους IV. ix. 3.
τῇ μὲν, τῇ δὲ VI. xiii. 3.
τηνικαῦτα I. x. 3.
τηρούντων IX. vi. 4. τηρηθείη VIII. i. 1.
τιτρωσκόμενοι I. viii. 16.
τίθεμεν I. vii. 7, 14. viii. 2. x. 15. xii. 8. VII. iv. 4. X. vi. 1. θέσθαι V. x. 6. τιθῇ V. iii. 9. τιθέντες I. vi. 7. VIII. xii. 7. X. iii. 4. θείη I. vi. 10. vii. 11. xiii. 11. ἐτίθεμεν I. ix. 8. ἐτίθεσαν X. ix. 20. τιθέασι III. i. 27. θέμενοι III. iii. 11. τιθέμεθα III. v. 20. θεῖμεν IV. iii. 10. θέσαν VI. vii. 2. τιθέασι VIII. i. 6. iii. 4. IX. iv. 1. ἔθεμεν VII. iv. 2. xi. 2. θετέον VII. iii. 1. τιθέντας VII. i. 5.
τίκτειν VII. v. 3.
τιμᾶν IV. iii. 23. IX. i. 9. τιμῶσι I. v. 4. III. v. 7. IX. i. 9. τιμηθησόμενα IV. iii. 36. τιμωμένῳ I. v. 4. τιμᾶσθαι I. v. 5. IV. iii. 18. iv. 3. VIII. viii. 1, 2. xiv. 3. τιμῶντος IV. i. 15. τιμῶντα IV. i. 20. τιμῶν IV. i. 26. τιμῶντας X. viii. 13. τετιμῆσθαι V. v. 14. τιμώμενοι VIII. viii. 2. τιμῶνται VIII. xi. 3. τιμᾶται VIII. xiv. 3. τιμώμενα X. vi. 4. τιμητέος IV. iii. 20. τιμῆται IX. i. 5. ἐτίμα IX. i. 9.
τιμῇ IV. ii. 18. iii. 27. VIII. viii. 2. τιμὴν I. iv. 3. v. 4, 5. vii. 5. II. vii. 7, 8. IV. iii. 11, 18, 37. iv. 5. V. ii. 6. VII. iv. 2, 5. VIII. viii. 2. xiv. 3. IX. ii. 9. τιμαὶ I. vi. 10. x. 3. III. vi. 9. ix. 3. τιμὰς I. vi. 11. II. vii. 8. III. viii. 3. IV. iii. 11, 15.

19. iv. 2, 3, 5. vii. 11. V. ii. 12. VII. i. 7. iv. 2, 6. VIII. viii. 2. xiv. 2. τιμὰς III. i. 2. viii. 1. IV. iii. 10, 17. 18. VIII. ix. 5. IX. ii. 8. viii. 9, 10. X. vii. 6. τιμὴ IV. iii. 10, 17, 18. V. vi. 7. VII. iv. 5. VIII. xiii. 2, 3. IX. i. 7. τιμαῖς VIII. xiv. 4. IX. viii. 4.

τιμήματι VIII. x. 3. τιμημάτων VIII. x. 1.

τίμιον I. xii. 8. τιμίων I. xii. 5, 7. τίμια IV. ii. 11. X. vi. 4, 5. viii. 8. τιμιωτέρα I. xiii. 7. τιμιώτερον VII. i. 2. IX. iii. 2. τιμιώταται I. x. 10. τιμιώτατον IV. ii. 10. τιμιωτάτων VI. vii. 3, 5.

τιμιότητι X. vii. 8.

τιμοκρατία VIII. x. 2, 3. τιμοκρατίας VIII. x. 3.

τιμοκρατικὴν VIII. x. 1. xi. 5. τιμοκρατικῷ VIII. x. 6.

τιμωροῦνται III. v. 7. τιμωρησόμενοι III. viii. 12. τιμωρεῖσθαι IV. v. 12.

τιμωρητικὸς IV. v. 4.

τιμωρία IV. v. 10. τιμωρίας IV. v. 11. V. ix. 12. X. ix. 4, 10. τιμωρίαν VII. vi. 1.

τινες VII. x. 2. τινῶν V. iii. 4. τινας VI. vii. 3. τισι VIII. vi. 4. X. v. 7. τινι V. v. 11. IX. i. 8. τινὸς V. iii. 4. iv. 5. v. 1.

τμῆμα, τμήματι V. iv. 8.

τοίνυν V. iii. 4. v. 10, 17. VII. vi. 5. IX. ii. 5.

τοιάσδε IV. vii. 12. τοιάδε V. i. 20. ii. 13. IX. ii. 1. τοιόνδε III. v. 20. VI. xii. 10. VII. iii. 6. τοιῶσδε III. xi. 1. VII. xiv. 7. τοιοῖσδε X. ix. 15.

τοῖχον V. xi. 6.

τοιχωρυχεῖ V. xi. 6.

τοξευτὰς IV. i. 40.

τολμηρὰ III. viii. 11.

τομὴν V. ix. 5.

τάξονται I. ii. 2.

τόποι, τόπους VIII. x. 1. τόπῳ I. vi. 3. X. iv. 3.

τοσαῦθ' V. v. 10.

τοσαῦτα I. iii. 4. vi. 16. vii. 18. x. 16. xi. 5. II. vii. 15. ix. 9. III. ix. 7. IV. v. 3. V. iv. 12. v. 9, 15. ix. 15. VI. xiii. 1. VIII. iii. 4. ix. 1. xii. 7. xiv. 4. IX. i. 5, 8, 9. xii. 4. τοσαύτας IX. x. 5. τοσαύτου IX. i. 9. τοσαύτῃ VIII. xiii. 11. τοσαύτης I. iii. 2. τοσαῦτα IV. i. 45. VII. iii. 14. VIII. xiii. 4. X. viii. 10. τοσούτων IV. iii. 7. VIII. xiii. 4. τοσούτῳ VIII. i. 2. IX. i. 4. viii. 1. X. vii. 8.

τότε I. x. 2, 7. II. iv. 2. III. i. 6. v. 14. V. iv. 8. VIII. vii. 2.

τοὐναντίον V. v. 18. VI. iv. 6. X. i. 2. v. 5.

τοὔνομα IV. ii. 1. v. 9. V. v. 11. VI. x. 4.

τουτέστι V. iii. 12.

τραγῳδίζοντες X. v. 4.

τραγῳδίαις I. xi. 4.

τραύματα III. ix. 4.

τρεῖς I. v. 2. II. vii. 11. IV. viii. 12. τριῶν II. iii. 7. viii. 1. V. viii. 6. VI. vi. 2. VIII. ii. 3. τρία II. v. 1. VI. ii. 1. vi. 2. VII. i. 1. VIII. iii. 1. x. 1.

τρέφεσθαι I. xiii. 11. VIII. viii. 3. τρεφομένους I. xiii. 11. τραφῆναι VIII. xii. 5. X. ix. 11. τραφέντα X. ix. 8.

τρέχειν V. ix. 16. δραμεῖν II. vi. 2.

τριγλύφου X. iv. 2.

τρίγωνον VI. iii. 9. v. 6.

τριηραρχεῖν IV. ii. 11.

τριηράρχῳ IV. ii. 2.

τρίτον I. v. 2, 7. τρίτη VIII. x. 1. τρίτου V. iii. 9. τρίτων II. iv. 3. VII. xi. 3.

τριττῶν VIII. xiii. 1.

τριχῇ I. viii. 2.

τρίψουσι III. x. 11.

τρόπος VII. ii. 2. IX. viii. 10. τρόπον I. i. 4. iii. 4. vi. 8. vii. 19. viii. 10. x. 13. II. vii. 9. ix. 4. III. iii. 11. IV. i. 32. V. i. 3, 4, 13. v. 17, 19. x. 2. xi. 10. VI. i. 5. iii. 4, 5. xiii. 1. VII. iii. 7. v. 5, 8. x. 2, 3. X. iv. 6, 8. τρόπῳ IV. i. 38. VII. iii. 6. τρόπους III. viii. 1. VII. iii. 6.

τρωτὸν III. iii. 4.

τροφὴ V. v. 12. X. v. 8. τροφῆς III. xi. 1. VIII. xi. 2. IX. ii. 8. X. ix. 9, 13. τροφῇ I. vi. 4. V. v. 10. IX. x. 2. τροφὴν II. ii. 8. V. v. 10. VII. iv. 2. X. ii. 1. iii. 6. viii. 9. ix. 8.

τροχιζόμενον VII. xiii. 3.

τρυφὴ VII. vii. 5. τρυφῆς VII. i. 4.

τρυφῶν VII. vii. 5.

Τρώεσσι III. viii. 3.

τρώξεις VII. v. 3. τρώσῃ V. viii. 6. τρώσαντας III. viii. 10.

τυγχάνομεν I. ii. 2. τυγχάνουσι I. v. 3. V. i. 1. VI. vi. 1. VIII. xiii. 4.

τυχεῖν I. viii. 14. x. 4. II. ix. 4. VI. ix. 5. 6. X. ix. 8, 9. τετυχηκέναι II. vii. 3. τυγχάνειν II. viii. 7. VI. xii. 9. τευξόμεθα II. viii. 9. ἔτυχε III. iv. 2, 3. v. 14. V. v. 18. ix. 9. VII. xiii. 2. IX. i. 2. τυγχάνει III. xi. 5. V. iii. 5. vii. 7. VI. ix. 5. xi. 7. VIII. viii. 6. IX. i. 4. X. ix. 15. τέτευχε III. xi. 7. τυγχάνων IV. iii. 17. VIII. xiii. 2. τύχωσι IV. iii. 21. V. iv. 7. τυγχάνῃ IX. i. 4. τεύξεται VI. ix. 4. τευξόμενοι V. iv. 7. τυγχάνομεν VI. i. 1. τύχῃ VII. iii. 10. ix. 2. τεύξεσθαι VIII. viii. 2. τυχόντων I. x. 14. xiii. 13. III. xi. 2. x. 2. IV. iii. 17. IX. ix. 3. τυχόντα I. x. 15. III. xi. 3. τυχὸν III. iv. 4. VI. xii. 10. X. iii. 5. τυχοῦσι IV. i. 17. vi. 8. VII. xiv. 6. τυχὸν IV. i. 36. X. vi. 8. τυχόντος X. iii. 5. ix. 17. τευκτικὴ VI. ix. 4.

Τυδεΐδης III. viii. 2.

τύπῳ I. ii. 3. iii. 4. xi. 2. II. ii. 3. vii. 5. III. iii. 20. v. 21. ix. 7. V. i. 3. X. vi. 1. τύποις X. ix. 1.

τύπτει V. viii. 3. τύπτειν V. i. 14. τύπτοι V. viii. 3. VII. vi. 2. vii. 3. τύπτοντες III. viii. 5. τύπτεσθαι III. ix. 3. τυπτόμενον V. viii. 3. τυπτόμενος III. viii. 11.

τυραννικὴ VIII. x. 4.

τυραννὶς VIII. x. 2, 3. τυραννίδι VIII. xi. 6. τυραννίδα VIII. x. 3. τυραννίσι VIII. xi. 8.

τύραννον III. i. 4. V. vi. 5. VIII. x. 2, 3. τύραννοι V. vi. 7. τυράννους IV. i. 23, 42. τυράννοις X. vi. 3.

τυφλῷ III. v. 15.

τύχη III. iii. 7. VI. iv. 5. τύχην I. vi. 11. II. iv. 2. III. iii. 5. VII. xiii. 2. 4. τύχῃ I. ix. 6. IV. i. 21. τύχην I. ix. 1, 5. x. 12. VI. iv. 5. τύχαι I. ix. 11. τύχαις I. ix. 11. x. 8, 9, 14. τύχας I. x. 7, 11, 13. xi. 1.

τυχόντος IV. iii. 22. IX. viii. 9.

Υ.

ὑβρίζει VII. vi. 4. ὑβρίζειν V. i. 14. ὑβρίζων VII. vi. 4.

ὕβρις VII. vi. 1. ὕβρει VII. vii. 6. ὕβριν III. vi. 5. IV. iii. 32.

ὑβρισταὶ IV. iii. 21.

ὑγιάζειν V. ix. 16. ὑγιάσει III. iii. 11.

ὑγιαίνειν I. viii. 14. III. ii. 9. VI. xii. 2. X. iii. 9. iv. 6. viii. 9. ὑγιαίνομεν III. ii. 9. ὑγιαίνων V. i. 4. ὑγιαίνοντι X. v. 9.

ὑγίεια I. i. 3. vii. 1. V. xii. 5. X. iv. 6. ὑγιείας II. ii. 6. III. i. 24. V. i. 4. VI. xiii. 8. ὑγίειαν I. iv. 3. vi. 16. II. ii. 6. III. xi. 8. V. ix. 15. VI. v. 1. vii. 7. xii. 2, 5. VII. xii. 4. X. iii. 3.

ὑγιεινὸν V. xi. 7. VI. vii. 4. ὑγιεινὰ II. ii. 3. III. iv. 4. V. i. 4. VI. vii. 7. xii. 1. VII. xii. 4. X. iii. 8. ὑγιεινῶν VI. x. 1.

ὑγιεινοῖς V. i. 4.

ὑγιὴς III. v. 14. ὑγιοῦς VII. xiv. 7.

ὑγρᾶς III. xi. 1. ὑγρῷ VIII. viii. 7.

ὑδέρῳ VII. viii. 1.

ὕδωρ VII. ii. 10. ὕδατα VI. viii. 7.

υἱὸν III. i. 17. VIII. vii. 1. xiv. 4. υἱῷ VIII. vii. 1. xiv. 4. υἱεῖς VIII. x. 4. X. ix. 18. υἱέσι VIII. vii. 2. x. 4. υἱῶν VIII. xi. 2.

ὑλακτοῦσιν VII. vi. 1.

ὕλη III. viii. 11. V. x. 4. ὕλην I. iii. 1. vii. 18. II. ii. 3.

ὑμνούμενοι IX. x. 6.

ὑπάλλαγμα V. v. 11.

ὑπαναστάσει IX. ii. 9.

ὑπάρχει I. iv. 7. viii. 14. x. 10. 16. III. v. 19. vi. 12. ix. 5. x. 10. IV. iii. 20. v. 7. vii. 2. V. vi. 9. ix. 10. VI. i. 5. VII. iii. 7. VIII. iii. 7. v. 5. vi. 7. IX. iv. 5, 7. viii. 2. ix. 3, 4, 5. X. iii. 4. vii. 8. viii. 8, 13. ix. 6. ὑπάρχουσι VI. xiii. 1. VIII. xii. 6. ὑπάρχειν I. viii. 5. ix. 7. V. iii. 7. ix. 7. VI. xiii. 1. VIII. iii. 7, 9. xii. 7. IX. iv. 5, 7. ix. 1. 10. x. 4. X. iii. 2. viii. 9, 10. ὑπάρχοι X. vi. 2. ix. 21. ὑπάρχῃ IX. i. 3. ὑπάρξουσι VI. xiii. 6. ὑπάρξειν IX. vi. 1. ὑπάρξαι I. ix. 4. V. ix. 19. ὑπάρξει I. x. 11. 16. VIII. vi. 4. IX. iii. 6. ὑπάρξας IV. iii. 24. ὑπαρχούσῃ VI. xiii. 6. ὑπάρχοντα I. viii. 1. IV. i. 34. vii. 4. IX. i. 3. ii. 9. ix. 8. ὑπάρχουσαν I. viii. 9. ὑπάρχον I. x. 7. IX. ix. 9. ὑπαρχόντων I. x. 13. IV. ii. 12. vii. 2, 10. V. viii. 3. X. ix. 5. ὑπηργμένων VIII. xiv. 4. ὑπάρχοντος X. iv. 7.

ὑπείκειν X. ix. 7.

ὑπεναντίον V. x. 2.

ὑπὲρ V. v. 4.

ὑπεραγαπῶσι IX. vii. 2.

ὑπεραποθνῄσκειν IX. viii. 9.
ὑπερβάλλει II. vii. 4. IV. i. 29. ii. 20. iii. 3. ὑπερβάλλουσι II. vii. 4. viii. 2. III. vii. 12. xi. 4. IV. i. 38. 40. iii. 8. ὑπερβάλλειν II. vi. 16. IV. i. 18. 23. 31. ii. 6. VII. iv. 5. ὑπερβάλλοντα II. ii. 6. ὑπερβαλλόντων II. vii. 2. III. vii. 7. VII. vii. 7. ὑπερβάλλων II. vii. 2. 8. 10. 13. 14. 15. III. vii. 7. 10. IV. i. 31. ii. 20. iii. 35. VIII. xiii. 2. ὑπερβάλλουσαν VII. xiv. 4. ὑπερβάλλουσα VII. vi. 5. xiii. 4. ὑπέρβαλλον VII. x. 4. ὑπερβάλλουσαι IV. ii. 4. ὑπερβάλλοντες IV. viii. 3. ὑπερβάλλοντας VII. i. 3. iv. 2. ὑπερβάλλοντος VIII. xiv. 4. ὑπερβαλλουσῶν VII. vii. 6.
ὑπερβεβλημένως III. x. 4.
ὑπερβολή II. vi. 10. 12. 14. 19. 20. vi. 3. 4. 6. 7. 10. 13. viii. 6. 8. III. xi. 5. IV. i. 38. ii. 4. iv. 2. 4. v. 2. vii. 15. viii. 2. V. v. 18. ix. 17. VII. iv. 5. xiv. 2. IX. iv. 6. x. 5. ὑπερβολῆς II. ii. 6. 7. vi. 4. 9. 19. 20. IV. i. 38. VI. i. 1. VII. vi. 1. ὑπερβολῇ IV. v. 9. VII. xiv. 2. VIII. vi. 2. X. viii. 9. ὑπερβολήν II. vi. 8. 15. 19. viii. 1. ix. 1. 9. III. x. 3. IV. v. 12. V. ix. 17. VI. i. 1. VII. i. 2. iv. 2. viii. 3. xiv. 2. 7. IX. iii. 5. x. 1. ὑπερβολαί II. vi. 18. IV. i. 3. 29. v. 14. VII. iv. 5. vii. 2. ὑπερβολάς II. viii. 2. IV. vii. 9. V. v. 12. VII. iv. 3. 4. vii. 2. xii. 7. xiv. 4. IX. i. 6.
ὑπερέχει II. vi. 9. IV. ii. 1. V. iv. 8. 10. 11. 12. X. vii. 8. ὑπερέχον IV. iii. 9. VIII. xii. 5. ὑπερέχεται II. vi. 6. V. iv. 11. ὑπερέχειν IV. iii. 21. 25. 26. ὑπερέχοντος IV. iii. 24. ὑπερεχομένου ibid. ὑπερεῖχε V. iv. 10. ὑπερέχοντι VIII. vi. 6. xiv. 2. ὑπερέχηται VIII. vi. 6. ὑπερεχόμενος VIII. vi. 6. viii. 1. ὑπερέχουσι VIII. vii. 4. IX. vii. 6. ὑπερέχων VIII. x. 2.
ὑπερόπται IV. iii. 18. 21.
ὑπεροχή I. vii. 18. ὑπεροχῆς I. vii. 14. ὑπεροχῇ IV. iii. 19. VIII. xi. 1. 3. ὑπεροχήν V. v. 10. VIII. vii. 1. 2. xiii. 1. xiv. 1. ὑπεροχαῖς VIII. xiii. 1.
ὑπερτείνει III. i. 7. ὑπερτείνῃ III. viii. 9. IX. ii. 5. xi. 4.
ὑπερφιλῶν IX. i. 2.
ὑπηκόους I. xiii. 2.
ὑπηρεσίας VIII. vi. 3.
ὑπηρετεῖν IV. iii. 26. ὑπηρετοῦσι VIII. viii. 5. ὑπηρετητέον IX. ii. 1.
ὕπνοι I. xiii. 13. ὕπνον I. xiii. 12. ὕπνους ibid.
ὑπό I. i. 4.
ὑπόγυια III. vi. 10.
ὑπόδημα I. x. 13. V. v. 8. ὑποδήματα V. v. 10. ὑποδημάτων IX. i. 1.
ὑποδοχάς IV. ii. 15.
ὑποζύγιον X. ix. 10.
ὑποθέσεως IV. ix. 7. V. v. 15. ὑποθέσεσι VII. viii. 4.
ὑπόκειται II. iii. 6. ὑποκείσθω II. ii. 2. V. i. 3. VI. i. 5. ὑποκειμένην I. iii. 1. vii. 18. ὑποκειμένων V. i. 5.
ὑποκρινομένων VII. iii. 8.
ὑποκρίσεις III. x. 4.
ὑποκριτῶν III. ii. 8. VII. iv. 6.
ὑπολαμβάνει VII. ii. 9. ὑπολαμβάνοντα VII. ii. 1. ὑπολαμβάνων VII. ii. 1. ὑπολαμβάνουσι I. iv. 2. VIII. ii. 4. IX. iv. 2. 7. ὑπολαμβάνειν I. v. 1. viii. 9. ὑπολάβοι I. v. 6. 8. ὑπολαμβάνοντες I. vii. 5. ὑπέλαβε V. viii. 9. ὑπολάβῃ IX. iii. 2. ὑπολαβεῖν X. viii. 11. ὑπειλήφαμεν I. x. 7. ὑπειλήφαμεν X. viii. 7. ὑπειλήφασιν ibid. ὑποληπτέον VII. i. 4. iii. 8. iv. 6. X. viii. 12.
ὑπόληψις VI. vi. 1. ix. 7. VII. ii. 4. ὑπολήψει VI. iii. 1. ὑπόληψιν VI. v. 6. VII. iii. 4. 11.
ὑπολείπων VII. xii. 2.
ὑπομονητικώτερος III. vi. 6.
ὑπομένει III. vii. 6. 13. IV. viii. 8. VIII. xiv. 3. IX. xi. 4. ὑπομένων II. ii. 7. iii. 1. III. vii. 5. ὑπομένειν II. ii. 8. 9. III. viii. 1. 14. ix. 2. xi. 5. ὑπομένουσι III. i. 7. ὑπομεῖναι ibid. ὑπομενεῖ III. vii. 2. ὑπομένουσι III. vii. 9. IV. i. 41. 43. ὑπομείνας III. i. 7. VIII. vi. 4. ὑπομένοντας VII. xiv. 7. ὑπομένῃ VIII. xiii. 9. ὑπονοοῦντας X. viii. 7. ὑπομενετέον III. i. 9.
ὑπόνοια IV. viii. 6.
ὑποπτεύουσι III. viii. 16.
ὑποσημαίνει IV. ii. 1. ὑποσημαίνειν III. ii. 12.
ὑποσχέσεις IX. i. 4.
ὑποτιθεμένου II. iv. 2. [illegible] VI. xii. 9.

ὑποτοπῆσαι I. vii. 17.
ὑπουργία IX. i. 7.
ὑποφαίνεται I. vi. 8.
ὕστερον I. vi. 2. vii. 17. II. i. 4. vii. 5, 6. III. xii. 5. IV. ii. 4. ix. 8. V. ii. 11. iv. 14. vii. 7. VII. i. 4. IX. vii. 2. X. iv. 1, 9.
ὑφάντης I. vi. 16. ὑφάντῃ IX. i. 1.
ὑφηγημένον II. vii. 9.

Φ.

φαγεῖν II. vi. 7. VII. v. 7. φαγὼν VII. v. 3. φαγόντι X. iii. 9.
φαίνεται I. i. 2. ii. 5, 8. iii. 4. v. 4, 6, 8. vi. 16. vii. 1, 3, 6, 8, 9, 11, 12. viii. 5, 15. ix. 3. xi. 1, 2. xii. 2, 4, 17, 18. xiii. 12, 15. II. iii. 7. viii. 2, 5, 8. III. i. 8. ii. 2, 16. iii. 12. iv. 3, 4, 5. v. 6, 17, 18, 19. ix. 3. x. 1, 7. IV. i. 41. iv. 5. vi. 9. vii. 9, 10, 15, 17. ix. 2. x. 1. VI. vii. 4. xii. 10. VII. xiv. 3. VIII. v. 3. vii. 3. x. 1, 4, 5, 6. xi. 1. xii. 8. xiv. 3. IX. i. 8, 9. iv. 7, 10. v. 1. vi. 2. vii. 1. viii. 11. xi. 2. xii. 1. X. iv. 11. v. 1, 7, 10. vi. 4, 6. vii. 8. viii. 3. ix. 18. φανεῖται VI. v. 6. φανείη X. v. 2, 3, 8. viii. 7, 11. φαίνονται X. viii. 7. φαίνοιτο I. iv. 7. IV. iii. 15. VIII. xii. 3. X. viii. 7. φαίνονται I. v. 3. xi. 6. xii. 3. III. viii. 6, 16. x. 8, 9. IV. iv. 6. vii. 14, 16. VI. xiii. 1. VII. ix. 5. xii. 1. xiv. 3. VIII. ii. 4. iv. 2. vi. 5, 7. viii. 6. ix. 5, 6. xii. 1. IX. ii. 7. X. ii. 5. ix. 3, 18, 20, 21. φανῇ VII. xiv. 3. VIII. iii. 8. φαίνηται III. iii. 13. φαίνεσθαι III. vii. 8. VII. xiv. 4. φαινομένῃ V. viii. 10. φαινόμενον III. ii. 7. iv. 3, 4. VIII. ii. 2. III. v. 10. φαινομένου III. iii. 11. iv. 1. v. 17. φαινόμενα III. viii. 14. VII. i. 5. IX. iv. 1, 2. X. iii. 8. φαινόμεναι X. v. 10. φαινομένοις VII. ii. 2.
Φάλαρις VII. v. 7. Φάλαριν VII. v. 2.
φανερόμισον VI. iii. 28.
φανερὸν II. iii. 7. V. ii. 6, 10. ix. 10. x. 8. xi. 1, 7. VI. iii. 2. vii. 4. viii. 8. xii. 10. VII. ii. 2. iv. 1. vi. 3. viii. 4, 5. xiii. 7. VIII. i. 2. X. ii. 2. φανερὸν I. iv. 3. φανεροῖς II. ii. 6. φανερὰ IV. iii. 36. vii. 15, 16. V. i. 5. φανερώτερον IV. i. 28. VIII. x. 2. IX. ix. 8. φανερωτέραν II. ii. 8. φανερώτατα VI. vii. 4. φανεροὶ IV. v. 8. φανερὸν VII. ix. 5.
φανερόφιλον IV. iii. 28.
φανερῶς IV. iii. 28.
φαντασία VII. vi. 1. φαντασίας III. v. 17. φαντασίαν VII. iii. 11. φαντασίᾳ VII. vii. 8.
φαντάσματα I. xiii. 13.
φαρμακεία V. ii. 13.
φαρμακεύειν V. ix. 16.
φάρυγγα III. x. 10.
φάσει VI. ix. 3. φάσεις VI. xi. 6.
φάσκων VIII. i. 6. φάσκοντες VII. xiii. 3. xiv. 5.
φαῦλοι IV. i. 31. iii. 15. V. iv. 3. VI. ix. 4. xii. 9. VII. viii. 5. ix. 4. xiv. 2. IX. iv. 10. viii. 1. φαύλη I. xiii. 13. VII. ii. 6, 7. viii. 5. φαῦλον IV. ix. 7. V. iv. 3. xi. 8. VII. xiv. 5. X. i. 2. ix. 10. φαύλου III. i. 7. IV. ix. 6. IX. viii. 4. φαύλης II. i. 5. VII. xiv. 4. φαύλῳ III. iv. 4. IV. vii. 10. IX. iii. 3. φαύλῃ X. v. 6. φαῦλα II. v. 3. VII. xiv. 6. VIII. iv. 6. IX. iv. 10. X. v. 6. φαῦλαι II. iii. 5. VII. i. 6. ii. 6. iv. 5. xi. 3. xii. 1. xiii. 2. φαῦλος I. x. 13. II. iii. 1. vi. 18. IV. ix. 6. V. xi. 7. VI. viii. 7. VII. i. 6. xii. 4. X. ix. 11. φαύλων VII. i. 6. xiii. 2. xiv. 4. VIII. viii. 5. IX. iv. 7. xii. 3. X. i. 2. ix. 4. φαύλους III. v. 3. IV. ix. 4. VIII. iv. 2. IX. iv. 7, 8. viii. 7. ix. 6. X. ii. 4. vi. 4. φαύλοις VIII. iv. 2. IX. vi. 4. φαύλας VII. ii. 6. ix. 5, 6. xii. 4. X. viii. 7. φαυλότεροι IV. i. 4. φαυλότατα VII. ii. 5.
φαυλότης VII. vi. 7. VIII. x. 3. φαυλότητι X. v. 6.
Φειδίαν VI. vii. 1.
φειδωλοὶ IV. i. 10.
φέρειν I. x. 13. IV. iii. 21. φέρῃ I. x. 12. IV. vi. 7. οἴσει I. x. 11. ἐνεγκεῖν II. vi. 2. φέρουσι VIII. vi. 4. ἔφερον X. ix. 3. φέρομεν III. xii. 5. IV. iv. 4. v. 1. φέροντι V. v. 14. φέρονται X. viii. 12. φέρεσθαι II. i. 2. X. ii. 1. φερόμενος II. i. 2. φερόμενα III. viii. 10.
φεύγει II. vi. 8. VII. iv. 4. xi. 4. xii. 7. xiv. 2. IX. xi. 4. φεύγοι VII. xiii. 7. φεύγων II. ii. 7. III. vii. 13. VII. iv. 3. φεύγειν II. iii. 5. III. vii.

11. viii. 9. IV. iii. 15. X. i. 15. VII. iii. 10. vii. 3. xii. 7. VIII. v. 2. φεύγουσι III. iv. 6. viii. 9, 14, 16. VIII. xiv. 4. IX. iv. 8, 9. X. i. 1. ix. 4. φεύγοντα III. vii. 13. φεύγοντες III. viii. 4. IV. vii. 14. X. ii. 5. φυγεῖν III. ii. 12. φυγέειν III. viii. 4. φευκτέον IX. iv. 10.

φευκτὸν III. xii. 1. VII. iv. 6. xiii. 1. X. ii. 2. φευκτῷ VII. xiii. 1. φευκταί VII. vi. 5. φευκτὰ III. i. 26. X. ii. 5. φευκτῶν VII. i. 1. X. v. 6.

φήμη VII. xiii. 5.

φημὶ VII. x. 4. φησὶ II. iii. 2, 10. III. xi. 1. V. ix. 7. VI. iv. 5. vii. 2. IX. ix. 7. φαμὲν I. vii. 14. viii. 14. xiii. 18. II. ix. 7. III. ii. 9. IV. v. 13. V. i. 12. ii. 1. VI. i. 1. vii. 6. xi. 1. xii. 9. VII. ii. 10, 11. iv. 6. X. ii. 4. iv. 7. φασὶ I. xiii. 12. II. ix. 4. III. i. 17. vii. 7. IV. i. 39. V. iv. 8. 14. vi. 6. VI. vii. 4, 5. ix. 2. xiii. 3. VII. i. 2, 6, 7. ii. 1, 3. v. 2. vi. 3. xi. 1. xii. 3. xiv. 5. VIII. i. 6. ii. 3. ix. 4. xii. 3, 5. xiii. 10. xiv. 1. IX. i. 5. vi. 1. viii. 2. ix. 1. X. ii. 5. iii. 2. ix. 10. φαῖεν III. vii. 4. VII. xiii. 6. φάναι I. xiii. 19. III. i. 24. VI. ii. 2. VII. iii. 9. xii. 3. ἔφη IX. i. 4. φήσειε VII. ii. 5. φαίη III. i. 11. ii. 7. VI. xiii. 8. VII. xiii. 1. IX. v. 3. vii. 2. φήσει III. viii. 2. ἔφαμεν V. v. 1. IX. i. 6. ἔφαμεν VI. i. 4. φατέον III. i. 10. iv. 4. v. 5. V. viii. 4. X. v. 11.

φθαρτικὴ VI. v. 6.

φθαρτὰ VII. xiv. 8.

φθείρει II. ii. 6. III. xii. 2. VII. viii. 4. X. v. 3. ix. 23. φθείρεται II. i. 6. ii. 7. iii. 1. φθείρεσθαι II. ii. 6. φθειρομένης II. vi. 9. φθείρειν IV. i. 5. φθείρουσι X. v. 5.

φθίνει VII. viii. 1.

φθονερὸς II. vii. 15.

φθόνος II. vi. 18. φθόνου II. vii. 15. φθόνον II. vii. 2. X. vi. 5.

φθορὰ IV. i. 5. X. iii. 5. φθοραί II. ii. 8. VIII. x. 1. X. v. 10. φθοραῖς III. vi. 12.

φιλαλήθης IV. vii. 8.

φιλανθρώπους VIII. i. 3.

φιλαρέτῳ I. viii. 10.

φίλαυλοι X. v. 3.

φίλαυτος IX. viii. 6. φίλαυτον IX. viii. 3, 5, 7, 11. φιλαύτοις IX. viii. 4. φιλαύτους IX. viii. 1, 4, 5.

φιλεῖν IV. vi. 5. VII. iv. 5. VIII. ii. 2. iii. 7. vii. 2. viii. 1, 3, 4. xiii. 2. IX. iii. 1. vii. 1, 6. viii. 1, 2. φιλοῦντα IV. i. 11. φιλεῖ VIII. ii. 2. v. 5. φιλῇ IX. i. 3. ἐφίλουν IX. i. 3. φιλοῦσι VIII. ii. 2, 3. iii. 1, 5. v. 5. vii. 1. viii. 3, 6. xii. 2, 3. IX. v. 3. vii. 2. xi. 4. φιλοῦνται VIII. iii. 2. φιλεῖσθαι VIII. i. 2. vii. 2. viii. 1, 2, 3, 6. IX. iii. 2. vii. 6. φιλοῦντες VIII. iii. 1, 2, 3. v. 5. vii. 1. φιλοῦντι VIII. iii. 7. φιλοῦντα VIII. xiii. 2. φιλούμενος VIII. iii. 2. φιλουμένοις VIII. v. 5. φιλητέον IX. iii. 3. viii. 2.

φιληδέσιν VIII. iv. 4. x. 6. xi. 1.

φίλησις VIII. v. 5. vii. 2. IX. v. 1. vii. 2, 6. φιλήσει VIII. ii. 3. IX. v. 1. φίλησιν VIII. vii. 2. φιλήσεις VIII. iii. 1. vii. 1.

φιλητικὸν III. x. 2.

φιλητὸς VIII. iii. 8. φιλητοῦ VIII. i. 2. φιλητὸν VIII. ii. 1, 2. v. 4. IX. i. 2. iii. 3. iv. 9, 10. vii. 5, 6. φιλητοί VIII. iii. 9. φιλητοῖς VIII. iii. 1. φιλητὸν ὂν VIII. viii. 6. φιλητὰ VIII. i. 2. iii. 7. X. v. 9.

φιλία II. vii. 13. VIII. i. 4, 7. ii. 3. iii. 3, 4, 5, 6, 7, 9. iv. 3. v. 4, 5. vi. 1. vii. 2. viii. 2, 4, 6. ix. 1. xi. 3, 4, 5, 6, 7. xii. 1, 6, 7. xiv. 1, 3. IX. i. 7. iv. 5, 6. v. 1. vi. 2. xii. 1, 3. φιλίας IV. vi. 5. VII. xiv. 9. VIII. i. 1, 4, 7. iii. 1, 3, 9. iv. 4, 6. v. 1. vi. 1. vii. 1, 2. viii. 4. xi. 6, 7. xiii. 2, 5, 11. xiv. 2, 4. IX. i. 3. iii. 1, 3. iv. 6. v. 3. x. 1, 5. xii. 4. X. vi. 1. ix. 1. φιλίᾳ IV. vi. 4. VIII. i. 4. iv. 3. vi. 4. vii. 3. ix. 3. xii. 7. xiii. 2. xiv. 1. IX. v. 1. φιλίαν II. v. 2. VIII. ii. 3, 5. v. 1. vi. 2. xiv. 1, 3. IX. i. 1. iii. 5. iv. 1. v. 3, x. 6. φιλίαι VIII. iii. 1, 2. iv. 1. vi. 4, 7. vii. 1. ix. 6. xi. 8. IX. i. 3. iv. 1. φιλιῶν VIII. ix. 2. xiii. 1. φιλίαις VIII. vii. 2. xiv. 1. IX. i. 1. iii. 4.

φιλικὸν VIII. i. 4. IX. iv. 9. φιλικοῦ IX. x. 3. φιλικῷ VIII. xiii. 6. φιλικαί VIII. v. 2. φιλικὰ VIII. iii. 9. vi. 1. xii. 7. IX. iv. 1. vii. 6. viii. 2. φιλικώτατον IX. x. 3.

φιλικῶς VIII. v. 1. IX. iv. 10. vi. 1.

φιλίππῳ I. viii. 10.

φιλοδικαίῳ I. viii. 10.
φιλοθεώρῳ I. viii. 10.
φιλοικοδόμοι X. v. 2.
φιλοκάλοις I. viii. 11. φιλόκαλον IV. iv. 4.
φιλοκίνδυνος IV. iii. 23.
φιλοκόλακες VIII. viii. 1.
Φιλοκτήτης VII. vii. 6. Φιλοκτήτῃ VII. ii. 7. ix. 4.
φιλομαθὴς X. iv. 10.
φιλομαθία III. x. 2.
φιλόμουσοι X. v. 2.
φιλομύθους III. x. 2.
Φιλόξενος III. x. 10.
Φιλοπάτωρ VII. iv. 5.
φίλος II. vii. 13. VII. vi. 1. VIII. v. 5. vii. 6. viii. 1. IX. iii. 3, 5. iv. 5, 10. v. 3. viii. 2. ix. 7, 10. xi. 3. X. ii. 1. iii. 11. φίλοι VIII. xiii. 9. xiv. 1. IX. i. 7. viii. 1. ix. 2, 5, 10. xi. 6. φίλῳ VIII. ii. 3, 6. vii. 6. xii. 8. xiii. 2, 7. IX. ii. 1. iii. 4. φίλον IV. iii. 29. vi. 4. VIII. i. 3. v. 5. vi. 2. xii. 8. xiii. 9. xiv. 1. IX. iii. 3. iv. 1, 5. x. 5. viii. 2. ix. 1, 10. x. 6. xi. 1, 2, 5, 6. xii. 2. X. ix. 18. φίλε VII. x. 4. φίλοι I. viii. 16. VIII. iii. 3, 5, 6, 9. iv. 2, 4, 5, 6. vi. 1. vii. 4, 5, 6. viii. 4, 5. xiii. 1, 2. IX. iii. 1, 4. iv. 5. viii. 9. x. 6. φίλων I. vii. 7. viii. 15. xi. 1, 6. xiii. 18. III. iii. 13. IV. i. 43. VIII. i. 1, 4. iv. 3. viii. 4. ix. 1. xiii. 1. IX. iv. 1. viii. 2, 9. ix. 1, 3, 4, 5, 10. x. 3. xi. 1, 2, 5, 6. xii. 2. X. ix. 18. φίλοιν I. vi. 1. φίλοις I. vii. 6. III. x. 2. IV. v. 10. VIII. iii. 6, 7, 9. v. 3. vi. 4. 5. viii. 5. IX. iii. 5. xi. 4. xii. 1. X. ix. 14. φίλους I. vi. 1. vii. 7. xi. 3. VIII. i. 1, 2, 5, 6, 7. ii. 4. iii. 8. iv. 2, 4. vi. 4. ix. 1, 3. IX. iii. 1, 4. iv. 1. v. 3. vi. 4. ix. 2, 4. x. 1, 4. xi. 3, 4, 5. X. vii. 6. φίλῳ IX. iv. 1. viii. 9, 10. φιλτάτοις X. ix. 19.
φιλοσοφεῖν II. iv. 6. φιλοσοφοῦντες ibid. φιλοσοφοῦντος VII. xi. 1.
φιλοσοφία X. ix. 29. φιλοσοφίας I. vi. 13. IX. i. 7.
φιλοσόφους I. vi. 1.
φιλοστοργότεροι IX. viii. 7.
φιλοτιμία II. vii. 8. III. x. 2. IV. iv. 5. φιλοτιμίαν IV. iv. 5. VIII. viii. 1.
φιλότιμος, φιλοτίμου II. vii. 8. φιλότιμον II. vii. 8. IV. iv. 3, 4.
φιλοτοιοῦτον I. viii. 10. φιλοτοιούτου IV. iv. 4. φιλοτοιούτων III. xi. 4.
φιλοφίλων VIII. viii. 4.
φιλοχρήματοι IV. i. 37.
φοβερὸν III. vii. 1. φοβερὰ II. ii. 9. III. vi. 2. vii. 3, 7, 8, 9, 13. viii. 14. ix. 1. X. viii. 7. φοβερῶν II. ii. 9. III. vi. 6. xii. 2. φοβερώτερον VII. vi. 7. φοβερώτατον III. vi. 6.
φοβεῖται III. vi. 5. vii. 11. φοβεῖσθαι II. i. 7. vii. 2. III. vi. 3, 4. vii. 3. 10. viii. 11. φοβούμενος II. ii. 8. v. 3. III. vi. 3. vii. 5. φοβούμεθα II. v. 4. III. vi. 2, 3. φοβηθῆναι II. vi. 10. φοβήσεται III. vii. 2. φοβοῖτο III. vii. 1. φοβούμενοι III. viii. 9. IV. ix. 2. φοβουμένου IV. iii. 28.
φόβον IV. ix. 1. φόβῳ IV. ix. 2. X. ix. 4. φόβος II. v. 2. III. i. 4. vi. 2. viii. 4. IV. i. 39. V. viii. 4. φόβοις III. viii. 15. φόβους II. vii. 2. III. vi. 1. ix. 1.
Φοινίσσαις IX. vi. 2.
φόνοι X. vii. 6.
φορὰ X. iv. 3.
φορτικὸς X. viii. 7. φορτικὸν IV. iii. 27. φορτικοὶ IV. viii. 3. φορτικώτατοι I. v. 2.
φρονεῖ IX. iv. 3. φρονεῖν I. vi. 10. VII. xi. 4. X. vii. 8. φρονοῦντας VII. vi. 9. φρονοίη VI. viii. 4.
φρόνησις I. viii. 6. VI. iii. 1. v. 3, 8. vi. 1, 2. vii. 6, 7. viii. 1, 2, 3, 5, 8, 9. ix. 7. x. 2, 3. xi. 7. xii. 1, 6, 10. xiii. 1, 2, 5. X. viii. 3. ix. 17. φρονήσεως I. vi. 11. VI. v. 1, 7, 8. xiii. 2, 3, 6, 7. VII. ii. 5. x. 2. X. ii. 3. viii. 3. ix. 12. φρονήσει VI. x. 1. xiii. 6. VII. xii. 5. X. viii. 3. φρόνησιν I. xiii. 20. VI. v. 6, 7. vi. 2. vii. 3. x. 3. xi. 3. xii. 6, 7. xiii. 4. X. viii. 3. φρονήσεις VI. xiii. 3.
φρόνιμος II. vi. 15. VI. v. 2. viii. 4, 5. xi. 2. VII. ii. 5. x. 1, 2. xi. 4. xii. 7. φρόνιμον VI. vii. 4. xi. 3. xii. 2, 10. xiii. 6. VII. i. 7. x. 1. xii. 7. φρόνιμοι VII. x. 2. φρονίμου VI. v. 1. vii. 6. VII. ii. 5. φρονίμων I. v. 5. VI. ix. 7. xi. 6. φρόνιμα VI. vii. 4. X. ii. 4. φρονίμους VI. v. 1, 2, 5. vii. 5. xi. 2. xii. 9. VII. i. 7.
φροντίζειν IV. i. 34. vi. 5. φροντίζοντες IV. vi. 2.
φυγὴ VI. ii. 2. φυγὴν III. viii. 3. φυγὰς II. iii. 7. VI. vii. 1.

φυλακή IV. i. 7.
φυλακτικὸν IV. i. 20. φυλακτικὰ I. vi. 8. V. i. 13.
φύλαξ V. vi. 5.
φυλάττειν IV. i. 39. φυλάξασθαι III. viii. 7. φυλακτέον II. ix. 6.
φυλάττει VIII. ix. 5. φυλάττουσι IX. ii. 9.
φυλακτικοὶ VIII. xii. 1.
φῦναι III. v. 17. ἔφυ III. v. 17. πέφυκεν I. vii. 11. viii. 14. ix. 5, 7. x. 12. xiii. 14. II. ii. 6. iii. 5. III. v. 17. VI. xii. 8. VIII. vi. 2. ix. 3. X. iv. 8. πεφύκασι I. vii. 22. II. iii. 4. X. ix. 4. πεφυκέναι I. xii. 2. III. v. 17. VIII. xii. 3. πεφυκότα I. xiii. 10. VIII. xii. 3. πεφυκὸς I. xiii. 15. VI. i. 5. IX. ix. 3. πεφυκότων II. i. 2. πεφυκόσι II. i. 3. πεφύκαμεν II. viii. 8. ix. 4. ἐνεφύκει V. vi. 9.
φυσικὸν VI. viii. 6. φυσικὴ III. xi. 1, 3. VI. xiii. 1, 2. VII. viii. 4. φυσικὸν III. v. 19. xi. 2. V. vii. 1. ix. 12. IX. vii. 4. X. ii. 4. φυσικὴν VII. xii. 2. φυσικῇ VIII. xiv. 4. φυσικοὶ VII. xiv. 5. φυσικῶν VII. x. 4. φυσικὰς VI. xiii. 6. φυσικαῖς III. xi. 3. VII. vi. 2. φυσικὰ V. vii. 5. viii. 7. VI. xi. 5. VIII. i. 7. X. v. 2. φυσικαὶ VI. xiii. 1. VII. vi. 6. φυσικωτάτη III. viii. 12. φυσικώτερον VII. vi. 2. VIII. i. 6. IX. vii. 2. ix. 7.
φυσικῶς VII. iii. 9.
φυσιολόγων VII. iii. 12.
φύσις I. iii. 4. xiii. 15. II. vi. 4, 9. III. iii. 7. V. v. 19. x. 6. VII. v. 4. xiii. 6. xiv. 8. VIII. v. 2. X. viii. 9. φύσεως VI. xi. 6. VII. v. 6. vi. 1, 6. x. 4. xii. 2, 3. xiv. 4, 7. IX. ix. 7. X. ix. 6. φύσει I. iii. 2. vi. 2. vii. 6. viii. 11. II. i. 2, 3, 4. v. 5. III. iii. 4. iv. 3. v. 15, 18, 19. V. v. 11. vii. 2, 3, 4, 7. viii. 3. x. 4. VI. vii. 5. xi. 5. xiii. 1. VII. iv. 5. v. 1, 3, 6. x. 4. xii. 2. xiii. 6. xiv. 7, 8. VIII. xi. 2. xii. 7. IX. ix. 3, 5, 7, 9, 10. X. v. 6. vii. 9. ix. 6, 14. φύσιν I. ix. 5. II. i. 3. iii. 5. III. i. 7. v. 15. xi. 3. xii. 2. V. vii. 5. VI. iv. 4. vii. 4. VII. vii. 6. x. 4. xi. 4. xii. 3. xiv. 5, 6, 8. VIII. xii. 7. IX. xi. 4. X. iii. 6. vii. 1. φύσεις VII. v. 1. xii. 1.
φυτικὸν I. xiii. 18. φυτικῷ I. xiii. 11.
φυτοῦ X. vi. 2. φυτοῖς I. vii. 12.
φωνὴ IV. iii. 34. φωνῆς III. x. 7. φωνῇ ibid. φωνὴν II. ix. 6.

X.

χαίρει III. x. 2. xi. 7. VII. xi. 4. xiv. 8. IX. ix. 6. X. v. 10. χαίρειν II. iii. 2, 9. vii. 15. III. x. 3, 6, 7, 11. xi. 4. VII. v. 2. ix. 5. xi. 2. xiv. 5. VIII. vi. 1. IX. vii. 6. X. i. 1. iii. 12. viii. 13. ix. 6. χαίρουσι VIII. vi. 1, 4. χαίρουσι III. x. 5, 7, 9. xi. 4. VII. ix. 3. xii. 2. xiv. 2, 5. VIII. ix. 2. vi. 1. viii. 2. xiii. 3. IX. xi. 4. χαίροιεν VIII. xii. 7. ἔχαιρε IV. vii. 10. χαίρων I. viii. 12. II. iii. 1. IV. vii. 12. IX. v. 3. χαίροντα I. viii. 12. χαίροντες III. x. 3. xi. 7. VII. xi. 4. xiv. 8. IX. ix. 6. X. v. 10. χαίροντας III. x. 4, 5, 6. VIII. v. 3. χαιρόντων IV. viii. 4. χαίρουσαι VIII. viii. 3.
χαλεπαίνει VII. vi. 1. χαλεπαίνειν IV. v. 1. χαλεπαίνοντας II. ix. 7. IV. v. 11, 13.
χαλεπὸς IX. ix. 5. χαλεπὸν II. iii. 8. vi. 14. ix. 4, 7. III. i. 9. ix. 7. IV. iii. 16, 26. V. i. 18. ix. 15. IX. x. 5. X. ix. 8. χαλεποὶ IV. v. 12. χαλεποὺς IV. v. 11. χαλεπὰ III. x. 8. VI. vii. 5. χαλεπώτερον II. iii. 10. III. i. 9. ix. 2.
χαλεπότης VII. v. 5. xi. 2. χαλεπότητα V. ii. 2.
χαλινοποιητικὴ I. i. 4. v. 8. vii. 1, 5. xii. 8. xiii. 8. III. i. 11.
χαλκεῖον V. ix. 7.
χαμαιλέοντα I. x. 8.
χαρὰν II. v. 2.
χαρίεις IV. viii. 9, 10. VIII. xiii. 2. χαρίεντες I. iv. 2. v. 4. xiii. 7. IV. vii. 16. viii. 4. χαριέστεροι IV. vii. 14.
χαρίζεται IX. viii. 6. χαρίζονται IX. viii. 4. χαρίζεσθαι IX. iii. 5. χαριζόμενον, χαρισαμένῳ V. v. 7. χαριστέον IX. ii. 3. χαριζόμενος IX. viii. 6.
χάρις IV. i. 8. χάριτος V. v. 7. ix. 12. χάριν I. i. 4. IV. vii. 11. VI. xii. 2, 10. VIII. ix. 4. xii. 7. IX. i. 4. ii. 1. iv. 1. viii. 1. xii. 2. X. ii. 2. vi. 6. ix. 10. χάριτας IX. vii. 1. χαρίτων V. v. 7.
χαῦνος IV. iii. 6, 13, 35. χαῦνοι IV. iii. 36.
χαυνότης II. vii. 7. χαυνότητος IV. iii. 37.
χειμῶσι III. i. 5.

χείρ V. ix. 11. χειρὸς I. vii. 11. VIII. xiii. 6. χεῖρα V. viii. 3. VIII. xiii. 6. χειρὶ V. ix. 14.
χειροτέχναι VI. viii. 2.
χειροτονητέον IX. ii. 1.
χείρων II. iii. 4. IV. vii. 17. VI. xii. 3. VII. vii. 3. VIII. xiv. 1. χείρονι VIII. xiii. 1. χεῖρον III. i. 6. IV. iii. 37. vii. 1. V. i. 14. x. 8. xi. 7. χείρους III. viii. 4, 16. IV. iii. 35. v. 12. VII. vii. 1. χείριστη VIII. x. 2. xi. 6.
χελιδὼν I. vii. 16.
χιὼν I. vi. 11.
χορηγῶν IV. ii. 20. κεχορηγημένον I. x. 15. κεχορηγημένων X. vii. 4. κεχορηγημένους X. viii. 11. χορηγεῖν IV. ii. 11.
χορηγίας X. viii. 4.
χρεία III. iii. 14. IV. i. 6. V. v. 11, 13. IX. xi. 6. X. viii. 4, 6. χρείας V. v. 11. VIII. vi. 1. χρείᾳ V. v. 13. VIII. i. 1. IV. xi. 6. χρειῶν V. v. 15. VII. iv. 2. χρείαις VIII. xiii. 10. X. viii. 1.
χρεὼν I. ii. 6. iii. 4. x. 1. IX. viii. 2. X. viii. 7.
χρὴ I. vii. 18. xiii. 19. VI. xii. 7. IX. iii. 3. viii. 11. X. vii. 8. viii. 12.
χρήσεως VIII. xiii. 7.
χρήματα II. vii. 6. IV. i. 2, 5, 6, 7, 14, 20, 21, 26. ii. 1. vi. 9. V. ii. 6. VII. iv. 5. VIII. ix. 3. xiv. 3. IX. i. 7. vii. 7. viii. 9. χρημάτων II. vii. 4. III. iii. 13. vi. 4. IV. i. 1, 7, 24. iv. 2. vi. 9. V. ii. 12. iv. 2. VII. iv. 2. VIII. ix. 5. xiv. 1. X. viii. 4. χρήμασι III. x. 2. IV. ii. 1. V. ii. 2. IX. viii. 4.
χρηματίζεσθαι VIII. xiv. 3.
χρηματισμὸν VII. xii. 4.
χρηματιστὴς I. v. 8.
χρηματιστικὴν III. iii. 8.
χρῆσθαι I. x. 13. II. ii. 6. III. v. 22. viii. 7. x. 9. IV. i. 6. V. i. 15. VI. x. 3. VII. iii. 7. VIII. vi. 5. X. ix. 2. χρῶνται VIII. x. 4. χρησάμενον I. ix. 11. ἐχρησάμεθα II. i. 4. χρησάμενοι II. i. 4. χρῆται IV. i. 6. V. iii. 9. iv. 3. VI. x. 3. xiii. 8. VII. x. 3. χρήσεται IV. i. 6. χρώμενοι IV. vii. 16. VIII. xiii. 4. χρωμένοις I. ii. 7. χρώμενος II. iii. 10. V. i. 18. VII. iii. 5. χρωμένων VII. xii. 3. VIII. xi. 6. χρώμενος VII. iii. 6. χρωμένῳ X. ix. 23. χρωμένῳ VII. x. 4. χρηστέον I. xiii. 9. IX. iii. 4.
χρήσιμοι VI. xii. 2. VIII. iii. 3. vi. 6. χρησίμη I. vii. 19. χρήσιμον I. v. 8. vi. 3. III. i. 2. VIII. i. 2. iii. 1, 3. iv. 1, 2, 4, 5, 6. vi. 3, 4, 7. viii. 6. xii. 6, 7. xiii. 1, 4, 5, 11. IX. i. 3. iii. 1. v. 3. vii. 6. χρήσιμοι VI. xii. 1. VIII. vi. 5. viii. 6. IX. vii. 2. χρήσιμα I. ix. 7. χρησίμων IV. i. 6. VIII. vi. 4. IX. vii. 6. xi. 2. χρησίμοις VIII. ii. 4. vi. 5. IX. ix. 4. χρησιμώτατοι X. i. 4.
χρῆσις I. x. 12. IV. i. 7. V. i. 15. ii. 10, 13. χρήσει I. viii. 9. χρῆσιν IX. ii. 9. v. 3. x. 2.
χρηστοὶ VII. ii. 6.
χρονιζομένην IX. v. 3.
χρόνιον VIII. iv. 1.
χρονιωτέρας X. v. 5.
χρόνος I. vii. 16, 17. χρόνου II. i. 1. IV. v. 10. VI. viii. 5. VII. iii. 8. xii. 2. X. iv. 2. χρόνῳ I. vi. 3. x. 14. VIII. iv. 3. vi. 3. X. iv. 2, 3, 4. χρόνον I. iii. 17. x. 5, 15. II. ix. 7. III. viii. 16. IV. v. 3, 7, 10, 11, 13. VI. ix. 2, 6. xii. 1. VIII. iii. 9. vi. 4. viii. 5. xii. 8. xiii. 6. IX. viii. 9. X. iv. 1. χρόνοις X. v. 6.
χρόνια V. ix. 7.
χρυσὸς IV. ii. 10. χρυσοῦ, χρυσὸν X. v. 8.
χρώμασι III. x. 3.
χωλὸν III. x. 9.
χώρας II. vii. 8.
χωρίζεται IV. i. 38. χωρίσαντες I. vi. 9. χωρισθῇ V. vi. 8. χωρίζονται VI. xiii. 6. χωρίζεσθαι X. v. 7. χωρισθέντες VIII. vii. 5. κεχωρίσθαι X. v. 7. κεχωρισμένα VIII. v. 1. κεχωρισμένη X. viii. 3.
χωριστὸν I. vi. 13.
χωρὶς VIII. xiv. 4. X. ii. 3.
χωρισμὸν X. iv. 11.

Ψ.

ψέγομεν IV. iv. 3. V. ii. 2. ψέξει IX. viii. 5. ψέγειν X. i. 3. ψέγοντες IV. iv. 4. ψεγόμεθα II. v. 3, 5. ψέγεται II. v. 3. vi. 12. ix. 8. IV. v. 5, 13. V. viii. 2. VII. iv. 2. ψέγονται III. i. 7. VII. iv. 5. ψέγονται IV. iii. 31. ψέγοντες IV. iv. 4. ψέγων X. i. 3.
ψεκτὸς II. ix. 8. IV. v. 13. vii. 11.

ψεκτὸν III. xi. 5. IV. vii. 6. V. xi. 7. ψεκτοὶ IV. vii. 6. ψεκταὶ IV. v. 4. vi. 3. X. v. 6. ψεκτὰ II. vii. 11. ψεκτῶν VII. i. 6. ii. 4. iv. 6.
ψεύδεσθαι VII. ix. 4. ψευδόμενος VII. ii. 7, 8. ψευδόμενοι IV. vii. 6. ψευδομένου IV. vii. 1.
ψευδής. ψευδεῖ VI. ix. 5. VII. ii. 7. ix. 1. ψευδεῖς VI. iv. 6. ψευδῆ VI. ix. 5.
ψευδομαρτυρία V. ii. 13.
ψεῦδος IV. vii. 6, 8. VI. ii. 3. ψεύδει I. viii. 1. III. ii. 10. v. 4. IV. vii. 10, 12. ψευδοῦς VII. xiv. 3.
ψεύστης IV. vii. 12.
ψηφίζονται VII. x. 3.
ψήφισμα V. x. 7. VI. viii. 2. ψηφίσματος V. x. 6. ψηφίσματα VII. ix. 3.
ψηφισματώδη V. vii. 1.
ψιμμυθίῳ I. vi. 11.
ψόγον I. x. 11. ψόγοι III. i. 9. ψόγων III. i. 1.
ψοφοδεὴς VII. v. 6. vi. 1.
ψυχὴ VI. iii. 1. IX. iv. 9. viii. 2. ψυχῆς I. vii. 14, 15. ix. 7. xiii. 1, 6, 7, 8, 11, 13, 15, 16. II. iii. 5. III. v. 15. V. xi. 9. VI. i. 3, 4, 5, 8. xi. 7. xii. 6, 10. IX. viii. 4. ψυχῇ I. vi. 12. xiii. 16. II. v. 1. VI. ii. 1. VIII. xi. 6. ψυχὴν I. viii. 2, 3. II. iv. 6. VII. iii. 9. IX. iv. 3. X. ix. 6.
ψυχικαὶ III. x. 2. ψυχικῶν I. viii. 10. xii. 6. ψυχικὰς I. viii. 2.
ψύχους VII. iv. 3.

Ω.

ὧδε II. vi. 4. VII. iii. 9.
ὡδὶ V. ix. 14, 16. VII. iii. 2.
ὠμοῖς VII. v. 2.
ὠνεῖσθαι V. iv. 13. ὠνοῦνται V. vii. 5.
ὠνὴ V. ii. 13.
ὠνίοις, IX. i. 8.
ὥρα X. iv. 8. ὥραις VIII. iv. 1.
ὡς IV. vii. 11. viii. 2. V. ii. 10. iii. 6. vii. 3. ix. 12. VI. i. 1. VII. i. 4. vi. 5, 7. viii. 2. x. 3. xii. 2.
ὥς IV. viii. 1. V. viii. 3. ix. 4. xi. 2. VI. ix. 6. VII. iii. 2.
ὡς ἂν II. vi. 20.
ὡσαύτως II. iii. 11. V. ii. 9. VII. iv. 4. v. 4.
ὡς ἐπὶ τὸ πολὺ I. iii. 4. III. i. 9.
ὥσπερ I. iii. 1. iv. 5. vii. 10, 14. viii. 9, 12. ix. 10. xii. 3. xiii. 7, 17, 18, 19. II. i. 4. ii. 1, 3, 4, 6, 7. iv. 1, 6. vi. 9, 20. vii. 11. viii. 2, 4. III. i. 17. iii. 11. iv. 4, 5. v. 5, 14, 17, 20, 22. viii. 4, 8, 10. xi. 5. xii. 8. IV. i. 20, 23. ii. 1, 6, 12, 15, 20. iii. 27, 37. iv. 1, 2, 4. vii. 12. viii. 3. V. i. 7. iv. 8, 9. v. 1, 11, 13. vi. 8. vii. 2. viii. 3, 10. ix. 1, 3, 13, 16. x. 7. xi. 4, 7, 9. VI. iii. 3. iv. 6. v. 7. vii. 2, 3. viii. 2, 8. x. 3. xii. 1, 2, 7. xiii. 1, 8. VII. i. 2, 5. ii. 1. iii. 13. iv. 2, 6. v. 3, 4, 8. vi. 1, 2, 6, 7. vii. 6, 8. viii. 1, 2, 3. ix. 3, 5. x. 3, 4. xii. 3. xiii. 1, 2. xiv. 4, 5, 6, 8. VIII. iv. 4. v. 1. vi. 2. xi. 1, 6. IX. ii. 3. iv. 5, 9. v. 3. vi. 2, 3. vii. 3. viii. 6. ix. 5, 10. x. 3. xi. 2. xii. 1. X. ii. 1. iii. 4, 9. iv. 7, 9. v. 7, 8, 11. vi. 4. viii. 7, 13. ix. 6, 10, 14, 17, 20.
ὥστε I. ii. 1, 7. vi. 2, 10. vii. 1, 3. viii. 2, 11. xi. 5, 6. II. iii. 2, 10. vii. 15. viii. 5. III. v. 2, 10. xi. 6. xii. 3. IV. ii. 6. ix. 5, 6. V. i. 8, 13. ii. 5, 9. iii. 9. iv. 4, 6, 12, 14. v. 10, 12, 17. vi. 4. viii. 2, 10. ix. 2, 9. x. 1, 7. xi. 4. VI. i. 6. ii. 2. iv. 2. v. 2, 6. vii. 2, 3, 7. ix. 4, 5. xi. 6. xii. 7, 10. xiii. 2. VII. i. 2. ii. 6, 9. iii. 6, 7, 8, 11. vi. 1, 3. vii. 3. viii. 5. ix. 1, 3. x. 3. xii. 2. xiii. 2, 7. xiv. 3, 8. VIII. i. 2. iv. 1. viii. 4. xiii. 9. xiv. 4. IX. vii. 5. viii. 7. ix. 9. xii. 1. X. v. 4, 6. viii. 7, 8, 13.
ὠφέλεια IV. vi. 9. VIII. iv. 2. xiii. 11. ὠφελείας II. vii. 13. VIII. v. 3. vi. 7. viii. 6. ὠφελείᾳ VIII. xiii. 4, 10. ὠφελείαις VIII. xiii. 1.
ὠφελεῖ IV. i. 32. ὠφελοῦνται VIII. xi. 6. xiii. 11. ὠφεληθῇ IX. i. 8. ὠφεληθεὶς IX. viii. 7. ὠφελήσειν IX. xi. 5. ὠφελεῖσθαι IX. xi. 6. ὠφελοῦνται X. vi. 3. ὠφελουμένων VIII. xiv. 3. ὠφεληθήσονται I. vi. 16.
ὠφέλιμον V. ix. 17. VI. ix. 6. VIII. iii. 4. xiii. 8. ὠφελίμων V. v. 18. ὠφελίμοις IX. vi. 4. ὠφέλιμα VI. vii. 5. VIII. x. 2. xiii. 8. X. ix. 21. ὠφέλιμοι IV. i. 11. VIII. iii. 4, 6. ὠφελίμων I. vi. 9. IV. iii. 33. ὠφελιμώτερον VIII. xiv. 1. ὠφελιμώτερον VIII. vii. 2.
ὠχριῶσι IV. ix. 1.

II.

INDEX

OF

GREEK WORDS COMMENTED UPON.

ἀβέβαιον ii. 310.
ἀγαθοί 'nobles' i. 92.
ἀγόμενος ii. 262.
ἀθανασία ii. 16.
ἀΐδιον ii. 19.
αἰδώς in Hesiod i. 86, 506.
αἱρετόν and φευκτόν ii. 316.
αἴσθησις i. 451.
αἰσχροπραγεῖν ii. 58.
ἀκόλαστοι ii. 54.
ἀκρίβεια i. 350, 391, 400, 425. ii. 19.
ἀκροχειρίζεσθαι ii. 13.
ἀκρόχολοι ii. 82.
ἀλεκτρυών i. 123.
'Αλήθεια, work of Protagoras i. 123.
ἄλλος idiomatic i. 482.
ἀμετρία ii. 319.
ἀναβολή ii. 277.
ἀναισθησία i. 510.
ἄνθρωπος ii. 210. fem. ii. 213.
ἀόριστος i. 202–3, 423. ii. 304.
ἀπείπασθαι ii. 280.
ἄπειρον, ἰέναι εἰς i. 422.
ἁπλῶς and κατὰ πρόσθεσιν i. 414. ἁπλῶς ἀγαθά ii. 101.
ἀπό ii. 205.
ἀποδέχεσθαι ii. 258, 260.
ἀπολαυστικός, i. 432.
ἀπομάσσω ii. 311.
ἀποτετορνευμένα i. 317.
ἀπορίαι i. 380, 395.
ἀρετή i. 388, 449, 455, 477.
ἄρρενα 'masculines' i. 123.
ἀρχή i. 387, 393, 431. γνώσεως καὶ γενέσεως 470. ἐν ἀρχῇ ii. 249.
ἀρχιθέωρος ii. 67.
ἀρχιτεκτονικός i. 421.
ἄσωτος ii. 58.

αὐθάδης ii. 85.
αὐθέκαστος ii. 87.
αὐλοί i. 444.
αὐτάρκης i. 190. αὐτάρκεια i. 445. ii. 301.
αὑτοῦ, δι' ii. 283. καθ' ii. 255.
αὐτῶν, ἐπὶ τῶν ii. 294.
ἀφαιρέσεως, ἐξ, &c. ii. 171.

βάναυσοι ii. 67.
βάρος ii. 309.
βίαιος i. 435.
βίος i. 432, 449.
βούλεται ii. 58, 81, 272.
βούλησις ii. 23.
βωμολόχοι ii. 90.

γαστρίμαργος ii. 50.
γένεσις i. 235, 420.
γένος i. 426.
γνώμη ii. 178.
γνώριμα ἁπλῶς, ἡμῖν i. 431.

δέ in apodosis i. 421.
δέον i. 422.
δειλοί 'commonalty' i. 92.
δεινός ii. 185.
δεκάζω i. 511.
δι' αὑτῶν, ii. 116.
διαβάλλω ii. 259.
διαγωγή ii. 90.
διάθεσις i. 504.
διαιρετόν i. 497.
διακεῖμαι, i. 495.
διαμένω ii. 286.
διάνοια ii. 174.
διάστασις ii. 292.
διαφθείρομαι ii. 287.
δίκαιον i. 349. etymology ii. 114.

δικαιοπραγία ii. 122.
διόρθωμα ii. 113.
διότι ii. 170.
διπλάσιον i. 438.
δίψαι ii. 246.
δοκεῖ i. 343.
δυάς, δυὰς ἀόριστος i. 438.
δύναμις i. 231 sqq. 'art' i. 420.

ἐγγυητής, νόμος ii. 121.
ἐγκύκλιοι λόγοι i. 408. ἐγκύκλιον i. 435.
ἐγκώμιον i. 470.
ἐθισμός i. 451.
ἔθος i. 480, ii. 343.
εἶδος i. 441.
εἶναι i. 501, ii. 104.
εἰκών ii. 86.
ἐνέργεια i. 230–251. etymology 233. this and δύναμις Megarian 233. 'energy' 387. ii. 296. ἐνέργεια τῶν ἀρετῶν ii. 26.
ἐντελέχεια i. 234.
ἐξαγωγή i. 333. ii. 121.
ἐξαμβλόω ii. 329.
ἕξις i. 240, 387. 319, ii. 204.
ἐξουσία ii. 339.
ἐξωτερικοὶ λόγοι i. 397–408.
ἐπαγωγή i. 451.
ἐπαρκέω ii. 286.
ἐπείσακτος ii. 302.
ἐπίδειξις i. 128.
ἐπίδοσις i. 510.
ἐπιεικής, ἐπιείκεια ii. 139, 272.
ἐπιζητέω i. 453.
ἐπιθυμίαν λαμβάνειν ii. 228.
ἐπιπολάζω i. 430.
ἐπιστήμη i. 421. ἐπιστήμων 'artistic' ii. 68.
ἔργον i. 191, 447. τὰ ἔργα ii. 298.
ἔρως etymology ii. 292.
ἐσθλοί 'nobles' i. 92.
ἔσχατον ii. 168, 172.
ἑταιρική ii. 307.
εὐδαίμων i. 465.
εὐθυνοῦντα i. 460.
εὕρεσις i. 321.
εὐτράπελος ii. 99.

ζωή i. 432.

ἤ in questions i. 420.
ἤ indefinite ii. 111, 182.
ἥδεσθαι and ἡσθῆναι ii. 320.
ἡδύ ii. 179.

ἡδονὴ οἰκεία and ἀλλοτρία ii. 328.
ἦθος i. 480.

θεῖαι i. 424.
θεοφιλής ii. 342.
θέσις i. 434.
θεωρέω ii. 154, 203.
θήλεα 'feminines' i. 122.
θυμός ii. 42.

ἰδέα, prob. Democritean word i. 201, 441. 'form' ii. 100.
ἵστασθαι i. 422, ii. 173.
ἴσον i. 419.

καθόλου i. 437.
καί 'or' ii. 152.
καινὰ τοῦ πολέμου ii. 40.
κοινῇ 'commonly' i. 92.
καλόν i. 422, ii. 9.
καλοκἀγαθία ii. 75, 181.
κάρδοπος i. 123.
καταβέβληνται i. 436.
κατάστασις ii. 236.
κατέχω ii. 215.
κατοκώχιμος ii. 344.
κενὰ τοῦ πολέμου ii. 40. κενότερον i. 502.
κίνησις i. 235.
κλῆσις ii. 100.
κληρωτός ii. 270.
κοινός i. 484. κοινότερον 502.
κρίσις ii. 58.
κύριος i. 423, ii. 299.

Λεσβία οἰκοδομή ii. 140.
λογικός i. 507.
λογιστικόν ii. 149.
λόγος i. 485. 'inference' ii. 163. forms of λόγος classified by Protagoras i. 122. ὀρθὸς λόγος i. 485. λόγον ἔχειν i. 400. κατὰ λόγον i. 78, 448. μετὰ λόγου i. 448, ii. 162.

μαθηματικά, τὰ i. 476.
μακάριος i. 465.
μάλιστα i. 419.
μανθάνειν ii. 177.
μαντεύομαι i. 433.
μέθοδος i. 419.
μελαγχολικοί ii. 223.
μεσότης, μέσον i. 251–262. μέσος δικαστής ii. 114.
μεσίδιοι ii. 114.

μεθόριος ii. 259.
μοναδικὸς ἀριθμὸς ii. 111.

νέμεσις i. 86, 506.
νοῦς παθητικὸς and ποιητικὸς i. 297.
ναυτίλης ii. 238.

ξένος ii. 306.

ο inserted and omitted ii. 188.
οἷος 'individual' i. 448.
ὅλη ἀρετὴ ii. 183.
ὁμόνοια ii. 293.
ὁμώνυμα i. 442.
ὄναρ ii. 156.
ὀργανικὸς ii. 8.
'Ορθοέπεια, work of Protagoras i. 122.
ὅρος, Eudemian term i. 60. ii. 147.
ὅσιον i. 438.
ὅταν with aorist ii. 120.
οὗ ἕνεκα i. 495.
οὐσία i. 500.

πάθη i. 387.
παιδεία, i. 426.
παιδεραστία ii. 214, 292.
πάνυ, οὐ πάνυ, ἀλλὰ πάνυ ii. 59.
παρὰ i. 428.
παράβασις ii. 270.
πάσχειν ii. 119, 327.
περίαπτον i. 456.
Πέρσαις, ἐν ii. 127.
Πλάτων with and without article i. 430.
πλοῦς δεύτερος i. 511.
ποίησις distinguished by Prodicus from πρᾶξις i. 124.
ποιητικοῖς ii. 206.
ποιοῦν ii. 119, 327.
πότερον i. 420.
πραγματεία i. 484.
πρακτὰ i. 422. πρακτικὸς 447.
πρᾶξις distinguished by Prodicus from ποίησις i. 124. in Eudemus 420. ii. 150.
πράττειν εὖ i. 429.
προαίρεσις ii. 15.
προηγμένα i. 317.
προΐεσθαι ii. 29.
προσαιρούμενον ii. 288.
προϋπαρχὴ ii. 285.
προϋπάρχειν ii. 70.

σεμνότης ii. 85.
σκεύη 'neuters' i. 122.
σκοπὸς Eudemian term, ii. 142.
σοφία ii. 164.
σοφιστὴς i. 105–113.
σοφοί i. 429.
σπουδάζω ii. 291.
στρατιῶται ii. 41.
συγγράμματα ii. 349.
συλλογιστέον i. 467.
συμβάλλομαι i. 468.
συμβεβηκὸς ii. 259.
συμμετρία ii. 320.
συμφέρον ii. 11.
σὺν in composition ii. 40.
συναίτιον ii. 31.
συνάπτω ii. 257.
συναριθμεῖσθαι i. 446.
σύνεσις ii. 176.
συνεχὲς i. 421.
σύνθετον, τὸ ii. 239.
συνώνυμος ii. 105.
σχεδὸν i. 419.
σωφροσύνη ii. 47. etymology 160.

τέλειον i. 190, 239, 449.
τέλος i. 220–230, 420, 466. 'morality' of an action ii. 7, 36. τὸ κατὰ τὴν ἕξιν τέλος ibid.
τεχνάζειν ii. 157.
τέχνη i. 420, 421, 428.
τί ἦν εἶναι i. 500.
τις frequently omitted ii. 8, 46.
τοιούτων περί, ἐκ i. 426.
τομαὶ καὶ καύσεις ii. 321.

ὑβρίζω ii. 218.
ὕλη, πρώτη and ἐσχάτη i. 234. opposed to form 425.
ὑπάρχοντα i. 452.
ὑπερβολὴ ii. 262.
ὑπόθεσις ii. 226.
ὑποκείμενον i. 425, ii. 99. ὑποκεῖσθαι i. 485.
ὑφηγεῖσθαι i. 504.

φαινόμενα ii. 197.
φαντασία ii. 30, 216.
φάρυγξ ii. 49.
φευκτὸν and αἱρετὸν ii. 316.
φιλαυτία ii. 300.
φιλόκαλοι, φιλοκαλεῖν i. 455.
φρόνησις i. 183, 441; ii. 158, 238.
φρόνιμος i. 499.
φύσει i. 456. φύσις i. 481.

χαρίεις ii. 276.

ψευδόμενος ii. 200.
ψυχὴ i. 294–302.

III.

INDEX OF MATTERS.

'Actuality,' i. 230-251.
Æschylus, ii. 12.
Agathon, i. 126.
Albinus, prætor, i. 341.
Alcidamas of Elæa, i. 122, 185.
Alexander the Great, i. 325, 399.
Amafinius, i. 346.
Anacreon, i. 82.
Anaxagoras of Clazomenæ, i. 103, 110, 140, 281, 453. His 'happy man,' ii. 341.
Anaxandrides of Rhodes, ii. 231.
Anaximenes of Miletus, i. 89.
Andronicus Rhodius, i. 6. His recension is 'our Aristotle,' i. 9. Principles on which it was made, i. 17.
Antimoerus of Mende, i. 114.
Antipater, Stoic, i. 307. Another, i. 343.
Antiphon of Rhamnus, i. 108.
Antisthenes, i. 171, 172.
Anytus, accuser of Socrates, i. 115, 162.
Apellicon, i. 6.
Apollodorus, i. 2, 180.
Apollonides, Stoic, i. 344.
Aquinas, Thomas, i. 373.
Aratus, i. 337.
Archedemus, Stoic, i. 307.
Archelaus, philosopher, i. 149, 160, 284.
Archytas, pseudo-, i. 102.
Arete, i. 174.
Aristippus of Cyrene, i. 169, 173.
Aristophanes, *Clouds* quoted, i. 106, 113, 122, 142.
Aristotle, Dates of life, i. 2.

I. *General.* Period of composition of his works, i. 3. Employed his school in co-operation, 4, 70. Fate of his writings, according to Strabo, 5-18. Used prooems, 20. Sometimes ends with a line of poetry, 47. Deferred treating of Justice, 50. Most of his works unfinished, 68. Order of his extant writings, 70. Often begins with a historical sketch, 73. His tone and style of writing, 215. Deficient in humour, 216. Made philosophy scientific, 219. Introduced technical formulæ, 188, 220. Constantly defers metaphysical questions, 270, 275. Order of his writings, 271. Promised works on *Physiology of Plants*, and on *Health and Disease*, 68, 273. His *Metaphysics* a fragment, 274. His merits as a Physicist, 277. Was unappreciated previous to the recension of Andronicus, 8. His Dialogues prized by the ancients, 10. Catalogue of his works by Diogenes, 9. His *Ethics* soon superseded, 371. Preservation of his works, 372. Study of him in the Middle Ages, 373, 375. Translated into Latin, 373. Recognised as the great Encyclopædist, 374. His phraseology adopted into modern languages, 387. Why he is worth being studied, 388. His ethical method, 391-396. Was he a dogmatist? 396. In *Pol.* vii. i. has given us an extract from one of his own dialogues, 405. Virtually separated ethics from politics, 408. His loose writing, ii. 48, 50, 262, 285. Junctures in his works, i. 43; ii. 32, 94, 248, 280, 311. Interpolations, i. 447; ii. 51, 254, 301.

II. *Aristotle's relation to Plato.* Was he Plato's pupil? i. 180.

Codified the results of Plato, 181. His debt to Plato, 188-198. Criticises him, 198-214. Criticises Idea of Good, 204-212. His early polemic against Plato, 212. His captious and unsatisfactory attitude towards him, 188, 396. Sets aside *Republic* and *Laws*, ii. 350. Suggestions adopted from Plato:—on Education, ii. 314. Courage, ii. 32, 33, 37. Liberality, ii. 61. Communities arise from mutual needs, ii. 117. Money, ii. 119. *ἀγχίνοια*, ii. 174. *φρόνησις* and *σύνεσις*, ii. 177. Questions about Friendship, ii. 252, 253. Fluctuations of bad men, ii. 290. Intellectual pleasures, ii. 322. Proper and foreign pleasure, ii. 328. Archers, i. 422. Mathematicians, *ib.* *μαντεύομαι*, i. 434. *ἔργον*, i. 447. *τετράγωνος*, i. 464. *ἀπορία*, i. 469. Dealing, i. 472. Derivation of *ἦθος*, i. 481. Dye of education, i. 491. Boxer who eats much, i. 498. Crooked timbers, i. 511. Tuning lyre, ii. 147. 'Mind's eye,' ii. 181. *Corruptio optimi*, ii. 187. *σοφὸς ἀνήρ*, ii. 194.

III. *Logic.* Aristotle prided himself on being the discoverer of the Syllogism, i. 262. Logic not a part of philosophy, i. 271.

IV. *Metaphysics.* Unity of Thought and Being, ii. 304. His nominalism, i. 211. Four Causes, i. 220. The Potential and the Actual, i. 230-251. Absolute and Relative Knowledge, i. 433. *ἀρχαί*, how obtained, i. 451. Knowledge better than search, ii. 337. Metaphysics identical with Theology, i. 287. Aristotle's ideas of God, i. 287-294. He is indeterminate on the question of a future life, i. 299-302.

V. *Physics.* His physical treatises, i. 273. Nature, i. 278-284. Chance, i. 279. Necessity, i. 280. Teleology, i. 282. Chain of Nature, i. 284. Man and nature, i. 285. Heavenly Bodies, i. 272, 286. Stars more divine than man, ii. 166. Secular catastrophes, i. 288. Nature desires good, ii. 263. Makes nothing in vain, i. 422. Man and nature, i. 284.

Life defined, i. 255. Life sweet, ii. 304. Scale of life, i. 294. Senses of brutes, ii. 48. Moral qualities of brutes, ii. 187, 207, 218. Purer senses, ii. 330. Separate senses and common sense, ii. 172. Sleep and dreams, i. 474. Youth like wine, ii. 246. Psychology a branch of physics, ii. 226. Aristotle's psychology a development of Plato's, i. 192. Soul, i. 294-298. Division of mind, i. 419. Resemblance of subject and object, ii. 149. Two kinds of reason, i. 296-298. Permanence of mental states, i. 463. Attention, ii. 327. Immortality, i. 298-302.

VI. *Ethics.* Four treatises on, i. 18. Aristotle's ethical method, i. 391-396. Advance on Plato—accumulation of experience and new formulæ, i. 185. Abstract terms ethicised, i. 220. Virtue not predicable of God, i. 292. Boys have no virtue, i. 460. No doctrine of moral obligation, i. 377. Condemns suicide, ii. 37. Evil self-destructive, ii. 82.

Book 1. End, Chief Good, Happiness; Psychology.—Doctrine of *τέλος*, i. 220-230. Partly Cyrenaic, i. 228. Ends in Plato, i. 444. Chief good must be *αὐτάρκης* (Platonic), i. 190. Cannot be added to (Platonic), *ib.* Cannot be painful, ii. 263. To be found in man's *ἔργον* (Platonic), i. 191. Happiness, i. 249.

Book 2. Habit, and Definition of Virtue.—Virtue can be taught, i. 166. Doctrine of habit implicitly Socratic, *ib.* Habit second nature, ii. 231. *ἕξις*, i. 240. 'Mean' (Platonic), i. 254. Ignorance, ii. 11.

Book 3. Will and the Virtues: Courage, Temperance.—Will, i. 285. Question of Free-will not entered on, i. 376. List of Virtues, i. 213.

Book 4. Liberality, Magnificence, Great-souledness, Ambition, Mildness, *φιλία*, *ἀλήθεια*, εὐτραπελία, αἰδώς, Anger, ii. 216.

Book 5. Justice. — Aristotle deferred writing on, i. 49. Relation of the Eudemian account of, to Aristotle, ii. 95. Natural and Conventional, ii. 126. Justice a proportion, ii. 109, 110, 124.

Book 6. Moral Standard and Intellectual Virtues.—φρόνησις partly Platonic, i. 192. φρόνησις as standard, Cynic, i. 171.

Book 7. Incontinence and Moral struggle; Pleasure.—Practical Syllogism, i. 262-269. Three motives, ii. 150.

Books 8-9. Friendship,—partly suggested by Plato, i. 196.

Book 10. Pleasure; Speculation; Transition to Politics.—Pleasure, i. 246-249. Prominence of Pleasure suggested by Cyrenaics, i. 177. Plato's view of, i. 194. Pleasure and pain, i. 488. Pleasure not chief good, ii. 234. Amusements, ii. 333. Philosophy above morality, ii. 338. Duty of aspiration, ii. 337.

VII. *Politics.* Political ideas in *Eth. Nic.* i. 409-412. Ethics subordinate to Politics, i. 424. Philosophy the end of state, i. 227. Necessity of Politics to Ethics, ii. 343-351. Law universal, ii. 101, 141. Division of the science, ii. 168. Best form of government, ii. 128. Tyranny worst form, ii. 125. Various forms, ii. 269-272. State prior in idea to family, ii. 275. Limited size of state, ii. 306. Legislation higher part of Politics, ii. 347. Praises Sparta, ii. 345. Bad Political Economy, ii. 66. Value and Price, ii. 118. Money, ii. 119, 121. Slavery, i. 385. Slave, ii. 334. Contempt for potentates, ii. 341.

VIII. *Rhetoric and Art.* His account of the rise of Rhetoric, i. 121. Regarded it as the art of Composition, i. 123. The Ludicrous, ii. 92. Law of art, i. 255. Artistic view of virtue, *ib.* Musical ear, i. 257; ii. 301.

IX. *Religion.* Practical religion not discussed by him, i. 26. Providence, i. 222, 293; ii. 342. God, i. 287-294; ii. 247. 'The gods,' ii. 128, 275. God's life is thought, ii. 330. This doubted in the *Great Ethics*, i. 36. Prayer, ii. 101.

X. *Lost Writings.* 'Dialogues,' i. 8, 10, 14, 400-408. Συναγωγὴ τεχνῶν, i. 121. Dialogue called *Eudemus*, i. 300. Περὶ Ποιητῶν, i. 402. Πολιτικός, &c., i. 404. Νήρινθος, or Κορίνθιος, i. 406. 'Exoteric' writings, i. 398. Πολιτεῖαι, ii. 350.

XI. *Spurious Writings, De Virtutibus et Vitiis*, i. 19, 38. See also *Eudemian Ethics* and *Magna Moralia*. *De Mundo*, i. 17. *De Xenophane*, &c., i. 137. *De Motu Animalium*, i. 263. *Categoriæ*, i. 438.

Arnold, Dr., quoted, i. 389.

Arrian, i. 360.

Aspasius, i. 32.

Athenians, no naval feeling, ii. 35. Their social freedom, ii. 345.

Athenodorus, Stoic, i. 307. Another, *ib.* 344.

Atticus, Platonist, i. 31.

Aurelius, Marcus, i. 363-365.

Averroes, i. 298, 373.

Bacon, quoted, i. 15; ii. 135. His 'believing Christian,' i. 312. His disparagement of Aristotle, i. 277, 395. His 'forms,' i. 300.

Balbus, Lucilius, i. 343.

Barea Soranus, i. 347.

Bentham, i. 368.

Berkeley, 'Theory of Vision,' i. 239.

Bernays, his theory of the 'Exoteric discourses,' i. 400-406.

Bias of Priene, i. 69.

Boethius, i. 8.

Brasidas, ii. 127.

Buckle, quoted, i. 380.

Buddhism, i. 385.

Burke, quoted, ii. 38.

Butler compared with the Stoics, i. 319. His 'self-love,' ii. 300. Quoted, ii. 335.

Cæranus, Stoic, i. 348.

Callicles, i. 149, 150.

Cannibalism, ii. 213.

Carneades, Academic, i. 340.

Casaubon, i. 63.

Catiline, ii. 59.
Cato the Censor, i. 340. Cato of Utica, i. 343.
Chorus, comic and tragic, ii. 71.
Chrysippus, Stoic, i. 314, 315, 321, 325, 329-332; ii. 200.
Cicero,—no real acquaintance with Aristotle, i. 7. Mentions *Eth. Nic.* i. 8. Mentions 'Commentaries,' i. 398. Quotes Συναγωγὴ τεχνῶν, i. 121. Hears Posidonius, i. 343. His philosophy, i. 345. Quoted, i. 460.
Cleanthes, i. 307, 312-314. His hymn, i. 327, 337.
Cleobulus of Lindus, i. 91.
Clitomachus, i. 341.
Comedy new, ii. 91.
Comte, his 'Religion of Humanity,' i. 383. Compared with Aristotle, i. 385.
Convention and Nature, i. 149-151; ii. 126-127.
Corax, i. 121.
Coriscus, name used as example, i. 132.
Corruption, human, i. 357, 509.
Crantor, Academic, i. 218.
Crates, of Thebes, i. 173, 312.
Critolaus, Peripatetic, i. 340.
Cronus, Megarian, i. 312.
Customs, variety of, ii. 127.
Cynics, i. 170-173, 195, 312.

Dante, quoted, i. 374, 436.
Darwin, Mr., his genesis of the Moral Nature, i. 382.
Delian epigram, i. 456.
Demetrius, Peripatetic, i. 344.
Democritus of Abdera, i. 103, 140, 149, 158, 278, 284, 306, 490.
Demodocus of Leros, ii. 225.
Dicaearchus of Messana, quoted, i. 88.
Diogenes Laertius, his catalogue of the writings of Aristotle, i. 9-15.
Diogenes of Sinope, i. 172.
Diogenes of Babylon, i. 307, 340.
Diogenes of Seleucia, i. 307.
'Duty,' i. 262, 323, 422.

Ecclesiastes, traces of Stoicism in, i. 335.
Editors of Aristotle, their additions and interpolations, i. 17, 42, 43, 44, 46, 64, 70.
Education, systematic, begins with the Sophists, i. 120.
Egnatius Celer, i. 347, 360.
Eleatic 'one,' i. 440.
Empedocles, i. 140, 278, 281, 282; ii. 149.
Epaphroditus, i. 360.
Epicharmus, quoted, ii. 337.
Epictetus, i. 359-363.
Epicurism, contrasted with Stoicism, i. 310. In the Roman world, i. 345.
Epicurus, i. 300. Grote's defence of, i. 311.
Ethics, not a separate science before Aristotle, i. 73. Eras of Morality, i. 75. Origin of Morals, i. 74. Unconscious era, i. 78. Influence of the Sophists upon morals, i. 142. Predominance of Ethics in Post-Aristotelian philosophy, i. 304. Supersession of Aristotelian Ethics, i. 371.
Eubulides, Megarian, ii. 200.
Eudemus of Rhodes, pupil of Aristotle, i. 30. Ancient notices of, i. 30-32. Names of his writings, i. 31.
Eudemian Ethics, origin of name, i. 41. Neglected by commentators, i. 19. Commencement of, examined, i. 22. Contents and characteristics of, i. 23-30. Quoted as the work of Eudemus by Aspasius, i. 32. Separate Ethics from Politics, i. 25. Religious tone of, i. 26-28. Endeavour to improve upon Aristotle, i. 27; ii. 40. Deficient in clearness, i. 29. Cannot have been written by Aristotle, i. 68.
Three books common to them and the *Nicomachean Ethics*, i. 23. Refer to *Eudemian Ethics*, i. 56. Not referred to in *Eth. Nic.* x., i. 49. Supposed references to them in other works of Aristotle, i. 50-55. Referred to in *Eudemian* treatise, i. 58. Differ in doctrine and formulæ from *Eth. Nic.*, i. 60-63. Hypotheses concerning them, i. 63, 64. Treatise on Pleasure (Book VII.), i. 63, 194, 249. Theory of Justice (Book V.), ii. 96. Full of logical formulæ, ii. 99, 150. Of subject of incontinence, ii. 135. Of physiology, ii. 130, 171, 206. Differ from Aristotle, ii. 98, 107, 157, 176, 180, 184, 240. Resemble or quote *Eth. Nic.* ii. 117, 138, 171, 181, 182, 186, 206, 209,

219, 230, 233, 234, 241, 245, 247. Resemble or quote *Eth. Eud.* ii. 98, 100, 101, 104, 129, 130, 146, 147, 148, 150, 151, 167, 168, 183, 184, 185, 194, 198, 209, 212, 219, 226, 228, 232, 235, 243. Borrow from *Organon*, ii. 153–156. *Metaphysics*, ii. 156–158, 167, 201. *De Animâ*, ii. 149, 150, 152, 162. *Politics*, ii. 109, 110, 113.

Eudoxus of Cnidus, i. 217; ii. 242, 315–316.

Euthydemus, i. 169.

Euxine, ii. 213.

Evenus of Paros, ii. 251.

'Evolution' theory, i. 381.

Freedom of Will, i. 376.

Fritzsche, Dr., editor of *Eudemian Ethics*, i. 31. Thinks Book V. Aristotle's, VI. and VII. Eudemian, i. 64. On the style of Eudemus, ii. 169.

Gender, transition to neuter, i. 464.

Goats sacrificed to Theban Zeus, ii. 127, 286.

Goethe, views of, i. 167, 245. Quoted, ii. 142, 246.

Good, chief, great question of Greek ethics, i. 101, 151.

Gorgias of Leontium, i. 118, 121, 124–126, 129, 133, 136–141.

Hampden, Bishop, quoted, ii. 193.

Harper, story of, ii. 282.

Hegel, his Moralität and Sittlichkeit, i. 77, 448; ii. 200.

Hegesias, i. 177.

Heiresses, ii. 271.

Heraclitus of Ephesus, i. 103, 201, 306. His pride, i. 428; ii. 203. On anger, i. 491. On senses, ii. 207. Harmony of opposites, ii. 253. Tastes of the ass, ii. 331.

Herbert, George, quoted, ii. 337, 341.

Herillus, Stoic, i. 307.

Hermæum, ii. 41.

Hesiod, morality of, i. 85–88, 251.

Hipparchus, son of Pisistratus, i. 82.

Hippias of Elis, i. 118, 119, 124, 146.

Hobbes, ii. 60.

Homer, morality of, i. 83–85. Plato's opinion of, i. 83, 437.

Honour, i. 433, 434; ii. 74, 266, 279.

Imperfect tense, in reference to something previously said, ii. 126, 208, 288. To general occurrences, i. 430.

Individual merged in State, i. 150.

Instruments, ii. 273.

Isocrates, i. 110–112, 118, 137; ii. 337.

Jealousy, notion of divine, i. 90.

Josephus, i. 335.

Jowett, Professor, quoted, i. 180.

Justinian, i. 367.

Kant, antinomies of, i. 139. Subjective idealism of, i. 140. Charges Aristotle with eudæmonism, i. 223; and with imperfect definition of virtue, i. 257. His theory of pleasure, i. 248; of foundation of morals, i. 337. On freedom, ii. 20. On love of enemies, ii. 34. On kindness *versus* justice, ii. 64.

Laconia invaded by Thebans, ii. 76.

Lælius, C., i. 341.

'Law,' in morals, i. 258–261. Roman law and Stoicism, i. 365–369.

Lightfoot, Canon, on St. Paul and Seneca, i. 336.

Locke, quoted, ii. 323.

Lucilius, epistles of Seneca addressed to, i. 352.

Lucretius, i. 345.

Lyceum, Aristotle's place of teaching, i. 2.

Marcellinus, friend of Seneca, i. 358.

Maxims, basis of popular morality, i. 82. Of the Seven Sages, i. 91.

Mayo, Dr. Thomas, quoted, ii. 191.

Megarians, on the actual and potential, i. 233. On the 'one,' i. 440.

Melitus, or Meletus, accuser of Socrates, i. 163.

Milesians, ii. 225.

Mimnermus of Colophon, i. 89.

Monopsychism, Averroes' doctrine of, i. 298.

Monotheism, i. 328.

Moralia, Magna, origin of name, i. 41. Neglected by commentators, i. 19. Contents and characteristics of, i. 11–38. Contain matter from Theo-

phrastus, i. 34. Quoted, i. 510; ii. 189, 197.
Mosaic code, retaliation enjoined by, ii. 117.
Mothers, love of, ii. 267, 288.
Musonius Rufus, Stoic, i. 348, 360.
Mysteries, i. 100.

Neleus of Scepsis, i. 8.
Neoptolemus, ii. 198.
Nicomachus father of Aristotle, i 31. Son of Aristotle, i. 39-40. Perhaps edited his father's *Ethics*, i. 41. Mentioned by Cicero, i. 8.

'Obligation,' i. 378.
'One,' i. 440.
Opinion of the many, Aristotle's relation to, i. 101.

Paetus, i. 349.
Paley, i. 282.
Panaetius, i. 324, 342.
Parliaments, French, ii. 22.
Parmenides, i. 140.
Patricius, quoted, i. 103, 375.
Paul, Saint, born in the head-quarters of Stoicism, i. 336. Stoical terms in his speech at Athens, i. 337. In his epistles, i. 338-339. Not known to Seneca, i. 339.
Peripatetic School, decline of, i. 11-12. Tendencies after the death of Aristotle, i. 13-14, 25. Imitation of the style of Aristotle, i. 29. Approximation to Stoics, i. 37. Worked in co-operation with Aristotle, i. 70.
Persaeus, Stoic, i. 307.
Petit, Samuel, i. 32.
Phanias, pupil of Aristotle, i. 31.
Pharisees, influenced by Stoicism, i. 335.
Philetas of Cos, ii. 200.
Philo, Megarian, i. 312.
Philolaus, i. 232.
Phocylides, i. 251.
Pindar, morality of, i. 96-98. His eschatology, i. 97.
Pittacus of Mitylene, i. 89; ii. 28, 293.
Plato.
I. *General*. Dialogues exhibit successive phases of his mind, i. 178-179. Not dogmatic, i. 179-180. A poet and dialectician, i. 181. His presentation of Socrates, i. 157. His tone, i. 215. His untechnical language, i. 219.
II. His doctrine of *Ideas*, i. 199-204. Origin of the doctrine, i. 200. Not a settled theory with him, i. 199. Attacked by himself in *Parmenides*, i. 200. Idea of Good, i. 203. A principle for ethics, i. 204, 443. Criticised by Aristotle, i. 204-212; ii. 436-443.
III. *Physics*. Matter, an 'undefined duad,' i. 153. Heavenly bodies, i. 286. Purer senses, ii. 330. Division of mind, i. 167, 192.
IV. *Ethics and Politics*. Contempt for unphilosophic virtue, i. 78. Different moral points of view in the *Republic*, i. 76. Develops the principle of Socrates, i. 182. Treats of the cardinal virtues, *ib.* Separates Wisdom from the rest, i. 183. Unifies the virtues, i. 185. Identifies virtue with knowledge, i. 118; and vice with ignorance, *ib.* Future rewards and punishments, i. 187. Influenced by Pindar, i. 187. His theory of Pleasure, i. 246-247. Not chief good, ii. 234, 317, 320. Intellectual pleasures, ii. 322. Justice, ii. 104. Justice a proportion, ii. 109. Implies its contrary, ii. 137. Injustice worse than being injured, ii. 142. Injustice better if voluntary, i. 168. 'Pigeon-house,' ii. 203. Praise of Sparta, ii. 345. Community of wives from Cynics, i. 173.
V. *Religion*. Providence, ii. 342. Prayer, ii. 101. Being made like to God, i. 193. Eschatology, i. 187. His influence on the Stoics, i. 332-333.
VI. *Art*, full of law and harmony, i. 254. His view of Rhetoric, i. 128.
VII. *Doubtful Works*. *Hipparchus*, i. 81. *Menexenus*, i. 466. *Περὶ δικαίου*, ii. 26.
Plutarch, i. 5, 6, 8, 305, 315, 321; ii. 62.
Polemo, i. 218, 312.
Polus of Agrigentum, i. 122, 151.
Polygnotus, painter, i. 312.

Pompey, i. 341.
Porphyry, on Andronicus, i. 6, 8, 17. On the three ethical treatises, i. 31.
Posidonius, Stoic, i. 342.
Poste, Mr., quoted, i. 70; ii. 226.
Present tense in quotations, i. 430.
'Principles' in morals, i. 269.
Prodicus of Ceos, i. 123. His apologue, i. 144.
Proportion, arithmetical, ii. 113.
Protagoras, i. 115, 117, 122. On grammar, i. 123. Not an eristic, i. 133. His boast, *ib.* His philosophy, i. 134-136. His teaching virtue, i. 143. First taught for money, ii. 282.
Protarchus, i. 280.
Protasis, complex, i. 467.
Pythagoras, his metaphor, i. 432.
Pythagoreans, i. 102, 158, 216, 252, 259, 295, 440; ii. 116, 261.

Ransom, ii. 127.
Renouvier, quoted, i. 103, 172.
Rhetoric, created by Sophists, i. 121-126. General considerations on, i. 126-128. Roman tendency to, i. 345.
Rubellius Plautus, i. 348.

Salt, proverb about, ii. 258.
Sardanapalus, his epitaph, i. 433.
Scævola, i. 366.
Scythian malady, ii. 222.
Seneca, i. 349-359.
Seven Wise Men, i. 88-91.
Sextius, Stoic, i. 346.
Shakespeare quoted *Eth. Nic.* i. 428. On courage, ii. 43. Murderers, ii. 46. 'Kept not time,' ii. 71. Anger, ii. 81. Love, ii. 292.
Sicyonians, ii. 44.
Sight, ii. 323.
Simonides of Ceos, i. 76, 82, 92, 93, 510; ii. 62.
Socrates, i. 142, 154-170. On courage, ii. 40. Various opinions, ii. 188, 195, 197.
Solon, i. 89, 90, 228, 301, 460-466. Called 'the first Sophist' by Isocrates, i. 112.
Sophists, Grote's defence of, i. 104, 152. History of the name, i. 105-113. Not merely a few particular persons, i. 113. Plato's view of, i. 115-117. Itinerant teachers, i. 117. Their gains, i. 118. Their rhetoric, i. 121-126. Earlier and later Sophists, 129-132. Their eristic, i. 132-133. Not a philosophical sect, i. 133. Excesses of Sophistry, i. 141. Their influence upon morals, i. 142-150. Aristotle's view of, i. 151. Summary with regard to, i. 153.
Sophocles, quoted, i. 463; ii. 199.
Sosithens, comic poet, i. 313.
Sotion, Stoic, i. 346.
Spengel, Professor Ludwig, his theory as to the three ethical treatises, i. 19. On the Great Ethics, i. 37, 38. On the order of Aristotle's writings, i. 272. Quoted, i. 486, 499.
Speusippus, i. 216-217, 460; ii. 207, 234, 237-240, 315.
Sphærus, Stoic, i. 307.
Spinoza, i. 370. Quoted, ii. 337.
Stewart, Dugald, i. 378.
Stilpo, Megarian, i. 312.
Stoics, their Semitic origin, i. 306-309. Formation of their doctrine, i. 304-334. Reaction of their doctrine on the East, i. 334-339. Stoicism in the Roman world, i. 339-349. Merits and defects of Stoicism, i. 369.
Suicide, i. 334, 358; ii. 141.
'Suitable,' i. 324.
Swedenborg, his clairvoyance, i. 155.
Sybarites, ii. 222.
Syllogism, do we always reason in? ii. 216.
Symonds, Mr. J. A., quoted, i. 80, 90, 97.

Tennyson, quoted, ii. 224.
Thales of Miletus, i. 89; ii. 166.
Theatres, sweetmeats in, ii. 329.
Theodectes, ii. 329.
Theognis of Megara, i. 91-94. Quoted, ii. 03, 344.
Theophrastus, i. 8, 13, 30, 34, 41, 398.
Thrasea, i. 349.
Thrasymachus of Chalcedon, i. 76, 148, 150.
Thucydides, i. 107, 113, 124, 153.
Tickling, ii. 223.
Tigellinus, i. 348.
Tisias, i. 121.

Tyler, Mr. T., on *Ecclesiastes*, quoted, i. 335, 336.
Tyndall, Professor, his criticism on Aristotle, i. 277.

Utility, i. 377.

Vatican Scholium, ii. 240.

Wordsworth, quoted: Duty, i. 259. Happy Warrior, ii. 45.

Xenocrates, i. 217, 312, 454.
Xenophon, i. 109, 113, 154, 156, 161, 162, 163, 169, 502; ii. 275.

Zaleucus, his law of retaliation, ii. 117.
Zeno, founder of Stoics, i. 307, 311–312.
Zeno, of Sidon, i. 307.

THE END.

www.ingramcontent.com/pod-product-compliance
Lightning Source LLC
Chambersburg PA
CBHW020537300426
44111CB00008B/698

* 9 7 8 3 7 4 2 8 2 6 4 3 5 *